# SOCIAL PSYCHOLOGY

This fully revised and updated edition of **Social Psychology** is an engaging exploration of the question, "what makes us who we are?" presented in a new, streamlined fashion. Grounded in the latest research, *Social Psychology* explains the methods by which social psychologists investigate human behavior in a social context and the theoretical perspectives that ground the discipline.

Each chapter is designed to be a self-contained unit for ease of use in any classroom. This edition features new boxes providing research updates and "test yourself" opportunities, a focus on critical thinking skills, and an increased emphasis on diverse populations and their experiences.

**John D. DeLamater** was Conway-Bascom Professor of Sociology-Emeritus at the University of Wisconsin-Madison until his death in 2017. John received his education at the University of California, Santa Barbara, and the University of Michigan. He earned his Ph.D. in Social Psychology in 1969. He began teaching an undergraduate course in social psychology in 1970, and graduate courses and seminars in the area beginning in 1981. He led a seminar on teaching for graduate students, and won several teaching awards, including the Chancellor's Award for Distinguished Teaching, during his career. He was also the co-editor of the *Handbook of Social Psychology, 2nd edition*, published by Springer. He had been a co-author of this text since its first edition.

**Jessica L. Collett** is Professor of Sociology at the University of California, Los Angeles. This very book, in a much earlier edition, inspired her own interest in social psychology during her time as an undergraduate at Winthrop University. After Winthrop, she went on to study social psychology at the University of Arizona, where she received her Ph.D. in Sociology in 2006. She is an award-winning instructor, most recently receiving the Charles E. Sheedy Award for Excellence in Teaching from the College of Arts and Letters at the University of Notre Dame. She regularly teaches social psychology at both the undergraduate and graduate levels, as well as courses on social inequality and socialization and the life course.

# NINTH EDITION

# SOCIAL PSYCHOLOGY

JOHN D. DELAMATER AND JESSICA L. COLLETT

Routledge
Taylor & Francis Group

NEW YORK AND LONDON

Ninth edition published 2019
by Routledge
711 Third Avenue, New York, NY 10017

and by Routledge
2 Park Square, Milton Park, Abingdon, Oxon, OX14 4RN

*Routledge is an imprint of the Taylor & Francis Group, an informa business*

First edition published by Harcourt 1986
Eighth edition published by Westview 2015

*Library of Congress Cataloging-in-Publication Data*
Names: DeLamater, John D., author. | Collett, Jessica L., author.
Title: Social psychology / John D. DeLamater & Jessica L. Collett.
Description: 9th Edition. | New York : Routledge, 2018. | Revised edition of
   Social psychology, [2015] | Includes bibliographical references and index.
Identifiers: LCCN 2017058007 (print) | LCCN 2017059066 (ebook) |
   ISBN 9781351015837 (Master Ebook) | ISBN 9781351015820 (Web pdf) |
   ISBN 9781351015813 ( ePub) | ISBN 9781351015806 (Mobipocket) |
   ISBN 9781138498709 (hardback : alk. paper) | ISBN 9780813350684 (pbk. : alk. paper) |
   ISBN 9781351015837 (ebk)
Subjects: LCSH: Social psychology.
Classification: LCC HM1033 (ebook) | LCC HM1033 .D45 2018 (print) | DDC 302—dc23
LC record available at https://lccn.loc.gov/2017058007

ISBN: 978-1-138-49870-9 (hbk)
ISBN: 978-0-8133-5068-4 (pbk)
ISBN: 978-1-351-01583-7 (ebk)

Typeset in Bembo
by Apex CoVantage, LLC

Visit the eResources: www.routledge.com/9780813350684

Printed and bound in the United States of America by Sheridan

For John; who dedicated his life to sharing social psychology and his other intellectual and personal interests with others, in hopes of making the world a better place. His commitment to teaching, to mentoring, and to this book leaves a lasting legacy. He is missed by many, but lives on in our hearts and minds.

## ABOUT THIS BOOK

We are pleased to welcome you to the ninth edition of this textbook! When revising a textbook, the authors always seek to build on the strengths of the prior editions, introducing new material reflecting developments in the field and changes in our larger society, while maintaining thorough coverage of the subject examined in the book. As in past editions, we seek to cover the full range of phenomena of interest to social psychologists. Not only do we address intrapsychic processes in detail, but cover social interaction and group processes, as well as larger-scale phenomena, such as the impact of social structure on physical and mental health, and intergroup conflict. Our goal in writing this book is, as it has always been, to describe contemporary social psychology and to present the theoretical concepts and research findings that make up this broad and fascinating field. We have drawn on work by a wide array of social psychologists, including those with sociological and psychological perspectives, drawing on both classic works and more recent studies. Throughout the book we have used the results of empirical research—surveys, experiments, observational and qualitative studies, and meta-analyses—to illustrate this wide range of social psychological ideas.

## ABOUT THE AUTHORS

The late John D. DeLamater was Conway-Bascom Professor of Sociology-Emeritus at the University of Wisconsin-Madison until his death in December 2017. He received his education at the University of California, Santa Barbara, and the University of Michigan. He earned his Ph.D. in Social Psychology in 1969. He began teaching undergraduate courses in social psychology in 1970 and graduate courses and seminars in the area in 1981. Committed to teaching, he led a seminar on teaching for graduate students in his department, and won several teaching awards, including the Chancellor's Award for Distinguished Teaching, during his career. He was also the co-editor of the *Handbook of Social Psychology, 2nd edition*, published by Springer. His research and writing focused on the effects of life-course transitions on sexuality. He published papers on the effects of having a child, of dual-career couples, of divorce, and of influences on sexual desire and sexual behavior among men and women over 45. At the end of his career, he was investigating sexual behavior in later life, specifically the changes experienced by men and women in their sexual relationships and how they respond to them. Amazingly, he was one of the original creators of this text and co-authored all nine editions.

Jessica L. Collett is Professor of Sociology at the University of California, Los Angeles. This very book, although a much earlier edition, inspired her own interest in social psychology during her time as an undergraduate at Winthrop University. After Winthrop, she went on to study social psychology at the University of Arizona, where she received her Ph.D. in Sociology in 2006. She is an award-winning instructor, most recently receiving the Charles E. Sheedy Award for Excellence in Teaching from the College of Arts and Letters at the University of Notre Dame where she was on the faculty from 2006–2018. She regularly teaches social psychology at both the undergraduate and graduate levels, as well as courses on social inequality and socialization and the life course. Her research focuses on small group processes, self and identity, and the connection between the two. In recent years, she has turned attention toward fathers, exploring how they learn what it means to be a father and how their conceptions of fatherhood not only influence their involvement in family life, but also their self-esteem and emotional outcomes.

## NEW TO THIS EDITION

The last edition of the text, the eighth, included 17 chapters, and an organization that closely paralleled earlier editions. When we solicited feedback on the eighth edition, some reviewers requested that we separate the lengthy chapter that included both self and self-presentation (Chapter 4). These are core topics and deserve their own chapters. Accordingly, they are separate chapters in this edition (4 and 5), although we did not lengthen either of them a great deal. We received feedback that even the eighth edition was too much material to get through in one academic term, and so, after much deliberation, we have dropped the final chapter on "Collective Behavior and Social Movements." Some reviewers over the years have suggested this change and some users have told us they do not assign it. We also moved the chapter on deviance from 16 to 13, reasoning that it fits better among chapters discussing individuals than coming after chapters on small groups.

The ninth edition also contains updated research, data, and examples throughout the book, new boxes providing research updates and "test yourself" opportunities, and an increased emphasis on diverse populations and their experiences. As in the past, we have made a special effort to incorporate research that reports differences among participants who vary on race, gender, and sexual orientation, but of course are limited by what is available, and point out these limitations.

In preparing the ninth edition, we paid especially careful attention to every instance of gendered language. We opted for the pronouns "they" and "them." Where appropriate, we eliminated the use of words like "boys," "girls," "men," and "women." After all, most of the social psychological concepts and principles we discuss are common to most people. One exception is in the descriptions of samples used in the research we summarize. We also eliminated language reflecting assumptions, e.g., about the gender composition of "couples." We have undoubtedly missed a few cases, and welcome feedback pointing us to them.

## CONTENT AND ORGANIZATION

As in past editions, the first chapter covers major theoretical perspectives in contemporary social psychology. It provides an introduction to dual-process theories and evolutionary perspectives from psychology, as well as symbolic interaction, group processes, and social structure and personality from sociology. In this edition we returned to including a table in this introductory chapter that summarizes and compares these theoretical perspectives.

Chapter 2, Research Methods, has been reorganized. It now reflects the widely recognized distinction between quantitative and qualitative research methods. Following the discussion of characteristics of research, it presents three quantitative techniques: surveys, diary methods (new to this edition), and experiments. The next section discusses qualitative methods, including observational research and archival analysis. The remainder of the chapter retains the material and organization of past editions.

The remainder of the book is divided into four loose but substantive sections. Section 1 focuses on individual social behavior. It includes chapters on socialization, self, self-presentation, emotions, social perception and cognition, and attitudes. Section 2 is concerned with social interaction, the core of social psychology. Each of the chapters in this section discusses how persons interact with others and how they are affected by this interaction. These chapters cover such topics as communication, social influence and persuasion, altruism and prosocial behavior, aggression, interpersonal attraction, and deviant behavior and the importance of interaction in creating and responding to it. Section 3 provides extensive coverage of groups. It includes chapters on group cohesion, conformity, and intergroup conflict, as well as an overview of the dominant research focuses in the social psychological studies of groups today, including status characteristics and expectation states theory, decision making in groups, social exchange, and distributive and procedural justice. Section 4 considers the relations between individuals and the wider society. Chapter 17 examines the impact of social structure on the individual, especially on physical and mental health.

## EASE OF USE

Although we have attempted to present the material in this book in a logical sequence that will appeal to many instructors, there are, of course, many different ways in which an instructor can organize an introductory course in social psychology. Therefore, we have written each chapter as a self-contained unit. Later chapters do not presume that the student has read earlier ones (although we insert appropriate cross-references to allow students to easily find related material in other chapters). This compartmentalization enables instructors to assign chapters in any sequence.

Chapters share a standard format. To make the material interesting and accessible to students, each chapter's introductory section articulates four or five learning objectives. These are restatements of the focal questions that we used in earlier editions to orient the reader. These establish the issues discussed in the chapter. The remainder of the chapter consists of four or five major sections, each designed to achieve one of the objectives. A summary at the end of each chapter reviews the key points. Thus, each chapter introduces several key issues/objectives related to the topic and then considers these in a framework that enables students to easily learn the major ideas.

In addition, the text includes several learning aids. Tables emphasize the results of important studies. Figures illustrate important social psychological processes. Photographs dramatize essential ideas from the text. Boxes in each chapter highlight interesting or controversial issues and studies and also discuss the applications of social psychological concepts in daily life. Some boxes are identified as "Research Update"; these boxes have been updated by including the latest research. Other boxes are identified as "Test Yourself"; these contain a questionnaire that the student can complete to find out their standing on the measure of interest. Key terms appear in bold. A glossary of key terms appears at the end of the book.

A major feature in the ninth edition is an emphasis on developing critical thinking skills. Critical thinking is an important goal of a quality education; it refers to the ability to use cognitive skills and strategies to increase the probability of a desirable outcome. Diane Halpern is an expert on critical thinking and developing these skills, and we drew heavily on her writings. Critical thinking is logical, rational, and free of self-deception. As the student learns about social psychology, they will learn that there are a number of important ways in which our everyday thinking is biased, and ways in which we engage in self-deception. Developing critical thinking skills and using them in daily life should lead the student to make better decisions and therefore lead a better life.

At the end of each chapter there is a section called Critical Thinking Skill. Each teaches a particular skill with an application to social psychology, and will have applications throughout the student's life. Let's get going!

## ACKNOWLEDGMENTS

Throughout the writing of the various editions of this book, many colleagues have reviewed chapters and provided useful comments and criticisms. We express sincere appreciation to the many reviewers of the previous editions, and specifically to those involved in this ninth edition's review process: Lesa Johnson, University of Nebraska-Lincoln; Andrea Laurent-Simpson, Texas Woman's University; Stephen Merino, University of Texas-Pan American; Terri L. Orbuch, Oakland University; and Deborah Ramirez-Tinoco, Bakersfield College.

We also thank the many students who used the previous editions and who provided us

with feedback about the book; we applied this feedback to improve the presentation, pace, and style of the new edition.

Finally, we express thanks to the professionals at Westview and Routledge who contributed to the process of turning the manuscript into a book. James Sherman, acquisitions editor at Westview, worked with us in the earlier stages and Samantha Barbaro, Senior Editor at Taylor & Francis, stepped in during the final stages and, with the help of Erik Zimmerman, oversaw the transformation of manuscript into printed pages. Our appreciation to them all. Although this book benefited greatly from feedback and criticisms, the authors accept responsibility for any errors that may remain.

## POSTSCRIPT FROM JESSICA L. COLLETT

Sadly, John D. DeLamater passed away before this revision appeared in print. I chose not to edit the preface and to use the pronoun "we" throughout, as John and I wrote this book together and John is very much alive and present in the text.

# INTRODUCTION TO SOCIAL PSYCHOLOGY

## LEARNING OBJECTIVES

By the end of this chapter you will be able to:

- Define social psychology and list the core concerns of the field.

- Understand five broad theoretical perspectives common in social psychology and describe the strengths and weaknesses of each.

- Comprehend the interdisciplinary nature of social psychology.

## INTRODUCTION

Many of us are curious about the world around us. We ask ourselves questions, or pose them to friends, relatives, coworkers, or professors: What leads people to fall in and out of love? Why do people cooperate so easily in some situations but not in others? What effects do major life events like graduating from college, getting married, or losing a job have on physical or mental health? Where do stereotypes come from and why do they persist even in the face of contradictory evidence? Why do some people conform to norms and laws while others do not? What causes conflict between groups? Furthermore, why do some conflicts subside and others progress until there is no chance of reconciliation? Why do people present different images of themselves in various social situations, whether online or in person? Why are so many political and business leaders men? And why are they often paid more money than women when they work in the same positions? What causes harmful or aggressive behavior? What motivates helpful or altruistic behavior? Why are some people more persuasive and influential than others? Perhaps questions such as these have puzzled you, just as they have perplexed others through the ages. You might wonder about these issues simply because you want to better understand the social world around

you. Or you might want answers for practical reasons, such as increasing your effectiveness in day-to-day relations with others.

Answers to questions such as these come from various sources. One such source is personal experience—things we learn from everyday interaction. Answers obtained by this means are often insightful, but they are usually limited in scope and generality, and they can also be misleading. Another source is informal knowledge or advice from others who describe their own experiences to us. Answers obtained by this means are sometimes reliable, sometimes not. A third source is the conclusions reached by philosophers, novelists, poets, and men and women of practical affairs who, over the centuries, have written about these issues. Often their answers have filtered down and become commonsense knowledge. We are told, for instance, that joint effort is an effective way to accomplish large jobs ("Many hands make light work") and that bonds among family tend to be stronger than those among friends ("Blood is thicker than water"). These principles reflect certain truths and may sometimes provide guidelines for action.

Although commonsense knowledge may have merit, it also has drawbacks, not the least of which is that it often contradicts itself. For example, we hear that people who are similar will like one another ("Birds of a feather flock together") but also that persons who are dissimilar will like each other ("Opposites attract"). We are told that groups are wiser and smarter than individuals ("Two heads are better than one") but also that group work inevitably produces poor results ("Too many cooks spoil the broth"). Each of these contradictory statements may hold true under particular conditions, but without a clear statement of when they apply and when they do not, these sayings provide little insight into relations among people. They provide even less guidance in situations in which we must make decisions. For example, when facing a choice that entails risk, which guideline should we use—"Nothing ventured, nothing gained" or "Better safe than sorry"?

If sources such as personal experience and commonsense knowledge have only limited value, how are we to attain an understanding of social interactions and relations among people? One solution to this problem—the one pursued by social psychologists—is to obtain knowledge about social behavior by applying the methods of science. That is, by making systematic observations of behavior and formulating theories that are subject to testing, we can develop a valid and comprehensive understanding of human social relations. In this book we present some of social psychologists' major findings from systematic research. In this chapter, we lay the foundation for this effort by introducing you to the field of social psychology and its major theoretical perspectives.

## WHAT IS SOCIAL PSYCHOLOGY?

### A Formal Definition

We define **social psychology** as the systematic study of the nature and causes of human social behavior. This definition has three main components. First, social psychology's primary concern is *human* social behavior. This includes many things—individuals' activities in the presence of others and in particular situations, the processes of social interaction between two or more persons, and the relationships among individuals and the groups to which they belong. Importantly, in this definition, behavior moves beyond action to also include affect (emotion) and cognition (thoughts). In other words, social psychologists are not only interested in what people do, but also what individuals feel and think (Fine, 1995).

Second, social psychologists are not satisfied to simply document the nature of social behavior; instead, they want to explore the *causes* of such behavior. This differentiates social psychology from a field like journalism. Journalists describe what people do. Social psychologists are not only interested in what people do but also want to understand why they do it. In social psychology, causal relations among variables are important building blocks of theory, and, in turn, theory is crucial for the prediction and control of social behavior.

Third, social psychologists study social behavior in a *systematic* fashion. Social psychology is a social science that employs the scientific method and relies on formal research methodologies, including surveys, diary research, experiments, observational research, and archival research or content analysis. These research methods are described in detail in Chapter 2.

### Core Concerns of Social Psychology

Another way to answer the question "What is social psychology?" is to describe the topics that social psychologists actually study. Social psychologists investigate human behavior, of course, but their primary concern is human behavior in a social context. There are five core concerns, or major themes, within social psychology: (1) the impact that one individual has on another; (2) the impact that a group has on its individual members; (3) the impact that individual members have on the groups to which they belong; (4) the impact that one group has on another group; (5) the impact of social context and social structure on groups and individuals. The five core concerns are shown schematically in Figure 1.1.

**Impact of Individuals on Individuals.** Individuals are affected by others in many ways. In everyday life, interactions with others may significantly influence a person's understanding of the social world. Much of this happens simply by observation. Through listening to others and watching them, an

## BOX 1.1  Test Yourself: Is Social Psychology Simply Common Sense?

Because social psychologists are interested in a wide range of phenomena from our everyday lives, students sometimes claim that social psychology is common sense. Is it? Five of the following commonsense statements are true. The other five are not. Can you tell the difference?

1.  **T   F**   When faced with natural disasters such as floods and earthquakes, people panic and social organization disintegrates.

2.  **T   F**   Physically attractive individuals are usually seen as less intelligent than physically unattractive individuals.

3.  **T   F**   The reason that people discriminate against minorities is prejudice; unprejudiced people don't discriminate.

4.  **T   F**   People tend to overestimate the extent to which other people share their opinions, attitudes, and behavior.

5.  **T   F**   Rather than "opposites attract," people are generally attracted to those similar to themselves.

6.  **T   F**   "Putting on a happy face" (i.e., smiling when you are really not happy) will not make you feel any different on the inside.

7.  **T   F**   People with few friends tend to live shorter, less healthy lives than people with lots of friends.

8.  **T   F**   The more certain a crime victim is about their account of events, the more accurate the report they provide to the police.

9.  **T   F**   If people tell a lie for a reward, they are more likely to come to believe the lie when given a small reward rather than a large reward.

10. **T   F**   The more often we see something—even if we don't like it at first—the more we grow to like it.

True: 4, 5, 7, 9 & 10.

---

individual learns how they should act, what they should think, and how they should feel.

Sometimes this influence is more direct. A person might persuade another to change their beliefs about the world and their attitudes toward persons, groups, or other objects. Suppose, for example, that Mia tries to persuade Andrew that all nuclear power plants are dangerous and undesirable and, therefore, should be closed. If successful, Mia's persuasion attempt could change Andrew's beliefs and perhaps affect his future actions (picketing nuclear power plants, advocating non–nuclear sources of power, and the like).

Beyond influence and persuasion, the actions of others often affect the outcomes individuals obtain in everyday life. A person caught in an emergency situation, for instance, may be helped by an altruistic bystander. In another situation, one person may be wounded by another's aggressive acts. Social psychologists have investigated the nature and origins of both altruism and aggression as well as other interpersonal activity such as cooperation and competition.

Also relevant here are various interpersonal sentiments. One individual may develop strong attitudes toward another (liking, disliking, loving, hating) based on who the other is and what they do. Social psychologists investigate these issues to discover why individuals develop positive attitudes toward some people but negative attitudes toward others.

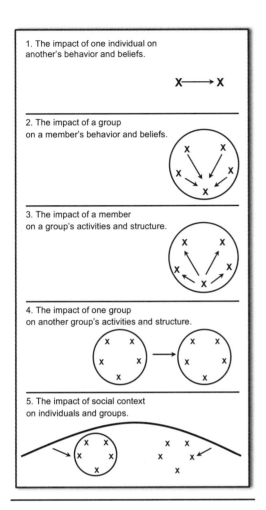

1. The impact of one individual on another's behavior and beliefs.

2. The impact of a group on a member's behavior and beliefs.

3. The impact of a member on a group's activities and structure.

4. The impact of one group on another group's activities and structure.

5. The impact of social context on individuals and groups.

**FIGURE 1.1** The Core Concerns of Social Psychology

**Impact of Groups on Individuals.** Social psychology is also interested in the influence groups have on the behavior of their individual members. Because people belong to many different groups—families, work groups, seminars, and clubs—they spend many hours each week interacting with group members. Groups influence and regulate the behavior of their members, typically by establishing norms or rules. Group influence often results in conformity, as group members adjust their behavior to bring it into line with group norms. For example, college fraternities and sororities have norms—some formal and some informal— that stipulate how members should dress, what

meetings they should attend, whom they can date and whom they should avoid, and how they should behave at parties. As a result of these norms, members of particular groups behave quite similarly to one another.

Groups also exert substantial long-term influence on their members through socialization, a process through which individuals acquire the knowledge, values, and skills required of group members. Socialization processes are meant to ensure that group members will be adequately trained to play roles in the group and in the larger society. Although we are socialized to be members of discrete groups (sororities and fraternities, families, postal workers), we are also socialized to be members of social categories (woman, Latinx, working class, American). Outcomes of socialization vary, from language skills to political and religious beliefs to our conception of self.

**Impact of Individuals on a Group.** A third concern of social psychology is the impact of individuals on group processes and products. Just as any group influences the behavior of its members, these members, in turn, may influence the group itself. For instance, individuals contribute to group productivity and group decision making. Moreover, some members may provide leadership, performing functions such as planning, organizing, and controlling, necessary for successful group performance. Without effective leadership, coordination among members will falter and the group will drift or fail. Furthermore, individuals and minority coalitions often innovate change in group structure and procedures. Both leadership and innovation depend on individuals' initiative, insight, and risk-taking ability.

**Impact of Groups on Groups.** Social psychologists also explore how one group might affect the activities and structure of another group. Relations between two groups may be friendly or hostile, cooperative or competitive.

These relationships, which are based in part on members' identities and may entail group stereotypes, can affect the structure and activities of each group. Of special interest is intergroup conflict, with its accompanying tension and hostility. Violence may flare up, for instance, between two families disputing land rights or between racial groups competing for scarce jobs. Conflicts of this type affect the interpersonal relations between groups and within each group. Social psychologists have long studied the emergence, persistence, and resolution of intergroup conflict.

**Impact of Social Context on Individuals and Groups.** Social psychologists realize that individuals' behavior is profoundly shaped by the situations in which they find themselves. If you are listening to the radio in your car and your favorite song comes on, you might turn the volume up and sing along loudly. If you hear the same song at a dance club, you are less inclined to sing along but instead might head out to the dance floor. If your social psychology professor kicks off the first day of class by playing the song, chances are you won't sing or dance. In fact, you might give your fellow students a quizzical look. Your love for the song has not changed, but the social situation shapes your role in the situation (club-goer, student) along with the expected behaviors based on that role. These contextual factors influence your reaction to the music.

These reactions are based, in part, on what you have learned through your interactions with others and through socialization in groups, the social influences discussed in the previous sections. However, as we grow and develop, the rules, belief systems, and categorical distinctions that have profound influence on our everyday lives seem to separate from these interactions. We forget that these things that feel or appear natural were actually socially constructed (Berger & Luckmann, 1966).

## Sociology, Psychology, or Both?

Social psychology bears a close relationship to several other fields, especially sociology and psychology.

Sociology is the scientific study of human society. It examines social institutions (family, religion, politics), stratification within society (class structure, race and ethnicity, gender roles), basic social processes (socialization, deviance, social control), and the structure of social units (groups, networks, formal organizations, bureaucracies).

In contrast, psychology is the scientific study of the individual and of individual behavior. Although this behavior may be social in character, it need not be. Psychology addresses such topics as human learning, perception, memory, intelligence, emotion, motivation, and personality.

Social psychology bridges sociology and psychology. In the mid-twentieth century, early in the history of social psychology, sociologists and psychologists worked closely together in departments and on research. In fact, top programs offered degrees in "Social Relations" or "Social Psychology" rather than Sociology or Psychology. However, over time, the interests of sociological social psychologists and psychological social psychologists diverged somewhat. For a period, collaboration became rather uncommon. Although that is beginning to change and more sociological and psychological social psychologists are collaborating again (for example, the work of Feinberg, Willer, and colleagues described in Figure 10.2 and Box 11.1 of this text), most students still earn degrees in one of the two disciplines with a specialization or concentration in social psychology. That said, many still see social psychology as interdisciplinary.

Both sociologists and psychologists have contributed to social psychological knowledge. Sociological social psychologists use surveys, experiments, and observational techniques to gather data. These investigators are most interested in the relationships between individuals and the groups to which they belong. They emphasize such processes as socialization, conformity and deviance, social interaction, self-presentation, within-group processes, leadership, and cooperation and competition. Social psychologists working in the psychological tradition rely heavily on laboratory experimental methodology but increasingly use surveys and questionnaires. They are much less likely than sociological social psychologists to use observational methods outside the laboratory. Their primary concern is how social stimuli (often other persons) affect an individual's behavior and internal states. They emphasize such topics as the self, person perception and attribution, attitudes and attitude change, personality differences in social behavior, social learning and modeling, altruism and aggression, and interpersonal attraction.

Thus, sociologically oriented and psychologically oriented social psychologists differ in their outlook and emphasis. As we might expect, this leads them to formulate different theories and to conduct different programs of research. Yet these differences are best viewed as complementary rather than as conflicting. Social psychologists of all kinds are generally interested in individuals as social beings and social psychology as a field is richer for the contributions of both approaches.

## THEORETICAL PERSPECTIVES IN SOCIAL PSYCHOLOGY

Yesterday at work, Warren reported to his boss that he would not be able to complete an important project on schedule. To Warren's surprise, the boss snapped back angrily and told him to complete the task by the following Monday—or else! Warren was not entirely sure what to make of this behavior, but he decided to take the threat seriously.

That evening, talking with his girlfriend, Madison, Warren announced that he would have to work overtime at the office, so he could not go with her to a party on Friday as originally planned. Madison immediately got mad at Warren—she definitely wanted to go, she did not want to go alone, and he had promised several times to come along—and walked out of his apartment, slamming the door as she left. By now, Warren was distressed and a little perplexed.

Reflecting on these two events, Warren noticed they had some characteristics in common. To explain the behavior of his boss and his girlfriend, he formed a general proposition: "If you fail to deliver on promises made to another, that person will get mad at you." He was happy with this simple formulation until the next day, when the car behind him at the stoplight started honking. He looked up and realized the light had turned green. As he moved forward, the car behind him passed him and the driver gave him an angry look. Warren thought about this event and concluded that his original theory needed some revision. Although he had not promised the driver behind him anything, the driver had become angry and aggressive because of Warren's actions. His new theory included a chain of propositions: "If someone expects something that does not happen, they will become frustrated. If someone is frustrated, they will become aggressive. If someone is aggressive, they will lash out at either the source of the frustration or a convenient surrogate."

In his own way, Warren had started to do informally the same thing social psychologists do more elaborately and systematically. Starting from some observations regarding social behavior, Warren attempted to formulate a theory to explain the observed facts. As the term is used here, a **theory** is a set of interrelated propositions that organizes and explains a set of observed phenomena. Theories usually pertain not just to some particular event but rather to whole classes of events. Moreover, as Warren's example indicates, a theory goes beyond mere observable facts by postulating causal relations among variables. In other words, it describes not only what people do but also why they do it. If a theory is valid, it enables its user to explain the phenomena under consideration and to make predictions about events not yet observed.

In social psychology, no single theory explains all phenomena of interest; rather, the field includes many different theories. Many of these theories are discussed in this book. **Middle-range theories** identify the conditions that produce specific social behavior. One such theory is the frustration-aggression hypothesis, not unlike Warren's theory above, which describes the connection between expectations, frustration, and aggression. However, social psychology also includes **theoretical perspectives**. Broader in scope than middle-range theories, theoretical perspectives offer general explanations for a wide array of social behaviors in a variety of situations. These general explanations are rooted in explicit assumptions about human nature. Theoretical perspectives serve an important function for the field of social psychology. By making certain assumptions regarding human nature, a theoretical perspective establishes a vantage point from which we can examine a range of social behaviors. Because any perspective highlights certain features and downplays others, it enables us to "see" more clearly certain aspects or features of social behavior. The fundamental value of any theoretical perspective lies in its applicability across many situations; it provides a frame of reference for interpreting and comparing a wide range of social situations and behaviors.

Social psychology can be organized into a number of distinct theoretical perspectives. For sociologists who study social psychology, these theoretical perspectives are situated in three traditions—symbolic interactionism, group processes, and social structure and personality. James House (1977) referred to these as the three "faces" of social psychology, each with a unique perspective and emphasis. These faces as well as related theoretical perspectives are explained below. Also below is an introduction to theoretical perspectives that have dominated psychological social psychology over the last 20 years: cognitive theories (including both the dual-process model of information processing and social identity theory) and evolutionary theory.

## Symbolic Interactionism

The theoretical perspective that guided much of the early work of sociological social psychologists—and that is still important today—is symbolic interactionism (Charon, 1995; Stryker, 1980, 1987). Although it is sometimes called **symbolic interaction theory**, symbolic interactionism is actually a perspective that guides the development of more specific theories (McCall, 2013). The basic premise of symbolic interactionism is that human nature and social order are products of symbolic communication among people. Society (from cultures to institutions to ourselves) is produced and reproduced through our interactions with others by means of language and our interpretation of that language. There are three main premises of symbolic interaction (Blumer, 1969):

1. We act toward things on the basis of their meanings.
2. Meanings are not inherent but are negotiated in interaction with others.
3. Meanings can be modified and changed through interaction.

People can communicate successfully with one another only to the extent that they ascribe similar meanings to objects. An object's meaning for a person depends not so much on the properties of the object itself but on what the person might do with the object.

In other words, an object takes on meaning only in relation to a person's plans. Consider an empty glass bottle. Standing alone, a bottle has no meaning. The meaning of the bottle comes from how you plan to use it. If there is liquid in it, it becomes a vessel for a beverage. Placed in the recycling bin, it becomes waste. But if someone pulls it out of the recycling and puts flowers in it, it becomes a vase. Use it in a bar fight, it might be a weapon. Placed on its side at the center of a table filled with people, it becomes a game piece for Spin the Bottle. We learn the meanings of things—whether bottles or smiles or pieces of linen and cotton printed with black and green ink—through interaction with others. These meanings can change and shift over time based on social interaction.

According to symbolic interactionism, we derive the meaning of objects from how we (or others) plan to use those objects. The same bottle can be a vessel for liquid, waste, a vase, a weapon, or a game piece. Depending on how people intend to use the table the bottle is on, its meaning can also vary—from a table, to a desk, to a seat, to a place to lie down for a nap. © Tamas Panczel, Eross/Shutterstock

**Negotiating Meanings.** Symbolic interactionism views humans as proactive and goal seeking. People formulate plans of action to achieve their goals. Many plans, of course, can be accomplished only through cooperation with other people. To establish cooperation with others, meanings must be shared and consensual. If the meaning of something is unclear or contested, an agreement must be developed through give-and-take before cooperative action is possible. For example, if a man and a woman have begun to meet after work for drinks and, one night, as they are leaving the bar, she invites him to her apartment, exactly what meaning does this proposal have? One way or another, they will have to achieve some agreement about the purpose of the visit before joint action is possible. In symbolic interaction terms, they would need to develop a consensual definition of the situation. The coworkers might achieve this through explicit negotiation or through tacit, nonverbal communication. She might explain that she wants to show him her new guitar or to make him a cup of coffee before he drives home or kiss him to suggest she might be interested in something more romantic. But without some agreement regarding the definition of the situation, the man may have difficulty deciding whether to accept the invitation; the woman, sensing the man's discomfort, may find herself behaving in an atypically awkward manner. Either way, cooperative action will be difficult.

Symbolic interactionism portrays social interaction as having a tentative, developing quality. Meanings can change over time or across situations. On the way home from his first day of kindergarten, a young boy was describing a little girl from his class—Maeve—to his mother. It was clear the boy was fond of Maeve as he spoke of her big brown eyes, long straight hair, pink lips, and chubby cheeks. But when he proceeded to tell his mother that Maeve looked like a dog, his mother was taken aback. To her, calling a woman a dog was an insult. The reverence in her son's voice suggested he would never insult Maeve, so the mother was confused. Thinking more about it, the mother realized that to her son, calling Maeve a dog was a compliment rather than an insult. There was nothing the young boy loved more than to cuddle up with the family dog. To him, a dog was something to love and cherish. He had not yet learned that dog was an insult, but his mother knew he would in time. To fit their actions together and achieve consensus, people interacting with one another must continually negotiate new meanings or reaffirm old meanings. In the same way that the mother had to work to determine the boy's meaning to have interaction proceed smoothly, the coworkers will have to negotiate a working consensus to effectively

communicate and interact. In this process, each person formulates plans for action, tries them out, and then adjusts them in light of others' responses. Thus, social interaction always has some degree of unpredictability and indeterminacy.

For an interaction among persons to proceed smoothly, there must be some consensus with respect to the **situated identity**—who one is in relation to the others in the situation—of each person. In other words, every person involved in the interaction must know who they are in the situation and who the other people are. In the example of the coworkers: Are they friends, are they dating, or are they simply coworkers? Only by answering this question in some detail can each person understand the implications (meanings) that others have for their plan of action.

This comic strip illustrates the negotiation of meaning between Calvin and his imaginary friend, Hobbes. They each have different labels for the same physiological reactions. Through interaction, Calvin learns that he had mistaken for cooties a feeling that Hobbes explains to him is actually love. CALVIN AND HOBBES © 1986 Watterson. Used by permission of Universal Uclick. All rights reserved.

**The Self in Relationship to Others.** As we grow, we learn that the **self** is also a social object and its meaning is also developed and negotiated in interaction. As we interact with people, we try to imagine how they see us so we can come to understand not only how they see us, but also how we should see ourselves (Cooley, 1902). To do this, we engage in a process of **role taking**: we imagine ourselves from the other person's viewpoint. This serves two purposes. First, role taking makes cooperative action possible. Based on previous experience, we can imagine how another would react in any given situation. Consider a teenager whose mother has just asked him whether he completed his homework. Before answering, he will try to imagine the situation from his mother's perspective. If he tells her he played video games instead, she will be disappointed or even angry. If he lies and says it is all done, she will be satisfied—at least until she finds out the truth, and then she will be even angrier. By role taking, he can effectively guide subsequent interaction. However, there is a second important purpose of role taking. In imagining how he appears to his mother, the teenager is acquiring self-meanings. If he failed to do the homework, opting instead to play video games, he may see himself as lazy or unmotivated because that is how he imagines someone else (like his mother) would see him. If he lied about it, he might see himself as a liar. The self occupies a central place in symbolic interaction theory (see Box 1.2 for two theories of the self: role theory and identity theory). Individuals strive to maintain self-respect in their own eyes, but because they are continually engaging in role taking, they see themselves from the viewpoint of the others with whom they interact. To maintain self-respect, they must meet the standards of others, at least to some degree.

Of course, an individual will care about the opinions and standards of some persons more than those of others. The persons about whose opinions they care most are called **significant others**. Typically, these are people who control important rewards or who occupy central positions in groups to which the individual belongs. Because their positive opinions are highly valued, significant others have more influence over the individual's behavior than others might.

Inherent in the above discussion is symbolic interactionism's assertion that a person can act not only toward others but also toward oneself. That is, an individual can engage in self-perception, self-evaluation, and self-control just as they might perceive, evaluate, and control others. The ability to act toward oneself, taking the role of both subject and object, is a uniquely human trait. George Herbert Mead, a forefather of symbolic interactionism, referred to this ability as the **reflexive self** (1934).

In sum, the symbolic interactionist perspective has several strong points. It recognizes the importance of the self in social interaction. It stresses the central role of symbolic communication and language in personality and society and the socially constructed nature of meanings. It addresses the processes involved in achieving consensus and cooperation in interaction. It illuminates why people try to maintain a positive image of self and avoid embarrassment. Many of these topics are discussed in detail in later chapters. The self, self-presentation, and impression management are discussed in Chapters 4 and 5, embarrassment and other social emotions in Chapter 6, symbolic communication and language are taken up in Chapter 9, and Chapter 13 addresses the importance of labeling on self and others.

**Limitations of Symbolic Interaction Theory.** Critics of symbolic interactionism point to various shortcomings. One criticism concerns the model of the individual implicit in symbolic interaction theory. The individual is depicted as a specific personality type—an other-directed person who is concerned primarily with maintaining self-respect by meeting others' standards—but, in reality,

## BOX 1.2  Symbolic Interaction in Action: Roles and Identities

We do not infer who we are based solely on our actions—as the teenager might when he opts for video games instead of homework or lies to his mother; our definitions of self—as captured in roles and identities—also guide our actions. **Roles** consist of a set of rules (that is, expectations held by others), tied to social positions, that function as plans or blueprints for behavior. **Identities** are categories—sometimes based on roles, other times based on group membership or personal characteristics—that specify the positions we hold in society and groups. Both of these concepts are tied to contemporary social psychological theories rooted in symbolic interactionism.

According to **role theory** (Biddle, 1979, 1986; Heiss, 1981; Turner, 1990):

1.  People spend much of their lives participating as members of groups and organizations.
2.  Within these groups, people occupy distinct positions (fullback, advertising executive, police sergeant, and the like).
3.  Each of these positions entails a role, which is a set of functions performed by the person for the group. A person's role is defined by expectations (held by other group members) that specify how they should perform.
4.  Groups often formalize these expectations as norms, which are rules specifying how a person should behave, what rewards will result for performance, and what punishments will result for nonperformance.
5.  Individuals usually carry out their roles and perform in accordance with the prevailing norms. In other words, people are primarily conformists—they try to meet others' expectations.
6.  Group members check each individual's performance to determine whether it conforms to the group's norms. If an individual meets others' role expectations, they will receive rewards in some form (acceptance, approval, money, and so on). If they fail to perform as expected, however, group members may embarrass, punish, or even expel that individual from the group. The

anticipation that others will apply sanctions ensures performance as expected.

Role theory implies that if we have information about the role expectations for a specified position, we can then predict a significant portion of the behavior (as well as the beliefs and attitudes) of the person occupying that position. If we want to change a person's behavior, role theory argues that it is first necessary to change or redefine their role (Allen & Van de Vliert, 1982). As an example, if someone is interested in you romantically—taking on the role of suitor or admirer—and you are not interested in that person in that way, what might you do? If you decide to tell them how much you value them as a friend or what a great *friend* they are, you are attempting to cast them in a new role, hoping their behavior follows suit.

Identity theory (Burke & Stets, 2009; Stryker, 1980; Stryker & Burke, 2000) also emphasizes the importance of self-meanings in guiding behavior. However, identity theorists extend beyond role identities to include three additional types of self-designations—person, social, and group identities. Olevia might be a student (role identity), but she is also a sister (another role identity), moral (person identity), a member of the Black Student Association (a group identity), and a woman (social identity). All five of these influence her behavior. Although our identities are often consistent, sometimes they come in conflict. Identity theory understands that because individuals occupy more than one identity at a time, their influence on our behavior is not as clear-cut as role theory might suggest. Therefore, much of the research in identity theory works to predict which identity we will enact in a given situation. Identity theory postulates that we are more likely to enact identities that we see as central to who we are; this centrality or salience is based in part on how much we have invested in the identity, the quality and quantity of social ties that we have through that identity, our need for identity support, and the situational opportunities (Stryker & Serpe, 1994).

individuals' attunement and concern toward others varies. A second criticism of symbolic interactionism is that it places too much emphasis on consensus and cooperation and, therefore, neglects or downplays the importance of conflict. The perspective does recognize, however, that interacting people may fail to reach consensus despite their efforts to achieve it. The symbolic interactionist perspective is at its best when analyzing fluid, developing encounters with significant others; it is less useful when analyzing self-interested behavior or principled action.

## Group Processes

Social psychologists have long been interested in the ways individuals interact in groups. Throughout this text you will learn about ground-breaking social psychological experiments that explored the role of groups on individual behavior. Some of the most notable are the work of John Darley and Bibb Latané on helping in emergencies (Chapter 11) and Solomon Asch's research on majority influence in groups (Chapter 15). Like much of this early research, contemporary work on group processes tends to favor the experimental method over surveys or observational methods. Today's group processes researchers tend to draw on a number of theoretical perspectives and theories as they explore the foundations, perceptions, and implications of inequality in interaction.

The theoretical perspectives relevant to groups are described in detail in Chapters 15 and 16, but two of the main orienting frameworks—social exchange and status—are introduced below.

**Social Exchange.** Like with symbolic interaction, there are many who refer to the exchange perspective as a theory. However, that is technically incorrect. Social exchange is a framework, within which a number of middle-range theories are situated

(power-dependence theory, affect theory, reciprocity theory) (Cook, Cheshire, Rice, & Nakagawa, 2013). The **social exchange** perspective (Cook, 1987; Homans, 1974; Kelley & Thibaut, 1978) has a unique set of concepts and assumptions that connect the various theories subsumed under the framework. In social exchange there are (1) *actors* who exchange (2) *resources* using an (3) *exchange process* while situated in an (4) *exchange structure* (Molm, 2006). These resources can be tangible goods or behaviors (an individual might give money or a simple "thank you" in exchange for a cookie) and can be exchanged through different processes—a student might receive a cookie as a gift from a professor or they might purchase it in a negotiated transaction, by exchanging money for the cookie, at a bakery. These exchanges occur in relations between actors (students, professors, cashiers). According to this perspective, social relationships are primarily based on the exchanges of goods and services among persons.

The social exchange perspective assumes that individuals have freedom of choice and often face social situations in which they must choose among alternative actions. Any action provides some rewards and entails some costs. There are many kinds of socially mediated rewards—money, goods, services, prestige or status, approval by others, and the like. The theory posits that individuals are hedonistic—they try to maximize rewards and minimize costs. Consequently, they choose actions that produce good profits and avoid actions that produce poor profits. You may hold the door for someone just behind you, as it takes little time and could foster gratitude, but opt not to hold it open for someone more than a few steps away, as any benefit would not be enough to make up for the time it takes. This view might seem overly rational and calculated, but social exchange theory suggests that these choices are actually often unconscious and are the result of **conditioning**—learning as the result of positive or negative responses to behavior (Mazur, 1998; Skinner, 1953).

People will be more likely to perform a specific behavior if it is followed directly by the occurrence of something pleasurable or by the removal of something aversive; likewise, people will more likely refrain from performing a particular behavior if it is followed by the occurrence of something aversive or by the removal of something pleasant. This interplay between action and outcome reinforces or discourages exchange behavior. Individuals become embedded in ongoing exchange relationships—whether with friends, colleagues, business owners, or others—because they experience positive outcomes. They stop exchanging with particular others when the exchanges stop providing these positive reinforcements and there are alternative relations available that might provide comparable benefits.

Exchange theory also predicts the conditions under which people try to change or restructure their relationships. A central concept involved is **equity** (Adams, 1963). A state of equity exists in a relationship when participants feel that the rewards they receive are proportional to the costs they bear. For example, a chef may earn more money than a line cook and receive better benefits on the job. But the line cook may nevertheless feel the relationship is equitable because the chef bears more responsibility and has a higher level of education and training.

If, for some reason, a participant feels that the allocation of rewards and costs in a relationship is inequitable, the relationship is potentially unstable. People find inequity difficult to tolerate—they may feel cheated or exploited and become angry. Social exchange theory predicts that people will try to modify an inequitable relationship. Most likely, they will attempt to reallocate costs and rewards so that equity is established. However, they may also leave the relationship in search of one with a more equitable arrangement.

**Status.** Social psychologists are also interested in status differences. The chef has more than just a higher salary and better benefits compared to the line cook; they also have higher **status**—levels of esteem and perceived competence (Ridgeway, 2006). Sociological social psychology has explored how social differences in society—based on categories like gender, race, and education—become status differences. Why is it that men, across a range of domains, are held in greater esteem and thought to be more competent than women? Why is it that Whites are assumed, often unconsciously, to be more effective leaders and more skilled at any number of tasks than Blacks? Understanding the process through which status differences originate and are sustained in society and how they might decline (for example, how Irishness has lost its significance in the United States) offers important insight into inequality not only between groups but also within them (Ridgeway, 2011).

Social psychologists are interested in the emergence of status differences within groups. To illustrate, imagine you are assigned to work with a group of students from your social psychology class on a project. If you all were strangers but varied on status dimensions like gender, race, or year in school, how would that affect your behavior in groups? Over time, differences in contribution are likely to emerge. Some of the group members would talk more. Among those who contributed more, some have more influence. If they made suggestions, these ideas would be more likely to be accepted by the group. Group members would also be less likely to interrupt these members while speaking. Based on status research, these integral members are more likely to possess attributes that are high status (White, male, juniors and seniors). They are afforded more influence in groups because we tend to hold higher performance expectations of high-status individuals. We assume they will perform better on any number of tasks unless we have explicit information that suggests otherwise or the task was explicitly seen as a domain of a lower-status group. For example, if we knew that Rich—the senior, White man in our group—was flunking social psychology, we would have lower expectations of his competence on the group task. Likewise, if the class was apparel and textiles rather than social psychology and the group task was related to sewing, the group would draw on the cultural belief that women would perform better on such tasks and defer to Monica.

In sum, the group processes tradition focuses on a number of interesting topics that are integral aspects of social life. Both social exchange and status, for example, are ubiquitous in our daily interactions, and the usefulness of theorizing on these processes is clear. The tradition recognizes the importance of the groups and relationships in shaping individuals' experiences. It explores processes both within and between groups. It also addresses inequality, a core sociological concern. Many topics of interest to this tradition are discussed in detail in later chapters. The role of groups in socialization processes is covered in Chapter 3, and the importance of social categories as shaping individual experiences is discussed in Chapter 7. Processes within and between groups, including group conflict and cohesion, are discussed in Chapters 15 and 16.

**Limitations of Group Processes.** The main criticism of the group processes tradition and related theories is that they are based, in large part, on research that was conducted in laboratories, with North American college students as participants. There are concerns that any results from WEIRD—Western, Educated, and from Industrialized, Rich, Democratic countries—research participants are not generalizable to people from other social groups or cultures (Henrich, Heine, & Norenzayan, 2010) and that the way people behave in the artificial situations presented in the laboratory

are not indicative of how individuals would respond in everyday situations. This is especially true for a perspective oriented toward understanding inequality. Although these concerns are certainly important to keep in mind, as you will see in this book, the theories tested and developed in the laboratory are often based on "real world" events. Furthermore, a growing number of social psychologists are incorporating non-laboratory-based methods to diversify their research participants and settings (Correll, Benard, & Paik, 2007; Price & Collett, 2012; Zhu, 2013). Chapter 2 discusses the value of various research methods in social psychology.

## Social Structure and Personality

The third tradition in social psychology argues that we are each situated in unique positions in the social structure (Schnittker, 2013). For example, Professor Collett is a married White woman with a son who is applying to college. She grew up outside of Seattle, graduating high school in the early 1990s. Neither of her parents graduated college. They opened a small restaurant when Professor Collett was in elementary school, and she spent a lot of time hanging out—and later working—in the family business. Social psychologists who adopt a social structure and personality approach believe these attributes and experiences situate Professor Collett in a particular position in the social structure and influence her personality—her attitudes, values, and goals, among other things.

You might assume, for example, that Professor Collett values education, because she teaches college. You might also see how this value is instrumental in encouraging her son to pursue a college degree. You might think that as a woman she prefers HGTV to ESPN or that she is more nurturing than aggressive. Because she is from the Seattle area, you may think she is liberal or likes coffee or the rain. As a product of the early 1990s, you could imagine she is more fond of Nirvana or Pearl Jam than Macklemore. Would you be surprised if you heard that she did not apply to college as a high school student, or can you imagine that her parents' education level and exposure to a family business might have influenced her orientation toward college and work as a young person? Although social psychologists are interested in describing general trends rather than a particular individual's personality, sociological social psychologists who work in this tradition are exploring the effect of gender, marital and parental status, race, education and occupation, age, and other attributes on people's lives.

The seminal work in social structure and personality (SSP) was conducted by Melvin Kohn and Carmi Schooler (Kohn, 1969; Kohn & Schooler, 1973). Described in more detail in Chapters 3 and 17, this research found important social class differences in child rearing—with middle- and upper-class parents valuing self-direction and curiosity over conformity, for example. Think back to the definition of social psychology on p. 3. Rather than to simply note the connection, Kohn and Schooler sought out the cause of the patterns. They noted that working-class parents were more likely to be employed in manufacturing jobs that rewarded conformity while middle- and upper-class parents were more likely to be employed in sectors and positions that rewarded self-direction, creativity, and curiosity. Kohn and Schooler argued that rewards at work reinforced these values in the parents, and through their child-rearing styles at home, the parents subsequently passed these values on to their children. These values likely influenced their children's work orientations as well, which would ultimately affect the types of work they would be drawn to and recreate the connection between class, work, values, and parenting for the next generation (Kohn & Schooler, 1982).

As noted above, social class is only one of many aspects of social structure of interest to social psychologists. Additionally, personality—as conceived by those who work in this tradition—extends beyond values and beliefs to behavior and both physical and mental health. Many of these topics are covered in the chapters to follow. Chapter 3 discusses socialization as the process through which we come to acquire values. Chapters 7 and 8 describe how our positions in social structure can influence the way we perceive events and the attitudes we hold. The connection between social structure and both prosocial (altruism and helping) and antisocial (aggression) behavior is covered in Chapters 11 and 12. Finally, Chapter 17 takes the social structure and personality approach as its focus, introducing a wide array of research in the tradition.

**Limitations of Social Structure and Personality.** Although some assert that the social structure and personality tradition is the most sociological of the social psychological approaches because of its consideration of macrosociological structures (Kohn, 1989), SSP does have its critics. The main criticism launched is that much of the research only describes a relationship—attractive people are happier than unattractive people, married people live longer than single people, groups with members who are similar tend to be more cohesive—and falls short of providing a mechanism like Kohn and Schooler did, an explanation of why one thing leads to another. As you will see as you progress through this book, however, this is a somewhat unfair criticism. There are a number of causal mechanisms suggested throughout social psychology. However, the SSP tradition's reliance on survey methods makes causal inferences difficult. The social structure and personality approach is also criticized because it fails to account for individuals who deviate from trends and averages. Not everyone from Seattle is liberal and plenty of women prefer sports to home decorating.

## Cognitive Perspectives

For social psychologists, the basic premise of **cognitive theory** is that the mental activities of the individual are important determinants of social behavior (Operario & Fiske, 1999). These mental activities, called **cognitive processes**, include perception, memory, judgment, problem solving, and decision making. Cognitive theory does not deny the importance of external stimuli, but emphasizes that the link between stimulus and response is not direct; rather, the individual's cognitive processes intervene between external stimuli and behavioral responses. You do not scream at the sight of a snake simply because it is a snake. You do so because your mind interprets the snake as dangerous and screaming is a response to danger or fear. In other words, individuals not only actively interpret the meaning of stimuli but also select the actions to be made in response, even when they may not realize it.

Historically, the cognitive approach to social psychology has been influenced by the ideas of Koffka, Kohler, and other theorists in the Gestalt movement of psychology. Central to Gestalt psychology is the principle that people respond to configurations of stimuli rather than to a single, discrete stimulus. In other words, people understand the meaning of a stimulus only by viewing it in the context of an entire system of elements (the gestalt) in which it is embedded. A chess master, for example, would not assess the importance of a chess piece on the board without considering its location and strategic capabilities vis-à-vis all the other pieces currently on the board. To comprehend the meaning of any element, we must look at the whole of which it is a part.

Cognitive theorists depict humans as active in selecting and interpreting stimuli (Fiske & Taylor, 1991; Moskowitz, Skurnik, & Galinsky, 1999). According to this view, people do more than react to their environment; they actively structure their world cognitively. However, social psychologists also realize that humans are cognitive misers. Because individuals cannot possibly attend to all the complex stimuli that surround them, they select only those stimuli that are important or useful to them and ignore the others. They also actively control which categories or concepts they use to interpret the stimuli in the environment. There are a wide range of cognitive tactics available for people to draw from, and individuals choose the approach they take (Operario & Fiske, 1999). Humans are "motivated tacticians" (Fiske & Taylor, 1991). This means, of course, that various individuals can form dramatically different impressions of the same complex stimulus in the environment.

Consider, for example, what happens when several people view a vacant house displaying a bright "for rent" sign. When a building contractor passes the house, they pay primary attention to the quality of the house's construction. They see lumber, bricks, shingles, glass, and some repairs that need to be made. Another person, a potential renter, sees the house very differently. They note that it is located close to their job and wonder whether the neighborhood is safe and whether the house is expensive to heat in winter. The property manager trying to find a renter for the house construes it in still different terms—cash flow, occupancy rate, depreciation, mortgage, and amortization. One of the young children living in the neighborhood has yet another view; observing that no person has lived in the house for several months, they are convinced the house is haunted.

**Cognitive Structure and Schemas.** Central to the cognitive perspective is the concept of **cognitive structure**, which refers broadly to any form of organization among cognitions (concepts and beliefs). Because a person's cognitions are interrelated, cognitive theory gives special emphasis to exactly how they are structured and organized in memory and how they affect a person's judgments.

Social psychologists have proposed that individuals use specific cognitive structures called *schemas* to make sense of complex information about other persons, groups, and situations. The term **schema** is derived from the Greek word for "form," and it refers to the form or basic sketch of what we know about people and things. For example, our schema for "law student" might be a set of traits thought to be characteristic of such persons: intelligent, analytic and logical, argumentative (perhaps even combative), and thorough with an eagle eye for details, strategically skillful in interpersonal relations, and (occasionally) committed to seeing justice done. This schema, no doubt, reflects our own experience with lawyers and law students as well as our conception of which traits are necessary for success in the legal profession. That we hold this schema does not mean we believe that everyone with this set of characteristics

is a law student or that every law student will have all of these characteristics. We might be surprised, however, if we met someone who impressed us as unmethodical, illogical, withdrawn, inarticulate, inattentive, sloppy, and not very intelligent and then later discovered they were a law student.

Schemas are important in social relations because they help us interpret the environment efficiently. Whenever we encounter a person for the first time, we usually form an impression of what they are like. In doing this, we not only observe the person's behavior but also rely on our knowledge of similar persons we have met in the past; that is, we use our schema regarding this type of person. Schemas help us process information by enabling us to recognize which personal characteristics are important in the interaction and which are not. They structure and organize information about the person, and they help

We have schemas about older women and schemas of rock bands, with very little overlap. When we encounter individuals, images, or situations that do not match schemas we have, like in this photo, we take notice. We may be confused, but can also find such enigmas humorous, like this Granny Rock Band. © Alija/iStock

us remember information better and process it more quickly. Sometimes they fill gaps in knowledge and enable us to make inferences and judgments about others.

To illustrate further, consider a law school admissions officer who faces the task of deciding which candidates to admit as students. Because it would take too long to attend to every piece of information they have on each candidate, they process applications drawing on a schema for "strong law student candidate" that is based on traits believed to predict success in law school and beyond. The admissions officer pays close attention to information regarding candidates that is relevant to their schema for law students, and they likely ignore or downplay other information. LSAT scores do matter, whereas eye color does not; undergraduate GPA does matter, whereas ability to throw a football does not; and so on.

Schemas are rarely perfect as predictive devices, and the admissions officer probably will make mistakes, admitting some candidates who fail to complete law school and turning down some candidates who would have succeeded. Moreover, another admissions officer with a different schema might admit a different set of students to law school. Schemas also figure centrally in our stereotypes and discriminatory attitudes. If, for example, an admissions officer includes only the race "White" in their schema for successful law students, they will be less likely to admit African Americans. Despite their drawbacks, schemas are more efficient ways to process social information than having no systematic framework at all. Thus, they persist as important cognitive mechanisms even when less than perfect. Schemas will be discussed in more detail in Chapter 7.

**Dual-Process Theory of Information Processing.** Much of the recent work in psychological social psychology incorporates dual-process models. Like the approaches outlined earlier, the dual-process theory is a theoretical perspective that subsumes a number of specific theories. Theories associated with this theoretical perspective are all based on the notion that we process information two (hence the use of dual) ways—automatically and deliberately—and this influences perception, impression formation, and attributions (Chapter 7), attitudes (Chapter 8), persuasion (Chapter 10), attraction (Chapter 14), and stereotyping (Chapters 7 and 15), among other social psychological processes.

The automatic process of perception occurs so quickly that individuals fail to even notice it. This automaticity relies on the use of **heuristics**—cognitive shortcuts using readily accessible information based on experience—that aid in information processing. Schemas, as outlined above, are a good example. Individuals have learned, over time, the content of a variety of schemas. We have ideas about women and men, law students and grandmothers, Blacks and Whites. When we encounter someone new, we use heuristics to classify them into a category using salient physical features, behaviors, or labels provided to us through means of an introduction or setting. Once classified, heuristics also help us determine what to expect from them and how to treat them—without giving any conscious thought to the categorization or these expectations. These processes are automatic and require little effort.

However, if we decide to keep processing, a more conscious and deliberate process occurs. This high-effort systematic processing as it relates to forming impressions of people we encounter is shown in Figure 1.2. This process takes place if the person is of even minimal relevance to us. If you are walking down the street late at night, for example, you want to know whether you can trust the person who is walking toward you. Are they a threat? Are they benevolent? Additional processing takes place because you are seeking out a more accurate judgment than what is provided through unconscious processing alone. It can also occur because the information presented to us is so inconsistent with our heuristics (grandmothers do not fit our schema for band members like those in the photo on p. 18; the person walking toward us is a Black man whistling a concerto by Vivaldi [Steele, 2010]). Based on this dual-processing view, we are not doomed to be cognitive misers who act on autopilot throughout our lives. We are capable of more elaborate processing, but we must have reason to set that high-effort processing in motion (Moskowitz, Skurnik, & Galinsky, 1999).

**Social Identity Theory.** Social identity theory grew out of a concern that psychology had become too reductionist and was only concerned with individuals. This perspective argues that while we sometimes think, feel, and act as individuals, most of our behavior stems from the social groups that we belong to (Operario & Fiske, 1999). **Social identity theory** argues that individuals' identification with societal structures—groups, organizations, cultures—guides cognitive processes (Markus, Kitayama, & Heiman, 1996). Identification is central here. If someone does not identify with a group, it is not psychologically real (Hogg, 2006). If someone does identify with a group—as Rachel Dolezal did when she viewed herself as Black—that social identity is likely more important for the individual than how they may be classified by others. This is why social identity theory is a cognitive theory. Self-categorization—a cognitive process—is instrumental in social identity processes (Turner, 1987).

We categorize ourselves and others into groups using a type of schema called a prototype. We decide that we are a member of a group because we fit a schema of typical group members. This categorization affects our self-concept, of course, but it also influences our perceptions of others. We view ourselves and those who we classify as fellow group members more positively. Because of this, we feel a sense of camaraderie and cohesion with our social groups. However, the same processes lead us to feel distinct from those who are not in our social group, and the cognitive shortcuts we take in classification tend to exaggerate the differences between us and them.

Social identity processes appear throughout the text. Chapter 4 describes the importance of social identities in self-concepts. Chapter 7 covers prototypes and stereotypes. Chapter 15 discusses both inter- and intragroup dynamics like cohesion and conformity, ethnocentrism, and discrimination.

In sum, cognitive theory is an incredibly active area in psychological social psychology, and it continues to produce many insights and striking predictions regarding individual and social behavior. It is among the more popular and productive approaches in social psychology.

**Limitations of Cognitive Perspectives.** One drawback of cognitive theories is that they simplify—and sometimes oversimplify—the way in which people process information, an inherently complex phenomenon. Another drawback is that cognitive phenomena are not directly observable; they must be inferred from what people say and do. This means that compelling and definitive tests of theoretical predictions from cognitive theory are sometimes difficult to conduct. However, methodological advances—including the ability to subliminally prime subjects, to measure millisecond reaction times, and to use fMRI scans and readings from EEGs—are making such research increasingly possible (Operario & Fiske, 1999).

## Evolutionary Theory

The final theoretical perspective introduced in this chapter is evolutionary theory. Although it is not one of the main perspectives in contemporary social psychology, it is found throughout the topics in this book and, therefore, is still an important perspective to understand

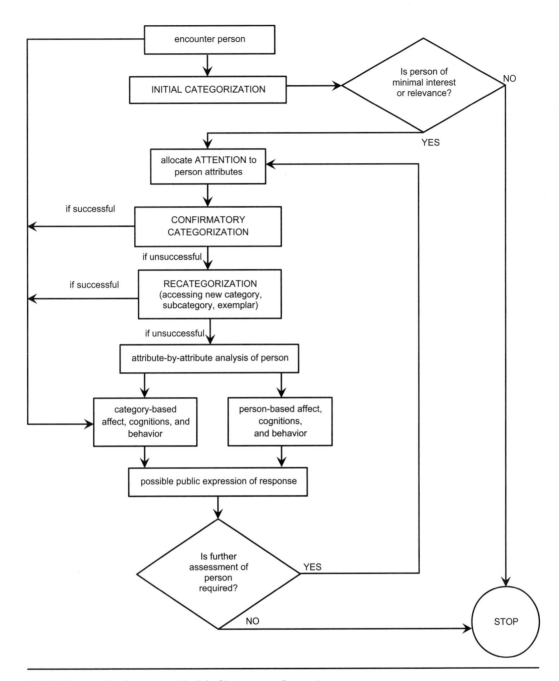

**FIGURE 1.2** The Continuum Model of Impression Formation

This model illustrates the dual processes at work when we form impressions of people we encounter. The initial categorization is low effort and occurs immediately upon perception of the person. If the person we encounter is relevant to us, this sets in motion a high-effort process in which we allocate additional attention to the person to try to confirm our original categorization or to recategorize the person. These categorizations guide our responses (affect, cognition, and behavior) to the person. However, if we are unable to categorize (or recategorize) the person we encounter, we will conduct an attribute-by-attribute analysis of the person to determine how to respond to them and whether additional attention is needed.

*Source:* Adapted from Figure 11.1 in Fiske, Lin, & Neuberg (1999), *The Continuum Model: Ten Years Later.*

moving forward. When we think of Charles Darwin and evolution, we most often think of the development of physical characteristics. How, for example, did humans develop binocular vision or the ability to walk upright? How did some animals develop an acute sense of smell, whereas others depend for survival on their ability to see at low levels of light? Evolutionary psychologists—and sociobiologists—do not stop with strictly physical characteristics, however. They extend evolutionary ideas to explain a great deal of social behavior, including altruism, aggression, mate selection, sexual behavior, and even such seemingly arcane topics as why presidents of the United States are taller than the average man (Buss & Kenrick, 1998).

**Evolutionary Foundations of Behavior. Evolutionary psychology** locates the roots of social behavior in our genes and, therefore, intimately links the psychological and social to the biological (Buss, 1999; Symons, 1992; Wilson, 1975). In effect, social behavior, or the predisposition toward certain behaviors, is encoded in our genetic material and is passed on through reproduction. In physical evolution, those characteristics that enable the individual to survive and pass on their genetic code are ones that will eventually occur more frequently in the population. For instance, animals whose camouflage coloring allows them to escape predators will be more likely to survive and produce offspring—who will then receive the advantageous coloring from their parents. Animals of the same species whose camouflage coloring is less efficient will be more likely to be caught and killed before they can reproduce. Thus, over time, the camouflaged animals increase in number relative to the others, who will fade from the population over the generations.

The same process, argue evolutionary psychologists, occurs with respect to social behaviors. Predispositions for certain behaviors are coded in genes, and these preprogrammed

mental modules affect the behavior of our genetically similar offspring (Donald, 1991). Consider one area of research that has received a great deal of attention by evolutionary psychologists: mate selection. Psychologists have observed that men strongly value physical attractiveness and youthful appearance in a potential mate, whereas women focus more on the mate's ability to provide resources for herself and their offspring (Buss, 1994). Why does this difference occur? From an evolutionary perspective, it must be that the different strategies differentially enable men and women to produce successful offspring. The source of the difference lies in the span of fertility—men can continue to reproduce nearly their entire lives, whereas women have a much more constricted period in which they can have children. Therefore, men who prefer to mate with women past their childbearing years will not produce offspring. Over time, then, a genetic preference for older women will be eliminated from the population because these men will not reproduce. Men who prefer younger women will reproduce at a much higher rate, and thus this social behavior will dominate men's approach to mating.

Conversely, women are less concerned with a mate's age because even much older men can produce offspring. Women's concerns about successful reproduction are focused on the resources necessary for a successful pregnancy and for ensuring the proper development of the child. This is particularly true in developed countries, where success and longevity are the result of more than good genes (Mace, 2014). According to Buss and Kenrick (1998), women select mates who have the resources and willingness to assist during the pregnancy and after. Women who do not prefer such men or do not have the ability to identify them will be less likely to have successful pregnancies and child-rearing experiences. Therefore, women's preference for resource-providing men will eventually dominate in the population.

## BOX 1.3 Research Update: The Differential Susceptibility Hypothesis

You have likely heard of the nature versus nurture debate—the discussion over whether we are the way we are because of our biology and physiology (nature) or our environment and experiences (nurture). As you will see in this book, many social psychologists would contend that it is both— that we act according to meanings that we have acquired through social interaction, and within the constraints of our environment, but that we are able to do so because of our physiological development and mental capacities.

Researchers today are considering a particularly interesting combination of the two. According to the **differential susceptibility hypothesis**, our genes make some of us more susceptible to our environmental conditions than others (Belsky, Bakermans-Kranenburg, & van IJzendoorn, 2007). In other words, some of us are genetically predisposed to be more susceptible to social influence than others of us are.

It is important to note that it is not particular genes. It is not as if there is a gene that some people have and others don't that is related to susceptibility. Instead, it is specific variants of genes—also called alleles—that we all have, that affect the predisposition to influence. Everyone has both dopamine receptor genes (DRD4) and serotonin transporter genes (5HTT) inherited from their mothers and fathers. For some people, one or more of these genes are short. For others, they may be long. Particular variants have been tied to outcomes of interest to social psychologists. For example, exposure to

racial discrimination appears most likely to lead to later adolescent behavioral problems among young men with the short 5HTT allele (Brody et al., 2006).

Looking at a group of children who had been abused by their parents or caregivers, researchers found that young adults with long DRD4 genes or short 5HTT genes were more aggressive than others who had also been abused but who had short DRD4 or long 5HTT genes (Belsky et al., 2007). This is where the differential hypothesis emerged. Rather than link those variants to aggression, the researchers posited that some abuse survivors were more aggressive because they were more susceptible to the adverse conditions they were raised in. If this hypothesis was true, children with those same alleles raised in positive environments would be even less likely to be aggressive than those without the variants who were raised in positive environments.

Tests of this hypothesis showed that the results were just as the researchers imagined. In other words, young people who seem most responsive to adversity are also the ones who would benefit most from interventions, whether in educational settings, counseling, or strategies to improve family life. Individuals with genetic variants that had originally been categorized as problematic actually hold tremendous promise, as they may be more likely than many of their peers to flourish in positive environments.

Adapted from Simons et al., 2011.

---

Using this basic notion of evolutionary selection, evolutionary psychologists have developed explanations for an extremely wide variety of social behaviors. For example, altruistic or prosocial behaviors initially seem to provide a paradox for evolutionary theory. Why would an individual reduce their chances of survival and reproduction

by helping others? One answer, as demonstrated in a number of studies, is that individuals are most likely to assist those to whom they are genetically related (Dawkins, 1982). Because individuals share genetic material with those they assist, they help pass on their own genetic code even if they do not do it directly or their own chances of survival are compromised by doing so (Meyer, 2000).

Evolution also helps to explain parenting practices. For example, men tend to be somewhat less invested in parenting than women because they invest less in producing offspring—a single sexual act versus nine months of gestation and giving birth. Adults are also more likely to abuse their stepchildren than their biological children (Daly & Wilson, 1998). Again, evolutionary psychologists would argue that this difference can be traced to the fact that parents share genetic material with their biological children but not with their stepchildren (Piliavin & LePore, 1995). These and many other topics will be examined using evolutionary ideas throughout the book, particularly in Chapters 3 (Socialization Through the Life Course), 7 (Social Perception and Cognition), 11 (Altruism and Prosocial Behavior), 12 (Aggression), and 14 (Interpersonal Attraction and Relationships).

**Limitations of Evolutionary Theory.** Although the perspective continues to guide some social psychological work, the evolutionary perspective never eclipsed other theoretical approaches to social psychology and has been subject to a fair amount of criticism (Caporeal, 2001; Rose & Rose, 2000). The most persistent critique accuses evolutionary psychologists of circular reasoning (Kenrick, 1995). Typically, the evolutionary psychologist observes some characteristic of the social world and then constructs an explanation for it based on its supposed contribution to genetic fitness. The logic of the argument then becomes: Why does this behavior occur? Because it improves the odds of passing on one's genes. But how do we know it improves those odds? Because it occurs. This logical trap is, in some sense, unavoidable because we cannot travel back in time to observe the actual evolution of social behavior.

Mothers tend to be more invested in parenting and nurturing children than fathers because they invest more in producing offspring (nine months of gestation, giving birth, and potentially nursing the newborn versus men's single sexual act). © yulkapopkova/iStock

The problem appears most clearly when we consider the possibility of alternative outcomes. For example, we may observe that men are more accepting of casual sex than women. The evolutionary explanation for this difference between men and women is that men can maximize the survival of their genetic material by spreading it as widely as possible. Women, however, need to know who the father of their children is and extract support from him to ensure the successful transmission of their own genes. Suppose, however, that women were actually more accepting of casual sex than men. This could also easily be explained by the evolutionary perspective. A man cannot be certain that a child is his, so a strong commitment to a monogamous relationship would help ensure that it is actually his genes that are being passed to a child. Women, however, are always 100 percent sure whether their own genes are passed down to their children, so in terms of genetic fitness, it should not matter to them who is the father. Because these after-the-fact explanations are always easy to construct and difficult to prove, it can be very difficult to judge them against competing arguments. Therefore, although the evolutionary perspective has a number of supporters, it still has major obstacles to overcome before achieving widespread acceptance as a useful explanation for social behavior. At the same time, accounts that downplay evolution and instead emphasize genes and their interaction with environment in explaining behavior (see Box 1.3) are beginning to increase (Freese & Shostak, 2009).

## Five Complementary Perspectives

The five theoretical perspectives discussed here—symbolic interaction, group processes, social structure and personality, cognitive perspectives, and evolutionary theory—differ with respect to the issues they address, the concepts they draw on, and the behavior they attend to (see Table 1.1). The first three begin with society and consider how social forces influence the individual, favoring external—structural and interactional—processes. The latter two perspectives, however, tend to privilege internal (cognitive or physiological) processes because they start with the individual (Stryker, 2001). However, these perspectives should be seen as complementary rather than

**TABLE 1.1** Comparison of Theoretical Perspectives in Social Psychology

| DIMENSION | SYMBOLIC INTERACTION | GROUP PROCESSES | SOCIAL STRUCTURE AND PERSONALITY | COGNITIVE THEORIES | EVOLUTIONARY THEORY |
|---|---|---|---|---|---|
| Central Concepts | Meaning, interaction, self, role, identity | Relation, exchange, status, equity, justice, context | Position, personality | Cognitions, cognitive structure, heuristics, dual-process | Genes, biology, fitness |
| Primary Behavior Explained | Behavior, interaction as a sequence of acts establishing and based on meanings | Power, status, inequality, exchange processes | Values, beliefs, achievement, health, life outcomes | Formation and changes of beliefs and attitudes, effects cognitive processes | Reproduction, investment, survival |
| Assumptions about Human Nature | Humans act according to meanings; use role taking to guide action and self-perception | Reinforcement produces patterns; interaction produces and reinforces inequality | Our social location influences important life outcomes in patterned ways | People are cognitive beings who act on the basis of their cognitions | People seek to perpetuate their own genes; the fittest survive |

competing. For example, cognitive theories stress the importance of schemas and cognitive structure in determining judgments and behavior but connect with symbolic interaction in arguing that the contents of these schemas and cognitive structures are learned in social interaction and with social structure and personality in that these schemas and cognitive structures are based on positions and roles individuals hold in social structures.

Because of the overlap, in the chapters that follow, insight from these perspectives is most often presented without explicit mention of the guiding theoretical perspective. Social psychology is a collective enterprise, with sociologists and psychologists routinely drawing on each other's work (Thoits, 1995). This textbook is unique in the way it bridges these two disciplines—giving voice to both sociological social psychology and the more psychological approaches—and presents social psychology to a new generation of students as a collective enterprise with much of interest to people regardless of their disciplinary orientation.

This chapter considered the fundamental characteristics of social psychology and important theoretical perspectives in the field.

**What Is Social Psychology?** There are several ways to characterize social psychology. (1) By definition, social psychology is the systematic study of the nature and causes of human social behavior. When thinking about behavior, social psychologists are not only interested in what people do but also what they feel and think. (2) Social psychology has several core concerns, including the impact of one individual on another individual's behavior and beliefs, the impact of a group on a member's behavior and beliefs, the impact of a member on the group's activities and

structure, the impact of one group on another group's activities and structure, and the impact of social context on individuals and groups. (3) Social psychology has a close relationship with other social sciences, especially sociology and psychology. Although they emphasize different issues and often use different research methods, both psychologists and sociologists have contributed significantly to social psychology, and it can be an interdisciplinary enterprise.

**Theoretical Perspectives in Social Psychology.** A theoretical perspective is a broad theory based on particular assumptions about human nature that offers explanations for a wide range of social behaviors. This chapter discussed five theoretical perspectives: symbolic interaction, group processes, social structure and personality, cognitive perspectives, and evolutionary theory. (1) Symbolic interaction theory holds that human nature and social order are products of communication among people. It stresses the importance of the self, of role taking, and of consensus in social interaction. It is most useful in explaining fluid, contingent encounters among people. (2) The group processes perspective focuses its attention on interaction in social groups or networks. It mainly draws on experimental research to demonstrate how the structure of groups influences individual behavior and experiences within groups. (3) Social structure and personality argues that individuals' positions in the social structure influence their thoughts, feelings, and behaviors. Some argue that it is the most sociological of the approaches because it considers how macrosociological structures influence individuals. (4) Cognitive theories hold that such processes as perception, memory, and judgment are significant determinants of social behavior. Differences in cognitions, including the use of low-effort or high-effort cognitive processing, help to illuminate why individuals may behave differently from one another in any given situation. (5) Evolutionary theory posits that social behavior is a product of long-term evolutionary adaptation. Behavioral tendencies exist in human beings because these behaviors aided our ancestors in their attempts to survive and reproduce.

### Critical Thinking Skill:
### An Introduction to Critical Thinking

A variety of stakeholders, including employers and graduate and professional program faculty and administrators, are interested in college graduates with well-developed critical thinking skills. To help students develop these skills, this chapter and all that follow will include sections labeled Critical Thinking Skill. These exercises will not only improve your critical thinking skills as applied to social psychology but will also give you the tools to engage critical thinking in other classes and in other areas of your life.

According to Diane Halpern, an expert in critical thinking:

> Critical thinking is the use of those cognitive skills and strategies that increase the probability of a desirable outcome. It is purposeful, reasoned, and goal directed. It is the kind of thinking involved in solving problems, formulating inferences, calculating likelihoods, and making decisions. Critical thinking also involves evaluating the thinking process—the reasoning that went into the conclusions we have arrived at or the kinds of factors considered in making a decision. (Halpern, 2002, p. 93)

Critical thinking is logical and fact based. Critical thinkers work to overcome bias and avoid self-deception. Most importantly, critical thinking is a skill set that we can acquire and can use throughout our lives. Once we acquire the ability, we can think critically in a range of situations to make better decisions and experience positive outcomes (Halpern, 1998).

Each Critical Thinking Skill exercise will engage a particular critical thinking skill as applied to social psychology. However, you will find that these skills will have applications throughout your life and that becoming a critical thinker will have benefits far beyond this course.

**Understand Diverse Causal Forces.** Most of us pay little attention to our everyday behaviors, feelings, and thoughts. Consider a trip to the movies. In American culture, we tend to sit quietly in a theater, laugh during comedies and cry during dramas, and think popcorn, candy, and soda are appropriate movie-viewing foods. We like to believe that we choose all of these actions freely, but do we?

As the theoretical perspectives covered in this chapter suggest, very little of what we do in our everyday life is based on individual actors making truly unique decisions. One of the best ways to see the social nature of our psychology—to learn social psychology—is to begin to question the motivation behind actions we often take for granted, "to recognize the social significance in mundane behaviors" (Fine, 1995, p. 6). Being attuned to the sources of our thoughts, feelings, and behavior is also important to critical thinking because understanding ourselves helps us understand our biases and reasoning.

Let's begin by thinking about a mundane behavior we all engage in: eating. I would bet that you gave little thought to what you ate for breakfast today (or if you decided to eat breakfast at all). However, the choice was actually socially significant. According to Gary Alan Fine, there are four dimensions at play in human action: body, mind, others, and culture.

I will use myself as an example. Today I had a cup of coffee and a bowl of cereal with milk for breakfast. I ate because my *body* signaled it was hungry, with a growling in my stomach. My *mind* interpreted this growling as a sign that I should eat. I learned to interpret sensations like the growling stomach in interaction with *others*. My mother always told me to eat breakfast, and she and others taught me, whether explicitly or implicitly, what an appropriate breakfast is and that the caffeine in coffee would wake me up. In this way, others influenced the way my mind processes information by teaching me to categorize foods as appropriate or inappropriate for breakfast. *Culture* also influences what we see as breakfast foods. Even though I know that soup would satiate my hunger, I was less likely to choose it or to crave it because of my cultural background. Whereas someone from an Asian culture might eat soup for breakfast, Americans traditionally do not. Cultural beliefs also shift over time. My grandparents would never have eaten cold cereal for breakfast. They would have eaten their cereal piping hot.

By stopping to think not only about why I ate breakfast (although that, too, is worth considering similarly) but also about why I chose what I did for breakfast, I can see how little physiological processes, innate cognition, or my own unique thoughts and desires had to do with my action. Instead, I recognize the social influences in shaping what I think, feel, and do. What did you eat for breakfast? How did these four dimensions or a subset of them influence that action? Similarly, what did you decide to wear today? Where are you reading this chapter? Are you doing anything else while studying? What other mundane behaviors can you see as socially significant by using this same framework?

When we stop to evaluate the sources of our mundane behaviors, we are not only recognizing the importance of social psychological processes and interaction; we are also training ourselves to evaluate all actions—whether mundane or not—to better interpret and understand them and those who engage in them.

# RESEARCH METHODS IN
# SOCIAL PSYCHOLOGY

## LEARNING OBJECTIVES

By the end of this chapter you will be able to:

- Explain the four objectives of social psychological research and the nature of research hypotheses.

- Describe steps researchers take to increase the validity of their findings.

- Describe the defining characteristics of quantitative research methods such as surveys and experiments, and qualitative methods such as observation and archival research, and be able to compare them.

- Explain the issues that are raised when we undertake research on diverse groups within U.S. society or with members of other cultures.

- Understand the ethical issues that are important in the conduct of social psychological research, and describe the safeguards available to protect the rights of participants.

## INTRODUCTION

Social psychology relies on empirical research, which is the systematic investigation of observable phenomena (behavior, events) in the world. Researchers try to collect information about behavior and events in an accurate and unbiased form. This information, which may be either quantitative or qualitative, enables social psychologists to describe reality in detail and to develop theories about social behavior.

When conducting empirical research, investigators usually employ a **methodology**, which is a set of systematic procedures that guide the collection and analysis of data. In a typical study, investigators begin with a question or hypothesis amenable to investigation. Next they develop a research design. Then, they go into a research setting and collect the data. Next, they code and analyze the data

to test hypotheses and arrive at various conclusions about the behaviors or events under investigation. Throughout this process, investigators follow specific procedures to ensure the validity of the findings.

When investigators report their research to the wider community of social psychologists, they describe not only the results but also the methodology used to obtain the results. By reporting their methods, they make it possible for other investigators to independently verify their findings.

Independent verification of research findings is one of the hallmarks of any science. Suppose, for instance, that an investigator were to report some unanticipated empirical findings that ran contrary to established theory. Other investigators might wish to replicate the study to see whether they can obtain the same findings in other settings with different participants. Through this process, investigators with differing perspectives can identify and eliminate biases in the original study. If the results are replicable, they are more likely to be accepted by other social psychologists as reliable, general findings.

In this chapter, we will discuss the research methods used in contemporary social psychology. This discussion will provide a foundation for understanding and evaluating the empirical studies discussed throughout this book.

## CHARACTERISTICS OF EMPIRICAL RESEARCH

There are several issues common to all forms of empirical research. Specifically, we will consider the objectives that typically underlie empirical research, the nature of the hypotheses that guide research, and the factors that affect the validity of research findings.

### Objectives of Research

Investigators conduct social psychological studies for a variety of reasons. Their objectives usually include one or more of the following:

describing reality, identifying correlations between variables, testing causal hypotheses, and developing and testing theories.

In some studies, the central objective is simply to describe reality in accurate and precise terms. An investigator may wish to describe the features of a social process. Description is often the paramount goal when a researcher investigates a phenomenon about which little or nothing is known. Even when investigating more familiar phenomena, a researcher may wish to ascertain the frequency with which a particular attitude or behavior occurs in a specified group or population. For instance, during election years, researchers routinely conduct public opinion polls to learn how Americans feel about political candidates, issues, and parties. Their goal is to describe public sentiment with great accuracy and precision.

A second objective of research is to ascertain whether a correlation exists between two or more behaviors or attributes. Researchers might conduct a survey, for example, to find out whether growing older is associated with changes in a person's sexual behavior (Karraker & DeLamater, 2013) or whether social class is related to how parents raise their children (Lareau, 2011). Although a correlation between variables may reflect an underlying causal relation, two variables can be correlated without one causing the other; this will happen, for instance, if both are caused by a third variable. Correlation alone is not sufficient evidence for causation.

A third objective of research, then, is to discover the causes of some behavior or event. When pursuing this goal, the researcher first develops a causal hypothesis, which is a statement that differences or changes in one behavior or event produce a difference or change in another behavior or event. For instance, an investigator might hypothesize that studying for an exam in groups will produce higher grades than studying for the exam individually. After specifying the hypothesis, the investigator collects data to test the hypothesis. To

support the hypothesis of causality, this test must show that differences or changes in one variable produce differences or changes in the other. Moreover, the design of the test must preclude or eliminate plausible alternative (noncausal) interpretations of the data. Frequently, the best way to test a causal hypothesis is by an experiment, a topic discussed in greater detail further on.

A fourth objective of social psychological research is to test existing theories and to develop new ones. A **theory** is a set of interrelated propositions that organizes and explains a set of phenomena (see Chapter 1 for examples). Frequently, a theory will serve as a basis for predicting future events. Tests of theories resemble tests of hypotheses, except that several interrelated hypotheses are assessed at once. In some cases, investigators juxtapose theories that make different predictions, and the results of the test may enable them to reject one theory in favor of another.

## Research Hypotheses

In broad terms, a **hypothesis** is a conjectural statement of the relation between two or more variables. Many social psychological studies begin with one or more hypotheses. To test whether a hypothesis is correct, an investigator will first ask what observations would be expected if the hypothesis is true; then, they will take some observations or measures of reality and compare these with what is expected under the hypothesis. If a discrepancy is noted, it constitutes evidence against the hypothesis and may lead to its rejection.

There are various types of hypotheses. Some hypotheses are noncausal in nature; for example, "Variables X and Y are correlated, such that high levels of X occur with low levels of Y" (negative correlation). Or, "Obesity is associated with increased sexual risk-taking" (Akers et al., 2016). Noncausal hypotheses make statements about observed relations between variables.

Other hypotheses are explicitly causal in nature. For instance, a causal hypothesis relating two variables might take the form "X causes Y" or "Higher levels of X produce lower levels of Y" or "Exhibitionism will positively affect SNS [Social Networking Site] use" (Mantymaki & Najmul Islam, 2016). Sometimes, of course, causal hypotheses are more explicit and qualified in scope; for example, "If conditions A and B are present, then an increase of 1 unit in X will cause a decrease of 6 units in Y."

Causal hypotheses always include at least two variables—an independent variable and a dependent variable. An **independent variable** is any variable considered to cause or have an effect on some other variable(s). A **dependent variable** is any variable caused by some other variable. The dependent variable changes in response to changes in the independent variable. In the preceding example where X causes Y, X is the independent variable and Y is the dependent variable.

Another important type—the **extraneous variable**—is any variable that is not expressly included in the hypothesis but that nevertheless has a causal impact on the dependent variable. Extraneous variables are widespread in social psychology because most dependent variables of interest have more than one cause.

## Validity of Findings

One cannot take for granted that the findings of any given study will have validity. Consider a situation where an investigator is studying deviant behavior. In particular, they are investigating the extent to which cheating by college students occurs on exams. Reasoning that it is more difficult for people monitoring an exam to keep students under surveillance in large classes than in smaller ones, they hypothesize that a higher rate of cheating will occur on exams in large classes than in small. To test this hypothesis, they collect data on cheating in both large classes and small ones and then analyze the data. The results show that more cheating per student occurs in the larger classes. Thus, the data apparently support the investigator's research hypothesis.

A few days later, however, a colleague points out that all the large classes in the study used multiple-choice exams, whereas all the small classes used short answer and essay exams. The investigator immediately realizes that an extraneous variable (exam format) is confounded with the independent variable (class size) and may be operating as a cause in the data. The apparent support for their research hypothesis (more cheating in large classes) may be nothing more than an artifact. Perhaps the true effect is that more cheating occurs on multiple-choice exams than on essay exams, irrespective of class size.

We say that the findings of a study have **internal validity** if they are free from contamination by extraneous variables. Internal validity is a matter of degree; findings may have high or low internal validity. Obviously, the investigator's findings about the effect of class size on cheating have low internal validity due to the possibly confounding effect of exam format. Internal validity is very important. Without internal validity, a study cannot provide clear, interpretable results.

To achieve results with higher internal validity, the investigator might repeat the study with an improved design. For instance, our investigator might repeat their study with only one exam format (say, multiple choice) in both large and small classes. Then they could test whether class size affects the rate of cheating on multiple-choice exams. By holding constant the extraneous variable (exam format), their new design will have greater internal validity. Better still, they might use a more complex design that includes all four logical possibilities (that is, small class/multiple choice; small class/essay; large class/multiple choice; large class/essay). They could analyze the data from this design to estimate separately the relative impacts of class size and exam format on cheating. In effect, this design converts an extraneous variable (exam format) into a second independent variable. Although better, it is not a perfect design, because other extraneous variables could still be operating as causes of cheating—and they may be confounded with class size and exam format.

As important as internal validity is, it is not the only concern of the investigator. Another concern is external validity. **External validity** is the extent to which a causal relationship, once identified in a particular setting with a particular population, can be generalized to other populations, settings, or time periods. Even if an investigator's results have internal validity, they may lack external validity; that is, they may hold only for the specific group and setting studied and not generalize to others. For instance, if the investigator studying cheating and class size conducted their study in a 2-year college, there is no assurance that the findings (whatever they turn out to be) would also apply to students in other settings, such as high schools or 4-year colleges or universities. In general, external validity is important and desirable, because the results of a study often have general importance only if they generalize beyond the particular setting in which they appeared.

## RESEARCH METHODS

Two general types of methods are used by social psychologists. **Quantitative methods** collect information in ways that produce numbers which can then be analyzed by applying statistical techniques. Major techniques in this category include surveys, secondary data analysis, diary studies, and experiments. **Qualitative methods** broadly refer to those that rely on verbal or textual materials to represent the phenomenon of concern. These include observational research, which records information about naturally occurring events, archival research, which studies previously collected data, and content analysis of documents

and video and audio recordings. We discuss each of these methods in turn.

### Surveys

A survey is a procedure for collecting information by asking members of some population a set of questions and recording their responses. The survey technique is very useful for identifying the average or typical response to a question, as well as the distribution of responses within the population. It is also useful for identifying how groups of respondents differ from one another. For instance, Prince-Gibson and Schwartz (1998) used a survey to test a set of hypotheses about gender differences in values. They predicted that men would more strongly value power, achievement, hedonism, and stimulation, whereas women would value benevolence, conformity, tradition, and security. The hypotheses were tested using data from a probability sample of the Israeli Jewish population. Contrary to predictions, there were no significant differences in the mean ratings of the importance of these values given by men and women. Because some earlier research conducted in the 1970s and 1980s did report such differences, the authors concluded that their results suggest that men's and women's values are converging.

**Purpose of a Survey.** Investigators often conduct surveys to obtain self-reports from individuals about their own attributes—that is, their attitudes, behavior, and experiences. Information of this type enables investigators to discover the distribution of attributes in the population and to determine whether a relationship exists between two or more attributes of interest.

One form of survey—the public opinion poll—has become very common in the United States. Several organizations specialize in conducting surveys that measure the frequency and strength of favorable or unfavorable attitudes toward public issues, political

Working from a schedule of questions, the survey interviewer carefully records the answers given by a respondent. © wdstock/iStock

figures and institutions, and candidates for office. These polls play a significant role in American politics, for their findings increasingly influence public policy and the positions taken by political figures (Halberstam, 1979; Ratzan, 1989). Presidential candidates used the results of such polls to guide their decisions during the 2016 election campaign, and they will do so again in 2020.

Investigators also often use surveys to obtain data about various social problems. For instance, government agencies and individual researchers have conducted surveys on sexual activity and pregnancy risk among single women (Lindberg & Singh, 2008) and on alcohol and drug use by teenagers (Substance Abuse and Mental Health Services Administration, 2012). Information about the extent of such activities and the people involved in them is requisite to developing effective social policies.

Finally, investigators often conduct surveys with the primary objective of making basic theoretical contributions to social psychology. For instance, many studies of socialization processes and outcomes (see Chapter 3), psychological well-being, discrimination and prejudice, attitude-behavior relationships (see Chapter 8), and collective behavior have used survey methods.

**Types of Surveys.** There are two basic types of surveys—those based on interviews and those based on questionnaires. In an **interview**, a person serves as an interviewer and records the answers from the respondents. To ensure that each respondent in the study receives the same questions, the interviewer usually works from an interview schedule. This schedule indicates the exact order and wording of questions. In certain studies, however, the interviewer has flexibility in determining the exact order and wording of questions, but they are expected to make sure that certain topics are covered. One advantage of using an interview is that the interviewer can adjust the questioning to the respondent. That is, they can look for verbal or nonverbal signs that the respondent does not understand a question and repeat or clarify the question as needed (Moore, 2004).

In a **questionnaire**, the questions appear on paper or an electronic screen, and the respondent reads and answers them at their own pace. No interviewer is present. One advantage of questionnaires over interviews is that questionnaires cost less to administer. The cost of a national survey using trained personnel to conduct face-to-face interviews is rather large; it can run to as much as $250 to $300 or more per completed interview, although this varies with the length of the interview and other factors. In contrast, the same survey using questionnaires mailed to respondents would cost considerably less—maybe as little as $15 per completed form. The same survey posted online may cost only $2–3 per completed survey. The major disadvantage of questionnaires lies in the **response rate**—the percentage of people contacted who complete the survey. Whereas an interview study can obtain response rates of 75 to 80 percent or more, mailed questionnaires rarely attain more than a 50 percent response rate. Online surveys may have as little as a 20 percent response rate. Because a high response rate is very desirable, this is a significant disadvantage for mailed questionnaires and online surveys.

A compromise is the telephone interview. This is the standard method used by public opinion polling organizations, such as Gallup and Roper. Investigators are using it in basic research as well. The telephone interview uses a trained interviewer to ask the questions, but it sacrifices the visual feedback available in a face-to-face interview. It is cheaper (about $60 per completed interview, depending on length) than the face-to-face interview, although it typically involves a somewhat

lower response rate (about 65 percent). Many surveys now use computer-assisted telephone interviewing (CATI). With CATI, the computer randomly selects and dials telephone numbers (RDD, random digit dialing). Once a potential respondent is on the line, the interviewer takes over and conducts the interview. They read some questions and enter the answers directly into the computer when the respondent gives them. In listing questions to ask, the computer may alter later questions in light of earlier answers by the respondent. A major drawback of RDD is that it can only be used to contact landline phones, and thus misses potential respondents who rely on cell phones, notably younger persons.

The latest innovation is the web survey, using the Internet to collect survey data. Researchers prepare a questionnaire using specially designed software and post it on the web. Potential participants are recruited either directly through targeted e-mail, or by banners on relevant webpages. The software may allow some tailoring of the later questions to the person's earlier answers, an advantage over the printed survey.

Potential advantages include the opportunity to recruit people with specific characteristics, or unique populations (Wright, 2005). Thus, a researcher in a racially homogenous community can recruit members of other racial/ethnic groups from around the United States (or indeed the world) for a study of prejudice. A researcher on a college campus can move beyond the study of students and recruit a more representative sample of adults of all ages. Further, one can recruit a large sample with a minimum of effort. For example, one web survey of gays, lesbians, and bisexuals yielded 2,800 completed surveys in just two months (Mustanski, 2001). Another advantage is that data are recorded in digital form, eliminating the need for coding handwritten material, facilitating a shortened analysis phase.

Disadvantages include sampling issues. Respondents to online surveys self-select and may not represent the spectrum of people in the group/population of interest. E-mail lists may include duplicates and inactive addresses, inflating the apparent size of the group. Also, there is no guarantee that the person completing the survey is the person who was invited.

The quality of data depends on the percentage of the sample members who complete the research. Response rates for printed/mailed surveys are low, sometimes less than 30 percent. Researchers believe that participants are more likely to complete a web survey because it is readily accessible and uses a technology that is now widely used, especially by younger people. Web surveys of undergraduate students at a single university may achieve a completion rate of 60 percent. At the same time, Internet users are not a random sample of the population, and so the sample may be biased by age, income, or education. In 2013, persons over 65, persons earning less than $50,000 per year, and Blacks and Hispanics were less likely to have Internet access (File & Ryan, 2014).

**Measurement Reliability and Validity.** In any form of research, the quality of measurement is an important consideration. Of primary concern are the reliability and the validity of the instruments. **Reliability** is the extent to which an instrument produces the same results each time it is employed to measure a particular construct under given conditions. Reliability is a matter of degree; some instruments are highly reliable, whereas others are less so. Obviously, investigators prefer instruments with high reliability and try to avoid those with low reliability.

There are several ways to assess the reliability of an instrument. The first is to see if people's responses to an instrument are consistent across time. In this approach, called the *test-retest method*, an investigator applies the measuring instrument to the same respondents on two different occasions, and then they compare the first responses with the second responses. If the correlation between the first and second responses is high, the instrument has high reliability; if the correlation is low, the instrument has only low reliability.

A second way to assess the reliability of an instrument is to see if people's responses are consistent across items that measure the same construct. This approach is called the *split-half method*. To illustrate, suppose we have a scale of 20 questions measuring psychological well-being. These questions ask the respondent about psychological states, such as how often they are sad, nervous, depressed, tense, or irritable, and how often they have trouble concentrating, working, or sleeping. Assume that we administer all the questions to 300 men. To use the split-half method, we would randomly divide the 20 questions into two groups of 10, calculate a score for each respondent on each group of 10, and compute a correlation between the two scores. A high correlation (if it occurs) provides confirmation that the scale is reliable.

Just as findings must be valid, as discussed above, so must our measures. Does the instrument actually measure the theoretical concept we intend to measure? There are several types of validity, including face validity, criterion validity, and construct validity. First, an instrument has *face validity* if its content is manifestly similar to the behavior or process of interest. If a researcher wishes to measure the frequency of sexual intercourse, for example, the question "How often do you engage in sexual intercourse?" has face validity. The question "How often do you have sex?" has lower face validity, since "sex" includes behaviors other than intercourse.

Second, an instrument has *criterion validity* if we can use it to predict respondents' standing on some other variable of theoretical or practical interest. Suppose, for example, that an investigator is concerned with traffic safety on the roads and that they develop an instrument to distinguish good drivers from bad drivers. To establish the instrument's predictive validity, the investigator first administers the instrument to young people getting their driver's license and then, several years later, checks their driving records for moving violations. If the drivers' scores on the instrument correlate highly with their level of subsequent violations, the instrument has criterion validity.

Third, an instrument has *construct validity* if it provides a good measure of the theoretical concept being investigated by the research. In general, an instrument will have construct validity if it measures what people understand the concept to mean and if it relates to other variables as predicted by the theory under consideration. Establishing the construct validity of an instrument can be difficult, especially if the underlying theoretical construct is highly abstract in nature. Suppose, for example, that an investigator's theory includes an abstraction like "intellectual development." The measurement of this concept is somewhat problematic, for there is no readily observable referent, no single behavior or occurrence that the investigator can point to as indicative of intellectual development. The usual method of establishing the construct validity of an instrument is to show that the pattern of correlations between respondents' scores on the instrument and their scores on other variables is what would be expected if the underlying theory holds true.

**The Questions.** The phrasing of questions used in any measure requires close attention by investigators. Subtle differences in the form, wording, and context of survey questions can produce differences in responses (Schwarz, Groves, & Schuman, 1998). Creating good survey questions is part art and part science, but there are certain guidelines. First, the more precise and focused a question, the greater will be its reliability and validity. If a question is expressed in vague, ambiguous, abstract, or global terms, respondents may interpret it in different ways, and this in turn will produce uncontrolled variation in responses. A second consideration in formulating survey

questions is the exact choice of words used. It is best to avoid jargon or specialized terminology unless one is interviewing a sample of specialists. Likewise, it is important to adjust questions to the educational and reading level of the respondents. A third consideration is the length of questions. Several studies have shown that questions of moderate length elicit more complete answers than very short ones (Anderson & Silver, 1987; Sudman & Bradburn, 1974). A fourth consideration is whether the topic under investigation is potentially a threatening or embarrassing one (sex, alcohol, drugs, money, and so on). In general, threatening questions requiring quantified answers are better asked by presenting a range of alternative answers (say, 0, 1–5, 6–10) than by asking a question requiring an exact number (Rea & Parker, 1997).

**Measuring Attitudes.** Perhaps the most common purpose of surveys is to measure people's attitudes toward some event, person, or object. Because attitudes are mental states, they cannot be directly observed. Therefore, to find out someone's attitude, we usually ask them.

The most direct way of finding out someone's attitude is to ask a direct question and record the person's answer. This is the way most of us study the attitudes of the people with whom we interact. It is also the technique used by newspaper and television reporters. To make the process more systematic, social psychologists use several methods, including the single-item measure, Likert scales, and semantic differential techniques.

*Single Items.* The single-item scale usually consists of a direct positive or negative statement, and the respondent indicates whether they agree, disagree, or are unsure. Such a measure is economical; it takes a minimum of time and space to present. It is also easy to score. The major drawback of the single item is that it is not very precise. Of necessity, it must be general and detects only gross differences in attitude. Using the single-item measure in

Box 2.1, we could separate people into only two groups: those who favor premarital abstinence and everybody else.

*Likert Scales.* Often, we want to know not only how each person feels about the object of interest but also how each respondent's attitude compares with the attitudes of others. The Likert scale, a technique based on summated ratings, provides such information (Likert, 1932).

Box 2.1 includes a two-item Likert scale. Each possible response is given a numerical score, indicated in parentheses. We would assess the respondent's attitude by adding their scores for both items. For example, suppose you strongly agree with item 1 (+2) and strongly disagree with item 2 (+2). Your score would be 4, indicating strong opposition to premarital intercourse. Your roommate might strongly disagree with the statement that people should wait until they marry (−2) and might also disagree that premarital sex strengthens a marriage (+1). The resulting score of −1 indicates a slightly positive view of premarital intercourse. Finally, someone who strongly disagrees with item 1 (−2) and agrees with item 2 (−1) would get a score of −3 and could be differentiated from a person who received a score of −4.

Typically, a Likert scale includes at least four items. The items should be counterbalanced— that is, some should be positive statements, and others should be negative ones. Our two-item scale in Box 2.1 has this property; one item is positive, and the other is negative. The Likert scale allows us to order respondents fairly precisely; items of this type are commonly used in public opinion polls. Such a scale takes more time to administer, however, and involves a scoring stage as well.

*Semantic Differential Scales.* Like most attitude scales, the single-item and Likert scales measure the denotative or dictionary meanings of the object to the respondent. However, objects also have a connotative meaning, a set of psychological meanings that vary from one respondent to another. For instance, one person may have had very positive experiences with sexual intercourse, whereas another person's experiences may have been very frustrating.

The semantic differential scale (Osgood, Suci, & Tannenbaum, 1957) is a technique for measuring connotative meaning. In using it, an investigator presents the respondents with a series of bipolar adjective scales. Each of these is a scale whose ends are two adjectives having opposite meanings. The respondent rates the attitude object on each scale. After the data are collected, the researcher can analyze them by various statistical techniques. Analyses of such ratings frequently identify three aspects of connotative meaning: evaluation, potency, and activity. Evaluation is measured by adjective pairs such as *good–bad* and *positive–negative;* potency, by *weak–strong* and *light–heavy;* and activity, by *fast–slow* and *exciting–boring.*

The example in Box 2.1 includes two bipolar scales measuring each of the three dimensions. Scores are assigned to each scale from +3 to −3; they are then summed across scales of each type to arrive at evaluation, potency, and activity scores. In the example shown, scores on each dimension could range from −6 (*bad, weak,* and *slow*) to +6 (*good, strong,* and *fast*).

One advantage of the semantic differential technique is that researchers can compare an individual's attitudes on three dimensions, allowing more complex differentiation among respondents. Another advantage is that because the meaning it measures is connotative, it can be used with any object, from a specific person to an entire nation. This technique is also used to assess the meaning of role identities (*mother, doctor*) and role behaviors (*hug, cure*) (Heise, 1979; Smith-Lovin, 1990). Its disadvantages include the fact that it requires more time to administer and to score.

**The Sample.** Suppose a survey researcher wants to ascertain the extent of prejudice toward Blacks among White adults in the United States. These White adults constitute

# BOX 2.1 The Measurement of Attitudes

Suppose you want to assess attitudes toward premarital sexual behavior. Here are three direct techniques you could employ.

## Single Item

The single item is probably the most common measure of attitudes. An example of this type is:

I think people should wait until they are married to have sex.

_____ Yes
_____ No
_____ Not sure

## Likert Scale

The **Likert scale** consists of a series of statements about the object of interest. The statements may be positive or negative. The respondent indicates how much he or she agrees with each statement. For example:

1. I think people should wait until they are married to have sex.

_____ Strongly agree (+2)
_____ Agree (+1)
_____ Undecided (0)
_____ Disagree (−1)
_____ Strongly disagree (−2)

2. I think having sex before marriage strengthens the marriage.

_____ Strongly agree (−2)
_____ Agree (−1)
_____ Undecided (0)
_____ Disagree (+1)
_____ Strongly disagree (+2)

## Semantic Differential Scale

The semantic differential scale consists of a number of dimensions on which the respondent rates the attitude object. For example:

Using the table below, rate how you feel about premarital sexual intercourse on each of the following dimensions.

**Semantic Differential Scale**

| good | ____ | ____ | ____ | ____ | ____ | ____ | ____ | bad |
|---|---|---|---|---|---|---|---|---|
| | (3) | (2) | (1) | (0) | (−1) | (−2) | (−3) | |
| weak | ____ | ____ | ____ | ____ | ____ | ____ | ____ | strong |
| | (−3) | (−2) | (−1) | (0) | (1) | (2) | (3) | |
| fast | ____ | ____ | ____ | ____ | ____ | ____ | ____ | slow |
| | (3) | (2) | (1) | (0) | (−1) | (−2) | (−3) | |
| negative | ____ | ____ | ____ | ____ | ____ | ____ | ____ | positive |
| | (−3) | (−2) | (−1) | (0) | (1) | (2) | (3) | |
| light | ____ | ____ | ____ | ____ | ____ | ____ | ____ | heavy |
| | (3) | (2) | (1) | (0) | (−1) | (−2) | (−3) | |
| exciting | ____ | ____ | ____ | ____ | ____ | ____ | ____ | boring |
| | (3) | (2) | (1) | (0) | (−1) | (−2) | (−3) | |

## Using Social Media to Measure Attitudes

The measures discussed above are direct; the respondent is aware that you are measuring their attitudes. Social media provide us with an indirect method, e.g., the number of posts on Facebook or the number of tweets about an attitude object. For example, researchers drew a sample of 113,985 tweets by 30,995 users, and found that the percentage of free-text tweets was highly correlated (.558) with votes cast for candidates in the U.S. House elections in 2010 (McKelvey, DiGrazia, & Rojas, 2014).

the **population** of interest—that is, the set of all people whose attitudes are of interest to the researcher. It would be virtually impossible—and enormously expensive—to interview all people in the population of White adults, so the researcher instead selects a sample, or representative subset, from that population to interview.

Sample selection is one of the most important aspects of any type of survey. In some cases, investigators may use a particular sample simply because it is readily available; samples of this type are known as *convenience samples*. A sample consisting of students taking a class, occasionally used in social science research, is a convenience sample. Convenience samples have a major drawback—they usually lack external validity and do not enable the investigator to generalize the findings to any larger population. For this reason, it is better research practice to select some other type of sample—one that is representative of the underlying population. Only when the sample is representative can the results obtained from it (for example, information regarding racial prejudice obtained from survey respondents) be generalized to the entire population. The nature of the sample, therefore, has a major impact on the external validity of the survey.

Two types of systematic samples are commonly used in social psychological surveys. One is the **simple random sample**, wherein the researcher selects units—usually individuals—from the population such that every unit has an equal probability of being included. To use this technique, the researcher needs a complete list of members of the population. At a university, for example, they might obtain a list of all students from the registrar. At the city or county level, they might use voter registration lists. A frequent problem, especially when the population being studied is large, is the absence of a complete list. Under these circumstances, researchers usually fall back on some substitute, such as a telephone directory. Of course, this will limit the population to which one can generalize, because

people who are poor or who move frequently may not have telephones, others may choose not to list their numbers in the directory, and others may only have cell phones. In 2012, only 66 percent of adults in the United States had a landline phone. Persons under 25 and Hispanics were least likely to have such phones (Blumberg & Luke, 2012).

Working from a complete list of the population, the researcher draws a random sample. A common way to do this is to number the people on the list consecutively and then use a table of random numbers to choose people for the sample. Once the researcher has drawn a random sample, they must take steps to ensure that all the members of the sample are interviewed; in other words, the researcher must strive for a high response rate. Without a high response rate, the results of the survey will not be generalizable to the whole population. Bias may result if the people who participate in the study differ in some significant way from those who refuse to participate.

If the population is very large, the investigator may not be able to list all its members and draw a random sample. Under these conditions, researchers frequently employ a **stratified sample**. That is, they divide the population into groups according to important characteristics, select a random sample of groups, and then draw a sample of individuals within each selected group. For example, public opinion polls designed to represent the entire adult population of the United States often use stratified samples. The population is first stratified on the basis of region (Northeast, Midwest, South, Southwest, and West). Next, the population within each region is stratified into urban versus rural areas. Within urban areas, there may be still further stratification by size of urban area. The result will be numerous sampling units—population subgroups of known regional and residential type. Some units are then selected for study in proportion to their frequency in the entire population. Thus, one would sample more urban units from the Northeast than from the South or Midwest; conversely, one would select more rural units in the latter regions. Finally, within each sampling unit, people are selected randomly to serve as respondents. Using this technique, one can represent the adult population of the United States with a sample of 1,500 people and obtain responses accurate within plus or minus 3 percent.

**Causal Analysis of Survey Data.** Social psychologists have long used computers to aid in the descriptive analysis of survey data. In recent years, however, some social psychologists have begun to use more sophisticated techniques to aid in the causal interpretation of survey data. Analysis techniques of this type (such as LISREL, path analysis, and structural equation modeling) require the investigator to postulate a pattern of cause-and-effect relations among a set of variables (Bollen, 1989; Jöreskog & Sörbom, 1979). The computer then estimates coefficients of effect from the data. These coefficients indicate the strength of the relationships among the variables, and they provide a test of whether the causal linkages postulated by the theory are indeed present in the data. Using this approach, an analyst can test many alternative hypotheses. Typically, some hypotheses will turn out to be inconsistent with the data, and the analyst can reject these in favor of alternative hypotheses that survive the test. One difficulty with this approach is that for problems involving many variables (say, a dozen or more) there often exist numerous alternative hypotheses that are plausible. Although this process will eliminate many hypotheses, more than one may survive as tenable.

**Panel Studies.** One useful extension of the survey technique is the longitudinal survey or **panel study**, in which a given sample of respondents is surveyed at one point in time and then resurveyed at a later point. For instance, in a panel study, a sample of respondents would be surveyed by telephone interview or questionnaire (this is called the first wave of the panel). Then, at some future time (say, one year later), the same respondents would be surveyed again (the second wave); the questionnaire items in the second wave will be similar to—or an extension of—those used in the first wave. If desired, the same respondents could be surveyed again at a still later point in time (the third wave), and so on. In principle, there is no upper limit on the number of waves that might be included in a panel study, although there are practical constraints, such as the dollar cost of running the panel and the difficulties in tracking down members of the sample at various times. The waves in a panel study can be spaced either closely together or far apart in time, depending on the study's purpose.

In general, data from a panel study lend themselves somewhat more readily to causal interpretation than data from a simple cross-sectional survey. The waves in the panel study provide a natural temporal ordering among the variables, which usually provides increased clarity when interpreting the results causally.

**Secondary Data Analysis.** There are a number of very well-done panel studies focused on a variety of topics and populations. Among those relevant to social psychologists are The National Longitudinal Study of Adolescent to Adult Health (Add Health), The National Longitudinal Surveys of Youth, 1979, 1997 (NLSY, Bureau of Labor Statistics), and the United States Census and American Community Surveys (ACS). All of these make data available to qualified researchers for detailed analyses. This research is referred to as secondary data analysis, analysis of data the researcher did not collect. As the collection of data has become increasingly expensive, more and more researchers have turned to such analyses.

**Strengths and Weaknesses of Surveys.** Surveys can provide, at moderate cost, an accurate and precise description of the characteristics of a specific population. When a social psychological researcher uses measures that are reliable and valid, employs a sampling design that guarantees representativeness, and takes steps to ensure a high response rate, the survey can produce a clear portrait of the attitudes and social characteristics of a population.

Surveys also provide an effective means to study the incidence of various social behaviors. A survey or diary study asking people to report their behavior is usually more efficient and cost-effective than observational studies of actual behavior. This is especially true for behavior that occurs only infrequently or in private settings.

Surveys are frequently used to test predictions based on symbolic interaction theory, such as predictions about influences on personal identity and self-esteem. These methods are also used to test hypotheses about attitude structure and function based on cognitive theory.

There are also certain drawbacks to the survey technique. Both questionnaires and interviews rely on self-reports by respondents. Under certain conditions, however, self-reports can be invalid sources of information. First, some people may not respond truthfully to questions about themselves. This is not usually a major problem, but it can become troublesome if the survey deals with activities that are highly personal, illegal, or otherwise embarrassing to reveal. Second, even when respondents want to report honestly, they may give wrong information due to imperfect recall or poor memory. This can be a nettlesome problem, especially in surveys investigating the past (for example, historical events or childhood). As an illustration, consider the question "When were you last vaccinated?" This may seem simple and straightforward, but it often produces incorrect responses because many people cannot remember the relevant dates. Third, some respondents answering self-report questions have a tendency to fall into a response set. That is, they answer all questions the same way (for example, always agree or

disagree) or they give extreme answers too frequently. If many respondents adopt a response set, this will introduce bias into the survey's results.

## Diary Research

Diary research refers to a variety of procedures that elicit reports of ongoing/recent activities from participants. Participants may be asked to provide information when events occur, or at specific times, e.g., daily. The researcher is able to collect data as events occur in their natural setting, as opposed to after the fact as in a survey. In turn, this should reduce or eliminate errors due to memory and the passage of time since the event (Bolger, Davis & Rafaeli, 2003). Diary methods have been used for decades to study media use patterns (remember the Nielsen ratings of broadcast TV programs?) and time use. More recently, they have been used to study what people spend money on, what they eat, when and how far they travel, and what housework and childcare activities they engage in, to name a few.

Mark (2014) conducted diary research to study the *in situ* relationship between sexual desire and sexual satisfaction. Both members of 87 heterosexual couples provided ratings of the degree to which they felt sexual desire for their partner (a five-point scale) and the quality of each sexual experience (a nine-point scale) during the preceding 24 hours. Each participant was instructed to log on to the researcher's website every day and complete the ratings. Data were collected for 30 days from each couple. The results indicated that higher daily desire predicted higher daily satisfaction for both women and men. These data provide a window into sexual relationship dynamics that would be hard to collect in any other way.

Surveys and interviews ask direct questions about activities such as sexual behavior, alcohol and drug use, and church attendance. Researchers have recognized for decades that answers to such questions may be biased by the respondent's desire to appear to be a particular kind of person (or not). One way to conceptualize this is that such questions elicit thoughts about one's identity. If I ask you how many times you exercised in the last week, you may think, "Well, I am a person who exercises whenever I can" and reply, "Four times." If you identify as a couch potato, you may say "Not at all." Diary methods provide an alternative, by simply asking you to report what you did each day. Brenner and DeLamater (2016) asked students to report every major change in their activity for a five-day period. Reports were submitted by a text message, and participants were asked to report the new activity as soon as they could. The researchers analyzed reports of exercise, comparing them with data from an online survey of how often the same students exercised, and records of entry to campus exercise facilities. Diary data submitted via text message were more accurate.

## Experiments

The other quantitative research method widely used in social psychology is the experiment. It is the most highly controlled of the research methodologies, and it is a powerful method for establishing causal relations between variables. For a study to be a true **experiment**, it must have two specific characteristics:

1. The researcher must manipulate one or more of the independent variables that are hypothesized to have a causal impact on the dependent variable(s) of concern.
2. The researcher must assign the participants randomly to the various treatments—that is, to the different levels of each of the independent variables.

The term **random assignment** denotes the placement of participants in experimental treatments on the basis of chance, as by flipping a coin or using a table of random numbers. Random assignment is desirable because it mitigates the effects of extraneous variables. By using random assignment, the researcher creates groups of participants that are equivalent in all respects except their exposure to different levels of the independent variables. This removes the possibility that these groups will differ systematically on extraneous variables such as intelligence, personality, or motivation. Thus, random assignment enables the investigator to infer that any observed differences between groups on the dependent variable are due only to the effects of the independent variable(s) (or chance), not to extraneous variables (Haslam & McCarty, 2004).

Whereas researchers manipulate the independent variables in an experiment, they simply measure the dependent variable(s). Experimenters can measure dependent variables in many ways. For example, they can monitor participants' neural or physiological arousal, administer short questionnaires that assess participants' attitudes, record the interactions that occur between participants, or score the participants' performance on tasks. The exact type of measurement used in the experiment will depend on the nature of the dependent variable(s) of interest.

**Laboratory and Field Experiments.** It is useful to distinguish between laboratory experiments and field experiments. Laboratory experiments are those conducted in a setting where the investigator can control much of the participants' physical surroundings. In the laboratory, the investigator can determine which stimuli, tasks, information, or situations the participants will face. This control enables the experimenter to manipulate the independent variables, to measure the dependent variables, to hold constant some known extraneous variables, and to implement the random assignment of participants to treatments. For instance, if an investigator is studying the impact of verbal communication on group productivity in a laboratory setting, they may wish to restrict the interaction among participants. To do this, they might limit communication to written notes or verbal messages sent by electronic equipment. This practice not only would eliminate the possibly contaminating influence of nonverbal communication, but also would permit the content of any messages to be analyzed later by the experimenter.

Field experiments, in contrast with laboratory experiments, are studies where investigators manipulate variables in natural, nonlaboratory settings. Usually, these settings are already familiar to the participants. Investigators have used field experiments to study topics ranging from pay inequity in large bureaucratic organizations to altruistic behavior on street corners and in subway cars. Compared with laboratory experiments, field experiments have the advantage of high external validity. When conducted in natural and uncontrived settings, they usually have greater mundane realism than laboratory experiments. Moreover, participants in field experiments may not be aware of their status as experimental participants—a fact that reduces participants' reactivity. The primary weakness of field experiments, of course, is that in natural settings, experimenters sometimes have difficulty manipulating independent variables exactly as they would wish and often have little control over extraneous variables. This means that the internal validity of field experiments is often lower than in comparable laboratory experiments.

**Conduct of Experiments.** To illustrate how investigators conduct experiments, consider the following laboratory study, which sought to determine the impact of certain independent variables on whether one person will help another in an emergency (Darley & Latané, 1968). The investigators conducted the study at a university in New York City. Male and female students came to the laboratory to discuss problems they had encountered in adjusting to the university. The experimenters placed each participant in a separate room and instructed them to communicate with other participants via an intercom. The rationale given was that this procedure would permit them to remain anonymous while discussing personal problems.

The independent variable was the number of other persons who the participant believed were participating in the discussion (and who would, therefore, later witness an emergency). Depending on experimental treatment, participants were told there were one, two, or five other participants. Participants were randomly assigned to the various levels of this independent variable.

The discussion proceeded with each participant speaking in turn over the intercom for two minutes. Thus, depending on the experimental treatment, the participant heard the voices of one, two, or five others. In reality, the participant was hearing a tape recording of other people, not the voices of actual participants. (This was the real reason for putting participants in separate rooms and having them communicate via intercom.) One of these recorded voices admitted somewhat hesitantly that they were subject to nervous seizures. In their second turn, they started to speak normally, but suddenly their speech became disorganized. Soon, they lapsed into gibberish and choking sounds and then into silence. Evidently, an emergency was occurring. The participant realized that all participants could hear it, although the intercom prevented them from talking to one another.

The dependent variables were whether the participant would leave the room to offer help and how quickly they would do so. The experimenter timed the speed of the participant's response from the beginning of the victim's speech. The results verified the research hypothesis that the greater the number of witnesses, the less likely a participant was to offer help to the victim.

Experiments enable the investigator to manipulate independent variables and measure behavior in various ways. Many studies have replicated Darley and Latané's pioneering bystander intervention research, discussed in the text. Some have been field experiments, where an emergency is staged in a public area. As the photo suggests, most find that the more witnesses, the less likely anyone is to help. © Renato Seiji Kawasaki/ Shutterstock

This carefully controlled experiment allowed a straightforward test of the hypothesis. The manipulated independent variable (number of witnesses) and the measured dependent variable (speed of helping response) were unambiguous. Confounds from extraneous variables could be ruled out due to the random assignment of participants to treatments. From these results, we can conclude that the number of witnesses has a causal effect on the speed of helping response.

Note, however, that although the experiment showed the causal effect to hold, it did so only under the conditions prevailing in the laboratory. The causal effect may or may not hold under other conditions. This can be problematic if the conditions that existed in the laboratory setting are uncommon in daily life. (When, for instance, was the last time you discussed personal issues over an intercom with five strangers in other rooms?) Thus, from this study alone, it is not clear whether we can generalize the cause-and-effect findings from the laboratory to everyday, face-to-face situations. The relationship between the number of others present and a person's reaction to an emergency might be different in other situations.

Although this experiment provides some answers regarding intervention in emergencies, it also raises further questions. Why, for instance, should the number of witnesses present affect a person's willingness to help in an emergency? The researchers conducting this study were aware of this question and, based on data from a brief questionnaire administered after the experiment, they proposed that participants in larger groups were slower to help because the responsibility for helping was more diffuse and less focused than in smaller groups. Although this diffusion of responsibility hypothesis is interesting, we must note that this experiment did not demonstrate it to be either true or false. The experiment showed only that under the conditions in the laboratory, the number of witnesses present affected the participants' helping behavior.

**Strengths and Weaknesses of Experiments.** The strength of experimental studies lies in their high level of internal validity. This makes experiments especially well suited for testing causal hypotheses. Experiments excel over other methods (surveys, field observation, and so on) in this respect.

Experiments have high internal validity precisely because they control or offset all factors other than the independent variable that might affect the dependent variable. Techniques to accomplish this include (1) randomly assigning participants to treatments, (2) holding constant known extraneous variables, and (3) incorporating extraneous variables as factors in the research design—that is, manipulating them as independent variables, so that they are not confounded with the main independent variables of interest. Another technique is (4) measuring extraneous variables and including them in the data analysis as covariates of the independent variables.

In principle, investigators can design both laboratory experiments and field experiments to have high internal validity. In practice, however, laboratory experiments often have higher internal validity than comparable field experiments. This happens because researchers have more control over extraneous variables in the laboratory than in the field. Field experiments, however, often surpass laboratory experiments with respect to external validity.

Experiments have been used to test many causal hypotheses drawn from social exchange theory and cognitive theory. Hundreds of experiments have been conducted in an effort to identify the causes of racial and ethnic prejudice.

On the other hand, there are many social phenomena investigators cannot study by this method. Oftentimes, they lack the capacity to manipulate the independent variables of interest or to implement random assignment. Numerous ethical, financial, and practical considerations in everyday life restrict what investigators can manipulate experimentally. For example, we cannot randomly assign children to various types of parental socialization.

Even when the independent variable(s) can be manipulated, experiments face several threats to internal validity. First, there is the possibility that the experimental manipulation may fail. This might occur, for example, if the participants interpret the manipulation as meaning something other than what the researcher intended. The usual remedy for this problem is to use manipulation checks— measures taken after the manipulation that show whether the participants perceived the manipulation as intended. Use of manipulation checks is routine and widespread in social psychological experiments. Similar checks are used in surveys to ensure that participants understood directions or questions as intended.

Another threat to the internal validity of experiments is the existence of *subject-expectancy effect*s. For instance, participants often bring a stereotyped role expectation or mental set to the experiment. If something in the experimental situation activates that expectation, the participants may emit the role-defined behavior. To prevent this, some designs disguise the nature of the research and the research hypothesis by providing a cover story—a plausible, albeit false, description of its purpose.

Another threat to internal validity is *experimenter effects*. This refers to the possibility that an experimenter may expect participants to behave in a particular manner (aggressively,

## BOX 2.2   Using Research to Answer Questions

- What makes people fall in love? What makes them fall out of love?
- What causes harmful or aggressive behavior?

In Chapter 1, we suggested that social psychology answers these questions by applying the methods of science. So how might we answer these questions, using the research methods discussed in this chapter?

Consider the questions about love. First, we need to define *love*. One approach would be to study how people experience this emotion. To do that, we could conduct interviews. We could ask open-ended questions, such as:

- Have you ever been in love?
- How did you know you were in love?
- What does it feel like to be in love?

We would want to ask these questions of an appropriate sample, so we might choose young adults (college students?). After gathering answers from many respondents, we would study the answers carefully, looking for common themes in the answers to each of the three questions. Common themes might include being obsessed with the person, and feeling passionate emotion. In order to create a quantitative measure that we could use in research, we would create a scale, such as the one in Box 14.3, which measures these and other aspects of love.

Now we can turn to the question of what makes people fall in love. Again, we want to study people's experience. So we might use the

method of collecting personal narratives or stories, and conducting a content analysis of the stories. We could request that people "Write a description of the most recent love relationship that you experienced. Describe how you met, what happened in the early days and weeks of the relationship, how you fell in love, and where your relationship is now." Obviously, we would want these narratives from people who are or have recently been in love; we might recruit such people by newspaper ads or flyers on bulletin boards or posts on websites.

We would read a sample of the stories and try to develop a set of coding categories that capture the content of the stories. For example, categories for describing how people met could include school, work, party, bar, dating or relationship apps, concert, sports event, introduction by friends/relatives, and religious services. Then we would train at least two coders to use our categories and "score" each narrative. Suppose the results showed that one-half of the women and one-third of the men met through an introduction; what would that suggest about how people fall in love? What if 40 percent of the men and women met using a dating app? Research studying how heterosexual and same-sex couples met found that 21 and 70 percent respectively met online (see Figure 14.1).

So a variety of research methods can be fruitfully applied to the study of a phenomenon like love. Each method provides us with insight into the phenomenon, and each is useful for answering some questions but not others.

cooperatively, and so on) and may unwittingly telegraph these expectations to the participants (Rosenthal, 1966, 1980). The expectations communicated to participants will likely influence their behavior. This can be a serious problem, especially if the expectations conveyed by the experimenter change as a function of the experimental treatment. People designing an experiment can use several

techniques to minimize or eliminate experimenter effects. First, they can restrict the experimenters' contact with the participants and standardize their behavior in the experimental setting. This will limit the opportunities to transmit expectations. Second, they can keep the research personnel "blind" regarding the hypotheses under study and the treatment to which each participant is assigned. Third, they can use a research design with two or more groups of experimenters, each holding a different hypothesis concerning the study. Analysis of the data from such a design will show whether experimenter effects are present or absent.

Beyond internal validity, experiments also face problems with external validity. Some experiments take place in settings that seem artificial to participants and have low apparent realism. This is often true of laboratory experiments, although less true of field experiments. One useful distinction is that between mundane realism and experimental realism (Aronson, Ellsworth, Carlsmith, & Gonzales, 1990). Mundane realism is the extent to which the experimental setting appears similar to natural, everyday situations. Experimental realism, in contrast, is the impact the experimental situation creates—that is, the degree to which the participants feel involved in the situation.

Low mundane realism need not imply low experimental realism. A laboratory study can have low mundane realism but high experimental realism. Participants were highly involved, for example, in the previously discussed study where the experimenters staged an emergency in the laboratory. Many participants were nervous and expressed concern when they came out of their room looking for the supposed victim. Most expressed surprise when they later learned that the seizure was simulated, not genuine.

There is no single solution to the problem of establishing high experimental realism. Some investigators use a combination of laboratory experiments and field experiments when investigating a phenomenon. This approach is often successful, for the field experiments provide the mundane realism that the laboratory experiments lack. Other investigators simply note that they are more concerned with experimental realism than with mundane realism. If the situation is real and involving to the participants, they maintain,

then the behavior of the participants is real and worthy of study.

## Qualitative Methods

The methods discussed so far produce data that are expressed in numerical form, and thus are amenable to various statistical analytic techniques. At the same time, numbers do not capture the richness of human behavior. We noted above that some participants in the experiment involving a staged emergency came out of their rooms nervously, unsure what to do. Others came out confidently, taking decisive action. We can capture these nuances by observing their behavior, not simply measuring the number of seconds until the door opened.

*Observational research*—often termed a **field study**—involves making systematic observations about behavior as it occurs naturally in everyday settings. Typically, the data are collected by one or more researchers who directly observe the activity of people and record information about it. Field studies have been used to investigate many forms of social behavior in their natural settings. For instance, researchers have observed and recorded data about social interaction between judges and attorneys in the courtroom (Maynard, 1983), between teachers and students in the classroom (Galton, 1987), between couples in informal settings (Zimmerman & West, 1975), between working-class boys and girls in grade school (Thorne, 1993), and between street vendors and passersby in Greenwich Village (Duneier, 2001). Other studies have focused on socialization. Lois (2003) spent 3½ years observing a volunteer search and rescue group, studying the process by which individuals became willing to routinely risk their lives—often in dangerous situations such as blizzards—to save others.

Because field studies investigate social behavior in its natural setting, researchers usually make efforts to minimize or limit the extent to which they intrude on that behavior. In fact, field studies are usually less intrusive than surveys or experiments. Whereas a survey often intrudes on people by asking for self-reports and an experiment involves manipulation of the independent variable(s) and random assignment to treatment, a field study involves nothing more intrusive than recording an observation about the behavior of interest.

Field studies differ in how the observers collect and record information. In some studies, observers watch carefully while the phenomenon of interest is occurring and then make notes about their observations from memory at a later time. The advantage of recording afterward is that the observer is less likely to arouse curiosity, suspicion, or antagonism in the participants. In other studies, the observers may record field notes or make audiotapes at the same time that they observe the behavior. In still other field studies, researchers make audio or video recordings of interactions, and then analyze the recordings later (Whalen & Zimmerman, 1987). Audio and video recordings may seem a superior alternative to the use of human observers (who may have selective perception), but this is not always the case. The use of recordings maximizes the information obtained, but it can also inadvertently influence behavior if the participants discover that they are being recorded.

**Participant Observation.** When the behavior of interest occurs in public settings, such as restaurants, courtrooms, or retail stores, researchers can simply go to the setting and observe the action directly. The researchers do not need to interact with the people being observed or reveal their identities. However, when the behavior of interest is private or restricted in nature (such as intimate sexual activity, use of illegal drugs, or recruiting new members for a cult), observation is usually more difficult. To investigate activities of this type, researchers use the technique of participant observation. Using this method, members of the research team not only make systematic observations of others' behavior but also interact with them and play an active role in the ongoing events. Frequently, the fact of being an active participant enables the investigators to approach and observe behavior that otherwise would be inaccessible. In participant observation, researchers usually do not engage in overt coding or any other activity that would disrupt the normal flow of interaction. In some instances, they may even need to use an assumed identity, lest their true identity as investigators disrupt the interaction.

One study (Pascoe, 2012) used observational techniques combined with interviews to study masculinity and sexuality in high school. The researcher identified herself as a researcher interested in studying high school culture. She "hung out" in various locations in the school building and on the grounds and observed interaction and recorded conversations. She also attended school functions. She supplemented her observations with 50 interviews with students and school personnel. Her data led her to conclude that masculinity and femininity are performances that students carefully cultivate and are not reducible to the characteristics of the physical body.

**Unobtrusive Measures.** Field studies sometimes use unobtrusive measures, which are measurement techniques that do not intrude on the behavior under study and that avoid causing a reaction from the people whose behavior is being studied (Webb, Campbell, Schwartz, & Sechrest, 1981). For example, some unobtrusive measures rely on the physical evidence left behind by people after they have exited from a situation. One illustration is the analysis of inventory records and bar bills to unobtrusively measure the alcohol consumption patterns at various nightclubs and bars (Lex, 1986). Another investigator discovered that the rate at which vinyl floor tiles needed replacement in the Chicago Museum of Science and Industry was a good indicator of the popularity of exhibits (Webb, Campbell, Schwartz, & Sechrest, 1999).

**Strengths and Weaknesses of Observational Studies.** Like any research method, such studies have both strengths and weaknesses. A major strength is that observational techniques allow researchers to study social activity in real-world settings. Careful observation can provide a wealth of information about behavior as it actually occurs in natural settings. These data can be used to investigate ideas about social interaction drawn from role theory or symbolic interaction theory. Moreover, because these techniques are relatively unintrusive, investigators can use them to investigate sensitive or private behaviors—such as drug use or sexual activity—that would be difficult to address through intrusive methods like surveys or experiments.

Weaknesses of field studies include their sensitivity to the specific recording methods used. Observations documented after the fact are often less reliable and valid than those documented on the spot or those based on audio or video recordings. Furthermore, the validity of the observations may depend in part on the identities that the investigators publicly project while making their observations; validity may be destroyed if the researchers have been operating covertly and the subjects suddenly discover that they are under observation. Then, too, the external validity of field observation studies can be problematic, because research of this type frequently focuses on only one group or organization, or on a sample of interactions selected for convenience.

In some cases, field investigators do not get informed consent from the people being observed prior to the collection of data. Permission for using the data is sought only after the behavior has been observed or the conversations recorded. Some people construe this as a serious drawback and object to participant observation on ethical grounds. Of course, this concern has to be weighed against the fact that if permission were sought in advance, the behavior under investigation might never occur or might take a different form.

**Archival Research and Content Analysis.** Although social psychological researchers often prefer to collect original data, it is sometimes possible to test hypotheses and theories by using data that already exist. The term **archival research** denotes the acquisition and analysis (or re-analysis) of information collected previously by others. When archival data of suitable quality exist, a researcher may decide that analyzing them is preferable to collecting and analyzing new data. Archival research usually costs less than alternative methods.

There are many sources of archival data. In the United States, one important source is government agencies. The Census Bureau makes available much of the data it has collected over the years. Census data are a rich source of information about the U.S. population; they often include repeated measures taken at different points in time, which allow an investigator to assess historical trends. The Bureau of Labor Statistics, the Federal Bureau of Investigation, and other agencies also release data to investigators. A second important source of archival data in the United States is the data banks maintained at various large universities. These archives serve as locations where researchers can deposit data they have collected so others can use them. They include, among others, the Interuniversity Consortium for Political and Social Research and the Data Archive on Adolescent Pregnancy and Pregnancy Prevention. There are also several archives of public opinion data, enabling researchers to track attitude change across time. Foremost among these is the General Social Survey-NORC archive. A third source of archival data—less used by social psychologists but still important—is formal organizations such as insurance companies and banks. These typically entail over-time data with respect to various measures of financial and economic performance, or individual and family well-being. A fourth source of archival information for research is news media. Media reports are a rich source of information about past events. For instance, an investigator wishing to study the reactions of those affected by a natural disaster, such as the impact of Hurricane or "Superstorm" Sandy (October 2012), one of the costliest in U.S. history, might use newspapers and television footage as sources of data. Other types of printed material (for example, corporate annual reports) can also provide archival data usable in research.

In some cases, an investigator relying on newspaper articles, government documents, or annual reports as archival sources can use quantitative data directly as they appear. All the investigator has to do is extract the information and analyze it by computer. In other cases, however, the investigator faces the problem of how to interpret and code the information from the source. Under these circumstances, they may use **content analysis**, which involves undertaking a systematic scrutiny of documents or messages to identify specific characteristics and then making inferences based on their occurrence. For example, if newspapers serve as the source, one could use content analysis to code the reportage from newspaper articles into a form suitable for systematic statistical analysis.

Researchers have used content analysis to investigate a wide variety of topics. Some studies, for instance, have analyzed the content of personal advertisements on the Internet placed by gay men, lesbians, and heterosexual men and women (Lever, Grov, Royce, & Gillespie, 2008). Other studies have addressed such issues as whether the depiction of older people is distorted in American media (Dahmen & Cozma, 2009) and the relationship between the mortality rates associated with a disease, for example, AIDS, and newspaper coverage of that disease (Adelman & Verbrugge, 2000).

When a researcher conducts a content analysis, the first step is to identify the informational unit to be studied—is it the word, the sentence, the paragraph, or the article? The second step is to define the categories into which the units will be sorted. A third step is to code the units in each document into the categories, and the final step is to look for relations within the categorized data.

As an example of content analysis, consider a study of the relationship between rhetorical forms of speech and applause from the audience (Heritage & Greatbatch, 1986). The investigators hypothesized that political speakers will use certain rhetorical forms—for example, a three-element list—to signal the audience when to applaud. The raw data in this study were the texts of 476 speeches delivered by British political leaders at party meetings. The researchers carefully defined the rhetorical devices and identified their use in the speeches. Then they counted the number of times that the speakers used each device and noted whether the audience responded immediately to each use with applause. The results showed that applause was much more likely to occur immediately after the use of certain rhetorical devices (such as a three-element list) than at other points in the speech.

**Strengths and Weaknesses of Archival Research and Content Analysis.** One significant advantage of archival research is its comparatively low cost. By reusing existing information, the investigator avoids the cost of collecting new data. A second advantage is that by using information already on hand, an investigator may complete a study more quickly than otherwise. A third advantage is that an investigator can test hypotheses about phenomena that occur over extended periods of time. In some cases, authorities have kept records (such as marriage licenses) for decades or even centuries, and these can serve as a basis for investigating various questions (such as who marries whom).

**TABLE 2.1** Strengths and Weaknesses of Research Methods

| | METHOD | | | | |
|---|---|---|---|---|---|
| | SURVEY | OBSERVATIONAL STUDY | ARCHIVAL RESEARCH | LABORATORY EXPERIMENT | FIELD EXPERIMENT |
| Internal Validity | Moderate | Low | Low | High | Moderate |
| External Validity | Moderate | Moderate | Moderate | Moderate | High |
| Investigator Control | Moderate | Moderate | Low | High | Moderate |
| Intrusiveness of Measures | Moderate | Moderate | Low | Moderate | Low |
| Difficulty of Conducting Study | Moderate | Moderate | Low | Moderate | High |
| Ethical Problems | Few | Many | Few | Some | Some |

*Note:* Entries in the table indicate the strength of the research methods with respect to the various concerns (validity, control, intrusiveness, and the like).

One major disadvantage is the lack of control over the type and quality of information that is available. An investigator must work with whatever others have collected. This may or may not include data on all the variables the investigator wishes to study. Moreover, there may be doubts regarding the quality of the original research design or the procedures used for collecting data. A second disadvantage is that creating a reliable and valid content analysis scheme for use with records can be difficult, especially if the records are complex.

A third disadvantage is that some sets of records contain large amounts of inconsistent or missing information. Obviously, this will hinder the study and limit the validity of any findings.

### Comparison of Research Methods

We have discussed a variety of research methods. Table 2.1 summarizes the strengths and weaknesses of each research method. As this table indicates, no one method of empirical investigation is best for all purposes. A method's appropriateness depends on the phenomenon under study and on the research characteristics most important to the investigator.

Surveys, which provide a useful way of obtaining an accurate description of the attributes of some population, usually have at least moderate internal and external validity, and they pose few ethical problems. Laboratory experiments, which can be especially useful in testing causal hypotheses, are generally high in internal validity, but they may pose some ethical problems (especially if deception is used). Observational techniques will tend to have comparatively low internal validity and may confront a variety of ethical issues, but they may still be the best way to investigate previously unexplored social phenomena in their natural settings.

### Meta-Analysis

Social psychologists have been conducting empirical research for more than a century. There have been dozens and sometimes hundreds of studies of some phenomena. Unfortunately, the results of different studies on a specific question do not always agree. For instance, some studies show that contact with members of a group produces more positive attitudes (reduces prejudice) toward that group; other studies find that contact has no effect on attitudes. Meta-analysis allows an investigator to bring order out of this apparent chaos.

**Meta-analysis** is a statistical technique that allows the researcher to combine the quantitative results from all previous studies on a question to determine what, collectively, they say. In conducting a meta-analysis, the researcher performs three steps:

1. The researcher locates all previous studies on the question. Today, this is typically done using computerized searches of libraries and databases. It should also include a canvas of researchers known to have worked in the area to identify unpublished research.
2. For each study, the investigator computes a statistic that measures how big the difference was, say, between those who did and those who did not interact with members of the group, and what the direction of the difference was (whether those who had contact were more or less prejudiced). This statistic is called *d*. The formula for it is

$$d = \frac{M_c - M_{nc}}{s}$$

where $M_c$ is the mean or average score for the participants who had contact and $M_{nc}$ is the average score for those who did not; *s* is the standard deviation of the scores of all participants. The standard deviation is a measure of how much variability there is in the scores. The *d* statistic tells us—for this one study—how big the difference between the two groups of participants was relative to the variability in scores.
3. The researcher averages all the values of *d* over all the studies that were located. This average *d* value tells what the direction of the difference is in attitudes between those who do and do not

have contact with the group and how large the difference is for all the studies combined. A general guide is that a *d* of .20 is a small difference, a *d* of .50 is a moderate difference, and a *d* of .80 is a large difference.

Meta-analyses have become especially important in light of the "replication crisis." One of the hallmarks of science is reproducibility of results, successful replication. If results cannot be replicated they are not reliable or valid. A team of researchers worked to carefully replicate 100 experimental and correlational studies published in three major psychology journals, including the *Journal of Personality and Social Psychology*. Ninety-seven percent of the original studies reported significant results; significant results were found in only 36 percent of the replications (Open Science Collaboration, 2015). This calls into question the validity of the original results. Where numerous studies of a phenomenon have been conducted, meta-analyses provide a solution. We include the results of numerous meta-analyses throughout the book.

## RESEARCH IN DIVERSE POPULATIONS

For much of the twentieth century, the participants in research by social psychologists were often White, often middle-class, and often college students. In the past 30 years, there has been increasing interest in studying racial and ethnic minority groups in the United States, and members of other cultures around the world. It is important that research in such groups meets the standards of internal and external validity discussed earlier. This requires that we give careful consideration to the methods we use and be willing to adapt or change them.

Much research is based on theory. The theories and assumptions on which we base studies of diverse groups should take into account

## BOX 2.3  Crowdsourcing Social Psychological Research

*Crowdsourcing* refers to "the practice of obtaining needed services, ideas, or content by soliciting contributions from a large group of people, and especially from an online community" (http://en.wikipedia.org/wiki/Crowdsourcing). Employers needing services, and so forth, post requests for workers to provide what they need, with or without compensation. Online solicitation of contributions can provide access to a large number of people who may complete the task very quickly. One widely used online platform is Amazon's Mechanical Turk (AMT). Requesters can post various tasks using templates provided by the software, solicit workers to complete the tasks, and offer compensation to those who complete it. The task is referred to as a HIT (human intelligence task). Social psychologists are employing AMT to conduct both online surveys and experiments.

A researcher can post a survey on AMT just as they would post it on a university server. The researcher creates a description of the HIT, which is posted on a list. Persons looking for work read the list and select the HITs they want to complete. The researcher can list prerequisites for completing the HIT, such as age, gender, and so on. AMT includes a payment mechanism. The researcher can deposit an amount of money in an online account, specify the compensation to be provided, and AMT will transfer the compensation to the worker's account upon completion of the task. If they want to, the requester can specify that the worker's contribution be reviewed for quality/completeness before payment is transferred, giving the researcher some quality control.

It is also possible to conduct experiments on AMT. If the independent variable can be manipulated by exposing groups of participants to different information—different texts, images, decision-making problems—and measuring the dependent variables (DVs) with questions or scales, it can be done online. In this case, each experimental condition is one HIT, and the researcher specifies how many "assignments" (participants) are allowed for each HIT. Again, the researcher can specify prerequisites, or even have potential workers complete a screening questionnaire or practice items. For example, one could conduct a bystander effect experiment on AMT by providing a story or video of a person suffering a seizure or being attacked; there could be four versions, varying the setting (university classroom, shopping mall) or gender of person needing help. The DV would be measured by a series of questions about whether the participant would intervene or help. Many laboratory experiments are now presented "live" to participants on laptop computers using digitized materials and recording the responses. It is easy to transfer such protocols to the AMT platform.

AMT has several advantages as a research site. It provides access to a very large participant pool (more than 100,000 people) and a streamlined recruitment procedure (Buhrmester, Kwang, & Gosling, 2011). Research indicates that AMT participants are demographically diverse, certainly more diverse than an undergraduate subject pool. A comparison of data collected via AMT with data collected from a national population-based sample found that the results were very similar (Weinberg, Freese, & McElhattan, 2014). Participation rates are affected by task length and compensation rate. A final advantage is fast cycles of developing theory, collecting data, revising theory, and collecting more data (Mason & Suri, 2012). As with other methods, there are pitfalls that can undermine the quality of the research. Surveys posted on AMT sometimes attract primarily women with younger children (who are at home during the day). There are several guides specifying best practices for using AMT; one of the most comprehensive is http://wiki.wearedynamo.org/index.php/Guidelines_for_Academic_Requesters

the cultural history and present social and economic circumstances of the group(s) being studied. For example, Orbuch and colleagues (2002), in developing a longitudinal study of divorce among Black and White couples, assumed that the risk of divorce for Black couples is influenced by past and present social and economic conditions faced by Blacks, which may differ from those of Whites. Also the measures must be linguistically equivalent—that is, be worded so that they are understood in the same way by all participants; if the participants speak a different primary language from that of the instrument, a careful process of translation and independent back translation should be employed to produce equivalent instruments. Measures should be standardized or interpreted using data from the population(s) being studied; for example, researchers should not use score distributions obtained from majority samples to interpret the scores of minority populations unless they have been shown to be equivalent. In this example (Orbuch, Veroff, Hassan, & Horrocks, 2002), the measures of positive interaction and of conflict had been used in the earlier waves of the research, and their applicability to both Blacks and Whites had been demonstrated.

If the researcher's intent is to characterize groups or cultures, the samples studied must be representative. If they are not, it should be noted in any reports of the research, and the results should be interpreted accordingly. Whereas the samples in this study (Orbuch et al., 2002) were not representative of Blacks or Whites, they did appear to represent the population of couples marrying for the first time in both groups. Finally, the research team should include either researchers who are members of the group(s) or persons who are culturally competent based on supervised training and experience (CNPAAEMI, 2000).

*Culture* refers to an intersubjective (shared) set of schema, attitudes, and values that members use to perceive and understand the world. When we conduct research, it is important that the results reflect the culture of the group(s) being studied. Some suggest that this requires that quantitative research be supplemented with methods focused on the cultural meanings that group members attribute to the quantitative measures. For example, a study of differences in gender role used scores on the Bem Sex-Role Inventory to compare a sample of European-American women with a sample of Women of Color (Landrine, Klonoff, & Brown-Collins, 1995). There were no significant differences between the groups in self-rating on traits such as "feminine," "assertive," and "independent." Following the self-rating items were questions designed to measure the meaning of these words to the respondent. Responses to these questions revealed differences in meaning between the groups. The most common meaning of "assertive" among European-American women was "standing up" for themselves, while among Women of Color it meant saying what was on their mind. Thus, understanding differences across groups requires research designs that will capture relevant aspects of the cultures of the groups.

## ETHICAL ISSUES IN SOCIAL PSYCHOLOGICAL RESEARCH

As important as the methodological issues are the ethical issues involved in research on humans. There is a consensus among investigators and others affiliated with the scientific community that people who participate in research have certain rights that must be respected. In some cases, protecting those rights requires investigators to limit or modify their research practices.

In the following discussion of ethical issues, we focus first on potential sources of harm to participants. Then we discuss various safeguards, such as risk-benefit analysis and informed consent, to protect participants' rights. Finally, we consider potential benefits to participants in research.

## Potential Sources of Harm

Harm to participants in research can take a variety of forms, including physical harm, psychological harm, and harm from breach of confidentiality. We will discuss each of these.

**Physical Harm.** Exposure to physical harm in social psychological research is uncommon. Investigations to measure the effects of stress do sometimes employ an exercise treadmill or tasks where participants immerse one hand in ice water. As a precaution, investigators usually screen prospective participants to exclude those with relevant medical conditions. At the onset of a study, investigators are expected to inform the participants about any risks so that they can decide whether they might be harmed by participating. In studies involving physical stress, investigators typically monitor participants for adverse effects throughout the research.

**Psychological Harm.** A more common risk in social psychological research is psychological harm to participants. This risk is present in studies where participants receive negative information about themselves. For example, a not uncommon experimental manipulation is to give participants false feedback about their physical attractiveness, about others' reactions to them, or about their performance on various tests or tasks. Investigators can use such feedback to raise or lower participants' self-esteem, to induce feelings of acceptance or rejection by others, or to create perceptions of success or failure on important tasks. These manipulations are effective precisely because they do influence the participants' self-perception.

Negative feedback may cause psychological stress or harm, at least temporarily. For this reason, some investigators believe that such techniques should not be employed in research. Others believe, however, that they are acceptable and may be used if alternative, less harmful manipulations are not available.

When false feedback is used, an investigator can limit any long-term harmful effects by giving the participants a thorough debriefing after the study, providing the participants with a full description of the study, and emphasizing the falsity of the feedback. Debriefing should be done immediately after the study to minimize the time that participants labor under false impressions.

**Breach of Confidentiality.** Confidentiality is another important issue, especially in survey and observational research. Interviewers and observers are frequently able to identify participants, and they may recall details regarding the participants' behavior or responses to questions. Were confidentiality to be breached, the effects might be damaging to the participants. This concern arises especially in surveys inquiring about sexual behaviors, past physical or psychiatric illnesses, or other sensitive personal matters. It also arises in observational studies of deviant or criminal activities.

One important precaution against breach of confidentiality is to avoid including on the research team any people who are apt to have social contacts with respondents in other settings. Furthermore, many investigators refuse to attach any identifying information such as names and addresses to data after they have been collected. Another approach is to keep any identifying information separate from questionnaires or behavioral records to prevent breaches of confidentiality. An important precaution is to never store data that are not anonymous on laptop or other portable devices. Numerous breaches have occurred as a result of stolen or lost digital devices.

Observational research often deals with a specific group or organization. During their investigation, researchers may gather information about the organization itself and about various members. When these findings are published, the investigators typically refer to the organization by a pseudonym and to

## BOX 2.4 Ethical Considerations in Research Design

Before conducting a given study, investigators and members of review boards ask certain ethical questions about the proposed research design and its impact on participants. Among the most commonly asked ethical questions are the following:

1. Is it possible that participants in the study might be harmed physically, for example, by strenuous exercise?
2. Does the study give participants false information about themselves or use any other form of deception?
3. Does the study induce participants to engage in behavior that might threaten their self-respect?
4. If the investigators make audio- or videotapes of the participants, will they obtain permission from the participants to use the tapes as a data source?
5. What steps will the investigators take to preserve the confidentiality of information obtained about the participants?
6. Will the investigators tell potential participants in advance about the foreseeable risks that their participation may entail?
7. Will participants have a chance to ask questions about the study before they consent to participate?
8. Will the investigators inform the participants that they have the right to terminate their participation at any time?
9. At the end of the study, will the investigators fully debrief the participants and tell them about the real nature of the study and its procedures?

members by role only. This practice usually suffices to prevent outsiders from identifying the organization and its members, although it may not prevent members from identifying each other. There are obvious risks to members' positions, reputations, or jobs within the organization if compromising information becomes known to other members. Box 2.4 lists some of the major ethical questions that apply to many studies.

### Institutional Safeguards

As noted earlier, researchers can take various steps to prevent harm to participants. Although many people feel that voluntary self-regulation by researchers suffices to protect the rights and interests of the participants, others feel that some agency other than the researcher should review proposed research designs. Accordingly, most institutions have developed and put into place safeguards against potentially harmful effects of research. The two most important safeguards are conducting a **risk-benefit analysis** and obtaining informed consent from all participants.

**Risk–Benefit Analysis.** The federal government is a major provider of funds for research in the social and biomedical sciences. Many federal departments and agencies have adopted common criteria for the review of research involving human participants (the Common Rule, 45 Code of Federal Regulations 46 A). Under these regulations, investigators and institutions are responsible for minimizing the risks, of whatever type, to participants in research. The rules encourage researchers to develop designs that expose participants to no more than "minimal risk"—meaning risk no greater than that ordinarily encountered in daily life or during the performance of routine physical or psychological examinations or tests (U.S. Department of Health and Human Services, 2010).

Furthermore, the regulations require each institution that receives funds from federal agencies to establish an institutional review board (IRB) responsible for reviewing proposed research involving human participants. The IRB (sometimes called a human subjects committee or research ethics committee) assesses the extent to which participants in each proposed study will be placed at risk. As noted earlier, many social psychological studies involve no foreseeable risks to participants, but if the members of the board believe that participants might be harmed—physically, psychologically, or by breach of confidentiality—a detailed assessment must be made. That is, the review board conducts a risk-benefit analysis, which weighs potential risks to the participants against anticipated benefits to the participants and the importance of the knowledge that may result from the research. The review board will not approve research involving risk to participants unless it concludes that the risk is reasonable in relation to the benefits.

**Informed Consent.** The other major safeguard against risk is the requirement that investigators obtain **informed consent** from all individuals, groups, or organizations that participate in research studies. Informed consent exists when potential participants or respondents, on being informed by the investigators what their participation will involve, agree willingly to participate in the research. Specifically, six elements are essential to informed consent. (1) The researchers should give potential participants an explanation of the purposes of the research and a brief description of the procedures to be employed; however, they need not and usually do not tell the participants the hypothesis of the research. (2) The investigators should inform participants about any foreseeable risks of participation. (3) The researchers should provide a description of any benefits to the participant or others. (4) The investigators should provide information about which

medical or psychological resources, if any, are available to participants who are adversely affected by participation. (5) The researchers should offer to answer questions about the study whenever possible. (6) The researchers should inform potential participants that they have the right to terminate their participation at any time.

In many survey and observational settings, investigators implement informed consent by giving this information to respondents orally. In experiments, especially those involving some risk to participants, investigators usually obtain written consent from each participant.

## Potential Benefits

In the process of obtaining informed consent, participants are usually told that they will not benefit directly from the research. Although that is often true, there are exceptions. Field trials of new forms of treatment for physical or psychological problems may directly benefit participants if the new form of treatment proves to be effective. Similarly, participants in some studies may gain insight into themselves and others. For example, a longitudinal study of couples in premarital relationships included measures of how the men and women were affected. Many participants reported that they paid more attention to evaluating their relationship, and those who reported paying more attention reported more satisfaction with their relationship at the end of the yearlong study (Hughes & Surra, 2000).

Some people believe that being questioned about one's sexual behavior is upsetting, especially to youth. In one study, 15- to 25-year-olds completed such a questionnaire. Later, they rated how distressing and positive the experience had been. Few reported being distressed, and 89 percent said surveys like this should be carried out. Persons who were distressed were those who reported experiencing sexual coercion in the past (Kuyper, Wit, Adam, & Woertman, 2012).

## SUMMARY

This chapter discussed the research methods used by social psychologists to investigate social behavior, activity, and events.

**Characteristics of Research.** (1) Objectives of research include describing reality, identifying correlations between variables, testing causal hypotheses, and testing theories. (2) Research is usually guided by a hypothesis, which may specify a causal relationship between two or more variables. (3) Ideally, the findings of empirical research should be high in both internal validity and external validity.

**Research Methods.** Social psychologists use a variety of quantitative and qualitative methods to study human social behavior. The principal quantitative methods are surveys and experiments. (1) A survey involves systematically asking questions and recording the answers from respondents. Investigators use surveys to gather self-reported information about attitudes and activities. The quality of the data obtained in a survey depends on the reliability and validity of the measures used. (2) An experiment involves the manipulation of one or more independent variables and the random assignment of participants to experimental conditions or treatments. Some experiments are conducted in a laboratory, where the investigator has a high degree of control, whereas others are conducted in natural settings. Qualitative methods include observational techniques and archival methods. (3) Naturalistic observation involves collecting data about naturally occurring events. In a field study, observers view an event or activity as it occurs and then record their observations. (4) Archival research involves the analysis of existing information collected by others. Sources of archival data include the Census Bureau and other federal agencies, data archives, and newspapers. Investigators use content analysis to study textual material such as speeches or reports.

**Ethical Issues in Research.** (1) There are several potential sources of harm to participants in research. These include physical harm, psychological harm, and breach of confidentiality. There are various steps that individual investigators can take to prevent or minimize such harm. (2) There are also institutional safeguards against harm. These safeguards require investigators to minimize risks to participants and to obtain informed consent from participants. Institutional review boards monitor research designs to ensure that these conditions are met by investigators. (3) In some cases, participants in research may benefit directly from their participation.

### *Critical Thinking Skill:*
### *Understanding the Importance of Sampling*

Every type of research in social psychology involves a sample. Surveys involve asking questions of a sample of persons drawn from some population (students, adult voters, visitors to an Internet website, and so on). Experiments involve participants recruited/sampled from some population, often students at a college or university. Ethnographic and observational studies involve a sample of settings (such as bars) or persons (for example, McDonald's employees). The character of the sample has a major impact on the conclusions one can make from the research.

A researcher was interested in studying the culture of alcohol consumption on the campus where they taught. In particular, they wanted to compare Black and White male students' attitudes and consumption patterns. They decided to approach several Black student groups and several White student groups to recruit men to be interviewed. They contacted two Black and two White fraternities, two Black and two White eating clubs, and two Black and two White professional groups (business students and engineering students). They distributed fliers to members of each group describing the research, and asked interested men to call them. They interviewed five men from each of the six groups, for a total of 30 men. The researcher found that about two-thirds of the men drank four or more drinks on one or more nights each week, and that drinking didn't seem to vary by race/ethnicity.

What can we conclude from this study? Can we conclude that there is no difference in alcohol attitudes and behavior by race among college students generally? By race among students at this college? That business and engineering students are equally likely to drink? Think about these questions and then answer them. When you have finished, read on.

The sample in this study is a volunteer sample. The participants volunteered based on a flier that described the study as a study of drinking. It is likely that most of the volunteers were men who currently drank. A nondrinker would probably think the researcher wasn't interested in talking to him. The men are all from the same college; we certainly can't infer anything about men at other colleges and universities. And these men were all recruited from social groups on the campus, and so they probably aren't representative of Black and White male students on the campus. In fact, it takes money to belong to a fraternity or eating club. The researcher may have found that college students who have money drink a lot; not an especially newsworthy result!

So whenever you read a report of the results of research, find out the nature of the sample before you draw any conclusions. A sample that is representative of some group or population is usually a prerequisite for valid research.

# SOCIALIZATION THROUGH THE LIFE COURSE

By the end of this chapter you will be able to:

- Define the four basic perspectives in the study of socialization.

- Describe the major socializing agents in contemporary U.S. society.

- Explain the processes through which socialization occurs.

- Describe the outcomes of socialization in childhood and adolescence.

- Define the basic influences on the adult life course.

## INTRODUCTION

My daughter is the percussionist in her middle school band. At the first session in September when the director asked for volunteers, six boys shouted, "Me!" "I want to do it!" and so on. Then the director asked, "Who can play the piano?" Kimberly and two other girls raised their hands. The band director auditioned the three girls. He wanted a percussionist who could read music; a really good idea.

Kimberly got the position. She jumped right in, practicing on the bass drum, the snare drum, and the chimes after school; we had to pick her up when she finished because she missed the bus. She brought the drums home sometimes on weekends (I had to pick her up and transport the instruments on Friday, and return her and the instruments on Monday morning). I was amazed. I had no musical talent at all, and here she was improving every week.

I had gone to a small school. The administration wanted a big band. I knew I had no talent or even training but *everybody* had to audition. The band director gave me a clarinet and said, "Just move your fingers in time to the music." I lasted

about two concerts, after which he grudgingly conceded that I couldn't play at all and dismissed me from the band. Of course, the 95 percent of the students who were still in the band made my life hell for several weeks. So I was really pleased that Kimberly not only made the band, but was practicing and improving and getting good! I could hardly believe it. She wasn't like me at all. But I was really proud!

In late October, the band gave their first public concert. I was in the second row. It was great! They played the "Star Spangled Banner," then a couple of short pieces, a march by John Philip Souza, "The Tempest," and finished with the *Pirates of the Caribbean* theme. It was awesome!! I was so proud of her. The audience, mostly parents of the band members, loved it. I waited outside the band room after the concert.

She was the last band member to come out. I saw her, smiled, and walked toward her with my arms out. I hugged her. She started crying. "Dad, I was awful." I was stunned. I stuttered and said, "No, you were great." She said, "I missed my cue once, and my timing was off in the Souza." I said, "I didn't notice, and I am sure no one else did."

She *is* like me—a perfectionist. It is wonderful that she has musical talent. She also got my perfectionism.

One of the striking features of social life is that there is great continuity from one generation to the next—continuity both in physical characteristics and in behavior. Genetic inheritance is one source of continuity. But a major contributor to intergenerational similarity is **socialization**, the ways in which individuals learn and re-create skills, knowledge, values, motives, and roles appropriate to their positions in a group or society.

How does an infant become "human"—that is, an effective participant in society? The answer is, through socialization. As we grew from infancy, we interacted continually with others. We learned to speak a language—a prerequisite for participation in society. We learned basic interaction rituals, such as greeting a stranger with a handshake and a loved one with a kiss. We also learned the socially accepted ways to achieve various goals, both material (food, clothing, shelter) and social (respect, love, help of others). As we learned these, we used them; as we used them, we re-created them—adapted them to our particular circumstances.

It is obvious that socialization makes us like most other members of society in important ways. It is not so obvious that socialization also produces our individuality. The sense of self and the capacity to engage in self-oriented acts (discussed in Chapter 4) are a result of socialization.

The first part of this chapter will examine childhood socialization. By childhood, we mean the period from birth to adolescence. Childhood is a social concept, shaped by historical, cultural, and political influences (Corsaro, 2011). In contemporary American society, we define children as immature—in need of training at home and of a formal education. The second part examines socialization beyond childhood, such as gender roles and historical variations that affect the person.

## PERSPECTIVES ON SOCIALIZATION

Which is the more important influence on behavior—nature or nurture, heredity or environment? This question has been especially important to those who study children. Although both influences are important, one view emphasizes biological development (heredity), whereas another emphasizes social learning (environment).

### The Developmental Perspective

The human child obviously undergoes a process of maturation. They grow physically, develop motor skills in a relatively uniform sequence, and begin to engage in various social behaviors at about the same age as most other children.

Some theorists view socialization as largely dependent on processes of physical and psychological maturation, which are biologically determined. Gesell and Ilg (1943) documented the sequence in which motor and social skills develop and the ages at which each new ability appears in the average child. They viewed the development of many social behaviors as primarily due to physical and neurological maturation, not social factors. For example, toilet training requires voluntary control over sphincter muscles and the ability to recognize cues of pressure on the bladder or lower intestine. According to developmental theory, when children around age 2½ develop these skills, they learn by themselves without environmental influences.

Table 3.1 lists the sequences of development of various abilities that have been identified by observational research. The ages shown are approximate; some children will exhibit the behavior at younger ages, whereas others will do so later.

As an example, consider the development of responsiveness to other persons. As early as 4 weeks, many infants respond to close physical contact by relaxing. At 16 weeks, babies can discriminate the human face and usually smile in response. They also show signs of recognizing the voice of their usual caregiver. By 28 weeks, the infant clearly differentiates faces and responds to variations in facial expression. At 1 year, the child shows a variety of emotions in response to others' behavior. A toddler will seek interaction with adults or with siblings by crawling or walking toward them and tugging on clothing. Thus, recognition of, responsiveness to, and orientation toward adults follow a uniform developmental pattern. The ability to interact with others depends in part on the development of visual and auditory discrimination.

**TABLE 3.1** The Process of Development

|  | 16 WEEKS | 28 WEEKS | 1 YEAR | 2 YEARS | 3 YEARS |
|---|---|---|---|---|---|
| Visual Activity | Follows objects with eyes; eyes adjust to objects at varying distances | Watches activity intently; hand–eye coordination | Enjoys watching moving objects (like TV pictures) | Responds to stimuli in periphery of visual field; looks intently for long periods | |
| Interpersonal | Smiles at human face; responds to caregiver's voice; demands social attention | Responds to variation in tone of voice; differentiates people (fears strangers) | Engages in responsive play; shows emotions, anxiety; shows definite preferences for some persons | Prefers solitary play; rudimentary concept of ownership | Can play cooperatively with an older child; strong desire to please; gender differences in choice of toys, materials |
| Vocal Activity | Vocalizes pleasure (coos, gurgles, laughs); babbles (strings of syllable-like sounds) | Vocalizes vowels and consonants; tries to imitate sounds | Vocalizes syllables; practices two to eight known words | Vocalizes constantly; names actions; repeats words | Uses three-word sentences; likes novel words |
| Bodily Movement | Can hold head up; can roll over | Can sit up | Can stand; can climb up and down stairs | Can run; likes large-scale motor activity— push, pull, roll | Motion fluid, smooth; good coordination |
| Manual Dexterity | Touches objects | Can grasp with one hand; manipulates objects | Manipulates objects serially | Good control of hand and arm | Good fine-motor control— uses fingers, thumb, wrist well |

*Source:* Adapted from Caplan & Caplan, 1973; and *Infant and Child in the Culture of Today* (1943) by Arnold Gesell and Frances L. Ilg. Used with permission of the Gesell Institute of Human Development.

Responsiveness to another person develops early in life. By 16 weeks of age, a child smiles in response to a human face. By 28 weeks, a child can distinguish caregivers from strangers. © video1/iStock

Development continues throughout life. Important physical and hormonal changes occur during puberty, pregnancy, and menopause/later life and impact motivation and behavior. Recognition of this lifelong process is one aspect of the life course perspective, discussed later in this chapter.

## The Social Learning Perspective

Whereas the developmental perspective focuses on the unfolding of the child's own abilities, the social learning perspective emphasizes the child's acquisition of cognitive and behavioral skills in interaction with the environment. Successful socialization requires that the child acquire considerable information about the world. The child must learn about many physical or natural realities, such as what animals are dangerous and which things are edible. Children also must learn about the social environment. They must learn the language used by people around them to communicate their needs to others. They also need to learn the meanings their caregivers associate with various actions. Children need to learn to identify the kinds of persons encountered in their immediate environment. They need to learn what behaviors they can expect of people, as well as others' expectations for their own behavior.

According to the social learning perspective, socialization is primarily a process of children learning the shared meanings of the groups in which they are reared (Shibutani, 1961). Such variation in meanings gives groups, subcultures, and societies their distinctiveness. Although the content—what is learned—varies from group to group, the processes by which social learning takes place are universal. This viewpoint emphasizes the adaptive nature of socialization. The infant learns the verbal and interpersonal skills necessary to interact successfully with others. The processes by which this occurs are the concern of **reinforcement theory**. Having acquired these skills, children can perpetuate the meanings that distinguish their social groups and even add to or modify these meanings by introducing innovations of their own (Corsaro, 2011).

Recent research on socialization has considered both the importance of developmental processes and the influence of social learning. The developmental age of the child obviously determines which actions the child can perform. Infants less than 6 months old cannot walk. All cultures have adapted to these developmental limitations by coordinating the performance expectations placed on children with the maturation of their abilities. However, developmental processes alone are not sufficient for the emergence of complex social behavior. In addition to developmental readiness, social interaction—learning—is necessary for the development of language. This is illustrated by the case of Isabelle, who lived alone with her deaf-mute mother until the age of 6½. When she was discovered, she was unable to make any sound other than a croak. Yet within two years after she entered a systematic educational program, her vocabulary numbered more than 1,500 words and she had the linguistic skills of a 6-year-old (Davis, 1947).

Thus, both nature and nurture influence behavior. Developmental processes produce a readiness to perform certain behaviors. The content of these behaviors is determined primarily by social learning—that is, by cultural influences.

## The Interpretive Perspective

Socialization occurs primarily through social interaction. Whereas the social learning perspective emphasizes the process of learning—for example, the role of reinforcement in the acquisition of behavior—the interpretive perspective (Corsaro, 2011) focuses on the interaction itself. Drawing on symbolic interaction theory (see Chapter 1), this perspective views the child's task as the *discovery* of the meanings common to the social group (such as the family or a school band). This process of discovery requires communication with parents, other adults, and other children. Especially important is the child's participation in **cultural routines**, which are recurrent and predictable activities that are basic to day-to-day social life (Corsaro & Fingerson, 2003). Greeting rituals, common games, and mealtime patterns are examples of such cultural routines. These routines provide members with a sense of security and of belonging to a group. At the same time, their predictability enables children to use them to display their developing cultural knowledge and skills. A good example is Kimberly, who we met in the introduction. There are cultural routines for playing a musical instrument, but Kimberly, like other young musicians, develops her own particular style in playing the snare drum.

According to this perspective, socialization is a process of interpretive reproduction. Children don't simply learn culture. In daily interaction, children use the language and interpretive skills that they are learning or discovering. As they become more proficient in communicating and more knowledgeable about the meanings shared in the family and school, children attain a deeper understanding of the culture. Children, through interaction, acquire and reproduce the culture.

When children communicate with one another (as in school or at play), they do not simply imitate the acquired culture. They use what they have learned to create their own somewhat unique peer culture. Children take a traditional game such as one group chasing another group and change the rules to fit their needs and the physical and social context in which they are enacting the game. In the 1950s the two groups were often cowboys and Indians; in the 2000s in some neighborhoods they were cops and perps (Goffman, 2015). The changed rules become part of a new routine of chase. Thus, from an early age, children are not just imitating culture, but recreating it.

## The Impact of Social Structure

A fourth perspective emphasizes the influence of social structure. Socialization is not a random process. Teaching new members the rules of the game is too important to be left to chance. Socialization is organized according to the sequence of roles that newcomers to the society ordinarily pass through. In American society, these include familial roles, such as offspring, and roles in educational institutions, such as preschooler, elementary school student, and high school student. These are age-linked roles; we expect transitions from one role to another to occur at certain ages. Distinctive socialization outcomes are sought for those who occupy each role. Thus, we expect young children to learn language and basic norms governing such diverse activities as eating, dressing, and bowel and bladder control. Many preschool programs will not enroll a child who has not learned the latter.

Furthermore, social structure designates the persons or organizations responsible for producing desired outcomes. In a complex society such as ours, there is a sequence of roles and a corresponding sequence of socializing agents. From birth through adolescence, the family is primarily responsible for socializing the child. From ages 6 to 12, a child is an elementary school student; we expect elementary school teachers to teach the basics to their students. When the adolescent becomes a high school student, there is yet another group of agents to further develop their knowledge and abilities. In adulthood, we become partners and coworkers, and need to learn these roles from persons in related roles.

This perspective is sociological; it considers socialization as a product of group life. It calls our attention to the changing content of and responsibility for socialization throughout the individual's life. This theme is fundamental to the life course perspective, discussed later in this chapter.

These perspectives are not contradictory or mutually exclusive. Each points to a different influence on the unique person that each of us becomes. (See the Critical Thinking Skill at the end of this chapter.)

## AGENTS OF CHILDHOOD SOCIALIZATION

Socialization has four components. It always involves (1) an agent—someone who serves as a source for what is being learned; (2) a learning process; (3) a target—a person who is being socialized; and (4) an outcome—something that is being learned. This section will consider the four primary agents of childhood socialization—family, peers, school, and mass media. Later sections will focus on the processes and outcomes of childhood socialization.

## Family

At birth, infants are primarily aware of their own bodies. Hunger, thirst, or pain creates unpleasant and perhaps overwhelming bodily tensions. The infant's primary concern is to remove these tensions and satisfy bodily needs. To meet the infant's needs, adult caregivers must learn to read the infant's signals accurately (Ainsworth, 1979). Also, infants begin to perceive their principal caregivers as the source of need satisfaction. These early experiences are truly interactive (Bell, 1979). The adult learns how to care effectively for the infant, and the infant forms a strong emotional attachment to the caregiver.

**Is a Mother Necessary?** Does it matter who responds to and establishes a caring relationship with the infant? Must there be a single principal caregiver in infancy and childhood for effective socialization to occur?

Psychoanalytic theory (as originally framed by Freud) asserts that an intimate emotional relationship between infant and caregiver (almost always the mother at the time Freud wrote) is essential to healthy personality development. This was one of the first hypotheses to be studied empirically. To examine the effects of the absence of a single, close caregiver on children, researchers have studied institutionalized infants. In the earliest reported work, Spitz (1945, 1946) studied an institution in which six nurses cared for 45 infants under 18 months old. The nurses met the infants' basic biological needs. However, they had limited contact with the babies, and there was little

evidence of emotional ties between the nurses and the infants. Within one year, the infants' scores on developmental tests fell dramatically from an average of 124 to an average of 72. Within two years, one-third had died, 9 had left, and the 21 who remained in the institution were severely developmentally delayed. Research on children who lived in orphanages for an average of 16 months following birth found that at age 4½, they had significant difficulty matching facial expressions of emotion with stories, compared to children from control families (Fries & Pollak, 2004). These findings dramatically support the hypothesis that an emotionally responsive caregiver is essential.

Thus, infants need a secure **attachment**—a warm, close relationship with an adult that produces a sense of security and provides stimulation—to develop the interpersonal and cognitive skills needed for proper growth (Ainsworth, 1979). Moreover, being cared for in such a relationship provides the foundation of the infant's sense of self.

For many decades, the gender rules in American society made mothers primarily responsible for raising children. Fathers' parental responsibility was to work outside the home and provide the income needed by the family. The division of labor in many families conformed to these definitions. As a result of these structural arrangements, some analysts concluded that a warm, intimate, continuous relationship between a child and its mother is essential to normal child development (Bowlby, 1965). Perhaps only in the mother–infant relation can the child experience the necessary sense of security and emotional warmth. According to this view, other potential caregivers have less emotional interest in the infant and may not be adequate substitutes.

Research on parent–child interaction indicates that if mothers are sensitive to the child's needs and responsive to their distress in the first year of life, the child is more likely to develop a secure attachment (Demo &

Cox, 2001). This is true in both two-parent and mother-only families. Infants who are securely attached to their mothers in the first two years of life evidence less problem behavior and more cooperative behavior from ages 4 to 10. Thus, secure mother–infant attachment is associated with positive outcomes.

What about children raised by single fathers? Research examined variations in physical health by family structure, in a sample of more than 67,000 children (Ziol-Guest & Dunifon, 2014). The outcomes measured were whether the child had a physical or mental health condition that limited participation in daily activities, was in good physical health, and good mental health (five-item scale). Children living with single fathers had slightly higher scores on all three compared to children living with single mothers. Children living with their biological father were in better health than children living with a stepfather. Thus, it may be the case that the gender of the adult caregiver may not matter.

A related question is whether children need or benefit from having both a male and a female parent—that is, does the gender of parents matter? Researchers (Biblarz & Stacy, 2010) compared studies of two-parent families with same or different gender co-parents with studies of single-parent families. The relationships between parenting practices and child outcomes reported in studies of heterosexual families were also found in lesbian families, and in the few studies of gay co-parents that have been published. In general, in single-parent families, children fared better with a single mother than a single father, but such families differ on important dimensions like circumstances of formation, gender of child, and income.

Since 1960, gender role definitions have been changing. Married women with children are increasingly working outside the home (see Figure 3.3). The effect of maternal employment on the child is a major continuing public concern.

**Effects of Maternal Employment.** What effect does maternal employment have on children? A meta-analysis of 69 studies found mostly nonsignificant effects on children's achievement outcomes—IQ, test scores—and child behavior problems (Lucas-Thompson, Goldberg, & Prause, 2010). Early employment was most beneficial in single-parent families. Employment during the child's first year had a small negative effect.

The Fragile Families and Child Wellbeing survey is a longitudinal study of children born in 1999, with an oversample of non-marital births. Researchers collected data from White, Black, and Hispanic families. Researchers analyzed the relationship between maternal employment during the child's first year and several outcomes at 3 years of age. Maternal employment was associated with lower vocabulary scores in White, but not Black or Hispanic families, and with higher levels of behavior problems in Hispanic families (Berger, Brooks-Gunn, Paxson, & Waldfogel, 2008). These outcomes were not related to maternal stress or parenting behaviors.

A major argument had been that employment reduces the time mothers spend with children, which in turn could affect quality of parenting. A study of a nationally representative sample of individuals and families collected time diaries measuring how and with which adults children from birth through 12 spent their time (Hsin & Felfe, 2014). The results show that maternal employment is associated with reduced time spent on unstructured activities, but no reduction in time spent on educational activities. Thus, working mothers trade quantity of time for quality of time.

There have been dozens of studies of the effects of maternal employment on achievement outcomes in children and adolescents. A meta-analysis of 68 studies looked at four educational outcomes: tests of achievement, tests of intellectual functioning, grades, and teacher ratings of cognitive competence (Goldberg, Prause, Lucas-Thompson, & Himsel, 2008).

## BOX 3.1   Test Yourself: Attachment in Children and Adults

Which of the following best describes your feelings about relationships?

1. I find it relatively easy to get close to others and am comfortable depending on them and having them depend on me. I don't often worry about being abandoned or someone getting too close to me.
2. I am somewhat uncomfortable being close to others; I find it difficult to trust them completely, difficult to allow myself to depend on them. I am nervous when anyone gets too close, and often, love partners want me to be more intimate than I feel comfortable being.
3. I find that others are reluctant to get as close as I would like. I often worry that my partner doesn't really love me or won't want to stay with me. I want to merge completely with another person, and this desire sometimes scares people away. (Hazan & Shaver, 1987)

Each of these statements represents one attachment style, an individual's characteristic way of relating to significant others (Hazan & Shaver, 1987). The first describes a secure style, the second an avoidant style, and the third an anxious/ambivalent style.

The roots of the individual's style may be found in childhood. Ainsworth (1979) identified three styles of attachment in caregiver–child interactions. The attachment style of a young child is assessed by observing how the child relates to their caregiver when distressed (by, for example, a brief separation in a strange environment). The secure child readily approaches the caregiver and seeks comfort. The avoidant child does not approach the caregiver and appears detached. The anxious/ambivalent child approaches the caregiver and expresses anger or hostility toward them. Children as young as 2 years behave consistently in one of these ways when distressed.

According to the prototype hypothesis, we bring the style we developed as children into our intimate adult relationships. Early experiences with intimacy create internal working models of relationships that influence relationship behaviors later in life (Simpson & Rholes, 2010). Surveys of adults (for example, Hazan & Shaver, 1987) have found that about 55 percent describe themselves as secure, 25 percent as avoidant, and 20 percent as anxious/ambivalent. Attachment style influences our responses to other people (Feeney, 1999). It leads us to pay attention to certain aspects of a person (for example, their trustworthiness), creates biases in memory (we remember events consistent with our style), and affects how we explain relationship events. A secure person will ignore an event (their partner talking to an attractive person) that would make an anxious person feel jealous. Attachment style also influences relationship quality. Men and women who describe themselves as secure report that their romantic relationships involve interdependence, trust, and commitment (Simpson, 1990). Adults who describe themselves as avoidant say that they do not trust others and are afraid of getting close (Feeney & Noller, 1990). Those who are anxious/ambivalent report intense emotions toward the partner and a desire for deep commitment in a relationship.

Research using cross-sectional Internet survey data found that attachment bonds in adult relationships emerge within the first year; a longitudinal study of romantically involved persons found that there was little change in attachment to the partner over a one-year period (Heffernan, Fraley, Vicary, & Brumbaugh, 2012). A longitudinal study of a sample of heterosexual dating couples, ages 18 to 25, brought couples into the laboratory and had them engage in a conflict resolution task; participants completed self-report measures of attachment, and their interaction during the task was rated by observers. These measures were repeated about one year later. Both self-rated and observer-rated attachment security at Time 1 predicted scores at Time 2 (Holland & Roisman, 2010). Results of both studies suggest that attachment in relationships is stable over time.

Comparing children of mothers who worked (including part- and full-time) with children of mothers who did not, there were no significant differences on the four outcomes. Part-time work was positively associated with all four outcomes; there were more positive effects for girls than for boys.

The effects of maternal employment on older children depend partly on work characteristics. Nonstandard work (for example, working nights or rotating shifts) can negatively affect parent–child closeness and delay cognitive development (Crosnoe & Cavanagh, 2010). Mothers' exposure to physical hazards at work also negatively affects cognitive development, and exposure to work-related stressors has a negative effect on behavior (Felfe & Hsin, 2012). Fathers' exposure to physical hazards and stressors may have similar effects.

What about the effects of child care? It depends on the type, quality, and amount of care. A large-scale research project conducted at 10 sites around the United States followed 1,000 children from birth. At age 4½, children who experienced higher-quality care and whose care was provided in a center had significantly better cognitive skills and language performance; quality was measured using observers who completed a standardized observational record. Children who received more hours of care between the ages of 3 months and 4½ years were given higher ratings on behavior problems (on the 113-item Child Behavior Checklist) by care providers. Twenty-four percent of the sample were children of color; it appears that the results do not vary by ethnicity (NICHD Early Child Care Research Network, 1997a, 1997b, 2002; Belsky, 2006).

Researchers have continued to follow these youth. At age 15, both quality and quantity of nonrelative child care at young ages were linked to adolescent outcomes. Higher-quality care predicted higher cognitive and academic achievement, and youth reports of fewer school and emotional problems (Vandell et al., 2010).

**Fathers' Involvement with Children.** The broadening of maternal role definitions to include work outside the home has been accompanied by changes in expectations for fathers. This ideology of fatherhood, promoted by television and film, encourages active involvement of fathers in child care and child rearing (Parke, 1996). Some men have adopted these expectations for themselves. Fathers typically engage in more play activities than caregiving with infants and young children. A longitudinal study of 2,900 mothers and fathers assessed frequency of *play* (reading, telling stories, singing) and *caregiving* (e.g., washing, dressing, putting to sleep) when the child was 9 months, 2 years, and 4 years old (Planalp & Braungart-Rieker, 2016). Fathers who identified with the father role more strongly engaged in both types of activities more often, and increased their involvement more over time. A meta-analysis of 21 studies including children from 3 to 8 years old assessed fathers' engagement with the child in both home activities and school work. Results indicated a positive relationship between father engagement and the development of children's cognitive/academic skills, prosocial skills, and self-regulation (McWayne, Downer, Campos, & Harris, 2013). These patterns are found in European-American, African-American, and Hispanic two-parent families.

Several variables influence the extent of fathers' involvement with their children. Maternal attitudes are one important factor; a father is more involved when the mother encourages and supports his participation. Maternal employment is another influence. Husbands of employed women are more involved in child care and in some cases provide full-time care for the child. Also, a study found that lower levels of stress on the job and greater support from coworkers for being an active father were associated with greater involvement (Volling & Belsky, 1991). Thus, research suggests that work stressors have negative effects on both fathers' and mothers' involvement in child rearing. Research on Mexican-American families finds that a positive relationship between mother and father was related to quality fathering (Formoso, Gonzales, Barrera, & Dumka, 2007). Finally, parental education is positively related to time spent with children by both fathers and mothers (Guryan, Hurst, & Kearney, 2008).

**Child Rearing in a Diverse Society.** There is diversity in the living arrangements of children in the United States today. Table 3.2 indicates the living arrangements of all children in 2014 (U.S. Bureau of the Census, 2014). Sixty-eight percent of all children lived with two parents. Eighty-seven percent of the married couples lived with only their biological children, compared to 51 percent of the cohabiting couples (Vespa, Lewis, & Kreider, 2013). Twenty-four percent lived with a single mother; note that more than 2.8 million children are living with a single father. These arrangements vary by race/ethnicity. Compared to White (15%), Asian (9%), and Hispanic (27%), more African-American children lived with their mother (48%). Asian children were most likely (82%) to live with married, biological parents, compared to White (68%), Hispanic (61%), and Black (31%) (Kreider & Ellis, 2011). These differences result in differences in the norms, values, and daily lives of the children.

Studies of socialization have focused on child-rearing techniques or parenting styles and their impact on cognitive and social development. Research has consistently found that authoritative parenting—characterized by high levels of warmth combined with control—benefits children. Reliance by parents on this style is associated with greater achievement in school and positive relations with other adults and peers. Authoritarian styles, including physical punishment, and permissive styles are more likely to be associated with poor adjustment in childhood (Demo & Cox, 2001).

Spanking of children aged 1 to 3 is more likely when the child is fussy or has behavior problems, the mother is experiencing psychological distress, and the family is of low socioeconomic status (SES) (Hahlweg et al., 2008). In a large, ethnically diverse sample, spanking at ages 1 and 2 is associated with behavior problems at school entry (Slade & Wissow, 2004). In low-income White, African-American, and Mexican-American families, spanking at age 1 predicts aggressive behavior at age 2 and lower mental development scores at age 3 (Berlin et al., 2009).

The negative outcomes reported by research to be associated with physical punishment and authoritarian styles of parenting lead some observers to conclude that these are improper child-rearing techniques. Minority researchers challenge the validity of this conclusion for

**TABLE 3.2** U.S. Children's Living Arrangements, 2014

| ARRANGEMENT | WHITE | BLACK | ASIAN | HISPANIC | OTHER/MIXED |
|---|---|---|---|---|---|
| Two parents, married | 74% | 34% | 85% | 58% | 55% |
| Two parents, cohabiting | 3 | 5 | 2 | 7 | 7 |
| Mother, currently or formerly married | 11 | 15 | 7 | 14 | 12 |
| Mother, never married | 4 | 33 | 2 | 13 | 15 |
| Father | 4 | 4 | 2 | 3 | 4 |
| Other: grandparent, relative | 3 | 6 | 2 | 4 | 6 |
| Number of children, millions | 38.4 | 11.1 | 3.6 | 17.8 | 5.1 |

*Source:* U.S. Bureau of the Census, America's Families and Living Arrangements, 2014, Table C3. www.census.gov/hhes/families/data/cps2014C.htm

minority families (McLoyd, Cauce, Takeuchi, & Wilson, 2001). White and Black mothers living in poverty are more likely to use physical punishment, partly due to chronic financial stress (Demo & Cox, 2001). Research by Deater-Deckard and Dodge (1997) suggested that physical discipline is more common in African-American families and that they define it as positive parenting. Other research (Chao, 1994) has suggested that Asian-American parents rely on providing training and clear and concrete guidelines for behavior, and that this should not be seen as authoritarian.

With respect to values, White parents emphasize the development of autonomy (Alwin, 1990), which is consistent with the mainstream culture's emphasis on individualism and independence. Minority children are more likely to be socialized to value cooperation and interdependence (Demo & Cox, 2001). African-American parents tend to emphasize assertiveness, whereas Mexican-American families emphasize family unity and solidarity with the extended family. Asian-American parents teach children to value family authority. Thus, as we would expect, socialization in distinctive communities tends to emphasize the values of those communities (Richman & Mandara, 2013).

Contemporary scholars stress that the meaning and the impact on the child of a parenting technique varies depending upon cultural background, family structure, and social context. This suggests that we should focus on specific techniques and not group differences in their use (Crosnoe & Cavanagh, 2010). Scholars also point to diversity within racial categories, rendering generalizations about a group, such as Blacks or Hispanics, questionable (Burton et al., 2010).

**Effects of Divorce.** What percentage of couples divorce? That turns out not to be an easy question to answer (Kennedy & Ruggles, 2014). The age-standardized rate based on the American Community Survey was 19 per 1,000 married women in 2011. The divorce rate was high among 20- and 30-year-olds in the 1980s and 1990s; as those people have aged, the divorce rate has climbed among persons in their 40s, 50s and 60s. The rate in the past decade among young persons has declined. This suggests that the Baby Boom generation was the source of much of the marital instability in recent decades. Another statistic is that in 2011, 22 percent of women and 21 percent of men have ever been divorced (Stanton, 2015).

The probability of marital disruption is much lower for a woman with a college education. About one-half of divorces involve children under the age of 18 years, though this may change with the recent decline in divorce rates among young couples. Divorce usually involves several major changes in the life of a child: a change in family structure, a change in residence, a change in the family's financial resources, and perhaps a change of schools. Therefore, it is difficult to isolate the effects of divorce—the change in family structure—independently of these other changes. Research consistently finds that the number of transitions a child experiences is positively associated with undesirable outcomes (Cherlin, 2010). An additional confounding fact is that divorce is not a one-time crisis; it is a process that begins with marital discord while the couple is living together, continues through physical separation and legal proceedings, and ends, if ever, when those involved have completed the uncoupling process (Amato, 2001).

Research comparing children of divorced with children of married parents has consistently found that the children of divorced parents score lower on measures of academic success (such as grades), psychological adjustment, self-esteem, and long-term health, among other outcomes (Amato, 2001). These effects appear to be mediated by the type of maternal or paternal parenting the children receive following the divorce (Bastaits & Mortelmans, 2016). Some research (for example,

Hetherington, 1999) has reported that these deficits were present several years before the divorce, leading to the suggestion that children's problems contribute to the discord that leads to divorce. However, if we view the divorce as a process, children's problems prior to the divorce could be caused by the marital discord. A few studies report positive consequences for some children. Some offspring, especially daughters, develop very positive relationships with custodial mothers (Arditti, 1999).

Although most people acknowledge the undesirability of divorce, it is often justified with the argument that it is less harmful than growing up in a family with chronic marital, social, and perhaps economic problems. Is this true? A longitudinal study in Great Britain followed thousands of children from birth to age 33, enabling researchers to compare adults whose parents divorced when they were 7 to 16, 17 to 20, or 21 to 33 years of age (Furstenberg & Kiernan, 2001). The results show that men and women whose parents divorced when they were 7 to 16, compared to men and women whose parents divorced when they were older, completed less schooling and earned higher scores on an index of psychological symptoms; women were more likely to drink heavily as adults. The researchers also found higher rates of early and nonmarital pregnancy among those whose parents had divorced early. All of these results have been reported in studies of persons in the United States (Demo & Acock, 1988; Garfinkel & McLanahan, 1986). Reduced educational attainment and early parenthood and marriage result in a higher rate of poverty among adults raised in single-parent families (McLanahan & Booth, 1989).

A review of research on low-income families (often single-parent families) concludes that the need for the parent(s) to work long hours in order to earn enough money shifts the burden of family labor onto one or more children, usually girls. This labor includes caring for younger siblings, cooking, and cleaning; it prevents the person providing it from focusing on education and taking advantage of extracurricular and other opportunities, and may funnel her into early childbearing and marriage (Dodson & Dickert, 2004). Very few studies have been done of the effects of divorce in non-European-American families. We don't know whether we would find the effects described here in racial and ethnic minority groups.

## Peers

As the child grows, peers become increasingly important as socializing agents. The peer group differs from the family on several dimensions. These differences influence the type of interaction and thus the kinds of socialization that occur.

The family consists of persons who differ in status or power, whereas the peer group is composed of relative equals. From an early age, the child is taught to treat parents with respect and deference. Failure to do so will probably result in discipline. Interaction with peers is more open and spontaneous; the child does not need to be deferential or tactful. Thus, children at the age of 4 years bluntly refuse to let children they dislike join their games. With peers, they may say things that adults consider insulting, such as "You're ugly," to another child. This interactional give-and-take is a basic aspect of the friendship process (Corsaro & Fingerson, 2003).

Membership in a particular family is ascribed, whereas peer interactions are voluntary (Gecas, 1990). Thus, peer groups offer children their first experience in exercising choice over whom they relate to. The opportunity to make such choices contributes to the child's sense of social competence and allows interaction with other children who complement the developing identity.

Unlike the child's family, peer groups in early and especially middle childhood (aged

## BOX 3.2  Peer Culture

American society is highly segregated by age. Most of us spend most of our time with people of about the same age. This is especially true in childhood and adolescence, because age segregation is the fundamental organizing principle of our schools. Research provides important sights into the nature of *peer culture*, "a stable set of activities or routines, artifacts, values and concerns that are produced and shared in interaction with peers" (Corsaro, 2011), and its significance for socialization.

Children in American society learn about the role of friends and the expectations associated with that role. Friendship involves shared activities in specific spaces (Corsaro, 2011). Kids' understanding of this role provides a basis for evaluating their relationships with other children. They exercise their understanding by frequently asking, "We're friends, right?" As children begin to play in groups, maintaining access to the group becomes an issue. Children become concerned with issues of inclusion and exclusion—who is in the group and who is not. For many children in the U.S., these concerns emerge when they enter preschool. These issues remain important ones throughout childhood and into adolescence (Adler & Adler, 1995).

Peer groups reflect the desire of children to gain some control over the social environment and to use that control in concert with other children (Corsaro & Eder, 1995). Children become concerned with gaining control over adult authority, and they learn that a request or plea by several children is more likely to be granted. In elementary school, children develop a strong group identity, which is strengthened by minor rebellions against adult authority. Thorne (1993) observed that in one fourth/fifth-grade classroom, most of the students had contraband—small objects such as toy cars and trucks, nail polish, and stuffed animals—which were prohibited by school rules. By keeping these items in desks and by displaying or exchanging them at key moments during class, the kids were displaying resistance, a form of nonconformity challenging the academic regime and rules in the classroom (McFarland, 2004). Both children and adolescents assert themselves by making fun of and mocking teachers and administrators.

Peer groups play a major role in socializing young persons to gender role norms. As children move through elementary school, they

6 to 10) are usually homogeneous in sex and age. A survey of 2,299 children in third through twelfth grade measured the extent to which they belonged to tightly knit peer groups, the size of such groups, and whether they were homogeneous by race and gender (Schrum & Creek, 1987). The proportion belonging to a group peaked in sixth grade and then declined. The size of peer groups declined steadily from third through twelfth grade. Boys' groups are generally larger than girls' groups (Rose & Rudolph, 2006). A study of third through eighth graders found, controlling for the number of boys and girls in each grade, substantial sex homogeneity in

both boys' and girls' networks (Neal, 2010). Sex homophily was consistent from grades three through nine; significant homophily by race developed in seventh grade. Other research indicates that friendships of seventh- to twelfth-grade Black, Hispanic, and White students tend to be homogeneous by race (Quillian & Campbell, 2003).

Peer associations make a major contribution to the development of the child's identity. Children learn the role of friend in interactions with peers, contributing to greater differentiation of the self (Corsaro & Rizzo, 1988). Peer and other relationships outside the family provide a basis for

increasingly form groups that are homogeneous by gender. For instance, in one study, Thorne (1993) observed that there is a geography of gender in the school yard. Boys generally were found on the playing fields, whereas girls were concentrated in the areas closer to the building and in the jungle gyms. Children who violated these gender boundaries risked being teased or even ridiculed. Thorne identified several varieties of **borderwork**, which is "interaction across—yet interaction based on and even strengthening—gender boundaries" (1993, p. 64). These activities involve the themes of gender and aggression—themes common to heterosexual relationships in American society. There is also the implicit message that boys and their activities are more important than girls and their activities.

In another study, Eder (1995) and her colleagues observed peer relationships in a middle school for three years. During the sixth, seventh, and eighth grades, young adolescents shift their focus from gender role norms to norms governing male–female relationships. Boys learn from other boys the "proper" view of girls; in some but not all groups, the prescribed view was that girls were objects of sexual conquest. Girls learn to view boys as potential participants in romantic relationships. Public teasing and ridicule of those who violate norms—common in elementary school—are replaced by gossip and exclusion from the group as sanctions for violations of group norms in middle school. Policing of sexual and romantic relationship norms increasingly takes the forms of bullying and insults—"slut-shaming"—as youth move into high school (Miller, 2016).

Eder (1995) also observed that the status hierarchy in the school generally reproduced the class structure of the wider community. Status was accorded to students based on popularity. One became popular by being visible. The most visible students were those on athletic teams and the cheerleader squad. Participating in these activities required money, as they were not funded by the school. Furthermore, the teams and cheerleaders relied on parents to transport them to games, giving an advantage to students who had one parent who did not work or parents whose jobs allowed them to take time off for such activities. Not surprisingly, the popular, visible students were those from middle-class families.

establishing independence; the child ceases to be exclusively involved in familial roles—offspring, cousin. Alternative, nonfamilial identities such as friend may provide a basis for actively resisting parental socialization efforts (Stryker & Serpe, 1982). For example, a parent's efforts to enforce certain rules may be resisted by a child whose friends make fun of children who behave that way. As suggested in Box 3.2, children actively resist adult culture through peer interaction and talk (Kyratzis, 2004). Playing house may provide an occasion for mimicking a parent through the use of parent-like words and tone.

Research also indicates that peer interactions are important influences on a child's satisfaction or dissatisfaction with their body (Tatangelo, McCabe, Mellor, & Mealey, 2016). A meta-analysis found that 20 to 70 percent of children under age 6 express dissatisfaction with their bodies. Peer teasing and modeling are associated with children's dissatisfaction with their bodies. Parents also influence body image by verbal statements and their own appearance-related behavior.

Although peer culture tends to be concerned with the present, it plays an important role in preparing children and adolescents for role transitions. An observational study of

Italian preschoolers found that the transition to elementary school was a common topic of discussion and debate (Corsaro & Molinari, 2000).

## School

Unlike the peer group, school is intentionally designed to socialize children. In the classroom, there is typically one adult and a group of children of similar age. There is a sharp status distinction between teacher and student. The teacher determines what skills are taught and relies heavily on instrumental learning techniques, with such reinforcers as praise, blame, and privileges to shape student behavior (Gecas, 1990). School is the child's first experience with formal and public evaluation of performance. Every child's behavior and work is evaluated by the same standards, and the judgments are made public to others in the class as well as to parents.

We expect schools to teach reading, writing, and arithmetic, but they do much more than that. Teachers use the rewards at their disposal to reinforce certain personality traits, such as punctuality, perseverance, and tact. Schools teach children which selves are desirable and which are not. Thus, children learn a vocabulary that they are expected to use in evaluating themselves and others (Denzin, 1977). The traits chosen are those thought to facilitate social interaction throughout life in a particular culture or society. In this sense, schools civilize children.

A key feature of social life in the United States is making statements or "claims" about reality and supporting them with evidence. Each of us engages in such discourses many times each day. In legislative arenas and courtrooms, there are multiple perspectives, each with its claims and supporting arguments contending for adherents. Schools, especially public speaking and debate classes and clubs, are the settings in which youth learn and hone these skills (Fine, 2000).

Social comparison has an important influence on the behavior of schoolchildren. Because teachers make public evaluations of the children's work, each child can judge their performance relative to the performance of others. These comparisons are especially important to the child because of the homogeneity of the classroom group. Even if the teacher de-emphasizes a child's low score on a spelling test, the child interprets the performance as a poor one relative to those of classmates. A consistent performance will affect a child's image of self as a student.

An observational study of children in kindergarten, first, second, and fourth grades documented the development of social comparison in the classroom (Frey & Ruble, 1985). In kindergarten, comparisons were made to personal characteristics—for example, liking ice cream. Comparisons of performance increased sharply in first grade; at first, comparisons were blatant, but they became increasingly subtle in second and fourth grades.

## Mass Media

In recent decades the **mass media** have become very influential agents of socialization. Media portrayals—social media, television programs, videos, films, Internet sites, print articles—present information about every aspect of daily life and the world around us. These images shape our perception of people, places, and events, and thus influence our attitudes toward these objects. The images also shape our *scripts,* our images of the people and behaviors that are appropriate in various types of relationships.

Media portrayals shape the child's image of self, including satisfaction or dissatisfaction with their bodies and physical features (Tatangelo et al., 2016). These portrayals also influence their expectations about and treatment of others based on gender (and of course, race and age). Older children and adolescents learn schemas and scripts for various types of relationships from watching familial, romantic, and work relationships unfold on the movie or television screen and on YouTube. For example, Ward and Friedman (2006) have shown that adolescents' attitudes and sexual behavior are associated with viewing sexual content on television. Prime-time television in particular portrays a heterosexual script that includes not only behavioral but cognitive and emotional guidelines for people in romantic relationships (Kim et al., 2007).

In the discussion of aggression we will summarize the correlational and experimental evidence linking exposure to portrayals of violence in the mass media with aggressive and violent behavior (see Chapter 12). There is also concern that viewing aggressive pornography contributes to violence against girls and women. Another concern is the link between frequent playing of violent video games and active shooter incidents or mass murder. Anecdotal evidence suggests that some recent incidents in which many people died from gunfire were perpetrated by persons with extensive exposure to "shooter" video games.

Media have an especially powerful socializing effect because many children and adolescents are exposed to media content several hours per day. According to a survey of a nationally representative sample of children 6 and under, 75 percent watch TV, 32 percent watch videos, 16 percent use a computer, and 11 percent play video games (Rideout & Hamel, 2006). More than 40 percent of 2- to 6-year-olds spend two or more hours with screen media per day. The average number of hours per day spent in media activities by youth aged 8 to 18 is shown in Figure 3.1. Note that children 8 to 10 are exposed to media content almost 8 hours per day, while older children spend more than 11 with media.

## PROCESSES OF SOCIALIZATION

How does socialization occur? We will examine three processes that are especially important: instrumental conditioning, observational learning, and internalization.

## Instrumental Conditioning

When you got dressed this morning, chances are you put on a shirt or blouse, pants, a dress, or a skirt that had buttons, hooks, or zippers. When you were younger, learning how to master buttons, hooks, zippers, and shoelaces undoubtedly took considerable time, trial and error, and slow progress accompanied by praise from adults. You acquired these skills through **instrumental conditioning**, a process wherein a person learns what response to make in a situation in order to obtain a positive reinforcement or avoid a negative reinforcement. The person's behavior is instrumental in the sense that it determines whether they are rewarded or punished.

The most important process in the acquisition of many skills is a type of instrumental learning called **shaping** (Skinner, 1953, 1957). Shaping refers to learning in which an agent initially reinforces any behavior that remotely resembles the desired response and later requires increasing correspondence between the learner's behavior and the desired response before providing reinforcement. Shaping thus involves a series of successive approximations in which the learner's behavior comes closer and closer to resembling the specific response desired by the reinforcing agent.

In socialization, the degree of similarity between desired and observed responses required by the agent depends in part on the learner's past performance. In this sense, shaping is interactive in character. In teaching children to clean their rooms, parents initially reward them for picking up their toys. When children show they can do this consistently, parents may require that the toys be placed on certain shelves as the condition for a reward. Shaping is more likely to succeed if the level of performance required is consistent with the child's abilities. Thus, a 2-year-old may be praised for drawing lines with crayons, whereas a 5-year-old may be expected to draw recognizable objects or figures.

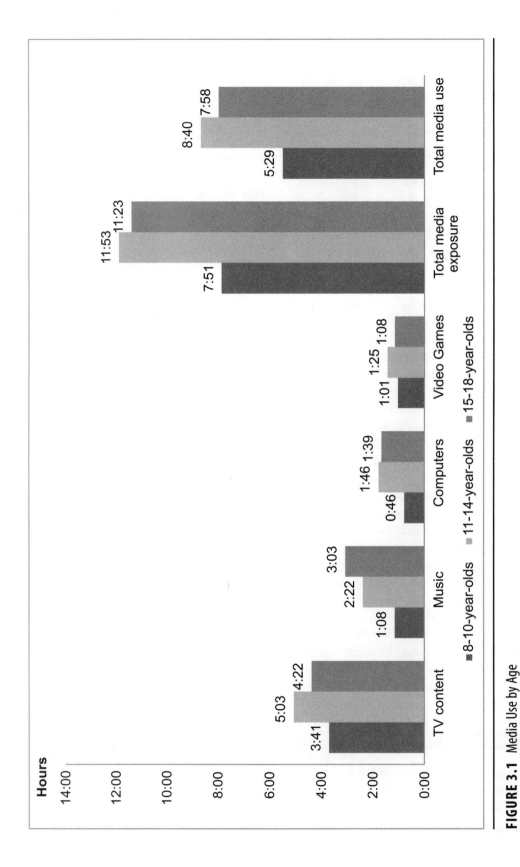

**FIGURE 3.1** Media Use by Age

*Source:* Rideout, Foehr, & Roberts (2010). *Generation M2: Media in the Lives of 8- to 18-year-olds.* Menlo Park, CA: Kaiser Family.

Shaping is a process through which many complex behaviors, such as playing the violin, are learned. Initially, the socializer (teacher or parent) rewards behavior that resembles the desired response. As learning progresses, greater correspondence between the behavior and the desired response is required to earn a reward, such as praise.© Bill Oxford/iStock

**Reinforcement Schedules.** When shaping behavior, a socializing agent can use either positive reinforcement or negative reinforcement. Positive reinforcers are stimuli whose presentation strengthens the learner's response; positive reinforcers include food, candy, money, or high grades. Negative reinforcers are stimuli whose withdrawal strengthens the response, such as the removal of pain (Shaw & Costanzo, 1982).

In everyday practice, it is rare for a learner to be reinforced each time the desired behavior is performed. Instead, reinforcement is given only some of the time. In fact, it is possible to structure when reinforcements are presented to the learner, using a reinforcement schedule.

There are several possible reinforcement schedules. The fixed-interval schedule involves reinforcing the first correct response after a specified period has elapsed. This schedule produces the fewest correct responses per unit of time; if the learner is aware of the length of the interval, they will respond only at the beginning of the interval. It is interesting that many schools give examinations at fixed intervals, such as the middle and end of the semester; perhaps that is why many students study only just before an exam. The variable-interval schedule involves reinforcing the first correct response after a variable period. In this case, the individual cannot predict when reinforcement will occur, so they respond at a regular rate. Grading a course based on several surprise or "pop" quizzes uses this schedule. Observers have suggested that variable-interval reinforcement is the reason we check e-mail and Facebook every chance we get; we never know when we will receive good news.

The fixed-ratio schedule provides a reinforcement following a specified number of correct, nonreinforced responses. Paying a worker on a piece rate, such as five dollars for every three items produced, uses this pattern. If the reward is sufficient, the rate of behavior may be high. Finally, the variable-ratio schedule provides reinforcement after several non-rewarded responses, with the number of responses between reinforcements varying. This schedule typically produces the highest and most stable rates of response. An excellent illustration is the gambler, who will insert quarters in a slot machine for hours, receiving only occasional, random payoffs.

**Punishment.** By definition, **punishment** is the presentation of a painful or discomforting stimulus or the removal of a positive stimulus (by a socializing agent) that decreases the probability that the preceding behavior (by the learner) will occur. Punishment is one of the major child-rearing practices used by parents. The Gallup organization interviewed a nationally representative sample of parents in 1995 (Straus & Field, 2003; Straus & Stewart, 1999). The percentage of parents who reported using corporal punishment—pinching, slapping, spanking, or hitting—during the preceding year varied by the age of the child. The use of corporal punishment was reported by 94

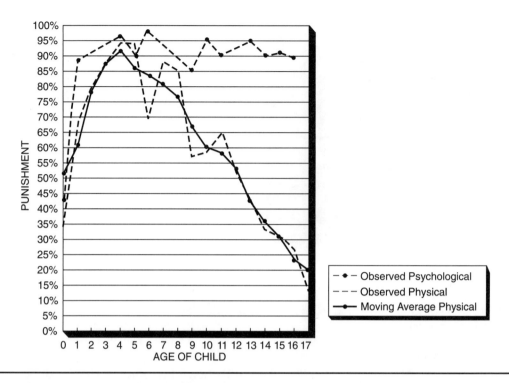

**FIGURE 3.2** Percentage of Parents Who Use Physical Punishment and Psychological Punishment

The Gallup organization interviewed a representative sample of 991 parents in 1995. Each parent was asked whether and how often they used physical punishment (spanked the bottom; slapped hand, arm, or leg; pinched; shook; hit on the bottom with an object; or slapped head, face, or ears) and psychological punishment (shouted, yelled, or screamed; threatened to hit or spank; swore or cursed; threatened to kick out of the house; or called names, such as dumb or lazy). Most parents reported using both types. The use of physical punishment peaked with 4-year-old children and then declined steadily through age 17. By contrast, the use of psychological punishment was reported to be as common with 17-year-olds as with 1-year-olds (90 percent).

*Source:* Straus & Field, 2003; Straus & Stewart, 1999

percent of the parents of 3- and 4-year-olds; the prevalence declined steadily from age 5 to age 17. The use of psychological techniques—shouting, name calling, threatening—was reported by more than 85 percent of parents of children of all ages. The results are displayed in Figure 3.2.

Punishment is obviously widely used in the United States, suggesting that our culture is tolerant of or encourages its use. So, does punishment work? Research indicates that it is effective in some circumstances but not in others. One aspect is timing. Punishment is most effective when it occurs in close proximity to the behavior. A verbal reprimand delivered as the child touched the toy was more effective than a prior warning or a reprimand following the action (Aronfreed & Reber, 1965). Also, the effectiveness may be limited to the situation in which it is given. Because punishment is usually administered by a particular person, it may be effective only when that person is present. This probably accounts for the fact that when their parents are absent, children may engage in activities that their parents earlier had punished (Parke, 1969, 1970).

Another factor in the effectiveness of punishments is whether they are accompanied by a reason (Parke, 1969). Providing a reason allows the child to generalize the prohibition to a class of acts and situations. Yelling "No!" as a child reaches out to touch the stove may suppress that behavior. Telling the child not to touch it because it is "hot" enables them to learn to avoid hot objects as a group. Finally, consistency between the reprimands given by parents and their own behavior makes punishment more effective than if parents do not practice what they preach (Mischel & Liebert, 1966).

What about the long-term consequences of punishment? Clearly, parents and caregivers need to control children's behavior. At the same time, they need to recognize that corporal punishment may be associated with subsequent antisocial behavior by children. Punishment should focus on the behavior and not the child, and should be balanced by praise and rewards.

**Self-Reinforcement and Self-Efficacy.** Children learn hundreds, if not thousands, of behaviors through instrumental learning. The performance of some of these behaviors will remain **extrinsically motivated**—that is, they are dependent on whether someone else will reward appropriate behaviors or punish inappropriate ones. However, the performance of other activities becomes **intrinsically motivated**—that is, performed in order to achieve an internal state that the individual finds rewarding (Deci, 1975). Research has demonstrated that external rewards do not always improve performance. Providing a reward for a behavior that is intrinsically motivated, such as drawing, may actually reduce the frequency or quality of the activity (Lepper, Greene, & Nisbett, 1973).

Closely related to the concept of intrinsic motivation is **self-reinforcement**. As children are socialized, they learn not only specific behaviors but also performance standards. Children learn not only to write but to write neatly. These standards become part of the self; having learned them, the child uses them to judge their own behavior and thus becomes capable of self-reinforcement (Bandura, 1982). The child who has drawn a house and comes running up to their father with a big smile, saying, "Look what I drew," has already judged the drawing as a good one. If their father agrees, their standards and self-evaluation are confirmed.

Successful experiences with an activity over time create a sense of competence at the activity, or self-efficacy (Bandura, 1982). This, in turn, makes the individual more likely to seek opportunities to engage in that behavior. The greater one's sense of self-efficacy, the more effort one will expend at a task and the greater one's persistence in the face of difficulty. For instance, a young girl who perceives herself as a good basketball player is more likely to try out for a team. Conversely, experiences of failure to perform a task properly, or of the failure of the performance to produce the expected results, create the perception that one is not efficacious. Perceived lack of efficacy is likely to lead to avoidance of the task. A boy who perceives himself as poor at spelling will probably not enter the school spelling bee.

## Observational Learning

Children love to play dress-up. Some kids put on skirts, step into high-heeled shoes, and totter around the room; others put on jackets and drape ties around their necks. Through observing adults, children have learned the patterns of appropriate dress in their society. Similarly, children often learn interactive rituals, such as shaking hands or waving goodbye, by watching others perform the behavior and then doing it on their own.

**Observational learning**, or modeling, refers to the acquisition of behavior based on the observation of another person's behavior and of its consequences for that person (Shaw & Costanzo, 1982). Many behaviors and skills are learned this way. By watching another person (the model) perform skilled actions, a child can increase their own skills. The major advantage of modeling is its greater efficiency compared with trial-and-error learning.

Does observational learning lead directly to the performance of the learned behavior? No; research has shown that there is a difference between learning a behavior and performing it. People can learn how to perform a behavior by observing another person, but they may not perform the behavior until the appropriate opportunity arises. Considerable time may elapse before the observer is in the presence of the eliciting stimulus. A father in the habit of muttering "damn" when he spills something may, much to his chagrin, hear his 3-year-old daughter say "damn" the first time she spills milk. Children may learn through observation many associations between situational characteristics and adult behavior, but they may not perform these behaviors until they occupy adult roles and find themselves in such situations.

Even if the appropriate stimulus occurs, people may not perform behaviors learned through observation. An important influence is the consequences experienced by the model following the model's performance of the behavior. For instance, in one study (Bandura, 1965), nursery school children watched a film in which an adult model punched, kicked, and threw balls at a large, inflated rubber Bobo doll. Three versions of the film were shown to three groups of children. In the first, the model was rewarded for their acts: a second adult appeared and gave the model soft drinks and candy. In the second version, the model was punished: the other adult spanked the model with a magazine. In the third version, there were no rewards or punishments. Later, each child was left alone with various toys, including a Bobo doll. The child's behavior was observed through a one-way mirror. Children who had observed the model who was punished were much less likely to punch and kick the doll than the other children.

Did these other children not learn the aggressive behaviors, or did they learn them by observation but not perform them? To answer this question, the experimenter returned to the room and offered a reward for each act of the model that the child could reproduce. Following this offer, the children in all three groups were equally able to reproduce the acts performed by the model. Thus, a child is less likely to perform an act learned by observation if the model experienced negative consequences.

Whether children learn from observing a model also depends on the characteristics of the model. Children are more likely to imitate high-status and nurturant models than models who are low in status and nurturance (Bandura, 1969). Preschool children given dolls representing peers, older children, and adults consistently chose adult dolls as people they would go to for help and older children as people they would go to for teaching (Lewis & Brooks-Gunn, 1979). Children also are more likely to model themselves after nurturant persons than after cold and impersonal ones. Thus, socialization is much more likely to be effective when the child has a nurturant, loving primary caregiver.

Observational learning or imitation is an important process through which children learn appropriate behaviors. © Images_Bazaar/iStock

## Internalization

Often, we feel a sense of moral obligation to perform some behavior. At other times, we experience a strong internal feeling that a particular behavior is wrong. Usually, we experience guilt if these moral prescriptions or prohibitions are violated.

**Internalization** is the process by which initially external behavioral standards (for example, those held by parents) become internal and subsequently guide the person's behavior. An action is based on internalized standards when the person engages in it without considering possible rewards or punishments. Various explanations have been offered of the process by which internalization occurs, but all of them agree that children are most likely to internalize the standards held by more powerful or nurturant adult caregivers.

Internalization is an important socializing process. It results in the exercise of self-control. People conform to internal standards even when there is no surveillance of their behavior by others and, therefore, no rewards for their conformity. People who are widely admired for taking political or religious actions that are unpopular—for standing up for their beliefs—often do so because those beliefs are internalized.

## OUTCOMES OF SOCIALIZATION

Persons being socialized acquire new skills, knowledge, and behavior. In this section, we discuss some specific outcomes of the socialization process, including gender role, linguistic and cognitive competence, moral development, and orientation toward work.

## Gender Role

"Congratulations, you have a girl!" Such a pronouncement by a birth attendant may be the single most important event in a new person's life. The gender assigned to the infant—boy or girl—has a major influence on the socialization and life experiences of that child.

Every society has differential expectations regarding the characteristics and behavior of men and women. In U.S. society, men traditionally have been expected to be competent—competitive, logical, able to make decisions easily, ambitious. Women have been expected to be high in warmth and expressiveness—gentle, sensitive, tactful (Broverman et al., 1972). Parents employ these or other expectations as guidelines in socializing their children, and differential treatment begins at birth. Infants labeled male are handled more vigorously and roughly, whereas those labeled female are given more cuddling (Lamb, 1979). Boys and girls are dressed differently from infancy and often are given different kinds of toys to play with.

Moreover, mothers and fathers differ in the way they interact with infants. Mothers engage in behavior oriented toward fulfilling the child's physical and emotional needs (Baumrind, 1980), whereas fathers engage the child in rough-and-tumble, physically stimulating activity (Walters & Walters, 1980). Fathers also engage sons in more rough-and-tumble play than daughters. These differences are found in European-American, African-American, and Hispanic families (Parke, 1996). Thus, almost from birth, infants are exposed to models of masculine and feminine behavior. Mothers and fathers differ in their talk to young children; mothers talk more than fathers, and mothers' talk is socioemotional (supportive or negative), whereas fathers' talk is instrumental (Leaper, Anderson, & Sanders, 1998). An observational study of mothers' interactions with 5- to 12-month-old males and females analyzed behaviors during discipline events; mothers' interactions with males were significantly longer and used more affectionate terms, perhaps because male infants reacted more negatively to discipline than female infants (Ahl, Fausto-Sterling, Garcia-Coll, & Seifer, 2013).

Infants quickly develop a sense of their own body as a differentiated entity in the world (Rochat, 2010). By age 2, most children have a firmly established gender identity, a conception of the self as male or female (Money & Ehrhardt, 1972). Boys and girls show distinct preferences for different types of play materials and toys by this age. Between the ages of 2 and 3, differences in aggressiveness become evident, with boys displaying more physical and verbal aggression than girls (Hyde & Else-Quest, 2012). This difference is stable across ages 3, 4, and 5 (Lussier, Corrado, & Tzoumakis, 2012). In data from nine countries, boys aged 7 to 10 were found to engage in more physical and relational aggression than girls (Lansford et al., 2012). By age 4, the games typically played by boys and girls differ; groups of girls play house, enacting familial roles, whereas groups of boys play space rangers. In middle childhood, gender-segregated play appears to be almost universal (Edwards, Knoche, & Kumru, 2001).

We noted early in this chapter the importance of "nature" in understanding children's development. Research involving almost 4,000 twin and non-twin sibling pairs (Iervolino et al., 2005) identified both genetic and shared environmental (family) influences on sex-typed behavior (play activities) for both boys and girls. In related research, Hines and colleagues (2002) measured women's blood levels of testosterone during pregnancy, and gender role behaviors when the children were 3½ years old. There was a positive relationship between testosterone and male-typed behavior among girls, but not among boys.

Parents are an important influence on the learning of **gender role**—the behavioral expectations associated with one's gender. Children learn gender-appropriate behaviors by observing their parents' interaction. Children also learn by interacting with parents, who reward behavior consistent with their expectations and punish behavior inconsistent

with them. The child's earliest experiences relating to members of the other gender occur in interaction with the opposite-gender parent. A woman may be more likely to develop the ability to have warm, psychologically intimate relationships with men if her relationship with her father was of this type (Appleton, 1981).

Many of the activities parents engage in with their children provide occasions for gender socialization. An observational study of parent–child interactions in a major zoo found that many parents gendered the animals children were observing and associated the animals and their behaviors with human gender stereotypes (Garner & Grazian, 2016). In addition, adults disciplined boys and girls differently, encouraging them to behave in conventionally gendered ways.

Obviously, boys are not all alike in our society, and neither are girls. The specific behaviors and characteristics that the child is taught depend partly on the gender role expectations held by the parents. These in turn depend on the network of extended family—grandparents, aunts and uncles, and other relatives—and friends of the family. The expectations held by these people are influenced by the institutions to which they belong, such as churches and work organizations (Stryker & Serpe, 1982). With regard to religion, research suggests that the differences among denominations in socialization techniques and in outcomes such as gender role attitudes have declined in recent decades (Alwin, 1986). The data suggest that church attendance is more influential than the denomination to which one belongs.

Gender role definitions vary by culture. Some research suggests that Latino families teach more traditional expectations for behavior of boys and girls compared to other groups in U.S. society. These families also encourage a strong sense of family obligation, which has benefits but may tie offspring physically to the family, limiting educational and occupational mobility (Crosnoe & Cavanagh, 2010). Other research finds that as education and women's labor-force participation increase, families have more egalitarian views of behavior and decision making (Ginorio, Gutierrez, Cauce, & Acosta, 1995). It is important to remember that "Latino" encompasses people from several different cultural backgrounds, including Mexican-American, Puerto Rican, and Cuban. Asian cultures are patriarchal, and parents may socialize female children to restrictive norms designed to serve the family rather than express their individuality (Root, 1995). Again, "Asian" includes persons of Chinese, Taiwanese, Japanese, Korean, and Vietnamese descent; these cultures may differ in the prevailing gender role definitions.

Schools also teach gender roles. Teachers may reward appropriate gender role behavior. A more subtle influence on socialization is the content of the stories that are read and told in preschool and first-grade classes. Many of these stories portray men and women as different. In the past, men were depicted as rulers, adventurers, and explorers; women were wives (Weitzman, Eifler, Hokada, & Ross, 1972). A study of award-winning books for children published from 1995 to 1999 found men and women equally represented as main characters, but men played a greater variety of roles and were seldom shown engaging in child care, shopping, or housework (Gooden & Gooden, 2001). An analysis of 200 children's picture books found that boys and men were title characters twice as often as girls and women, and the latter were more often portrayed as nurturing, in indoor scenes, and appeared to have no paid employment (Hamilton, Anderson, Broaddus, & Young, 2006). A study of illustrations in a sample of 56 contemporaneous coloring books found that males were more active, and more likely to be portrayed as adults, and as superheroes (Fitzpatrick & McPherson, 2010).

A minority of children, some as young as 2 or 3 years of age, are not comfortable living and being treated by adults as the gender they were assigned at birth. They begin to engage in gender nonconforming behavior, such as rejecting clothing associated with their assigned gender. These behaviors may be met by increasing pressure from parents to conform, causing conflict. Some of these individuals, as children or adolescents, transition to living at least part-time as the other gender, i.e., become *transgender* (Grossman, D'Augelli, & Salter, 2006). Interviews with 31 *transwomen* (male-to-female persons, average age 17.5) found that they felt, acted, or were told they were different at 8 or 9 years of age. About two-thirds were told by their parents to stop acting like "sissies" and that they needed counseling. More gender atypical persons reported parental abuse. *Transmen* (female-to-male persons) report that their mothers emphasized the need for conformity to feminine roles, limiting their dress and behavior options (Dietert & Dentice, 2013). Both reported that as they moved into interaction with other children, peers also demanded conformity with gender role expectations, and often harassed them for deviating from those norms (see Box 3.2). Thus, these youth face great pressure to fit into the dominant gender binary.

A major influence on gender role socialization is the mass media. Media provide images of masculinity and femininity that can readily be imitated. Researchers analyzing the contents of television programs, television advertising, feature films, and other media report that portrayals of men and women and girls and boys reinforce traditional definitions of gender roles. A content analysis of 175 episodes of 41 animated TV series found that masculine characters were portrayed as independent, athletic, ambitious, and aggressive, whereas feminine characters were shown as dependent, emotional, domestic, and romantic (Thompson & Zerbinos, 1995). A content analysis of 160 hours of children's cartoons found that superheroes are defined in masculine terms (Baker & Raney, 2007). A study of the fiction in *Seventeen* and *Teen*, the two highest-selling magazines for teenage girls at the time, found that the stories reinforced

Children and adolescents learn gender-role expectations and behavior through interaction with adults. Meeting their hero, basketball player Dwyane Wade, may have a lifelong impact on these boys/girls/youth. © AP Photo/J. Pat Carter

traditional messages (Peirce, 1993). Half of the conflicts were about relationships, and half the young women relied on someone else to solve their problems. Adult men in the stories were doctors, lawyers, and bankers; adult women were nurses, clerical workers, and secretaries.

Perhaps the most stereotyped portrayals of gender are found in music videos. An analysis of music videos broadcast in 2004 on MTV and MTV2 found that gender displays reinforced stereotypes of women as sex objects, and males as aggressive and females as submissive (Wallis, 2010). Another study of 120 videos revealed that videos of African-American musical genres (rap, hip-hop) or featuring black performers were much more likely to portray sexual content and women in provocative dress, compared to videos of White musical genres (rock, pop) (Turner, 2011).

Research documents the impact of these portrayals on young media consumers. Researchers asked 190 first- and second-graders to name their three favorite television programs. They analyzed portrayals of gender in the six programs named most often. Male characters were more likely to answer questions, boss others, and achieve goals. Boys who preferred stereotypic male characters were more likely to value hard work. Boys who preferred female counterstereotypic content were more likely to report attraction to male characters; girls who preferred female counterstereotypic content were more likely to report attraction to female characters (Aubrey & Harrison, 2004). A study of African-American high school students surveyed their media usage and gender role attitudes. Later, students viewed either four music videos with stereotypic portrayals of gender or four nonstereotypic ones.

More frequent viewing of music videos was associated with more traditional gender role attitudes. Youth who viewed stereotypic videos expressed more traditional views of gender and sexual relationships (Ward, Hansbrough, & Walker, 2005). Clearly, gender role portrayals are related to gender role attitudes of children and adolescents.

During childhood and adolescence, youth are explicitly taught and rewarded for behavior consistent with gender role norms. They also observe models behaving in a variety of ways. Children do not simply mimic their parents, siblings, or MTV performers. As the interpretive perspective suggests, children learn gender role behaviors and then re-create them, adapting them to their individual social contexts. Williams (2002) refers to this process as trying on gender—experimenting, resisting, and rehearsing ways to be feminine or masculine. Some children combine behaviors and self-presentations in novel, gender nonconforming ways.

## Linguistic and Cognitive Competence

Another important outcome of socialization is the ability to interact effectively with others. We discuss two specific competencies: language and the ability to cognitively represent the world.

**Language.** Using language to communicate with others is a prerequisite for full participation in social groups (Shibutani, 1961). The child's acquisition of speech reflects both the development of the necessary perceptual and motor skills and the impact of social learning (Bates, O'Connell, & Shore, 1987).

The three main components of language are the sound system (phonology), the words and their associated meanings (lexicon), and the rules for combining words into meaningful utterances (grammar). Young children appear to acquire these in sequence, first mastering meaningful sounds, then learning words, and finally learning sentences. In reality,

acquiring speech is a process that involves all three at the same time and continues throughout childhood.

Language acquisition in the first three years passes through four stages (Bates et al., 1987). The pre-speech stage lasts for about 10 months and involves speech perception, speech production, and early intentional communication. In the first few weeks of life, infants can perceive all of the speech sounds. They begin producing sounds at 2 to 3 months, and begin producing sounds specific to their parents' language at 4 to 7 months. Speech production involves imitation of the sounds they hear. With regard to intentional communication, observational data indicate that vocal exchanges involving 4-month-old infants and their mothers are patterned (Stevenson, Ver Hoeve, Roach, & Leavitt, 1986). Vocalization by *either* infant or mother was followed by silence, allowing the other to respond. Vocalization by one was likely to be followed by vocalization by the other, a pattern like that found in adult conversation.

The first intentional use of gestures occurs at about 9 months. At this age, infants orient visually to adults rather than to desired objects, such as a cookie. Furthermore, if an initial gesture is not followed by the adult engaging in the desired behavior, the infant will repeat the gesture or try a different gesture.

The second or first word stage occurs at 10 to 14 months and involves the infant's recognition that things have names. The first words produced are usually nouns that name or request specific objects (Marchman, 1991). Obviously, this ability to use names reflects cognitive as well as linguistic development.

At about 18 months, there is a vocabulary burst, with a doubling in a short time of the number of words that are correctly used. The suddenness of this increase suggests that it reflects the maturation of some cognitive abilities. This, in turn, is followed by an increase in the complexity of vocalizations, leading to the first sentence stage at 18 to 22 months. Examples of such sentences include "See truck, Mommy" and "There go one." Such speech is telegraphic—that is, the number of words is greatly reduced relative to adult speech (Brown & Fraser, 1963). At the same time, such utterances are clearly more precise than the single-word utterances of the 1-year-old child.

The fourth stage, grammaticization, occurs at 24 to 30 months. The child's use of language now reflects the fundamentals of grammar. Children at this age frequently overgeneralize, applying rules indiscriminately. For example, they will add an appropriate ending to a novel word although it is incorrect: "He runned." Such usage indicates that the child understands that there are rules. At about the same age, a child puts series of acts in the conventional sequence—for example, undressing a doll, bathing it, drying it, and dressing it. Perhaps both activities reflect the maturation of an underlying ability to order arbitrary units.

An important process in learning to make grammatically correct sentences is speech expansion. That is, adults often respond to children's speech by repeating it in expanded form. In response to "Eve lunch," the mother might say "Eve is eating lunch." One study showed that mothers expanded 30 percent of the utterances of their 2-year-old children (Brown, 1965). Adults probably expand on the child's speech to determine the child's specific meaning. Speech expansion contributes to language acquisition by providing children with a model of how to convey more effectively the meanings they intend.

The next stage of language development is highlighted by the occurrence of private speech, in which children talk to themselves, often for extended periods. Private speech begins at about age 3, increases in frequency until age 5, and disappears by about age 7. Such private talk serves three functions. First, it contributes to the child's developing sense of self. Private speech is addressed to the self as object, and it often includes the application of meanings to the self, such as "I'm a girl." Second, private speech helps the child develop an awareness of the environment. It often consists of naming aspects of the physical and social environment. The repeated use of these names solidifies the child's understanding of the environment. Children also often engage in appropriate actions as they speak, reflecting their developing awareness of the social meanings of objects and persons. Thus, a child may label a doll a "baby" and dress it and feed it. Third, children engage in more private speech during novel or open-ended tasks than during tasks where the teacher or parent tells them what to do (Kyjonkova & Lacinova, 2010), or self-selected activity (Winsler, Carlton, & Barry, 2000), suggesting that its use facilitates self-regulation of behavior by the child.

Gradually, the child begins to engage in dialogues, either with others or with the self. These conversations reflect the ability to adopt a second perspective. Thus, by age 6, when one child wants a toy that another child is using, the first child frequently offers to trade. They know that the second child will be upset if they merely take the toy. This movement away from a self-centered view also may reflect maturational changes. Dialogue requires that the child's own speech meshes with that of another.

Language is important in the socialization of gender. A meta-analysis of observational studies of parents' use of language in interaction with their children identified several differences between mothers and fathers in types of communication. For example, mothers were more supportive and less directive compared to fathers. Moreover, mothers and fathers differed in the way they talked to sons and to daughters (Leaper, Anderson, & Sanders, 1998). Thus, children are socialized to gender differences in language use as they observe and interact with their parents/caregivers.

Language socialization involves much more than learning to talk. It also involves learning to think, how to behave, and how to feel and express feelings (Garrett & Baquedano-Lopez, 2002). As the interpretive perspective suggests, language learning occurs in the routine, everyday interaction of children and adults. It is responsive to and reflects local values, patterns of social organization, and (sub)cultural features.

**Cognitive Competence.** Children must develop the ability to represent in their own minds the features of the world around them. This capacity to represent reality mentally is closely related to the development of language.

The child's basic tasks are to learn the regularities of the physical and social environment and to store past experience in a form that can be used in current situations. In a complex society, there are so many physical objects, animals, and people that it is not possible for a child (or an adult) to remember each as a distinct entity. Things must be categorized into inclusive groupings, such as dogs, houses, or girls. A category of objects and the cognitions that the individual has about members of that category (for example, "dog") makes up a schema. Collectively, our schemas allow us to make sense of the world around us.

Young children must learn schemas (see Chapter 1). Learning language is an essential part of the process, because language provides the names around which schemas can develop. It is noteworthy that the first words that children produce are usually nouns that name objects in the child's environment. At first, the child uses a few very general schemas. Some children learn the word *dog* at 12 to 14 months and then apply it to all animals—to dogs, cats, birds, and cows. Only with maturation and experience does the child develop the abstract schema "animals" and learn to discriminate between dogs and cats.

Researchers can study the ability to use schemas by asking children to sort objects, pictures, or words into groups. Young children (aged 6 to 8) rely on visual features, such as color or word length, and sort objects into numerous categories. Older children (aged 10 to 12) increasingly use functional or superordinate categories, such as foods, and sort objects into fewer groups (Olver, 1961; Rigney, 1962). With age, children become increasingly adept at classifying diverse objects and treating them as equivalent.

These skills are very important in social interaction. Only by having the ability to group objects, persons, and situations can one determine how to behave toward them. Person schemas and their associated meanings are especially important to smooth interaction. Even very young children differentiate people by age (Lewis & Brooks-Gunn, 1979). By about 2 years of age, children correctly differentiate babies and adults when shown photographs. By about 5, children employ four categories: little children, big children, parents (aged 13 to 40), and grandparents (aged 40-plus).

As children learn to group objects into meaningful schemas, they learn not only the categories but also how others feel about such categories. Children learn not only that Catholics are people who believe in the Trinity of Father, Son, and Holy Spirit, but also whether their parents like or dislike Catholics. Thus, children acquire positive and negative attitudes toward the wide range of social objects they come to recognize. The particular schemas and evaluations that children learn are influenced by the social class, religious, ethnic, and other subcultural groupings to which those who socialize them belong.

## Moral Development

In this section, we discuss moral development. Specifically, we focus on the acquisition of knowledge of social rules and on the process through which children become capable of making moral judgments.

**Knowledge of Social Rules.** To interact effectively with others, people must learn the social rules that govern interaction and in general adhere to them. Beliefs about which behaviors are acceptable and which are unacceptable for specific persons in specific situations are termed **norms**. Without norms, coordinated activity would be very difficult, and we would find it hard or impossible to achieve our goals. Therefore, each group, organization, and society develops rules governing behavior.

Early in life, an American child learns to say "Please," a French child "S'il vous plaît," and a Serbian child "Molim te." In every case, the child is learning the value of conforming to arbitrary norms, in this case governing requests. Learning language trains the child to conform to linguistic norms and serves as a model for the learning of other norms. Gradually, through instrumental and observational learning, the child learns the generality of the relationship between conformity to norms and the ability to interact smoothly with others and achieve one's own goals.

What influences which norms children will learn? The general culture is one influence. All American children learn to cover parts of the body with clothing in public. The position of the family within the society is another influence. Parental expectations reflect social class, religion, and ethnicity. Thus, the norms that children are taught vary from one family to another. Interestingly, parents often hold norms that they apply distinctively to their own children. Mothers and fathers expect certain behaviors of their own sons or daughters but may have different expectations for other people's children (Elkin & Handel, 1989). For instance, they may expect their own children to be more polite than other children in interaction with adults. Parental expectations are not constant over time; they change as the child grows older. Parents expect greater politeness from a 10-year-old than from a 5-year-old. Finally, parents adjust their expectations to the particular child. They consider the child's level of ability and experiences relative to other children; they expect better performance in school from a child who has done well in the past than from one who has had problems in school. In all of these ways, each child is being socialized to a somewhat different set of norms. The outcome is a young person who is both similar to most others from the same social background and unique in certain ways.

When children begin to engage in cooperative play at about 4 years of age, they begin to experience normative pressure from peers. The expectations of age-mates differ in two important ways from those of parents. First, children bring different norms from their separate families and, therefore, introduce new expectations. Thus, through their peers, children first become aware there are other ways of behaving. In some cases, peers' expectations conflict with those of parents. For example, many parents do not allow their children to play with toy guns, knives, or swords. Through involvement with their peers, children may become aware that other children routinely play with such toys. As a result, some children will experience normative conflict and discover the need to develop strategies for resolving such conflicts.

A second way that peer norms differ from parental norms is that the former reflect a child's perspective (Elkin & Handel, 1989). Many parental expectations are oriented toward socializing the child for adult roles. Children react to each other as children and are not concerned with long-term outcomes. Thus, peers encourage impulsive, spontaneous behavior rather than behavior directed toward long-term goals. Peer norms emphasize participation in group activities, whereas parental norms may emphasize homework and other educational activities that may contribute to academic achievement.

When children enter school, they are exposed to a third major socializing agent—the teacher. In school, children are exposed to universalistic rules—norms that apply equally to all children. The teacher is much less likely

At school, children get their first exposure to universal norms—behavioral expectations that are the same for everyone. Although parents and friends treat the child as an individual, teachers are less likely to do so. © monkeybusinessimages/iStock

than the parents to make allowances for the unique characteristics of the individual; children must learn to wait their turn, to control impulsive and spontaneous behavior, and to work without a great deal of supervision and support. In this regard, the school is the first of many settings where the individual is treated primarily as a member of the group rather than as a unique individual. As noted in Box 3.2, children may engage in resistance in response to the authority structure in a school.

**Moral Judgment.** We not only learn the norms of our social groups, we also develop the ability to evaluate behavior in specific situations by applying certain standards. The process through which children become capable of making moral judgments is termed **moral development**.

How do children evaluate acts as good or bad? One of the first people to study this question in detail was Piaget, a Swiss developmental psychologist. Piaget read a child stories in which the central character performed an act that violated social rules. In one story, for example, a young girl, contrary to rules, was playing with scissors and made a hole in her dress. Piaget asked the children to evaluate the behaviors of the characters (that is, to indicate which characters were naughtier) and

then to explain their reasons for these judgments. Based on this work, Piaget concluded there were three bases for moral judgments: amount of harm/benefit, actor's intentions, and the application of agreed-upon rules or norms (Piaget, 1965).

Kohlberg (1969) extended Piaget's work by analyzing the reasoning by which people reach moral judgments. He uses stories involving conflict between human needs and social norms or laws. Here is an example:

> In Europe, a woman was near death from cancer. One drug might save her, a form of radium that a druggist in the same town had recently discovered. The druggist was charging $2,000, ten times what the drug cost him to make. The sick woman's husband, Heinz, went to everyone he knew to borrow money, but he could only get together about half of what it cost. He told the druggist that his wife was dying and asked him to sell it cheaper or let him pay later. But the druggist said no. The husband got desperate and broke into the man's store to steal the drug for his wife (Kohlberg, 1969).

Respondents are then asked, "Should Heinz have done that? Was Heinz right or wrong? What obligations did Heinz and the druggist have? Should Heinz be punished?"

Kohlberg proposed a developmental model with three levels of moral reasoning, each level involving two stages. He argued that the progression from stage 1 to stage 6 is a standard or universal one, and that all children begin at stage 1 and progress through the stages in order. Most adults reason at stages 3 or 4. Few people reach stages 5 or 6. Kohlberg's model is an impressive attempt to specify a universal model of moral development. However, it has limitations. First, like Piaget, Kohlberg locates the determinants of moral judgment within the individual. He does not recognize the influence of the situation. Studies of judgments of aggressive behavior (Berkowitz, Mueller, Schnell, & Pudberg, 1986), of driving while intoxicated (Denton & Krebs, 1990), and of decisions about reward allocation (Kurtines, 1986) have found that both moral stage and type of situation influenced adult moral judgment.

Second, Kohlberg's model has been criticized as sexist—not applicable to the processes that women use in moral reasoning. Gilligan (1982) identifies two conceptions of morality: a morality of justice and a morality of caring. A justice orientation is concerned with adherence to rules and fairness, whereas a caring orientation is concerned with relationships and meeting the needs of others. Gilligan argues that the former is characteristic of men and is the basis of Kohlberg's model. She believes the latter is more characteristic of women. A meta-analysis of studies testing predictions from the two models indicates that there is a significant but modest tendency for women to base judgments on caring criteria and for men to base judgments on considerations of justice (Jaffee & Hyde, 2000).

Notice that Piaget and Kohlberg studied the development of morality by asking children to describe their reactions to scenarios, to talk. We have just seen that linguistic competence takes several years to develop. Is it possible that children notice and dislike unfairness before they can talk? Researchers gave pairs of 3- to 5-year-old children unequal numbers of stickers as a reward for cleaning up blocks from the floor. The adult carefully counted out four stickers for one child and two for the other. After a short delay, the adult asked a series of questions about the distribution. Children as young as 3 reacted negatively to the unfair distribution, often nonverbally, but children did not explicitly talk about fairness until the age of 5 or 6 (LoBue et al., 2011). Thus, reactions to unfairness occur at younger ages than previously thought, suggesting that early moral intuition may have an evolutionary base (Brownell, 2013). Based on these and other results, Haidt (2012) has proposed that (moral) intuition comes first, and reasoning comes second. An event triggers an intuitive, emotional reaction which points toward a corresponding judgment; moral reasoning occurs when we try to communicate/explain our judgment to others, or convince them to adopt our judgment. Reasoning relies on language, and so it comes second. The intuitive, emotional reaction may well have a biological/neural base, whereas reasoning has a social one.

Recent research on children's moral judgment also finds that evaluations of an action as "right" or "wrong" are influenced by their attributions of emotion, that is, beliefs about how the transgressor will feel after the action (Malti, Gasser, & Gutzwiller-Helfenfinger, 2010). In a sample of 5-, 7- and 9-year-olds, older children were more likely to employ moral reasons in judging transgressions, and to attribute feeling guilty to the transgressor. Other research shows that prosocial moral reasoning increases from adolescence (ages 15 to 16) to young adulthood (ages 25 to 26) (Eisenberg et al., 2005).

## Work Orientations

Work is of central importance in social life. In recognition of this, occupation is a major influence on the distribution of economic and other resources in many societies. We identify others by their work; its importance is evidenced by the fact that one of the first questions we ask a new acquaintance is "What do you do?"

Socialization related to work begins in the family. By the age of 2, many children are aware that adult caregivers "go work" and ask why. A common reply is "Mommy goes to work to earn money." A study of 900 elementary school children found that 80 percent of first-graders understood the connection between work and money (Goldstein & Oldham, 1979). The child, in turn, learns that money is needed to obtain food, clothing, and toys. The child of a physician or nurse might be told "Mommy goes to work to help sick people." The child of a construction worker might be told "I go to work to build houses for people." Thus, from an early age the child is taught the social meaning of work.

Adults in different occupations should have different orientations toward work, and these orientations should influence how they socialize their children. Based on this hypothesis, extensive research has been conducted on the differences between social classes in the values transmitted through socialization (Kohn, 1969). Fathers are given a list of traits, including good manners, success, self-control, obedience, and responsibility, and asked to indicate how much they value each for their children. Underlying these specific characteristics, a general dimension—"self-direction versus conformity"—is usually found. Data from fathers of 3- to 15-year-old children indicate that the emphasis on self-direction and reliance on internal standards increases as social class increases. The relationship of values and social class is found not only in samples of American fathers but also in samples of Japanese and Polish fathers (Kohn et al., 1990).

These differences in the evaluations of particular traits reflect differences in the conditions of work. In general, middle-class occupations involve the manipulation of people or symbols, and the work is not closely supervised. Thus, these occupational roles require people who are self-directing and who can make judgments based on knowledge and internal standards. Working-class occupations are more routinized and more closely supervised. Thus, they require workers with a conformist orientation. Kohn argues that fathers value those traits in their children that they associate with success in their occupation.

Do the differences in the value parents place on self-direction influence the kinds of activities in which they encourage their children

to participate? A study of 460 adolescents and their mothers (Morgan, Alwin, & Griffin, 1979) examined how maternal emphasis on self-direction affected the young person's grades in school, choice of curriculum, and participation in extracurricular activities. The researchers reasoned that parents who valued self-direction would encourage their children to take college-preparatory courses, because a college education is a prerequisite to jobs that provide high levels of autonomy. Similarly, they expected mothers who valued self-direction to encourage extracurricular activities, because such activities provide opportunities to develop interpersonal skills. The researchers did not expect differences in grades. The results confirmed all three predictions. Thus, parents who value particular traits in their children do encourage activities that they believe are likely to produce those traits. We met Kimberly in the introduction; her mother started her in piano lessons in fourth grade because mom valued music, and that gave Kimberly the skills required when the band director needed a percussionist.

Young people also are affected by their perceptions of adult work experience. A survey of 154 parent–youth dyads found that parents' reports of their experiences at work were related to the youth's perceptions of that parent's success at work. Youth who viewed work as a positive experience were more engaged in schoolwork (Lee & Porfeli, 2015).

There is considerable segregation of occupations in the U.S. by gender (see Chapter 17). Research has documented an association between gender socialization in the family and entry into a male-typed or a female-typed occupation (Lawson, Crouter, & McHale, 2015). Family experiences were assessed at age 10, and occupational attainment 15 years later. Mothers' traditional attitudes toward women's roles were associated with a greater likelihood of sons entering male-typed occupation. Spending more time with fathers was associated with daughters' reduced likelihood of entering a female-typed occupation, and son's greater likelihood of entering a male-typed occupation.

Occupational choices are also associated with sexual orientation in the United States, according to data from 9,000 men and women aged 18 to 56. Heterosexual men were significantly more likely to prefer such jobs as athlete, auto mechanic, electrician, high school coach, and police officer. Gay men's preferences were more likely to include actor, artist, beautician, nurse, and novelist. Heterosexual women were more likely to prefer accountant, beautician, and CEO (Ellis & Ratnasingam, 2006).

## THE LIFE COURSE

Socialization continues throughout one's life. Maturation and social learning, parents, peers and media, and social structural position continue to influence development as a social actor. In adulthood, prior experience and the cultural capital (education, wealth, and status) derived from it become important, as do historical events. A viewpoint that integrates all of these is the life course perspective. First, an introduction.

"I still can't get over Liz," said Meghan. "I sat next to her in almost every class for 3 years, and still, I hardly recognized her. Put on some weight since high school, and dyed her hair. But mostly it was the defeated look on her face. When she and Hank announced they were getting married, they were the happiest couple ever. But that lasted long enough for a baby. Then there were years of underpaid jobs. She works part-time in sporting goods at Sears now. Had to take that job when her real estate work collapsed in the recession of 2008."

Jim had stopped listening. How could he get excited about Meghan's Lincoln High School reunion and people he'd never met? But Meghan's mind kept racing. A lot had happened in 25 years.

Vito—Still larger than life. Football coach at the old school, and assistant principal too. Must be a fantastic model for the tough kids he works with. That scholarship to Indiana was the break he needed.

José—Hard to believe he's in a mental hospital! He started okay as an engineer. Severely burned in a helicopter crash, and then hooked on painkillers. Just fell apart. And we voted him Most Likely to Succeed.

Precious—Thinking about a career in politics. She didn't start college until her last kid entered school. Now she's an urban planner in the mayor's office. Couldn't stop saying how she feels like a totally new person.

Tom—Head nurse at Westside Hospital's emergency ward. Quite a surprise. Last I heard, he was a car salesman. Started his nursing career at 28. Got the idea while lying in the hospital for three months after a car accident.

Maria—Right on that one, voting her Most Ambitious. Finished Yale Law, clerked for the New York Supreme Court, and just promoted to senior partner with Kennedy, Sanchez, and Ortega. Raised two kids at the same time. Having a husband who writes novels at home made life easier. Says she was lucky things were opening up for women just when she came along.

Meghan's reminiscences show how different lives can be—and how unpredictable. When we think about people like Liz or José or Tom, change seems to be the rule. There is change throughout life for all of us. But there is continuity too. Maria's string of accomplishments is based on her continuing ambition, hard work, and competence. Vito is back at Lincoln High—once a football hero, now the football coach. Even José had started on the predicted path to success before his tragic helicopter crash.

As adults, each of us will experience a life characterized both by continuity and by change. This section examines the **life course**—the individual's progression through a series of age-linked social roles embedded in social institutions (Elder & O'Rand, 1995), and the important influences that shape the life course that one experiences. Our examination of the life course is organized around three broad questions:

1. What are the major components of the life course?
2. What are the major influences on progression through the life course? That is, what causes people's careers to follow the paths they do?
3. In what ways do historical trends and events modify the typical life course pattern?

## Components of the Life Course

Lives are too complex to study in all their aspects. Consequently, we will focus on the three main components of the life course: (1) careers, (2) identity and self-esteem, and (3) stress and satisfaction. By examining these components, we can trace the continuities and changes that occur in what we do through the life course.

**Careers.** A **career** is a sequence of roles—each with its own set of activities—that a person enacts during their lifetime. Our most important careers are in three major social domains: family and friends, education, and work. The idea of a career comes from the work world, where it refers to the sequence of

jobs held. Liz's work career, for example, consisted of a sequence of jobs as waitress, checkout clerk, clothing sales, real estate agent, and sporting-goods sales.

The careers of one person differ from those of another in three ways—in the roles that make up the careers, the order in which the roles are performed, and the timing and duration of role-related activities. For example, one woman's family career may consist of roles as infant, child, adolescent, spouse, parent, grandparent, and widow. Another woman's family career may include roles as stepsister and divorcée but exclude the parent role. A man's career might include the roles of infant, child, adolescent, partner, and uncle. The order of roles also may vary. "Parent" before "spouse" has very different consequences than "spouse" before "parent." Furthermore, the timing of career events is important. Having a first child at 36 has different life consequences than having a first child at 18. Research indicates that marrying before age 23 is strongly associated with returning to school as an adult (Hostetler, Sweet, & Moen, 2007). Finally, the duration of enacting a role may vary. For example, some couples end their marriages before the wedding champagne has gone flat, whereas others go on to celebrate their golden wedding anniversary.

Societies provide structured career paths that shape the options available to individuals. The cultural norms, social expectations, and laws that organize life in a society make various career options more or less attractive, accessible, and necessary. In the United States, for example, educational careers are socially structured so that virtually everyone attends kindergarten, elementary school, and at least a few years of high school. Thereafter, educational options are more diverse—night school, technical and vocational school, apprenticeship, community college, university, and so on. But individual choice among these options is also socially constrained. The norms and expectations of our families and peer groups strongly influence our educational careers; so do the economic resources available to us.

Events in the family affect the child's/adolescent's educational career, via linkages between adults and child(ren). Changes in family structure (exit or entry of mother/stepmother or father/stepfather) is a stressor that affects the child's attachment to school and grade point average (GPA) (Heard, 2007). The timing of the event matters; changes occurring at age 6 or younger have greater impact than changes from age 7 to adolescence. Duration also matters; the number of years spent in a mother-stepfather or single-parent (mother or father) home is negatively related to GPA in grades 7 through 11.

A person's total life course consists of intertwined careers in the worlds of work, family, and education (Elder, 1975). The shape of the life course derives from the contents of these careers, from the way they mesh with one another, and from their interweaving with those of family members. Sally's classmates, Maria and Precious, enacted similar career roles: both finished college, held full-time jobs, married, and raised children. Yet the courses of their lives were very different. Maria juggled these roles simultaneously, helped by a husband who was able to work at home. Precious waited until her children were attending school before continuing her education and then adding an occupational role. The different content, order, timing, and duration of intertwining careers make each person's life course unique.

Why and when do people move? A rarely studied phenomenon is the housing or residential career. A person may move upward—into a larger, more expensive, or single-family residence—or downward—into a smaller, lower-quality, or multifamily dwelling. This residential career is interwoven with educational, family, and occupational careers. In fact, a move is usually associated with events in these other realms. With regard to

Some parents are able to blend work roles and family roles by working at home. As further advances occur in telecommunications, more women and men may choose this option. However, some major companies have barred employees from working off-site. © Fertnig/iStock

family careers, entering cohabitation or marriage often involves a move up for one or both partners; a separation or divorce often involves moves down. Comparing married and cohabiting couples, couples who divorced experienced a larger drop in housing quality (Feijten & van Ham, 2010).

**Identities and Self-Esteem.** As we engage in career roles, we observe our own performances and other people's reactions to us. Using these observations, we construct **role identities**—conceptions of the self in specific roles. The role identities available to us depend on the career paths we are following. When Liz's work in real estate collapsed, she got a job in sales at Sears; she was qualified to sell sporting goods because of her prior work experience.

As we will see in Chapter 4, identities are negotiated. To become a parent, one must negotiate with a partner, or with persons representing alternative paths (artificial insemination, surrogates, adoption) to parenthood. Many gay men see the identity of prospective father as incompatible with the identity of gay man. However, some gay men are fathers. Interviews focused on how this identity change occurred; consideration by a man of parenthood was triggered by caring for a child, meeting a gay or lesbian parent, or contact with an adoption agency (Berkowitz & Marsiglio, 2007). Adoption of the identity was the product of negotiations with intimate partners, birth mothers, lawyers, and other agents of organizations associated with reproduction.

As we enact major roles, especially familial and occupational roles, we evaluate our performances and thereby gain or lose **self-esteem**—one's sense of how good and worthy one is. Self-esteem is influenced by one's achievements; Maria has high self-esteem as a consequence of being the first in her family to earn a law degree, and a senior partner in a prestigious law firm. Self-esteem is also influenced by the feedback one receives from others.

Identities and self-esteem are crucial guides to behavior, as discussed in Chapter 4. We therefore consider identities and self-esteem as the second component of the life course.

**Stress and Satisfaction.** Performing career activities often produces positive feelings, such as satisfaction, and negative feelings, including stress. These feelings reflect how we experience the quality of our lives. Thus, stress and satisfaction are the third component of the life course.

An important influence on the amount of stress or satisfaction experienced by a partner in a dual-earner relationship is the balance between marital and work roles. A study of dual-earner couples found that couples who shared in making decisions and in which both spent time doing household or housekeeping tasks experienced equity (see Chapter 14) (Bartley, Blanton, & Gilliard, 2005). Couples in which one person exerted unilateral influence and did a disproportionate share of housework perceived less equity and experienced stress.

Changes in career roles, such as having a baby, adopting a child, or changing jobs, place emotional and physical demands on the person. Life events, such as moving or serious conflict with a parent or lover, may have similar effects. These are referred to as stressful life events. These may have positive effects such as motivating career or housing improvements; when the person responds to stress as a positive challenge, it is referred to as *eustress*. At other times, the demands made on a person exceed the individual's ability to cope with them; such a discrepancy is called **stress** (Dohrenwend, 1961). People who are under stress often experience psychological (anxiety, tension, depression) and physical (fatigue, headaches, illness) consequences (Wickrama, Lorenz, Conger, & Elder, 1997).

These feelings vary in their intensity in response to life course events (see Chapter 17). Levels of stress, for example, change as career roles become more or less demanding (parenting roles become increasingly demanding as children enter adolescence), as different careers compete with one another (family versus occupational demands), and as unanticipated setbacks occur (one's employer goes bankrupt). Levels of satisfaction vary as career rewards change (salary increases or cuts) and as we cope more or less successfully with career demands (meeting sales quotas, passing exams) or with life events (a heart attack or a car accident).

The extent to which particular events or transitions are stressful depends on several factors. First, the more extensive the changes associated with the event, the greater the stress. For example, a change in employment that requires a move to an unfamiliar city is more stressful than the same new job located across town. Second, the availability of social support—in the form of advice and emotional and material aid—increases our ability to cope successfully with change. To help their members, families reallocate their resources and reorganize their activities. Thus, parents lend money to young couples, and older adults provide care for their grandchildren so their children can work.

Personal resources and competence influence how one copes with stress. Coping successfully with earlier transitions prepares individuals for later transitions. Men who develop strong ego identities in young adulthood perceive events later in their lives as less negative (Sammon, Reznikoff, & Geisinger, 1985). *Life course mastery* refers to the belief that an individual has directed and managed the trajectories of their life. Influences on this sense of mastery were studied through face-to-face interviews with more than 1,100 persons aged 65 and older (Pearlin, Nguyen, Schieman, & Milkie, 2007). Attaining occupational prestige (see Chapter 17) and accumulated wealth were positively related to sense of life course mastery. Experiences of unfair treatment in educational or work settings, and number and severity of periods of economic hardship, were negatively related to it.

## Influences on Life Course Progression

At the beginning of this section, we noted many events that had important impacts on the lives of Meghan's classmates: loss of a job due to economic recession, a helicopter crash, a car accident, having a baby, and graduating from a prestigious law school. These are **life events**—episodes that mark transition points in our lives and involve changes in roles. They provoke coping and readjustment (Hultsch & Plemons, 1979). For many young people, for example, the move from home to college is a life event marking a transition from adolescence to young adulthood. This move initiates a period during which students work out new behavior patterns and revise their self-expectations and priorities.

There are three major influences on the life course: (1) biological aging, (2) social age grading, and (3) historical trends and events. These influences act on us through specific life events (Brim & Ryff, 1980). Some life events are carefully planned—a trip to Europe, for example. Other events, no less important, occur by chance—like meeting one's future spouse in an Amsterdam hostel.

**Biological Aging.** Throughout the life cycle, we undergo *maturation*—biological changes in body size and structure, in the brain and central nervous system, in the endocrine system, in our susceptibility to various diseases, and in the acuity of our sight, hearing, taste, and so on. These changes are rapid and dramatic in childhood. Their pace slows considerably after adolescence, picking up again in old age. Even in the middle years, however, biological changes may have substantial effects. The shifting hormone levels associated with menstrual periods in women and with aging in men and women, for example, are thought by many to affect mood and behavior (Sommer, 2001).

Biological aging is inevitable and irreversible, but it is only loosely related to chronological age. Puberty may come at any time between 8 and 17, for example, and serious decline in the functioning of body organs may begin before age 40 or after age 85. The neurons of the brain die off steadily throughout life and do not regenerate. Yet intellectual functioning—long assumed to be determined early in life and to decline with aging—is now known to be capable of increase over the life course. Even in old age, mental abilities can improve with opportunities for learning and practice (Baltes & Willis, 1982).

A major life event or transition for employed people is retirement. Many people base retirement decisions on biological age, retiring at

62 or 65 or 70. There are two other ways in which one can exit the labor force: suffering work-related disability or dying. Research on a sample of more than 7,200 women aged 50 to 80 used data collected in 1992 to identify variables associated with work status in 2004 (Brown & Warner, 2008). White, Black, and Hispanic women were equally likely to die before leaving the labor force, but Black and Hispanic women were 65 percent more likely to leave due to disability. Not surprisingly, women without health insurance, who rated their health as poor, or who reported greater limitations on their functioning in 1992 were more likely to subsequently experience disability. This, in turn, reflects their access to resources.

Biologically based capacities and characteristics limit what we can do. Their impact on the life course depends, however, on the social significance we give them. How does the first appearance of gray hair affect careers, identities, and stress, for instance? For some, this biological event is a painful source of stress. It elicits dismay, sets off thoughts about mortality, and instigates desperate attempts to straighten out family relations and to make a mark in the world before it is too late. Others take gray hair as a sign to stop worrying about trying to look young, to start basing their priorities on their own values, and to demand respect for their experience. Similarly, the impact of other biological changes on the life course—such as the growth spurt during adolescence, or menopause in middle age—also depends on the social significance given them.

**Social Age Grading.** Which members of a society should raise children, and which should be cared for by others? Who should attend school, and who should work full-time? Who should be single, and who should marry? Age is the primary criterion that every known society uses to assign people to such activities and roles (Riley, 1987). Throughout life, individuals move through a sequence of age-graded social roles. Each role consists of a set of expected behaviors, opportunities, and constraints. Movement through these roles shapes the course of life.

Each society prescribes a customary sequence of age-graded activities and roles. In American society, many people expect a young person to finish school before they enter a long-term relationship. Many people expect a person to marry before they have or adopt a child. There are also expectations about the ages at which these role transitions should occur. These expectations vary by race and ethnicity; Hispanic adolescent girls expect to marry and have a first child at younger ages (22, 23) than Whites (23, 24) or Blacks (24, 24) (East, 1998). These age norms serve as a basis for planning, as prods to action, and as brakes against moving too quickly (Neugarten & Datan, 1973).

Pressure to make the expected transitions between roles at the appropriate times means that the life course consists of a series of normative life stages. A **normative life stage** is a discrete period in the life course during which individuals are expected to perform the set of activities associated with a distinct age-related role. The order of the stages is prescribed, and people try to shape their own lives to fit socially approved career paths. Moreover, people perceive deviations from expected career paths as undesirable.

Not everyone experiences major transitions in the socially approved progression. Consider the transition to adulthood; the normative order of events is leaving school, performing military service, getting a job, and getting married. Analyzing data about the high school class of 1972 collected between 1972 and 1980, researchers found that half of the men and women experienced a sequence that violated this "normal" path (Rindfuss, Swicegood, & Rosenfeld, 1987). Common violations included entering military service before one finished school and returning to school after a period of full-time employment.

In some cases, violating the age norms associated with a transition has lasting consequences. The transition to marriage is expected to occur between the ages of 19 and 25. Research consistently finds that making this transition earlier than usual has long-term effects on marital as well as occupational careers. A survey of 63,000 adults allowed researchers to compare men who married as adolescents with men of similar age who married as adults (Teti, Lamb, & Elster, 1987). Because the sample included people of all ages, the researchers could study the careers of men who married 20, 30, and 40 years earlier. Men who married as adolescents completed fewer years of education, held lower-status jobs, and earned less income. Furthermore, the marriages of those who married early were less stable. These effects were evident 40 years after marriage. Early marriage has similar effects on women. Women who marry before age 20 experience reduced educational and occupational attainment, and are more likely to get divorced (Teti & Lamb, 1989).

Movement from one life stage to another involves a **normative transition**—socially expected changes made by all or most members of a defined population (Cowan, 1991). Although most members undergo this institutional passage,

Violating the age norms associated with a major transition, such as the transition to parenthood, may have lasting consequences. Having a baby at age 16 may force a young woman to leave school and limit her to a succession of poorly paid jobs.
© alphalight1/Pixabay

each individual's experience of it may be different, reflecting their past experience. Normative transitions are often marked by a ceremony, such as a bar/bat mitzvah, graduation, commitment ceremony, wedding, baby shower, or retirement party. But the actual transition is a process that may occur over a period of weeks or months. This process involves both a restructuring of the person's cognitive and emotional makeup and of their social relationships. The cognitive and emotional restructuring may not occur until months after the ceremony marking the event.

Transitions from one life stage to another influence a person in three ways. First, they change the roles available for building identities. The transition to adulthood brings major changes in roles. Those who marry or have their first child begin to view themselves as partners and parents, responsible for others. Second, transitions modify the privileges and responsibilities of persons. Age largely determines whether we can legally drive a car, be employed full-time, serve in the military, or retire. Third, role transitions change the nature of socialization experiences. The content of socialization shifts from teaching basic values and motivations in childhood, to developing skills in adolescence, to transmitting role-related norms for behavior in adulthood (Lutfey & Mortimer, 2003). The power differences between socializee and socializing agents also diminish as we age and move into higher education and occupational organizations. As a result, adults are more able to resist socialization than children (Mortimer & Simmons, 1978).

**Historical Trends and Events.** Recall that Meghan's classmate Maria attributed her rapid rise to senior law partner to lucky historical timing. Maria applied to Yale Law School shortly after the barriers to women had been broken, and she sought a job just when affirmative action came into vogue at the major law firms. Meghan's friend Liz attributed her setback as a real estate broker to an economic recession coupled with high interest rates that crippled the housing market. As the experiences of Maria and Liz illustrate, historical trends and events are another major influence on the life course. The lives of individuals are shaped by trends that extend across historical periods (such as increasing equality of the sexes and improved nutrition) and by events that occur at particular points in history (such as recessions, wars, earthquakes, and tsunamis).

The title of the report says it all: "For first time in modern era, living with parents edges out other living arrangements for 18- to 34-year-olds" (Fry, 2016). A major marker of the transition to adulthood is the establishment of an independent residence. In the past, many youth couldn't wait to "move out" when they got a full-time job or went to college. But recent social changes—postponement of marriage, poor employment opportunities due to the recession of 2008–2009, and falling wages, especially for men—have resulted in more than 30 percent of young men and women remaining with or returning to live with parents. Note that poor employment prospects and low wages make it more difficult to establish a long-term relationship and your own residence.

*Birth Cohorts.* To aid in understanding how historical events and trends influence the life courses of individuals, social scientists have developed the concept of cohorts (Ryder, 1965). A **birth cohort** is a group of people who were born during the same period. The period could be one year or several years, depending on the issue under study. What is most important about a birth cohort is that its members are all approximately the same age when they encounter particular historical events. The birth cohort of 1970 graduated from college about 1992, the beginning of a decade of sustained economic growth. Most of the graduates got good jobs and experienced several years of growth in their average annual household income (www.demos.org/data-byte/changes-average-annual). Between

1990 and 2000, incomes grew between 10 and 28 percent. This growth facilitated establishing relationships and families and purchasing homes. In contrast, the cohort of 1980 graduated about 2002, the beginning of a decade of economic shocks—9/11, major corporate bankruptcies, and the recession of 2008. During that decade, average annual household incomes declined between 5 and 15 percent. This cohort had a more difficult time establishing families and settling into adulthood due to economic hardship.

A person's membership in a specific birth cohort locates that person historically in two ways. First, it points to the trends and events the person is likely to have encountered. Second, it indicates approximately where an individual is located in the sequence of normative life stages when historical events occur. Life stage location is crucial because historical events or trends have different impacts on individuals who are in different life stages.

To illustrate, consider the effects of the economic collapse of several large corporations in 2001 and 2002. Enron and Arthur Andersen virtually collapsed; several other firms went out of business; and Kmart, Tyco, and others downsized. Tens of thousands of workers and managers aged 30 to 60 were laid off. Some people in their 50s found it impossible to get new jobs, perhaps due to age discrimination, and experienced prolonged unemployment. Some persons in their 30s and 40s returned to school and subsequently entered new fields. Workers who kept their jobs were left with insecurity and increased workloads. Persons just finishing college—the birth cohort of 1980—found fewer employment opportunities than those who graduated in 1995. Of course, not all members of a cohort experience historical events in the same way. Members of the class of 2002 who majored in liberal arts faced more limited opportunities than those earning professional degrees.

Placement in a birth cohort also affects access to opportunities. Members of large birth cohorts, for example, are likely to be disadvantaged throughout life. They begin their education in overpopulated classrooms. They then must compete for scarce openings in professional schools and crowded job markets. As they age, they face reduced retirement benefits because their numbers threaten to overwhelm the Social Security system. Table 3.3 presents examples of how the same historical events affect members of different cohorts in distinct ways. These historically different experiences mold the unique values, ideologies, personalities, and behavior patterns that characterize each cohort through the life course. Within each cohort, there are differences too. For example, the wars in Iraq and Afghanistan led to a father's or mother's absence for some children but not for others.

*Cohorts and Social Change.* Due to the differences in their experiences, each birth cohort ages in a unique way. Each cohort has its own set of collective experiences and opportunities. As a result, cohorts differ in their career patterns, attitudes, values, and self-concepts. As cohorts age, they succeed one another in filling the social positions in the family and in political, economic, and cultural institutions. Power is transferred from members of older cohorts with their historically based outlooks to members of younger cohorts with different outlooks. In this way, the succession of cohorts produces social change. It also causes intergenerational conflict about issues on which successive cohorts disagree (Elder, 1975).

Occasionally, a major event or trend occurs that is profoundly discontinuous with the past; examples include the attacks on the World Trade Center and the Pentagon on September 11, 2001, the wars in Iraq and Afghanistan that began in 2003, and Hurricane Harvey that made landfall in Texas in August 2017. Cohorts that are in late adolescence or early adulthood when such events occur may be profoundly affected by them and, in consequence, may develop a generational identity—a strong identification with their own generation and a sense of difference from older and younger cohorts (Stewart, 2002). This identity may shape their lives, influencing their choice of work, political views, and family relationships.

**TABLE 3.3** History and Life Stage

| TREND OR EVENT | COHORT OF 1990–1995 | | COHORT OF 2000–2005 | |
|---|---|---|---|---|
| | LIFESTAGE WHEN EVENT OCCURRED | SOME LIFE COURSE IMPLICATIONS OF EVENT | LIFESTAGE WHEN EVENT OCCURRED | SOME LIFE COURSE IMPLICATIONS OF EVENT |
| Economic Expansion (1992–2000) | Childhood | Raised in dual-career family. Good schools. | _____ | |
| Terrorist Attacks (9/11/01) | Youth | Shaken sense of security. Uncertainty about the future. Increased stress. | Infant | Few affected directly. |
| War in Iraq (2003–2011) | Adolescent | Crowded schools. School violence. | Childhood | Military service disrupts families. |
| War in Afghanistan (2001–2014) | | Military service disrupts families | | |
| Recession (2008–2010) | Transition to adulthood | High youth unemployment. Difficulty launching into workforce. | Youth | Family economic hardship. Limited resources. |
| Sluggish Recovery (2010–2016) | Young Adult | Large student debt. Limited incomes. Living with parents. | Adolescent | School funds cut. Reduced social safety net. |

In this section, we have provided an overview of changes during the life course. Based on this discussion, it is useful to think of ourselves as living simultaneously in three types of time, each deriving from a different source of change. As we age biologically, we move through developmental time in our own biological life cycle. As we pass through the intertwined sequences of roles in our society, we move through social time. And as we respond to the historical events that impinge on our lives, we move together with our cohort through historical time.

We have emphasized the changes that occur as individuals progress through the life course. However, there is also stability. Normative transitions usually involve choices, and individuals usually make choices that are compatible with preexisting values, selves, and dispositions (Elder & O'Rand, 1995). More than 90 percent of all Americans experience the normative transition of marriage. Most persons choose when and whom they marry. Longitudinal research indicates that we choose a spouse who is compatible with our own personality, thus promoting stability over time (Caspi & Herbener, 1990).

Thus, each person's life course experience/trajectory includes periods of stability and changes. Periods of gradual change are interrupted by normative transitions, which are often predictable, and unpredictable life events—accidents, illnesses, sudden economic changes, relationship status changes. The person will eventually adjust to the changes, though the experience may be very stressful. Engelman and Jackson (2017) suggest that rather than gradual change, the life course may better be thought of as a punctuated equilibrium, with stability represented by equilibrium, punctuated by both expected and unexpected changes.

Many elderly people participate in organized activities, such as this exercise group. As long as they remain healthy and economically independent, most elderly people maintain their social involvements, activities, and self-esteem. © monkeybusinessimages/iStock

## Historical Variations

Unique historical events—wars, depressions, medical innovations—change life courses. And historical trends—fluctuating birth and divorce rates, rising education, varying patterns of women's work—also influence the life courses of individuals born in particular historical periods.

No one can predict with confidence the future changes that will result from historical trends and events. What we can do is to examine how major events and trends have influenced life courses in the past. Two examples will be presented: the historical trend toward greater involvement of women in the occupational world, and the effects of historical events on different cohorts of high school graduates. The goals of this section are (1) to emphasize the influence of historical trends on the typical life course, and (2) to illustrate how to analyze the links between historical events and the life course.

**Women's Work: Gender Role Attitudes and Behavior.** There has been a substantial increase in the percentage of women who work outside the home in the United States since 1960 (see Figure 3.3). We will consider the role of attitudes and of economic changes in this trend.

*Gender Role Attitudes.* In the past five decades, attitudes in the U.S. toward women's roles in the world outside the family have changed dramatically. The historical trend in attitudes has been away from the traditional division of labor (paid occupations for men and full-time homemaking for women) to a more egalitarian view.

Consider the following statements. Do you agree with them?

1. It is much better for everyone involved if the man is the achiever outside the home and the woman takes care of home and family.

2. Women should take care of running their homes and leave the running of the country up to men.
3. Most men are better suited emotionally for politics than are most women.

These are typical of attitude statements included in one or more large-scale surveys of adults during the 1970s, 1980s, and 1990s. In the 1970s, two-thirds or more of the people surveyed agreed with the first statement, and one-third agreed with the second and third statements. However, by 1998, only one-third agreed with statement 1, and statements 2 and 3 were endorsed by only 15 and 21 percent, respectively (Davis, Smith, & Marsden, 2000). This shift from traditional to egalitarian gender role attitudes has been quite strong among women. Hispanic women are often characterized as having more traditional gender role attitudes. However, young, well-educated, working Latinas have more egalitarian attitudes, similar to White women (Ginorio, Gutierrez, Cauce, & Acosta, 1995). Many Asian women struggle with conflicts between traditional attitudes common in their cultures and the more egalitarian attitudes found in the United States (Root, 1995).

**Workforce Participation.** This historical trend is not limited to attitudes. Women's actual participation in the workforce has been on the increase for almost a century. Figure 3.3 shows the percentage of women employed outside the home since 1960. The proportion of married women who are employed grew steadily from 1960 to 1995; from 1995 to 2005, employment levels remained stable. Among young single women, the employment level, already very high in 1960, remained high. From 2005 to 2012, rates for all four groups declined several percent, but rebounded by 2015. In 2015, rates of employment for Black, Hispanic, and White women were essentially the same. In 2008–2010, rates for Asian women varied considerably, from 49

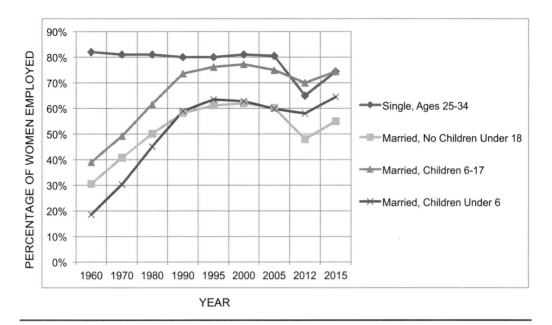

**FIGURE 3.3**  Women's Employment: 1960–2015

The percentage of married women who are employed rose steadily from 1960 to 1995. Single women 25–34 maintained virtually the same high level of employment throughout this period, with about 80 percent employed. Among married women, the level of employment rose slowly for those with no children and more rapidly among those with children under 18. The patterns shift between 2005 and 2010 and 2010 to 2015. The recession of 2008–2009 pushed some women out of the labor market, as they lost their jobs, but also sent others in, as they sought employment to make up for their partners' lost wages.

*Source:* U.S. Bureau of the Census and Bureau of Labor Statistics. Data for 2015 from Bureau of Labor Statistics, 2016.

percent for Japanese women, to 55 percent for Asian Indian women, to 67 percent for Filipinas (Allard, 2011).

Why have women joined the workforce in ever greater numbers throughout the twentieth century? Has the spread of egalitarian attitudes been an important source of influence? Probably not. The idea that wives and mothers should not work except in cases of extreme need was widely held until the 1940s. Yet women's employment increased steadily between 1900 and 1940. The change in gender role attitudes occurred largely in the 1970s, yet women's employment rose rapidly during the two decades preceding these attitude changes. It therefore seems likely that gender role attitude changes have not been a cause of the increased employment of women

but a response to it—an acceptance of what more and more women are, in fact, doing. Of course, as these attitudes change, that facilitates additional women entering the labor force.

What, then, are the causes? Perhaps most convincing is the argument that the types of industries and occupations that traditionally demand female labor are the ones that have expanded most rapidly in this century. Light industries like electronics, pharmaceuticals, and food processing have grown rapidly, for example, and service jobs in education, health services, and secretarial and clerical work have multiplied. Many of these occupations were so strongly segregated by sex that men were reluctant to enter them (Oppenheimer, 1970). Moreover, male labor was scarce during much of the century due to rapidly expanding industry and commerce. The majority of the slack was taken up by a large pool of unemployed married women. These women could be pulled into the workforce at a lower wage because they were often supplementing their family income.

The changes noted in the preceding paragraph led to increased job opportunities for women. Other factors influenced women's desire to work outside the home. One of these was continuing inflation and rising interest rates; in many families, two incomes became necessary to make ends meet.

Other factors that may have promoted the increased employment of women include rising divorce rates, falling birth rates, rising education levels, and the invention of labor-saving devices for the home. None of these factors alone can explain the continuing rise in the employment of women over the century. However, at one time or another, each of these factors probably strengthened the historic trend, along with changes in gender role attitudes.

The specific changes in women's work behavior demonstrate that the timing of a person's birth in history greatly influences the course of their life. Whether you join the workforce depends in part on historical trends during your lifetime. So does the likelihood that you will get a college education, marry, have children, divorce, die young or old, and so on.

**Impact of Events.** Life course researchers are also interested in the impact of events on those who experience them. One dimension of impact is the magnitude of the event—that is, the number of people who are affected. The events of September 11, 2001, in the United States affected millions of people across the United States and in other parts of the world. The closing of a school affects hundreds of people in the community where the school is located.

How an event affects people depends on the life stage at which it is experienced.

**TABLE 3.4** The Impact of Social Events on the Person

| LIFESTAGE WHEN EVENT IS EXPERIENCED | FOCUS OF IMPACT OF EVENT |
| --- | --- |
| Childhood | Values and attitudes |
| Adolescence, young adulthood | Identities, opportunities |
| Adulthood | Behavior, opportunities |
| Later adulthood | New life choices, revised identity |

*Source:* Adapted from Stewart, 2000.

One model of this relationship is displayed in Table 3.4. In one sense, events have the greatest impact on children, by influencing their basic values and attitudes. The effects of an event on adolescents and young adults may be on one or more of their identities and on the social and economic opportunities they experience. A helicopter accident had a profound effect on the opportunities of José (whom we met earlier), leaving him partially paralyzed. Events may affect an adult's behavior, but they are unlikely to influence their identity or basic values. On the other hand, for those at midlife, some events, such as a major illness or the loss of a job, may create new identities and opportunities.

The impact of an event may also vary depending on the person's location in the social structure—that is, class, gender, and race. Consider the closing of a high school in Oak Valley, a prosperous Midwestern community. In the mid-1960s, the community and the school were racially integrated; about 50 percent of the students were African-American. As the civil rights movement gathered momentum in the United States, it affected the identities and behavior of some of the students; some African-American students adopted distinctive dress and grooming patterns. The principal of the high school responded by imposing a dress code prohibiting facial hair; some students, parents, and faculty interpreted his action as racist. There was a walkout by African-American students and their supporters, and public protests; some parents demanded action by the Oak Valley school board. Eventually, the board decided to close the school (Stewart, 2002).

A team of researchers has been studying two cohorts of persons who were students at the school: members of the classes of 1955, 1956, and 1957, and of the classes of 1968 and 1969 (Stewart, 2000; Stewart, Henderson-King, Henderson-King, & Winter, 2000). The research involves three methods—ethnographic observation, surveys, and in-depth interviews with selected persons. The team is interested in how the social structure—that is, race, class, and gender—shaped the students' lives in interaction with their experiences at the high school. Note that these people went to the same school in the same neighborhood, and many knew one another. The researchers could talk to each participant about the same people and events, being attentive to differences from one person to another in interpretation and experience. Many of the graduates still live in Oak Valley. The researchers also read newspapers and other documents from the 1950s and 1960s and interviewed people who were teachers, administrators, ministers, and other community members during this period.

The 1950s graduates, asked 45 years later about the significance of events in their lives, rated past events like World War II high in meaning to them personally. They viewed their years in high school as idyllic; both African and European Americans described the school as a successful "melting pot," where differences were accepted and there was no conflict. There also were no major differences in the descriptions of men and women. In contrast, the 1960s cohort rated then-current events such as the civil rights and women's movements as highly meaningful personally. Reflecting the significance of race, African Americans rated the civil rights movement as much more meaningful than

did European Americans. Both Blacks and Whites described Midwest High in terms of the diversity of students and teachers. Probing deeper, differences by race reappeared; African Americans discussed discrimination, racism, and the dress code, whereas European Americans discussed their fear of violence.

Turning to gender, African-American men spoke of the school with pride and noted the power of the community in the response to the dress code. These men successfully resisted a code they viewed as racist. One said, "My experience left little to be desired." African-American women spoke of the good teachers and the friends they made, but also about their limited social life as Black women and about racism. One said the worst thing about high school was "not being accepted or even noticed by many students." White men discussed the diversity of the student body; they also sometimes pointed to a breakdown of authority in the school. One said the worst thing was "getting beat up a couple of times." Like Black women, White women discussed friendships, but they also discussed the breakdown of authority, recalling instances of sexual harassment.

Thus, the social structure interacts with events to determine their impact on persons. Carrying out an intensive study of specific events, such as the imposition of the dress code and subsequent events at Midwest High, makes us aware that the same events may be perceived very differently depending on the perceiver's race and gender.

## SUMMARY

This chapter has discussed the life course and gender roles in American society. Socialization is the process through which infants become effective participants in society. It makes us like all other members of society in certain ways (shared language) but distinctive in other ways (identities).

**Perspectives on Socialization.** (1) One approach to the study of socialization emphasizes biological development; it views the emergence of interpersonal responsiveness and the development of speech and of cognitive structure as influenced by maturation. (2) Another approach emphasizes learning and the acquisition of skills from other persons. (3) A third approach emphasizes the child's discovery of cultural routines as they participate in and re-create them. (4) A fourth approach emphasizes the influence of social structure, which specifies who is responsible for socializing children, adolescents, and other types of persons, and what they should be taught.

**Agents of Childhood Socialization.** There are four major socializing agents in childhood. (1) The family provides the infant with a strong attachment to one or more caregivers. This bond is necessary for the infant to develop interpersonal and cognitive skills. Family composition and social class affect socialization by influencing the amount and kind of interaction between parent and child. Ethnic and racial groups differ in the child-rearing techniques they use and in the values they emphasize. (2) Peers provide the child with equal status relationships and are an important influence on the development of self. (3) Schools teach skills—reading, writing, and arithmetic—as well as traits like punctuality and perseverance. (4) Mass media provide children and adolescents with powerful images of some of the identities available in the society and scripts for various types of relationships and behaviors.

**Processes of Socialization.** Socialization is based on three different processes. (1) Instrumental conditioning—the association of rewards and punishments with particular actions—is a basis for learning both behaviors and performance standards. Studies of the effectiveness of various child-rearing techniques indicate that rewards do not always make a desirable behavior more likely to occur, and punishments do not always eliminate an undesirable behavior. The use of corporal punishment appears to increase the likelihood of later antisocial behavior. Through instrumental learning, children develop the ability to judge their own behaviors and to engage in self-reinforcement. (2) We learn many behaviors and skills by observation of models. We may not perform these behaviors, however, until we are in the appropriate situation. (3) Socialization also involves internalization—the acquisition of behavioral standards, making them part of the self. This process enables the child to engage in self-control.

**Outcomes of Socialization.** (1) The child gradually learns a gender role—the expectations associated with being a boy or a girl. Whether the child is independent or dependent, aggressive or passive, depends on the expectations communicated by parents, kin, and peers. Some children do not fit into the dominant gender binary; their efforts to develop a gender expression may result in bullying and abuse. (2) Language skill is another outcome of socialization; it involves learning words and the rules for combining them into meaningful sentences. Related to the learning of language is the development of thought and the ability to group objects and persons into meaningful categories. (3) The learning of social norms involves parents, peers, and teachers as socializing agents. Children learn that conformity to norms facilitates social interaction. Children also develop the ability to make moral judgments. (4) Children acquire motives—dispositions that produce sustained, goal-directed behavior. Orientations toward work are influenced primarily by parents; middle-class families emphasize self-direction, whereas working-class families emphasize conformity.

**Components of the Life Course.** To aid our understanding of adult lives, we focused on three components of the life course. (1) The life course consists of careers—sequences of roles and associated activities. The principal careers involve work, family, and friends. (2) As we engage in career roles, we develop role identities, and evaluations of our performance contribute to self-esteem. (3) The emotional reactions we have to career and life events include feelings of stress and of satisfaction.

**Influences on Life Course Progression.** There are three major influences on progression through the life course. (1) The biological growth and decline of body and brain set limits on what we can do. The effects of biological developments on the life course, however, depend on the social meanings we give them. (2) Each society has a customary, normative sequence of age-graded roles and activities. This normative sequence largely determines the bases for building identities, the responsibilities and privileges, and the socialization experiences available to individuals of different ages. (3) Historical trends and events modify an individual's life course. The impact of a historical event depends on the person's life stage when the event occurs.

**Historical Variations.** The historical timing of one's birth influences the life course through all stages. (1) Between 1960 and 2005 women's participation in the workforce increased dramatically, and attitudes toward women's employment became much more favorable. It is likely that the changes in attitudes reflect the changes in labor force participation, rather than the reverse. The likelihood that women will experience pressures and opportunities to work outside the home is now greater at every life stage. (2) Events also influence the life course of those affected by them. The impact of an event depends on its scope and on the life stage and social structural location of the persons influenced by it.

### Critical Thinking Skill: Understanding the Difference Between Truth and Validity

In this chapter we introduced several theories about how a person becomes an effective member of society: the developmental perspective, the social learning perspective, the interpretive perspective, and the life course perspective. A common reaction by students is to ask "So which one is right?" or "Which one is the best?" These questions reflect the belief that a theory is correct or incorrect, right or wrong. Truth can be defined as consistent with facts or reality. The belief that some things are true and others are not is one that most of us rely on as we navigate the world, so we often try to sort out truth from falsity.

However, this belief will not serve us well if we apply it to evaluating theory. A theory is an abstraction, a simplification, an intentional focus on one or a few elements of a complex situation in order to make sense of that situation. Every observer of children notes that they develop the skills needed to interact successfully with adults. But the explanation the observer provides depends upon their theoretical lens. The developmental perspective says that this reflects the development of the brain so that it can process complex information, the development of motor control over posture, speech, and so on, and the maturation of vocal organs. The learning theorist would say that this reflects learning language via social learning and reinforcement, and interactional skills by observation of other children and adults interacting. The interpretive theorist would point out that they practiced many times per day interacting with other children, and developed their own unique brand of speech and gestures. Each theorist's interpretations are consistent with some of the reality they are observing in the child's behavior, so in this sense, each theory is "true." So asking "Which one is true?" doesn't help us evaluate the different theories.

Instead, we evaluate theories in terms of their validity. We look for *evidence*. We use the theory to generate testable questions or hypotheses, collect data or observations that are relevant to the hypotheses, and evaluate the consistency between the observations or data and the hypotheses. We described this process in detail in Chapter 2. To the extent that the evidence is consistent with the theory each time the theory is tested, we develop confidence that the theory is valid. Evidence that is not consistent, or evidence reported by one researcher/group that cannot be confirmed by subsequent research, gives us less confidence in the validity of the theory. In writing this book, we pay careful attention to the consistency of evidence, and often don't include theories or ideas because the evidence for them isn't consistent. So the next time you meet a new theory, what question will you ask?

# SELF AND SELF-ESTEEM

## LEARNING OBJECTIVES

By the end of this chapter you will be able to:

- Define the self and describe how it develops.

- Explain the process by which we acquire unique identities and use them to locate ourselves in the world.

- Understand how our identities guide our plans and behavior.

- Explain the origins of our self-evaluations, how they affect our behavior, and how we protect our self-esteem.

## INTRODUCTION

He is a stranger to himself, a mystery to everyone else. Police call him Al, so at least he has a name, even if he knows it isn't his own.

Al's earliest memory takes him to the morning of September 10, when he woke up frightened and disoriented on the sidewalk in front of the World Trade Center in downtown Denver. Every memory before that moment is gone. "I want my past," Al says. "I want who I was. I don't care about anything else."

He learns something new about himself every day. He has discovered that he likes lasagna and "when it's warm outside." But he can't remember how to cook and isn't sure if he knows how to drive. When Al was examined, doctors found no drugs or alcohol in his system, or any sign of a head injury. Mental health experts who have interviewed Al believe he is suffering from retrograde amnesia.

He is expecting to go on national news shows in hopes someone will recognize him. Some clues come forward. Al was wearing a ring, a watch, yellow baseball cap, and glasses when he was found. He had a cigarette lighter and $8 in his pocket. Police have unsuccessfully tried to trace where his watch and ring were purchased. They ran his fingerprints through FBI databases, but no matches were found.

"I feel totally lost," Al said. "I feel totally alone, very depressed, very anxious about everything." Al now lives in a transitional housing facility where he spends much of his time contemplating what he doesn't have—family, friends, his past, his identity (Bernuth, *The Denver Post,* October 22, 2006).

"Who am I?" Few human beings in Western societies live out their lives without pondering this question. Some people pursue the search for self-knowledge and for a meaningful identity eagerly; others pursue it desperately. College students in particular are often preoccupied with discovering who they are. Few, however, have experienced existential uncertainty to the degree faced by Al.

Each of us has unique answers to this question, answers that reflect our **self-schema** or self-concept, the organized structure of cognitions or thoughts we have about ourselves. The self-schema comprises our perceptions of our social identities and personal qualities and our generalizations about the self based on experience.

One way to assess the contents of self-schemas is by asking people to answer the question "Who am I?" This is the focus of Box 4.1. Before you read on, take a few moments and respond to this question yourself in the space provided in the box. For comparison, read the answers of a 9-year-old boy and a female college sophomore to the question "Who am I?" Their responses are listed at the bottom of the box.

## THE NATURE AND GENESIS OF SELF

### The Self as Source and Object of Action

We can behave in a wide variety of ways toward other persons. For example, if George is talking to Keisha, he can perceive her,

## BOX 4.1  Test Yourself: Measuring Self-Concepts

In order to study self-concepts, we need ways to measure them. Several methods have been used. For example, one approach asks people to check those adjectives on a list (intelligent, aggressive, trusting, and so on) that describe themselves (Sarbin & Rosenberg, 1955). In another approach (Osgood, Suci, & Tannenbaum, 1957), people rate themselves on pairs of adjectives (strong–weak, good–bad, active–passive): Are they more like one of the adjectives in the pair or more like its opposite? Another technique, developed by Miyamoto and Dornbusch (1956), asks people whether they have more or less of a characteristic (self-confidence, likableness) than members of a particular group (such as fraternities, sororities, and so on). In yet another technique, people sort cards containing descriptive phrases (interested in sports, concerned with achievement) into piles according to how accurately they think the phrases describe them (Stephenson, 1953).

Each of these popular methods provides respondents with a single standard set of categories to use in describing themselves. Using the same categories for all respondents makes it easy to compare the self-concepts of different people. These methods have a weakness, however. They do not reveal the unique dimensions that individuals use in spontaneously thinking about themselves. For this purpose, techniques that ask people simply to describe themselves in their own words are especially effective (Kuhn & McPartland, 1954; McGuire & McGuire, 1982).

Instructions for the "Who am I?" technique for measuring self-concepts (Gordon, 1968) are provided below. You can try this test yourself.

In the 15 numbered blanks, write 15 different answers to the simple question "Who am I?" Answer as if you were giving the answers to yourself, not to somebody else. Write the answers in the order they occur to you. Don't worry about "logic" or "importance."

1. _____     9. _____
2. _____    10. _____
3. _____    11. _____
4. _____    12. _____
5. _____    13. _____
6. _____    14. _____
7. _____    15. _____
8. _____

The following responses have been obtained from two persons, Josh and Arlene (Gordon, 1968).

| JOSH: A 9-YEAR-OLD MALE | ARLENE: A FEMALE COLLEGE SOPHOMORE |
| --- | --- |
| a boy | a person |
| do what my mother says, mostly | member of the human race |
| Louis's little brother | daughter and sister |
| Josh | a student |
| have big ears | people-lover |
| can beat up Andy | people-watcher |
| play soccer | creator of written, drawn, and spoken (things) creations |
| sometimes a good sport | |
| a skater | music enthusiast |
| make a lot of noise | enjoyer of nature |
| like to eat | partly the sum of my experiences |
| talk good | always changing |
| go to third grade | lonely |
| bad at drawing | all the characters in the books I read a small part of the universe, but I can change it I'm not sure? |

evaluate her, communicate with her, motivate her to action, attempt to control her, and so on. Note, however, that George also can act in the same fashion toward himself—that is, he can engage in self-perception, self-evaluation, self-communication, self-motivation, and self-control. Behavior of this type, in which the individual who acts and the individual toward whom the action is directed are the same, is termed *reflexive behavior*.

For example, if George, a student, has an important term paper due Friday, he engages in the reflexive process of self-control when he pushes himself ("Got to work on that history paper now"). He engages in self-motivation when he makes a promise to himself ("You can go out for pizza and a movie Friday night"). Both processes are part of the self. To have a self is to have the capacity to engage in reflexive actions—to plan, observe, guide, and respond to our own behavior (Bandura, 1982; Mead, 1934).

Our understanding of reflexive behavior and the self is drawn from symbolic interaction theory (see Chapter 1). By definition, the **self** is the individual viewed as both the source and the object of reflexive behavior. Clearly, the self is both active (the source that initiates reflexive behavior) and passive (the object toward whom reflexive behavior is directed). The active aspect of the self is labeled the *I*, and the object of self-action is labeled the *me* (James, 1890; Mead, 1934).

It is useful to think of the self as an ongoing process (Gecas & Burke, 1995). Action involving the self begins with the I—with an impulse to act. For example, George wants to see Keisha. In the next moment, that impulse becomes the object of self-reflection and, hence, part of the me ("If I don't work on that paper tonight, I won't get it done on time"). Next, George responds actively to this self-awareness, again an I phase ("But I want to see Keisha, so I won't write the paper"). This, in turn, becomes the object to be judged, again a me phase ("That would really hurt my grade").

So George exercises self-control and sits down to write. The I and me phases continue to alternate as every new action (I) becomes in the next moment the object of self-scrutiny (me). Through these alternating phases of self we plan, act, monitor our actions, and evaluate outcomes (Markus & Wurf, 1987).

Mead (1934) portrays action as guided by an internal dialogue. People engage in conversations in their minds as they regulate their behavior. They use words and images to symbolize their ideas about themselves, other persons, their own actions, and others' probable responses to them. This description of the internal dialogue suggests there are three capacities human beings must acquire in order to engage successfully in action: they must (1) develop an ability to differentiate themselves from other persons, (2) learn to see themselves and their own actions as if through others' eyes, and (3) learn to use a symbol system or language for inner thought. In this section, we examine how children come to differentiate themselves and how they learn to view themselves from others' perspectives. We also discuss how language learning is intertwined with acquiring these two capacities.

## Self-Differentiation

To take the self as the object of action, we must—at a minimum—be able to recognize ourselves. That is, we must distinguish our own faces and bodies from those of others. This may seem elementary, but infants are not born with this ability. At first, they do not even discriminate the boundaries between their own bodies and the environment. Cognitive growth and continuing tactile exploration of their bodies contribute to infants' discovery of their physical uniqueness. So does experience with caregivers who treat them as distinct beings. Studies of when children can recognize themselves in a mirror suggest that most children are able to discriminate their own image from others' by about 18 months

(Bertenthal & Fischer, 1978). Research indicates that children become capable of representing self–other contingencies (for example, "If I do X, she does Y") at 18 to 24 months old (Higgins, 1989).

Children must learn not only to discriminate their physical selves from others, but also to discriminate themselves as social objects. Mastery of language is critical in children's efforts to learn the latter (Denzin, 1977). Learning one's own name is one of the earliest and most important steps in acquiring a self. As Allport (1961) put it,

> By hearing his name repeatedly the child gradually sees himself as a distinct and recurrent point of reference. The name acquires significance for him in the second year of life. With it comes awareness of independent status in the social group. (p. 115)

A mature sense of self entails recognizing that our thoughts and feelings are our private possessions. Young children often confuse processes that go on in their own minds with external events (Piaget, 1954). They locate events in their own dreams, for example, in the world around them. The distinction between self and nonself sharpens as social experience and cognitive growth bring children to realize that their own private awareness of self is not directly accessible to others. By about age 4, children report that their thinking and knowing goes on inside their heads. Asked further, "Can I see you thinking in there?" they generally answer, "No," demonstrating their awareness that self-processes are private (Flavell, Shipstead, & Croft, 1978).

Changes in the way children talk also reveal their dawning realization that the self has access to private information. At first, children's speech patterns are the same whether they are talking aloud to themselves or directing their words to others. Gradually, however, they begin to distinguish speech to self from speech to others (Vygotsky, 1962). Speech

To take the self as the object of our action—observing and modifying our own behavior—we must be able to recognize ourselves. Although infants are not born with this ability, they acquire it quickly. © Plus/iStock

to self becomes abbreviated until it is virtually incomprehensible to the outside listener, whereas speech to others becomes more elaborated over time. "Cold" suffices for Shanice to tell herself she wants to take off her wet socks. But no one else would understand this without access to her private knowledge. When addressing others, Shanice would expand her speech to include whatever private information they would need to understand ("Gotta change my wet socks. They're making me cold").

Access to private information about the self leads to systematic differences in adults' self-descriptions compared to descriptions of others (McGuire & McGuire, 1986).

Descriptions of the self focus on what one does—on physical action and on cognitive and affective reactions to others. Descriptions of others focus on who the person is—as evidenced in their visible behavior and characteristics. Furthermore, people perceive themselves as more complex than other people (Sande, Goethals, & Radloff, 1988). Did your responses in Box 4.1 reflect these characteristics of self-descriptions?

## Role Taking

Recognizing that one is physically and mentally differentiated from others is only one step in the genesis of self. Once we can differentiate ourselves from others, we also can recognize that the other person sees the world from a different perspective. The second crucial step in the genesis of self is **role taking**—the process of imaginatively occupying the position of another person and viewing the self and the situation from that person's perspective (Hewitt, 2000).

Role taking is crucial to the genesis of self because through it the child learns to respond reflexively. Imagining others' responses to the self, children acquire the capacity to look at themselves as if from the outside. Recognizing that others see them as objects, children can become objects (me) to themselves (Mead, 1934). They can then act toward themselves to praise ("That's a good girl"), to reprimand ("Stop that!"), and to control or regulate their own behavior ("Wait your turn").

Long ago, Cooley (1909) noted the close tie between role taking and language skills. One of the earliest signs of role-taking skills is the correct use of the pronouns *you* and *I*. To master the use of these pronouns requires taking the role of the self and of the other simultaneously. Most children firmly grasp the use of *I* and *you* by the middle of their third year (Clark, 1976). This suggests that children are well on their way to effective role taking at this age. Studies indicate that children develop the ability to infer the thoughts and expectations of others between ages 4 and 6 (Higgins, 1989).

## The Social Origins of Self

Our self-schema, the cognitive component of self, is produced in our social relationships. Throughout life, as we meet new people and enter new groups, our view of self is modified by the feedback we receive from others. This feedback is not an objective reality that we can grasp directly. Rather, we must interpret others' responses in order to figure out how we appear to them. We then incorporate others' imagined views of us into our self-schema.

To dramatize the idea that the origins of self are social, Cooley (1902) coined the term **looking-glass self**. The person imagines how they appear to someone, how the other judges that appearance, and experiences pride or shame as a result. Thus, for Cooley, the origins of both the self-schema and self-esteem are social. The most important looking glasses for children are their parents and immediate family and, later, their playmates. They are the child's **significant others**—the people whose reflected views have greatest influence on the child's self. As we grow older, the widening circle of friends and relatives, school teachers, clergy, and fellow workers provides our significant others. The changing images of self we acquire throughout our lives depend on the social relationships we develop. As children use digital devices, these provide another source of feedback about the self.

**Play and the Game.** Mead (1934) identified two sequential stages of social experience leading to the emergence of the self in children. He called these stages *play* and the *game*. Each stage is characterized by its own form of role taking.

In the **play** stage, young children imitate the activities of people around them. Through such play, children learn to organize different activities into meaningful roles (nurse, police officer, firefighter). For example, using their imaginations, children carry sacks of mail, drop letters into mailboxes, greet homeowners, and learn to label these activities as fitting the role of "mail carrier." At this stage, children take the roles of others one at a time. They do not recognize that each role is intertwined with others. Playing mail carrier, for example, the child does not realize that mail carriers also have coworkers and a postmaster to whom they must relate. Nor do children in this stage understand that the same person simultaneously holds several roles—that mail carriers are also parents, store customers, and golf partners.

The **game** stage comes later, when children enter organized activities such as complex games of house, school, and team sports. These activities demand interpersonal coordination because the various roles are differentiated. Role taking at the game stage requires children to imagine the viewpoints of several others at the same time. For Michael to play center effectively, for example, he must adopt the perspectives of the guards and members of the defensive team as he dribbles the ball and decides whether to pass it or go for three. In the game, children also learn that different roles relate to one another in specified ways. Michael must understand the specialized functions of each position, the ways the players in different positions coordinate their actions, and the rules that regulate basketball.

**The Generalized Other.** Repeated involvement in organized activities lets children see that their own actions are part of a pattern of interdependent group activity. This experience teaches children that organized groups of people share common perspectives and attitudes. With this new knowledge, children construct a **generalized other**—a conception of the attitudes and expectations held in common by the members of the organized groups with whom they interact. When we imagine what the group expects of us, we are taking the role of the generalized other. We are also concerned with the generalized other when we wonder what people would say or what society's standards demand. As children grow older, they control their own behavior more and more from the perspective of the generalized other. This helps them to resist the influence of impulse or of specific others who just happen to be present at the moment.

Over time, children internalize the attitudes and expectations of the generalized other, incorporating them into their self-concepts. But building up self-concepts involves more than accepting the reflected views of others. We may misperceive or misinterpret the responses that others direct to us, for example, due to our less-than-perfect role-taking skills. Others' responses may themselves be contradictory or inconsistent. Also, we may resist the reflected views we perceive because they conflict with our prior self-concepts or with our direct experience. A boy may reject his peers' view that he is a "wuss," for example, because he previously thought of himself as brave and could still visualize his experience of beating up a bully.

By playing complex games such as baseball, children learn to organize their actions into meaningful roles and to imagine the viewpoints of others at the same time. Role taking enables the third baseman to coordinate effectively with teammates, for example, to tag a runner out. © jpbcpa/iStock

**Online Communication and the Self.** Since 1995, there has been a rapid expansion in computer-mediated communication (CMC). People communicate using e-mail, text messaging, FaceTime, Skype, participation in chat rooms and interest groups, and via personal webpages and social networking sites (for example, Facebook, Snapchat). We will discuss the relationship between CMC and other forms of communication, and the role of CMC in self-presentation and in relationships, in other sections. Here we focus on CMC as a potential influence on the development of self.

The self is heavily influenced by feedback from others. Our discussion so far has implicitly assumed feedback in face-to-face interaction. One difference between CMC and "real life" is that in CMC, the interaction partner is not physically present; thus, when we use e-mail, instant messaging (IM), or Facebook, nonverbal cues (facial expressions, body language, and paralinguistic cues) are not available (Zhao, 2005). These are often the cues we use to assess the feedback we receive from others; without them, assessing the personal meaning of their statements is more difficult. Thus, we may be more skeptical of others' messages, and less likely to use them as a looking glass. On the other hand, teens are particularly heavy users of CMC (Ramirez & Broneck, 2009), and are in the life stage where feedback from others is especially influential.

The self constructed through online interaction may be termed the *digital self*. It has four characteristics (Zhao, 2005). First, it is *inwardly oriented*; people may use CMC to communicate about their inner world of thoughts and feelings. Second, like the self more generally, it is a *narrative* or a story—that is, a self-presentation that is expected by others to be coherent and consistent. Third, it is *retractable*; in real life, our various selves all inhabit the same body, and cannot easily be detached. In CMC, you can delete a self, and it is gone (or at least not ordinarily visible to others). Retracting a self will be more costly to the extent that it is salient, that the individual has invested time and resources in it, and receives valued rewards from it. Finally, the digital self is *multiplied*; one can have several, diverse selves. According to

one survey, more than one-half of teens who use CMC have more than one screen name or e-mail account (Lenhart, Rainie, & Lewis, 2001). The digital self is not constrained by geographic and institutional factors; this can be very important in allowing people with uncommon or stigmatized characteristics, such as survivors of breast cancer or persons struggling with issues of gender identity or sexual orientation, to contact similar others and form support networks.

Research suggests that online self-disclosure tends to be superficial. A study including students (ages 18 to 39) and nonstudents (ages 18 to 37) found that they were more likely to disclose information about their interests than their beliefs and intimate feelings (Attrill & Jalil, 2011). This constrains the feedback that one receives, and thus its influence on the self.

An important dimension of one's self is its clarity, the degree to which the elements of it are clearly articulated and consistent. Such a self serves as a secure basis for choosing behaviors and relating to others. To the extent that the self is developed in interaction, the more influences on it, the less clear it may be. Online communication has vastly expanded the number of persons who can potentially influence one's self. Researchers hypothesized that the more time an adolescent spent online, the less clear their self would be. A study of seventh- through ninth-graders that measured these and several other concepts found that scores on an Internet addiction scale were strongly associated negatively with a measure of self-clarity (Israelashvili, Kim, & Bukobza, 2012).

**Self-Evaluation.** As Cooley recognized, the views of ourselves that we perceive from others usually include positive or negative evaluations. These evaluations also become part of the self we construct. Actions that others judge favorably contribute to positive self-concepts. In contrast, when others disapprove or punish our actions, the self-concepts we derive may be negative.

We also form self-evaluations when reflecting on the adequacy of our role performances—on the extent to which we live up to the standards we aspire to. Our self-evaluations most commonly focus on our competence, self-determination, moral worth, or unity. Self-evaluations also influence the ways we express our role identities. A musician, for example, will pursue opportunities to perform in public more persistently if they see themself as competent than if they think they are never quite good enough. Self-evaluations are so important that a later section of this chapter will be devoted to them.

## IDENTITIES: THE SELF WE KNOW

In Box 4.1, Arlene described herself as a person, daughter, student, people-lover, and creator of things. This is the self she knows, a self that includes specific identities. **Identities** are the meanings attached to the self by one's self and others (Gecas & Burke, 1995). When we think of our identities, we are actually thinking of various plans of action that we expect to carry out. When Arlene identifies herself as a student, for example, she has in mind that she plans to attend classes, write papers, take exams, and so on. If Arlene does not engage in these behaviors, she will have to relinquish her student identity.

In this section, we consider four questions about the self we know: (1) How do our roles influence the identities we include in our self? (2) How do group memberships influence the self we know? (3) What evidence is there that the self we know is based on the reactions we perceive from others? (4) How do the aspects of self that people note vary from one situation to another?

### Role Identities

Each of us occupies numerous positions in society—student, friend, son or daughter,

customer. Each of us, therefore, enacts many different social roles. We construct identities by observing our own behavior and the responses of others to us as we enact these roles. For each role we enact, we develop a somewhat different view of who we are—an identity. Because these identities are concepts of self in specific roles, they are called **role identities**. The role identities we develop depend on the social positions available to us in society. As a result, the self we know is linked to society fundamentally through the roles we play. It reflects the structure of our society and our place in it (McCall & Simmons, 1978; Stryker, 1980). Role identities highlight the impact on self of social structure via reciprocal relationships with occupants of complementary roles.

Do societal role expectations strictly dictate the contents of our role identities? Apparently not. Consider, for example, the role expectations for a college instructor. Some instructors deliver lectures, whereas others lead discussions; some encourage questions, whereas others discourage them; some assign papers, and others do not. As this example indicates, role expectations usually leave individuals some room to improvise their own role performances. It is probably more accurate to think of people as "making" their roles—that is, shaping them—rather than as conforming rigidly to role expectations (Turner, 1978). Societal expectations do dictate the goals of role performance; instructors must instruct using means that are consensually agreed on (Burke, 2004).

Several influences affect the way we make the roles we enact. Conventional role expectations in society set a general framework. Within the boundaries set by these expectations, we can fashion our actual role performances to reflect our personal characteristics and competencies. We can select behaviors that highlight our strengths, and cover our weaknesses. Because each person makes roles in a unique, personal fashion, we each derive somewhat different role identities even if we occupy similar social positions. Consequently, our role identities as student, ball player, and so on differ from the role identities of others who also occupy these positions.

In describing themselves, people frequently mention the styles of interpersonal behavior (introverted, cool) that distinguish the way they fashion their unique role performances. People also mention the emotional or psychological styles (optimistic, moody) that characterize these performances. Individual preferences point to specific ways in which people express their role identities. For example, a person who sees themself as a musician expresses this role identity differently depending on whether they prefer Bach or rock. Body image—the aspect of the self we recognize earliest—remains important throughout life. Beyond this, our self extends to include our material possessions, such as our clothing, house, car, music collection, and so on (James, 1890).

## Social Identities

A second source of identities is membership in social categories or groups based on criteria such as gender, nationality, race/ethnicity, sexual preferences, or political affiliation (Howard, 2000). A definition of the self in terms of the defining characteristics of a social group is a **social identity** (Hogg, Terry, & White, 1995; Tajfel & Turner, 1979). Each of us associates certain characteristics with members of specific groups. These characterizations—Chicago Bulls fans are loud, mothers are nurturant—define the group. If you define yourself as a member of the group, these characteristics become standards for your thoughts, feelings, and actions. If your interactions with others, whether members or not, confirm the importance of these attributes, they become part of the self you know. Research indicates that cognitive representations of the self and of the groups to which the person belongs are closely linked (Smith & Henry, 1996).

Social identities highlight the impact on self of social structure via consensually defined social groupings (Deaux & Martin, 2003). Note that one need not interact with other members to identify as a member of the group.

Social groups are often defined in part by reference to other groups. The meaning of being a Young Republican is related to the meaning of being a Young Socialist and a Young Democrat. The meaning of being a man in American society is closely related to the meaning of being a woman. Thus, when membership in a group becomes a salient basis for self-definition, perceptions of relevant outgroups are also made salient. Often there is an accentuation effect—an emphasis on perceived differences and unfavorable evaluations of the out-group and its members (Hogg, 2013). Thus, negative stereotypes directed at persons of a different gender, race, or religion are often closely related to the self-concept of the person who holds them. Research indicates that both in-group favoritism and out-group hostility are reinforced in conversations between group members (Harasty, 1997).

## Research on Self-Concept Formation

Two of the key theoretical ideas discussed so far are that (1) the formation of the self-schema involves the adoption of role and social identities, and (2) a person's self-concept is shaped by the reactions that they receive from significant others during social interaction. Each of these ideas has been the focus of empirical research.

**The Adoption of Role and Social Identities.** Self-schemas are formed in part by adopting identities. The identities available to us depend on the culture. One difference between cultures is whether a culture is individualist or collectivist (Triandis, 1989). **Individualist cultures** emphasize individual achievement and its associated identities such as president, team captain, idealist, and outstanding player. **Collectivist cultures** emphasize values that promote the welfare of the group and its associated identities such as son (family), Catholic (religion), Italian (ethnicity), and American. According to research, the self-schemas of persons in individualist cultures (such as the United States) include more individual identities, whereas those of persons in collectivist cultures include more group-linked identities (Triandis, McCusker, & Hui, 1990).

The adoption of a role identity involves socialization into the group or organization of which the role is a part. A study of members of a volunteer search and rescue group, Peak, identified three stages of membership: new, peripheral, and core (Lois, 2003). New members were often attracted by the desire to meet people, develop and exercise their outdoor skills, or be a hero. To make the transition to (be accepted by others as) a peripheral member, they had to suppress self-oriented attitudes and behavior and acknowledge the importance of the team. They also had to learn survival skills and rescue techniques, demonstrating humility and persistence in the process. To make the transition to core member, they had to accept the roles offered by the team (sometimes very unglamorous ones) and demonstrate that they were skilled by leading training sessions. As members progressed through these stages, they increasingly shared in the sense of "we-ness," and their membership became an important social identity. They ultimately achieved the role of hero by becoming a committed member of the team, not by performing acts of individual heroism.

Adopting a social identity involves self-categorization—the defining of the self as a member of a social category such as Irish American, Black American, or feminist (Stets & Burke, 2000). Whereas enacting a role identity involves behavior conforming to a role, enacting a social identity involves adopting

Social identities are often displayed by wearing items of clothing displaying the group's name or logo. Sports fans are especially likely to wear branded clothing after a major victory! © vnews.tv/Shutterstock

styles of dress, behavior, and thought associated with the social category. Successful adoption may require consensus by other members of the category that you can claim the identity (Wong, 2002). Whether one identifies with a social category in which one can claim membership depends on how easily one can be identified as a member of that group, for example, by name or skin color (Lau, 1989). It also depends on the general visibility and status of that group or category in society.

**Reflected Appraisals.** The idea that the person bases the self-schema on the reactions they perceive from others during social interaction is captured by the term *reflected appraisal*. Studies of this process (Marsh, Barnes, & Hocevar, 1985; Miyamoto & Dornbusch, 1956) typically compare people's self-ratings on various qualities (such as intelligence, self-confidence, physical attractiveness) with the views of themselves that they perceive from others. The studies also compare self-ratings with actual views of others. The results of these studies support the hypothesis that it is the perceived reactions of others rather than their actual reactions that are crucial for self-concept formation (Felson, 1989). A study of 12- and 14-year-olds got self-descriptions from the youth and one of their parents, teachers, and a peer chosen by the youth. Agreement in self/parent, self/teacher, and self/peer descriptions increased with age, and was greater among girls than boys (van Aken, van Lieshout, & Haselager, 1996). The concept of reflected appraisals refers to the content of one's self-schema; Cooley's looking-glass self describes the process by which these appraisals become a part of the self. Research has focused on the differential effect of various significant others on one's appraisal of self in particular roles or domains. Felson (1985; Felson & Reed, 1986) has studied the relative influence of parents and peers on the self-perceptions of fourth- through eighth-graders about their academic ability, athletic ability,

and physical attractiveness. The results indicate that parents affect self-appraisals in the areas of academic and athletic ability, whereas peers are an important influence on perceived attractiveness. One aspect of attractiveness is weight. Although there is an objective measure of weight (that is, pounds, or pounds in relation to height), it is the social judgment ("too fat," "too thin," or "just right") that is incorporated into the self-concept. A study of adolescent health obtained self-appraisals of weight from 6,500 adolescents, as well as appraisals from their parents and a physician (Levinson, Powell, & Steelman, 1986). These young people were generally unhappy with their weight, with boys judging themselves to be too thin and girls judging themselves to be overweight. For both, parental appraisal was significantly related to the young person's judgment, whereas the physician's rating was not. Research on a large sample of young adult athletes found that self-perceptions of athletic competence were strongly related to the athlete's perception of appraisals by coaches, teammates, and parents (Trouilloud & Amiel, 2011). However, athletes' perceptions of their future were negatively related to others' appraisals.

A study of married couples with one child examined the relative influence of self-appraisal and partner's appraisal on two types of behavior: caregiving (traditionally female) and breadwinning (traditionally male) (Maurer, Pleck, & Rane, 2001). The hypothesis was that self-appraisal would be more influential for gender-consistent behavior (male breadwinning, female caregiving), whereas partner's appraisal would be more influential for noncongruent behavior (male caregiving, female breadwinning). The results generally supported the hypothesis. Thus, the appraisals of those presumed to be more knowledgeable about the role were more important.

Typically, a person's self-ratings are related more closely to their perceived ratings by others than to the actual ratings by others. Why is this so? Three reasons are especially important. First, others rarely provide full, honest feedback about their reactions to us. Second, the feedback we do receive is often inconsistent and even contradictory. Third, the feedback is frequently ambiguous and difficult to interpret. It may be in the form of gestures (shrugs), facial expressions (smiles), or remarks that can be understood in many different ways ("Dude!"). For these reasons, we may know little about others' actual reactions to us. Instead, we must rely on our perceptions of others' reactions to construct our self-concepts (Schrauger & Schoeneman, 1979).

Evidence that self-concepts are related to the perceived reactions of others does not in itself demonstrate that self-concepts are actually formed in response to these perceived reactions. However, one study (Mannheim, 1966) does suggest such an impact of the perceived reactions of others on self-concepts. The investigators in this study asked college dormitory residents to describe themselves and to report how they thought others viewed them. Several months later, self-concepts were measured again. In the interim, students' self-concepts had moved closer to the views they had originally thought that others held. Change toward the perceived reactions of others had indeed occurred. Similarly, a longitudinal study of delinquent behavior found that parental appraisals of youth as delinquent were associated with subsequent self-appraisals as delinquent; self-appraisal as delinquent was in turn related to delinquent behavior (Matsueda, 1992).

**Identity and Multiracial Heritage.** In a racially diverse society, social identity based on racial heritage is a significant component of self-schema. According to the reflected appraisal model, it is perceived reactions of others that influence self-perception. Also, successful adoption of an identity requires acceptance by others of one's claims. Thus, an important influence on racial identity should be responses of others based on one's appearance. The racial identity of some persons seems obvious—that is, their skin color and physical features fit the social stereotype of what Asians, Blacks, or Whites look like. But the racial identity of others is not obvious. People with ambiguous appearance are frequently asked "What are you?" and may come to hate having to answer that question one more time (Navarro, 2005). To study multiracial identity, Khanna (2004) recruited adults who had one Asian parent and one White parent. She predicted that (apparent) phenotype or appearance (How would others categorize you, Asian or White?) would be the most important influence on racial identity. But what about persons whose phenotype is ambiguous? Khanna predicted that cultural exposure, language proficiency, eating foods, and celebrating holidays would influence identity—that is, identifying oneself as "Asian." Both hypotheses were confirmed. A study of hundreds of Asian and Latino students entering UCLA found that speaking the ethnic language at home and having high school friends of the same ethnicity were the main predictors of strong ethnic identity (Sears, Fu, Henry, & Bui, 2003).

Note that these studies focus on participation in a racial or ethnic culture as determinates of racial identity. However, the theory of reflected appraisals predicts that it is the labeling of one's race by others in interaction that is the main influence. Persons with ambiguous appearance may get inconsistent or mixed messages; as one mixed Asian/White woman put it, people "never can really figure it out" (Sims, 2016). How does this inconsistency affect identity formation? From interviews with 30 mixed-race adults in the U.S. and the U.K. Sims (2016) revealed that the consistent inconsistency in others' reactions to them was taken as validation of their mixed-race status which, under certain social conditions such as weak cultural norms of hypodescent, facilitated mixed-race identity formation.

## The Situated Self

If we were to describe ourselves on several different occasions, the identities, personal qualities, and self-evaluations mentioned would not remain the same. This is not due to errors of reporting; rather, it demonstrates that the aspects of self that enter our awareness and matter most to us depend on the situation. The **situated self** is the subset of self-concepts chosen from our identities, qualities, and self-evaluations that constitutes the self we know in a particular situation (Hewitt, 2000). Markus and Wurf (1987) refer to the current, active, accessible self-representations as the *working self-concept.*

The self-concepts most likely to enter the situated self are those distinctive to the setting and relevant to the ongoing activities. Consider a Black woman for whom being Black and being a woman are both important self-concepts. When she interacts with Black men, she is more likely to think of herself as a woman. When she interacts with White women, she is more likely to be aware that she is Black. Similarly, whether gender is part of

your situated self depends in part on the gender composition of others present (Cota & Dion, 1986). Male and female college students placed in a group with two students of the opposite gender were more likely to list gender in their self-descriptions than members of all-male or all-female groups. Thus, self-concepts that are distinctive or peculiar to the social setting tend to enter into the situated self.

Our activities also determine the self-concepts that constitute the situated self. A job interview, for example, draws attention to your competence; a party makes your body image more salient. The self we experience in our imaginings and in our interactions is always situated, because setting characteristics and activity requirements prime or make distinctive and relevant particular self-concepts.

### IDENTITIES: THE SELF WE ENACT

How does the self influence the planning and regulation of social behavior? The general answer to this question is that we are motivated

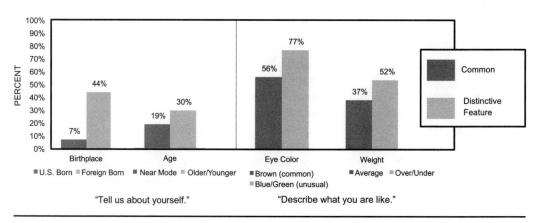

**FIGURE 4.1** Students Spontaneously Mention a Distinctive Feature as Part of Their Self-Concept

A group of 252 sixth-graders from 10 classrooms were asked to describe themselves. Students mentioned a particular feature (for example, birthplace) more often if that feature distinguished them from their classmates. Because these are characteristics on which we stand out from our social groups, attracting more notice and social comment, we are more likely to build them into our self-concepts.

*Source:* Adapted from "Trait Silence in the Spontaneous Self-Concept" by W. J. McGuire and A. Padawer-Singer, *Journal of Personality and Social Psychology, 33,* 743–754. © 1976 by the American Psychological Association.

to plan and to perform behaviors that will confirm and reinforce the identities we wish to claim for ourselves in the situation (Burke & Reitzes, 1981; Markus & Wurf, 1987). In elaborating on this answer, we will examine three more specific questions: (1) How are behaviors linked to particular identities? (2) Of the different identities available to us, what determines which ones we choose to enact in a situation? (3) How do our identities lend unity and consistency to our behavior?

## Identities and Behavior

Each of us makes dozens of decisions every day; most of them influence our behavior. These decisions are influenced by explicit and implicit egotism—that is, giving undue prominence to the self. A study of major life decisions (where to live, choice of career) suggests that these decisions are influenced by our names (Pelham, Mirenberg, & Jones, 2002). We tend to choose places and occupations with names that resemble our own. According to this study, it is not an accident that Susie sells seashells by the seashore.

Identities that are important to the person can motivate behavior that is consistent with or validates that identity. A longitudinal study of almost 800 seventh-, ninth-, and eleventh-graders measured how much each student identified with (from "not at all" to "very much like me") the characteristics "popular" and "troublemaker." The researchers expected that these identities at Time 1 would be related to sexual debut between Times 1 and 2. Among boys, identifying with both was associated with initiating sex. Among girls, identification with "troublemaker" was associated with sexual debut (Longmore, Manning, & Giordano, 2006).

The link between identities and behaviors is through their common meanings (Burke & Reitzes, 1981). If members of a group agree on the meanings of particular identities and behaviors, they can regulate their own

behavior effectively. They can plan, initiate, and control behavior to generate the meanings that establish the identities they wish to claim. If members do not agree on these meanings, however, people have difficulty establishing their preferred identities. If Imani sees no connection between competitiveness and femininity, for example, she will have trouble establishing a feminine identity in the eyes of friends who think being feminine means being noncompetitive.

According to **identity control theory** (Burke, 1991), an actor uses the social meaning of an identity as a reference point for assessing what is occurring in the situation. The identities of the other actors and elements of the situation also have shared meanings. The behaviors of others and situational elements are evaluated by the actor according to whether they maintain their identity. Subsequent behaviors are selected and enacted in order to maintain one's identity in this situation. The (shared) meaning of an identity operates like a thermostat; if reflected appraisals or situational elements are inconsistent with identity, an actor will behave in ways designed to restore it (Smith-Lovin & Robinson, 2006).

Consider a person whose identity is a "considerate professor." When students hand in assignments on time, that identity is reinforced. Occasionally, when an apparently hardworking student asks for an extension of a due date, it is consistent with their identity as "considerate" to grant the request. But if numerous students ask for extensions for reasons that seem trivial, they may "crack down" and refuse to give an extension to anyone, enacting the "professor" identity.

Since the meanings of role-identity elements, actions, and other identities are widely shared, Burke and other researchers use quantitative techniques to assess them. Adapting the techniques developed by Osgood (see Box 2.1), the meaning of an identity element or action is assessed on the dimensions of affect, evaluation, and potency. Researchers can compare these values across roles or groups or cultures to assess the impact of context on meanings.

Social identities are associated with category or group memberships. There are widely held meanings or stereotypes associated with many categories and groups. Thus, claiming a social identity creates a pressure to accept these stereotypes as self-descriptive. This can have a powerful impact on behavior. We may voluntarily adopt behavior or traits associated with positive stereotypes, such as adopting the food preferences associated with "veganism." On the other hand, we may avoid engaging in behaviors we associate with disliked out-groups. Researchers found that American-Indian, African-American, and Mexican-American college students and eighth-graders viewed healthy behaviors (for example, good diet, exercise) as White and middle class, and were less likely to engage in them. Minority students were more likely to identify unhealthy behaviors as consistent with in-group identity (Oyserman, Fryberg, & Yoder, 2007). This is a good example of a negative consequence of enacting a group identity. (See Chapter 5—self-presentation.)

We may be influenced by negative stereotypes as well; *stereotype threat* refers to a situation in which one is at risk of confirming as self-characteristic a negative stereotype about a group to which one belongs (see Chapter 7). For instance, Blacks may underperform in an academic testing situation because they believe that others stereotype them as "dumb," which creates anxiety that disrupts their performance. Their poor performance validates the stereotype, but the performance reflects their anxiety, not their ability.

On the other hand, some group members will obviously violate any stereotype of the group. We noted earlier that characteristics that distinguish us from others are more likely to be part of our self-concept. Indeed, research indicates that people are more likely to include in their self-schema areas in which their performance is counterstereotypic—that is, distinctive (von Hippel, Hawkins, & Schooler, 2001).

## Choosing an Identity to Enact

Each of us has many different identities. Each identity suggests its own lines of action. These lines of action are not all compatible, however, nor can they be pursued simultaneously in a single situation. If you are at a family reunion in your parents' home, for example, you might wish to claim an identity as a helpful son or daughter, an aspiring rap artist, or a witty conversationalist. These identities suggest different, even conflicting, ways of relating to the other guests. What influences the decision to enact one rather than another identity? Several factors affect such choices.

**The Hierarchy of Identities.** The many different role identities we enact do not have equal importance for us. Rather, we organize them into a hierarchy according to their **salience**—their relative importance to the self-schema. This hierarchy exerts a major influence on our decision to enact one or another identity (McCall & Simmons, 1978; Stryker, 1980). First, the more salient an identity is to us, the more frequently we choose to perform activities that express that identity (Stryker & Serpe, 1981). Second, the more salient an identity, the more likely we are to perceive that situations offer opportunities to enact that identity. Only a person aspiring to the identity of a rap artist, for example, will perceive a family reunion as a chance to demonstrate their skill. Third, we are more active in seeking opportunities to enact salient identities (say, searching for an open-mic session). Fourth, we conform more to the role expectations attached to the identities that we consider the most important.

What determines whether a particular identity occupies a central or a peripheral position in the salience hierarchy? In general, the importance we attach to a role identity is affected by (1) the resources we have invested in constructing the identity (time, effort, and money expended, for example, in learning to be a sculptor); (2) the extrinsic rewards that enacting the identity has brought (for example, purchases by collectors, acclaim by critics); (3) the intrinsic gratifications derived from performing the identity (for example, the sense of competence and aesthetic pleasure obtained when sculpting a human figure); and (4) the amount of self-esteem staked on enacting the identity well (for example, the extent to which a positive self-evaluation has become tied to being a good sculptor). As we engage in interaction and experience greater or lesser success in performing our different identities, their salience shifts.

**Social Networks.** Each of us is part of networks of social relationships (see Chapter 17). These relationships may stand or fall depending on whether we continue to enact particular role identities. The more numerous and significant the relationships that depend on enacting an identity, the more committed we become to that identity (Callero, 1985). Consider, for example, your role as a student. Chances are that many of your relationships—with roommates, friends, instructors, and perhaps a lover—depend on your continued occupancy of the student role. If you left school, you could lose a major part of your life. Given this high level of commitment, it isn't surprising that for many students, being forced to leave school is traumatic.

The more commitment we have to a role identity, the more important that identity will be in our salience hierarchy. For instance, adults for whom participating in religious activities is crucial for maintaining everyday social relationships rank their religious identity as relatively important compared with their parent, spouse, and worker identities (Stryker & Serpe, 1981). Similarly, the importance rank that undergraduates give to various identities

(student, friend, son or daughter, athlete, religious person, and dating partner) depends on the importance to them of the social relationships maintained by enacting each identity (Hoelter, 1983).

Online networks provide us with opportunities to enact identities. Some provide us with opportunities to enact and get feedback about our professional identities, for example, Social Psychology Network or LinkedIn. Others such as eHarmony or Chemistry provide opportunities to enact identities related to meeting potential partners and intimate relationships. Obviously your posts on LinkedIn will be quite different from those on AVEN (Asexuality Visibility and Education Network)!

**Need for Identity Support.** We are likely to enact those of our identities that most need support because they have recently been challenged. For instance, suppose that someone has recently had difficulty getting a date. That person may now choose actions calculated to elicit responses indicating they are an attractive dating partner. They may change their physical appearance and dress to make them more stylish. Researchers randomly selected men and women to be given feedback whether they were masculine or feminine; women were not affected by being told they were masculine, but men told they were feminine expressed more support for war, purchasing an SUV, and homophobia (Willer, Conlon, Rogalin, & Wojnowicz, 2013). We also tend to enact identities likely to bring intrinsic gratifications (such as a sense of accomplishment) and extrinsic rewards (such as praise) that we especially need or miss at the moment. For example, if, after hours of solitary study, you feel a need for relaxed social contact, you might seek gratification by going to a student union or a bar to find someone to chat with.

**Situational Opportunities.** Social situations are restrictive; they let us enact only some identities profitably, not others. Thus, in a

The more important an identity is to us, the more consistently we act to express it, regardless of others' reactions. Are any of your identities so important that you would express them by wearing such distinctive clothing as this high schooler? © Odua Images/Shutterstock

particular situation, the identity we choose to enact depends partly on whether the situation offers opportunities for profitable enactment. Regardless of the salience of your identity as musician, if no one wants to listen to your music, there will be no opportunity to enact that identity.

In a series of studies, Kenrick et al. (1990) asked students to rate the extent to which various personal qualities could be displayed in each of six different settings. The traits were adjustment, dominance, intellectual ability, likableness, social control, and social inclination. The students agreed that one can display intellectual ability in academic settings but not in recreational ones. Behaviors expressive of dominance can be displayed in athletic and business settings but not in religious ones. Finally, there are opportunities to display adjustment and social inclination in recreational settings but not in church.

## Identities as Sources of Consistency

Although the self includes multiple identities, people usually experience themselves as a unified entity. One reason is the influence of the salience hierarchy. Another reason is that we use several strategies that verify our perceptions of self.

**Salience Hierarchy.** Our most salient identities provide consistent styles of behavior and priorities that lend continuity and unity to our behavior. In this way, the salience hierarchy helps us to construct a unified sense of self from our multiple identities.

The hierarchy of identities influences consistency in three ways. First, the hierarchy provides us with a basis for choosing which situations we should enter and which ones we should avoid. A study of the everyday activities of college students (Emmons, Diener, & Larsen, 1986) found clear patterns of choice and avoidance in each student's interactions; these patterns were consistent with the student's characteristics, such as sociability.

Second, the hierarchy influences the consistency of behavior across different situations. In another study, each person was asked to report the extent to which each of 10 affective states and 10 behavioral responses occurred in various situations over a 30-day period (Emmons & Diener, 1986). The results indicated a significant degree of consistency across situations.

Third, the hierarchy influences consistency in behavior across time. Serpe (1987) studied a sample of 310 first-year college students, collecting data at three points during their first semester in college. The survey measured the salience at each point of five identities: academic ability, athletic/recreational involvement, extracurricular involvement, personal involvement (that is, friendships), and dating. There was a general pattern of stability in salience. Change in salience was more likely for those identities where there was greater opportunity for change, such as dating.

Although the self-concept exhibits consistency over time, it may change (Demo, 1992). Life transitions may change situations one encounters. This creates a need to exit from one or more roles, adopt new roles, and change the salience hierarchy. During times such as adolescence, break up of a long-term relationship, and retirement, we are likely to feel a weakened sense of unity and a confusion about how to behave. This has been called an *identity crisis* (Erikson, 1968). To overcome such confusion, we must reorganize our identity hierarchy, giving greater importance to identities based on our newly available or remaining social positions. A retiree may successfully reorganize the hierarchy, for example, by upgrading identities based on new hobbies (gardener) and on continuing social ties (witty conversationalist).

**Self-Verification Strategies.** We experience ourselves as consistent across time and situations because we employ several strategies that verify our self-perceptions (Banaji & Prentice, 1994).

One set of strategies consists of behaviors that lead to self-confirming feedback from others. First, we engage in selective interaction; we choose as friends, roommates, and intimates people who share our view of self. Second, we display identity cues that elicit identity-confirming behavior from others. In a hospital setting, most people treat a person wearing a white coat with a stethoscope around the neck as a physician. Third, we behave in ways that enhance our identity claims, especially when those claims are challenged. In one study, White students who viewed themselves as unprejudiced were led to believe they were prejudiced toward Blacks. When they were subsequently approached by a Black panhandler, they gave them more money than did students whose egalitarian identity had not been threatened (Dutton & Lake, 1973).

Another set of strategies involves the processing of feedback from others. As noted in the next section, we often do this in ways that make others' responses to us seem to support our self-concept.

There are limits to the extent to which we engage in self-verifying strategies. There are times when we want accurate feedback about our abilities or about another person's view of our relationship with them. When we want such feedback, and we have the necessary cognitive resources (attention, energy), we evaluate feedback from others by comparing it with our self-representations (Swann & Schroeder, 1995). This evaluation may lead to changes in behavior, such as moving toward a goal or a desired identity, or to a change in self-representation.

## Self-Awareness and Self-Discrepancies

In this section, we discuss two additional ways in which the self affects our behavior. These include (1) ways in which focusing attention on the self influences the relationship between our identities and our behavior; and (2) the effect of self-discrepancies on emotional state and behavior.

**Effects of Self-Awareness.** While eating with friends, reading a book, or participating in conversation, your attention is usually directed toward the objects, people, and events that surround you. But what happens if, on looking up, you discover a photographer, iPhone focused on you, snapping away? Or what if you suddenly notice your image reflected in a large mirror? In such circumstances, most of us become self-conscious. We enter a state of **self-awareness**—that is, we take the self as the object of our attention and focus on our own appearance, actions, and thoughts. This corresponds to the "me" phase of action (Mead, 1934).

Numerous circumstances cause people to become self-aware. Mirrors, cameras, and recordings of ourselves cause self-awareness because they directly present the self to us as an object. Unfamiliar situations and blundering in public also cause self-awareness, because they disrupt the smooth flow of action and interaction. When this happens, we must attend to our own behavior more closely, monitoring its appropriateness and bringing it into line with the demands of the situation. In general, anything that reminds us that we are the objects of others' attention will increase our self-awareness.

How does self-awareness influence behavior? When people are highly self-aware, they are more likely to be honest and to more accurately report on their mood state, psychiatric problems, and hospitalizations (Gibbons et al., 1985). In general, people who are self-aware act in ways more consistent with personal and social standards (Wicklund, 1975; Wicklund & Frey, 1980). Their behavior is controlled more consciously by the self. In the absence of self-awareness, behavior is more automatic or

habitual. Society gains control over its members through the self-control that individuals exercise when they are self-aware (Shibutani, 1961). This is because the standards to which people conform are largely learned from significant groups in society. Self-awareness is thus often a civilizing influence.

These findings suggest that groups enhance their social control over individual behavior when they expose individuals to conditions—like an attentive audience, unfamiliar circumstances, or socially awkward tasks—that increase awareness of the public self. Interestingly, these are precisely the conditions used by many groups—fraternities, sororities, military organizations—in initiation rituals.

**Effects of Self-Discrepancies.** Research has shown that the relationships between components of one's self-schema influence one's emotional state and behavior. There are three components of the self-schema: self as one is (actual), as one would like to be (ideal), and as one ought to be (ought). When we evaluate ourselves, we typically use the ideal self or the ought self as the reference point. When the actual self matches the ideal self, we feel satisfaction or pride. However, when there is a **self-discrepancy**—that is, a component of the actual self is the opposite of a component of the ideal self or the ought self—we experience discomfort (Higgins, 1989).

According to self-discrepancy theory, the two types of discrepancies produce two different emotional states. Someone who has an actual–ideal discrepancy will experience dejection, sadness, or depression. Someone who perceives an actual–ought discrepancy will experience fear, tension, or restlessness. The theory predicts that the larger the discrepancy, the greater the discomfort.

In a study designed to test these hypotheses (Higgins, Klein, & Strauman, 1985), students were asked to list up to 10 attributes each of the actual self, the ideal self, and the ought self. Discrepancy was measured by comparing two lists (say, the actual and the ideal); a self-state listed in both was a match, whereas a self-state listed on one list with its antonym (opposite) listed on the other was a mismatch. The self-discrepancy score was the number of mismatches minus the number of matches. Discomfort was measured by several questionnaires. The results showed that as the actual–ideal discrepancy increased, the frequency and intensity of reported dissatisfaction and depression increased. As the actual–ought discrepancy increased, the frequency and intensity of reported fear and irritability increased.

Self-discrepancy scores also are related to behavior. Discrepancies may lead to problematic behaviors in an effort to cope. A study of satisfaction with one's body and of eating disorders found that a form of actual–ideal discrepancy was associated with bulimic behaviors, whereas an actual–ought discrepancy was associated with anorexic behaviors (Strauman et al., 1991). A study of 100 women found that a number of discrepancies was associated with both depressive symptoms and eating disorders. When experiencing symptoms was controlled, actual–potential discrepancies were associated with eating disorders (Sawdon, Cooper, & Seabrook, 2007). Research involving 112 female undergraduates found that exposure to ads portraying thin women increased body dissatisfaction and levels of depression, and lowered self-esteem. Women with high body-image self-discrepancy were more likely to experience these effects (Bessenoff, 2006).

Alternatively, discrepancies may lead to changes intended to align behavior with the standard. Interviews with fathers in 61 couples assessed personal definitions of fatherhood and the degree of specificity of standards (Collett, Vercel & Boykin, 2015). Fathers with more specific standards, e.g., "teach my son sports," were more likely to experience discrepancies between performance and standards; at the same time, the standard provided a goal for their efforts to reduce the discrepancy. Fathers with vague, general standards, e.g., "be there", were less likely to perceive a discrepancy. Also, it is easier to perceive oneself as meeting a vague, general standard. Perhaps not surprisingly, fathers with more specific standards generally engaged in more carework.

## SELF-ESTEEM

Do you have a positive attitude about yourself, or do you feel you do not have much to be proud of? Overall, how capable, successful, significant, and worthy are you? Answers to these questions reflect **self-esteem**, the evaluative component of self-concept (Gecas & Burke, 1995).

This section addresses four questions: (1) How is self-esteem assessed? (2) What are the major sources of self-esteem? (3) How is self-esteem related to behavior? (4) What techniques do we employ to protect our self-esteem?

### Assessment of Self-Esteem

Our overall self-esteem depends on (1) which characteristics of self are contingencies of self-esteem, and (2) how we evaluate each of them. Some of our specific role and social identities and personal qualities are important to us; characteristics of self or categories of outcomes on which a person stakes self-esteem are **contingencies** of self-esteem (Crocker & Wolfe, 2001). Others are unimportant. For instance, you may consider yourself an excellent student and a worthy friend, an incompetent athlete and an unreliable employee, and not care about your social identity as Basque French. According to theory, our overall level of self-esteem is the product of these individual evaluations, with each identity weighted according to its salience (Rosenberg, 1965; Sherwood, 1965).

Ordinarily, we are unaware of precisely how we combine and weigh the evaluations of our specific contingencies. If we weigh our positively evaluated identities and traits as more important, we can maintain a high level of overall self-esteem while still admitting to certain weaknesses. If we weigh our negatively evaluated identities heavily, we will have low overall self-esteem even though we have many valuable qualities.

There are several approaches to measuring self-esteem. Probably the most widely used is the Rosenberg Self-Esteem Scale (see Box 4.2). It consists of 10 statements about feelings toward and evaluations of oneself, and assesses the extent of agreement or disagreement with each. A second approach is the attempt to measure implicit self-esteem—the unaware, automatic evaluation of the self—by assessing the person's evaluation of objects and qualities associated with the self (Greenwald & Farnham, 2000). A third technique involves using trained coders to assess autobiographical narratives; the coder reads the narrative and assigns two overall ratings, each on a 9-point scale. The coder rates the degree of self-liking and of self-confidence evident in the narrative (Anderson, 2006).

## Sources of Self-Esteem

Why do some of us enjoy high self-esteem, whereas others suffer low self-esteem? To help answer this question, consider three major sources of self-esteem—family experience, performance feedback, and social comparisons.

**Family Experience.** As one might expect, parent–child relationships are important for the development of self-esteem. From an extensive study of the family experiences of fifth- and sixth-graders, Coopersmith (1967) concluded that four types of parental behavior promote higher self-esteem: (1) showing acceptance, affection, interest, and involvement in children's affairs; (2) firmly and consistently enforcing clear limits on children's behavior; (3) allowing children latitude within these

limits and respecting initiative (such as older children setting their own bedtime and participating in making family plans); and (4) favoring noncoercive forms of discipline (such as denying privileges and discussing reasons, rather than punishing physically). Findings from a representative sample of 5,024 New York high school students corroborate these conclusions (Rosenberg, 1965). Note that these results are consistent with our discussion of socialization techniques in Chapter 3.

Family influences on self-esteem confirm the idea that the self-concepts we develop mirror the view of ourselves communicated by significant others. Children who see that their parents love, accept, care about, trust, and reason with them come to think of themselves as worthy of affection, care, trust, and respect. Conversely, children who see that their parents do not love and accept them may develop low self-esteem. A longitudinal study of adolescents found that excessive parental shaming and criticism were associated with low self-esteem and depression (Robertson & Simons, 1989).

Research also suggests that self-esteem is produced by the reciprocal influence of parents and their children on each other (Felson & Zielinski, 1989). Children with higher self-esteem exhibit more self-confidence, competence, and self-control. Such children are probably easier to love, accept, reason with, and trust. Consequently, they are likely to elicit responses from their parents that further promote their self-esteem.

As young people move into adolescence, their overall or global self-esteem becomes linked to the self-evaluations tied to specific role identities. A study of 416 sixth-graders found that evaluations of self as athlete, son or daughter, and student were positively related to global self-esteem (Hoelter, 1986). Also, the number of significant others expands to include friends and teachers in addition to parents. The relative importance of these others appears to vary by gender. A study of 1,367

## BOX 4.2  Test Yourself: The Rosenberg Self-Esteem Scale

| STATEMENT | STRONGLY AGREE | AGREE | DISAGREE | STRONGLY DISAGREE |
|---|---|---|---|---|
| 1. I feel that I am a person of worth, at least on an equal plane with others. | | | | |
| 2. I feel that I have a number of good qualities. | | | | |
| 3. All in all, I am inclined to feel that I am a failure. | | | | |
| 4. I am able to do things as well as most other people. | | | | |
| 5. I feel I do not have much to be proud of. | | | | |
| 6. I take a positive attitude toward myself. | | | | |
| 7. On the whole, I am satisfied with myself. | | | | |
| 8. I wish I could have more respect for myself. | | | | |
| 9. I certainly feel useless at times. | | | | |
| 10. At times I think I am no good at all. | | | | |

Scores are calculated as follows:

*For items 1, 2, 4, 6, and 7:*

Strongly agree = 3
Agree = 2
Disagree = 1
Strongly disagree = 0

*For items 3, 5, 8, 9, and 10 (which are reversed in valence):*

Strongly agree = 0
Agree = 1
Disagree = 2
Strongly disagree = 3

*Your score on the Rosenberg Scale:*

The scale ranges from 0 to 30. Scores between 15 and 25 are within normal range; scores below 15 suggest low self-esteem.

*Source:* Morris Rosenberg, *Society and the Adolescent Self-Image,* 1989. Revised edition. Middletown, CT: Wesleyan University Press.

high school seniors found that the perceived appraisals of friends had the biggest impact on girls' self-esteem, whereas the perceived appraisals of parents had the biggest impact on boys' self-esteem (Hoelter, 1984). For both boys and girls, teachers' appraisals were second in importance.

A longitudinal study assessed whether the actual appraisals of peers or the perceived appraisals of peers were more influential on the person's self-esteem (Gruenenfelder-Steiger, Harris, & Fend, 2016). Self-esteem was assessed at ages 12, 13, 14, and 15 using items from the Rosenberg scale; at each age perceived peer approval was highly correlated with self-esteem (.28 to .52), while ratings by one's peers were correlated at .15 or less at each age. Thus, perceptions of others' approval has much more influence on our self-esteem than their actual liking for us. Both popular (Pipher, 1994) and academic (American Association of University Women, 1992) works have argued that a substantial difference between male and female self-esteem emerges in adolescence. Various causes have been suggested, such as the devaluing of female roles in U.S. society, the development of body consciousness and concern with appearance among girls, and the preferential treatment of boys by teachers. A meta-analysis of studies involving more than 146,000 participants of all ages finds a small difference in overall self-esteem favoring boys that is larger but not substantial in adolescence (Kling, Hyde, Showers, & Buswell, 1999). Furthermore, the difference declines from ninth grade to twelfth grade (Falci, 2011), and there is no gender difference at age 30 (Erol & Orth, 2011).

Although there are not large differences in boys' and girls' self-esteem, it would be a mistake to think that some boys don't experience self-esteem issues. Boys may also struggle with body consciousness and concern about their appearance, lack of athletic prowess, and other ways in which they fall short of the idealized male image. Socialization to traditional role expectations and the media attention given to celebrities may set all youth up for issues with self-esteem.

**Performance Feedback.** Everyday feedback about the quality of our performances—our successes and failures—influences our self-esteem. We derive self-esteem from experiencing ourselves as active causal agents who make things happen in the world, who attain goals and overcome obstacles (Franks & Marolla, 1976). In other words, self-esteem is based partly on our sense of efficacy—of competence and power to control events (Bandura, 1982). People who hold low-power positions (such as clerks, unskilled workers) have fewer opportunities to develop efficacy-based self-esteem because such positions limit their freedom of action. Even so, people seek ways to convert almost any kind of activity into a task against which to test their efficacy and prove their competence (Gecas & Schwalbe, 1983). In this way, they obtain performance feedback useful for building self-esteem. Note, however, that the criterion a person chooses may not be one that others would choose; a shipping clerk may gauge competence by the number of orders entered in the database per hour, without regard to frequent errors in the addresses.

**Social Comparison.** To interpret whether performances represent success or failure, we must often compare them with our own goals and self-expectations or with the performances of others. Getting a B on a math exam, for example, would raise your sense of math competence if you had hoped for a C at best, but it would shake you if you were counting on an A. The impact of the B on your self-esteem also would vary depending on whether most of your friends got As or Cs.

Social comparison is crucial to self-esteem, because the feelings of competence or worth we derive from a performance depend in large part on with whom we are compared, both

Few athletes win an Olympic gold medal. Those who do, like Simone Biles in 2016, often experience great exhilaration. But for all of us, an inner sense of self-esteem depends on experiencing ourselves as causal agents who make things happen, overcome obstacles, and attain goals. © Leonard Zhukovsky/Shutterstock

by ourselves and by others. Even our personal goals are largely derived from our aspirations to succeed in comparison with people whom we admire. We are most likely to receive evaluative feedback from others in our immediate social context—our family, peers, teachers, and work associates. We are also most likely to compare ourselves with these people and with others who are similar to us (Festinger, 1954; Rosenberg & Simmons, 1972). This reasoning suggests that the self-esteem of minority persons may benefit from being in a consonant environment, that is, one where most people are from the same group; a longitudinal study of a national sample of Blacks found that as the percentage of Blacks in the college attended increased, post-college self-esteem increased (St. C. Oates, 2004). A study of Chinese adults in Los Angeles County also found context effects on self-esteem; participation in Chinese culture, for example, speaking Chinese, eating ethnic foods, and celebrating ethnic festivals, was associated with higher self-esteem for persons living in predominantly Chinese neighborhoods, but not for Chinese living in predominantly White neighborhoods (Schnittker, 2002).

Losing one's job is generally interpreted as a serious failure in our society. A national survey of American employees reveals that job loss undermined self-esteem, but the size of the drop in self-esteem depended on social comparison (Cohn, 1978). In neighborhoods with little unemployment, persons who lost their jobs suffered a large drop in self-esteem. In neighborhoods where many others were unemployed too, the drop was less. This difference points to the importance of the immediate social context for defining success or failure.

## Self-Esteem and Behavior

People with high self-esteem often behave quite differently from those with low self-esteem. At the same time, we should not overestimate the effects of self-esteem (Baumeister, 1998).

Compared with those having low self-esteem, children, teenagers, and adults with higher self-esteem are socially at ease and popular with their peers. They are more confident of their own opinions and judgments, and more certain of their perceptions of self (Campbell, 1990). They are more vigorous and assertive in their social relations, more ambitious, and more academically successful. During their school years, persons with higher self-esteem participate more in extracurricular activities, are elected more frequently to leadership roles, show greater interest in public affairs, and have higher occupational aspirations. Persons with high self-esteem achieve higher scores on measures of psychological well-being (Rosenberg, Schooler, Schoenbach, & Rosenberg,1995). Adults with high self-esteem experience less stress following the death of a spouse and cope with the resulting problems more effectively (Johnson, Lund, & Dimond, 1986).

The picture of people with low self-esteem forms an unhappy contrast. People low in self-esteem tend to be socially anxious and ineffective. They view interpersonal relationships as threatening, feel less positively toward others, and are easily hurt by criticism. Lacking confidence in their own judgments and opinions, they yield more readily in the face of opposition. They expect others to reject them and their ideas, and they have little faith in their ability to achieve. In school, they set lower goals for themselves, are less successful academically, less active in the classroom and in extracurricular activities, and less popular. People with lower self-esteem appear more depressed and express more feelings of unhappiness and discouragement. They more frequently manifest symptoms of anxiety, poor adjustment, and psychosomatic illness.

Self-esteem influences our attributions regarding events in our close relationships. College students in dating relationships were recruited to participate in research. Their self-esteem was measured, and then they imagined two scenarios. In one, the dating partner was in a good mood; in the other, the partner was in a bad mood. When the partner's mood was negative and the cause ambiguous, those with low self-esteem felt more responsible, more rejected, and more hostile (Bellavia & Murray, 2003).

Most of these contrasts are drawn from comparisons between naturally occurring groups of people who report high or low self-esteem. It is, therefore, difficult to determine whether self-esteem causes these behavior differences or vice versa. For example, high self-esteem may enable people to assert their opinions more forcefully and, thus, to convince others.

But the experience of influencing others, in turn, may increase self-esteem. Thus, reciprocal influence, rather than causality from self-esteem to behavior, is probably most common (Rosenberg, Schooler, & Schoenbach, 1989).

## Protecting Self-Esteem

What grade would you like to get on your next exam in social psychology—an A or a C? Your answer depends in part on whether your self-esteem is high or low. We often think that everybody wants to get positive feedback from others, to have others like them, to be successful—that is, to experience self-enhancement. As noted in the previous section, people with high self-esteem expect to perform well and usually do. People with low self-esteem, on the other hand, expect to perform poorly and usually do. People are motivated to protect their self-esteem whether it is high or low—that is, to experience *self-verification* in the feedback they receive. Most people have high self-esteem and want self-enhancing feedback. Some people have low self-esteem; to verify their self-evaluation, they want self-derogating feedback.

Research with sixth- through eighth-graders assessed their perception of their strengths and their weaknesses, making them salient. They were then given the choice of self-enhancing or self-verifying feedback. These early adolescents preferred self-verification (Rosen, Principe, & Langlois, 2013). A meta-analysis of research on feedback found that context makes a difference; when the risk of rejection is high, people prefer self-enhancing feedback (Kwang & Swann, 2010).

People use several techniques to maintain their self-esteem. We will examine four of them (McCall & Simmons, 1978).

**Manipulating Appraisals.** We choose to associate with people who share our view of self and avoid people who do not. For example, a study of interaction in a college sorority revealed that women associated most frequently with those they believed saw them as they saw themselves (Backman & Secord, 1962). People with negative self-views seek people who think poorly of them (Swann & Predmore, 1985). Another way to maintain our self-esteem is by interpreting others' appraisals as more favorable or unfavorable than they actually are. For instance, college students took an analogies test and subsequently were given positive, negative, or no feedback about their performance (Jussim, Coleman, & Nassau, 1987). Each student then completed a questionnaire. Students with high self-esteem perceived the feedback—whether positive or negative—as more positive than students with low self-esteem.

**Selective Information Processing.** Another way we protect our self-esteem is by attending more to those occurrences that are consistent with our self-evaluation. In one study, participants high or low in self-esteem performed a task; they were then told either that they succeeded or that they failed at the task. On a later self-rating, all the participants gave biased ratings. High-self-esteem participants who succeeded increased their ratings, whereas their low-self-esteem counterparts did not. Low-self-esteem participants who failed gave themselves lower ratings, whereas high-self-esteem participants who failed did not (Schlenker, Weigold, & Hallam, 1990).

Memory also acts to protect self-esteem. People with high self-esteem recall good, responsible, and successful activities more often, whereas those with low self-esteem are more likely to remember bad, irresponsible, and unsuccessful ones.

**Selective Social Comparison.** When we lack objective standards for evaluating ourselves, we engage in social comparison (Festinger, 1954). By carefully selecting others with whom to compare ourselves, we can further protect our self-esteem. We usually compare ourselves with persons who are similar in age, sex, occupation, economic status, abilities, and attitudes (Suls & Miller, 1977; Walsh & Taylor, 1982). We generally rate ourselves more favorably than we rate our friends (Suls, Lemos, & Stewart, 2002). We tend to avoid comparing ourselves with the class valedictorian, homecoming queen, or star athlete, thereby forestalling a negative self-evaluation.

**Selective Commitment to Identities.** Still another technique to protect self-esteem involves committing ourselves more to those self-concepts that provide feedback consistent with our self-evaluation, downgrading those that provide feedback that challenges it. This protects overall self-esteem because self-evaluation is based most heavily on those identities and personal qualities that are contingencies of self-esteem. This process may also lead us to change roles, exiting those that are associated with negative feedback.

People tend to enhance self-esteem by assigning more importance to those identities (religious, racial, occupational, family) they consider particularly admirable (Hoelter, 1983). They also increase or decrease identification with a social group when the group becomes a greater or lesser potential source of self-esteem (Tesser & Campbell, 1983). In one study, students were part of a group that either succeeded or failed at a task (Snyder, Lassegard, & Ford, 1986). On measures of identification with the group, students belonging to a successful group claimed closer association with the group (that is, basked in the reflected glory), whereas those in an unsuccessful group distanced themselves from the group. Similarly, students are more apt to wear clothing that displays their university affiliation following a football victory than after a defeat. They also identify more with their school when describing victories ("We won") than defeats ("They lost"), thereby enhancing or protecting self-esteem (Cialdini et al., 1976).

## BOX 4.3  Minority Status and Self-Esteem

Members of racial, religious, and ethnic minorities might have special issues related to self-esteem. Because of prejudice, minority group members may see a negative image of themselves reflected in appraisals by members of majority groups. When they make social comparisons of their own educational, occupational, and economic success with that of the majority, they are likely to compare unfavorably. Therefore, we might assume that members of minority groups will interpret their performances and failures to achieve as evidence of a basic lack of worth and competence— that they will have low self-esteem.

Is this hypothesis true? Hundreds of studies have sought to determine whether minority status undermines self-esteem in America (Porter & Washington, 1993; Wylie, 1979). The vast majority of studies offer little support for the conclusion that minorities (racial, religious, or ethnic) have significantly lower self-esteem. Further research suggests that self-esteem among racial and ethnic minorities has two components. One is *group self-esteem*—how the person feels as a member of a racial or ethnic group. The other

is *personal self-esteem*—how the person feels about the self (Porter & Washington, 1993).

A meta-analysis of data from more than 120 sources found that Blacks score significantly higher than Whites on global measures of personal self-esteem (Gray-Little & Hafdahl, 2000). Reflected appraisals from significant others affect minority group members just as they do majority group members. The self-esteem of Black schoolchildren is strongly related to their perception of what their parents, teachers, and friends think of them. These appraisals are not negative (Rosenberg, 1973, 1990). Living in segregated neighborhoods, minority group children usually see themselves through the unprejudiced eyes of their own group, not the prejudiced eyes of members of other groups. Similarly, the self-esteem of Black adults is related to the quality of their relationships with family and friends and their involvement in religion (Hughes & Demo, 1989).

What about other racial/ethnic groups? A meta-analysis of data from 354 samples of people of all ages, including Hispanics, Asians, and Native Americans (Twenge & Crocker, 2002),

People who want to verify their low self-esteem behave differently. Low-self-esteem participants who were members of a successful group downplayed their connection to the group and minimized their contribution to its success. Low-self-esteem participants were more likely to link themselves to the successful group when they were not members of it (Brown, Collins, & Schmidt, 1988).

All four techniques for protecting self-esteem described here portray human beings as active processors of social events. People do not accept social evaluations passively or allow their self-esteem to be buffeted by the cruelties and kindnesses of the social environment. Nor do successes and failures directly

affect self-esteem. The techniques described here testify to human ingenuity in selecting and modifying the meanings of events in the service of self-esteem.

## SUMMARY

The self is the individual viewed both as the source and the object of reflexive behavior.

**The Nature and Genesis of Self.** (1) The self is the source of action when we plan, observe, and control our own behavior. The self is the object of action when we think about who we are. (2) Newborn infants lack a sense of self. Later, they come to recognize that they are

again found Blacks' mean scores on global measures to be somewhat higher than Whites'; the means of the other three groups were somewhat below the means of Whites.

Recent research has assessed self-esteem levels across the life course. Analyzing data from a longitudinal sample of 7,100 persons aged 14–30 (Add Health data), researchers found that self-esteem increases for everyone from adolescence into young adulthood. Hispanics had lower self-esteem in adolescence than Blacks or Whites, but subsequently experienced a larger increase. At age 30, Blacks and Hispanics had higher self-esteem than Whites (Erol & Orth, 2011). Data from 3,600 adults aged 25 to 75+ showed that Blacks and Whites had similar levels of self-esteem until age 65. Beyond 65, Blacks' self-esteem dropped more sharply than Whites' (Shaw, Liang, & Krause, 2010).

Group self-esteem, on the other hand, is not associated with reflected appraisals. Among Black Americans, group self-esteem includes Black consciousness, Black racial identity, and support for independent Black politics. High group self-esteem among Blacks is associated with higher education and more frequent contact with Whites, not with relationships with family and friends (Demo & Hughes, 1990). Research indicates that Puerto Ricans, Mexican Americans, and Asian Americans have high levels of group self-esteem (Porter & Washington, 1993). Other data suggest that when members of these groups receive negative feedback from members of other groups, they attribute it to racial prejudice (Crocker, Voelkl, Testa, & Major, 1991).

But what about the effects of social comparisons? Many minority group members are disadvantaged in terms of education, occupation, and income. Minority individuals do compare themselves with the majority, but they often do not blame themselves for their disadvantaged position. Minorities can protect their personal self-esteem by blaming the system of discrimination for their lesser accomplishments. Indeed, minority statuses such as race, religion, and ethnicity show virtually no association with self-esteem (Jacques & Chason, 1977; Rotheram-Borus, 1990). Social failure affects self-esteem only when people attribute it to poor individual achievement (Rosenberg & Pearlin, 1978).

physically separate from others. As they acquire language, they learn that their own thoughts and feelings are also separate. (3) Through role taking, children come to see themselves through others' eyes. They can then observe, judge, and regulate their own behavior. (4) Children construct their identities based on how they imagine they appear to others. Both face-to-face and online interactions influence the development of self. They also develop self-evaluations based on the perceived judgments of others.

**Identities: The Self We Know.** The self we know includes multiple identities. (1) Some identities are linked to the social roles we enact. (2) Some identities are linked to our membership in social groups or categories. These identities may be associated with in-group favoritism and out-group stereotyping. (3) We form self-concepts primarily through learning and adopting role and social identities. The self we know is primarily influenced by the perceived reactions of others. (4) The self we know varies with the situation. We attend most to those aspects of our selves that are distinctive and relevant to the ongoing activity.

**Identities: The Self We Enact.** The self we enact expresses our identities. (1) We choose behaviors to evoke responses from others that will confirm particular identities. To confirm identities successfully, we must share with others our understanding of what these behaviors and identities mean. Adopting these meanings may lead to poorer performance when we experience stereotype threat. (2) We choose which identity to express based on that identity's salience, need for support, and situational opportunities for enacting it. (3) We gain consistency in our behavior over time by striving to enact important identities. We also employ several strategies that lead to verification of our self-conceptions.

**Self-Esteem.** Self-esteem is the evaluative component of self. Most people try to maintain positive self-esteem. (1) Overall self-esteem depends on the evaluations of our specific role identities. (2) Self-esteem derives from three sources: family experiences of acceptance and discipline, direct feedback on the effectiveness of actions, and comparisons of our own successes and failures with those of others. (3) People with higher self-esteem tend to be more popular, assertive, ambitious, and academically successful, better adjusted, and happier. (4) We employ numerous techniques to protect self-esteem. Specifically, we seek reflected appraisals consistent with our self-view, process information selectively, carefully select those with whom we compare ourselves, and attribute greater importance to qualities that provide consistent feedback.

### Critical Thinking Skill: Understanding the Influences on Your Self-Esteem

In this chapter we learned that one's self-esteem is an important influence on an individual's life. The evidence indicates that high self-esteem is associated with many desirable personal and interpersonal outcomes, whereas low self-esteem is associated with reduced self-confidence and achievement and poor social adjustment. This evidence has led to a great deal of interest in how to raise the self-esteem of persons whose self-esteem is low. The result is a cottage industry of books and self-help programs that promise to improve your self-esteem, confidence, success, and physical attractiveness. As is often the case when confronted with such pop social psychology, we need to apply our critical thinking skills.

Who is/are the authors of the book or program? Do they have any training in the field? Do they have advanced degrees? If so, were they earned at reputable educational institutions, or mail-order degree mills? Is the material or program evidence-based? Has the evidence been peer-reviewed? Are they experienced in working with the issues they address? Are their claims or promises about outcomes plausible? All of these questions reflect the application of good critical thinking skills.

We have also reviewed research investigating the influences on self-esteem. Let's go back to that review and see what it suggests about ways to raise self-esteem. For most people, the family is the earliest influence on self-esteem, and it remains influential for many people throughout their lives. Hopefully, members of your family communicate positive messages about your worth as a person and value your accomplishments. Sometimes, however, reflected appraisals from family members are negative; that occurs when they hold standards that, in their judgment, you are not meeting. These situations provide an opportunity for you to decide what is important to you, what your contingencies—dimensions of self that are important to you—are. This may require seeking information and support from others who perhaps hold different standards. This role is often played by support groups, either in person or online.

The other important source we discussed is performance feedback. What is the mix of successes and failures in your life? If, in your assessment, the failures outweigh the successes, one way to improve your self-esteem is to change the mix. If you have been working at learning tennis for two years and still are not good enough to make the team, think about trying a different activity, perhaps swimming or running. If you are a chemistry major and working very hard to earn Cs, consider changing your major. If you are in a relationship and your partner is critical of you much of the time, it's possible you should change partners. Often, when we are not succeeding, we try harder. But if we lack the skills necessary to succeed at that particular task, trying harder won't make things better. Creating new goals that are compatible with our strengths may be much more effective and create a situation where we can replace failure with success.

# SELF-PRESENTATION AND IMPRESSION MANAGEMENT

By the end of this chapter you will be able to:

- Understand what is conveyed through self-presentation in everyday life, and describe the personal and situational factors that influence self-disclosure.

- Explain the impression management tactics we use when we claim an identity such as "attractive potential partner" or "competent student," and why we choose one tactic rather than another.

- Evaluate whether people can detect when others are using impression management tactics against them, and potential cues that reveal deception.

- Describe some of the consequences that occur when people fail to project the identities they desire.

## INTRODUCTION

Strolling down the aisle of the exhibition hall at the food fair, you notice the man in the next booth. He sees you at the same time and says, "Come on up. We're going to do it for you one more time." As you get closer, you see that he is surrounded by bowls of salsa and of coleslaw and piles of vegetables. On the table in front of him is a hard-plastic, hand-operated food processor—the Quick Chopper.

"Let me show you how to work these real quick, all right? You guys seen these on TV before? Cool. You didn't see me on TV, did you, *The Hunt,* Sunday night? Now the blades are the best part."

He makes it look effortless. He chops tomatoes, green peppers, and onions, all the while keeping up a steady banter. "Folks," he calls out, "come on up here. Help me get a crowd together. Sir, come on up here. You don't have to buy a thing,

sir. Nobody else has." Other potential customers approach the booth.

He finishes the onions. "And then salt it to taste. This is my daddy's recipe, by the way. He's from Cuba. My mother's from Iceland. I'm an Ice Cube. What can I tell you? That's cool." A woman reaches into her purse. "Did you want to go ahead and get that now, ma'am? Cash, check, or charge? Folks, come on up here. Grab him by the hand. Hi there. I'll get your change, ma'am."

It looks easy. But it isn't. Bill Daniels and other product demonstrators who work food fairs spend weeks in training before they hit the stage. They are learning the art of "retailtainment"—how to run the demonstration, take the money, run the credit cards, keep talking the whole time, roll over the audience, and start another demonstration smoothly. Much harder than it looks, but very rewarding if you are good at it; you can earn $70,000 per year working long weekends. The successful ones have learned the art of tactical impression management and are making it pay (National Public Radio, 2002).

Although few of us make our living by creating such a finely tuned impression, we all present particular images of who we are. When we shout or whisper, dress up or dress down, smile or frown, we actively influence the impressions others form of us. In fact, presenting some image of ourselves to others is an inherent aspect of all social interaction. The term **self-presentation** refers to the processes by which individuals attempt to control the impressions that others form of them in social interaction (Leary, 1995; Leary & Kowalski, 1990; Schlenker & Weigold, 1992). The individuals involved may be aware of these processes or not.

For certain purposes, it is useful to distinguish between authentic self-presentation, ideal self-presentation, and tactical self-presentation (Baumeister, 1982; Kozielecki, 1984; Swann, 1987). In authentic self-presentation, our goal is to create an image of ourselves in the eyes of others that is consistent with the way we view ourselves (our real self; see Chapter 4). In ideal self-presentation, our goal is to establish a public image of ourselves that is consistent with what we wish we were (our ideal self). In tactical self-presentation, our concern is to establish a public image of ourselves that is consistent with what others want or expect us to be. We may do this, for instance, by claiming to have some attributes they value, even if we really do not have them.

Persons engaging in tactical self-presentation usually have some ulterior motive(s) in mind. In some cases, they want others to view them positively because it will enable them to get some reward(s) that others control. Bill Daniels, for example, is earning money to support his lifestyle. In other cases, they are trying to pass as specific kinds of persons in hopes of gaining access to individuals and situations that are otherwise unavailable. If an undercover narcotics agent is trying to set up a sting, for example, the agent needs to infiltrate the drug operation, create the impression of being an experienced drug runner, and gain the confidence of the bad guys. In tactical self-presentation, a person cares only about the impact of the image presented to others, not about whether that image is consistent with the real self or ideal self. When a person uses self-presentation tactics calculated to manipulate the impressions formed by others, we say that they are engaging in **tactical impression management**.

Of course, there are hybrid situations in which a person uses several forms of self-presentation simultaneously. For instance, a woman might try to remain largely authentic in self-presentation (that is, giving others a correct impression of her) but also try to hide a few little flaws, for example, by using makeup to create a youthful appearance (so that others form a positive impression of her).

This chapter considers the ways in which people actively determine how others perceive them.

## SELF-PRESENTATION IN EVERYDAY LIFE

In this section, our primary concern is authentic self-presentation, although we must recognize that many processes in authentic self-presentation also are involved in tactical self-presentation. In everyday settings, people routinely project specific identities, and they must take care that others understand and accept their identity claims. For example, when a temporarily out-of-work individual meets a potential employer during a job interview, they may naturally strive to create a positive first impression and claim the identity of "productive worker." However, they have to be careful to create an authentic impression and not to claim too much. If hired, it would be quite difficult to maintain a false image for very long when the person has to perform on the job.

Successful self-presentation involves efforts (1) to establish a workable definition of the situation and (2) to disclose information about the self that is consistent with the claimed identity. We discuss each of these topics in turn.

### Definition of the Situation

For any interaction to be successful, participants in that situation must share some understandings about their social reality. Symbolic interaction theory (Blumer, 1962; Charon, 1995; Stryker, 1980) holds that for social interaction to proceed smoothly, people must somehow achieve a shared **definition of the situation**—an agreement about their situated identities, what their goals are, what actions are proper, and what their behaviors mean. In some interactions, they can establish a shared definition by actively negotiating the meaning of events (McCall & Simmons, 1978; Stryker & Gottlieb, 1981). In other interactions, people may invoke preexisting event schemas to provide a definition of the situation. Event schemas are particularly relevant when the event is of a common or recurring type, such as classes, job interviews, funerals, first dates, and the like.

To establish a definition of the situation, people must agree on the answers to two questions: (1) What type of social occasion is at hand? That is, what is the frame of the interaction? (2) What identities do the participants claim, and what identities will they grant one another? We consider these issues in turn.

**Frames.** The first requirement in defining the situation is for people to agree regarding the type of social occasion in which they are participating. Is it a commitment ceremony/ wedding? A family reunion? A job interview? The type of social occasion that people recognize themselves to be in is called the *frame of the interaction* (Goffman, 1974; Manning & Cullum-Swan, 1992). More strictly, a **frame** is a set of widely understood rules or conventions pertaining to a transient but repetitive social situation that indicates which roles should be enacted and which behaviors are proper. When people recognize a social occasion to be a commitment ceremony or wedding, for example, they immediately expect that two partners and someone authorized to perform the ceremony will be present. They also know that the other guests attending are mostly friends and relatives of the couple and that it is acceptable—indeed, appropriate—to congratulate both persons.

Participants usually know the frame of interaction in advance, or else they discover it quickly once interaction commences. Sometimes, however, there will be conflict and they must negotiate the frame of interaction. When parents send their wayward teenager to a physician for a talk, for example, the discussion may begin with subtle negotiations about whether this is a psychiatric interview or merely a friendly chat. Once established, the frame limits the potential meanings that any particular action can have (Gonos, 1977). If the persons involved define the situation as a psychiatric interview, for example, any jokes the teenager tells may end up being interpreted as

symptoms of emotional problems or resistance to the interview, not as inconsequential banter.

**Identities.** Another issue in defining a situation is for people to agree on the identities they will grant one another and, relatedly, on the roles they will enact. That is, people must agree on the type of person they will treat each other as being (Baumeister, 1998). The frame places limits on the identities that any person might claim. For example, a teenager in a psychiatric interview cannot easily claim an identity as a "normal, well-adjusted kid." And employers would find it incongruous and bizarre if a young person tried to claim the identity of "vegan" in a job interview.

Each person participating in an interaction has a **situated identity**—a conception of who one is in relation to the other people involved in that situation (Alexander & Rudd, 1984; Alexander & Wiley, 1981). Identities are "situated" in the sense that they pertain to the particular situation. For instance, the identity projected by a person while discussing a film ("insightful critic") differs from the identity projected by the same person when asking for a small loan ("reliable friend"). Situated identities usually facilitate smooth interaction. For this reason, people sometimes support situated identities claimed by others in public settings even though they may not accept them privately (Muedeking, 1992). To avoid unpleasant arguments, for example, you might relate to your friend as if they were an insightful or reliable person even though privately you believe they are not.

Much of the time, our identities are not self-evident to others because their perceptions of us filter through the person schemas and stereotypes they bring to a situation. These schemas bias the identities they perceive and grant to us. Thus, even if the identity claimed by us is authentic—in the sense of being consistent with our self-concept—we may need to highlight or dramatize it (Goffman, 1959b). For instance, consider some adolescents who are innocent of any wrongdoing. If they display their usual nonchalant, defiant image when stopped by police, they risk being detained or arrested. They are more likely to avoid arrest if they dramatize their innocence by presenting a polite, deferential demeanor (Piliavin & Briar, 1964). Failure to dramatize one's innocence may account for some of the violence that has occurred in police–citizen interactions in recent years in the U.S.

## Self-Disclosure

A primary means we use to make authentic identity claims is to reveal certain facts about ourselves. When we first meet someone, we usually discuss only safe or superficial topics and reveal rather little about ourselves. Eventually, however, as we get to know the other better, we disclose more revealing and intimate details about ourselves. This might include information about our needs, attitudes,

experiences, aspirations, and fears (Archer, 1980). This process of revealing personal aspects of one's feelings and behavior to others is termed **self-disclosure** (Derlega, Metts, Petronio, & Margulis, 1993; Jourard, 1971).

Self-disclosure is usually reciprocal. There is a widely accepted social norm that one person should respond to another's disclosures with disclosures at a similar level of intimacy (Rotenberg & Mann, 1986; Taylor & Belgrave, 1986). This is termed the *norm of reciprocity in disclosure*. Most people follow it, although strict reciprocity in disclosure is more common in new relationships or developing friendships than in established ones where people already know a lot about one another (Davis, 1976; Won-Doornink, 1979). Furthermore, we are more likely to reveal more personal information to those we initially like and find attractive (Collins & Miller, 1994).

Self-disclosure usually leads to liking and social approval from others. People who reveal a

These chess players seem to be building trust and liking through reciprocal self-disclosure, an important process in authentic self-presentation. © Kali Nine LLC/iStock

lot of information about themselves tend to be liked more than people who disclose at lower levels (Collins & Miller, 1994). This holds especially true if the content of the self-disclosure complements what their partner has revealed (Daher & Banikiotes, 1976; Davis & Perkowitz, 1979).

Although self-disclosure usually produces liking, there is such a thing as revealing too much about oneself. Self-disclosure that violates the audience's normative expectations may actually produce dislike. For instance, self-disclosure that is too intimate for the depth of the relationship (such as a new acquaintance describing the details of their latest bladder infection) will not strengthen the friendship and may just create the impression that the discloser is indiscreet or maladjusted (Cozby, 1972). Likewise, self-disclosure that reveals negatively valued attributes (such as a person discussing their prison record for felonious assault) or profound dissimilarities with the partner (such as a believer revealing their strong religious commitment to a nonbeliever) may produce disliking (Derlega & Grzelak, 1979). Constant updates of one's Facebook profile may result in disclosing more than your friends want to know. Posting pictures of yourself in which you appear drunk may cause conflict with family and friends and cost you a job in the future.

Perhaps not surprisingly, the level of self-disclosure is related to loneliness. Young adults low in self-disclosure feel more lonely and isolated than those high in self-disclosure (Mahon, 1982). Lonely persons tend to have fewer skills in self-presentation and are less effective in making themselves known to others than are nonlonely persons (Solano, Batten, & Parish, 1982). The self-disclosure style of lonely persons may impair the normal development of social relations.

## TACTICAL IMPRESSION MANAGEMENT

As we noted previously, self-presentation is inherent in social situations. Most people strive

to create images of themselves that are authentic or true—that is, consistent with their own self-concept. These processes are automatic: The person is not conscious of them, they involve limited or no cognitive effort, and they are autonomous and involuntary (Schlenker, 2003).

Nevertheless, under certain conditions, individuals may make a conscious effort to present themselves in such a way as to create narrow, exaggerated, or misleading images in the eyes of others. The use of conscious, goal-directed activity to control information to influence impressions is called *tactical impression management*.

There are various reasons we might engage in tactical impression management (Jones & Pittman, 1982; Tetlock & Manstead, 1985). One is to make others like us more than they would otherwise (ingratiation). Other reasons for impression management are to make others fear us (intimidation), respect our abilities (self-promotion), respect our morals (exemplification), or feel sorry for us (supplication).

One aspect of the self that often requires management is the expression of emotion. The frame of a situation defines some emotions as appropriate and others as inappropriate. Service workers such as airline flight attendants and food servers are required to be polite to customers and to conceal anger, even if the customer is being unreasonable or insulting (Hochschild, 1983). Professional hockey players, on the other hand, are required to act aggressively on the ice and even physically attack an opponent if provoked. An important part of the socialization into some professions involves learning to manage emotions; for instance, mortuary science students must learn to suppress negative reactions to dead bodies, bodily fluids, and disfigurement (Cahill, 1999). Some situations, such as the loss of a spouse, a job, or some other salient identity or resource, may elicit very strong emotions that the person has difficulty managing. One reaction to such loss is aggression directed at others (see Chapter 12). Alternatively, the person may seek professional help from a therapist, counselor, or support group. Support groups frequently provide a redefinition of the event (for instance, a divorce is an opportunity to start over—"turn your scar into a star") and an identity for the person that encourages emotions that are consistent with the group's ideology (Francis, 1997).

In this section, we examine some of the tactics used in impression management. In particular, we discuss managing appearances, ingratiation, aligning actions, and altercasting.

## Managing Appearances

People often try to plan and control their appearance. As used here, the term *appearance* refers to everything about a person that others can observe. This includes clothes, grooming, overt habits such as smoking or chewing gum, choice and arrangement of personal possessions, verbal communication (accents, vocabulary), and nonverbal communication. Through the appearances we present, we show others the kind of persons we are and the lines of action we intend to pursue (DePaulo, 1992; Stone, 1962).

**Physical Appearance and Props.** Many everyday decisions regarding appearance—which clothes to wear, how to arrange our hair, whether and what to shave, and so on—stem from our desire to claim certain identities. In some situations, we arrange our clothing and accessories to achieve certain effects. This would be true, for example, if we were attending a party or going to a football game. It is also true when we go to a job interview, as illustrated in a study of female

Physical appearance is important in impression management. If impression management is to be successful, one's appearance in the eyes of the audience must be consistent with the identity one claims. If this performer lacked their makeup and costume, they would have a hard time convincing an audience of their identity as a mime.
© Anneka/Shutterstock

job applicants (von Baeyer, Sherk, & Zanna, 1981). Some applicants in this study were led to believe that their (male) interviewer felt that the ideal female employee should conform closely to the traditional female stereotype (passive, gentle, and so on); other applicants were led to believe that he felt the ideal female employee should be nontraditional (independent, assertive, and so on). The results showed that applicants managed their physical appearance to match their interviewer's stereotyped expectations. Those expecting to meet the traditionalist wore more makeup and used more accessories, such as earrings, than those planning to meet the nontraditional interviewer.

An important aspect of personal appearance is the location and visibility of hair on the body. U.S. social norms dictate groomed hair on the head unless one is bald; hair on parts of the body such as underarms and legs is expected on some persons (bikers) but not others (competitive swimmers). In fact, some women who do not shave these areas are subject to harassment and ridicule (Hawkins, 2004). A person may refuse to shave parts of the body as a matter of principle, of not yielding to an arbitrary grooming norm, and may want this act of independence to be visible to others. But others react with "How do you expect people to like you if you look like that?" and a man may pointedly ask a woman "Are you a lesbian?" This is an example of gender policing, sanctioning by others of behaviors that violate gender role norms.

Visible tattoos as a type of intentional personal adornment are becoming increasingly popular; one source estimates that in 2015, 9.5 million people in the United States have tattoos, most of them between ages 18 and 50 (Harris Poll, 2016). Several studies have compared college students with and without tattoos on various measures; in these studies, 12 to 33 percent of the participants report having one or more tattoos. Those with tattoos do not differ in personality characteristics or reported childhood experiences from those

without (Forbes, 2001). Men and women with tattoos do report significantly more risk-taking behavior and greater use of alcohol and drugs (Drews, Allison, & Probst, 2000; Dukes & Stein, 2011), and earlier experience with sexual intercourse (Gueguen, 2012). Studies of students' reactions to tattoos find that both men and women have significantly more negative reactions to a woman with a visible tattoo (Degelman & Price, 2002); also, participants with more conservative gender attitudes rank her more negatively (Hawkes, Senn, & Thom, 2004).

In a survey of 1,400 high school students, 9 percent of boys and 7 percent of girls reported tattoos, and 42 percent of girls reported piercings (not including ear lobes) (Dukes & Stein, 2011). Girls with piercings were less school oriented and reported more substance use. Apparently, unconventional body markers are associated with unconventional behavior.

The impression an individual makes on others depends not only on clothes, makeup, and grooming, but also on props in the environment. The impression Ashley makes on her friends and acquaintances, for instance, will depend in part on the props she uses—the titles in the pile of books she places on her desk, the music she selects for her playlist, the wine she serves, and the like. A study of the impact of cleanliness of an apartment on perceptions of the resident found that persons with dirty apartments were given significantly lower ratings on agreeableness, conscientiousness, and intelligence, and higher ratings on openness and neuroticism. Ratings did not vary by the gender of the rater (Harris & Sachau, 2005). Thus, others make inferences about one's character and interests from the props that surround them.

**Regions.** Goffman (1959b) draws a parallel between a theater's front and back stages and the regions we use in managing appearances. He uses the term **front regions** to denote settings in which people carry out interaction

This person's body language clearly displays his embarrassment. Covering the eyes and trying to block photos with the hand are common gestures people make when an important social identity that they have claimed for themselves is discredited. © igorstevanovic/Shutterstock

performances and exert efforts to maintain appropriate appearances vis-à-vis others. One example of a front region is a restaurant's dining room, where servers smile and courteously offer to help customers. **Back regions** are settings inaccessible to outsiders in which people knowingly violate the appearances they present in front regions. Behind the kitchen doors, the same servers shout, slop food on plates, and even mimic their customers. In general, persons use back regions to prepare, rehearse, and rehash the performances that occur in front regions.

Front and back regions are often separated by physical or locational barriers to perception, like the restaurant's kitchen door. These barriers facilitate impression management, because they block access of outsiders to the violations of images that occur in back regions. Any breakdown in these barriers will undermine the ability of persons to manage appearances.

In recent years, for example, such breakdown has occurred regarding national political figures. Because the mass media are pervasive, they sometimes catch presidents, senators, and corporate officers off guard. National figures are shown expressing views and performing actions they would strongly prefer to keep hidden from the public. American presidents find it difficult to project a heroic identity when the media publicize one choking on a pretzel, another collapsing while jogging, and a third losing the TV remote. It was much easier to be a hero in the days of Jefferson or Lincoln, before the invention of electronic media that penetrate the barriers between front and back regions (Meyrowitz, 1985).

### Ingratiation

Most people want to be liked by others. Not only do we find it inherently pleasant, but being liked may gain us a promotion or a better grade, and it may save us from being fired or flunked. How do we persuade others to like us? Whereas much of the time we are authentic and sincere in our relations with others, occasionally we may resort to **ingratiation**—attempts to increase a target person's liking for us (Wortman & Linsenmeier, 1977). The original theory (Jones, 1964) included the assumption that these attempts are conscious, but subsequent work has broadened the definition to include attempts that occur automatically due to social learning (Jones & Wortman, 1973).

Certain preconditions make ingratiation more likely. Individuals may try to ingratiate themselves when they depend on the target person for certain benefits and believe or assume that the target person is more likely to grant those benefits to someone they like. Moreover, people are more likely to use ingratiation tactics when the target is not constrained by regulations and can therefore exercise their discretion in distributing rewards (Jones, Gergen, Gumpert, & Thibaut, 1965). In organizational settings, when roles are ambiguous, so that members are uncertain whether they are doing a good job, they may engage in ingratiation in an effort to ensure that they are perceived as competent and to receive rewards (Kacmar, Carlson, & Bratton, 2004).

There are a number of ingratiation tactics. Three of them are intended to increase the other's liking for an actor—that is, are other-focused. These are opinion conformity (that is, pretending to share the target person's views on important issues), other enhancement (that is, outright flattery or complimenting of the target person), and supplication (that is, convincing others you are deserving).

**Opinion Conformity.** Faced with a target person who has discretionary power, an ingratiator may try to curry favor by expressing insincere agreement on important issues. This tactic, termed *opinion conformity*, is often successful because people tend to like others who hold opinions similar to their own (Byrne, 1971). Of course, obvious or excessive opinion conformity on issue after issue would quickly arouse a target's suspicion, so a clever ingratiator will mix conformity on important issues with disagreement on unimportant issues.

Opinion conformity sometimes requires us to tailor the content of the opinions we express to match a target person's general values rather than any specific opinions they may hold. There is evidence that persons tend to show more ingratiation responses of all kinds toward their boss than toward a stranger or a friend (Bohra & Pandey, 1984). However, a meta-analysis of 69 studies (Gordon, 1996) indicates that ingratiation attempts directed upward (that is, toward persons of higher status) are less likely to be effective in promoting liking than are ingratiation attempts directed laterally (that is, toward persons of equal status) or downward (that is, toward persons of lower status). High-status targets, aware that others may have a motive to ingratiate, may be somewhat more vigilant than equal- or low-status targets.

**Other Enhancement.** A second ingratiation tactic is other enhancement—that is, using flattery on the target person. To be effective, flattery cannot be careless or indiscriminate. More than two centuries ago, Lord Chesterfield (1774) stated that people are best flattered in those areas where they wish to excel but are unsure of themselves. This hypothesis was tested in a study in which female participants were told that their supervisor valued either efficiency or sociability (Michener, Plazewski, & Vaske, 1979). The supervisor was a target for ingratiation because the participants' earnings depended on the evaluations they received from her. Before the supervisor made these evaluations, the participants had an opportunity to flatter her. The experimenter asked them to rate the supervisor's efficiency and sociability, and indicated that the supervisor would see the ratings. The results showed that the supervisor's assumed values channeled the form of flattery the participants used. Those who believed the supervisor valued efficiency publicly rated her higher on efficiency than on sociability, whereas those who believed she valued sociability publicly rated her higher on sociability than on efficiency. Thus, the participants were discriminating in their use of praise; moreover, they avoided extreme ratings that might suggest insincerity.

Ingratiation works. Research shows that targets of flattery are more likely to believe it—and to like the flatterer—than observers (Gordon, 1996). A set of experiments were conducted to identify which of several plausible reasons—vanity of the target, reduced ability to make accurate attributions, or the desire to like the other person—account for the target's reactions. The results suggest that it is the target's vanity; people like to be evaluated positively (Vonk, 2002). Other enhancement can also take forms other than flattery; one example, playing dumb, is discussed in Box 5.1.

**Supplication.** A third other-focused tactic is **supplication**—convincing a target person that you are needy and deserving (Baumeister, 1998). This is the tactic that roadside panhandlers use. By dressing in ragged clothes, they convey their need for money; by holding a sign that suggests a good use of the money ("Vet needs money to feed kids"), they attempt to convey that they are deserving. Students sometimes use this tactic in attempts to get an instructor to change a grade: "But I studied really hard and I knew a lot more than was on the exam." Whereas some people choose to use this tactic, others are forced to do so, for example, to get benefit payments from government or charitable agencies. In the latter case, the supplicant may feel embarrassed or angry, and will have to manage their emotional display.

**Selective Self-Presentation.** The fourth, self-focused ingratiation tactic is selective self-presentation, which involves the explicit presentation or description of one's own attributes to increase the likelihood of being judged attractive by the target. There are two distinct forms of selective self-presentation:

self-promotion (Baumeister, 1998) and self-deprecation. When using self-promotion, a person advertises their strengths, virtues, and admirable qualities. If successful, this tactic creates a positive public identity and gains liking by others. A field study of job interviews in a campus placement office assessed the degree to which each applicant (61 men, 58 women, 91 percent White) used opinion conformity and self-promotion during the interview; the interviewer's perception of the applicant's fit to the job was assessed following the interview. The results indicated that opinion conformity enhanced perceived fit and influenced hiring recommendations, whereas self-promotion had little effect (Higgins & Judge, 2004).

In contrast, when using self-deprecation, a person makes only humble or modest claims. Self-deprecation can be an effective way to increase others' approval and liking, especially when it aligns the ingratiator with such important cultural values as honesty and objectivity in self-appraisal.

To be effective, however, self-deprecation must be used in moderation. Excessively harsh and vigorous public self-criticism may gain expressions of support from others, but these expressions run the risk that others may actually believe them and form a negative private evaluation of the person using them (Powers & Zuroff, 1988). A more effective form of self-deprecation is an assured, matter-of-fact modesty that understates or downplays one's substantial achievements. In one experiment, members of a group were asked to evaluate other members following the group's success or failure at a task (Forsyth, Berger, & Mitchell, 1981). Group members reported greater liking for those who took blame for the group's failure or credited others for the group's success (self-deprecation) than for those who blamed others for failure and claimed credit themselves for the group's success (self-enhancement). These results suggest that when observers have evidence about someone's performance—whether favorable

## BOX 5.1  Research Update: Playing Dumb

"Playing dumb" is an ingratiation tactic used with some frequency in interaction. When playing dumb, impression managers pretend to be less intelligent or knowledgeable than they really are. By playing dumb, they present themselves as inferior, thereby giving the target person a sense of superiority. Thus, playing dumb is a form of other enhancement.

Although popular belief and early research suggested that women are more prone than men to playing dumb (Wallin, 1950), a national survey of American adults indicated just the opposite (Gove, Hughes, & Geerken, 1980). Significantly more men than women said that they had pretended at least once to be less intelligent or knowledgeable than they really were. Men reported playing dumb more often than women in most of the situations examined, including work. Experimental research indicates that it is only in groups including both men and women that women are more deferent (play dumb) than men; in all-male and all-female groups, rates of deference are similar (Hopcroft, 2009). A review of research on the use of impression management tactics in organizations found that both men and women use them, and use tactics consistent with gender-role expectations (Guadagno & Cialdini, 2007).

What leads people to play dumb? The data indicate that people who use this technique tend to be young, highly educated men (Gove et al., 1980). In contemporary American society, these persons are likely to hold lower-status positions in competitive occupations where knowledge is valued (junior executives, law clerks, graduate students, and the like). Because of their youth, many of these people are located at the bottom of an occupational ladder they aspire to climb.

These people interact with superiors in settings where intelligence and knowledge are prized. Under these circumstances, one's relatively low status may require deferring to superiors despite one's own knowledge and ability. People may stand to gain by hiding any intellectual superiority they feel—that is, by playing dumb.

Among college students, both men and women report playing dumb with dates, friends, and partners (Thornton, Lovley, Ryckman, & Gold, 2009). Measures of both hypercompetitiveness—desire to win—and competition avoidance were associated with more frequent use of the tactic.

Alternatively, playing dumb may be a defensive tactic, used to avoid action (Ashforth & Lee, 1990) or work (McLuhan, Pawluch, Shaffir, & Haas, 2014). The actor may attempt to avoid acting or taking on a task by pleading ignorance or incompetence; this tactic is sometimes referred to as "putting on the cloak of incompetence". Again, this may be more common in a highly structured, competitive organization, where midlevel personnel are motivated to avoid irritating others in order to enhance their long-term prospects. Another motive is to save one's face. In the twenty-first century, playing dumb has become a common tactic for avoiding responsibility for corporate misconduct and fraud (Steffy, 2005). On trial for fraudulent financial practices, a CEO pleads ignorance, arguing that they didn't know what the CFO (chief financial officer) or the auditors were doing. In this case, the actor is playing dumb in an effort to avoid significant penalties rather than to enhance others' liking for them.

Interestingly, some researchers use the tactic to facilitate their work. When ethnographic and observational researchers enter a new site, such as a museum or a massage parlor, they can legitimately ask an insider to explain who the actors are and what is going on. They often discover that insiders are happy to cooperate, and so continuing to play dumb may help them enlist new participants and collect additional data (Scott, Hinton-Smith, Harma, & Broome, 2012).

or unfavorable—self-deprecation can be an effective tactic of ingratiation.

## Aligning Actions

During interaction, occasional failures of impression management are inevitable. Others may sometimes catch us performing actions that violate group norms (such as "dissing" other group members) or break laws (such as running a red light). Such actions potentially undermine the identities we have been claiming and disrupt smooth interaction. When this occurs, people engage in **aligning actions**—attempts to define their apparently questionable conduct as actually in line with cultural or group norms. Aligning actions repair cherished identities, restore meaning to the situation, and reestablish smooth interaction (Hunter, 1984; Spencer, 1987). In this section, we discuss two important types of aligning actions—disclaimers and accounts.

**Disclaimers.** When people anticipate that their planned actions will disrupt smooth social interaction, invite criticism, or threaten their established identity, they often employ disclaimers. A **disclaimer** is a verbal assertion intended to ward off any negative implications of impending actions by defining these actions as irrelevant to one's established identity (Bennett, 1990; Hewitt & Stokes, 1975). By using disclaimers, they suggest that although the impending acts ordinarily imply a negative identity, theirs is an extraordinary case. For example, before making a bigoted remark, a person may point to extraordinary credentials (for example, "I am close friends with many Mexican people, but . . ."). Disclaimers are also used prior to acts that would otherwise undermine one's identity as moral (for example, "I know there are deserving poor, but I don't . . .") or as mentally competent (for example, "Call me crazy, but . . ."). These disclaimers emphasize that although the speakers

are aware the act could threaten their identity, they are appealing to a higher morality or to a superior competence.

Still other disclaimers plead for a suspension of judgment until the whole event is clear: "Please hear me out before you jump to conclusions." When individuals are not certain how others will react to new information or suggestions, they are more likely to preface their actions with hedging remarks (such as "I'm no expert, but . . ." or "I could be wrong, but . . ."). Such remarks proclaim in advance that possible mistakes or failures should not reflect on one's crucial identities.

**Accounts.** After individuals have engaged in disruptive behavior, they may try to repair the damage by using accounts. **Accounts** are the explanations people offer to mitigate responsibility after they have performed acts that threaten their identities (Harvey, Weber, & Orbuch, 1990; Scott & Lyman, 1968; Semin & Manstead, 1983). There are two main types of accounts: excuses and justifications. Excuses reduce or deny one's responsibility for the unsuitable behavior by citing uncontrollable events (for example, "I'm late because my car broke down"), coercive external pressures (for example, "My boss made me do it"), or compelling internal pressures (for example, "I suddenly felt sick and couldn't concentrate on the exam"). Presenting an excuse is intended to reduce the observer's tendency to hold the individual responsible or to make negative inferences about the actor's character (Riordan, Marlin, & Kellogg, 1983; Weiner, Amirkhan, Folkes, & Verette, 1987). Excuses also preserve the individual's self-image and reduce the stress associated with failure (Snyder, Higgins, & Stucky, 1983). Justifications admit responsibility for the unsuitable behavior but also try to define the behavior as appropriate under the circumstances (for example, "Sure I hit him, but he hit me first") or as prompted by praiseworthy motives (for example, "It was for her own good; she needs to learn . . .").

Justifications are intended to reduce the perceived wrongness of the behavior.

Persons are more likely to accept accounts when the content appears truthful and conforms with the explanations commonly used for such behavior (Riordan et al., 1983). Accounts are honored more readily when the individual who gives them is trustworthy, penitent, and of superior status, and when the identity violation is not serious (Blumstein, 1974). Thus, we are more likely to accept a psychiatrist's quiet explanation that they struck an elderly mental patient because they kept shouting and would not talk than to accept a delinquent's defiant use of the same excuse to explain why they struck an elderly person.

A staple of public life in many countries is the political scandal: allegations that a politician has engaged in some improper or illegal behavior. The politician typically either denies the allegation outright ("I did not have sex with that woman") or offers an excuse ("I did not know that my housekeeper was in the United States illegally") or a justification ("I did accept $200,000 from that group. I did so on the advice of my lawyer that it was legal"). How effective are these responses? Does their effectiveness vary depending on the transgression and the politician's gender? To answer these questions, researchers prepared four newspaper stories involving hiring an illegal alien, engaging in sex with a superior, accepting illegal gifts, and engaging in sex with a subordinate. Within each, gender was varied. Within each, the politician's response was denial, an excuse, or a justification. The results (mean ratings by undergraduates and adults from the community) show that denials and justifications were associated with more favorable ratings than were excuses. Contrary to predictions, respondents did not judge female politicians more harshly than men for the same offense. However, respondents did judge more harshly persons whose offense was consistent with gender stereotypes: men accepting illegal contributions and having sex with a subordinate,

and women hiring an illegal alien and having sex with a superior (Smith, Powers, & Suarez, 2005). Thus, had President Bill Clinton been a woman, he might have escaped impeachment!

## Altercasting

The tactics discussed so far illustrate how people claim and protect identities. The actions of one person in an encounter will place limits on who the others can claim to be. Therefore, to gain an advantage in the interaction, we might try to impose identities on others that complement the identities we claim for ourselves. We might also pressure others to enact roles that mesh with the roles we want for ourselves. **Altercasting** is the use of tactics to impose roles and identities on others. Through altercasting, we place others in situated identities and roles that are to our advantage (Weinstein & Deutschberger, 1963).

In general, altercasting involves treating others as if they already have the identities and roles that we wish to impose on them. Teachers engage in altercasting when they tell a student, "I know you can do better than that." This remark pressures the student to live up to an imposed identity of competence. Altercasting can entail carefully planned duplicity. An employer may invite subordinates to dinner, for example, casting them as close friends in hopes of learning employee secrets.

People frequently use altercasting to put someone on the defensive. "Explain to the voters why you used a personal e-mail server," says the challenger, altercasting the public official as violating government regulations. Should the official rise to their own defense, they admit that the charge merits discussion and that the negative identity may be correct. Should the official remain silent, it implies acceptance of the altercast identity. Putting one's rivals on the defensive is an effective technique, because a negative identity is difficult to escape.

The news about self-presentation and impression management is not all good; these

## BOX 5.2 Research Update: The Downside of Self-Presentation

Self-presentation facilitates smooth interaction, and impression management tactics may benefit the user. However, these practices also may have harmful effects.

*Self-Presentation May Be Hazardous to Your Health.* Leary and his colleagues (Leary, Tchividjian, & Kraxberger, 1994; Martin, Leary, & Rejeski, 2000) study the relationship between concern with how others perceive you and risky behavior. We usually want others to evaluate us favorably and support the identities we claim in interactions. We want to avoid failures in self-presentation because they are painful and because they tarnish others' images of us. These motives may lead to behaviors that jeopardize our physical health.

Teen pregnancy and sexually transmitted infections (STIs) are major public health problems and can be traumatic or life threatening to those affected by them. There are 750,000 pregnancies among teens and 4 million new cases of STIs among people under 25 in the United States each year. Most of these could be prevented by the correct and consistent use of condoms. Why don't sexually active young people, many of whom are aware of these risks, use condoms? Research indicates that self-presentational concerns are a major reason (Leary et al., 1994). Some men and women are afraid to buy condoms because others will infer they are sexually active. Some are afraid to produce a condom during sexual interaction for fear they will appear prepared (gasp!) for sexual activity. Some are afraid to suggest condom use because it might suggest that they are unfaithful or that they think their partner is unfaithful.

Consider skin cancer. The incidence of skin cancer increases every year in the United States. A major cause is excessive exposure to ultraviolet radiation. Many people intentionally expose themselves to this radiation by using tanning booths and sunbathing. Why? To enhance others' impressions of their attractiveness. Research indicates that people who are concerned with others' impressions or high in body consciousness are more likely to sunbathe or use tanning facilities (Leary et al., 1994). More than 25 percent of teenage girls use tanning devices each year;

the rate doubles from age 14 to 15, and again from age 15 to 17 (Balk, Fisher, & Geller, 2013). In an experiment, coeds whose mating interests were primed by showing them photos of attractive young men were significantly more willing to use tanning facilities and take potentially dangerous diet pills (Hill & Durante, 2011).

Numerous other risky behaviors result in part from the desire to make a favorable impression on others, including excessive dieting and eating disorders; alcohol, tobacco, and drug use; and excessive use of steroids by athletes. Teens may engage in risky behavior in order to be accepted by their friends. Numerous teens die every year as a result of showing off, whether by driving recklessly or diving into shallow water.

*Deception May Be Hazardous to Your Relationships.* Many of us engage in selective self-presentation—that is, accentuating our positive features and withholding information or avoiding issues that might create negative impressions. Research indicates that we are most likely to engage in these practices in our romantic relationships. Obviously, we engage in these practices in an effort to preserve the relationship and to avoid costly interactions, such as conflict with or punishment by our partner. A study of 128 heterosexual couples found that many men and women reported using "misleading communication" with their partners for such purposes (Cole, 2001). However, they also reported using these practices when they perceived that their partner was using these tactics. And people who reported using deception or who perceived that their partner was dishonest reported lower levels of satisfaction with and commitment to their relationships.

One of the processes at work in this situation is the norm of reciprocity. Just as there is reciprocity in self-disclosure, there is reciprocity in withholding information and intentionally using misleading communication (that is, lying) in close relationships. These behaviors, motivated by a desire to preserve the relationship, can lead to a downward spiral and the eventual dissolution of the relationship.

may have negative effects on health and relationships, as outlined in Box 5.2.

## Impression Management Online

The widespread use of computer-mediated communication (CMC) has dramatically changed patterns of interaction and communication. We consider its use in everyday communication in Chapter 9. Here we consider its role in self-presentation and impression management. CMC has multiplied the opportunities to engage in tactical self-presentation. As senders using Facebook, Instagram, Tinder, and other digital channels, CMC users can selectively present themselves; they have complete control over the content and timing of messages (Walther, 2007). The writer and the receiver are physically isolated from each other, so the receiver does not have access to nonverbal cues, which are often less controlled and therefore more revealing (see the next section of this chapter). Thus, messages and postings can be carefully crafted and manipulated (Lee, 2006).

A study of one user group included observation and analysis of messages for 2½ years (Lee, 2006). Members took a variety of steps to limit information about themselves. For example, 27 of the 66 members used a remailer to secure their privacy; only 5 included the URL of their personal webpage in their postings. Members based their "knowledge" of other members by inference from e-mail address and domain, name, signature, and message content. Members often tested identity inferences indirectly, by basing a communication on an inference about, for example, gender, and seeing how the recipient reacted. Over time, "regulars" revealed age, gender, careers, and hobbies. The researcher concludes that regulars carefully controlled interaction and employed a variety of protective practices.

Creating and posting a personal webpage or space is "conspicuous self-presentation that assumes external observation" (Schau

& Gill, 2003). Researchers drew a sample of 326 sites and performed a content analysis on them; they also interviewed the creators of 35 of these sites. Creators carefully select and embed text, photos and drawings, icons, and hyperlinks. Hyperlinks may be used to tell one's story, such as links to schools attended and past/present employers. Some pages include references to or links to retailers, providing information about preferred clothing, makeup, or jewelry. The researchers observed variation in whether and how the site referenced the creator's physical body. One woman intentionally used the word *sexy* and professional photos of herself in lingerie on her site; other creators carefully avoided any reference to appearance or the body. People began to create a website in response to a life transition (graduation, career change), a desire for personal growth or experience, or to advocate for something. As they became more experienced through viewing other sites and getting feedback on their own, they continuously upgraded or fine-tuned it, or created new sites, indicating the importance of intentionality in the construction of sites. The self presented on these sites was often an idealized or imagined self; the creators sometimes visually enhanced images of the body, for example, by careful attention to pose. So websites or spaces allow one to explore changing identities and monitor the feedback; obviously this could lead in some cases to a change in identity in the real world.

Social networking sites (SNS) are the most used form of CMC. Their use is especially widespread among young adults. Two potential benefits are interpersonal connectivity (communicating/maintaining contact with others), and the opportunity to experiment with the self (Mantymaki & Najmul Islam, 2016). Two potential negatives are enhancing one's exhibitionism and narcissism. Longitudinal data from 191 Facebook users found that social connectivity (e.g., "Using Facebook helps me stay in touch") and the user's exhibitionism (e.g., "I like to be the center of attention") are the major drivers of SNS use (number of visits per day and length of visits).

Researchers studied the use of SNS by 37 online daters (Ellison, Hancock, & Toma, 2011). These men and women are trying to construct a site that will appeal to potential partners for several months into the future. Thus, they were less concerned about the accuracy of the profile. Their criterion for what they posted was whether the self presented could be produced in the future. Thus, they perceived their presented self as a "promise" (losing 10 pounds, quitting smoking, reducing alcohol consumption, earning more money) that could be fulfilled if they met the right person. Promises, promises.

## DETECTING DECEPTIVE IMPRESSION MANAGEMENT

Up to this point, we have discussed various techniques used by impression managers to project identities and control relationships. Now we will shift our focus to the person (target) toward whom impression management tactics are directed. Impression managers intentionally try to create a particular image. This image may or may not be challenged by the person targeted. In some cases, the target will accept a false image because they have little to gain by questioning the sincerity of the impression manager. Consider the "white lie" of the guest to the host: "it was a wonderful party." The telling of the lie is motivated by a norm requiring politeness, and supports the claimed identities of both "gracious guest" and "successful host." Millions of insincere "white lies" are told and not challenged by recipients or hearers every day. In other cases, however, the accurate detection of deception is crucial for protecting our own interests. In attempting to win a contract, for example, builders may claim to be reliable businesspeople and skilled artisans even when they are total frauds.

For the homeowner about to make a down payment, it is literally worth thousands of dollars to determine whether the builder's hearty handshake belongs to a responsible contractor or to a fly-by-night operator.

How do people go about trying to unmask the impression manager? In general, they attend to two major types of information: (1) the ulterior motives the other person may have for an action, including a verbal statement, and (2) the cues that accompany the action. In this section, we discuss both of these.

### Ulterior Motives

The recognition that another person has a strong ulterior motive for their behavior usually colors an interaction. Many young people are interested in connecting with others. When a fellow student has flirted with you a few times, and one day says, "You look really nice today," you may discount the compliment because you know that they have an ulterior motive. Ironically, the very conditions that increase the temptation to use deception also make the target more vigilant. As noted earlier, ingratiators are especially prone to use such tactics as flattery or opinion conformity when the target person controls important rewards and can use discretion in distributing them. Unhappily for ingratiators, these same conditions alert the target to be vigilant and to expect deception. This state of affairs, termed the *ingratiator's dilemma*, means that ingratiators must be doubly careful to conceal their ulterior motives and avoid detection under conditions of high dependency. The terrorist must work very hard to prevent an alert Transportation Security Administration (TSA) agent from unmasking them and barring them from the concourse. As documented by Gordon (1996) based on a meta-analysis, ingratiation attempts that are transparent tend to be relatively ineffective, sometimes to the point of backfiring. Ingratiators usually understand this, and indeed, there is some evidence that ingratiators avoid using tactics such as opinion conformity under conditions of blatant power inequality; they are more likely to use them under conditions that are less likely to alert the target (Kauffman & Steiner, 1968).

## Nonverbal Cues of Deception

**Cues Indicating Deception.** When people interact face-to-face, they send messages through verbal (words), paralinguistic (voice quality), and kinesic or body language (facial expressions, gestures) channels (see Chapter 9). The multichannel nature of communication can pose problems for impression managers, because the meanings transmitted through some of these channels are more controllable than those transmitted through others. For instance, if an impression manager is trying to deceive a target, they may tell a lie verbally but then inadvertently reveal their true intentions or emotions through nonverbal channels. The term *nonverbal leakage* denotes the inadvertent communication of true intentions or emotions through nonverbal channels (Ekman & Friesen, 1969, 1974).

An impression manager will generally have a high level of control over their verbal expression (choice of words) and a fair amount of control over facial expressions (smiles, frowns, and so on). The deceiver may have less control, however, over body movements (arms, hands, legs, feet) and over voice quality and vocal inflections (the pitch and waver of their voice). The nonverbal channels that are least controllable—voice quality and body movements—are the ones that leak the most information (Blanck & Rosenthal, 1982; DePaulo & Rosenthal, 1979).

Several studies have demonstrated that the fundamental pitch of the voice is higher when someone is lying than when telling the truth (DePaulo, Stone, & Lassiter, 1985; Ekman, Friesen, & Scherer, 1976). The difference is fairly small—individuals cannot discriminate just by listening. Other vocal cues associated with deception include speech hesitation (liars hesitate more), speech errors (liars stutter and stammer more), and response length (liars give shorter answers; DePaulo et al., 1985; Zuckerman, DePaulo, & Rosenthal, 1981). Notice that interrogators on TV crime dramas use these cues to catch the villain lying.

Certain facial and body cues are also associated with deception. The musculature of a smile is slightly different when people are lying than when they are telling the truth. Lying smiles contain a trace of muscular activity usually associated with expression of disgust, fear, or sadness (Ekman, Friesen, & O'Sullivan, 1988) (see Box 5.3).

A meta-analysis of research on nonverbal cues identified 54 studies with relevant results (Sporer & Schwandt, 2007). To serve as a cue of deception useful in interaction, the behavior would have to be visible to the typical observer; therefore, the analysis focused on 11 different behaviors involving the head or body. Only three behaviors were reliably associated with deception by the actor: nodding the head, foot and leg movements. All three were negatively related to deception, in contrast to the widespread assumption that nonverbal behaviors increase while lying. However, reduced rates of behavior are consistent with the hypothesis that intentional liars would attempt to control nonverbal leakage.

**Accuracy of Detection.** Most of us rarely concern ourselves with the possibility of deception as we interact with others. But attacks by terrorists who gain access to airplanes or other venues lead us to realize that, in some situations, the costs of undetected deception are high indeed. As a result, there is much greater interest in the question "How good are observers at detecting acts of deception?" Although some people believe they can always detect deception when it is used by an impression manager, research suggests the contrary. The results of most experiments reveal that observers are not especially adept at correctly

## BOX 5.3 Test Yourself: Can You Detect the Deception?

Research indicates that most lay people are not very accurate in detecting deception. How about you? Can you tell the difference between Nicolas Cage's fake and genuine smiles?

On the surface, fake and genuine smiles may look quite similar, but there are distinct differences between the two. To learn more and to test yourself on spotting fake smiles, go to www.ekmaninternational.com/paul-ekman-international-plc-home/news/can-you-spot-a-fake-smile

Nicolas Cage © EdStock/iStock

identifying when others are lying. Rates of detection are generally somewhat better than chance but not especially good in absolute terms (Ekman & O'Sullivan, 1991; Zuckerman et al., 1981). This occurs in part because observers often use the wrong cues or do not rely on the most useful kinds of information in judging whether someone is lying.

Difficulty in liar detection is illustrated by a study in which travelers at an airport in New York were asked to participate in a mock inspection procedure (Kraut & Poe, 1980). Some of these travelers were given "contraband" to smuggle past inspection, whereas others carried only their own legitimate luggage. All participants were instructed to present themselves as honest persons. As motivation, the researchers offered travelers prizes up to $100 for appearing honest. Later, professional customs inspectors and lay judges watched videotaped playbacks of each of the travelers and tried to decide which travelers ought to be searched. The results showed that both the customs inspectors and the inexperienced judges failed to identify a substantial proportion of the travelers who were smuggling contraband. The rate of detection, even by the customs inspectors, was no better than chance. Interestingly, however, the professional inspectors and the inexperienced judges agreed on which travelers should be searched. That is, the inspectors and the lay judges used the same (invalid) behavioral cues as indicative of deception. Travelers were more likely to be selected for search if they were young and lower-class, appeared nervous, hesitated before answering questions, gave short answers, avoided eye contact, and shifted their posture frequently. Unfortunately for the inspectors, these cues were imperfect indicators of deception. The results of this experiment remind us of the difficulties facing immigration and customs officials in airports and at border crossings.

Why aren't observers better at detecting deception? First, paralinguistic and nonverbal behaviors that do reveal deception—such as high vocal pitch and reduced leg movement—are imperfect indicators. They do arise from deception, but they can also result from conditions unrelated to deception, such as excitement or anxiety. In such circumstances, the innocent will appear guilty, and observers will make mistakes in detection. Second, there are certain cues that are commonly believed to reveal deception but that actually do not (DePaulo et al., 1985). These cues include speech rate (people think liars talk slower), smiling (people think liars smile less), gaze (people think liars engage in less eye contact), and postural shifts (people think liars shift more). If observers rely heavily on these cues, they will make mistakes in detection. Third, certain skilled impression managers are able to give near-flawless performances when deceiving. One study (Riggio & Friedman, 1983) finds evidence that certain people can give off what seem to be honest emotional cues (such as facial animation, some exhibitionism, few nervous behaviors) even when they are deceiving. If an impression manager has this capability, they will appear innocent, again causing mistakes in detection by observers. Fourth, we note that face-to-face interaction is a two-way street; impression managers not only exhibit behavior, but they also observe the reactions of their audiences. The feedback from audiences in face-to-face situations is fairly rich, and it often provides impression managers with a clear indication whether their attempts at deception are succeeding.

If they are not succeeding, they may be able to adjust or fine-tune their deceptive communications to be more convincing.

The picture is not entirely bleak, however. First, members of some groups are accurate at catching liars. Law enforcement officers, judges, and professional psychologists were shown videotapes of the head and shoulders of ten persons; each person was speaking about an issue they felt strongly about, and half of them were lying about their position. Federal officers (most from the CIA) attained an accuracy score of 73, while sheriffs, federal judges, and clinical psychologists interested in deception attained scores of 67 to 62. Law enforcement officers and academic psychologists attained the lowest scores (Ekman, O'Sullivan, & Frank, 1999). Second, observers' success in detecting deception can be increased by special discrimination training (Zuckerman, Koestner, & Alton, 1984).

Thus, success in detecting deception can be affected by the instructions given to observers. For instance, one study (DePaulo, Lassiter, & Stone, 1982) varied the instructions given to observers in face-to-face interaction. When given instructions to pay particular attention to auditory cues and to downplay visual cues, observers were more successful in discriminating truth from deception than when they were given instructions to pay attention to both visual and auditory cues. By emphasizing auditory and downplaying visual cues, observers more fully attended those cues that are least under an impression manager's control, such as voice quality. In general, lack of attention to verbal content and paralinguistic cues seriously impairs the ability to detect deception (Geller, 1977; Littlepage & Pineault, 1978). A meta-analysis of the effects of training (Hauch, Sporer, Michael, & Meissner, 2016) found that the most effective type of training focused on training observers to monitor content including whether the message was logically structured and the number of details included. Truthful messages are more likely to have a logical structure and contain numerous details about the event or subject.

Notice that nonverbal cues play an important role in detecting false or inaccurate images. It is precisely these cues that are lacking in online communication, making it easier to engage in deceitful or fraudulent interactions online.

## INEFFECTIVE SELF-PRESENTATION AND SPOILED IDENTITIES

Social interaction is a perilous undertaking, for it is easily disrupted by challenges to identity. Some of us may recover when a challenge occurs, but others will be permanently saddled with spoiled identities. In this section, we discuss what happens when impression management fails. First, we consider embarrassment—a spontaneous reaction to sudden or transitory challenges to our identities. Second, we examine cooling-out and identity degradation, which are deliberate actions aimed at destroying or debasing the identities of persons who fail repeatedly. Third, we analyze the fate of those afflicted with stigmas—physical, moral, or social conditions that may spoil their identities permanently.

### Embarrassment and Saving Face

**Embarrassment** is the feeling we experience when the public identity we claim in an encounter is discredited (Edelmann, 1987; Semin & Manstead, 1982, 1983). It is usually experienced in social interaction (Ho, Fu, & Ng, 2004). Many people describe it as an uncomfortable feeling of exposure, mortification, awkwardness, and chagrin (Miller, 1992; Parrott & Smith, 1991). It may entail such physiological symptoms as blushing, increased heart rate, and increased temperature (Edelmann & Iwawaki, 1987).

Whereas we experience embarrassment when our own identity is discredited, we also experience embarrassment when the identities of people with whom we are interacting are discredited (Miller, 1987). In this sense, embarrassment is contagious. It may be more acute when our own adequate performance serves as a frame of reference that highlights the inadequacy of others' performances (Bennett & Dewberry, 1989). We feel embarrassment at others' spoiled identities because we have been duped about the assumptions on which we built our interaction with them, including our unwarranted acceptance of their identity claims (Edelmann, 1985; Goffman, 1967). For example, someone who claims to be an outstanding ballplayer will experience embarrassment when they drop the first three routine fly balls to center field, but the manager who let them play in a crucial game also will feel embarrassment and chagrin for accepting the ballplayer's claim of competence.

**Sources of Embarrassment.** Investigators have analyzed hundreds of cases of embarrassment to ascertain the conditions that produce this feeling (Gross & Stone, 1970; Miller, 1992; Sharkey & Stafford, 1990). The results show that any of several conditions can precipitate embarrassment. To begin with, people feel embarrassed if it becomes publicly apparent that they lack the skills to perform in a manner consistent with the identity they claim. This is the plight, for example, of the math professor who suddenly discovers that they cannot solve the demonstration problem they have written on the chalkboard. Closely related to lack of skill is cognitive shortcoming, such as forgetfulness. A host's inability to remember others' names during introductions at a small party can cause embarrassment for all concerned.

Another condition that precipitates embarrassment is violation of privacy norms. If one person barges unaware into a place where they do not belong (such as a residential bathroom occupied by another), both persons are likely to experience embarrassment at the violation of privacy. The sudden and unexpected conversion of a back region into a front region is embarrassing for those whose identities are tarnished or discredited.

A further condition that often precipitates embarrassment is awkwardness or lack of poise. A person can lose poise if they trip, stumble, spill coffee, or miscoordinate physically with others. Loss of control of equipment (a dentist dropping the drill), of clothing (a speaker whose clothing tears, revealing too much), or of one's own body (trembling, burping, or worse) also will destroy poise. In general, poise vanishes and embarrassment increases whenever we lose control over those aspects of our self-presentation that we ordinarily manage routinely.

A study of Japanese undergraduates (Higuchi & Fukada, 2002) found that the causes of embarrassment include disruption of social interaction, fear of negative evaluation by others, inconsistency with self-image, and loss of self-esteem. The first two were rated as most important when the event occurred in the presence of others (criticism by an instructor during class, falling in public), and the last two as most important when the individual considered a prior event in private (failing to support a friend, failing an examination). In an experiment, male and female university students viewed slides of nudes and erotic couples either alone or with two strangers. Participants self-reported greater embarrassment when others were present, but careful analysis of videotapes showed fewer instances of nonverbal indicators of embarrassment, such as face touches and downward gazes, in the public condition (Costa, Dinsbach, & Manstead, 2001). It may be that we try to control nonverbal indicators in the presence of others.

**Responses to Embarrassment.** A continuing state of embarrassment is uncomfortable for everyone involved. For this reason, it is usually in everyone's interest to restore face—that is, to eliminate the conditions causing embarrassment. The major responsibility for restoring face lies with the person whose actions produced the embarrassment, but interaction partners frequently try to help the embarrassed person restore face (Levin & Arluke, 1982). For instance, if a party guest slips and falls while demonstrating dancing prowess, the partner might help save face by remarking that the floor tiles seem newly waxed and very slippery. Mutual commitment to supporting each other's social identities is a basic rule of social interaction (Goffman, 1967).

To restore face, the embarrassed person will often apologize, provide an account, or otherwise realign their actions with the normative order (Knapp, Stafford, & Daly, 1986; Metts & Cupach, 1989). When providing accounts, people will either make excuses that minimize their responsibility or offer justifications that define their behavior as acceptable under the circumstances. If the interaction partners accept these accounts—and partners have been known to accept the lamest excuses rather than endure continuing embarrassment—a proper identity is restored. If accounts are unavailable or insufficient, the embarrassed individual may offer an apology for the discrediting behavior and admit that their behavior was wrong. We have seen this pattern—discrediting behavior, excuse, excuse rejected by the public, a public apology—hundreds of times involving celebrities, politicians, and entertainers. In this way, the person reaffirms threatened norms and is committed to maintaining social relationships (Feinberg, Willer, & Keltner, 2012). Research suggests that blushing is particularly important in restoring the normative order. Observers rated videotapes of a public gaffe; an actor who visibly blushed following the incident was judged less negatively, as less responsible, and as more trustworthy than an actor who did not blush (Jong, 1999). The results suggest that blushing communicates to others that the actor is attached to the social rules in question despite the violation.

Embarrassment is usually unpleasant. Thus actors will often engage in actions designed to deflect it. Consider the person who enters the drug store to buy a product associated with intimate sexual activity. Presenting that product by itself to the cashier may be embarrassing because it broadcasts one's intent to engage in the activity. To mitigate the embarrassment, the person might also purchase several other personal care products to minimize the prominence of the safe-sex product (Blair & Roese, 2013).

When our behavior discredits a particular, narrow identity, we can sometimes restore face through an exaggerated reassertion of that identity. A person whose masculine identity is threatened by infantile behavior, for example, might try to reassert courage and strength. In a test of this hypothesis (Holmes, 1971), some male participants were asked to suck on a rubber nipple, a pacifier, and a breast shield—all embarrassing experiences. Other participants were asked to touch surfaces such as sandpaper and cloth. The men were next asked how intense an electric shock they would be willing to endure later in the experiment. Men who had faced the embarrassing experiences indicated willingness to endure more intense shocks than men who had faced no threat to their masculine identity. By taking the intense shocks, the embarrassed men could present themselves as tough and courageous, thereby reasserting their threatened masculinity.

Sometimes people embarrass others intentionally and make no effort to help them to save face. A study of self-reports of intentional embarrassment found that embarrassors reported that their goal was to negatively sanction the target, while targets reported that the embarrassor's goal was self-satisfaction (Sharkey, Kim, & Digs, 2001). In such circumstances, the embarrassed persons are likely to react aggressively. They may vigorously attack the judgment or character of those who embarrassed them. Some research indicates that an aggressive response to embarrassment is more

likely between status unequals than between status equals (Sueda & Wiseman, 1992). Alternatively, the embarrassed persons may assert that the task on which they failed is worthless or absurd (Modigliani, 1971). Finally, they may retaliate against those who embarrassed them intentionally. Retaliation not only reasserts an image of strength and achieves revenge, it also forestalls future embarrassment by showing resolve to punish those who discredit us. Thus, a politician asked an embarrassing question by a reporter on national television may later tweet an unflattering comment about the reporter. In these ways, embarrassment may lead to interpersonal aggression.

## Cooling-Out and Identity Degradation

When people repeatedly or glaringly fail to meet performance standards or to present appropriate identities, others cease to help them save face. Instead, they may act deliberately to modify the offenders' identities or to remove them from their positions in interaction. Failing students are dropped from school, unreliable employees are let go, tiresome suitors are rebuffed, people with severe mental illness are institutionalized. Persons will modify an offender's identity either by cooling-out (Goffman, 1952) or by identity degradation (Garfinkel, 1956), depending on the social conditions surrounding the failure.

The term **cooling-out** refers to gently persuading a person whose performance is unsuitable to accept a less desirable, though still reasonable, alternative identity. A counselor at a community college may cool-out a weak student by advising them to switch from pre-med to an easier major, for example, or by recommending they seek employment after completing community college rather than transfer to a university. Persons engaged in cooling-out seek to persuade offenders, not to force them. Cooling-out actions usually protect the privacy of offenders, console them, and try to reduce their distress. Thus, the counselor meets privately with the student, emphasizes the attractiveness of the alternative, listens sympathetically to the student's concerns, and leaves the final choice up to them.

The process of destroying the offender's identity and transforming them into a lower social type is termed **identity degradation**. Degradation establishes the offender as a nonperson—an individual who cannot be trusted to perform as a normal member of the social group because of reprehensible motives. This is the fate of a once-powerful politician convicted of crimes associated with the sexual abuse of at least one of his students 40 years earlier when he was a wrestling coach. His sentencing was accompanied by a long, powerfully worded statement by the judge. Identity degradation imposes a severe loss on the offender, so it usually is done forcibly. Identity degradation often involves a dramatic ceremony—such as a criminal trial, sanity hearing, or impeachment proceeding—in which a denouncer acts in the name of the larger society or the law (Scheff, 1966). In such ceremonies, persons who had previously been treated as free, competent citizens are brought before a group or individual legally empowered to determine their "true" identity. They are then denounced for serious offenses against the moral order. If the degradation succeeds, offenders are forced to give up their former identities and to take on new ones like "criminal," "insane," or "dishonorably discharged."

Two social conditions strongly influence the choice between cooling-out and degradation: (1) the offender's prior relationships with others, and (2) the availability of alternative identities (Ball, 1976). Cooling-out is more likely when the offender has had prior relations of empathy and solidarity with others and when alternative identity options are available. For example, during a breakup, lovers who have been close in the past can cool-out their partners by offering to remain friends. Identity degradation is more likely when prior relationships entailed little intimacy or when

respectable alternative identities are not readily available. Thus, persons found guilty of sexually molesting youth are degraded and transformed into child molesters—immoral, subhuman creatures.

Observers have pointed out that in U.S. society, there are public degradation ceremonies for various types of offenders—trials and sentencing hearings, competency hearings, press conferences where one admits wrongdoing. However, there are no ceremonies when these persons return to society, and so they remain stigmatized. Redemption rituals could ease the reentry process. To be successful, they should be community based and public, and eliminate the person's "official" record (Fader, 2011).

## Stigma

A **stigma** is a characteristic widely viewed as an insurmountable handicap that prevents competent or morally trustworthy behavior (Goffman, 1963b; Jones et al., 1984). There are several different types of stigmas. First, there are physical challenges and deformities—missing or paralyzed limbs, ugly scars, blindness, or deafness. Second, there are character defects—dishonesty, sexual attraction to inappropriate targets, psychological derangements, or treacherous beliefs. These may be inferred from a known record of crime, imprisonment, sexual abuse of children or partners, mental illness, or radical political activity, for example. Third, there are characteristics such as race, sex, and religion that—in particular segments of society—are believed to contaminate or morally debilitate all members of a group.

We discussed earlier the relationship between identity salience and self-esteem. Research involving 300 persons with various concealable stigmatized identities (for example, history of mental illness, victim of rape, of domestic violence, substance abuse) indicated that the amount of distress experienced was related to how much stigma the person expected, and the centrality (how important is it?) and salience (how often do you think about it?) of the identity (Quinn & Chaudoir, 2009).

Once recognized during interaction, stigmas spoil the identities of the persons having them. Stigmas operate via reflected appraisals; nonstigmatized persons convey expectations and negative evaluations of the stigmatized person (Kaufman & Johnson, 2004). No matter what their other attributes, stigmatized individuals are likely to find that others will not view them as fully competent or moral. As a result, social interaction between nonstigmatized and stigmatized persons is shaky and uncomfortable.

**Sources of Discomfort.** Discomfort arises during interaction because both are uncertain what behavior is appropriate. Nonstigmatized persons may fear, for example, that if they show direct sympathy or interest in the stigmatized person's condition, they will be intrusive (for example, "Is it difficult to write with your artificial hand?" "Can you dance with that artificial leg?"). Yet if they ignore the defect, they may make impossible demands (for example, "Would you help me move the refrigerator?"). To avoid being hurt, stigmatized individuals may vacillate between shame-faced withdrawal (avoiding social contact) and aggressive bravado ("I can do anything anyone else can!"). Uncomfortable interactions may be very common for veterans of military service with visible physical limitations, and may make more difficult their reintegration into society.

Another source of discomfort is the threat, a sense of anxiety or even danger that nonstigmatized persons experience during interaction with stigmatized individuals (Blascovich et al., 2001). They may fear that associating with a stigmatized person may discredit them (for example, "If I befriend a convicted criminal, people may wonder about my trustworthiness"). Interestingly, stigmatized persons can use this discomfort in their

presence to elicit a positive response to appeals. Confederates soliciting donations for charities were more successful when seated in a wheelchair than in a regular chair (Norton, Dunn, Carney, & Ariely, 2012).

**Effects on Behavior and Perceptions.** Persons without visible stigma react toward stigmatized persons with an attitude of ambivalence (Katz, 1981; Katz, Wackenhut, & Glass, 1986). Toward a person with quadriplegia, for instance, people have feelings of aversion and revulsion but also of sympathy and compassion. This ambivalence creates a tendency toward behavioral instability, in which extremely positive or extremely negative responses may occur toward the stigmatized person, depending on the specific situation.

When interacting with stigmatized individuals, people alter their usual behavior. They gesture less than usual, refrain from expressing opinions that reflect their actual beliefs, maintain less eye contact, and terminate the encounters sooner (Edelmann, Evans, Pegg, & Tremain, 1983). Moreover, nonstigmatized persons speak more rapidly in interactions with stigmatized persons than in other interactions, ask fewer questions, agree less, make more directive remarks, and allow the stigmatized persons fewer opportunities to speak (Bord, 1976). By limiting the responses of the stigmatized person, people reduce uncertainty and diminish their own discomfort. Negative messages are likely to be expressed nonverbally; nonstigmatized persons often monitor their speech and try to restrain or suppress negative remarks, but nonverbal leakage may carry the day (Hebl & Dovidio, 2005).

For their part, stigmatized persons also have difficulty interacting with persons who are not stigmatized. Remarkably, the mere belief that we have a stigma—even when we do not—leads us to perceive others as relating to us negatively. In a dramatic demonstration of this principle (Kleck & Strenta, 1980), some female participants were led to believe

that a woman with whom they would interact had learned that they had a mild allergy
(a nonstigmatizing attribute). Other female
participants believed that the woman would
view them as disfigured due to an authentic-
looking scar that had been applied to their
faces with stage makeup (a stigmatizing attribute). In fact, the interaction partner had no
knowledge of either attribute. In the allergy
condition, the partner had received no medical information whatsoever. In the scar condition, there was actually no scar to be seen,
because the experimenter had surreptitiously
removed the scar just before the discussion.
After a six-minute discussion with the interaction partner, the participants described their

partners' behavior and attitudes. Those participants who believed they had a facial scar
remarked more frequently that their partners
had stared at them. They also perceived their
partners as more tense, more patronizing, and
less attracted to them than the nonstigmatized
participants did. Judges who viewed videotapes of the interaction perceived none of
these differences. This is not surprising, as the
partner knew nothing about either disability.
However, these results show that people who
believe they are stigmatized perceive others as
relating negatively to them. This occurs even
if the others are not, in fact, doing anything
negative or irregular. These findings are illustrated in Figure 5.1.

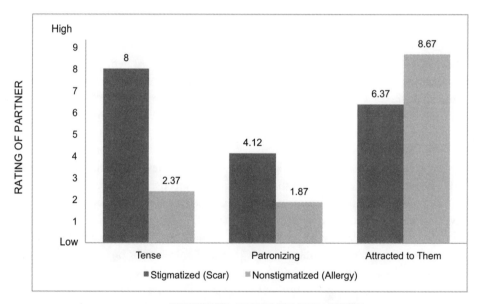

PERCEIVED ATTRIBUTE OF PARTNER

**FIGURE 5.1** Perceptions of Interaction Partners by Stigmatized and Nonstigmatized Individuals

In this study, some female students were led to believe that a large facial scar stigmatized them in the eyes of their
female interaction partner. Others were led to believe their partner knew they had a mild allergy—a nonstigmatized
characteristic. In fact, interaction partners were unaware of either of these characteristics. Nonetheless, students
who believed they were stigmatized perceived their partners as substantially more tense and patronizing and as less
attracted to them. This suggests that the mere belief that we are stigmatized leads us to perceive others as behaving
negatively toward us.

*Source:* Adapted from "Perceptions of the Impact of Negatively Valued Physical Characteristics on Social Interaction" by Kleck &
Strenta, *Journal of Personality and Social Psychology,* 39, 861–873. © 1980 by the American Psychological Association.

When people believe they are stigmatized, they tend not only to perceive the social world differently but also to behave differently. In one study, for instance, one group of mental patients believed that the person with whom they were interacting knew their psychiatric history, whereas another group thought their stigma was safely hidden (Farina et al., 1971). Patients in the first group performed more poorly on a cooperative test and found the task more difficult. Moreover, outside observers of the interaction perceived these patients to be more anxious, more tense, and less well adjusted.

**Coping Strategies.** Stigmatized persons adopt various strategies to avoid awkwardness in their interactions with others and to establish the most favorable identities possible (Gramling & Forsyth, 1987). Persons who are disabled or physically challenged often must choose between engaging in interaction (thereby disclosing their stigma) or withdrawing from interaction (concealing their stigma; Lennon, Link, Marbach, & Dohrenwend, 1989). A stutterer, for instance, may refrain from introducing themselves to strangers; were they to do so, there is a risk of stumbling over their name and drawing attention to the stigma (Petrunik & Shearing, 1983). Men with spinal cord injury have a visible physical limitation. They also cannot engage in sexual intimacy using the traditional script. Some took control of the circumstances and enlisted their partners' active cooperation (helping them undress, positioning their bodies). Others rarely disclosed their difficulties and relied on their drugs and performance to maintain the semblance of the script. A third group simply stopped engaging in partnered sexual activity (Bender, 2012).

In interaction, stigmatized persons often try to induce nonstigmatized persons to behave tactfully toward them and to build relationships around the aspects of their selves that are not discredited. Their strategies depend on whether their stigma can be defined as temporary—such as a broken leg on the mend or a passing bout of depression—or whether it must be accepted as permanent, such as blindness or stigmatized racial identity (Levitin, 1975). Persons who are temporarily stigmatized focus attention on their disability, recounting how it befell them, detailing their favorable prognosis, and encouraging others to talk about their own past injuries. In contrast, people who are permanently stigmatized often try to focus attention on attributes unrelated to their stigma (Davis, 1961). They often use props to highlight aspects of the self that are unblemished, such as proclaiming their intellectual interests (say, by carrying a heavy book), their political involvements (say, by wearing campaign buttons), or their hobbies (say, by toting a knitting bag).

In cases where a stigma does not force excessive dependency, permanently stigmatized individuals often try to strike a deal with others. They will behave in a nondemanding and nondisruptive manner in exchange for being treated as trustworthy human beings despite their stigma. Under this arrangement, they are expected to cultivate a cheerful manner, avoid bitterness and self-pity, and treat their stigma as a minor problem with which they are coping successfully (Hastorf, Wildfogel, & Cassman, 1979).

Everyone gains some benefit from handling stigmas in this way. Stigmatized persons avoid the constant embarrassment of indelicate questions, inconsiderateness, and awkward offers of help. They gain some acceptance and enjoy relatively satisfying interaction in most encounters. Persons without stigma gain because this resolution assuages the ambivalence they feel toward stigmatized persons and spares them the true pain the stigmatized person suffers.

Some persons are stigmatized because of some individual characteristic—birth defect, illness, disfigurement due to an accident, or history of deviant or criminal behavior. They often rely on these strategies. Others are stigmatized because they are members of certain groups—that is, because of a shared social identity: bipolar disorder, obesity, or racial/ethnic minority status (Crocker & Major, 1989). In these cases, stereotypes that are widely shared by both stigmatized and stigmatizers shape the attitudes and behavior of members of both groups, including the identities claimed in interaction (Renfrow, 2004). These persons have an additional coping strategy; they can attribute the stigma they experience to the prejudiced attitudes of others and base their self-perception on traits on which they rank well. They may also seek out relationships with others who share the stigma in an effort to experience positive reflected appraisals (Kaufman & Johnson, 2004). This is the basis for the widespread success of support groups for members of these groups.

The widespread advertising of medications for depression, bipolar disorder, and other forms of emotional disorders on television contributes to the stereotypes of the mentally ill (Smardon, 2007). On the one hand, the ads typically portray milder cases, and so in one sense they trivialize emotional disorders. On the other hand, persons taking a drug such as Prozac have a basis for forming a social network and supporting others who experience the condition or take the drug.

Another coping strategy is *passing*, distancing oneself from the stigmatized identity by hiding information (Renfrow, 2004). The person may hide the identity from persons without stigma while cultivating discreet associations with others who share the stigma; this will prevent negative appraisal and provide the person with positive appraisals by the others. Millions of college students have used this strategy to gain access to bars and alcoholic beverages before they reach the legal drinking age. Or the person may distance themself from other stigmatized persons and associate with normals or withdraw from interaction (the

closeted minority person); the latter strategy may result in great psychological distress. The central emotion in passing is fear: fear of the consequences of being identified by others as stigmatized leads to passing, and fear of discovery dominates the passing experience.

Persons may attempt to cope with stigma by seeking therapy (Kaufman & Johnson, 2004). Physical and occupational therapy may reduce or remove the debilitating effects of accidents, loss of limbs, or loss of abilities. Psychological or behavioral therapy may change the beliefs and behavior that accompany mental illness, or unnatural passions. A final strategy is to join a social movement intended to change the perceptions and stereotypes of normals.

## SUMMARY

**Self-Presentation in Everyday Life.** Self-presentation refers to our attempts—both conscious and unconscious—to control the images we project of ourselves in social interaction. Some self-presentation is authentic, but some may be tactical. Successful presentation of self requires efforts to control how others define the interaction situation and accord identities to participants. (1) In defining the situation, people negotiate the type of social occasion considered to be at hand and the identities they will grant each other. (2) Self-disclosure is a process through which we not only make identity claims but also promote friendship and liking. Self-disclosure is usually two-sided and gradual, and it follows a norm of reciprocity.

**Tactical Impression Management.** People employ various tactics to manipulate the impressions that others form of them. (1) They manage appearances (bodily adornment, clothes, possessions, and so on) to dramatize the kind of person they claim to be. (2) They ingratiate themselves with others through such tactics as opinion conformity, other enhancement, and selective presentation of their admirable qualities. (3) When caught performing socially unacceptable actions, people try to repair their identities through aligning actions, which are attempts to align their questionable conduct with cultural norms. They explain their motives, disclaim the implications of their conduct, or offer accounts that excuse or justify their actions. (4) They altercast others, imposing roles and identities that mesh with the identities they claim for themselves. (5) Impression management is a major component of online communication. In e-mail, text messages, personal webpages, and online dating profiles, people intentionally select content to create a certain image in the mind of the receiver/viewer.

**The Downside of Self-Presentation.** (1) Self-presentational motives such as the desire to be liked by or obtain rewards controlled by others may lead to behavior that is risky to your health, such as unprotected sexual intercourse or alcohol or drug abuse. (2) The desire to maintain romantic relationships may lead to withholding information from or lying to your partner; people who report deceiving their partner or who perceive their partner as deceptive report reduced commitment to their relationship.

**Detecting Deceptive Impression Management.** Observers attend to two major types of information in detecting deceitful impression management. (1) They assess others' possible ulterior motives. If a large difference in power is present, an impression manager's ulterior motives may become transparent to the target, making tactics like ingratiation difficult. (2) They scrutinize others' nonverbal behavior. Although detection of deceit is difficult, observers are more accurate when they concentrate on leaky cues, such as tone of voice, and the content of communication—length, amount of detail. Some professionals are quite accurate in detecting deception.

**Ineffective Self-Presentation and Spoiled Identities.** Self-presentational failures lead to several consequences. (1) People experience embarrassment when their identity is discredited. Interaction partners usually help the embarrassed person to restore an acceptable identity. Otherwise, embarrassed persons tend to reassert their identity in an exaggerated manner or to attack those who discredited them. (2) Repeated or glaring failures in self-presentation lead others to modify the offender's identity through deliberate actions. They may try to cool-out offenders by persuading them to accept less desirable alternative identities, or they may degrade offenders' identities and transform them into lesser social types. (3) Many physical, moral, and social conditions stigmatize individuals and permanently spoil their identities. Interaction between stigmatized and nonstigmatized persons is marked by ambivalence and is frequently awkward and uncomfortable. In general, people pressure stigmatized individuals to accept inferior identities, whereas stigmatized individuals seek to build relationships around the aspects of their selves that are not discredited. Some persons with stigma attempt to pass to avoid the negative reflected appraisals they would receive from others.

### Critical Thinking Skill: Defending Against Everyday Persuasive Techniques

The foundation of our efforts at self-presentation is our desire to have certain other people like and accept us, and treat us in particular ways. We want friends, we want a committed relationship, we want harmony with our roommates, and so we are motivated to conform to their expectations by presenting ourselves in certain ways. The means by which they communicate their expectations is often by using everyday persuasion techniques.

Imagine that you have not been in a relationship for several months. One day a close friend inquires about your "love life." You reply honestly, "I don't have one these days." The friend replies, "Well, maybe you're having trouble because of the way you look." "What do you mean?" "Well, you don't look healthy; you're not trim, and your skin is awfully white. I think you need to get some tan. Three times a week in a tanning bed will work wonders!"

This is an example of everyday persuasion. A well-meaning friend or coworker or roommate is trying to persuade you to solve a problem in the way they think will work. In this situation, many of us are tempted to follow the suggestion. They mean well, you like the person, you don't want to be critical or start an argument. You are inclined to accept in order to maintain a good relationship. But is it a good idea? They are suggesting tanning sessions to increase your attractiveness. Will it? Being tan is certainly considered attractive in your social group. But there is a good deal of evidence that tanning, especially in tanning beds, is related to increased risk of skin cancer in later life. And we reviewed evidence that persons who are concerned with others' impressions are more likely to use tanning facilities. So your inclination to accept the persuasive attempt probably reflects a heightened concern with self-presentation, not the merits of the suggestion.

As we suggest in a later Critical Thinking Skill (Chapter 9), direct, honest communication is best in this situation. If you aren't sure your friend's suggestion is a good idea, you could say, "Thanks for that suggestion. I'll check it out." Then you can gather information about the effects of using tanning beds by going to recognized health care information sites like the one maintained by the Mayo Clinic (http://newsnetwork.mayoclinic.org/discussion/fda-gets-tough-on-tanning-beds/). If you conclude it isn't a good idea, you can ignore the advice. If your friend asks later, you can say that you learned there is a link between tanning bed use and skin cancer. That might lead to an interesting conversation!

# EMOTIONS

## LEARNING OBJECTIVES

By the end of this chapter you will be able to:

- Identify various emotions and psychological emotional states and distinguish emotions and emotional expressions that are universal human traits from those specific to social or cultural contexts.

- Describe where emotions originate from, including the physiological, psychological, and social bases of emotions, as well as the importance of social context.

- Explain how, and why, people psychologically and socially control the expression of emotions through both suppression and production.

## INTRODUCTION

Robert Yu is a kindergarten teacher in a suburb of Columbus, Ohio, facing a Monday morning of teaching 25 energetic 5-year-olds for three hours. Robert is a very dedicated teacher and always strives to give his best to his students. He is usually energized for class and always follows well-developed lesson plans. His students love him and look forward to school every day.

Unfortunately, Robert is coming off a very difficult weekend. On Friday afternoon, he was denied a loan for a new house he hoped to buy, and on Saturday he was in a serious car accident caused by a teenager who was texting rather than paying attention. No one was hurt, but Robert's car was damaged beyond repair and towed to the junkyard. To top it all off, his favorite basketball team lost its final game of the season and, thus, was eliminated from the playoffs. On Monday morning, Robert woke up in his shabby apartment, rode the bus to work, and proceeded to pay off a bet he had made on the basketball game with another teacher. Needless to say, he was not in a very good mood when he headed down the hall to his classroom.

But Robert still wanted to do a good job with the children in his class, so he decided to hide his feelings and put on a cheerful face. He bounced into the room acting as though absolutely nothing was wrong and he was just as happy as he could be. The students and the teacher's aide thought Mr. Yu was in a great mood. They all reacted very positively toward him, and everyone had a great day in the classroom. As things progressed, Robert himself began feeling much better and, at the end of the day, decided that this was one of the best days he'd ever had in the classroom.

In the space of a few days, Robert experienced a wide range of emotions. He started off the weekend feeling fine, but was severely disappointed when he found out about his loan. When his car was hit, his first emotion was fear, but that quickly turned to anger toward the other driver. Later, he started watching the basketball game with excited anticipation, rode a roller coaster of ups and downs as the game progressed, and came close to tears when the game was over. By the time he walked into work Monday morning, he felt positively depressed. However, he managed to recover—very much by his own doing—during the course of teaching that morning.

How can we explain Robert's diverse emotional experiences and the changes from one emotional state to another? During the basketball game, for example, Robert vacillates quickly between anger, sadness, disgust, joy, and satisfaction, all because of a few images on a television screen. On Monday morning, he is able to consciously choose behaviors that end up actually changing his mood. What is involved, both on an individual level and a social level, in producing these emotional states and the rapid progression from one to another? Given that Robert is not an inherently unstable individual, we need to understand the social context of his interactions to understand his emotional states.

## DEFINING EMOTIONS

To talk about emotions, we first need to know exactly what we mean by that term. This can be difficult because emotions are not particularly easy to define. To complicate things, there are other related terms that are partially synonymous with emotion, including sentiment, affect, mood, and, of course, feelings (Smith-Lovin, 1995). Each of these terms is used in everyday conversation to refer to the experience of emotion, but social psychologists use them in specific ways, so we first need to distinguish between them.

**Affect** is the most general of the terms. It refers to virtually any kind of subjective positive or negative evaluation of an object. This includes short-term reactions like the anger you might feel toward another person after being the target of an insult. It also includes longer-term orientations such as the pleasant association many people have with the Christmas season. Affect is usually described not just in terms of direction (also called emotional valence), but also strength and the level of activity associated with it (Osgood, Suci, & Tannenbaum, 1957). In other words, it is not just whether one generally feels positive or negative toward something—perhaps a student, sports team, or riding the bus, in Robert Yu's case—but also how intense and dynamic that orientation is.

Emotions are often treated as a subset of affect. Usually, **emotions** are thought of as short-lived reactions to a stimulus. To distinguish emotions from other human stimulus-impulse reactions, sociologist Peggy Thoits (1989) delineates four components of emotions: (1) a situational stimulus, (2) physiological changes, (3) expressive gesturing of some kind, and, most importantly, (4) a label to identify a cluster of the first three. Being

slapped by one's girlfriend plus elevated temperature and heart rate plus a furrowed brow and a clenched fist equals anger. Being slapped by one's girlfriend plus elevated heart rate plus laughter and smiling equals humorous teasing. Various culturally defined combinations produce what we typically think of and experience as an emotion.

Emotions tend to be related to goals. Whether we are frustrated by a blocked goal, joyful upon achieving one, anxious as we approach one, embarrassed that we failed at one, or motivated by an emotion to pursue a goal (such as fleeing from a fearful situation), emotions and goals are intimately entwined (Frijda & Mesquita, 1994).

Sentiment is very close to emotion in meaning, but when social psychologists use the term sentiment, they emphasize the social aspect of emotion. Early social psychologists used sentiment to refer to the components of human responses that separate them from analogous responses that animals would have. For example, Cooley (1909) contrasts love and lust. Although lust is instinctive, we learn what love is through social interaction. In other words, sentiment relies not just on the responses of the individual to the stimulus but also on how other human beings understand that stimulus (to see this in action, you might revisit the Calvin and Hobbes comic strip, p. 10). In later years, social psychologists largely accepted that social elements are a key piece of a range of emotions and the earlier idea of sentiment became less distinguishable from that of emotion (Stets, 2003). Today, social psychologists often use the term **sentiment** to distinguish immediate emotional responses from longer-term emotional states such as love, grief, and jealously (Gordon, 1990). These sentiments can endure for days, weeks, and even years after the initial event that triggered them.

Moods are also more enduring than emotions. Whereas we might experience one emotion and move on to another in a matter of seconds or minutes (Ekman, 1992), a **mood** is a general psychological condition that characterizes our experience and emotional orientation for hours or even days. When an emotion or sentiment occurs, we have a very good sense of where it is directed or what stimulus caused it. Moods, however, are diffuse; they can be widely directed at anything that comes in our path—regardless of whether it has anything to do with the origin of the bad mood. In other words, although both sentiments and moods tend to be long lasting, sentiments are tied to an object or actor, while moods describe an individual's state of mind.

Returning to the experiences of the kindergarten teacher, Robert, almost all of the events described involve affect—some were stronger, such as when he was in the car accident, and some were weaker, such as when he paid his gambling debt. He also experienced many short-term emotional states. Some had a great deal of social content (such as the disappointment of losing the loan), and others had much less social content (such as the initial fear and shock when hit by another car). These events accumulated, and by the time he got to work on Monday, although he loves his job and his students, he had been experiencing a morose mood for a number of hours.

## CLASSICAL IDEAS ABOUT THE ORIGINS OF EMOTION

Where do emotions come from? Much of the earliest scientific work on emotions focuses on the nonsocial origins of emotions. Although these perspectives are now viewed as quite incomplete, we review them here because they provide some of the essential building blocks used in later understandings of emotions.

The beginnings of the study of emotion are found in the work of Charles Darwin, especially in his influential book, *The Expression of the Emotions in Man and Animals*. At the time, many believed that humans had a number of unique characteristics not shared by other animals—including facial expressions. Darwin, on the other hand, thought that if humans and other animals had common ancestors, there ought to be some similarities in emotional expression as well. His book pointed out fascinating continuities in the emotional expressions made by humans and by other animals, including monkeys and dogs, and described some facial expressions and gestures that Darwin thought were universal across cultures (Darwin, 1998).

The theory Darwin developed about emotional expression was based on these similarities across cultures and species. If some emotions and emotional expressions were universal, then they must be genetically encoded. And if they are genetically encoded, then they must have value that enhances genetic survival. Thus, emotional gestures, for example, were residual expressions related to threat or sexual attraction. The act of gritting and showing our teeth when angry could be a derivative of the act of biting in a battle for survival.

Although Darwin focused on the *expression* of emotions, other early thinkers were more concerned about the *internal sources* of emotions. Lange and James (1922) separately proposed a biological approach to emotions that focused heavily on the physiological responses to stimulus. In this model, the stimulus is followed by the biological reaction, and then the individual cognitively processes the physiological sensation and interprets it as an emotion. The physiological component of the emotional experience (for example, increased blood pressure) helps us to identify the emotion (anger) rather than anger causing the physiological change.

Sigmund Freud (1962) believed that repressed childhood sexual desires were the sources of emotions (principally anxiety and guilt). Although many of Freud's ideas have been discredited over time, he did contribute to the study of emotions in several ways. First, he drew attention to the ways emotions could develop unconsciously. Individuals can hide their feelings from themselves and yet still have these emotions affect the way they think and act. Second, he drew attention to the role an individual's past experience plays in helping to understand the meaning of emotions and the physical sensations that accompany them. Recognizing the past context of emotional reactions was an important step toward understanding the social forces that shape and define emotions.

## FACIAL EXPRESSIONS AND THE UNIVERSALITY OF EMOTIONS

The classic perspectives discussed above point to one of the more persistent questions in the study of emotions: Are some emotions genetically encoded in human biology? If so, are emotions universal human experiences that are similar across cultural and geographic boundaries as well as over historical epochs? When we feel anger, for example, are we feeling the same physiological and psychological sensations people experienced hundreds and thousands of years ago or experience in other parts of the world? Darwin's work hypothesized that at least some (but not all, he believed) emotions are universal—not just among humans but also across some different species—and others have researched these questions in more detail. In this subsequent work on the universality of emotions, scholars have focused a great deal of attention on facial expression of emotion.

### Facial Expressions as Emotions

Many facial expressions we make are involuntary—we perform them without thought or conscious effort. If we are trying to hide our emotions, we often try to look away or hide our face because we know we are involuntarily revealing our feelings (Goffman, 1959b). Other emotion displays are conscious.

For example, we might express an emotion to emphasize a point, to appear friendly and welcoming, or to threaten others.

Social psychologists have used this distinction between involuntary and voluntary facial displays to study the issue of emotional universality. If involuntary facial expressions are (1) produced by the same emotional state across individuals and are (2) identified by many observers as meaning the same thing, then we have reason to believe they are universal expressions of emotions (Ekman, Sorenson, & Friesen, 1969). Furthermore, if these emotional expressions are consistent across all world cultures, then Darwin's view of emotion is supported.

Paul Ekman has worked on this very problem for almost 50 years, finding support for the universality of particular emotional expressions. In his initial studies, Ekman showed photographs of varied facial expressions to thousands of people across a number of different cultures and asked them to identify the related emotions. He found six emotions that were widely recognized across groups, even in a preliterate culture in New Guinea (Ekman & Friesen, 1971, Ekman et al., 1969). These six fundamental emotions were happiness, sadness, surprise, fear, anger, and disgust (Ekman & Friesen, 1975). In the 1980s, a seventh universal emotion emerged: contempt (Ekman & Friesen, 1986).

To move beyond his work that suggested there was widespread agreement on the *interpretation* of emotional expression, Ekman attempted to explore the universality of emotional expression itself. Most notably, he asked members of the Fore, the primitive, preliterate culture he studied in New Guinea, to act out their facial expression in different scenarios, such as "Your child has died and you are sad," or "You are angry and about to fight." After returning to the United States, Ekman asked college students to look at the photographs and film clips he had taken of the Fore acting out these scenarios. Despite vast cultural

**TABLE 6.1** Single-Emotion Judgment Task: Percentage of Participants Within Each Culture Who Chose the Predicted Emotion

| NATION | HAPPINESS | SURPRISE | SADNESS | FEAR | DISGUST | ANGER |
|--------|-----------|----------|---------|------|---------|-------|
| Estonia | 90 | 94 | 86 | 91 | 71 | 67 |
| Germany | 93 | 87 | 83 | 86 | 61 | 71 |
| Greece | 93 | 91 | 80 | 74 | 77 | 77 |
| Hong Kong | 92 | 91 | 91 | 84 | 65 | 73 |
| Italy | 97 | 92 | 81 | 82 | 89 | 72 |
| Japan | 90 | 94 | 87 | 65 | 60 | 67 |
| Scotland | 98 | 88 | 86 | 86 | 79 | 84 |
| Sumatra | 69 | 78 | 91 | 70 | 70 | 70 |
| Turkey | 87 | 90 | 76 | 76 | 74 | 79 |
| United States | 95 | 92 | 92 | 84 | 86 | 81 |

*Source:* Adapted from P. Ekman and W. V. Friesen, "Single Judgment Emotion Task," *Journal of Personality and Social Psychology, 53,* 712–717. Copyright © 1987 by the American Psychological Association. Adapted with permission.

differences across a number of dimensions, the American students were able to accurately identify many of the expressed emotions in the photos, including happiness, anger, disgust/contempt, and sadness. They struggled with surprise and fear, two emotions that Ekman discovered the Fore had trouble distinguishing from one another (Ekman, Friesen, and Ellsworth 2013).

Critics argued that this study still captured the universality of emotion recognition and not of emotional expression. To combat these claims, Ekman did another study where he videotaped Japanese and American participants as they watched an emotional film (Ekman, 1972). He found that the expressions among the two groups throughout the viewing were not only similar but also the same expressions expected based on Ekman's previous research on universal emotion displays. Later research on people who were born blind further supports Ekman's claim. Even though they never visually learned from other people how to express emotions, blind people still smile, laugh, and frown in much the same way as sighted people do (Eibl-Eibesfeldt, 1979).

In an effort to generate a systematic method to help further this research, Ekman and his colleagues (Ekman & Friesen, 1978) developed the Facial Action Coding System (FACS), a methodology to classify visible facial behavior. Each of the fundamental emotions involves movement among a particular configuration of facial muscles. Ekman calls these **action units** (AU) and argues that any facial movement, even those unrelated to emotion, can be described using the action units that produced it. For example, happiness involves the "cheek raiser" (AU 6) and "lip corner puller" (AU 12). These configurations are not only crucial for the expression of each emotion but also what we use to determine the emotions of others. The interpretation of these action units is, in part, why younger people have difficulty interpreting emotion displays in the elderly (Hess, 2013). A study of young people found that those who were shown older people with neutral expressions—with no emotion—were more likely to rate the faces as angry or sad, not because of stereotypes they had about the elderly's emotional states, but because wrinkles cause the mouth to drop or the forehead to crinkle (Garrido et al., 2013).

| Upper Face Action Units | | | | | |
|---|---|---|---|---|---|
| AU 1 | AU 2 | AU 4 | AU 5 | AU 6 | AU 7 |
| Inner Brow Raiser | Outer Brow Raiser | Brow Lowerer | Upper Lid Raiser | Cheek Raiser | Lid Tightener |
| *AU 41 | *AU 42 | *AU 43 | AU 44 | AU 45 | AU 46 |
| Lid Droop | Slit | Eyes Closed | Squint | Blink | Wink |
| Lower Face Action Units | | | | | |
| AU 9 | AU 10 | AU 11 | AU 12 | AU 13 | AU 14 |
| Nose Wrinkler | Upper Lip Raiser | Nasolabial Deepener | Lip Corner Puller | Cheek Puffer | Dimpler |
| AU 15 | AU 16 | AU 17 | AU 18 | AU 20 | AU 22 |
| Lip Corner Depressor | Lower Lip Depressor | Chin Raiser | Lip Puckerer | Lip Stretcher | Lip Funneler |
| AU 23 | AU 24 | *AU 25 | *AU 26 | *AU 27 | AU 28 |
| Lip Tightener | Lip Pressor | Lips Part | Jaw Drop | Mouth Stretch | Lip Suck |

Specific combinations of these action units (AU) have been categorized as emotional expressions that are fundamental across cultures (Ekman & Friesen, 1978). AU 6 ("cheek raiser") and AU 12 ("lip corner puller") combine for an expression of happiness, while AU 1 + AU 4 + AU 15 are a universal expression of sadness. © Paul Ekman Group, LLC

Recent technological developments have made real-time coding of facial expressions by computer software possible (Bartlett et al., 2006). Although this is useful across a variety of domains, including emotions research, the technological advances are of particular interest to advertisers. When computers or smartphones are able to recognize the emotions that users are feeling based on facial expressions, they can measure the efficacy of particular media—whether it be a commercial or movie trailer—at eliciting the desired emotion. They could also offer users advertising content based on their specific emotions (Bosker, 2013). A similar technology is also being developed in collaborations between psychiatrists and computer programmers to help screen, diagnose, and monitor users' mental health states (Glenn & Monteith, 2014).

## Criticisms and Limitations

Although most of the research about the facial expressions of emotions seems to support the notion that some emotions are universal across cultures, the research has its limitations as well. There are two main concerns about the methods. The first concerns the highly contrived circumstances of the experiments and contends that the results are in some ways elicited from the participants (Barrett 2012; Zajonc, 1998). This may be, in part, because Ekman's own background—as a White American—had an unintended effect on his studies' design as well as his respondents' behavior. The second argues that the research that asks participants to identify the emotion expressed using a selection of possible emotion labels is more like a matching or multiple-choice test, which is likely to end up with much higher degrees of agreement than if the participants could give any emotional description they wish to the facial expression. Subsequent research has tried to address these concerns and has generally supported Ekman's findings (see Haidt & Keltner, 1999).

There are two important limitations to Ekman's approach to keep in mind:

First, just because subjects who see a certain facial expression associate it with a particular emotion does not mean that the particular emotion is always expressed that way or even expressed on the face at all. For instance, we might recognize a smiling face as expressing happiness, but we do not smile every time we are happy. A study of sports fans who were watching their favored team win found that even during periods of intense happiness, these individuals often did not smile (Fernández-Dols & Ruiz-Belda, 1995). Furthermore, some people are very good at faking their emotional displays and can smile very convincingly, even when they are angry or sad. Remember the story of Robert, who convinced his coworkers and students that he was in a very good mood. We will explore the selective display of emotion in more detail later in this chapter.

Second, Ekman's studies of emotional universality also examined a very limited set of emotions. Seven emotions (happiness, sadness, anger, fear, disgust, surprise, and contempt) appear repeatedly in emotion studies (Ekman & Friesen, 1986). There is no reason to believe that these are the core emotions. Whereas Ekman's approach focuses on those emotions that have uniquely identifiable facial expressions, other social psychologists who had subjects generate a list of emotions in a free-form way find five categories of basic emotions: love, joy, anger, sadness, and fear (Shaver, Schwartz, Kirson, & O'Connor, 1987).

There may be other universal emotions missing from the list. For example, using Ekman's emotional display approach, Keltner and colleagues have demonstrated that a particular expression of embarrassment is widely recognized by others (Haidt & Keltner, 1999; Keltner, 1996). When we are embarrassed, we tend to avert our gaze, move our heads down, and touch our faces (see photo on p. 157 for an example). Future research may find that additional emotions, beyond the seven currently identified, also have universal recognition.

## CULTURAL DIFFERENCES IN BASIC EMOTIONS AND EMOTIONAL DISPLAY

Not all emotion is universal. Because of the importance of labels in emotion (Thoits, 1989), cultural expression and language influence the experience of emotion. For example, Shaver, Wu, and Schwartz (1992) discerned a unique category called "sad love" in Chinese culture that combined notions about unrequited love and nostalgia. The German culture has a word for vicarious embarrassment (being embarrassed for someone else): *fremdschämen*. Although Americans may understand these emotions and have similar feelings from time to time, they cannot label emotions as such because they lack the language or label to do so. Emotional language is powerful. Labeled emotions are easier to interpret, meaning that individuals are better equipped to address them (perhaps using the emotion to motivate action or to deem it irrelevant) (Kashdan, Barrett, & McKnight, 2015). In other words, having a word for what we are experiencing helps us process that emotion.

## Emotional Socialization

Cultural forces can influence emotion in other ways. For example, cultural values influence how children are socialized to experience and express emotions through a process called **emotional socialization** (Friedlmeier, Corapci, & Cole, 2011; Matsumoto, 1990). In some cultures, children are taught **individualistic emotion competence**. For example, in the United States and many European countries, parents are accepting of "ego-focused" emotions—like anger and pride—that support children's independence. In these cultures, the individual person is seen as a key social unit. Individuals have goals, accomplishments, and behaviors that are separate from group membership, and so parents encourage the experience of emotions related to individualism.

In other cultures, individuals are seen in terms of their membership in their family and are much more affected by the interconnected behaviors, accomplishments, and failures of others in their groups. They are less independent and more interdependent in their social relationships and identities. In these cultures, including many East Asian countries, caregivers cultivate "other-focused" emotions—like sympathy and shame—to build **relational emotion competence**. In preschools, for example, young children are taught to control these emotions and to be interpersonally sensitive. For example, in Japan, teachers foster *omoiyari* (empathy) by having children consider *sabishii-sa* (loneliness) (Hayashi, Karasawa, & Tobin, 2009). The "ego-focused" emotion

expressions valued in other cultures are seen as potentially harmful to relationships and so are therefore discouraged.

As a result of this socialization, there are cultural differences in the experience and expression of happiness. In individualist cultures, individuals are most likely to express happiness about individual achievements and attributes. If the individual is good at something or has a characteristic that causes a positive reaction, then that individual has reason to be happy and to express it. When relational emotion norms are emphasized, on the other hand, individuals express happiness in situations that emphasize their connectedness with others, like positive engagement with a social group (Mesquita & Karasawa, 2002).

These cultural influences also affect the potency of emotional experience. One study comparing individuals in the United States and Japan found that the Japanese experience engaging emotions (friendliness or guilt) more strongly than they experience disengaging emotions (pride or anger). Americans were the opposite, experiencing emotions like pride more potently than guilt (Kitayama, Mesquita, & Karasawa, 2006).

Although most of the research exploring the difference between individualistic and relational (or collectivist) cultural orientations compare Americans, who often value individualism, and Japanese participants, whose Confucian values emphasize relationships, these orientations are seen across cultural contexts. For example, interdependence is high in Eskimo culture because groups depend heavily on the relationships among group members for survival. Their emotion norms reflect this, with an emphasis on group harmony and an aversion to anger (Briggs, 1970). Australia, on the other hand, emphasizes autonomy and assertiveness (Eid & Diener, 2001). As a result, anger and the expression of it are seen as a normal part of healthy social interaction and a way to signal assertiveness (Safdar et al., 2009).

## Emotional Display

The expression of anger and other emotions is related to **display rules** (Ekman, 1972). These cultural norms direct us to modify our facial expressions to ensure they are appropriate for the social situation. Display rules are typically learned in childhood and sometimes become habits that automatically control facial muscles. Display rules may modify facial expressions of emotion in one of several ways. They may require (1) greater intensity in the expression of an emotion, (2) less intensity in the expression of an emotion, (3) complete neutralization of the emotional expression, or (4) masking one emotion with a different one.

Perhaps as a result of more subdued emotional expression, research finds that the Japanese are more sensitive to indirect emotional cues than people in the United States. In one study, research subjects were presented with a curious mix of words with unpleasant meaning that were read using positive vocal cues and pleasant words conveyed using negative emotional cues. The results demonstrated that Japanese participants were much more attentive to the vocal cues, whereas the Americans were more attentive to the words themselves (Ishii, Reyes, & Kitayama, 2003). Thus, whereas collectivist cultures might work at reducing the expression and interpretation of negative emotions, they are actually more sensitive to them than those from individualistic cultures.

Looking across cultures, we can witness an incredible range in the expression of grief and mourning. In almost all cultures, mourning a death involves sadness and tears. Given the wide variety of funeral and bereavement practices, it can be difficult to draw clear distinctions among the practices of collectivist and individualistic cultures. However, some of the most dramatic cultural mourning acts are associated with social groups in which there are strong interdependent relationships. These practices can range from elaborate wailing episodes to the suicide of a widow or

widower. Individualistic societies view these kinds of practices as extremely strange and instead carry a belief that although mourning and grief after a death is normal, there are limits. Mourners who cannot get over a death are considered unstable and may end up being isolated until they can recover.

These cultural differences in the experience and expression of emotions complicate theories about the universality of basic emotions. For the most part, social psychologists agree that some emotions are universal and that they are physiologically connected to distinctive facial expressions, and yet the expression of even the most primary emotions is heavily influenced by cultural norms and can vary a great deal from place to place. If people are to communicate emotions effectively in everyday interaction, they must learn and use the display rules of their own culture. In addition, some emotions are far more conditioned on social processes than others. Social psychologists who study emotion are much more focused on these kinds of social-emotional processes than on the biological links.

## THE SOCIAL PSYCHOLOGY OF EMOTIONS

A social psychological approach to emotions moves beyond the notion that emotions are simply natural reactions to things that happen in the world around us. The above discussions demonstrate that although some aspects of emotion may be biologically hardwired, others are influenced by cultural norms and experiences. Social psychologists also argue that much of our emotional experience is a matter of interpretation. When we experience a physiological reaction that is part of an emotion, before we can decide which emotion is involved, we have to interpret the physical sensation in its social context.

Consider the feeling of being slightly nauseous and having sweaty palms. There are

## BOX 6.1  Research Update: Social Status and Anger

There are also differences on patterns of emotions within cultures, but across different social groups. For many years, social psychologists who studied emotions posited contradictory expectations about the relationship between social status (based on dimensions like class, education, or occupation) and the experience of anger. Some researchers argued that status and anger are inversely related, while others believed that status and anger are positively related.

There are a number of social psychological explanations for an inverse relationship, where people of high status experience less anger than those of lower status. To put it another way, why higher-status people would experience more positive emotion. For example, higher-status individuals are less likely to face obstacles than lower-status individuals (Kemper, 1978), they are viewed more positively and are therefore more influential in interactions (Lucas & Lovaglia, 1998), and they are more likely to have been socialized by their parents and others to suppress negative emotion (Hochschild, 1983).

There are also convincing reasons for why the reverse might be true and anger and status are positively related, with higher-status people experiencing anger more, and not less, often. Because anger is an emotion that signals mastery and dominance, it is seen as legitimate for higher-status people to employ it in interaction (Ridgeway & Johnson, 1990). This makes high-status people more likely to use it more frequently than those of lower status. Higher-status people are also more inclined to blame others if they are unable to get their way and that could contribute to increases in both the experience and expression of anger (Conway, DiFazio, & Mayman 1999).

Rather than position these two accounts against one another, two researchers combined them in the same analysis and considered them in tandem (Collett & Lizardo, 2010).

The results suggest that these findings from previous research are complementary rather than competing. Individuals at both ends of the status hierarchy (those who are either very high or quite low on occupational status) are more likely to experience anger than those who are in the middle. In fact, individuals at the top and bottom of the status ladder experience anger, on average, 36 more days a year than those in the middle. What may be most interesting, however, is that the two status groups differ on the type of anger they experience and the likely cause of it. Lower-status individuals are more likely to experience anger that is trans-situational. It endures across social situations and is due to chronic stressors in the day-to-day experience of those at the bottom of the status ladder. In other words, the anger is continuous and often directed at impersonal targets like objects or circumstances, rather than other people. Unfortunately, without a tangible object to direct their anger toward, it is difficult for lower-status individuals to discharge and therefore tends to endure. High-status people, on the other hand, experience encounter-based anger. They get angry with specific others, most often people of lower status than themselves who fail to afford them the status they feel they deserve. They are more likely to get angry at relatively unfamiliar others in specific situations. Because they are able to focus and direct their anger in a specific situation, high-status people's anger is likely to dissipate more quickly than the anger of lower-status individuals.

In sum, while rates of anger may be the same for those of high and low status, social psychological research suggests that the causes and the consequences of this emotion can be quite different.

*Source:* Collett & Lizardo, 2010.

many potential interpretations of these physical symptoms. Perhaps you are a first-year medical student feeling disgusted upon seeing your first cadaver. Maybe you are grief stricken at the unexpected death of a cherished pet. Then again, perhaps you are excited about an upcoming date. Or it could be that you are nervously heading into an exam for which you are unprepared. When we think more closely about emotions, we find that they are often just plausible explanations for our physiological reactions, and how we interpret them depends very much on what is happening in our social world. To the degree that we are actively experiencing, interpreting, and constructing our social world, we are also interpreting and constructing our emotions.

## Theories of Emotion

An early theory on the social roots of emotions was Schachter's **two-factor theory of emotion** (Schachter, 1964). This theory proposes that emotional experience is the result of the following two-step sequence:

1. An event in the environment produces a physiological reaction.
2. We notice the physiological reaction and search for an appropriate explanation.

In an early study of two-factor theory of emotion (Schachter & Singer, 1962), researchers gave students an injection of epinephrine, a drug that produces mild physiological arousal. The experimenters told one group of participants that this injection would probably cause them to experience a pounding heart, flushed face, and trembling. They told a second group nothing about the drug's effects. All students then waited with a confederate who, though appearing to be another participant, was actually employed by the researchers. Depending on the experimental treatment, the confederate behaved either euphorically (for example,

shooting crumpled paper at a waste basket, flying paper airplanes, playing with a hula hoop) or angrily (for example, reacting with hostility to items on a questionnaire and finally tearing it up).

According to the theory, students in the informed group would not need to seek an explanation for their own arousal because they knew their symptoms were drug induced. Students in the uninformed group, however, lacked an adequate explanation for their symptoms and thus would need to search the environment for cues to help them label their feelings. The results confirmed these predictions. Students in the uninformed group adopted the label for their arousal suggested by their environment. That is, those who waited with the euphoric confederate described themselves as happy, whereas those who waited with the angry confederate described themselves as angry. The self-descriptions of the informed group, however, were largely unaffected by the confederate's behavior.

Inherent in this theory is the assumption that physical arousal is a general state. In other words, arousal does not substantially differ from one emotional state to another. Because one arousal state is not physiologically distinguishable from another, virtually any emotion can be attached to the arousal state. Students experiencing the same physiological reaction to the drug could interpret that reaction as either happiness or anger. Which emotion becomes attributed to the arousal depends on the context.

Numerous later studies have expanded these findings to additional emotions (Kelley & Michela, 1980). They show that people who are unaware of the true cause of their physiological arousal can be induced to view themselves as anxious, guilty, amused, or sexually excited by placing them in environments that suggest these emotions (Dutton & Aron, 1974; Zillmann, 1978). Environmental conditions strongly influence people's labeling of their physiological arousal.

Other research suggests that the emotional label sometimes even precedes the awareness of arousal (Leventhal, 1984; Pennebaker, 1980). Our social context suggests that we should be experiencing a particular emotion, and only then do we search our bodily sensations for signs that will verify our belief. If environmental cues give us reason to believe we are angry, we attend to our flushed face and racing heart and verify our anger. If the cues suggest we are happy, we attend to our feelings of alertness and trembling and confirm our happiness. At any given time, our physiological state may afford evidence to support several emotional labels. Once the emotional label is applied, it can induce further physiological arousal that provides additional confirmation of the emotional label we have applied. Put another way, our expectations can help generate that affective response.

As the study of emotions has developed, researchers have come to better understand the centrality of the social situation in defining emotions. As the two-factor theory posits and the empirical research on the topic demonstrates, our immediate emotional reactions are products of internal physical processes that must also be recognized and interpreted in light of the present social context. This is true of not only immediate emotional reactions that are tied to arousal but also complex, enduring feelings like love and jealousy. These emotional states last even after physical arousal has passed (Gordon, 1990). Each is a pattern of sensations, emotions, actions, and cultural beliefs that are appropriate to a social relationship.

Peggy Thoits's (1989) *four-factor model* described in the beginning of this chapter expanded Schachter's two-factor theory. In her model, in addition to situational cues and a physiological response, to experience an emotion there must also be emotional expression and a label for the particular emotion. In other words, in Thoits's model someone's heightened heart rate (physiological response) at the sight

of a bear (situational cues) is recognized as fear (label for the emotion) and their raised brow, wide eyes, and scream (expressions of fear) demonstrate that fear to themself and others.

**The Importance of Others in Emotional Experiences.** At times, it is people in our social circles who define our emotions for us. Like us, they consider physiological reactions, social contexts, and our behavior to determine how we might be feeling and then communicate this to us. On the first day of kindergarten, a young child might describe to their father that they feel strange. When he asks them what they mean by strange, they would try to describe their physical symptoms or emotions but may not have acquired the cognitive or linguistic skills to say "lightheaded" or "anxious" or even to interpret the physiological arousal as an indicator of an emotional state. If they describe the feeling as a bee buzzing through their body, from up in their head to down in their stomach, their father would likely explain to them that they are feeling excited or nervous and that such an emotion is completely normal in a new situation. From then onward, the young child would understand that the buzzing response should be interpreted as a sign of nervousness or excitement and that those types of emotions are expected when they try something new.

This emotional socialization occurs throughout our lives. In a study of a university-based evangelical Christian religious group, Amy Wilkins (2008a, 2008b) found that members of the group claimed to be happier than non-Christians. Rather than see this emotion as a positive mental health effect stemming from participation in the group, Wilkins saw it as originating in the culture of the group. She found that members of "Unity" (the pseudonym Wilkins gave the group) often talked about emotion, particularly happiness, and new members were taught to think of themselves as happy and learned how to actively produce that emotional response. Group members linked emotion to religiosity. They taught recruits that an important part of signaling a connection with God and differentiating themselves from nonmembers was experiencing elation. This prompted new members to both interpret their physiological responses as signs of happiness and to work to elicit positive feelings so they could feel a sense of belongingness and, thus, separate themselves from non-Christians.

**Context in Interpreting the Emotions of Others.** Just as individuals use context to determine their own emotional states, they use context to determine how others are feeling. In fact, context is routinely encoded in the perception of emotion (Barrett & Kensinger, 2010). Social psychologists conducted an experiment where they asked participants to determine either the specific emotion or the affective significance (positive, negative, or neutral) of a facial expression that was coupled with a context. Participants who were asked to label an emotional expression were much more likely to remember the context (a scene like a desert or a coffee shop) than those who were only asked to determine the affective significance of an expression. In other words, the facial expressions themselves provided all the information that the participants needed to determine general affect. However, to determine the particular emotion, participants relied on context clues and, therefore, were more likely to remember them when prompted by experimenters.

## Emotion Work

There are times when individuals want to either experience or express emotions that they might not currently feel, particularly if they want to elicit emotions that are consistent with the social context. Have you ever tried to psych yourself up for a performance, sporting event, or examination? Have you ever forced yourself

to have a good time at a party even though you were tired? Maybe you have tried to feel grateful for a gift that you really didn't like or displayed a stiff upper lip despite severe disappointment. These are all instances of **emotion work**—attempts to change the intensity or quality of feelings to bring them into line with the requirements of the occasion (Hochschild, 1983).

We manage emotions in two ways: through evocation and suppression. In some situations, it is advantageous to evoke an emotion that is currently absent or at least beyond what one is really feeling. A mother who is tired after a long day in the office might put on her happy face when she picks her twins up from daycare. Although the mother might be glad to see her children, she will work to smile wider and express more excitement and cheer than she is actually feeling to appear involved and interested. This may be, in part, because she thinks that a good mother should be very happy to see her children and she wants to live up to that expectation for herself, her children, and the daycare workers. At other times, emotion work (also called emotion management) involves suppressing an emotion that is seen as inappropriate. A medical student who is examining a patient for the first time might suppress their disgust, embarrassment, or arousal so as to appear professional in front of the patient and their adviser (Smith & Kleinman, 1989).

Emotion work occurs because we are subject to **feeling rules**—rules that dictate what people with our role identities ought to feel in a given situation. If we are receiving a gift, the feeling rule is that we should feel grateful. If we are at a party, we should be having fun. Social psychologists have attempted to identify feeling rules by presenting scenarios to subjects and asking about appropriate or expected emotions. Many times, there was a high degree of agreement about which emotions should be present in certain social situations—evidence that there indeed are emotional expectations or feeling rules (Heise & Calhan, 1995). If our feelings are not in line with the current feeling rules and we were to unintentionally express our true feelings, we would be violating the norms of the situation. Therefore, we try to not only express the right feeling but also *feel* the right feelings. Efforts to change the experience of emotion stem, in part, from a desire to be consistent. It causes dissonance to feel sad while smiling on the outside.

To examine this phenomenon of intentional efforts to alter the experience of emotion, Arlie Hochschild conducted a study of flight attendants (1983). Generally speaking, airline flight attendants are expected to feel calm and cheerful as they interact with passengers. But suppose a group of flight attendants has been working for ten hours, serving hundreds of people on three different flights. Fatigue and irritation may be the main feelings they are experiencing, but they must work directly on their own emotions to evoke feelings of cheerfulness and to suppress feelings of irritation. In fact, Hochschild showed that this kind of emotion work—to display upbeat, positive, energetic personas—was a fundamental requirement of the job and flight attendants were trained to perform it.

There are two types of emotion management strategies: surface acting and deep acting. Surface acting only changes the expression of emotion (smiling and exchanging pleasantries). Recall our story about Rob the kindergarten teacher at the beginning of the chapter. Although he did not feel like it at all, feeling rules demanded that he act energetic and cheerful in front of his class. Deep acting, on the other hand, transforms our emotional state (Larson & Yao, 2005). Deep acting can occur through behavioral or cognitive effort. To evoke suitable emotions and suppress unsuitable ones we may simply adopt an appropriate

Mixed martial arts competitors engage in emotion work to cultivate a convincing manhood. They not only suppress fear of injury, pain, or embarrassment, but also evoke confidence with their bodies and language to attempt to intimidate competitors (Vaccaro, Schrock, & McCabe, 2011). © Nicholas Piccillo/Shutterstock

physical posture. Slumping over in a chair is unlikely to evoke feelings of cheerfulness, but standing up straight and walking briskly can. We might also take a series of deep breaths or begin to breathe quickly to produce the required feeling. Taking a more cognitive than behavioral approach, we might imagine a situation that produces the required feeling. In a strategy that combines behavioral and cognitive strategies, flight attendants may take a deep breath to relax and reduce irritation, while imagining how good it will feel to be home tonight to increase energy.

Actively pursuing these strategies allows us to gain some control over our feelings. In fact, research has found that these portrayals of emotions can change the actual emotions the person is feeling under the surface of their performance. For example, Hochschild found that flight attendants who appeared to be happy and agreeable even while fatigued and irritable tended to become happier as they continued the act. This is similar to Rob, who found that the longer he acted cheerful for his class, the more cheerful he actually became.

Emotional performances influence affect in a number of ways. First, according to the **facial feedback hypothesis**, our facial muscles not only reflect emotion, but can also influence the one we feel (Adelmann & Zajonc, 1989). This is why people will sometimes tell others who are down to smile, as they may actually begin to feel better. Second, we may begin to feel better when we act happy because of cognitive consistency effects (see Chapters 7 and 8), in which we are motivated to bring our attitudes in line with our behaviors. If we are smiling, we want our attitudes to be in line with that positive emotion. Third, we can also begin to feel better because when we act cheerfully, people in turn interact with us in the way they would with a cheerful person. Their behavior reflects positively on us and can enhance our mood.

When emotion work is done for pay and the emotion is one of the important goods a worker is producing—such is the case, in no uncertain terms, for flight attendants—it is called **emotional labor**. Research suggests that the demands for emotion work—and occupations that require emotional labor—are not evenly distributed. Those who have higher status in a social situation have more freedom in expressing their emotions. A boss or a parent can easily express anger or irritability in circumstances in which lower-level employees and children are expected to follow the feeling rules more closely. In effect, a person's status allows different feeling rules. Emotion work can also become a commodity, in that people who are proficient at it can be rewarded. For example, employers can demand emotion work from their employees as a part of their job requirements. Since Hochschild's seminal research on flight attendants and bill collectors, many other social psychologists have examined emotion management in workplaces such as Disneyworld and Disneyland (Reyers & Matusitz, 2012; Van Maanen, 1991), medical schools and offices (Larson & Yao, 2005; Smith & Kleinman, 1989), and police departments (Schaible & Gecas, 2010).

It can be taxing to manage emotions day in and day out. Workers whose jobs require significant emotional labor are prone to emotional exhaustion and job burnout. However, the types of strategies workers employ have different effects. Surface acting—which is more common in sales or service work and other industries where interactions with customers are brief—tends to produce greater job-related stress than deep acting does (Grandey, 2003). There is also variation within the service sector and across cultures. In the United States, where "service with a smile" is an expectation, service workers tend to be more dissatisfied than in cultures where emotion management is a choice rather than a requirement, including France and China (Allen, Diefendorff, & Ma, 2014).

Emotion work is not always effective. **Emotional deviance** (Thoits, 1990) is when we are unable to effectively manage our emotions and instead project an emotion that is inappropriate (or too high or low an intensity of an emotion). In 2010, a flight attendant engaged in emotional deviance when he lost his patience with a passenger who ignored his instructions and, in doing so, had accidentally struck the flight attendant with a piece of luggage. Rather than make light of what happened—or smile and brush off the incident, as one might expect from a flight attendant—Steven Slater took to the plane's public address system and angrily cursed out the flier. Although some emotional deviance is expected in social life, persistent or pronounced emotional deviance can be seen as a sign of mental illness (Thoits, 1985). While his behavior may have stemmed in part from the negative implications of emotional labor, a subsequent mental health evaluation found that Slater was suffering from a clinical disorder and had a series of alcohol-abuse problems that also likely contributed to his inability to regulate his emotional reaction that day.

## SOCIAL EMOTIONS

Although many emotions have both social and nonsocial components, there are certain emotions that simply cannot be understood or even defined without reference to the social world. These emotions are called **social emotions**, and they are defined as emotions that (1) involve an awareness of oneself in the social context, (2) emerge out of interaction with at least one other actor, and (3) are often experienced in reference to some kind of societal standard (Barrett, 1995; Stets, 2003). For many social emotions, it is necessary to place oneself in the role of others to experience the emotion (Shott, 1979).

To understand this rather complex definition, think about the notion of empathy. To experience emotional empathy, you first have to be aware that you have some kind of connection to a person who is experiencing an emotion. For example, when we feel empathy

for someone who is feeling pain, we are at least partially recognizing that we are involved and perhaps even responsible for easing the person's pain. (The notion that helping can reduce empathic suffering is explored in greater detail in Chapter 11.) Second, there must be someone else in the social environment who is experiencing some kind of emotion in order for us to experience empathy. By definition, then, empathy is social. Third, when one experiences empathy, one is reminded of society's standards. If the object of our empathy is feeling pain, we may evaluate, based on societal standards, our own obligation to intervene to ease their pain. If their pain is minimal and the risk of harm to ourselves is great, we are not obligated to intervene and, therefore, may experience minimal empathy.

Parents experience strong empathic responses to the emotional states of their children. They find it easy both to recognize distress in their offspring and to put themselves in the place of their children. © iofoto/123rtf

In this section, we will examine the social bases of five emotions to illustrate how important social interaction is in experiencing and defining some of our most important social processes. There are many other social emotions, but here we focus on guilt, shame, love, jealousy, and embarrassment.

## Guilt

We feel guilt when we judge that we have done something we should not have done. Guilt is, therefore, inherently evaluative. We are not necessarily a bad person if we have done something that causes us guilt, but we are certainly less good than we could be. Where do the standards come from that we use to judge ourselves? They come from others in our social groups or environment. Guilt, therefore, involves a self-reflexive judgment in which we see ourselves through other people's eyes. When we feel guilt, we are engaged in an appraisal of ourselves using standards that we may have accepted but were constructed by others. Guilt also implies action. Just like so many social psychological processes, guilt involves an uncomfortable feeling. Individuals who feel guilt need to do something to eliminate it so they can return to a more pleasant psychological state. They attempt to engage in some kind of reparative activity so they can be forgiven by someone who has the power to release them from guilt (Stets, 2003). Thus, not only is the negative emotion itself inherently social, so is the method of dealing with it.

Returning for a moment to our story about Rob, the kindergarten teacher, suppose in his frustration he had blown up at his teacher's aide for not getting the children settled for story time. After yelling at his aide, Rob may feel guilty for the unnecessary outburst, which made the aide feel underappreciated; the aide may feel guilty for not following classroom procedures properly; and if the children observed the outburst, they might also feel guilty for not getting into the story-time

circle quickly enough. In each instance of guilt, there is a social standard of behavior (for Rob, for the aide, and for the children) that has been violated. Each guilty party can reduce or eliminate the guilt by, for example, apologizing to the offended party and receiving forgiveness.

Guilt has a number of social functions, the first of which is socialization (Hoffman, 2001). When a parent disapproves of a child's behavior, the result is a feeling of discomfort. If the parent can then induce the child to realize that the source of the discomfort is the child's own behavior, then the child will feel a sense of guilt. The child can then be taught to avoid the guilt by avoiding the behavior. Closely related, people can use guilt as a method to get what they want from others. If they can induce others to feel guilty about doing or not doing something, they may be able to change the target's behavior (Stets, 2003). Partners can use guilt as a pressure strategy for sexual coercion (Hartwick, Desmarais, & Hennig, 2007) and panhandlers use various methods of making their targets feel guilty for refusing to help them (Basil, Ridgway, & Basil, 2008).

Finally, although we often think guilt has a negative impact on social relationships, social psychologists have found that it actually functions to support and strengthen relationships. It does this in two ways. First, it distributes the negative consequences of a bad social interaction. If I do something that hurts you, you are bearing all of the costs of the social exchange. But if I feel guilty about it, I also have to bear some costs—so guilt evens out the suffering to some degree (Baumeister, Stillwell, & Heatherton, 1994). Second, when we feel guilt and act to correct whatever problem caused the guilt, we are sending a powerful message to those who we harmed—we are telling them that we value the relationship and that we don't want our own poor behavior to damage it. If Rob apologizes to his classroom aide, his actions may actually endear him more to her than if he had never yelled at her in the first place.

## Shame

A counterpart to the emotion of guilt is shame. Although both emotions share certain characteristics—a person feeling either of these emotions has committed some kind of offense against another—shame is a much deeper and longer-lasting state than guilt. When we feel guilty, it is typically tied to a single incident that is easy to identify and oftentimes has an easily identifiable response that will relieve the guilt. If, for example, you steal something and feel guilty, you can return what you stole or replace it. Shame, however, is not so much about an incident or transgression as it is about how you evaluate yourself as a person. When you feel shame, there is a deep sense of the self not as someone who has just done something wrong but as someone who is a bad person (Thoits, 2011). There is something wrong with your intrinsic character, and it is not something that can be easily rectified (Babcock & Sabini, 1990). As a result, the response to shame is not as simple as repairing the damage done to the social relationship. The more likely response to shame is to flee. Shamed individuals want to run away from the situation, hide from everyone, or just disappear completely (Barrett, 1995; Tangney, 1995). Given that shame threatens the very core of an individual's self-regard, it is a very intense emotional experience—much more so than that of guilt.

Because shame is such an intense emotion, people are all the more motivated to try to escape it. One way of reducing shame is to escape the blame for the problems that caused it. Those who have been shamed sometimes try to accomplish this by blaming others. The result can be a volatile "shame–anger cycle" (Scheff & Retzinger, 2001) that escalates tension and shame. Imagine that a woman, Karla, insults her husband, Leo, by telling him that he is a worthless human being, as evidenced by his repeated failure to hold down a job. If Leo were to accept this appraisal, he would

become ashamed. Escaping shame is a powerful motivator, so Leo responds by getting angry and insulting Karla with a retaliatory slur that implies she is the reason he has lost his job. He claims that he had to leave work early many times to deal with their son because she was an incompetent mother. Each partner now feels shame and sees the other person as the source of the problem. Shame leads to more anger through a retaliatory cycle. Oftentimes this is exactly the kind of interaction pattern that leads to intimate partner abuse and violence.

## Love

Despite our immediate sense that love is a happy, positive emotion, it is important to remember that it is not always so. As discussed earlier, in the section on culture and emotion, some Asian cultures actually identify a separate emotion that might be called "sad love," which usually involves some unrequited feelings of love. Nevertheless, most people experience love as a positive, mood-enhancing emotion.

Love is covered in greater detail in Chapter 14 (Interpersonal Attraction and Relationships), including different types of love that are experienced across a wide range of intensity. It is a complex emotion or, more appropriately, a set of related emotions. Love is, however, an inherently social emotion as it involves at least two people—one who loves and one who is the object of the love. Growing up, we learn that to love someone implies a willingness to sacrifice something for the object of our affection (Nikolajeva, 2012).

The type of love involved and the experience of it depends very heavily on the relationship to the object of love and the reaction to any expression of love. Friends have different experiences of love than spouses, teenage boyfriends and girlfriends have different experiences of love than a couple who has been married for 30 years. Even within a single loving relationship, there can be significant asymmetry. A parent, for example, shares love with a child, but the adult's experience of love is considerably different from the child's. The differences in all of these experiences of love are not derived from some kind of natural reaction but rather from the different expectations associated with the role of parent, child, boyfriend, girlfriend, husband, wife, best friend, and so on. Parents have responsibilities for the growth, development, and well-being of their children that indicate a caretaking element in their concept of parental love, an element their children do not share. Other role demands produce very different conceptions

## BOX 6.2 Finding Emotion in Love Songs

Taylor Swift, who is perhaps one of the most successful musicians of the last decade, has earned quite a reputation when it comes to love and heartbreak. Many of her most popular songs provide vivid descriptions of her experiences in relationships—whether before they started, during their ups and downs, or after they have ended. Swift is not alone in singing about love and loss. In fact, 75 percent of the Top 40 songs since the 1930s have been love songs (Scheff, 2011). In his 2011 book, *What's Love Got to Do With It? Emotion and Relationships in Popular Songs*, social psychologist Thomas Scheff describes how love songs reflect, reinforce, and shape listeners' definitions of love. Take Swift's "You Are In Love" (*1989*, 2014) as an example. After describing daily life with a boyfriend, Swift writes:

> One night he wakes, strange look on his face
> Pauses, then says, you're my best friend
> And you knew what it was, he is in love

In doing so, she reinforces the idea that romantic love is not only about attraction, but also about commitment and understanding that we expect among friends and family. In other lyrics from the same song, she paints a picture of what "true love" looks like and how it feels. Other love songs, whether romantic or platonic, demonstrate similar themes.

Of course, many love songs are not about "true love" at all. Instead, they describe feelings of infatuation. These songs allude to love at first sight, where only a single glance is needed to fall deeply in love. We see this in "Everything Has Changed" (*Red*, 2012) when Swift describes everything changing with someone saying hello and introducing himself, as he held the door for her:

> All I know is you held the door
> You'll be mine and I'll be yours
> All I know since yesterday is everything has changed

In many of these songs, the object of affection does not reciprocate. They might not even realize that someone is interested in them. Swift details this experience in her 2008 hit "You Belong With Me" (*Fearless*, 2008). Interestingly, most infatuation songs leave the ending of the story ambiguous, letting the listener imagine it as either a passing moment or the beginning of a love affair.

Love songs also introduce other emotions that are tied to love or are meant to somehow signal or explain such feelings, including pride, fear or anxiety, grief, shame, and anger. Relationships that generate a sense of connectedness and satisfaction demonstrate pride. We see this when Swift speaks of how she and another are in tune with each other, despite their troubles, in "Style" (*1989*, 2014):

> You got that James Dean daydream look in your eye
> And I got that red lip, classic thing that you like
> And when we go crashing down, we come back every time
> 'Cause we never go out of style, we never go out of style

of love, not only in different types of relationships but also across cultures.

## Jealousy

Jealousy, a negative emotional reaction we feel when something good happens to someone else that may or may not be tied to love, is also an inherently social emotion (Ben-Ze'ev, 2000). Because an individual cannot, by definition, experience jealousy without the participation of someone else, the emotional state is dependent on the social context. One situation that often produces

On the flip side of pride is shame. Shame is inherent in songs that describe a sense of disconnection, loneliness, or unworthiness. Swift shares her own experience of the shame that stems from unequal investment in a relationship and in each other in "Come In With the Rain" from *Fearless* (2008):

I've got you down, I know you by heart
And you don't even know where I start

Shame is not the only negative emotion in love songs. In a line from "You Are In Love" that precedes the segment described earlier in this box, Swift talks of letting go of "your fears and your ghosts." In doing so, she acknowledges some of the negative affect that can accompany the thrill of love. As a public figure who wears her heart on her sleeve and spends much of her time in the public sphere, these are experiences that Swift knows well. In "I Know Places" (*1989*, 2014) she sings:

It's a bad sign, bad sign
Something happens when everybody finds out
See the vultures circling dark clouds
Love's a fragile little flame, it could burn out

Love songs like this one that focus on fear, whether centrally or in passing, allude to anticipation of rejection or loss and the shame and embarrassment that result from those situations.

The majority of love songs are not about love or infatuation at all, but are instead about heartbreak (Scheff, 2011). Grief and anger are two prominent emotions in these songs. Songs focused on grief include themes of loss, rejection, tears, or sadness. Swift expressed her sadness at losing someone she cared for and a sense of shame from feeling disconnected:

Hey, all you had to do was stay
Had me in the palm of your hand
Then, why'd you have to go and lock me out
    when I let you in
    ("All You Had to Do Was Stay," *1989*, 2014)

Finally, in one of her most popular songs—and a song purportedly about a friend rather than a love, demonstrating how these themes of love songs apply to both romantic and platonic relationships—Swift sings of her anger:

Did you think we'd be fine? Still got scars on
    my back from your knife
So don't think it's in the past, these kinda
    wounds they last and they last.
Now did you think it all through? All these
    things will catch up to you
And time can heal but this won't, so if you're
    coming my way, just don't
    ("Bad Blood," *1989*, 2014)

Anger in songs often manifests as desire for revenge or hope for pain. Because anger is one of the most policed emotions, many love songs soften it with sarcasm. Perhaps this is what Swift is doing in "Blank Space" (*1989*, 2014) when she writes:

Got a long list of ex-lovers
They'll tell you I'm insane.
'Cause you know I love the players
And you love the game

jealousy is when a relationship moves from a dyad (group of two) to a triad (group of three), causing a person to lose a significant relationship with someone they were close to. The third person, who may threaten an individual's relationship with the second person, is the object of the jealousy of the first person. A good example of this dynamic is the change that a couple experiences with the birth or adoption of a child. The mother may sense that the father loves the baby more than he loves her, and she may feel somehow displaced and, therefore, jealous of the baby. Later on, if the child grows close to the mother, the father may feel envious of the bond the two of them share and become jealous of the mother. Research on siblings shows that toddlers direct jealousy toward one another when a mother shifts her attention from playing with one child to the other (Draghi-Lorenz, Reddy, & Costall, 2001). This kind of dynamic can be observed in virtually any kind of paired relationship. Breakups of a romantically involved couple are another example. If the girlfriend, for example, leaves the relationship and starts dating a new partner, the girlfriend who is left behind may feel jealous of the new girlfriend.

If social emotions exist for a reason, what could be the functions of jealousy? We typically think of jealousy as being a destructive force—a green-eyed monster—that we must struggle to control. But if jealousy is really born of social forces and is not completely natural, it must have some useful purpose. One function may be to draw oneself back into a social interaction. When we express jealousy, we are signaling to others in the environment that we have been left out, that we want to be included, and that they are in some way responsible for helping to reintegrate us into the social relationship. A child who expresses jealousy when his mother is attending to some other child is sending the message that he wants to interact with her. If she responds, as parents often do, by increasing her interaction

with him—perhaps picking him up or drawing him into activities with the other child—then the expression of jealousy has been rewarded and, thereby, reinforced.

Jealousy can also signal to others in the environment that the jealous person has some kind of claim on the object in question (be it a person or a physical item). If, for example, a young girl expresses jealousy that her brother is getting to play with a favored toy, it would indicate that she is making a claim on the toy: she has a right to play with it, she deserves more time with the toy and he deserves less, and she wants to exercise that claim by playing with the toy. Thus, jealousy and envy help to establish turf boundaries around objects and around people.

## Embarrassment

Another social emotion is embarrassment—an uncomfortable feeling of mortification or exposure. We become embarrassed when we fail to live up to an image or identity that we are trying to claim to an audience. For example, a math professor will likely experience embarrassment if they make a simple calculation error on the board in front of the class. The embarrassment the professor feels is inherently social because it stems from their imagination of how they appear to students who realize the mistake. They may worry that the mistake threatens students' impressions of the professor's competence as a math professor, thus threatening the professor's identity. Lacking the skills necessary for an identity is only one source of embarrassment. As covered in Chapter 5, embarrassment can also come from a violation of privacy norms or awkwardness or lack of poise. Because of our ability to imagine ourselves in the eyes of others, we can feel embarrassed even when we are alone as we take the perspective of the generalized other or think about what others might think of us if they were to witness what we had done.

Embarrassment is also social because it is contagious; an additional source of embarrassment is the embarrassment of others. In a study of empathic embarrassment, groups of women observed another woman perform either a very embarrassing or an ambiguous task (Marcus, Wilson, & Miller, 1996). Most observers reported feeling embarrassed as they observed another perform the embarrassing task. Some observers of the innocuous task also reported feeling embarrassed, suggesting that people vary in their readiness to perceive emotion in others (empathy). Indeed, individuals vary a great deal in their ability to read, understand, and respond to the emotional cues and behavior of others. Those who are skilled in this process are said to have high **emotional intelligence** (see Box 6.3). High levels of empathy and emotional intelligence increase the likelihood that we will experience vicarious (or empathic) embarrassment.

Because of our ability to experience others' embarrassment, we work to help others save face in interaction. In a study of street-corner ciphers (impromptu rap sessions), Lee (2009) found that if a performer seemed at risk for messing up during a freestyle performance, others would engage in collateral face-saving. If a rapper "fell off" and lost rhythm, someone else would "jump in" and begin rapping to keep the flow going in the cipher. Other onlookers would also use strategies to encourage the audience to turn their attention toward the person who jumped in. Both these tactics help minimize the embarrassment experienced by the rapper who fell off and the vicarious embarrassment of the onlookers.

Another indication of the social nature of embarrassment is the way it maps onto social organization (Goffman, 1956). For example, we are more likely to experience embarrassment in groups rather than when we are alone or with just one other person (Parrott & Smith, 1991; Tangney, Miller, Flicker, & Barlow, 1996). Embarrassment is also more common when we are among unfamiliar others, whose favorable impressions of us might seem more dependent on our performances in any

one social situation. Falling short of an identity claim among family or close friends, on the other hand, is less likely to cause embarrassment because they would have more information to draw from in judging us. We are also more likely to experience embarrassment in front of a diverse audience than in a more homogeneous one. For example, teenagers are much more likely to experience embarrassment among a mixed-gender group than if they are with their same gender peers (Lizardo & Collett, 2013).

## SUMMARY

**Defining Emotions.** Affect is a general label that encompasses any kind of evaluation of an object. Affect varies in direction, intensity, and activity. Emotions are short-lived reactions to stimuli involving cognitive reactions, physiological reactions, expressive gesturing, and a label we associate with a cluster of the first three elements. Today's social psychologists use the term "sentiment" to refer to longer-term emotional states directed at a person or object. Moods are general psychological conditions that can last for hours or even days.

**Classical Ideas about the Origins and Expression of Emotion.** Charles Darwin believed some emotions and their expression were universal not only among human beings but also across species. These ideas were developed to support his theories of evolution. Work by Paul Ekman and others generally supports the universality of particular emotional expressions, specifically: happiness, sadness, surprise, fear, anger, and disgust, and more recently, contempt. But there are also significant differences in the experience and expression of emotions across cultures. Some of these differences stem from language; others from cultural values. Collectivist cultures process and display emotion in ways that protect and reinforce social bonds. Individualist

## BOX 6.3  Test Yourself: What's Your Emotional IQ?

Think you're smart? Think you're street smart? Maybe you are, but will those smarts help negotiate all social situations? Maybe not, say social psychologists who study emotional intelligence. A best-selling book called *Emotional Intelligence: Why It Can Matter More Than IQ* (Goleman, 1996, 2006), claims that an individual's ability to understand the emotional content in social interactions constitutes a unique dimension of intelligence that is substantially different from the different kinds of intelligences measured by IQ that had traditionally been the focus of the psychological literature on intelligence.

According to psychologists, emotional intelligence consists of four capacities:

1. Being able to accurately perceive emotions (one's own and others)
2. Being able to use emotional information in rational thinking
3. Being able to understand the meaning of emotions
4. Being able to manage emotions (both one's own and those of others).

These four capacities have been tied to success and failure in a number of social environments, including family and marital relationships, managing employees and coworkers, intergroup relations, and even personal health (Goleman, 2006).

A number of measures have been developed to assess emotional intelligence (see Brackett & Mayer, 2003; Lopes, Salovey, Côté, & Beers, 2005). One, developed by the Hay Group, is called the Emotional Competence Inventory (ECI). As with most other measures, the ECI is too long to be reproduced here, but some sample items give a preliminary sense of how emotional intelligence is typically measured.

1. *You are on an airplane that suddenly hits extremely bad turbulence and begins rocking from side to side. What do you do?*
   A. Continue to read your book or magazine or watch the movie, trying to pay little attention to the turbulence.
   B. Become vigilant for an emergency, carefully monitoring the stewardesses and reading the emergency instructions card.
   C. A little of both a and b.
   D. Not sure—never noticed.

2. *You are in a meeting when a colleague takes credit for work you have done. What do you do?*
   A. Immediately and publicly confront the colleague over the ownership of your work.
   B. After the meeting, take the colleague aside and tell her you would appreciate in the future that she credits you when speaking about your work.
   C. Nothing—it's not a good idea to embarrass colleagues in public.
   D. After the colleague speaks, publicly thank her for referencing your work and give the group more specific detail about what you were trying to accomplish.

3. *You are a customer service representative and have just gotten an extremely angry client on the phone. What do you do?*
   A. Hang up. It doesn't pay to take abuse from anyone.
   B. Listen to the client and rephrase what you gather he is feeling.
   C. Explain to the client that he is being unfair, that you are only trying to do your job, and you would appreciate it if he wouldn't get in the way of this.
   D. Tell the client you understand how frustrating this must be for him, and offer a specific thing you can do to help him get his problem resolved.

4. *You are a college student who had hoped to get an A in a course that was important for your future career aspirations. You just found out you got a C on the midterm. What do you do?*
   A. Sketch out a specific plan for ways to improve your grade and resolve to follow through.
   B. Decide you do not have what it takes to make it in that career.
   C. Tell yourself it really doesn't matter how much you do in the course; concentrate instead on other classes where your grades are higher.

D. Go see the professor and try to talk her into giving you a better grade.

5. *You are a manager in an organization that is trying to encourage respect for racial and ethnic diversity. You overhear someone telling a racist joke. What do you do?*
   A. Ignore it—the best way to deal with these things is not to react.
   B. Call the person into your office and explain that their behavior is inappropriate and is grounds for disciplinary action if repeated.
   C. Speak up on the spot, saying that such jokes are inappropriate and will not be tolerated in your organization.
   D. Suggest to the person telling the joke that he go through a diversity training program.

6. *You are an insurance salesman calling on prospective clients. You have left the last 15 client meetings empty-handed. What do you do?*
   A. Call it a day and go home early to miss rush-hour traffic.
   B. Try something new in the next call, and keep plugging away.
   C. List your strengths and weaknesses to identify what may be undermining your ability to sell.
   D. Sharpen up your résumé.

7. *You are trying to calm down a colleague who has worked herself into a fury because the driver of another car has cut dangerously close in front of her. What do you do?*
   A. Tell her to forget about it—she's okay now and it is no big deal.
   B. Put on one of her favorite tapes and try to distract her.
   C. Join her in criticizing the other driver.
   D. Tell her about a time something like this happened to you and how angry you felt until you saw the other driver was on the way to the hospital.

8. *A discussion between you and your partner has escalated into a shouting match. You are both upset and, in the heat of the argument, start making personal attacks that neither of you really mean. What would be the best thing to do?*
   A. Agree to take a 20-minute break before continuing the discussion.

B. Go silent, regardless of what your partner says.
   C. Say you are sorry, and ask your partner to apologize too.
   D. Stop for a moment, collect your thoughts, then restate your side of the case as precisely as possible.

9. *You have been given the task of managing a team that has been unable to come up with a creative solution to a work problem. What is the first thing you do?*
   A. Draw up an agenda, call a meeting, and allot a specific period of time to discuss each item.
   B. Organize an off-site meeting aimed specifically at encouraging the team to get to know each other better.
   C. Begin by asking each person individually for ideas about how to solve the problem.
   D. Start out with a brainstorming session, encouraging each person to say whatever comes to mind, no matter how wild.

10. *You have recently been assigned a young manager in your team and have noticed that he appears to be unable to make the simplest of decisions without seeking advice from you. What do you do?*
   A. Accept that he "does not have what it takes to succeed around here" and find others in your team to take on his tasks.
   B. Get an HR manager to talk to him about where he sees his future in the organization.
   C. Purposely give him lots of complex decisions to make so he will become more confident in his role.
   D. Engineer an ongoing series of challenging but manageable experiences for him, and make yourself available to act as his mentor.

**Scoring: Question 1.** Either A, B, or C–10 points; **2.** B–5, D–10; **3.** B–5, D–10; **4.** A–10, C–5; **5.** B–5, C–10, D–5; **6.** B–10, C–5; **7.** C–5, D–10; **8.** A–10; **9.** B–10, D–5; **10.** B–5, D–10. Higher scores suggest greater emotional intelligence.

*Source:* Hay Acquisition Company 1, Inc. Copyright © 1999–2005, used with permission.

cultures display emotions in ways that broadcast individual states and draw attention to the individual as the key social unit.

**The Social Psychology of Emotions.** Social psychologists argue that much of our emotional experience is a matter of interpretation. Theories of emotion describe the sequence through which we recognize and label emotions by drawing on the situation and expressions. Others can also help us label our emotions, both teaching us how to interpret specific cues and helping us do so in interaction. We use context not only to interpret our own emotions, but also the emotions of others. Social environments also define feeling rules, which dictate which emotions are appropriate for particular roles in that social context.

Individuals often engage in emotion work, in which they attempt to suppress or evoke particular emotions to bring their emotional expression and experience in line with situational expectations. Some occupations require workers, like flight attendants, to market their emotions as a commodity. If we fail to manage our emotions effectively and express or experience an emotion that is inappropriate in any given situation, we are engaged in emotional deviance.

**Social Emotions.** Many emotions, like empathy, cannot be defined or experienced without reference to the social context in which they exist. Guilt and shame require the judgments of others. Love requires an object of affection. Jealousy requires another person to compare oneself to, and embarrassment requires an audience (even an imagined one).

### Critical Thinking Skill: Effortful Consideration of Ideas

William Shakespeare famously said, "All the world's a stage, and all the men and women merely players." By this point in the text, you have ample evidence that this is a perspective

in social psychology as well. For example, the last chapter (Chapter 5) introduced you to the importance of self-presentation and impression management in everyday life, and the current chapter extended this by discussing the role of emotion management in social interactions. Although students seem to intuitively understand this material and enjoy these topics, it is important that they see beyond Shakespeare's stage. It is not simply that we are acting in social life; these performances have enduring effects. To consider this requires additional effort but provides great payoff.

As Thomas and Thomas (1928) wrote, if persons define situations as real, they are real in their consequences. If you put on a suit to present yourself as a respectable young man when meeting your girlfriend's parents for the first time, they are likely to accept that image and treat you as respectable. If you work to evoke tears at your godmother's funeral despite your excitement over your favorite team's win earlier that day, others around you will likely accept that performance as reality and empathize with you further. In other words, your expression of emotion might influence their own emotional experience.

To push this further, these performances can ultimately affect you as well. If your girlfriend's parents treat you as respectable, their treatment might influence your behavior and actually encourage you to live up to their expectations. If others at the funeral begin to express more sadness in response to your own, you may experience more "real" emotion.

Consider some of your recent performances. Given what you know about social psychology thus far—symbolic interaction, socialization, the self, deep acting—can you think of how they might have come to affect you and not just those around you?

Although it might be easy to assume that the performative nature of social life discounts the importance of our socially constructed reality, the effortful consideration of the effects of these performances provides a more nuanced view of social psychological processes and social life.

# SOCIAL PERCEPTION AND COGNITION

## LEARNING OBJECTIVES

By the end of this chapter you will be able to:

- Describe the categorization process that we use to make sense of the flood of information that surrounds us, and identify various types of schemas we draw on.

- Understand how we form impressions of others based on specific qualities and the way we integrate the information into a coherent, overall impression.

- Explain the attribution process we use to determine the causes of other people's behavior (and our own), along with the errors we commonly make in judging the behavior of others, and the source of those errors.

- Recognize the criteria we use to make attributions for our own success and failure, as well as the difference between an internal locus of control and an external one and the emotional and behavioral implications of these perceptions.

## INTRODUCTION

It is 10 p.m., and the admitting physician at the psychiatric hospital is interviewing a respectable-looking man who has asked for treatment. "You see," the patient says, "I keep hearing voices." After taking a full history, the physician diagnoses the man with schizophrenia and assigns him to an inpatient unit. The physician is well trained and makes the diagnosis with apparent ease. Yet, to diagnose someone's mental condition correctly is a difficult problem in social perception. The differences between paranoia, schizophrenia, depression, and normality are not always easy to discern.

A classic study conducted by Rosenhan (1973) demonstrates this problem. Eight pseudo-patients who were actually research investigators gained entry into mental hospitals by claiming to hear voices. During the intake interviews, the pseudo-patients gave true accounts of their backgrounds, life experiences, and present (quite ordinary) psychological condition. They falsified only their names, occupations, and their complaint of hearing voices. Once in the psychiatric unit, the pseudo-patients immediately stopped simulating symptoms of schizophrenia. They reported that the voices had ceased and talked normally with other patients. The other patients began to suspect that the investigators were not really mentally ill, but the staff continued to believe they were. The nurses and orderlies made note of the pseudo-patients' "strange" behavior, including a tendency to line up very early for meals and to spend significant amounts of time writing in their notebooks. Although such behavior would not be seen as odd for healthy researchers with little else to do, the staff considered it evidence of mental illness. Because of these enduring beliefs, upon discharge, the pseudo-patients were still diagnosed with schizophrenia, although now it was "schizophrenia in remission."

A man voluntarily checking into a psychiatric hospital may pose a confusing problem for the hospital staff. Is he really "mentally ill" and in need of hospitalization, or is he "healthy"? Is he no longer able to function in the outside world, or is this a temporary state? Is he on drugs?

To try to answer these questions, the admitting physician gathers information about the person and classifies it as indicating illness or health. Then the doctor combines these facts to form a general diagnosis (paranoia, schizophrenia, or depression) and determines what treatment the person needs. While performing these actions, the doctor is engaging in **social perception**. Broadly defined, social perception refers to constructing an understanding of the social world from the data we get through our senses. More narrowly defined, it refers to the processes by which we form impressions of other people's traits and personalities.

In making her diagnosis, the physician not only forms an impression about the traits and characteristics of the new patient, but she also tries to understand the causes of that person's behavior. She tries, for instance, to figure out whether the patient acts as he does because of some internal dispositions or because of external pressures from the environment. Social psychologists term this process **attribution**. In attribution, we observe others' behavior and then infer backward to causes—intentions, abilities, traits, motives, and situational pressures—that explain why people act as they do.

Social perception and attribution are not passive activities. We do not simply register the stimuli that impinge on our senses; rather, our expectations and cognitive structures influence what we notice and how we interpret it. This is closely tied to the dual-process model introduced in Chapter 1. The intake physician at the psychiatric hospital, for example, does not expect to encounter researchers pretending to be mentally ill; instead, she expects to meet people who are mentally ill. Thus, even before the interaction begins, the doctor has categorized the patient as mentally ill. With that categorization firmly in place, the doctor falls victim to **confirmation bias**, focusing on information relevant to that condition and ignoring or downplaying information that is inconsistent with a diagnosis of mental illness (Nickerson, 1998). In other words, her interpretation is influenced by her expectation that the patient is a real patient. Most of the time, the impressions we form of others are sufficiently accurate to permit smooth interaction. After all, few people who are admitted to psychiatric hospitals are researchers faking mental illness. Yet social perception and attribution can be unreliable. Even highly trained observers can misperceive, misjudge, and reach the wrong conclusions.

In February 1999, police officers in New York City were attempting to track down a serial rapist. Sketches of the rapist had been circulated to the police, so they had some idea what the rapist looked like. Four White officers patrolling the Bronx encountered Amadou Diallo, a Black man, and thought he resembled the sketches of the rapist. As Diallo was entering his apartment building, the police officers ordered him to stop. Diallo stopped and began to reach for his wallet to produce his identification. The police officers interpreted this action quite differently, however. Believing he was reaching for a gun, the officers opened fire. They fired a total of 41 shots, and Diallo died immediately. Diallo was not the rapist and had no criminal record—the officers' snap judgments were wrong.

The image of a Black man in a bad neighborhood, reaching into his pocket as he was being stopped by the police, provided too many dangerous cues that caused the officers to act immediately. Many have wondered whether the police officers would have been slower to act if Diallo had been White. Did race help activate a dangerous image in the police officers' minds and encourage them to respond aggressively? Thirteen years later, the shooting of an unarmed Trayvon Martin prompted similar questions. George Zimmerman, a neighborhood watch coordinator, shot Martin, a 17-year-old African American, during a confrontation in Zimmerman's gated community. Just moments before the shooting, Zimmerman called the local police department because he was concerned about Martin's behavior: "There is a really suspicious guy . . . This guy looks like he's up to no good. Or he's on drugs or something. It's raining and he's just walking around, looking about" (CNN, March 20, 2012). The case received national attention, with many asking whether it was racially motivated. Did an African-American teen in a hoodie elicit different reactions from what he would have if he been wearing something else? If Martin had been White, would Zimmerman have interpreted his actions—"walking through [the neighborhood], looking about"—as less threatening?

As concerns over potential police bias spread, social psychologists were developing tools to determine whether there was a widespread implicit, or unconscious, association linking Blacks and perceived threat (Correll, Hudson, Guillermo, & Ma, 2014). In one study, subjects were asked to act as police officers and decide whether to shoot at suspected criminals. The suspected criminals were either holding a gun (in which case the officer should shoot) or were holding a neutral object such as a cell phone (in which case the officer should not shoot). The results showed that the subjects were more likely to mistakenly shoot a suspect holding a cell phone—a harmless object—if the suspect was Black. They were also more likely to mistakenly hold back from shooting a suspect holding a gun if the suspect was White (Plant, Peruche, & Butz, 2005). Research replicated with actual police officers produced similar results (Correll et al., 2007). Findings like these, alongside additional shootings of unarmed Black men, fueled both the Black Lives Matter movement and research on how to counter deep-seated stereotypes (Plant & Peruche, 2005).

In this chapter, we outline processes of social perception and attribution that are not only the basis of this contemporary social issue, but are also ubiquitous in our daily lives and experiences.

## SCHEMAS

The human mind is a sophisticated system for processing information. One of our most basic mental processes is **categorization**— our tendency to perceive stimuli as members of groups or classes rather than as isolated, unique entities. For instance, at the theater, we see an attractive woman on stage wearing a short dress and dancing on her toes; rather than viewing her as a novel entity, we immediately categorize her as a "ballerina."

How do we go about assigning people or things to categories? For instance, how do we know the woman should be categorized as a ballerina and not as an "actress" or a "cheerleader"? To categorize some person, we usually compare that person to our prototype of the category. A **prototype** is an abstraction that represents the "typical" or quintessential instance of a class or group—as least to us. It is the best example of the category. Perhaps your prototypical quarterback is Tom Brady. Others may have a different prototype for the same category, like Joe Montana or Peyton Manning. Although he is an outstanding quarterback, few might think of Russell Wilson as a prototypical quarterback, in part because of his race. Although the number is growing, there have been very few Black quarterbacks in the history of the NFL. Usually, prototypes are specified in terms of a set of common attributes among members of a category. For example, the prototype of a "quarterback" may be someone who is tall, White, athletic, intelligent, and who has had a successful career, perhaps even winning a Super Bowl.

Categorizing people, objects, situations, events, and even the self becomes complicated because the categories we use are not isolated from one another; rather, they link together and form a structure. For instance, we may think of a person (Jonathan) not only as having various attributes (tall, wealthy) but also as bearing certain relations to other persons or entities (friend of Kareem, stronger than Bill, owner of a Lexus). These other persons or entities will themselves have attributes (Kareem: thin, athletic, Black; Bill: short, fat, balding; Lexus: silver, two-door, new). They also have relations with still other persons and entities (Kareem: coworker of Bill, husband of Lisa; Bill: friend of Lisa, owner of a Prius). In this way, we build a cognitive structure consisting of persons, attributes, and relations.

To better understand these cognitive structures and how they may be connected, think about a time when you had a thought that appeared to come out of nowhere. Perhaps you and your friend were talking about your social psychology course and you suddenly remember that you need new shoes. Chances are, there is some connection between that thought of shoes and something that either you or your conversation partner said. Maybe as you thought about social psychology you imagined sitting in the classroom, bringing to mind the young woman who you sit behind, connecting social psychology and the young woman. Then you remembered admiring the shoes that she wore to class last week, connecting the young woman and her shoes. You compare her shoes to your own and decide you need to shop for a new pair. Although new shoes and social psychology seem unrelated, they may be connected through various relationships in your cognitive structure.

Social psychologists use the term **schema** to denote a well-organized structure of cognitions about a specific social entity such as a person, group, role, or event. Schemas usually include information about an entity's attributes and about its relations with other entities. To illustrate, suppose Chandra, who is somewhat cynical about politics, has a schema about the role of "member of Congress." In Chandra's schema, the member of Congress will insist they serve the needs of their constituents but will actually vote for the special interests of those who contributed most to their campaign, will run TV advertisements containing half-truths at election time, will spend more time in Washington, DC, than in their home district, will put avoiding scandal above ethics, will vote for large pay raises and retirement benefits for themself, and, above all, will never do anything to lessen their own power.

Someone else, of course, may hold a less cynical view of politics than Chandra and have a different schema about the role of "member of Congress." But, like Chandra's, this schema will likely incorporate such elements as the congressional representative's typical activities, relations, motives, and tactics. Whatever their

exact content, schemas enable us to organize and remember facts, to make inferences that go beyond the facts immediately available, and to assess new information (Augoustinos & Innes, 1990; Fiske & Linville, 1980).

## Types of Schemas

There are several distinct types of schemas, including person schemas, self-schemas, group schemas, role schemas, and event schemas (Eckes, 1995; Taylor & Crocker, 1981).

*Person schemas* are cognitive structures that describe the personalities of others. Person schemas can apply either to specific individuals (such as Barack Obama, Lady Gaga, your father) or to types of individuals (such as introvert, class clown, sociopath). Person schemas organize our conceptions of others' personalities and enable us to develop expectations about others' behavior.

*Self-schemas* are structures that organize our conception of our own characteristics (Markus, 1977, 1983). For instance, if you conceive of yourself as independent (as opposed to dependent), you may see yourself as individualistic, unconventional, and assertive. To behave in a manner consistent with your self-schema, you may refuse to accept money from your parents, refuse to ask others for help with schoolwork, take a part-time job, or dye your hair an unusual color. Self-schemas are discussed in detail in Chapter 4.

*Group schemas*—also called stereotypes—are schemas regarding the members of a particular social group or social category (Stangor & Schaller, 2000). Stereotypes indicate the attributes and behaviors considered typical of members of that group or social category. These are rigid conceptions and widely shared by members of a culture or community. American culture uses a wide variety of stereotypes about different races (Blacks, Asians), religious groups (Protestants, Catholics, Jews, Muslims), and ethnic groups (Arabs, Irish, Latinos, Italians).

*Role schemas* indicate which attributes and behaviors are typical of persons occupying a particular role in a group. Chandra's conception of the role of a congressional representative illustrates a role schema. Role schemas exist for most occupational roles—nurses, cab drivers, store managers, and the like—but they also exist for other kinds of roles in groups: group leader, captain of a sports team. Role schemas are often used to understand and predict the behaviors of people who occupy particular roles. For example, knowing that Russell Wilson is a quarterback gives us a good idea of what he will do during a football game.

*Event schemas* (also called *scripts*) are schemas regarding important, recurring social events (Abelson, 1981; Schank & Abelson, 1977). In our society, these events include weddings, funerals, sports matches, job interviews, cocktail parties, and hook-ups. An event schema specifies the activities that constitute the event, the predetermined order or sequence for these activities, and the persons (or role occupants) participating in the event. Scripts can be revealed by asking people to describe what typically happens during an event.

One type of script of interest to both social psychologists and college students alike is a hook-up script (Cohen & Wade, 2012). Hooking up—or engaging in a casual physical encounter—has replaced dating on many college campuses (Simon & Gagnon, 2003). As shown in Table 7.1, when asked to describe a "typical" hook-up, students tend to agree on a number of important characteristics (Paul & Hayes, 2002): Hook-ups tend to occur between strangers or acquaintances rather than friends. Although someone may go out intending to hook up, in most cases hooking up with a particular person is not planned. Men usually initiate the encounter, and the couples tend to meet one another at parties. Alcohol or drugs are often involved, and hook-up partners seldom talk about what is happening (or what has happened, after the hook-up ends). Although most hook-ups are one-time encounters, couples will occasionally engage in multiple hook-ups with the same person (Bogle, 2007). However, unlike a couple who is dating exclusively, a couple who is hooking up—even repeatedly—has no obligations toward one another. The component of the hook-up script in which there is the least agreement among young people is what exactly "hooking up" implies (Glenn & Marquardt, 2001). Hooking up can range from kissing to intercourse. This ambiguity is one of the reasons the term "hooking up" appeals to young people, particularly women. Because it has a casual tone and could imply simply kissing or heavy petting, using the term can save women from potential damage to their reputations that may come from being seen as too promiscuous. Although people might sometimes ask for details, when a friend tells us that they attended a cousin's wedding or hooked up with a co-ed this past weekend, we usually fill in the gaps based on knowledge from our event schemas (and schemas for cousins and co-eds). However, in part because of **gender schemas**—characteristics and behavior that we expect from men versus women—both men and women respect women less when they hook up frequently than they do men who hook up as often (Allison & Risman, 2013)

## Schematic Processing

**Why Do We Use Schemas?** Although schemas may produce reasonably accurate judgments much of the time, they do not always work. Wouldn't it be better for us to rely less on schemas, perhaps to avoid the kind of tragic mistake the police made with Amadou Diallo and other unarmed Black men or to not jump to conclusions about a friend's promiscuity (or chastity)? Perhaps, but we come to rely on schemas because they give us a way to efficiently organize, understand, and react to the complex world around us. It is simply impossible to process all the information present in each interaction. We have to find a way to focus on what is most important in defining

**TABLE 7.1**   Illustrative Descriptions of a Typical Hook-up (quotes from student questionnaires)

|  | FROM A 20-YEAR-OLD WOMAN | FROM A 21-YEAR-OLD MAN |
|---|---|---|
| *Who is involved?* | A guy and a girl who are somewhat attracted to each other but are strangers. It can also be a guy and a girl who are acquaintances and under the right conditions hook up. | Any two people who find each other attractive or just there. |
| *What leads to the hook-up? Is planning involved? Who instigates the hook-up?* | The two may talk, flirt, dance together, drink together, make glances at each other. They are close to each other. Planning can be involved if one person scopes out the other or plans certain things to say. Usually the guy instigates the hook-up, but sometimes it is mutual instigation. | Sometimes investigation is done. One of the people may inquire about the other person in hopes of initiating the hook-up. Most often, however, the hook-up just kind of happens. The girl lets it be known (with eye contact or extremely friendly behavior) that she wants it, and generally the guy must then go and give it to her. |
| *Where does it happen?* | In rooms, at clubs, at parties. It can happen in a stairwell. | Anywhere possible. Most often on a couch or in adjacent chairs. Maybe in a bed if you're lucky. |
| *Are alcohol or other drugs involved?* | Sometimes, actually often. From my experiences, hook-ups always happen at parties . . . Many situations involve alcohol and drugs because people lose inhibition and wear beer goggles, increasing the likelihood of hooking up. | Alcohol is almost always involved. This helps the guy with his confidence to initiate the hook-up. |
| *What sexual behaviors take place? Are precautions taken to prevent transmission of sexually transmitted diseases (STDs)?* | It depends. Some people just kiss. Others go further into oral sex and sexual intercourse. Usually in oral sex, precautions aren't taken to prevent the transmission of STDs. Sometimes in sex, condoms are used. In situations with alcohol and drugs, condoms are often forgotten. | Condoms are sometimes used if intercourse takes place. But a lot of hook-ups go to oral sex, in which case no preventative measures are used. |
| *What communication takes place between the hook-up partners? Do they talk about what is happening?* | Usually not a lot. They mainly just hook up or communicate with sexual noises. | Sometimes partners may say, "I can't believe I'm doing this. I don't even know you!" But this is generally only the females, and the males are just hoping this will not put a premature end to the hook-up. |

*Source:* Adapted from Paul & Hayes, 2002.

*Note:* These representative highlights demonstrate the consistency among students' event schemas for hook-ups and illustrate the tremendous agreement (and some differences) between men and women.

the situation so we can respond appropriately. Schemas help us do this in several ways: (1) they influence our capacity to recall information by making certain kinds of facts more salient and easier to remember, (2) they help us process information faster, (3) they guide our inferences and judgments about people and objects, and (4) they allow us to reduce ambiguity by providing a way to interpret ambiguous elements in the situation. Once we have applied a schema to the situation, our decisions about how to interact in it become much more straightforward (Mayer, Rapp, & Williams, 1993).

**Schematic Memory.** Human memory is largely reconstructive. That is, we do not usually remember all the precise details of what transpired in a given situation—we are not a camera capturing a video, instantly recording all the images and sounds. Instead, we typically remember some of what happened, enough to identify the appropriate schema and then rely on that schema to fill in other details. Schemas organize information in memory and, therefore, affect what we remember and what we forget (Hess & Slaughter, 1990; Sherman, Judd, & Park, 1989). When trying to recall something, people often remember better those facts that are consistent with their schemas. For instance, one study (Cohen, 1981) investigated the impact of an occupational role schema on recall. Participants viewed a video of a woman celebrating her birthday by having dinner with her husband at home. Half the participants were told the woman was a librarian; the other half were told she was a waitress in a local diner.

Some characteristics of the woman were consistent with the schema of a librarian: she wore glasses, had spent the day reading, liked classical music, and received a romantic novel as a gift. Other characteristics of the woman, however, were consistent with the schema of a diner waitress: she drank beer, had a bowling ball in the room, ate chocolate birthday cake, flirted with her husband, and received a nightgown as a gift. Later, when participants tried to recall details of the video, they recalled most accurately those facts consistent with the woman's occupational label. That is, participants who thought she was a librarian remembered facts consistent with the librarian schema, whereas those who thought she was a waitress remembered facts consistent with the diner-waitress schema.

What about memory for material inconsistent with schemas? Several studies have tested the recall of three types of information: material consistent with schemas, material contradictory to schemas, and material irrelevant to schemas. The results show that people recall both schema-consistent and schema-contradictory material better than schema-irrelevant material (Cano, Hopkins, & Islam, 1991; Higgins & Bargh, 1987). One way social psychologists have investigated this is by creating a chain of communication—like the children's game "telephone"—to see how stories morph over time. These studies suggest that when individuals retell stories there is an initial boost in the memorability of information that contradicts schemas (also called schema-violations), in part because the information is surprising (Gocłowska, Baas, Elliot, & De Dreu, 2017). However, with time and across transmissions, individuals tend to include more schema-consistent information than information that is contradictory. This includes adding consistent information that was not initially present (Hunzaker, 2016).

In general, people remember schema-contradictory material better when the schema itself is concrete (for example, spends money wisely, tells lies frequently, brags about her accomplishments) rather than abstract (for example, practical, dishonest, egotistical) (Pryor, McDaniel, & Kott-Russo, 1986).

**Schematic Inference.** Schemas affect the inferences we make about persons and other social entities (Fiske & Taylor, 1991). That is, they supply missing facts when gaps exist in our knowledge. If we know certain facts about a person but are ignorant about others, we fill in the gaps by inserting suppositions consistent with our schema for that person. For example, knowing your roommate is head of the campus PETA (People for the Ethical Treatment of Animals) chapter, you can infer they will not want to spend time with your new friend who enjoys hunting or to celebrate their birthday dinner at a Brazilian Steakhouse. Of course, the use of schemas can lead to erroneous inferences. If the schema is incomplete or does not correctly mirror reality, some mistakes are likely. For instance, the police officers who confronted Amadou Diallo applied a schema that was incorrect. Their schema for "a Black man who puts his hand in his pocket as he is being confronted by the police" includes the element that the suspect would be reaching for a gun in his pocket. From this, they inferred that he would try to shoot at them, and they reacted according to that erroneous inference.

We often use schemas without giving them a lot of thought. Think back to the beginning of this chapter and reading about the doctor in the mental hospital. As you were imagining the scenario, how was the doctor dressed? In a white lab coat? Did you have an assumption about the doctor's gender before it was mentioned? You did not learn the doctor was a woman until late in the scenario. If you were surprised when you read the feminine pronouns, it is likely because you imagined the doctor as a man.

This same schema is the foundation of a common riddle: "A father and son have a car accident and are both badly hurt. They are taken to separate hospitals. When the boy is taken in for an operation, the surgeon says 'I cannot do the surgery because this is my son.' Who is the surgeon?" Although the riddle stumped many more people when it emerged in the 1980s, people who hear it today often still pause before realizing that the surgeon is the boy's mother.

Schemas—especially well-developed schemas—can also help us infer new facts. For instance, if a physician diagnoses a patient as having the flu, they can make inferences about how the patient contracted the disease, which symptoms might be present, what side effects or complications might arise, and what treatment will be effective. For another person who has no schema regarding this disease, these inferences would be virtually impossible.

**Schematic Judgment.** Schemas can influence our judgments or feelings about persons and other entities. The schemas themselves

Because of schematic inferences, if we hear a story about a doctor with no other identifying information, we assume that doctor is a man and may imagine him in a white lab coat. Similarly, without additional information, we assume nurses are women dressed in scrubs. © cyano66/iStock

may be organized in terms of evaluative dimensions; this is especially true of person schemas. For example, Chandra's schemas for members of Congress had a negative valence, predisposing her to view any congressperson unfavorably. The complexity of a schema—or the variety of attributes included in a schema—also affects our evaluations of other persons. The complexity of schemas is directly tied to diversity of experience with the group (Crisp & Turner, 2011). The more members of a group we interact with, the less uniform we see group members (perhaps their personality, values, and so forth), and the more complex our schema of the group is. However, less complex schemas lead to more extreme judgments and evaluations. This is called the **complexity-extremity effect**.

For instance, in one study (Linville & Jones, 1980), White college students evaluated a person applying for admission to law school. Depending on treatment, the applicant was either White or Black and had an academic record that was either strong or weak. The results showed an interaction effect between academic record and race. Participants rated a weak Black applicant more negatively than a weak White applicant, but they rated a strong Black applicant more positively than a strong White applicant. Judgments about Black applicants were more extreme—in both directions—than those about White applicants. This is because participants' schema for their own in-group (White) was more complex than their schema for the out-group (Black). Because these White students had more experience with a variety of Whites, it was difficult to infer competence based solely on this quality, and the schema was more complex. Further research (Linville, 1982) shows that the complexity-extremity effect also holds for other attributes, such as age. College students have less complex schemas for older persons than for persons their own age, so they are more extreme in judgments of older persons.

**Drawbacks of Schematic Processing.** Although schemas provide certain advantages, they also entail some corresponding disadvantages. First, people are overly accepting of information that fits consistently with a schema. Perceivers show a confirmation bias, like the doctor mentioned earlier, when collecting new information relevant to schemas (Higgins & Bargh, 1987; Snyder & Swann, 1978). That is, when gathering information, perceivers tend to ask questions that will elicit information supportive of the schemas rather than questions that will elicit information contradictory to the schemas. Consider the intake process of Rosenhan's study at the mental hospital. The doctors asked particular questions of the researchers, assuming they were mentally ill, that biased responses toward confirmation of that belief. The nurses and orderlies interpreted information about pseudo-patients' behavior in ways that confirmed their schemas and ignored or downplayed information suggesting that the pseudo-patients were actually not ill, because it contradicted their existing schemas.

Second, when faced with missing information, people fill in gaps in knowledge by adding elements that are consistent with their schemas. Sometimes these added elements turn out to be erroneous or factually incorrect. When this happens, it will, of course, create inaccurate interpretations or inferences about people, groups, or events. As an example, research on eyewitness accounts of crimes finds that witnesses draw on event schemas of "typical crimes" when recalling specific incidents. This can distort memories in schema-consistent ways, leading to misinformation in reporting (Holst & Pezdek, 1992). Furthermore, as witnesses share their accounts of events, listeners who were not privy to the scene are likely to interpret events in ways that are influenced by their own existing beliefs (Allport & Postman, 1947). This introduces further distortion.

We make snap judgments about the personalities of individuals based on stereotypes we have of the groups we think they belong to. These images are of the same man, with him dressed in business attire in one and showing off his tattoos in the other. If you only saw the photo on the left, what would you assume about him? What about if you only saw the photo on the right? © alvarez/iStock

Third, because people are often reluctant to discard or revise their schemas, they occasionally apply schemas to persons or events even when the schemas do not fit the facts very well. Forced misapplication of a schema may lead to incorrect characterization and inferences, and this in turn can produce inappropriate or inflexible responses toward other persons, groups, or events. A teacher who believes a child is lazy because they are not getting the class reading done may be less inclined to engage with the child in class or encourage the child's parents to have them tested for dyslexia or ADD (attention deficit disorder), leaving the young child's reading skills unlikely to improve regardless of their cause (see the discussion of self-fulfilling prophecies on p. 230).

## PERSON SCHEMAS AND GROUP STEREOTYPES

### Person Schemas

As noted earlier, person schemas are cognitive structures that describe the personalities of other individuals. There are several distinct types of person schemas. Some person schemas are very specific and pertain to particular people. For example, Sarah is a 17-year-old high school student, and Joan is her mother.

After years of interacting with Joan, Sarah has an elaborate schema of her mother. She can usually predict how Joan will react to new situations, information, or problems and plan accordingly. She can also interpret specific behavior. When Sarah returns home to see Joan baking a pie, she asks her mother who is coming to visit, as it is only on such occasions that her mother bakes. We often also have individual schemas for public figures (for instance, Oprah Winfrey, former talk show host, actor, advocate for women, Black, extremely wealthy) or for famous historical figures (for instance, Abraham Lincoln, political leader during the Civil War, honest, determined, opposed to slavery, committed to holding the Union together).

Other person schemas are very abstract and focus on the relations among personality traits. A schema of this type is an **implicit personality theory**—a set of unstated assumptions about which personality traits are correlated with one another (Grant & Holmes, 1981; Sedikides & Anderson, 1994) and behaviors associated with various personality traits (Skowronski & Carlston, 1989). If you learn that a child is gifted, do you automatically assume the child has other attributes? Recent research explored the beliefs that teachers in Germany associate with giftedness (Baudson & Preckel, 2013). When a student was described as "gifted," teachers assumed the student was also likely to be emotionally deficient. Although teachers believed gifted students would be more open to new experiences than students of average ability, they also saw them as more introverted, less emotionally stable, and less agreeable. These beliefs are considered implicit, or automatic, because we seldom subject our person schemas to close examination and are usually not explicitly aware of the schemas' contents. Therefore, the teachers were likely unaware of their biased judgments of gifted students and how these implicit assumptions were influencing their behavior toward the students in class.

**Implicit Personality Theories and Mental Maps.** As do all schemas, implicit personality theories enable us to make inferences that go beyond the available information. Instead of withholding judgment, we use them to flesh out our impressions of a person about whom we have little information. For instance, if we learn someone has a warm personality, we might infer they are also likely to be sociable, popular, good-natured, and so on. If we hear that somebody else is cold, we may infer they are humorless, pessimistic, and unsociable, even though we lack evidence that they actually have these traits.

We can depict an implicit personality theory as a mental map indicating the way traits are related to one another. Figure 7.1 displays such a mental map. This figure, based on judgments made by college students, shows how various personality traits stand in relation to one another (Rosenberg, Nelson, & Vivekananthan, 1968). Traits thought to be similar are located close together within our mental map, meaning we expect people who have one trait to have the other. Traits thought to be dissimilar are located far apart, meaning we believe they rarely occur together in one person.

If your mental map resembles the one portrayed in Figure 7.1, you think that people who are wasteful are also likely to be unintelligent and irresponsible (see the lower left part of the map). Similarly, you think that people who are persistent are also likely to be determined and skillful (the upper right part of the map).

Using data like that presented in Figure 7.1, early researchers reasoned there were two distinct evaluative dimensions—social and intellectual—upon which trait dimensions fell. For instance, the traits "warm" and "cold" differ mainly on the social dimension, whereas "frivolous" and "industrious" differ on the intellectual dimension (Rosenberg & Sedlak, 1972). Traits usually tend to be either good on both dimensions (like "important") or bad on both dimensions (like "unreliable," explaining a common bias in impression formation). We

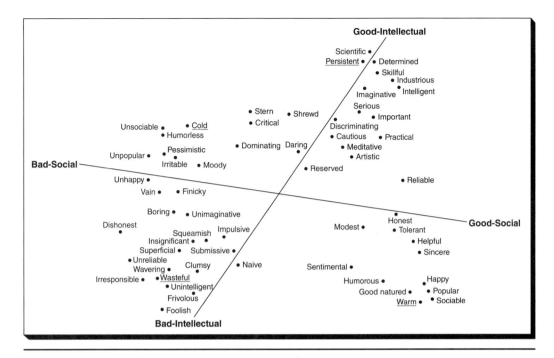

**FIGURE 7.1** Relationships among Attributes: A Mental Map

Each of us has an implicit theory of personality—a theory about which personality attributes tend to go together and which do not. We can represent our theories of personality in the form of a mental map. The closer attributes are located to each other on our mental map, the more we assume these attributes will appear together in the same person. The mental map shown above was created based on the mental maps of American college students.

*Source:* Adapted from Rosenberg, Nelson, & Vivekananthan, 1968.

tend to judge persons who have several good traits as generally good and persons who have several bad traits as generally bad. Once we have a global impression of someone as, say, generally good, we assume that other positive traits (located nearby in the mental map) also apply. This tendency for our general or overall liking for a person to influence our subsequent assessment of more specific traits of that person is called the **halo effect** (Lachman & Bass, 1985; Thorndike, 1920). The halo effect produces bias in impression formation; it can lead to inaccuracy in our ratings of others' traits and performances (Cooper, 1981; Fisicaro, 1988).

In the decades since Rosenberg's mental map was published, social psychologists have worked to refine the dimensions and test impression formation across different cultures and groups. There is growing consensus that the two universal dimensions are better conceived of as warmth and competence (rather than social and intellectual). As early research (Asch, 1946, discussed later in this chapter) found, warmth is a highly influential trait in impression formation, and it appears to take precedence over competence, both in how rapidly it is judged and how much weight it carries in impressions (Fiske, Cuddy, & Glick 2007). Immediately upon encountering someone else, we must determine whether they are more likely to harm or help us. To do so, we gauge their level of warmth because it is the dimension that is tied to our perceptions of another's intent. The warmth dimension captures traits like friendliness, helpfulness, and sincerity. The competence dimension, how-ever, is related to ability and includes traits like intelligence, creativity, and skill. Although everyone lends primacy to the warmth dimen-sion in forming impressions, women and individuals from collectivist cultures appear particularly cued in to warmth (Abele, 2003).

Our impressions influence how we treat others. In hiring, for example, those who are warm but not competent are directed toward service positions, where sociability is key. Those who are competent but cold are often placed in technical jobs, while those who are incompetent and cold may be placed in par-ticularly low-status positions (like janitor). Those who are both warm and competent are most likely to become managers (Cuddy, Glick, & Beninger, 2011).

Impressions also affect the emotions we feel toward others. We are likely to pity those who we consider high on warmth but low on com-petence and envy those who are high on com-petence and low on warmth. We admire those who we believe are high on both dimensions and hold contempt for those who are seen as low on both (Cuddy, Fiske, & Glick, 2007). Similar emo-tions are directed toward groups that we classify using the same two dimensions. We envy the rich (high-competence, low-warmth), admire the middle class (high-competence, high-warmth), pity the elderly (low-competence, high-warmth), and have contempt for welfare recipients (low-competence, low-warmth).

## Group Stereotypes

- "Politicians are liars and cheaters, with no compassion for ordinary people."
- "Asian women are 'tiger moms,' demand-ing perfection from their kids."
- "People on welfare are lazy, wasteful, and unemployed."
- "Arabs and Muslims are terrorists who hate America."
- "Jocks might be strong and athletic, but they're stupid and arrogant."

An unfortunate reality in our society is that we have all heard remarks like these—categorical, extreme, inaccurate characterizations. Each of these is an example of a group schema or ste-reotype. A **stereotype** is a set of characteris-tics attributed to all members of some specified group or social category (McCauley, Stitt, & Segal, 1980; Taylor, 1981). Just like other types of schemas, stereotypes simplify the complex social world. Rather than encouraging us to treat each member of a group individually, stereotypes encourage us to think about and treat all politicians, welfare recipients, or jocks the same way. By helping us quickly place people into categories, stereotypes enable us to form impressions of people and predict their behavior with only minimal information—the groups to which they belong.

Stereotypes, however, involve overgeneral-ization. They lead us to think that all members of a particular group or social category possess certain attributes. Although stereotypes might contain a kernel of truth—some members of the stereotyped group may have some of the imputed characteristics—it is almost never the case that all members have those characteris-tics. For this reason, stereotypes often lead to inaccurate inferences. Consider, for instance, all the feminists you know. Perhaps one of them is—as the stereotype suggests—a radi-cal who would like to have the gender binary completely eradicated, and maybe another is lesbian. It is certainly false, however, that all your feminist acquaintances are as politically active or eschew relationships—romantic or otherwise—with men. It is also false that all feminists are women.

Throughout our daily lives, we are constantly categorizing people whom we encounter into existing groups to conserve mental attention. Walking down the street, we pass men and women, Blacks and Whites, young people and the elderly. Without much conscious thought, we sort these strangers into groups based on distinguishing char-acteristics and then draw on group schemas (stereotypes) to decide how to respond to others without giving our actions much consideration (Fiske & Neuberg, 1990). We tend to not notice the work that our minds are doing until we encounter someone who does not neatly fit into one of our group schemas: an individual whose gender, race, or age is ambiguous. In these situations, because we need to gather additional information, processing takes longer and becomes more conscious. If it is difficult to determine a person's gender from a cursory glance, we may look for other nonverbal or vocal clues. If we are unable to classify someone, we grow increasingly uncomfortable. Thinking back to moments when we sought such clarification and considering how seldom such moments occur demonstrates the ubiquity of categorization and stereotypes in our everyday lives.

**Common Stereotypes.** In American society, many widely known stereotypes pertain to ethnic, racial, and gender groups. Ethnic (national) stereotypes held by Americans might include, for example, the view that Mexicans are undocumented immigrants who struggle to speak English, the French are cultured and romantic, and Vietnamese people are hardworking and friendly. Investigators have studied ethnic, racial, and gender stereotypes for many years, and the results show that the content of stereotypes changes over time (Diekman, Eagly, Mladinic, & Ferreira, 2005). For instance, few of us now believe—as many once did—that the typical Native American is a drunk, the typical African American is superstitious, or the typical Chinese American is conservative and inscrutable. Stereotypes may not have disappeared over time, but they have changed content (Dovidio & Gaertner, 1996).

Just as stereotypes about ethnic and racial groups are commonly held in our society, so are stereotypes about gender groups. Usually, our first judgment when meeting people involves classifying them as men or women. This classification is likely to activate an elaborate stereotype. This stereotype depicts men as more independent, dominant, competent, rational, competitive, assertive, and stable in handling crises. It characterizes women as more emotional, sensitive, expressive, gentle, helpful, and patient (Ashmore, 1981; Martin, 1987; Minnigerode & Lee, 1978). Research on the nature of these gender stereotypes is discussed in Box 7.1. In fact, two other boxes in this textbook (9.2 and 17.1) also discuss gender stereotypes, reflecting the important and pervasive effects of gender in our society.

Within gender, stereotypes are linked to subtle cues like titles and surnames. For instance, research conducted in the 1980s found that women labeled "Ms." were seen as more achieving, more masculine, and less likable than women labeled "Mrs." (Dion & Schuller, 1991). These impressions were consistent with the high-competence, low-warmth stereotype of feminists in general (Fiske, Cuddy, Glick, & Xu, 2002), who were often associated with the term. However, today's college students are more likely to see "Ms." as related to marital status rather than concerns about sexism and, therefore, rate "Ms." as positively as "Mrs." or "Miss" (Lawton, Blakemore, & Vartanian, 2003).

Perhaps a more contemporary example related to the nuances of titles is the use of hyphenated surnames. Research finds that women who hyphenate their surnames after marriage are assumed to be well educated and more likely to have a career, as well as more friendly, good-natured, industrious, and intellectually curious than married women who do not hyphenate. Men with hyphenated surnames are also perceived as good-natured, as well as more nurturing and more committed to their marriages than married men who do not hyphenate (Forbes, Adams-Curtis, White, & Hamm, 2002).

Gender, ethnicity, and race are only a handful of the groups stereotyped in our culture.

## BOX 7.1 Test Yourself: Gender Schemas and Stereotypes

One of the most consistent findings on stereotypes is that many people believe men and women have different personality traits. What are the traits believed to be typical of each gender? Where do these gender stereotypes come from?

Studies of gender stereotyping have established a number of characteristics that people associate differently with men and women. In the chart below, 20 characteristics are listed that are consistently associated with men or women. To see how aware you are of these stereotypes, fill out the chart by indicating which of the traits listed are more typical of men and which are more typical of women. Also indicate if you consider each trait as a desirable or undesirable characteristic.

The Bem Sex Role Inventory (BSRI; Bem, 1974) is a widely used measure of sex-role stereotyping and self-perceptions. Although there has been some weakening of the distinctions between stereotypes of men and women over time, gender differences endure (Bergen & Williams, 1991; Holt & Ellis, 1998). The first five traits (defends beliefs—individualistic) are seen as more typical

of men, whereas the next five (cheerful—childlike) are considered more typical of women. Although there are subtle differences, the first seven traits are seen as desirable for both men and women. The next three (gullible, shy, and childlike), however, are rated as both feminine and generally undesirable (Colley, Mulhern, Maltby, & Wood, 2009). The next five (affectionate—compassionate) are seen as feminine and more desirable for women than for men, while the last five (assertive—has leadership abilities) are considered more desirable for men than for women. In general, research finds that traits associated with men are more desirable than those associated with women (Broverman et al., 1972). Did your evaluations of trait desirability favor the male stereotyped traits? If not, you may fit in with the trend among educated respondents toward valuing some traditionally feminine traits more positively and some more traditionally masculine traits more negatively (Der-Karabetian & Smith, 1977; Lottes & Kuriloff, 1994; Pleck, 1976). If this trend continues, even if sex and gender stereotypes persist, women may be evaluated less negatively than before.

People also stereotype groups defined by occupation, age, political ideology, mental illness, hobbies, musical tastes, majors, school attended, and so on (Miller, 1982; Rahn, 1993; Rentfrow & Gosling, 2007; Rothbart, 1996).

**Consequences of Stereotypes.** Although stereotypes are overgeneralizations, we still constantly use them and are often unaware of their impact on our judgments of others (Bornstein & Pittman, 1992; Hepburn & Locksley, 1983). And although there is nothing inherent in stereotypes that requires them to be negative, many stereotypes do contain negative elements that disparage or diminish the group stereotyped. Even stereotypes that are positive ("Asians excel at math"; "Blacks are

gifted athletes") may have negative implications. For example, on many college campuses there is the assumption that Black students are student-athletes who were admitted for athletic talents rather than academic ones. Stereotypes like this affect members of stereotyped groups through a process called **stereotype threat** (Steele, 1997, 2010). Stereotype threat occurs when a member of a group suspects that they will be judged based on a common stereotype that is held of that group. Fear of confirming that stereotype interferes with a successful performance. To test for this kind of effect, Steele and Aronson (1995) gave Stanford University students a very difficult test using questions from the Graduate Record Examination in literature. Even though the White and

| TRAIT | MOST TYPICAL OF | | DESIRABLE | |
|---|---|---|---|---|
| | MEN | WOMEN | YES | NO |
| Defends beliefs | _____ | _____ | _____ | _____ |
| Athletic | _____ | _____ | _____ | _____ |
| Strong personality | _____ | _____ | _____ | _____ |
| Makes decisions easily | _____ | _____ | _____ | _____ |
| Individualistic | _____ | _____ | _____ | _____ |
| Cheerful | _____ | _____ | _____ | _____ |
| Loyal | _____ | _____ | _____ | _____ |
| Gullible | _____ | _____ | _____ | _____ |
| Shy | _____ | _____ | _____ | _____ |
| Childlike | _____ | _____ | _____ | _____ |
| Affectionate | _____ | _____ | _____ | _____ |
| Flatterable | _____ | _____ | _____ | _____ |
| Tender | _____ | _____ | _____ | _____ |
| Eager to soothe hurt feelings | _____ | _____ | _____ | _____ |
| Compassionate | _____ | _____ | _____ | _____ |
| Assertive | _____ | _____ | _____ | _____ |
| Competitive | _____ | _____ | _____ | _____ |
| Independent | _____ | _____ | _____ | _____ |
| Dominant | _____ | _____ | _____ | _____ |
| Has leadership abilities | _____ | _____ | _____ | _____ |

Black students who participated were matched on ability, when participants were told that the test was a measure of intellectual ability, the Black students scored much lower than the White students. However, when researchers told the students that the test was part of a study to understand how people solved problems and that it did not measure ability, the stereotype threat was removed and the Black and White students did equally well. Subsequent research suggests that part of the negative effect of stereotype threat stems from people in a negatively stereotyped group overthinking questions, changing answers, and becoming less efficient at test-taking (Steele, 1999).

Speaking of stereotypes of Blacks' athleticism, social psychologists tested stereotype threat related to athletic performance (Stone, Lynch, Sjomeling, & Darley, 1999). Researchers recruited Black and White students to take an athletic test (simply ten rounds of miniature golf) in the laboratory. Black students who were told that this task was a diagnostic of "natural athletic ability" performed significantly better than those who were told that the task measured "sports intelligence." White participants, however, performed better in the "sports intelligence" condition than the "natural athletic ability" condition. Although stereotypes about Whites are generally more favorable than those about Blacks, students were aware of the stereotype that favors Blacks over Whites in athletic ability, and this caused differences in performance.

Stereotypes are particularly harmful when they are used to limit access to important social roles—for example, when an individual applies for a job or for admission to college.

To explore the effect of gender stereotypes on women's underrepresentation in science, a group of scientists asked science faculty at research-intensive universities to rate the materials of a student applying for a lab manager position (Moss-Racusin et al., 2012). The scientists used an experimental design and created fake applications that were randomly assigned a masculine (John) or feminine (Jennifer) name. Other than the name, the application materials sent out were identical. Both men and women faculty who received John's application rated the applicant as significantly more competent and hireable than those who received Jennifer's (identical) application. Faculty also reported that they would offer a higher starting salary and more mentoring to John than to Jennifer. None of the faculty actively disliked women. In fact, faculty perceived Jennifer as a more likeable applicant than John. However, the pervasive gender stereotypes of women being less competent at science unintentionally influenced the raters' evaluations. This is just one study of many suggesting that stereotypes can negatively affect work-related outcomes (see also Correll, Benard, & Paik, 2007).

**Origins of Stereotypes.** How do various stereotypes originate? Some theorists suggest that stereotypes arise out of direct experience with some members of the stereotyped group (Campbell, 1967). We may once have known an Italian who was passionate, someone from Japan who was polite, or a southerner who was bigoted. We then build a stereotype by generalizing—that is, we infer that all members of a group share the attribute we know to be characteristic of some particular members.

Other theorists (Eagly & Steffen, 1984) suggest that stereotypes derive in part from a biased distribution of group members into social roles. Consider professional athletes. After professional sports integrated, Blacks quickly dominated a number of popular sports. In 2016, 70 percent of professional football players and 74 percent of professional basketball players were African American (Institute for Diversity and Ethics in Sports, 2016). The impressive athletic performances mean that Blacks also dominate the sports coverage in newspapers, online, and on television (Davis & Harris, 1998). Roles have associated characteristics—professional sports players are athletically gifted—and eventually those characteristics are attached to the persons occupying the roles. The overwhelming athletic success and related images contribute to and help maintain the stereotype that Blacks are athletically superior to other racial groups. If a social group is concentrated in roles with negative characteristics, an unflattering stereotype of that group may emerge that ascribes the negative characteristics of the role to members of the group.

Stereotyping may also be a natural outcome of social perception (McGarty, Yzerbyt, & Spears, 2002). When people have to process and remember a lot of information about many others, they store this information in terms of group categories rather than in terms of individuals (Taylor, Fiske, Etcoff, & Ruderman, 1978). In trying to remember what went on in a classroom discussion, you may recall that several women spoke and an older student expressed a strong opinion, although you cannot remember exactly which women spoke or who the older student was. Because people remember behavior by group category rather than by individual, they attach the behavior to the groups (Rothbart et al., 1978). Remembering that women spoke and an older student expressed a strong opinion, you might infer that in general, women are talkative and older students are opinionated. You would not form these stereotypes if you recalled these attributes as belonging to individuals rather

When schematic categories are not salient, we view persons as individuals and their behaviors as unique. However, when we view persons as category members, we tend to interpret their behavior as stereotypic and representative of the entire category or group. Comic courtesy of xkcd.com

than remembering them as attached to group membership.

**Errors Caused by Stereotypes.** Because stereotypes are overgeneralizations, they foster various errors in social perception and judgment. First, stereotypes lead us to assume that all members of a group are alike and possess certain traits. Yet individual members of a group obviously differ in many respects. One person wearing a hard hat may shoulder you into the stairwell on a crowded bus; another may offer you their seat. Second, stereotypes lead us to assume that all the members of one group differ from all the members of another group. Stereotypes of football players and ballet dancers may suggest, for instance, that these groups have nothing in common. But both groups contain individuals who are athletic, hardworking, intelligent, and so on. If we see the two groups as nonoverlapping, we neglect to realize that there are ballet dancers who also play football like we might overlook that surgeons can also be mothers.

Although stereotypes can produce inaccurate inferences and judgments in simple situations, they are especially likely to do so in complex situations when our minds are attending to a lot of stimuli. This is because we rely on stereotypes for efficiency (Sherman, Lee, Bessenoff, & Frost, 1998). If an observer uses a stereotype as a central theme around which to organize information relevant to a decision, they may neglect information that is inconsistent with the stereotype (Bodenhausen & Lichtenstein, 1987). A process like this can contribute to bias in educational admissions or hiring decisions, like with the White students' ratings of law school applicants and faculty's ratings of lab assistant applications discussed earlier. With a large amount of detailed material to be read, our minds take shortcuts wherever they can. The stereotype that favors men with regard to scientific competence (and disfavors women) may overshadow specific evidence of competence from the applications. Similarly, police officers are more likely to shoot unarmed suspects—and not shoot armed ones—when they are experiencing greater cognitive load, or more things vying for their attention, as is often the case when they are on patrol (Correll et al., 2014; Kleider,

Parrott, & King, 2010). Severe stress activates the fight/flight system and leads to a narrow cognitive focus, sometimes referred to as "tunnel vision."

Research also indicates that people of higher status have a tendency to use stereotypes more than people of lower status. This seems to occur because people of higher status have more people competing for their attention and, thus, have more incentive to use shortcuts. They may also be able to afford to make more mistakes because of their power (Goodwin, Gubin, Fiske, & Yzerbyt, 2000). High-status individuals are not hurt by an inaccurate judgment, whereas a lower-status person's fate depends on an accurate reading of the higher-power person's mood, attitudes, and so forth. This dynamic occurs even when subjects are randomly assigned to higher- and lower-status roles (Richeson & Ambady, 2003).

Although stereotypes involve overstatement and overgeneralization, they resist change even in the face of concrete evidence that contradicts them. This occurs because people tend to accept information that confirms their stereotypes and ignore or explain away information that disconfirms them (Lord, Lepper, & Mackie, 1984; Snyder, 1981; Weber & Crocker, 1983). Suppose, for example, that Oscar stereotypes gay men as effeminate, nonathletic, and artistic. If he stumbles into a gay bar, he is especially likely to notice the men in the crowd who fit this description, thereby confirming his stereotype. But how does he construe any rough-looking, athletic men who are there? It is possible that these individuals might challenge his stereotype, but reconstructing schemas is a lot of work, and Oscar is more likely to find a way around this challenge. He might scrutinize those who don't fit his stereotype for hidden signs of effeminacy. He might underestimate their number or even assume they are straight. He may also engage in **subtyping**, a process through which perceivers create subcategories of stereotyped groups who serve as exceptions to

the rule without threatening the overarching stereotype (e.g., these are "atypical gay men"). Through cognitive strategies like these, people explain away contradictory information and preserve their stereotypes.

## IMPRESSION FORMATION

Information about other people comes to us from various sources. We may read facts about someone. We may hear something from a third party. We may witness their behavior. We may interact directly with the other and form an impression of that person based on their appearance, dress, speech style, or background. We even infer personality characteristics from people's facial features (Hassin & Trope, 2000; Zebrowitz et al., 1998). Regardless of how we get information about someone, we as perceivers must find a way to integrate these diverse facts into a coherent picture. This process of organizing diverse information into a unified impression of the other person is called **impression formation**. It is fundamental to person perception.

### Trait Centrality

In a classic experiment, Asch (1946) used a straightforward procedure to show that some traits have more impact than others on the impressions we form. Undergraduates in one group received a list of seven traits describing a hypothetical person. These traits were *intelligent, skillful, industrious, warm, determined, practical,* and *cautious*. Undergraduates in a second group received the same list of traits but with one critical difference: the trait "warm" was replaced by "cold." All participants then wrote a brief paragraph indicating their impressions and completed a checklist to rate the stimulus person on such other characteristics as *generous, wise, happy, good-natured, humorous, sociable, popular, humane, altruistic,* and *imaginative*.

Students had no difficulty performing the task. They were able to weave the trait information into a coherent whole and construct a composite sketch of the stimulus person. Importantly, the overall impressions students formed changed dramatically when substituting the trait "warm" for the trait "cold." When the stimulus person was "warm," the students typically described him as happy, successful, popular, and humorous. But when he was "cold," they described him as self-centered, unsociable, and unhappy. The terms "warm" and "cold" had a larger impact than other traits on the overall impression formed of the stimulus person (for example, Asch also tried "polite" and "blunt").

We say that a trait has a high level of **trait centrality** when it has a large impact on the overall impression we form of that person. In Asch's study, the warm/cold trait displayed more centrality than the polite/blunt trait because differences in warm/cold produced larger differences in participants' ratings.

A follow-up study (Kelley, 1950) replicated the warm/cold finding in a more realistic setting. Students in sections of a psychology course read trait descriptions of a guest lecturer before he spoke. These descriptions contained adjectives similar to those Asch used (that is, *industrious, critical, practical, determined*), but they differed regarding the warm/cold variable. For half the students, the description contained the trait "warm"; for the other half, it contained "cold." The lecturer subsequently arrived at the classroom and led a discussion for about 20 minutes. Afterward, the students were asked to report their impressions of him. The results showed large differences between the impressions formed by those who read he was "warm" and those who read he was "cold." Those who had read he was "cold" rated him as less considerate, sociable, popular, good-natured, humorous, and humane than those who had read he was "warm." Because all students saw the same guest instructor in the classroom, the differences in their impressions could stem only from the use of "warm" or "cold" in the profile they had read.

How could a single trait embedded in a profile have such an impact on impressions of someone's behavior? Several theories have been advanced, but one plausible explanation holds that the students used a schema—a mental map—indicating what traits go with being warm and what traits go with being cold. Looking again at Figure 7.1, we note the locations of the attributes "warm" and "cold" on the map and the nature of the other attributes close by. If the mental maps used by the participants in the Asch (1946) and Kelley (1950) studies resembled Figure 7.1, it becomes immediately clear why they judged the warm person as more sociable, popular, good-natured, and humorous; these traits are close to "warm" and remote from "cold" on the mental map.

### First Impressions

Even before studying social psychology, you surely noticed the effort individuals make to create a good impression when interviewing for a new job, entering a new group, or meeting an attractive potential date. This effort reflects the widely held belief that first impressions are especially important and have an enduring impact.

In fact, this belief is supported by a body of systematic research. Observers forming an impression of a person give more weight to information received early in a sequence than to information received later. This is called the **primacy effect** (Luchins, 1957).

What accounts for the impact of first impressions? One explanation is that after forming an initial impression of a person, we interpret subsequent information in a way that makes it consistent with our initial impression. Having established that your new roommate is neat and considerate, you interpret the dirty socks on the floor as a sign of temporary forgetfulness rather than as evidence of sloppiness and lack of concern. Thus, the schema into which an observer assimilates new information influences the interpretation of that information (Zanna & Hamilton, 1977).

A second explanation for the primacy effect holds that we attend very carefully to the first bits of information we get about a person, but we pay less attention once we have enough information to make a judgment. It is not that we interpret later information differently; we simply use it less. This explanation assumes that whatever information we attend to most has the biggest effect on our impressions (Dreben, Fiske, & Hastie, 1979).

What happens if we make an effort to attend to all information equally? In such cases, recent information exerts stronger influence on our impression than information gleaned earlier (Crano, 1977), an occurrence known as the **recency effect** (Jones & Goethals, 1971; Steiner & Rain, 1989). Jurors, for example, are asked to take the perspective that an individual on trial is innocent until proven guilty and instructed to weigh all the evidence presented at trial. Research shows the sequencing of the presentation of that evidence is important. Two groups witnessing identical courtroom arguments came to different verdicts based on whether it was the prosecution or defense who presented last (Furnham, 1986). When the defendant's case came second, perceptions of innocence increased significantly. A recency effect may also occur when so much time has passed that we have largely forgotten our first impression, or when we are judging characteristics that change over time, like performance or moods. For example, research on student course evaluations—often collected after a four- or five-month-long course—show that students rely heavily on the classes that just occurred versus those at the start of the semester that may be difficult to remember after so much time has passed (Dickey & Pearson, 2005).

Perceivers' own moods also influence what information they attend to. Those in good moods seem to favor early information, while the primacy effect is eliminated for those who are experiencing a bad mood (Forgas, 2011).

## Impressions as Self-Fulfilling Prophecies

Whether correct or not, the impressions we form of people influence our behavior toward them. Recall, for instance, the study in which students read that their guest instructor was "warm" or "cold" before meeting him (Kelley, 1950). Not only did the students form different impressions of the instructor, but they also behaved differently toward him. Those who believed the instructor was "warm" participated more in the class discussion than those who believed he was "cold." In a classic study, Rosenthal and Jacobson (1968) found that teachers act differently toward students who they expect to succeed—giving them more time, attention, and approval than other students—thereby creating more opportunity for those students to rise to the teachers' expectations and unintentionally disadvantaging the children for whom the teachers have lower expectations.

When our behavior toward people reflects our impressions of them, we cause them to react in ways that confirm our original impressions. When this happens, our impressions become **self-fulfilling prophecies** (Darley & Fazio, 1980). For example, if we ignore someone because we think they are dull, they will probably withdraw and add nothing interesting to the conversation, living up to our initial impressions. Because our own actions evoke appropriate reactions from others, our initial impressions—whether correct or incorrect—are often confirmed by the reactions of others.

The self-fulfilling prophecy can influence desirability in dating. Researchers took the actual dating profiles of 100 men (both unattractive and attractive) from an online dating website and separated the photos from the text (Brand, Bonatsos, D'Orazio, & DeShong, 2012). Fifty women then rated both the photos and the profile texts independently. Even without the photos attached, the women rated the attractive men's profile texts as more appealing than those of the unattractive men. The researchers argued that the confidence these men had established in their earlier dating history was the key factor. Having been treated as more attractive in previous interactions, these men came to act in a way that was more appealing even long after those previous dating experiences had ended.

## Heuristics

In most social situations, our impressions could be guided by a number of different schemas. How do we make decisions on how to characterize these situations? The answer comes in the form of another type of mental shortcut called a **heuristic** (Tversky & Kahneman, 1974). Heuristics provide a quick way of selecting schemas that—although far from infallible—often help us make an effective choice amid considerable uncertainty.

**Availability.** One factor that determines how likely we are to choose a particular schema is how long it has been since we have used that particular schema, influencing how vivid or salient it is (Arkin & Duval, 1975). If we have recently used a particular schema, it is easier for us to call up that schema for use in the current situation. Schemas more available to us may also be ones we use more often. Suppose you were asked whether there are more words in the English language that begin with the letter *r* or if there are more words in which the third letter is an *r*. Given our experience categorizing words by first letter, most people find it much easier to think of examples of words that begin with *r* than whose third letter is *r*; thus, it seems as if there are more words that begin with *r* (Manis, Shedler, Jonides, & Nelson, 1993).

**Representativeness.** A second heuristic we often use is called the representativeness

heuristic (Tversky & Kahneman, 1974). In this case, we take the few characteristics we know about someone or something and determine whether that person or object is likely to be a member of a particular category (Dawes, 1998; Thomsen & Borgida, 1996). We use this type of heuristic when we judge the musical tastes of others (Lonsdale & North, 2012). The closer one is to a stereotypical country music fan—based on age (older), race (White), religion (Christian), and political beliefs (conservative)—the more likely we are to believe they listen to country music (Lonsdale, 2009). This heuristic holds even when fewer than half of the Whites (43%) in the United States consider themselves country music fans—and even with almost 10 percent of country fans as people of color—because people tend to discount statistical information in the face of the representativeness heuristic (Kahneman & Tversky, 1973; National Endowment for the Arts, 2008).

**Anchoring and Adjustment.** When faced with making a judgment on something we know very little about, we grasp any cues we can find to help us make a decent guess. Oftentimes, we will use some particular standard as a starting point and then try to determine whether we should guess higher or lower than that starting point. Such a starting point is called an *anchor*, and our modification relative to the anchor is called *adjustment* (Mussweiler, Strack, & Pfeiffer, 2000; Tversky & Kahneman, 1974). Suppose you were asked on an exam to provide the population of Chicago. If you did not know that population but you did know the population of New York City, you might use the population of New York as an anchor and, thinking that Chicago must be somewhat smaller than New York, adjust the New York value downward to produce your guess.

When using this heuristic, however, we do not always have meaningful anchors. If a number is in our head for any reason, we are likely to use it as an anchor even if it has nothing whatsoever to do with the situation we are facing (Cadinu & Rothbart, 1996; Wilson, Houston, Etling, & Brekke, 1996). Suppose an employer is conducting an annual evaluation of employees and has the power to give employees a raise of anywhere from 0 to 40 percent depending on their performance. If the boss just attended a retirement party for someone who worked in the firm for 30 years, they may unconsciously use this value as an anchor and end up giving relatively high raises. If, however, the boss just attended the birthday party of a 5-year-old niece, five may be used as the anchor, and although the boss may adjust up from five, the raises are likely to be considerably lower than if 30 were used as the anchor. These anchoring effects tend to occur even if we are explicitly warned not to allow arbitrary anchors to affect our decisions (Griffin, Gonzalez, & Varey, 2001).

Perhaps most often, we use ourselves as an anchor when judging social situations (Markus, Smith, & Moreland, 1985). We have a tendency to do this even when we know we are unusual. If you are a very generous person who always tips at least 25 percent at a restaurant and are asked whether your friend Emily is miserly or charitable, you would be likely to use your own rather unusual behavior as an anchor and report that she is tightfisted because you know she typically tips "only" 20 percent (when 15 percent is the standard for acceptable service).

## ATTRIBUTION THEORY

When we interact with other people, we observe only their actions and the visible effects those actions have. As perceivers, we often want to also know why others act as they do. To figure this out, we must usually make inferences beyond what we observe. For instance, if a coworker performs a favor for us, why are they doing it? Are they doing it because they

are fundamentally a generous person? Or are they manipulative and pursuing some ulterior motive? Does their social role require them to do it? Have other people pressured them into doing it? To act effectively toward them and to predict their future behavior, we must first figure out why they behave as they do.

The term *attribution* refers to the process an observer uses to infer the causes of another's behavior: "Why did that person act as they did?" In attribution, we observe another's behavior and infer backward to its causes—to the intentions, abilities, traits, motives, and situational pressures that explain why people act as they do. Theories of attribution focus on the methods we use to interpret another person's behavior and to infer its sources (Kelley & Michela, 1980; Lipe, 1991; Ross & Fletcher, 1985).

### Dispositional versus Situational Attributions

Fritz Heider (1944, 1958), whose work was an early stimulus to the study of attribution, noted that people in everyday life use commonsense reasoning to understand the causes of others' behavior. They act as "naive scientists" and use something resembling the scientific method in attempting to discern causes of behavior. Heider maintained that regardless of whether their interpretations about the causes of behavior are scientifically valid, people act on their beliefs. For this reason, social psychologists must study people's commonsense explanations of behavior and events so we can understand their behavior.

The most crucial decision observers make is whether to attribute a behavior to the internal state(s) of the person who performed it—this is termed a **dispositional attribution**—or to factors in that person's environment—a **situational attribution**. For example, consider the attributions an observer might make when learning that their neighbor is unemployed. They might judge that the neighbor is out of work because they are lazy, irresponsible, or unskilled. These are dispositional attributions, because they attribute the causes of behavior to the neighbor's internal states or characteristics. Alternatively, the observer might attribute the neighbor's unemployment to the scarcity of jobs in their line of work, to employment discrimination, to the depressed condition of the economy, or to the evils of the capitalist system. These are situational attributions because they attribute the neighbor's behavior to external causes.

What determines whether we attribute an act to a person's disposition or to the situation? One important consideration is the strength of situational pressures on the person. These pressures may include normative role demands as well as rewards or punishments applied to the person by others in the environment. For example, suppose we see a judge give the death penalty to a criminal. We might infer that the judge is tough (a dispositional attribution). However, suppose we learn that the law in that state requires the death penalty for the criminal's offense. Now we would see the judge not as tough but as responding to role pressures (a situational attribution).

This logic has been formalized as the **subtractive rule**, which states that when making attributions about personal dispositions, the observer subtracts the perceived impact of situational forces from the personal disposition implied by the behavior itself (Trope & Cohen, 1989; Trope, Cohen, & Maoz, 1988). Thus, considered by itself, the judge's behavior (imposing the death penalty) might imply that they are tough in disposition. The subtractive rule, however, states that the observer must subtract the effect of situational pressures (the state law) from the disposition implied by the behavior itself. When the observer does this, they may conclude the judge is not especially tough or overly inclined to impose the death penalty. In other words, using the subtractive rule in this situation served to weaken the dispositional attribution and strengthen the situational attribution.

There are other times, however, when applying the subtractive rule (by accounting for the situational influences) actually strengthens or augments the dispositional attribution—not unlike what happens when we subtract a negative number in arithmetic. This happens, for instance, when someone engages in an activity that their environment discourages or punishes. What if we learned that the judge in the previous example gave the death penalty even though they were the first to give the death penalty for such a crime or even after the jury suggested a lesser punishment or that the judge would face difficulty being reelected because of their decision? These situational factors would strengthen our dispositional attribution. The judge is more than tough; they are harsh.

Another factor that may influence our attributions is our attention to situational pressures and structural constraints. Social science students, whose coursework and training encourages them to think beyond the individual and to consider social structure, are more likely to blame the system for individuals' problems with unemployment and poverty than are either business or engineering students (Guimond, Begin, & Palmer, 1989; Guimond & Palmer, 1990). Some might argue that this is a selection effect; students who embrace system-blame are somehow drawn toward the social sciences. However, Figure 7.2 shows that students begin college with quite similar levels of system-blame, and it is over time that differences emerge. In a sense, as students are socialized into the norms of their disciplines, they acquire a particular view of the social world and reality—a type of cultural lens.

Culture plays an important role in the attribution process. As discussed in Chapter 6, one important dimension of cultural difference is the degree to which a culture is individualist or collectivist (Norenzayan & Nisbett, 2000; Triandis, 1995). Individualist cultures emphasize the individual and value individual achievement; collectivist cultures emphasize the welfare of the

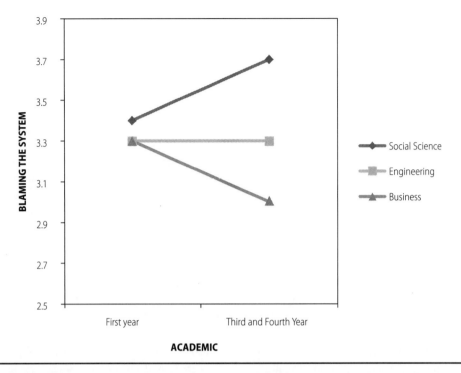

**FIGURE 7.2** Situational Attributions for Poverty and Unemployment, by Field of Study and Academic Year

Students enter college with similar levels of "system-blame" for poverty and unemployment. College classes increase the likelihood of making situational attributions among social science students and decrease such attributions among business students. Because engineering classes are unlikely to engage discussions of poverty or unemployment, engineering students' views remain unaffected over the course of study.

*Source:* Adapted from Guimond & Palmer, 1990.

family, ethnic group, and perhaps work group over the interests of individuals. This difference in emphasis turns out to have a substantial impact on the orientation toward dispositional versus situational attributions for behavior. Individualist cultures focus on the individual—thus, their members are predisposed to make individualist or dispositional attributions. In collectivist cultures, the focus on groups draws some attention to context—thus, members of these cultures are more likely to include situational elements in their attributions.

### Inferring Dispositions from Acts

Although Heider's analysis and the subtractive rule are useful in identifying some conditions under which observers make dispositional attributions, they do not explain which specific dispositions observers will ascribe to a person. Suppose, for instance, that you are on a city street during the Christmas season and you see a young, well-dressed man walking with a woman. Suddenly, the man stops and tosses several coins into a Salvation Army pot. From this act, what can you infer about the man's dispositions? Is he generous and altruistic? Or is he trying to impress the woman? Or is he perhaps just trying to clear out some nuisance change from his coat pocket?

When we try to infer a person's dispositions, our perspective is much like that of a detective. We can observe only the act (a man gives coins to the Salvation Army) and the effects of that act (the Salvation Army receives more resources, the woman smiles at the man, the man's pocket is no longer cluttered with coins). From this observed act and its effects, we must infer the man's dispositions.

According to one prominent theory (Jones, 1979; Jones & Davis, 1965), we perform two major steps when inferring personal dispositions. First, we try to deduce the specific intentions that underlie a person's actions. In other words, we try to figure out what the person originally intended to accomplish by performing the act. Second, from these intentions we try to infer what prior personal disposition would cause a person to have such intentions. If we think the man intended to benefit the Salvation Army, for example, we infer the disposition "helpful" or "generous." However, if we think the man had some other intention, such as impressing his girlfriend, we do not infer he has the disposition "helpful." Thus, we attribute a disposition that reflects the presumed intention. Thinking back to impression formation, we may use this disposition to form a (presumed) broad understanding of the man.

Several factors influence observers' decisions regarding which effect(s) the person is really pursuing and, hence, what dispositional inference is appropriate. These factors include the commonality of effects, the social desirability of effects, and the normativeness of effects (Jones & Davis, 1965).

**Commonality.** If any given act produced one and only one effect, then inferences of dispositions from acts would always be clear-cut. Because many acts have multiple effects, however, observers attributing specific intentions and dispositions find it informative to observe the actor in situations that involve choices between alternative actions.

Suppose, for example, that a person can engage either in action 1 or in action 2. Action 1, if chosen, will produce effects a, b, and c. Action 2 will produce effects b, c, d, and e. As we can see, two of these effects (b and c) are common to actions 1 and 2. The remaining effects (a, d, and e) are unique to a particular alternative; these are noncommon effects. The unique (noncommon) effects of acts enable observers to make inferences regarding intentions and dispositions, but the common effects of two or more acts provide little or no basis for inferences (Jones & Davis, 1965).

Thus, observers who wish to discern the specific dispositions of a person try to identify effects that are unique to the action chosen. Are there other ways the man may have impressed his date or cleared his pockets? Research shows that the fewer noncommon effects associated with the chosen alternative, the greater the confidence of observers about their attributions (Ajzen & Holmes, 1976).

**Social Desirability.** In many situations, people engage in particular behaviors because those behaviors are socially desirable. Yet people who perform a socially desirable act show us only that they are "normal" and reveal nothing about their distinctive dispositions. Suppose, for instance, that you observe a guest at a party thank the hostess when leaving. What does this tell you about the guest? Did they really enjoy the party? Or were they merely behaving in a polite, socially desirable fashion? You cannot be sure—either inference could be correct. Now suppose instead that when leaving, the guest complained loudly to the hostess that they had had a miserable time at such a dull party. This would likely tell you more about them because observers interpret acts low in social desirability as indicators of underlying dispositions (Miller, 1976).

**Normative Expectations.** When inferring dispositions from acts, observers consider the normativeness of behavior. Normativeness is the extent to which we expect the average person to perform a behavior in a particular setting. This includes conformity to social norms and to role expectations in groups (Jones & McGillis, 1976). Actions that conform to norms are uninformative about personal dispositions, whereas actions that violate norms lead to dispositional attributions. An observer could be confident that a Michigan fan who cheered for their team while sitting in the middle of Notre Dame's student section is much more passionate about football (a dispositional attribution) than if the same fan were acting similarly in the heart of the Michigan student section. If every person passing by the Salvation Army pot dropped coins in, the man's actions would communicate less about his own generosity.

## BIAS AND ERROR IN ATTRIBUTION

According to the picture presented thus far, observers scrutinize their environment, gather information, form impressions, and interpret behavior in rational, if sometimes unconscious, ways. In actuality, however, observers often deviate from the logical methods described by attribution theory and fall prey to biases. These biases may lead observers to misinterpret events and to make erroneous judgments. This section considers several major biases and errors in attribution.

### Overattribution to Dispositions

At the time of the Cuban Missile Crisis, the Cuban leader Fidel Castro was generally unpopular, even feared, in the United States. In an interesting study done shortly after the crisis, Jones and Harris (1967) asked participants to read an essay written by another student. Depending on the experimental condition, the essay either strongly supported the Cuban leader or strongly opposed him. Moreover, the participants received information about the conditions under which the student wrote the essay. They were told either that the essay was written by a student who was assigned by the instructor to take a pro-Castro or anti-Castro stand (no-choice condition) or that the essay was written by a student who was free to choose whichever position they wanted to present (choice condition). The participants'

task was to infer the writer's true underlying attitude about Castro. In the conditions in which the writer had free choice, participants inferred that the content of the essay reflected the writer's true attitude about Castro. That is, they saw the pro-Castro essay as indicating pro-Castro attitudes and the anti-Castro essay as indicating anti-Castro attitudes. In the conditions in which the writer was assigned the topic and had no choice, participants still thought the content of the essay reflected the writer's true attitude about Castro, although they were less sure that this was so. Participants made these internal attributions even though it was possible the writer held an opinion directly opposite of that expressed in the essay. In effect, participants overestimated the importance of internal dispositions (attitudes about Castro) and underestimated the importance of situational forces (role obligations) in shaping the essay.

The tendency to overestimate the importance of personal (dispositional) factors and to underestimate situational influences is called the **fundamental attribution error** (Higgins & Bryant, 1982; Ross, 1977; Small & Peterson, 1981). This tendency was first identified by Heider (1944), who noted that most observers ignore or minimize the impact of role pressures and situational constraints on others and interpret behavior as caused by people's intentions, motives, or attitudes. This bias toward dispositional factors was labeled "fundamental" because it was documented in study after study over the years and assumed to be universal. However, more recent research suggests that the bias is less universal than it originally seemed. The tendency was mistakenly considered fundamental because early social psychological research relied almost exclusively on American and Western European participants in surveys and experiments. Members of these cultures have a more independent view of the self (Markus & Kitayama, 1991) than those in Eastern cultures, who were seldom studied. Contemporary social psychologists, now more attentive to cultural differences, find that members of collectivist cultures (e.g., China, India, Taiwan) tend to favor situational explanations over dispositional ones—the reverse of the fundamental attribution error (Smith & Bond, 2003). Although the term remains the same, through cross-cultural research social psychologists realize that the bias is not as fundamental as it once seemed. Specifically, individuals in collectivist cultures see individuals as more malleable to situational pressures than those who privilege individualism.

Overemphasizing the importance of disposition is especially dangerous when it causes us to overlook the advantages of power built into social roles. For instance, we may incorrectly attribute the successes of the powerful to their superior personal capabilities, or we may incorrectly attribute the failures of persons without power to their personal weaknesses.

## Focus-of-Attention Bias

A closely related error is the tendency to overestimate the causal impact of whomever or whatever we focus our attention on; this is called the **focus–of–attention bias**. A striking demonstration of this bias appears in a study by Taylor and Fiske (1978). The study involved six participants who observed a conversation between two persons (Speaker 1 and Speaker 2). Although all six participants heard the same dialogue, they differed in the focus of their visual attention. Two observers sat behind Speaker 1, facing Speaker 2; two sat behind Speaker 2, facing Speaker 1; and two sat on the sides, equally focused on the two speakers. Measures taken after the conversation showed that observers thought the speaker they faced not only had more influence on the tone and content of the conversation but also had a greater causal impact on the other speaker's behavior. Observers who sat on the sides and were able to focus equally on both speakers attributed equal influence to them.

We perceive the stimuli that are most salient in the environment—those that attract our attention—as most causally influential. Thus, we attribute most causal influence to people who are noisy, colorful, vivid, or in motion. We credit the person who talks the most with exercising the most influence; we blame the person who we see run past us when we hear a rock shatter a window. Although salient stimuli may be causally important in some cases, we overestimate their importance (Krull & Dill, 1996; McArthur & Post, 1977).

The focus-of-attention bias provides one explanation for the fundamental attribution error. The person behaving is the active entity in the environment. Because many of us in the United States are socialized to direct our attention more to people who act than to the context, we attribute more causal importance to people than to their situations.

## Actor-Observer Difference

Actors and observers make different attributions for behavior. Observers tend to attribute actors' behavior to the actors' internal characteristics, whereas actors believe their own behavior is due more to characteristics of the external situation (Jones & Nisbett, 1972; Watson, 1982). This tendency is known as the **actor–observer difference**. Thus, although other customers in a market may attribute the mix of items in your grocery cart (beer, vegetables, candy bars) to your personal characteristics (hard-drinking, vegetarian, chocolate addict), you will probably attribute it to the requirements of your situation (preparing for a party) or the qualities of the items (nutritional value or special treat).

In one demonstration of the actor-observer difference (Nisbett, Caputo, Legant, & Maracek, 1973), male students wrote descriptions explaining why they liked their girlfriends and why they chose their majors. Then, as observers, they explained why their best friend liked his girlfriend and chose his major. When explaining their own actions, the students emphasized external characteristics like the attractive qualities of their girlfriends and the interesting aspects of their majors. However, when explaining their friends' behavior, they downplayed external characteristics and emphasized their friends' internal dispositions (preferences and personalities).

Two explanations for the actor-observer difference in attribution are that actors and observers have different visual perspectives and different access to information.

**Visual Perspectives.** The actor's natural visual perspective is to look at the situation, whereas the observer's natural perspective is to look at the actor. Thus, the actor-observer difference reflects a difference in the focus of attention. Both the actor and the observer attribute more causal influence to what they focus on. Consider a classroom of students watching a math professor struggle with a simple equation on the board. The students may think of their math professor as incapable because they are the students' visual focus. The

professor, who cannot see themself and whose visual attention is turned toward the classroom, blames the disrespectful behavior of the students in their class.

If the actor-observer difference in attributions were due simply to a difference in perspective, it should be possible to reverse the actor-observer difference by making the actor see the behavior from the observer's viewpoint and the observer see the same behavior from the actor's viewpoint. To test this, Storms (1973) gave individuals the other's point of view by videotaping a conversation between two people, using two separate cameras. One camera recorded the interaction from the visual perspective of the actor, the other from the perspective of the observer. Storms then showed actors the videotape made from the observer's perspective, and he showed observers the videotape made from the actor's perspective. As predicted, reversing the visual perspectives reversed the actor-observer difference in attribution; finding ways to make individuals more self-aware can, therefore, reduce the actor-observer bias (Fejfar & Hoyle, 2000).

In most classrooms, students are visually focused on the professor, whereas the professor is visually focused on the students. These visual perspectives influence attributions. If a lecture is not going well, the professor may blame the class's inattention and apathy, but the students are more likely to blame the professor and his lack of teaching ability or enthusiasm. © BraunS/iStock

**Information.** A second explanation for the actor-observer difference is that actors have information about their own past behavior and the context relevant to their behavior that observers lack (Johnson & Boyd, 1995). Thus, for example, observers may assume that certain behaviors are typical of an actor when in fact they are not. This would cause observers to make incorrect dispositional attributions. An observer who sees a model stumble on a runway may assume the model always behaves this way—resulting in a dispositional attribution of being uncoordinated. However, if the model knows they have never tripped before, they would probably not interpret their current behavior as evidence of a clumsy nature. Consistent with this, research shows that observers who have a low level of acquaintance with the actor tend to form more dispositional attributions and fewer situational attributions than those who have a high level of acquaintance with the actor (Prager & Cutler, 1990).

Even when observers have some information about an actor's past behavior, they often do not know how changes in context influence the actor's behavior. This is because observers usually see an actor only in limited contexts. Suppose that students observe a professor delivering witty, entertaining lectures in class week after week. The professor knows that in other social situations they are shy and withdrawn, but the students do not have an opportunity to see this. As a result, the observers (students) may infer dispositions from apparently consistent behavior that the actor (the professor) knows to be inconsistent across a wider range of contexts.

## Motivational Biases

Up to this point, we have considered attribution biases based on cognitive factors. That is, we have traced biases to the types of information that observers have available, acquire, and process. Motivational factors—a person's needs, interests, and goals—are another source of bias in attributions.

When events affect a person's self-interests, biased attribution is likely. Specific motives that influence attribution include the desire to defend deep-seated beliefs, to enhance one's self-esteem, to increase one's sense of control over the environment, and to strengthen the favorable impression of oneself that others have.

The desire to defend cherished beliefs and stereotypes may lead observers to engage in biased attribution. Observers may interpret actions that correspond with their stereotypes as caused by the actor's personal dispositions. For instance, they may attribute a female executive's outburst of tears during a crisis to her emotional instability because that corresponds to their stereotype about women. At the same time, people attribute actions that contradict stereotypes to situational causes. If the female executive manages the crisis smoothly, the same people may credit this to the effectiveness of her male assistant. When observers selectively attribute behaviors that contradict stereotypes to situational influences, these behaviors reveal nothing new about the persons who perform them. As a result, the stereotypes persist (Hamilton, 1979). Social psychologists refer to our tendency to view our initial assumption as correct despite evidence to the contradictory as **belief perseverance** (Ross, Lepper, & Hubbard, 1975).

Motivational biases may also influence attributions for success and failure. People tend to take credit for acts that yield positive outcomes, whereas they deflect blame for bad outcomes and attribute them to external causes (Bradley, 1978; Campbell & Sedikides, 1999; Ross & Fletcher, 1985). This phenomenon, referred to as the **self-serving bias**, is illustrated clearly by athletes' reporting of the results of competitions (Lau & Russell, 1980; Ross & Lumsden, 1982). Whereas members of winning teams take credit for winning ("We won"), members of losing teams are more likely to attribute the outcome to an external cause—their opponent ("They won," not "We lost"). Students are similar. In a study in which college students were asked to explain the grades they received on three examinations (Bernstein, Stephan, & Davis, 1979), students who received As and Bs attributed their grades much more to their own effort and ability than to good luck or easy tests. However, students who received Cs, Ds, and Fs attributed their grades largely to bad luck and the difficulty of the tests.

Various motives may contribute to this self-serving bias in attributions of performance. For instance, attributing success to personal qualities and failure to external factors enables us to enhance or protect our self-esteem. Regardless of the outcome, we can continue to see ourselves as competent and worthy. Moreover, by avoiding the attribution of failure to personal qualities, we maximize our sense of control. This in turn supports the belief that we can master challenges successfully if we choose to apply ourselves because we possess the necessary ability.

## ATTRIBUTIONS OF SUCCESS AND FAILURE

Given motivational biases, how do observers (and actors) decide which of these is the "real" cause of success or failure? For students, football coaches, elected officials, and anyone else whose fate rides on evaluations of their performance, attributions for success and failure are vital. As observers realize, however, attributions of this type are problematic. Whenever someone succeeds at a task, a variety of explanations can be advanced for the outcome. For example, a student who passes a test could credit their own intrinsic ability ("I have a lot of intelligence"), their effort ("I really studied for that exam"), the easiness of the task ("The exam could have been much more difficult"), or even luck ("They just happened to test us on the few chapters I read").

## Observing Success and Failure

These four factors—ability, effort, task difficulty, and luck—are general and apply in many settings. When observers look at an event and try to figure out the cause of success or failure, they must consider two things. First, they must decide whether the outcome is due to causes within the actor (an internal or dispositional attribution) or due to causes in the environment (an external or situational attribution). Second, they must decide whether the outcome is a stable or an unstable occurrence. That is, they must determine whether the cause is a permanent feature of the actor or the environment or whether it is labile and changing.

Ability, for instance, is usually considered internal and stable. That is, observers usually construe ability or aptitude as a property of the person (not the environment), and they consider it stable because it does not change from moment to moment. In contrast, effort is internal and unstable. Effort or temporary exertion is a property of the person that changes depending on how hard they try. Task difficulty depends on objective task characteristics, so it is external and stable. Luck or chance is external and unstable. These attributes and relationships are shown in Table 7.2. Only after observers make judgments regarding internality–externality and stability–instability can they reach conclusions regarding the cause(s) of the success or failure.

### TABLE 7.2   Perceived Causes of Success and Failure

| | LOCUS OF CONTROL | |
|---|---|---|
| DEGREE OF STABILITY | INTERNAL | EXTERNAL |
| Stable | Ability | Task difficulty |
| Unstable | Effort | Luck |

*Source:* Adapted from Weiner, Heckhausen, Meyer, & Cook, 1972.

**Determinants of Attributed Causes.**
Whether observers attribute a performance to internal or external causes depends on how the actor's performance compares with that of others. We usually attribute extreme or unusual performances to internal causes. For example, we would judge a tennis player who wins a major tournament as extraordinarily able or highly motivated. Similarly, we would view a player who performs unusually poorly compared to others as weak in ability or unmotivated. In contrast, we usually attribute average or common performances to external causes. If defeat comes to a player halfway through the tournament, we are likely to attribute it to tough competition or perhaps bad luck.

Whether observers attribute a performance to stable or unstable causes depends on how consistent the actor's performance is over time (Frieze & Weiner, 1971). When performances are very consistent, we attribute the outcome to stable causes. Thus, if a tennis player wins tournaments consistently, we would attribute this success to their great talent (ability) or perhaps to the uniformly low level of their opponents (task difficulty). When performances are very inconsistent, however, we attribute the outcomes to unstable causes rather than stable ones. Suppose, for example, that our tennis player is unbeatable one day and a pushover the next. In this case, we would attribute the outcomes to fluctuations in motivation (effort) or to random external factors such as wind speed, court condition, and so on (luck).

**Consequences of Attributions.** Attributions for performance are important because they influence both our emotional reactions to success and failure and our future expectations and aspirations. For instance, if we attribute a poor exam performance to lack of ability, we may despair of future success and give up studying; this is especially likely if we view ability as given and out of our control. Alternatively, if we attribute the poor

exam performance to lack of effort, we may feel shame or guilt, but we are likely to study harder and expect improvement. If we attribute the poor exam performance to bad luck, we may experience feelings of surprise or bewilderment, but we are not likely to change our study habits, because the situation will not seem controllable; despite this lack of change, we might nevertheless expect improved grades in the future. Finally, if we attribute our poor performance to the difficulty of the exam, we may become angry, but we will not strive for improvement (McFarland & Ross, 1982; Valle & Frieze, 1976; Weiner, 1985, 1986).

## Locus of Control

A social psychological concept closely related to the attributions that we may make for success and failure is **locus of control**, or the perceived cause of events in one's life (Rotter, 1966). Individuals are classified as having an *internal* locus of control if they believe they have control over many of their life outcomes—like getting into college, finding a mate, or being promoted—and an *external* locus of control when they feel powerless over such outcomes. These orientations (sometimes referred to as internality or externality) have profound effects on people's thoughts and behaviors (Lefcourt, 1991). For example, people with an internal locus of control tend to exercise more and eat healthier than those with an external locus of control (Steptoe & Wardle, 2001); they also drive more safely (Huang & Ford, 2012).

Locus of control is acquired through reinforcement (see Chapter 3), as part of social learning (Rotter, 1966). However, because of differential socialization and experiences across domains, it sometimes varies across spheres (Paulhus, 1983). For example, after being rewarded for her hard work with good grades, Jade may feel efficacious in college, believing she has control over her GPA and trajectory toward graduate school and her

## BOX 7.2  Test Yourself: Academic Attributions and Locus of Control

Although there are locus of control scales that measure more general attitudes (most notably, Rotter, 1966), the Multidimensional Multiattributional Causality Scale (Lefcourt, 1981) gives insight into students' academic locus of control and their attributional tendencies toward achievement. The original scale includes 48 items (Lefcourt, 1979). In the interest of space, we provide a selection of items focused on academic achievement so you can test yourself.

For the following statements, select whether you agree, disagree, or think it depends.

Scoring: Give yourself 2 points for each time you "agree," 1 point for each time you chose "it depends," and 0 for each time you selected "disagree." Determine your attributions for academic success by adding the scores in each group (*Ability*: 1, 3, 6; *Effort*: 7, 10, 11; *Context/ Task Difficulty*: 4, 5, 12; *Luck*: 2, 8, 9). To determine whether you are oriented more toward an internal or external locus of control, add your scores for ability + effort (internal) and context/ task difficulty + luck (external) and compare the two.

| | AGREE | IT DEPENDS | DISAGREE | STATEMENT |
|---|---|---|---|---|
| 1. | | | | I feel that my good grades reflect directly on my academic ability. |
| 2. | | | | Sometimes my success on exams depends on some luck. |
| 3. | | | | If I were to fail a course, it would probably be because I lacked skill in that area. |
| 4. | | | | Some of my good grades may simply reflect that these were easier courses than most. |
| 5. | | | | In my experience, once a professor gets the idea that you're a poor student, your work is much more likely to receive poor grades than if someone else handed it in. |
| 6. | | | | When I get good grades, it is because of my academic competence. |
| 7. | | | | In my case, the good grades I receive are always the direct result of my efforts. |
| 8. | | | | Sometimes I have to consider myself lucky for the good grades I get. |
| 9. | | | | Some of my lower grades have seemed to be partially due to bad breaks. |
| 10. | | | | I can overcome the obstacles in the path of academic success if I work hard enough. |
| 11. | | | | Poor grades inform me that I haven't worked hard enough. |
| 12. | | | | Some of my good grades in courses were due to the teacher's easy grading scheme. |

career. However, given that no one she has voted for has ever been elected to office, she may feel powerless in the realm of politics and government. Based on the relationship between locus of control and behavior, Jade would be likely to do her homework and study for an upcoming exam, but probably would not call a congressperson or take time off from her studies to vote.

Because of this potential variation, there are a number of customized scales to measure individuals' domain-specific perceptions of control (Donovan & O'Leary, 1978; Furnham, 2010; Wallston, 2005), including a scale related to academic achievement (Lefcourt, 1981; see Box 7.2 for sample items). Studies that use this scale find that students with an internal locus of control have lower levels of academic stress than those with an external locus of control (Abouserie, 1994). They are also less likely to procrastinate or to experience test anxiety, and have higher GPAs (Carden, Bryant, & Moss, 2004).

Over the last 50 years, externality has increased significantly among young Americans (Twenge, Zhang, & Im, 2004). In other words, young people today are much less likely to have an internal locus of control than their parents. Given the negative implications of externality—including poor school achievement, increased depression, decreased self-control, and increased delinquency— this trend is disturbing. It could also explain declining voter participation among college-age Americans (Bronfenbrenner et al., 1996) and record levels of anxiety (Twenge, 2000).

Another negative effect of an external locus of control is **learned helplessness** (Hiroto, 1974; Twenge et al., 2004). Learned helplessness occurs when individuals focus on past failures and conclude that they are incapable of achieving success. Imagine how you would feel about a final exam if you had not done well on the other two exams during the term, despite attending class and studying for them. With a sense that nothing that you could possibly do will help you pass the final, you might be inclined to skip class or to watch the basketball game with friends rather than study.

In one experiment (Trice & Woods, 1979), researchers asked students in a Statistics class to solve a series of math problems during class. Unbeknownst to the students, one group of students was given a series of unsolvable math problems, while another received solvable ones. Two days after working on these, both groups were given the same set of solvable math problems and asked to solve as many as they could in four minutes. Students who had been working on the unsolvable math problems in the previous class period completed significantly fewer problems in that short time than those who had previously worked on solvable problems. This suggests that a sense of powerlessness causes people to underperform even when offered an opportunity to do so.

In an effort to combat the negative implications of helplessness, social psychologists have begun to explore the importance of perspective in responses to failure (Duckworth, 2016; Dweck, 2007). Individuals who adopt a growth mindset—viewing intelligence as malleable and something that can be cultivated— are less susceptible to helplessness in the face of failure than those who have a fixed mindset and believe that their intelligence and ability are set and unlikely to change (Dweck, 2007). Importantly, these mindsets are learned and can be unlearned, decreasing one's susceptibility to learned helplessness and increasing one's potential for success.

## SUMMARY

Social perception is the process of using information to construct understandings of the social world and form impressions of people.

**Schemas.** A schema is a well-organized structure of cognitions about some social entity. (1) There are several distinct types of schemas: person schemas, self-schemas, group schemas (stereotypes), role schemas, and event schemas (scripts). (2) Schemas organize information in memory and, therefore, affect what we remember and what we forget. Moreover, they guide our inferences and judgments about people and objects.

**Person Schemas and Group Stereotypes.** (1) One important type of person schema is an implicit personality theory—a set of assumptions about which personality traits go together with other traits. These schemas enable us to make inferences about other people's traits. We can depict an implicit personality theory as a mental map. (2) A stereotype is a fixed set of characteristics attributed to all members of a given group. American culture includes stereotypes for ethnic, racial, gender, and many other groups. Because stereotypes are overgeneralizations, they cause errors in inference; this is especially true in complex situations.

**Impression Formation.** (1) Research on trait centrality using the "warm/cold" variable illustrates how variations in a single trait can produce a large difference in the impression formed by observers of a stimulus person. (2) Information received early usually has a larger impact on impressions than information received later; this is called the primacy effect. (3) Impressions become self-fulfilling prophecies when we behave toward others according to our impressions and evoke corresponding reactions from them. (4) Impressions are informed by schemas that are selected through mental shortcuts called heuristics.

**Attribution Theory.** Through attribution, people infer an action's causes from its effects. (1) One important issue in attribution is locus of causality—dispositional (internal) versus situational (external) attributions. Observers follow the subtractive rule when making attributions to dispositions or situations. (2) To attribute specific dispositions to an actor, observers observe an act and its effects and then try to infer the actor's intention with respect to that act. Observers then attribute the disposition that corresponds best with the actor's inferred intention.

**Bias and Error in Attribution.** (1) Observers frequently overestimate personal dispositions as causes of behavior and underestimate situational pressures; this bias is called the fundamental attribution error. (2) Observers also overestimate the causal impact of whatever

their attention is focused on. (3) Actors and observers have different attribution tendencies. Actors attribute their own behavior to external forces in the situation, whereas observers attribute the same behavior to the actor's personal dispositions. (4) Motivations—needs, interests, and goals—lead people to make self-serving, biased attributions. People defend deep-seated beliefs by attributing behavior that contradicts their beliefs to situational influences. People defend their self-esteem and sense of control by attributing their failures to external causes and taking personal credit for their successes.

**Attributions of Success and Failure.** Observers attribute success or failure to four basic causes—ability, effort, task difficulty, and luck. They attribute consistent performances to stable rather than to unstable causes, and they attribute average performances to external rather than internal causes. These attributions are related to individuals' locus of control and influence their responses to failure, including learned helplessness.

### *Critical Thinking Skill: Understanding Stereotyping*

Although our culture makes it seem as though there are vast differences between men and women, the scientific data show a very different picture. Men and women are actually quite similar on most, though not all, psychological characteristics, including behaviors such as math performance and leadership (Hyde, 2005). If men and women are so similar, why do people like to believe they are so different?

The answers lie in stereotypes and motives for stereotyping. As noted in the chapter, a stereotype is a generalization about a group of people (e.g., men) that distinguishes those people from another group (e.g., women). Gender stereotypes abound. Women are talkative, and men have little to say. Women are submissive, whereas men are dominant. Women are best suited for the humanities and social sciences, whereas men excel at science and math. When we collect rigorous scientific data, it turns out that some stereotypes are fairly accurate and some are not. For example, it turns out that although men tend to dominate task-oriented groups and women acquiesce (Ridgeway, 2011), gender difference in talkativeness is tiny (Leaper & Smith, 2004) and girls and boys perform equally on standardized math tests (Hyde et al., 2008) (see also Box 17.1).

*If so many stereotypes turn out not to be accurate, why do people continue to stereotype?* Although this chapter introduced cognitive efficiency as a possible explanation, another motivation is self-enhancement.

We make ourselves feel better by denigrating people from another group. For example, if we say or think, "Teenagers are so irresponsible," by implication we, as adults, are much more responsible. Although when people stereotype for cognitive efficiency, the stereotypes can be positive or negative, when people stereotype for self-enhancement purposes, the stereotypes tend to be negative.

*How does this illuminate potential reasons for gender stereotyping?*

Good critical thinking involves understanding why people stereotype and acknowledging that stereotypes are often not accurate. The next time you hear someone (or yourself!) making a stereotyped comment (whether based on gender, race, age, or other differences), ask yourself two questions: (1) What is the person's/your goal in stereotyping? and (2) Is this a stereotype that is supported by scientific data?

# ATTITUDES

By the end of this chapter you will be able to:

- Understand what attitudes are and identify their core components and articulate where they originate from, how they are formed, and the functions they serve.

- Describe how attitudes are organized and connected and be able to apply a variety of consistency theories to better understand your own and others' attitudes and the relationships between them.

- Understand the link between attitudes and behavior and identify and explain the variety of internal and external forces that influence attitudes and behavior.

## INTRODUCTION

We are bombarded with thoughts, opinions, and claims throughout our daily lives. Your grandfather tells you, "The Yankees are awesome!" and your roommate laments, "My human sexuality class is incredibly boring." Your older sister texts to say, "I like my new job." You hear a morning show commentator argue that "Something needs to be done about the nation's debt," while a politician claims "Marijuana should be legal everywhere" in a stump speech. A viral tweet, in response to calls to crack down on gun control after a school shooting, claims "Guns don't kill people; people kill people."

What do these statements have in common? Each represents an **attitude**—a predisposition to respond to a particular object in a generally favorable or unfavorable way (Ajzen, 1982). A person's attitudes influence the way in which they perceive and respond to the world (Allport, 1935; Thomas & Znaniecki, 1918). For example, attitudes influence attention—the person who likes the New York Yankees is more likely to notice news stories

about the team and its players. Attitudes also influence behavior—the person who thinks marijuana should be legal is more likely to smoke it regardless of the current law.

Attitudes do not exist in isolation. The person who believes that the nation's debt is too high likely has a whole set of beliefs about the role of government in the economy. They are more likely to support austerity measures, to think that the government needs to cut items from its budget, and to believe entitlement programs like Medicaid or Medicare should be reformed. Because attitudes can influence behavior, holding this attitude about the nation's debt might influence who someone votes for or whether they will call or e-mail their congressperson before an important vote on the debt ceiling. If attitudes influence behavior, is it possible to change behavior by changing attitudes? Politicians, auto manufacturers, restaurants, and others spend billions of dollars every year trying to create favorable attitudes. If they succeed, do these attitudes affect our behavior? What about when your parents or friends try to influence your attitudes? Are you less likely to smoke if your parents tell you it is a dirty and dangerous habit, or perhaps more inclined to become vegetarian if your friends tell you about the documentary they watched on industrial animal farming?

## THE NATURE OF ATTITUDES

An attitude exists in a person's mind; it is a mental state. Every attitude is about something, the "object" of the attitude. This section introduces the components, sources, and functions of attitudes.

### The Components of an Attitude

Consider the statement: "My human sexuality class is incredibly boring." This attitude has three components: (1) beliefs or cognitions,

(2) an affective evaluation, and (3) a behavioral predisposition.

**Cognition.** An attitude is based on a set of **cognitions**, knowledge structures or beliefs associated with the attitude object (Pratkanis & Greenwald, 1989). The student who doesn't like their human sexuality class perceives it as involving certain content, taught by a particular person, using a particular method of instruction. Often we cannot prove whether particular beliefs are true or false, as many are opinions. For example, economists, politicians, and constituents disagree on whether the nation's debt is too high, with people on both sides equally convinced they are right.

**Affective Evaluation.** An attitude is also based on how someone feels about an object. This is the attitude's affective or evaluative component. "It's incredibly boring" indicates that the course arouses an unpleasant emotion in the student. Stronger negative emotions include dislike, hatred, or even loathing: "I can't stand punk rock." Of course, the evaluation may be positive: "Thai food is delicious" or "I like Jimmy Fallon." The evaluative component of an attitude has both a direction (positive or negative) and an intensity (ranging from very weak to very strong).

**Behavioral Predisposition.** An attitude also involves a predisposition to respond or a behavioral tendency toward the object. Referring to a sexualities course as "incredibly boring" implies a tendency to avoid the class. "I like my new job" suggests an intention to go to work. People who hold a specific attitude are inclined to behave in ways that are consistent with that attitude.

**Relationships among the Components.** Cognitive, affective, and behavioral components all have the same object, so we would expect them to form a single, relatively consistent whole. However, these three components are distinct; if they were identical, we would not need to distinguish among them (Kothandapani, 1971).

Some attitudes are primarily driven by the affective component of the attitude: "I am scared of snakes" (Edwards, 1990). We call these affect-based, as fear is an emotion. Even if someone tried to influence the cognitive components of this attitude, perhaps assuring you that most snakes are not poisonous or that poisonous snakes are more scared of you than you are of them, this is unlikely to change this attitude. If you have a phobia of snakes, you will jump at the sight of one. These affect-based attitudes are difficult to change with cognitive reasoning.

Other attitudes are cognition-based, with the cognitive components of that attitude taking priority: "The Toyota Prius is the best hybrid car." Whether you are aesthetically drawn to the car, which would be a more evaluative component, is less important than what you know or believe—the cognitive component of your attitudes—about the car. It is reliable, gets good gas mileage, and has a lower carbon footprint than other models. It is not that how you feel about the car is unimportant; rather, it is simply that the affect-based evaluation is not central to this attitude.

Greater consistency between the cognitive and affective components is associated with greater attitude stability and resistance to persuasion (Chaiken & Yates, 1985). If you both like the appearance of the Prius and believe it is the best hybrid car based on its other attributes, your positive attitude toward it is unlikely to change. You are also more likely to purchase a Prius than other hybrid cars because greater consistency between attitude components is also associated with a stronger relationship between attitude and behavior.

## Attitude Formation

Where do attitudes come from? How are they formed? The answer lies in the processes of socialization (discussed in Chapter 3). Attitudes may be formed through reinforcement (instrumental conditioning), through associations of stimuli and responses (classical conditioning), or by observing others (observational learning).

Attitudes toward our classes and jobs might be formed through instrumental conditioning—that is, learning based on direct experience with the object. If you experience rewards related to some object, your attitude will be favorable. Thus, if your work provides you with good pay, a sense of accomplishment, and compliments from your coworkers, your attitude toward it will be quite positive. Conversely, if you associate negative emotions or unpleasant outcomes with some object, you will dislike it. If you experience frequent embarrassment in your human sexuality class or have struggled to stay awake while doing the course reading and scored poorly on every test and assignment, you are likely to have a very negative attitude toward the course.

However, only a small portion of our attitudes are based on direct contact with objects. You also have attitudes about objects that you have never personally experienced. These attitudes may have been acquired through classical conditioning. In this process, a stimulus gradually elicits a response through repeated association with other stimuli. Children learn at an early age that "lazy," "dirty," "stupid," and many other characteristics are undesirable. Children themselves are often punished for being dirty or hear adults say, "Don't be stupid!" If they hear their parents (or others) refer to members of a particular group as lazy or stupid, children increasingly associate the group name with the negative reactions these terms initially elicited (Staats & Staats, 1958). Advertisers use this type of conditioning when they associate products or brands with positive feelings—whether warmth, excitement, or happiness—to influence brand evaluations (Pham, Geuens, & De Pelsmacker, 2013). Coca-Cola is well known for its emotional storytelling in ads. In 2016 they launched their "Taste the Feeling" advertising campaign. Strategically shifting from their previous "Open Happiness" campaign, the new ads are intended to link Coca-Cola with the range of emotions people experience in "everyday moments" from a first date to an afternoon with friends (Schultz, 2016).

These learned associations play an important role in our automatic (low-effort) processing and unconscious reactions to stimuli (Moskowitz, Skurnik, & Galinsky, 1999). In other words, attitudes affect our behavior regardless of whether we realize we have them (see Box 8.1 and photos on p. 252).

We also learn attitudes more directly by observing others and interacting with them. For example, we acquire many of our attitudes from our parents. Research shows that children's attitudes toward gender roles, politics, religion, and racial groups are frequently similar to those held by their parents (Glass, Bengston, & Dunham, 1986; Sinclair, Dunn, & Lowery, 2005). This is in part because of observational learning, but the similarity between parents' and children's attitudes may also be a product of instrumental learning because parents typically reward their children—consciously or unconsciously—for adopting the same or similar attitudes. Friends are another important source of our attitudes. The attitude that marijuana should be legal, for example, may be learned through interaction with peers.

Many of us grow up in homogeneous settings, within families that are similar to us and among neighbors and friends who hold both similar attributes (race, social class) and attitudes. However, when we attend college, we often encounter people—both students and faculty—who are quite different from us. This is one of the reasons significant attitude shifts frequently occur during young adulthood. A classic study of Bennington College women by Newcomb (1943) demonstrated the impact of peers on the political attitudes of college students. Although the majority of these women grew up in wealthy, politically conservative

## BOX 8.1  Research Update: The Implicit Associations Test

Social psychologists understand that people are sometimes unwilling—and often unable—to report their attitudes on surveys. Although people's unwillingness may stem from concerns about political correctness, an inability to report attitudes has been attributed to people's limited awareness of those attitudes. When it comes to attitudes—in the words of dual-process theories—some of them are low-effort rather than high-effort.

Although these automatic or implicit attitudes are beyond our consciousness, they profoundly influence our perceptions and behavior. For social scientists to fully explore the impact of implicit attitudes on social life, they had to find a way to measure them. To do that, they developed the Implicit Associations Test (IAT).

The IAT is a computerized test that measures individuals' response latencies when they encounter attitude-consistent and attitude-inconsistent stimuli. For example, if someone holds the attitude that men are more inclined toward math and science and that women are more inclined toward the humanities and liberal arts, they should be able to process information linking men and math (attitude-consistent) more quickly than they would women and science (attitude-inconsistent). The easier information is to process, the shorter one's response latency.

To test this, the IAT has subjects complete a number of blocks. First, respondents are asked to use two keys (often E and I) to classify exemplars of two contrasted concepts (for example, men and women's names). The next block will, once again, ask respondents to use the keys to classify exemplars of contrasted concepts (for example, algebra and English). The third and fourth blocks are combined tasks, in which all four exemplars are shown in various combinations, and respondents are explicitly instructed on how to classify objects (to categorize men's names and science and math subjects using E and women's names and humanities and liberal arts classes using I). If they hold implicit attitudes that are consistent with these pairings, they should be able to complete this task more quickly (and with fewer errors) than they will in the final when the same key will be used for women's names as for science and math and another key for both men's names and humanities and liberal arts.

If a respondent possesses an attitude—even an unconscious one—they have a mental association between the affective or cognitive component of the attitude (academic strengths) and the attitude object (gender). The implicit association is able to gauge that mental association by comparing individuals' response latencies in the third and fourth blocks and then considering the number of errors (Greenwald, Nosek, & Banaji, 2003).

The IAT has been used to measure a variety of implicit attitudes in the U.S. population—including racial stereotypes, ageism, and gender roles—but has also been used to measure the biases of specific groups (for example, doctors and police officers) whose implicit associations may have life or death consequences (Correll, Hudson, Guillermo, & Ma, 2014; Moskowitz, Stone, & Childs, 2012). The test is particularly useful for socially sensitive topics, in which respondents' concerns about impression management might distort their self-report responses. Research finds that the IAT is often more predictive of behavior than self-reports.

You can try the IAT yourself by visiting http://implicit.harvard.edu.

*Source:* Adapted from Greenwald, Poehlman, Uhlmann, & Banaji, 2009.

families, most of the faculty—and a number of students—at Bennington had very liberal political attitudes. The study demonstrated that first-year students who maintained close ties with their families and did not become involved in campus activities remained conservative. However, women who became active in the college community and interacted more frequently with other students and with faculty gradually became more liberal.

Another source of attitudes is the media. The media provide interpretive packages or frames about objects that may influence viewers' and readers' attitudes. By portraying events and actors in certain ways, news outlets and the entertainment industry can produce cognitive images that influence attitudes. For example, television coverage of racially charged riots depicting a racial group as being volatile, dangerous, or unreasonable fosters negative attitudes toward that group (Myers & Caniglia, 2004). Similarly, portrayals of families of various social classes—such as *The Real Housewives* or *The Middle*—shape viewers' attitudes toward those groups, whether positive or negative (Kendall, 2011).

Although research on media influence has traditionally focused on television and films, interest in the effects of social media and the Internet more generally is growing rapidly. Social media and websites are especially influential because they transmit information quickly and easily and people spend so much time online. Unfortunately, even web-savvy audiences have trouble distinguishing between fact and fiction online. Studies show high school and college students cannot tell the difference between "real news" and "fake news" on Facebook, do not suspect potential bias in tweets from activist groups, and are unable to differentiate a mainstream source from a fringe source (Stanford History Education Group, 2016). This lack of online reasoning skills, coupled with "fake news," was seen as influential in the outcome of the 2016 U.S. presidential election and the U.K. vote to exit the European Union (Kucharski, 2016).

**Photos below:** Implicit associations were likely at play when the same behavior (taking

A young man walks through chest-deep flood water after looting a grocery store in New Orleans on Tuesday, August 30, 2005. Flood waters continue to rise in New Orleans after Hurricane Katrina did extensive damage when it made landfall on Monday. © AP Photo/Dave Martin

Two residents wade through chest-deep water after finding bread and soda from a local grocery store after Hurricane Katrina came through the area on August 29, 2005, in New Orleans, Louisiana. Katrina was downgraded to a category 4 storm as it approached New Orleans. © Chris Graythen/Getty Images

items from stores) was described in one news agency photo caption (left) as "finding" when attributed to Whites and in another caption (right) as "looting" when attributed to Blacks.

## The Functions of Attitudes

We acquire attitudes through learning, but there would be no reason to retain them—and to draw on them so frequently—if they did not serve at least some important functions (Katz, 1960; Pratkanis & Greenwald, 1989).

The first is the heuristic function (see Chapter 7). Once they are developed, attitudes provide a simple and efficient means of evaluating objects (Fazio, 1995). Attitudes help us decide whether objects are something we want to approach or avoid (Ajzen & Sexton, 1999). As discussed in Chapter 7, because the world is too complex for us to completely understand, we group people, objects, and events into categories or schemas and develop simplified attitudes that allow us to treat individuals as members of a category. Our attitudes about that category (the attitude object) provide us with a basis for making inferences about that category's members and influence our behavior toward them (Fiske, Lin, & Neuberg, 1999). Reacting to every member of the group in the same way is more efficient, even if less accurate and satisfying, than trying to learn about each person as an individual.

Attitudes about groups are often associated with intense emotions. A strong like or dislike for members of a specific group is called a **prejudice**. Prejudice and stereotyping (discussed in Chapter 7) go together, with people using their stereotyped beliefs to justify prejudice toward members of the group. The emotional component of prejudice can lead to intergroup conflict (see Chapter 14).

Second, attitudes define the self and maintain self-worth. Some attitudes express an individual's basic values and reinforce their self-image. Think about your musical tastes, your attitudes toward particular music. What does your dislike of rap or your love of country or your tolerance of "anything but heavy metal" say about you (Bryson, 1996)? We tend to adopt attitudes we see as consistent with our identities. For example, many political conservatives in our society have negative attitudes toward abortion, immigration, and government-sponsored entitlement programs that help the poor. Thus, a person whose self-concept includes conservatism might adopt these attitudes because they align with that self-image.

Even if an individual never gave a particular attitude much thought, they will see attitudes as symbolic of their identification with or membership in particular groups or subcultures. A first-year student at Notre Dame who never gave a thought to football might suddenly adopt the attitude that the Fighting Irish are the best football team ever simply because it is consistent with their self-image as a member of the Notre Dame community. The attitudes "Guns don't kill people; people kill people" and "The only way to stop a bad guy with a gun is a good guy with a gun" are widespread among members of the National Rifle Association (NRA). Holding these attitudes may be both a prerequisite to acceptance by other group members and a symbol of loyalty to the group.

Finally, some attitudes protect the person from recognizing certain thoughts or feelings that threaten their self-image. Imagine you received a negative performance review at work. In order to maintain a positive self-image, you may adopt attitudes that shift the blame toward other entities (van Dellen, Campbell, Hoyle, & Bradfield, 2011). If you originally held a positive attitude toward your job or your manager, you might adopt a more negative one instead, thinking "that job is not fulfilling" or "my manager fails to appreciate me." This protective mechanism has also been used to explain the number of Whites who believe that we live in a post-racial society in the United States (a context where racism and racial bias do not exist) or are skeptical of White privilege (Margolin, 2015). Admitting racism or privilege exist could prompt Whites to feel that their success was not earned, threatening their self-esteem.

Experiences that threaten a person's self-esteem are particularly likely to lead to more negative attitudes toward other groups among people who have high self-esteem because if self-esteem is already low, there is no reason to shift attitudes to protect it (Crocker, Thompson, McGraw, & Ingerman, 1987).

## ATTITUDE ORGANIZATION

### Attitude Structure

Have you ever tried to change another person's attitude toward an object (global warming) or a behavior (recycling)? If you have, you probably discovered that the person had a counterargument for almost every argument you put forth. They probably had several reasons why their attitude was correct. This tendency flows from how attitudes are arranged in our minds. Attitudes are usually embedded in a cognitive structure, linked with a variety of other attitudes. Not only would changing one attitude require shifting a slew of other attitudes, but the other attitudes also work as a support structure to keep the original attitude intact.

We can often determine the cognitive structure attitudes are embedded in by asking someone why they hold a particular attitude. Consider the following fictional exchange between an interviewer for the campus newspaper and Joaquin, a current student:

INTERVIEWER: Why do you think same-sex marriage should be legal?
JOAQUIN: Because the Constitution's Bill of Rights says that all Americans should have equal rights and protections. To exclude same-sex couples from the rights and

protections of marriage is unfair.
INTERVIEWER: Are there any other reasons?
JOAQUIN: Well, I think children do best in homes with two parents, and marriage would encourage more people to stay together and raise their children.
INTERVIEWER: Any other reasons?
JOAQUIN: Um . . . yeah. I believe that who we are attracted to is not usually a choice. I have always been attracted to women. I was born that way. Why is someone who is attracted to the same sex any different? Shouldn't we all be able to marry who we love?

This exchange indicates Joaquin's reasons for his attitude. More than that, it illustrates the two basic dimensions of attitude organization: vertical and horizontal structure (Bem, 1970).

**Vertical Structure.** Attitudes are organized hierarchically. Specific beliefs and attitudes tend to be dependent on other, more fundamental, beliefs. Such a structure is portrayed in Figure 8.1.

Working backward from the attitude of interest—Joaquin's support for the Supreme Court's 2015 decision on same-sex marriage—it is clear that Joaquin's favorable attitude toward marriage equality (at the top of the cognitive structure) is rooted in a belief that all citizens of the United States should have equal rights and protections (in the middle of the cognitive structure) and this belief in equality stems from his acceptance of the Constitution (at the base of the cognitive structure). The unquestioning acceptance of the credibility of some authority, such as the Constitution, is a **primitive belief** (Bem, 1970).

The same primitive belief, such as a belief in the Constitution, is often the basis for a large number of specific beliefs (Bem, 1970). For example, Joaquin probably supports the democratic political system in the United States, freedom of speech, and race and gender

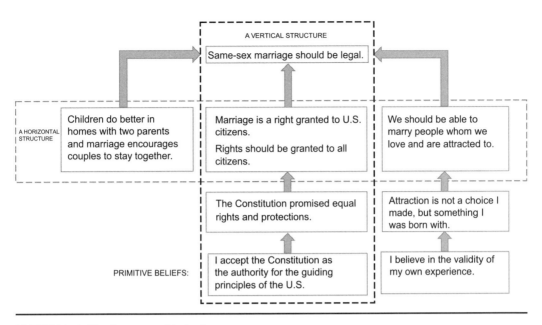

**FIGURE 8.1** The Structure of Attitudes

equality. Changing a primitive belief may result in widespread changes in the person's attitudes. If Joaquin were to align himself with the Chinese Communist Party and declare the U.S. Constitution untenable and unreasonable, the change in his primitive beliefs will likely lead to changed attitudes toward many objects, including his views of democracy, freedom of speech, and equality.

Joaquin has another primitive belief in his cognitive structure, a belief in the validity of his own experience. Joaquin realizes that he did not choose who he is attracted to. His belief that this is true of others, and his opinion that everyone should be able to marry people whom they love and are attracted to, is another vertical link supporting his attitude about same-sex marriage.

**Horizontal Structure.** When the interviewer asked Joaquin why he supports same-sex marriage, Joaquin gave an additional reason: his belief that it is best for children to be raised in homes with two adults and that marriage encourages couples to stay together.

When an attitude is linked to more than one set of underlying beliefs—that is, when there are two or more different justifications for it—the linkages are termed *horizontal*. Attitudes with a horizontal structure are more difficult to change than those supported by a single belief. Even if you show Joaquin statistical evidence that couples are no more likely to stay together if married than if simply cohabiting, his belief in equality and the roots of romantic attraction make it unlikely his attitude toward same-sex marriage will change.

**COGNITIVE CONSISTENCY**

Alysia lives a "green" life. She composts and recycles. She has her own garden and thinks organic produce is better than nonorganic options. She identifies as an environmentalist and believes she is intentional about her consumption and waste patterns. These beliefs (we should be intentional consumers) and attitudes (organic is better than nonorganic) fit together. Many of her attitudes and behaviors are also consistent with what she perceives as green or environmentalist. For example, she prefers to give handmade, wooden toys to her nieces for gifts rather than mass-produced plastic toys, and she likes to purchase her clothes at thrift stores and second-hand shops.

Consistency among a person's cognitions—that is, their beliefs and attitudes—is widespread. If you have liberal political values, you probably favor housing assistance programs for people living in poverty. If you value public education, you are likely to support a property-tax increase to generate additional revenue for the local schools or choose to send your children to public schools rather than to a private school in the area. Cognitions are usually consistent because people are motivated to maintain that consistency. If an inconsistency develops between cognitive elements—for example, if you value public education yet oppose a tax increase or decide to enroll your children in private school—you will be motivated to restore harmony between those elements. Several theories of attitude organization are based on this principle of consistency.

## Balance Theory

One important consistency theory is **balance theory**. This theory was originally formulated by Heider (1958) and later elaborated by Rosenberg and Abelson (1960) to explain how we seek consistency in cognitive structures.

Balance theory is concerned with cognitive systems like this one: "I'm going to vote for Cam Nguyen. Like me, she is also in favor of reducing taxes." This system contains three elements—the speaker, another person (candidate Cam Nguyen), and an impersonal object (taxes). According to balance theory, two types of relationships may exist between elements—*unit relations* and *sentiment relations*. Unit relations describe the relationship

between two elements (ownership, proximity) that are nonevaluative (just because you own a car does not necessarily mean that you like it and being far from someone physically does not necessarily mean you dislike them). Sentiment relations, on the other hand, are evaluative and based on positive or negative evaluation. For example, a positive sentiment relation may result from a social relationship (such as friendship or marriage) between elements. A negative sentiment relation indicates a negative evaluation of that other element— "I don't like my ex-husband" or "I hate those greedy politicians."

Using these terms, let's analyze the above example. We can depict this system as a triangle (see Figure 8.2). Balance theory is concerned with the elements and their interrelations from the speaker's viewpoint. In our first example (Figure 8.2A), the speaker favors reduced taxes, perceives Cam Nguyen as favoring reduced taxes, and, therefore, intends to vote for Nguyen. This system is balanced. By definition, a balanced state is one in which all three sentiment relations are positive or in which one is positive and the other two are negative. For example, this system would also be balanced if the speaker still favored reduced taxes (+) and, therefore, decided not to vote for Cam Nguyen (−) because Nguyen was opposed to reducing taxes (−) (Figure 8.2B). This is the type of system behind the phrase "the enemy of my enemy is my friend."

**Imbalance and Change.** According to balance theory, an imbalanced state is one in which two of the relationships between elements are positive and one is negative. This is easiest to illustrate with friendships. Consider Haley and Ellen, who are starting their junior year in high school. They have been friends since fifth grade and spend all their free time together. This past summer, Haley grew close to Aaliyah, another girl at their high school, while working together at a local day camp.

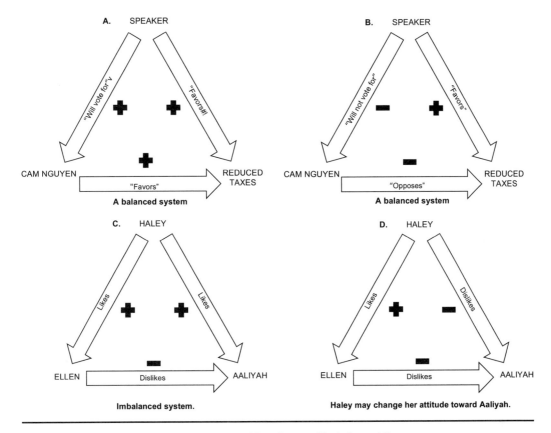

**FIGURE 8.2** Balanced Cognitive Systems and Resolution of Imbalanced Systems

When the relationships among all three cognitive elements are positive (A) or when one relationship is positive and the other two are negative (B), the cognitive system is balanced. When two relationships are positive and one negative, the cognitive system is imbalanced. In (C), Ellen's negative attitude toward Aaliyah creates an unpleasant psychological state for Haley. Haley can resolve the imbalance by deciding she does not want to be friends with Aaliyah (D), deciding she does not like Ellen anymore, or persuading Ellen to like Aaliyah.

Ellen thinks Aaliyah is a gossip and does not like her. Figure 8.2C illustrates the situation from Haley's viewpoint. Haley feels positively toward Ellen and Aaliyah, but Ellen feels negatively toward Aaliyah. Thus, there is an imbalance.

In general, an imbalanced situation like this is unpleasant (as is a situation where all three relations are negative). Balance theory assumes that people will try to restore balance among their attitudes to ease tension. There are three basic ways to do this.

First, Haley may change her attitudes so the sign of one of the relations is reversed (Tyler &

Sears, 1977). For instance, she may decide that she really does not like Aaliyah (Figure 8.2D). Alternatively, Haley may decide that she and Ellen have grown apart and she does not like her as much as she used to, or she may persuade Ellen to give Aaliyah a chance and to get to know her better so she can see how wrong her initial impressions are. Each of these involves changing one relationship so the system of beliefs contains either zero or two negative relationships.

Second, Haley can restore balance by changing a positive or negative relation to a null relation (Steiner & Rogers, 1963). Haley may decide that Ellen doesn't know anything about Aaliyah and her attitude toward her is irrelevant.

Third, Haley can restore balance by differentiating the attributes of the other person or object (Stroebe, Thompson, Insko, & Reisman, 1970). For instance, Haley may distinguish between types of friends—work friends, who you share few personal details with, and close friends, who you can trust with anything. Ellen might be correct in her belief that Aaliyah is a gossip. However, Haley believes she can be friends with both if she is careful what she shares with Aaliyah so as to protect herself (and if she tells Ellen that this is her intention).

Which technique will a person use to remove the imbalance? Balance is usually restored by whatever means are easiest (Rosenberg & Abelson, 1960). If one relationship is weaker than the other two, the easiest mode of restoring balance is to change the weaker relationship (Feather, 1967). Because Haley and Ellen have been friends for over five years, it would be very difficult for Haley to change her sentiments toward Ellen; it would be easier for her to change her attitude toward Aaliyah. However, Haley really likes both girls and would prefer to maintain both friendships. Therefore, she may attempt to change Ellen's attitude. If this influence attempt fails, theory suggests that Haley will probably change her own attitude toward Aaliyah.

## Theory of Cognitive Dissonance

Another major consistency theory is the **theory of cognitive dissonance**. Whereas balance theory deals with the relationships among three cognitions, dissonance theory deals with consistency between two or more elements (behaviors and attitudes). For example, given Alysia's attitude toward intentional, environmentally sound consumption, we would never expect her to buy a Hummer or a large, luxury car. If she did, then her behavior would be inconsistent with her attitudes, and this would likely cause her dissonance.

There are two situations in which dissonance commonly occurs: (1) after a decision, or (2) when one acts in a way that is inconsistent with one's beliefs.

**Postdecisional Dissonance.** Taylor will begin his sophomore year of college next week. He needs to work part time so he can pay for school. After two weeks of searching for work, he receives two offers. One is a part-time job doing library research for a faculty member he admires, and it pays $8 per hour with flexible working hours. The other is a job in a restaurant as a busser that pays $12 per hour but has set working hours—5 p.m. to 11 p.m., Thursdays, Fridays, and Saturdays. He has no experience bussing tables.

Taylor has a hard time choosing between these jobs. Both are located near campus, and he thinks he would like either one. Whereas the research job offers flexible hours, the busser's job pays more and offers him the opportunity to meet interesting people. In the end, Taylor chooses the bussing job, but he is experiencing dissonance.

Dissonance theory (Festinger, 1957) assumes there are three possible relationships between any two cognitions. Cognitions are consistent or consonant if one naturally or logically follows from the other. They are dissonant when one is inconsistent with the other. The logic involved is psycho-logic (Rosenberg & Abelson, 1960)—that is, logic as it appears to the individual, not logic in a formal sense. Two cognitive elements also may be irrelevant; one may have nothing to do with the other. In Taylor's case, the decision to take the position clearing tables is consonant with (1) the job's convenient location, (2) the higher pay, and (3) the opportunities to meet people, but it is dissonant with the fact that (1) he is unsure of his ability to bus tables and (2) he has to work weekend

## BOX 8.2  Selling with Cognitive Dissonance

Cognitive dissonance is a ubiquitous part of our daily lives. We encounter it almost wherever we go and in almost whatever we do. One social interaction in which we are very likely to encounter cognitive dissonance is when we encounter a salesperson—particularly one who uses high-pressure sales techniques. These techniques are especially common in settings where employees work on commission, including car dealerships, many retail settings, and insurance companies. Although there is a growing interest in soft selling—when salespeople use subtle persuasion to encourage customers to buy—the hard sell still exists. In the hard sell, salespeople harness the power of cognitive dissonance and use it to increase the chances of convincing the customer to buy. How do they do this?

First, salespeople often make use of a technique called the "foot-in-the-door" (Freedman & Fraser, 1966). In this case, the salesperson attempts to get the customer to agree to some kind of small request and, having established a pattern of compliance, will ask the customer to do bigger things, including purchasing the product. Salespeople might offer you a free sample, request an appointment, ask you to fill out paperwork, or encourage you to take a test drive. This is one of the reasons so many businesses will offer free estimates to potential clients. Once the small request is fulfilled, an inconsistency is produced if you do not go ahead and buy the product (Burger, 1999). Your refusal to buy causes some dissonance because it is inconsistent with your previous compliant behavior. Not buying is even more difficult if, through this process, you find you actually like the product. It is much more difficult to turn down a car you loved to test drive than one that you did not enjoy driving. Of course, this is not always enough to get you to buy, but it can reduce sales resistance.

A second technique, often used by unscrupulous salespeople, is called "low-balling" (Burger & Petty, 1981; Weyant, 1996). In this technique, the salesperson will offer the buyer a very good price on a product. The buyer agrees, and the salesperson sets about to do all the paperwork. Before it is completed, though, the salesperson "discovers" that they have made an error and that the price is going to be higher than initially promised. Under these circumstances, the buyer has a tendency to accept the higher price; after all, they have already agreed to buy—why should a few more dollars make that much of a difference? Interestingly, though, social psychologists have found that buyers will often pay more than their original upper limit when confronted with the low-balling technique (Cialdini, 1993; Cialdini, Cacioppo, Basset, & Miller, 1978). If you walk into a cell-phone store thinking you are willing to spend $200 on a new phone and you are low-balled with an offer of $175, you are enticed and begin to imagine having the new phone. When the salesperson comes back, saying they made a mistake and that the phone is actually $225, you are likely to pay that rather that hold out for a different phone under $200.

In a third technique that involves consistency, salespeople usually work very hard to get us to like them (Gordon, 1996). In fact, they are often trained in many specific techniques to get buyers to feel like they are friends with the salesperson. It is no surprise that we are more likely to buy things from people we like than from people we do not like, but why does this occur? One reason is that refusing a request from someone we like is inconsistent with our liking them. When a friend asks us to purchase candy for a fundraiser, turning them down can be difficult because such behavior is incompatible with the friendship. Salespeople can use this underlying tendency to increase compliance as well (Jones, 1964). This is a delicate process, however. When customers sense insincerity from salespeople, the interaction is less likely to result in a sale (Basso, dos Santos, & Gonçalves, 2014).

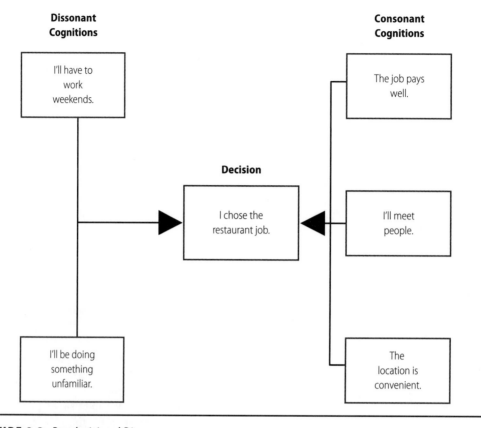

**FIGURE 8.3** Postdecisional Dissonance

Whenever we make a decision, there are some cognitions—attitudes, beliefs, knowledge—that are consonant with that decision and other cognitions that are dissonant with it. Dissonant cognitions create an unpleasant psychological state that we are motivated to reduce or eliminate. In this example, Taylor has chosen a job and is experiencing dissonance. Although three cognitions are consistent with his decision, two other dissonant cognitions are creating psychological tension.

nights and will miss out on hanging out with his friends (see Figure 8.3).

Having made the choice, Taylor is experiencing **cognitive dissonance**, a state of psychological tension induced by dissonant relationships between cognitive elements. Some decisions produce a large amount of cognitive dissonance, others very little. The magnitude of dissonance experienced depends in part on the proportion of elements that are dissonant with a person's decision. In Taylor's case, there are three consonant and only two dissonant cognitions, so he will only experience moderate dissonance. The magnitude is also influenced by the importance of the elements. He will experience less dissonance after taking the bussing job if hanging out with his friends on the weekends is not important to him, but more dissonance if an active social life is.

Dissonance is an uncomfortable state. To reduce dissonance, the theory predicts, Taylor will change his attitudes by changing either the cognitive elements themselves or the importance of the elements. For example, he may decide that having a thriving social life should no longer be a priority as he enters this season of his life.

It is hard to change cognitions. He chose the restaurant job, and he made a commitment to work weekend nights and to take a job he had no experience in. Alternatively, Taylor can rationalize his choice by changing the relative importance of his cognitions. He can emphasize the importance of one or more of the consonant cognitions and deemphasize one or more of the dissonant cognitions. Although he has to do a job that is unfamiliar to him, he can emphasize the fact that it pays well. Although he would prefer to be able to go out on weekends, he can decide that this is less important because the restaurant job will still allow him to meet interesting people.

Decisions often result in dissonance (Brehm, 1956). Regardless of the job he decided to take, Taylor would have to work to reduce dissonance. If he had decided, instead, to do research for his professor, he would still experience dissonance because he chose to forgo the more lucrative position even though he needs money to stay in school. He would still try to rationalize his choice to reduce dissonance. It would probably work. If you asked him soon after he started his job if he would make the same decision again, he would likely say he would (Wee, 2013).

Postdecisional dissonance can have powerful effects. Elias Dinas (2013) argues that such dissonance and the cognitive efforts individuals use to reduce that dissonance influence voters' party identification. Although some may believe that party identification comes before voting, influencing who one votes for, Dinas argues that consistency theories provide a compelling argument for how voting might lead to party identification. Voting demands constituents choose from a number of alternatives. When someone has a number of objects to choose from, they are more likely to try to rationalize their final choice. They might rationalize a vote for a political candidate by seeing that candidate as more attractive somehow and begin to align with the party the candidate represents. Once aligned, the constituent is more likely to vote for candidates in that party, and each vote choice further fortifies the voter's identification with the political party.

**Counterattitudinal Behavior.** Dissonance can also occur when we behave in ways that are inconsistent with our attitudes. Such situations may involve forced compliance—that is, pressures on a person to comply with a request to engage in counterattitudinal behavior (Joule & Azdia, 2003).

Imagine you have volunteered to serve in a psychology experiment. You arrive at the lab and are told you are participating in a study of performance. You are given a pegboard and told to turn each peg exactly one-quarter turn. After you have turned the last peg, you are told to start over, to turn each peg another one-quarter turn. Later, you are told to remove each peg from the pegboard and then to put each peg back. After an hour of such activity, the experimenter indicates you are finished. The experimenter says, "We are comparing the performance of participants who are briefed in advance with that of others who are not briefed. You did not receive a briefing. The next participant is supposed to be briefed, but my assistant who usually does this couldn't come to work today." He then asks you to help out by telling a waiting participant that the tasks you have just completed were fun and exciting. For your help, he offers you either $1 or $20.

In effect, you are being asked to lie—to say the boring and monotonous tasks you just performed were enjoyable. If you actually tell the next participant the tasks are fun, you may experience cognitive dissonance afterward. Your behavior (telling someone the tasks are fun) is inconsistent with your attitude about the tasks (that they are boring). Moreover, lying to the next participant is dissonant with your beliefs about yourself (that you are moral and honest). To reduce dissonance, you can change one of the cognitions. Which one will you change? You cannot change your awareness that you told the next participant the task is fun. The only cognition open to change is your attitude toward the task, which can change in the direction of greater liking for the task.

The theory of cognitive dissonance predicts (1) that you will change your attitudes toward the tasks (like them better), and (2) that the amount of change will depend on the incentive you were paid to tell the lie. Specifically, the theory predicts that greater attitude change will occur when the incentive to tell the lie is low ($1) rather than high ($20), because you will experience greater dissonance under low incentive than you would under high incentive and will, therefore, be more motivated to change your attitude.

These predictions were tested in a classic experiment by Festinger and Carlsmith (1959). Participants in the experiment completed the boring peg task and, when asked by the experimenter to brief the next participant, most agreed. The participants told the next person who arrived at the laboratory that the experimental tasks were interesting and they had fun doing them. A secretary then asked each participant to fill out a postexperimental questionnaire on which they would rate the experiment and the tasks. These ratings provided the measures of the dependent variable.

Control participants, who did not brief anyone and were not offered money, rated the tasks as very unenjoyable and did not want to participate in the experiment again. What about the participants who were paid money to tell a lie? For those receiving $20, the situation was not very dissonant. The money provided ample justification for engaging in counterattitudinal behavior (lying). You could think to yourself that you were being paid to act, not to tell the truth. In the $1 condition, however, the participants experienced greater dissonance because they did not have the justification for lying that the large amount of money provided. These participants could not deny they lied, so they reduced dissonance by

changing their attitude—that is, by increasing their liking for the task and the experiment. The results of this study confirmed the predictions from dissonance theory. Participants in the high-incentive ($20) condition rated the task and experiment negatively on the postexperimental questionnaire, whereas those in the low-incentive ($1) condition rated the task and experiment positively.

Dissonance occurs only in some situations (Wicklund & Brehm, 1976). To experience dissonance, a person must be committed to a belief or course of action (Brehm & Cohen, 1962). Moreover, the person must believe that they chose to act voluntarily and are, thus, responsible for the outcome of the decision (Linder, Cooper, & Jones, 1967). This is shown in the case of Taylor, who chose the job bussing tables. If the owner of the restaurant were Taylor's father, who demanded he work for him, Taylor would have had little or no postdecisional dissonance because he could blame his father for the choice he made. Likewise, if the experimenter had forced the participants to lie—rather than asking whether they would be willing to help—the level of dissonance would have been lower.

Researchers have found that some individuals—referred to as maximizers—are more prone to postdecisional dissonance than others. Maximizers are individuals who always strive to make the best possible decision. Conversely satisficers are people who will be content with an option as long as it is good enough (Schwartz, 2004). Standing in front of the cereal aisle, a satisficer would simply be focused on choosing a box of cereal they like. A maximizer would be focused on choosing the best of all the cereal options. When it comes to making choices, maximizers engage in more predecision fact finding, perceive more time pressure, experience more postdecisional dissonance and dissatisfaction, and are more likely to change their initial choices if given the opportunity to do so than are satisficers (Chowdhury, Ratneshwar, & Mohanty, 2009; Misuraca & Teuscher, 2013).

Psychologists find that hand washing helps ease the postdecisional dissonance people feel after making a choice between two alternatives (Lee & Schwarz, 2010). They believe that physical cleansing helps people feel psychologically cleansed, like they have wiped the slate clean. © snokid/iStock

## THE RELATIONSHIP BETWEEN ATTITUDES AND BEHAVIOR

### Do Attitudes Predict Behavior?

We have seen how our behavior can affect our attitudes and how people sometimes change their attitudes when their behavior appears to contradict those attitudes. However, many people think of attitudes as the source of behavior. We often assume that when we know a person's attitude toward an object or another person (a colleague, a political issue, a sports team), we can predict how that person will behave toward the object. If you know Haley likes Aaliyah, you would expect her to accept an invitation to Aaliyah's barbecue. If you know that Joaquin supports same-sex marriage, you would expect him to vote for a candidate who made protecting gay rights part of their platform. If you know that I am a New York Mets fan, you would expect me not only to cheer for the Mets but also to root for any team playing against the Yankees. We like to predict others' behaviors so we can decide how to behave toward that person in order to achieve our own goals. But can we truly predict someone's behavior if we only know their attitudes?

In 1930, the social scientist Richard LaPiere traveled around the United States by car with a Chinese couple. At that time, there was considerable prejudice against the Chinese, particularly in the West. The three travelers stopped at more than 60 hotels, auto camps, and tourist homes as well as more than 180 restaurants. They kept careful notes about how they were treated. In all their travels and stops, they were only denied service once. Later, LaPiere sent a questionnaire to each place, asking whether they would accept Chinese guests. He received responses from 128 of the establishments; 92 percent of them indicated that they would *not* serve Chinese guests (LaPiere, 1934). Some say that the hosts LaPiere and the couple encountered may have been influenced by the fact that LaPiere himself was a White man and perhaps hosts would have acted differently had the couple been alone. However, "Uncertain, depends upon the circumstances" was an available response that only 8 percent of the responding establishments selected. Evidently there can be a great discrepancy between what people do and what they say.

Since LaPiere's ground-breaking research, many studies on the topic have found only a modest correlation between attitude and behavior (Glasman & Albarracín, 2006). Several reasons have been suggested for this tenuous relationship. In this section, we consider four of these: (1) the accessibility and activation of the attitude, (2) the characteristics of the attitude, (3) the correspondence between attitude and behavior, and (4) situational constraints on behavior.

### Accessibility and Activation of the Attitude

Each of us has thousands of attitudes. Most of the time, a particular attitude is not within our conscious awareness. Moreover, much of our behavior is mindless or spontaneous (Fazio, 1990). We act without thinking—that is, without considering our attitudes. For an attitude to influence behavior, it must be activated; it must be brought from memory into conscious awareness. The most accessible attitudes are most easily activated.

Attitudes become activated when something in the environment triggers them, like encountering the attitude object (Fazio & Towles-Schwen, 1999). For example, earlier sections of this chapter may have activated your attitudes toward many objects, such as the Yankees, snakes, same-sex marriage, and voting. These triggers are particularly effective if the attitude was originally formed through direct experience with the object (Fazio, Powell, & Herr, 1983). Thus, one way to activate attitudes is to arrange situations in which persons are exposed to the relevant objects. Soft lighting, a cozy fire, and glasses of wine are all associated with a romantic evening; we often set up these cues in the hope of activating someone's positive attitudes toward romance and intimacy.

Attitudes differ in the ease with which they can be activated because they differ in accessibility. Some attitudes, such as stereotypes or a fear of snakes, are highly accessible and are activated automatically by the perception of the stereotyped object or the snake (Devine, 1989). These are often called implicit attitudes (Greenwald, Poehlman, Uhlmann, & Banaji, 2009). Other attitudes are situated deeper in our memory, making them less accessible and, therefore, activated more slowly (Fazio, Sanbonmatsu, Powell, & Kardes, 1986). It takes more than a brief encounter to activate these attitudes. You might be able to provide an almost immediate reaction if someone asked you about your favorite (or least favorite) restaurant in town, but it would take you longer to access an attitude toward a restaurant you were less familiar with. The more accessible an attitude is, the greater its influence on categorizing and judging objects (Smith, Fazio, & Cejka, 1996). Applying this to restaurants again, you are more likely to compare new restaurants you visit to your favorite place in town than to places you are less familiar with because your attitude about the former is more accessible than the latter.

Evidence also suggests that the more accessible an attitude, the more it is likely to guide future behavior. This was shown, for example, in a study of the impact of accessibility on voting

in the 1984 presidential election (Fazio & Williams, 1986). In June and July 1984, 245 people were questioned about their attitudes toward two presidential candidates (Ronald Reagan and Walter Mondale). The latency of the answer—how quickly the person replied to the question about each candidate—was used as a measure of accessibility. After the election, each person was asked whom they voted for. The more accessible the attitude—that is, the more quickly the person replied to the original question about the candidate—the more likely the person was to vote for that same candidate in November.

## Characteristics of the Attitude

The relationship between attitude and behavior is also affected by the nature of the attitude itself. Four characteristics of attitudes may influence the attitude-behavior relationship: (1) the degree of consistency between the affective (evaluative) and the cognitive components, (2) the extent to which the attitude is grounded in personal experience, (3) the strength of the attitude, and (4) the attitude's stability.

**Affective-Cognitive Consistency.** The beginning of the chapter introduced three components of attitudes: cognition, affective evaluation, and behavioral predisposition. When we consider the relation between attitude and behavior, we are looking at the relationship between the first two components and the third. As shown earlier with the example of a Prius, the degree of consistency between the affective and cognitive components influences the attitude-behavior relationship. That is, the greater the consistency between the two components, the greater the strength of the attitude-behavior relation.

Social psychologists find that affective-cognitive consistency predicts intentions to help the poor (Tagler & Cozzarelli, 2013). Individuals' affective evaluations of the poor—if they described their feelings toward the poor as positive or negative—were most likely to influence intentions to help the poor if individuals' cognitions about the poor were consistent with those affective evaluations. For example, if respondents who viewed the poor positively also believed that poverty was caused by structural forces (see the discussion of attributions for poverty in Chapter 7), their affective evaluation and cognitions were consistent. If respondents thought that laziness or lack of effort contributes to poverty yet still viewed the poor positively, this suggested attitude inconsistency. When asked about willingness to volunteer or to support policies to help the poor, the group with affective-cognitive consistency wanted to do more for the poor than those with inconsistent attitudes.

Affective-cognitive consistency not only predicts behavior but also increases the resistance of attitudes to change. When individuals have high affective-cognitive consistency, they tend to discredit information that is discrepant with their attitude or to minimize its importance. This makes attitudes more resistant to change.

**Direct Experience.** Suppose you have a positive attitude toward an activity based on having done it once, and your roommate has a positive attitude based on hearing you rave about it. Which of you is more likely to accept an invitation to engage in that activity?

One study (Regan & Fazio, 1977) provides an answer to this question. The behavior of interest was the proportion of time spent playing with several kinds of puzzles. Participants in the direct-experience condition played with sample puzzles; those in the indirect experience condition were given only descriptions of the puzzles. Researchers then asked participants to respond to some attitude measures and later gave participants an opportunity to play with the puzzles. Not surprisingly, they discovered that the average correlation between attitude and behavior was much higher for participants who had direct experience than for those who did not.

Attitudes based on direct experience are more predictive of subsequent behavior for a number of reasons (Fazio & Zanna, 1981). First, the best predictor of future behavior is past behavior; the more frequently you have hiked or camped in national parks, the more likely you are to visit them in the future (Stewart & Craig, 2001). Second, direct experience makes more information available about the attitude object itself (Kelman, 1974). If we are using information we have about an attitude object to determine our behavior, there is likely to be a strong link between attitude and behavior (Fazio & Towles-Schwen, 1999). Individuals who spend more time engaged in appreciative outdoor recreation—nature walks, backpacking, or day-hiking—not only have more environmental knowledge than those who spend less time, they are also more likely to engage in pro-environmental behavior. Third, attitudes based on direct experience with the object may be held with greater certainty—leading us to the third factor in the likelihood that attitudes influence behavior, attitude strength.

**Strength.** Suppose you ask two friends which candidate they like in the upcoming election. One replies, "I'm voting for X!" The other hedges a bit, saying, "Well, maybe I'll vote for Y." Which person's behavior do you think you could predict? In general, the greater the strength of an attitude, the more likely it is to influence behavior.

Studies of the link between attitudes toward candidates and subsequent voting behavior find that many of the errors in predictions occur among those who report indifference to the election—that is, people who hold weak or uncertain attitudes (Schuman & Johnson, 1976). This may have contributed to forecasters' inability to anticipate Donald Trump's win in the 2016 election. Both Clinton and Trump were unpopular and many Americans were indifferent, perhaps complicating predictions based on polling. Furthermore, given what we learned at the beginning of the chapter, forecasters may have underestimated how much more certain attitudes based on affective evaluations (for example, whether a candidate was likable or warm) are than attitudes based on cognition (for example, whether they were experienced or a good fit for the position) (Edwards, 1990).

The relevance of an attitude—the extent to which the issue or object directly affects the person—also influences the strength of the attitude. Framing an issue in relevant terms, say, tuition increases on your college campus, brings to mind important consequences for you, such as the need for greater income or having to take out additional student loans. Framing it in irrelevant terms, say, tuition increases on campuses in Russia, may elicit no thought of personal consequences (Lieberman & Chaiken, 1996). When an issue is relevant to an individual, there will be a much stronger relationship between attitudes and voting on the issue (Crano, 1997). This is, in part, because personal relevance increases attitude strength. Individuals who have a gay family member or friend are more likely not only to hold a more favorable attitude toward gays and lesbians but also to be more certain about that attitude (Herek & Capitanio, 1996).

**Attitude Stability.** Most studies attempting to predict behavior from attitudes measure people's attitudes first and their behavior weeks or months later. A modest or small correlation may mean a weak attitude-behavior relationship—or it could mean people's attitudes have changed in the interim period. If the attitude changes after it is measured, the person's behavior may be consistent with their present attitude, although it appears inconsistent with the measure of the attitude.

In general, we would expect that the longer the time between the measurement of attitude and that of behavior, the more likely the attitude will change and the smaller the attitude-behavior relationship will be. In a study designed to test this possibility (Schwartz, 1978), an appeal was mailed to almost 300 students to volunteer as tutors for blind children. Earlier, students had filled out a questionnaire measuring general attitudes toward helping others, including questions about tutoring blind children. Some students had filled out the questionnaire six months earlier; some, three months earlier; some, both three and six months earlier; and still others had not seen the questionnaire. The correlation between

attitude toward tutoring and actually volunteering was greater over the three-month period than over the six-month period. Thus, to avoid problems of temporal instability, the amount of time between the measurement of attitudes and that of behavior should be brief.

However, some attitudes evidence a remarkable degree of stability. Marwell, Aiken, and Demerath (1987) studied the political attitudes of 220 White young people who spent the summer of 1964 organizing Blacks in the South to vote. They measured the same attitudes of two-thirds of these activists two decades later, in 1984. The extreme radical attitudes these people held in 1964 had softened in the intervening 20 years, but in general these people remained liberal and committed to the needs of disadvantaged groups. This stability of their attitudes likely stemmed from the direct experience the activists had with the issues from their time in the South.

## Attitude-Behavior Correspondence

Attitudes are more likely to predict behavior when the two are at the same level of specificity (Schuman & Johnson, 1976). For example, suppose you have invited a casual acquaintance to dinner, and you want to plan the menu. You know they like an Italian restaurant in town, so you infer they like Italian food. But can you predict with confidence that they will eat spinach noodles with clam sauce? Probably not. A favorable attitude toward a type of cuisine does not mean the person will eat every dish of that type.

Many studies have attempted to predict from general attitudes to specific behaviors (Ajzen, 1991; Green, 1972). For instance, some studies of families have tried to predict men's specific contributions to housework and child rearing (how often he vacuums or changes diapers, for example) from their gender role attitudes. Perhaps not surprisingly, there is little congruence. Although many men express egalitarian gender role attitudes, this is generally not reflected in their specific gender role behavior (Araji, 1977). A general attitude is a summary of many feelings either about an

Although most Americans have attitudes about abortion, only a minority act on their beliefs like these demonstrators. People with strong attitudes, whether pro or con, are more likely to engage in such behavior. © DJMcCoy/iStock

object under a variety of conditions or about a whole class of objects. Logically, it should not predict behavior in any particular single situation. However, it might predict a composite measure of several relevant behaviors (Weigel & Newman, 1976). For example, although a man with egalitarian attitudes may do little more vacuuming than a man with more traditional gender role attitudes, he may be engaged in other egalitarian behaviors or have a less-gendered division of labor on the whole in his household than the more traditional man.

What about predicting a specific behavior, such as whether your Italian food loving guest will eat spinach noodles and clam sauce? Just as general attitudes best predict a composite index of behavior, we need a specific measure of attitude to predict a specific behavior. We can think of an attitude and a behavior as having four elements: an action (eating), an object or target (spinach noodles and clam sauce), a context (in your home), and a time (tomorrow night). The greater the degree of **correspondence**—that is, the number of elements that are the same in the attitude and the behavior—the better we can predict behavior from attitudes (Ajzen &

Fishbein, 1977). If you know that your casual acquaintance likes to eat (correspondent action) spinach noodles (correspondent object) for dinner (correspondent time) at the Italian restaurant (noncorrespondent context), you can better predict their behavior than if all you know is that they like to eat (correspondent action) at the Italian restaurant (noncorrespondent context).

## Situational Constraints

If you believe tuition increases at your college are necessary to maintain the quality of your education—to retain the best faculty, provide ready access to books, journals, and computers, and so on—and you attend a meeting of Students for Educational Quality, your behavior reflects your attitude.

Suppose, however, that you oppose tuition increases but find yourself in a conversation with a date who expresses support for the increases. Would you voice your opposition—that is, behave in a manner consistent with your attitudes—or not? Your reaction would probably depend partly on the strength of your attitude (Pratkanis & Greenwald, 1989). If you are strongly opposed to tuition increases, you may speak your mind. But if you are moderately opposed, you may decide to avoid an argument and behave in a way that is inconsistent with your attitude. In LaPiere's study discussed earlier, for instance, hotel and restaurant employees confronted by a White man and a Chinese couple may have felt compelled to serve them rather than run the risk of creating a scene by refusing to do so.

**Situational constraint** refers to the way in which others' anticipated reactions to our attitudes—either positive or negative—influence behavior. Situational constraints guide behavior across situations (Ajzen, 2005). Two factors increase its influence. First, the greater the agreement among others about how we should behave, the greater the situational constraint on persons whose attitudes are inconsistent with the situational norms (Schutte, Kendrick, & Sadalla, 1985). In other words, you would be more likely to share your opposition in conversation with one friend who supported the increases than you would if you were in a group of four in which the other three were in support and you were the only opposed. Second, the more one self-monitors—strategically constructing their public image (as discussed in Chapter 5)—the more one is likely to agree with an audience's attitudes (Klein, Snyder, & Livingston, 2004).

Consequently, the less visible our behavior is to others, the more likely our behavior and attitudes will be consistent (Acock & Scott, 1980). With respect to attitudes about race and gender, many scholars who study prejudice have noted a shift in how people express prejudicial attitudes. As the social environment has become less accepting of overt expressions of racism and sexism, people may have responded to the situational constraints by hiding their attitudes and finding different, more subtle ways of expressing prejudice (Gawronski & Strack, 2004). This has shifted how we measure attitudes related to racism, sexism, and other socially sensitive attitudes (see Box 8.1) and how we think about sexism (and racism) in society (see Box 8.3).

## BOX 8.3 Test Yourself: Ambivalent Sexism Inventory

On January 21, 2017, women—and many men and children—marched throughout the world in an effort to bring attention to sexism. However, not all women believed that such a march was necessary. One vocal opponent wrote a post on social media detailing why she had chosen not to march. She wrote that she did not feel like a second-class citizen because she was a woman. In fact, she felt respected by men. Others agreed, arguing that Donald Trump made it abundantly clear that he respected women throughout his campaign, citing comments like this one that Trump made in 2015: "I cherish women. I want to help women. I'm going to do things that no other candidate will be able to do [for women]" (Krieg, 2016).

Social psychologists assert that such comments actually demonstrate that sexism—prejudice or discrimination based on a person's sex—is alive and well; it has simply changed shape. Over time, sexism has shifted from overt and hostile forms to a subtle, less recognizable one (Fiske, 1998; Glick & Fiske, 2001; Nelson, 2002). This less hostile form, known as benevolent sexism, can sometimes be disguised as respect for women.

Rather than assert that men are in leadership positions because women are somehow less deserving or should be held in contempt, benevolent sexism suggests that women are simply different. They should be cherished, provided for, and protected, and it is men's responsibility to do that. In attempts to shield women, men practicing this type of sexism feel they can and should control women. Benevolent sexism is particularly

| 0 DISAGREE STRONGLY | 1 DISAGREE SOMEWHAT | 2 DISAGREE SLIGHTLY | 3 AGREE SLIGHTLY | 4 AGREE SOMEWHAT | 5 AGREE STRONGLY |
|---|---|---|---|---|---|

1. _____ No matter how accomplished he is, a man is not truly complete as a person unless he has the love of a good woman.

2. _____ Many women are actually seeking special favors, such as hiring practices that favor them over men, under the guise of asking for "equality."

3. _____ In a disaster, women ought to be rescued before men.

4. _____ Most women interpret innocent remarks or acts as being sexist.

5. _____ Women are too easily offended.

6. _____ Many women have a quality of purity that few men possess.

7. _____ Feminists want women to have more power than men.

8. _____ Most women fail to appreciate fully all that men do for them.

9. _____ Women seem to gain power by getting control over men.

10. _____ Women should be cherished and protected by men.

11. _____ Every man ought to have a woman whom he adores.

12. _____ A good woman should be set on a pedestal by her man.

13. _____ Women exaggerate problems they have at work.

14. _____ Women, compared to men, tend to have a superior moral sensibility.

15. _____ Men should be willing to sacrifice their own well-being in order to provide financially for those who are dependent on them.

16. _____ Once a woman gets a man to commit to her, she usually tries to put him on a tight leash.

17. _____ Women, as compared to men, tend to have a more refined sense of culture and good taste.

18. _____ Men are incomplete without women.

19. _____ Many women get a kick out of leading men on.

20. _____ When women lose to men in a fair competition, they typically complain about being discriminated against.

To determine your Hostile Sexism score, average items 2, 4, 5, 7, 8, 9, 13, 16, 19, 20.
To determine your Benevolent Sexism score, average items 1, 3, 6, 10, 11, 12, 14, 15, 17, 18

insidious because it does not seem like prejudice to male perpetrators, because it is not contemptuous, and because women may find it alluring, disarming, and difficult to resist. In fact, although women are significantly more likely than men to reject hostile sexism, they are much more accepting of benevolent sexism—with rates in the United States quite similar to men (Glick et al., 2000).

The survey above measures two forms of sexism—hostile and benevolent. How do you score? Can you tell the difference between them?

*Source:* Adapted from Glick & Fiske, 2001.

## Reference Groups

Several studies have assessed the impact of reference groups on the attitude-behavior relationship. Such research involves measuring participants' attitudes and behaviors toward some object and then asking them to indicate the positions of various social groups regarding that object.

One survey assessed adults' attitudes toward drinking alcoholic beverages and the degree to which their friends approved of drinking (Rabow, Neuman, & Hernandez, 1987). When attitudes and social support were congruent—that is, when the respondents' and their friends' views about drinking were the same—there was a much stronger relation between attitudes and behavior than when attitudes and social support were not congruent. We are much more likely to act in ways that are consistent with our attitudes when people who we perceive as members of our in-group hold similar attitudes (Terry & Hogg, 1996; White, Hogg, & Terry, 2002).

---

### SUMMARY

**The Nature of Attitudes.** (1) Every attitude has three components: cognition, affective evaluation, and a behavioral predisposition toward some object. (2) We learn attitudes through reinforcement, through repeated associations of stimuli and responses, and by observing others. (3) Attitudes are useful; they may serve heuristic and knowledge functions, and they define and maintain self.

**Attitude Organization.** An attitude is usually embedded in a larger cognitive structure and is based on one or more fundamental or primitive beliefs. Attitudes derived from primitive beliefs form a vertical structure. When multiple underlying beliefs support an attitude, these beliefs have a horizontal structure that help the attitude persist.

**Cognitive Consistency.** Consistency theories assume that when cognitive elements are inconsistent, individuals will be motivated to change their attitudes or behavior to restore harmony. Balance theory assesses the relationships among three cognitive elements and suggests ways to resolve imbalance. Dissonance theory identifies two situations in which inconsistency often occurs: after a choice between alternatives or when people engage in behavior that is inconsistent with their attitudes. The theory also cites two ways to reduce dissonance: by changing one of the elements or by changing the importance of the cognitions involved.

**The Relationship between Attitudes and Behavior.** The attitude-behavior relationship is influenced by five variables: accessibility and activation of the attitude, characteristics of the attitude, attitude-behavior correspondence, situational constraints, and reference groups. (1) For an attitude to influence behavior, it must be activated, and the person must use it as a guide for behavior. (2) The relationship is stronger if affective-cognitive consistency is high and if the attitude is based on direct experience, is strong and relevant, and is stable. (3) The relationship is stronger when the measures of attitude and behavior correspond in action, object, context, and time. (4) Situational constraints may facilitate or prevent the expression of attitudes in behavior. (5) Attitudes are more likely to influence behavior if reference groups hold similar attitudes.

### Critical Thinking Skill:
### Analyzing Attitudes

This chapter opened your eyes to the components of attitudes and made you think about where they come from, how they relate to one another, and how your attitudes may—or may not—influence your behavior. What are some of the ways this knowledge might change the way you think about or respond to your own attitudes and those of others?

It is important to recognize the central role our beliefs play in shaping our attitudes. For example, you are likely to have a more positive attitude toward environmentally conscious living if you believe humans are causing climate change and that climate change has a negative impact on our world, our lives, or on future generations. It is also important to consider where those beliefs come from and why we hold them.

Other critical thinking exercises in this book encourage you to gather evidence and investigate claims. These are certainly important. However, critical thinking also requires you to consider why you hold the beliefs you do in the first place. For example, why would someone think humans are causing climate change? Not everyone does. And why might someone believe climate change is having a negative impact on the world? Some argue that certain crops in certain locations are benefiting from higher temperatures.

What is your attitude about climate change? Try to write it down in a short paragraph. What are the sources of your attitude? Is it influenced by the attitudes or behavior of your family members—about cars, lighting in your home, recycling behaviors? Do you recall media images or advertising that might have influenced it? How about where you live—do you live on the Gulf Coast or in Alaska where there have been major oil spills, or in Montana? Do you think your attitude would be different if you lived somewhere else?

Your attitude is supported by the structure of related attitudes. Create a diagram like the one in Figure 8.1. Place your attitude in the box at the top. Now think about the beliefs you hold that may relate to your attitude about the environment. What are the beliefs that influence the attitude? Where might those beliefs originate from—family, religion, education, media? How are they part of your time and place in culture? Questions like these help us understand our own views and the views of others, thereby increasing critical thinking.

# SYMBOLIC COMMUNICATION
# AND LANGUAGE

## LEARNING OBJECTIVES

By the end of this chapter you will be able to:

- Describe the nature of language, and how we use it.

- Compare the major types of nonverbal communication and explain how nonverbal communication combines with language to convey emotions and ideas.

- Understand how social relationships shape communication, and how communication expresses or modifies social relationships.

- Describe the rules and skills people use to maintain a smooth flow of conversation.

## INTRODUCTION

Imagine that you wake up tomorrow morning and you cannot speak. How would you manage to get through the day? How would it affect your interactions with roommates, partners, professors, employers? Now, imagine that you wake up the next day and you can speak again! But you can't move your arms or hands. How would that influence your ability to interact with those same people? Communication is a basic ingredient of every social situation. Without communication, interaction breaks down; indeed, it would be simply impossible to participate in a class, purchase something, or arrange a birthday party or any other social occasion.

**Communication** is the process whereby people transmit information about their ideas, feelings, and intentions to one another. We communicate through spoken and written words, through voice qualities and physical closeness, through gestures and posture. Often, communication is deliberate: we smile, clasp our beloved in our arms, and whisper, "I love you." Other times, we communicate meanings that are unintentional. A Freudian slip, for instance, may tell our listeners more than we want them to know.

Because people do not share each other's experiences directly, they must convey their ideas and feelings to each other in ways that others will notice and understand. We often do this by means of symbols. **Symbols** are arbitrary forms that are used to refer to ideas, feelings, intentions, or any other object.

Symbols represent our experiences in ways that others can perceive with their sensory organs—through sounds, gestures, pictures, even fragrances. But if we are to interpret symbols as others intend them to be understood, their meanings must be socially shared. To communicate successfully, we must master the ways for expressing ideas and feelings that are accepted in our community.

Symbols are arbitrary stand-ins for what they represent. A green light could as reasonably stand for "stop" as for "go," the sound *luv* as reasonably for negative as for positive feelings. The arbitrariness of symbols becomes painfully obvious when we travel in foreign countries. We are then likely to discover that the words and even the gestures we take for granted fail to communicate accurately. A North American who makes a circle with thumb and index finger to express satisfaction to a waiter may be in for a rude surprise if they are eating at a restaurant in Ghana, where the waiter may interpret this gesture as a sexual invitation. In Venezuela, it may be interpreted as a sexual insult! The traveler may then have serious difficulties straightening out these misunderstandings because they and the waiter lack a shared language of verbal symbols to discuss them.

Language and nonverbal forms of communication are amazingly complex. They must be understood and used with flexibility and creativity. Most of us fail on occasion to communicate our ideas and feelings with accuracy or to understand others' communications as well as we might wish. Yet, considering the problems a communicator must solve, most people do surprisingly well. This chapter begins with an examination of language, moves on to nonverbal communication, then analyzes the impacts of communication and social relationships on each other. Finally, this chapter considers the delicate coordination involved in our most common social activity—conversation.

## LANGUAGE AND VERBAL COMMUNICATION

Although people have created numerous symbol systems (such as mathematics, music, painting), language is the main vehicle of human communication. All people possess a spoken language. There are thousands of different languages in the world (Katzner, 1995). This section addresses several crucial topics regarding the role of language in communication. These include the nature of language, three perspectives on how people attain understanding through language use, and the relation between language and thought (see Box 9.1).

### Linguistic Communication

Little is known about the origins of language, but humans have possessed complex spoken languages since earliest times (Kiparsky,

Signing by an interpreter for a speaker involves using hand movements to communicate the words. Signing for a rapper is much harder because music is more than words. It requires the interpreter to study the music in advance, and to use facial expressions and body language to convey the sounds and energy of the performance. © TK

1976; Lieberman, 1975). **Spoken language** is a socially acquired system of sound patterns with meanings agreed on by the members of a group. We will examine the basic components of spoken language and some of the advantages of language use.

**Basic Components.** Spoken languages include sounds, words, meanings, and grammatical rules. Consider the following statement of one roommate to another: "Wherewereyoulastnight?" What the listener hears is a string of sounds much like this, rather than the sentence "Where were you last night?" To understand a string of sounds and to produce an appropriate response, people must recognize the following components: (1) the distinct sounds of which the language is composed (the phonetic component); (2) the combination of sounds into words (the morphologic component); (3) the common meaning of the words (the semantic component); and (4) the conventions for putting words together built into the language (the syntactic component, or grammar). We are rarely conscious of manipulating all these components during conversation, though we do so regularly and with impressive speed.

Unspoken languages, such as Morse code, computer programming languages, and sign languages, lack a phonetic component, although they do possess the remaining components of spoken language. People who use sign languages, for example, use upper body movements to signal words (morphology) with shared meanings (semantics), and they combine these words into sentences according to rules of order (syntax). For a communication system to be considered a language, morphology, semantics, and syntax are all essential. Linguists study these components, seeking to uncover the rules that give structure to language. Social psychologists are more interested in how language fits into social interaction and influences it and in how language expresses and modifies social relationships (Giles, Hewstone, & St. Clair, 1981).

## BOX 9.1  Research Update: The Linguistic Relativity Hypothesis

Does the language we speak influence the way we think about and experience the world? The most famous theory on this question—the Sapir-Whorf linguistic relativity hypothesis—holds that language "is not merely a reproducing instrument for voicing ideas, but is itself a shaper of ideas, the program and guide for the individual's mental activity" (Whorf, 1956).

According to the strong form of the linguistic relativity hypothesis, language determines our perceptions of reality, so we cannot perceive or comprehend distinctions that don't exist in our own language. Orwell's description of Newspeak, the language developed by the totalitarian rulers in his novel *Nineteen Eighty-Four*, portrays in frightening terms how language restricts thought:

> Don't you see that the whole aim of Newspeak is to narrow the range of thought? In the end we shall make thought crime literally impossible because there will be no words in which to express it. . . . Every year fewer and fewer words, and the range of consciousness always a little smaller. . . . The revolution will be complete when the language is perfect. (George Orwell, *Nineteen Eighty-Four*, 1949, pp. 46–47.)

Orwell's description suggests that language determines thought through the words it makes available to people. We cannot talk about objects or ideas for which we lack words. The ways we think about the world are determined by the way our language slices up reality. Thus, people who speak different languages should perceive the world differently.

The strong form of the linguistic relativity hypothesis has not fared well in research (Wolff & Holmes, 2011). Consider some of the facts. Some languages have only two basic words (*dark* and *white*) to cover the whole spectrum of colors. Yet people from these and all other known language groups can discriminate between and communicate about whatever large numbers of colors they are shown (Heider & Olivier, 1972). Most likely, any concept can be expressed in any language, though not with the same degree of ease and efficiency. Before either TV or the word *television* existed, for example, someone undoubtedly referred to the concept of "a device that can transmit pictures and sounds over a distance." When new concepts are encountered, people invent words (*laser*) or borrow them from other languages (*sabotage* from French, *goulash* from Hungarian).

Thus, the strong linguistic relativity hypothesis that language determines thought has found

---

**Advantages of Language Use.** Words—the symbols around which languages are constructed—provide abundant resources with which to represent ideas and feelings. The average adult native speaker of English knows the meanings of some 35,000 words, and actively uses close to 5,000. Because it is a symbol system, language enhances our capacity for social action in several ways.

First, language frees us from the constraints of the here and now. Using words to symbolize objects, events, or relationships, we can communicate about things that happened last week or last year, and we can discuss things

that may happen in the future. The ability to do the latter allows us to coordinate our behavior with the activities of others. In thinking about losing your voice for the day, it may have occurred to you that it would be very difficult to make appointments, schedule a meeting, or plan a trip.

Second, language allows us to communicate with others about experiences we do not share directly. You cannot know directly the joy and hope your friend feels at bearing a child, nor the grief and despair at their mother's death. Yet your friend can convey a good sense of those emotions and concerns to

little support. But there is considerable evidence that language influences our perception of the world. Each language facilitates particular forms of thinking because it makes some events and objects more easily codable or symbolizable. In fact, the availability of linguistic symbols for objects or events has been shown to have two clear effects: (1) it improves the efficiency of communication about these objects and events, and (2) it enhances success in remembering them.

Counting is difficult for people whose language does not include numbers. The Piraha, a group living in the Amazon, have only two words for numbers, words that mean *one* and *two*. When an experimenter lined up several batteries and asked a member of the tribe to match it, the member did well when the line contained two or three, but had a difficult time if there were more than three batteries in the experimenter's line (Frank, Everett, Fedorenko, & Gibson, 2008; Gordon, 2004).

Language influences what we pay attention to. Native speakers of Ndonga (spoken in parts of Africa) and of English were compared on three color cognition tasks. Ndonga has no terms for orange, pink, and purple. Participants were presented with colors that exploited this fact. Speakers of both performed well at sorting colors based on similarity. However, they differed in performance on a task that required them to search for specific colors; native speakers of English were better (Pilling & Davies, 2004). This same influence of language was demonstrated in experiments using speakers of English. Participants who were primed with (shown) abstract terms focused on general features in a categorization task, whereas those primed using concrete terms focused on specific aspects in performing the task (Stapel & Semin, 2007).

The availability of linguistic symbols also affects memory for objects and persons. This was shown in a study that involved subjects who spoke English or Chinese (Hoffman, Lau, & Johnson, 1986). This study used English- and Chinese-language descriptions of two people whose traits could be easily labeled in English but not in Chinese and of two other people whose traits could be easily labeled in Chinese but not in English. Three groups of participants read the descriptions: English monolinguals, Chinese-English bilinguals who read in Chinese, and Chinese-English bilinguals who read in English. The participants' memory of the descriptions was assessed. The results showed that memory was much better when the information about the target conformed to labels in the participant's language of processing.

Thus, language plays an important role in influencing our thought and in our perceptions of reality.

you through words, even in writing, because these shared symbols elicit the same meanings for you both.

Third, language enables us to transmit, preserve, and create culture. Through the spoken and the written word, vast quantities of information pass from person to person and from generation to generation. Language also enhances our ability to go beyond what is already known and to add to the store of cultural ideas and objects. Working with linguistic symbols, people generate theories, design and build new products, and invent social institutions.

We turn now to three models of communication: the encoder-decoder model, the intentionalist model, and the perspective-taking model. We will consider how each model views the communication process and discusses communication accuracy.

### The Encoder-Decoder Model

Language is often thought of as a medium of communication that one person uses to transmit information to another. The **encoder-decoder model** views communication as a process in which an idea or feeling is encoded

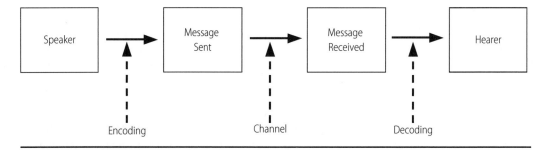

**FIGURE 9.1** The Encoder-Decoder Model

According to the encoder-decoder model, communication originates in the speaker's desire to convey an idea or feeling. They encode the message into a set of symbols and transmit it to the hearer. The hearer decodes the message. The more codable the idea or feeling in the language, the more accurate the communication.

into symbols by a source, transmitted to a receiver, and decoded into the original idea or feeling (Krauss & Fussell, 1996). This process is portrayed in Figure 9.1.

**Communication Process.** According to this model, the basic unit of communication is the message, which has its origin in the desire of the speaker to communicate. A message is constructed when the speaker encodes the information they wish to communicate into a combination of verbal and nonverbal symbols. The message is sent via a channel, whether by face-to-face interaction, telephone, electronic communication, or in writing. The listener must decode the message in order to arrive at the information they believe the speaker wanted to communicate.

**Communication Accuracy.** The goal of communication is to accurately transfer the message content from speaker to listener. The speaker hopes to create in the listener the mental image or feeling that the speaker intends to convey. The listener is also motivated to achieve accuracy, in order to coordinate their behavior with that of the speaker. **Communication accuracy** refers to the extent to which the message inferred by the listener matches the message intended by the speaker. According to this model, the primary influence on accuracy

is *codability*, which is the extent of interpersonal agreement about what something is called. Codability is partly a function of language. Early research focused on the codability of colors (Lantz & Stefflre, 1964). In this research, one person (the encoder) was shown a color and asked to describe that color in words. This verbal message was then sent to a second person (the decoder), who tried to use the verbal description to identify the color intended by the encoder. Some colors are much more easily coded in the English language (fire-engine red) than others (the reddish color of a sunset). By extension, some ideas and feelings are easily expressed in English, whereas others are much more difficult to put into words. In general, messages that are easily coded will be more accurately transmitted.

Codability involves agreement about what something is to be called. It also depends on the extent to which speaker and listener define symbols (such as words or gestures) in the same way. This in turn depends on the language to which each was socialized. Thus, a common cause of miscommunication is differences in language between speaker and listener. This is obvious when we try to converse with someone from a different country. It is less obvious, but perhaps just as important, when we converse with someone of a different race, class, or gender (Maynard & Whalen, 1995).

At times, the processes of encoding and decoding are very deliberate or mindful (Giles & Coupland, 1991). If we are preparing a speech, we may consciously consider alternative ways to phrase a message and alternative gestures to use when communicating. Listening to a speaker, we may pay careful attention to the words used, the speed and volume of the spoken message, the gestures, and the posture of the speaker in order to decide which message is the correct one. We are often mindful of the encoding and decoding process in novel situations or in communicating about novel topics.

Communication is not always a process of consciously translating ideas and feelings into symbols and then transmitting these symbols deliberately in hopes that the listener will interpret them correctly. Much communication occurs without any self-conscious planning. In familiar or routine situations, we often rely on a conversational script—a sequentially organized series of utterances that occur with little or no conscious thought. Thus, when you enter a restaurant, you can interact with the server without much mental effort, because you both follow a conversational script that specifies what each of you should say and in what sequence. Communication accuracy is typically high in situations governed by conversational scripts. When you order food in a fast-food outlet, you usually get exactly what you want with minimum effort.

If conversation is scripted, listeners will probably not pay careful attention to the idiosyncratic features of a message. They will tend to remember the generic content of a message but not its unusual characteristics. In a field experiment testing this prediction, students were approached by a stranger who asked for a piece of paper. Prior to the request, one-half of the students were asked to pay attention to the request; the other half were not forewarned. Later, the forewarned students were more likely to remember the specific words used in the request than the unprepared students (Kitayama & Burnstein, 1988).

## The Intentionalist Model

The encoder-decoder model emphasizes messages consisting of symbols whose meaning is widely understood. It directs our attention to the literal meaning of verbal messages. Often, however, messages are not interpreted literally. For example, in many theaters, the feature film is preceded by the message "Please, silence during the show." But are members of the audience expected to be silent? No. They can laugh if the film is a comedy, boo at the villain, and applaud when the bad person gets what they deserve. Most of us understand this message in terms of its intention: we should not whisper or talk to those seated near us. For this type of communication, we need a different model.

According to the **intentionalist model**, communication involves the exchange of communicative intentions, and messages are merely the means to this end (Krauss & Fussell, 1996). The speaker selects the message they believe is most likely to accomplish their intent. "Please, silence during the show" is intended to keep us from disturbing other members of the audience, and that is how we understand it.

**Communication Process.** The origin of communication is the speaker's intent to achieve some goal or to have some effect on the listener. But there is not a fixed, one-to-one relation between words and intended effects, so the speaker can use a variety of messages or utterances to achieve their intended effect. For example, imagine you are studying in your living room, and you want your roommate to bring you something to drink. Table 9.1 lists some of the utterances you might use to make the request. Which one would you choose?

According to the intentionalist model, decoding the literal meaning of a message is only part of the process of communication. The hearer must also infer the speaker's underlying intention in order to respond

**TABLE 9.1** "Get Me a Drink of Lemonade."

| | |
|---|---|
| 1. | Get me a glass of lemonade. |
| 2. | Can you get me some lemonade? |
| 3. | Would you get me some lemonade? |
| 4. | Would you get me something to drink? |
| 5. | Would you mind if I asked you to get me some lemonade? |
| 6. | I'm thirsty. |
| 7. | Did you buy some lemonade at the store? |
| 8. | How is that lemonade we bought? |

appropriately. To the question "How is that lemonade we bought?" a satisfactory response to the literal message is "Good." If the communication is to be successful, however, your roommate needs to infer your intention— that they bring you a glass of lemonade. Both selecting a message to convey your intention and inferring another's intention from their utterance are carried out according to social conventions.

**Communication Accuracy.** According to this model, accuracy in communication is accuracy in understanding the intentions of the speaker. To achieve accuracy requires more sophisticated processing than merely knowing the meaning of the words. When inferring the speaker's intention, the listener needs to take into account the context, especially (1) the status or role relationship between speaker and listener, and (2) the social context in which the communication occurs. If you and your roommate are lovers, you might choose a less polite form of the request, such as option 2 in Table 9.1, and you would expect a less polite response than if the two of you are simply sharing the residence. If your parents are visiting at the time, your request to them is likely to take a different form, such as option 3.

According to **speech act theory**, utterances both state something and do something (Searle, 1979). In Table 9.1, utterances 1 to 6 state the speaker's desire for a drink (or

specifically for lemonade), whereas utterances 7 and 8 do not. But all eight of the utterances perform an action; each has the force of a request. The significance of an utterance is not its literal meaning, but what it contributes to the work of the interaction in which it occurs (Geis, 1995). The use of language to perform actions is rule-governed; these rules influence both the creation and the interpretation of speech acts. To achieve accurate communication, both speaker and listener must be aware of these rules. Miscommunication is caused not only by the lack of shared meaning of symbols, but also by a lack of shared understanding of the rules governing the use of speech to perform actions.

To determine whether the message has achieved the intended effect, the speaker relies on the feedback provided by the listener's reaction. If the reaction indicates that the listener interpreted the message accurately, the speaker may elaborate, change the topic, or end the interaction. However, if the reaction suggests that the listener inferred a meaning different from the intended one, the speaker will often attempt to send the same message, perhaps using different words and gestures.

**The Cooperative Principle.** Mutual understanding is a cooperative enterprise. Because language does not convey thoughts and feelings in an unambiguous manner, people must work together to attain a shared understanding of each other's utterances (Goffman, 1983). A speaker must cooperate with a listener by formulating the content of speech acts in a manner that reflects the listener's way of thinking about objects, events, and relationships.

In turn, the listener must cooperate by actively trying to understand. They must go beyond the literal meanings of words to infer what the speaker is really saying. A listener must make a creative effort to cope with a speaker's tendency to formulate speech acts indirectly. Without such an effort, a listener would not understand speech acts that leave out words ("Paper come?"), abbreviate familiar terms ("See ya in calc"), and include vague references ("He told him he would come later").

According to Grice (1975), listeners assume that most talk is based on the **cooperative principle**. That is, listeners ordinarily assume that the speaker is behaving cooperatively by trying to be informative (giving as much information as is necessary and no more), truthful, relevant to the aims of the ongoing conversation, and clear (avoiding ambiguity and wordiness).

The cooperative principle is more than a code of conversational etiquette. It is crucial to the accurate transmission of meaning. Often, a listener can reach a correct understanding of otherwise ambiguous talk only by assuming that the speaker is trying to satisfy this principle. Consider, for example, how the maxim of relevance enables the conversationalists to understand each other in the following exchange:

JUAN: I'm exhausted.
MARIA: Fred will be back next Monday.

On the surface, Maria's statement seems unrelated to Juan's declaration. In some contexts, we might infer that Maria has changed the subject, indirectly sending the message that she does not care about his physical state. In fact, however, Maria is stating that she and Juan won't have to work as hard after their colleague Fred returns to the office next week. But why does she expect that Juan will understand this? Because she expects him to assume that she is adhering to the relevance maxim— that her comment relates to what he said.

The cooperative principle is also crucial for speech forms like sarcasm or understatement to succeed. In sarcasm or understatement, speakers want listeners to recognize that their words mean something quite different from their literal interpretation. One way we signal listeners that we intend our words to imply

something different is by obviously violating one or two component maxims of the cooperative principle while holding to the rest. Consider Carrie's sarcastic reply when asked what she thought of the lecturer: "He was so exciting that he came close to keeping most of us awake the first half hour." By flouting the maxim of clarity (responding in an unclear, wordy way) while still being informative, truthful, and relevant, Carrie implies that the lecturer was in fact a bore.

Violation of the maxim of clarity may signal that a communication is false, or fraudulent. The publication of scientific papers that are later withdrawn because they are fraudulent, e.g., based on fake data, is an increasingly serious problem in numerous scientific disciplines, including social psychology (Van Noorden, 2011). Researchers identified 253 publications that were retracted because they were based on fraudulent data, and compared their writing style with 253 unretracted publications (Markowitz & Hancock, 2015). Fraudulent papers were written much less clearly, with lower readability scores (a standard measure) and greater use of jargon, making it harder to evaluate them. Looking at the larger issue of clarity in science, six researchers have identified 50 terms commonly used in psychology and related fields that should be avoided (Lilienfeld et al., 2015). The list includes terms that are inaccurate (e.g., "brainwashing"), frequently misused (e.g., "closure"), ambiguous (e.g., "interaction"), and almost any term with the prefix "neuro-".

### The Perspective-Taking Model

A third model is based on symbolic interaction theory (see Chapter 1). It views the process of communication as both creating and reflecting a shared context between speaker and listener. This approach maintains that symbols do not have a meaning that is invariant across situations (see Box 9.1). According to the **perspective-taking model**, communication involves the exchange of messages using symbols whose meaning grows out of the interaction itself.

**Communication Process.** Communication involves the use of verbal and nonverbal symbols whose meaning depends on the shared context created by the participants. The development of this shared context requires reciprocal role taking, in which each participant places the self in the role of the other in an attempt to view the situation from the other's perspective. The context created by the ongoing interaction changes from minute to minute; each actor must be attentive to these changes in order to communicate successfully as both speaker and listener.

**Communication Accuracy.** In the perspective-taking model, communication is much more than transmitting and receiving words with fixed, shared meanings. Conversationalists must select and discover the meanings of words through their context. In ordinary social interaction, the meanings of whole sentences and conversations may be ambiguous. Speakers and listeners must jointly work out these meanings as they go along.

Successful communication depends on **intersubjectivity**; each participant needs information about the other's status, view of the situation, and plans or intentions. Strangers rely on social conventions and rules about interpersonal communication. They categorize other participants and use stereotypes as a basis for making inferences about the plans and intentions of the other person(s) who are present in the setting. Notice that this practice perpetuates stereotypes via the self-fulfilling prophecy (see Chapter 7). Persons who know each other can draw on their past experience with each other as a basis for effective communication.

**Interpersonal Context.** According to this model, both the production and the interpretation of communication are heavily influenced by the interpersonal context in which they occur (Giles & Coupland, 1991). This context influences communication through norms, cognitive representations of prior similar situations, and emotional arousal.

Every social situation invokes norms regarding communicative behavior. These norms specify what topics are appropriate and inappropriate for discussion, what language is to be used, and how persons of varying status should be addressed. Depending on these norms, we use one or another of various speech repertoires, ways of communicating the same literal message that vary in words, tone, and so on (Giles & Coupland, 1991). Imagine a man who wishes another person to close a door. To his son in his home, he might say, "Close the door." To his son at work, he might say, "Please close the door, Tom." To an employee, he could say, "Would you close the door?" These different ways of making a request reflect differences in speech rules, which depend on the relationship between speaker and listener, and on the setting.

Each new situation evokes representations of prior similar situations and the language one has used or heard in them (Chapman et al., 1992). These conversational histories provide us with the contents of our speech repertoires. Each of us has a set of things we say when we meet a stranger our own age at a party; these are opening lines that in the past have been effective in facilitating conversation with strangers at parties. If, instead, you met the same stranger on a plane, you might use different speech acts.

The processing of messages by listeners is also influenced by these contextual factors. Listeners interpret messages in light of the rules operating in situations, their past experience, and the emotions elicited in them. When speaker and listener have the same understanding of the normative demands, communication should be quite accurate. Similarly, if a situation evokes the same representations and emotions in both, it is likely that the listener will accurately interpret the speaker's message. Communication across group and cultural boundaries is often difficult precisely because speaker and listener differ in their assumptions and experiences, even though they may speak the same language.

Members of a group share a **linguistic intergroup bias** (Maass & Arcuri, 1992). That is, there are subtle and systematic differences in the language we use to describe events as a function of our group membership and the group to which the actor or target belongs. We describe other members of our own group behaving properly and members of out-groups behaving improperly at very abstract levels (say, "Jim [in-group member] is helpful"; "George [out-group member] is aggressive"). This encourages positive stereotypes of us and negative stereotypes of them. When in-group members behave badly or out-group members behave well, we describe the events concretely ("Jim pushed that guy out of his way"; "George held the door for a woman carrying a baby"). This technique encourages an attribution to the individual rather than to the group. Research with Danish youth found evidence that the influence of this bias increased significantly from age 8 to age 19 (Werkman, Wigboldus, & Semin, 1999).

**Sociolinguistic Competence.** To attain mutual understanding, language performance must be appropriate to the social and cultural context. Otherwise, even grammatically acceptable sentences will not make sense. "My parent eats raw termites" is grammatically correct and meaningful; it reflects linguistic competence. But as a serious assertion by a North American, this utterance would draw amazed looks. It expresses an idea that is incongruous with American culture, and listeners would have difficulty interpreting it. In a termite-eating culture, however, the same utterance would be quite sensible. This example shows that successful communication requires **sociolinguistic competence**— knowledge of the implicit rules for generating socially appropriate sentences. Such sentences make sense to listeners, because they fit with the listeners' social knowledge (Hymes, 1974).

Speech that clashes with what is known about the social relationship to which it refers suggests that a speaker is not sociolinguistically competent (Grimshaw, 1990). Speakers are expected to use language that is appropriate to the status of the individuals they are discussing and to their relationship of intimacy. For example, competent speakers would not state seriously, "The janitor ordered the president to turn off the lights in the Oval Office." They know that low-status persons do not "order" those of much higher status; at most, they "hint" or "suggest." Referring to a relationship of true intimacy, sociolinguistically competent speakers would not say, "The lover bullied the beloved." Rather, they would select such socially appropriate verbs as "coaxed" or "persuaded." In short, competent speakers recognize that social and cultural constraints make some statements interpretable and others uninterpretable in a given situation.

Thus, successful communication is a complex undertaking. A speaker must produce a message that has not only an appropriate literal meaning, but also an intention or goal appropriate to the relationship and setting. The message must reflect the present degree of intersubjectivity between speaker and hearer, consistent with the interactional context. The message must also signify the statuses of the participants (Geis, 1995). Given these requirements, it is remarkable that each of us communicates successfully many times each day.

## NONVERBAL COMMUNICATION

In the introduction, we asked you to think about what it would be like to communicate without using words. Imagine that you are looking out of a window of your third-floor dorm room or apartment. You notice a man on the sidewalk below, dressed immaculately in a three-piece suit, pacing back and forth. He looks up and sees you and immediately begins to gesture. He points to you, then to some other window, and then to his watch. His movements are quick and sharp. His face is tense. What is he trying to communicate to you?

Even without the use of words, most of us can make some inferences about the man's message and emotional state. We do so by interpreting his nonverbal communication. This section examines three questions concerning nonverbal communication: (1) What are the major types of nonverbal communication? (2) What is communicated by the human face? (3) What is gained and what problems arise when nonverbal and verbal communication are combined in ordinary interaction?

### Types of Nonverbal Communication

By one estimate, the human face can make some 250,000 different expressions (Birdwhistell, 1970). In addition to facial expressions, nonverbal communication uses many other bodily and gestural cues. Four major types of nonverbal cues (summarized in Table 9.2) are described next.

**Paralanguage.** Speaking involves a great deal more than the production of words. Vocal behavior includes loudness, pitch, speed, emphasis, inflection, breathiness, stretching or clipping of words, pauses, and so on. All the vocal aspects of speech other than words are called **paralanguage**. This includes such highly communicative vocalizations as moaning, sighing, laughing, and even crying. Shrillness of voice and rapid delivery communicate tension and excitement in most situations (Scherer, 1979). Various uses and interpretations of paralinguistic and other nonverbal cues will be examined later in this chapter. For now, see how many distinct meanings you can give to the sentence "Asad is on the phone again" by varying the paralinguistic cues you use.

**Body Language.** The silent movement of body parts—scowls, smiles, nods, gazing, gestures, leg movements, postural shifts, and so on—all constitute **body language**. Because body language entails movement, it is known as *kinesics* (from the Greek *kinein* meaning "to move"). Whereas paralinguistic cues are auditory, we perceive kinesic cues visually. The body movements of the man in our example were probably particularly useful to you in interpreting his feelings and intentions. Researchers investigated the use of

**TABLE 9.2** Types of Nonverbal Communication

| TYPE OF CUE | DEFINITION | EXAMPLES | CHANNEL |
|---|---|---|---|
| Paralanguage | Vocal but nonverbal behavior involved in speaking | Loudness, speed, pauses in speech | Auditory |
| Body language (kinesics) | Silent motions of the body | Gestures, facial expressions, eye gaze | Visual |
| Interpersonal spacing (proxemics) | Positioning of body at varying distances and angles from others | Intimate closeness, facing head-on, looking away, turning one's back | Primarily visual; also touch, smell, and auditory |
| Choice of personal effects | Selecting and displaying objects that others will associate with you | Clothing, makeup, room decorations | Primarily visual; also auditory and smell |

head tilts to the side and shoulder shrugs during debates (Debras & Cienki, 2012). Head tilts served to point to other persons or objects, to call attention to them, whereas shrugs were markers of disengagement.

The handshake is a common nonverbal behavior. There are a variety of beliefs about the meaning of a handshake, depending on whether it is firm or limp, dry or damp. Research on how we interpret handshakes involved four trained coders (two men, two women); each shook hands twice with 112 men and women and rated the participants on four measures of personality. The man or woman with a firm handshake was rated by the coders as extroverted and emotionally expressive and given low ratings on shyness. Women who shook hands firmly were also rated as open to new experience (Chaplin et al., 2000). Thus, a handshake can make a strong or weak first impression and influence future interactions.

In some groups and social settings, the hug has replaced the handshake. The hug, formerly a gesture signaling intimacy, is now much more widely used, often exchanged by friends or just acquaintances. Of particular interest is the rapid spread of the bro hug, a handshake accompanied by pulling the other person toward you and exchanging a hug, involving two men. Anderson & McCormack (2015) suggest that the spread of this gesture reflects decreasing homophobia among young men.

**Interpersonal Spacing.** We also communicate nonverbally by using **interpersonal spacing** cues—positioning ourselves at varying distances and angles from others (for example, standing close or far away, facing head-on or to one side, adopting various postures, and creating barriers with books or other objects). Because proximity is a major means of communication between people, this type of cue is also called *proxemics*. When there is very close positioning, proxemics can convey information through smell and touch as well.

What types of communication by wait staff influence your emotional reactions in a restaurant? Researchers surveyed several hundred diners in family restaurants in Seoul, Korea; diners completed a 31-item questionnaire while waiting for dessert. The survey assessed diners' reactions to the server's verbal, paralinguistic, kinesic, and proxemic behaviors. The results indicated that eye contact, smiles, bodily positioning, and touch determined whether the customer reported a positive or negative experience; the server's language and paralanguage were not related to diners' impressions (Jung & Yoon, 2011).

**Choice of Personal Effects.** Though we usually think of communication as expressed through our bodies, people also communicate nonverbally through the personal effects they select—their choices of clothing, hairstyle, makeup, eyewear (contact lenses), and the like. A uniform, for example, may communicate social status, political opinion, lifestyle, and occupation, revealing a great deal about how its wearer is likely to behave (Joseph & Alex, 1972). You may have made assumptions about the status and lifestyle of the man in our sketch based on the fact that he wore a three-piece suit. The deliberate use of bodily hair and tattoos to influence the impressions of others is discussed in Chapter 5.

Clothing can convey a great deal of information about the wearer. Interviews with 38 young people found that clothing choices conveyed information about group membership (Piacentini & Mailer, 2004). The wearing of gold jewelry signaled membership in one group, whereas dressing in "joggies" and "trackies" indicated membership in a very different group. Wearing expensive, branded clothing conveyed one's social class status to other students and staff in the school. Clothing was also chosen to fit and communicate the role that the person was performing.

In spaces that a person controls, such as a bedroom, dormitory room, or office, objects that are displayed will be associated with the person. Persons who enter the space will make inferences about the occupant based on what objects are displayed, their relative position or prominence, and so on. A survey of eighth- and ninth-graders focused on the contents of their bedrooms found gender differences in the objects and decorations; boys' rooms contained sports equipment and things they had built, whereas girls' rooms contained stuffed animals and photographs of people/family members (Jones et al., 2007). Girls' rooms were much more likely to contain makeup tables and have matching bedspread, curtains, and rugs. Similar differences have been found in the living spaces of college students and recent graduates (Gosling, Craik, Martin, & Pryor, 2005). Furniture in residences reflects and displays the patterns of social interaction preferred by residents. Furniture creates and constrains possibilities for interaction, and is often purchased and arranged for that purpose. A study of the tables purchased by Australians found that purchasers of a rectangular table used it to display the family hierarchy, with adults sitting at the short ends; a round table was purchased and used by two people who preferred an equalitarian style of interaction (Bjorkvall & Karlsson, 2011).

For the most part, nonverbal cues, like language, are learned rather than innate. As a result, the meanings of particular nonverbal cues may vary from culture to culture. One example is the meaning of nodding one's head up and down. In some cultures, including American, it means "Yes." In others, it means "No." Other features of nonverbal communication may have universal meanings, however. These universals are based on our biological nature.

## Digital/Computer-Mediated Communication

The preceding discussion implicitly assumes that communication is face-to-face. In the past

The meaning of a gesture can vary greatly from one culture to another. or one social setting to another. A good example is the gesture in this photo. It is widely known as "Hook em horns" and is used to show support for the University of Texas Longhorns. In a different context, it is used by several professional wrestlers during matches to mock their opponents. Rockers like this person use it to encourage the audience at a concert to "rock on." In several other cultures, including Italy, Brazil and Spain, this gesture directed at a man signals that his partner is cheating on him! © Fernando Cortes/Shutterstock

century, new forms of communication aided by technology have become widely used. The first was the telephone, which allowed communication at a distance; it involves spoken language and paralanguage, but body language, proxemics, and the impact of personal effects are lost. There is less shared context for the communication, unless the actors know each other. More recently the cell phone has freed communicators from connection to "landlines" and allows communication from almost anywhere at any time. This is an advantage in increasing the spontaneity and sense of connection, but a disadvantage to the extent that it happens at inappropriate times such as during a meeting, a performance, a class, or a religious service.

The development and adoption of computer-mediated communication (CMC) has been especially rapid. E-mail and texting (SMS, or short message service) are almost universal in certain segments of U.S. society. In CMC, communication is entirely by written language, removing the paralingual cues, kinesics, and proxemics—that is, aural and visual feedback (Kiesler, Siegel, & McGuire, 1984). We noted earlier that these are very important in providing context, which aids in interpreting the words, and is often the mode by which emotion is communicated. This obviously makes many messages harder to code, potentially restricting the topics of communication, and increases risk of inaccuracy. The widespread use of emoticons is an effort to compensate for the difficulty of conveying emotion, as is the use of textual devices such as CAPITAL LETTERs to indicate shouting. CMC also involves the limited *digital self* (discussed in Chapter 4), rather than the embodied person.

E-mail and text are also asynchronous, meaning that there is no immediate feedback from others. As we note later in the chapter, *back-channel feedback* (eye contact, smiles, nods) makes an important contribution to accuracy of communication, and to the smooth flow of interaction (a relationship). The absence of immediate feedback makes the time lag between the sending of a message and receiving an answer potentially meaningful to the sender: "Why did they wait one hour/one day/one week to respond to my invitation?" The lack of a synchronous connection is taken advantage of when a communicator uses e-mail or text to send "bad news." College students acknowledge using text messages instead of face-to-face contacts to break up with a partner (Harrison & Gilmore, 2012).

Perhaps not surprisingly, in class discussions of texting this is a common complaint! Students also report sending messages at times some would consider inappropriate, such as while on a date, interacting with friends or family, on an airplane in flight, or even while having sex. In other words, CMC users regularly violate the temporal and spatial boundaries that separate intimate life, social activities, work, and religion (Kiesler, Siegel, & McGuire, 1984). These breaches suggest that CMC encourages disinhibition and lack of attention to ongoing social activity. A number of social commentators have pointed to negative impacts on our lives and relationships of disengagement from the world around us due to time spent on social media (Oswalt, 2014).

Teens aged 13 to 17 are major users of technology (Lenhart et al., 2015). In particular, digital communication plays an important role in making and maintaining friendship ties. A Pew study found that more than half of teens surveyed reported texting daily with friends. Twenty-three percent reported connecting with friends daily via social media, compared to 25 percent who reported daily face-to-face contact with friends.

## What's in a Face?

The face is an important communication channel. Typically, we pay attention to the face of persons with whom we interact. Moreover, the face is capable of many nonverbal behaviors; one dictionary lists 98 behaviors, of which 25 involve the face (Rashotte, 2002). They include baring the teeth, closing one's eyes, frowning, grinning, licking the lips, nodding, tilting the head, raising one's eyebrows, and smiling. The physical features of the face combined with these movements convey a variety of messages, including information about social identities, personality, and emotions (see Chapter 6).

The physical features of the face, including skin color, often provide cues to racial or ethnic identity. The features, in combination with grooming, makeup, and jewelry, virtually always indicate gender. Thus, inferences about two important social identities are made the moment we see someone's face, and these inferences shape our interaction with that person.

Physiognomy, the art of "reading" faces, is based on the belief that personality traits can be inferred from facial features. In research designed to test this, participants were given photographs and descriptions of a target person. The photographs were selected based on ratings by other participants on the confidence, charisma, and dominance of the person in the photo; one-half of the photos were of people rated high on these, and the other half were of people rated low on them. Participants were asked to rate the target on 13 personality scales. When the verbal description was ambiguous, the characteristics of the photo significantly influenced ratings (Hassin & Trope, 2000). This research suggests that people do make inferences about personality based on facial features. The idea that there are basic facial expressions implies that we interpret facial expressions without reference to context. In fact, research has demonstrated that identical facial expressions are interpreted differently, depending upon context. In a specific context, we expect certain facial expressions, and we compare the expression(s) displayed to what we expect in interpreting it (Aviezer et al., 2008).

Later in this chapter, we discuss research on facial maturity and how it influences interaction.

## Combining Nonverbal and Verbal Communication

When we speak on the telephone or shout to a friend in another room, we are limited to communicating through verbal and paralinguistic channels. When we wave to arriving or departing passengers at the airport, we use only the kinesic channel. Often, communication is multichanneled. Information is conveyed simultaneously through verbal, paralinguistic, kinesic, and proxemic cues.

What is gained and what problems are caused when different communication channels are combined? If they appear to convey consistent information, they reinforce each other, and communication becomes more accurate. But if different channels convey information that is inconsistent, the message may produce confusion or even arouse a suspicion of deception. In this section, we examine some outcomes of apparent consistency and inconsistency among channels.

**Reinforcement and Increased Accuracy.** The multiple cues we receive often seem redundant, each carrying the same message. A smile accompanies a compliment delivered in a warm tone of voice; a scowl accompanies a vehemently shouted threat. But multiple cues are seldom entirely redundant, and they are better viewed as complementary (Poyatos, 1983). The smile and warm tone convey that the compliment is sincere; the scowl and vehement shout imply that the threat will be carried out. Thus, multiple cues convey added information, reduce ambiguity, and increase the accuracy of communication (Krauss, Morrel-Samuels, & Colasante, 1991).

Taken alone, each channel lacks the capacity to carry the entire weight of the messages exchanged in the course of a conversation. By themselves, the verbal aspects of language are insufficient for accurate communication. Paralinguistic and kinesic cues supplement verbal cues by supporting and emphasizing them. The importance of paralinguistic cues is illustrated in a study of students from a Nigerian secondary school and teachers' college (Grayshon, 1980). Although these students took courses in English and knew the verbal language well, they did not know the paralinguistic cues of British native speakers. The students listened to two British recordings with identical verbal content. In one recording, paralinguistic cues indicated that the speaker was giving the listener a brush-off. In the other recording, paralinguistic cues indicated that the speaker was apologizing. Of 251 students, 97 percent failed to perceive any difference in the meanings the speaker was conveying. Failure to distinguish a brush-off from an apology could be disastrous in everyday communication. Accurate understanding requires paralinguistic as well as verbal knowledge.

Our accuracy in interpreting events is greatly enhanced if we have multiple communication cues rather than verbal information alone. The value of a full set of cues was demonstrated in a study of U.S. undergraduates' interpretations of various scenes (Archer & Akert, 1977). Participants observed scenes of social interaction that were either displayed in a video broadcast or described verbally in a transcript of the video broadcast. Thus, students received either full, multichannel communication or verbal cues alone. Afterward, students were asked to answer questions about what was going on in each scene—questions that required going beyond the obvious facts. Observers who received the full set of verbal and nonverbal cues were substantially more accurate in interpreting social interactions. For instance, of those receiving multichannel cues, 56 percent correctly identified which of three women engaged in a conversation had no children; this compared with only 17 percent of those limited to verbal cues. These findings convincingly demonstrate the gain in accuracy from multichannel communication.

**Resolving Inconsistency.** At times, the messages conveyed by different channels appear inconsistent with one another. This makes communication and interaction problematic. What would you do, for example, if your instructor welcomed you during office hours with warm words, a frowning face, and an annoyed tone of voice? You might well react with uncertainty and caution, puzzled by the apparent inconsistency between the verbal and nonverbal cues you were receiving. You would certainly try to figure out the instructor's true feelings and desires, and you might also try to guess why the instructor was sending such confusing cues.

The strategies people use to resolve apparently inconsistent cues depend on their inferences about the reasons for the apparent inconsistency (Zuckerman et al., 1981). Inconsistency could be due to the communicator's ambivalent feelings (Mongrain & Vettese, 2003), to poor communication skills, or to an intention to deceive. A large body of research has compared the relative weight we give to messages in different channels when we do not suspect deception.

In one set of studies, people judged the emotion expressed by actors who posed contradictory verbal, paralinguistic, and facial signals (Mehrabian, 1972). These studies showed that facial cues were most important in determining which feelings are interpreted as true. Paralinguistic cues were second, and verbal cues were a distant third. Later research exposing receivers to more complete combinations of visual and auditory cues replicated the finding that people rely more on facial than on paralinguistic cues when the two conflict. This preference for facial cues increases with age from childhood to adulthood, indicating that it is a learned strategy (DePaulo et al., 1978).

People also use social context to help them judge which channel is more credible (Bugenthal, 1974). They consider whether the facial expression, tone of voice, or verbal content is appropriate to the particular social situation. If people recognize a situation as highly stressful, for example, they rely more on the cues that seem consistent with a stressful context (such as a strained tone of voice) and less on cues that seem to contradict it (such as a happy face or a verbal assertion of calmness). If the emotional expression is ambiguous, situational cues determine the emotion that observers attribute to the person (Carroll & Russell, 1996). For example, a person in a frightening situation displaying an expression of moderate anger was judged to be afraid. In short, people tend to resolve apparent inconsistencies between channels in favor of the channels whose message seems most appropriate to the social context.

## SOCIAL STRUCTURE AND COMMUNICATION

So far, this chapter has examined the nature of verbal, nonverbal, and digital communication. How do social relationships shape communication? And how does communication express, maintain, or modify social relationships? These questions pinpoint social psychology's concern with the reciprocal impacts of social structure and communication on each other. This section examines four aspects of these impacts. First, it discusses gender differences in communication. Second, it considers the links between styles of speech and position in the social stratification system. Third, it analyzes the ways in which communication creates and expresses the two central dimensions of relationships—status and intimacy. Finally, it examines the social norms that regulate interaction distances and some of the outcomes when these norms are violated.

### Gender and Communication

A fundamental question about how social structure influences communication is whether there are systematic differences between men and women in communication style. Many empirical studies have been conducted since 1970. Typically, each study focuses on one or two aspects of interaction and compares men and women on it. The most widely studied aspect has been interruptions. Research by Zimmerman and West (1975) reported that in casual conversation of mixed-gender

dyads, men interrupted women much more frequently than the reverse. Other research suggested that women's speech involves more frequent use of tag questions ("It's really hot, isn't it?"), hedges ("In my opinion, . . ."), and disclaimers ("I may be wrong but . . ."). These three are often linked and have been said to indicate that women's speech is more tentative than men's. Some studies report that women are more likely to use intensifiers ("It's really hot, isn't it?"). In the nonverbal realm, women smile more often than men and are less likely to look at the other person as they interact. These and other findings of gender differences are the basis for the assertion that there are vast differences in style of interaction between men and women. In addition to academic researchers who take this position, it has been popularized in books such as *You Just Don't Understand: Women and Men in Conversation* (Tannen, 1991) and *Men Are from Mars, Women Are from Venus* (Gray, 1992) (see Box 9.2). The early academic interpretation of these differences was that they reflect the fact that men have greater power than women. Thus, interruptions, declarative statements instead of tentative ones, and speech without intensifiers all reflect the possession of power—that is, the stratification system of the society.

Research on gender differences in communication has gotten more sophisticated in recent years. Instead of descriptive research comparing men and women on a small number of behaviors, researchers now study these processes in specific social contexts. Thus, researchers study how gender and contextual variables such as type of relationship, group task, or authority structure interact to influence communication. For example, studies in the 1970s and 1980s found that when men attempted to change the topic of conversation, they succeeded 96 percent of the time; in contrast, attempts by women succeeded only 36 percent of the time (Fishman, 1983). This was interpreted as reflecting the difference in status of men and women. But if we take a broader

## BOX 9.2  Gender Differences in Communication

Two of the best-selling books of the 1990s, *You Just Don't Understand* (Tannen, 1991) and *Men Are from Mars, Women Are from Venus* (Gray, 1992), proclaim that there are important differences in the way men and women communicate. According to Tannen, men and women have different goals in conversation. Men intend to exert control, maintain their independence, and enhance their status; women want to establish and maintain relationships. Men engage in conversational dominance, women in conversational maintenance. (Does this sound like the gender stereotypes discussed in Box 7.1?)

Lakoff (1979) called attention to the greater use by women of tag questions—statements that are between an assertion ("male" speech style) and a question. For example, "Richard is here, isn't he?" Lakoff and others argue that tag questions express a lack of confidence in the speaker—a desire to avoid commitment to a statement and potential conflict. Empirical results with regard to gender differences in the use of tag questions are conflicting: in some studies, women use them more; in other studies, men use them more; and in some studies, there are no differences. Also, if we look at the functions of tag questions in conversation, we see that there are several: they may express uncertainty, but they also may express solidarity ("You were really sad about losing her, weren't you?") or politeness ("Sit down, won't you?"). A closer look suggests that it is too simplistic to interpret the use of tag questions as an indication of lack of confidence, regardless of the gender of the person using them (Aries, 1996).

Another oft-discussed difference is in the use of back-channel feedback—small vocal comments a listener makes while a speaker is talking. Women use less intrusive responses than men to indicate attention or agreement during conversation. Women prefer head nods and "M-hmn" rather than the more assertive "Yeah" or "Right." Women also make more such responses than men. Again, research shows that gender interacts with other variables. Back-channel responses occur more often in cooperative than in competitive interactions, and carry different meaning depending on whether they are inserted in the middle (showing active attention) or at the end of a long utterance (indicating an end to the topic). Back-channel comments are not consistently associated with power or dominance.

There are also gender differences in nonverbal behavior. Men tend to signal dominance through freer staring, pointing, and walking slightly ahead of the women they are with. Women are more likely to avert or lower their eyes and move out of a man's way when they are passing him (LaFrance & Mayo, 1978; Leffler, Gillespie, & Conaty, 1982). However, when men are in subordinate positions to women, they avert their eyes or move out of her way. Thus, the gender difference is really a difference in the numbers of men and women who occupy superordinate positions. An observational study of 799 instances of intentional touch found that in public situations—at shopping malls, outdoors on a college campus—men are more likely to touch women. In greeting or leave-taking situations—at bus stations and airports—there was no asymmetry by gender (Major, Schmidlin, & Williams, 1990).

Thus, a comprehensive review of the literature on gender differences in communication leads to the conclusion that speech patterns, conversational style, and nonverbal behavior vary not only by gender but by characteristics of the context, such as the goals of the interaction and the roles of the participants. Anyone is capable of displaying "masculine" or "feminine" styles of communication when it is appropriate.

look, we see that (1) there are several types of topic shifts in interaction, and (2) any group of three or more people tends to develop an internal status structure that is influenced by the setting, task, and characteristics of the specific people present. A more recent study of six-person task-oriented groups found that topic shifts are more sensitive to the internal status structure of the group than to gender (Okamoto & Smith-Lovin, 2001). Moreover, topic shifts often occurred following a lapse in the discussion or an obvious conclusion to the current topic, suggesting that they are not displays of power.

Research on other aspects of communication has reached similar conclusions. A study of nonverbal behavior recruited participants in a company's headquarters; 42 employees each participated in two interactions with another, randomly chosen employee. As a result, the dyads varied in the corporate status of participants. There were 10 all-male, 9 all-female, and 25 mixed-gender dyads. During each interaction, the pair was given two tasks. Interaction was video- and audiotaped, and the tapes were coded by trained observers. The data were analyzed by gender and by corporate status. Some nonverbal behavior varied by gender and some varied by status. The differences associated with status did not correspond to the differences associated with gender. Although women smiled more, there were no differences in smiling by status. There were no stable differences across gender or status, suggesting that the differences observed reflected local or corporate practices and participants' motives (Hall & Friedman, 1999).

In short, men and women do not form two different, homogeneous groups with respect to communication style (Cameron, 1998). Generalizations about gender and communication require taking into account the context and particular local (group, organizational) communication practices (Eckert & McConnell-Ginet, 1999).

## Social Stratification and Speech Style

The way we speak both reflects and re-creates our social relationships (Giles & Coupland, 1991). Every sociolinguistic community recognizes variation in the way its members talk. One style is usually the preferred or standard style. In addition to this preferred style, there are often other, nonpreferred styles.

**Standard and Nonstandard Speech.** Consider an example of each style. As you enter a theater, a young man approaches you. He asks, "Would you please fill out this short survey for me?" Depending on your mood, you might comply with his request. But what if he asked, "Wud ja ansa sum questions?" Many people would be less likely to comply with this request.

The first request employs standard American English. **Standard speech** is defined as characterized by diverse vocabulary, proper pronunciation, correct grammar, and abstract content. It takes into account the listener's perspective. Note the inclusion of "please" in the first request, which indicates that the speaker recognizes that he is asking for a favor. **Nonstandard speech** is defined as characterized by limited vocabulary, improper pronunciation, incorrect grammar, and directness. It is egocentric; the absence of "please" and "for me" in the second request makes it sound like an order, even though it is phrased as a question.

In the United States, as in many other countries, speech style is associated with social status (Giles & Coupland, 1991). The use of standard speech is associated with high socioeconomic status and with power. People in positions of economic and political power are usually very articulate and grammatically correct in their public statements. In contrast, the use of nonstandard speech is associated with low socioeconomic status and low power.

These variations in speech are often used in mass media to index social class (Stamou,

2011). An analysis of a very popular Greek TV series describes the standard speech used by Constantine, a 40-something professor. He uses a formal speech style, peppered with obsolete language forms and ancient Greek proverbs. He lives with Helen, a 40-something barmaid, who uses everyday and colloquial speech, and throws in expressions from youth language ("pissed off"). Their consistent use of these styles contrasts with two other characters, both lawyers, who switch from one style to the other depending on the occasion. Given the class gulf between them, it is not surprising that Constantine and Helen don't cohabit happily ever after. You can probably think of a TV series or film that uses speech style to mark social class.

Speech style is also influenced by the interpersonal context. In informal conversations with others of equal status, such as at some parties or in bars, we often use nonstandard speech, regardless of our socioeconomic status. In more formal settings, especially public ones, we usually shift to standard speech. Thus, our choice of standard or nonstandard speech gives listeners information about how we perceive the situation.

Studies in a variety of cultures have found systematic differences in how people evaluate speakers using standard and nonstandard speech. In one study, students in Kentucky listened to tape recordings of young men and women describing themselves. Four of the recordings, two by men and two by women, were of speakers with "standard" American accents. Four others, identical in content, were of speakers with Kentucky accents. On the average, students gave the standard speakers high ratings on status and the nonstandard speakers low ratings on status (Luhman, 1990).

Is mumbling macho? Women's speech has somewhat greater phonetic distinctiveness than men's; women speak with more dispersed vowels (better enunciation) and more precise articulation of consonants. Radio DJs report altering their speech to fit the audience, so they might use more masculine styles when broadcasting heavy metal and country music, and less masculine styles when playing popular and classical music. Eight on-air DJs were recorded on XM satellite radio; one-minute samples were created for each, and rated by male and female undergraduates on ten Likert scales. Recordings were also analyzed using acoustic computer software. Those DJs whose speech was acoustically less distinctive (that is, they mumbled more) were rated as significantly more masculine by the listeners. As predicted they were the DJs on the heavy metal and country music channels (Heffernan, 2010).

**African-American Vernacular English.** African-American Vernacular English (AAVE, AAE) is one of many dialects found in the United States. It is rooted in history, and shares features with other dialects found in the U.S. South. The use of dialect by members of a group is a marker of social and personal identity (see Chapter 4) and an expressive resource in interaction. Dialects often involve differences in pronunciation and in grammar (Rickford et al., 2015), and are therefore considered nonstandard speech. A dialect may involve limited vocabulary, and may not allow for elaboration and qualification of ideas. As a result, some analysts advocate so-called *deficit theories*, which claim that people who use dialects or nonstandard speech are less capable of abstract and complex thought. These theories also claim that nonstandard speech styles are typical of lower-class, Black, and other culturally disadvantaged groups in the United States, Great Britain, and other societies. Combining these two claims, deficit theorists argue that the children from disadvantaged groups perform poorly in school because their restricted language makes them cognitively inferior. Their poor academic performance in turn leads to unemployment and poverty in later life.

The strongest criticism of deficit theories has come from Labov (1972). Based on interviews in natural environments, he demonstrated that "Black English" is every bit as rich and subtle as standard English. Black English differs from standard English mainly in surface details like pronunciation ("ax" = *ask*) and grammatical forms ("He be busy" = *He's always busy*). Nonstandard speech may appear impoverished because nonstandard speakers feel less relaxed in the social contexts where they are typically observed (such as schools or interviews), and so they limit their speech. Anxiety may be the reason the young man asked "Wud ja ansa sum questions?" Social researchers or other "outsiders" who observe nonstandard speakers may also inhibit their language (Grimshaw, 1973). When interviewed by a member of their own race, for instance, Black job applicants used longer sentences and richer vocabularies and employed words more creatively (Ledvinka, 1971). Overall, speech differences between groups have not been shown to reflect differences in cognitive ability (Thorlundsson, 1987), and deficit theories have not received much empirical support.

In 1996, the Oakland, California, school board adopted a resolution stating that Black English, which the resolution called **ebonics** (ebony phonics), is a distinctive language. The board decided to provide some instruction in ebonics to facilitate the education of students and encourage "their mastery of English language skills." The board's action set off a national debate. Numerous scholars and organizations now recognize the legitimacy and cultural value of this language, now referred to as African-American Vernacular English (Rodriguez, Cargile, & Rich, 2004). Some teachers use AAVE in an effort to enhance the comprehension and learning of African-American students (Bohn, 2003). For example, one seventh-grade teacher in a predominantly minority school encourages students to journal and write poetry in AAVE, which facilitates self-expression, and requires students to produce an "errorless draft" of a paper adhering to all the conventions of Standard English (SE) (Hill, 2009). A field researcher in one high school in Washington, DC, observed that for many African-American students, AAVE was the preferred speech style; they associated ASE (American Standard English) with White, majority culture, and its history of oppressing Blacks (Fordham, 1999). For these students, ASE is the nonstandard vernacular, and they "dissed" (disrespected) those Blacks who used it. These students "leased" ASE—that is, used it when they had to while in school, from 9:00 a.m. to 3:00 p.m., but not outside the school building. Two researchers collected essays from 52 African-American tenth-graders (Godley & Escher, 2012). Twenty-three (45 percent) argued that only AAVE should be spoken in the classroom, because they were more proficient and comfortable speaking it. Eighteen said both AAVE and ASE should be spoken; they said AAVE facilitates group work and brainstorming, and that SE should be used for "practicing" communication in future contexts. Ten students argued that only ASE should be spoken, to prepare them for future academic and professional endeavors. These results parallel the broader debate among educators, activists, and politicians about what role AAVE should play in education.

We noted earlier that evaluation of speakers is influenced by their speech style. Do people evaluate speakers of AAVE differently? In a carefully designed experiment, majority and minority students evaluated recordings of speakers using strong AAVE (11 features), moderate AAVE (6 features), or U.S. Standard English (USE). Listeners rated the strong AAVE speakers as less attractive and lower-status than the speakers of moderate AAVE. They rated speakers of moderate AAVE as lower in attractiveness and status than speakers of USE (Rodriguez, Cargile, & Rich, 2004). Other research has attempted to identify the specific features that cause listeners to distinguish AAVE from USE; the results are inconclusive (Thomas & Reaser, 2004).

What about speech patterns in other ethnic groups? Some observers have suggested that there is an Asian-American Vernacular English, a dialect widespread among Asian Americans. A closer look indicates that there is not. One reason is that people of many different backgrounds are included in this group: Chinese American, Taiwanese American, Vietnamese American, North Korean American, South Korean American, etc. There is no evidence that there are atypical patterns of grammar and pronunciation shared by all of these persons. There may be dialects spoken within one or more of these groups; research on this question has not been carried out. Similarly, there is no evidence of Hispanic or Latino/a vernacular English. People who live in the U.S. and speak Spanish are also from a broad range of backgrounds: Mexico, numerous South American countries, Puerto Rico, Cuba, etc. (Stanlaw, Adachi, & Salzmann, 2017).

## Communicating Status and Intimacy

The two central dimensions of social relationships are status and intimacy. Status is concerned with the exercise of power and control. Intimacy is concerned with the expression of affiliation and affection that creates social solidarity (Kemper, 1973). Verbal and nonverbal communication express and maintain particular levels of intimacy and relative status in relationships. Moreover, through communication we may challenge existing levels of intimacy and relative status and negotiate new ones (Scotton, 1983).

Communication can signal our view of a relationship only if we recognize which communication behaviors are appropriate for an expected level of intimacy or status, and which are inappropriate. The following examples suggest that we easily recognize when communication behaviors are inappropriate. What if you:

- used vulgar slang during a job interview?

- repeatedly addressed your mother as Mrs. X?
- draped your arm on your professor's shoulder as they explained how to improve your test answers?
- looked away each time your beloved gazed into your eyes?

Each of these communication behaviors would probably make you uncomfortable, and they would doubtlessly cause others to think you inept, disturbed, or hostile. Each behavior expresses levels of intimacy or relative status easily recognized as inappropriate to the social relationship. In the following section, we survey systematically how specific communication behaviors express, maintain, and change status and intimacy in relationships.

**Status.** Forms of address clearly communicate relative status in relationships. Inferiors use formal address (title and last name) for their superiors (for example, "When is the exam, Professor Levine?"), whereas superiors address inferiors with familiar forms (first name or nickname; for example, "On Friday, Pat"). Status equals use the same form of address with one another. Both use either formal (Ms./Mr./Mrs.) or familiar forms (Alexa/Mateo), depending on the degree of intimacy between them (Brown, 1965). When status differences are ambiguous, individuals may even avoid addressing each other directly. They shy away from choosing an address form because it might grant too much or too little status.

A shift in forms of address signals a change in social relationships, or at least an attempted change. During the French Revolution, in order to promote equality and fraternity, the revolutionaries demanded that everyone use only the familiar (*tu*) and not the formal (*vous*) form of the second-person pronoun, regardless of past status differences. Presidential candidates try to reduce their differences with voters by inviting the use of familiar names

Kinesic and proxemic cues are all we need to decipher the status relations displayed in this photo. His position, half sitting in a relaxed posture with active hand gestures, tells us which one is the boss; their seated postures, direct eye contact, and uniform smiles identify the employees. © pixdeluxe/iStock

(Hillary/The Donald). In cases where there is a clear status difference between people, the right to initiate the use of the more familiar or equal forms of address belongs to the superior (for example, "Why don't you drop that 'Professor' stuff?"). This principle also applies to other communication behaviors. It is the higher-status person who usually initiates changes toward more familiar behaviors such as greater eye contact, physical proximity, touch, or self-disclosure.

We each have a speech repertoire, different pronunciations, dialects, and a varied vocabulary from which to choose when speaking. Our choices of language to use with other people express a view of our relative status and may influence our relationships. People usually make language choices smoothly, easily expressing status differences appropriate to the situation (Gumperz, 1976; Stiles et al., 1984).

Teachers in a Norwegian town, for instance, were observed to lecture to their students in the standard language (Blom & Gumperz, 1972). When they wished to encourage student discussion, however, they switched to the local dialect, thereby reducing status differences. Note how your teachers also switch to more informal language when trying to promote student participation.

An experiment involving groups composed of a manager and two workers studied the effect of authority and gender composition of the group on verbal and nonverbal communication (Johnson, 1994). The researcher created a simulated retail store; the manager gave instructions to the subordinates and monitored their work for 30 minutes. The interaction was coded as it occurred. Authority affected verbal behavior: subordinates talked less, were less directive, and gave less feedback compared to superiors, regardless of gender. Gender affected the nonverbal behaviors of smiling and laughing: women in all-female groups smiled more than men in all-male groups.

Paralinguistic cues also communicate and reinforce status in relationships. An experimental study of influence in three-person groups systematically varied the paralanguage of one member (Ridgeway, 1987). This member, a confederate, was most influential when she spoke rapidly, in a confident tone, and gave quick responses. She was less influential when she behaved dominantly (that is, spoke loudly, gave orders) or submissively (that is, spoke softly, in a pleading tone). A subsequent study found that a person who spoke in a task-oriented style (that is, rapid speech, upright posture, eye contact) or a social style (that is, moderate volume, relaxed posture) was more influential (Carli, LaFleur, & Loeber, 1995). Persons who spoke using dominant or submissive paralanguage were less influential. Thus, engaging in the paralinguistic behaviors appropriate to the statuses of group members—in these experiments equals—enhances one's influence; engaging in behaviors inappropriate to one's status (say, like a superior toward equals) reduces one's influence.

Body language also serves to express status. When status is unequal, people of higher status tend to adopt relatively relaxed postures with their arms and legs in asymmetrical positions. One such position is the "manspread," involving a man sitting on a crowded transit vehicle with his legs spread widely, taking up two seats as a result. Those of lower status stand or sit in more tense and symmetrical positions. The amount of time we spend looking at our partner, and the timing, also indicate status. Higher-status persons look more when speaking than when listening, whereas lower-status persons look more when listening than when speaking. Overall, inferiors look more at their partners, but they are also first to break the gaze between partners. Finally, superiors

are much more likely to intrude physically on inferiors by touching or pointing at them (Dovidio & Ellyson, 1982; LaFrance & Mayo, 1978; Leffler, Gillespie, & Conaty, 1982).

An important phenomenon that both expresses and produces status differences is *silencing*. In many interactions, being silent is not a passive state reflecting the absence of a desire to communicate. The silence of one or more of the actors may reflect an active state produced by the ongoing interaction. A common form of silencing involves not replying to a comment or question addressed to you, which may silence the other person. Bodily movement may contribute to silencing, as when you turn away from someone and pick up the TV remote, or leave the room. Silencing can be an especially complex process when it occurs in a group setting, as illustrated by a detailed analysis of the silencing of one student during a classroom discussion (Leander, 2002). In response to a teacher's question about equal rights for women, one woman, Chelle, sitting in the back of the room, says quietly, "No, we don't have equal rights." A young man in front of her gestures with his thumb over his shoulder and says, "We got somebody back here who says they don't have equal rights." The young man, by gesturing rather than looking at Chelle, and by invoking we–they (in-group vs. out-group identities), is attempting to silence her. Both students are sitting near friends, and the friends become engaged in the conversation, so that interacting groups are now attempting to control the discourse. This contest by the groups is facilitated by seating arrangements, and participants turn their bodies and direct their gaze in ways that signal alignment. Other techniques employed included speaking over a member of the other group, and ridicule of an example given by one of the women. Thus, silencing is a complex interactional process involving language, gaze, gesture, bodily orientation, and symbolic invocation of group ties within the setting.

**Intimacy.** Communication also expresses another central dimension of relationships—intimacy. The exchange of title and last names is common for strangers. One way we signal intimacy or solidarity is by addressing each other with first names. In other languages, speakers express intimacy by their choice of familiar versus formal second-person pronouns. As noted earlier, the French can choose between the familiar *tu* or the formal *vous*; the Spanish have *tu* or *usted*; the Germans *du* or *sie*; and so on.

Choice of language, or *code switching*, is a strategy that is employed in a variety of situations. Deliberate choice of a language may play a central role in the construction of ethnicity (De Fina, 2007). Members of *Il Circolo*, an Italian-American community with 48 members (men), gathered monthly for dinner and cards. All spoke both English and Italian, and some also spoke a dialect. Public communication, verbal and written, and club business during dinner was conducted in English. Informal conversation, including talk during card games, was typically in Italian; if the men knew the dialect, that language might be used. The dialect and Italian were spoken to emphasize the men's common ethnic background.

Code switching may also reflect the desire to maintain or revitalize an ethnic community. Young adults of Mayan descent living in Guatemala were less likely to use Spanish, compared to older (Mayan) adults. The youth spoke in the Mayan dialect more often to demonstrate their resistance to Spanish culture and to revitalize the Mayan language (Barrett, 2008). Note the similarity to the use of AAVE by Black high school students to resist White U.S. culture discussed earlier.

Code switching is a common occurrence in language classes where native speakers of one language are learning a second language. Observation in high school English-as-a-second-language classes for immigrants from China (Liang, 2006), and Spanish classrooms where 10- to 12-year-old native speakers of

Spanish were learning Catalan (Unamuno, 2008), found that students switched back to native language when it facilitated completion of class assignments. Thus, the goals of interaction influence language choice.

You can even observe code switching in CMC. Swiss of German descent who visited Internet chat rooms often used dialect instead of German in their messages. Frequency of dialect use reflected not only the preference of individual message senders, but also the relative use of dialect in the thread—that is, context (Siebenhaar, 2006). This is especially remarkable because a written version of the dialect was rarely used prior to the Internet.

The intimacy of a relationship is clearly reflected in and reinforced by the content of conversation. As a relationship becomes more intimate, we disclose more personal information about ourselves. Intimacy is also conveyed by conversational style. In one study (Hornstein, 1985), telephone conversations were recorded and later analyzed; the conversations were between strangers, acquaintances, and friends. Compared to strangers, friends used more implicit openings ("Hi," or "Hi, it's me"), raised more topics, and were more responsive to the other conversationalist (for example, asked more questions). Friends also used more complex closings (for example, making concrete arrangements for the next contact). Conversations of acquaintances were more like those of strangers.

The **theory of speech accommodation** (Beebe & Giles, 1984; Giles, 1980) illustrates an important way in which people use verbal and paralinguistic behavior to express intimacy or liking. According to this theory, people express or reject intimacy by adjusting their speech behavior during interaction to converge with or diverge from their partner's. To express liking or evoke approval, they make their own speech behavior more similar to their partner's. To reject intimacy or communicate disapproval, they accentuate the differences between their own speech and their partner's.

A detailed analysis of 18 interviews illustrates speech accommodation based on both ethnicity and familiarity (Scanlon & Wassink, 2010). A 65-year old, middle-class, African-American woman interviewed 14 African-American and 4 White adults who grew up in the same multiethnic neighborhood. She had known some of the interviewees growing up in that neighborhood but not others. Her speech patterns were recorded and analyzed acoustically for use of features common to AAVE. She was more likely to use tokens common to AAVE in interviews with African Americans; she rarely used them in interviews with Whites—that is, she used SE patterns with them. Also, she was more likely to match speech patterns with persons she had known growing up than with strangers.

Adjustments of paralinguistic behavior demonstrate speech accommodation during conversations (Taylor & Royer, 1980; Thakerar, Giles, & Cheshire, 1982). Individuals who wish to express liking tend to shift their own pronunciation, speech rate, vocal intensity, pause lengths, and utterance lengths during conversation to match those of their partner. Individuals who wish to communicate disapproval modify these vocal behaviors in ways that make them diverge more from their partner's. Researchers recruited 100 romantically involved couples. Following an initial 3-minute conversation, couples were separated and randomly assigned to one of five conditions; one member was instructed to engage in very low, low, high, or very high intimacy in a subsequent 3-minute interaction, or were given no instruction. The second interaction was videotaped, and the frequency of 11 behaviors reflecting intimacy was coded for each participant. As expected, the partner adjusted their behavior by reciprocating the behaviors exhibited by the confederate. Reciprocity was especially evident on verbal expressions of intimacy and nonverbal indicators of

involvement, for example, facial pleasantness (Guerrero, Jones, & Burgoon, 2000).

Among bilinguals, speech accommodation may also determine the choice of language (Bourhis, Giles, Leyens, & Tajfel, 1979). To increase intimacy, bilinguals choose the language they believe their partner would prefer to speak. To reject intimacy, they choose their partner's less preferred language.

If greater intimacy leads to accommodation, can accommodation lead to greater intimacy? Research suggests that extreme accommodation, in the form of mimicry, leads to behaviors associated with greater intimacy. Using the methodology of the field experiment, 60 groups of customers in a restaurant were randomly assigned to one of two conditions. In one condition, a waitress literally repeated the orders of her customers; in the other, she merely acknowledged the orders by saying "Okay" or "Coming up." Customers whose orders were mimicked were more generous, giving significantly larger tips than those in the other condition (van Baaren, Holland, Steenaert, & van Knippenberg, 2003). In a related experiment conducted in a laboratory, the experimenter mimicked the posture (bodily orientation, positions of arms and legs) of one-half of the participants during a 6-minute interaction; those whom she mimicked were more likely to help her later when she dropped some pens (van Baaren, Holland, Kawakami, & van Knippenberg, 2004).

Accommodation is evident even in very subtle paralinguistic cues. Using audiotapes of interviews by talk-show host Larry King of 25 guests (stars, athletes, politicians), analyses indicated voice convergence between partners (Gregory & Webster, 1996). Lower-status persons accommodated their voices to higher-status persons. Moreover, student ratings of the status of Larry King and of his guests were correlated with the voice characteristics that showed convergence.

The ways we express intimacy through body language and interpersonal spacing are well recognized. For instance, research supports the folklore that lovers gaze more into each other's eyes (Rubin, 1970). In fact, we tend to interpret a high level of eye contact from others as a sign of intimacy. We communicate liking by assuming moderately relaxed postures, moving closer and leaning toward others, orienting ourselves face-to-face, and touching them (Mehrabian, 1972). Increasing emotional intimacy is often accompanied by increasing body engagement, from an arm around the shoulders to a full embrace (Gurevitch, 1990). There is an important qualification to these generalizations, however. Mutual gaze, close distance, and touch reflect intimacy and promote it only when the interaction has a positive cast. If the interaction is generally negative—if the setting is competitive, the verbal content unpleasant, or the past relationship antagonistic—these same nonverbal behaviors intensify negative feelings (Schiffenbauer & Schiavo, 1976).

**The Case of "Dude".** Let's apply the themes in this section to a concrete case. Language is continually evolving; some words and phrases fall into disuse (remember "valley girl"?) while new ones appear, like "dude." Think about the last time you used "dude" in conversation; to whom were you talking, and what was the context? Research using diaries, surveys of students, and analysis of conversations yields a snapshot of its use (Kiesling, 2004). "Dude" is used primarily by young men in conversation with other young men, suggesting that it is a marker of youth and masculinity. Further, men rarely use the term in conversation with parents and professors; its use indexes a relationship between persons of equal status. Like many terms that are adopted widely by youth, "dude" has many uses, as a greeting ("What's up, dude?"), an exclamation ("Dude!"), to one-up someone ("That's lame, dude"), and to express anger (DUDE!!). Thus, like all use of speech, the use of this term is governed by sociolinguistic norms,

and reflects group membership and the status and intimacy of the relationship between the conversationalists.

## NORMATIVE DISTANCES FOR INTERACTION

American and Northern European tourists in Cairo are often surprised to see men touching and staring intently into each other's eyes as they converse in public. Surprise may turn to discomfort if the tourist engages an Arab man in conversation. Bathed in the warmth of his breath, the tourist may feel sexually threatened. In our own communities, in contrast, we are rarely made uncomfortable by the overly close physical approach of another. People apparently know the norms for interaction distances in their own cultures and they conform to them. What are these norms, and what happens when they are violated?

### Normative Distances

Edward Hall (1966) has described four spatial zones that are normatively prescribed for interaction among middle-class Americans. Each zone is considered appropriate for particular types of activities and relationships. Public distance (12 to 25 feet) is prescribed for interaction in formal encounters, lectures, trials, and other public events. At this distance, communication is often one way, sensory stimulation is very weak, people speak loudly, and they choose language carefully. Social distance (4 to 12 feet) is prescribed for many casual social and business transactions. Here, sensory stimulation is low. People speak at normal volume, do not touch one another, and use frequent eye contact to maintain smooth communication. Personal distance (1.5 to 4 feet) is prescribed for interaction among friends and relatives. Here, people speak softly, touch one another, and receive substantial sensory stimulation by sight, sound, and smell. Intimate distance (0 to

18 inches) is prescribed for giving comfort, making love, and aggressing physically. This distance provides intense stimulation from touch, smell, breath, and body heat. It signals unmistakable involvement.

Many studies support the idea that people know and conform to the normatively prescribed distances for particular kinds of encounters (LaFrance & Mayo, 1978).

When we compare different cultural and social groups, both similarities and differences in distance norms emerge. All cultures prescribe closer distances for friends than for strangers, for example. The specific distances for preferred interactions vary widely, however. With regard to personal distance, research using participants from several cultural groupings found that Anglo-Saxons (people from the United States, the United Kingdom, and Canada) preferred the largest zone or distance, followed by Asians and Caucasians (Western Europe), with Mediterraneans and Latinos preferring the smallest zone (Beaulieu, 2004). Women tend to interact with one another at closer distances than men do in Western cultures (Sussman & Rosenfeld, 1982), whereas two men interact at close distances in some Muslim countries (Hewitt & Alqahtani, 2003). Social class may also influence interpersonal spacing. In Canadian school yards, lower-class primary school children were observed to interact at closer distances than middle-class children, regardless of race (Scherer, 1974). Members of the same group chose to sit closer together to perform a task than members of different groups (Novelli, Drury, & Reicher, 2010). Observational research on Boy Scout and Girl Scout troop meetings suggests that maintaining the appropriate physical and emotional distance from peers is associated with peer acceptance (Stiles & Raney, 2004).

Differences in distance norms may cause discomfort in cross-cultural interaction. People from different countries or social classes may have difficulty in interpreting the amount of intimacy implied by each other's interpersonal spacing and in finding mutually comfortable interaction distances. Cross-cultural training in nonverbal communication can reduce such discomfort. For instance, Englishmen were liked more by Arabs with whom they interacted when the Englishmen had been trained to behave nonverbally like Arabs—to stand closer, smile more, look more, and touch more (Collett, 1971).

Two aspects of interpersonal spacing that clearly influence and reflect status are physical distance and the amount of space each person occupies. Equal-status individuals jointly determine comfortable interaction distances and tend to occupy approximately equal amounts of space with their bodies and with the possessions that surround them. When status is unequal, superiors tend to control interaction distances, keeping greater physical distance than equals would choose. Superiors also claim more direct space with their bodies and possessions than inferiors (Gifford, 1982; Hayduk, 1978; Leffler et al., 1982).

**Violations of Personal Space.** What happens when people violate distance norms by coming too close? In particular, what do we do when strangers intrude on our personal space?

The earliest systematic examination of this question included two parallel studies (Felipe & Sommer, 1966). In one, strangers approached lone male patients in mental hospitals to a point only 6 inches away. In the other, strangers sat down 12 inches away from lone female students in a university library. The mental patients and the female students who were approached left the scene much more quickly than the other patients and students who were not approached. After only 2 minutes, 30 percent of the patients who were intruded on had fled, compared with none of the others. Among the students, 70 percent of those whose space was violated had fled by the end of 30 minutes, compared with only 13 percent of the others. The results of this study are shown in Figure 9.2.

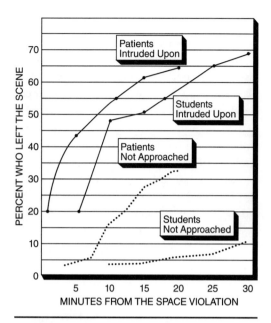

**FIGURE 9.2**  Reactions to Violations of Personal Space

How do people react when strangers violate norms of interpersonal distance and intrude on their personal space? A common reaction is illustrated here. Strangers sat down 12 inches away from lone female students in a library or approached lone male patients in a mental hospital to within 6 inches. Those who were approached left the scene much more quickly than control subjects who were not approached. Violations of personal space often produce flight.

*Source: Social Problems* by N. J. Felipe and R. Sommer. Copyright 1966 by University of California Press—Journals. Reproduced with permission of University of California Press—Journals in the format Textbook and extranet posting via Copyright Clearance Center.

Research in a university library in Pakistan replicated the study of invasions involving students. A female invader, dressed like a student, selected a person sitting alone (51 men, 50 women) and sat down within three feet (Khan & Kamal, 2010). She remained seated for 10 minutes, or until the other person left the table ("flight"). Observers recorded other reactions: stare/glance, browse books, lean away, use cell phone, initiate conversation, or no reaction. Ninety-four percent of the men and women reacted (in a control condition,

only 6 percent of students sitting alone performed any of the behaviors in a 10-minute period). The most common reactions were stare/glance and use cell phone. Men who fled on average left within 2 minutes, whereas for women (the same gender as the invader) it was 9 minutes.

The reaction to violations depends in part on the setting in which they occur. Whereas violations of space norms at library tables may lead to flight, violations in library aisles lead to the person spending more time in the aisle (Ruback, 1987). Similarly, intrusion into the space of someone using a public telephone is associated with the caller spending more time on the phone (Ruback, Pape, & Doriot, 1989). It is possible that when you are looking for a book or talking on the phone, a violation of distance norms is distracting, so it takes you longer to complete your task.

Staring is a powerful way to violate another's privacy without direct physical intrusion. Staring by strangers elicits avoidance responses, indicating that it is experienced as an intense negative stimulus. When stared at by strangers, for instance, pedestrians cross the street more rapidly, and drivers speed away from intersections more quickly (Ellsworth, Carlsmith, & Henson, 1972; Greenbaum & Rosenfeld, 1978).

As the energy crisis worsens, more people are considering alternatives to the car as a means of transportation. Yet many people are unwilling to use mass transit, even when it is more convenient and equally fast. Why? Possibly because on crowded buses, streetcars, and commuter trains, passengers experience violations of personal space. Interviews with auto users identified influences associated with the decision to drive versus use transit; one theme was negative affect due to violations of personal space on transit vehicles (Mann & Abraham, 2006). Research involving 139 passenger train commuters found that both self-reports of stress and increases in salivary cortisol, a hormonal indicator of stress, were related to local seating density within the rail coach. People

Despite the crowded circumstances, the people on this subway train are maintaining some privacy. Strangers feel uncomfortable when they must intrude on each other's personal space. To overcome this discomfort, they studiously ignore each other, avoiding touch, eye contact, and verbal exchanges. © IMNATURE/iStock

experienced adverse reactions when they had to sit close to others (Evans & Wener, 2007).

In the contemporary world, crowded public transportation facilities like airplanes and airports are also very noisy. Travelers are likely to encounter violations of their aural space, by the noise of crowds, jet engines, crying infants, noisy teens, loud cell phone conversations, and so on. Perhaps this accounts for the marketing success of noise-canceling headphones (Hagood, 2011). They allow the user to at least create a quiet space, if not an uncrowded one.

## CONVERSATIONAL ANALYSIS

Although conversation is a common daily activity, we all have trouble communicating at times. The list of what can go wrong is long and painful: inability to get started, irritating interruptions, awkward silences, failure to give others a chance to talk, failure to notice that listeners are bored or have lost interest, changing topics inappropriately, assuming incorrectly that others understand, and so on. This section examines the ways people avoid these embarrassing and annoying blunders. To maintain smooth-flowing conversation requires knowledge of certain rules and communication skills that are often taken for granted. We will discuss some of the rules and skills that are crucial for initiating conversations, regulating turn taking, and coordinating conversation through verbal and nonverbal feedback.

### Initiating Conversations

Conversations must be initiated with an attention-getting device—a summons to interaction. Greetings, questions, or the ringing of a telephone can serve as the summons. But conversations do not get underway until potential partners signal that they are attending and willing to converse. Eye contact is the crucial nonverbal signal of availability for face-to-face interaction. Goffman (1963a) suggests that eye contact places a person under an obligation to interact: when a waitress permits eye contact, she places herself under the power of the eye-catcher.

The most common verbal lead into conversation is a **summons-answer sequence** (Schegloff, 1968). Response to a summons ("Jack, you home?" "Yeah") indicates availability. More important, this response initiates the mutual obligation to speak and to listen that produces conversational turn taking. The summoner is expected to provide the first topic—a conversational rule that little children exasperatingly overlook. Our reactions when people violate the summons-answer sequence demonstrate its widespread acceptance as an obligatory rule. When people

ignore a summons, we conclude either that they are intentionally insulting us, socially incompetent, or psychologically absent (sleeping, drunk, or crazy).

Telephone conversations exhibit a common sequential organization. Consider the following conversation between a caller and a recipient:

0. (ring)
1. Recipient: Hello?
2. Caller: This is John.
3. R: Hi.
4. C: How are you?
5. R: Fine. How are you?
6. C: Good. Listen, I'm calling about . . .

The conversation begins with a summons-answer sequence (lines 0, 1). This is followed by an identification-recognition sequence (lines 2, 3); in this example, the recipient knows that the caller, John, recognizes his voice, so he

Flirting is a complex behavior that conveys interest in being approached by another person. These young people are using posture, smiles, and direct gaze to attract each other's attention. © Lise Gagne/iStock

does not state his name. Next, there is a trading of "How are you?" sequences (lines 4 through 6). Finally, at line 6, John states the reason for the call. This organization is found in many types of telephone calls. However, in an emergency, when seconds count, the organization is quite different (Whalen & Zimmerman, 1987). Consider the following example:

0. (ring)
1. R: Mid-City Emergency.
2. C: Um, yeah. There's a fire in my garage.
3. R: What's your address?

Notice that the opening sequence is shortened; both the greeting and the "How are you?" sequences are omitted. In emergency calls, the reason for the call is stated sooner. Note also that the recognition element of the identification-recognition sequence is moved forward, to line 1. Both of these changes facilitate communication in an anonymous, urgent situation. However, if the dispatcher answers a call and the caller says, "This is John," that signals an ordinary call. Thus, the organization of conversation clearly reflects situational contingencies.

## Regulating Turn Taking

A pervasive rule of conversation is to avoid bumping into someone verbally. To regulate turn taking, people use many verbal and nonverbal cues, singly and together, with varying degrees of success (Duncan & Fiske, 1977; Kendon, Harris, & Key, 1975; Sacks, Schegloff, & Jefferson, 1978).

**Signaling Turns.** Speakers indicate their willingness to yield the floor by looking directly at a listener with a sustained gaze toward the end of an utterance. People also signal readiness to give over the speaking role by pausing and by stretching the final syllable of their speech in a drawl, terminating hand gestures, dropping voice volume, and tacking

relatively meaningless expressions (such as "You know") onto the end of their utterances. Listeners indicate their desire to talk by inhaling audibly as if preparing to speak. They also tense and move their hands, shift their head away from the speaker, and emit especially loud vocal signs of interest (such as "Yeah," "M-hmn").

Speakers retain their turn by avoiding eye contact with listeners, tensing their hands and gesticulating, and increasing voice volume to overpower others when simultaneous speech occurs. People who persist in these behaviors are soon viewed by others as egocentric and domineering. They have violated an implicit social rule articulated by columnist Richard Armour: "It's all right to hold a conversation, but you should let go of it now and then" (Shepherd, 2007).

Verbal content and grammatical form of speech also provide important cues for turn taking. People usually exchange turns at the end of a meaningful speech act, after an idea has been completed. The first priority for the next turn goes to any person explicitly addressed by the current speaker with a question, complaint, or other invitation to talk. People expect turn changes to occur after almost every question, but not necessarily after other pauses in conversation (Hanni, 1980). It is difficult to exchange turns without using questions. When speakers in one study were permitted to use all methods except questions for signaling their desire to gain or relinquish the floor, the length of each speaking turn virtually doubled (Kent, Davis, & Shapiro, 1978).

**Turn Allocation.** Much of our conversation takes place in settings where turn taking is more organized than in spontaneous conversations. In class discussions, meetings, interviews, and therapy sessions, for example, responsibility for allocating turns tends to be controlled by one person, and turns are often allocated in advance. Prior allocation of turns reduces strains that arise from people either competing for speaking time or avoiding their responsibilities to speak. Allocation of turns also increases the efficiency of talk. It can arrange a distribution of turns that best fits the task or situation—a precisely equal distribution (as in a formal debate) or just one speaker (as in a football huddle).

Much of the early work on the structure of conversation was based on English-language talk. More recently, researchers have examined talk within a broader range of languages and communities/cultures. These comparative studies are leading to the identification of a generic series of problems in conversation, and an understanding of how the solution varies, reflecting local/cultural context (Sidnell, 2007).

## Feedback and Coordination

We engage in conversation to attain interpersonal goals—to inform, persuade, impress, control, and so on. To do this effectively, we must assess how what we say is affecting our partner's interest and understanding as we go along. Both verbal and nonverbal feedback help conversationalists in making this assessment. Through feedback, conversationalists coordinate what they are saying to each other from moment to moment. The responses called **back-channel feedback** are especially important for regulating speech as it is happening. These are the small vocal and visual comments that a listener makes while a speaker is talking, without taking over the speaking turn. They include such responses as "Yeah," "M-hmn," short clarifying questions (such as "What?" "Huh?"), brief repetitions of the speaker's words or completions of their utterances, head nods, and brief smiles. When conversations are proceeding smoothly, the fine rhythmic body movements of listeners (such as swaying, rocking, blinking) are precisely synchronized with the speech sounds of speakers who address them (Condon & Ogston, 1967). These automatic listener movements are another source of feedback that indicates to speakers whether they are being properly tracked and understood (Kendon, 1970).

Both the presence (or absence) and the timing of back-channel feedback influence speakers. In smooth conversation, listeners time their signs of interest, agreement, or understanding to occur at the end of long utterances, or when the speaker turns their head toward them. When speakers are denied feedback, the quality of their speech deteriorates. They become less coherent and communicate less accurately. Their speech becomes more wordy, less organized, and more poorly fitted to the situation (Bavelas, Coates, & Johnson, 2000). Lack of feedback causes such deterioration because it prevents speakers from learning several things about their partners. They cannot discern whether their partners (1) have relevant prior knowledge they need not repeat; (2) understand already so they can wrap up the point or abbreviate; (3) have misinformation they should correct; (4) feel confused so they should backtrack and clarify; or (5) feel bored so they should stop talking or change topics.

Alerted to the possible loss of listener attention and involvement by the absence of feedback, speakers employ attention-getting devices to evoke feedback. One such attention-getting device is the phrase "You know." Speakers frequently insert "You know" into long speaking turns immediately prior to or following pauses if their partner seems to be ignoring their invitation to provide feedback or to accept a speaking turn (Fishman, 1980).

Another device a speaker can use to regain the attention of another participant is to ask them a question. Such displays of uncertainty (for example, "What was the name of that character on *Game of Thrones*?") restructure the interaction by getting listeners more involved (Goodwin, 1987). If the speaker shifts their gaze to a specific person as they ask the question, it will draw that person into the conversation.

The fact that feedback influences the quality of speech has another interesting consequence. Listeners who frequently provide their conversational partners with feedback also understand their partner's communication more fully and accurately. Through their feedback, active listeners help shape the conversation to fit their own needs. The information needed varies on several dimensions, one of which is precision; recall that the cooperative principle assumes the actors provide relevant precision. In responding to an invitation, it may be sufficient, if exaggerated, to say, "I don't have any money," but in bankruptcy court, counsel or the judge will want greater precision. When we fail to provide relevant precision, we will be challenged by an alert listener (Drew, 2003). This reinforces a central theme of this chapter: accurate communication is a shared social accomplishment.

Feedback is important not only in conversations, but also in formal lectures. Lecturers usually monitor members of the audience for feedback. If listeners are looking at the speaker attentively and nodding their heads in agreement, the lecturer infers that their message is understood. On the other hand, quizzical or out-of-focus expressions suggest failure to understand. Similarly, members of the audience use feedback from the lecturer to regulate their own behavior; a penetrating look from the speaker may be sufficient to end a whispered conversation between listeners.

An important form of feedback in many lectures is applause. Speakers may want applause for a variety of reasons, not just ego gratification. Sometimes, lecturers subtly signal the audience when to applaud; audiences watch for such signals in order to maintain their involvement. For instance, an analysis of 42 hours of recorded political speeches suggests that there is a narrow range of message content that stimulates applause (Heritage & Greatbatch, 1986). Attacks on political opponents, foreign persons, and collectivities; statements of support for one's own positions, record, or

party; and commendations of individuals or groups generate applause. These devices occur regularly in speeches by U.S. political figures. When these messages are framed within particular rhetorical devices, applause is from two to eight times more likely. For example:

SPEAKER: Governments will argue [pause] that resources are not available [short pause] to help disabled people. [long pause] The fact is that too much is spent on the munitions of war, [long pause] and too little is spent [applause begins] on the munitions of peace.

In this example, the speaker uses the rhetorical device of contrast or antithesis. Using this device, the speaker's point is made twice. Audiences can anticipate the completion point of the statement by mentally matching the second half with the first. This rhetorical device is an "invitation to applaud," and in the example the audience begins to applaud even before the speaker completes the second half.

## SUMMARY

Communication is the process whereby people transmit information about their ideas and feelings to one another.

**Language and Verbal Communication.** Language is the main vehicle of human communication. (1) All spoken languages consist of sounds that are combined into words with arbitrary meanings and put together according to grammatical rules. (2) According to the encoder-decoder model, communication involves the encoding and sending of a message by a speaker, and the decoding of the message by a listener. Accuracy depends on the codability of the idea or feeling being communicated. (3) In contrast, the intentionalist model argues that communication involves the speaker's desire to affect the listener, or the transmission of an intention. The context of the communication influences how messages are sent and interpreted. (4) The perspective-taking model argues that communication requires intersubjectivity—the shared context created by speaker and listener. Thus, communication is a complex undertaking; to attain mutual understanding, conversationalists must express their message in ways listeners can interpret, take account of others' current knowledge, and actively work to decipher meanings.

**Nonverbal Communication.** A great deal of information is communicated nonverbally during interaction. (1) Four major types of nonverbal communication are paralanguage, body language, interpersonal spacing, and choice of personal effects. (2) CMC involves only written language, eliminating paralinguistic and visual cues that contribute to accuracy and regulation of interaction. It also encourages disinhibition. (3) The face is an important channel of communication; it provides information that observers use to infer social identities and personal characteristics. (4) Information is usually conveyed simultaneously through nonverbal and verbal channels. Multiple cues may add information to each other, reduce ambiguity, and increase accuracy. But if cues appear inconsistent, people must determine which cues reveal the speaker's true intentions.

**Social Structure and Communication.** The ways we communicate with others reflect and influence our relationships with them. (1) Gender is related to communication style; its impact depends on the interpersonal, group, or organizational context. (2) In every society, speech that adheres to rules governing vocabulary, pronunciation, and grammar is preferred or standard. Its use is associated with high status or power and is evaluated favorably by listeners. Nonstandard speech is often used by lower-status persons and evaluated negatively. (3) We express, maintain, or challenge the levels of relative status and intimacy in our relationships through our verbal and nonverbal behavior. Status and intimacy influence and are influenced by forms of address, choice of dialect or language, interruptions, matching of speech styles, gestures, eye contact, posture, and interaction distances. (4) The appropriate interaction distances for particular types of activities and relationships are normatively prescribed. These distances vary from one culture to another. When strangers violate distance norms, people flee the scene or use other devices to protect their privacy.

**Conversational Analysis.** Smooth conversation depends on conversational rules and communication skills that are often taken for granted. (1) Conversations are initiated by a summons to interaction. They get underway only if potential partners signal availability, usually through eye contact or verbal response. (2) Conversationalists avoid verbal collisions by taking turns. They signal either a willingness to yield the floor or a desire to talk through verbal and nonverbal cues. In some situations, turns are allocated in advance. (3) Effective conversationalists assess their partner's understanding and interest as they go along through vocal and visual feedback. If feedback is absent or poorly timed, the quality of communication deteriorates. An effective speech also involves coordination between speaker and audience; the timing of applause is a joint accomplishment.

### Critical Thinking Skill: Understanding the Importance of Clear Communication

Our lives consist of our relationships with other people—parents or caregivers, siblings, lovers, friends, supervisors, coworkers. The quality of our lives rests on the quality of these relationships. And what does the quality of a relationship depend on? Communication. As we discuss in Chapter 14, an essential aspect of developing a relationship is self-disclosure. Self-disclosure involves telling the other person personal information about yourself—that is, communicating (also see Chapter 5).

For many people, good, satisfying relationships are those in which we get some of our needs met, whatever the needs may be—help, emotional support, information, money, or sexual pleasure. In order for that to happen, the other person has to know what our needs are and how to satisfy them. We often wish the person would know without our having to tell them; we wish they could read our minds. Or we think, "If you were really a good mother/friend/lover, you would know what I want." Some reflection, or critical thinking, will reveal these beliefs to be false.

In order for another person to meet our needs, we must communicate clearly and honestly. This can be harder than it sounds. Our communication usually follows well-rehearsed scripts, as in ordering food in a restaurant, talking individually with an instructor, or flirting at a party. We rely on social conventions, but these may not communicate clearly who we are and what we want. Look at the "Get me a drink" example earlier in this chapter. "Did you buy some lemonade at the store?" is a pretty indirect request if your goal is to have your roommate bring you some lemonade. "Yes" or "No" is a sufficient response, leaving you mildly frustrated. Clear, direct communication—"Please bring me a glass of lemonade"—is much more likely to get you a glass of lemonade.

Communication involves not only words but also paralanguage—the way one speaks: warmly, coldly, with hostility; loudly or softly; fast or slow. As we noted, these cues may communicate the speaker's emotional state.

Perhaps you have been in conversations where the words didn't match the person's mood; or you tried to hide your anger. When your coworker asks if you are mad that they are late for your meeting or for work, you may say "No!" but your tone and the loudness of your voice may give you away. Your effort to avoid clear, honest communication may not work.

Communication also involves nonverbal behavior and body language. A tense body, arms folded across the chest, and avoidance of eye contact probably indicate anger or withdrawal from the conversation. On the other hand, relaxed posture, a smile, and a nodding head indicate engagement and desire to communicate.

Clear communication requires effort and critical thinking. First, you need to understand yourself. What do you want to say?

Once you identify your intention, think about how best to communicate it. Be aware that social scripts and conventions may not provide the means for clear, honest communication. Use direct language. Choose the context: time and place. Consider the other person's communication style. Be direct, and try to match your words to your paralinguistic and nonverbal cues.

Now it's time to apply this skill. Think about a circumstance in your life that could be improved by clear communication—at home, at school, at work, in a relationship. What is the circumstance or problem? What is your goal? What do you want to achieve? Now think about ways that you could communicate clearly to the other(s) involved. What language would clearly convey what you want? What would be a good time and place to talk about it? Next is the hard part: do it. Recognize that clear communication takes practice; it may not work the first time. In fact, things may get worse before they get better. But you may also be surprised to learn that the other(s) want to do things differently as much as you do!

# SOCIAL INFLUENCE AND PERSUASION

By the end of this chapter you will be able to:

- Evaluate whether a communication will likely be successful in persuading a target to change their beliefs or attitudes by considering characteristics of the source, target, and the message itself.

- Describe the conditions under which threats and promises prove most successful in gaining compliance and the conditions under which targets are likely to obey an order from someone in authority.

- Identify how individuals might resist persuasion attempts and maintain their original attitudes.

## INTRODUCTION

Consider some examples of social influence:

- In front of her condominium, Julie is met by Erika, a neighbor. Erika has heard that a waste management company plans to open a new landfill only a mile from their complex. Trying to mobilize opposition, Erika argues that the landfill would pose dangers to health and lower property values. She asks Julie to attend a meeting with her and to sign a petition against the landfill. Somewhat alarmed by this development, Julie finds Erika's view persuasive, and she agrees to sign.
- One evening, the owner of a 24-hour convenience store is confronted by a man wearing a ski mask and brandishing a pistol. The man threatens, "Hand over your money or I'll blow you away!" Facing a choice between two undesirable alternatives—losing his money or his life—the victim opens

the cash register and hands over its contents.
- During a military action in Afghanistan, a U.S. commander orders a platoon of soldiers to attack a series of caves where terrorists are thought to be hiding. The danger involved is great. Night has fallen, the entire area is covered with antipersonnel mines, and the enemy has been firing on the troops from the hills. Despite these obstacles, the troops move out as ordered.

These stories illustrate various forms of **social influence**. By definition, social influence occurs when one person (the **source**) engages in some behavior (such as persuading, threatening, promising, or issuing orders) that causes another person (the **target**) to behave differently from how they would otherwise behave. In the preceding illustrations, the sources were Erika (persuading Julie), the thief (threatening his victim), and the infantry commander (ordering the troops to enter a dangerous situation).

Social influence leads to a variety of outcomes. In some cases, the influencing source may produce **attitude change**—a change in the target's beliefs and attitudes about some issue, person, or situation. Attitude change—like Julie's above—is a fairly common result of social influence. In other cases, however, the source may not really care about changing the target's attitudes but only about securing compliance. **Compliance** occurs when the target's behavior conforms to the source's requests or demands, as is the case with both the convenience store owner and platoon. Some social-influence attempts, of course, produce both attitude change and compliance.

Not all influence attempts are effective. Many produce little or no change in the target's attitudes or behavior. Although orders issued by direct authority frequently obtain compliance, at other times, their targets may respond with defiance or open revolt. Recognizing that influence attempts vary in their degree of success, this chapter outlines the conditions under which influence attempts are most effective.

## Forms of Social Influence

Influence attempts can be either open or covertly manipulative (Tedeschi, Schlenker, & Lindskold, 1972). This chapter largely focuses on open influence, when the target understands that someone is trying to change their attitudes or behavior. In manipulative influence, the attempt is hidden from the target. Manipulative influence strategies like ingratiation and tactical self-presentation were covered in Chapter 5.

There are many forms of open influence. Among the more important forms are (1) the use of persuasive communication to change the target's attitudes or beliefs, (2) the use of threats or promises to gain compliance, and (3) the use of orders based on legitimate authority to gain compliance.

When attempting to persuade, the source uses information to change the target's attitudes and beliefs about some issue, person, or situation. Certain types of information are more useful than others in bringing about persuasion. For instance, Erika's persuasion attempt is more likely to succeed if she can introduce facts that Julie did not already know about the landfill and its effects; likewise, success is more likely if the source can advance compelling and valid arguments the target had not previously considered. Having the right type of information is important in effective persuasion.

Influence attempted by means of threats or promises is based on punishments and rewards rather than on information. If a threat is to produce compliance, the target must believe that the source can impose punishment. The convenience store owner was more likely to hand over the money in the register because

the brandished pistol substantiated the robber's threat. The same is true for influence based on promises, except that it involves the control of rewards rather than punishments. If the target believes that the source has no real control over the punishments or rewards involved, the threat or promise is unlikely to succeed.

Influence through the use of orders from an authority or officeholder is based on the target accepting the authority's legitimacy. Influence of this type is especially common within formal groups or organizations. When attempting influence by invoking legitimate authority, the source makes demands on the target that are vested in their role within the group. Such an attempt will succeed only if the target believes the source actually holds a position of authority and has the right to issue orders of the kind involved in the influence attempt. The chain of command in the military helps explain why a platoon would willingly walk toward danger.

## PERSUASION

Day in and day out, we are bombarded with messages intended to persuade us. As an example, consider what happens to Maria Castillo on a typical day. Early in the morning, Maria's clock radio comes on. Before Maria can get out of bed, a cheerful announcer is trying to sell her a new breakfast sandwich. Her Facebook and Twitter feeds are filled with messages from friends urging others to get out and vote for a particular candidate in the upcoming election. As she sits on the bus, she reads the advertisements overhead. The cashier at the coffee shop asks her if she would like to donate her change to help a local charity. Once at her desk, Maria checks her e-mail and finds a message from her favorite clothing store offering free shipping on any purchases today. Minutes later, a coworker drops by to ask Maria whether she would like to buy wrapping paper for his daughter's school fundraiser. At lunch, a friend mentions her plans to attend a concert the following weekend and urges Maria to come along. In midafternoon, she listens to an argument from a coworker who wants to change some paperwork procedures in the office. When she arrives home in the evening, Maria opens her mail. One letter is a carefully worded appeal from a charitable organization asking her to volunteer her time. Other letters are junk mail fliers asking for money or offering discounts at local restaurants and stores. Later that night, when Maria is watching television, advertisers bombard her endlessly with ads for their products—insurance, light beers, cosmetics, and imported sports cars.

All these messages Maria received have something in common: they seek to persuade. **Persuasion** may be defined as changing the beliefs, attitudes, or behaviors of a target through the use of information or argument. Persuasion is widespread in social interaction and assumes many different forms (McGuire, 1985). The Elaboration Likelihood Model in Figure 10.1 demonstrates the persuasion process—based on the dual-process theory introduced in Chapter 1—and is referenced throughout this section. As we are inundated with messages, we are only motivated and able to process some. This section introduces various facets of message-based persuasion, including the communication-persuasion paradigm and the characteristics of sources, messages, and targets that affect the persuasiveness of a message.

### Communication-Persuasion Paradigm

Consider the question, "Who says what to whom with what effect?" This question is one way of organizing modern research on persuasion. In this question, the "who" refers to the source of a persuasive message, the "whom" refers to the target, and the "what" refers to the content of the message. The phrase "with what effect" refers to the various responses of the target to the message. These elements (source, message, target, response) are fundamental components of the **communication-persuasion paradigm.** Figure 10.2 displays this paradigm and shows how these components are interrelated. First, the properties of the source may influence how the target audience will construe the message. For instance, characteristics such as the expertise and trustworthiness of the source can affect whether a target changes attitudes. Second, the properties of the message itself can have a significant impact on its persuasiveness. For instance, whether a message carries a fear appeal or presents only one-sided arguments can affect whether a persuasion attempt is successful. Third, the characteristics of the target are also important. For instance, what a target already believes about an issue as well as the extent of the target person's involvement in the issue and commitment to a position can affect whether a message will be rejected or will lead to attitude change.

### The Source

Suppose we ask 25 persons selected at random to read a persuasive communication (such as a newspaper editorial) that advocates a position on a plant-based diet. We tell this group that the message came from a Nobel Prize-winning biologist. At the same time, we ask 25 other persons to read the same message, but we tell this group that it came from a cook at a local fast-food establishment. Subsequently, we ask both groups to indicate their attitude toward the position advocated in the message. Which group of persons will be more persuaded by the communication? Most likely, the persons who read the message ascribed to the prize-winning biologist will be more persuaded than those who read the message ascribed to the fast-food cook.

Why should the source's identity make any difference? The identity of the source provides the target with information above and beyond the content of the message itself. Because

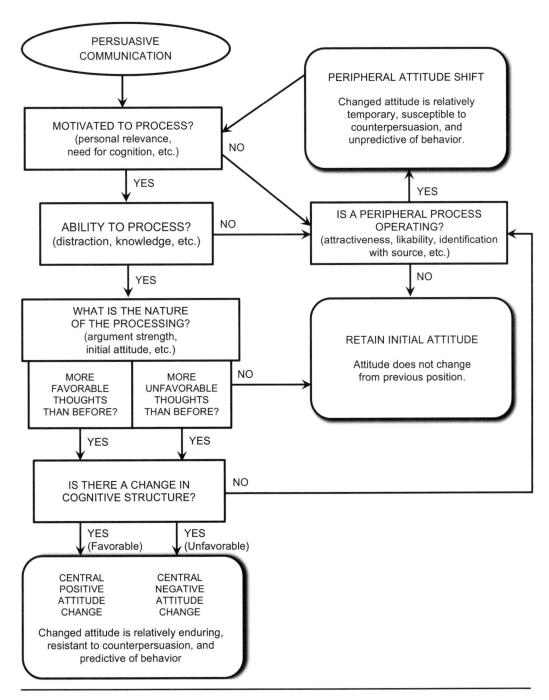

**FIGURE 10.1**  The Elaboration Likelihood Model

A popular dual-process theory of persuasion is the Elaboration Likelihood Model. Depending on an individual's motivation and ability to process a persuasion attempt, one of two routes is activated. Persuasion in the peripheral process relies on heuristics (attractiveness, likability, shared identity) and tends to lead to weaker attitude change. The central persuasion process requires more thought and attention (higher levels of elaboration of the argument) and results in more enduring attitude change.

*Source:* Adapted from Petty & Wegener. In Chaiken & Trope (Eds.), *Dual-Process Theories in Social Psychology*, 41–72. Figure 3.1. Copyright 1999 by the Guilford Press.

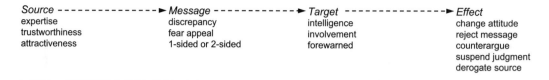

**FIGURE 10.2**  The Communication-Persuasion Paradigm

some sources are more credible than others, the target may pay attention to the source's identity when deciding whether to believe the message. **Communicator credibility** denotes the extent to which the target perceives the communicator as a believable source of information. Note that the communicator's credibility is "in the eye of the beholder"—a given source may be credible for some audiences but not for others. Many consider Fox News a credible source; others do not.

A variety of factors influence the extent to which a source is credible. Two of these, the source's expertise and the source's trustworthiness, are of special importance.

**Expertise.** Generally, a message from a source with a high level of relevant expertise will bring about greater attitude change than a similar message from a source with a lower level of expertise (Clark, Wegener, Habashi, & Evans, 2012; Hass, 1981). This may occur because targets may be more accepting and less critical of messages from high-expertise sources. It can also be because there is more consideration—conscious processing in dual-process theories—to what an expert said (Chaiken & Maheswaran, 1994).

The impact of source expertise is illustrated by a study of participants' reactions to online health information (Hu & Sundar, 2010). The information came from either a doctor (Chris Park, MD, a high-credibility source) or layperson (Chris Park, low-credibility source). One message discouraged the use of sunscreen so as to prevent against Vitamin D deficiency and another advocated consuming raw milk instead of pasteurized milk. Participants

believed that both messages were more credible when they came from a doctor than from a layperson.

The source's expertise interacts with the target's involvement and knowledge about the topic in determining attitude change. When the target has little involvement—meaning that the issue is of little personal importance—or limited prior knowledge on a given issue, messages from highly expert sources produce more attitude change than those from less expert sources. But the more personally relevant the issue is to the target or the more knowledgeable the target is about the issue, the less likely it is that communicator expertise will make much difference in persuasion (Stiff, 1986). When involvement and knowledge are high, the target is already likely to engage in detailed processing and elaboration, so the content of the message itself rather than the source's expertise drives the processing that should lead to attitude change (Petty & Cacioppo, 1979, 1990).

In some cases, a persuasion attempt from a low-credibility source that originally fails has a sleeper effect and a target can later be persuaded. However, this only occurs if the target noted the important arguments in the message and has forgotten that they originally considered the source to be noncredible (Kumkale & Albarracín, 2004).

**Trustworthiness.** Although expertise is an important factor in communicator credibility, it is not the only one (Tormala, Briñol, & Petty, 2007). Under some conditions, a highly expert source may not be very credible. As an example, suppose your car is running poorly,

As an automobile owner listens to the message from the garage mechanic, he assesses not only the quality of the argument but also the credibility of the communicator. The mechanic may have expertise, but can he be trusted?
© savas keskiner/iStock

so you take it into a garage for a tune-up. A mechanic you have never met before inspects your car. They identify several problems, one of which involves major repair work on the engine. The mechanic offers to complete this work for $870 and claims that your car will soon fall apart without it. The mechanic may be an expert, but can you accept their word that the expensive repair is necessary? How much do they stand to gain if you believe their message?

As this example shows, the target pays attention not only to a source's expertise but also to their motives. If the message appears highly self-serving and beneficial to the source, the recipient may distrust the source and discount the message (Hass, 1981). In contrast, communicators who argue against their own vested interests seem especially candid and trustworthy. For example, suppose that mechanic told you that they could repair your car for $870,

but that a mechanic down the street could repair it for $50 less and more quickly because their garage specializes in engines and would have all the needed parts already in stock. The mechanic's remarks would probably be unexpected, but you would likely think that $820 is a fair deal and would not wonder if your car really needed the repairs. A source who argues against their vested interest will seem particularly honest and trustworthy because they are violating our expectations. This will make that source particularly persuasive (Priester & Petty, 1995; Walster [Hatfield], Aronson, & Abrahams, 1966).

Trustworthiness also depends on the source's identity, because this carries information about the source's goals and values. A source perceived as having goals similar to the audience—like Erika, who is both a condo-owner and single woman like Julie—will be more persuasive than one perceived as having dissimilar goals (Chaiken, 1980). A study exploring consumer reactions to religious symbols in advertising (for example, an ichthys or cross) demonstrates this identity effect. The researchers (Taylor, Halstead, & Haynes, 2010) found that, in general, religious symbols enhanced consumer evaluations and purchase intentions, but the positive effect was largest for evangelical Christians. This was, in part, because the symbols signaled attitude similarity and trustworthiness to Christian consumers. However, the reverse was true among less religious young adults. This group reported they were less likely to purchase goods or services from a business that used a religious symbol than businesses that did not. Also related to similarity, endorsements from men increase men's intent to purchase goods, while endorsements from women increase women's intent to do so (Caballero, Lumpkin, & Madden, 1989).

**Attractiveness and Likability.** The physical attractiveness of the source—determined at a glance, without great cognitive effort—can also affect the persuasiveness of a message. Advertisers regularly select attractive individuals as spokespersons for their products in television and magazine advertisements because we pay more attention to messages from attractive sources, and higher levels of attention facilitate greater persuasion (Chaiken, 1986). Moreover, because physical attractiveness leads to liking, we like attractive persons more and, thus, are sometimes more positively disposed to accept products or positions they advocate (Eagly & Chaiken, 1975; Praxmarer, 2011). Whatever the source of likability (similarity, attractiveness, or simple contact), likability tends to increase persuasive influence because we want to maintain and enhance relationships with those we like (Cialdini, 2001).

A source's attractiveness can have greater effect when combined with other factors, like message strength. Strong arguments tend to be detailed, compelling, and substantiated by fact (Wood, Kallgren, & Preisler, 1985).

Conversely, weak arguments are of lower quality. In a study investigating the impact of persuasive advertisements for sun-tanning oil, the participants received a message that contained either strong or weak arguments and came from either an attractive or an unattractive female spokesperson (DeBono & Telesca, 1990). Results showed that, in general, the attractive source was more persuasive than the unattractive one. But the attractive source was especially persuasive when the message arguments were strong rather than weak. When the arguments were weak, attractiveness made very little difference in persuasion.

**Effect of Multiple Sources.** According to **social impact theory** (Latané, 1981)—a general framework applicable to both persuasion and obedience—the impact of an influence attempt is a function of the source's strength (that is, social status or power), immediacy (that is, physical or psychological distance), and the number of influencing sources. A target will be more influenced when the sources are strong (rather than weak), when the sources are physically close (rather than remote), and when the sources are numerous (rather than few).

Social scientists are increasingly interested in how this theory works in online forums and with reviews (Kim & Hollingshead, 2015). In one interesting test of two of the factors (immediacy and number of sources) using Facebook (Egebark & Ekström, 2011), researchers posted identical status updates in real Facebook accounts (with the users' permission) and then varied the numbers of "likes" that the updates had and who the likes were from. For each of these status updates, friends of the users either saw that (1) one unknown user had liked the status update, (2) three unknown users had liked the status update, or (3) one of their peers—a mutual friend, with a number of friends in common with the user—had liked the status update. Consistent with social impact theory's predictions, friends of the users were more than twice as likely to like (or comment on) a status update that had first been liked by at least three people (number of sources) or liked by a mutual friend (immediacy) than they were to like a status update that had only one like from a stranger. These results are consistent with previous studies that suggest a message presented by several different sources is more persuasive than the same message presented by a single source (Harkins & Petty, 1987). This is especially true when the arguments presented in the message are strong rather than weak. Strong messages coming from multiple sources receive greater scrutiny and increased issue-relevant thinking from the target, which leads to attitude change; however, weak messages from multiple sources may receive added scrutiny but will produce no extra attitude change (Harkins & Petty, 1981).

Certain qualifications apply to this multiple-source effect. First, for multiple sources to have more impact than a single source, the target must perceive the multiple sources to be independent of one another. If the target believes that the sources colluded in sending their messages, the added impact of multiple sources will vanish and the communication will have no more effect than if it came from a single source (Harkins & Petty, 1983). Second, there is an upper limit to the multiple-source effect (Tanford & Penrod, 1984). Adding more and more sources will increase persuasion, but only up to a point. For instance, positive Amazon reviews from three independent sources will be more persuasive than the same positive review from a single source, but a message coming from, say, 15 sources may not be appreciably more persuasive than the same message coming from 12 sources, and 1,500 reviews are not likely any more persuasive than 1,200.

## The Message

Persuasive messages differ dramatically in their content. Some contain arguments that are highly factual and rational, whereas others contain emotional appeals that motivate action by arousing fear or greed. Messages differ in their detail and complexity (simple versus complex arguments), the strength of their presentation (strong versus weak arguments), and their balance (one-sided versus two-sided arguments). These properties affect how a person will scrutinize, interpret, and elaborate a message.

**Message Discrepancy.** Suppose a woman told you that Elizabeth II, the Queen of England, is 5 feet 4 inches tall. Would you believe her? What if she said 5 feet 10 inches tall—would you believe that? How about 6 feet 3 inches? Or 7 feet 6 inches? You may not know how tall the queen actually is, but you probably have a rough idea. Although you might believe 5 feet 10 inches, you would probably doubt 6 feet 3 inches and certainly doubt 7 feet 6 inches. The last message—asserting the queen is 7 feet 6 inches tall—is highly discrepant from your beliefs.

By definition, a **discrepant message** is one advocating a position that is different from what the target believes (Fink & Cai, 2013). Discrepancy is a matter of degree; some messages are highly discrepant, like the queen being as tall as Yao Ming, others less so. To cause a change in beliefs and attitudes, a message must be at least somewhat discrepant from the target's current position; otherwise, it would just reaffirm what the target already believes through a confirmation bias (see Chapter 7). Up to a certain point, greater message discrepancy will lead to greater change in attitudes (Jaccard, 1981). A message that is moderately discrepant will be more effective in changing a target's beliefs and attitudes than a message that is only slightly discrepant. Of course, it is possible for a message to be so discrepant that the target will simply dismiss it. To say that the Queen of England is 7 feet 6 inches tall is just not believable.

There is an important interaction between message discrepancy and source expertise.

Sources with high credibility produce more attitude change at higher levels of discrepancy than do sources with low credibility. In other words, a target is more likely to accept a highly discrepant message from a high-credibility source than from a low-credibility source. If the BBC told you that Queen Elizabeth was over 7 feet tall, you would be more likely to believe it than if a server at a local restaurant did. This is particularly true if the argument is strong rather than weak and there was some sort of detail or evidence that increased the likelihood that it is factual (Clark et al., 2012). Highly discrepant messages from a low-credibility source are ineffective because the target will quickly derogate the source (what does a waitress know about Queen Elizabeth?).

In one experiment on the importance of discrepancy, participants were given a written message on the number of hours of sleep that people need each night to function effectively (Bochner & Insko, 1966). In some cases, the message was attributed to a Nobel Prize-winning physiologist (high credibility), whereas in other cases it was attributed to a YMCA director (medium credibility). The arguments contained in the message were identical for all participants, with one important exception. In some cases the message proposed that people need eight hours of sleep per night; in others, the message proposed seven hours; in others, six hours; and so on down to zero hours of sleep per night. Most participants began the experiment believing that people need approximately eight hours of sleep each night. Therefore, these messages differed in level of discrepancy. The results showed that the more discrepant the position advocated by the high-credibility source (the Nobel Prize winner)—in other words, the fewer hours suggested—the greater the amount of attitude change. Only when this source argued for the most extreme position (zero hours of sleep) did the participants refuse to believe the message. The same pattern appeared for the medium-credibility source (the YMCA director), except that their

effectiveness peaked out at moderate levels of discrepancy (three hours of sleep per night) and the medium-credibility source was less effective with very extreme positions (two hours of sleep or less). Thus, this study demonstrates that sources with higher credibility produce greater amounts of attitude change at higher levels of discrepancy.

**Fear Arousal.** Most messages intended to persuade incorporate either rational appeals or emotional appeals. Rational appeals are factual in nature; they present specific, verifiable evidence to support claims. Rational appeals frequently address a need already felt by the audience and provide the missing solution; that is, these messages are drive reducing. Emotional appeals, in contrast, try to arouse basic drives and to stimulate a need where none was present. These messages are drive creating.

Perhaps the most common emotional appeals are those involving fear. Fear-arousing messages are especially useful when a source is trying to motivate the target to take some specific action. A political candidate, for example, may warn that if voters elect the opponent to office, the nation will become embroiled in international conflict or they will lose access to affordable health care. Likewise, in an anti-smoking advertisement on TV, a victim dying of throat cancer and emphysema warns young persons that if they start smoking cigarettes, they may end up as diseased victims themselves. In each of these cases, the source is using a fear-arousing communication. Messages of this type direct the target's attention to some negative or undesired outcome that is likely to occur unless the target takes certain actions advocated by the source (Higbee, 1969; Ruiter, Kok, Verplanken, & van Eersel, 2003).

Studies have shown that arousing high levels of fear produces more change in attitude than arousing low levels of fear (Witte & Allen, 2000). If a message arouses fear and the targets believe that attending to the message will show

## BOX 10.1  Susceptibility to "Fake News"

"Fake news" may seem to have come out of nowhere during the 2016 election, but the phrase has actually been around over 100 years (Merriam-Webster, 2017). Meaning exactly what the phrase's two words imply—false or counterfeit material reported in a news-related periodical or program—contemporary usage often refers to political stories. Both the term and this type of news are spreading like wildfire because social media platforms make sharing fake news easy and consuming it on those platforms discourages processing the information carefully.

Although both liberals and conservatives are susceptible to "fake news" and political bias (Ditto et al., 2017), evidence is mounting that conservatives are particularly susceptible (Lazer et al., 2017). What accounts for this difference along political lines?

For one thing, conservative sources are abundant. Online political and news outlets are multiplying; with conservative sources far outnumbering liberal ones, conservatives have more to filter. Individuals across the political spectrum are also experiencing information overload, decreasing our ability to process messages. While these outlets and overload are important factors, the primary cause of difference between liberals and conservatives appears to be a perfect storm between targets and messages.

People across the political spectrum tend to be more sensitive to risks than benefits. For example, an audience is more likely to be motivated to develop strategies to combat rape if they learn that 85 percent of attempts at rape are successful rather than 15 percent of rape attempts are unsuccessful. However, research suggests that conservatives tend to be more sensitive to threat than liberals (Fessler, Pisor, & Holbrook, 2017). They fear dangerous influences may threaten U.S. society—whether immigration, same-sex marriage, sex education, or liberal policies. Because it seems better to err on the side of caution—to believe a threat exists that may not rather than ignoring a potential threat that may be—individuals who are fearful or believe that the world is more dangerous are likely to believe politicians' and others' alarmist claims as a survival strategy. Conservatives are not only more susceptible to negative stimuli than liberals, when faced with potential threats they also have stronger physiological and psychological responses (Hibbing, Smith, & Alford, 2014). With "fake news" on both sides of the political spectrum largely oriented around threat and negativity, it is no wonder that conservatives are more likely to believe it and pass it along.

Noting this difference is not to say that one political ideology is better than another one or that liberals are smarter or better educated than conservatives—social psychological research suggests that neither is true. In fact, it is extremely useful to protect oneself against a potential threat. However, it is not necessary to live in fear—consumed by negative events—to protect against them. An understanding of both the elaboration likelihood model (Figure 10.1) and communication-persuasion paradigm (Figure 10.2) will decrease your susceptibility to fake news, and by considering the social psychological factors behind the proliferation, you can resist it.

them how to cope with this fear, then they may analyze the message carefully and change their attitudes (Petty, 1995). Fear-arousing communications have been effective in persuading people to do many things, including reducing cigarette smoking and encouraging safe driving practices (Lewis, Watson, Tay, & White, 2007; Thompson, Barnett, & Pearce, 2009).

The impact of fear-arousal on persuasion is clearly demonstrated by a study in which college students received messages advocating tetanus vaccinations (Dabbs & Leventhal, 1966). These messages described tetanus as easy to catch and as producing serious, even fatal consequences. The message also indicated that the vaccine, which could be obtained easily, provided effective protection against the disease. Depending on experimental treatment, the participants received either high-fear, low-fear, or control communications. In the high-fear condition, the messages described tetanus in extremely vivid terms, thereby creating a high level of fear and apprehension. In the low-fear condition, the messages described tetanus in less detailed terms, thereby creating no more than low to moderate fear. In the control condition, the message provided little detail about the disease, thereby arousing no fear.

To determine the message's effectiveness, the students were asked whether they thought it was important to get a tetanus shot and whether they actually intended to get one. The responses showed that students exposed to the high-fear message had stronger intentions to get shots than those exposed to the other messages. Moreover, records kept at the university health service indicated that students receiving the high-fear message were more likely to actually be vaccinated during the following month than students who received the other messages.

Although this study shows the effectiveness of fear, fear-arousing messages are effective only when certain conditions are met. First, the message must assert that if the target does not change behavior, they will suffer serious negative consequences. Second, the message must show convincingly that these negative consequences are highly probable. Third, the message must recommend a specific course of action that, if adopted, will enable the target to avoid the negative consequences. Fear played an important part in motivating students to be vaccinated. However, giving them a specific way to do so was imperative. A message that predicts negative consequences but fails to assure the target that they can avoid them by taking specific action will produce little attitude change. Instead, it will leave the target feeling that the negative consequences are inevitable regardless of what they may do (Maddux & Rogers, 1983).

Some studies suggest, however, that fear-arousing messages can fail if they are too strong and create too much fear. If people feel very threatened, they may become defensive and deny the reality or the importance of the threat rather than think rationally about the issue (Johnson, 1991; Lieberman & Chaiken, 1992). In this sense, a message arousing moderate fear may prove more effective than one arousing extremely high fear.

Recent research on cultural orientations and the persuasiveness of fear appeals finds that such appeals are most effective when the messages reflect receivers' internalized cultural beliefs (Lee & Park, 2012). Anti-smoking public service announcements (PSAs) that emphasized the health risks of smoking to the participants themselves ("When you smoke, you suffer") were more effective among participants with an individualistic orientation, as is common in the United States, whereas PSAs with identical imagery and facts but that framed smoking as a threat to participants' family members ("When you smoke, they suffer.") were more effective among those with a collectivist cultural orientation.

**One-Sided versus Two-Sided Messages.** When a source uses rational rather than emotional appeals, other message characteristics also come into play. One is the number of viewpoints, or sides, represented in the message. A one-sided message emphasizes only those facts that explicitly support the position advocated by the source ("Sun tanning causes skin cancer" or "Sun tanning causes wrinkles"). A two-sided message, in contrast, presents not only the position advocated by the source but also opposing viewpoints ("Sun tanning helps to maintain healthy Vitamin D levels, but causes skin cancer" or "Sun tanning gives you an attractive glow, but causes wrinkles").

Which is more effective—a one-sided message or a two-sided message? The answer depends heavily on the target audience.

One-sided messages have the advantage of being uncomplicated and easy to grasp. They are more effective when the audience already agrees with the source; they also tend to be effective when the audience does not know much about the issue because they keep the audience blind to opposing viewpoints. Two-sided messages are more complex, so they attract more attention and are processed more thoroughly than one-sided messages (Petty & Cacioppo, 1986). They also have the advantage of making the source appear less biased and more trustworthy (Eisend, 2007). Such messages tend to be more effective when the audience initially opposes the source's viewpoint or knows a lot about the alternative positions (Kimmel, 2004). In the case of the sun-tanning messages above, the most effective of the four messages (two one-sided, two two-sided) in decreasing individuals' intentions to sun tan was the two-sided appearance-focused appeal: "Sun tanning gives you an attractive glow, but causes wrinkles" (Cornelis, Cauberghe, & De Pelsmacker, 2014). Because most people who sun tan do so for appearance-focused benefits rather than health-focused (to increase Vitamin D levels), the statement that tapped into the existing motivation was more effective than the message less consistent with individuals' experiences or motives.

Research suggests that the most effective two-sided messages are *refutational appeals* (Eisend, 2006). In these messages, sources provide both the positive and negative arguments, but then provide information that either discounts or denies the negative one. An example of an actual ad, used in early research (Sawyer, 1973), was: "Why pay $1.98 for a ballpoint pen? You can get them for $0.49, $0.69, or for free. The kind that skip, stutter, etc. and run out of ink. You pay $1.98 for a Parker, but you never have to buy another." The ad begins with why it is ridiculous to pay almost $2.00 for a pen when less expensive ones are available (negative). It then refutes that statement, clarifying that the less expensive pens are inferior (refutation), and explains that the Parker pen is worth the price (positive).

## The Target

So far, we have discussed how the characteristics of the source and the content of the message affect persuasion. Characteristics of the target also play a role in persuasion.

**Intelligence.** One important characteristic that affects susceptibility to persuasion is the target's level of intelligence. Individuals who are more intelligent tend to be more resistant to influence for a number of reasons. Intelligent targets generally know more about any given issue than less intelligent targets (Rhodes & Wood, 1992). Even if they know little or nothing about the issue, bright people are better able to critically evaluate the source, the source's specific appeal, and the message itself (Wood, Kallgren, & Preisler, 1985). They are more skeptical of simple solutions to complex problems and are more comfortable thinking analytically (van Prooijen, 2017). Importantly, this is not only a matter of innate intelligence (IQ), but also knowledge acquired through experience and education that does not always map on to intellect (see Chapter 17). In a study of susceptibility to phishing, the group most susceptible to such scams was 18- to 25-year-olds. Despite their comfort with technology, people in this age group had lower levels of education and less experience with e-mail than those who were older (Sheng et al., 2010).

The ideal level of intelligence varies with the message. It is easiest to persuade someone with low levels of intelligence if the message is simple and straightforward. However, people of moderate intelligence are better persuaded by more complex messages (Briñol & Petty, 2012).

**Involvement with the Issue.** One important attribute of targets is the extent of their involvement with a particular issue (Johnson &

Eagly, 1989; Petty & Cacioppo, 1990). Personal involvement with an issue fundamentally affects the way a message is processed (Chaiken & Maheswaran, 1994). When highly involved with an issue, a target will want to scrutinize the message closely and think carefully about its content. In contrast, an uninvolved target is less motivated to think carefully about the message. If any change in attitude occurs, it will result more from peripheral factors, such as source expertise or trustworthiness, than from the arguments themselves.

Suppose, for example, that someone advocates an increase in the degree requirements at your school, specifically proposing students pass a comprehensive exam in their major areas in order to graduate. The proposed change would take effect at the beginning of the next year. Many students would be very involved with this issue because the change would affect the difficulty of completing their degrees. Now, suppose the source advocated instead that the change take place ten years in the future rather than next year. Current students would probably have little interest in this proposal because they will finish college long before any changes take effect.

In one study, researchers presented a scenario like the one just described to a group of college students (Petty, Cacioppo, & Goldman, 1981). Three independent variables were manipulated in this study. The first variable was personal involvement with the issue. Half the participants were told that the new policy would take effect next year at their college (high involvement), whereas the other half were told that the policy would take effect ten years in the future (low involvement). The second was the strength of the message's argument. Half the participants received eight strong and cogent arguments in favor of the proposal; the other participants received eight weak and superficial arguments. The third variable was the expertise of the source. Half of the participants were told that the source of the message was a professor of education

at Princeton University (high expertise); the other half were told that the source was a student at a local high school (low expertise).

In the high-involvement condition, the target's attitude toward exams was determined primarily by the strength of the arguments. Strong, cogent arguments produced significantly more attitude change than weak, superficial ones. The expertise of the source had no significant impact on attitude change. In the low-involvement condition, attitudes were determined primarily by the source's expertise, with the high-expertise source (the Princeton professor) producing more attitude change than the low-expertise source (the local high school student). The strength of the arguments had little effect on this group.

Thus, involvement with the issue moderated which factor was most important for attitude change. For participants with high involvement, the strength of the argument was more important than source expertise because participants cared about the issue and scrutinized arguments more closely. For those with low involvement, source expertise was more important because the participants had little motivation to scrutinize the arguments.

**Personality.** Some people have a high need for cognition, meaning they enjoy puzzling through problems and thinking about issues (Cacioppo, Petty, Feinstein, & Jarvis, 1996). This plays an important role in persuasion attempts. Those who do enjoy these thinking tasks are motivated to examine arguments more carefully and thoroughly than those who have a low need for cognition (Shestowsky, Wegener, & Fabrigar, 1998). Thus, they are more likely to engage with the content of argument and more likely to ignore the peripheral cues—like attractiveness or likability of the source—making them resistant to persuasion (Haugtvedt & Petty, 1992). When facing an audience of people with a high need for cognition (for example, college professors), it is wise to carefully construct a solid set of arguments that will stand up to the scrutiny of full engagement.

Other personality traits also affect individuals' susceptibility to persuasion. One popular model of personality in psychology that considers a range of personality traits is the **five-factor model** (Costa & McCrae, 1992; Digman, 1990) or "Big Five." The model takes a wide variety of personality traits and organizes them into five factors, or categories. These factors and examples of associated traits are agreeableness (warmth, friendliness), conscientiousness (efficiency, dependability), extraversion (outgoingness, assertiveness), openness (curiosity, insight), and emotional stability (confidence, sensitivity), which is sometimes referred to as neuroticism. Research finds that individuals who are low on emotional stability—for example, those who feel socially anxious or depressed—are more susceptible to persuasion (Hovland, Janis, & Kelley, 1953), as are those who are high on openness (Gerber et al., 2013). There is less consensus on the effects of extraversion, agreeableness, or conscientiousness and their relationship to susceptibility to social influence.

It is difficult to pinpoint general connections between the five factors and susceptibility to influence in part because persuasive messages vary tremendously. Therefore, some of the most interesting research on personality and persuasion focuses on connecting targets to messages (Alkiş & Temizel, 2015). If sources understand personality differences, they can construct arguments specifically targeted toward different groups. Imagine a new smartphone on the market. To influence someone high in conscientiousness, a company could create an ad campaign that caters to order and efficiency. Perhaps something along the lines of, "A phone that works with your schedule" (Hirsh, Kang, & Bodenhausen, 2012). To market the same product effectively to individuals high in extraversion, the company could tell potential buyers "With this phone, you'll always be where the excitement is" or, to

consumers high on openness, "A phone that pushes the envelope of innovation."

Targets also vary in their perceptions of what distinguishes right from wrong, what social psychologists call **moral foundations** (Haidt, 2012). Some people prioritize fairness in determining whether something is ethical, while others value loyalty above all else, or emphasize respect, purity, or caring. These foundations tend to map on to political leanings, with liberals embracing caring (and protection from harm) and fairness, and conservatives focused on loyalty, respect for authority, and purity (Caprara et al., 2006). To explore the role of these foundations in political persuasion—and why we are so bad at convincing people to change their minds about particular issues—two social psychologists devised a creative series of studies (Feinberg & Willer, 2015).

In the first study, they asked liberals and conservatives to craft arguments to persuade someone on the other end of the political spectrum in an effort to change that person's mind about a contemporary political issue. The vast majority of participants incorporated moral arguments into their messages. However, the foundations of the arguments they wrote favored their own moral beliefs rather than those of the opposition. As an example, a liberal trying to convince a conservative to support same-sex marriage incorporated the two moral foundations more common among liberals (care and fairness) in their argument: "Why would we punish people for being born a certain way? They deserve the same rights as other Americans." Such arguments would carry little weight among individuals with different moral foundations, including many conservatives.

In a later experiment, the researchers tested whether the opposition could be influenced with arguments that were more closely aligned with their own moral foundations. To test this, they created pairs of arguments for a set of political issues, one situated in moral

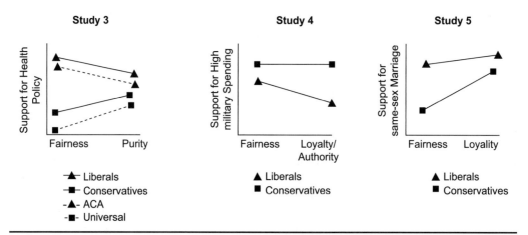

## FIGURE 10.3 LINKING PERSUASIVE MESSAGES AND TARGETS

These figures illustrate the importance of framing for the persuasiveness of arguments. Arguments for policies generally supported by liberals (health care and same-sex marriage) were more persuasive for conservatives when framed in moral values associated with conservativism (purity, loyalty, and authority). Conversely, liberals' support for high military spending was higher when the argument was framed in fairness, a moral foundation widespread among liberals, than supported with appeals to authority or loyalty.

*Source:* Feinberg & Willer, 2015.

foundations more common among conservatives and another reflecting liberal values. Results shown in Figure 10.3 demonstrate the potential of arguments when aligned with a target's moral compass. Reading an argument in support of increased military spending—an issue that is significantly more popular among conservatives—that was framed in fairness, focusing on how the military is an institution that helps reduce inequality in the United States, made liberals much more supportive of such a policy. The same thing happened for conservatives who read an argument in support of same-sex marriage when it was described as an issue of loyalty ("Same-sex couples are proud and patriotic Americans"). Note that moral framing did not affect support among participants predisposed to endorse a particular policy. Because a liberal is likely to support same-sex marriage or a conservative to support increased military spending, they are not motivated to scrutinize the specific argument and are likely to retain their initial attitude regardless of the argument's basis (see Figure 10.2).

**Distraction.** Even people with a high need for cognition who are strongly involved in an issue will sometimes have trouble paying attention to arguments. This can occur because the audience is distracted by any number of things—perhaps they aren't feeling well, maybe there is street noise that makes it hard to hear, perhaps the speaker has an annoying habit that bothers the listener, and so on. Anything that prevents the target from giving full attention to the argument will impair the target's ability or motivation to evaluate an argument or appeal effectively and, therefore, influence the persuasion attempt (Albarracín, 2002). Given the discussion so far, it will be no surprise to learn that when we are distracted, we are more likely to use peripheral cues when forming our opinions. Our distraction prevents us from fully engaging and appreciating the details of the argument and we fall back on peripheral indicators such as the attractiveness of the speaker (Petty & Brock, 1981; Petty & Wegener, 1999).

## COMPLIANCE WITH THREATS AND PROMISES

Attitude change is not the only outcome of social influence. At times, we are less concerned with what people think and more concerned with what they do. When a target conforms to a source's requests or demands, these are acts of compliance. With compliance, the fundamental concern is producing a particular behavior from the target, irrespective of whether the target's beliefs and attitudes change. Of course, in some cases, compliance can be obtained indirectly by changing attitudes—if someone can change what we believe, they might also change how we behave. But persuasion is not necessary to change behavior. French and Raven (1959; Raven, 1992) proposed six kinds of social power that can be used to induce compliance—some of which require actual persuasion and some of which do not (see Box 10.2). In this section, we examine two in more detail: threats and promises.

Consider a homeowner, Richard Sorenson, who lives in an area of Michigan where it snows heavily. One cold day in January, a snowstorm dumps 12 inches of snow on his driveway and sidewalk. Although Richard has been the person in his household who has always shoveled the snow, he believes his teenage son is now old enough to take on the task and has been considering the best way to shift the responsibility. He could approach his son and say, "I'll give you $20 if you shovel the snow out of the driveway." This would be an attempt to gain compliance in the form of a promise: Richard promises to pay $20 in return for a specified performance. Or he could use a threat: "Shovel the snow or else I won't let you use the car for a week." Here, compliance is demanded or Richard will levy a penalty.

Influence based on promises and threats differs from persuasion attempts in a fundamental way. When using persuasion, the source tries to change the way a target views the situation. Sorenson, for example, might have attempted to persuade his son that shoveling snow is a great workout for building muscles in the upper body or actually a lot of fun. These appeals, if successful, would change how the teen looks at the situation, but they would not actually change the situation itself. With promises or threats, on the other hand, the source does restructure the situation. By promising to pay money for a clear driveway or threatening punishment if it is not done, Sorenson has added a new reinforcement contingency to the situation—money in return for snow removal or the inconvenience of walking if it is not removed. In both cases, he hopes the looming reinforcement will induce his son to comply, but which approach will be most effective?

### Effectiveness of Threats and Promises

A **threat** is a communication from one person (the source) to another (the target) that takes the general form, "If you don't do X [which I want], then I will do Y [which you don't want]" (Boulding, 1981; Fink et al., 2003).

When a source issues a threat, the sanction threatened can be virtually anything—a physical beating, the loss of a job, a monetary fine, the loss of love. The important point is that for a threat to be effective, the target must want to avoid the sanction. If Richard's son has plans to stay home all week or knows his friends will give him rides, he will not care if his father withholds car privileges.

In the context of compliance, a **promise** is similar to a threat, except that it involves contingent rewards, not punishments. A person using a promise says, "If you do X [which I want], then I will do Y [which you want]." Notice that a promise involves a reward controlled by the source. Richard Sorenson promises a payment of $20 if his teenage son clears the driveway and sidewalk. People frequently use promises in exchanges, both monetary and nonmonetary.

## BOX 10.2  Social Power and Compliance

Suppose a high school student did not do well on her midterm exams and her father wants to try to influence her to study harder for her winter finals. The father can choose from a number of different tactics to try to produce compliance. These tactics can be organized by the type of power the father might use to influence the daughter. According to a model forwarded by French and Raven (1959; Raven, 1992), there are six major social bases of power that can be used in such a situation.

*1. Promise of Reward.* One way of inducing compliance is to promise a reward if the target performs the desired behavior. The father might tell his daughter, "If you spend two hours a day studying for the next two weeks, I will buy you a new cell phone." Oftentimes, explicit agreements about behavior and rewards are made, but other times they are more subtle, such as when we work hard to gain approval from our parents even though we have never explicitly agreed on such an arrangement.

*2. Coercion through Threat.* In contrast to the reward strategy, the father might use the threat of a negative outcome to induce compliance. "If you don't do better on your exams next time, you will not go on the spring break trip you are planning." As with rewards, the threats do not necessarily have to be explicit in order to be effective.

*3. Referent Power.* Referent power uses our desire to be accepted by members of valued social groups. When we seek acceptance, we may be more likely to comply with the demands of the group or we may try to become more similar to the group by imitating the behavior of its members (see Chapter 15). To use referent power, the father could identify people whom his daughter admires and then point out how studious those people are: "Your older sister spends at least two hours a day studying."

*4. Legitimate Power.* The social positions people occupy often supply them with power over other individuals, and this hierarchical arrangement is often accepted by both the higher-power and lower-power persons involved (see Chapter 16). Bosses have the power to tell employees what to do, parents have the power to tell children what to do, and police officers have the power to tell motorists what to do. When authority is accepted as a right associated with a social role, it is called legitimate power. The father in our example could invoke legitimate power by saying, "I'm the parent, and one of my jobs as a parent is to make sure you study. So get to work!" If the daughter accepts the traditional authority arrangement, she will head off to study, even if she does not really want to.

*5. Information.* Sometimes, we can actually change people's attitudes about the behavior we want them to exhibit, and the behavior change will then follow in order to produce consistency with the attitude. One way of doing this is to provide information about the effects of the behavior. "The grades you have now are not going to be high enough for you to get into college. The average grades of entering students at State College last year were in the B range. You currently only have a C average."

*6. Expertise.* Information can play a less direct role in compliance as well. There are many times in life when we do not need to know all information about the behavior as long as we think the person telling us what to do is an expert. We assume that because the person is an expert, they know what they are talking about and, thus, we will comply with their request. When a doctor prescribes drugs, we usually take them even if we don't know exactly how they work because we can rely on the expertise of the doctor. In the case of the father and the high school student, he might refer to an expert on studying who claims that an additional two hours of studying per day will raise a student's GPA by a full letter grade.

By issuing a promise, the source creates a set of options for the target. Suppose, for example, that Richard makes the promise, "I'll give you $20 if you clear the snow from the driveway." In response, his son can (1) comply with the source's request and clear the driveway, (2) refuse to comply and let the matter drop, or (3) make a counteroffer, such as "How about $30? It's a long driveway, and the snow is very deep" (Boulding, 1981; Payan & McFarland, 2005).

The range of possible responses to threats and promises raises a fundamental question: Under what conditions will threats and promises be successful in gaining compliance, and under what conditions will they fail? Certain characteristics of threats and promises, such as their magnitude and credibility, affect the probability that the target will comply.

**Magnitude of Threats and Promises.** In promises, the greater the magnitude of the reward offered by a source, the greater the probability of compliance by the target (Balliet, Mulder, & Van Lange, 2011). For example, a factory supervisor might obtain compliance from a worker by offering a large incentive: "If you are willing to work the late shift next month, I'll approve your request for four extra days of vacation in September." The worker's reaction might be less accommodating, however, if their supervisor offered only a trivial incentive: "If you work the late shift next month, I'll let you take your coffee break five minutes early today."

A similar principle holds for threats. Other factors being equal, targets will dismiss threats that entail trivial consequences and comply with threats that entail large and serious consequences (Miranne & Gray, 1987). Consistent with this, researchers find that the more severe the possible punishments for cheating, the more likely students are to adhere to an honor code (McCabe, Treviño, & Butterfield, 2001).

**Credibility of Threats and Promises.** Suppose you own a little puppy that often runs wild. Your not-so-nice neighbor hates dogs. One day, they issue a threat: "If you don't keep your dog off my property, I will call animal control." This threat is troublesome, because your dog romps on their property frequently. But would your neighbor really do what they say, or are they merely bluffing? You will comply and tether your dog if the threat is real, but you do not want to comply if it is merely a bluff. Unfortunately, there is no surefire, risk-free way to find out whether the threat is credible. The only true way to test your neighbor's credibility is to call their bluff—that is, to refuse to comply. Then, if your neighbor were merely bluffing, that fact will quickly become evident. Of course, if they were not bluffing, you will suffer the consequences.

Bluffing or not, any source who makes a threat wants the target to believe the threat is credible and to comply with their demand. They do not want the target to call their bluff. After all, a successful threat is one that obtains compliance without actually having to be carried out. If the target refuses to comply, the threatener must either admit they are bluffing or incur the costs of carrying out the threat.

To judge the credibility of a threat, targets gauge the cost to the source of carrying out the threat. Threats that cost a lot to carry out are less credible than those costing less. Calling animal control would require very little of your neighbor's time. Targets also estimate the credibility of a threat based on the social identity of the source. A threat involving physical violence, for example, will be more credible if it comes from a karate expert wearing a black belt than if it comes from the proverbial 97-pound weakling. Finally, previous behavior affects the credibility of the threat. If your neighbor has called animal control to pick up other neighbors' dogs, you are more likely to take their threat seriously. Although threats are seen as most

A robber holds a pharmacist at gunpoint. Targets are more likely to comply when threats are both large and credible. © stevecoleimages/iStock

credible when they are consistently followed through with, credibility can be established with only occasional enforcement because even that increases the perception that this is one of the times when the source will follow through.

## OBEDIENCE TO AUTHORITY

We have all witnessed situations in which—without the use of threat, promises, or persuasion—one person issues an order and another person complies. For example, a baseball umpire tosses an unruly manager out of the game and orders him to leave the field; the manager, after showing his resentment by throwing his cap to the ground and kicking first base, grudgingly complies. The umpire does not attempt to persuade the manager to leave voluntarily; he simply issues an order directing the manager to leave. The capacity of the source (the umpire) to influence the target

(the manager) stems from the rights conferred by their roles within the game. Under the rules of the game, the umpire has the right to throw the manager out of the game for disruptive behavior.

When persons occupy roles within a group, organization, or larger social system, they accept certain rights and obligations vis-à-vis other members in that social unit. Typically, these rights and obligations give one person authority over another with respect to certain acts and performances. **Authority** refers to the capacity of one member to issue orders to others—that is, to direct or regulate the behavior of other members by invoking rights that are vested in their role. When the umpire tosses the manager out of the game, the basis of his power is legitimate authority. When the manager complies, he is obedient to authority and social norms.

Orders by police officers, decisions by judges, directives by parents, and exhortations by clergymen—all these entail authority and the invocation of norms. A source can exercise authority only when, by virtue of the role that they occupy in a social group, others accept their right to prescribe behavior regarding the issue at hand (Kelman & Hamilton, 1989; Raven & Kruglanski, 1970). The greater the number of persons the source can directly or indirectly influence in this manner and the wider the range of behaviors over which the source has jurisdiction, the greater that individual's authority is within the group (Michener & Burt, 1974).

## Experimental Study of Obedience

Obedience to authority is often beneficial because it facilitates coordination among persons in groups or collective settings. Civil order hinges on obedience to orders from police officers and judicial officials, and effective performance in work settings often depends on following bosses' or employers' directives. However, if obedience to authority is unquestioning, it can produce disquieting or undesirable outcomes.

At the 2012 Sundance film festival, a number of viewers walked out of the showing of *Compliance*, a docudrama recounting the disturbing events that transpired at a Kentucky restaurant in 2004. The audience was shocked and uncomfortable to learn how far someone might go as they yielded to requests from an authority figure.

It was a busy Friday night when a man posing as "Officer Scott" called the local McDonald's and asked an assistant manager, Donna Summers, for help with a police investigation. Scott told Summers that one of her employees had been accused of theft. He gave a vague description of an employee, who Summers recognized as a young woman working the front counter. Scott claimed that there were no officers available to come conduct the investigation and so he would need her assistance. He assured Summers that her general manager was aware of the situation and that he had given permission for her to help the officer. Scott asked Summers to take the employee to the office. He then began to give her instructions on how to proceed: first asking Summers to search the employee's possessions, then to strip search her. When things picked up in the restaurant and Summers was needed up front, Scott asked her to bring in someone else who she could trust to continue with the procedure. Summers asked her fiancé, Walter Nix, to come to the restaurant and help. For the next two hours, Scott demanded that Nix have the employee engage in acts of humiliation, including a body cavity search and performing a sex act. When Nix became uncomfortable with the situation and told his fiancée that he needed to leave, a still-rushed Summers asked the restaurant's maintenance man to help out. When the maintenance man realized what was happening in the restaurant's office, he refused to play any part in it. His reaction sparked something in Summers. She became suspicious and called the store's general manager to see whether he had, in fact, talked with Scott. He had not. The call had been a hoax. Summers and Nix were not the only unknowing accomplices who had complied with disturbing commands from an unknown caller. Similar events—most likely from the same perpetrator—occurred throughout the United States.

Social psychological research also documents the disconcerting outcomes of obedience to authority. In one study, hospital nurses received orders from doctors to administer a drug to a patient. The order came by telephone, and the nurses involved did not previously know the doctor giving the order. The drug was one seldom used in the hospital; hence, it was not very familiar to the nurses. The dosage the doctor prescribed was heavy and substantially exceeded the maximum listed on the package. Nevertheless, the results showed that nearly all the nurses in this study were ready to follow orders and administer the drug at the dosage prescribed by the doctor they spoke with (Hofling et al., 1966).

Of course, the conditions in this study—like conditions in the Kentucky McDonald's—were very favorable for obedience; under different conditions, obedience rates will not be so high. Subsequent research has indicated, for instance, that when nurses are more familiar with the medicine involved and are able to consult freely with their colleagues, the rates of obedience are considerably lower (Rank & Jacobson, 1977).

In some cases, obedience to authority can produce very negative consequences, especially if the orders involve actions that are morally questionable or reprehensible. History provides many examples, such as the My Lai Massacre during the Vietnam War, at which soldiers obeyed Lieutenant Calley's orders to kill innocent villagers, or the activity of the Third Reich of Nazi Germany during the 1930s and 1940s that produced the Holocaust. In complying with the dictates of Hitler's authoritarian government, some German citizens committed acts that most people consider morally unconscionable—beatings, confiscation of property, torture, and murder of millions of people. This may seem like madness, but Hannah Arendt (1965) has argued that most participants in the Holocaust were not psychotics or sadists who enjoyed committing mass murder but ordinary individuals exposed to powerful social pressures.

To explore the limits of obedience to legitimate authority, Stanley Milgram carried out a program of experimental research in a laboratory setting (Milgram, 1965, 1974, 1976; Miller, Collins, & Brief, 1995). Milgram created a hierarchy in which one person (the experimenter, who assumed the role of authority) directed another person (the participant) to engage in actions that ostensibly hurt a third person (a confederate, who played the role of victim). The primary goal of this research was to understand the conditions under which participants would follow morally questionable orders to hurt the confederate.

At the outset, Milgram (1963) recruited 40 adult men to serve as participants. These men, contacted through newspaper advertisements, were adults (aged 20 to 50) with diverse occupations (labor, blue collar, white collar, and professional). When a participant arrived for the experiment, he met a gentle, 47-year-old male accountant. This person, though ostensibly another participant who had responded to the same advertisement, was actually a confederate. The experimenter told the participants that the purpose of the research was to study the effects of punishment (that is, electric shock) on learning. One of the participants would occupy the role of learner, while the other occupied the role of teacher. Participants drew a slip of paper to determine their roles; unknown to the participant, the drawing was rigged so the confederate was always selected as the learner. The participant and the confederate were led into an adjacent room where the learner was strapped into an "electric chair," and electrodes were attached to his wrist. He mentioned that he had some heart trouble and expressed concern that the shock might prove dangerous. The experimenter, who was dressed in a lab coat, replied that the shock would be painful but would not cause permanent damage.

The experimenter then led the participant to the main room and had him sit in front of a large machine and intercom. The participant, in the role of teacher, read pairs of words over an intercom system to the confederate in the adjacent room, and the confederate was supposed to memorize these. After reciting the entire list of paired words, the participant then tested the confederate. Going through the list again, the participant read aloud the first word of each pair and four alternatives for the second word of the pair, much like a multiple-choice exam. The confederate's task was to select the correct alternative response for each item.

Consistent with the cover story that the study was investigating the effects of punishment on learning, the experimenter ordered the participant to shock the learner whenever he made an incorrect response. This shock was to be administered by the machine in front of him, an electric generator that had 30 voltage levels, ranging from 15 to 450 volts. The participant was directed to set the first shock at the lowest level (15 volts) and then, with each successive error, increase to the next higher voltage. That is, the participant was to increase the voltages from 15 to 30 to 45, and so on up to the 450-volt maximum. On the shock generator, the lowest voltage level (15 volts) was labeled *slight shock*; a higher level (135 volts) read *strong shock*; higher still (375 volts) read *danger: severe shock*; the highest level (450 volts) was ominously marked *XXX*. In actuality, this equipment was a dummy generator, and the confederate never received any actual shocks, but its appearance was quite convincing to participants.

Soon after the session began, it became apparent that the confederate was a slow learner. Although he got a few answers right, his responses were incorrect on most trials. The participants reacted by administering ever-higher levels of shock, as they had been ordered to do. When the shock level reached 75 volts, the confederate (who was still in the adjacent room) grunted loudly. At 120 volts, he shouted that the shocks were becoming painful. At 150 volts, he demanded to be released from the experiment ("Get me out of here! I won't be in the experiment anymore! I refuse to go on!"). At 270 volts, his response to the shock was an agonized scream. (Actually, the shouts and screams that participants heard from the adjacent room came from tape recordings so the learner's response was uniform for all participants.)

Whenever a participant expressed concern or dismay about the procedure, the experimenter urged him to persist ("The experiment must continue" and "You have no other choice—you must go on."). At the 300-volt level, the confederate shouted in desperation that he wanted to be released from the electric chair and would not provide any further answers to the test. In reaction, the experimenter directed the participant to treat any refusal to answer as an incorrect response. At the 315-volt level, the learner gave out a violent scream. At the 330-volt level, he fell completely silent, and from that point on nothing more was heard from him. Stoically, the experimenter directed the participant to continue toward the 450-volt maximum, even though the learner did not respond.

Before the experiment, Milgram had asked psychology students and psychiatrists what percentage of participants would likely deliver shocks up until the highest voltage. The average prediction was less than 5 percent. In the end, 26 of the 40 participants (65 percent) continued to the end of the shock series (450 volts). Although they could have refused to proceed, not a single participant stopped before administering 300 volts. Despite the tortured reactions of the confederate, most participants followed the experimenter's orders.

Understandably, this situation was very stressful for the participants, and many felt some concern for the learner's welfare. As the shock level rose, the participants grew increasingly worried and agitated. Some began to sweat or laugh nervously, and many pleaded with the experimenter to check the learner's condition or to end the study immediately. A few participants became so distressed that they refused to follow the experimenter's orders. The overall level of compliance in this study, however, was quite high, reflecting the enormous impact of directives from a legitimate authority.

Being put in a situation in which you are required to shock someone—even with the ability to leave and even later discovering during debriefing that it was all a ruse—is disturbing and can lead to post-traumatic stress. Milgram faced tremendous criticism for his experiments, including concerns about his methods and the detrimental psychological effects on the participants (Griggs & Whitehead, 2015). Institutional Review Boards at universities, hospitals, and other organizations now evaluate detailed plans for any research that involves human subjects, weighing the risks and potential benefits, and must approve the plans before research can begin (see Chapter 2). For over 50 years, Milgram's experiment was largely unreplicated because such boards believed the risks outweighed the benefits, especially given what was already known from Milgram's research.

In 2015, however, psychologists in Poland were given permission to conduct a modern-day replication if they used lower shock levels than Milgram and had the potential to generate important new knowledge. The experiment itself was much like Milgram's. Participants could deliver ten increasingly high levels of shock to a learner by pressing buttons on a computer console. This time, however, some of the participants (both teachers and learners) were women. In the end, 90 percent of the participants delivered the maximum level shock (Doliński et al., 2017). Given the maximum was at a lower level than Milgram's, these results are quite similar. However, there was a gender difference. Although the number of participants was too small to draw a definitive conclusion, it appears that participants were much less likely to follow the experimenter's commands when the learner was a woman than when the learner was a man.

## Factors Affecting Obedience to Authority

As Milgram's results show, persons in authority usually obtain compliance with their orders, especially when these are accepted as legitimate or backed by potential force. Nevertheless, orders from an authority can set off

The lines of authority become salient as a military commander gives orders to his recruits. © panda3800/ shutterstock

a complex process that can lead to various responses (Blass, 1991). Compliance does not always occur, and subordinate members sometimes defy orders from an authority. Although most participants in Milgram's research obeyed orders, some refused to comply. Other studies have reported similar effects: obedience is the most common response to authority, but defiance does occur (Gibson, 2014; Rochat & Modigliani, 1995). This raises a basic question: Under what conditions will people comply with authority, and under what conditions will they refuse? What factors affect the probability that group members will comply with authority?

Certain factors affecting compliance are straightforward. For instance, other things being equal, a direct display of authority symbols—like a uniform or badge—will increase compliance (Bushman, 1988). In one study (Sedikides & Jackson, 1990), visitors at the bird exhibit of the Bronx Zoo were approached by a person who told them not to touch the handrail of the exhibit. They were significantly more likely to obey this directive when it came from a person dressed in a zookeeper uniform than when it came from a person dressed in casual clothes. The use of authoritative symbols may also have played a part in the Milgram studies, in which the experimenter wore a gray lab coat.

Another factor that matters is whether the person in authority can back up their demands with punishment in the event of noncompliance. Although this was not an explicit factor in Milgram's studies, a body of research suggests that greater magnitudes of potential punishment lead to higher levels of compliance (Grasmick & Bursik, 1990).

Milgram (1974) extended his basic experiment to study some other factors that affect compliance with orders. For instance, one variation manipulated the degree of surveillance by the experimenter over the participant (Milgram, 1965, 1974). In one condition, the experimenter sat a few feet away from the

participant during the experiment, maintaining direct surveillance; in another condition, after giving basic instructions, the experimenter departed from the laboratory and issued orders by telephone from a remote location. The results show that the number of obedient participants was almost three times greater in the face-to-face condition than in the order-by-telephone condition. In other words, obedience was greater when participants were under direct surveillance than under remote surveillance. During the telephone conversations, some participants specifically assured the experimenter they were raising the shock level when, in actuality, they were using only the lowest shock and nothing more. This tactic enabled them to ease their conscience while at the same time avoiding a direct confrontation with authority.

In another variation, Milgram (1974) manipulated the participant's physical proximity to the victim. The findings showed that bringing the victim closer to the participant—and, therefore, increasing the participant's awareness of the learner's suffering—substantially reduced the participant's willingness to administer shock. In the extreme case, when the victim was seated right next to the participant, obedience decreased substantially. These results raise important concerns about the use of drones in warfare and targeted killing, as the physical—and potentially psychological—distance between the drone operator and the target (and possible civilian casualties) is greater than any previous weaponry allowed (Powers, 2017). Preliminary studies suggest that using technology to generate distance—in the laboratory and when participants thought they were harming insects—increased participants' killing behavior (Rutchick et al., 2017).

Obedience to authority is also affected by the participant's position in a larger chain of command. Kilham and Mann (1974) used a Milgram-like situation in which one participant (the executant) actually pushed the buttons to administer shock, while another participant (the transmitter) simply conveyed the orders from the experimenter. The results showed that obedience rates were approximately twice as high among transmitters as among executants. In other words, persons positioned closer to the authority but farther from the unhappy task of throwing the switch were more obedient.

## RESISTING INFLUENCE AND PERSUASION

It is important to note that we are not simply hapless victims of the persuasion and compliance efforts of other people. Social psychologists have identified a number of factors that enhance our ability to resist persuasion. In this section, we discuss three contributors to resistance: inoculation, forewarning, and reactance.

### Inoculation

Interested in how persons develop resistance to persuasion, McGuire (1964) proposed that targets can be inoculated against persuasion. He specified various **attitude inoculation** treatments that would enable target persons to defend their beliefs against persuasion attempts, not unlike when a patient receives a small dose of a pathogen so that they can develop antibodies. By exposing a target to weak attacks of an attitude and allowing the target to refute them, this inoculation builds up the target's resistance and prepares the target to resist stronger attacks on their attitudes in the future.

To test attitude inoculation's protective effects in the lives of college students, researchers conducted a study to determine whether inoculation might help students resist predatory marketing from credit card companies (Compton & Pfau, 2004). Although most students have a negative attitude toward debt, credit card companies target them and are generally successful at convincing students not only to sign

up for credit cards, but also to carry high-interest debt on those cards. To inoculate students against card companies' persuasive recruitment, researchers actually gave students counterarguments for why credit card debt is not a problem for college students: "Credit cards keep college students safe by providing financial means in emergencies, like car troubles" (a strong counterargument) or "Most students are responsible users of credit cards, so student credit card use is not a major problem or concern" (a weak counterargument). They then quickly followed these statements with attitude-consistent refutations, informing participants of the dangers of credit cards and providing examples of the problems they have caused in the lives of college students. They found that when counterarguments matched refutations in strength—that is, when a strong counterargument is followed with a strong refutation, or a weak counterargument is followed by a weak refutation—students were not only resistant to subsequent persuasion, but were motivated to tell others about the dangers of credit cards.

### Forewarning

A second aid to resisting influence is simply warning people that they are about to be exposed to a persuasion attempt. It is not necessary to provide information to refute the arguments for this effect to occur—if we are warned that our attitudes will be coming under attack, we begin to develop our own counterarguments (Freedman & Sears, 1965). This is especially true if we care about the topic, as that motivates us to construct a counterargument (Chaiken, Giner-Sorolla, & Chen, 1996). Although social psychologists once believed that the more time there was between the forewarning and the persuasion attempt, the stronger the resistance would be (Chen, Reardon, Rea, & Moore, 1992), a meta-analysis (see Chapter 2) of research on the topic finds that forewarning is more effective when the appeal, or the potential effects of persuasion, seem more immediate (Wood & Quinn, 2003). Immediacy is important because a sense of threat—and related motivation—dissipates over time.

A combination of forewarning and refutational defenses is particularly effective. As an example, exposing middle school students to public service announcements that included both warning of an impending threat to their existing beliefs ("No matter how much you want to stay a non-smoker, the truth is that the pressure to smoke in junior high will be higher than at any other time in your life") and demonstrated refutations to counterarguments (*Smoking is cool.* "It is definitely not cool for friends to expect you to do something stupid. Real friends respect your decision to live a healthy life because they will want what's best for you") effectively protected anti-smoking attitudes and curbed dangerous behaviors, particularly among the most vulnerable (Pfau, Van Bockern, & Kang, 1992).

## Reactance

Sometimes, persuasion attempts can go too far. When trying to convince people to change their attitudes, we may become too heavy-handed and actually produce a reaction in the direction opposite to that we intended. This phenomenon is called **reactance**—or the boomerang effect—and it occurs when the target of the persuasion attempt begins to feel that their independence and freedom are being threatened (Brehm, 1966). This prompts both anger and negative cognitions (Quick, Shen, & Dillard, 2013). Feeling the need to reassert control, the targets will behave in a way counter to the persuasion attempt in order to demonstrate their independence. Reactance effects have been demonstrated in a variety of studies, including efforts to encourage college students to floss more and drink less alcohol (Dillard & Shen, 2005).

## SUMMARY

Social influence occurs when behavior by one person (the source) causes another person (the target) to change an opinion or to perform an action they would not otherwise perform. Important forms of open influence include persuasion, use of threats and promises, and exercise of legitimate authority.

**Persuasion.** Persuasion is a widely used form of social influence intended to produce attitude change. (1) The communication-persuasion paradigm points to many factors—properties of the source, the message, and the target—that affect whether a message will change beliefs and attitudes. (2) Certain attributes of the source affect a message's impact. Sources who are credible (that is, highly expert and trustworthy) are more persuasive than sources who are not. Attractive sources are more persuasive than unattractive ones, especially if message arguments are strong. A message coming from multiple, independent sources will have more impact than the same message from a single source. (3) Message characteristics also determine a message's effectiveness. Highly discrepant messages are more persuasive when they come from a source having high credibility. Fear-arousing messages are most effective when they specify a course of action that can avert impending negative consequences. One-sided messages have more impact than two-sided messages when the target already agrees with the speaker's viewpoint or is not well-informed. (4) Attributes of the target also determine a message's effectiveness. Targets who are highly involved with an issue, who like thinking issues through in detail, and who are not distracted tend to scrutinize messages closely and are more influenced by the strength of the arguments than by peripheral factors. Messages that are matched to targets' personality and moral orientations are particularly effective.

**Compliance with Threats and Promises.**
Threats and promises are influence techniques used to achieve compliance (not attitude change) from the target. In using threats
and promises, the source alters the environment of the target by directly manipulating
reward contingencies. The effectiveness of a
threat depends on both the magnitude of the
punishment involved and the probability that
it will be carried out. Greater compliance
results from high magnitude and high probability. Similar effects hold true for promises,
although these involve rewards rather than
punishments.

**Obedience to Authority.** *Authority* refers
to the capacity of one group member to
issue orders or make requests of other members by invoking rights vested in their role.
(1) Research on obedience to authority
shows that participants will comply with
orders to administer extreme levels of electric shock to an innocent victim. (2) Obedience to authority is more likely to occur
when the authority is dressed in uniform,
when the authority can back up orders with
punishments, when participants are under
direct surveillance by the person issuing
orders, when participants are distant from
rather than close to the victim, and when
participants are transmitters rather than executants of a command.

**Resisting Influence and Persuasion.**
Resistance to persuasion attempts can be
increased through inoculation processes, in
which targets are exposed to some of the
source's arguments before the persuasion
attempt occurs and provided with counterarguments. Persuasion can also be reduced by
warning the target that a persuasion attempt is
going to occur. Finally, if a persuasion attempt
is too heavy-handed, targets may feel their
freedom is threatened and attempt to reestablish their independence by defying the persuasion attempt.

*Critical Thinking Skill:*
*Evaluating Persuasive Messages*

As this chapter illustrated, we are inundated
with persuasive statements throughout our
daily lives. Some of these are messages worth
being persuaded by; others are not. Critical thinking can help you discern between
the two.

Think about your dentist's regular encouragement to brush and floss regularly. This message is consistent with toothpaste, mouthwash,
and toothbrush ads encouraging you to practice good dental hygiene (and use their product in doing so). There is nothing inherently
wrong about any of these messages. Certainly
no one would argue that we should neglect
our teeth and gums.

However, you may be exposed to similar
persuasive messages from friends who regularly encourage you to go out drinking to have
a good time. This message is consistent with
the commercials and other advertisements
that show glamorous-looking people having a good time while drinking alcohol. Like
the dental hygiene messages, the messages of
advertisers and an individual whom you know
might be consistent with one another, offering multiple sources of information in support
of their claims. However, there are important
differences in the two sets of messages. Based
on what you learned in this chapter, what are
some of the ways these persuasive attempts
differ? Think of these before you continue.

You might have thought about the reliability and trustworthiness of the source. Your
dentist has little to gain by having you take
better care of your teeth. In fact, you would
spend more time in the dentist's office—and
pay more for your dentist's services—if you did
not heed their advice and neglected your teeth.

You might have also thought about the purpose of the message. Your friends might genuinely care about you and whether you have a
good time, but they also want to have others
to hang out with when they go out, and if

they drink regularly, they want others to drink regularly too in order to make them feel more normal. It might be self-serving to encourage you to join them. Advertisers, whether selling vodka or mouthwash, have their bottom line in mind, so they are sources to be skeptical of. Consider whether a message is biased or self-serving.

You might have also considered the source's evidence and credentials. Your dentist knows quite a bit about dental hygiene. Messages from advertisers for oral hygiene products often include supporting evidence: "Kills 99% of germs in clinical tests," "4 out of 5 dentists recommend." What evidence do your friends or the alcohol advertisers have that people have a better time out at the bars than elsewhere? Is there an assumption that people are having a good time? Do your friends or the alcohol advertisers make any effort to prove this claim or substantiate it? Thinking critically, you should evaluate a message's argument. Is it compelling? Are the ideas presented in a logical, reasoned way that follow from one another and lead to a particular conclusion?

# ALTRUISM AND PROSOCIAL BEHAVIOR

## LEARNING OBJECTIVES

By the end of this chapter you will be able to:

- Understand the difference between types of prosocial behavior and the underlying motivations that influence when, how, and why we help others.

- Explain how our personal characteristics and values, as well as those of others and the specific situations we are in, impact helping behavior, and identify why we may not all seek help or respond positively to receiving it.

- Describe the model that determines whether or not a bystander will intervene and offer help in the case of an emergency.

## INTRODUCTION

Jennifer Beyer, age 22, was driving along Old River Road in Appleton, Wisconsin, on a cold day in February. She was on the way to visit a friend, but when a soaking wet child flagged her down, she pulled over immediately. Shivering and frightened, Jeff Laszewski hurriedly explained that he and his friend, 9-year-old Colin Deeg, had been playing on the frozen Fox River when the ice gave way. Jeff had managed to climb back onto the ice and make it to shore, but Colin was still in the water and couldn't get out.

Starting down the river bank, Jennifer saw Colin splashing in the frigid water. At the point where others may have stopped due to the great personal risk, she went onto the frozen river to rescue him. Inching her way onto the ice, she tried to use her scarf to pull Colin out, but the ice cracked and she plunged into the water. At this point, Colin was still conscious but fading fast. In the meantime, Jeff reached another adult, Cyndy Graf, who quickly dialed 911 for help and then ran to the river.

Jennifer grabbed Colin to keep him from going under and tried to get him out of the water. This proved impossible, however. Colin soon passed out and the weight of his wet clothes made him too heavy to push onto land. Jennifer's limbs were numb with cold by the time police arrived and fire teams reached the river with rescue equipment, but she had kept Colin's head above water and prevented him from drowning. Officers rushed the pair to nearby St. Elizabeth's hospital, where doctors used a bypass machine to warm Colin's blood, which had dropped in temperature to 78 degrees. Jennifer was treated for hypothermia. A week later, Colin was doing fine.

Jennifer Beyer's story is extraordinary for its valor and heroism, but everyday life is filled with smaller tales of people helping others in need. Individuals help others in many ways. They may give someone a ride, help change a flat tire, donate blood, make contributions to charity, return lost items to their owners, assist victims of accidents, and so on. Of course, the mere fact that someone needs help does not mean others will rush to give aid. Humans are capable of vastly different responses to persons in need. Although Jennifer Beyer went onto the ice to rescue Colin Deeg, many others would not have taken that risk. Some will not even stop to help a stranded motorist or make contributions to charitable causes. Thus, a challenge for social psychologists is to explain variations in helping behavior. When will people help others, when will they refuse to, and why?

## KEY CONCEPTS

When discussing the positive end of social behaviors, social psychologists use three interrelated terms. **Prosocial behavior** is a broad category of actions considered beneficial to others and as having positive social consequences. These include donating to charity, intervention in emergencies, cooperation, sharing, volunteering, sacrifice, and the like. This contrasts with antisocial behavior that is aggressive, violent, or destructive. **Helping** is prosocial behavior that has the consequence of providing some benefit to or improving the well-being of another person (Dovidio, Piliavin, Schroeder, & Penner, 2006). Intent is unimportant. There is no requirement that the helper intends to benefit another person with their action. Furthermore, the helper can also benefit from helping; under this definition, helping behavior may involve either selfish or egoistic motives. Another type of prosocial behavior is altruism. Although there is some disagreement on what behaviors count as altruistic (Kalmijn & De Graaf, 2012), here we define **altruism** as helping that is intended to provide aid to someone else without expectation of any reward (other than the good feeling that may result) and that comes at a cost to the helper. Note that, for altruism, intentions do matter. Under this definition, the helper must intend to benefit the other (Schroeder, Penner, Dovidio, & Piliavin, 1995). In fact, this must be the primary goal of the altruistic action (Batson, 2011).

## MOTIVATION TO HELP

What motivates one person to help another? There are at least three major views on the issue, each rooted in different conceptions of human nature. The first view depicts humans as egoistic or selfish beings, concerned primarily with their own gratification. Helping originates from some ulterior, self-serving motive. Potential helpers weigh the costs and benefits of helping to decide whether they will do so. The second view depicts humans as more generous and unselfish beings, capable of real concern for the welfare of others. For instance, a bystander may rush to rescue an accident victim to relieve the victim's pain and anguish.

Our human ability to empathize with others motivates us to alleviate their distress. The third view, from evolutionary psychology, sees prosocial behavior as an evolved trait that helps ensure individuals will pass along their genes to the next generation. In this section, we look at these three views in more detail.

### Egoism

One view of human nature regards us all as fundamentally selfish beings, concerned primarily with our own gratification. This seemingly simple seed is used throughout the social sciences to explain a huge variety of social behavior, including prosocial acts. Although this view acknowledges that helping behavior occurs with considerable frequency, it treats helping as originating from some ulterior, self-serving consideration (Gelfand & Hartmann, 1982). For instance, a student might help a peer with a difficult assignment to get admiration and approval from the other, to avoid feelings of guilt or shame, to obligate the other to them, or to bolster their own self-esteem. Helping behavior motivated by self-gratification is called **egoism**.

Even in the most other-oriented, charitable behavior, there is little doubt that considerations of reward and cost influence decisions to give or withhold help. Every helping act imposes some costs on the helper (danger, loss of time, financial costs, expenditure of effort). In general, the greater these costs, the less likely persons are to help (Kerber, 1984; Shotland & Stebbins, 1983). Would you be more likely to help someone study for an exam you are also studying for than for an exam you took last semester? If you are also studying for the exam, ensuring someone else understands the material takes little additional time and might actually help you understand the material better (in addition to the potential benefits of helping another student outlined above). Helping someone study for an exam for a class that you are not enrolled in, however, comes at a cost; it takes away valuable time that you could spend studying another subject and offers you fewer direct benefits.

There may also be some costs to potential helpers for *not* helping (public disapproval by others, embarrassment and loss of face, and condemnation by the victim). The evaluation of these costs is important in determining helping behavior, and many theorists believe individuals will generally not give help unless they think the rewards (even if not immediate) will outweigh the costs (Lynch & Cohen, 1978; Piliavin, Dovidio, Gaertner, & Clark, 1981).

The rewards that motivate potential helpers are many and varied. They may include such things as gratitude from the victim, admiration and approval from others, financial rewards and prizes, and recognition for efforts. People will help more if they anticipate rewards such as status enhancement (Bienenstock & Bianchi, 2004; Kerber, 1984). Even small rewards—like the small chocolate that the local Goodwill offers with every donation—tend to increase individuals' helping behavior. Getting something in return helps people make a self-interested justification for the behavior (Holmes, Miller, & Lerner, 2002; Perlow & Weeks, 2002).

The form of help that someone offers may depend on the specific rewards they seek, and these may, in turn, depend on their own needs. Contributors to Wikipedia, for example, value the knowledge and prestige they derive from contributing. Both support their desire to see themselves as intellectuals, as well as competent and credible content creators (Rafaeli & Ariel, 2008).

## Altruism and Empathetic Concern

People often react to the distress of others on an emotional level and offer help in response. The term **empathy** refers to the vicarious experience of an emotion that is congruent with—or possibly identical to—the emotion that another person is experiencing (Barnett, 1987; Eisenberg & Miller, 1987). For example, when a mother sees her child in pain, she may experience a very similar emotion to the child. There is considerable evidence that feelings of empathy for a person in need will lead to helping behavior (Batson et al., 1981; Dovidio, Allen, & Schroeder, 1990; Eisenberg & Miller, 1987; Fultz et al., 1986).

**The Empathy-Altruism Model.** The *empathy-altruism model* proposes that adults can experience two distinct states of emotional arousal while witnessing another's suffering: distress and empathy. Distress involves unpleasant emotions such as shock, alarm, worry, and upset at seeing another person suffer. Empathy, however, entails such emotions as compassion, concern, warmth, and tenderness toward the other (Batson, 1987, 1991; Batson & Coke, 1981; Batson & Oleson, 1991). These states of emotional arousal give rise to different motivations, but both can lead to helping behavior. If the bystander experiences distress at seeing another suffering, they may be motivated to reduce this distress (egoism). This contrasts with the situation in which a bystander experiences empathy when witnessing the suffering of another. Feelings of this type may cause the bystander to help the victim, but this help is motivated fundamentally by a desire to reduce the other's distress (altruism). The empathy-altruism model has received support from many experiments. Typically, the participants in these studies witness a person in distress and must decide whether to offer help. The independent variables in these studies are the level of empathy and the ease of escape from the situation. When empathy is high, the frequency of helping behavior is also high, irrespective of whether it was easy to avoid the situation. However, when distress is high, the frequency of helping behavior drops off substantially when escape is easy; participants

Who will volunteer at the food pantry? Who will donate goods? Personal characteristics sometimes drive the decision to help, but cost-benefit calculations, cultural norms, situational factors, and even genetics also play important roles. © Steve Debenport/iStock

leave the situation rather than absorbing the costs of helping (Batson et al., 1983). Distress can be alleviated by leaving the situation; empathy cannot.

Altruistically motivated helping, fueled by empathy, appears to lead to more sustained giving than helping that is motivated by egoism (Piferi, Jobe, & Jones, 2006). In a study on the motivations for helping after the September 11 terrorist attacks, researchers found that individuals who gave money, blood, goods, or other forms of assistance because of other-focused motives (giving to reduce another's discomfort) were almost four times more likely to still be giving support one year later than those whose original motivation was to reduce personal distress (egoistic motives). This effect likely stems from differences in emotional arousal. The events of September 11 emotionally affected people throughout the United States. Those who gave to reduce their own distress reduced their emotional arousal with their initial gift, discharging that emotional distress. However, those who gave to reduce others' distress did not stop empathizing with victims who continued to struggle long after the attacks.

## Evolutionary Perspectives

A third view on prosocial behavior takes an evolutionary perspective. The basic notion driving this theory is that any genetically determined physical attribute or trait that helps an individual survive will be passed on to the next generation. Eventually, individuals with the attribute will become more numerous than those without. The evolutionary perspective often points to others in the animal kingdom to demonstrate its propositions. For example, helping behaviors and even altruistic, self-sacrificing behaviors are common in nature. Ground squirrels, for instance, frequently sound alarm calls when a predator approaches. These calls warn other squirrels of the threat, but they also draw the attention of the predator to the individual sounding the alarm, thereby increasing the chances of that individual being killed (Sherman, 1980). Other animals sacrifice themselves to predators to protect the larger group (Wilson, 1971).

Evolutionary psychology and a related theoretical perspective called *sociobiology* (Archer, 1991; Buss, 1999; Ketelaar & Ellis, 2000; Wilson, 1975, 1978) suggest that helping makes sense in an evolutionary context if we understand that the "fittest" animal is the one that passes on its genes to subsequent generations. This can happen either by the animal itself producing offspring or by the animal's close relatives, such as brothers, sisters, and cousins (who share many of its genes), producing offspring. Investment in offspring is important too, particularly in developed countries where success and longevity are tied to more than good genes. An increasing understanding that *quality* of offspring may be more important for survival than *quantity* is one explanation for decreasing fertility rates (Mace, 2014).

Parents' and nonparents' behavior is influenced by these evolutionary processes. For example, the *fa'afafine*—a group of men in Samoa who are less likely to have their own

## BOX 11.1   Research Update: Gossip as Prosocial Behavior

Gossip is a complex social behavior; although it is very common, it is also widely criticized. An evolutionary perspective would argue that gossip exists because it serves a purpose. According to psychologist Robin Dunbar, that purpose is a prosocial one. Dunbar (1996) hypothesized that gossip became more and more prominent as a linguistic practice as humans began to live in larger and larger groups. Without being able to directly observe others' behavior, group members would use gossip to track one another's reputation as trustworthy group members.

A team of social psychologists tested Dunbar's assumption about the prosociality of gossip in a series of experiments. Feinberg, Willer, Stellar, & Keltner (2012) put participants in situations in which they watched another participant (the transgressor) act selfishly. The researchers then gave the participants the opportunity to gossip about the transgressor to the participant who would interact with the transgressor next in the experiment. More than half the students chose to gossip, and 96 percent of those gossip messages moved beyond serving a selfish, personal end. Examples of prosocial gossip messages were: "[He] didn't send anything back last round. I'd advise not sending anything" or "Try to keep all

the money you can, because [she] will not give you much in return."

Using a battery of self-reports and heart rate monitors, the researchers explored why gossip—and, particularly, prosocial gossip—was so common. They found that people with a more prosocial orientation, whose personality reflected more other-directed concerns, tend to gossip more than those with an egoistic orientation and that participants would gossip even if there was no potential of harm toward the transgressor and when it was costly to gossip. What made gossip so attractive?

Results suggest that witnessing the unfair acts of transgressors evoked negative arousal, especially among more prosocial individuals. The more negative affect participants felt, the more compelled they were to engage in prosocial gossip. Furthermore, engaging in prosocial gossip actually reduced their levels of negative affect. This was especially true for more prosocial individuals.

Gossip also had an important effect on behavior. Participants behaved more cooperatively when they knew that observers could potentially gossip about them.

*Source:* Adapted from Feinberg, Willer, Stellar, & Keltner, 2012.

biological offspring than other men, not unlike gay men in other contexts—devote more time and resources to nieces and nephews than other uncles or aunts give, especially when they are not in a romantic relationship themselves (Vanderlaan & Vasey, 2012). So although it is true that altruistic behavior will not have survival value for an individual, altruistic acts can increase the survival of one's genes if directed toward others who share the same genes (Hamilton, 1964; Meyer, 2000).

Another sociobiological account for the perpetuation of altruistic behavior is reciprocation. If all the members of a group engage in

helping behavior, they will all be better off in the long run (Hardy & van Vugt, 2006). If, for example, animals take turns playing the role of sentry and warning the group of approaching predators, many more members of that group will survive and reproduce than if none of them had warned the group.

Evolutionary approaches to altruism have produced a considerable body of interesting research and theoretical propositions. For example, animals should be most altruistic toward those that most closely resemble them genetically—that is, they should help immediate family members more than distant cousins, and distant cousins more than outsiders or strangers (Burnstein, Crandall, & Kitayama, 1994; Rushton, Russell, & Wells, 1984). Second, parents will tend to behave altruistically toward healthy offspring, who are likely to survive and pass on their genes, but less altruistically toward sick or unhealthy offspring, who are likely to die before reproducing (Dovidio et al., 1991). Third, helping behavior should only favor those who can still reproduce. Thus, helping behavior should be targeted more toward young women than to older women who are past the age of menopause (Kruger, 2001).

Although interesting, the sociobiological perspective is controversial, especially as applied to humans. By the above model, animals and humans would help only close relatives. Yet we know humans often help others who are unrelated—even total strangers. To explain altruism among unrelated persons, it is necessary to rely on cultural constructs, such as religious values, that define unrelated others as appropriate recipients of help. There are also alternative explanations for findings attributed to evolutionary accounts (Buss & Kenrick, 1998; Caporeal, 2001; Dovidio et al., 1991). For example, Sime (1983) examined people in a fire emergency and found that they were much more likely to endanger themselves by searching for family members than by searching for friends. Rather than attributing this behavior to genetic kin selection, however, we may just as likely assume that people would sacrifice more to save someone they love than someone who is simply an acquaintance because losing the former would cause them more distress (an egoism account). At best, it appears evolution is an incomplete explanation for altruism.

## CHARACTERISTICS OF THE NEEDY THAT FOSTER HELPING

Social psychologists' understanding of prosocial behavior focuses not only on those who help and why, but also who is likely to be the recipient of generosity. When in need, some people have a much better chance of receiving help than others do, as our willingness to help others depends on a variety of factors. Important among these are whether we know and like them, whether they are similar to or different from us, and whether we consider them truly deserving of help.

### Acquaintanceship and Liking

We are especially inclined to help people whom we know and to whom we feel close. Studies of reactions following natural disasters, for example, indicate that whereas people generally become very helpful toward others, they tend to give aid first to needy family members, then to friends and neighbors, and last to strangers (Amato, 1990; Form & Nosow, 1958). Research suggests this tendency stems, in part, from an increased ability to empathize with those we know well (Maner & Gailliot, 2007). We are better able to take their perspective and vicariously experience their emotional distress. More intense emotion and empathy motivate altruistic helping. Relationships also increase helping because they involve relatively stronger normative obligations and greater costs if we fail to help (Marion & Burke, 2016). Even a brief acquaintanceship is sufficient to make us more likely to help someone (Pearce, 1980). A simple introduction or comment, and sometimes less, is enough to transform a complete stranger into a "familiar stranger" (Milgram, 1977) and increase the likelihood of helping. One famous study created a situation at a beach where the researchers staged the theft of a radio while its owner was swimming. Most people—about 80 percent—did nothing to try to stop the thief or to intervene in any manner. However, when the owner of the radio asked the person next to them to keep an eye on the radio while they were swimming, almost all of them confronted the person stealing the radio (Moriarty, 1975). We are also more likely to help someone we like than to help someone we do not like. This effect occurs whether our positive feelings about the other are based on their physical appearance, personal characteristics, or friendly behavior (Mallozzi, McDermott, & Kayson, 1990). We are also more likely to help someone who likes us than to help someone who does not (Baron, 1971).

## Similarity

In general, we are more likely to help others who are similar to ourselves than to help others who are dissimilar (Dovidio, 1984). For example, a regular cyclist is more likely to stop to help a cyclist with a flat tire than to help a stranded motorist. Privileging similar others, we are more likely to help those who resemble us in race, attitudes, political ideologies, and even mode of dress (Dovidio & Gaertner, 1981; Hornstein, 1978).

Much of the effect of similarity is a product of perceived group membership. Although groups and group processes will be discussed in more detail in Chapters 15 and 16, people tend to help in-group members (people who share a particular characteristic) more than out-group members (people who are different from them on a particular characteristic).

Our propensity to help similar others extends to a range of in-groups, including fans of our favorite sports teams. In a creative study, a group of researchers choreographed an accident in which a confederate fell down and feigned a painful injury in the presence of a subject (Levine, Prosser, Evans, & Reicher, 2005). Prior to the accident, the researchers had asked subjects about their favorite soccer team. This not only primed their identity as fans of their favorite team, but also gave researchers important information to use later. After the survey, subjects were directed to walk to a different location for the second part of the soccer study to watch a video about soccer teams. Along the way, they passed the confederate, who fell and pretended to be hurt.

The manipulation in the experiment was simple. The injured confederate wore one of three shirts: a shirt identified with the subjects' favorite team, a shirt identified with the main rival of the subjects' favorite team, or a neutral shirt that did not identify with any team at all. The outcome of interest was whether the subjects stopped to help and, if so, how much help was offered. The results were surprisingly stark. Confederates wearing the favorite team's shirt received help from the subjects over 90 percent of the time, whereas those wearing a plain shirt or the rival team's shirt received help less than one-third of the time.

One reason individuals are more likely to help members of their in-group is because individuals are better able to ascribe emotions to in-group members. Remember, emotions and empathy are a key reason that we are more likely to help people whom we know. Even when we do not know others in our in-group, we assume they are similar to us and we think that we know how they feel. In a study of helping after Hurricane Katrina, researchers had White, Black, and Latino participants read a fictionalized account of a mother who had lost her child during the hurricane (Cuddy, Rock, & Norton, 2007). Names cued readers into the victims' race (Tanesha/Amanda and Tyrell/Joshua). After reading the news story, participants were asked to describe the emotions the mothers were experiencing and whether they planned to volunteer or had already volunteered time toward Hurricane Katrina relief efforts.

Of primary interest to the researchers was the role of emotion in helping. They distinguished between two types of emotions—primary and secondary—to determine their relative effects. Primary emotions are emotions that are a direct result of an external cue. They are closely related to the situation at hand. For example, the moment an intimate relationship ends—the breakup—causes a rush of emotion that can be directly attributed to the breakup. You might experience sadness, hurt, and frustration. Secondary emotions are the more enduring effects of these immediate emotions. The rush of sadness may give way to insecurity, anxiety, or depression.

Results showed that participants inferred similar primary emotions—sadness, distress, pain, fear, and so on—for in-group and out-group members. In other words, whether a Black or White participant read the story of Tanesha or Amanda, they believed the mothers would feel similar levels of sadness. However, when participants were asked to rate secondary emotions—grief, sorrow, mourning, guilt, and so on that would persist long after the loss—differences emerged. Specifically, participants inferred lower levels of secondary emotions to out-group members, thinking they would experience less grief than someone in their in-group. Importantly, empathizing with someone in need based on these secondary emotions has more of an influence on helping than simply empathizing on primary emotions.

## Deservingness

After Hurricane Katrina decimated parts of New Orleans, some Americans felt that the residents who stayed in the city during the storm did not deserve help. After all, it seemed like they decided to ignore officials' orders to evacuate. Whether we see someone as deserving help has important implications for our desire to act on their behalf.

Suppose you received a call asking you to help elderly people who had just suffered a sharp reduction in income after losing their jobs. Would it matter whether they lost their jobs because they were caught stealing and lying or because their work program was being phased out? A study of Wisconsin residents who received such a call showed that respondents were more likely to help if the elderly people had become dependent because their program was cut than because they had been caught stealing (Schwartz & Fleishman, 1978).

What matters in this situation is the potential helpers' causal attribution regarding the origin of need (such attributions were covered in Chapter 7). Potential helpers respond more favorably when a person's need is caused by circumstances beyond their control. Such people are true "innocent victims" who deserve help. In contrast, needs caused by a person's own actions, misdeeds, or failings elicit little desire to help (Frey & Gaertner, 1986; Weiner, Perry, & Magnusson, 1988). For instance, one study found that people who erroneously believed that children with juvenile diabetes were somehow responsible for the disease—because they were lazy, unhealthy, or obese—were less sympathetic to those suffering it than respondents who understood that it is not preventable (Vishwanath, 2014). Similarly, bystanders who believe a victim is somehow responsible for a sexual assault (see Box 12.3) feel less responsibility to intervene (Burn, 2009).

In the United States, we tend to commit the fundamental attribution error (the tendency to overemphasize personality in making attributions) and assume that those in need are somewhat to blame for their situation and to downplay or ignore the importance of circumstances outside of their control that may have led to the need or made it difficult to overcome it. Needs thought to stem from illegitimate sources—including individual choices—undermine helping by inhibiting empathic concerns, blocking our sense of normative obligation, and increasing the possibility of condemnation rather than social approval for helping.

Even in emergencies, potential helpers are influenced by whether they consider a victim deserving. Consider responses to an emergency staged by experimenters on the New York City subway (Piliavin, Rodin, & Piliavin, 1969). Shortly after the subway train left the station, a young man (a confederate) collapsed to the floor and lay staring at the ceiling during the seven-and-a-half minute trip to the next station. In one experimental condition,

We are less likely to stop to help someone passed out on a sidewalk or in a park when we see situational cues like alcohol or assume they are homeless. Such cues allow us not only to interpret the situation as a non-emergency, even if it may be one, but alcohol also encourages onlookers to attribute blame to the passed out person, making them seem less deserving of help. © 1000 Words/Shutterstock

the man carried a cane and appeared disabled. In another condition, he carried a liquor bottle and reeked of whiskey. Bystanders helped the seemingly disabled man immediately, but waited several minutes, on average, before helping the man who appeared drunk.

This effect is also found with large-scale disasters (Wiepking & van Leeuwen, 2013). In one study (Zagefka et al., 2011), respondents read a news article about a widespread famine. Half read a version that attributed the famine to an armed conflict and the other half read a version that blamed changes in climate. After reading the article, respondents were asked if they would like to donate to help those affected by the famine. People who thought the famine was a natural disaster (climate) donated more and more often than those who believed it was somehow caused by humans (conflict).

## NORMATIVE FACTORS IN HELPING

Would you intervene in a heated argument between a man and a woman you believe are married? In one experiment (Shotland & Straw, 1976), participants unexpectedly witnessed a realistic fight between a man and a woman in an elevator. The man attacked the woman, shaking her violently, while she struggled and resisted. In one treatment, the man and woman were depicted as strangers; the woman screamed, "Get away from me! I don't know you!" In the other treatment, she screamed, "Get away from me! I don't know why I ever married you!" This simple variation greatly affected the participants' propensity to help. Whereas 65 percent of the subjects intervened in the stranger fight, fewer than 20 percent intervened in the married fight.

This difference may have been due, in part, to the participants' perceptions of a greater likelihood of injury to the woman in the stranger fight than in the married fight. They assumed that an attack by a stranger might progress further than an attack by a husband. However, this reticence may have also been due to normative expectations. The participants who witnessed the married fight said they hesitated to take action because they were not sure their help was wanted. Almost all the participants who did not intervene said they felt the fight was "none of my business." Clearly, "wife" and "husband" are social roles, and some widely understood norms regulate the relations between wives and husbands (and outsiders). One of these is that, except in the case of physical abuse, outsiders should basically mind their own business and let married couples resolve disputes as they will. When the woman in the elevator identified herself as the man's wife, this norm suddenly became relevant and changed the meaning of intervention. To intervene in the fight would be an intrusion on the marital relationship and might invite reprisals from the husband, the wife, or both, putting either the participants or wife in danger. Fear of eliciting an attack on oneself when intervening makes men—who see themselves as more able to protect themselves in such an attack—more likely to intervene when they see a woman being abused than other women are (Laner, Benin, & Ventrone, 2001). Individuals may also intervene in relationships in a less direct or dangerous way, by speaking to the wife (or girlfriend) when her partner is not around so that the conversation remains confidential. For more information on domestic violence, including its definition and potential outlets for help, visit ncadv.org.

## Norms of Responsibility and Reciprocity

Cultural norms mandate helping as appropriate under some conditions, and they suggest it is inappropriate under others. When

mandated as appropriate, helping becomes an approved behavior, supported by social sanctions and integrated into broad social norms.

**Social Responsibility Norm.** The **social responsibility norm** is a general norm stating that individuals should help others who are dependent on them. People often mention their sense of what they "ought to do"—their internalized standards—when asked why they offer to help (Berkowitz, 1972). For example, Simmons (1991) reports the words of a bone marrow donor prior to giving: "This is a life and death situation and you must do anything you can to help that person, whether it is family, friends, or [someone] unknown" (p. 14). The word "must" in this statement suggests that a norm is operative.

Because it is applicable in many situations, the social responsibility norm is readily activated. Some research suggests that simply informing individuals that another person—even a stranger—is dependent on them is enough to elicit help (Berkowitz, Klanderman, & Harris, 1964). Recognize, however, that there are stronger and weaker versions of the social responsibility norm. Although the norm that we must help dependent kin or friends in need is widely held, the belief that we must help needy strangers or unknown persons is not as universally accepted. Although the awareness of a stranger's dependency will sometimes elicit help, it does not always do so. Speeding passersby, for example, frequently disregard stranded motorists they notice on the roadside. Bystanders watch, apparently fascinated but immobile, during rapes and other assaults. Thousands of people reject charity appeals every day.

In a classic study of the social responsibility norm, social psychologists tried to remind individuals of their obligation to others and then gave them an opportunity to help someone in need (Darley & Batson, 1973). The researchers asked a group of theological students to write and record a talk. Some were told to prepare remarks on the parable of the Good Samaritan, while others wrote about job opportunities. On the way to record their talk, the students passed a man slumped in a doorway. Although the students who wrote about the Good Samaritan were presumably thinking about the virtues of altruism as they passed the man, they helped the stranger only slightly more than the students who had prepared a talk on the unrelated topic. Although this brief reminder of the importance of helping others was not enough for a meaningful difference in theology students' reactions, research suggests that experience with helping others in need can cultivate a social responsibility norm in individuals. For example, service learning courses and programs that integrate community service into students' educational experience have been shown to increase helping behaviors and participants' sense of social responsibility long after the specific courses have ended (Durlak et al., 2011).

**The Norm of Reciprocity.** Another cultural standard, the **norm of reciprocity**, states that people should (1) help those who have helped them and (2) not help those who have denied them help for no legitimate reason (Schroeder et al., 1995; Trivers, 1983). Imagine your roommate's car has broken down and they ask you for a ride to the grocery store to pick up a few things. You are much more likely to help them if they did a favor for you the last time you needed one. However, if they turned down a previous request to help you—say, when you needed a ride to campus from the bus station after returning from winter break—you are much less likely to agree. This reciprocity norm applies to anyone who has previously received some benefit from another. The norm is found in different cultures around the world (Gergen, Ellsworth, Maslach, & Siepel, 1975). Small kindnesses that create the conditions for reciprocity are a common feature of family, friendship, and work relationships (Spitzmuller & Van Dyne, 2013).

Reciprocity is especially likely when the person expects to see the helper again (Carnevale, Pruitt, & Carrington, 1982; Nguyen, Seers, & Hartman, 2008). People try to match the amount of help they give to the quantity they received earlier. By matching benefits, people maintain equity in their relationships and avoid becoming overly indebted to others. Understanding the norm of reciprocity, those in need are less likely to ask for help when they believe they will not be able to repay the aid in some form (Nadler, 1987, 1991). That said, people do not reciprocate every benefit they receive. Whether we feel obligated to reciprocate depends in part on the intentions we attribute to the person who helped us. We feel more obligated to reciprocate if we perceive that the original help was given voluntarily rather than coerced and that one's action was chosen consciously rather than an accident (Desmet, De Cremer, & van Dijk, 2010; Greenberg & Frisch, 1972).

### Personal Norms

Although broad norms like social responsibility and reciprocity undoubtedly affect helping behavior, they are, by themselves, often inadequate for predicting helping. There are several reasons for this. First, these norms are simply too general to dictate our behavior given the variety of contingencies we encounter. Second, not everyone in society accepts these norms to the same degree; some individuals internalize them to a greater extent than others do. Third, the social norms that apply to any given situation occasionally conflict with one another. For example, the social responsibility norm may obligate us to help an abused wife, but the widely accepted norm against meddling in others' marriages tells us not to intervene.

Therefore, it is important to understand **personal norms**—feelings of moral obligation to perform specific actions that stem from an individual's internalized system of values

## BOX 11.2 Research Update: Cooperative Games and Prosocial Behavior

Cooperative games—where players work together to achieve a common goal—are becoming increasingly popular. In *Pandemic*, players are disease specialists with unique roles (scientists, researchers, field medics) who work together to contain and cure deadly plagues. One player drives the kart in *Mario Kart: Double Dash!!* while a partner deploys a variety of items to slow competitors down to help their team win the race. Four players, each performing a different, integral role, team up to execute a heist in *Grand Theft Auto Online*.

These games and others like them appeal to Millennials—the cohort born between the late 1970s and late 1990s—who tend to be more cooperative and affiliative than previous generations (Howe & Strauss, 2009). However, is it possible that playing these games could also have an effect on players' behavior toward others? Could experience with cooperative games make players more cooperative outside of games?

To test the effects of cooperative games on prosocial behavior, social psychologists Tobias Greitemeyer and Christopher Cox (2013) invited college students to play video games in a laboratory. When the students arrived, they were paired with another student who they did not know. The two were led to a room with side-by-side computers and screens. The pair were randomly assigned to play either separate single-player games or a team-player condition of the same game (*Mario Kart: Double Dash!!*) while seated next to one another. After playing the game for

15 minutes, the pair was separated, given a short survey, and asked to participate in a second stage of the experiment.

In the second stage, players were given five poker chips. They were told that they could either keep the chips or give them away to the person who they had been playing video games with. Any chips the participants kept would be worth 50 cents, while any chips given to their partner would double in value and be worth $1 to the other player. Participants were told that the other player had the same number of chips with similar values and therefore faced an identical decision. They then had to decide how many chips to give to their partner.

Participants who had played a cooperative version of the game with the other participant gave away significantly more chips (4.15) than the participants who played single-player games (2.94). Using the survey results, the researchers showed that this prosocial behavior stemmed from the increased bond the pairs who played the cooperative game felt. This bond enhanced trust between them and this trust encouraged them to act prosocially toward one another.

There is an important caveat. The game used in this experiment was a neutral video game. Whether cooperative or not, violent games tend to decrease rates of helping and empathy (Anderson et al., 2010).

*Source:* Adapted from Greitemeyer and Cox, 2013.

(Schwartz & Howard, 1981, 1984). These help explain not only the conditions under which norms are likely to motivate helping, but also individual differences in helping in particular situations.

These personal norms may stem from role identities (Piliavin, Grube, & Callero, 2002). We are driven to act in ways consistent with our identities to experience ourselves as authentic

and to uphold those identities (see Chapter 4). For example, a religious person might help because it is "the Christian thing to do" or because they believe in the golden rule: "Do unto others as you would like done to you." Similarly, someone who has adopted an identity as a "blood donor" is more likely to give blood than someone who has not (Piliavin & Callero, 1991) and someone who describes themselves as moral is more likely to act ethically when offered the opportunity (Stets & Carter, 2011). Helping is most likely to occur when conditions simultaneously foster the activation of personal norms and suppress any defenses that might neutralize personal norms.

## Gender Norms

Although there are not significant gender differences in how much people help, there are significant differences in the ways men and women help. These differences are related to gender role norms and expectations (Piliavin & Unger, 1985). For example, research findings suggest that men are more likely than women to intervene and offer assistance in emergency situations that entail danger (Eagly & Crowley, 1986). Acting heroically by confronting risk and danger is often considered part of the traditional male role. Women, however, are more likely to help in situations requiring nurturance, caretaking, and emotional support, in part because they tend to experience more empathy in those situations than men do (Zagefka & James, 2015). Women are more likely to help children they witness being abused than men are (Laner, Benin, & Ventrone, 2001) and women care for children and aging parents more on a day-to-day basis than men do, fulfilling an important help-giving function (Brody, 2004). Women are also more likely than men to provide their friends with personal favors, emotional support, and informational counseling (Eisenberg & Fabes, 1991; Otten, Penner, & Waugh, 1988). These differences in men's and women's forms of helping are consistent with expectations for femininity and masculinity.

## SITUATIONAL INFLUENCES

Prosocial behavior is influenced by not only normative factors but also situational influences on potential helpers. For example, we are more likely to help when we feel we have time

to. In the earlier study of theological students who were on their way to give a speech on the parable of the Good Samaritan (Darley & Batson, 1973), being in a hurry had a much stronger effect on whether the students stopped to help than the topic of the speech did. Students who were in a hurry offered much less help than those who were not, in part because they felt a sense of social responsibility toward those who were waiting on them instead of the person who needed their help (Batson et al., 1978). In this section we consider a handful of other such factors: experiences with models and audiences of helping, mood, and the potential costs of helping (or not).

## The Presence of Others

Later in this chapter we will discuss how others can suppress our likelihood of helping in emergency situations. However, there are also important ways that others increase prosocial behavior, including acting as models or serving as valued audiences.

**Modeling.** A key influence in helping is the presence of behavioral models—someone else who is helping. The presence of a behavioral model tends to increase helping for several reasons. First, a model demonstrates what kinds of actions are possible or effective in the situation. Others who previously did not know how to help can emulate the model. As an example, even if a young college student wants to help a stranded motorist on the highway, they might not know anything about cars and, therefore, be unsure of how they might assist the motorist. However, if the student had previously been in a car with someone else who, in a similar instance, made note of the mile marker and pulled out their cell phone and called highway patrol to notify the police of the stranded motorist and their location, the student would have a model of a possible behavior and would be more likely to respond similarly if a comparable situation occurred.

Second, a helping model conveys the message that to offer help is appropriate in the particular situation. A model may, for example, increase the salience of the social responsibility norm. Once aware of this norm, others may decide to help. A popular series of insurance commercials demonstrated this nicely, showing the sense of responsibility spreading through the city. It begins with a mother watching as a man stops to pick up her child's toy. She makes note of this and, later, in a restaurant, pushes a coffee cup—teetering on the edge of a table and at risk of falling—back toward the center of the table. A passerby witnesses this act of kindness and later stops to help a man up from a wet sidewalk. The commercial continues through a long series of models and observers who eventually become models for another observer.

Finally, a model provides information about the costs and risks involved in helping—a consideration that is especially important in situations involving danger. By offering help under conditions of danger or potential damage to self, models demonstrate to others that the risks incurred are tolerable or justified.

**Audience.** Others sometimes increase helping by serving as an audience. For example, people tend to give more when their donations will be public rather than private. Online fundraising websites like GoFundMe or YouCaring will often list contributors—and their donation amounts—knowing that visitors will be inclined to give more than they would have if there was no running tally (Wiepking & Heijnen, 2011). Even an imagined audience can be effective, as studies find that images of eyes—for example, on donation containers or nearby posters and signs—increase a variety of prosocial behaviors (Powell, Roberts, & Nettle, 2011). Audience effects are particularly strong when individuals are trying to uphold or restore their reputation (Zagefka & James, 2015).

## Mood

As discussed in Chapter 6, a mood is a transitory feeling, such as being happy and elated or being frustrated and depressed. Both good and bad moods can help or hinder a person's likelihood of helping another.

**Good Moods and Helping.** When individuals are in a good mood, they are more likely to help others—either through spontaneous helping or complying with requests for help—than when they are in a neutral mood (Salovey, Mayer, & Rosenhan, 1991). There are several reasons that being in a good mood increases our propensity to help others. First, people who are in a good mood are less preoccupied with themselves and less concerned with their own problems. This allows them to focus more attention on the needs and problems of others. This increases helping through empathy, as discussed earlier in the chapter. Second, people in a good mood often feel relatively fortunate compared to others who are deprived. They recognize that their good fortune is out of balance with others' needs and use their resources to restore balance by helping (Rosenhan, Salovey, & Hargis, 1981). Third, people in a good mood want to retain the warm glow of happiness. Helping can offer a "helper's high" and increase positive affect (Snippe et al., 2017). Thus, if someone can maintain or even increase their own positive feelings through prosocial behavior, they will do so.

That said, good moods may also inhibit helping in particular situations. Those in a good mood may avoid forms of helping that threaten to interrupt or end their good mood (Cunningham, Steinberg, & Grev, 1980).

**Bad Moods and Helping.** The effects of a bad mood—feeling sad or depressed—can have rather complex effects on helping. Under some conditions, a bad mood inhibits helping. Under other conditions, however, it promotes helping (Carlson & Miller, 1987; Rosenhan et al., 1981).

Bad moods can suppress helping because they lessen the salience of others' needs. In contrast to those in a good mood, people in a bad mood are concerned about their own problems and less likely to notice others' needs than are people in a neutral or good mood. When others' needs do not grab the attention of a potential helper, help is less likely to be given (Aderman & Berkowitz, 1983; Rogers, Miller, Mayer, & Duval, 1982). People in a bad mood also often see themselves as less fortunate than others. Feeling relatively impoverished, they may resist using their own resources to help others, lest they become even more disadvantaged (Rosenhan et al., 1981).

However, bad moods can sometimes increase helping. One explanation for this is the *negative-state relief hypothesis* (Cialdini, Kenrick, & Baumann, 1982; Cialdini et al., 1987). This hypothesis assumes that (1) individuals experiencing unpleasant feelings will be motivated to reduce them, and (2) people have learned since childhood that helping others will improve their own mood, often through the receipt of thanks or praise. In other words, people in bad moods will help others to boost their own spirits. This is an egoistic rather than altruistic motive for helping because individuals are offering help primarily to relieve their own sadness, but the effect is the same. Consistent with the hypothesis, a negative mood will only motivate helping if people believe that doing so will improve their mood (Manucia, Baumann, & Cialdini, 1984) and there is not an accessible alternative way to relieve the bad mood (Schaller & Cialdini, 1988).

## Costs

When making a decision to help, people usually make a calculation about the potential costs and benefits of their action. Cost calculations for helping involve both the costs to the helper and the needs of the victim.

Helpers may be willing to endure higher costs to themselves if the costs to the victim of not receiving help are extremely high (Dovidio et al., 1991; Piliavin et al., 1981). Jennifer Byer realized that Colin would likely die if she did nothing. This potential cost was so great that she was willing to risk falling into the frozen river herself to prevent it.

Bystanders often consider several kinds of costs to themselves in emergency situations. First, bystanders consider the cost of giving direct help. This includes the costs to them if they offer help—lost time, exposure to danger, expenditure of effort, exposure to disgusting experiences, and the like. Second, bystanders consider the cost of not giving help. Costs borne by the bystanders if the victim receives no help include the burden of unpleasant emotional arousal while witnessing another's suffering and the costs associated with one's personal failure to act in the face of another's need (self-blame, possible blame from others, embarrassment, and the like). The greater the cost of giving direct help, the less likely one is to offer assistance (Darley & Batson, 1973).

Helping can also be financially costly. Research shows that income is positively related to financial giving, meaning that the more money someone has, the more they will give away. However, poor people tend to give a much larger portion of their income to charity than wealthy people do. They also tend to engage more in other types of prosocial behavior (Piff et al., 2010), in part because they are more attuned to the needs of others and their own experiences of need foster compassion for others who are suffering.

## BYSTANDER INTERVENTION IN EMERGENCY SITUATIONS

Some of the earliest and most interesting social psychological research on helping was inspired by the tragic murder of a young woman named Catherine (Kitty) Genovese. Shortly before 3:20 a.m. on March 13, 1964, Kitty was attacked near her apartment in Queens. An influential *New York Times* article published soon after Kitty's death described a number of neighbors who heard Kitty screaming and did little or nothing to intervene in the 35 minutes between her first scream and a single call to the local police station. According to the article, 37 people had witnessed the stalking and stabbing but they had done little to help Kitty.

Later investigations suggest that far fewer people had actually been eye-witnesses to the stabbing and many assumed what they heard was a domestic dispute. More people also claim to have called the police and a young woman went barreling down the stairs to try to help Kitty after her assailant left, holding her until the police arrived. Despite these differences that emerged between the initial account and what people now believe about

Genovese's death, the initial article's narrative about a neighborhood that did nothing as a young woman was brutally attacked was instrumental in social psychologists' understanding of bystander intervention (Gallo, 2015). The tragic story quickly became front page news in New York and across the country, setting off a flurry of social psychological research. The fundamental questions raised by Kitty's murder were, "Under what conditions will bystanders and witnesses intervene in an emergency and give help?" and, "Why do people help in some emergency situations but not in others?"

## The Decision to Intervene

The term **bystander intervention** denotes a (quick) response by a person witnessing an emergency to help another who is endangered

Would you intervene in this knife fight? High potential costs inhibit bystander intervention in this fight. Most bystanders would feel little responsibility for either man and would wish to avoid entanglement in the fight that is still in progress. © Cathy Yeulet/123rf

by events. Whether and how to intervene in an emergency is a complex decision because providing assistance often places the helper in considerable danger. These decisions require integration of a great deal of information about self and the environment. Given the often short time frame to process that information, it is relatively easy for the decision-making process to break down, thus preventing emergency intervention.

Latané and Darley (1970) produced a five-step model of this decision-making process. If any of these steps fail, the decision-making process ends and the bystander does not provide assistance.

1. The bystander must notice the situation. Some studies have manipulated how preoccupied potential helpers were, and unsurprisingly, those who were more caught up in their own thoughts were less likely to notice the emergency situation and, therefore, less likely to respond (Darley & Batson, 1973).

2. Once the bystander has noticed the situation, they must interpret it as an emergency. Most emergency situations are quite ambiguous, and failure to interpret them as emergencies will produce inaction among bystanders.

3. The bystander must decide that they have some personal responsibility in the situation. If bystanders interpret the situation to be "none of their business" or that it is someone else's responsibility to intervene, they will not respond.

4. The bystander must believe that they know how to help. Sometimes, the assistance required is something very simple, like dialing 911 for assistance. Other times, the situation is more complex. When witnessing an epileptic seizure, most people have no idea how to respond, and so they do nothing. People with medical training are much

more likely to attempt to provide assistance at accident sites than are those without medical knowhow (Cramer, McMaster, Bartell, & Dragna, 1988).

5. The bystander must make the decision to act. Even if all of the first four conditions are fulfilled, people often will hesitate to act because they are afraid of negative consequences to themselves. Typically, people engage in some kind of risk calculation before they act in emergency situations (Fritzsche, Finkelstein, & Penner, 2000). For example, we are often hesitant to break up a fight between other individuals because we are afraid of getting hurt accidentally—or even that the two combatants will turn on us.

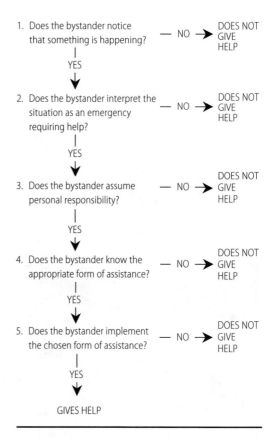

**FIGURE 11.1** Decisions Leading to Intervention in an Emergency

## The Bystander Effect

In emergency situations, potential helpers are influenced by their relationship to other bystanders (Dovidio, 1984; Latané & Darley, 1970). This influence is apparent at each step in the decision-making process. To investigate the nature of bystander influence, researchers conducted a variety of laboratory studies that simulated emergencies of one kind or another (see Chapter 2). For instance, in an early experiment (Latané & Rodin, 1969), participants heard a loud crash from the room next door, followed by a woman screaming, "Oh my God, my foot! I . . . can't move it. Oh my ankle. I . . . can't get this thing off me." In another experiment (Darley & Latané, 1968), participants engaged in a discussion over an intercom suddenly heard someone in the group begin to choke, gasp, and call for help, apparently gripped by an epileptic seizure.

In each experiment, the number of people who were supposedly present when the emergency occurred varied. Participants either believed they were alone with the victim or that one or more bystanders were present. Time and again, the same finding emerged: as the number of bystanders increased, the likelihood that any one of them would help decreased (Latané & Nida, 1981). Bystanders helped most often and most quickly when they were alone with the victim. In other words, simply knowing that other potential helpers were also present inhibited intervention in an emergency. Furthermore, as the number of bystanders increases, the likelihood that any one bystander will help a victim decreases. Social psychologists termed this the **bystander effect**.

Theorists have identified several distinct processes that contribute to the bystander effect. These include social influence regarding the definition of the situation, evaluation apprehension, and diffusion of responsibility (Latané, Nida, & Wilson, 1981; Piliavin et al., 1981). Each of these processes affects specific steps in the decision-making process.

**Interpreting the Situation.** One important element of emergencies is the ambiguity of the situation. In retrospect, the Kitty Genovese situation does not seem that ambiguous at all, but in the heat of the moment, people are often not certain how to respond to unusual situations. Was she really stabbed? Is this a domestic argument that is being dramatized to embarrass one party? Is she acting as bait so the two of them can mug someone else? These and other questions delay reactions and stall a decision to act. During that pause, people look to the reactions of others for cues about what is going on and how to react. If others appear calm, the bystander may decide that nothing special is happening or that whatever is happening requires no help. Likewise, the failure of others to act may signal to the bystander that there is no appropriate way to help. In this way, they inhibit each other from helping.

Bystanders often try to appear calm, avoiding overt signs of worry until they see whether others are alarmed. Through such cautiousness, onlookers unintentionally encourage one another to define the situation as not problematic. The larger the number of apparently unruffled bystanders, the stronger their inhibiting influence is on one another. This effect is illustrated in Figure 11.2, using data from an experiment in which a false epileptic seizure was portrayed.

Because bystanders often suppress intervention by influencing the definition of the situation with their reactions, research suggests that the number of bystanders does not inhibit individual helping when reactions reveal that others are indeed alarmed (Darley, Teger, & Lewis, 1973) or when the need for help is so unambiguous that others' reactions are unnecessary to define the situation (Clark & Word, 1972).

**Evaluation Apprehension.** Bystanders are not only interested in others' reactions; they also realize that other bystanders are an audience for their own reactions. As a result,

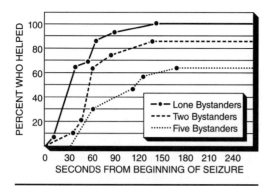

## FIGURE 11.2 The Bystander Effect

Students who were discussing, via intercom, their adjustment to college life heard one participant begin to choke, then gasp and call for help, as if he were undergoing a serious nervous seizure. Students intervened to help the victim most quickly and most often when they believed they were the lone bystander to witness the emergency. More than 90 percent of lone bystanders helped within the first 90 seconds after the seizure. Among those who believed other bystanders were present, however, fewer than 50 percent intervened in the first two minutes and fewer than 70 percent did so even after four minutes. The bystander effect refers to the fact that the greater the number of bystanders in an emergency, the less likely any one bystander will help.

*Source:* Adapted from Darley & Latané, "Bystander Intervention in Emergencies: Diffusion of Responsibility," *Journal of Personality and Social Psychology*, 8, 377–383. Copyright 1968 by the American Psychological Association.

bystanders may feel evaluation apprehension—concern about what others expect of them and how others will evaluate their behavior. Evaluation apprehension can either inhibit or promote helping. On the one hand, evaluation apprehension increases bystanders' reluctance to step in and help because they fear that others will view their intervention as foolish, inappropriate, or wrong. On the other hand, evaluation apprehension promotes helping if there are no cues to suggest that other witnesses oppose intervention or if there is a sense of mutual awareness that some intervention is necessary (Schwartz & Gottlieb, 1976). Evaluation apprehension affects step 4 (choosing

a way to react or help) and step 5 (deciding whether to implement a chosen course of action).

**Diffusion of Responsibility.** When one and only one bystander witnesses an emergency, the responsibility to intervene is focused wholly on that individual. But when there are multiple bystanders, the responsibility to intervene is shared, as is the blame, if the victim is not helped. Therefore, a witness is less likely to intervene when others are present. The process wherein a bystander does not take action because others share the responsibility for intervening is called **diffusion of responsibility**. In the decision sequence, diffusion of responsibility operates primarily as step 3 (bystander decides whether they have the responsibility to act).

Diffusion of responsibility occurs only when a bystander believes that the other witnesses are capable of helping. We are less likely to expect witnesses who are too far away to take effective action or who are too young to cope with the emergency to help (Bickman, 1971; Ross, 1971). However, the tendency to diffuse responsibility is particularly strong if a bystander feels less competent than others who are present. Bystanders helped less, for example, when one of the other witnesses to a seizure was a premed student with experience working in an emergency ward (Pantin & Carver, 1982; Schwartz & Clausen, 1970).

## SEEKING AND RECEIVING HELP

Although the bulk of this chapter focused on giving help rather than receiving it, recipients' reactions to receiving help—and people's willingness to seek help in the first place—are important topics that also deserve attention. It seems obvious that the expected response to helping is gratitude and appreciation. But that is not always the case. In fact, help can elicit resentment, hostility, and anxiety.

## Help and Obligation

When help is sought and received, resources are transferred from one person to another. If the norm of reciprocity is salient in the situation, the person receiving help may feel obligated or indebted to the helper (Greenberg & Westcott, 1983). In consequence, needy persons (in non-emergency situations) sometimes experience a dilemma. On the one hand, they can ask for help and possibly endure some embarrassment or social obligation; on the other hand, they can suffer through the difficulties of trying to solve their problems on their own (Gross & McMullen, 1983). In cases in which the recipient has the opportunity and ability to reciprocate, there may be no problem. But in cases in which this is more difficult, it may create a lingering sense of indebtedness in the needy toward the helper (Nadler, 1991; Wills, 1992), and they may develop resentment and negative sentiments toward the benefactor (Clark, Gotay, & Mills, 1974; Gross & Latané, 1974). One way to discharge this negative affect that stems from being unable to reciprocate directly is to pay it forward in some way to protect one's self-image (Alvarez & Leeuwen, 2015).

## Threats to Self-Esteem

In studying people's reactions to receiving help, theorists have proposed that an important determinant of whether help is appreciated or resented is the extent to which the help undermines the recipient's self-esteem (Nadler, 1991; Nadler & Fisher, 1986; Shell & Eisenberg, 1992). Although helping provides relief, it can also impair a recipient's self-esteem and sense of self-reliance. The avowed purpose of food stamps, for instance, has been to aid impoverished individuals and to help families escape hunger while they establish themselves as self-supporting. Yet food stamps and other forms of assistance are sometimes stigmatized. Intentionally or otherwise, helpers may communicate the message that those who need and accept help are inferior in status and

ability because they fail to display self-reliance and achievement (DePaulo & Fisher, 1980; Rosen, 1984). Efforts to police benefits and restrict the foods that food stamps can purchase exacerbate these perceptions (Lister, 2015). Furthermore, accepting benefits challenges the norm of self-reliance—an expectation that individuals should take care of themselves and their dependents. Thus, potential recipients can feel embarrassed, which can deter some who qualify for such benefits from requesting them (Haynes-Maslow et al., 2015). Similarly, students might be reticent to ask for help for fear that their professor or peers will consider them incompetent or unintelligent.

## Similarity of Help Provider

Surveys regarding help seeking for personal and psychological problems indicate that we are most likely to ask people who are similar to us for assistance (Wills, 1992). However, the helper's similarity to the recipient is a complex factor in help giving and help seeking. Help that implies an important inadequacy is often more threatening to our self-esteem when we receive it from those who are similar to us in attitudes or background than from those who are dissimilar (Nadler, 1987; Nadler & Fisher, 1984). You may be more embarrassed to get statistics tutoring from a fellow sociology major than you would be from a graduate student seeking a Ph.D. in mathematics. People who accept aid from helpers similar to themselves on a task central to their self-concept report lower self-esteem, less self-confidence, and more personal threat than when they accept aid from dissimilar helpers (Nadler, Halabi, Harapz-Gorodeisky, & Ben-David, 2010).

## OTHER FORMS OF PROSOCIAL BEHAVIOR

Although much of this chapter focused on helping specific others, there are more organizationally based forms of prosocial behavior that are also of interest to social psychologists. This final section highlights two specific types: philanthropy and volunteering.

## Philanthropy

Charitable giving, or philanthropy, includes both small-scale donations (dropping your change in the plastic container at the grocery store counter) or large monetary donations (making a large gift to endow an annual scholarship at your local university). Such giving is particularly prevalent in churches and religious organizations, in which there is a tithing norm that encourages members to donate 10 percent of their income to charity or the church. In part because of the large amount of religious charitable giving, the United States is considered a "giving culture" (Wright, 2001). However, researchers suggest that this culture is sustained, in part, because people in the United States tend to feel that they have something to gain by giving, whether tax credits and deductions, enhanced social status, or something else.

People are more likely to give when certain factors are present. In addition to some discussed earlier (for example, an awareness of need and perceptions of deservingness), research suggests that individuals are more motivated to donate money when they are directly asked to contribute. In other words, we are more likely to give when we are approached and made aware of the opportunity to give (Bryant, Jeon-Slaughter, Kang, & Tax, 2003). We are also more likely to give when the organization who needs contributions reflects values that are similar to our own (Wiepking, 2010) and when we feel that our gift can make an important difference (Parsons, 2003). Giving not only helps charitable organizations but has also been shown to result in an enhanced mood—"a warm glow"—after giving (Meier, 2006).

## Volunteering

Volunteering—freely giving time for the benefit of another person, group, or organization—also benefits organizations (Wilson, 2000). It has four distinct attributes that set it apart from other forms of prosocial behavior: *longevity* (it is usually institutionalized, ongoing, and quite often repeated), *planfulness* (it is thought out before being done), *nonobligatory* (it is not motivated by a concern for a specific individual with whom one has a relationship), and is done in *an organizational context* (most volunteering is not an individual acting alone) (Penner, 2002).

Certain qualities of individuals make them much more likely to volunteer. For example, greater social integration—being embedded in social networks—increases both the chances that someone will be asked to volunteer and their likelihood of agreeing to do so (Penner, Dovidio, Piliavin, & Schroeder, 2005). Being socially integrated might also give individuals greater awareness of problems that need attention. Research also suggests that those who are married, religious, and/or well educated are more likely to volunteer, as are women and those of higher social classes (Wilson, 2000; Wilson & Janoski, 1995; Wilson & Musick, 1997). Although findings are mixed, it appears that volunteering is beneficial to one's health, particularly mental health and well-being (Greenfield & Marks, 2004).

## SUMMARY

Prosocial behavior is any behavior that helps others. Helping is a specific type of prosocial behavior that benefits specific others. Altruism, another kind of prosocial behavior, is voluntary behavior intended to benefit another with no expectation of external reward. This intent is an important component of altruism.

**Motivation to Help.** Actors often engage in some kind of calculation of costs and benefits before engaging in prosocial behavior and will often help others for some type of reward (egoism). However, helping without intention of benefit (altruism) typically stems from humans' ability to experience empathy.

Prosocial behavior may also be passed from parent to child through evolutionary processes that enhance the persistence of an individual's genes in future generations. Even self-sacrifice can be beneficial in perpetuating one's genes if targeted at those who share genetic material. If the net costs are too high, however, they will not act.

**Helpers and Targets.** Many characteristics of individuals affect the chance of receiving help from another. Acquaintanceship and liking can increase the chances of helping behavior. Similarity between helpers and targets can substantially increase the chances of helping behavior. Potential helpers also consider whether the target deserves help. Innocent individuals are more likely to receive help.

**The Contexts of Prosocial Behavior.** External factors, both norms and situational influences, can have powerful effects on prosocial behavior. We are more likely to help those who are dependent on us (the norm of social responsibility) and those who have helped us in the past (the norm of reciprocity). Personal norms that facilitate helping and determine how we help are often related to salient role and social identities, including gender. The presence of a model who demonstrates prosocial behavior facilitates helping and an audience can increase the likelihood of someone helping, particularly if they hope to build or repair a reputation. However, moods have mixed effects. In deciding when to help, we weigh the benefits and costs both to the persons in need and to ourselves. Individuals can learn about the costs and benefits through a social learning process.

**Bystander Intervention in Emergency Situations.** Prior to actually giving help in emergencies, bystanders go through a decision sequence. A bystander must realize that something is happening, interpret the situation as an emergency, decide that they have the responsibility to act, know or recognize

an appropriate form of assistance, and decide to implement the chosen behavior. Ambiguous social situations cause participants to look for cues that might lead toward helping. The *bystander effect* occurs when persons depending on others for these cues can fail to provide help while everyone waits for cues from others that action is required. The more observers there are to an emergency, the less likely any one person is to act because of a diffusion of responsibility.

**Seeking and Receiving Help.** Help is not always sought after or easily accepted by the targets because they are sometimes reticent to bear the obligations the help entails and because the assistance may threaten their self-esteem. The more similar a target is to a helper, the more embarrassing it may be to accept assistance.

**Other Forms of Prosocial Behavior.** Volunteering and philanthropy are prosocial behaviors that tend to benefit organizations rather than individuals.

### *Critical Thinking Skill: Creative Thinking*

Throughout this book, you have been exposed to research that may or may not relate to your personal experience. Although it might be interesting to you, you might ask what you can or cannot do with that information in your own life.

Take, for example, research suggesting that heterosexual married couples who engage in prosocial behaviors, like small acts of kindness and displays of respect and affection, and who are willing to forgive each other's faults or mistakes, experience more marital satisfaction and are less likely to imagine divorcing their partner (Dew & Wilcox, 2013). You likely know people who are married, so you could share this information with them in hopes of improving their relationship or helping to explain why they are so happily married. But could it have further-reaching influence? What might you take from it if you are not married?

To engage in critical creative thinking, we search for alternative applications of what we have learned.

The most obvious application would be to nonmarried couples. Whether cohabiting or simply dating, whether heterosexual or same-sex, these same behaviors from the Dew and Wilcox (2013) study likely strengthen intimate relationships and lessen the chances of either person imagining ending the relationship. Can you think of examples of this?

But what about other types of relationships? Can you use these findings and the basis for them to enhance your platonic friendships or to create a better relationship with your mother or your daughter? What types of kindnesses, displays of respect, and forgiveness would be applicable in those relationships? What about your relationships with your neighbors or coworkers? Could you share the findings with your employer to help them think of ways they might increase employee satisfaction and reduce turnover?

Scientists often use this type of creative thinking to consider what questions to explore next. A sociologist reading this research might consider recruiting a sample of same-sex couples and asking similar questions to determine whether the relationship between prosocial behaviors and relationship satisfaction and commitment was as strong or perhaps stronger in those couples (Carrington, 1999). However, even if you are not planning to conduct your own research, you can still benefit from this creative thinking. Considering alternative applications not only helps you understand the material but also encourages you to engage with the world in a deliberate way.

# AGGRESSION

## LEARNING OBJECTIVES

By the end of this chapter you will be able to:

- Understand what motivates people to act aggressively.

- Describe the characteristics of aggressors, targets, and situations that influence aggression.

- Evaluate potential ways to reduce the frequency of aggressive behavior in individuals and society.

- Examine important contemporary issues in interpersonal aggression, specifically those related to sexual assault and the link between media and violence.

## INTRODUCTION

- In November 2011, four young men assaulted a 15-year-old girl at a party. One of the boys took pictures of the assault that he passed on to his friends and their fellow schoolmates. The photos soon made their way onto social media websites, including Facebook. The girl in the photo, Rehtaeh Parsons, was taunted by her peers. She was bombarded with texts and messages. Some called her a slut, others asked to have sex with her, some claimed she only cried rape because she regretted that her actions became public. In April of 2013, unable to handle the bullying anymore, Rehtaeh committed suicide.
- Under investigation for murdering his wife, Josh Powell was allowed a supervised visit with his two young sons, Charlie, 7, and Braden, 5. As soon as the social worker and his children pulled up to his rental house, the boys ran toward the front door, anxious to see their father. Powell let the boys in, locked the social worker out, and proceeded to attack the boys with a hatchet. As the social worker called authorities to report Powell for locking her out, Powell set the house on fire, killing his sons and himself in a murder-suicide.
- On the morning of December 12, 2012, a young man shot his mother in the head as she slept in her bed. He then drove to Sandy Hook Elementary, a school he had attended as a boy. After breaking in to the locked school and main office, he killed the principal, school psychologist, and lead teacher. He then entered a first grade classroom, killing the teacher and all but one of the children. Meanwhile, Rick Thorne, the school custodian, ran through the school, locking open doors, and clearing hallways. At the end of the rampage, the gunman had killed 20 children, 6 staff-members, and himself, leaving no indication of what motivated him.

These disturbing incidents are stark demonstrations of persons' ability to inflict pain and death on others. This chapter focuses on how social psychology can help us understand these incidents and the many acts of aggression that occur in the United States and throughout the world.

Defining aggression seems simple: aggression is any behavior that hurts another, whether physically or emotionally. But, thinking about this further, you likely recognize that it is not the outcome so much as the intention that is important. For example, would you consider a surgeon an aggressor if a heart transplant patient died on the operating table despite heroic efforts to save the patient's life? Following Krebs (1982), we define **aggression** as any behavior *intended* to harm another person (the target). Importantly, this harm must be something the target wants to avoid. According to this definition, a bungled assassination is an act of aggression, whereas

American culture tends to associate physical violence with aggression and ignores psychological and emotional abuse as additional types of aggression. If social service agencies and others can broaden individuals' conception of abuse, they can encourage more victims to seek help. © SolStock/iStock

heart surgery—approved by the patient and intended to improve their health—is clearly not aggression, even if the patient dies.

Aggression should not be equated with physical violence. Aggressive actions vary widely. The intended harm may be physical, psychological, or social—ranging from homicide or battery, to emotional abuse and cyberbullying, to active neglect or harming a target's reputation.

## AGGRESSION AND THE MOTIVATION TO HARM

As the examples in the introduction show, human beings have a remarkable capacity to harm others—even those they love or are expected to protect. Why do people turn against others? What motivates human aggression? There are at least four possible answers: (1) people are instinctively aggressive; (2) people become aggressive in response to frustrating events; (3) people experiencing negative emotion aggress against others; and (4) people learn to use aggression as a means of obtaining what they want. This section considers each of these in turn.

## Aggression as Instinct

A deep history of psychological thought, going back at least to Sigmund Freud (1930, 1950), has considered aggression to be a basic human **instinct**—that is, an innate behavior that seems to emerge even without socialization or training. To Freud, the innate urge to destroy is as natural as our need to breathe. This instinct constantly generates hostile impulses that demand release. We often release these hostile impulses by aggressing against others, but we can also turn violently against ourselves (suicide) or suffer internal distress (physical or mental illness).

If our aggressive impulses are innate, that means they must be passed to us through our genetic code and are a result of long evolutionary processes. According to Lorenz (1966, 1974), the aggressive instinct has evolved because it contributed to an animal's survival. For instance, in many species, the strongest and most aggressive animals occupy the top positions in the group's social hierarchy. To fight for position in this hierarchy is adaptive in a Darwinian sense, for it gives the animal control over food, shelter, and other resources needed to survive as well as access to mating partners.

Proponents of instinct theories are pessimistic about the possibility of controlling human aggression. At best, they believe, aggression can be channeled into approved competitive activities such as athletics, academics, or business. In these types of activities, there are social rules to govern the expression of aggression intended to prevent competition from degenerating into destructiveness. Quite often, however, socially approved competition stimulates aggression: football and hockey players start throwing punches, soccer fans riot violently, and businesspeople destroy competitors or cheat the public through ruthless practices.

Although the propensity for aggression can be passed through human generations and aggression is common in social life, most social psychologists have not seen instinct theories of aggression as particularly useful. One reason is that generalizing findings about animal behavior to human behavior is hazardous. Moreover, cross-cultural studies suggest that human aggression lacks two characteristics that are typical of instinctive behavior in animals—universality and periodicity. The need to eat and breathe, for example, are universal to all members of a species. Aggression, in contrast, is not universal in humans. It pervades some individuals and societies but is virtually absent in others. Thus, our biological makeup provides only the capacity for aggression, not an inevitable urge to aggress.

## Frustration-Aggression Hypothesis

A second possible explanation for aggressive behavior is that aggression is an internal state that is elicited by certain events. The most famous view of aggression as an elicited drive is the **frustration-aggression hypothesis** (Dollard et al., 1939). This hypothesis asserts that (1) every frustration leads to some form of aggression and (2) every aggressive act is due to some prior frustration. In contrast to instinct theories, this hypothesis states that aggression is instigated by external, environmental events.

In one early demonstration (Barker, Dembo, & Lewin, 1941), researchers showed children a room full of attractive toys. They allowed some children to play with the toys immediately while others were made to wait 20 minutes. The children who waited behaved much more destructively during play, smashing the toys on the floor and against the walls. Here, aggression is a direct response to **frustration**—that is, to the blocking of a goal-directed activity. By blocking the children's access to the tempting toys, the researchers frustrated them. This, in turn, elicited an aggressive drive that the children expressed by destroying the researchers' toys. More recent research suggests that the link between frustration and aggression may be an important cause for the positive link between some video games and violence. More competitive games and activities tend to increase aggressive behavior, supporting the role of frustration—from losing in a competitive situation—on increasing aggression (Adachi & Willoughby, 2013).

Several decades of research have led to modifications of the original hypothesis (Berkowitz, 1978). First, studies have shown that frustration does not always produce aggressive responses (Zillmann, 1979)—frustrated individuals often restrain themselves due to fear of punishment (Catalano, Novaco, & McConnell, 1997) or concerns about damaging their reputation (Haidt, 2012). Second, aggression can occur without prior frustration (Berkowitz,

Aggressive acts often stem from frustration. Both the mother who yells at her children and a coach who yells at a referee do so because they are frustrated, one with her children fighting and the other with the referee's call. *Left*: © asiseeit/iStock *Right*: © Steve Debenport/iStock

1989). The ruthless businessperson or scientist may attempt to sabotage competitors due to the desire for wealth and fame, even though the competitors have not blocked their goal-directed activity.

The frustration-aggression hypothesis implies that the nature of the frustration influences the intensity of the resulting aggression. Two factors that intensify aggression are the strength and the arbitrariness of frustration.

**Strength of Frustration.** The more we desire a goal and the closer we are to achieving it, the more frustrated and aroused we become if blocked. If someone cuts ahead of us just as we reach the front of a very long line, our frustration will be especially strong and result in a more aggressive response than if we were further back. Researchers demonstrated this with a field experiment (Harris, 1974). They had confederates cut ahead of people in lines at theaters, restaurants, and grocery checkout counters. The confederate cut in front of either the second or the twelfth person in line. Trained observers recorded the reactions of the person. As predicted, people at the front of the line responded more aggressively. They directed more than twice as many abusive remarks toward the confederate than people at the back of the line.

Cases of "road rage" also exemplify the frustration-aggression hypothesis and the relationship between the intensity of frustration and intensity of aggression. Road rage most commonly occurs when one motorist engages in a behavior that causes frustration in another driver, blocking the driver's attempt to reach a goal, such as arriving on time for an appointment or securing an available parking spot. This frustration may lead to many types of aggression. Social psychologists distinguish between driver aggression (honking, tailing, making obscene gestures) and driver violence (chasing the other car or its driver, throwing objects, or shooting at them). Mild frustration tends to cause the former, whereas stronger frustration

causes the latter. Research finds that men and women are equally likely to report engaging in driver aggression in response to frustrating events, but only men reported driver violence (Hennessy & Wiesenthal, 2001).

**Arbitrariness of Frustration.** People are also apt to feel more hostile when they believe the frustration is arbitrary, unprovoked, or illegitimate than when they attribute it to a reasonable, accidental, or legitimate cause.

In a study demonstrating this principle, researchers asked students to make appeals for a charity over the telephone (Kulik & Brown, 1979). The students were frustrated by refusals from all the potential donors (in reality, confederates). In the legitimate frustration condition, potential donors offered good reasons for refusing (such as "I just lost my job"). In the illegitimate frustration condition, they offered weak, arbitrary reasons (such as "charities are a rip-off"). As shown in Figure 12.1, individuals exposed to illegitimate frustration were more emotionally aroused than those exposed to legitimate frustration. They also directed more verbal aggression against the potential donors.

### Aversive Emotional Arousal

Research suggests that negative experiences tied to something other than frustration may also cause aggression (Averill, 1983). Legitimate actions by others and unavoidable accidents can trigger aggressive reactions. Physical pain, such as stubbing one's toe, and verbal and physical attacks could arouse us and elicit an aggressive response. Insults—especially those involving traits that we value, perhaps intelligence, honesty, ethnicity, or attractiveness—may also provoke aggression. Bullying by classmates contributed to Columbine and other more recent school shootings by students.

Accidents, attacks, and insults tend to increase aggression because they all arouse **aversive affect**—negative emotion that people seek to

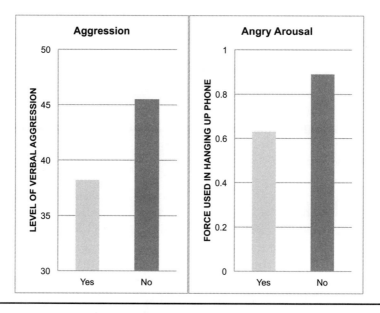

**FIGURE 12.1** Effect of Legitimacy of Frustration on Aggressive Responses

*Source:* Adapted from "Frustration, Attribution of Blame, and Aggression" by Kulik and Brown, Journal of Experimental Social Psychology, 15: 183–194. Copyright 1979, with permission from Elsevier.

reduce or eliminate (Berkowitz, 1989). When persons act aggressively in response to this negative affect, the aggression is often instrumental. That is, it is intended to reduce or eliminate the cause of the affect. Often, this aversive affect is anger, but it can be pain or other types of discomfort. For example, one of the reasons violence is higher in the summer months is because the higher temperatures produce discomfort and people look for a way to discharge this aversive affect (Anderson, Anderson, & Deuser, 1996). Turning on the air conditioner, yelling at your little sister, kicking the dog, or shooting someone who insults you are instrumental actions to deal with the discomfort.

Aggression resulting from aversive affect is called **affective aggression**. Affective aggression is more common among persons who believe that acting aggressively will make them feel better (Bushman, Baumeister, & Phillips, 2001). If someone believes that acting aggressively will not decrease the negative affect, they will engage in other instrumental actions to try to decrease the discomfort and related emotions.

**Social Learning and Aggression**

**Social learning theories** provide a fourth explanation for aggressive behavior. Two processes by which aggression can be learned are **imitation** and **reinforcement**.

**Imitation.** Many people learn their aggressive behaviors by observing others commit aggressive acts and then enacting these same behaviors themselves. In one experiment, children observed an adult playing with a five-foot-tall, inflated rubber Bobo doll (Bandura, Ross, & Ross, 1961). In one experimental condition, the adult engaged in aggressive behavior toward the doll, including punching and kicking it and sitting on it. These actions, accompanied by the shouting of aggressive words and phrases, continued for nine minutes. Later, each child was intentionally frustrated and then left alone in a room with various toys, including a smaller Bobo doll. The children who had observed the aggressive model were much more aggressive toward the doll than those who had observed a non-aggressive model. They engaged in aggressive behavior such as kicking the doll and made comments similar to those they had observed.

Many children learn aggressive behavior from their parents. Children who are spanked or slapped for transgressions are learning that if someone's behavior breaks rules or makes you angry, it is okay to punish them physically. A longitudinal study of 717 boys found that boys who experienced harsh parenting practices at ages 10 to 12 were more likely to be involved in violent dating relationships at age 16 (Lavoie et al., 2002). Much of the other aggressive behavior within the family—including psychological, sexual, and emotional abuse—can also be explained with social learning theory (Abbassi & Aslinia, 2010). People who abuse their intimate partners or children often grew up in families in which they either witnessed or were the targets of abuse. Growing up in a family in which some members abuse others teaches the child that not only is it acceptable to engage in physical and psychological aggression but that occupants of certain roles—such as husbands, girlfriends, or children—are appropriate targets for aggression.

**Reinforcement.** A social learning theory account for aggression suggests such responses are acquired and maintained—like any other social behavior—through experiences of reinforcement and reward (Bandura, 1973). Individuals learn early on that aggression can be associated with desired outcomes, thereby reinforcing the behavior. Muggers may attack a person to take their money. One child knocks down another to obtain the toy they desire. Students bully other students to gain esteem or deference from their peers.

Significant others are an important source of reinforcement. In a study of college students, researchers found that men and women embedded in social networks of friends, family, partners, and others who condone or reward violence in intimate relationships were significantly more

likely to engage in dating violence (Sellers, Cochran, & Branch, 2005). Even if we do not consciously consider the rewards we might gain, we can learn that aggression leads to individual gain, thus reinforcing the behavior.

## CHARACTERISTICS OF TARGETS THAT INFLUENCE AGGRESSION

The preceding section introduced four potential sources of a motivation to aggress. Once aroused, such motives incline us toward aggressive behavior. Whether aggression occurs, however, also depends on the characteristics of the **target**—the person toward whom the aggressive behavior is directed. In this section, we discuss four target characteristics related to aggression: gender and race, attributions for the aggressor's attack, and retaliatory capacity.

### Gender and Race

Aggression does not occur at random. If it did, we would observe aggressive behaviors by all kinds of people directed at targets of both genders, all ethnic groups, and all ages. In fact, aggression is patterned. Most notably, aggressive behavior usually involves two people of the same race or ethnicity. This is true of aggression within the family, as most families are racially and ethnically homogeneous, but it is also true of violent crimes such as assault, sexual assault, and murder. Table 12.1 reports FBI murder statistics that demonstrate this within-race tendency.

The relationship between aggression and gender depends on the type of aggressive behavior. Most murders and **aggravated assaults**—an attack by one person on another with the intent of causing bodily injury—involve two men. As Table 12.1 reports, men were responsible for almost 90 percent of murders, of both men and women, committed in 2013.

In cases of abuse within the family, both genders are targets. Boys and girls are equally likely to be abused by a parent. Women abuse their

**TABLE 12.1**  Race, Ethnicity, and Sex of Murder Victim by Race, Ethnicity, and Sex of Offender, 2013

| | TOTAL | RACE OF OFFENDER | | | ETHNICITY OF OFFENDER | | | SEX OF OFFENDER | |
| --- | --- | --- | --- | --- | --- | --- | --- | --- | --- |
| | | WHITE | BLACK | OTHER | HISPANIC/ LATINO | NOT HISPANIC/ LATINO | UNKNOWN | MALE | FEMALE |
| *Race of Victim* | | | | | | | | | |
| White | 3,005 | 83.5% | 13.6% | 1.6% | 17.7% | 31.4% | 50.8% | 87.7% | 8.7% |
| Black | 2,491 | 7.6% | 90.1% | 0.8% | 3.0% | 32.4% | 64.5% | 88.5% | 10.0% |
| Other | 159 | 20.1% | 16.9% | 60.4% | 6.3% | 39.6% | 54.1% | 89.5% | 9.9% |
| *Ethnicity of Victim* | | | | | | | | | |
| Hispanic/Latino | 588 | 82.6% | 14.8% | 0.8% | 74.7% | 20.9% | 4.4% | 92.2% | 7.0% |
| Not Hispanic/ Latino | 1,891 | 46.4% | 49.1% | 0.9% | 8.0% | 88.4% | 3.6% | 90.3% | 8.7% |
| Unknown | 3,244 | 42.9% | 51.9% | 2.7% | 0.9% | 1.1% | 98.0% | 86.6% | 11.0% |
| *Sex of Victim* | | | | | | | | | |
| Male | 3,976 | 43.7% | 52.1% | 2.5% | 11.5% | 31.5% | 56.9% | 88.1% | 10.3% |
| Female | 1,679 | 59.0% | 36.2% | 3.7% | 9.4% | 33.4% | 57.0% | 90.2% | 8.7% |

*Source:* FBI Homicide Data, 2013.

*Note:* This table is based on incidents where some information about offenders and victims is unknown by law enforcement. Because of the small numbers, when the offender sex and race are reported as unknown these data are excluded from the table. However, data on unknown ethnicity is included because these numbers are much larger.

romantic partners as often as men abuse theirs (Archer, 2006). However, the types of abuse are different. Although men and women are equally likely to engage in *aggressive* behavior, men engage in significantly more *violent* behavior. Women are more likely to slap, kick, bite, or to try to hit their partner with an object. Men are more likely to beat up their partner and to push, grab, or shove. Because of these different tactics, men are more likely to cause injury to their partner—including same-sex partners—than women (Archer, 2000). Women are also more likely to be killed by a current or former intimate partner than men. In fact, women who are murdered are more likely to be killed by an intimate partner (once again, current or former) than another family member, friend, acquaintance, or stranger (Cooper & Smith, 2011). Similar patterns of intimate partner violence (IPV) are found among Black, Latino, White, and multiracial women, but rates are significantly higher among Native Americans and lower among Asian and Pacific Islanders (Tjaden & Thoennes, 2000).

These patterns suggest that the display of aggression is channeled by social beliefs and norms. Beliefs and norms in U.S. society encourage men to direct physical and sexual aggression toward women and other men. For example, masculine gender norms encourage men to be dominant over women (Connell, 2005). These gender norms also associate masculinity with status and toughness, motivating men to use aggression to gain the respect of others (Thompson & Pleck, 1986). Men in our society frequently compete with each other for various rewards, such as influence or status in a group, companionship, or other symbols of success. These competitions often lead to insults that provoke anger or direct physical challenges. There are norms in some groups, cultures, or subcultures that require men to defend themselves in such situations. For example, observers have often described the American South as having a norm that requires men to defend themselves against insults—a "culture of honor" (see Box 12.1).

## BOX 12.1 Research Update: The Culture of Honor

Students were milling around the cafeteria of Spring High School—just outside of Houston, Texas—before school on a September morning. Some were eating breakfast, others catching up on their homework, many simply talking with friends before the first bell rang. Just outside the cafeteria, Joshua Broussard "bumped" into Luis Alfaro as he moved through the crowded hallway. The two exchanged words. Moments later, Alfaro pulled out a knife and attacked Broussard. As students scattered, Broussard collapsed in the school hallway and died.

The attack at Spring High School is not unusual. A large number of the homicides that occur in any given year are triggered by arguments, and many of these disputes are over trivial matters, including offensive comments or name calling. However, what is most interesting about the incident is its similarity to a series of social psychological experiments conducted 20 years earlier on the "culture of honor" (Cohen, Nisbett, Bowdle, & Schwarz, 1996).

In those experiments, both "Northerner" and "Southerner"[1] students from the University of Michigan were invited to the laboratory for what they believed was an experiment on response times and human judgment. Upon arrival, they were asked to fill out initial paperwork and take it to a table at the end of a long, narrow hallway. Unbeknownst to the participants, the experimental treatment actually occurred during the walk to this table. As some of the participants made their way down the hallway, a confederate bumped the unsuspecting student and called him an "asshole." Observers situated in the hallway, ostensibly working on their homework, made note of the participants' responses. Participants then participated in a series of judgment tasks to gauge their reactions to the incident.

Comparisons of the reactions of Southerners and Northerners supported the idea of a "culture of honor" in the South. Social scientists argue that individuals from places with a "culture of honor" are more likely to perceive a benign incident as an interpersonal threat. Furthermore, once offended or insulted, those who accept a "culture of honor" will feel the need to restore honor by retaliating against the insult. Sure enough, Southerners who were bumped by the confederate were more likely to see the insult as a cause for anger rather than amusement and to see violence as an appropriate reaction to an "affront." Whereas Northerners were able to brush off the insult and remain unaffected, Southerners who were insulted were primed for aggression and would act out if given the right stimulus. Later studies found that Southerners were also more prepared to aggress on a physiological level, with higher cortisol and testosterone levels than Northerners who had also been insulted.

A tremendous amount of research on the culture of honor conducted since these early studies supports these findings. Social psychologists more recently considered this concept in relation to school violence and found that high school students in culture-of-honor states—including Texas—were more likely to bring a weapon to school and were at higher risk of school shootings than were students in other states (Brown, Osterman, & Barnes, 2009). Although many attributed the tragedy at Spring High to gang violence, the culture of honor may have also played an important role in the events of that September morning.

[1] Students were classified as "Southern" if they lived in one of the following states for at least six years: Delaware, Maryland, West Virginia, Virginia, North Carolina, South Carolina, Georgia, Florida, Kentucky, Tennessee, Alabama, Mississippi, Arkansas, Louisiana, or Texas. All other students, except those who lived in Washington, DC, were considered "Northern." On average, those classified as "Southern" had lived 87 percent of their lives in the South, whereas those classified as "Northern" had spent only 4 percent of their lives in the South.

## Attribution of Intent

Direct attacks, both verbal and physical, often produce an aggressive reaction. Nevertheless, we withhold retaliation when we perceive that an attack was not intentional (Krieglmeyer, Wittstadt, & Strack, 2009). We are unlikely to respond aggressively, for example, to a man crashing his grocery cart into our car in the parking lot if we realize he was trying to save a child from an oncoming car. However, to redirect aggression, we must first realize the man's intention. We are much more likely to aggress, and to aggress more strongly, following harm when we attribute the attack to the actor's intentions rather than to accidental or legitimate external pressures (De Castro et al., 2002).

The general aggression model (Anderson & Bushman, 2002), based on a dual-process model (see Chapter 1), proposes that after an initial immediate appraisal (or attribution) of an attack or hostile situation, a reappraisal of the situation only occurs if there are sufficient resources (for example, time or cognitive capacity) and the initial appraisal is somehow deemed unsatisfactory or incomplete.

These appraisals and related attributions have important implications for responses to aggression. In one study of 70 abused women, some living with a violent partner blamed themselves for the abuse. They attributed it to their incompetence, unattractiveness, or talking back to the partner. Other women blamed situational factors, such as their partner's stress. The women most likely to leave their abusive partners were those who blamed him—rather than themselves or the situation—for the abuse (Andrews & Brewin, 1990).

An important influence on attributions is whether an attacker apologizes. An apology often states or implies that the harm another caused was unintentional. In one study, an experimenter made mistakes that caused the participant to fail at the tasks. When the experimenter apologized, the participants

refrained from acting aggressively toward her (Ohbuchi, Kameda, & Agarie, 1989). However, it is important for the apology to be perceived as authentic. When victims feel an apology is inauthentic or forced, this can actually increase retaliatory aggression (Struthers et al., 2008; Zechmeister, Garcia, Romero, & Vas, 2004).

One way that apologies may lessen resulting aggression is by providing additional information—accounts of external causes of the offending action—that facilitate a reappraisal. For example, in one study where respondents received negative feedback on an essay—ostensibly from a fellow student, but actually a programmed response—they were significantly less aggressive when they were told that the rater had just broken up with their partner than when they were not given an explanation (Barlett & Anderson, 2011). However, it is important to note that as the severity of the harm increases, the effectiveness of apologies decreases.

Some individuals are more likely to make hostile attributions of intent than others, particularly in situations where another's intentions are ambiguous. Potential risk factors for young people include being rejected by one's peers or subjected to harsh parenting practices (De Castro et al., 2002).

## Retaliatory Capacity

One of the qualities of the target that one considers in calculating the costs (and benefits) of aggression—and therefore whether to behave aggressively—is the likelihood of retaliation.

In one experiment testing the effect of possible retaliation on aggressive behavior, participants were told that they would deliver electric shocks to another person, but that they could select the shocks' intensity. In one condition, participants were told that after they delivered the shocks, the experiment would be over. In another condition, participants were told that after they had delivered shocks, they would change places with the other person. In other words, they would be in a position in which the other person would be delivering shocks (and could retaliate). Participants in the latter condition delivered significantly less intense shocks than in the former condition (Prentice-Dunn & Rogers, 1980). These findings help explain why anonymous cyber-bullying is described as more severe than nonanonymous forms of bullying (Sticca & Perren, 2013). In May 2017, Yik Yak, a popular school gossip and messaging app with an anonymous platform had to close down, in part because of its inability to control rampant bullying and harassment. Bullies may be inclined to engage in more aggressive acts when they use fake aliases or post on anonymous websites because the risk of retaliation is significantly smaller.

Threat of retaliation may also be responsible for instances of **displaced aggression**—defined as aggression toward a target that exceeds what is justified by provocation by that target. Displaced aggression often occurs because aggression instigated by a threatening source is displaced onto a less powerful or more available target who had no responsibility for the initial response (Umberson, Williams, & Anderson, 2002). Displaced aggression is a common explanation for aggression directed toward partners, children, or pets—"She is taking her bad day out on us."—but does it actually occur? A meta-analysis of social psychological research on the subject provides substantial evidence that displaced aggression is quite real (Marcus-Newhall, Pedersen, Carlson, & Miller, 2000). Individuals who score high in displaced aggression (see Box 12.2) self-report higher rates of domestic abuse and road rage (Denson, Pedersen, & Miller, 2006). Displaced aggression may partially account for higher incidences of domestic violence in poor and working-class households (Umberson, Anderson, Glick, & Shapiro, 1998), as frustration with a lack of control over events outside the home, whether related to work or in other interactions, ends up directed toward

family members (see the discussion of spillover from work to home in Chapter 17). Similar processes can also help explain why children who are bullied are more likely to be bullies themselves (Salmivalli & Nieminen, 2002).

Research on displaced aggression also finds that the more negative the insult, attack, or frustration and the more similar the instigator and the target (in appearance, group membership, and so forth), the greater the likelihood that displaced aggression will occur (Marcus-Newhall et al., 2000) and the less regret and/or more satisfaction an aggressor will experience (Sjöström & Gollwitzer, 2015).

## SITUATIONAL IMPACTS ON AGGRESSION

A number of specific characteristics of situations make aggression more likely. Five covered in this chapter are potential rewards, presence of models, norms, stress, and aggressive cues.

### Potential Rewards

Three types of rewards that promote aggression are direct material benefits, social approval, and attention.

The material benefits that armed robbers and human traffickers obtain by using violence support their aggression. If the material benefits are reduced—say, by vigorous law enforcement—this type of aggressive violence will decline.

Social approval is a second common reward for aggressive acts. Although aggression is generally condemned, virtually every society has norms that approve aggression against particular targets in particular circumstances. Soldiers are honored for shooting the enemy in war and children are praised for defending their siblings in a fight.

Attention is the third type of reward for aggressive acts. The teenager who taunts or bullies a classmate basks in the spotlight of attention from peers, even as they are reproached

## BOX 12.2 Test Yourself: Displaced Aggression

Although nearly everyone has engaged in displaced aggression—taking anger out on someone or something other than the person or object that triggered the aggression—there are people who appear particularly prone to do so. They possess a displaced aggression personality trait. In 2006, a group of social psychologists developed and tested a displaced anger questionnaire (DAQ) to determine individuals' propensity for displaced aggression. Below are some of the items from the DAQ.

For each statement below, choose how characteristic the statement is of you, ranging from extremely characteristic to extremely uncharacteristic:

1. "Sometimes I can't help thinking about times when someone made me mad."

   Extremely characteristic    1   2   3   4   5   6   7    Extremely uncharacteristic

2. "I move on to other things after an anger episode has happened."

   Extremely characteristic    1   2   3   4   5   6   7    Extremely uncharacteristic

3. "When someone or something makes me angry, I am likely to take it out on another person."

   Extremely characteristic    1   2   3   4   5   6   7    Extremely uncharacteristic

4. "When feeling bad, I take it out on others."

   Extremely characteristic    1   2   3   4   5   6   7    Extremely uncharacteristic

5. "When angry, I have taken it out on people close to me."

   Extremely characteristic    1   2   3   4   5   6   7    Extremely uncharacteristic

6. "Sometimes I get upset with a friend or family member even though that person is not the cause of my anger or frustration."

   Extremely characteristic    1   2   3   4   5   6   7    Extremely uncharacteristic

7. "I take my anger out on innocent others."

   Extremely characteristic    1   2   3   4   5   6   7    Extremely uncharacteristic

8. "If someone made me angry, I would tell them how I feel."

   Extremely characteristic    1   2   3   4   5   6   7    Extremely uncharacteristic

9. "When things don't go the way I plan, I take out my frustration on the first person I see."

   Extremely characteristic    1   2   3   4   5   6   7    Extremely uncharacteristic

10. "Sometimes I get so upset by work or school that I become hostile toward family or friends."

    Extremely characteristic    1   2   3   4   5   6   7    Extremely uncharacteristic

11. "If I have had a hard day at work or school, I'm likely to make sure everyone knows about it."

    Extremely characteristic    1   2   3   4   5   6   7    Extremely uncharacteristic

12. "After being irritated or annoyed, I am extremely short-tempered for the rest of the day."

    Extremely characteristic    1   2   3   4   5   6   7    Extremely uncharacteristic

**Scoring:** First, change your scores on #2 and #8 to the reverse (1 = 7, 2 = 6, 3 = 5, 5 = 3, 6 = 2, 7 = 1), as they were reverse coded so that higher scores demonstrate lower levels of displaced anger. Add your scores for each of your responses and divide them by 12 (or the number of questions you answered) to determine your average. For most age groups, an average greater than 4.2 suggests a displaced aggression trait. An average score of 1.8 or less suggests low displaced aggression propensity and a score between 1.9 and 4.1 suggests an average propensity.

*Source:* Adapted from Denson, Pedersen, & Miller (2006).

by school authorities. Research conducted in elementary school classrooms shows that even though aggressive children are generally disliked by their peers, the aggressive behavior at school is positively reinforced with laughter and interest from classmates (Powers & Bierman, 2013).

## Modeling

A second situational factor that increases aggression is the presence of behavioral models. Just as aggressive behavior is learned by observing and then imitating a model (Bandura, Ross, & Ross, 1961), a model's aggressive behavior in a specific situation may encourage others to behave in similar ways. This "peer contagion" (Dishion & Dodge, 2005) has been found not only among elementary students and teenagers but also among adults.

Just as the previous chapter discussed the importance of models in demonstrating types of helping acts that are possible, aggressive models demonstrate possible negative behaviors. Aggressive models provide three types of information that influence observers. First, models demonstrate specific aggressive acts that are possible in a situation. Second, models provide information about the appropriateness of aggression—about whether it is normatively appropriate in a setting. Finally, models provide information about the consequences of acting aggressively.

In 2016, a series of clown sightings that started in South Carolina spread through the United States, into Canada, and throughout the world. Law enforcement largely blamed social media and the viral sharing of pictures and videos of clowns in unexpected places like school grounds or wooded areas. The notoriety of these clowns, coupled with their success in wreaking havoc and shutting down schools with few arrests or consequences, encouraged others to follow suit and the spread of sightings increased. Not surprisingly, observers are more likely to imitate aggressive behaviors that yield some type of reward and avoid punishment.

These models matter little when observers are not motivated to do harm. But people who feel provoked and who are suppressing any urge to aggress often lose their inhibitions after observing an aggressive model. They are the most likely to imitate aggression. In other words, the news coverage of school shootings like Columbine is unlikely to cause an observer who is not motivated to do harm to consider bringing a gun to school or to hurt a classmate. However, such coverage might provoke someone who has an underlying urge to harm their peers by showing them that lashing out violently at school is not only possible but also perhaps both common and rewarded through mass media attention (Coleman, 2004). Concerns about "copycat" shooters and suicides is one reason for a push to end the nonstop media coverage of these events, particularly coverage focused on the shooter rather than the victims.

## Norms

Just as there is a positive norm of reciprocity (see Chapter 11), there is also a *negative norm of reciprocity*. This norm—"an eye for an eye, a tooth for a tooth"—justifies retaliation for attacks. Research on the culture of honor (see Box 12.1) suggests that the belief that one should respond to an attack on one's family property or self with aggression—and even killing—varies across cultural groups. There is also evidence that men are more likely to endorse this honor ideology than women are (Barnes, Brown, & Osterman, 2012). Such norms influence behavior.

The negative reciprocity norm requires that the retaliation be proportionate to the provocation (Taylor, 1967). In an experiment on this norm, participants engaged in a competitive reaction time task in a laboratory. After each trial, the faster person could direct a noxious blast of noise at the slower person (Bushman, Baumeister, & Stack, 1999). The experiment was rigged so the participant received the noise on one-half of the trials (randomly selected) and could deliver noise on the other half. Over time, the participant increasingly matched the noise level delivered to them—clear evidence of reciprocity.

In the heat of anger, however, we are likely to overestimate the strength of another's provocation and to underestimate the intensity of our own response. Fear has similar implications (Toch, 1996). When angry or fearful, we are more likely to misinterpret responses that have no aggressive intent as intentional provocation. Thus, even when people strive to match retaliation to provocation, aggression may escalate. The Black Lives Matter movement argues that stereotypes like those discussed in Chapter 7—including that Black men are aggressive, threatening, or criminal—may exacerbate perceptions of provocation. This not only leads police officers to infer greater threat from Black men, but also to respond with excessive, and sometimes deadly, force.

## Stress

Stress also increases the likelihood of aggressive behavior. Social stressors, such as chronic unemployment and the experience of discrimination are related to aggression because of their effects on frustration and negative affect like anger and fear. During the Great Recession, unemployment and economic hardship were positively related to intimate partner violence and controlling behavior. The effect was particularly pronounced in periods or places of rapid job loss that evoked uncertainty or fear (Schneider, Harknett, & McLanahan, 2016).

There are several other sources of stress within couples that may lead to IPV. Some potential stressors include: a short relationship duration (that is, the couple doesn't know each other well), a mismatch in gender role definitions (one has traditional views, the other more progressive views), substance abuse, and large numbers of children. These are related to intimate violence in part

through their relationship to more frequent disagreements as well as a more heated disagreement style that causes disagreements to escalate (DeMaris et al., 2003). This process of escalation occurs, in part, because the longer an argument or fight continues, the more likely each person is to introduce past grievances rather than focusing solely on the issue at hand. The negative mood evoked also elicits memories associated with previous negative emotions that enter awareness.

Stress can also stem from living conditions. Research finds that IPV is more frequent and more severe in economically disadvantaged neighborhoods (Benson & Fox, 2004), even among those who are better off financially than their neighbors (Fox & Benson, 2006). These same processes suggest, though, that neighborhood characteristics can also reduce intimate violence. Research linking survey data, census data, and homicide data for the city of Chicago found that, even in disadvantaged neighborhoods, if residents share a sense of collective efficacy (for example, "people in this neighborhood can be trusted") and a sense that neighbors could be counted on, rates of intimate violence were lower (Browning & Cagney, 2003). Such sentiments could be interpreted as indicators of lower levels of stress stemming from the neighborhood environment.

Other situational stressors can also produce high levels of aggression. Several studies have shown that temperature is related to the occurrence of a number of violent crimes, including assault, sexual assault, murder, and riots (Anderson et al., 2000). As discussed earlier in this chapter, this is, in part, because temperatures increase discomfort and feelings of hostility (Anderson, 2001). Research finds that climate controls like air conditioning have the potential to curb heat-related violence, but access to such technologies is not uniform and their reach is limited (Rotton & Cohn, 2004). Interestingly, taking into account the time of day—because more crime occurs at night, but temperatures tend to be lower then—rates of violence peak at a temperature between 80 and 90 degrees (Cohn & Rotton, 2005). Temperatures beyond that lead to reduced violence, perhaps because people want to escape the heat and break off interaction with others (Cohn & Rotton, 1997).

Heat also influences aggression indirectly by increasing the prevalence of aggressive thoughts that may subsequently lead to aggressive behavior. Researchers found that exposure to words related to hot temperatures (sunburn, boils, roasted, hot, sweats), regardless of the actual temperature in the laboratory, resulted in more aggressive thoughts and hostile perceptions than exposure to either cold (frostbite, freezes, cold, shivers) or neutral words unrelated to temperature (DeWall & Bushman, 2009).

## Aggressive Cues

Situations that produce aggression often start out in ways that are ambiguous to those involved in them. Should that insult be interpreted as a good-natured joke or a challenge to a man's masculinity? Is a jovial conversation between your boyfriend and another woman perfectly innocent, friendly banter, or an unwelcome attempt at flirting? Observers and participants involved in such incidents need help from the environment to figure out what is happening and how they should respond.

Aggressive cues in the environment can increase the likelihood of an aggressive response (Berkowitz, 1989). These cues may intensify the aggressive motivation or lower inhibitions even if they are not directly involved in the immediate situation. For example, people who have been aroused or frustrated respond more aggressively when in the presence of a gun than in the presence of neutral objects, even when the object has nothing to do with the aggression (Carlson, Marcus-Newhall, & Miller, 1990). The so-called **weapons effect** occurs when people

are already aroused. The effect involves cognitive priming; the sight of a weapon makes more accessible, or primes, aggression-related concepts or scripts for behavior (Anderson, Benjamin, & Bartholow, 1998).

**Rumination** is a self-focused attention toward one's distress and the possible causes and consequences of the distress rather than ways to overcome it. Someone who is ruminating about a negative event may respond aggressively to a mildly annoying event (Marcus-Newhall et al., 2000). If your roommate is thinking of an incident in which their professor embarrassed them in class earlier in the day as they stir the spaghetti sauce on the stove, they might snap at you for asking when they will be finished cooking. If your roommate is instead thinking of the weekend ahead, they will be more likely to simply tell you that dinner will be done in a few minutes. Ruminators could also be especially sensitive to aggressive cues or at risk of misinterpreting ambiguous information.

To test the effect of ruminating on aggression, social psychologists had a group of undergraduates participate in a three-part experiment (Bushman et al., 2005). In the first part of the experiment, the provocation phase, the participants were asked to solve difficult anagrams (for example, to unscramble NVTNIMEREON to spell ENVIRONMENT) while loud and distracting music played in the background. After a few minutes, the research assistant collected the anagram sheets, turned off the music, and left to score the sheet. When the research assistant returned, they informed the participants that their score was well below average and they really should repeat the task but added—in an exasperated tone—that repeating the first part would be a waste of time and they should just proceed to part two. For part two, a random group of participants were assigned to the rumination phase and asked to respond to a number of self-focused phrases ("what kind of person you are," "why people treat you the way they do") while others responded to externally focused or mood-enhancing phrases. In the final part of the experiment, the trigger phase, all the participants played a trivia game. When the research assistant read the trivia questions too quickly, mispronounced some of the names (pronouncing Leonardo da Vinci as Leon Divinsky), and occasionally mixed up the possible responses, participants who had been in the rumination condition reacted significantly more aggressively—recommending the research assistant not be hired for a permanent position and experiencing more negative emotions—than did those who had been assigned to the other groups in part two or who had not experienced an annoying trigger in the final part of the experiment (see Figure 12.2).

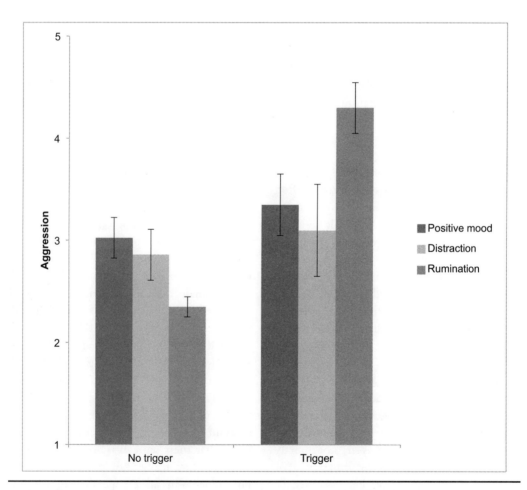

**FIGURE 12.2** The Interaction between Rumination and a Mild Annoyance on Aggression

When participants were prompted to ruminate about an aggressive provocation, a subsequent minor trigger caused a significantly more aggressive reaction than for those who were provoked but not asked to ruminate or for those who ruminated but were not exposed to the minor trigger.

*Source:* Figure 1, Bushman et al., (2005)."Chewing on It Can Chew You Up: Effects of Rumination on Triggered Displaced Aggression." *Journal of Personality and Social Psychology, 88,* 969–983.

## REDUCING AGGRESSIVE BEHAVIOR

Aggressive behavior is often costly to individuals and the groups and society to which they belong. Given the problems associated with aggressive behavior, reducing aggression has been an important topic of research. Four strategies that hold some promise and relate to previous sections of this chapter are reducing frustration, providing opportunities for catharsis, punishing aggressive behavior, and providing nonaggressive models.

### Reducing Frustration

Given that frustration is so central to aggression, we might be able to reduce aggressive behavior by reducing the frequency or strength of frustration. A major source of frustration in American society, for example, is inadequate resources. Studies comparing crime rates across different cities (e.g., Land, McCall, & Cohen, 1990) and nations (Gartner, 1990) find that economic deprivation is the best predictor for crime. Many cases of robbery, assault, and murder are motivated simply by a desire for money or property. Frustration and, therefore, aggression could be reduced if everyone had access to life's necessities.

Many of the frustrations we experience arise from conflicts with other people. Thus, another way to reduce aggressive behavior is to provide people with alternative means of resolving interpersonal conflicts. Recent innovations in dispute resolution involve the increasing use of professionally trained mediators and the training of selected community members in conflict-resolution techniques (Braithwaite, 2002). These innovations have also been implemented in schools. Conflict resolution programs using peers as mediators and training students and teachers in problem-solving methods were introduced partly in response to the rise in mass shootings (Wike & Fraser, 2009).

### Catharsis

Infuriated by a day of catering to the whims of her boss, Christina turned on her teenage son as he drove her home. "Why must you drive like a maniac?" she snapped in a fit of displaced aggression. Miguel was stunned. He was driving a sedate 35 miles per hour and had done nothing to provoke his mother's aggression. Did Christina feel better after venting her anger on Miguel? Could it reduce frustration?

Many people believe that letting off steam is better than "bottling up" hostility. A very old psychological concept captures this idea (Aristotle, *Poetics*, Book 6). **Catharsis** is the notion that one can reduce aggressive arousal by performing aggressive acts. The catharsis hypothesis states that we can purge ourselves of hostile emotions by experiencing these emotions while acting aggressively. A broader view suggests that by observing aggression as an involved spectator to drama, television, or sports, we also release aggressive emotions.

Misdirected or displaced aggression, such as kicking the dog or yelling at Miguel, seldom results in catharsis. For catharsis to occur, the aggressive act must be directed at the source of the frustration and not someone else. We also must feel that the aggression we display will be viewed as acceptable by others, and we cannot feel guilty about it afterward. In part because of these strict conditions, studies show that catharsis and venting are generally ineffective ways of reducing anger or related aggression (Augustine & Hemenover, 2009).

In fact, with few exceptions, research has shown that performing aggressive acts will increase future aggression, not reduce it (Bushman, 2002). This is true whether the initial aggression is a verbal attack, a physical attack, or even aggressive play (Bushman, Baumeister, & Stack, 1999). For example, research finds higher rates of both psychological and physical dating violence among collegiate athletes involved in contact sports (wrestling, basketball) versus those in noncontact sports (track and field, swimming) (Burns, 2009).

## Punishment

Punishment is often used to control aggression because of a widely held belief that punishment is an effective deterrent. Threats can indeed be effective in eliminating aggression (see Chapter 10), but only under certain narrowly defined conditions (Baron, 1977). For threats to inhibit aggression, the anticipated punishment must be great and the probability that it will occur very high. Even so, threatened punishment is largely ineffective when potential aggressors are extremely angry.

Actual (not just anticipated or threatened) punishment can also control aggression, but again, strict conditions must be met: (1) the punishment must follow the aggressive act promptly, (2) it must be seen as the logical outcome of that act, and (3) it must not violate legitimate social norms. Unless these conditions are met, people perceive punishment as unjustified, and this increases the likelihood that they will respond with anger or aggression.

Although research demonstrates the importance of these conditions for deterrence, the criminal justice system often fails to meet these conditions. The probability that any single criminal act will be punished is low, simply because most criminals are not caught. Even when criminals are caught, punishment rarely follows the crime promptly. Moreover, few criminals see the punishment as a logical or legitimate outcome of their act. Finally, criminals often have much to gain through their aggression. Perceived benefits are as, if not more, important than possible costs in predicting crime (Baker & Piquero, 2010). As a result, the criminal justice system is not very effective in deterring criminal aggression.

### Nonaggressive Models

Just as aggressive models may increase aggression, nonaggressive models may reduce it (Baron, 1983). Mahatma Gandhi, who led the movement to free India of British colonialism, used pacifist tactics that have since been imitated by protesters around the world. Parents and peers also serve as positive models. Parents who use nonpunitive child-rearing practices and who serve as nonviolent models help socialize children to be nonviolent adults (Anwar, Fry, & Grigaitytė, 2018). Young men who live in violent neighborhoods are less likely to connect violence with masculinity, or to be violent themselves, if they belong to a peer group that promotes nonviolence (Barker, 1998).

## AGGRESSION IN SOCIETY

Over the last two decades, there has been increasing recognition that aggressive behavior is at the heart of several major social problems. This awareness is due, in part, to the widespread publicity given to certain incidents like school shootings and other mass murders. But, fortunately, mass murders are rare. Much more common are other types of interpersonal violence, in which one person directs physical aggression toward another with the intent to injure or kill the target. The #metoo movement is working to bring increased attention to this type of aggression.

This final section of this chapter discusses three specific aspects of interpersonal violence. First, it looks at the causes and consequences of sexual assault. Next, it examines the impact of pornography on sexual assault. Finally, it discusses whether television programming and video games contribute to violence.

### Sexual Assault

**Sexual assault** is an umbrella term for "any type of sexual contact or behavior that occurs without the explicit consent of the recipient," including rape, incest, forcible sodomy or fondling, child molestation, and attempted rape (U.S. Department of Justice, 2017). Women are ten times more likely to be victims of sexual assault than men and 99 percent of reported cases involve a male offender (Breiding et al., 2014). Although most of the victims of sexual assaults by men are women, men—particularly incarcerated men—also report being assaulted by other men (Stemple & Meyer, 2014). Like other forms of assault, most cases involve offenders and victims from the same racial or ethnic group.

There are a number of motivations for sexual assault. In some cases, the offender is motivated by sexual desire. In other cases, the offender's intent is to dominate, humiliate, or injure the victim. Sexual assault is one form of sexual aggression; sexual aggression is really a continuum, ranging from the use of bribes through verbal pressure, the intentional use of alcohol or drugs, physical force, and kidnapping, to sexual murder (Jewkes, Sen, & Garcia-Moreno, 2002). As an example of gender differences on the sexual aggression continuum, in a study of sexual coercion among new members of fraternities and sororities, men were as likely as women to report being coerced into unwanted sexual contact. However, only women reported being physically forced to do so (Larimer, Lydum, Anderson, & Turner, 1999).

Sexual aggression stems from a variety of factors. One is a specific set of cultural beliefs and practices that create conditions encouraging rape. In a rape-prone society, the sexual assault of women by men is allowed or overlooked (Sanday, 1981, 2003). Rape-prone societies share several characteristics. First, there are high levels of interpersonal violence. Second, there is an ideology of male dominance that subordinates women, suggesting that women are the property of men and should be subject to men's control. Third, men and women are regularly separated (during religious rituals, for

example) in rape-prone societies. The United States is a rape-prone society. Rates of violent crime are high. Men continue to dominate women politically, economically, and sexually despite measurable shifts toward gender equality. There is also a continuing separation of men and women in certain spheres (athletic programs, workplaces).

Rape-proneness has also been applied to college campuses. Researchers find that when fraternities or men's dorms are allowed to have parties, whereas sororities and women's dorms are not, men are able to structure the party and control the movement and behavior of their guests (Boswell & Spade, 1996). Men also regulate and distribute the alcohol, an important factor in sexual assault on college campuses (Logan, Walker, Cole, & Leukefeld, 2002). With men as hosts, women are also expected to be nice and to defer to men in interaction, ultimately supporting male dominance in the situation and contributing to the rape-prone environment of campus parties (Armstrong, Hamilton, & Sweeney, 2006). Particular beliefs and values support a *rape culture*, where both men and women come to see sexual violence as given rather than something that can be controlled or eradicated (Buchwald, Fletcher, & Roth, 2005).

**Perpetrators of Sexual Assault.** Of course, despite the importance of cultural characteristics, beliefs, and values, ultimately individuals, rather than societies or cultures, commit sexual assault. Therefore, a second approach to determining the causes of sexual assault is to identify characteristics that may help account for sexually aggressive behavior (Malamuth, Sockloskie, Koss, & Tanaka, 1991). Research suggests that some men are sexually aggressive—that is, they rely on aggressive behaviors in their relationships with women (Malamuth, Heavey, & Linz, 1993). These men tend to score highly on measures of the desire to dominate women, hostility toward women, and distrust of women. They also have a variety of attitudes that facilitate aggression toward women, including more traditional gender attitudes and an acceptance of rape myths (see Box 12.3) (Burt 1980; McMahon, 2010). These men have an impersonal view of sex, where it is detached from emotional closeness. They prefer casual sex to long-term, monogamous relationships and see sex as a game to win (DeGue & DiLillo, 2004). They also tend to be sexually aroused by portrayals of rape (Check & Malamuth, 1983) and are prone to misperceiving women's friendliness as sexual interest (Abbey, McAuslan, & Ross, 1998).

Men's tendency to be sexually aggressive is stable over time. Researchers collected data on 423 young men, including measures of hostility toward women and attitudes supportive of violence. Ten years later, they reinterviewed a number of the men and their female partners (Malamuth et al., 1995). The characteristics measured ten years earlier predicted later reports of sexual aggression from both men and their partners. This research suggests that men who commit sexual assault have learned a script for interactions that includes the use of verbal abuse or physical force to exercise influence over or obtain sexual gratification from a woman (Huesmann, 1986). Research suggests that this script is learned in childhood (Jacobson & Gottman, 1998), likely when the child observes aggression frequently, is reinforced for aggressive behavior, and is the victim of physical, sexual, or emotional abuse (Romano & De Luca, 2001). Once learned, this script is used to regulate behavior in various situations.

In addition to specific gender attitudes and experiences, research suggests alcohol consumption and abuse are also significant predictors of the perpetration of sexual violence (Carr & VanDeusen, 2004). In experimental studies on the relationship between alcohol and sexual aggression, researchers administer alcoholic or nonalcoholic beverages to participants in the laboratory to explore its effect in particular situations. In one experiment, researchers exposed sober and intoxicated men to the same rape scenario—where a man used force to have sex with an acquaintance. Results showed that men who had been drinking found the male character's use of force more acceptable and could imagine themselves acting in a similar manner (Abbey, 2011). Importantly, the effect of alcohol was strongest for men who possess characteristics that predispose them to sexual violence (e.g., hostility toward women, impersonal view of sex, and others introduced earlier in this section).

**Victims of Sexual Assault.** Victims of sexual assault are primarily women between the ages of 15 and 24. Some women—although an overwhelming minority of all victims—are assaulted by men they do not know. These assaults by strangers often occur outdoors, in parks, deserted parking lots, or in the victim's residence. The offenders in these cases are often opportunistic, attacking any woman who is available or appears to be vulnerable.

Much more often, women are assaulted by someone they know. This may be a man they are dating, or a neighbor, coworker, or friend. The victims in most sexual assault cases are young, single women—often high school or college students. A recent study found that 78 percent of unwanted sexual contact on a college campus took place while "hooking up" (Flack et al., 2007). White students tend to be more involved in rape-prone fraternities on campus and in the hook-up culture, putting them at a higher risk of sexual assault than are other racial groups on campuses (Armstrong, Hamilton, & Sweeney, 2006). However, what is perceived as a higher risk could simply be the result of Whites being more likely to report rape than members of other racial groups.

Alcohol does not only affect perpetration of sexual assault, but also victimization.

## BOX 12.3  Test Yourself: Rape Myths

Among the causes of sexual aggression are cultural beliefs that encourage rape. These beliefs are *rape myths*—prejudicial, stereotyped, and false beliefs about rape, rape victims, and persons who commit rape (Burt, 1980). Examples of these myths are "She asked for it," "He didn't mean to," and "It wasn't really rape." These beliefs create a climate that encourages sexual assault and is suspicious of and hostile toward victims.

Various scales have been designed to assess these beliefs (e.g., Burt, 1980). Below are some of the items from a scale specifically intended for college students (McMahon, 2010).

Read each statement and circle the appropriate response: Strongly Agree (SA), Agree (A), Don't know (?), Disagree (D), or Strongly Disagree (SD).

1. If a girl goes to a room alone with a guy at a party, it is her own fault if she is raped.

   **SA  A  ?  D  SD**

2. If a girl doesn't physically fight back, you can't really say it was rape.

   **SA  A  ?  D  SD**

3. When girls go to parties wearing slutty clothes, they are asking for trouble.

   **SA  A  ?  D  SD**

4. It shouldn't be considered rape if a guy is drunk and didn't realize what he was doing.

   **SA  A  ?  D  SD**

5. If both people are drunk, it can't be rape.

   **SA  A  ?  D  SD**

6. Rape happens when a guy's sex drive goes out of control.

   **SA  A  ?  D  SD**

7. A lot of times, girls who say they were raped agreed to have sex and then regret it.

   **SA  A  ?  D  SD**

8. Rape accusations are often used as a way of getting back at guys.

   **SA  A  ?  D  SD**

9. If a girl doesn't say "no" she can't claim rape.

   **SA  A  ?  D  SD**

10. When guys rape, it is usually because of their strong desire for sex.

    **SA  A  ?  D  SD**

**Scoring:** Scores for each question range from 1 (strongly agree) to 5 (strongly disagree). Scores should be totaled for a cumulative score. Higher scores indicate greater rejection of rape myths. A man with a lower score likely believes that if he engages in sexual activity with a woman who comes home with him on the first date after they have both been drinking, it is not rape even if she offers some resistance. This is one of the dangers of rape myths. They provide scripts that legitimize sexual activity to which the woman may not have overtly consented. Another type of rape myth—that claims of rape are not true—is related to rape culture environments where such claims are not believed and, therefore, sexual assault is not punished. The above scale captures five types of myths: "She asked for it" (1, 3), "It wasn't really rape" (2, 9), "He didn't mean to" (6, 10), "Alcohol is to blame" (4, 5), and "She lied" (7, 8).

There have been many studies on the correlates of endorsing rape myths. One review summarizes the findings of 72 studies (Anderson, Cooper, & Okamura, 1997). Men, older people, and persons from lower socioeconomic backgrounds are more likely to hold such attitudes. Acceptance of rape was associated with traditional beliefs about gender roles, an adversarial view of male–female relationships, and conservative political beliefs. These results are consistent with the theory that rape myth acceptance is the result of socialization to gender types and conservative beliefs.

Alcohol is a factor in more than half of all sexual assaults (whether involving alcohol consumption by the perpetrator, victim, or both) (Abbey, 2002). Both surveys and experiments provide evidence that people are more likely to engage in risky behavior—including entering a risky situation—when they have been drinking. In fact, some men use alcohol or drugs intentionally to make a woman more likely to take risks voluntarily (Abbey et al., 2001).

When responsibility for a sexual assault is placed on the victim rather than the perpetrator, it is referred to as **victim-blame**. Those engaged in victim-blame argue that a woman's flirting or provocative dress can somehow lead a man to believe that a woman is consenting to sexual contact or intercourse. Men tend to perceive more sexual intent in women's behavior than other women do (Farris, Treat, Viken, & McFall, 2008).

Victims internalize many of the same cultural beliefs that perpetrators do regarding sexual assault. According to one survey of 14- to 17-year-olds, teenagers of both genders believe that a man is justified in forcing a woman to have intercourse if she gets him sexually excited, leads him on, or has dated him for a long time (Goodchilds & Zellman, 1984). Other influential cultural beliefs include that men cannot stop once they have started to become sexually aroused, that husbands cannot rape their wives, and that women actually enjoy rape (Edwards et al., 2011; Ryan, 2011).

Misperceptions and cultural beliefs influence women's interpretation of forced, non-consensual sexual activity. Many women who experience sexual assault do not perceive the experience as rape (Kahn, Mathie, & Torgler, 1994). This may be because their experience—being assaulted by someone they know during a date after some sexual foreplay—does not match their script for rape: a violent attack by a stranger (Ryan, 1988). In one study, researchers asked women to write a description "of events before, during, and after a rape" and to describe their past experiences with assault. There were some women who reported that they had been forced to have sex but who also replied "no" to the question, "Have you ever been raped?" These women were more likely to describe rape as an attack by a stranger than were women who reported that they had been raped. Similarly, women's script for a loving relationship is one of equality and romance, which encourages individuals to overlook their partner's bad behavior, with an emphasis on male rather than female sexual drive (Lloyd & Emery, 2000). An experience of aggression does not fit this script and so it may be ignored (see Chapter 7). The #metoo movement attempted to change the script, thus encouraging more victims to come forward to share their stories and experiences.

## Pornography and Violence

On August 1, 2013, Ariel Castro was sentenced to life plus 1,000 years for the kidnapping, rape, and assault of three women whom he held captive in his home in Cleveland, Ohio. At the sentencing hearing, Castro blamed his behaviors on an addiction to pornography and joined a growing number of perpetrators—including Ted Bundy, a serial murderer who confessed to killing at least 24 young women—who have used pornography addiction as a defense for their heinous actions. Such claims generate great interest in the connection between pornography and violence, a link that social psychologists have conducted considerable research to explore (Ryan, 2011).

**Nonaggressive Pornography.** Various studies have shown that the effect of pornography on behavior depends on what the pornography portrays. Pornography that explicitly depicts adults engaging in consenting sexual activity is termed **nonaggressive pornography** or erotica. Reading or viewing nonaggressive pornography creates sexual arousal (Byrne &

Kelley, 1984), usually through the mechanism of cognitive and imaginative processing.

Nonaggressive pornography by itself does not produce aggression toward women (Donnerstein & Linz, 1998). However, when the viewer's inhibitions are lowered—as they may be if he is intoxicated—or if a man is already at risk for sexual aggression, it may do so (Vega & Malamuth, 2007). Research finds that when men are angered or frustrated and then view nonaggressive pornographic images, they show more aggressive behavior toward women (Donnerstein & Barrett, 1978). The mechanism is thought to be transfer of arousal: the sexual arousal that results from viewing pornography is added to the arousal induced by the anger, resulting in sexual aggression.

Hollywood films, while not considered pornography, increasingly include apparently consensual sexual activity that is degrading or humiliating to women. For example, a study of James Bond films found that both the sexual activity and harm to women shown in the films has been increasing steadily over time (Neuendorf et al., 2010). An experiment explored the effect of viewing scenes that objectified women. Men and women who participated in the experiment saw either selections from highly sexualized films (*9½ Weeks* and *Showgirls*) or scenes from animated cartoons. Participants subsequently read and evaluated a magazine story about a date rape or a stranger rape. Men who saw the sexualized film clips were more likely to say that the victim of the date rape enjoyed it and "got what she wanted" (Milburn, Mather, & Conrad, 2000). These results have important implications given the rise of depictions of sexual violence toward women in advertising and print media (Cortese, 2016).

**Aggressive Pornography.** Exposure to **aggressive pornography**—explicit depictions of sexual activity in which force is threatened or used to coerce a woman to engage in sex—also influences behavior, especially aggression toward women (Malamuth, 1984; Malamuth, Addison, & Koss, 2000). Unlike erotica, aggressive pornography has lasting effects on both attitudes and behavior. In a study of its effects on attitudes (Donnerstein, 1984), men viewed one of three films featuring either aggression, nonaggressive sexual activity, or aggressive sexual activity. Following the film, the participants completed several attitude scales, including one that measured acceptance of rape myths. Men who saw the films depicting aggression or aggressive sexual activity scored higher on the rape myth acceptance scale (see Box 12.3) than did men who saw the film depicting nonaggressive sexual activity. They also indicated greater willingness to use force to obtain sex. The fact that both films depicting aggression, even nonsexual aggression, affected attitudes more than the nonaggressive film suggests that it is aggression rather than explicit portrayals of sex that influences attitudes toward sexual aggression. Experimental research like this is important for demonstrating the effects of viewing pornography to counter the argument that the relationship between pornography and aggression only goes the other direction: that men who consume pornography already have aggressive tendencies toward women and are, therefore, attracted to aggressive pornography (Malamuth, Addison, & Koss, 2000). Although that certainly may be the case, exposure to pornography also influences sexual aggression.

In another experimental study (Donnerstein & Berkowitz, 1981), male participants were either angered or treated neutrally by a male or female confederate. The participants then viewed one of four films: a neutral film, a nonaggressive pornographic film, or one of two aggressive pornographic films. In the latter films, a young woman is shoved around, tied up, stripped, and raped. In one version, she finds the experience disgusting, whereas in the other she is smiling at the end. Following the film, the men were given an opportunity to aggress against a male or female confederate by delivering electric shocks. The films did not affect aggression toward the male confederate. However, participants who saw the aggressive films delivered more intense electric shocks to the female confederate. Note that aggressive films led to increased violence toward the female confederate and not the male confederate. This suggests the film created an association in the viewer's mind between the victim in the film and the woman who angered him, suggesting that women are appropriate targets and increasing aggression toward the female confederate. These films may also reduce inhibitions to aggression by suggesting that aggression directed toward women has positive outcomes.

One important question is whether we can generalize from the results of laboratory research to natural settings. Does the viewing of aggressive pornography in nonlaboratory settings contribute to violence against women? One study examined the influence of intentional exposure to X-rated material on sexually aggressive behavior among 10- to 15-year-olds (Ybarra et al., 2011). After accounting for other potential influences related to both exposure and sexual aggression (for example, substance abuse and being a victim of sexual aggression), researchers found that boys and girls who were exposed to violent X-rated material were six times as likely to report perpetrating a sexually aggressive behavior as were those who had either not viewed X-rated material or who had only been exposed to nonviolent X-rated material.

## Media Violence and Aggression

If one thing has changed about American lifestyles over the past century, it is the amount of time spent consuming entertainment and news through visual media, whether online, on television, or in theaters. These media are replete with violence, sex, and aggressive behaviors of all kinds. Given the ubiquity of media and the widespread belief that violence—sexual,

physical, and psychological—is increasing around the world, both researchers and the public are interested in the effects media exposure has on behavior.

**Violent Television and Aggression.** Evelyn Wagler was carrying a two-gallon can of gasoline back to her stalled car. She was cornered by six young men who forced her to douse herself with the fuel. Then, one of the men tossed a lighted match. She burned to death. Two nights earlier, a similar murder had been depicted on national television.

Violence pervades television. Both heroes and villains perform aggression on television. Not just humans, but also cartoon characters, torment each other in astonishingly creative ways. During prime-time television, three to five violent incidents occur per hour of programming, and 20 to 25 violent incidents occur per hour during Saturday morning children's shows (American Psychological Association, 1993). In all, 60 percent of television programs and 70 percent of the programming intended for children contains violence (Wilson et al., 2002). By age 18, the average American child is likely to have seen about 200,000 violent acts on television, including 40,000 homicides (Plagens, Miller, Foote, & Yoffe, 1991). Only one-quarter of these violent acts results in any punishment for the perpetrators (National Television Violence Study, 1996). Although research suggests that watching violent television is correlated with aggressive behavior (Anderson et al., 2003; Coyne et al., 2011), correlation is not the same as causation.

Does exposure to television violence encourage viewers to behave aggressively? Experimental research—where one group is exposed to violent media in a controlled setting while another group is not and then both groups' behavior and attitudes are measured—suggests that there is a causal connection (Comstock, 1984; Friedrich-Cofer & Huston, 1986; Murray & Kippax, 1979). This research also points to five processes that explain why exposure to media violence might increase aggressive behavior (Huesmann & Moise, 1996).

*Imitation.* Viewers learn specific techniques of aggression from media models. Social learning evidently played a role in the violent attack on Evelyn Wagler.

*Cognitive priming.* Portrayals of violence activate aggressive thoughts and pro-aggression attitudes. The activation of an attitude increases the likelihood that it will be expressed in behavior.

*Legitimization/justification.* Exposure to violence that leads to goal attainment and has positive outcomes (for example, punishes wrongdoers) legitimizes aggression and makes it more acceptable (Bushman & Huesmann, 2001).

*Desensitization.* After observing violence repeatedly, viewers become less sensitive to aggression. This makes them less reluctant to hurt others and less inclined to ease others' suffering.

*Arousal.* Viewing violence on television produces excitement and physiological arousal, which may amplify aggressive responses in situations that would otherwise elicit milder anger.

Moreover, these results have been found in experiments with boys and girls of all ages, races, social classes, and levels of intelligence as well as in many countries (Huesmann & Moise, 1996). A meta-analysis of all the research available at the time reports that virtually every study—whether cross-sectional (n = 86), longitudinal (n = 46), or experimental (n = 152)—finds a significant relationship between exposure to media violence and aggression (Anderson & Bushman, 2002). This is true of television, movies, and online media (Ybarra et al., 2008).

Violence on the Internet takes a number of forms, including violent videos, like some posted on YouTube or Snapchat, or violent images and scenarios depicted in photos and ads showing physical and sexual aggression.

Other violence online takes the form of psychological violence. "Hate pages" are devoted to harassing and degrading specific groups, and cyber-bullying runs rampant on Facebook and other social media sites. Users—particularly adolescents who are highly susceptible to peer pressure—frequently imitate this displayed aggression, both on- and offline (Ybarra et al., 2008).

However, the relationship between violent media and aggression is not one directional. A growing body of evidence suggests that the link between aggression and media usage is actually circular (Slater, Henry, Swaim, & Anderson, 2003). Because aggressive children are relatively unpopular with their peers, they spend more time watching television as well as online and playing video games. If these media experiences include violence, this exposes these young people to more violence, teaches them aggressive scripts and behaviors, and reassures them that their behavior is appropriate. When they then try to enact these scripts in interactions with others, they become even more unpopular and are driven back to television—and the vicious cycle continues.

Despite all this evidence on the connection between media violence and violent behavior, scientists have been unable to convince film and television producers to decrease the amount of violence shown in television and movies. In fact, over time, film ratings have relaxed to allow more violent content in PG-13 films than was allowed in previous years (Leone & Barowski, 2011). To approach the issue from another side, researchers have turned their attention toward developing interventions to limit the negative effects of media violence (Rosenkoetter, Rosenkoetter, & Acock, 2009).

Social psychologists have used experimental methods—both in the field and the laboratory—to test strategies that parents, teachers, and others might use to counteract the deleterious effects of violent media

(Rosenkoetter, Rosenkoetter, & Acock, 2009). Previous work suggests that aggression is lower among individuals who are high in empathy (Dean & Malamuth, 1997). Drawing on this, researchers tried to induce empathy among viewers. When adults ask children to empathize with the victim, children are less accepting of aggression and find the aggression in cartoons less humorous (Nathanson & Cantor, 2000). Adults can also reduce children's imitation of aggression by making negative comments about the violence. A neutral comment, however, is no less effective than no comment at all (Cantor & Wilson, 2003).

Interventions are most effective when they are long term. A year-long program for elementary students that emphasized the ways that television distorts the reality of aggression not only resulted in less positive attitudes about violence on television but also reduced identification with violent heroes and led children to watch less violent programming. Participating in the program also lowered aggressive behaviors among boys, who watch more violent programming than girls do (Rosenkoetter, Rosenkoetter, Ozretich, and Acock, 2004; Dodge, Coie, & Lynam, 2006).

### Violent Video Games and Aggression.

One late summer afternoon, an 8-year-old boy shot Marie Smothers, his elderly caregiver, in the back of the head as she sat in her living room watching television. Media reports claimed the shooting was intentional and blamed the violent video game *Grand Theft Auto*—which the boy had been playing just moments before he killed Smothers—for his violent actions. Although it is difficult to determine the causes of acts of aggression, research suggests that there is a relationship between both short- and long-term exposure to violence in video games and aggression (Anderson et al., 2010). Both men and women who report playing violent video games are more likely to report engaging in various

Technological advances have greatly expanded young people's access to media, including violent media, and have limited adults' knowledge of what young people are exposed to and the opportunity to discuss the images together. © wavebreakmedia/Shutterstock

aggressive behaviors (Bushman, Baumeister, & Stack, 1999).

Recent research suggests that the relationship between violent video games and violent behavior is not direct. Resulting aggression is less about imitation and more about heightened negative arousal. Technological advances have improved the sound effects and graphics, making video games more engrossing than they were in the past (Ivory & Kalyanaraman, 2007). Playing violent video games leads to both physiological (heart rate, body temperature) and emotional arousal (anger, hostility) (Anderson et al., 2010) that increase aggression. Features of games either dampen or amplify the arousing effects. For example, both more visible blood in games and controllers in the shape of a realistic gun tend to heighten arousal and hostility (Barlett, Harris, & Baldassaro, 2007; Barlett, Harris, & Bruey, 2008). Competition in video games also amplifies aggression by priming competitive schemas (Adachi & Willoughby, 2011, 2013).

Ongoing exposure to violence also desensitizes players to violence, making it seem more normal and natural (Krahé, 2013). Connecting this type of media consumption to sexual assault, research finds that playing a video game that sexualized and objectified women—with provocative dress—increased men's rape acceptance and led them to judge rape victims more negatively than did playing an identical game with fully clothed women as characters (Stermer & Burkley, 2012).

## SUMMARY

Aggression is behavior intended to harm another person that the target person wants to avoid.

**Aggression and the Motivation to Harm.** There are four main theories regarding the motivation for aggression. (1) People are instinctively aggressive. (2) People become aggressive in response to events that are frustrating. (3) People aggress against others as a result of aversive emotion. (4) People are motivated by rewards and learn to use aggression as a means of obtaining what they want.

**Characteristics of Targets that Affect Aggression.** Once aggressive motivation has been aroused, target characteristics influence whether aggressive behavior occurs. Aggressive behavior is more likely if the target is of the same race or ethnicity. The target's gender also influences the response. When we are attacked, our response is influenced by

the attributions we make about the attacker's intentions. We are less likely to engage in aggression toward a target who we believe is capable of retaliation. We may, however, engage in displaced aggression against another.

**Situational Impacts on Aggression.** Situational conditions influence aggressive behavior. Rewards that encourage aggression include material benefits, social approval, and attention. Aggressive models provide information about available options, normative appropriateness, and consequences (or lack thereof) of aggressive acts. The negative reciprocity norm encourages aggressive behavior in certain situations. Aggressive behavior is more likely when stressors, such as high temperature, are present. Aggressive behavior is also more likely in the presence of aggressive cues, especially weapons.

**Reducing Aggressive Behavior.** Frustration levels could be reduced by guaranteeing everyone the basic necessities, therefore limiting aggression motivated by rewards. Catharsis may follow aggressive acts and be seen as a way to reduce frustration, but is largely ineffective. Punishment is effective in controlling aggression only when it promptly follows the aggressive act, is seen as the logical outcome of that act, and does not violate social norms. Nonaggressive models reduce the likelihood of aggression and can offset the effect of aggressive models.

**Aggression in Society.** Interpersonal violence is a serious problem in American society. Rates of sexual assault and acceptance of the behavior are influenced by societal characteristics, such as male domination of women, and by scripts that encourage male aggression toward women. Nonaggressive pornography and aggressive pornography both influence attitudes and behavior, although the latter to a much higher degree. Experimental research shows that observing violence in film, on television, and online, increases aggressive attitudes and behavior in everyday settings. The link between video games and aggression is less direct than originally thought.

### Critical Thinking Skill:
### Applying Scientific Research
### to Policy Decisions

Gun violence in the United States has many people concerned. However, both politicians and citizens are divided on how best to curb this violence. Some argue that only police and the military should have guns, others argue that automatic weapons should be restricted or guns should be harder to purchase, while still others assert that access to guns is not the problem and that other measures should be taken. How should the average citizen or policymaker decide their stance on this critical issue? The best way to make a good decision is to use the best available scientific evidence and think clearly about it. The evidence might come from correlational methods, like field studies and surveys, or from experiments.

The current discourse around gun violence centers on access. To determine whether the widespread availability of guns increases gun violence using a correlational method, a scientist might compare rates of lethal gun violence (deaths related to gunshot wounds) in countries where gun ownership is legal to the rates in countries where citizens are not allowed to buy guns through legal channels. The researchers would then see whether there is a correlation between accessibility and lethal gun violence. Suppose the correlation is positive and significant—that is, the more accessible guns are to citizens (legal to own, easy to purchase, and so forth), the larger the number of people who die from gun-related violence each year. This evidence provides support for policies that

limit access to guns. However, because it is a correlational study, it cannot tell us whether access actually influences violence.

Another way to get at the question would be with an experiment. In a field experiment, scientists might choose two cities with similar rates of gun violence that are similar on other characteristics (racial diversity, economic inequality, education and income levels, and so forth). They would then have politicians institute a law that limited access to firearms in one of the cities. By tracking gun violence in the two cities, they could gauge whether restricting access lessened violence. However, there are a number of confounding factors that make such an experiment problematic and the findings difficult to interpret.

Alternatively, scientists could run a laboratory experiment in which they put subjects in a situation—something like a video game—in which they either had easy access to a gun or a gun was difficult or costly to acquire. The researchers could then expose subjects to frustrating situations in which they had the opportunity to use the gun or deal with their aggression in another way and then compare the likelihood that subjects would choose responses other than gun violence. Although laboratory experiments allow scientists significant control over conditions, the problem here is that it is a video game. Furthermore, in such a research setting, participants are acutely aware that their behavior is being tracked. Perhaps the findings would not generalize to a natural environment.

What are the benefits and limitations of the above studies? What are other studies you might conduct?

We can be most confident of a conclusion if there is converging evidence from multiple studies, both correlational and experimental. Considering these hypothetical studies together would give us more confidence in our ultimate decision because each study addresses some of the limitations of the others.

How can these studies inform a policy decision? At this point, a good policy decision would involve a cost-benefit analysis. Reducing citizens' access to guns might make those citizens more vulnerable to the violent attacks of others. Gun manufacturers and retailers would lose money if their only clients were police and military. These are costs. What are other costs? However, fewer gun deaths—whether accidental or intentional—would be a benefit. Are there other benefits?

In general, when making policy decisions when scientific evidence is available, we should evaluate the quality of that evidence and then weigh the costs and benefits of implementing policies based on the evidence.

# DEVIANT BEHAVIOR AND SOCIETAL REACTION

## LEARNING OBJECTIVES

By the end of this chapter you will be able to:

- Compare five major theoretical perspectives on deviance and describe several causes of deviance.

- Explain why the reactions of observers are important influences on deviance.

- Answer the question, "Why do some people repeatedly behave badly?"

- Explain the influence of gender, race, and social class on authorities' reactions to instances of deviance.

## INTRODUCTION

Megan and Hanna wandered through the boutique, stopping briefly to look at blouses and then going to the lingerie section. Each looked at several bra and panty sets. Hanna kept returning to a burgundy set priced at $69.50. Finally, she picked it up, glanced quickly around her, and dropped it into her shoulder bag.

The only other shopper in the vicinity, a well-dressed man in his 40s, saw Hanna take the clothing. He looked around the store, spotted a clerk, and walked toward her. Megan stammered to Hanna, "I, uh, I don't think we should do this."

"Oh, it's okay. Nothing will happen," Hanna replied, before walking quickly out of the store. Moments later, Megan followed her. As Hanna entered the mall, the clerk stepped up to her, took her by the elbow, and said, "Come with me, please."

Shoplifting episodes like this one occur many times every day in the United States. Shoplifting is one type of **deviant behavior**— behavior that violates the norms that apply in a given situation. In addition to crime, deviance includes, for example, cheating, substance use or abuse, fraud, corruption, delinquent behavior, harassment, and behavior considered symptomatic of mental illness.

There are two major reasons why social psychologists study deviant behavior, one theoretical and one practical. First, social norms and conformity are the basic means by which the orderly social interaction necessary to maintain society is achieved. By studying nonconformity, we learn about the processes that produce social order. For example, we might conclude that Hanna took the lingerie because there were no store employees nearby, suggesting the importance of surveillance in maintaining order. Second, social psychologists study deviant behavior to better understand its causes. Deviant behaviors such as alcoholism, drug addiction, and crime are perceived as serious threats to society. Once we understand their causes, we may be able to develop better programs that reduce or eliminate deviance or that help people change their behavior.

Norms are created by groups, organizations, and societies to encourage behaviors that contribute to social order and discourage behaviors that challenge it. Not surprisingly, citizens, politicians, and social scientists tend to focus on *negative deviance*, such as the examples listed above. But violations of norms sometimes have positive outcomes. *Positive deviance* refers to intentional behaviors that depart from the norms in honorable ways (Spreitzer & Sonenshein, 2004). Examples include outstanding athletes, musicians, and geniuses. Athletic ability, musicianship, and intelligence all range from way below to way above average (the statistical norm). Much of the material in this chapter is concerned with negative deviance. Ask yourself as we go along whether the same ideas would apply to positive deviance.

We first consider why people break rules.

## THE VIOLATION OF NORMS

When we read or hear that someone is accused of assault, or embezzling money from their employer, or hacking into confidential files, we often ask, "Why?" In Hanna's case, we would ask, "Why did she take that lingerie?" In this section, we consider first the nature of norms and then look at several theories about the causes of deviant behavior. These include anomie theory, control theory, differential association theory, and routine activities theory.

## Norms

Most people would regard Hanna's behavior in the department store as deviant because it violated social norms. Specifically, she violated laws that define taking merchandise from stores without paying for it as a criminal act. Thus, deviance is a social construction; whether a behavior is deviant or not depends on the norms or expectations for behavior in the situation in which it occurs.

In any situation, our behavior is governed by norms derived from several sources (Suttles, 1968). First, there are purely "local" and group norms. Thus, roommates and families develop norms about what personal topics can and cannot be discussed at meals. Second, there are subcultural norms that apply to large numbers of persons who share some characteristic. For example, there are racial or ethnic group norms governing the behavior of Blacks or persons of Polish descent that do not apply to other Americans. A subculture that is particularly relevant to the discussion of deviance is the subculture of violence, which will be discussed later. Third, there are societal norms, such as those requiring certain types of dress or those limiting sexual activity to certain relationships and situations. Thus, the norms that govern our daily behavior have a variety of origins, including family and friends; socioeconomic, religious, or ethnic subcultures; and the society in general.

The repercussions of deviant behavior depend on which type of norm an individual violates. Violations of local norms may be of concern only to a certain group. Failing to do the dishes when it is your turn may result in your roommate being angry, although your friends may not care about that deviance. Subcultural norms are often held in common by most of those with whom we interact, whether they are friends, family members, or coworkers. Violations of these norms may affect most of one's day-to-day interactions. Violations of societal norms may subject a person to action by formal agencies of control, such as the police or the courts. At other points in this book, we discuss the violation of local norms (see Chapter 5) and group norms (see Chapter 15). In this chapter, we focus on the violation of societal norms and on reactions to norm violations.

## Anomie Theory

Anomie is a fundamental concept in sociology. Emile Durkheim introduced the term in 1893, and employed it in his analysis of *Suicide* (1897). It refers to a weakening of the influence of social norms on individual behavior. Merton (1957) developed the **anomie theory** of deviance, suggesting that deviance arises when people striving to achieve culturally valued goals, such as wealth, find that they do not have any legitimate way to attain these goals. These people then break the rules, often in an attempt to attain these goals illegitimately.

**Anomie.** Every society provides its members with goals to aspire to. If the members of a society value religion, they are likely to socialize their youths and adults to aspire to salvation. If the members value power, they will teach people to seek positions in which they can dominate others. U.S. culture extols wealth as the appropriate goal for most members of society, and the means to happiness. In every society, there are also norms that define acceptable ways of striving for goals, called **legitimate means**. In the United States, legitimate means for attaining wealth include getting an education, working hard at a job to earn money, or starting a business, and making wise investments.

A person socialized into U.S. society will most likely desire material wealth and will strive to succeed in a desirable occupation—to become a sales rep, teacher, nurse, business executive, doctor, or the like. The legitimate means of attaining these goals are to obtain a formal education and to climb the ladder of occupational prestige (see Chapter 17). The person who has access to these means—who can afford to go to college and has the accepted skin color, ethnic background, and gender—can attain these socially desirable goals.

What about those who do not have access to the legitimate means? As Americans, these people will desire material wealth like everyone else, but they will be blocked in their strivings. Because of the way society is structured, certain members are denied access to legitimate means. Government decisions regarding budgeting, building schools, or closing schools determine the availability of education to individuals. Similarly, certain members of society are denied access to jobs. Not only individual characteristics, such as lack of education, but also social factors, such as the profitability of making autos in Janesville, WI, determine who is unemployed.

A person who strives to attain a legitimate goal but is denied access to legitimate means will experience *anomie*—a state that reduces commitment to norms or the pursuit of goals. There are four ways a person may respond to anomie; each is a distinct type of deviance. First, an individual may reject the goals, and give up trying to achieve success, but continue to conform to social norms. This adaptation is termed *ritualism*. The poorly paid stock clerk who never misses a day of work in 45 years is a ritualist. They are deviant because they have given up the struggle for success. Second, the individual might reject both the goals and the means, withdrawing from active participation in society by *retreatism*. This may take the form of drinking, drug use, withdrawal into mental illness, or other kinds of escape. Third, one might remain committed to the goals but turn to disapproved or illegal ways of achieving success. This adaptation is termed *innovation*.

Earning a living as a burglar, commercial sex worker, or drug dealer is an innovative means of attaining wealth. Finally, one might attempt to overthrow the existing system and create different goals and means through *rebellion*.

Shoplifting is a form of innovation. Like other types of economic crime, it represents a rejection of the normatively prescribed means (paying for what you want) while continuing to strive for the goal (possessing merchandise). According to anomie theory, Hanna, the shoplifter, has been socialized to desire wealth but does not have access to a well-paying job due to her poor education. As a result, she steals what she wants because she does not have the money to pay for it.

Another influence on an individual's adaptation is access to deviant roles. Using a means of goal achievement—whether legitimate or illegitimate—requires access to two structures (Cloward, 1959). The first is a **learning structure**—an environment in which an individual can learn the information and skills required. A shoplifter needs to learn how to conceal objects quickly, how to spot electronic anti-theft devices, and so forth. The second is an **opportunity structure**—an environment in which an individual has opportunities to play a role, which usually requires the assistance of those in complementary roles. Anomie theory assumes that anyone can be an innovator—through shoplifting, prostitution, or professional theft. But not everyone has access to the special knowledge and skills needed to succeed as a commercial sex worker (Heyl, 1977; World Bank, 2008) or a black-market banker (Weigand, 1994). Just as access to legitimate means to achieve goals is limited, so is access to illegitimate means. Only those who have both the learning and opportunity structures necessary to become a shoplifter, commercial sex worker, or embezzler can use these alternative routes to success (Coleman, 1987).

The opportunities for deviance available to a person depend on age, gender, kinship, ethnicity, and social class (Cloward, 1959). These

Most Americans are socialized to strive for economic success. But some people do not have access to legitimate employment, so they seek wealth by alternative, sometimes illegal means, such as commercial sex work. © RapidEye/iStock

characteristics, with the possible exception of class, are beyond the individual's control. Thus, commercial sex work in our society primarily involves young, physically attractive persons. People who do not have access to the learning or opportunity structures necessary for deviance cannot succeed either through legitimate or through illegitimate means. Such failure often produces retreatism, such as drug addiction, alcoholism, and mental illness.

We ask you to consider whether the ideas presented in this chapter apply to positive as well as negative deviance. The importance of access to learning and opportunity structures to engage in a behavior certainly does. To be an Olympic athlete, play in a major symphony, or be a headline performer, one has to first get the necessary training, i.e., have access to a learning structure. One needs a trainer/coach/teacher; it might be a parent, private instructor, or a neighborhood ensemble. One then needs the opportunity to perform, first on neighborhood or community teams or stages, then regional, etc. In some arenas, one needs the fabled "break," being discovered by a professional scout, maestro, or being available the night the star is too ill to perform. Also, in many arenas, one's age, gender, ethnicity, and social class make the difference between access and lack of access.

**Anomie and Social Class.** Anomie theory emphasizes access to education and employment. Those who have access to both should not engage in deviant behavior. Those who do not have access to one or both should experience anomie and are likely to engage in deviance. A survey of 1,614 youths aged 15 to 18 measured commitment to success goals ("making a lot of money") and perceived access to college education (Farnworth & Leiber, 1989). Respondents who said they wanted to make a lot of money but did not expect to complete college were much more likely to report delinquent behavior. Research with a sample of low-income minority ninth through twelfth graders found that those with high career aspirations were much less likely to report alcohol and substance use and risky sexual behavior (Dudovitz, Chung, Nelson, & Wong, 2017).

One measure of access to legitimate means is the unemployment rate. According to the theory, as unemployment increases—reducing access to legitimate means—rates of deviance also should increase. One study analyzed the relationship between unemployment rates and crime rates in the United States for each year of the 1948–1985 period (Devine, Sheley, & Smith, 1988). There was a strong relationship: as unemployment increases, so does crime. The relationship is stronger for economic crime (burglary) than for violent crime (murder). An analysis of increases and decreases in the homicide rate from 1970 to 2000 in major U.S. cities found that increases and decreases in relative deprivation (percentage of families living in poverty, median family income) was related to number of murders (McCall, Parker, & MacDonald, 2008). Evidence of a direct connection between unemployment and economic crime comes from a longitudinal study in which ex-addicts, ex-offenders, and "dropout" youths reported their legal and illegal income for up to three years; as the unemployment rate in the city increased, youths reported greater income from illegal activities–economic crimes (Uggen & Thompson, 2003).

Researchers have found that it is both relative and absolute socioeconomic standing that determines whether one experiences anomie. One aspect of relative deprivation is inequality compared to your neighbors. Stucky and colleagues (2016) measured income, and within-neighborhood income inequality using the Gini coefficient. This measures the dispersion of income between the wealthiest and poorest persons in the sample. Overall, lower neighborhood income was associated with higher rates of reported property and violent crime; greater income inequality within the neighborhood was independently associated with greater reported crime. Thus, both absolute deprivation (low income) and **relative deprivation** (low income relative to others in your neighborhood) are related to crime.

Stucky and colleagues also investigated the role of race (White vs. Black comparison) and ethnicity (White vs. Hispanic comparison). Controlling for the effect of absolute and relative deprivation, income and income inequality, a greater percentage of neighborhood residents who were Black predicted higher rates of assault and murder, but was not related to property crime. The percentage of neighborhood residents who were Hispanic was unrelated to crime rates. The results suggest that the additional stresses associated with being Black result in higher rates of violence; among Hispanics, the strong tradition of reliance on the family and the Catholic Church may provide greater resilience in the face of stress.

Anomie theory directs our attention to the importance of social class. Because lower-class members are more frequently excluded from quality education and jobs, the theory predicts that they will commit more crimes. Data collected by police departments and the FBI generally confirm this prediction, showing that a disproportionate number of those arrested for crimes are poor, minority men. This has led some to conclude that crime and social class are inversely related—that the highest crime rates are found in the lower social strata (Cloward, 1959).

However, there is a class bias built into the official statistics on crime. Not all illegitimate economic activities are included in these statistics. Whereas data on burglary, robbery, and larceny are compiled by police departments, data on income tax evasion, price fixing, and insider trading are not. Police and FBI statistics are much more likely to include "street" crimes than the kinds of economic crimes committed by the wealthy, corporate executives, and stockbrokers. The latter are called *white-collar crime*—activities that violate norms of trust, usually for personal gain (Shapiro, 1990). To embezzle or misappropriate funds or engage in insider trading of stocks, one needs access to a position of trust. Such positions usually are filled by middle-class and upper-class persons. These crimes are facilitated by the social organization of trust; the acts of trustees are invisible, hidden in a network of often electronic connections between organizations. Widespread crimes of this type in the investment and banking industries caused the economic crisis of 2008–2010. Thus, although specific crimes may vary by class, illegitimate economic activity may be common to all classes.

**General Strain Theory.** One limitation of anomie theory is that it does not specify the mechanism by which the lack of access to legitimate means produces delinquent or criminal behavior. One attempt to do so is Agnew's general strain theory (Agnew, 1992; Agnew & White, 1992). Agnew proposes that emotion connects the experience of strain with deviant behavior; strain elicits negative affective states—frustration, anger, or fear—that create the motivation to act. These actions may be deviant or criminal. Such actions include crimes that provide access to the goal (robbery, burglary, selling drugs), aggression against people perceived as responsible for the strain (abuse, assault), or drug and alcohol use to escape the emotions. The role of emotion can explain incidents such as an angry former employee returning to the workplace and killing supervisor(s) and former coworkers.

A longitudinal study of high school youths provides data to test the theory. Youths in the ninth, tenth, and eleventh grades in three primarily White communities were interviewed three times in 2 years. The research measured life stress and family conflict, anger and anxiety, aggressive delinquency (damaging property, carrying a weapon, fighting) and nonaggressive delinquency (stealing, joyriding, running away), and marijuana use. The results indicated that life stressors and family conflict were related to delinquency and marijuana use. As predicted by the theory, family conflict was related to anger, and anger was related to engaging in aggressive delinquency. However, anger was not related to nonaggressive delinquency or marijuana use, and anxiety was not related to any of the behaviors (Aseltine, Gore, & Gordon, 2000). Thus, the results provide only modest support for the key predictions.

A longitudinal study of youths living in Dade County, Florida, yielded a sample with substantial numbers of African Americans and Hispanics, as well as Whites. To the extent that there are differences by racial/ethnic group in criminal behavior, general strain theory suggests that these are caused by differences between groups in strain. The research measured three types of strain: recent life events (in the preceding 12 months), chronic stressors (for example, unemployment, relationship, child care, residence), and lifetime major events (for example, abandonment, school failure, divorce, physical or sexual assault) (see Chapter 17). It also included measures of social support. Using data from 898 young men, analyses indicated that strain as measured by recent life events was related to criminal activity, and that greater involvement of African Americans in crime was associated with greater exposure to major lifetime events (Eitle & Turner, 2003).

A survey of a random sample of residents of Raleigh, North Carolina, tested strain theory with an adult population. Respondents were asked to report the likelihood they would commit violence, a property violation (for example, theft), a minor offense, or illegal drug use. A measure of strain predicted likelihood of offending. However, the relationship was not mediated by negative emotions (feeling upset, angry, depressed) (Tittle, Broidy, & Gertz, 2008).

## Control Theory

If you were asked why you don't shoplift clothing from stores, or do drugs or drop out of school, you might reply, "Because my parents (or lover, or friends) would kill me if they found out." According to **control theory**, social ties influence our tendency to engage in deviant behavior. We often conform to social norms because we are sensitive to the wishes and expectations of others. This sensitivity creates a bond between the individual and other persons. The stronger the bond is, the less likely the individual is to engage in deviant behavior.

There are four components of the social bond (Hirschi, 1969). The first is attachment—ties of affection and respect for others. Attachment to parents is especially important, because they are the primary socializing agents of a child. A strong attachment to them leads the child to internalize social norms (see Chapter 3). The second component is commitment to long-term educational and occupational goals. Someone who aspires to go to law school is unlikely to commit a crime, because a criminal record would be an obstacle to a career in law. The third component is involvement. People who are involved in sports, Scouts, church groups, and other conventional activities simply have less time to engage in deviance. The fourth component is belief—a respect for the law and for persons in positions of authority.

We can apply control theory to the shoplifting incident described in the introduction.

Hanna does not feel attached to law-abiding adults; therefore, she was not concerned about their reactions to her behavior. Nor did she seem deterred by commitment when she said, "Nothing will happen." Hanna's deviant act reflects the absence of a bond with conventional society.

The relationship between delinquency and the four components of the social bond has been the focus of numerous studies. Several studies have found a relationship between a lack of attachment and delinquency; young people from homes characterized by a lack of parental supervision, communication, and support report more delinquent behavior (Hoffmann, 2002; Hundleby & Mercer, 1987; Messner & Krohn, 1990). A lack of attachment to school, measured by grades, is also associated with delinquency. Boys and girls who do well in school are less likely to be delinquent. Regarding commitment to long-term goals, research indicates that youths who are committed to educational and career goals are less likely to engage in property crimes such as robbery and theft (Johnson, 1979; Shover, Novland, James, & Thornton, 1979). Findings relevant to the third component, involvement, are mixed. Whereas involvement in studying and homework is negatively associated with reported delinquency, participation in athletics, hobbies, and work is unrelated to reported delinquency. Involvement in religion, as reflected in frequent church attendance and rating religion as important in one's life, is associated with reduced delinquency (Sloane & Potrin, 1986). Finally, evidence suggests that conventional beliefs reduce the frequency of delinquent behavior (Gardner & Shoemaker, 1989).

Control theory asserts that attachment to parents leads to reduced delinquency. Implicitly, the theory assumes that parents do not encourage delinquent behavior. Although this assumption may be correct in most instances, there are exceptions. Studies suggest that some parents encourage delinquent and criminal behaviors. Some parents explicitly teach their children how to shoplift, commit burglaries, and steal cars and trucks (Butterfield, 2002). A longitudinal study of criminal convictions in a Dutch sample found that same-sex parents' convictions significantly predicted sons'/ daughters' convictions (van De Rakt, Nieuwbeerta, & Apel, 2009). However, same-sex siblings' convictions were the strongest predictor. These data provide a stringent test, since the outcome measure is convictions. These are cases in which crime really does "run in the family." In these instances, parental (and sibling) attachment leads to increased delinquency and crime. The influence of gender suggests the importance of learning and imitation.

Does a lack of attachment to parents in childhood relate to adult deviant behavior? Yes. Research consistently shows that children who are physically and sexually abused are more likely to be involved as adults in violent and property crime, prostitution, and alcohol and substance abuse (Macmillan, 2001). The strength of adult social bonds is also related to adult criminal behavior. One study assessed month-to-month variations in circumstances that could strengthen or weaken the bond, and related this variation to the occurrence of criminal behavior (Horney, Osgood, & Marshall, 1995). The circumstances were starting/

These youth are playing in a league soccer tournament. Participation in such group activities increases attachment to and involvement in conventional society, reducing the likelihood of delinquency. © FatCamera/iStock

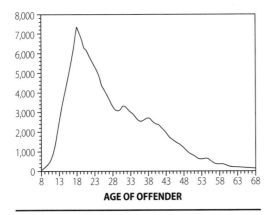

**FIGURE 13.1** The Relationship between Age and Crime

Involvement in delinquency and crime varies across the life course, responding to changes in economic conditions, changes in social roles, and opportunities. While rates of offenses vary by gender and race, the shape of the curve is the same across these groups.

*Source:* Stolzenberg & D'Alessio, "Co-offending and the Age-Crime Curve," *Journal of Research in Crime and Delinquency,* 45, 65–86, 2008.

stopping school, starting/stopping work, and starting/stopping living with a girlfriend or wife. Interviews were conducted with 658 men in prison who had committed felonies. Increases in criminal behavior were closely related to changes that reduced the men's bonds to others—stopping school or work, and stopping living with a girlfriend or wife.

A well-established finding in the study of delinquency and crime is the "age-crime curve"—rates of offending rise sharply in adolescence, peak in young adulthood, and decline steadily thereafter (Stolzenberg & D'Alessio, 2008; see Figure 13.1). Most offenses are committed by men, but the curve is the same for women's offenses. Typical adolescent offenses include vandalism, auto theft, and burglary. Persons aged 18 to 28 are more likely to be involved in drug violations and homicide. Middle-aged persons are more frequently involved in gambling and white-collar offenses. These variations suggest life course

changes in attachments and opportunities lead to different types of offenses, and to desistance as one ages.

One longitudinal study indicates that the strength of the social bond influences whether adults engage in deviant behavior (Sampson & Laub, 1990). The researchers studied 500 boys aged 10 to 17 who were in a correctional school and 500 boys of the same age from public school. Each boy was followed until he was 32. Generally, strong ties to social institutions were associated with reduced rates of crime, alcohol abuse, gambling, and divorce. In adolescents, the important attachments were to family and school. In young adults, the influential ties were to school, work, or marriage. In later adulthood, the important ties were to work, marriage, and parenthood.

What about women? Would work, marriage, and parenthood be associated with desistance from crime among women who were serious delinquents in adolescence? A study comparing women and men who were in institutions during adolescence found that neither job stability nor marriage was associated with adult desistance. In narratives of their lives, women were more likely than men to describe their children and religious transformation as the forces for change (Giordano, Cernkovich, & Rudolph, 2002). Moreover, it was not the fact of having children or a good job that was important; it was a transformation in the woman's identity or her thinking about those aspects of her life. These results are consistent with symbolic interaction theory and its emphasis on meaning constructed by the person in interaction with others (see Chapter 1).

Ethnographic research on women who smuggle drugs from Mexico to the United States illustrates how strong adult attachment to male family members, lovers, or spouses may lead to a woman's involvement in crime. Some of these women were coerced by these others into smuggling, whereas others perceived involvement as a means of increasing their income and independence from men (Campbell, 2008).

## Differential Association Theory

Vince and Arturo were roommates in the Phi Kappa Sly house. They were both taking Human Sexuality, and the first exam was in three days. Arturo asked Vince if he wanted to study with him. Vince replied, "I'm just going to review the old exams in the file the night before." Arturo replied, "But that's cheating!" Vince said, "I got to get an A. I saw Butch and George using the file last night." Arturo said, "Well, I want to learn the material, so count me out." Arturo studied for several hours and got an A−; Vince looked at old exams for one hour and got a C.

Vince's behavior reflects a conflict between two sets of norms. His college has rules defining cheating as academic misconduct. Academic work such as writing papers and preparing for tests should be done by the student, not by relying on paper or exam files or materials on the Internet. Arturo's behavior reflects this set of norms. Some fraternity members, on the other hand, believe academic work is not important, and help their brothers minimize effort by maintaining an exam file. Butch's and George's behavior represents this set of norms. Vince is not insensitive to the expectations of others. In fact, he is highly sensitive to the expectations of his "brothers."

This view of deviance is the basis of **differential association theory**, developed by Sutherland. He argued that although the law provides a uniform standard for deviance, one group may define a behavior as deviant, whereas another group defines it as desirable. Some groups believe cheating is wrong because (1) it violates academic regulations, (2) it claims credit for work that is not your own, and (3) it is unfair to other students who do their own work. Other groups believe it is acceptable because (1) it saves time, (2) the professor will never know, and (3) everybody

(like Butch and George) is doing it. The latter are referred to as *neutralizing beliefs* (Rettinger & Kramer, 2009; Sykes & Matza, 1957); they neutralize the influence of definitions/beliefs unfavorable to the behavior.

Attitudes about behaviors are learned through associations with others, usually in primary group settings. People learn motives, drives, and techniques of engaging in specific behaviors. What they learn depends on with whom they interact—that is, on their differential associations. Whether someone engages in a specific behavior depends on how frequently they are exposed to attitudes and beliefs that are favorable toward that behavior.

The principle of differential association states that a "person becomes delinquent because of an excess of definitions favorable to violation of the law over definitions unfavorable to violation of the law" (Sutherland, Cressey, & Luckenbill, 1992). Studies designed to test this principle typically ask individuals questions about their attitudes toward a specific behavior and about their participation in that behavior. One study revealed that the number of definitions favorable to delinquency accurately predicted which young men reported delinquent behavior (Matsueda, 1982). The larger the number of definitions a youth endorsed, the larger the number of delinquent acts he reported having committed in the preceding year. A subsequent study found that associating with delinquent peers was also related to delinquent behavior (Heimer & Matsueda, 1994).

Research on cheating by students found that direct knowledge of cheating by other students is the most powerful predictor of cheating (O'Rourke et al., 2010). Thus, seeing Butch and George use the exam file was probably a major influence on Vince's behavior.

Certain groups within the United States hold a set of beliefs that justify the use of physical aggression in certain situations. This set of beliefs is referred to as the *subculture of violence* (related to the culture of honor introduced in Chapter 12). Within this subculture, violence is considered appropriate when used as a means of self-defense and protection of one's home, or to defend one's reputation. A review of state laws governing spouse abuse, corporal punishment, and capital punishment found that Southern states have laws that are more accepting of violence (Cohen, 1996). Several studies report a relationship between these beliefs and behavior. Felson, Liska, South, and McNulty (1994) studied young men in 87 high schools. The young men were asked whether aggressive responses were appropriate in three situations involving insults or threats. Those young men who endorsed the use of violence were much more likely to report involvement in eight types of interpersonal violence, including striking a parent or teacher, fighting, and using weapons in disputes. Endorsing the use of violence was also associated with delinquency within the school, including cheating, tardiness, and truancy.

That this is a widespread, (sub)cultural belief is evident in the popularity of "stand your ground" laws. These laws allow a person to use any level of force they believe necessary in the face of a (perceived) threat of bodily harm. Twenty-eight states have adopted such laws, and eight additional states follow the principle in various legal practices. In July 2017, a Florida Circuit Court judge ruled that Florida's law violates the Florida Constitution.

The theory of differential association does not specify the process by which people learn criminal or deviant behavior. For this reason, Burgess and Akers (1966) developed a modified theory of differential association. This modified version emphasizes the influence of positive and negative reinforcement on the acquisition of behavior (see Chapter 3). Much of this reinforcement comes from friends and associates.

A survey of 3,056 high school students was conducted to test the theory (Akers, Krohn, Lanza-Kaduce, & Radosevich, 1979). In particular, it assessed the relationship between differential association, reinforcement, and adolescents' drinking behavior and marijuana use. Differential association was measured by three questions: "How many of your (1) best friends, (2) friends you spend the most time with, and (3) friends you have known longest smoke marijuana and/or drink?" The survey also assessed students' definitions of drug and alcohol laws. Both social reinforcement (whether the adolescent expected praise or punishment for use from parents and peers) and nonsocial reinforcement (whether the effects of substance use experienced by the person were positive or negative) were measured. The findings of this survey showed that differential association was closely related to the use of alcohol or drugs. The larger the number of friends who drank or smoked marijuana, the more likely the student was to drink alcohol or smoke marijuana. Reinforcement was also related to behavior; those who used a substance reported that it had positive effects. The students' definitions were also related to those with whom they associated; if their friends drank or used marijuana, they were more likely to have positive attitudes toward the behavior and negative attitudes toward laws defining that behavior as criminal. Finally, students' attitudes were consistent with their behavior. Those who opposed marijuana use and supported the marijuana laws were much less likely to use that substance.

A similar study (Akers, LaGreca, Cochran, & Sellers, 1989) focused on drinking among older persons. Interviews were conducted with 1,410 people aged 60 and over. The measures used were the same or similar to those used with adolescents. The results were essentially the same. The drinking behavior of persons 60 and older was related to the drinking behavior of spouse, family, or friends; reinforcements; and an individual's attitudes toward drinking.

Survey data collected at one point in time often cannot be used to test hypotheses about cause-effect relationships. However, survey data collected from the same people at two or more times can be. Stein, Newcomb, and Bentler (1987) analyzed data from 654 young people who were surveyed three times at 4-year intervals that began when they were in junior high school. The measures included peer drug use, adult drug use, and community approval of drug use. The results showed that adolescents who believed that both peers and adults were using drugs were more likely to become drug users.

Persons who are members of a group should be most heavily influenced by it. A study analyzing longitudinal data collected over a 6-year period, from adolescence into young adulthood (Pollard et al., 2013), differentiated three positions: member (more than 50 percent of friends are members of same group), liaison (has friends in more than one group), and isolate (only one tie to the group/network). Members of a group with one or more binge drinkers at Time 1, in high school, were much more likely to become long-term heavy bingers. This may reflect the point noted above, that observing deviance is the best predictor of engaging in the behavior.

Thus, differential association emphasizes interacting with groups and learning pro-conformity or neutralizing beliefs with regard to the behavior. Learning emphasizes modeling and imitation in learning the behavior (see Chapter 3) and reinforcement, a positive or negative experience including feedback from others. A meta-analysis considered the results of 133 studies testing the relationship between these and crime or deviant behavior. The results indicate that measures of interaction and beliefs are consistently stronger in cross-sectional but not longitudinal studies (Pratt et al., 2013).

In addition to being modeled by peers or family, deviant behaviors can sometimes be provoked by media coverage, as detailed in Box 13.1.

An important characteristic of social networks is density—the extent to which each member of the network or group knows the other members. Networks that are dense should have more influence on their members' behavior; if all of your friends drink alcohol, it will be hard for you to "just say no." A study of a nationally representative sample of seventh to twelfth graders found that peers' delinquency has a stronger association with an adolescent's delinquency when the friendship network is dense (Haynie, 2001).

Because each person usually associates with several groups, the consistency or inconsistency in definitions across groups is also an important influence on behavior (Krohn, 1986). *Network multiplexity* refers to the degree to which individuals who interact in one context also interact in other contexts. When you interact with the same people at church, at school, on the athletic field, and at parties, multiplexity is high. When you interact with different people in each of these settings, multiplexity is low. When multiplexity is high, the definitions of an activity will be consistent across groups; when it is low, definitions may be inconsistent across groups. Thus, differential associations should have the greatest impact on attitudes and beliefs when multiplexity is high. A survey of 1,435 high school students measured the extent to which individuals interacted with parents and with the same peers in each of several activities (Krohn, Massey, & Zielinski, 1988). Students who participated jointly with parents and peers in various activities were less likely to smoke cigarettes.

## Routine Activities Perspective

So far, we have considered characteristics of the person (motivation, beliefs) and of their associations with others (parents, friends). These have been shown to be related to delinquency, assault, murder, burglary, economic crimes, suicide, and alcohol and drug use. The **routine activities perspective** focuses on a third class of influences—how these behaviors emerge from the routines of everyday life (Felson, 1994).

Each instance of deviant behavior requires the convergence of the elements necessary for the behavior to occur. Crimes such as burglary, larceny, or robbery require the convergence of an offender and a likely target (residence, store, or person) and the absence of some guardian who could intervene. In the illustration at the beginning of the chapter, the shoplifting incident involves such a convergence: Hanna, the lingerie, and the absence of a clerk or security guard. Illegal consumption requires two offenders (seller and user), a substance, and a setting with no guardian; "crack houses" provide the latter in many large cities. Without such convergence, deviance will not occur. We can understand another aspect of deviance if we analyze everyday activity from the perspective of how it facilitates or prevents such convergences. This perspective calls our attention to the contributions of situations to behavior.

One class of situations that facilitates deviance is unstructured socializing with peers in the absence of an authority figure (Osgood et al., 1996). The presence of peers makes it likely that definitions will be shared, including definitions favorable to particular forms of deviance. The absence of an authority figure or guardian reduces the likelihood of punishment for deviance. Lack of structure makes time available for deviance. What situations have these characteristics? They include cruising in a car with friends, going to parties, and "hanging out" with friends. Data from a longitudinal study of a national sample of 1,200 persons aged 18 to 26 allowed researchers to relate involvement in these situations to deviance. Frequency of participation in them was related to alcohol and marijuana use, dangerous driving, and criminal behavior. Changes across five waves of data collection in an individual's participation in these activities were related to changes in their involvement in deviance.

Researchers have consistently noted that men are much more likely to commit criminal acts than women. This is not only true of street crime but also of economic crimes involving violation of trust, such as insider trading. The routine activities perspective explains this as due to gender role socialization, which teaches women different norms and definitions; to lack of access to tutelage in various forms of deviance; and to restrictions on activities that keep women out of certain settings (Steffensmeier & Allan, 1996). Thus, few women commit either burglary or insider trading because of their lack of access in everyday life to the apprenticeships where one learns these behaviors. Similarly, we are not surprised that the corporate executives of Enron, WorldCom, and other companies who committed fraud in the period 1995–2003 were men; the "glass ceiling" prevented most women from occupying such roles.

Research on youths aged 9 to 19 living in 12 high-poverty neighborhoods demonstrates that some elements simultaneously increase and decrease the likelihood of criminal activity. Carrying a gun in such a neighborhood makes it available for use in a crime, but also available to defend oneself in case of attack. Similarly, employment creates a conventional attachment and provides income by a legitimate means, but also creates the risk of injury or death during a robbery (Spano, Freilich, & Bolland, 2008).

The anomie, control, differential association, and routine activities perspectives are not incompatible. Anomie theory suggests that culturally valued goals and the opportunities available to achieve these goals are major influences on behavior. Opportunities to learn and occupy particular roles are influenced by age, social class, gender, race, and ethnic background—that is, by the structuring of everyday life based on these variables. According to control theory, we are also influenced by our attachments to others and our commitment to attaining success. Our position in the social structure and our attachments to parents and

## BOX 13.1  The Power of Suggestion

Rape, robbery, murder, and other types of deviant behavior receive a substantial amount of coverage in newspapers and on radio and television. One function of publicizing deviance is to remind us of norms—to tell us what we should not do (Erikson, 1964). But is this the only consequence? Could the publicity given to particular deviant activities increase the frequency with which they occur? In some cases, the answer appears to be yes.

Research on the relationship between the publicity given to suicides and suicide rates indicates that the two are positively correlated (Phillips, 1974). Phillips identified every time a suicide was publicized in three major U.S. daily newspapers during the years 1947–1968. Next, he calculated the number of expected suicides for the following month by averaging the suicide rates for that same month from the year before and the year after. For example, the suicide of a Ku Klux Klan leader on November 1, 1965, was widely publicized. Phillips calculated the expected number of suicides (1,652) by averaging the total number of suicides for November 1964 (1,639) and November 1966 (1,665). In fact, there were 1,710 suicides in November 1965; the difference between the observed and the expected rates (58) could be due to suggestion via the mass media.

The results of this study showed that suicides increased in the month following reports of a suicide in major daily papers. Moreover, the more publicity a story was given—as measured by the number of days the story was on the front page—the larger the rise in suicides. If a story was published locally—in Chicago but not in New York, for example—a rise in suicides occurred only in the area where it was publicized.

Why should such publicity lead other persons to kill themselves? There must be some factor that predisposes a small number of persons to take their own lives following a publicized suicide. That predisposing factor may be anomie. According to this theory, suicide is a form of retreatism—of withdrawal from the struggle for success. Persons who don't have access to legitimate means or who are blocked by life circumstances are looking for some way to adapt to their situation. Publicity given to a suicide may suggest a solution to their problem.

These results were replicated by a study in Australia, which measured the amount of publicity in newspapers and on radio and TV given suicides during a one-year period (Pirkis et al., 2006). Media reports were more likely to be associated with increases in suicides if they were broadcast on television, the suicide was successful, and other suicides were reported on the same day.

When we think of suicide, we think of shooting oneself, taking an overdose of a drug, or jumping off a building. We distinguish suicide from accidents, in which we presume the person did not intend to harm themself. But the critical difference is the person's intent, not the event itself. Some apparent accidents may be suicides. For example, when a car hits a bridge abutment well away from the pavement on a clear day with no evidence of mechanical malfunction, this may be suicide.

If some auto accidents are, in fact, suicides, we should observe an increase in motor vehicle accidents following newspaper stories about a suicide. In fact, data from newspapers and motor vehicle deaths in San Francisco and Los Angeles verify this hypothesis (Phillips, 1979). Statistics show a marked increase in the number of deaths due to automobile accidents two and three days after a suicide is publicized, especially accidents involving a single vehicle. In the Detroit metropolitan area, an analysis of motor vehicle fatalities for the years 1973–1976 revealed an average increase in fatalities of 35 to 40 percent the third day after a suicide story appeared in the daily papers (Bollen & Phillips, 1981). Again, the more publicity, the greater the increase. Finally, if the person whose suicide is publicized was young, deaths of young drivers increase, whereas if the person killing themselves was older, the increase in fatalities involved older drivers.

Does an increase in suicide follow any publicized suicide, or are some suicides more likely to be imitated than others? Stack (1987) studied instances in which celebrities killed themselves. The effect of publicized celebrity suicide is gender- and race-specific. Suicide by a male celebrity was followed by an increase in the number of men who killed themselves but not in the number of women who took their lives, and vice versa. Similarly, an increase in suicides by Whites followed a publicized case involving a White celebrity, whereas rates among Blacks were unaffected. The fact that the effects of publicized suicide are age-, gender-, and race-specific is consistent with the concept of *imitation* (see Chapter 3).

Suicide was one of the first forms of deviant behavior to be linked to media publicity. As you can see, the methodology involves the calculation of an expected rate of an event based on comparison periods of time. Several studies by different researchers using this method report results confirming the hypothesized link between media portrayals and suicide. Recall from Chapter 2 that causal hypotheses are best tested by experiments. There is no ethical way to conduct experiments on the relationship between media exposure and suicide! However, experiments (and other methods) have been used to study the relationship between media exposure and another category of deviant behaviors, aggressive actions. That research is summarized in Chapter 12; we concluded that research shows that exposure of youth and adults to violence in film, on television, on the Internet, and in video games increases aggressive behavior in every day settings.

In the past decade, there has been growing concern about the impact of media coverage of mass shootings and subsequent similar events. The Columbine High School massacre in 1999 involved two students and resulted in the deaths of 13 persons and the injuries of 24 others. The perpetrators, Eric Harris and Dylan Klebold, committed suicide at the scene. Harris maintained a website for three years prior to the event, documenting his hatred of students and teachers and making statements about weapons and explosives. The investigation following the massacre revealed the site's existence nationally. According to *Mother Jones*, the Columbine massacre and information about it available through the media "has inspired at least 74 plots or attacks across 30 states" (Follman & Andrews, 2015). The magazine's editors are sufficiently concerned about the impact of media reports on behavior that they have not released all of the details of their investigation.

It is more difficult to definitively link one mass shooting to another than to document the effect of a specific suicide or portrayal of violence. Researchers have identified several characteristics on which mass shootings vary; the more characteristics on which events are similar, the more plausible the claim that they are related. Characteristics include setting (school, work, shopping mall, etc.), weapons (number, type), perpetrators (e.g., number, gender, age), and whether perpetrators commit suicide onsite. Since multiple incidents may be traced back to a single event, the theoretical concept used is *contagion*, the spread through a group of a visible and often unusual behavior. A team of researchers investigated mass killings, incidents in which four or more persons are killed, in the years 2006 to 2013, and school shootings, shootings in a school building or on campus, 1997–2013 (Towers et al., 2015). They focused on clustering of incidents in time and/or geographic location. They found that mass killings involving firearms are "incented" by similar events in the immediate past. "On average, the temporary increase in probability lasts 13 days, and each incident incites at least 0.30 new incidents."

There can be little doubt that media coverage may tell us what not to do, but it also tells us how to do it, in some cases in graphic detail.

peers determine our differential associations—the kinds of groups to which we belong. Within these groups, we learn definitions favorable to particular behaviors, and we learn that we face sanctions when we choose behaviors that group members define as deviant.

## REACTIONS TO NORM VIOLATIONS

When we think of murder, robbery, or sexual assault, we think of cases we have read about, or heard of on radio or television or from coworkers or family members. We frequently refer to police and FBI statistics as measures of the number of crimes that have occurred in our city or county. Our knowledge of alcohol or drug abuse depends on knowing or hearing about persons who engage in these behaviors. All of these instances of deviance share another important characteristic as well: in every case, the behavior was discovered by someone who called it to the attention of others.

Does it matter that these instances involve both an action (by a person) and a reaction (by a victim or an observer)? Isn't an act equally deviant regardless of whether others find out about it? Let's go back to Hanna's theft of the lingerie. Suppose Hanna had left the store without being stopped by the clerk. In that case, she and Megan would have known she had taken the lingerie, but she would not have faced sanctions from others. She would not have experienced the embarrassment of being confronted and accused of a crime. Moreover, she would have had some beautiful lingerie. But the fact is that she was stopped by the clerk. She will be questioned, the police will be called, and she may be arrested. Thus, the consequences of committing a deviant act are quite different when certain reactions follow.

Whether a rule violation becomes "known about" depends in part on the actor's social and economic resources (Jackson-Jacobs, 2004). Consider two cocaine users, both 21-year-old men. DuShawn lives in a deteriorating

neighborhood; he works at a car wash, and his earnings support his habit. When he isn't working, he hangs out with other users. Sometimes, he commits burglary to get more money. He shoots up in a "crack house," the only place where he can get some privacy and escape surveillance. He is at risk of assault by fellow users, who know he is a user; they want his money or his drugs. Doug is a junior at a university. He lives in an apartment near campus, where he can snort coke with little risk. His part-time job supplies the money. His schedule of classes and work make it relatively easy for him to restrict his use to leisure times in his apartment, alone or with carefully selected friends. Doug's legitimate and sufficient income, control over his life, and access to private space make it unlikely he will be arrested.

This reasoning is the basis of **labeling theory**—the view that reactions to a norm violation are a critical element in deviance. Only after an act is discovered and labeled "deviant" is the act recognized as such. If the same act is not discovered and labeled, it is not deviant (Becker, 1963).

If deviance depends on the reactions of others to an act rather than on the act itself, the key social psychological question becomes "Why do particular audiences choose to label an act as deviant, whereas other audiences may not?" Labeling theory is an attempt to understand how and why acts are labeled deviant. In the case of the stolen lingerie, labeling analysts would not be concerned with Hanna's behavior. Rather, they would be interested in the responses to Hanna's act by Megan, the customer, and the clerk. Only if an observer challenges Hanna's behavior or alerts a store employee does the act of taking the lingerie become deviant.

### Reactions to Rule Breaking

Labeling theorists refer to behavior that violates norms as **rule breaking**, to emphasize that the act by itself is not deviant. Most rule violations are "secret," in the sense that no one other than the actor (and on occasion, the actor's accomplices) is aware of them. Many cases of theft and tax evasion, many violations of drug laws, and some burglaries are never detected. These activities can be carried out by a single person. Other acts, such as robberies, assaults, and various illegal sexual activities, involve other people who will know about them, but who may not label the act as deviant. Instances of assault, domestic violence, rape, and sexual abuse of children are often not reported because the victim is unwilling or unable to do so. This is why intervention programs often emphasize increased reporting of the behavior and support for victims who come forward.

How will members of an audience respond to a rule violation? It depends on the circumstances, but studies suggest that people very often ignore it. People react to isolated episodes of unusual behavior in one of four ways. A common response is denial, in which the person simply does not recognize the behavior as a rule violation. In an analysis of accounts women gave of instances of intimate partner violence, one woman said "he came over and was intoxicated . . . and he *pushed* me" (Langan, Hannem, & Stewart, 2016). A second response is normalization, in which the observer recognizes that the act occurred but defines it as normal or common. Thus, women often react to excessive drinking by men as normal, assuming that many men drink a lot. Asked about behavior by her partner that some would consider verbal abuse, one woman said "I've been getting called names since grade school." Third, the person may recognize the act as a rule violation but excuse it, attributing its occurrence to situational or transient factors; this reaction is attenuation. We may react to an intimate's excessive drinking by attributing it to the stress of working overtime. Finally, people may respond to the rule violation by balancing it, recognizing it as a violation but

de-emphasizing its significance in light of the actor's good qualities; "Yes, she beats me, but she is a great mother to the kids."

The man who witnessed Hanna's behavior looked around, spotted the clerk, and reported the act. In doing so, he labeled the actor. Labeling involves a (re)definition of the actor's social status; the man placed Hanna into the category of "shoplifter" or "thief." The clerk, in turn, probably defined Hanna as "another shoplifter." Although labeling is triggered by a behavior, it results in a redefinition or typing of the actor. As we shall see, this has a major impact on people's perceptions of and behavior toward the actor.

## Determinants of the Reaction

What determines how an observer reacts to rule breaking? Reactions depend on three aspects of the rule violation, including the nature of the actor, the audience, and the situation.

**Actor Characteristics.** Reactions to a type of deviance, such as mental illness, depend on the specific behavior. Given a vignette describing a person who meets the diagnostic criteria for mental illness, adults are more unwilling to interact with (for example, have as a neighbor or coworker) someone who is dependent on drugs (72 percent) or alcohol (56 percent) than someone who has schizophrenia (48 percent) or depression (37 percent). People who view these behaviors as caused by stress are less likely to reject interaction with the person. The belief most closely associated with rejection is the belief that such persons are dangerous (Martin, Pescosolido, & Tuch, 2000). The extent to which different people have the same reaction depends on the degree of *normative consensus* about the act (Schmidtke, 2007). We noted that there are often both definitions favorable and unfavorable to a behavior; the greater the agreement that the act is undesirable/deviant/criminal, the more likely observers will label the actor.

Reaction to a rule violation often depends on who performs the act. First, people are more tolerant of rule breaking by family members than by strangers. Many of us probably know of a family attempting to care for a member whose behavior creates problems for them. Second, people are more tolerant of rule violations by persons who make positive contributions in other ways; note the discussion of balancing above. In small groups, tolerance is greater for persons who contribute to the achievement of group goals (Hollander & Julian, 1970). We seem to tolerate deviance when we are dependent on the person committing the act—perhaps because if we punish the actor, it will be costly for us. Third, a study of employee theft from restaurants found that coworkers were less likely to label the act as theft if they perceived the actor as more similar to themselves (Schmidtke, 2007). Fourth, we are less tolerant if the person has a history of rule breaking (Whitt & Meile, 1985).

Does gender affect reactions to deviant behavior? It depends on the behavior. An ingenious field experiment suggests that it does not affect responses to shoplifting. With the cooperation of stores, shoplifting events were staged near customers who could see the event. The experiment was conducted in a small grocery store, a large supermarket, and a large discount department store. The gender of the shoplifter, the appearance of the shoplifter, and the gender of the observer were varied. Neither the shoplifter's nor the customer's gender had an effect on the frequency with which the customer reported the apparent theft (Steffensmeier & Terry, 1973). Gender does affect reactions to persons who are mentally ill. People are more willing to interact with a woman who is described as having schizophrenia, depression, or drug or alcohol dependence than with a man described the same way. This is partly explained by the fact that women are perceived as less dangerous than men (Schnittker, 2000). We are less likely to label women than men for violations

of criminal law (Haskell & Yablonsky, 1983), women are less likely to be kept in jail between arraignment and trial, and they receive more lenient sentences than men. One explanation for this differential treatment is that women are subject to greater informal control by family members and friends, and so are treated more leniently in the courts. A study of the influences on pretrial release and sentence severity found that both men and women with families received more lenient treatment; the effect was stronger for women (Daly, 1987).

On the other hand, research suggests that psychiatrists are more likely to label women as having a personality disorder than men (Dixon, Gordon, & Khomusi, 1995). Case histories were prepared that included symptoms of clinical disorders (as defined in the then-current *Diagnostic and Statistical Manual of Mental Disorders*, "*DSM-III*"; American Psychiatric Association, 1981) and personality disorders (*DSM-III*, Axis II). Personality disorders are generally less serious and more ambiguously defined than clinical disorders. The case histories were identical except for gender: male, female, or unspecified. The psychiatrists' diagnoses of clinical disorders were not influenced by gender, but they were more likely to diagnose women as having personality disorders than men with the same symptoms.

**Audience Characteristics.** The reaction to a violation of rules also depends on who witnesses it. Because groups vary in their norms, audiences vary in their expectations. People enjoying a city park on a warm day will react quite differently to a nude man walking through the park than will a group of people in a nudist park. Recognizing this variation in reaction, people who contemplate breaking the rules—by smoking marijuana, drinking in public, or jaywalking, for example—often make sure no one is around who will punish them.

Social identity theory (see Chapter 4) suggests that the group membership of the deviant person and the audience both influence reactions. We are motivated to maintain a positive in-group identity, and one means we employ is to maximize the differences we perceive between our group and other groups. Thus, we negatively judge members of our in-group who deviate, especially if the deviation is negative. We judge favorably an out-group member who deviates from their group's norms. A laboratory experiment tested these predictions; the results supported them (Abrams, Marques, Brown, & Henson, 2000).

An important influence on whether a witness will label a rule violation is the level of concern in the community about the behavior. Citizens who are concerned about drug use as a social problem are probably more alert for signs of drug sales and use, and are more likely to label someone as a drug user. A major determinant of the level of concern is the amount of activity by politicians, service providers, and the mass media calling attention to the problem (Beckett, 1994). Political rhetoric, intense media attention, and public concern over a perceived threat may combine to create a *moral panic* (Fox, 2013), leading to demands that persons who are perceived as violating certain rules be labeled and punished/treated, e.g., "child molesters," crack users, or persons who send sexts.

Officials who routinely deal with suspects react very differently to suspected offenders than do most citizens. One study focused on officials working in a court-affiliated unit which evaluated suspected murderers following arrest. These officials had a stereotyped image of the type of person who commits murder (Swigert & Farrell, 1977). When lower-class male members of ethnic minorities committed murder, these officials believed that it was in response to a threat to their masculinity. For example, if an Italian-American truck driver was arrested for murder, they were likely to assume that he had killed the other man in response to verbal insults. This labeling based on a stereotype had important

consequences. Suspects who fit this stereotype were less likely to be defended by a private attorney, more likely to be denied bail, more likely to plead guilty, and more likely to be convicted on more severe charges.

Consider the example of a student with a drinking problem seeking help at a university counseling center. The treatment will depend on how counselors view student "troubles." Researchers found that the staff of one university clinic believed that students' problems could be classified into one of the following categories: problems in studying, choosing a career, achieving sexual intimacy, or handling personal finances; conflict with family or friends; and stress arising from sociopolitical activities. When a student came to the clinic because of excessive drinking, the therapist first decided which of these categories applied to this person's troubles; that is, which type of problem was causing this student to drink excessively. How the problem was defined in turn determined what the therapist did to try to help the student (Kahne & Schwartz, 1978).

**Situational Characteristics.** Whether a behavior is construed as normal or labeled as deviant also depends on the definition of the situation in which the behavior occurs. Marijuana and alcohol use, for example, are much more acceptable at a party than at work (Orcutt, 1975). Various sexual activities expected between spouses in the privacy of their home would elicit condemnation if performed in a public park in many parts of the United States.

Consider so-called gang violence. In some major cities, incidents in which teenage gangs assault each other are common. News media, police, and other outsiders often refer to such incidents as "gang wars." These events often occur in the neighborhoods where the gang members live. How do their parents, relatives, and friends react to such incidents? According to a study of one Chicano community, it depends on the situation (Horowitz, 1987).

Young men are expected to protect their families, women, and masculinity. When violence by community members results from a challenge to honor, the community generally tolerates it. On the other hand, if the violence disrupts a community event, such as a dance or a wedding, it is not tolerated.

We often rely on the behavior of others to help us define situations. Our reaction to a rule violation may be influenced by the reactions of other members of the audience. The influence of the reactions of others is demonstrated in a field experiment of intrusions into waiting lines (Milgram, Liberty, Toledo, & Wackenhut, 1986). Members of the research team intruded into 129 waiting lines with an average length of six persons. One or two confederates approached the line and stepped between the third and fourth person. In some cases, other confederates served as buffers; they occupied the fourth and fifth positions and did not react to the intrusion. When the buffers were present, others in the line were much less likely to react verbally or nonverbally to the intrusion.

A good deal of research suggests that interpersonal violence—especially assaults and murders—often involves two young men and is triggered by a verbal insult (Katz, 1988). An aggressive response by a male to an insult often reflects masculine overcompensation: reaction to a threat to one's masculinity with an exaggerated demonstration of masculinity (Willer, Conlon, Rogalin, & Wojnowicz, 2013). But whether a remark is an insult is a matter of social definition. Not surprisingly, fights are more likely to erupt following a remark when there is a male audience and when the men have been drinking (Felson, 1994). A remark is less likely to lead to a fight if the audience includes women.

## Consequences of Labeling

Assume that an audience defines an act as deviant. What are the consequences for the actor and the audience? We will consider four possible outcomes.

**Institutionalization of Deviance.** In some cases, individuals who label a behavior as deviant may decide that it is in their own interest for the person to continue the behavior. They may, in fact, reward that person for the deviant behavior. If you learn that a good friend is selling drugs, you may decide to use this person as a source and purchase drugs from them. Over time, your expectations will change; you will come to expect that person to have access to and sell drugs. If your drug-selling friend then decides to stop dealing, you may treat them as a rule breaker! Illegal activities by stockbrokers are likely to be ignored or encouraged by other employees and supervisors when all of them benefit economically from the activity (Zey, 1993). The process by which members of a group come to expect and support deviance by another member over time is called **institutionalization of deviance** (Dentler & Erikson, 1959).

Consider the following sworn statement by a former Enron employee, Timothy N. Belden:

> I was Director of Enron's California energy trading desk . . . [We] marketed and supplied electricity to Californian wholesale customers. . . . Beginning in approximately 1998, and ending in approximately 2001, I and other individuals in Enron agreed to devise and implement a series of fraudulent schemes through these markets. We designed the schemes to obtain increased revenue for Enron. . . .
>
> We exported and then imported amounts of electricity generated within California in order to receive higher, out-of-state prices from the [ISO] when it purchased "out of market." We scheduled energy that we did not have, or did not intend to supply. (*United States of America v. Timothy Belden,* U.S. District Court, Northern District of California, Doc. CR 02-0313 MJJ, October 17, 2002)

Note the repeated use of "we"; Belden and other Enron employees supported (and expected the support of) one another as they engaged in these deviant activities. It is possible that support for their criminal activities extended to the highest levels of the corporation.

Sadly, history repeats itself. The Federal Energy Regulatory Commission had charged JP Morgan Ventures Energy with the same manipulation of the electricity markets in the western United States in 2010 and 2011. Notice that JP Morgan acknowledged the violations and the assessment of a civil penalty of $285 million was issued July 30, 2013 (Docket Nos. IN11-8-000, IN13-5-000: Order Approving Stipulation and Consent Agreement). These activities clearly reflect differential association among corporate employees, and a corporate culture that prioritizes making money over obeying the rules.

**Backtracking.** Even when an audience reacts favorably to a rule violation, the actor may decide to discontinue the behavior. This second consequence of labeling is called *backtracking*. It may occur after the actor learns that others label the act as deviant. Though some audiences react favorably, the actor may wish to avoid the reaction of those who would not react favorably—and the resulting punishment. Many teenagers try substances like marijuana once or twice. Although their friends may encourage its continued use, some youths backtrack because they want to avoid their parents' or others' negative reactions.

**Effective Social Control.** An audience that reacts negatively to rule breaking and threatens or attempts to punish the actor may force the actor to give up further involvement in the deviant activity. This third consequence of labeling is known as *effective social control*. This reaction is common among friends or family members, who often threaten to end their association with an actor who continues to engage in deviance. Similarly, they may threaten to break off their relationship if the person does not seek professional help. In these

instances, the satisfaction of the actor's needs is contingent on changing their behavior. Members of the audience also may insist that the actor renounce aspects of their life that they see as contributing to future deviance (Sagarin, 1975). If excessive drinking is due to job-related stressors, for example, family members may demand that the person find a different type of employment. Displays of remorse may also lead to reduced punishment for an offense (Robinson, Smith-Lovin, & Tsoudis, 1994).

**Unanticipated Deviance.** Still another possibility is that the individual may engage in further or unanticipated deviance. Note the use of the term "unanticipated." Negative reactions by members of an audience are intended to terminate rule-breaking activity. However, such reactions may, in fact, produce further deviance. This occurs when the audience's response sets in motion a process that leads the actor to greater involvement in deviance. This process and its outcomes are the focus of the next section.

## LABELING AND SECONDARY DEVIANCE

Labeling a person as deviant may set in motion a process that has important and lasting effects on the individual. The process of societal reaction produces changes in the behavior of others toward the labeled individual and may lead to corresponding changes in their self-image. A frequent consequence of the process is involvement in secondary deviance and participation in a deviant subculture. In this section, we consider this process in detail.

### Societal Reaction

Earlier in this chapter, we mentioned that labeling is a process of redefining a person. By categorizing a person as a particular kind of deviant, we place that person in a stigmatized social status (see Chapter 5). The deviant person (sex addict, "bipolar," thief) is defined as undesirable—not acceptable in conventional society—and frequently treated as inferior. There are two important consequences of stigma: status loss and social discrimination (Link & Phelan, 2001). The loss of status causes a gradual change in self-conception; the person comes to perceive the self as a type of deviant. Discriminatory behavior by others not only affects one's self-concept but constrains one's behavior and opportunities (see discussion of learning and opportunity structures above).

**Changes in the Behavior of Others.** When we learn that someone is an alcoholic, a convicted "sex offender," or mentally ill, our perceptions and behavior toward that person change. For example, if we learn that someone has a drinking problem, we may respond to their request for a drink with "Do you think you should?" or "Why don't you wait until the food is served?" to convey our objection. We may avoid jokes about drinking in the person's presence, and we may stop inviting them to parties or gatherings where alcohol will be served.

A more severe behavioral reaction involves withdrawal from the stigmatized person (Kitsuse, 1964). For instance, the labeled shoplifter, alcoholic, or out(ed) gay teacher may be fired from their job. Behavioral withdrawal by others may occur because of hostility toward the deviant person, or it may reflect a sincere desire to help the person. For example, the employer who fires an alcoholic may do so because of dislike of alcoholics or because they believe that relief from work obligations will reduce the stress that may be causing the drinking problem.

Paradoxically, our reaction to deviance may produce additional rule breaking by the labeled person. We expect people who are psychologically disturbed to be irritable or unpredictable, so we avoid them to avoid an unpleasant interaction. The other person may sense that

Being caught in a deviant act has important consequences. This young woman may experience disrupted schooling and separation from family and friends as a result of being arrested. © filo/iStock

they are being avoided and respond with anger or distrust. This anger may cause coworkers to gossip behind their back; the person may respond with suspicion and become paranoid. When members of an audience behave toward a person according to a label and cause the person to respond in ways that confirm the label, they have produced a **self-fulfilling prophecy** (Merton, 1957). Lemert (1962) documents a case in which such a sequence led to a man's hospitalization for paranoia.

**Self-Perception of the Deviant.** Another consequence of stigmatized social status is that it changes the deviant person's self-image. A person labeled deviant often incorporates the label into their identity. This redefinition of oneself is due partly to feedback from others who treat the person as deviant. Moreover, the new self-image may be reinforced by the individual's own behavior. Repeated participation in shoplifting, for example, may lead Hanna to define herself as a thief.

Redefinition is facilitated by the social programs and agencies that deal with specific types of deviant persons. Such agencies pressure persons to acknowledge that they are deviant. Admitting that one purchased a term paper on the Internet will often lead student personnel workers and deans to go easy on a cheater, especially if it is a first offense. Failure to acknowledge the action may lead to suspension or dismissal from the college. Admitting that one is mentally ill is often a prerequisite for psychiatric treatment (Goffman, 1959a). Mental health professionals believe that a patient cannot be helped until the individual recognizes their problem. Employees of an agency that provided jobs for unemployed persons viewed their clients' employment problems as partly the result of individual failure (Miller, 1991). To receive agency services, clients had to agree with this view and change their behavior accordingly.

Thus, the deviant person experiences numerous pressures to accept a stigmatized identity. Acceptance of a stigmatized identity has important effects on self-perception.

Everyone has beliefs about what other people think of specific types of deviant persons. Accepting a label such as "thief," "drunk," or "bipolar" leads a person to expect that others will stigmatize and reject them, which in turn produces self-rejection. Self-rejection makes subsequent deviance more likely (Kaplan, Martin, & Johnson, 1986). In a study of junior high school students, data were collected three times at 1-year intervals. Self-rejection (that is, feeling that one is no good, a failure, rejected by parents and teachers) was related to more favorable dispositions (definitions) toward deviance and to an increased likelihood of associating with deviant persons 1 year later. A high disposition and associations with deviant peers were related to increased deviance—theft, gang violence, drug use, and truancy—1 year later (Kaplan, Johnson, & Bailey, 1987). Figure 13.2 summarizes these relationships. Delinquent behavior, in turn, is associated with reduced self-esteem (McCarthy & Hoge, 1984).

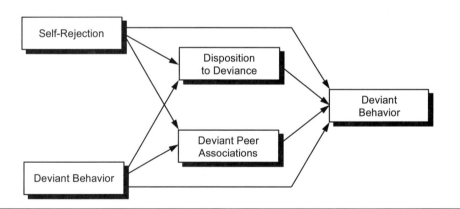

**FIGURE 13.2** The Relationship of Self-Rejection to Deviant Behavior

A person who engages in deviant behavior anticipates that others will reject them, which, in turn, can lead to self-rejection. A longitudinal study collected data from junior high school students three times, each 1 year apart. At Time 1, reported participation in deviance was positively related to self-rejection (feeling one is no good, a failure, rejected by parents and teachers). Self-rejection at Time 1 was associated with more favorable dispositions (attitudes) toward deviance but a decreased likelihood of associating with other deviants 1 year later (at Time 2). Favorable dispositions and deviant associations at Time 2, as well as deviance at Time 1, were related to increased deviance—theft, gang violence, drug use, and truancy—at Time 3.

*Source:* Kaplan, Johnson, & Bailey, "Deviant Peers and Deviant Behavior: Further Elaboration of a Model," *Social Psychology Quarterly*, 50(3), 281, 1987. Used with permission from the American Sociological Association.

In short, labeling may set in motion a cycle in which changes in the labeled person's behavior produce changes in other people's behavior, which in turn changes the deviant person's self-image and subsequent behavior. Self-fulfilling prophecies can also be positive. One study assessed the expectations of 98 sixth-grade math teachers for their students (N 1,539) (Madon, Jussim, & Eccles, 1997). Teachers' expectations (positive or negative) predicted performance much better for students who were low achievers. Also, teachers' overestimates—that is, positive expectations—predicted actual achievement better than their underestimates. Perhaps positive expectations inspire underachievers. Self-fulfilling prophecies may be important contributors to positive deviance, by opening up opportunities for training and performance at higher levels.

Although more attention has been given to situations in which others label the person, some persons become committed to deviance without such labeling. For example, some persons voluntarily seek psychiatric treatment; some of these cases reflect self-labeling (Thoits, 1985). People know that others view certain behaviors as symptoms of mental illness. If they observe themselves engaging in those behaviors, they may label themselves as mentally ill. A study of persons who had experienced a psychiatric disorder in the prior 12 months, measured by self-reports of symptoms, found that persons with more education, and who are not living in poverty, were more likely to voluntarily seek treatment (Thoits, 2005). This probably reflects in part greater information about mental illness and access to mental health services.

## Secondary Deviance

A frequent outcome of the societal reaction process is **secondary deviance**, in which a person engages increasingly in deviant behavior as an adjustment to others' reactions (Lemert, 1951). Usually, the individual becomes openly and actively involved in the deviant role, adopting the clothes, speech, and mannerisms associated with it. For example, initially, a person with a drinking problem may drink only at night and on weekends to prevent their drinking from interfering with work. Once the person adopts the role of "heavy drinker" or "alcoholic," however, they may drink continuously.

An attractive 19-year-old Latina woman working in an office answered an ad for models; at first, she modeled lingerie in provocative poses, somewhat tentatively and anxiously. At the urging of the photographer, and for more money, she did some nude shots, and as she got increasingly comfortable displaying her body, finally engaged in some explicit stills. Her parents found some of the photos and were horrified. They kicked her out, and within 6 months, she moved to San Fernando Valley and signed on with Vivid Entertainment. She became a fairly well-known actress in explicit films. She makes $1,500 per film and hangs with other actors and film producers in the community.

As an individual becomes openly and regularly involved in deviance, they may increasingly associate with others who routinely engage in the same or related activity. The individual may join a **deviant subculture**— a group of people whose norms encourage participation in the deviance and who regard positively those who engage in it. Subcultures provide not only acceptance but also the opportunity to enact deviant roles. Through a deviant subculture, the would-be drug dealer or commercial sex worker can gain access to customers more readily. This is exactly the process involving the woman described in the preceding paragraph.

Subcultural groups are an attractive alternative for deviant persons for two reasons. First, these persons are often forced out of nondeviant relationships and groups through others' reactions. As family and friends progressively break off relationships with them, they are compelled to seek acceptance else-where. Second, membership in subcultural groups may result from the deviant person's desire to associate with persons who are similar and who can provide them with feelings of social acceptance and self-worth (Cohen, 1966). Deviant persons are no different from others in their need for positive reflected appraisals.

Deviant subcultures help persons cope with the stigma associated with deviant status. We have already noted that deviant persons are often treated with disrespect and sanctioned by others for their activity. Such treatment threatens self-esteem and produces fear of additional sanctions. Subcultures help the deviant person cope with these feelings. They provide a vocabulary of motives—beliefs that explain and justify the individual's participation in the behavior.

The norms and belief systems of subcultures support a positive self-conception. In the early 1970s, a commercial sex workers' rights group, COYOTE (Cast Off Your Old, Tired Ethics), emerged in San Francisco. Although it has not obtained the legalization of prostitution, it has enhanced the self-images of its members (Weitzer, 1991). In 2012 it had branches in San Francisco and Los Angeles, and continued to advocate for sex workers' rights. Many people think that nudists are exhibitionists who take off their clothes to get sexual kicks. Nudists, on the other hand, consider themselves morally respectable and hold several beliefs designed to enhance that claim: (1) nudity and sexuality are unrelated, (2) there is nothing shameful about the human body, (3) nudity promotes a feeling of freedom and natural pleasure, and (4) nude exposure to the sun promotes physical, mental, and spiritual well-being. There are also specific norms—"no staring," "no sex talk," and "no body contact"—designed to sustain these general beliefs (Weinberg, 1976). "Nude is not lewd!" proclaims the banner on the Naturist Society home page. The belief systems of subcultures

Deviant subcultures create opportunities for people to enact roles not acceptable elsewhere in society. This nudist resort and pool provides a place where people can undress and swim and sunbathe in the nude without attracting attention or being arrested. © Photo courtesy of Domaine des Monts de Bussy, Camping Naturiste, France

provide the social support the person needs to maintain a positive self-image.

A study of the networks of persons having their first contact with the mental health system clearly documents these dynamics (Perry, 2011). Respondents reported experiences of people being anxious around them, unwilling to make friends, and cutting off relationships with them. Respondents diagnosed with schizophrenia and bipolar disorder, and who had high levels of symptoms, were more likely to report these reactions. At the same time, some respondents reported having supportive networks of people who knew about their illness and helped them to cope with it. People with more perceptible cognitive, emotional, and behavioral symptoms were more likely to report having a supportive core group, perhaps because the visible symptoms elicited concern in others.

Joining a deviant subculture often stabilizes participation in one form of deviance. It also may lead to involvement in additional forms of deviant behavior. For instance, many commercial sex workers become drug users through participation in a subculture.

## FORMAL SOCIAL CONTROLS

So far, this chapter has been concerned with **informal social control**—the reactions of family, friends, and acquaintances to rule violations by individuals. Informal controls are probably the major influence on an individual's behavior. In modern societies, however, there are often elaborate systems set up specifically to process rule breakers. Collectively, these are called **formal social controls**—agencies given responsibility for dealing with violations of rules or laws. Typically, the rules enforced are written, and, in some cases, punishments also may be specified. The most prominent system of formal social control in our society is the criminal justice system, which includes police, courts, jails, and prisons. A second system of formal social control is the juvenile justice system, which includes juvenile officers, social workers, probation officers, courts, and treatment or detention facilities. A third system of formal social control deals with mental illness. It includes mental health professionals, commitment procedures, and institutions for the mentally ill and mentally impaired.

### Formal Labeling and the Creation of Deviance

Most of us think of these agencies as reactive— as simply processing individuals who have already committed crimes or need psychiatric treatment. But these agencies do much more than take care of persons already known to be deviant. It can be argued that the function of formal social control agencies is to select members of society and identify or certify them as deviant (Erikson, 1964).

In the 1990s, crime control became big business in U.S. society. Federal and state governments provided funds to hire thousands of additional police officers, sheriff's deputies, and federal agents. Many states built new prisons. Additional officers and new prisons require large investments in new equipment.

It has been suggested that there is a crime control industry, with many people lobbying for its preservation and growth (Chambliss, 1994). More officers and prisons lead to more arrests and further increases in prison populations. Is this expansion due to real increases in crime? No. Crime has not increased substantially in the past 25 years. In fact, rates of violent crime were stable from 1973 to 1993; since 1993, they have fallen by more than 66 percent. Rates of property crime have been declining steadily since 1975, and also declined 63 percent between 1993 and 2014 (Truman & Langton, 2015). What has increased is political rhetoric on and mass media attention to the level of crime, leading the public to perceive an increase. Politicians have used this perception as a basis for fear campaigns to enlist support for the expansion of formal control systems. One consequence is that the United States now has one of the highest per capita rates of incarceration in the world: 693 persons per 100,000.

**Functions of Labeling.** Of what value is labeling people as "criminals," "delinquents," or "mentally ill"? There are three functions of labeling persons as deviant: (1) to provide concrete examples of undesirable behavior, (2) to provide scapegoats for the release of tensions, and (3) to unify the group or society.

First, the public identification of deviance provides concrete examples of how we should not behave (Cohen, 1966). When someone is actually apprehended and sanctioned for deviance, the norms of society are made starkly clear. For instance, the arrest of someone for shoplifting dramatizes the possible consequences of taking things that do not belong to us. Scandals involving sexual misconduct by high-profile politicians heighten awareness of politicians engaging in sexual harassment, sexting, and sexual activity with commercial sex workers.

According to the **deterrence hypothesis**, the arrest and punishment of some individuals for violations of the law deters other persons from committing the same violations. To what extent does general deterrence really affect people's behavior? Most analysts agree that the objective possibility of arrest and punishment does not deter people from breaking the law. Rather, conformity is based on people's perceptions of the likelihood and severity of punishment. Thus, youths who perceive a higher probability that they will be caught and that the punishment will be severe are less likely to engage in delinquent behavior (Jensen, Erickson, & Gibbs, 1978). Perceptions of risk are affected by personal experience; youths who have committed specific acts of delinquency but have not been punished perceive lower risk of sanction for those acts (Carmichael et al., 2005). Similarly, a study of theft of company property by employees found that those who perceived greater certainty and severity of organizational sanctions for theft were less likely to have stolen property (Hollinger & Clark, 1983).

For the punishment of some offenders to deter others, others must be aware of it. Again, research with youths found that those who had observed their peers getting away with delinquent acts perceived less risk of punishment, whereas those who observed peers receiving punishment following delinquent acts perceived greater risk (Matsueda, Kreager, & Huizinga, 2006). What about publicity? Does publicizing punishment influence perceived risk? In recent years, executions of murderers have been widely publicized. Does this publicity deter murder? Specifically, does coverage of executions on the evening news on network television lead to a reduction in homicide rates? A study of news coverage and homicide rates from 1976 through 1987 found no relationship (Bailey, 1990).

Perceived certainty of sanctions generally has a much greater effect on persons who have low levels of moral commitment (Silberman, 1976; Wright, Caspi, Moffit, & Paternoster, 2004). People whose morals define a behavior as wrong are not as affected by the threat of punishment. For example, personal moral beliefs are a more important influence on whether adults use marijuana than the fear of legal sanctions (Meier & Johnson, 1977). Adults who believe that the use of marijuana is wrong do not use it, regardless of their perception of the likelihood that they will be sanctioned for its use.

We have seen that personal experience or peers' experience of punishment is associated with greater perceived risk. This suggests that more vigorous or aggressive arrest practices (a "crackdown") should increase perceived risk, which in turn should reduce crime. A study of arrest practices in one precinct in New York City found that increases in the number of arrests per officer and total arrests for violent crimes produced decreases in cases of robbery and burglary. But the effect was not linear; beyond a threshold, further increases in arrests produced a larger number of robberies and burglaries. Also, arrest vigor did not produce decreases in assault, suggesting that deterrence effects of crackdowns occur for economic crimes and crimes in public, but not noneconomic crimes that occur in private (Kane, 2006).

A second function of the public identification of deviant persons is to provide a scapegoat for the release of tension. Many people face threats to the stability and security of their daily lives. Some fear the possibility that they will be victimized by aggressive behavior or the criminal activity of others. The existence of such threats arouses tension. Persons identified publicly as deviant persons provide a focus for these fears and insecurities. Thus, the publicly identified deviant person becomes the concrete threat we can deal with decisively.

This scapegoating process is illustrated among the Puritans, who came to New England in the 1600s to establish a community based on a specific Christian theology. As time passed, groups within the community

Nothing unites a community or a society like a common enemy. One function of publicity about major crimes is to create that cohesion. The widespread television and newspaper coverage of the San Bernardino mass shooting in December 2015 is a case in point. © "San Bernardino mass shooting" by "Renegade98" licensed under a Creative Commons Attribution 2.0 Generic (CC BY-SA 2.0). Accessed 15 September, 2017. https://www.flickr.com/photos/joshuatree/23112751399/in/photostream/

periodically challenged the ministers' claims that they were the sole interpreters of the theology. Furthermore, the community faced the threat of Native American attacks and the problems of daily survival in a harsh environment. In 1692, a group of young women began to behave in such bizarre ways as screaming, convulsing, crawling on all fours, and barking like dogs. The community focused attention on these women. The physicians defined them as "witches," representatives of Satan, and the entire community banded together in search of others who were under the "Devil's influence." The community imprisoned many persons suspected of sorcery and sent 22 persons to their deaths. Thus, the witch hunt provided a scapegoat—an outlet for people's fears and anxieties (Erikson, 1966).

A third function of the public identification of deviant persons is to increase the cohesion and solidarity of society. Nothing unites the members of a group like a common enemy

(Cohen, 1966). Deviant persons, in this context, are "internal enemies"—persons whose behavior threatens the morale and efficiency of a group. Should the solidarity of the group be threatened, it can be restored by identifying one member as deviant and imposing appropriate sanctions. Suppose you are given the case study of a boy with a history of delinquency who is to be sentenced for a minor crime. You are asked to discuss the case with three other persons and decide what should be done. One member of the group argues for extreme discipline, whereas you and the other two favor leniency. Suddenly, an expert in criminal justice, who has been sitting quietly in the corner, announces that your group should not be allowed to reach a decision. How might you deal with this threat to the group's existence? The reasoning just outlined suggests that the person who took the extreme position will be identified as the cause of the group's poor performance and that the other members will try to exclude them from future group meetings. A laboratory study used exactly this setup, contrasting the reaction of threatened groups to the person taking the extreme position with the reaction of nonthreatened groups. In the former condition, the person taking the extreme position was more likely to be stigmatized and rejected (Lauderdale, 1976).

Thus, controlled amounts of deviant behavior serve important functions. If deviance is useful, we might expect control agencies to "create" deviance when the functions it serves are needed. In fact, the number of persons who are publicly identified as deviant seems to reflect the levels of stress and integration in society (Scott, 1976). When integration declines, there is an increased probability of deviance. Eventually, the level and severity of deviance may reach a point where citizens will demand a "crackdown." Social control agencies will step up their activity, increasing the number of publicly identified deviant persons. This, in turn, will increase solidarity and lower stress, leading to an increase in the amount of informal control and a reduction in deviance.

**The Process of Labeling.** Labeling is not a simple, one-step procedure for formal agencies. The processing of rule breakers usually involves a sequence of decisions. At each step, someone has to decide whether to terminate the process or to pass the rule breaker on to the next step. Figure 13.3 shows the sequence of steps involved in processing criminal defendants.

Each of the control agents—police officers, prosecutors, and judges—has to make many decisions every day. Like anyone else, they develop cognitive schemas and rules that simplify their decision making (see Chapter 7). A very common police–citizen encounter occurs when an officer stops a motorist who has been drinking. What determines whether a driver who has been drinking is labeled a "drunken driver"? Officers on the street rely on a variety of subjective data, such as visible intoxication or the odor of alcohol (Myrstol, 2012), since the breathalyzer or blood or urine test are usually available only at the police station. Research suggests that police officers develop a series of informal guidelines that they use in deciding whether to arrest the motorist.

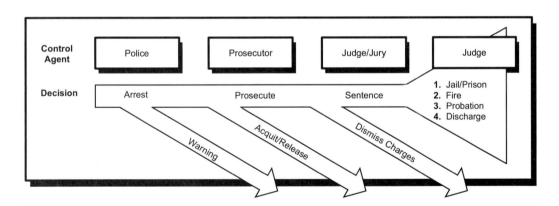

**FIGURE 13.3** Formal Social Control: Processing Criminal Defendants

Formal social control often involves several control agents, each of whom makes one or more decisions. The first step in the criminal justice system is an encounter with a law enforcement officer. If you are arrested, the case is passed to a prosecutor, who decides whether to prosecute. If your case goes to court, the judge or jury decides whether you are guilty. Finally, the judge renders a sentence. These decision makers are influenced by their own personal attitudes, cognitive schemas, role expectations, and the attitudes of others regarding their decisions. Much research is devoted to the social psychological aspects of decision making in the criminal justice system.

In one study of 195 police encounters with persons who had been drinking, arrests were more likely if the encounter occurred downtown and if the citizen was disrespectful (Lundman, 1974).

A study of policing and everyday life in skid row (Stuart, 2016) combined interviews, observation, and ride-alongs to document how officers interact with the men who live there. Officers engaged in harassment, stops, searches, and arrests, practices that seem random and inhumane to some observers. The officers' rationale was that these men were failed people who needed to be coerced into changing their lifestyles so they will get out of skid row. The officers embraced an ideology of therapeutic policing.

Prosecutors also develop informal rules that govern their decisions. For example, in one large Midwestern city, taking an object worth less than $100 is a misdemeanor, and conviction normally results in a fine. The theft of a more valuable object is a felony and results in a prison sentence. Because felony theft cases require much more time and effort, the prosecutor charged most persons arrested for shoplifting with misdemeanors, even if they had taken jewelry worth hundreds of dollars.

In many jurisdictions, probation officers are asked to prepare a presentencing report and to recommend a sentence for the convicted person. Research indicates that these officers have a set of typologies or schemas into which they sort persons (Lurigis & Carroll, 1985). Semi-structured interviews with probation officers in one community identified 10 schemas, including *burglar, addict, gang member, welfare fraud,* and *conman.* Each schema was associated with beliefs about the motive for the crime and the appropriate treatment and prognosis. When officers were asked to evaluate sample cases, those fitting a schema were evaluated more quickly and confidently. More experienced officers were more likely to use similar schemas (Drass & Spencer, 1987).

Each step in this process involves interaction between professionals and the alleged rule breaker—and often members of their family. The professional's goal is to have the rule breaker and other laypersons accept the label. Research on the labeling of children with developmental disabilities suggests that family members are more likely to accept a diagnosis if the professional elicits family members' schemas and frames the diagnosis/label in those terms (Gill & Maynard, 1995).

**Biases in Social Control.** Not all persons who violate the rules are labeled. Most social control agencies process only some of those who engage in rule-breaking behavior. In the study of police encounters with drunken persons, only 31 percent were arrested (Lundman, 1974). In some cases, control agents may be influenced by the demeanor of the rule breaker, by the agent's schema, or by where the violation occurs. This leads one to ask whether systematic biases exist in the social control system.

It has been suggested that control agents are more likely to label those people who have the least power to resist their certification as deviant (Quinney, 1970). This hypothesis predicts that lower-class persons and members of racial and ethnic minorities are more likely to be certified as deviant than upper-class, middle-class, and White persons. This hypothesis offers a radically different explanation for the correlation between crime and social class. Earlier in this chapter, we suggested that crime rates are higher for lower-class persons because they do not have access to nondeviant means of economic success. Here we are suggesting that crime rates are higher among lower-class persons because they are more likely to be arrested, prosecuted, and found guilty, even though the underlying rate of deviant activity may not vary as a function of social class.

Does social class or race influence how an individual is treated by control agents? One way to answer this question is by studying

Whether a police officer gives a citizen a traffic ticket or not depends partly on the demeanor of the citizen. Officers are more likely to ticket or arrest hostile, argumentative persons than polite and submissive ones. © Kali Nine LLC/iStock

police–citizen encounters through the ride-along method, in which trained observers ride in squad cars and systematically record data about police–citizen encounters. In the largest study of this kind, observers rode with some officers on all shifts every day for 7 weeks. Data were collected in Boston, Washington, and Chicago, and included 5,713 encounters. There was no evidence that Blacks were more likely to be arrested than Whites. Rather, arrests were more likely when a third party demanded an arrest, when the evidence was strong, and when the crime was serious (Black, 1980). A study of how police officers managed violent encounters between citizens found that arrest was more likely if the incident involved White persons; two men instead of one woman and one man, or two women; or if one person acted abusively toward the officer (Smith, 1987). On the other hand,

research that included ride-alongs in Washington, DC, suggests that at least in that city, Blacks are subjected to more intense police surveillance than other racial/ethnic groups (Chambliss, 1994).

Police officers frequently have to make a quick decision about whether someone is dangerous or a "criminal." As noted above, they rely on schemas they learn in training and on the job. Research indicates that they rely on nonverbal cues such as speech disruptions, inappropriate smiles, and avoidance of eye contact as indicators of nervousness or deception. An analysis of videotaped police–citizen encounters included interactions with 40 African-American, 40 Caucasian and 40 Hispanic persons who were innocent, and 40 from each group in which there was evidence that the suspect had committed a crime. While guilty White men and women did display more frequent speech disruptions, innocent African-American persons were more likely to display these nonverbal behaviors than guilty ones (Johnson, 2007).

What about decisions by prosecutors? Do they entail discrimination based on race or class? Prosecutors are generally motivated to maximize the ratio of convictions to trials. This may be one criterion that citizens use in evaluating the performance of an elected district attorney. Prosecutors develop beliefs about which cases are "strong"—that is, likely to result in conviction. A study of a random sample of 980 defendants charged with felonies found that prosecutors are more likely to prosecute cases involving serious crimes where the evidence is strong and the defendant has a serious prior police record. Race was not generally influential (Myers & Hagan, 1979).

Does the social class of an arrested person influence how they are treated by the courts? Several studies of the handling of juvenile cases report little evidence of class or race bias. A study of cases in Denver and Memphis found that the seriousness of the offense and the youth's prior record were the major determinants of the sentence given (Cohen & Kluegel, 1978). Two longitudinal studies, of 9,945 boys in Philadelphia (Thornberry & Christenson, 1984) and of cases in Florida (Henretta, Frazier, & Bishop, 1986), found that the most important influence on the disposition of a charge was the disposition imposed for a prior offense or offenses.

A common practice in adult criminal cases is plea bargaining, in which a prosecutor and a defendant's lawyer negotiate a plea to avoid the time and expense of a trial. A single action frequently violates several laws. For instance, if a driver who has been drinking runs a red light and hits a pedestrian who later dies, that incident involves at least three crimes: drunken driving, failure to obey a signal, and vehicular manslaughter. These offenses vary in seriousness and thus in their associated sentences. The prosecutor may offer not to indict the driver for manslaughter if a plea of guilty is entered to a drunken driving charge. The attorney may accept the offer, provided the prosecutor also recommends a suspended sentence.

Are the members of certain groups more likely to be tried or to get bigger reductions in sentences? An analysis of charge reduction or plea bargaining in a sample of 1,435 criminal defendants found that women and Whites received slightly more favorable reductions than men and Blacks (Bernstein, Kick, Leung, & Schulz, 1977). Another study of 1,213 men charged with felonies found that the characteristics of an offense—especially the seriousness of the crime and the strength of the evidence—were most important in determining the disposition. The outcomes of the cases were not related to age, ethnicity, or employment status (Bernstein, Kelly, & Doyle, 1977). A study of 296 women who killed another person found that whereas they were all initially charged with murder, in two-thirds of the cases, the charge was reduced to manslaughter or a lesser offense (Mann, 1996). Women in Southern cities and women who killed men were less likely to have the charge(s) reduced and received more severe sentences if convicted.

Among the persons convicted, do we find a class or racial bias in the length of the sentences given? One study focused on the sentences received by 10,488 persons in three Southern states: North Carolina, South Carolina, and Florida (Chiricos & Waldo, 1975). The researchers examined sentences for 17 different offenses and found no relationship between socioeconomic status or race and sentence length. Again, the individual's prior record was the principal variable related to sentence length. A study of a random sample of 16,798 felons convicted during the years 1976–1982 in Georgia looked at racial differences in sentencing (Myers & Talarico, 1986). In general, the seriousness of a crime was the principal influence on the sentence length. Another study of the influence of race on sentencing analyzed federal court proceedings (as opposed to state courts) for the years 1993–1996. The sentences given male defendants varied by race/ethnicity. For offenses of the same seriousness, there were small to moderate effects, with Whites receiving shorter sentences and Hispanics receiving longer ones; Blacks received intermediate sentences (Steffensmeier & Demuth, 2000).

Earlier, we discussed white-collar crime, which is often committed by middle-class and upper-class persons. Are white-collar offenders more likely to receive lenient sentences? A study of persons charged with embezzlement and tax, lending, credit, postal, and wire fraud found that within this group, high-status persons were no less likely to be imprisoned or to receive shorter sentences (Benson & Walker, 1988). The significant influences were the total amount of dollars involved and how widespread the offenses were. Blacks did receive longer sentences than Whites. It is sometimes argued that judges are lenient on high-status offenders because they suffer serious informal sanctions, such as the loss of a job. A study of the likelihood of job loss and the influence of job loss on sentence severity found no relationship (Benson, 1989). However, class position did influence job loss; high-status offenders and those whose frauds were larger in scale were less likely to lose their jobs.

Persons sentenced to prison may become eligible for parole. What influences decisions at this stage? A study in Alabama analyzed the influence of race. Alabama uses a two-stage process: a screening to determine who should be considered for parole, and a parole decision—whether to release the prisoner. Considering 762 cases, the results showed that race did not have a significant effect at either stage. At the preliminary stage, significant influences were seriousness of offense, time served, discipline while in prison, and parole officer's recommendation. The only significant influence on the decision was recommendations by prison personnel (Morgan & Smith, 2008).

## Long-Term Effects of Formal Labeling

How long does the official label of "deviant" stick to a person? Can it be shaken? In contrast to the trial or hearing in which a person is formally certified as deviant, there is no formal ceremony terminating one's deviant status (Erikson, 1964). People are simply released from prison or mental hospital, or the final day of probation passes—with no fanfare. Does the individual regain their former status upon release, or does deviant status in our society tend to be for life?

Some argue that ex-convicts, ex-patients, and others who have been labeled as deviant face continuing pressures from family, friends, employers, and coworkers that prevent them from readjusting to normal life. Such pressures constitute a reminder of their former deviant status.

One domain in which persons who have been officially labeled might face discrimination is employment. In the United States, a good job is essential to health and welfare as an adult. Labeling theory asserts that contact with authorities will reduce one's occupational attainment, independently of the rule-breaking or deviant behavior. Longitudinal data allowed a study of the effect of contact with authorities (suspended from school, stopped by police, charged, convicted, sentenced, jailed) at ages 15 to 23 on status (employed, status, income) during ages 29 to 37 (Davies & Tanner, 2003). For males, suspension or being stopped had little effect; the more serious forms of contact, especially being jailed, had significant negative effects on average hours worked, status of job, and income. For women, suspension had negative effects; also, being sentenced and jailed had substantial impact, with incarceration resulting in a reduction in annual income of more than 50 percent! Another study of data from more than 3,600 men compared those who had been incarcerated with men who had not (Western, 2002); overall, incarceration reduced subsequent earnings by 19 percent, and also resulted in slower wage growth in later years. The impact on Black and Hispanic men was about twice as large as the impact on White men.

Discrimination in employment following formal labeling may occur because others perceive these persons as "delinquents," "ex-cons," or "crazies," and expect them to behave in ways consistent with the label. A study of the impact of a criminal record on decisions by employers used the audit method, which involves sending matched pairs of people (testers) to apply for real job openings. The pairs differ on some characteristic, and the researcher observes whether employers respond differently to the two people. Two young White men and two young Black men, matched on age, physical appearance, and style, applied for the same jobs one day apart. One man of each race had a criminal record—a felony drug conviction that resulted in 18 months in prison. Each tester posed as the convicted felon in alternate weeks. The dependent variable was whether the employer called back the young man for an interview. Having a record had a significant effect. For the White pair, the man without the record was called 34 percent of the time, whereas the man with the record was called 17 percent of the time. Among the Black testers, the percentages were 14 percent and 5 percent (Pager, 2003). Thus, the combination of being Black and having a criminal record makes it unlikely one will be called for an interview. This, coupled with high rates of incarceration in the U.S., contributes to the high rates of unemployment in minority communities.

Questionnaires and interviews with men hoping to transition from AIDS disability back to work focused on issues of identity. The men countered the stigma of living with AIDS by developing a romanticized anticipatory identity as worker/gay man/recovered. As they sought re-employment, they experienced discrimination and shame, and had to adjust to medical and other constraints, producing an actualized identity at odds with the anticipatory one. The transition back into the worker role was thus very stressful for some (Ghaziani, 2004).

Another approach to studying the long-term effects is to compare persons who have and have not been labeled. A study of psychiatrically disturbed persons compared the income and employment status of those who had been treated (labeled) with the income and status of those who had not been treated. Treatment was negatively associated with both income and employment (Link, 1982). The impact seemed to depend partly on whether occupational competence was developed before or after the onset of the illness. Men who had no history of competent work performance had more difficulty obtaining employment following hospitalization. Men who had a history of occupational competence usually kept their jobs, even during periods when their work performance was seriously affected.

Some persons turn a career history of deviance into an occupational asset by becoming a "professional ex-" (Brown, 1991a). Individuals with histories of alcohol or drug abuse or other problem behaviors sometimes become counselors, working with others who are involved in these behaviors. Professionalizing rather than giving up the deviant identity is another way of going straight.

A study of the long-term impact of being labeled as mentally ill suggests that it is not the label by itself that has impact but the label combined with changes in self-perception (Link, 1987). The study compared samples of residents and clinic patients from the same area of New York City. Three samples involved people who had been labeled: first-treatment contact patients, repeat-treatment contact patients, and formerly treated community residents. The other two groups were untreated "cases" (people with symptoms) and a sample of residents. All participants completed a scale that measured the belief that mental patients are stigmatized and discriminated against. High scores on the measure were associated with reduced income and unemployment in the labeled groups but not in the unlabeled ones. Later research shows that when people enter treatment, those who expect discrimination use strategies such as keeping their condition secret or withdrawing from interaction (Link et al., 1989). This tends to cut them off from social support and interfere with their work performance.

A longitudinal study of recovery from mental illness obtained data from members of self-help groups ($N = 590$) and outpatients ($N = 90$) two times, 18 months apart. The results indicate that recovery is a complex process. As reported satisfaction with job status, income, place of residence, and time spent with family and friends increase, symptoms decrease. Decreases in symptoms over the 18-month period were associated with increases in self-esteem. In turn, we would expect increases in self-esteem to be associated with reduced symptoms and recovery (Markowitz, 2001). Thus, an important part of recovery is the quality of social, economic, and occupational roles available to the person.

The long-term effects of formal labeling on the reactions of others may be limited, because persons who have been labeled in the past engage in various tactics to prevent others from learning about their stigma. These tactics include selective concealment of past labeling, preventive disclosure to close friends, and various deception strategies (Miall, 1986). On the other hand, longitudinal research suggests that persons who have been publicly labeled and treated continue to anticipate rejection from others even though they no longer engage in the symptomatic behavior (Link et al., 1997). A longitudinal study of 88 persons released following an average of 8 years of hospitalization measured experiences with rejection following release. Those who reported a larger number of such experiences

subsequently attained low scores on mastery. Former patients' self-views appear to fluctuate, perhaps in response to alternating experiences of acceptance and stigma (Wright, Gronfein, & Owens, 2000). Thus, stigma may have lasting effects on a person's psychological well-being.

## SUMMARY

Deviant behavior is any act that violates the social norms that apply in a given situation.

**The Violation of Norms.** (1) Norms are local, subcultural, or societal in scope. The repercussions of deviant behavior depend on which type of norm an individual violates. (2) Anomie theory asserts that deviance occurs when persons do not have legitimate means available for attaining cultural success goals. Possible responses to anomie include ritualism, retreatism, innovation, and rebellion. General strain theory suggests that emotions link structural position and behavior. (3) Control theory states that deviance occurs when an individual is not responsive to the expectations of others. This responsiveness, or social bond, includes attachment to others, commitment to long-term goals, involvement in conventional activities, and a respect for law and authority. Research indicates that social integration is associated with reduced rates of deviance in adolescence and adulthood. (4) Differential association theory emphasizes the importance of learning through interaction with others. Individuals often learn the motives and actions that constitute deviant behavior just as they learn socially approved behavior. (5) The routine activities perspective calls attention to situations that facilitate the convergence of offenders and targets, in the absence of a guardian.

**Reactions to Norm Violations.** Deviant behavior involves not only acts that violate social norms but also the societal reactions to these acts. (1) There are numerous possible responses to rule breaking. Very often, we ignore it. At other times, we deny that the act occurred, define the act as normal, excuse the perpetrator, or recognize the act but de-emphasize its significance. Only after an act is discovered and labeled "deviant" is it recognized as such. (2) Our reaction to rule breaking depends on the characteristics of the actor, the audience, and the situation. People often have a stereotyped image of deviant persons; these stereotypes influence how audiences react to rule violations. (3) The consequences of rule breaking depend on the reactions of the audience and the response of the rule breaker. If members of the audience reward the person, the deviance may become institutionalized. Alternatively, the person may decide to avoid further deviance, in spite of others' encouragement. If the person is punished, they may either give up the behavior or respond with additional rule violations.

**Labeling and Secondary Deviance.** The process of labeling has two important consequences. (1) It leads members of an audience to change their perceptions of and behavior toward the actor. If they withdraw from the stigmatized person, they may create a self-fulfilling prophecy and elicit the behavior they expected from the actor. (2) Labeling often causes the actor to change their self-image and to come to define the self as deviant. This, in turn, may lead to secondary deviance—an open and active involvement in a lifestyle based on deviance. Such lifestyles are often embedded in deviant subcultures.

**Formal Social Controls.** Every society gives certain agents the authority to respond to deviant behavior. (1) In U.S. society, the major formal social control agents are the criminal justice, juvenile justice, and mental health systems. These agencies select persons and identify them as deviant through a sequence of decisions. In the criminal justice

system, the sequence includes the decisions to arrest, prosecute, and sentence the person. Various factors influence each step in decision making, including the strength of the evidence, the seriousness of the rule violation, and the individual's prior record, and sometimes gender and race. (2) Contrary to popular belief, people do not systematically stigmatize former deviant persons. Most families do not continue to stigmatize relatives following their release from mental hospitals, and most employers do not stigmatize ex-patients who have established competent work records. On the other hand, employers may stigmatize minority men with prison records, and stigma may have long-term effects on the ex-deviant person's psychological well-being.

### Critical Thinking Skill: Applying Stigmatizing Labels Critically

A major contribution of the labeling perspective on deviance is calling our attention to the fact that many of the words we use to describe people who engage in deviance are stigmatizing. Labels like "slut," "jd" (juvenile delinquent), "psycho," "child molester," and "murderer" carry a strong negative evaluation. If we use such labels in conversation, it changes the attitudes of others toward the person; eventually the label gets back to the person and may have a negative impact on their self-image and mental health. So it is really important that we use these labels only when they are accurate. Therefore, the issues are (1) to what does the label refer exactly, and (2) does the person actually have that characteristic?

One concern is that the meaning of some labels is ambiguous to begin with. The term *slut* is used to refer to someone who is sexually promiscuous; but what does that mean? In practice it probably means different things to different people. So whether a woman is a slut is subjective; it depends on the standards of the person doing the labeling. They may have very different standards than you do.

We also reviewed research in this chapter that indicates that often a person is labeled a slut, gay or lesbian, or an alcoholic based on indirect evidence. The person applying the label may not have observed relevant behavior—sex with multiple partners, or excessive drinking. Labeling is often based on dress—showing a lot of skin, wearing colorful clothing—hanging out with a certain group, working in a certain occupation, or being a type of athlete ("all ___ are lesbians").

Labels are communicated through social interaction. If a friend tells you that Jade is lesbian and you repeat the label to others, you are uncritically accepting another person's judgment—a judgment you might not agree with if you knew "the facts." This, of course, is gossip, which can ruin another person's reputation, possibly wrongly. People have been forced to change schools and jobs, lost relationships, and even committed suicide because of gossip.

A critical thinker should not accept without question the accuracy of such labels. At a minimum, we should inquire how the person applying the label knows it is accurate. If the answer is "So-and-so said so" or "Everybody knows!" we should be skeptical.

# INTERPERSONAL ATTRACTION AND RELATIONSHIPS

By the end of this chapter you will be able to:

- Define "availables" and "desirables," and list the influences on each.

- Explain the main determinants of liking or attraction to another person.

- Describe the process by which friendship and love develop between two people.

- Explain several different perspectives on love.

- Discuss influences on the course of a relationship.

- Describe processes involved in the termination of relationships.

## INTRODUCTION

Dan was looking forward to the new semester. Now that he was a junior, he would be taking more interesting classes. He walked into the lecture hall and found a seat halfway down the aisle. As he looked toward the front, he noticed a very pretty young woman removing her coat; as he watched, she sat down in the front row.

Dan noticed her at every class; she always sat in the same seat. One morning, he passed up his usual spot and sat down next to her.

"Hi," he said. "You must like this class. You never miss it."

"I do, but it sure is a lot of work."

As they talked, they discovered they were from the same city and both were economics majors. When the professor announced the first exam, Dan asked Mia if she wanted to study for it with him. They worked together for several hours the night before the exam, along with Mia's roommate. Dan and Mia did very well on the exam.

The next week, he took her to a film at a campus theater. The week after, she asked him to a party at her dormitory. That night, as they were walking back to her room, Mia told Dan that her roommate's parents had just separated and that her roommate was severely depressed. Dan replied that he knew how she felt because his older brother had just left his wife. Because it was late, they agreed to meet the next morning for breakfast. They spent all day Sunday talking about love, marriage, parents, and their hopes for the future. By the end of the semester, Mia and Dan were seeing each other two or three times a week.

At its outset, the relationship between Dan and Mia was based on **interpersonal attraction**—a positive attitude held by one person toward another person. Over time, however, the development of their relationship involved increasing interdependence and increasing intimacy.

The development and outcome of personal relationships involves several stages. This chapter discusses each of these stages.

## WHO IS AVAILABLE?

Hundreds or thousands of persons may go to school or live or work where you do. Most of them remain strangers—persons with whom you have no contact. Those persons with whom we come into contact, no matter how fleeting, constitute the field of **availables**—the pool of potential friends and lovers (Kerckhoff, 1974). What determines who is available? Is it mere chance that George rather than Bill is your roommate, or that Dan met Mia rather than Heather? The answer, of course, is no.

Two basic influences determine who is available. First, institutional structures influence our personal encounters. The admissions office of your school, the faculty committees that decide degree requirements, and the scheduling office all influence whether Dan and Mia enroll in the same class. Second, individuals' personal characteristics influence their choice of activities. Dan chose to take the economics class where he met Mia because of an interest in that field and a desire to go to graduate school in business. Mia took the course because she planned to major in econ, and it met at 10:00 a.m. (instead of 8:00 a.m.). Thus, institutional and personal characteristics together determine who is available.

Given a set of persons who are available, how do we make contact with one or two of these persons? Three influences progressively narrow our choices: routine activities, proximity, and familiarity.

## Routine Activities

Much of our life consists of a routine of activities that we repeat daily or weekly. We attend the same classes and sit in the same seats, eat in the same places at the same tables, shop in the same stores, ride the same bus, and work with the same people. These activities provide opportunities to interact with some availables but not with others. More important, the activity provides a focus for our initial interactions. We rarely establish a relationship by saying "Let's be friends" at a first meeting. To do so is risky, because the other person may decide to exploit us. Or that person may reject such an opening, which may damage our self-esteem. Instead, we begin by talking about something shared—a class, an ethnic background, a school, or the weather.

Most relationships begin in the context of routine activities. A study of college students found that relationships began with a meeting in a class, a dorm, or at work (36 percent); with an introduction by a third person (38 percent); or at parties (18 percent) or bars (14 percent). A study of 3,342 adults aged 18 to 59 asked how respondents met their sexual partners (Laumann, Gagnon, Michael, & Michaels, 1994).

One-third reported that they were introduced by a friend, and another third said they were introduced by family members or coworkers. Thus, social networks play an important role in the development of relationships. Studies of the friendship patterns of city dwellers have found that friends are selected from relatives, coworkers, and neighbors (Fischer, 1984). Thus, routine activities and social networks are important influences on the development of relationships.

How has the Internet affected where couples meet? A study of 2,462 heterosexual and 462 same-sex couples documents the changes (Rosenfeld & Thomas, 2012). Figure 14.1 displays the results. Since 1995, the percentage of couples meeting through family and friends has declined steadily, while the percentage meeting online has increased. The Internet has especially changed how same-sex couples meet.

## Proximity

Although routine activities bring us into the same classroom, dining hall, or workplace, we are not equally likely to meet every person who is present. Rather, we are more likely to develop a relationship with someone who is in close physical proximity to us.

In classroom settings, seating patterns are an important influence on the development of friendships. One study (Byrne, 1961a) varied the seating arrangements for three classes of about 25 students each. In one class, they remained in the same seats for the entire semester (14 weeks). In the second class, they were assigned new seats halfway through the semester. In the third class, they were assigned new seats every 3½ weeks. The relationships among students were assessed at the beginning and at the end of the semester. Few relationships developed among the students in the class where seats were changed every 3½ weeks. In the other two classes, students in neighboring seats became acquainted in greater numbers

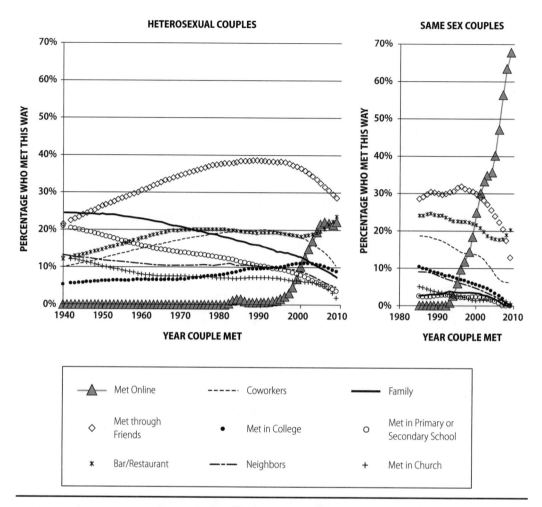

**FIGURE 14.1** The Impact of the Internet on Where People Meet

A unique data set allows us a glimpse at how the Internet has affected where people meet. A survey of 2,462 heterosexual couples and 462 same-sex couples asked where they met and the year they met. The results are displayed here. Among heterosexual couples, meeting through friends has become less important since 1995; in 2010, about 20 percent met on the Internet. Among same-sex couples, there have been dramatic declines in the importance of all the traditional sources, with almost 70 percent of those meeting in 2010 reporting they met on the Internet.

*Source:* M. J. Rosenfeld & R. J. Thomas (2012). "Searching for a mate: The rise of the Internet as a social intermediary." *American Sociological Review, 77,* 523–547.

than students in nonneighboring seats. Moreover, the relationships were closer in the class where seat assignments were not changed.

Similar positive associations between physical proximity and friendship have been found in a variety of natural settings, including dormitories (Priest & Sawyer, 1967), married student housing complexes (Festinger, Schachter, & Back, 1950), and business offices (Schutte & Light, 1978).

We are more likely to develop friendships with persons in close proximity because such relationships provide interpersonal rewards at the lowest cost. Interaction is easier with those

When we think about where people meet available partners, we often picture the singles bar. However, studies of heterosexual relationships have found that relatively few people met their partners at a bar. Much more common were meetings in classes, dorms, or workplaces. © Kzenon/Shutterstock

who are close by. It costs less time and energy to interact with the person sitting next to you than with someone on the other side of the room.

## Familiarity

As time passes, people who take the same classes, live in the same apartment building, or do laundry in the same place become familiar with each other. Having seen a person several times, sooner or later we will smile or nod. Repeated exposure to the same novel stimulus is sufficient to produce a positive attitude toward it; this is called the **mere exposure effect** (Zajonc, 1968). In other words, familiarity breeds liking, not contempt. This effect is highly general and has been demonstrated for a wide variety of stimuli—such as music, visual art, and comic strips—under many different conditions (Harrison, 1977).

Does mere exposure produce attraction? The answer appears to be yes. In one experiment, female undergraduates were asked to participate in an experiment on their sense of taste. They entered a series of booths in pairs and rated the taste of various liquids. The schedule was set up so that two participants shared the same booth either once, twice, five times, ten times, or not at all. At the end of the experiment, each woman rated how much she liked each of the other participants. As predicted, the more frequently a woman had been in the same booth with another participant, the higher the rating (Saegert, Swap, & Zajonc, 1973). Interestingly, the increase in liking as a function of frequency of exposure is greater for stimuli that are presented subliminally, of which the person is not consciously aware (Bornstein, 1992).

## WHO IS DESIRABLE?

We come into contact with many potential partners, but contact by itself does not ensure the development of a relationship. Whether a relationship of some type actually develops between two persons depends on whether each is attracted to the other. Initial attraction is influenced by social norms, physical attractiveness, and processes of interpersonal exchange. If the attraction is mutual, the interaction that occurs is governed by scripts.

### Social Norms

Each culture specifies the types of relationships that people may have. For each type, norms specify what kinds of people are allowed to have such a relationship. These norms tell us which persons are appropriate as friends, lovers, and mentors. In U.S. society, there is a **norm of homogamy**—a norm requiring that friends, lovers, and spouses be similar in age, race, religion, and socioeconomic status (Kerckhoff, 1974). Research shows that homogamy is characteristic of all types of social relationships from acquaintance to intimate (McPherson, Smith-Lovin, & Cook, 2001). Interviews with 832 students attending the same (all-White) high school obtained data on their romantic/sexual relationships (Bearman, Moody, & Stovel, 2004). The students' relationships were homophilous on IQ, family socioeconomic status (SES), getting drunk, sexual activity, and college plans.

A survey of 3,342 adults assessed the extent to which partners in relationships were similar on the following dimensions (Laumann et al., 1994): 75 to 83 percent were homophilous (similar) by age, 82 to 87 percent by education, 88 to 93 percent by race/ethnicity, and 53 to 72 percent by religion. Differences on one or more of these dimensions make a person less appropriate as an intimate partner and more appropriate for some other kind of relationship. Thus, a person who is much older

but of the same social class and ethnicity may be appropriate as a mentor—someone who can provide advice about how to manage your career. Potential dates are single persons who are of similar age, class, ethnicity, and religion. Same-sex couples are less likely to be homogeneous on race/ethnicity, age, and education, perhaps due to the limited availability of partners (Schwartz & Graf, 2007).

Norms that define appropriateness influence the development of relationships in several ways. First, each of us uses norms to monitor our own behavior. We hesitate to establish a relationship with someone who is defined by norms as an inappropriate partner. Thus, a low-status person is unlikely to approach a high-status person as a potential friend. For example, the law clerk who just joined a firm would not discuss their hobbies with the senior partner (unless they asked). Second, if one person attempts to initiate a relationship with someone who is defined by norms as inappropriate, the other person will probably refuse to reciprocate. If the clerk did launch into an extended description of the joys of restoring antique model trains, the senior partner would probably end the interaction. Third, even if both persons are willing to interact, third parties often enforce the norms that prohibit the relationship (Kerckhoff, 1974). Another member of the firm might later chide the clerk for presuming that the senior partner cared about their personal interests.

In the twenty-first century, interracial relationships continue to be rare in the United States. A study of adolescent friendships found that "best friends" are typically of the same race/ethnicity, particularly among Whites (92 percent) and Blacks (85 percent), compared to Hispanics (51 percent) and Asians (48 percent) (Kao & Joyner, 2004). In 2010, only 9.5 percent of married couples were interracial; of these, 38 percent were White–Hispanic, 8 percent were Black–White, and the rest were White–other (U.S. Bureau of the Census,

According to the matching hypothesis, people seek partners whose level of social desirability is about equal to their own. We frequently encounter couples who are matched—that is, who are similar in age, race, ethnicity, social class, and physical attractiveness. © Cathy Yeulet/123rf

2010). In 2013, 12 percent of newlyweds married someone of a different race (Pew Research Center, 2015). The norm of homogamy remains especially strong on this dimension (Blackwell & Lichter, 2004). Research on interracial romantic relationships found that non-White males reported more disapproval from their White female partners' family and friends than any other race/gender combination (Miller, Olson, & Fazio, 2004).

## Physical Attractiveness

In addition to social norms that define who is appropriate, individuals also have personal preferences regarding desirability. Someone may be normatively appropriate but still not appeal to you. Physical attractiveness can have a significant impact on desirability.

**Impact of Physical Attractiveness.** A great deal of evidence shows that given a choice of more than one potential partner, individuals will prefer the one who is more physically attractive (Hendrick & Hendrick, 1992). A study of 752 first-year college students, for example, demonstrates that most individuals prefer more attractive persons as dates (Walster [Hatfield], Aronson, Abrahams, & Rottman, 1966). As part of the study, students were invited to attend a dance. Before the dance, each student's physical attractiveness was secretly rated by four people, and each student completed a questionnaire. Although the students were told they would be paired by the computer, in fact, men and women were paired randomly. At the dance, during the intermission, students filled out a questionnaire that measured their impressions of their dates.

This study tested the **matching hypothesis**—the idea that each of us looks for someone who is of approximately the same level of social desirability. The researchers predicted that the students whose dates matched their own level of attractiveness would like their dates most. Those whose dates were very different in attractiveness were expected to rate their dates as less desirable. Contrary to the hypothesis, in this situation, students preferred a more attractive date, regardless of their own attractiveness. This same phenomenon, "reaching for the sky," is evident in the choices of users on OkCupid; both men and women send messages, on the average, to people who are more attractive than they are (Cooper, 2015). How can we explain the significance of attractiveness? One factor is simply aesthetic; generally, we prefer what is beautiful. Although beauty is, to a degree, "in the eye of the beholder," cultural standards influence our aesthetic judgments. A study of female facial beauty found substantial agreement among male college students about which features are attractive (Cunningham, 1986). These men rated such features as large eyes, small nose, and small chin as more attractive than small eyes, large nose, and large chin. What male features do women find attractive? Female college students rated men with large eyes, prominent cheekbones, and a large chin as more attractive (Cunningham, Barbee, & Pike, 1990). Research has also found a high level of agreement among men that certain female body shapes are more appealing than others (Wiggins, Wiggins, & Conger, 1968) and agreement among women about which male body shapes are attractive (Beck, Ward-Hull, & McLear, 1976). It is not an accident that every online dating site and digital matching app includes photos in user profiles. The increasing popularity of "swipe sites" like Tinder and Grindr, in contrast to sites like Match.com and eHarmony which provide more detailed profiles, suggests that appearance is the most important characteristic online (Khazan, 2013).

A second factor is that we anticipate more rewards when we associate with attractive persons. A man accompanied by an extremely attractive woman receives more attention and prestige from other persons than if he is seen with an unattractive woman, and vice versa (Sigall & Landy, 1973).

**The Attractiveness Stereotype.** A third factor is the **attractiveness stereotype**—the belief that "what is beautiful is good" (Dion, Berscheid, & Walster [Hatfield], 1972). We assume that an attractive person possesses other desirable qualities. Research consistently finds that we infer that physically attractive people possess more favorable personality traits and are more likely to experience successful outcomes in their personal and social lives (Berscheid & Reis, 1998; Lorenzo, Biesanz, & Human, 2010).

There are limits to the influence of this stereotype. A meta-analysis of more than 70 studies found that attractiveness has a moderate influence on judgments of social competence—how sensitive, kind, and interesting a person is (Eagly, Ashmore, Makhijani, & Longo, 1991). It has less influence on judgments of adjustment and intelligence, and no influence on judgments of integrity or concern for others. Also, the influence of attractiveness on judgments of intellectual competence is reduced when other information about the person's competence is available (Jackson, Hunter, & Hodge, 1995).

When we believe another person possesses certain qualities, those beliefs influence our behavior toward that person. Our actions may then lead them to behave in ways that are consistent with our beliefs (see Chapter 7). In one experiment, men were shown photographs of either an attractive or an unattractive woman. They were then asked to interact with that woman via intercom for 10 minutes. The woman was actually a student volunteer. Each conversation was tape-recorded and rated by judges. Women who were perceived as attractive by the men were rated as behaving in a more friendly, likable, and sociable way than women who were perceived as unattractive. This happened in part because the men gave the target person opportunities to act in ways that would confirm their expectations based on the attractiveness stereotype (Snyder, Tanke, & Berscheid, 1977). This is a good example of the self-fulfilling prophecy.

Each of us knows that physically attractive people may receive preferential treatment. As a result, we spend tremendous amounts of time and money trying to increase our own attractiveness to others. People purchase clothing, jewelry, perfumes, colognes, and hair color products in an effort to enhance their physical attractiveness. Our choice of products reflects current standards of what looks good.

Increasingly, people are using cosmetic surgery to enhance their appearance. Plastic surgeons can lift your eyelids; pin your ears; fill your wrinkles; reshape your nose, jaw, or chin; enlarge your breasts, pectorals, or penis; and suck the fat from your abdomen, thighs, or ankles. In 2015, over 12.8 million cosmetic procedures were performed by board certified persons in the United States, 1.9 million of them involving surgery (American Society for Aesthetic Plastic Surgery, 2015). The vast majority are elective—that is, intended to enhance appearance, reflecting the impact of the attractiveness stereotype. Ninety percent of the procedures are performed on women, reflecting the greater importance of attractiveness to them. Critics point out that the procedures don't always work; they may result in misshapen features, serious scarring, or even death. This is another example of the downside of self-presentational concerns (see Box 5.2).

Not everyone prefers attractive persons. Many of us were taught—and some of us believe—that "beauty is only skin deep," and "you can't judge a book by its cover." What kinds of people are influenced by another's attractiveness, and what kinds of people

"read the book" before making a judgment? Research suggests that people who hold traditional attitudes toward men and women are those whose judgments are much more likely to be influenced by beauty (Touhey, 1979).

**Evolutionary Perspective on Attractiveness.** According to the evolutionary perspective, men and women have an evolved disposition to mate with healthy individuals so that they will produce healthy offspring, who will in turn successfully mate and pass on their parent's genetic code. According to this view, facial and bodily physical attractiveness are markers for physical and hormonal health (Thornhill & Grammar, 1999). Thus, we prefer young, attractive partners because they have high reproductive potential.

Research based on this perspective argues that women and men face different adaptive problems in short-term (casual) mating compared to long-term mating and reproduction. These differences lead to different strategies or behaviors designed to solve these problems. In short-term mating, a woman may choose a partner who offers her immediate resources such as food or money (drinks, dinner?). In long-term mating, she will prefer a partner who appears willing and able to provide resources for the indefinite future (marriage?). A man may choose a sexually available woman for a short-term liaison and avoid such women when looking for a long-term mate. A study of mating strategies found that physical attractiveness and possession of resources were judged important in selecting a long-term mate, whereas sexual availability and giving gifts were judged more important in selecting a partner for a "one-night stand" (Schmitt & Buss, 1996). Moreover, both men and women are more selective when choosing a partner for a long-term relationship (Stewart, Stinnett, & Rosenfeld, 2000). It is not surprising, according to this perspective, that singles ads emphasize attractiveness and resources. It is also worth noting that mate-selection criteria do not vary much by age in the range from age 20 to age 60 (Buunk, Dijkstra, Fetchenhauer, & Kenrick, 2002).

**Attractiveness Isn't Everything.** Physical attractiveness may have a major influence on our judgments of others because it is readily observable. When we meet someone for the first time, one characteristic we can assess quickly is their attractiveness. If other relevant information is available, it might reduce or eliminate the impact of attractiveness on our judgments. In fact, an analysis of 70 studies found that when perceivers have other personal information about the target person, the effect of the attractiveness stereotype is smaller (Eagly et al., 1991).

## Exchange Processes

How do we move from the stage of awareness of another person to the stage of contact? Recall that in our introduction, Dan noticed Mia at every lecture. Because she was young and not wearing a wedding ring, Dan hoped that she was available. She was certainly desirable—she was very pretty and seemed like a friendly person. What factors does a person consider when deciding whether to initiate contact? One important factor in this decision is the availability and desirability of alternative relationships (Backman, 1990). Thus, before you chose to initiate contact with a partner, you probably considered whether there was anyone else who might be a better choice.

**Choosing Friends.** We can view each actual or potential relationship—whether involving a friend, coworker, roommate, or romance—as promising rewards but entailing costs. Rewards are the pleasures or gratifications we derive from a relationship. These might include companionship, a gain in knowledge, enhanced self-esteem, satisfaction of emotional needs, or sexual gratification. Costs are the negative aspects of a relationship, such as

time spent, physical or mental effort, embarrassment, anxiety, and money.

Exchange theory proposes that this is, in fact, the way people view their interactions (Blau, 1964; Homans, 1974). People evaluate interactions and relationships in terms of the rewards and costs that each is likely to entail. They calculate likely outcomes by subtracting the anticipated costs from the anticipated rewards. If the expected outcome is positive, people are inclined to initiate or maintain the relationship. If the expected outcome is negative, they are unlikely to initiate a new relationship or to stay in an ongoing relationship. Dan anticipated that a relationship with Mia would be rewarding; she would be fun to do things with, and others would be impressed that he was with such an attractive woman. At the same time, he anticipated that Mia would expect him to be committed to her and that he would have to spend time and money on her. He would also have less time to play pickup basketball.

What standards can we use to evaluate the outcomes of a relationship? Two standards have been proposed (Kelley & Thibaut, 1978; Thibaut & Kelley, 1959). One is the **comparison level** (CL), the level of outcomes expected based on the average of a person's experience in past relevant relationships. Each relationship is evaluated as to whether it is above or below that person's CL—that is, better or worse than the average of past relevant relationships. Relationships that fall above a person's CL are satisfying, whereas those that fall below it are unsatisfying.

If this were the only standard, we would always initiate relationships that appeared to promise outcomes better than those we already experienced and avoid relationships that appeared to promise poorer outcomes. Sometimes, however, we use a second standard. The **comparison level for alternatives** (CLalt) is the lowest level of outcomes a person will accept *in light of the available alternatives*. A person's CLalt varies depending on the outcomes that one believes can be obtained from the best of the available alternative relationships. The use of CLalt explains why we may sometimes turn down opportunities that appear promising or why we may remain in a relationship even though we feel that the other person is getting all the benefits.

Whether a person initiates a new relationship or not will depend on both the CL and the CLalt. An individual usually avoids relationships whose anticipated outcomes fall below the CL. If a potential relationship appears likely to yield outcomes above a person's CL, initiation will depend on whether the outcomes are expected to exceed the CLalt. Dan believed that a relationship with Mia would be very satisfying. He was seeing another woman, and that relationship was not gratifying. Thus, the potential relationship with Mia was above both CL and CLalt, leading Dan to initiate contact.

Whereas CL is an absolute, relatively unchanging standard, several factors influence a person's CLalt. These factors include the extent to which routine activities provide opportunities to meet people, the size of the pool of eligible persons, and one's skills in initiating relationships.

**Making Contact.** Once we decide to initiate interaction, the next step is to make contact. Sometimes we use technology, such as the telephone or e-mail. Often, we arrange to get physically close to the person. At parties and in bars, people often circulate, which brings them into physical proximity with many of the other guests.

Once in proximity, a stranger attracted to another person wants to communicate interest without making a commitment to interaction. In initial encounters, the problem can be resolved by using ambiguous cues. In opposite-sex encounters, the gender that has "more to lose" (the woman) will try to control the interaction; to do so, she will initially use nonverbal cues that the man may

not consciously perceive (Grammar, Kruck, Juette, & Fink, 2000). Researchers observed 45 male–female pairs of strangers (aged 18 to 23) left alone in a waiting room. Questionnaires completed later were used to assess each participant's interest in the other person. Women interested in the man were more likely to display several nonverbal cues, including short glances, coy smiles, and primping (adjusting clothing without a visible reason). Men interested in the woman were more likely to speak to her in the first 3 minutes (a direct cue); if she responded with head nods, his rate of speech increased. This pattern is probably repeated many times every day in airplanes, on trains and buses, and in classes and waiting rooms (see Box 14.1).

**Scripts.** The development of relationships is influenced by an event schema or script. A script specifies (1) the definition of the situation (a hook-up, date, or job interview), (2) the identities of the social actors involved, and (3) the range and sequence of permissible behaviors (see Chapter 7). Recall our discussion of symbolic interaction theory in Chapter 1.

The initiation of a relationship requires an opening line. Often, it is about some feature of the situation. At the beginning of this chapter, Dan initiated the conversation by commenting that Mia never missed the class. Two people waiting to participate in a psychology experiment may begin talking by speculating about the purpose of the experiment. The weather is a widely used topic for openings. Following a first contact or meeting, we may check out the other person online, at Facebook, LinkedIn, or similar sites.

Once initiated, scripts specify the permissible next steps. American society—or at least the subculture of college students—is characterized by a specific script for "first dates" (Rose & Frieze, 1993). When asked to describe "actions that a woman (man) would typically take" on a first date, both men and women identified a core action sequence: dress, be nervous, pick up date, leave (meeting place), confirm plans, get to

## BOX 14.1  Research Update: Flirting

A distinctive class of communicative behaviors is flirting, or courtship signaling (Birdwhistell, 1970). The term refers to a class of nonverbal behaviors exhibited by a man/woman that serve to attract the attention and elicit the approach of another man/woman (after Moore, 1985). The goal is to initiate a connection with another person, and gauge their interest in the initiator. A catalog of movements used by adult women to attract men has been developed by Moore (1985), and a catalog of movements used by men to attract women has been developed by Renninger, Wade, and Grammar (2004); both are based on naturalistic observation. Traditional flirting includes gestures such as hair tossing, licking lips, smiling, primping, touching hair or clothing, eye movements such as arching an eyebrow or direct glance, bodily movements that mirror another person's movement, or the wearing of revealing or seductive clothing (Whitty, 2004). Many of these behaviors are learned, and vary across cultures, and across contexts within a single culture.

Renninger and colleagues observed men in bars; each man was observed for 30 minutes, and each occurrence of 14 nonverbal behaviors that might attract a woman's attention was recorded. The average interobserver reliability was 0.84. The outcome, making contact, was defined as 1 minute or more of continual conversation. The results showed that men who engaged in short, direct glances at the woman, who used more space with their bodily position and movements, used fewer closed-body movements (for example, arms folded), and engaged in more nonreciprocated touching of other men were more likely to make contact.

While often it is the man who physically approaches and initiates verbal interaction, research indicates that women take the initiative, using nonverbal signals, in encouraging the man to initiate contact. Men (and women) are reluctant to approach another person without invitation because of the possibility of rejection. Evolutionary analyses of mating point out that since women make the greater investment in offspring, they are the choosers. Thus, women selectively encourage some men to approach but not others.

Women are said to be looking for a high-status male. The male behaviors identified by Renninger and colleagues as successful in producing contact, such as nonreciprocated touching and use of greater space, are thought to be behaviors that indicate high status (see Chapter 9).

Moore (1985) began her research by observing 200 White women, judged to be aged 18 to 35, and recording their nonverbal behavior. A woman not accompanied by a man was selected at random and observed for at least 30 minutes in settings where there were at least 20 men and women present. Observers recorded every behavior of the focal subject and its consequences. Flirting, or a nonverbal solicitation behavior, was defined as a behavior that resulted in a man's attention within 15 seconds. Subsequent research (Moore & Butler, 1989) describes behaviors that attract male attention and those that maintain his attention after interaction begins. Male attention is likely to follow a room-encompassing glance, a smile while looking at him, patting or smoothing the hair, the "lip lick," or a head toss. Once verbal interaction begins, male attention is maintained

know, evaluate, talk, laugh, joke, eat, attempt to make out/accept or reject, take date home, kiss, go home. In general, both men and women ascribed a proactive/aggressive role to the man and a reactive role to the woman. More recent research asked undergraduates to describe a "typical date"; in general, the descriptions were very similar to those reported 15 years earlier, indicating the persistence of the traditional, gendered script (Bartoli & Clark, 2006). Data from OkCupid indicate that the vast majority of first messages (i.e., initiations) sent by a user

by frequent head nods while he talks, leaning close to him, and touching or brushing part of the body against him.

Moore and Renninger, and others, provide contextual evidence for the assertion that these behaviors are courtship signals. If these behaviors are intended to attract male/female attention, we should observe them in contexts where such solicitations are likely, such as bars, but not in settings where no members of the other gender are present. Moore studied 10 women in each of four social settings: singles bar, university snack bar, university library, and women's center meeting. Again, focal sampling was employed; a woman was observed only if at least 25 people were present and she was not accompanied by a man. The display of courtship signals was clearly context-specific. Women were much more likely to engage in these behaviors in the singles bar, and least likely to engage in them at women's center meetings.

Once a couple begins to interact, flirting is reciprocal (Back et al., 2011). Three-minute interactions were videotaped in a speed-dating setting. Raters viewed the tapes and rated how much each person was flirting every 30 seconds. Flirting by one person was highly correlated with being flirted at by the other.

Most research on flirting has been done in romantic settings where the motivation is to meet someone. Hall and colleagues (2010) have described and developed a scale to measure five different flirting styles. Many of the nonverbal behaviors described so far reflect the physical style, intended to assess the other's sexual interest in the initiator. The sincere style is intended to create an emotional rather than sexual bond, and involves conversation and self-disclosure.

Note that this is the style reflected in Dan and Mia's interactions. The playful style involves flirting as fun, and is not intended to lead to the development of a relationship. Henningsen and colleagues (2008) assessed motives for flirting in samples of undergraduates (average age 20) and full-time workers (average age 33.5). Students viewed flirting as motivated by sexual interest or the desire to advance a relationship. Workers were more likely to view flirting as intended to achieve an instrumental goal, for example, get a coworker to do a favor or make a sale.

A review of the literature on sexting behavior by persons under 25 identified 88 relevant research studies (Cooper, Quayle, Jonsson, & Svedin, 2016). The research identified four motivations for creating and sending sexually suggestive text or photos. The most commonly cited reason was to flirt or gain romantic attention; many of these messages were directed to someone the sender was not currently in a relationship with. Thus, electronic media have added to the arsenal of flirting behaviors.

Do people stop flirting when they get into committed relationships? People in ongoing relationships do not need to initiate a relationship, but they do need to maintain it, and research suggests that flirting can contribute to achieving that goal as well. More than 160 married men and women, ages 19 to 74, completed a survey (Frisby & Booth-Butterfield, 2012). Both men and women reported substantial amounts of flirting behavior; they reported that flirting was motivated by desire for sexual activity with the spouse, and to create a private world not accessible to others. Both outcomes contribute to the maintenance of the relationship.

are from a man to a woman, regardless of the age of either person (Cooper, 2015).

Research has examined differences between Black and White undergraduates in the emphasis they place on certain aspects of dating (Jackson, Kleiner, Geist, & Cebulko, 2011). African

Americans place more importance on giving and receiving gifts, and meeting members of the date's family. Whites place greater emphasis on hanging out with the date's friends.

Since 2000, the "hook-up" has become increasingly common on college campuses, and

8

In the traditional dating script, males paid for the activity, but young men and women report that the female is increasingly paying, at least some of the time. © gchutka/iStock

some observers suggest it has replaced dating. Research suggests that hook-ups are very similar to dates (see Table 7.1). Men still initiate contact and direct activities, couples still talk and evaluate possible relationships/activities, leave the meeting place, and eventually go home (Eaton & Rose, 2011). The difference is that dates are perceived as the first stage in the development of a longer-term relationship, whereas the hook-up is not.

How do we learn these scripts, and the departures from them? One source is the mass media. Both men and women learn about relationships and how to handle them from popular magazines. A study of magazines oriented toward women (*Cosmopolitan*, *Glamour*, and *Self*) and men (*Playboy*, *Penthouse*, and *GQ*) found that they portrayed relationships in similar terms (Duran & Prusank, 1997). The

dominant focus in both types of magazines was sexual relationships. In women's magazines (January 1990 to December 1991), the themes were (1) women are less skilled at and more anxious about sex and (2) sex is enjoyed most in caring relationships. In men's magazines during the same period, the themes were (1) men are under attack in sexual relationships and (2) men have natural virility and strong sexual appetites. Also, the articles in women's magazines portrayed men as incompetent about relationships.

## THE DETERMINANTS OF LIKING

Once two people make contact and begin to interact, several factors will determine the extent to which each person will like the other. Two of these factors are considered in this section: similarity and shared activities.

### Similarity

How important is similarity? Do "birds of a feather flock together"? Or do "opposites attract"? These two aphorisms about the determinants of liking are inconsistent and provide opposing predictions. A good deal of research has been devoted to finding out which one is more accurate. The evidence indicates that birds of a feather do flock together—that is, we are attracted to people who are similar to ourselves (Markey & Markey, 2007). Probably the most important kind of similarity is **attitudinal similarity**—the sharing of beliefs, opinions, likes, and dislikes.

**Attitudinal Similarity.** A widely employed technique for studying attitudinal similarity is the attraction-to-a-stranger paradigm, initially developed by Byrne (1961b). Potential participants fill out an attitude questionnaire that measures their beliefs about various topics, such as life on a college campus. Later, participants receive information about a stranger as part of a seemingly unrelated study. The information they receive describes the stranger's personality or social background and may include a photograph. They also are given a copy of the same questionnaire they completed earlier, ostensibly filled out by the stranger. In fact, the stranger's questionnaire is completed by the experimenter, who systematically varies the degree to which the stranger's supposed responses match the participant's responses. After seeing the stranger's questionnaire, the participants are asked how much they like or dislike the stranger and how much they would enjoy working with that person

In most cases, the participant's attraction to the stranger is positively associated with the percentage of attitude statements by the stranger that agree with the participant's own attitudes (Byrne & Nelson, 1965; Gonzales, Davis, Loney, Lukens, & Junghans, 1983). We rarely agree with our friends about everything; what matters is that we agree on a high proportion of issues. This relationship between similarity of attitudes and liking is very general; it has been replicated in studies using both men and women as participants and strangers under a variety of conditions (Berscheid & Walster [Hatfield], 1978).

In the attraction-to-a-stranger paradigm, the participant forms an impression of a stranger without any interaction. This allows researchers to determine the precise relationship between similarity and liking. But what do you think the relationship would be if two people were allowed to interact? Would similarity have as strong an effect?

A study attempting to answer this question arranged dates for 44 couples (Byrne, Ervin, & Lamberth, 1970). Researchers distributed a 50-item questionnaire measuring attitudes and personality to a large sample of undergraduates. From the responses, they selected 24 couples whose answers were very similar (66 to 74 percent identical) and 20 couples whose answers were not similar (24 to 40 percent identical). Each couple was introduced and invited to spend the next 30 minutes together

at the student union. Each participant's attractiveness was rated. When they returned, each rated the other's sexual attractiveness, desirability as a date, and desirability as a marriage partner, and indicated how much they liked each other. The experimenter also recorded the physical distance between the two as they stood in front of his desk.

Both attitudinal similarity and physical attractiveness influenced liking. Partners who were attractive and who held highly similar attitudes were rated as more likable. Moreover, similar partners were rated as more intelligent and more desirable as a date and marriage partner. The couples high in similarity stood closer together after their date than the couples low in similarity—another indication that similarity creates liking.

At the end of the semester, 74 of the 88 participants in this study were contacted. Participants in the high attractiveness/high similarity condition were more likely to remember their partner's name, to report having talked to their partner, and to report wanting to date their partner than those in the low attractiveness/low similarity condition.

The story of Dan and Mia at the beginning of this chapter illustrates the importance of similarity in the early stages of a relationship. After their initial meeting, they discovered they had several things in common. They were from the same city. They had chosen the same major and held similar beliefs about their field and about how useful a bachelor's degree would be in that field. Each also found the other attractive; like the participants in the high attraction/high similarity condition, Dan and Mia continued to talk after their first meeting.

**Why Is Similarity Important?** Why does attitudinal similarity produce liking? One reason is the desire for consistency between our attitudes and perceptions. The other reason focuses on our preference for rewarding experiences.

Most people desire cognitive consistency—consistency between attitudes and perceptions of whom and what we like and dislike. If you have positive attitudes toward certain objects and discover that another person has favorable attitudes toward the same objects, your cognitions will be consistent if you like that person (Newcomb, 1971). When Dan discovered that Mia had a positive attitude toward his major, his desire for consistency produced a positive attitude toward Mia (see Balance Theory, Chapter 8). Our desire for consistency attracts us to persons who hold the same attitudes toward important objects.

Another reason we like persons with attitudes similar to our own is because our interaction with them provides three kinds of reinforcement. First, interacting with persons who share similar attitudes usually leads to positive outcomes (Lott & Lott, 1974). At the beginning of this chapter, Dan anticipated that he and Mia would get along well because they shared similar likes and dislikes.

Second, similarity validates our own view of the world. We all want to evaluate and verify our attitudes and beliefs against some standard. Sometimes, physical reality provides objective criteria for our beliefs. But often there is no physical standard, and so we must compare our attitudes with those of others (Festinger, 1954). Persons who hold similar attitudes provide us with support for our own opinions, which allows us to deal with the world more confidently (Byrne, 1971). Such support is particularly important in areas, such as political attitudes, where we realize that others hold attitudes dissimilar to our own (Rosenbaum, 1986).

Research indicates that similarity in mood is also an important influence on attraction. In the attraction-to-a-stranger paradigm, nondepressed participants prefer nondepressed strangers (Rosenblatt & Greenberg, 1988). In an experiment, male and female students interacted with a depressed or nondepressed person of the same sex. People in homogeneous pairs (both depressed or both nondepressed) were more satisfied with the interaction than people in mixed pairs (Locke & Horowitz, 1990). In another study, researchers measured the depression levels of people and of their best friends. Depressed people had best friends who were also depressed (Rosenblatt & Greenberg, 1991).

Third, we like others who share similar attitudes because we expect that they will like us. In one experiment, college students were given information about a stranger's attitudes and the stranger's evaluation of them (Condon & Crano, 1988). The participants' perceptions of the stranger's similarity to and evaluation of them were also assessed. The students were attracted to strangers whom they perceived as evaluating them positively, and that accounted for the influence of similar attitudes.

## Shared Activities

As people interact, they share activities. Recall that after Mia and Dan met, they began to sit together in class and to discuss course work. When the professor announced the first exam, Dan invited Mia to study for it with him. Mia's roommate was also in the class; the three of them reviewed the material together the night before the exam. Mia and Dan both got As on the exam, and each felt that studying together helped. The next week, they went to a movie together. Several days later, she invited Dan to a party.

Shared activities provide opportunities for each person to experience reinforcement. Some of these reinforcements come from the other person; Mia finds Dan's interest in her very reinforcing. Often, the other person is associated with a positive experience, which leads us to like the other person (Byrne & Clore, 1970). Getting an A on the examination was a very positive experience for both Dan and Mia. The association of the other person with that experience led to increased liking for the other.

Thus, as a relationship develops, the sharing of activities contributes to increased liking. This was shown in a study in which pairs of friends of the same sex both filled out attitude questionnaires and listed their preferences for various activities (Werner & Parmelee, 1979). The duration of the friendships averaged 5 years. The results of the study showed similarity between friends in both activity preferences and attitudes. A study of romantic relationships found that sharing of tasks or activities was a strong predictor of liking (Stafford & Canary, 1991). Thus, participation in mutually satisfying activities is a strong influence on the development and maintenance of relationships. The results of a series of five studies indicate that participation in novel and arousing activities rather than mundane and trivial pursuits is associated with relationship quality (Aron et al., 2000). As Dan and Mia got to know each other, their shared experiences—studying, seeing movies, going to parties—became the basis for their relationship, supplementing the effect of similar attitudes.

If shared activities are important, what happens when a couple does not do things together? This is not an idle question; many students and working adults are separated from their partner by distance, and may see each other (share activities) only occasionally. What about secret relationships, where contact is limited by the need to prevent others from learning about it? Some research suggests that secrecy will be associated with greater attraction (Wegner, Lane, & Dimitri, 1994). But if shared activities are important, absence will prevent the development of shared reinforcements and may increase costs, such as a sense of burden (a sense that the relationship is difficult to coordinate, requires a great deal of work, energy). A series of studies found that participants in secret relationships reported greater burden, less satisfaction, and lower relationship quality than persons in open ones (Foster & Campbell, 2005). People in secret relationships

also reported significantly less love for their partner. These results strengthen the conclusion that shared activities make an important difference.

## THE GROWTH OF RELATIONSHIPS

We have traced the development of relationships from the stage of zero contact through awareness (who is available) and surface contact (who is desirable) to mutuality (liking). At the beginning of this chapter, Dan and Mia met, discovered that they had similar attitudes and interests, and shared pleasant experiences, such as doing well on an examination, going to a movie, and later, going to a party.

Many of our relationships remain at the "minor" level of mutuality. We have numerous acquaintances, neighbors, and coworkers whom we like and interact with regularly but to whom we do not feel especially close. A few of our relationships grow closer; they proceed through "moderate" to "major" mutuality. Three aspects of this continued growth of relationships are examined in this section: self-disclosure, trust, and interdependence. As the degree of mutuality increases between friends, roommates, and coworkers, self-disclosure, trust, and interdependence also will increase.

### Self-Disclosure

Recall that when Dan and Mia returned from the party, Mia told Dan that her roommate's parents had just separated and that her roommate was very depressed. Mia said that she didn't know how to help her roommate—that she felt unable to deal with the situation. At this point, Mia was engaging in self-disclosure—the act of revealing personal information about oneself to another person. Self-disclosure usually increases over time in a relationship. Initially, people reveal things about themselves that are not especially intimate and that they believe the other will readily accept.

## BOX 14.2  Online Relationships: Are They Different?

Most of the literature reviewed so far in this chapter is based on or assumes face-to-face interaction. Internet technologies, especially instant messaging and chat rooms, which allow synchronous interaction, create the possibility of developing or sustaining intimate relationships without meeting face-to-face. How do the processes involved differ?

We discussed self-presentation online in Chapter 5. In face-to-face interaction, potential partners have access to a broad array of nonverbal cues in addition to verbal messages when forming an impression. Online, potential partners only have access to messages crafted by the person. Participants realize that self-presentation in the making contact stage is critical, because potential partners will use it to decide whether to explore possible relationships. So, in crafting a self-presentation, the person wants to emphasize positive characteristics; at the same time, if there is a possibility or hope of meeting, the presentation must be credible, if not authentic (Ellison, Heino, & Gibbs, 2006). Also, as in offline relationships, accurate self-disclosure is related to the development of intimacy, increasing motivation to be honest.

Research indicates that some online daters engage in misrepresentation. In an online survey of 6,581 Canadian users of such services, more than 25 percent reported misrepresenting themselves online; the most common areas were age (14 percent), marital status (10 percent), and appearance (10 percent) (Brym & Lenton,

2001). Ellison and colleagues (2006) interviewed 34 participants in Connect.com; half were male, most were in their 30s or 40s. They found that because participants wanted to create a positive impression, some described online a future, potential self, rather than the (current) self; they did not perceive this as misrepresentation. Another source of misrepresentation is limited self-awareness; as we saw in Chapter 4, we do not necessarily see ourselves as others see us.

Another study focused on accuracy of profiles posted on online dating sites. Researchers recruited subscribers to these sites; the sample was 50 percent male, and many participants were in their 20s. Participants were given a printed copy of their profile and asked to rate the accuracy of 15 informational items and of their photo. Upon completion of the ratings, the height and weight of the participant were measured, and age listed on the profile was compared with age on the driver's license. Differences were very common, and usually small. Men were more likely to lie about their height, women to lie about their weight; the more the person deviated from the average, the bigger the lie. Overall, the participants rated their profile photos as least accurate, and their reported relationship status as most accurate (Toma, Hancock, & Ellison, 2008).

Recognizing that others are motivated to present a positive image and may misrepresent themselves, participants in online dating carefully attend to subtle cues in others' messages. They scrutinize the writing for spelling or

Over time, they disclose increasingly intimate details about their beliefs or behavior, including information they are less certain the other will accept (Backman, 1990).

Self-disclosure increases as a relationship grows. In one study, same-sex pairs of previously unacquainted college students were brought into a laboratory setting and asked to get acquainted (Davis, 1976). They were

given a list of 72 topics. Each topic had been rated earlier by other students on a scale of intimacy from 1 to 11. The participants were asked to select topics from this list and to take turns talking about each topic for at least 1 minute while their partner remained silent. The interaction continued until each partner had spoken on 12 of the 72 topics. The results showed that the intimacy of the topic

grammatical mistakes, the style of the writing, and descriptors of the person. The inclusion/exclusion of sexual language is noted. Other aspects, such as user name, service provider, and time of day the message was sent, may influence inferences by the recipient.

Gibbs, Ellison, and Heino (2006) conducted an online survey of members of Match.com; 56 percent of the respondents were female, 93 percent were White, and many were in their 40s. Participants adapt their behavior/responses to the verbal and linguistic cues in messages they receive. The survey contained a three-item measure of relational goals: the importance of long-term dating, of meeting a special person, and of finding a life/marital partner. Those who rated these goals as more important reported that they were more honest and intentional in their online self-disclosures.

We noted earlier that the inclusion or exclusion of sexual language is considered significant by recipients of messages. Talk about sex can be sexually arousing, providing one motive for its inclusion. Expressions by another of sexual desire for you may give your self-esteem a boost. Also, if one's relational goal is a relationship that involves sexual intimacy, that needs to be communicated to potential partners (see Box 14.1). On the other hand, others may be turned off by direct, explicit statements of sexual interest. A study of 30-minute conversations from English and Spanish chat rooms examined the conversational negotiation of sexuality. Participants often embedded sexual content in a "play" frame, characterized by the use of emoticons and acronyms conveying laughter and joking, using verbal reproductions of humorous or childish pronunciations of sexual terms, and the taking on of alternative roles via humorous, or subtly sexual screen names. These techniques balance the inclusion of sexual content and adherence to constraints on public sex talk (Del-Teso-Craviotto, 2006).

The literature on the development of offline relationships reviewed in this chapter indicates that age, gender, and homophily are important influences on who we partner with. Do these matter online? Research suggests they are less important. A study of logs of social behavior in the virtual world *Second Life* found that people formed relationships with others who had relationships in common with them, not on the basis of age, gender, and homophily (Welles & Contractor, 2014).

Given the risks of selecting friends or partners with the limited information available online, having friends in common reduces your uncertainty about the other person. Are online friendships and social networks an extension of our offline social connectedness? Research indicates that the answer is no. Two surveys of Facebook users collected data from them on both online and offline connectedness—sense of attachment, friendship, and engagement with friends in each sphere (Grieve et al., 2013). The researchers found that Facebook connectedness was distinct from offline connectedness. They suggest that Facebook provides a distinct, alternative domain for developing social relationships for some persons.

Are online relationships different? The answer seems to be a qualified "Yes."

---

selected increased steadily from the first to the twelfth topic chosen. Research also indicates that greater self-disclosure during a 10-minute conversation was associated with an increase in positive affect—happiness, excitement—and attraction to the partner (Vittengl & Holt, 2000).

When Mia told Dan about the situation with her roommate, Dan replied that he knew how she felt, because his older brother had just separated from his wife. This exchange reflects reciprocity in self-disclosure; as one person reveals an intimate detail, the other person usually discloses information at about the same level of intimacy (Altman & Taylor, 1973). In the Davis (1976) study, each participant selected a topic at the same level of intimacy as the preceding one or at the next level

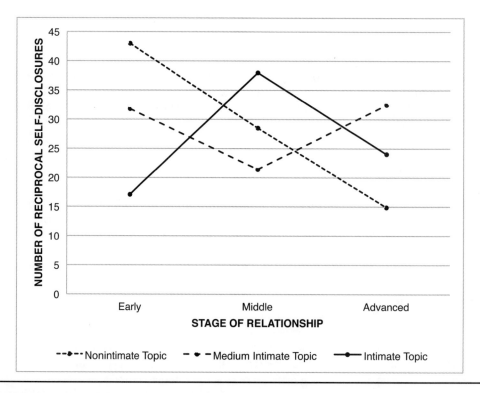

**FIGURE 14.2**  The Relationship between Reciprocity and Intimacy

Reciprocity—picking a topic of conversation that is as intimate as the last topic introduced by your partner—is the process by which relationships become more intimate. The extent of reciprocity depends on the intimacy of the topic and the stage of the relationship. Students talked with an acquaintance (early stage), friend (middle stage), or best friend (advanced stage). With topics that were not intimate (such as the weather), reciprocity declined steadily as the stage increased. With intimate topics, in contrast, reciprocity was greatest at the middle stage, less at the advanced stage, and least at the early stage of a relationship.

*Source:* Adapted from Won-Doornink Figure 4.

of intimacy. However, reciprocity decreases as a relationship develops. In another study, a researcher recruited students to be participants and asked each to bring an acquaintance, a friend, or a best friend to the laboratory (Won-Doornink, 1985). Each dyad was given a list of topics that varied in degree of intimacy. Each was instructed to take at least four turns choosing and discussing a topic. Each conversation was tape-recorded and later analyzed for evidence of reciprocity. The association between the stage of the relationship and the reciprocity of intimate disclosures was curvilinear—that is, there was greater reciprocity of intimate disclosures between friends

than between acquaintances but less reciprocity between best friends than among friends (see Figure 14.2).

Not all people divulge increasingly personal information as you get to know them. You have probably known people who were very open—who readily disclosed information about themselves—and others who said little about themselves. In this regard, we often think of men as less likely to discuss their feelings than women. However, research has shown that self-disclosure depends not only on gender but also on the nature of the relationship. In casual relationships (with men or women), men are less likely to disclose personal information than women (Reis, Senchak, & Solomon, 1985). In dating couples, the amount of disclosure is related more to gender role orientation than to gender. Men and women with traditional gender role orientations disclose less to their partners than those with egalitarian gender role orientations (Rubin, Hill, Peplau, & Dunkel-Scheker, 1980). Traditional gender roles are more segregated, with each person responsible for certain tasks, whereas egalitarian orientations emphasize sharing. An emphasis on joint activity leads to greater self-disclosure. In intimate heterosexual relationships, men and women do not differ in the degree of self-disclosure (Hatfield, 1982; Mitchell et al., 2008).

A study of self-disclosure by young adults inquired about the extent to which each had disclosed in a variety of domains, including sexual activities, shameful events, personal health, and feelings and traumas. Generally, there were no differences between men and women. African-American and young men were significantly less likely to disclose, but analyses suggested this was related to low income rather than to ethnicity and gender (Consedine, Sabag-Cohen, & Krivoshekova, 2007).

The work discussed so far is concerned with the intimacy of self-disclosure. But self-disclosure is a complex phenomenon and has several characteristics including content (information about self or about the relationship), amount, and emotional tone (Bradford, Feeney, & Campbell, 2002). Using diaries, researchers gathered data on 1,908 conversations lasting more than 10 minutes from both members of the couple. The results indicated that disclosures could be scored on these dimensions and that there were differences in intimacy and amount of disclosure related to the partner's attachment style.

## Trust

Why did Dan confide in Mia that his brother had just left his wife? Perhaps he was offering reciprocity in self-disclosure. Because Mia had confided in Dan, she expected him to reciprocate. But had he been suspicious of Mia's motives, he might not have. This suggests the importance of trust in the development of a relationship.

When we **trust** someone, we believe that person is both honest and benevolent (Larzelere & Huston, 1980). We believe that the person tells us the truth—or at least does not lie to us—and that their intentions toward us are positive. One measure of interpersonal trust is the interpersonal trust scale reproduced in Table 14.1. The questions focus on whether the other person is selfish, honest, sincere, fair, or considerate. We are more likely to disclose personal information to someone we trust. How much do you trust your partner? Answer the questions on the scale and determine your score. Higher scores indicate greater trust.

To study the relationship between trust and self-disclosure, researchers recruited men and women from university classes, from a list of people who had recently obtained marriage licenses, and by calling persons randomly selected from the telephone directory. Each person was asked to complete a questionnaire concerning their spouse or current or most recent date. The survey included the scale in Table 14.1. Researchers averaged the trust scores for seven types of relationships, ranging from divorced to newlyweds. As the relationship became more exclusive (casual, exclusive, cohabiting), trust scores increased significantly. Is there a relationship between trust and self-disclosure? Each person was also asked how much they had disclosed to the partner in each of six areas—religion, family, emotions, relationships with others, school or work, and marriage. Trust scores were positively correlated with self-disclosure—that is, the more the person trusted the partner, the greater the degree of self-disclosure.

Other research on interpersonal trust suggests that in addition to honesty and benevolence, reliability is an important aspect of trust. We are more likely to trust someone we feel is reliable—on whom we can count

**TABLE 14.1** Interpersonal Trust Scale

|  | STRONGLY AGREE | AGREE | SLIGHTLY AGREE | ? | SLIGHTLY DISAGREE | DISAGREE | STRONGLY DISAGREE |
|---|---|---|---|---|---|---|---|
| 1. My partner is primarily interested in their own welfare. | _____ | _____ | _____ | _____ | _____ | _____ | _____ |
| 2. There are times when my partner cannot be trusted. | _____ | _____ | _____ | _____ | _____ | _____ | _____ |
| 3. My partner is perfectly honest and truthful with me. | _____ | _____ | _____ | _____ | _____ | _____ | _____ |
| 4. I feel I can trust my partner completely. | _____ | _____ | _____ | _____ | _____ | _____ | _____ |
| 5. My partner is truly sincere in their promises. | _____ | _____ | _____ | _____ | _____ | _____ | _____ |
| 6. I feel my partner does not show me enough consideration. | _____ | _____ | _____ | _____ | _____ | _____ | _____ |
| 7. My partner treats me fairly and justly. | _____ | _____ | _____ | _____ | _____ | _____ | _____ |
| 8. I feel my partner can be counted on to help me. | _____ | _____ | _____ | _____ | _____ | _____ | _____ |

*Source:* Adapted from "The Dyadic Trust Scale: Toward Understanding Interpersonal Trust in Close Relationships," by Larzelere and Huston, *Journal of Marriage and Family*, 42(3). Copyright 1980 by the National Council on Family Relations, 3989 Central Ave. NE, Suite 550, Minneapolis, MN 55421. Reprinted by permission.

*Note:* For items 1, 2, and 6, Strongly Agree 1, Agree 2, Slightly Agree 3, and so on. For items 3, 4, 5, 7, and 8, the scoring is reversed.

(Johnson-George & Swap, 1982)—and predictable (Rempel, Holmes, & Zanna, 1985).

Many couples today are involved in long-distance relationships; they are committed to each other but do not live in the same city or state or even country. A longitudinal study of student couples who were exclusively dating compared couples in same-city and long-distance relationships (Cameron & Ross, 2007). Researchers reasoned that relational security, a sense of trust and faith in the partner, would be especially important in the survival of long-distance relationships. High relational security among both men and women predicted stability of all relationships one year later. Long-distance relationships were significantly more likely to break up; long-distance relationships in which the man reported lower relational security and higher negative affect (low self-esteem, optimism) at Time 1 were more likely to break up. Research with an ethnically diverse sample

of adults included 161 persons in long-distance (52 to more than 10,000 miles apart) nonmarital relationships (average duration 26 months). Measures included love for partner, fun with partner, sexual satisfaction, commitment, and perceived constraints/barriers to breaking up. Compared to persons from the same sample in close-proximity relations (living within 50 miles of the partner), persons in long-distance relationships reported significantly greater dedication to partner and fewer feelings of constraint. Over a 4-month follow-up period, people in long-distance relationships were as likely as those in close proximity to their partners to break up (Kelmer, Rhoades, Stanley, & Markman, 2013).

### Interdependence

Earlier in this chapter, we noted that people evaluate potential and actual relationships in terms of the outcomes (rewards minus costs) they expect to receive. Dan initiated contact with Mia because he anticipated that he would experience positive outcomes. Mia encouraged the development of a relationship because she, also, expected the rewards to exceed the costs. As their relationship developed, each discovered that the relationship was rewarding. Consequently, they increased the time and energy devoted to their relationship and decreased their involvement in alternative relationships. As their relationship became increasingly mutual, Mia and Dan became increasingly dependent on each other for various rewards (Backman, 1990). The result is strong, frequent, and diverse interdependence (Kelley et al., 1983).

Increasing reliance on one person for gratifications and decreasing reliance on others is called **dyadic withdrawal** (Slater, 1963). One study of 750 men and women illustrates the extent to which such withdrawal occurs. Students identified the intensity of their current heterosexual relationships, then listed the names of persons whose opinions they considered important. They also indicated how important each person's opinions were and how much they had disclosed to that person (Johnson & Leslie, 1982). As predicted, the more intimate their current heterosexual relationship, the smaller the number of friends listed by the respondent; there was no difference in the number of relatives listed. Furthermore, as the degree of involvement increased, the proportion of mutual friends of the couple also increased (Milardo, 1982). Other studies have found that as heterosexual relationships become more intimate, each partner spends less time interacting with friends, whereas interaction with relatives may increase (Surra, 1990).

Interdependence evolves out of the process of negotiation (Backman, 1990). Each person offers various potential rewards to the partner; the partner accepts some and rejects others. As the relationship develops, the exchanges stabilize. Shared activities are an important

potential source of rewards. Each person has activity preferences. As the relationship develops, the couple must blend their separate preferences into joint activities. A study of dating couples found that men liked sex, games, and sports better than women, whereas women preferred companionship, entertainment, and cultural activities (Surra & Longstreth, 1990). Some couples achieved a blend by taking turns, alternately engaging in activities preferred by each. Others cooperated, engaging in activities they both liked, such as preparing food and running errands. Some couples experienced continuing conflict over what to do.

A potential reward in many relationships is sexual gratification. As relationships develop and become more mutual, physical intimacy increases as well. The couple negotiates the extent of sexual intimacy, with the woman's preferences having a greater effect on the outcome (Lear, 1997). How important is sexual gratification in dating relationships? A study of 149 couples assessed the importance of various rewards in relationships of increasing intimacy (preferred date, going steady, engaged, living together, and married). Among intimate couples, sexual gratification was much more likely to be cited as a major basis for the relationship (Centers, 1975). Other surveys indicate that the more emotionally intimate a couple is, the more likely they are to engage in sexual intimacy (Christopher & Roosa, 1991).

## LOVE AND LOVING

It is fair to say that what we feel for our friends, roommates, coworkers, and some of the people we date is attraction. But is that all we feel? Occasionally, at least, we experience something more intense than a positive attitude toward others. Sometimes we feel, and even say, "I love you."

How does loving differ from liking? Much of the research in social psychology on attraction or liking is summarized earlier in this chapter. By contrast, there has been less research on love. Three views of love are considered in this section: the distinction between liking and loving, passionate love, and romantic love.

## Liking versus Loving

One of the first empirical studies of love distinguished between liking and loving (Rubin, 1970). Love is more than intense liking; it is the attachment to and caring about another person (Rubin, 1974). Attachment involves a powerful desire to be with and be cared about by another person. Caring involves making the satisfaction of another person's needs as significant as the satisfaction of your own.

Based on this distinction, Rubin developed scales to measure both liking and love. The liking scale evaluates one's dating partner, lover, or spouse on various dimensions, including adjustment, maturity, responsibility, and likability. The love scale measures attachment to and caring for one's partner, and intimacy (self-disclosure). These scales were completed by each member of 182 dating couples, both for her or his partner and best friend of the same sex (Rubin, 1970). The results showed a high degree of internal consistency within each scale and a low correlation between scales. Thus, the two scales do measure different things.

If the distinction between liking and loving is valid, how do you think you would rate a dating partner and your best friend on these scales? Rubin predicted high scores on both liking and love scales for the dating partner, lover, or spouse, and a high liking score but lower love score for the (platonic) friend. The average scores of the 182 couples confirmed these predictions. Research work by Davis (1985) also distinguishes between friendship and love. Friendship involves several qualities, including trust, understanding, and mutual assistance. Love involves all of these plus caring (giving the utmost to and being an advocate

for the other) and passion (obsessive thought, sexual desire).

## Passionate Love

Love certainly involves attachment and caring. But is that all? What about the agony of jealousy and the ecstasy of being loved by another person? An alternative view of love emphasizes emotions such as these. It focuses on **passionate love**—a state of intense physiological arousal and intense longing for union with another (Hatfield & Walster, 1978).

Cognitive and emotional factors interact to produce passionate love. Each of us learns about love from parents (Trotter, 2010), friends, and entertainment media (Ward, 2003). We learn with whom it is appropriate to fall in love, how it feels, and how we should behave when we are in love. We experience an emotion only when we are physiologically aroused. Thus, we experience passionate love when we experience intense arousal and the circumstances fit the cultural definitions we have learned.

Passionate love has three components: cognitive, emotional, and behavioral (Hatfield & Sprecher, 1986). The cognitive components include a preoccupation with the loved one, an idealization of the person or the relationship, and a desire to know the other and be known by them. Emotional components include physiological arousal, sexual attraction, and desire for union. Behavioral elements include serving the other and maintaining physical closeness to that person. A scale designed to measure passionate love is reproduced in Box 14.3. Notice that each item deals with one of these components.

Research in the United States using the passionate love scale finds that the items are closely related—that is, all of them measure a single factor (Hendrick & Hendrick, 1989). A study of 60 men and 60 women found that scores on the scale are related to the stage of the relationship. Passionate love increases substantially

## BOX 14.3  Test Yourself: Passionate Love

Think of the person you love most passionately right now. If you are not in love right now, think of the last person you loved passionately. If you have never been in love, think of the person you came closest to caring for in that way. Keep that person in mind as you complete this questionnaire. Try to record how you felt at the time when your feelings were the most intense.

Use the following scale to answer each item:

**1  2  3        4  5  6        7  8  9**

**Not at all true    Moderately true    Definitely true**

1. I would feel deep despair if _____ left me.

2. Sometimes I feel I can't control my thoughts; they are obsessively on _____.

3. I feel happy when I am doing something to make _____ happy.

4. I would rather be with _____ than anyone else.

5. I'd get jealous if I thought _____ were falling in love with someone else.

6. I yearn to know all about _____.

7. I want _____ physically, emotionally, and mentally.

8. I have an endless appetite for affection from _____.

9. For me, _____ is the perfect romantic partner.

10. I sense my body responding when _____ touches me.

11. _____ always seems to be on my mind.

12. I want _____ to know me—my thoughts, my fears, and my hopes.

13. I eagerly look for signs indicating _____'s desire for me.

14. I possess a powerful attraction for _____.

15. I get extremely depressed when things don't go right in my relationship with _____.

**Scoring**: Scoring is either kept continuous or broken into the following classifications (for the 15-item shortened version):

106–135   points = Wildly, even recklessly, in love.
86–105    points = Passionate, but less intense.
66–85     points = Occasional bursts of passion.
45–65     points = Tepid, infrequent passion.
15–44     points = The thrill is gone.

*Source:* Adapted from "Scale for Determining Passionate Love" by Hatfield and Sprecher, *Journal of Adolescence*, 9, 383–410. © Copyright 1986, with permission from Elsevier.

from the early stage of dating to the stage of an exclusive relationship. It does not increase further as the relationship moves from exclusively dating to living together or becoming engaged (Hatfield & Sprecher, 1986). A study of 197 couples at various stages of courtship, including recently married, found that passionate love did decline as the length of the relationship increased (Sprecher & Regan, 1998).

Passionate love is associated with other intense emotions. When our love is reciprocated and we experience closeness or psychological union with the other person, we experience fulfillment, joy, and ecstasy. Conversely, positive emotional experiences—excitement, sexual excitement—can enhance passionate love. The study of 197 couples found that passionate love and sexual desire were positively related (Sprecher & Regan, 1998). Interestingly, sexual desire and sexual activity are not related (Regan, 2000). Unrequited love, on the other hand, is often associated with jealousy, anxiety, or despair. Loss of a love can be emotionally devastating.

There are four widely used scales that measure love. A meta-analysis pooled the data from 81 studies, involving more than 19,000 participants, and analyzed the structure of the four scales (Graham, 2011). Three higher-order factors or dimensions underlying the items were identified: love, romantic obsession, and friendship. As relationship length increased, love scores increased and obsession scores decreased. These results are consistent with the research showing that passionate love generally decreases over time. Love scores were also positively related to relationship satisfaction.

An important question is whether passionate love is universal or only found in some (Western?) cultures. Analyses of answers to the 15-item scale (Box 14.3) using data from nine cultural groups (1,809 participants) identified a common-factor structure; the six dimensions included commitment/affection, security/insecurity, and self-/other-centered (Landis & O'Shea, 2000). More detailed analyses of the responses separating men and women identified variation in the relative importance of the factors across culture by gender groups.

## The Romantic Love Ideal

The studies and theories of love discussed so far assume that love consists of a particular set of feelings and behaviors. Furthermore, most of us assume that we will experience this emotion at least once in our lives. But these are very culture-bound assumptions. There are societies in which the state or experience we call "love" is unheard of. In fact, U.S. society is almost alone in accepting love as the major basis for marriage.

In U.S. society, we are socialized to accept a set of beliefs about love—beliefs that guide much of our behavior. The following five beliefs are known collectively as the **romantic love ideal**:

1. True love can strike without prior interaction ("love at first sight").

2. For each of us, there is only one other person who will inspire true love.
3. True love can overcome any obstacle ("Love conquers all").
4. Our beloved is (nearly) perfect.
5. We should follow our feelings—that is, we should base our choice of partners on love rather than on other, more rational considerations (Lantz, Keyes, & Schultz, 1975).

Researchers have developed a scale to measure the extent to which individuals hold these beliefs (Sprecher & Metts, 1989). When the scale was completed by a sample of 730 undergraduates, the results indicated that the first four beliefs are held by many young people. Interestingly, male students are more likely to hold these beliefs than female students.

Research suggests that the fourth belief, idealization of the partner, is an important influence on relationship satisfaction. Two studies of Dutch adults found that many of them believed that their relationship was better than the relationships of others, and that this belief was associated with reported happiness (Buunk & van der Eijnden, 1997). The perceived superiority of one's own relationship reflects strong commitment to that relationship, and is probably a resource in times of relational stress. In another study, researchers asked the members of dating (98) and married (60) couples to rate themselves, their partners, and their ideal partners on 21 interpersonal characteristics (Murray, Holmes, & Griffin, 1996a). Analyses indicated that the participant's ratings of the partner were more similar to the ratings of the self and the ideal partner than to the partner's self-ratings. Furthermore, people who idealized their partners and whose partners idealized them were happier. A longitudinal study found that over a 1-year period, partners came to share the individual's idealized image of them (Murray, Holmes, & Griffin, 1996b).

The romantic love ideal has not always been popular in the United States. A group of researchers conducted an analysis of best-selling magazines published during four historical periods (Lantz et al., 1975; Lantz, Schultz, & O'Hara, 1977). They counted the number of times the magazines mentioned one or more of the five beliefs that make up the romantic love ideal. The number of times the ideal was discussed increased steadily over time. These findings suggest that American acceptance of the romantic love ideal occurred gradually from 1741 to 1865. The romantic love ideal first really came into its own about the time of the Civil War.

## Love as a Story

When we think of love, our thoughts often turn to the great love stories: Romeo and Juliet, Cinderella and the prince, Julia Roberts and Richard Gere, King Edward VIII and Wallis Simpson, and *Pygmalion/My Fair Lady*. According to Sternberg (1998), these stories are much more than entertainment. They shape our beliefs about love and relationships, and our beliefs in turn influence our behavior.

> Zach and Tammy have been married 28 years. Their friends have been predicting divorce since the day they were married. They fight almost constantly. Tammy threatens to leave Zach; he tells her that nothing would make him happier. They lived happily ever after.
>
> Valerie and Leonard had a perfect marriage. They told each other and all of their friends that they did. Their children say they never fought. Leonard met someone at his office and left Valerie. They are divorced. (adapted from Sternberg, 1998)

Wait a minute! Aren't those endings reversed? Zach and Tammy should be divorced, and Valerie and Leonard should be living happily ever after, right? If love is merely the interaction between two people—how they communicate and behave—you're right; the stories have the wrong endings. But there is more to love than interaction; what matters is how each partner interprets the interaction. To make sense out of what happens in our relationships, we rely on our love stories.

A **love story** is a story (script) about what love should be like; it has characters, plot, and theme. There are two central characters in every love story, and they play roles that complement each other. The plot details the kinds of events that occur in the relationship. The theme is central; it provides the meaning of the events that make up the plot, and it gives direction to the behavior of the principals. The love story guiding Zach and Tammy's relationship is the "War" story. Each views love as war—that is, a good relationship involves constant fighting. The two central characters are warriors, fighting for what they believe, to maintain their independence. The plot consists of arguments, fights, threats to leave—in short, battles. The theme is that love is war; one may win or lose particular battles, but the war continues. Zach and Tammy's relationship endures because they share this view, and it fits their temperaments. Can you imagine how long a wimp would last in a relationship with either of them?

According to this view, falling in love occurs when you meet someone with whom you can create a relationship that fits your love story. Furthermore, we are satisfied with relationships in which we and our partner match the characters in our story (Beall & Sternberg, 1995). Valerie and Leonard's marriage looked great on the surface, but it didn't fit Leonard's love story. He left when he met his "true love"—that is, a woman who could play the complementary role in his primary love story.

Where do our love stories come from? Many of them have their origins in the culture—in folk tales, literature, theater, films, and television programs. The cultural context interacts with our own personal experience and characteristics to create the stories that each of us has (Sternberg, 1996). As we experience relationships, our stories evolve, taking account of unexpected events. Each person has more than one story; the stories often form a hierarchy. One of Leonard's stories was "House and Home"; home was the center of the relationship, and he (in his role of Caretaker) showered attention on the house and kids—not on Valerie. But when he met Sharon with her aloof air, ambiguous past, and dark glasses, he was hooked; she elicited the "Love Is a Mystery" story that was more salient to Leonard. He could not explain why he left Valerie and the kids; like most of us, he was not consciously aware of his love stories. It should be obvious from these examples that love stories derive their power from the fact that they are self-fulfilling. We create in our relationships events according to the plot and then interpret those events according to the theme. Our love relationships are literally social constructions. Because our love stories are self-confirming, they can be very difficult to change.

Sternberg and his colleagues have identified five categories of love stories found in U.S. culture, and several specific stories within each category. They have also developed a series of statements that reflect the themes in each story. People who agree with the statements "I think fights actually make a relationship more vital" and "I actually like to fight with my partner" are likely to hold the "War" story. Sternberg and Hojjat studied samples of 43 and 55 couples (Sternberg, 1998). They found that couples generally held similar stories. The more discrepant the stories of the partners, the less happy the couple was. Some stories were associated with high satisfaction—for example, the "Garden" story, in which love is a garden that needs ongoing cultivation. Two stories associated with low satisfaction were the "Business" story (especially the version in which the roles are Employer and Employee), and the "Horror" story, in which the roles are Terrorizer and Victim.

Love stories, or implicit theories of relationships (Franiuk, Cohen, & Pomerantz, 2002), are stable over time. Persons who believe there is a one-and-only love, or "soul mate," for them believe that finding the right person is the key to a satisfying relationship; people who believe that a successful relationship requires continuing work, Sternberg's "garden," believe that hard work is the key. So men and women in the first group emphasize the partner's characteristics in assessing their satisfaction with the relationship; if they decide their partner is not Ms. or Mr. Right, they may leave in search of the true love. Gardeners view the relationship as a work in progress and place less emphasis on the partner in assessing their satisfaction; if unhappy, they work harder and apply more water and fertilizer.

Sternberg states that love stories reflect the culture. Does that mean that the stories or themes he has identified are unique to U.S. culture? Researchers recruited 61 dating and 81 married couples in the United States (mostly White), and 46 dating and 94 married couples in China. A measure developed by Sternberg to measure preferences for themes was completed by the U.S. participants; a careful translation into Chinese was completed by the Chinese participants. Analyses revealed several components, including devotion/caring and pragmatism, that were common to both cultures. The themes of love as war and love as a fairy tale were unique to the United States. Love as the tending of a garden and the incomprehensibility of a lover were unique to China. Devotion/caring was the strongest predictor of relationship satisfaction (Jackson, Chen, Guo, & Gao, 2006).

## COMMITTED RELATIONSHIPS

Most persons will spend at least part of their adult lives in a long-term committed relationship. Such a relationship may take a number of forms in the contemporary U.S. It may involve "living-alone-together" (LAT), in which two people consider themselves in a long-term monogamous relationship but maintain separate residences. We discussed earlier long-distance relationships, where partners may be separated by many miles because of employment, family, or citizenship circumstances. But some people may literally live next door; Jorge and Ruth, both in their 70s, have adjoining apartments because they will lose economic benefits, Social Security and survivor benefits, if they move in together.

Cohabitation involves both the formation of a long-term relationship and sharing a residence. An unknown number of same-sex couples have lived together over the past 100 years. The number of cohabiting couples has increased substantially in the past 40 years, as it has become increasingly accepted as an alternative to marriage. These relationships are now recognized by law or ordinance in many communities, often referred to as "domestic partnerships." Couples who have experienced the development of a relationship, as described earlier in the chapter, may arrive at the point where they have negotiated a relationship that is mutually rewarding, are spending most of their time with each other, and have outgrown the club and bar social scene. Living together may be attractive because they can save time by eliminating traveling, by sharing housework, and have more disposable income by sharing expenses. Oh, and they may be in love! In the U.S. today, about two-thirds of young adults will experience at least one cohabiting union (Manning, 2013). Cohabitation is a distinct life course transition (see Chapter 3). It constitutes entry into an adult relationship with associated responsibilities, economic and social.

Marriage is a third committed relationship status. Until the 1980s, most heterosexual couples moved from dating to engagement to marriage, a clearly recognized pathway into a long-term committed relationship. This transition often followed completion of one's education, either high school or college. Since 1990 the median age of first marriage

has increased by at least two years for both men and women. However, the age of first union has not increased (Manning, Brown, & Payne, 2014); young people today move in together at the same age as they married in earlier years. So what has changed is the attractiveness or necessity of marriage, not the desire for a co-residential relationship. Several social trends have contributed to increased rates of cohabitation instead of marriage. One is the rapid increase in advanced educational and occupational opportunities for women, leading many to want to "keep their options open" while in their 20s. In addition, Manning and colleagues argue that willingness to marry requires the financial resources to support a family, and that increasing numbers of young men do not have them, due to high unemployment rates (especially among minority men) and the low pay associated with entry and service industry jobs.

Although these three (and other) relationship types are different in specific ways, entry into them is motivated by the desire of individuals for emotional and sexual intimacy (Sassler, 2010). Moreover, there is ample evidence that intimate relationships are very beneficial for emotional and physical health (see Chapter 17).

A unique study of the progression of relationships analyzed data from 2,774 men and women aged 18 to 39 who entered a sexual relationship (Sassler, Michelmore, & Holland, 2016). The longitudinal data allowed researchers to determine the state of each relationship 12 months after the couple initiated sexual activity. At the end of one year, 27 percent of the respondents were cohabiting, 23 percent were in a non-residential relationship, and 50 percent had broken up. Relationships involving a person under 25 were more likely to break up. Those experiencing disadvantage (i.e., did not live with a biological parent in adolescence) were more likely to transition to cohabiting. Those experiencing advantage (i.e., having a college-educated mother) were less likely to transition to cohabitation. Blacks were less likely than whites to transition rapidly to cohabitation.

How stable are relationships? Researchers analyzed data from same-sex cohabiting, different-sex cohabiting and different-sex married couples (Manning, Brown, & Stykes, 2016). The longitudinal design of the research allowed them to follow the couples at least for two years. Same-sex and different-sex cohabiting couples exhibited similar levels of stability. Within two years after moving in together, 33 percent of the different-sex cohabitors and 40 percent of the same-sex cohabitors had broken up. The average duration of the cohabitation was 12.4 months for different-sex couples and 10.4 months for same-sex couples. Marriages exhibited greater stability. At 24 months, less than 10 percent of the different-sex marriages had broken up. Stability was greater for couples with greater education (both had completed college), and an age difference between partners of less than five years. Another researcher analyzed stability in couple relationships, including those in same-sex marriages (Rosenfeld, 2014). The data set included more than 3,000 couples in both formal and informal unions. Controlling for duration of the relationship and marriage, there was no statistically significant difference in the longevity of relationships involving same-sex and heterosexual couples.

Which couples marry? With the widespread acceptance of cohabitation, one may wonder why couples marry. The answer may be affective and symbolic evaluations of marriage and, in particular, feelings about marriage relative to cohabitation. Research using data from a panel survey of young Dutch adults found that positive feelings toward marriage played a key role in the decision to marry (Billari & Liefbroer, 2016). More positive feelings were associated with being raised by religiously involved parents, and having parents who were married. Interestingly, men had more positive feelings than women did.

## BREAKING UP

### Progress? Chaos?

You may have noticed that much of the work we have reviewed assumes or implies that intimate relationships develop or progress in a linear way. We meet, disclose, trust, disclose more, trust more, become sexually intimate, become interdependent, fall in love, and (we hope) live happily ever after. This linear model underlies much of the work on relationships and relationship stability/instability. There is, however, an alternative model that may be (more) appropriate: chaos theory (Weigel & Murray, 2000). Chaos theory suggests that relationships do not develop in a steady linear progression. Instead, relationships may shift suddenly or spontaneously; they may go up (get better) or down (get worse). A small event (say, a missed phone call) may have a major impact; a traumatic event (say, a diagnosis of cancer) may have little or no effect. As a result, it may be impossible to predict the future of an individual relationship. Whether linear or not, few relationships last forever. Roommates who once did everything together lose touch after they finish school. Two women who were once best friends gradually stop talking. Couples fall out of love and break up. What causes the dissolution of relationships? Research suggests two answers: unequal outcomes and unequal commitment.

### Unequal Outcomes and Instability

Earlier in this chapter, we discussed the importance of outcomes in establishing and maintaining relationships. Our decision to initiate a relationship is based on what we expect to get out of it. In ongoing relationships, we can assess our actual outcomes; we can evaluate the rewards we are obtaining relative to the costs of maintaining the relationship. A survey of college students examined the impact of several factors on satisfaction with a relationship; one factor was the value of overall outcomes compared with a person's CL (Michaels, Edwards, & Acock, 1984). In an analysis of the reports of men and women involved in exclusive relationships, the outcomes being experienced were most closely related to satisfaction with the relationship. Several other studies report the same results (Surra, 1990).

The CLalt is also an important standard used in evaluating outcomes. Are the outcomes from this relationship better than those obtainable from the best available alternative? One dimension on which people may evaluate relationships is physical appearance. A relationship with a physically attractive person may be rewarding. Two people who are equally attractive physically will experience similar outcomes on this dimension. What about two people who differ in attractiveness? The less attractive person will benefit from associating with the more attractive one, whereas the more attractive person will experience less positive outcomes. Because attractiveness is a valued and highly visible asset, the more physically attractive person is likely to find alternative relationships available and to expect some of them to yield more positive outcomes.

This reasoning was tested in a study of 123 dating couples. Photographs of each person in the study were rated by five men and five women for physical attractiveness, and a relative attractiveness score was calculated for each member of each couple. Both men and women who were more attractive than their partners reported having more friends of the opposite sex—that is, alternatives—than men and women who were not more attractive than their partners. Follow-up data collected 9 months later indicated that dating couples who were rated as similar in attractiveness were more likely to be still dating each other (White, 1980). These results are consistent with the hypothesis that persons experiencing outcomes below CLalt are more likely to terminate the relationship.

But not everyone compares their current outcomes with those available in alternative relationships. Individuals in White's study who were committed—that is, cohabiting, engaged, or married—did not vary in the number of alternatives they reported. Also, their relative attractiveness was not related to whether they were still in the relationship 9 months later. Persons who are committed to each other may be more concerned with equity than with alternatives.

Weight is one aspect of physical attractiveness. A study of 1,405 adolescent and young adult couples investigated matching and trading (providing more of one input to compensate for less of another) in relationships involving obese persons (BMI greater than 30) (Carmalt, Cawley, Joyner, & Sobal, 2008). Obese men and women were less likely to have a physically attractive partner. The disadvantage was greater for women than men, and for Black women than for White women. Greater education, a more attractive personality, and better grooming (self-presentation) offset the disadvantage of obesity for some persons, resulting in a more attractive partner than would be expected.

Equity theory (Walster [Hatfield], Berscheid, & Walster, 1973) postulates that each of us compares the rewards we receive from a relationship to our costs or contributions. In general, we expect to get more out of the relationship if we put more into it. Thus, we compare our outcomes (rewards minus costs) to the outcomes our partner is receiving. The theory predicts that **equitable relationships**—in which the outcomes are equivalent—will be stable, whereas inequitable ones will be unstable.

This prediction was tested in a study involving 537 college students who were dating someone at the time (Walster [Hatfield], Walster, & Traupmann, 1978). Each student read a list of things that someone might contribute to a relationship, including good looks, intelligence, loving, understanding, and helping the other make decisions. Each student also read a list of potential consequences of a relationship, including various personal, emotional, and day-to-day rewards and frustrations. Each student was then asked to evaluate the contributions they made to the relationship, the contributions the partner made, the things they received, and the things the partner received. Each evaluation was made using an 8-point scale that ranged from extremely positive (+4) to extremely negative (−4). The researchers calculated the person's overall outcomes by dividing the rating of consequences by the rating of contributions. They calculated the perceived outcomes of the partner by dividing the rating of the consequences the partner received by the rating of the contributions the partner was making. By comparing the person's outcomes with the partner's perceived outcomes, the researchers determined whether the relationship was perceived as equitable.

Students were interviewed 14 weeks later to assess the stability of their relationships. Stability was determined by whether they were still dating their partner and by how long they had been going together (or how long they had gone together). The results clearly demonstrated that inequitable relationships were unstable. The less equitable the relationship was at the start, the less likely the couple was to be still dating 14 weeks later. Furthermore, students who perceived that their outcomes did not equal their partner's outcomes reported that their relationships were of shorter duration.

## Differential Commitment and Dissolution

Are outcomes (rewards minus costs) the only thing we consider when deciding whether to continue a relationship? What about emotional attachment or involvement? We often continue a relationship because we have developed an emotional commitment to the person and feel a sense of loyalty to and responsibility for that person's welfare. The importance of commitment is illustrated by the results of a survey of 234 college students (Simpson, 1987). Each student was involved in a dating

relationship and answered questions about ten aspects of the relationship. Three months later, each respondent was recontacted to determine whether they were still dating the partner. The characteristics that were most closely related to stability included length and exclusivity of the relationship and having engaged in sexual intimacy; all three are aspects of commitment. A review of research on premarital relationships concludes that commitment—the person's intent to remain in the relationship—is consistently related to stability (Cate, Levin, & Richmond, 2002).

A meta-analysis of the longitudinal studies of the stability of nonmarital romantic relationships included data from more than 37,000 participants in 137 studies (Le et al., 2010). Researchers assessed the relationships between 16 often-measured variables and stability; the average time between Time 1 and the last follow-up across studies was 145 weeks. The three major predictors of lasting relationships were greater commitment, greater love for the partner, and more positive illusions about the partner.

A study of 101 heterosexual dating couples tested the hypothesis that unequal involvement is related to greater instability. Each partner completed a questionnaire at baseline, and follow-up surveys at 6, 18, 30, and 42 months. At Time 5 (42 months), 41 of the couples were still together; 28 of the 41 were married. Perceptions of unequal emotional involvement were common; in 75 percent of the couples, at least one member reported that they, or the partner, were less involved. Less involved partners perceived themselves as more powerful—this reflects the "principle of least interest." Equal involvement was related to greater satisfaction (Sprecher, Schmeeckle, & Felmlee, 2006).

The importance of equal degrees of involvement is illustrated in another study. Couples were recruited from four colleges and universities in the Boston area (Hill, Rubin, & Peplau, 1976). Each member of 231 couples filled out an initial questionnaire and completed three follow-up questionnaires 6 months, 1 year, and 2 years later. At the time the initial data were collected, couples had been dating an average of 8 months; most were dating exclusively, and 10 percent were engaged. Two years later, researchers were able to determine the status of 221 of the couples. Some were still together, whereas others had broken up.

What distinguished the couples who were together 2 years later from those who had broken up? Couples who were more involved initially—who were dating exclusively, who rated themselves as very close, who said they were in love, and who estimated a high probability that they would get married—were more likely to be together 2 years later. Of the couples who reported equal involvement initially, only 23 percent broke up in the following 2 years. But of the couples who reported unequal involvement initially, 54 percent were no longer seeing each other 2 years later.

Not surprisingly, the breakup of a couple was usually initiated by the person who was less involved. Of those whose relationships ended, 85 percent reported that one person wanted to break up more than the other. There was also a distinct pattern in the timing of breakups; they were much more likely to occur in May through June, September, and December through January. This suggests that factors outside the relationship—such as graduation, moving, and arriving at school—led one person to initiate the breakup. Such changes, or life course transitions (see Chapter 3), are likely to increase the costs, such as the difficulty of meeting, or of continuing a relationship. Interestingly, other research shows that college students are also more likely to break up in the two weeks around Valentine's Day (Morse & Neuberg, 2004). This cultural event emphasizes what intimate relationships should be like; perhaps the hype leads participants in declining

Breaking up is very painful. It can be especially hard on the person who is more committed to the relationship. The person left behind may experience a variety of powerful, negative emotions. © Thomas Schweizer/Corbis

relationships to decide to quit, and perhaps to look for alternatives.

We suggested earlier that breaking up is costly. Who experiences greater costs? One study surveyed both rejectors and rejectees (Perilloux & Buss, 2008). Women were more likely to report loss of male protection and post-breakup stalking by the ex. Women also reported more negative emotions than men. Both men and women who were rejected experienced greater loss of self-esteem and depression than rejectors. In another study of students, greater distress was reported by rejectees, persons whose breakup was recent, and those who had not entered a new relationship (Field et al., 2011).

The dissolution of a relationship is often painful. But breaking up is not necessarily undesirable. It can be thought of as part of a filtering process through which people who are not suited to each other terminate their relationships. Furthermore, coping with and learning from the breakup may lead to personal growth and more successful relationships in the future (Tashiro, Frazier, & Berman, 2006).

## Responses to Dissatisfaction

Not all relationships that involve unequal outcomes or differential commitment break up. What makes the difference? The answer is, in part, the person's reaction to these situations. The level of outcomes a person experiences and their commitment to the relationship are influences on satisfaction with that relationship (Bui, Peplau, & Hill, 1996; Rusbult, Johnson, & Morrow, 1986). A study of 60 students and 36 married couples found that an important influence on satisfaction is the perception that your partner supports your attempts to achieve goals that are important to you (Brunstein, Dangelmayer, & Schultheiss, 1996). As long as the person is satisfied, whatever the level of rewards or commitment, they will want to continue the relationship. People

who are satisfied are more likely to engage in **accommodation**—to respond to potentially destructive acts by the partner in a constructive way (Rusbult et al., 1991). A study of Black and White married couples over 14 years found that reports of frequent conflict and of using insults, name-calling, and shouting in response to conflict (in other words, not engaging in accommodation) predicted subsequent divorce (Orbuch, Veroff, Hassan, & Horrocks, 2002).

An individual in an unsatisfactory relationship has four basic alternatives (Goodwin, 1991; Rusbult, Zembrodt, & Gunn, 1982): exit (termination), voice (discuss with your partner), loyalty (grin and bear it), and neglect (stay in the relationship but not contribute much). Which of these alternatives the person selects depends on the anticipated costs of breaking up, the availability of alternative relationships, and the level of reward obtained from the relationship in the past.

To assess the costs of breaking up, the individual weighs the costs of an unsatisfactory relationship against the costs of ending that relationship. There are three types of barriers or costs to leaving a relationship: material, symbolic, and affectual (Levinger, 1976). Material costs are especially significant for partners who have pooled their financial resources. Breaking up will require agreeing on who gets what, and it may produce a lower standard of living for each person. Symbolic costs include the reactions of others. A survey of 254 persons, 123 of whom were in relationships, measured the perception of friends' and family members' support for the relationship and commitment to it (Cox, Wexler, Rusbult, & Gaines, 1997). Persons who perceived more support were more committed, in both dating and married couples. Will close friends and family members support or criticize the termination of the relationship? A longitudinal study of dating couples found that lower levels of support by friends for the relationship were associated with later termination of it (Felmlee, Sprecher, & Bassin, 1990). Affectual costs involve changes in one's relationships with others. Breaking up may cause the loss of friends and reduce or eliminate contact with relatives—that is, it may result in loneliness. A study of married persons asked each to name "the most important factors keeping you together"; the most frequently mentioned barriers were children (31 percent of respondents), religion (13 percent), and financial need (6 percent) (Previti & Amato, 2003).

A second factor in this assessment is the availability of alternatives. The absence of an attractive alternative may lead the individual to maintain an unrewarding relationship, whereas the appearance of an attractive alternative may trigger the dissatisfied person to dissolve the relationship.

We noted at the beginning of this chapter that two factors influence who is available: personal characteristics and institutional structure. With regard to the first, people who are in relationships perceive opposite-sex persons of the same age as less physically attractive than do people who are not in relationships (Simpson, Gangestad, & Lerum, 1990). This devaluation of potential partners contributes to relationship maintenance. However, a longitudinal study found that the perceived quality of alternative partners increased among persons whose relationships subsequently ended (Johnson & Rusbult, 1989). With regard to institutional structures, the sex ratio in a community determines the number of eligible partners. Research combining survey data with census data for the area where the respondent lived found that the risk of divorce is greatest in areas where husbands or wives encounter numerous alternatives (South, Trent, & Shen, 2001).

A third factor is the level of rewards experienced before the relationship became dissatisfying. If the relationship was particularly rewarding in the past, the individual is less likely to decide to terminate it.

How important are each of these three factors? That is, which factors are most important in determining whether a dissatisfied person

responds by discussing the situation with their partner, waiting for things to improve, neglecting the partner, or terminating the relationship? In one study, participants were given short stories describing relationships in which these three factors varied. They were asked what they would do in each situation (Rusbult et al., 1982). The results showed that the lower the prior satisfaction—that is, the less satisfied and the less positive their feelings and caring for their partners—the more likely they were to neglect or terminate the relationship. The less the investment—that is, the degree of disclosure and how much a person stands to lose—the more likely participants were to engage in neglect or termination. Finally, the presence of attractive alternatives increased the probability of terminating the relationship. A later study of ongoing relationships yielded the same results (Rusbult, 1983).

A study of the stability of the relationships of 167 couples over a 15-year period also found that satisfaction, level of investments, and quality of alternatives predicted commitment. Relationships in which commitment was high were more likely to endure (Bui et al., 1996).

At the beginning of this section, we noted the influence of the linear model of relationship development and dissolution on our schema and on research. We have just reviewed a lot of literature on what leads couples to break up. One might think that breaking up reflects a permanent end to a relationship. However, one would be wrong! Researchers have identified a pattern referred to as **relationship churning**, a situation in which a couple is neither together nor stably broken up. Two churning states are at least temporary reconciliation following a separation or breakup, or engaging in sexual activity with an "ex" (Halpern-Meekin, Manning, Giordano, & Longmore, 2013). Churning may follow the breakup of dating, cohabiting, or marital relationships. Some couples may engage in one cycle of reconciliation and later break up again, this time for good. Other couples may experience multiple cycles. In a sample of 17- to 24-year-olds reporting on their most recent dating or cohabiting relationship, 48 percent of those reporting a breakup had experienced churning. Reconciliations were associated with reports of more conflict, more self-disclosure, and less commitment during the relationship. Reported sex with an ex was associated with reports of more conflict, more self-disclosure, and more commitment during the relationship. Thus, perhaps not surprisingly, churning is more likely in relationships that were more intimate prior to dissolution. Churning has also been documented in studies of marital dissolution, although with lower frequency than in these premarital relationships.

## SUMMARY

Interpersonal attraction is a positive attitude held by one person toward another person. It is the basis for the development, maintenance, and dissolution of close personal relationships.

**Who Is Available?** Institutional structures and personal characteristics influence who is available to us as potential friends, roommates, coworkers, and lovers. Three factors influence whom we select from this pool. (1) Our daily routines make some persons more accessible. (2) Proximity makes it more rewarding and less costly to interact with some people rather than others. (3) Familiarity produces a positive attitude toward those with whom we repeatedly come into contact.

**Who Is Desirable?** Among the available candidates, we choose based on several criteria. (1) Social norms tell us what kinds of people are appropriate as friends, lovers, and mentors. Homogamy—similarity in age, race, religion, and SES—is characteristic of intimate relationships in the United States. (2) We prefer a more physically attractive person, both for aesthetic

reasons and because we expect rewards from associating with that person. Attractiveness is more influential when we have no other information about a person. (3) We choose based on our expectations about the rewards and costs of potential relationships. We choose to develop those relationships whose outcomes we expect will exceed both comparison level (CL) and comparison level for alternatives (CLalt). We implement our choices by making contact; the development of the relationship is guided by a script.

**The Determinants of Liking.** Many relationships—between friends, roommates, coworkers, or lovers—involve liking. The extent to which we like someone is determined by three factors. (1) The major influence is the degree to which two people have similar attitudes. The greater the proportion of similar attitudes, the more they like each other. Similarity produces liking because we prefer cognitive consistency and because we expect interaction with similar others to be reinforcing. (2) Shared activities become an important influence on our liking for another person as we spend time with them. (3) We like those who like us; as we experience positive feedback from another, it increases our liking for them.

**The Growth of Relationships.** As relationships grow, they change on three dimensions. (1) There may be a gradual increase in the disclosure of intimate information about the self. Self-disclosure is usually reciprocal, with each person revealing something about themselves in response to revelations by the other. (2) Trust in the other person—a belief in their honesty, benevolence, and reliability—also increases as relationships develop. Trust may be especially important in long-distance relationships. (3) Interdependence for various gratifications also increases, often accompanied by a decline in reliance on and number of relationships with others.

**Love and Loving.** (1) Whereas liking refers to a positive attitude toward an object, love involves attachment to and caring for another person. Love also may involve passion—a state of intense physiological arousal and intense absorption in the other. (2) The experience of passionate love involves cognitive, emotional, and behavioral elements. Love increases as the length of the relationship increases, but passion may decline. (3) The concept of love does not exist in all societies; the romantic love ideal emerged gradually in the United States and came into its own about the time of the Civil War. (4) Love stories—scripts—shape our beliefs about love and relationships, and our beliefs influence how we behave in and interpret our relationships.

**Committed Relationships.** Most persons will spend at least part of their adult lives in a long-term committed relationship. The relationship may take the form of living-alone-together (LAT), cohabitation, or marriage. The decision to form the relationship is generally motivated by a desire for greater intimacy. A couple's choice may be influenced by where each one lives, age, economic considerations, or the degree to which each is committed to the relationship. Instability, breaking up, is associated with youth, less education, and a difference in age greater than five years.

**Breaking Up.** There are three major influences on whether a relationship dissolves. (1) Breaking up may result if one person feels that outcomes (rewards minus costs) are inadequate. A person may evaluate present outcomes against what could be obtained from an alternative relationship. Alternatively, a person may look at the outcomes the partner is experiencing and assess whether the relationship is equitable. (2) The degree of commitment to a relationship is an important influence on whether it continues. Someone who feels a low level of emotional attachment to and concern for their partner is more likely

to break up with that person. (3) Responses to dissatisfaction with a relationship include exit, voice, loyalty, or neglect. Which response occurs depends on the anticipated economic and emotional costs, the availability of attractive alternatives, and the level of prior satisfaction in the relationship. A breakup may not be permanent; it may be followed by churning, in which the ex-partners reconcile at least temporarily or resume having sex.

### Critical Thinking Skill: (Relationship) Decision Making and Problem Solving

In making good decisions, it helps to (1) identify your goal(s) in the situation; (2) list at least two possible actions or solutions to the problem; (3) evaluate the quality of each solution (Does it help you meet your goal? Does it have any negative aspects?); and (4) decide on the best one. Consider the following scenario.

> Britney, a student at your school, has been seeing Craig for a month. He seems to really like her, and she certainly is attracted to him. At a party on campus, she sees Shelly flirting with Craig and starts to worry that Shelly is trying to steal him. Back at her own apartment, Britney tries to decide what to do to keep Craig. They have not had intercourse yet, but have done just about everything else. She thinks maybe the thing to do is send him a nude photo of herself to arouse his interest and make herself seem hot.

What should Britney do? Apply the techniques listed above to consider what her best decision is. (1) What is her goal? (2) What are at least two possible solutions? (3) Evaluate each solution in terms of whether it helps her meet her goal and whether it has any negative aspects. Do this before you read on.

Britney's goal is to maintain and develop a relationship with Craig. One solution is to send him the nude photo. Another is to do nothing; doing "nothing" is doing something: waiting to see if there is a problem before doing something else. Did you think of other potential solutions? A third is to text him a positive, enthusiastic message without a photo. A fourth solution would be to make sure she sees him before class the next day and be friendly. It would be best if Britney takes out a piece of paper and systematically evaluates these options.

Here are some evaluations of each solution.

1. Send Craig the nude photo. It might help her achieve her goal of keeping him, but it might backfire if Craig forms a negative impression of her. A definite negative is that Britney cannot assume that Craig will keep the photo private. He might decide to forward it to his buddies, causing her great embarrassment.
2. Do nothing. This may not contribute positively to Britney's achieving her goal, but it also carries no risk. She can assess whether Craig behaves differently the next time she sees him.
3. and 4. Send a positive text or see him in person the next day. These are similar solutions; both involve making contact, an important part of attraction, as discussed earlier in the chapter. Positive contact is also important, as discussed by exchange theory. They differ in whether the contact is electronic or in person. Either one (or both) help Britney achieve her goal, and neither seems to have any negative aspects.

Overall, then, the key to making good decisions is to "Think first!" Be clear about your goal. Think of multiple solutions; don't stop after the first or most obvious one (especially if the obvious one involves lashing out angrily). Then carefully evaluate each possible solution. Choose the one that seems likely to help you achieve your goal and has few or no negative consequences.

# UNDERSTANDING

## GROUPS

By the end of this chapter you will be able to:

- Identify and describe the four attributes of groups and the sources and consequences of cohesion that unite members.

- Understand conformity and the specific types of influence that encourage group members to conform.

- Recognize the sources of intergroup conflict, the reasons conflict persists, and the effects the conflict has on intragroup processes.

## INTRODUCTION

Groups are everywhere. We all participate in them, spending a significant portion of our days engaging in group activities. Take Brandon Harris, for example. Brandon is the star cornerback on his university's football team. He is close to his parents and his two younger sisters and enjoys spending time with his extended family when he is home during school breaks. He regularly attends the local Islamic Society Mosque and is working closely with a group of students in his Business 102 class on a semester-long project. Although he thought about moving into the fraternity house, he has really enjoyed living in Reilly for the last few years. He thinks that dorm life keeps him grounded. He gets along well with his three roommates and found serving as treasurer of the dorm's council a valuable experience. During the off-season, Brandon also holds down a work-study job, shelving books in the library. He is friendly with the other work-study students and looks forward to the evenings he spends in the stacks. He and his girlfriend have been together since their first year of college, when they met in a sociology class. It has been a busy quarter for Brandon, and he is genuinely looking forward to spring break. He plans to kick it off with a long-awaited beach vacation with a group of his closest high school friends, a group he affectionately refers to as the Zoo Crew.

Brandon is clearly busy, but even if our own social lives are less active than his, groups are a pervasive part of our everyday experiences as well. We are members of families, work groups, sports teams, street gangs, classes and seminars, therapy and rehabilitation groups, classical quartets and rock groups, small military units, neighborhood clubs, church groups, and so on. Groups are important because they provide social support, a cultural framework to guide performance, and rewards and resources of all kinds. Without groups, most individuals would be isolated, unloved, disoriented, relatively unproductive, and very possibly hungry.

To better understand groups and the significant influence they have on our lives, this chapter provides the tools—both concepts and theories—used to classify and study groups. The next chapter (Chapter 16) delves more deeply into the within-group processes of interest to social psychologists.

## WHAT IS A GROUP?

We all have a notion of a "group," but our commonsense notion is too broad for use in social psychology (DeLamater, 1974). In this chapter and the next, the term **group** specifically refers to a social unit that consists of two or more persons with all of the following attributes:

1. *Membership.* To be a member of a group, we must identify ourselves as belonging to the group and must also be recognized by other members as belonging to the group (Lickel et al., 2000).
2. *Interaction among members.* Group members also must interact—communicating with one another

and influencing one another, whether in person, online, or through other mediums.

3. *Goals shared by members.* Group members may have goals that are the same, unique, or complementary. Regardless, group members should be interdependent with respect to goal attainment. In other words, progress by one member toward their objectives makes it more likely that another member will also reach their objectives.

4. *Shared norms.* Group members hold a set of expectations (that is, norms or rules) that place limits on members' behavior and guide action.

As this definition suggests, groups are not simply collections of individuals; rather, they are organized systems in which the relations among individuals are structured and patterned. For our purposes here, not all social units of two or more persons are groups. For example, persons in a theater crowd escaping in panic from a fire would not constitute a group. Although there may be some communication among them, there are no explicit normative expectations or a sense of shared membership among those present. Likewise, a commercial transaction between a customer and a cashier ringing up a basket of groceries would not qualify as a group interaction. In such a situation, there is no clear basis for group membership.

Social psychologists typically divide groups into two categories: primary and secondary (Cooley, 1909). **Primary groups** tend to be smaller groups with strong emotional ties and bonds that endure over time. They are more informal and intimate than other groups individuals belong to. Brandon's family and close friends—the Zoo Crew—are examples of primary groups. Conversely, **secondary groups** are more formal and impersonal. They tend to be organized around instrumental goals— like the group working on the Business 102

class project with Brandon or the other work-study students shelving books at the library— and have few emotional ties. Occasionally, secondary groups begin to take on some of the qualities of primary groups. For instance, over time the football team began to feel like family to Brandon, as team members' shared goals extended beyond the instrumental goals of winning a game or having an undefeated season toward something more intimate and diffuse, like encouraging one another and offering emotional support both on and off the field.

## GROUP COHESION

Whether primary or secondary, groups vary in their connectedness. Take the Jaguars—a recreational softball club—as an example of a tight-knit, secondary group. The Jaguars have a long record of championships in the city league. The Jaguar players take pride in their performance and are very committed to their team. At practice and during games, they are a model of enthusiasm and coordination. On the rare occasion when they have a losing streak, all of the team members voluntarily hold extra practice sessions to sharpen their skills and teamwork. The players like one another, and they enjoy playing together and celebrating their victories. Although they do not always agree on strategy, the Jaguars resolve their differences quickly. Several of the players consider teammates their best friends, and they often spend time together off the field. The Jaguars team rarely loses any of its players—not even its second-stringers.

The players of another team in the league— the Penguins—provide a very different story. The Penguins have finished in last place for the last three seasons. Occasionally, the Penguins have to forfeit a game because they cannot even field a team of nine players. The team is not a high priority for the players—they are often busy with other activities, and they often miss practice. The players seldom interact out-side of team activities. The Penguins' planning session last spring dissolved into chaos when the players could not agree on how to pay for some new equipment. The friction was so bad that there is doubt about whether the team will even participate in the league next year.

The Jaguars and the Penguins differ in a number of respects. For one thing, the Jag-uars win a lot more than the Penguins. But the teams also differ notably in their members' willingness to participate in the group. The Jaguar players care about their membership on the team and want to interact with one another, whereas the Penguin players seem to care much less. The Jaguars have a stronger grip on members' loyalty than the Penguins do, and the team has bonded together more firmly—the Jaguars have a higher level of group cohesion than the Penguins do.

**Group cohesion** refers to the extent to which group members desire to remain in a group and resist leaving it (Cartwright, 1968). A highly cohesive group generally maintains a firm hold over its members' time, energy, loyalty, and commitment. Cohesive groups are marked by strong ties among members, a positive emotional feeling about membership, and a tendency for members to perceive events in similar terms (Bollen & Hoyle, 1990; Lawler, Thye, & Yoon, 2000). Because members of a cohesive group desire to belong, the interactions among them will typically have a positive, upbeat character and reflect a "we" feeling.

## The Nature of Group Cohesion

There are a variety of motives for joining and staying in groups. Some people may belong to a group because they like the tasks they per-form in the group, because they enjoy inter-acting with the other members, because the group reflects their own values, or because the group helps them get something desirable (such as prestige, money, future opportunities,

protection, or social contacts). These varied motives lead to different levels and types of cohesion among the members (Carless & De Paola, 2000; Cota et al., 1995).

One of the fundamental types of group cohesion is *social cohesion* (Dion, 2000). A group has social cohesion if its members stay in the group primarily because they like one another as persons and desire to interact with one another (Aiken, 1992; Lott & Lott, 1965). All other things being equal, social cohesion will be greater when group members are similar. As discussed in Chapter 14, similar-ity increases liking; therefore, groups whose members have similar education, ethnicity, and status, and hold similar attitudes will have greater social cohesion.

The other major type of group cohesion is *task cohesion*. When a group has high task cohesion, its members remain together primar-ily because they are heavily involved with the group's task(s). Task cohesion will be greater if members find the group's task(s) intrinsically valuable, interesting, and challenging. It will also be greater if the group's objectives (and the related tasks) are clearly defined (Raven & Rietsema, 1957). Groups that succeed at achieving their goals (like the Jaguars) often have higher task cohesion than do groups that fail repeatedly (like the Penguins).

## Sources and Consequences of Cohesion

Social psychological research suggests that posi-tive emotions attributed to the group are an important source of cohesion (Lawler, Thye, & Yoon, 2000, 2008). For example, when the Jaguar players feel good after winning a game, they make attributions about the source of their happiness (see Chapter 7). Given that the team had to work together to win and the positive emotions came from winning, the players attri-bute their positive affect to the team and its joint action. Focusing on the group as an entity increases the group orientation of the mem-bers. The players are more likely to think of the

## BOX 15.1  Research Update: Adolescent Peer Groups, Cohesion, and Delinquency

Parents and teens alike realize the influence that peers have on adolescent behavior, but how are delinquent groups different than rule-abiding ones? Are delinquent peer groups more cohesive, making it easier for members to influence one another? Or are they less cohesive, because any antisocial personality characteristics that might drive delinquency also threaten connectedness? Recent work by social scientists (Kreager, Rulison, & Moody, 2011) tests these two possibilities by comparing attributes of adolescent friendship groups—including how tightly connected or cohesive the groups were—that have higher and lower average rates of delinquency.

To measure cohesion, the researchers gauged a variety of attributes of ninth graders' peer groups, including:

1. *Reciprocity*: whether a friendship choice indicated by one student to another is returned. In other words, Jack said he was Jill's friend, but does Jill reciprocate by listing Jack as her friend?

2. *Transitivity*: the extent to which group members form connected clusters where a "friend of a friend is a friend." If Jack is also friends with Jill's friend, Humpty, there is a "triangular" relationship between them that is common in cohesive groups.

3. *Structural cohesion*: the number of independent paths that connect members in a group. If all the group members are connected through Jill, the group is likely to become disconnected if she leaves. However, if there are a number of direct paths bringing members together—like the one between Jack

and Humpty—the group is likely to persist even if Jill or another member leaves.

With an interest in adolescent groups in particular, they also considered *average popularity* (popular groups had members who received a high number of friendship nominations relative to other students in the network) and *group centrality* (a measure of social status of the group).

Examining 900 different peer groups, the researchers found that groups high in delinquency were lower on the network measures related to both cohesion and status. Specifically, there were lower levels of reciprocity, transitivity, cohesion, popularity, and centrality in those delinquent groups than in others. When the researchers looked at peer groups who focused on drinking rather than other forms of delinquency, they found the reverse. These groups had more reciprocal and transitive ties than average groups and were more cohesive. They were also more popular and had higher centrality.

Importantly, once the researchers took into account characteristics of group members (particularly economic status and gender) these effects disappeared. In other words, because the less delinquent drinking groups tend to be of higher socioeconomic status and predominantly female, and groups with those characteristics also tend to be more cohesive and of higher social status, the link between group structure and delinquency is less about the network properties of groups and more about the characteristics of group members.

*Source:* Adapted from Kreager, Rulison, & Moody (2011).

team as an important unit and to invest further in the group (Lawler et al., 2000).

Implicit in the above is cohesion's relationship to interdependence. That is, the more that group members must rely on one another to achieve the goals that generate positive emotion,

the more likely they are to attribute any positive emotion they experience to the group (Lawler 2001; Lawler, Thye, & Yoon, 2008). If the Jaguars won because of the actions of a star player and not a group effort, the positive emotions associated with winning would be much less likely to strengthen group ties because the win would be attributed to the one player rather than any joint action of the team.

Cohesion begets increased cohesion. Given the opportunity, members of highly cohesive groups communicate more with one another than do members of less cohesive groups (Moran, 1966), and the interaction is of higher quality. Interaction among members in highly cohesive groups is usually friendlier, more cooperative, and includes more attempts to reach agreements and to improve coordination (Shaw & Shaw, 1962).

Members of high-cohesion groups also have more influence on one another than do members of low-cohesion groups (Lott & Lott, 1965). This is not only because members of high-cohesion groups try to influence one another more but also because they are more likely to be successful at doing so. Conformity—which we will cover in detail later in the chapter— is higher in cohesive groups than less cohesive ones (Sakurai, 1975; Wyer, 1966).

Members of groups with high cohesion are more likely to invest both time and energy into their groups (Lawler, Thye, & Yoon, 2000) because they want them to succeed. This helps explain why cohesion tends to increase the productivity and performance of groups (Carron, Colman, Wheeler, & Stevens, 2002). However, cohesion does not always contribute to success (Evans & Dion, 1991; Gully, Devine, & Whitney, 1995). Task cohesion (that is, members' commitment to the group's task) has a significant effect on group productivity, but other forms of cohesion, including social cohesion, do not seem to increase productivity (Chang & Bordia, 2001; Mullen & Copper, 1994). This may be because members of socially cohesive groups prefer to spend their time socializing rather than producing. Imagine a study group. Do you achieve more with a group of friends from the class who you like to socialize with, or with a group of relative strangers who are all committed to doing well on the exam?

Families are primary groups, with strong and intimate ties. Engaging in activities that require teamwork and generate positive emotions, like building a snowman together, increases cohesion among group members. The positive affect the activity generates is attributed to the group, enhancing a sense of "we-ness." Members of highly cohesive groups invest more time and energy into group activities than those in less cohesive groups. © ArtMarie/iStock

## GROUP GOALS

Groups can also be characterized by their goals. A **group goal** is an outcome group members view as desirable and important to attain. These goals can differ in terms of specificity, ranging from general statements about what the group does and why it exists to more specific targets and tasks that the group members attempt to achieve along the way to its larger goals. Primary groups tend to have more general or diffuse goals (like supporting or caring for one another). Conversely, secondary groups are likely to have specific goals (like winning football games or completing a course project).

## Group Goals and Individual Goals

Although individual and group goals may be related, they are not always the same, and these differences can be very important for the functioning of the group.

Most groups function best when there is compatibility between group goals and the individual goals of its members. The term **goal isomorphism** refers to a state in which group goals and individual goals are compatible in the sense that actions leading to group goals also lead to the attainment of individual goals. High isomorphism benefits the group because members are motivated to pursue group goals and to contribute resources and effort to the group (Sniezek & May, 1990). The common admonition among coaches—"There's no I in team"—is an effort to remind players that individuals' goals can sometimes interfere with group goals. A basketball player who refuses to pass might be trying to increase his own stats and notoriety, but this can be detrimental to the team's performance, causing them to lose points or keeping them from working effectively as a unit.

Groups use a number of strategies to heighten isomorphism. First, many groups, including sports teams, recruit selectively—that is, they only admit persons who strongly support the group's main goal(s). Second, groups use socialization and training. For example, a basketball coach might bench a star player who consistently hogs the ball in an effort to socialize him into being more of a team player or run drills in practice that incorporate a number of passes. Finally, increasing members' awareness that they belong to a group and making their identity as members more salient can enhance individuals' support for group goals (Mackie & Goethals, 1987). Using a common designation to label group members (Penguins, Tri-Delts, Zoo Crew) often makes a united identity salient (Dion, 1979). Other ways to increase the salience of group membership include increasing the proximity of members to one another, the experiences they share in common, and the amount of social contact and communication they have with one another (see Box 15.2; Turner, 1981).

## GROUP NORMS

A **norm** is a rule or standard that specifies how group members are expected to behave under given circumstances (Hechter & Opp, 2001). Most groups develop a variety of norms that regulate their members' activities. For example, a sports team may have norms specifying how many practices a teammate can miss before they are penalized or how to communicate with coaches and one another. Norms of these types will obviously have an impact on members' attendance and interaction styles. A group of college admissions officers may have norms that regulate how the officers make judgments; the nature of these norms will indirectly affect which applicants will be admitted and which will not. A family may have norms regulating who washes the dishes or mows the lawn.

### Functions of Norms

Norms serve a number of important functions for groups (Feldman, 1984). First, they foster coordination among members while in pursuit of group goals (Conte & Castelfranchi, 1995). Because norms are often oriented around a group's values, they prescribe behaviors that help the group attain important goals. When members conform to group norms, they know what to expect of one another, and can better coordinate. For example, if a family has established a norm of gathering together for Sunday dinner, this limits the needs to make explicit plans for the dinner or for family members to wonder whether they will be free for other activities on an upcoming Sunday.

Second, norms provide a cognitive frame of reference. That is, norms provide a basis for distinguishing good from bad and important from unimportant. They are especially useful in novel or ambiguous situations, where they serve as pointers on how to behave. Because norms are anchored in the group's values and culture, norms bring predictability and coherence to group activities. As an example, a high school teacher might develop particular norms for students in their class related to participation and considerateness. This not only allows students to distinguish good ways to participate from bad, but signals that participation is more important than something the teacher has not associated with normative expectations (perhaps what the students wear to class). Students may draw on these norms in unusual situations where they are uncertain how to behave, like when the class has a substitute teacher or is out on a field trip

Third, norms define and enhance the common identity of group members. This is especially true when group norms require members to behave differently from persons outside the group. Thus, norms that prescribe distinctive dress (for example, uniforms and hairstyles), behaviors (for example,

handshakes), or speech patterns (for example, dialects or vocabulary) will differentiate group members from nonmembers. These norms demarcate group boundaries and reinforce the group's distinctive identity.

## Conformity and Influence

When an individual adheres to group norms and standards, it is called **conformity**. Much of the behavior we witness in daily life involves conformity to one group norm or another.

**The Asch Conformity Paradigm.** In groups, influence flows in many directions—members influence other members and are influenced in turn. Of special importance, however, is the influence of the group's majority over individual members' behavior. Social psychologists use the term **majority influence** to refer to the processes by which a group's majority pressures an individual member to conform or to adopt a specific position on some issue.

The impact of majority influence on individual group members was illustrated in a series of classic experiments by Asch (1951, 1955, 1957). Using a laboratory setting, Asch created a situation in which an individual was confronted by a majority that agreed unanimously on a factual matter (spatial judgments)

Group norms can extend to any aspect of behavior, including dress and appearance. Bikers have a different dress code from corporate executives, but conformity is high in each group. *Left:* © hroe/iStock *Right:* © Squaredpixels/iStock

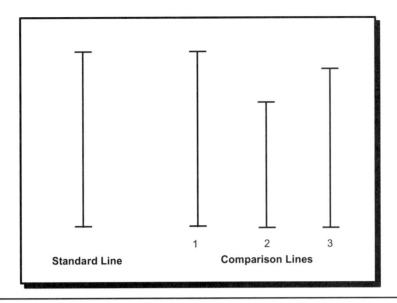

**FIGURE 15.1** Judgmental Task Used in Asch Conformity Studies

In the Asch paradigm, naive participants are shown one standard line and three comparison lines. The task is to judge which of the three comparison lines is closest in length to the standard line. By itself, this task appears easy. However, participants are surrounded by other persons (supposedly also naive participants but actually experimental confederates) who publicly announce erroneous judgments regarding the match between lines. Such a situation imposes pressure on the participant to conform to their erroneous judgments.

*Source:* Adapted from Asch, 1952.

but was obviously in error (see Figure 15.1). These studies showed that, within limits, groups can pressure their members to change their judgments and conform with the majority's position even when that position is obviously incorrect.

In the basic Asch experiment, a group of eight persons participated in an investigation of "visual discrimination." In fact, all but one of the participants in each group were confederates working for the experimenter. The remaining individual was a naive participant. In front of the experimental room, large cards displayed a standard line and three comparison lines, as shown in Figure 15.1. The participant's objective was to decide which of the three comparison lines was closest in length to the standard line.

The task seemed simple and straightforward: one of the comparison lines was the

same length as the standard line, whereas the other two were very different. The group of eight repeated this task 18 times, using a different set of lines each time. On each trial, the standard line matched one of the three comparison lines. During each trial of the experiment, the confederates announced their judgments publicly, one after another. The group was seated so that the confederates responded prior to the real participant, who also announced their opinion publicly. Although this task seemed easy, it turned out to be a difficult experience for the naive participant. On 6 of the 18 trials, the confederates gave a correct response, but on the other 12 trials, the confederates responded incorrectly. The confederates' erroneous responses put the naive participants in a trying position. On the one hand, they knew the correct response based on their own perception of the lines. On the other hand, they heard all the other persons (whom they believed to be sincere) unanimously announcing a different and incorrect judgment on two-thirds of the trials.

The results showed that majority opinion, even when obviously incorrect, strongly influenced the judgments the naive participants announced. In the 12 critical trials, nearly one-third of the responses by participants were incorrect (Asch, 1957). Only one-quarter of the participants showed no conformity and remained independent throughout; the remainder conformed, at least to some degree. One-third of the participants conformed on 50 percent or more of the critical trials. This is striking compared to the control condition. With no confederates present and participants recording their judgments privately on paper, the error rate was less than 1 percent.

Interviews conducted after the experiment revealed that most of the participants were quite aware of the discrepancy between the majority's judgments and their own. They felt puzzled and under pressure, and they tried to figure out what might be happening. Some wondered whether they had misunderstood the experimental instructions; others began to look for other explanations or to question their eyesight. Even those participants who did not conform to the majority felt some apprehension but eventually decided that the problem rested more with the majority than with themselves. The interviews indicated that participants' conformity in this study was of a particular type - public compliance without private acceptance: although many participants conformed publicly, they privately did not believe or accept the majority's judgment. In effect, they viewed public compliance as the best choice in a difficult situation.

**Why Conform?** Majority influence and conformity in groups stem from the fact that individual members are dependent on the majority cognitively, socially, and for utilitarian reasons. Members seek information about social reality and they depend on the majority to validate their understanding of and opinions about the group and the world. Going back to study groups, a participant is likely to accept a definition for a concept that is widely agreed upon during an exam review session. Individual members also want to obtain various rewards and benefits—including acceptance of their continuing membership in the group—and they depend heavily on the majority for these outcomes. The dependence of group members on the majority thus leads to the majority's exercise of influence in groups because it can withhold these outcomes from the minority. If a student attributes strong exam performance to participating in the study group, they will want to appeal to most of the other members.

**Types of Influence.** Many analyses distinguish between normative influence and informational influence (Deutsch & Gerard, 1955; Kaplan & Miller, 1987; Price, Nir, & Cappella, 2006). **Normative influence** occurs when a member conforms to expectations held by others (that is, to norms) in order to receive the social rewards or avoid the punishments that are contingent on meeting these expectations. Being liked and accepted by other members is one important reward in normative influence. To exercise influence of this type, a group will need to maintain at least some degree of surveillance over its members' behavior. The impact of normative influence is heightened, for instance, when members respond publicly rather than anonymously (Schultz, Tabanico, & Rendón, 2008).

Conformity to social norms may also be a utility-seeking activity, less in terms of directly avoiding punishments or currying favor but rather as a means to stabilize relationships and enhance the predictability of behavior in the group. Conforming to norms and enforcing them produces more predictable relationships among people, making exchanges in these relationships easier (Horne, 2004). If, for example,

Bob wishes to sell an item on eBay, he must follow the prescribed norms about describing his product accurately, adequately packaging his product for shipping, and charging reasonable shipping and handling costs. He is motivated to conform to the standards of the eBay community, not just because he will be sanctioned (by negative testimonials and perhaps even losing his account) if he does not, but also because following the norms enhances the trading system for everyone involved. It makes buying and selling behavior predictable, comfortable, and easy to manage.

**Informational influence** occurs when a group member accepts information from others as valid evidence about reality. This type of influence is likely when members need to reduce uncertainty—as in situations that involve ambiguity or when members are trying to solve a complex problem unfamiliar to them (Baron, Vandello, & Brunsman, 1996; Kaplan & Miller, 1987). Think back to your first time in the high school cafeteria. You might not have known what to expect, but there probably were not explicit instructions anywhere. You looked to what others were doing to determine how you should proceed. Members considered more expert or knowledgeable—in this case, upperclassmen—are especially likely to exercise informational influence during such tasks. This type of influence also occurs frequently in crisis situations when members must act immediately but lack knowledge about the appropriate action.

During the Asch line judgment task, *normative* influence operated prominently. Many of the participants who conformed in the experiment did so to avoid being embarrassed, ridiculed, or laughed at by the majority. They were seeking acceptance by the majority, or at least hoping to avoid outright public rejection. In one variation of the experiment, Asch retested his participants on the same stimuli with the majority group no longer present, and they gave correct answers. This suggests that their experience of judging lines in the presence of the majority did not permanently alter their understanding of the lines' lengths, suggesting that informational influence was not an influential factor.

Although *informational* influence was relatively unimportant in the Asch situation, we should not underestimate its importance in other situations. A famous study by Sherif (1935, 1936)—conducted years before Asch did his line judgment research—dramatically illustrates the impact of informational influence under conditions of uncertainty. Sherif's study used a physical phenomenon known as the autokinetic effect (meaning "moves by itself"). The autokinetic effect occurs when a person stares at a stationary pinpoint of light located at a distance in a completely dark room. For most people, this light will appear to move in an erratic fashion, even though the light is not actually moving at all. To study informational influence in groups, Sherif placed participants in a laboratory setting by themselves and asked them to estimate how far the light moved. In making these judgments, the participants were literally in the dark—they had no external frame of reference—and their estimates differed quite a bit. Whereas some thought the light was moving only one or two inches, others believed it was moving as much as eight or ten inches.

Shortly thereafter, Sherif put the same participants together in groups of three and placed them back in the autokinetic situation. Although the estimates the participants had made when alone were different, the estimates they made in groups converged on a common standard, providing evidence for the operation of informational influence. Lacking an external frame of reference and being uncertain about their own judgment, group members began to use one another's estimates as a basis for defining reality. Each group established its own arbitrary standard, and members used this as a frame of reference. This process of norm formation can be quite subtle, as group members are often unaware that other members are influencing their judgments (Douglas & Sutton, 2004). You may think that you are personally drawn to a new song or fashion trend, but you are likely underestimating how someone else's endorsement (a celebrity, a store or brand, or a radio DJ) is influencing your own opinion.

Additional evidence of informational influence emerged when, a week or two after their initial exposure, the participants in Sherif's experiments returned to the autokinetic situation alone. Results showed that the participants used the acquired group norm as the framework for their new, individual judgments. Although not all studies have found evidence of such enduring norm internalization, at least one study retested individual participants in the autokinetic task a year after their initial exposure to the group norm and found evidence that the group norm still influenced participants' judgments despite the passage of time (Rohrer, Baron, Hoffman, & Swander, 1954).

## Increasing Conformity

An individual's tendency to conform will be greater under some conditions than under others. Social psychologists have identified a number of factors that affect conformity in groups.

**Size of the Majority.** As the size of the unanimous majority increases, the amount of participants' conformity increases (Asch, 1955; Rosenberg, 1961). For example, a participant confronted by one other person in an Asch-type situation will conform very little; they will answer independently and correctly on nearly all trials. However, when confronted by two persons, the participant will experience more pressure and will agree with the majority's erroneous answer more of the time. Confronted by three persons, the participant will conform at a still higher rate. In his early studies, Asch (1951) found that conformity

to unanimous false judgments increased with majority size up to three members and then remained essentially constant beyond that point. Although some research (Bond & Smith, 1996; Clark & Maass, 1990) has questioned the exact point at which the effect of majority size begins to level off, there does seem to be some point at which additional persons do not further increase conformity.

**Unanimity.** If all other group members are united in their position, then the size of the majority will have an impact on the behavior of the participant—but what happens when the group's majority is not unanimous? Basically, lack of unanimity among majority members has a liberating effect on participants' behavior. A participant will be less likely to conform if another member moves away from the majority, breaking consensus (Morris & Miller, 1975). One explanation for this is that the member who abandons the majority provides validation and social support for the participant. If Kai believes he is the only one who thinks his employer's scheduling process is unfair, he is unlikely to say anything to his boss. However, if one or several other employees abandon the majority and make similar claims, their actions will reaffirm Kai's own perception of reality and reduce his tendency to conform to the majority. He will be much more comfortable speaking up.

Any breach in the majority—whether it provides social support or not—will reduce the pressure on the participant to conform (Allen & Levine, 1971; Levine, Saxe, & Ranelli, 1975). In one study (Allen & Levine, 1969), individuals participated in groups of five persons, four of whom were confederates. The participants made judgments on a variety of items. These included visual tasks similar to those used by Asch as well as informational items (for example, "In thousands of miles, how far is it from San Francisco to New York?") and opinion items for which there were no correct answers ("Agree or disagree: 'Most young people get too much education'"). Depending on the experimental condition, participants were confronted with either a unanimous majority of four persons (control condition), a majority of three persons and a fourth person who broke from the majority and gave the correct answer (social support condition), or a majority of three persons and a fourth person who broke from the majority but gave an answer even more erroneous than that of the majority (extreme erroneous dissent condition).

The control condition, which involved a unanimous majority, produced the highest level of conformity. The social support condition, in which the dissenter joined the participant, produced significantly less conformity than the control condition. Even the extreme erroneous dissent condition, in which the dissenter gave an answer that was more extreme and incorrect than the majority's, produced significantly less conformity. Thus, any breach in the majority reduces conformity because it calls into question the correctness of the majority's position and reduces the participant's tendency to conform.

**Attraction to the Group.** Members who are highly attracted to a group will conform more to group norms than will members who are less attracted to it (Mehrabian & Ksionzky, 1970). One explanation for this is that when individuals are attracted to a group, they also wish to be accepted personally by its members. Because acceptance and friendship are strengthened when members hold similar attitudes and standards, individuals who are highly attracted to a group conform more to the views held by the other members (McLeod, Price, & Harburg, 1966). However, attraction to a group will increase conformity only if that conformity leads to acceptance by others in the group (Walker & Heyns, 1962). If someone believes they will actually be rewarded for nonconforming behavior—perhaps wearing red sneakers when most people are wearing white—they will take the

risk and signal uniqueness in hopes of greater acceptance (Bellezza, Gino, & Keinan, 2014).

**Commitment to Future Interaction.** Members are more likely to conform to group norms when they anticipate that their relationship with the group will be permanent or enduring, as opposed to short term (Lewis, Langan, & Hollander, 1972). This is true regardless of whether members are attracted to a group (Forsyth, 1999). For example, even if you dislike your coworkers and your job, you are likely to continue to conform to group norms (coming in to work on time, being friendly, helping customers) when you know you will be continuing to work there for the foreseeable future.

**Competence.** Another factor affecting the likelihood of conformity is an individual member's level of expertise relative to that of other members. If members who are skilled at the group's task differ from the majority's view, they will resist pressure to the degree that they believe themselves to be more competent than the other group members (Ettinger et al., 1971). Interestingly, the extent to which a person believes that they are competent may be more important than the actual level of competence (Stang, 1972). Persons who, in fact, are not competent will still resist conformity pressure and perhaps try to persuade other members to change their positions if they believe they have more skill than others.

**Priming.** Two researchers combined the work of Sherif and Asch to do a study on the effects of priming in conformity. Louise Pendry and Rachael Carrick (2001) asked their subjects to count the number of beeps they heard—a task not as ambiguous as the Sherif autokinetic effect but still subject to considerable error by many subjects. Each time, the subjects actually heard 100 beeps, but the confederates (as in the Asch experiments) were instructed to lie and report between 120 and 125 beeps. Not

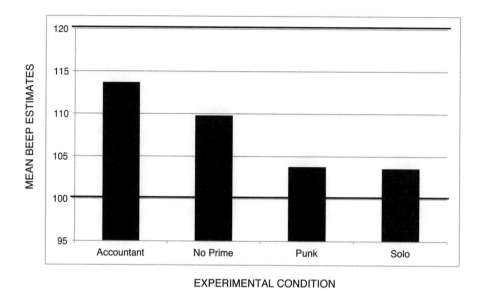

**FIGURE 15.2** Effect of Priming on Conformity

In an experiment that combined Asch (conformity paradigm) and Sherif (ambiguous situation), researchers found that priming influenced conformity. Participants primed to think about accountants conformed significantly more than any other group. Furthermore, participants who were primed with punk before the experiment did not differ from those who completed the task alone (without any type of influence).

*Source:* Adapted from Pendry & Carrick, 2001.

surprisingly, the subjects often conformed and reported much higher than 100 beeps.

However, what was most interesting was that the experimenters were able to manipulate conformity through a process of **priming**— brief exposure to a stimulus meant to influence the response to a second stimulus. The researchers exposed their subjects to either a "punk" stimulus (representing anarchy and nonconformity), an "accountant" stimulus (representing the neat and orderly conformist), or no stimulus (the control condition) by showing them a photo and asking them to read text that described the person in the text as either a punk rocker or an accountant. The results showed that the accountant-primed subjects conformed to the confederates' estimates of the number of beeps the most of the three groups. The group that received no prime conformed, but less so than the accountant-primed group. The punk-primed

group essentially did not conform at all. Their estimates were not significantly different from subjects who performed the beep-counting task in isolation (and thus had no conformity pressure). Similar effects have been found with religious priming (Van Cappellen, Corneille, Cols, & Saroglou, 2011).

## INTERGROUP CONFLICT

Processes *between* groups heavily influence processes *within* groups. Groups seldom exist in isolation as they do in the laboratory. Sports teams and gangs have rivals. Families and friendship groups have contemporaries. The United States is one of many countries in the world. One intergroup process with profound implications for groups is intergroup conflict.

The term **intergroup conflict** is often used in two distinct ways. First, we use it when referring to conflict between organized groups—each group consisting of members who interact with one another, who have well-defined role relationships, and who have interdependent goals. Second, we also use intergroup conflict to refer to what might be better described as conflict between persons belonging to different social categories. Although not necessarily members of organized groups, these people perceive themselves as members of the same social category and are involved emotionally in this common definition of themselves. For instance, conflict between members of ethnic or racial categories (such as neighborhood conflicts between Blacks and Hispanics in Miami) or political parties (Democrats and Republicans) is usually considered intergroup conflict, even though the individuals involved may not belong to organized groups.

## Effects of Intergroup Conflict on Within-Group Processes

Intergroup conflict produces changes in the internal structure of the groups participating in the conflict that can promote escalation and make conflict resolution more difficult (Coser, 1967). Three main changes that can occur are increased group cohesion, increased militancy of group leaders, and an alteration of norms in the group. Although these are most pronounced in delimited, or organized, groups, the examples in this section will show how this can also be true to some extent among members of social categories.

**Group Cohesion.** Research finds that when a group engages in conflict against another group or is threatened by another group, it will become more cohesive (Dion, 2000). During conflict, a group's boundaries will become more firmly etched, and its members will generally show higher levels of loyalty, commitment, and cooperativeness to the group (Sherif, 1966).

Why does intergroup conflict lead to higher cohesion? First, as the conflict escalates, a group's cause becomes more significant to its members, and thus they increase their commitment to it. Second, intergroup conflict frequently entails threats; if an out-group issues a threat, that action quickly identifies the out-group as an enemy. Having a common enemy heightens perceived similarity among in-group members and increases cohesion (Brown, 1988).

These positive effects are particularly likely in cohesive groups. A highly cohesive group will, in general, maintain a firm hold over its members' time, energy, loyalty, and commitment. With conformity and cooperation often greater in high-cohesion groups than in low-cohesion groups (Sakurai, 1975), cohesive groups are capable of taking well-coordinated action in pursuit of their goals. However, there are limits to this effect. If a group is embroiled in a conflict in which it cannot possibly prevail, members may give up all hope. When this occurs, cohesion can decline, and some members may leave the group. That said, under conditions in which success is still possible, in-group cohesion will usually increase when conflict develops with another group.

**Leadership Militancy.** Group leaders act differently under conditions of intergroup conflict than under conditions of peace. Under conflict, leaders have to direct the charge against the adversary. They plan the group's strategic moves, obtain resources needed for the conflict, coordinate members' actions, and serve as spokespersons in negotiations with the adversary. How well these activities are performed will have an important impact on a group's success or failure in intergroup conflict.

It is not uncommon for groups embroiled in heavy conflict to change leaders. If the campaign against an opposing group is not progressing well, rivals for leadership may emerge within the in-group. Frequently, these rivals will be angrier, more radical, and more militant than the existing leaders. This challenge from rivals will place the existing leaders under pressure. To defend against this threat, they may react by adopting a harder line and taking stronger action against the out-group. Under conditions of threat, group members are more receptive to influence from leaders and, therefore, are more accepting of this increased militancy (Hogg, 2001). Although existing leaders do not always react to threat in this way, they are especially prone to do so when their own position within the group is insecure or precarious (Rabbie & Bekkers, 1978).

**Norms and Conformity.** Intergroup conflict not only increases group cohesion and leadership militancy; it also changes group norms and goals. Once serious intergroup hostilities have begun, group members will grow concerned with winning (or surviving) the conflict. Some behaviors and activities the group considered valuable prior to the conflict may now seem useless or even detrimental to success in the conflict; if this happens, the group will reorder goal priorities and favor those behaviors that can help it win the conflict. Resulting changes in role definitions, task assignments, or a redistribution of status and rewards can increase tensions among members within the group (Leventhal, 1979). However, if the conflict is intense, concerns about group effectiveness and survival will overshadow concerns about equity and fairness.

Under severe conflict, the members will increase their demands on one another for conformity to group norms and standards. Enhanced coordination and task performance will help the group achieve success in the conflict. There will also be pressure to adopt the group's negative attitudes and stereotypes regarding the adversary. The importance of loyalty to the in-group will increase, and members will increasingly expect one another to display a distrusting, competitive orientation toward the out-group. Those who do not will be trusted less by the group and may even be ostracized or ejected from the group.

All three of these processes—increased cohesion, leadership militancy, and changing norms and conformity—were evident in the United States immediately following 9/11. The perceived threat from outside not only brought most of the country together, however briefly, but also allowed George W. Bush to get support to increase surveillance of citizens, significantly enhance airport security regulations, and devote more military personnel and monies to the War on Terror. Furthermore, those who refused to conform to related norms were often considered anti-American.

## SOURCES OF INTERGROUP CONFLICT

In the case of 9/11, intergroup conflict stemmed from a single aversive event, a series of terrorist attacks on U.S. soil. There are several other origins of intergroup conflict. Below we outline three potential origins: opposition of interest, discrimination and bias against an out-group, and threat. These factors are not mutually exclusive; in fact, they often work together to cause conflict between groups (Taylor & Moghaddam, 1987).

### Opposition of Interest

Overt conflict may develop because groups have an underlying opposition of interests; a benefit to one must come at a cost to the other. When opposition of interest prevents the groups from achieving their goals simultaneously, it can lead to antagonism and friction and, eventually, to open conflict.

Years ago, Muzafer Sherif and his colleagues conducted an important study of this type of intergroup conflict at Robbers Cave State Park in Oklahoma (Sherif, 1966; Sherif et al., 1961). The participants in this experiment were well-adjusted, academically successful, White, middle-class American boys, aged 11 and 12. These boys attended a two-week experimental summer camp and participated in camp activities, unaware that their behavior was under systematic observation. The research objective was to investigate how an underlying opposition of interest might lead to overt intergroup conflict. Therefore, the boys were divided into two groups, named the Eagles and the Rattlers.

The experiment progressed in several stages. The first stage, which lasted about a week, was designed to produce cohesion within each of the groups. The boys arrived at the camp on two separate buses and settled into cabins located a considerable distance apart. By design, contact within each group was high, but contact between the two groups was minimal.

The boys within each group engaged in various activities, many of which required cooperative effort for achievement. They camped out, cooked, worked on improving swimming holes, transported canoes over rough terrain to the water, and played various games. As they worked together, the boys in each group pooled their efforts, organized duties, and divided tasks of work and play. Eventually, the boys identified more and more with their own groups, and each unit developed a high degree of group cohesion and solidarity.

In the second stage, the experimenters induced conflict between the groups. Specifically, the camp staff arranged a tournament of games, including baseball, touch football, tug-of-war, and a treasure hunt. In this tournament, prizes were awarded only to the victorious group. Thus, one group could attain its goal only at the expense of the other—an opposition of interests.

The tournament started in the spirit of good sportsmanship, but as it progressed, the positive feelings faded. The good sportsmanship cheer that customarily follows a game, "two-four-six-eight, who do we appreciate," turned into "two-four-six-eight, who do we appreci-HATE." Intergroup hostility intensified, and members of each group began to refer to their rivals as "sneaks" and "cheats." After suffering a stinging defeat in one game, the Eagles burned a banner left behind by the Rattlers. When the Rattlers discovered this "desecration," they confronted the Eagles, and a fistfight nearly broke out. The next morning, the Rattlers seized the Eagles' flag. Name calling, threats, physical scuffling, and cabin raids by the opposing groups became increasingly frequent. When asked by the experimenters to rate each other's characters, a large proportion of the boys in each group gave negative ratings to all the boys in the other group. When the tournament was finally over, the two groups refused to have anything to do with each other.

This study was instrumental in advancing **realistic group conflict theory** (Campbell, 1965), a theory that provides one explanation for the development of intergroup conflict between the Eagles and the Rattlers. The basic propositions of realistic group conflict theory are (1) when groups are pursuing objectives in which a gain by one group necessarily results in a loss by the other, they have what is called an opposition of interest; (2) this opposition of interest causes members of each group to experience frustration and to develop antagonistic attitudes toward the other group; (3) as members of one group develop negative attitudes and unfavorable perceptions about members of the other group, they become more strongly identified with and attached to their own group; (4) as solidarity and cohesion within each group increase, the likelihood of overt conflict between groups increases, and even a very slight provocation can trigger direct action by one group against another.

Intergroup conflict stemming from an underlying opposition of interest is evident in contemporary events. Although an incredibly broad issue, disagreement over ownership of land in the West Bank, Gaza Strip, and East Jerusalem is central to the Israeli–Palestinian conflict, as only one group can own certain buildings or territory (Stephan & Renfro, 2002). Opposition of interest is also relevant to anti-immigrant sentiment in the United States and Europe that is rooted in a perception that immigrants are taking away jobs and resources from others (Schneider, 2008; Zarate, Garcia, Garza, & Hitlan, 2004).

## Discrimination and Bias against Out-Groups

Another factor in intergroup conflict is how strongly members identify with their own group. Even when an underlying opposition of interest is not present, strong group identification can, by itself, produce biased behavior toward out-groups.

People have a fundamental tendency to like their own group (the in-group) and to dislike competing or opposing groups (the out-groups) (Sumner, 1906). This is because of **ethnocentrism**—the tendency to regard one's own group as the center of everything and as superior to out-groups. Ethnocentrism involves a pervasive and rigid distinction between the in-group and one or more out-groups, with positive imagery and favorable attitudes regarding the in-group and negative imagery and hostile attitudes regarding the out-groups. For example, seeing the in-group as superior and the out-group as inferior, viewing the in-group as strong and the out-group as weak, and construing the in-group as honest and peaceful and the out-group as treacherous and hostile (LeVine & Campbell, 1972; Wilder, 1981).

Ethnocentric attitudes not only cause in-group members to devalue and demean out-group members; they also lead to **discrimination**—acts that treat members of certain out-groups in an unfair or disadvantageous manner. The simple process of social categorization—placing people into arbitrarily defined groups that have no important meaning—is sufficient to produce intergroup discrimination (Tajfel, 1982b; Tajfel & Billig, 1974).

Social psychologists working in the **minimal group paradigm** find that even arbitrary or trivial distinctions between groups trigger in-group and out-group processes. Even when explicitly informed that individuals were randomly assigned to groups by a coin toss, results show the same pattern as between well-entrenched groups: participants discriminate in favor of their own in-group and against the out-group. This bias is reflected both in attitudinal and evaluation measures and in the allocation of money and other rewards (Brewer, 1979; Brewer & Brown, 1998; Oakes & Turner, 1980; Tajfel, 1981).

Research in the minimal group paradigm consistently shows that even arbitrary group distinctions can trigger in-group and out-group processes like ethnocentrism and biased evaluations of group performance. Contact with members from the out-group can break down stereotypes and lessen intergroup conflict. Comic courtesy of xkcd.com

**Social identity theory**, developed by Tajfel and colleagues (Abrams & Hogg, 1990; Tajfel, 1981, 1982a; Tajfel & Turner, 1986), offers an account for discrimination even when there is no utilitarian value in those beliefs or behaviors. This theory starts by assuming that individuals want to hold a positive self-concept. With individuals' self-concepts derived from their identities, the social identities they possess—based on categories they belong to—are an important source of esteem (Aberson, Healy, & Romero, 2000; Rubin & Hewstone, 1998). To protect their view of self, individuals are motivated to view the groups they belong to favorably in comparison to out-groups. There are two underlying processes inherent in this account. The first is a categorization process that accentuates both the similarities between an individual and members of the group they belong to and the differences between the in-group and out-group. For example, if you identify as a Cleveland Cavaliers fan, you are imagining the things you have in common with others in that group. At the same time, you are distinguishing yourself from fans of the Golden State Warriors or other teams. The second is a self-enhancement process through which group members make comparisons between in-groups and out-groups in ways that favor the in-group to enhance perceptions of self. Cavaliers fans might view themselves as better sports fans than Warriors fans or think that Warriors fans are sore losers.

Although social identity theory helps explain conflict between either minimal or well-entrenched groups, two other theories focus on the latter and examine conflict that stems from the structural relationships between groups.

*Social dominance theory* (Sidanius & Pratto, 2001) argues that groups are organized hierarchically in culture (discussed in more detail in Chapter 16), resulting in unfair treatment toward groups situated lower in the hierarchy and generating conflict between groups. This discrimination can manifest itself in everyday interaction or institutional structures (Sidanius, Pratto, van Laar, & Levin, 2004). For example, protesters who took part in the Women's March in January 2017 argued that women were negatively affected not only by sexist or misogynistic treatment from men, but also by gendered policies (such as being charged more for health insurance and a restrictive national family leave policy). Bias can also result from better treatment of members of the higher status group, perhaps in the form of favoritism or deference.

*Group position theory* (Blumer 1958; Bobo, 1999) focuses on the perceived threat that one group poses for another group's status in society. Intergroup conflict emerges when a group fears its position compared to another may change in ways that threaten its prerogatives. For example, in a series of experiments social psychologists found that Whites' support for the Tea Party—a conservative political movement that protested the U.S. government under President Obama—was higher when participants were led to believe that Whites' standing in the United States was somehow under threat from other ethnic groups (Willer, Feinberg, & Wetts, 2016). Beliefs that Whites' relative incomes or share of the population were shrinking compared to other ethnic groups' led to racial resentment and support for race-related policies, like anti-immigration measures (Parker, 2016).

## Aversive Events

A single aversive event, like the 9/11 terrorist attack mentioned earlier, can provoke open hostilities between groups (Berkowitz, 1972; Konecni, 1979). An **aversive event** is a behavioral episode caused by or attributed to an out-group that entails undesirable outcomes for members of an in-group. The unexpected loss of a basketball game is an aversive event for fans of the home team, and it can trigger conflict extending far beyond the hardwood court. Although aversive events can assume many forms, they always involve outcomes that people would prefer to avoid, and they include such things as being physically or verbally attacked, being slighted or humiliated, or being subjected to a loss of income or property.

The idea that aversive events trigger overt intergroup conflict is based on the general frustration-aggression hypothesis (see Chapter 12). This hypothesis holds that frustration leads to annoyance or anger, which can quickly turn into aggression if the situational conditions are conducive (Berkowitz, 1989; Gustafson, 1989). The hypothesis is true for groups as well as individuals. If provoked by an aversive event seen to be caused by an out-group, an in-group will mobilize and attack the out-group. This response is most likely to happen when an underlying opposition of interest exists between groups, when easily identifiable characteristics (such as language, religion, or members' skin color) serve as a basis for differentiation between groups, and when members of one group already hold antagonistic attitudes and negative stereotypes regarding the other.

## PERSISTENCE OF INTERGROUP CONFLICT

Intergroup conflict persists, in large part, because of biased perceptions of the out-group. When in-group members hold mistaken perceptions of the out-group, disputes become increasingly difficult to resolve (see Chapter 7). These mistaken impressions arise from certain biases inherent in group perception, including the illusion that the out-group is homogeneous, an excessive reliance on stereotypes, errors in causal attribution, and biased evaluation of in-group performance relative to that of the out-group.

## Out-Group Homogeneity

There is a tendency for in-group members to overestimate the degree of similarity or homogeneity among out-group members (Linville, Fischer, & Salovey, 1989; Quattrone, 1986). Although in-group members perceive and appreciate the diversity within the in-group, individuals usually perceive less variability among members of the out-group (Mullen & Hu, 1989). In other words, they tend to perceive the out-group members as "all alike." This is referred to as the **illusion of out-group homogeneity**.

This perceptual bias is quite general and widespread. It has been observed in men's and women's perceptions of each other (Park & Rothbart, 1982), of young and elderly persons (Brewer & Lui, 1984), of people in different occupations (Brauer, 2001), of members of different religious groups (Jafar, 2017), and voters' perceptions of politicians (Simas, 2016), among other groups. This bias likely stems from limited contact with out-group members and richer contact with in-group members (Quattrone, 1986). Fewer experiences with an out-group make it less likely that the perceivers will have a chance to see or appreciate the extent to which out-group members differ from one another in important ways.

## Group Stereotypes and Images

In-group members tend to rely on stereotypes of the out-group. This can foster mistaken impressions of the out-group and its members as stereotypes which often exaggerate or accentuate the differences between an in-group and an out-group, making groups seem more different than they really are (Eiser, 1984). Stereotypes also tend to be depreciatory, ascribing negatively valued traits or characteristics to out-group members.

Individuals use these stereotypes as they overestimate similarities between themselves and their in-groups relative to themselves and their out-groups. Thus, the stereotypes created of out-groups tend to attribute characteristics to its members that are opposed to the individual's view of self and in-group: they are stingy, we are generous. These unrealistic contrasts between in-groups and out-groups exaggerate differences and promote intergroup conflict (Riketta, 2005).

As discussed in Chapter 7, stereotypes tend to be oversimplified and unrealistic (Linville & Jones, 1980). Relying on them puts in-group members at risk of neglecting or misinterpreting new information about the activities of the out-group, especially if it is inconsistent with the stereotype. For instance, if a peaceful overture by the out-group is difficult to understand in light of the in-group's stereotype of the out-group, the in-group members may incorrectly interpret the action as a veiled threat and react with hostility.

## Ultimate Attribution Error

Several studies have revealed a perceptual bias that Pettigrew (1979) has called the **ultimate attribution error**. When a member of our own in-group behaves in a positive or desirable manner, we are likely to attribute that behavior to the member's internal, stable characteristics (such as positive personality dispositions). If that same person behaves in a negative or undesirable manner, we will tend to discount it and attribute it to external, unstable factors (they were operating under unusual stress or having a bad day). However, when perceiving a member of an out-group, we display the opposite bias. Positive behaviors by out-group members are attributed to unstable, external factors (situational pressures or luck). Negative behaviors are attributed to stable, internal factors (undesirable personal traits or dispositions). In other words, you are more likely to blame the out-group for negative outcomes but are less likely to give it credit for positive outcomes (Hewstone, 1990). These attribution biases tend to maintain each side's negative

view regarding the character and motives of the other side.

## Biased Evaluation of Group Performance

Another common bias is for in-group members to rate the performance of their own group more favorably than that of the out-group, even when there is no objective basis for this difference (Hinkle & Schopler, 1986). One illustration of this bias appeared in the Robbers Cave study discussed earlier. When antagonism between the Eagles and the Rattlers was at its peak, the investigators arranged for the boys to participate in a bean-collecting contest. They scattered beans on the ground, and the boys collected as many as possible in one minute. Each boy stored his beans in a sack with a narrow opening, so he could not check the number of beans in it. Later, the experimenters projected a picture of the beans gathered by each boy on a screen in a large room. Boys from both groups tried to estimate the number of beans in each boy's collection. The projection time was very short and precluded counting. In reality, the experimenters projected the same number of beans (35) each time, although in different arrangements. The boys' estimates revealed a strong in-group bias; they overestimated the number of beans collected by members of their own group and underestimated the number collected by the out-group. This bias increases as the distinction between in-group and out-group becomes more salient (Brewer, 1979).

Bias in the evaluation of group performance can produce a variety of consequences. It can serve as a positive motivational device that strengthens the in-group's effort and boosts group morale (Worchel, Lind, & Kaufman, 1975). However, overvaluation of an in-group's relative performance can lead to faulty decision making or groupthink (Janis, 1982; see Chapter 16). Overestimation of a group's capacity relative to that of an adversary may also cause the in-group to become overconfident and, hence, too willing to continue a fight that realistically should be abandoned or settled.

## RESOLVING INTERGROUP CONFLICT

One cannot resolve intergroup conflict merely by "reversing" the processes that initially caused it. It is often impossible to eliminate the underlying opposition of interest, to diminish the ethnocentric identification with the in-group, or to forestall aversive events. Nevertheless, investigators and practitioners have developed various techniques to reduce or resolve intergroup conflict. In this section, we discuss two of them: superordinate goals and intergroup contact.

### Superordinate Goals

One of the most effective techniques for resolving intergroup conflict is to develop superordinate goals. A **superordinate goal** is an objective held in common by all groups in a conflict that cannot be achieved by any one group without the supportive efforts of the other group. Research confirms that, once introduced, superordinate goals usually reduce in-group bias and intergroup conflict (Gaertner et al., 1999).

When the conflict between the Eagles and the Rattlers was at its peak in the Robbers Cave experiment, the researchers introduced several goals that involved important shared needs. First, the researchers arranged for the system that supplied water to both groups to break down. To find the source of the problem and restore water to the camp, the two groups of boys had to work together. Next, the food delivery truck became stuck along the roadway. If the boys were to eat, they had to work together to free the heavy vehicle and push it up a steep grade. By inducing some cooperation between the groups, the superordinate goal structure also reduced hostility (Sherif et al., 1961).

The impact of superordinate goals on conflict reduction is not usually immediate but rather gradual and cumulative. The results are stronger when several goals are introduced one after another rather than a single goal (Blake, Shepard, & Mouton, 1964; Sherif et al., 1961).

Superordinate goals are effective for three reasons. First, they serve as a basis for restructuring the relationship between groups. They create cooperative interdependence between the in-group and the out-group. By changing a hostile win–lose situation into one of collaborative problem solving, with the possibility of a win–win outcome, a superordinate goal reduces friction between groups.

Second, superordinate goals also tend to increase interaction between in-group and out-group members. Increased contact by itself is generally not sufficient to reduce intergroup bias or hostility, but if some of the interaction with the out-group members is personalized rather than just task-oriented or if it provides information that reduces stereotyping, the superordinate goal will reduce bias and hostility (Brewer & Miller, 1984; Worchel, 1986).

Third, the introduction of a superordinate goal can generate a new, superordinate social identity shared by all members. The superordinate goal reduces the sharp distinction between the in-group ("us") and the out-group ("them"), and a new common identity applying to all members of both groups is created and attitudes toward one another will become more positive (Dovidio, Gaertner, Isen, & Lowrance, 1995). Former out-group members will increase in attractiveness, and the favoritism that in-group members originally afforded their own group will now be extended to the whole collective.

### Intergroup Contact

Even without a superordinate goal, an increase in contact and communication between members of opposing groups can also reduce intergroup conflict. According to the **intergroup**

**contact hypothesis**, increased contact should lessen stereotypes and reduce bias and, consequently, lessen antagonism between groups (Allport, 1954; Pettigrew & Tropp, 2006). For example, research finds that more contact with the homeless—whether having a homeless relative, interacting with them at a shelter, reading an article about the problem of homelessness, or even living in a neighborhood with a large homeless population—increases sympathy toward the group and fosters a willingness to sacrifice to help a homeless person (Lee, Farrell, & Link, 2004).

Although intergroup contact often reduces prejudice and conflict between groups in some cases, it does not always do so (Pettigrew, 1997). In some instances, increasing the level of intergroup contact can actually increase conflict (Brewer, 1986). This is particularly likely if individuals do not feel like they chose to have the contact or if participants feel threatened in the situation (Pettigrew & Tropp, 2013). This was certainly the case for the Black and White Titans players (see Box 15.2) when Coach Boone first made them sit together on the bus and at meals and to room together while at camp. The players not only felt forced to do something they did not want to do, but also worried that their roommate would be their competition for a starting position on the team once school started.

Given that contact is not always effective, social psychologists have worked to identify the conditions under which intergroup contact leads to reduced bias and conflict as well as the conditions under which it does not.

**Sustained Close Contact.** Findings suggest that contact between members of different groups is more effective in reducing conflict if the contact is sustained and personal rather than brief and superficial (Levin, van Laar, & Sidanius, 2003). Low levels of intimacy will have little effect on intergroup prejudice and stereotyping (Segal, 1965).

There are several reasons why sustained close contact tends to reduce prejudice and stereotyping. First, cognitive dissonance may produce attitude change. If individuals with negative attitudes find themselves subject to situational pressures that increase interaction, and if they consequently engage in positive actions toward members of an out-group, their behavior will be inconsistent with their attitudes, which may create a state of cognitive dissonance (see Chapter 8). The theory of cognitive dissonance predicts that these persons will end up changing their attitudes—becoming more positive toward the out-group—as a means of justifying to themselves their new behavior.

Second, during close contact, members of different groups may engage in self-disclosure. Higher levels of self-disclosure generally promote interpersonal liking, provided that the attributes one person reveals are viewed positively—or at least not negatively—by the other (Collins & Miller, 1994).

Third, sustained close contact between members of different groups can serve to break down stereotypes. Of course, contact with a single representative or "token" member of an out-group is usually not sufficient on its own to change group stereotypes because that person can too easily be viewed as an exception who is not representative of the entire out-group (Weber & Crocker, 1983). But close contact with multiple members of an out-group sustained over time may provide enough contrary information to compel a change in old stereotypes.

**Equal-Status Contact.** Intergroup contact is also more likely to reduce conflict when in-group and out-group members occupy positions of equal status than when they occupy positions of unequal status (Riordan, 1978; Robinson & Preston, 1976). One early demonstration of equal-status contact comes from a classic study conducted in the military during World War II (Mannheimer & Williams,

## BOX 15.2  Using *Remember the Titans* to Understand Intergroup Conflict Reduction

Many of the social psychological processes discussed in this book are illustrated in popular television shows and movies. Intergroup processes are no exception.

*Remember the Titans* follows the football team at Alexandria, Virginia's T. C. Williams High School during the 1971 season, its first as an integrated school and team. Herman Boone, played by Denzel Washington, is tasked with winning football games. However, he realizes that intergroup dynamics may stand in the way of that goal, and he employs specific strategies to reduce the conflict evident between the Black and White players.

The "coming together" of the Titans over the course of the film clearly illustrates three important sociological theories of intergroup conflict reduction—intergroup contact, superordinate goals, and shared identities.

Coach Boone began by trying to make Black and White students interact by having them sit together on the bus to camp, room together while there, and dine together at meals. When this contact failed at first to lessen the animosity between groups or forge an integrated community, Boone specifically instructs the players to spend time getting to know players of another race—things about their families, about their likes and dislikes. The stereotypes and generalizations prevalent between the groups become clear in the scenes that follow. At one point, a White player begrudgingly sits down to learn more about a Black player and asks, "What does your daddy do?" Before the player can answer, the White player says, "You do have a daddy,

right?" Only through ongoing, meaningful conversations are these stereotypes broken down.

Some of these conversations lead to close friendships. Scenes from the movie convey the importance of these friendships between group members, specifically because they offer numerous opportunities for anxiety reduction, empathy, and knowledge. Most notable is the friendship between the White team captain, Gerry Bertier, and a Black standout, Julius Campbell. When these two players move beyond superficial conversation to honestly assessing one another's strengths and weaknesses both on and off the field, their friendship begins. This relationship moves to a new level during a scene in the locker room at camp. One of the Black players makes a joke about Gerry Bertier's mama. Clearly upset, Gerry poises for a physically violent counterattack, but Julius comes and puts his hand on Bertier's shoulder and, smiling, shoots an insult back at the antagonist. This begins a round of "mama jokes" and exposes Bertier to this side of locker room banter that is apparently common among his Black teammates. The scene ends a few mama jokes later when another White player makes a joke that elicits raucous laughter and Bertier exclaims with good cheer, "Now that's a mama joke!"

Throughout the film, the shared goal of becoming an excellent football team and winning games provides a powerful superordinate goal for the players. Here, Boone himself plays a critical role as a no-nonsense authority figure. Superordinate goals are most effective when initiated by an authority figure or an individual or

1949). At that time, the U.S. Army was still largely segregated by race; only a few companies were integrated. This study showed that White soldiers changed their attitudes toward Black soldiers after the two racial groups fought in combat as equals, side by side. When asked how they felt about their company including Black as well as White platoons, only 7 percent

of the White soldiers from integrated units reacted negatively. In contrast, 62 percent of the soldiers in completely segregated White companies reacted negatively to the prospect of having Black platoons in their unit. Equal-status contact has been effective in reducing prejudice in other situations as well, including among schoolchildren from different racial

cause outside of the groups themselves (Johnson & Lewicki, 1969)—institutional support for the intergroup contact. Coach Boone makes it clear that he is such an authority figure—without vested interest in either racial group. He does not automatically side with the Black students because he is a Black man himself and does not stand for any behavior that gets in the way of winning. Early on, Boone informs his staff that he is there as a football coach, nothing else, and he came to win, and he tells his players that when they put on that Titan uniform, they better come out to win. Therefore, winning and overcoming any barriers to winning become the team's superordinate goal.

A pivotal moment in the establishment of this goal occurs during football camp. Boone rouses the team at three in the morning to take a run through the woods surrounding Gettysburg College. Despite a reminder from his assistant coach that this is a high school football team and not the Marines, Boone pushes the players harder. As the sun comes up, the team ends up at the field where the Gettysburg Battle was fought, and Boone turns to them and says,

> Fifty-thousand died fighting the same fight we're still fighting today. . . . Take a lesson from the dead. If we don't come together right now on this hallowed ground, we too will be destroyed. . . . Respect each other [and] learn to play this game like men.

Boone takes winning one game at a time and, with each achievement, gains more legitimacy with players and coaches alike, slowly breaking down the barriers between the racial groups and enhancing the positive effect of the superordinate goals.

Finally, integrating the in- and out-group (in this case, the Black and the White players) into a single group results in a reduction of bias. At a number of times in the film, Coach Boone reminds the team that they are in this together and they are all Titans. The viewer watches as the use of "they," "them," and "those people" lessens and there is an increase in the use of "we," "us," and "the Titans." However, the emergent shared identity is best illustrated with the team chants and choreographed dances emphasizing unity:

> Everywhere we go, people want to know . . .
> Who we are, who we are . . .
> So we tell them, so we tell them . . .
> We are the Titans, the mighty-mighty Titans.

Scenes of segregated stands of football spectators and conflict in the school as a whole remind the viewer that the players' shared identity as football players gives them a special perspective the other students lack. With time, however, the community and school come around. Students celebrate together, spectators sit together integrated by race, and town businesses proclaim that this is "Titan Country." Although the film occasionally departs from the specific historical reality of the Titans, as a narrative, it captures the spirit of social psychological research on conflict reduction in integrated schools; athletic teams really do serve an important role in school integration.

*Source:* Adapted from Collett, Kelly, & Sobolewski, 2010.

groups (Binder et al., 2009) and college students (Sidanius, Levin, van Laar, & Sears, 2008).

**Institutionally Supported Contact.** Finally, intergroup contact is more likely to reduce stereotyping and create favorable attitudes if it is backed by social norms that promote equality among groups (Adlerfer, 1982; Cohen, 1980; Williams, 1977). If the norms support openness, friendliness, and mutual respect, the contact has a greater chance of changing attitudes and reducing prejudice than if they do not.

Institutionally supported intergroup contact—that is, contacts sanctioned by an outside authority or by established customs—are more likely to produce positive changes than unsupported contacts. Without institutional support, members of an in-group may be reluctant to interact with outsiders because they feel doing so is deviant or simply inappropriate. With the presence of institutional support, however, contact between groups is more likely to be seen as appropriate, expected, and worthwhile.

In sum, intergroup contact tends to reduce conflict when it is anchored by institutional or authoritative support, when it is based on equal rather than unequal status, and when it is personal rather than superficial in character. Recent work shows that the relationship between contact and favorable attitude is reciprocal (Binder et al., 2009), meaning that it is not only that people who have more contact have less bias against out-groups, but also that people who are less biased are more likely to make contact.

## SUMMARY

**What Is a Group?** A group is a social unit that consists of two or more persons and has certain defining attributes, including recognized membership, interaction among members, shared goals and objectives, and norms that guide members' behavior. Primary and secondary groups differ on types of goals and level of intimacy. A cohesive group is one that can strongly attract and hold its members. Interdependence coupled with positive emotion enhances cohesion. Two important types of cohesion are social cohesion and task cohesion, and the level of a group's cohesion affects the interaction among members. Members in highly cohesive groups communicate more than those in less cohesive groups; they also exert more influence over one another, and their interaction is friendlier and more cooperative. A group goal is a desirable outcome that members strive collectively to bring about. Group goals differ from individual goals—outcomes desired by members for themselves.

**Conformity to Group Norms.** A norm is a rule or standard that specifies how group members are expected to behave under given circumstances. Group norms coordinate activity among members, provide a frame of reference that enables members to interpret their environment, and define the common identity of group members. Conformity means adherence by an individual to group norms and expectations. The Asch conformity paradigm uses a simple visual discrimination task to investigate conditions that produce individuals' conformity to the majority's judgment. Groups can use both normative influence and informational influence to exert pressure on individual members. Sherif's autokinetic effect studies illustrate the impact of informational influence on group members. Many factors affect the level of conformity in Asch-type situations. Conformity increases with group size up to three, and it is greater when the majority is unanimous than when it is not. Group members are also more likely to conform when they are highly attracted to a group and when conformity will lead to liking and acceptance by other members. Commitment to future interaction affects conformity. Finally, task competence affects conformity; members who oppose the majority's view will resist conformity pressures to the extent that they believe themselves to be more competent than other members.

**Intergroup Conflict.** Conflict between groups influences processes within groups. Conflict increases the level of cohesion of the in-group as members increase their commitment and unite to face a common adversary. However, it may also produce rivalry for leadership among in-group members, and this rivalry can produce more militant leadership. Conflict often changes the normative structure of the in-group and both increases the pressure on in-group members to conform and lessens the majority's tolerance of dissenters.

**Development of Intergroup Conflict.** Intergroup conflict has several origins. (1) Groups often have opposing interests that prevent them from achieving their goals simultaneously, leading to friction, hostility, and overt conflict. (2) A high level of in-group identification, accompanied by ethnocentric attitudes, may create discrimination between groups, which escalates conflict. (3) One group, by threatening or depriving another, may create an aversive event that turns submerged antagonism into overt conflict.

**Persistence of Intergroup Conflict.** Although some conflicts between groups dissipate quickly, others last for a long time. Several mechanisms support the persistence of intergroup conflict. Perception of the out-group by in-group members is often biased. This bias, caused by insufficient information regarding the out-group and excessive reliance on stereotypes, produces an incorrect understanding of the characteristics and intentions of out-group members and an overestimation of in-group capabilities.

**Resolution of Intergroup Conflict.** Several techniques can be used to reduce intergroup conflict. One is to introduce superordinate goals into the conflict. Because goals of this type can be achieved only through the joint efforts of opposing sides, they promote cooperative behavior and serve as a basis for restructuring the relationship between groups. Another technique is to increase intergroup contact. This approach is more effective in reducing bias and conflict when contact is sustained, close, based on equal status, and supported institutionally.

### Critical Thinking Skill: Promoting Higher-Order Cognitive Skills

As you read this chapter, are you stopping to ask yourself questions? What kinds of questions are you asking or would you ask someone else

if you were testing each other's understandings of the material? When you study the material, how are you engaging with it?

By this point in the semester, critical engagement—that is beneficial for both understanding and retention—should be coming naturally to you. However, this exercise is a good opportunity to step back and evaluate the types of questions you are asking yourself and the depth of the connections you are making (Bloom, 1956).

At the most basic level, questions test what you remember. Are the questions that you are asking things like, "What are the four attributes of a group?" or "What is the definition of a norm?" These questions simply ask you to recall data or information. Anyone could memorize these things without truly understanding them. It is slightly more cognitively demanding to also require evidence of understanding the information we retain. For example, "What is intergroup conflict? Describe how it affects group processes." Or "In your own words, summarize how the Titans were able to overcome intergroup conflict and to become a cohesive unit."

Higher-order questions require application, analysis, synthesis, or evaluation.

Application questions ask you to transfer the concepts you are learning to new situations. An example might be, "What is a group that you belong to? Demonstrate how it fits the four attributes of a group." The benefit of this question is that to answer it, you must have the knowledge of the four attributes of a group (a lower-order skill), but you are also using a higher-order process by applying the concepts to a novel situation that is personally relevant.

Questions that engage skills of analysis encourage you to divide material or information into its component parts and then demonstrate how to put it back together. If you asked yourself to "Use the tenets of Realistic Group Conflict Theory to explain a specific instance of enduring intergroup conflict in contemporary society," you must know the theory, including its individual propositions, and be able to engage each of those propositions in tandem to support your single example.

A question that requires synthesis pulls together seemingly separate or distinct knowledge to create a more complete picture or enhance an outcome: "The chapter discusses conformity as related to group norms, but how is conformity linked to other topics related to groups, including cohesion, goals, and intergroup conflict? How might making these connections enhance our understanding of conformity and groups?"

Finally, an evaluation question asks you to make judgments about the value of ideas, to develop opinions based on specific criteria. An example of such a question might be, "Imagine that your dorm's resident adviser approaches you for help. They heard you were taking a social psychology class and hope

you might have a solution for how to restore harmony between two roommates who can't seem to get along. If you were to give them a solution that is grounded in theory from this chapter, providing evidence of its effectiveness, what would it be?" This question should also prompt you to use creativity to solve a problem, another higher-order skill.

In sum, asking ourselves questions as we read is an invaluable way to stay alert and to learn material. However, we must also evaluate the types of questions we are asking. Although knowledge is important, higher-order questions require more critical thinking and reap more benefits for engagement, retention, and understanding.

What types of questions are you asking yourself? If they are currently higher-order questions, that is wonderful—keep it up! If not, how could you take what you learned here to shift your approach to studying?

# GROUP
# PROCESSES

## LEARNING OBJECTIVES

By the end of this chapter you will be able to:

- Describe how group leaders emerge in homogeneous and heterogeneous groups, the types of leadership roles they take, and the relationship between status and influence in groups and in social life more generally.

- Understand how groups make decisions and why they sometimes make the wrong decisions.

- Explain how relationships and interactions between people are related to power and dependence, as well as trust, commitment, and emotional attachment.

- Differentiate between the various principles individuals use to determine the fairness of outcomes and allocation processes and recognize possible responses to unfairness.

## INTRODUCTION

The trial has ended, and now it is time to deliberate. You think the defendant is probably guilty, but you want to hear how the others feel. Delivering a guilty verdict is not a trivial matter. You look around at the other jurors who are sitting at the table in the deliberation room.

- *Alex* is a senior at Yale, where he is apparently at the top of his class. He is heading to medical school after graduation.
- *Sophia* looks tired. She has talked about her three children and how difficult it has been to keep up with things around the house because of the long days in court. She misses staying home with her toddler while the twins are at school.

- *LaToya* is anxious to get back to work. She is concerned about how her oncology patients and their families are doing without her on the nursing rotation.
- *Charlotte* has been quiet during the meals the jury has shared, but you cannot help but notice how beautiful she is. You heard her tell Sophia that she just got a modeling contract in New York.
- *Martin* is vice president of a local grocery store chain. Judging by the wisps of gray in his sandy-brown hair, he is in his late 40s. With his confident demeanor, it is no surprise he has been so successful in business.

The judge has instructed you and the other jurors to select a foreperson, someone who will keep the jury on task and communicate with the court if necessary. The six of you look around at one another. Who will you choose? How will that choice affect the behavior of the jury and the group's ultimate decision?

## THE SYSTEMATIC STUDY OF GROUPS

Social psychologists have studied small groups like this jury for over 50 years. Their findings show that what happens next in that jury deliberation room is not based on chance but rather is the result of highly structured—and, therefore, predictable—group processes. Attributes of the group members (gender, race, age, occupation, attractiveness) and of the group itself (a collective task, a designated foreperson) influence both individuals' behavior in the group and the group's effectiveness at achieving its goals.

### Robert Bales

Although social psychologists have long been interested in groups and their influence on individuals (Allport, 1924; Cooley, 1902; Simmel,

1902), the systematic study of group processes did not begin until the mid-twentieth century, when Robert Bales (1950) began recording detailed accounts of interaction in small groups. He became interested in group processes as a research associate at Yale, working in alcohol studies. As part of that position, he observed therapeutic treatment groups for alcohol addicts. Watching these groups and the individuals who participated in them, Bales began to consider how individuals' behavior in groups stemmed not only from their personal characteristics but also from characteristics of the group. He formulated a method—Interaction Process Analysis (IPA)—to systematically document group members' behavior so he could better understand group-level patterns. With this method, Bales did not focus on the specific content of communication between group members; rather, he was interested in capturing the types of contributions group members made (a joke, a suggestion, a criticism), which group member made it, and to whom it was directed. Figure 16.1 shows his coding scheme.

Group processes researchers often study groups of students—or other community members (Milgram, 1974; Zimbardo, 1973)—in the laboratory to control as much of the situation as possible (see Chapter 2). Bales was no exception. The participants in much of his research were Harvard undergraduates whom he invited to a laboratory in the Harvard Social Relations department. Bales would have the groups work on a **collective task**—a task that cannot be achieved without the participation of all group members. In one such task, Bales had the groups discuss a case similar to the criminal cases that juries deliberate and then work to reach a unanimous agreement on a recommended punishment. Although a discussion is not generally seen as a collective task, making a unanimous decision is. As the group worked together, Bales and his research assistants would observe, meticulously categorize, and record every group-oriented behavior that group members made.

The small groups that Bales studied were **homogeneous**—that is, they were similar on a number of factors. They were all White, undergraduate men (Harvard was a men's college until 1977). They were typically sophomores, in their second year of study at the university.

Bales and his research team screened subjects to ensure that the students interacting in groups would not know one another. He wanted to be absolutely sure that the group dynamics he was studying were not influenced by anything beyond what he and his research team could manipulate and observe in the laboratory. Bales discovered that when members of these homogeneous groups of strangers started to discuss their problem, specific patterns emerged. For one, the initial equality among members disappeared, and distinctions quickly materialized between them.

Bales noted that some members participated more than others and exercised more influence regarding the group's decision. The most talkative member in the problem-solving groups typically initiated 40 to 45 percent of all communicative acts. The second-most active person initiated approximately 20 to 30 percent of all communication. This pattern is apparent in Table 16.1, which summarizes the percentage of acts initiated by each member for groups ranging from three to eight members. As the size of the group increased, the most talkative person still initiated a large percentage of the communicative acts, whereas the less talkative individuals were crowded out almost completely (Bales, 1970).

## Role Differentiation

These patterns remain tremendously stable once developed (Fişek, 1974). The group member who initiates the most communication during the beginning minutes of interaction is very likely to continue doing so throughout the interaction. Furthermore, these patterns tend to hold for the life of the

**TABLE 16.1** Percentage of Total Acts Initiated by Each Group Member as a Function of Group Size

| MEMBER NUMBER | GROUP SIZE | | | | | |
|---|---|---|---|---|---|---|
| | 3 | 4 | 5 | 6 | 7 | 8 |
| 1 | 44 | 32 | 47 | 43 | 43 | 40 |
| 2 | 33 | 29 | 22 | 19 | 15 | 17 |
| 3 | 23 | 23 | 15 | 14 | 12 | 13 |
| 4 | | 16 | 10 | 11 | 10 | 10 |
| 5 | | | 6 | 8 | 9 | 9 |
| 6 | | | | 5 | 6 | 6 |
| 7 | | | | | 5 | 4 |
| 8 | | | | | | 3 |

*Source:* Adapted from Bales, 1970, pp. 467–474.

*Note:* Data are based on a total of 134,421 acts observed in 167 groups consisting of 3 to 8 members.

group. If the same group meets for several sessions, the member who ranked highest in participation during the first session is likely to rank highest during subsequent sessions.

Of course, Bales was more interested in the quality of communications than the quantity. He wanted to know the specific types of contributions group members made and how these affected individuals' perceptions of their fellow group members. Observers scored the types of contributions (using the coding scheme illustrated in Figure 16.1), and then, at the end of the discussion period, group members filled out questionnaires and rated one another. Items included things like, "Who had the best ideas in the group?" "Who did the most to guide the group discussion?" and "Which group member was the most likable?"

Typically, there was high agreement among group members in their answers regarding ideas and guidance. In short, the person initiating the most communicative acts—generally the person who talked the most—was perceived as the group's task leader (guiding discussion, having the best ideas). But this task leader was not usually the best-liked member. In fact, they were sometimes the least-liked member. In most groups, the second-highest initiator was the best-liked member. Why does this occur?

In general, the highest initiator is someone who drives the group toward the attainment of its goals. Most of the acts this person initiates are task oriented (see the clustering of contributions on the left side of Figure 16.1). For this reason, social psychologists call the high initiator the group's **task specialist**. However, in an effort to get things done, the task specialist also tends to engage in negative behaviors. This type of leader might be pushy or even openly antagonistic. Even if it helps influence group opinion, this aggressive behavior can create tension.

Importantly, the negative behavior of the task specialist opens the door for some other member, the **social-emotional specialist**, to ease the tension and soothe hurt feelings in the group. The acts this person initiates are likely to be acts that release tension and encourage solidarity (see the positive social-emotional categories in Figure 16.1). The social-emotional specialist is the group member who exercises tact or tells a joke at just the right moment. This person helps to ease tensions and maintain good spirits within the group. Not surprisingly, the social-emotional specialist is often the best-liked member of the group.

Thus, in task groups, there are two basic functions—getting things done and keeping

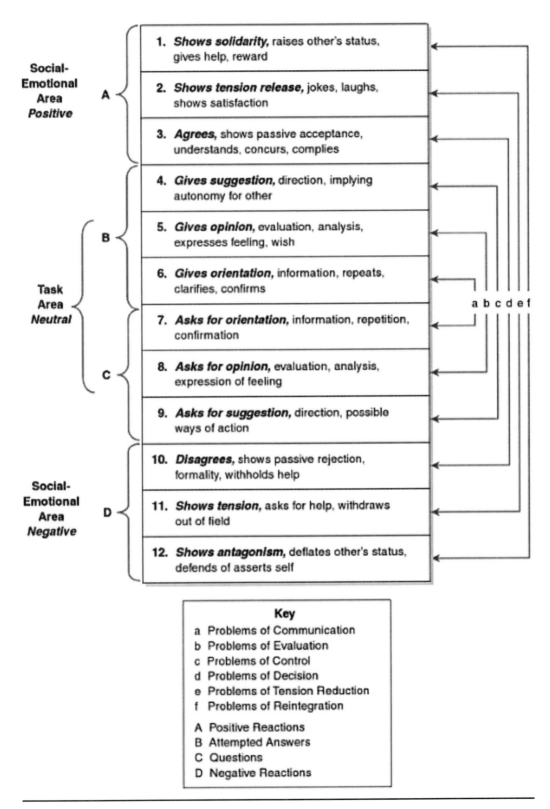

**FIGURE 16.1** Categorization Scheme for Interaction Process Observations

*Source:* Adapted from Bales, *Interaction Process Analysis: A Method for the Study of Small Groups*, 1950.

relations pleasant—that are typically performed by different members. When group members divide up functions in this manner, we say that **role differentiation** has occurred in the group. Although role differentiation is common, it is not inevitable. In 20 to 30 percent of case studies in the laboratory, a single member performs both the task-oriented and the social-emotional functions (Lewis, 1972). For groups in natural, nonlaboratory settings, the incidence of combined roles may be higher (Rees & Segal, 1984).

Both informal and formal groups tend to engage in role differentiation for efficiency. Usually, it is not productive for all members of a group to try to perform the same tasks. Instead, the group engages in a division of labor in which members are assigned different tasks, or roles.

A **role** is a cluster of rules or expectations indicating the set of duties to be performed by a member occupying a given position within a group; it describes the function that a group member serves for the group. Because group members hold role expectations regarding one another's performance, they feel justified in making demands on one another. For instance, the members of a sales group expect the salespeople to contact potential customers, to identify customers' needs, and to offer customers the products that meet these needs. If, for some reason, one of the salespeople suddenly stopped contacting customers, other members of the sales group would view it as a violation of role expectations and would likely take action to correct the situation.

## STATUS AND EXPECTATIONS

In their research on group participation, Bales and his graduate student researchers discovered a strange phenomenon. In some groups, role and status differences—measured by members' rate of participation, their influence over group decisions, and the types of acts they contributed—emerged rather slowly. In others,

it happened almost instantaneously. In trying to locate an explanation, the researchers realized that there was an important difference between these groups: some began the group task with more knowledge about one another than others.

Remember that Bales intended for these groups to be strangers. He was careful to ensure that the young men participating in a group had no prior interaction with one another. However, he had been less cautious once the men were in the laboratory. In some cases, there was time for the participants to chat before the experiment began. Think about the small talk you might make with other students in a waiting room. You might ask them where they are from, what year they are, and what they are majoring in. At Harvard, where almost all students live on campus for the entire four years of school, students would also ask one another what hall they lived in. These halls, not unlike fraternities, had reputations. The researchers realized that even though this information was completely unrelated to the task at hand, group members drew on it when determining who to turn to as a leader (Willer & Walker, 2007).

Think back to the jury at the beginning of the chapter. Given the little that you know about the jury members—the tidbits that you have picked up throughout the trial and based on what you can observe—who do you think is most likely to be chosen as foreperson? Social psychologists have studied decisions like these, and the groups—including juries—that they are made in, for decades. The sections that follow present some of their key insights about leadership and group processes in newly formed groups whose members are not identical in social attributes.

### Status Characteristics

We encounter groups, like the jury, that are composed of members who differ in gender, race, age, education, attractiveness, and occupations every day—PTAs, student committees, neighborhood associations, church groups, and so on. Social psychologists find that many of the within-group differences in participation and influence that emerge in heterogeneous groups are based on characteristics of group members.

A **status characteristic** is any social attribute of a person around which evaluations and beliefs about that person come to be organized. When a characteristic is imbued with status value, certain states of that status characteristic are afforded more esteem in a culture than are other states (Ridgeway & Walker, 1995). For example, in the United States, gender is a status characteristic, with men thought to be more competent than women; race is a status characteristic, with Whites perceived of as more capable than Blacks; education is a status characteristic, with graduate students believed to be more skilled than people who only completed high school and a student at Yale as more intelligent than a student from Southern Connecticut State University.

These cultural beliefs about status characteristics are carried into small-group settings, where they influence interactions. In problem-solving groups like the ones Bales studied, individuals of higher status are expected to make more contributions, and their contributions are perceived as more valuable. These expectations lead to the formation of a **power and prestige order** in groups, with those of lower status often deferring to those of higher status and those of higher status taking the lead in decision making (Berger & Webster, 2006).

**Types of Status Characteristics.** There are two types of status characteristics that guide performance expectations: diffuse and specific.

**Diffuse status characteristics** influence ideas about general competence. For example, in most cultures around the world, people assume that men are more competent than women across a range of tasks (analytic ability, conversation, driving). Men, therefore, benefit from greater esteem and are thought to be

more worthy of respect than women, not only in those domains, but also overall (Ridgeway, 2011). In fact, because of the *burden-of-proof process*, individuals tend to assume that diffuse status characteristics are relevant and operative across a range of situations unless those attributes are explicitly demonstrated to be unrelated to task performance (Berger, Cohen, & Zelditch, 1972). In other words, group members will assume that men will perform better at being a foreperson unless they are aware of evidence that gender is not at all related to the task or that women have actually been found to perform better on it.

**Specific status characteristics** (mathematical ability, athleticism) also influence performance expectations. However, these characteristics must be relevant to the task to influence expectations and can only be applied to a more circumscribed set of tasks. For example, if the trial was about a nurse who had accidentally administered the wrong drug to a patient, the group might decide that LaToya possessed a specific status characteristic (her experience as a nurse) that would make her more qualified to be foreperson—or to have informal influence over deliberations—than if the case was about tax evasion. If the jury faced a case of tax evasion, LaToya's nursing skills would seem irrelevant.

### Status Generalization

Studies show that persons with high standing on status characteristics are accorded more respect and esteem than are other members, and they are chosen more frequently as leaders. Their contributions to group problem solving are evaluated more positively, they are given more opportunities to participate in discussions, and they exert more influence over group decisions (Balkwell, 1991; Berger, Cohen, & Zelditch, 1972; Webster & Foschi, 1988). The tendency for members' status characteristics to affect group structure and interaction is called status generalization.

With gender a diffuse status characteristic, men are often afforded more influence in task groups regardless of the task at hand. However, if the group task is feminized—as some types of design might be—then women may be able to exert more influence in group decision making. © monkeybusinessimages/iStock

When **status generalization** occurs, a member's perceived status outside a group affects their status inside that group. That is, the members who hold higher status in society at large will tend to hold higher status in the group (Cohen & Zhou, 1991).

For example, you—like many Americans—might begin jury deliberations believing that Martin, as a professional man with experience, would be a more competent leader than Sophia, who is a stay-at-home mom. Because of the influence of status characteristics on the power and prestige order, you and the other jury members will likely decide that Martin should be foreperson. Although the foreperson is not a formal leadership role, you will find that you and the rest of the group increasingly defer to him. As a foreperson, he will likely talk more than other jurors (Ellison & Munro, 2010). The other members of the jury

are more likely to ask what he thinks, cede the floor to him when he wants it, and defer to him. They are also inclined to select the verdict that he suggests in deliberations. This is not just conjecture from students in laboratory experiments; these trends have been supported using research on mock jury deliberations, with juries composed of people from a typical jury pool (Strodtbeck, Simon, & Hawkins, 1965). Social psychologists found that men on these mock juries initiated more interactions than did women. Furthermore, those with occupations of higher status—both men and women—participated more than those of lower status. These behavioral trends were supported with a questionnaire mock jurors completed at the end of the session, providing perceptions of one another, including who was "most helpful in reaching the verdict." This measure of each member's influence—as perceived by the other members—was very similar to the observed rates of participation in groups. On average, male jurors were perceived as more helpful than female jurors, and jurors of high occupational status were perceived as more helpful than those of lower occupational status.

This jury study revealed the typical impact of status generalization: persons with higher standing in terms of gender and occupation in social life broadly became the group members with the higher status inside the group.

Although the findings in this study seem clear-cut, the interpretation in terms of status generalization is open to criticism. A critic might argue that a person's status inside a group is not a function of their status outside the group but is, instead, caused by the same qualities or personal traits that determine that person's status outside the group. One might hypothesize, for instance, that people of high intelligence translate their intelligence into both high occupational status and better contributions to the group. If this were the case, a person's standing inside a group would not be caused by their external occupational status; rather, both internal and external status would be caused by a third factor—intelligence.

To check the possibility of unseen, confounding factors, several studies have manipulated status characteristics experimentally. One of these studies (Moore, 1968) investigated pairs of female participants. Both women were shown a series of figures made up of smaller black-and-white rectangles. They were told that the test measured contrast sensitivity and their task was to judge which of the two colors—black or white—covered the greater area in each of the figures. This task was difficult because the black and white areas were in fact approximately equal, making the task ambiguous.

The participants, who were seated so they could not see or talk with each other, signaled their initial judgments to one another using a console with lights (these experiments are now conducted over computer networks).

The participants knew they would each make a final judgment after seeing each other's initial judgments. They were told that they should weigh their own answers against their partner's answers to make accurate final judgments.

What the participants did not know was that the lights on the consoles were, in fact, controlled by the experimenter. The experimenters were manipulating how often a participant learned that her partner's initial judgment was different from her own and then measuring how often the participant changed her judgment if that was the case.

All the participants in this experiment were students at a community college in the Bay Area. As a manipulation of status, one-half of the participants were told that their partner was a high school student (a lower-status partner), whereas the other half were told that their partner was from Stanford University (a higher-status partner). The results show that the women who believed their partner was higher status changed their answers on the judgmental task significantly more often than those who thought themselves to be higher status than their partner. In other words, they were likely to be influenced by those of higher status and more likely to resist influence from those of lower status. The random assignment of participants to experimental treatments eliminated the possibility that participants differed systematically in intelligence or ability on the contrast sensitivity task.

In the years since this experiment, research finds that many other status distinctions affect whether research participants are likely to change their initial responses or to stay with their original judgments. These include but are not limited to physical attractiveness, race and ethnicity, military rank, sexual orientation, age, and occupation (Webster & Foschi, 1988). Research on status effects has also extended beyond influence to examine other outcomes. For example, the research discussed in Box 16.1 explores how status affects hiring and salary decisions.

## BOX 16.1 Research Update: Motherhood as a Status Characteristic

A number of studies suggest that mothers with similar occupations, education, and training make, on average, less money than women without children. However, these studies rely on data that lacks measures of productivity. Perhaps mothers are paid less because they are taking more time off from work or are more distracted in their jobs than are nonmothers. To better understand the underlying mechanism for the pay gap between mothers and nonmothers, researchers would have to find a way to control for all the extraneous factors. A laboratory experiment allowed Shelley Correll and her colleagues to do just that.

Correll has always been interested in how cultural schemas influence performance expectations. Her earlier research (Correll, 2001, 2004) explored the link between stereotypes about women being less skilled at math than men and girls' self-assessments about mathematical ability and their plans to pursue math and science careers. In the case of mothers, Correll argued that cultural understandings of the motherhood role (warm, nurturing, devoted to her children) are in tension with the cultural understandings of the "ideal worker" role (rational, devoted to work). These schemas might lead evaluators,

perhaps unconsciously, to expect mothers to be less competent and less committed to their jobs (Blair-Loy, 2003; Ridgeway & Correll, 2004).

To test her ideas, Correll paid undergraduate participants to rate a pair of equally qualified, same-gender (either male or female), same-race (either Black or White) job applicants who differed on parental status. The job applicant files were created by Correll and her research team so they could be as similar as possible—with both candidates having similar education and experience along with equivalent skills, goals, and productivity levels—but the students believed the files they were reading were real. They thought that they were evaluating the candidates for a communications company that was interested in gathering input from college students who were heavy consumers of new communication technology. The only differences between the files were the names—this is how Correll cued race and gender—and parental status (the résumés of parents included a line about PTA involvement, and the mention of a family in an attached memo included children).

After reading each application, participants were asked to report their initial impressions of the applicants, to provide pros and cons for the

### Overcoming Status Generalization

Because group members often treat diffuse status characteristics as relevant to performance expectations even when they are not, status generalization can work to an individual's disadvantage (Forsyth, 1999). In a mixed setting with both men and women, for example, the women may find that they are not permitted to influence the group's decision significantly even though they are as qualified as—and may be more qualified than—men with respect to the problem under discussion. Because of the burden-of-proof process discussed earlier,

without a clear demonstration that gender is irrelevant to performance, verbal protests regarding gender equality may be to no avail (Pugh & Wahrman, 1983). Furthermore, status generalization is not only something that influences people's beliefs about others; it also influences performance expectations we hold for ourselves. Performance expectations tied to status can influence aspirations—leading fewer girls and young women to aspire to math careers, for example (Correll, 2001, 2004)—and performance (Lovaglia, Lucas, & Thye, 1998; see also the discussion of stereotype threat in Chapter 7). Because irrelevant diffuse status

|                                         | MOTHERS | NONMOTHERS | FATHERS | NONFATHERS |
|-----------------------------------------|---------|------------|---------|------------|
| Competence                              | 5.19    | 5.75       | 5.51    | 5.44       |
| Commitment                              | 67.0    | 79.2       | 78.5    | 74.2       |
| Salary Recommended ($)                  | 137,000 | 148,000    | 150,000 | 144,000    |
| Proportion Recommended for Management   | .691    | .862       | .936    | .851       |
| Likelihood of Promotion                 | 2.74    | 3.42       | 3.30    | 3.11       |
| Proportion Recommended for Hire         | .468    | .840       | .734    | .617       |

applicant, and then to complete an evaluation sheet that assessed applicants' competence and commitment and made recommendations on hiring, salary, additional training, and other job-related outcomes.

A selection of the results are summarized in the table.

The italicized numbers are those that differ significantly (more than expected by chance) from their counterparts (mothers from nonmothers, fathers from nonfathers). Even though their job-relevant file characteristics were identical, mothers were significantly disadvantaged on all measures. They were seen as less competent and less committed. The students recommended lower starting salaries and were less likely to recommend mothers for management, see them as promotable, or recommend them for hire. Interestingly, men experienced the reverse effect.

Whereas mothers suffered a "motherhood penalty," fathers were given a "fatherhood bonus" in which they were advantaged compared to their nonfather counterparts on all dimensions except perceptions of competence. In a follow-up audit study, Correll and her team sent the fake résumés to similar positions that were listed in the newspaper. Results support the experimental findings. Mothers received significantly fewer callbacks than did their childless peers.

The connection between perceptions of competence and motherhood suggests that motherhood does, indeed, act as a salient status characteristic in the workplace, and status processes and performance expectations play an important role in women's ongoing disadvantage across occupational spheres.

*Source:* Correll, Benard, & Paik, 2007.

characteristics can so easily place someone at a disadvantage, researchers have asked whether status generalization can be overcome or eliminated in face-to-face interaction.

Early research tried to overcome status generalization by raising the expectations of lower-status persons regarding their own performance on group tasks so they could, in turn, force a change in other people's expectations regarding their performance. In other words, maybe more women in college would study engineering if they were told that they were very likely to succeed in that major and the resulting career path. Unfortunately, this approach does

not work very well. Social psychologists discovered that to overcome status generalization, it is not enough to change the disadvantaged actors' expectations. Instead, everyone's performance expectations—not only those held by low-status group members but also those held by high-status group members—must be changed. One effective way to overcome status generalization, then, is to supply all group members—perhaps all engineering majors, or all college students—with information that contradicts performance expectations inferred from a diffuse status characteristic (Cohen & Roper, 1972; Riordan & Ruggiero, 1980).

However, it can be quite difficult to overcome status generalization because expectations and evaluations of status groups tend to reflect prevailing cultural stereotypes (Ridgeway, 2011). Although we may not think of ourselves as holding such views, as previous chapters suggest, these beliefs and their effect on our behavior in group settings are likely automatic and outside of consciousness (Fiske, Lin, & Neuberg, 1999).

Further complicating things, interactions in groups are not only based on cultural beliefs but also often serve to reinforce them. If Martin had been selected as the jury's foreperson and he had influenced the group's ultimate decision, you and the other jury members would likely leave the courthouse seeing him—and those who possess similar status characteristics—as a good leader. In other words, he would provide confirmation of your status beliefs. In this way status beliefs and their influence on the power and prestige order function as a type of self-fulfilling prophecy that thereby perpetuates inequalities based on status long after the specific encounter (Ridgeway and Smith-Lovin, 1999).

## Status Construction and Status Value

We acquire many of these cultural beliefs through socialization, but how is it that any particular attribute becomes imbued with status? According to Cecilia Ridgeway (2006, 2011), our beliefs about status are formed and reinforced in interaction, through the process of **status construction**. When people come upon a new type of nominal attribute, one that they have not learned status meanings for, they will look for clues about how that attribute's categories are organized in a status hierarchy. For example, if you know nothing about the fraternities on campus, you may look at fraternities' resources (attractiveness of pledges, wealth, popularity) to decide which fraternities

are higher or lower status. In effect, you are constructing your own status hierarchy, and these status beliefs will influence your performance expectations for the various groups. When you treat those groups based on those expectations and draw on these status beliefs in interaction, you create a status system.

We are also formulating and maintaining status meanings when we interact with others who are different on salient attributes that we are already aware of as status characteristics (race, gender, sexual identity) because we attend to evidence about status. We note that men have better-paying jobs and are afforded more authority, influence, and respect. We come to understand men as having higher status. When we carry these beliefs into interactions, we also carry them out of interaction—like you might if Martin impresses you as the leader of jury deliberations. This process continuously constructs and reconstructs the status system. Granted these interactions are also where status beliefs will be challenged or changed, but such shifts are rare given how status shapes interaction and the cognitive processes that reinforce existing beliefs (see Chapter 7).

Like attributes, objects can also acquire **status value**. Objects that are associated with high-status actors become more valuable than those linked to low-status actors (Thye, 2000). Within hours of the release of the first official family portrait of Prince William, Kate Middleton, and their son George, the $79 dress she wore for the photo shoot sold out. The next month, the company that made the dress doubled their sales figures. Although the publicity of the photo shoot played a role in the business's success, status value likely did as well. Once the dress—and brand—became associated with someone as high status as the Duchess, it became more valuable. Buyers believed that the particular dress the Duchess had worn was more valuable than other $79 dresses.

## GROUP DECISION MAKING

Social psychologists have also studied group decision making without a specific focus on status and individual influence. All other things aside, group decision making should be fairly easy and involves several basic steps (Janis & Mann, 1977). To make a decision effectively, group members need to (1) define a set of possible options, (2) gather all the relevant information about these options, (3) share this information among themselves, (4) carefully assess all the potential consequences of each option under consideration, and then (5) calculate the overall value of each option. Once this is done, (6) the group selects the most attractive option as the group's choice.

In practice, however, group decision making is not always so easy or straightforward, for the decision-making process can go awry in various ways. Information regarding certain options may prove hard to obtain, leading to incomplete or inadequate consideration of these options. Even if the individual members do have all the relevant information, they may fail to share it fully with one another (Stasser, 1992; Stasser & Titus, 1987). If members hold different values, they may disagree regarding which options are most attractive. This disagreement can spawn arguments and block consensus within the group. As the previous sections suggest, some group members may have more influence over the group, and conformity pressures (see Chapter 15) within the group may impel members to abbreviate or short-circuit the deliberation processes. If this happens, group discussion may lead to ill-considered or unrealistic decisions.

### Groupthink

Aberrations in decision making can plague any group, even those at the highest levels of business and government. The infamous Bay of Pigs invasion, for example, was planned by a small group of top government officials immediately after President John Kennedy took office in 1961. The group included what some considered to be the nation's "best and brightest" political leaders and strategists, along with President Kennedy and representatives of the Pentagon and the Central Intelligence Agency (CIA). This group decided to invade Cuba in April 1961, using a small band of 1,400 Cuban exiles as troops. The invasion was to be staged at the Bay of Pigs and assisted covertly by the U.S. Navy, Air Force, and CIA. As it turned out, the invasion was poorly conceived. The materials and reserve ammunition on which the exiles were depending never arrived because Castro's air force sank the supply ships. The exiles were promptly surrounded by 20,000 well-equipped Cuban soldiers, and within three days, virtually all the exiles had been captured or killed. The United States suffered a humiliating defeat in the eyes of the world, and Castro's communist government became more strongly entrenched on the Caribbean island.

How could it happen? How could a group of such capable and experienced men make a decision that turned out so poorly? In a post hoc analysis, Janis (1982) suggests that a specific group process, groupthink, may have led to the ill-fated decision. Although Janis's interpretation of events has been called into question, particularly since the release of recordings made during the Bay of Pigs briefings, the model he developed has largely endured (Esser, 1998).

**Groupthink** refers to a faulty mode of thinking by group members in which pressures for unanimity within the group overwhelm their desire to realistically evaluate alternative courses of action. In other words, the group members neglect to appraise alternatives critically and to weigh the pros and cons carefully because they fear disrupting the perception of consensus. Once groupthink sets in, the typical result is a poor decision.

**Symptoms of Groupthink.** By studying what happened during various important foreign policy decisions, Janis (1982) was able to ascertain certain symptoms that indicate when groupthink is operating. These include:

1. *Illusions of invulnerability.* Group members may think they are invulnerable and cannot fail, and therefore, they display excessive optimism and take excessive risks.
2. *Illusions of morality.* Members may display an unquestioned belief in the group's inherent superior morality, and this may incline them to ignore the ethical consequences of their decisions.
3. *Collective rationalization.* Members may discount warnings that, if heeded, would cause them to reconsider their assumptions.
4. *Stereotyping of the adversary.* Especially in the political sphere, the group may develop a stereotyped view of enemy leaders as too evil to warrant genuine attempts to negotiate or as too weak to mount effective counteractions.
5. *Self-censorship.* Members may engage in self-censorship of any deviation from the apparent group consensus, with each member inclined to minimize the importance of their own doubts.
6. *Pressure on dissenters.* The majority may exert direct pressure on any member who dissents or argues against any of the group's stereotypes, illusions, or commitments.
7. *Mindguarding.* There may emerge in the group some self-appointed "mind guards"—members who protect against information that might shatter the complacency about the effectiveness and morality of the group's decisions.
8. *Apparent unanimity.* Despite their personal doubts, group members may share an illusion that unanimity regarding the decision exists within the group.

Janis suggests that some of these symptoms were present during the decision-making process for the Bay of Pigs invasion. For example, there was an assumed air of consensus that caused members of the decision-making group to ignore some glaring defects in their plan. Although several of Kennedy's senior advisers had strong doubts about the planning, the group's atmosphere inhibited them from voicing criticism. Several members emerged as "mind guards" within the group; they suppressed opposing views by arguing that the decision to invade had already been made and that everyone should help the president instead of distracting him with dissension. Open inquiry and clearheaded exploration were discouraged. Even the contingency planning was unrealistic. For instance, if the exiles failed in their primary military objective at the Bay of Pigs, they were supposed to join the anti-Castro guerrillas known to be operating in the Escambray Mountains. Apparently, no one was troubled by the fact that 80 miles of impassable swamp and jungle stood between the guerrillas in the mountains and the exiles.

The Bay of Pigs invasion is not the only fiasco in which groupthink played an important role. Research shows that groupthink occurs and recurs in many groups. Groupthink was also involved in other high-level government decisions, including the failure to defend Pearl Harbor on the eve of World War II, the decision to escalate the Vietnam War, the decision to engage in the Watergate cover-up, and the decision to invade Iraq in 2003 (Badie, 2010; Rinehart & Dunwoody, 2005). Other studies argue that groupthink played a role in the *Challenger* disaster (Esser, 1995; Moorhead, Ference, & Neck, 1991), the Enron scandal (Sims & Sauser, 2013), the cover-up and handling of Penn State's sexual abuse (Cohen & DeBenedet, 2012; Wagner, 2013), and the mortgage crisis (Michaelson, 2009).

**Causes of Groupthink.** Various factors cause groupthink, including homogeneity of members, insulation of the group from its environment, lack of clear-cut rules to guide decision-making behavior within the group, and high levels of group stress or anxiety (Chapman, 2006; Manz & Sims, 1982; Moorhead & Montanari, 1986). Another contributing factor is promotional leadership—that is, a leader who actively promotes their own favored solution to the problem facing the group, to the neglect of other possible solutions (Ahlfinger & Esser, 2001; McCauley, 1989). Each of these factors contributes to groupthink and their simultaneous occurrence makes groupthink very probable. Janis also argued that groupthink is more likely to occur in high-cohesion groups than in low-cohesion groups, but there is only limited support for this hypothesis (Aldag & Fuller, 1993). More recent research finds that group identification—enough to generate conditions where normative or informational influence is likely and people are attracted to the group—significantly increases the likelihood of groupthink, even in less cohesive groups (Baron, 2005; Hogg & Hains, 1998).

**Avoiding Groupthink.** If groupthink produces poor decisions and outcomes, how can one guard against it? There are several ways to prevent groupthink from occurring (Janis, 1982).

1. A group's leader should encourage dissent and call on each member to express any objections and doubts.
2. A leader should be impartial and not announce a preference for any particular option or plan. By describing a problem rather than recommending a solution, a leader can foster an atmosphere of open inquiry and impartial exploration.
3. A group should divide itself into several independent subgroups, each working on the same problem and carrying out its deliberation independently. This will prevent the premature development of consensus in the main group.
4. After a tentative consensus has been reached, a group should hold a "second-chance" meeting, at which each member can express any remaining doubts before a firm decision is taken.
5. A group can appoint a "devil's advocate" who is responsible for challenging the positions of other group members whether or not they actually agree with them (Hirt & Markmann, 1995); although research finds that authentic dissent is most helpful (Nemeth, Brown, & Rogers, 2001).

These methods are effective because they increase the probability that a group will obtain all the information relevant to a decision and then evaluate that information with care. The net result of these steps will be a better, more realistic decision.

### Risky Shift, Cautious Shift, and Group Polarization

Even when group decision making is not dysfunctional and follows a fairly rational course, it can produce surprising consequences. For instance, there is some evidence that discussion in groups causes individuals to favor courses of action that are either riskier or more cautious than what they would choose if they made the decision alone (Stoner, 1968).

In an early experiment (Stoner, 1968), individuals responded to 12 different choice dilemmas entailing various degrees of risk. For example, one dilemma described "Mr. A, an electrical engineer with a secure job but a modest salary, who had been offered a potentially lucrative job at a newly founded company with an uncertain future" (Westfall, Judd, & Kenny, 2015). Respondents were asked how financially sound the new company would be for it to be acceptable for Mr. A to switch jobs. After responding to these choice

## BOX 16.2  Using Group Processes Concepts and Theories to Understand a Hazing Ritual Gone Wrong

Tim Piazza, a Beta Theta Pi pledge at Penn State, tragically died in February 2017. Later that same year, eighteen fraternity brothers were charged in the case—eight of them with manslaughter. As the media released court documents and specifics of the case, including a detailed timeline of the 12 hours between a drunken fall down a flight of stairs and the fraternity's 911 call, people all over the world were shocked. Why was a young man subject to these dangerous hazing rituals? How could so many people see someone suffering—including signs he was on the brink of death—and do nothing?

Social psychology offers tools to help us to understand hazing deaths like Piazza's. However, to use the knowledge for good, students must become comfortable applying the concepts to everyday life. That requires taking the concepts and theories, often presented in textbooks one by one, and considering how they operate in a world where the lines between the processes are seldom so clear. Here, we demonstrate the relevance of the social psychology of groups to the events in State College that night.

Groups and fraternities, like Beta Theta Pi, use initiation rituals to bring new members into the fold. Like boot camp for military recruits, these rituals not only help to reinforce the group (defining members, facilitating interaction, teaching norms), but are also thought to generate cohesion and help maintain role-differentiation as they distinguish veteran members from the incoming plebes (see Chapter 15). Although

initiation rituals do not need to be hazardous to socialize members, some groups use hazing rituals—rituals that tend to be more physically taxing, dangerous, and humiliating than most—in hopes of ensuring new members are truly committed to the group.

At Beta Theta Pi, hazing included a drinking-based obstacle course called "The Gauntlet" where pledges consumed large amounts of vodka, beer, and wine. Piazza emerged from the obstacle course at 10:30 p.m. on Thursday night, highly intoxicated. Although cameras show that he was initially helped by fraternity members, Piazza is soon staggering through the house alone. He passes fraternity brothers as he walks toward a staircase to the basement. He steps onto the staircase and trips, falling head first, down fifteen steps. Concerned for his safety, a group of fraternity members promptly intervene and carry a limp and bruised Piazza up the stairs to a couch.

As the men try to wake Piazza up, a newly initiated member—Kordel Davis—approached the group and pleaded that they call 911 as Piazza was clearly hurt and could have a brain injury. Showing a variety of symptoms of groupthink (see p. 518), the men literally push Davis—a perceived dissenter—aside and brush him off. When Davis approaches the fraternity's vice-president to try to reason with him, the vice-president tells Davis that he is over-reacting. The vice-president draws on *specific status characteristics* when he rationalizes taking a watch and wait approach

dilemmas alone, the participants assembled in groups of six and discussed each item until they reached a unanimous decision. The participants were then separated and asked again to review each item and indicate an individual decision. The basic finding was that the group decisions following discussion were, on the average, riskier than the decisions made

by individual members prior to the discussion. Moreover, the responses made individually after participating in the group were also riskier on average than the responses prior to discussion. This tendency to advocate more risk following a group discussion is termed a **risky shift**. Others researching the phenomenon often used Stoner's original set

because brothers who are kinesiology and biology majors—who he claims would therefore know more about Piazza's condition— think he will be fine. With a well-defined status hierarchy at play, Davis had little power or influence. He began to question his own interpretation of events, perhaps experiencing learned helplessness (see Chapter 7), and retreated.

The conditions favored groupthink. It was a high-stress environment. Beta Theta Pi was a "dry" fraternity that was supposed to be alcohol-free. Members feared there would be legal consequences for the fraternity and its members if people found out how much alcohol an underage Piazza had consumed under their watch. The fraternity's vice-president, a confident leader, openly rejected input. Text messages and group chats between the members suggested that they realized there was a problem, but no one reached out for help. Because of a perception of consensus, no one sought outside help. Instead, the brothers take turns slapping, striking, and shaking Piazza, trying to wake him up. At various times throughout the night Piazza rises, only to fall back and strike his head again. Throughout the night, fraternity members walking through the house encounter Piazza on the main floor. Some step over him, others help to move him out of the way; one films a Snapchat video. Despite Piazza writhing in pain, moaning, and crouching over and holding his head during some of these interactions, no one calls 911. Groupthink and a diffusion of responsibility (see Chapter 11) prevent the young men from taking action.

At 10 a.m. Friday morning, as members begin to wake, two brothers walk through the house searching for Piazza. They find him in the basement, unconscious and colorless. They carry him to the couch and, for the next 40 minutes, fraternity members try to revive Piazza and to dress his cold, stiff body while they debated what to do. Meanwhile, a young man used his cellphone to conduct Google searches with the phrases "falling asleep after head injury," "cold extremities in drunk person," and "binge drinking, alcohol, bruising or discoloration, cold feet and cold hands." At 10:48 a.m.—more than 12 hours after the hazing ritual began—a Beta Theta Pi brother dials 911. He does not tell the dispatcher that Piazza had fallen down the stairs, only that he was unconscious, breathing, and that alcohol had been involved.

Unaware of the extent of his injuries, the ambulance took Piazza to a local hospital where doctors determined he actually needed to be transported to Penn State's medical center. Meanwhile, in an attempt to protect their group, fraternity pledges and members were asked by fraternity leaders to clean the basement, delete conversations, and to keep quiet about what transpired. Piazza was pronounced dead at the medical center early Saturday morning, having suffered traumatic brain injury, severe internal bleeding, and a fractured skull.

The recounting of the events that led to Piazza's death and the charges against his fraternity brothers not only demonstrate how multiple social psychological concepts and theories in group processes may fit together, but also the important effects they have on our lives every day.

of dilemmas and produced similar findings (Cartwright, 1973).

Other studies, however, using similar tasks but different dilemmas, revealed something directly opposite to the risky shift (Moscovici & Zavalloni, 1969). On certain issues, when members are more likely to be cautious or risk avoidant, group discussion actually causes members to become even more cautious than they were initially (Fraser, Gouge, & Billig, 1971). This move away from risk following a group discussion is termed a **cautious shift**. So although group discussion leads to more extreme decisions, these are not necessarily riskier decisions.

Realizing that the type of dilemma is important, social psychologists now describe risky shift and cautious shift as forms of an underlying phenomenon called **group polarization** (Levine & Moreland, 1998). Polarization occurs when group members shift their opinions toward a position that is similar to—but more extreme—than their opinions before group discussion. This could be from a moderately risky position prior to a group discussion toward greater risk or from a moderately cautious position toward even greater caution after the group discussion (Myers & Lamm, 1976). In contemporary applications, this phenomenon accounts for how juries' dollar awards for damages are significantly higher than jurors' predeliberation recommendations (Schkade, Sunstein, & Kahneman, 2000) and the influence corporate board discussions have on raising—or lowering—CEO compensation to highly-skewed rates (Zhu, 2013).

## SOCIAL EXCHANGE

Around the same time that Bales was studying decision making and the types of interactions that occur in groups, George Homans (1958, 1961) was trying to develop a general theory of human behavior based on what we might observe in group interaction. As part of this general theory, Homans argued that interaction between people should be conceptualized as an exchange—a phenomenon he called "social exchange."

Conventional ideas about exchange tend to focus on tangible goods. For example, two college roommates might make a trade—Ryan lends Jason his car for the weekend and, in return, Jason gives Ryan his tickets to an upcoming concert. However, much of what we exchange in social life is intangible. You smile at a passerby and they smile back. You tell your friend that you like her new dress and she either expresses gratitude or deflects the compliment. In this framework, all interaction occurs through a **relation**—a connection between two people—with people

contributing benefits and potentially deriving them from the interaction. Because people are self-interested, Homans argued, the relative payoffs of relations shape interaction. For example, Ryan is less likely to lend Jason his car if Jason offers nothing—tangible or intangible—in return. Relative payoffs determine both Ryan and Jason's behavior.

The social exchange perspective (Cook, 1987; Homans, 1974; Kelley & Thibaut, 1978) focuses on (1) *actors* who exchange (2) *resources* using (3) an exchange *process* while

A popular application of exchange theory is to think of the "benefits" people bring to dating and marriage relationships. In one version of this, men offer status and financial resources in exchange for women's youth and beauty. Analyses of personal ads support gendered trends in benefits sought and offered. Heterosexual women tend to offer attractiveness in ads while seeking success in potential dates, and heterosexual men do the reverse, offering success while seeking attractiveness (Davis, 1990).
© leaf/iStock

situated in (4) an exchange *structure* (Molm, 2006) and assumes that individuals have freedom of choice and often face social situations in which they must choose among alternative actions. Ryan can decide whether or not he wants to lend Jason his car and Jason can choose whether and how to reciprocate.

Any action provides some rewards and entails some costs. Even if Jason gives Ryan nothing tangible in return, there could be benefits for Ryan. Jason could be indebted to Ryan. Ryan could feel good about himself for helping out a friend, or he might impress a guy he is interested in with his act of kindness. The costs can vary too. If Ryan will be unable to run his regular weekend errands or meet friends because he is without a car, these might be significant costs. If his car would sit idle all weekend if Ryan chose not to lend it to someone, the cost of lending it out is small. People tend to choose actions that produce good profits and avoid actions that produce poor profits or generate costs.

In this way, social exchange draws on operant psychology and reinforcement theories. These theories suggest that people will be more likely to perform a specific behavior if it is followed directly by the occurrence of something pleasurable or by the removal of something aversive; likewise, people will more likely refrain from performing a particular behavior if it is followed by the occurrence of something aversive or by the removal of something pleasant.

This view of human behavior might seem overly rational and calculated, but social exchange theory suggests that these choices to engage in or refrain from a line of action are often given little thought because they are the result of **conditioning**—learning as the result of positive or negative responses to behavior (Mazur, 1998; Skinner, 1953). Humans have the ability to learn the natural consequences of actions and to behave in ways that minimize costs and maximize rewards, either consciously or unconsciously (Emerson, 1972).

Social psychologists who study social exchange study mutually dependent and recurring exchange relationships. In other words, social psychology is less interested in a one-shot exchange, between people who will never see one another again (a gas station attendant and a motorist passing through town), than they are in the ongoing exchange relationship among friends like Ryan and Jason, who both derive benefits from their relationship with one another.

## Power and Dependence

In the same way that Robert Bales formalized the study of groups, Richard Emerson formalized the study of social exchange by taking Homan's ideas and testing and refining them in laboratory experiments.

One of Emerson's (1972) main contributions was his emphasis on the networks that exchange relationships are nested in (Thibaut & Kelley, 1959). Rarely are two people completely cut off from everyone else; there are always alternative exchange partners. Imagine that Ryan's other roommate, Max, also wants to borrow his car for the weekend. Ryan would find out what both Max and Jason had to offer before deciding to whom he would lend the car.

Emerson argued that individuals' positions in these networks, more than their personalities, influence their exchange behavior. This is true even when people are ignorant about the exchange structure and their relative position (Emerson, 1981). It might be hard to believe that a position rather than your personality can influence your behavior—especially a position that you are unaware of—but social psychological research shows it can. People who are in powerful positions will demand more benefits and get more from exchange than will individuals who are in weaker positions. But where does power come from? Social exchange argues that **power**—one's ability to direct or influence the behavior of others—is

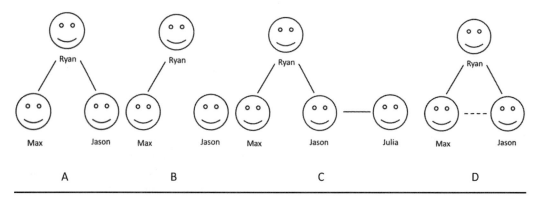

**FIGURE 16.2** Achieving Balance in an Exchange Relation

The relationship between Jason and Ryan is unbalanced in A because Ryan has Max as an alternative source of benefits. To achieve a more balanced relation Jason might decrease his interest in Ryan's car (B), find an alternative source of a car (C), or form a coalition with Max (D).

not an attribute of an actor but of a position. In exchange networks, power depends, in part, on the availability (and attractiveness) of alternative exchange partners (Molm, Peterson, & Takahashi, 2001; Skvoretz & Willer, 1993).

If both Max and Jason want to borrow Ryan's car, Ryan is in a powerful position. This power comes from Max's and Jason's dependence on him for a desired benefit (see Figure 16.2A). Remember, Jason was originally willing to trade the car for concert tickets. However, if he learned that someone else wanted the car, Jason would feel like he needed to increase the incentive for Ryan to choose to lend it to him. He might offer to do Ryan's laundry in addition to giving him the concert tickets.

According to Emerson (1962), there are four ways that Jason could decrease Ryan's power over him, leading to a relation with more power balance:

First, he could decide that he was not all that interested in borrowing Ryan's car for the weekend, perhaps convincing himself that he needed to stay on campus and study. Because Ryan's power stems from Jason's dependence, Ryan would no longer have power in the relationship if Jason were no longer motivated to exchange with him (see Figure 16.2B).

Second, Jason could find an alternative source for the benefit that Ryan has to offer. What if Jason's chemistry partner, Julia, also had a car on campus, and he could ask her instead? This would alter the structure that Ryan and Jason's exchange relationship is embedded in (see Figure 16.2C). This change in structure would decrease Ryan's power over Jason because it introduces an alternative for Jason, thereby decreasing his dependence on Ryan for the valued resource (a car).

Third, he could work to increase Ryan's interest in what he had to offer. If Ryan was as excited to go to the concert as Jason was to borrow the car, the exchange relation would be balanced. Of course, if Ryan was absolutely desperate to go to the concert and offered Jason the car as an incentive to give him the tickets, the power in the relation could be reversed, and Jason could be the one with the upper hand. In such a scenario, Ryan is more dependent on Jason for a desired outcome than Jason is on Ryan.

Finally, Jason could form a coalition with Max. They—either with or without Ryan's knowledge—could agree to share the car regardless of who Ryan gave it to. By forming a coalition, Max and Jason are decreasing Ryan's ability to play them against one another (see Figure 16.2D). They have become one collective actor and thereby increase their power relative to Ryan's by decreasing their dependence on him.

## Commitment and Trust

More recent work in exchange focuses less on power and dependence and more on the affective outcomes of exchange—how people feel about the people they exchange with—and how these feelings influence behavior. Two of these outcomes are trust and commitment. These are considered *emergent outcomes* because they develop over time in ongoing exchange relations.

Commitment can be measured in two ways in social exchange. The first is a behavioral measure. Using this metric, an individual is committed to an exchange partner if they repeatedly exchange with them even if there are alternative exchange partners available (Cook & Emerson, 1978). Take, for example, two colleagues who meet for lunch every Thursday. There are many other people in the office who go out to lunch and whom the two women enjoy spending time with, but these two women continue to meet at the same time and same place every Thursday. This recurrent behavior is interpreted as a sign of commitment to the exchange relation.

Another way to measure commitment is as an emotional attachment, a sense of liking of the exchange partner or partners (Lawler & Yoon, 1996). This sense of solidarity is important. People who have an emotional commitment to exchange relations are more likely to stay in the relationships (a sign of behavioral commitment) and to invest in them. For example, a study of teachers found that those who felt emotionally connected to the other teachers at their schools were more likely to invest their own time and money in professional development, from acting as a mentor to getting more training in instruction techniques (Price & Collett, 2012). These teachers

were also more committed to staying at their current school than were those who did not have the same emotional connection to their workplace and colleagues.

Trust is another emergent outcome of exchange. Successful social exchange requires that we trust an exchange partner to honor the terms of exchange. Returning to Ryan and Jason, Ryan and Jason must trust one another to follow through on their end of the agreement—either handing over the tickets or the car keys—for a successful exchange to occur. However, such exchanges also build trust. The more times that Ryan and Jason have honored previous agreements, the easier it is for them to trust one another in a subsequent exchange.

Trust usually evolves in relationships. Early transactions require little trust. As the relationship continues and partners demonstrate their trustworthiness, exchanges often require more and more trust (Molm, 2006). When you first meet a new person, you might share superficial things with them. However, as they increasingly demonstrate that they are accepting and honest, you will come to share more personal experiences with them. It is unlikely that Ryan would lend Jason his car for an entire weekend if they had just met; it is much more likely that Ryan and Jason have roomed together for a while. Jason has demonstrated that he is conscientious with the things he borrows from Ryan—his toothpaste, a pen, his flash drive, and then a leather jacket—and that he makes good on what he promises in return. This exchange history influences the trust Ryan and Jason have in one another.

## Forms of Exchange

There are a number of processes through which exchange occurs. Social psychologists find that, even with all else being equal, the form that an exchange takes has important effects on commitment, trust, and other affective and cognitive outcomes (Molm, Collett, & Schaefer, 2007). The four forms of exchange

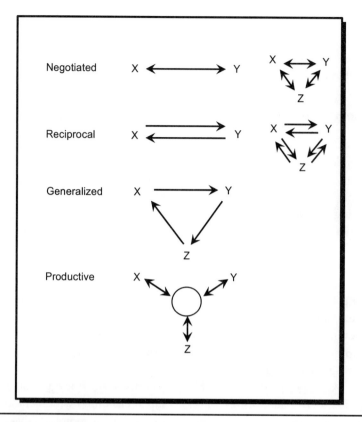

**FIGURE 16.3**  Forms of Exchange

These figures illustrate the four main exchange types—negotiated, reciprocal, generalized, and productive—in two- and three-person exchange networks.

social psychologists study most often are negotiated, reciprocal, generalized, and productive. These are illustrated in Figure 16.3.

**Negotiated Exchange.** In negotiated exchange, actors engage in a joint decision process, like bargaining, to establish and agree on the terms of exchange (Molm, 1997). If you and your professor decide that they will give you five extra credit points if you participate in a social psychology experiment, that is a negotiated exchange. Each person's obligation is clear.

**Reciprocal Exchange.** When we engage in an exchange with someone without direct negotiation—and in which the giving of

benefits is performed separately—this is considered reciprocal exchange. For example, you and a friend might have established a reciprocal trend in paying for the first round at happy hour. You paid for the first round two weeks ago, your friend picked up the tab last week, and now you are ready to take the check again. You might assume that your friend will pay again next week, but you cannot be sure. You are giving someone something without knowing when or even if they will reciprocate.

**Generalized Exchange.** Most people understand generalized exchange as the obligation to "pay it forward." In a generalized exchange relation, givers and receivers are not matched in pairs. With reciprocal exchange, the benefits and costs flow back and forth between two actors. With generalized exchange, the benefits (and costs) flow to an exchange partner and then to someone else and then to someone else (or perhaps back to you). If the person in front of you holds the door for you, and then you hold it for someone else, who holds it for yet another person, you are engaged in generalized exchange. Those who have been given a benefit give a benefit to someone else. These giving chains have taken drive-thru windows by storm in recent years, with customers paying for the car behind them at a variety of restaurants and all over the United States (Murphy, 2013).

**Productive Exchange.** The last form of exchange of interest to social psychologists is productive exchange. In productive exchange, there is a jointly produced good that exchange partners receive benefits from. An example might be a group project that a small group of students does for a class. Each group member ostensibly makes some individual contribution to the project and then benefits from the grade received for the group's work. Cooperation is key here, as individuals must coordinate efforts and combine resources to generate a collective good (Lawler, 2001); it is not something any single person could create on their own.

## Contemporary Exchange Theories

Two prominent theories explore the effects of form of exchange on affective and cognitive outcomes, including commitment, trust, and perceptions of fairness.

The **affect theory of social exchange** focuses on interdependence (Lawler, 2001). This theory proposes that the greater the perceptions of shared responsibility for the outcome—that is, the more the group had to work together to achieve it—the more likely that the exchange process will produce positive outcomes (solidarity, positive emotion,

commitment behaviors). Not surprisingly given its focus on shared responsibility, tests of this theory find that productive exchanges produce the most positive outcomes of the four types of exchange. However, the affect theory also predicts that negotiated exchange, with the joint decision process and shared responsibility inherent in bargaining, will foster more solidarity and positive emotion than reciprocal exchange. Results of studies testing this proposition are mixed (Lawler, Thye, & Yoon, 2008).

Rather than focus on interdependence, **reciprocity theory** is concerned with conflict, risk, and the expressive value of exchange. Reciprocity theory argues that the level of conflict inherent in an exchange process inhibits the development of trust and decreases the solidarity and positive affect between exchange partners. The back and forth nature of bargaining, like that in negotiated exchange, seems competitive. Therefore, generalized and reciprocal exchange strategies—forms that lessen the perception that exchange is competitive—will produce more trust and positive emotion than will negotiated exchange. When someone fails to live up to their end of a bargain in a negotiated exchange, this can easily be interpreted as an attempt to gain something at the expense of the other. In a relationship built on reciprocal exchange, on the other hand, failure to follow through is an act of omission rather than one of commission. This makes it less likely that the action (or lack thereof) will be seen as a transgression. Consider two of the examples above. If Ryan refuses to lend Jason his car after Jason has already given him the concert tickets and fulfilled his end of an explicit agreement, this has a different tenor than if you buy the first round at happy hour one week and your friend does not offer to do the same the next week.

Reciprocity theory also proposes that reciprocal and generalized exchanges entail more risk—because there is no guarantee of receiving something in return—and this increased risk encourages the development of trust. The structure of giving in reciprocal and generalized exchange also enhances affective outcomes because an act of giving (or reciprocity) for which there is no explicit agreement has expressive value beyond the instrumental benefits of the act (Molm, Collett, & Schaefer, 2007). Negotiated agreements lack this symbolic value.

Of course, many relationships are hybrids of negotiated and generalized exchange. In such cases, a history of successful reciprocal exchange helps to dampen potential conflict that may come from negotiation. It also increases the likelihood that negotiation is experienced as integrative and collaborative rather than conflictual (Molm, Whitham, & Melamed, 2012).

## EQUITY AND JUSTICE

On October 1, 2013, the U.S. government shut down. Although there were many issues plaguing Congress, the primary point of contention was whether the government should fund the Affordable Care Act—"Obamacare." One issue of concern was that if the government provided income-based subsidies for health care, this would benefit some Americans and not others. Why should the same health care be more expensive for some than for others? In 2017, in an attempt to address perceived inequality with new legislation, Republican leaders tried to cut Medicaid benefits that helped the poor access health care and to reduce taxes on the wealthy that helped make those benefits possible. Again, people were concerned about the decision. What would this mean for poor people who need health care they cannot afford without government assistance?

### Distributive Justice Principles

**Distributive justice** is the perceived fairness of a distribution of rewards. There are many principles that people use to judge distributive justice (Deutsch, 1985; Elliott & Meeker, 1986; Saito, 1988). The three that are most common are equity, equality, and relative need.

When group members follow the *equity principle*, they distribute rewards in proportion to members' contributions. For example, if three students started a business together, under the equity principle, the partner who invested the most resources in it (either initially or over time) would expect to take a larger share of the business's profits.

When group members use the *equality principle*, they distribute rewards equally among members, regardless of members' contributions. Using this principle, the three friends would divide the profits evenly, regardless of initial contribution or the hours each put into the business as it continued.

Finally, when they follow the *relative needs principle*, group members distribute rewards according to members' personal needs, regardless of contributions (Lamm & Schwinger, 1980). The most profits would go to the partner who had the most debts, the largest family, or some other measure of need. Because this is the least common principle in most Westernized cultures, instances of this principle—like an income-based subsidy for health care—are often met with skepticism or outright disdain.

When allocating rewards among members, a group may rely exclusively on one of these justice principles or may apply several of them simultaneously. Although these justice principles usually lead to different distributions of rewards, they can be combined. For example, the students above who are starting the business could divide the monthly profits they make from running their business equally but plan to divide any profits they make from the sale of the company based on an equity principle. In this case, each student's proportion of profits from the sale of the company would be equal to the proportion of the start-up funds they had initially provided.

Not surprisingly, the principles' relative importance varies from group to group and from situation to situation. For instance, the equality principle often prevails in situations in which members are concerned with solidarity and wish to avoid conflict (Leventhal, Michaels, &

Sanford, 1972). It is also more common in cultural settings that are relationship oriented rather than economically oriented (Mannix, Neale, & Northcraft, 1995). There is some evidence that women favor the equality principle over the equity principle more than men do (Leventhal & Lane, 1970; Watts, Messe, & Vallacher, 1982) and that friends are more likely to follow the equality norm than are strangers (Austin, 1980). Research findings also suggest that members of small (3-person) groups are more likely to favor equality than members of large (12-person) groups (Allison, McQueen, & Schaerfl, 1992).

The needs principle is frequently salient in close or intimate relationships involving friends, lovers, and relatives. The sandwich generation devotes much of their time and resources to elderly parents and children, as their needs are seen as more acute and important. However, this principle has also been invoked in other contexts. Karl Marx, for example, advocated the adoption of the needs principle in communist societies, in which individuals would contribute according to their abilities and receive according to their needs.

The equity principle is often used in work situations, where many persons want their share of rewards to reflect the importance of their contribution. For example, in an industrial work group in the United States, a worker normally would expect to receive better outcomes (salary, benefits) than others if their job required higher skill or more hours per week. Likewise, a woman would probably feel some inequity if she contributes more to the family than her partner but receives little help or love in return. As these examples suggest, equity judgments are made when one group member compares their own outcomes and inputs against those of another member (Brockner & Wiesenfeld, 1996; Homans, 1974; Walster [Hatfield], Walster, & Berscheid, 1978).

To make this more concrete, consider the case of two women employed by the same company. One of the women (Anita) receives a high outcome—a salary of $100,000 a year, four weeks of paid vacation, reserved parking in the company's lot, and a fancy corner office with thick rugs and a nice view. The other woman (Candace) is about the same age but receives a lesser outcome—a salary of $40,000 per year, no paid vacation, no reserved parking, and a cramped, noisy office with no windows.

Will Anita and Candace feel that this distribution of rewards is equitable? If their inputs to the company are identical, the arrangement will almost certainly be experienced as distressing, especially by Candace. For example, if both work a 40-hour week, have only high school educations, and have approximately equal experience, there is little basis for paying Anita more than Candace. Candace will probably feel angry because the reward distribution is inequitable, and Anita may feel uncomfortable or guilty.

But suppose instead that Anita's inputs are much greater than Candace's. Say that she works a 60-hour week, holds an advanced degree such as an M.B.A., and has 12 more years of relevant experience than Candace. Additionally, suppose that Anita's job involves a high level of stress because it entails the risk of serious failure and financial loss for the company. In this event, Anita not only has greater "investments" (that is, education and experience) but also is bearing greater immediate "costs" (60 hours of work a week plus high stress). Under these conditions, both Anita and Candace may feel that their outcomes, although not equal, are nevertheless equitable—and, therefore, fair.

## Responses to Inequity

Inequity produces distress (anger, guilt) and reduces productivity and commitment to the group. There are two distinct types of inequity: underreward and overreward. **Underreward** occurs when a person's outcomes are too low relative to their inputs; **overreward** occurs when a person's outcomes are too high relative to their inputs. Both increase the likelihood that there will be direct attempts to change the conditions that produce the inequity.

**Responses to Underreward.** Persons who are underrewarded typically become dissatisfied or angry (Austin & Walster [Hatfield], 1974; Hegtvedt & Isom, 2014). The greater the degree of underreward, the greater the dissatisfaction and desire to reestablish equity. There are four ways equity can be restored: (1) by increasing the outcomes to the underrewarded, (2) decreasing the inputs from the underrewarded, (3) decreasing the outcomes to the overrewarded, or (4) increasing the inputs from the overrewarded. For example, a person who feels their salary is too low compared to their peers might aggressively seek a pay raise (increasing outcomes). Alternatively, they might reduce their effort (decreasing inputs), which would also reduce group productivity (Lawler & O'Gara, 1967). Feelings of underreward have been connected to other negative outcomes, including increasing the likelihood that workers will steal from their employers or engage in other forms of work-related sabotage (Greenberg & Scott, 1996).

Not everyone responds to underreward behaviorally. Some engage in cognitive efforts to reduce feelings of distress (see Chapter 6). They might search for an external source to blame for the inequity—maybe there is a pay scale that caps what a new employee can make. When injustice can be attributed to an external source rather than an individual, people are less likely to address inequity behaviorally (Utne & Kidd, 1980).

**Responses to Overreward.** What happens when a person receives more than their fair share in a relationship? Will they be content just to enjoy the benefits? Although overreward tends to be less troubling to individuals than underreward because there is a higher threshold before an individual senses injustice, it can still create negative feelings (Greenberg, 1996; Miner 2002). This negative affect is often in the form of guilt rather than anger (Hegtvedt, 1990; Sweeney, 1990) and can also lead to the **imposter phenomenon**—a sense of phoniness, that one is undeserving of one's successes or accolades which must have been achieved based on luck or error (Clance & Imes, 1978). To reduce this distress, a person who feels guilty or phony may attempt to rectify the inequity by contributing more to the organization or group (McDowell, Boyd, & Bowler, 2007). For example, in a work situation, overrewarded members can strive to produce more or better products as a means of reducing inequity (Goodman & Friedman, 1971; Patrick & Jackson, 1991).

This process was investigated in a classic study in which students were hired to work as proofreaders (Adams & Jacobsen, 1964). In one condition, participants were told that they were not really qualified for the job—due to inadequate experience and poor test scores—but that they would nevertheless be paid the same rate as professional proofreaders (30 cents per page). In a second condition, participants were told that due to their lack of qualifications, they would be paid a reduced rate (20 cents per page). In a third condition, participants were told that they had adequate experience and ability for the job and that they would be paid the full rate (30 cents per page). Thus, the participants in the first condition viewed themselves as overrewarded, whereas those in the second and third conditions saw their pay as equitable. Measures of the quality of the students' work showed that the overrewarded students caught significantly more errors than the equitably paid students. In fact, the overrewarded students were so vigilant that they often challenged the accuracy of material that was correct. These results indicate that the overrewarded students increased their inputs, thereby restoring equity.

There is some evidence that overrewarded members tend to prefer to restore equity by increasing inputs like this, as it enables them to restore equity without sacrificing any of the outcomes they receive. However, overrewarded persons may also sacrifice some of their rewards to increase those of others. In these cases, the extent of the redistribution often will not be complete, and equity may be only partially restored (Leventhal, Weiss, & Long, 1969).

## Procedural Justice

Social psychologists increasingly find that the fairness of distributions, or outcomes, is only one measure of fairness. People also gauge the fairness of the procedures or processes that determine distributions, what many call **procedural justice**. There are two different components of procedural justice—instrumental and relational.

In instrumental terms, the justness of a process is related to the amount of control an individual feels they have in shaping the process and determining the outcome (Thibaut & Walker, 1975, 1978). The more control an individual has, the more just they believe the procedure is. If a teenager is allowed to give input on the punishment they receive for breaking curfew, they will see this as more just than if their parents decide this without consulting them. For example, if the parents ask what the teenager thinks is fair, the teenager will see the process as more just.

Procedural justice is important because the fairer an individual believes a process is, the fairer they will perceive the outcome to be (Tyler, Boeckmann, Smith, & Huo, 1997). In other words, the teenager will see the exact same punishment—perhaps a week without their cell phone or being grounded from the homecoming dance—as more fair if they are somehow involved in the process than if their parents simply announce the punishment.

In early research, these instrumental concerns—measures of control—dominated the research on procedural justice. However, over time the conception of procedural justice expanded beyond just giving participants control and began to consider whether processes make an individual feel included and valued. Social psychologists who attend to relational factors in processes would argue that including the teenager in discussions about punishment gives them *voice*—the opportunity to give their opinion (Greenberg & Folger, 1983). Having a say is important, even if it does not influence the outcome. In fact, people will perceive a process as fairer if they have such an opportunity, even if it comes after a decision has already been made (Lind, Kanfer, & Earley, 1990). If their parents let the teenager express disappointment rather than simply sending them to their room, the teenager will feel that the process was fairer. People are also more likely to rate a procedure as fair if it promotes relationships among group members, makes people feel included within a group, indicates standing in the group, and demonstrates neutrality (Lind & Tyler, 1988; Tyler & Lind, 1992).

Procedures are more likely to be seen as fair if they meet a number of criteria (Leventhal, Karuza, & Fry, 1980): suppression of bias, consistency, representation of all parties' interests, accuracy of information, ethicality, and correctability. For example, a teenager is more likely to see the process of choosing a punishment as fair if the parents ensure that they have all the information about why the teenager broke curfew (accuracy of information), they use the same process they would use for a sibling (suppression of bias) and one that is similar to those they have used previously (consistency), and they use a process that is seen as ethical (ethicality) and flexible enough that there is the possibility for change if there is a problem with the process or new information comes to light (correctability).

Procedural and distributive justice are related to other group processes in this chapter. For example, reward expectations theory (Berger, Fişek, Norman, & Wagner, 1998) suggests that status characteristics play an important role in perceptions of distributive justice—with people viewing it as fair to give high-status actors (Whites, men, college-educated) more rewards than lower-status actors (people of color, women, high-school graduates) in work groups (Fişek & Hysom, 2008).

Justice and fairness are also tied to social exchange, with recent work suggesting that people tend to perceive identical outcomes as more fair when they come from reciprocal exchange than when they are a result of negotiated exchange (Molm, Peterson, &

Takahashi, 2003). They also see exchange partners in reciprocal exchanges as more fair than
those in negotiated exchanges (Molm, Collett, & Schaefer, 2006). These effects are likely
because conflict increases attention to inequities (Deutsch, 2000), and conflict is lower in
reciprocal exchange than it is in negotiated
exchanges (Molm, 2010).

SUMMARY

**The Systematic Study of Groups.** Robert
Bales was the first to study groups in a systematic
fashion, using his Interaction Process Analysis
to document what type of contributions group
members made and to whom they directed those
communications. His research showed that status
and influence differences emerge, even in initially homogeneous groups, and then persist for
the life of the group. Over time, group members
take on particular roles in groups. Two roles that
influence group dynamics are the task specialist
and social-emotional specialist.

**Status Characteristics and Expectations.**
Most groups are not homogeneous. The diversity in groups affects within-group processes,
with those who are higher in status being
afforded more influence in groups. Status
characteristics are attributes that are connected
to group members' expectations and evaluations of people and performances through
a status generalization process. Diffuse status
characteristics are attributes that are thought
to influence performance on a wide range
of tasks, whereas specific status characteristics
only influence performance expectations if
they are explicitly connected to the group task.

**Group Decision Making.** There are a
series of steps that groups go through during
a group decision-making process. Sometimes
these processes go awry. One problem plaguing group decision making is groupthink, a
faulty mode of thinking that often leads to

ill-conceived outcomes. Social psychologists
have located a number of symptoms and causes
of groupthink as well as recommended ways
to avoid falling victim to groupthink. Group
decision making and discussion also lead to
group polarization, causing group members
to make either more cautious or more risky
decisions than they would alone.

**Social Exchange.** Social psychologists see
interaction as a process of exchange, whereby
individuals trade benefits and rewards with
one another in interaction. The central premise of social exchange is that actors exchange
resources using an exchange process while situated in an exchange network. These resources
can be tangible or intangible. Social exchange
theorists study attributes of relations and positions rather than individuals. Although early
research in social exchange focused on network structure, power, and dependence, more
recent research examines exchange forms,
trust, and commitment.

**Equity and Justice.** There are three distribution principles that shape justice evaluations—
equity, equality, and need. When individuals
feel they have been underrewarded or overrewarded, they experience distress and engage
in behavioral or cognitive efforts to restore a
perception of equity (in which an individual
gets what they deserve). Perceptions of fairness of procedures are also important in justice
evaluations. Procedures that afford participants control over the process and outcome
and make individuals feel like a valued part of
the group are seen as most fair.

*Critical Thinking Skill:*
*Understanding Theory as a Bridge*

Much of the research on group processes
relies on laboratory experiments. As we have
seen throughout this text, it is nearly impossible to create conditions in the laboratory that

approximate the world outside the laboratory (experimentalists tend to avoid the phrase "the real world" because the laboratory is very real). However, reproducing that outside world is not the goal of experiments (Zelditch, 1969); instead, experimental social psychologists are interested in testing theories—theories that are based on and apply to the life outside the laboratory.

Social psychologists consider a process they see in social life—for example, why you trust your current partner more than your last partner—and generate a theory about why that might be the case. Is it that their personality is different—they're inherently more trustworthy—or is there a social process at play? Thinking back on a previous relationship, perhaps you were together almost all the time, giving little opportunity for a partner to build trust in your absence. In your current relationship, you have your own life and your own interests and friends, and this gives you and your partner the opportunity to act in a trustworthy manner. You think that this difference might be one of the reasons you have greater trust now than previously. How could you test that?

If you were to create an experiment, you would have to think abstractly. What is it about being apart that facilitates trust in couples? What facilitates trust in other situations and relationships?

You might generate a theory—a statement of the relationship of facts about the social world—about the genesis of trust in relationships. Based on your experiences, you might decide that trust emerges from (1) situations of risk and uncertainty (for example, when a couple is not together) and (2) when the group members do not take advantage of the others' trust (for example, if a partner remains faithful).

In fact, Linda Molm had a similar theory. Instead of bringing couples into the laboratory, however, she brought students in and had some exchange points using processes with very low levels of risk and others with very high levels of risk (Molm, Schaefer, & Collett,

2009). Unbeknownst to the students, they were exchanging with computerized actors. Some were programmed to behave in a trustworthy manner, others in an untrustworthy manner. Molm found support for her theory. The highest levels of trust were among those students who exchanged points in a high-risk situation with partners who engaged in a trustworthy manner. She argued this supported her "theory of reciprocity."

To use Molm's theory as a bridge to connect the laboratory to life outside the laboratory, a researcher would not use the results of the experiment and explore whether exchanging points over computers led to different levels of trust in romantic relationships. Instead, they would use the theory and investigate whether acting in a trustworthy manner in a situation of risk outside of the laboratory also increases trust and enhances relationships. This is how theory can work as the bridge. It connects the outside world to the laboratory and the laboratory back to the outside world.

Although there are many examples of this from the text, one of the most famous is Latané and Darley's (1968, 1970) theory of bystander intervention. Their research was inspired by something they saw outside the laboratory—the way people reacted to the attack on Kitty Genovese. They came up with a theory about the diffusion of responsibility to explain why Kitty's neighbors failed to help her. They tested this theory in a series of laboratory experiments. None of the situations involved attacks or neighbors; they involved students and emergencies that might occur in a laboratory on campus. For those who apply the theory today, it is unimportant that Latané and Darley's research findings were related to billowing smoke or students' seizures. Using theory as the bridge, what the researchers learned can be used to explain countless situations in which individuals failed to act in an emergency—or when they did.

How might you use the theories in this chapter to understand life outside the laboratory?

# SOCIAL STRUCTURE AND PERSONALITY

By the end of this chapter you will be able to:

- Explain how location in society affects educational and occupational achievement.

- Describe the ways social location influences people's values.

- Compare the mechanisms by which social location influences physical and mental health.

- Discuss how social location influences a person's sense of belonging in society, or the lack thereof.

**INTRODUCTION**

*Fred* is 38, married, the father of two children, and sells pacemakers to hospitals. He travels 2 or 3 days a week and works at home the rest of the time in his $400,000 house in the suburbs. He earns almost $200,000 a year. Because his income is based entirely on commission, Fred worries about his sales falling off; but on the whole, he is satisfied with his life. His values are conservative, and he voted for Donald Trump in 2016.

*José* is also 38 and has a wife and two children. He runs a service station and works 6 days a week from early morning until 6:00 or 7:00 p.m. José and his family live in a small, three-bedroom house. Last year, he made about $65,000. He worries a lot about money and has been very tense the past year. He has liberal values and usually votes for Democratic candidates.

*Marie* is 39. She is nurse manager in a hospital pediatric unit. Last year, her salary was $94,500. Although she enjoys her young patients, she hates all the paperwork and the personnel problems. Some of her values are conservative, whereas others are liberal; she considers herself an Independent.

Fred, José, and Marie are three very different people. Each has a different occupation,

which produces differences in income and lifestyle. They differ in their *values*—in what they believe is important—and in the amount of stress they feel.

Where do these differences come from? Often, they are the result of one's location in society. Every person occupies a social **position**—a designated location in a social system (Biddle, 1986). The ordered and persisting relationships among these positions in a social system make up the **social structure** (House, 1981).

This chapter considers the impact of social structure on the individual. There are three ways in which social structure influences a person's life. First, every person occupies one or more positions in the social structure. Each position carries a set of expectations about the behavior of the occupant of that position, called a **role** (Rommetveit, 1955). Role expectations are anticipations of how a person will behave based on the knowledge of their position. Through socialization and personal experience, each of us knows the role expectations associated with our positions (Heiss, 1990). For example, Fred enacts several roles, including salesman, husband, and father. The expectations associated with these roles are a major influence on his behavior.

A second way that social structure influences the individual is through **social networks**—the sets of relationships associated with the various positions a person occupies. Each of us is woven into several networks, including those involving coworkers, family, and friends. Ties between the person and a family member or friend reflect a **primary relationship**—one that is personal, emotionally involving, and of long duration. Such relationships have a substantial effect on one's behavior and self-image (Cooley, 1902).

A third way in which social structure influences the individual is through **status**—the social ranking of a person's position. In every society, some positions are accorded greater prestige than others. Differences in ranking indicate a person's relative standing—their status—in the social structure. Each of us occupies several positions of differing status. In the United States, occupational status is especially influential. It is the major determinant of income, which has a substantial effect on one's lifestyle. One of the obvious differences between Fred and José, for instance, is their annual income.

Each person's location in the social structure is the most important determinant of many of their life experiences. This chapter focuses on the relationships between social location and several characteristics that determine the nature and quality of one's life, including education and occupation, values, health, and strength of connection to the society.

## STATUS ATTAINMENT

The individual's relative standing or status in the social structure is perhaps the single most important influence on their life. Status determines access to resources—to money and to influence over others. In the United States, occupation is the main determinant of status. This section considers the nature of occupational status, the determinants of the status that particular individuals attain or achieve, and the impact of social networks on the attainment of status.

### Occupational Status

Occupational status is a key component of social standing and a major determinant of income and lifestyle. Fred is a sales representative for a company that makes pacemakers and other electronic medical equipment. These items are in great demand, and few companies make them. Fred sells a single pacemaker for $6,250 and keeps 25 percent of the money as his commission. He needs to be on the road only 2 or 3 days per week to earn $200,000 a year. He has a beautiful suburban home and

two cars. José, by contrast, owns a service station. He works from morning until night pumping gas and repairing cars. His station is in a good location, but his overhead is high; he earned only $65,000 last year, and he worries that this year, that figure will be lower. José and his family live in a smaller, older house and have a 6-year-old car.

The benefits that Fred and José receive from their occupational statuses are clearly different. First, Fred earns almost three times as much money as José. This determines the quality of housing, clothing, and medical care his family receives. Fred also has much greater control over his own time. Within limits, he can choose which days he works and how much he works; this, in turn, affects the time he can spend with family and friends. José doesn't have much free time. Finally, Fred receives a great deal of respect from the people with whom he works. He controls a scarce resource, so doctors and hospital personnel generally treat him well. José, however, deals with people who are usually preoccupied or angry because their cars are not running properly. As a result, José's job is much more stressful.

In addition to these tangible benefits, occupational status is associated with prestige. Several surveys in the United States have found that there is widespread agreement about the prestige ranking of specific occupations. In these studies, respondents typically are given a list of occupations and asked to rate each occupation in terms of its "general standing" or "social standing." The average rating is often used as a measure of relative prestige. The prestige scores for the United States shown in Table 17.1 were taken from an occupational prestige scale of 0–100 (Nakao & Treas, 1994). Surprisingly, there is considerable agreement across diverse societies in the average ranking of occupations. Even adults in China give rankings similar to those displayed in Table 17.1 (Lin & Xie, 1988). This agreement may reflect the fact that modern societies develop a similar division of labor in

**TABLE 17.1** Occupational Prestige in the United States

| OCCUPATION | NAKAO-TREAS PRESTIGE SCORE |
|---|---|
| Physician | 86 |
| Lawyer | 75 |
| College or university professor | 74 |
| Registered nurse | 66 |
| Electrical engineer | 64 |
| Elementary school teacher | 64 |
| Police officer | 60 |
| Social worker | 52 |
| Dental hygienist | 52 |
| Office manager | 51 |
| Electrician | 51 |
| Housewife | 51 |
| Office secretary | 46 |
| Data-entry keyer | 41 |
| Farmer | 40 |
| Auto mechanic | 40 |
| Cosmetologist | 36 |
| Assembly-line worker | 35 |
| Housekeeper (private home) | 34 |
| Precision assembler | 31 |
| Truck driver | 30 |
| Cashier | 29 |
| Restaurant server | 28 |
| Garbage collector | 28 |
| Hotel housekeeper | 20 |
| Househusband | 14 |

*Source:* Hauser & Warren, 1997.

order to function effectively (van Leeuwen & Maas, 2010).

The social structure of the United States can be viewed as consisting of several groups or social classes. A **social class** consists of persons who share a common status in the society. There are various views regarding the nature of social classes in the United States. One view of social class emphasizes occupational prestige in conjunction with income and education in defining class boundaries. This approach ordinarily classifies people into upper upper, lower upper, upper middle, lower middle, working, and lower classes (Coleman & Neugarten, 1971). A very different approach emphasizes a relational view of class, especially the control, or lack of control, an individual has over their work and coworkers as the main determinant of class standing (Wright, Costello, Hachen, & Sprague, 1982).

**Intergenerational Mobility**

When a person moves from an occupation lower in prestige and income to one higher in prestige and income, they are experiencing **upward mobility**. To what extent is upward mobility possible in the United States? On the one hand, we have the rags-to-riches imagery in our culture: anyone who is determined and works hard can achieve economic success. This imagery is fueled by stories about the astonishing success of Oprah Winfrey, who spent her childhood living on a farm, as a media mogul, Bill Gates's success as founder and head of Microsoft, and so on. Many Americans believe that they can become rich in their lifetime (DiPrete, 2007). On the other hand, some argue that America is a caste society—that our eventual occupational and economic achievements are fixed at birth by our parents' social class, our ethnicity, and our gender. To be sure, every city has families that have been wealthy for generations and families that have been poor for as long. This suggests that the United States is characterized by castes—groups whose members are prevented by rigid class boundaries from changing their social status.

These two views of upward mobility in American society are concerned with intergenerational mobility—the extent of change in social status from one generation to the next. To measure intergenerational mobility, we compare the social status of adults with that of their parents. If the rags-to-riches image is accurate, we should find that a large percentage of adults attain a social status significantly higher than their parents'. If the caste society image is correct, we should find little or no upward mobility.

What are the influences on upward (intergenerational) mobility in American society? In this section, we consider the impact of four factors: socioeconomic background, education, gender, and social networks.

**Socioeconomic Background.** Occupational attainment in U.S. society rests heavily on educational achievement. To be a doctor, dental assistant, computer programmer, lawyer, or business executive, one needs the required education. To become a registered nurse, Marie (whom we met in the introduction) had to complete nursing school. Fred, our medical equipment salesman, earned a bachelor's degree in business.

Beyond education, what other factors influence occupational attainment? To answer this question effectively, we need to trace the occupational careers of individuals over their life course. Such longitudinal data are available from a research project begun in the 1950s (Sewell & Hauser, 1980). In 1957, all high school seniors in Wisconsin were surveyed, including measures of ability, high school grades, and post–high school plans. From this population, a random sample of 10,317 was selected for continuing study. In 1964, researchers obtained information from students' parents about post–high school education, military service, marital status, and current occupation. In 1975, 97 percent of the original sample were located, and most were interviewed by telephone. The interview focused on post–high school education, work history, and family characteristics. The data from this study enabled researchers to trace the impact of the characteristics of high school seniors on subsequent education, occupation, earnings, and work experience through adulthood. Researchers collected data from

survivors in 2011–12, when they were about 70 years old.

Figure 17.1 presents a diagram of the relationships found among the variables studied. The arrows indicate causal influences. Variables are arranged from left to right to reflect the order in which they affect the person through time. These results indicate that children from more affluent socioeconomic backgrounds have greater ability and higher aspirations in high school, which directly influence educational attainment. Children with higher ability get better grades, which reward them for their academic work and reinforce their aspirations. Children who do well are also encouraged by significant others, such as teachers and relatives, which also contributes to their high aspirations. These children are likely to choose courses that will prepare them for college. They are likely to spend more time on academic pursuits and less time on dating and social activities (Jessor, Costa, Jessor, & Donovan, 1983). As a result, they are likely to continue their education beyond high school and perhaps beyond college. Finally, high ability, encouragement of significant others, and high educational attainment lead to greater occupational status and earnings.

Note that socioeconomic background and grades have an indirect effect on occupational status. Parental socioeconomic status and an individual's grades are not directly related to occupational status in these results. Rather, status and grades influence occupational attainment through other variables— like aspirations—that do have a direct impact on occupational attainment (Sewell & Hauser, 1975). A meta-analysis of the interrelationship of intelligence and parental socioeconomic status (SES) on individuals' attainment included studies that measured all of the relevant variables and used a longitudinal design (Strenze, 2007). It used data from 85 data sets, involving 135 samples. An index of parental SES (education, occupation, and income), intelligence/ability measured while the individual was still

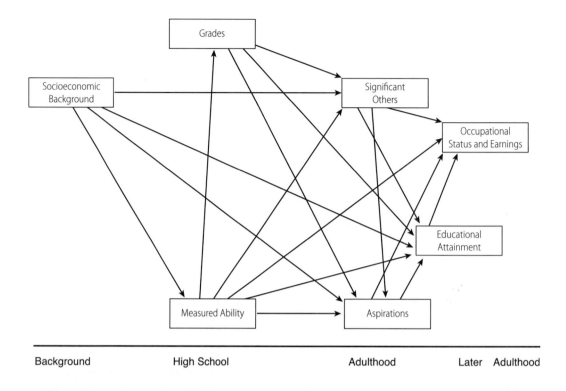

**FIGURE 17.1** The Determinants of Occupational Status Attainment

This figure summarizes the influences that determine educational and occupational status over the life course. Socioeconomic background (parents' education, occupation, and income) influences the child's ability, aspirations, and educational attainment. Ability influences grades, which, in turn, affect encouragement from significant others and aspirations for educational attainment. Adult occupational status is affected by education and also by ability, aspirations, and significant others' support.

*Source:* Adapted from William H. Sewell & Robert M. Hauser, "The Wisconsin Longitudinal Study of Social and Psychological Factors in Aspirations and Achievements," *Research in Sociology of Education and Socialization*, Vol. 1, 1980, pp. 59–99.

in school, and academic performance/grades predicted later educational and occupational attainment and income.

In the research summarized in Figure 17.1, the family characteristics studied are mothers' and fathers' socioeconomic standing—education, occupation, and income. How is it that variables such as your father's education and your mother's income influence your educational attainment? Parents often use their resources to create a home environment that facilitates doing well in school (Teachman, 1987). Thus, they provide such aids as a quiet place to study, money to purchase materials,

and a laptop or tablet computer. Moreover, they may provide cultural enrichment activities, such as attending concerts and sports events (DiMaggio & Mohr, 1985). A study of the daily activities of children aged 3 to 11 found that children of highly educated parents spent more time reading and studying and less time watching TV (Bianchi & Robinson, 1997). In high school, students whose parents have bachelor's degrees are more likely to study, and spend more hours studying (Allard, 2008).

Family structure also plays a role in the attainment process. An analysis of data from more than 29,000 Canadian students assessed the impact of family structure and youth characteristics at age 15 on educational attainment by age 26 (Wu, Schimmele, & Hou, 2015). Youth living with married, biological parents at age 16 were more likely to complete college or university by age 26, compared to children living in two-parent, single-parent, or alternative family forms. Greater attainment was associated with having college-educated parent(s) who monitored homework on a regular basis and had made financial preparations for the child to go to college. A study of a national sample of 30- to 59-year-old men and women compared those raised in original two-parent families with those raised in other family structures. Those raised in original families earned more as adults (Powell & Parcell, 1997). Among Blacks, the presence of two parents, both employed outside the home, is essential to mobility (McAdoo, 1997).

The experiences of Fred and José clearly reflect the importance of these processes. Fred's parents were upper middle class; they sent him to a good preschool at age 4 and encouraged him to learn to read. José's parents were working class; they encouraged him to get out and play. Fred did well in school; his grades were always high. José struggled with his schoolwork, especially math. By eighth grade, Fred had an excellent record, and his teachers gave him lots of encouragement; José's teachers, on the other hand, didn't pay much attention to him. Fred worked hard in high school, got good grades, and, with the support of his teachers and family, went to a university. After finishing high school, José went into the army, where he learned vehicle mechanics. When Fred finished college, he got a job in a medical equipment firm. Ten years after he graduated from high school, Fred was selling $200,000 worth of equipment per year and earning 20 percent commissions. After he finished his military service, José went to work in a gas station. Ten years after José graduated from high school, he was earning $28,000 per year working in a gas station.

Thus, there is some upward mobility in U.S. society, and one's socioeconomic background does not fix one's occupational attainment and earnings. Through greater education, many persons achieve an occupational status and income larger than would be expected based solely on their background. Thus, America is not a caste society. At the same time, one's socioeconomic background is not irrelevant to one's educational and occupational attainment. Not everyone can be a doctor, lawyer, or engineer. Opportunities for upward mobility are not unlimited.

**Education.** The research summarized in the preceding section clearly indicates the importance of education in determining one's occupational attainment and adult status. Thus, differences in the amount of education completed will result in differences in status. In U.S. society, there are large disparities in educational attainment by ethnicity. The percentage of all persons who have completed high school (and more) and college (and more) in 2015 are displayed in Table 17.2. Looking at

**TABLE 17.2** Educational Attainment by Ethnicity and Gender, 2015

|  | WHITE | | BLACK | | ASIAN | | HISPANIC | |
|---|---|---|---|---|---|---|---|---|
|  | MALE % | FEMALE % | MALE % | FEMALE % | MALE % | FEMALE % | MALE % | FEMALE % |
| High school graduate or more | 93.0 | 93.5 | 86.4 | 87.6 | 91.0 | 87.4 | 65.5 | 67.8 |
| College graduate or more | 36.3 | 36.1 | 20.6 | 24.0 | 56.8 | 51.5 | 14.3 | 16.6 |

*Source:* U.S. Census Bureau, CPS Historical Time Series Tables, Table A2.

5

the data, Asian Americans are the most educated (56.8 percent of men and 51.5 percent of women complete college), followed by Whites (36 percent of men and women), Blacks (20.6 percent, 24 percent), and Hispanics (14.3 percent, 16.6 percent). Not surprisingly, these differences translate into differences in occupations, which in turn create differences in income (see below) and lifestyle.

**Gender.** Is the process of status attainment different for men and women? According to the data obtained by the Wisconsin high school students study, the determinants of occupational status as depicted in Figure 17.1 are the same for both men and women. Using a prestige scale of 0–100, the first jobs held by women were, on the average, 6 points higher than the first jobs held by men. Women's first jobs were concentrated within a narrow range of prestige, whereas there was much greater variation in the prestige scores of first jobs held by men (Sewell, Hauser, & Wolf, 1980). Table 17.1 displays these differences in prestige. The first jobs that women held included registered nurse, schoolteacher, social worker, dental assistant, and secretary. The prestige scores of these jobs range from 66 to 46. In contrast, men's first jobs ranged from physician (86) to garbage collector (28).

When the researchers looked at 1975 occupations, they found that men had gained an average of 9 points in status in the 18-year period since their graduation from high school. Women, on the other hand, had actually lost status; the average prestige of current occupations for women was 2 points lower than the average prestige of their first jobs. The differential effect of life events on the work careers of men and women account for this differential attainment. Men experience upward mobility because they work continuously. Women's work careers are often interrupted by marriage and by raising children; when they return to work, they often return to the same job. Thus, women are less able

to build up enough continuous experience to gain raises and promotions. An analysis of differences in pay for recent entrants into careers in STEM fields (Science, Technology, Engineering, and Mathematics) found that women earn 31 percent less than men do; one-third of the difference is associated with being married and having children (Buffington, Cerf, Jones, & Weinberg, 2016). Moving also interferes with women's advancement, especially when the purpose of the move is to further the man's career (Shihadeh, 1991). Advancement for women is also more limited in occupations held largely by women. The top positions in schools, social work, airlines, and sales are more often held by men than by women.

Although the influence of social and individual factors such as socioeconomic background and ability on occupational attainment is similar for men and women, working men and women are not proportionately distributed across occupational categories. Look back at Table 17.1. As you look at each occupation in the list, which gender comes to mind? Chances are that when you think of electrical engineers, electricians, or auto mechanics, you picture men performing those jobs. In 2016, of those employed in these occupations, 90 percent, 98 percent, and 98 percent, respectively, were men (U.S. Bureau of Labor Statistics, 2017). Similarly, when you think of registered nurse or dental hygienist, you picture women in these roles; in 2016, of those employed in these occupations, 90 percent and 97 percent, respectively, were women. Many occupations consist overwhelmingly of either men or women; there is substantial occupational-level segregation by gender (Reskin & Padavic, 1994). As occupation is the basis of prestige and a major determinant of income, this segregation has serious consequences.

There are several processes that perpetuate occupational segregation. Our awareness of the gender composition of occupations through our daily experience and via media portrayals

 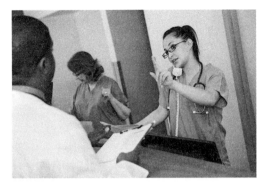

Segregation of occupations by gender is widespread in the United States; for example, most construction workers are men, whereas most nurses and unit clerks in hospitals are women. This segregation has serious consequences for a woman's earnings and occupational prestige. *Left:* © kozmoat98/iStock *Right:* © asiseeit/iStock

influences our aspirations. Further, cultural beliefs about gender differences in skills and abilities, for example that girls are less skilled than boys at math, influence educational decisions and career choices (Correll, 2004) in ways that maintain occupational segregation (men become engineers) (see Box 17.1).

Direct experience with occupational segregation begins in adolescence. Data from a sample of 3,101 tenth- and eleventh-grade students in suburban high schools provide concrete evidence (Greenberger & Steinberg, 1983). Adolescents' first jobs are segregated by sex, with girls earning a lower hourly wage. These differences reflect differential opportunity; employers hire primarily girls or primarily boys for a particular job (for example, laborer, fast-food sales), and they pay boys more. Performing different roles results in differences in the skills developed by gender.

In the preceding section, we discussed the differences in the first jobs typically held by men and women. These differences reflect both choice by the person, influenced by their education and beliefs about occupations, and the types of positions available to the person. A recent analysis of job satisfaction, using data from more than 300,000 men and women in the U.S., U.K., and Russia, finds that women's satisfaction increases as the proportion of men in the occupation decreases (Lordan & Pischke,

2016). Also, women's satisfaction is greater in occupations involving work with people and ideas, compared to jobs involving work with things (see discussion of Kohn's research later in this chapter). Apparently, Rosie doesn't like riveting! Job content is not related to men's satisfaction. The authors suggest that women may select occupations based on job content, which contributes to occupational segregation by gender.

What happens when a person of the other gender enters a segregated occupation? That person may experience stereotyping and harassment by coworkers or supervisors, like the 27-year-old male nurse assigned to a unit with 10 female staff, who reported frequent inappropriate comments to his face about his sexuality. Women working to earn Ph.D.s in astronomy have spoken publicly about harassment by faculty in the male-dominated field. Some have left the field (another reason why there are fewer women at the top!). On the other hand, the person may experience unusual rewards and rapid advancement. Elementary and middle school teachers are primarily women (78.5 percent in 2016); research comparing the outcomes of men and women elementary teachers found that men were more likely than women to be promoted to administrative positions (Cognard-Black, 2004); this practice is referred to as the "glass

## BOX 17.1   Can Girls Do Math? Cultural Beliefs and Occupational Segregation

The power of cultural beliefs was convincingly demonstrated by the controversy in early 2005 over remarks made by the then-president of Harvard University, Lawrence Summers. Speaking at a meeting of the National Bureau of Economic Research on January 14, Summers suggested three reasons why women are underrepresented "in high-end scientific professions. One is what I would call . . . the high-powered job hypothesis. The second is what I would call different availability of aptitude at the high end, and the third is what I would call different socialization and patterns of discrimination in a search" (Summers, 2005). In an elaboration of the second point, he suggested that, among those with the very highest abilities in science and math, the ratio of men to women was probably 5:1. Summers is restating a widely held cultural belief in the United States that girls/women are inferior at math and, by extension, will not succeed in occupations that require high mathematical ability. A professor of biology at MIT, Dr. Nancy Hopkins, walked out on Summers, and later discussed his remarks with a reporter.

One reason why many reacted to his remarks with indignation is that these beliefs become a self-fulfilling prophecy (see Chapter 7). Many teachers and guidance counselors (and many parents) believe girls are inferior at math and so they caution girls not to take advanced math or science courses. This, of course, restricts the number of girls who take the courses needed to later pursue degrees in these fields. This belief is held by many boys and girls, and influences the way they interact with one another. Furthermore, a girl who believes she is less skilled will not work as hard or be as persistent as a girl who believes she can do it, making it less likely that she will succeed (see Chapter 3, self-efficacy). If we really want to encourage members of a group to enter an occupational field in larger numbers, we need to stop constraining them by voicing and acting upon such beliefs. It is especially upsetting when someone of Summers's status, president of one of the oldest universities in the United States, voices them.

More important, Summers is wrong. There have been hundreds of studies of differences in mathematical and related skills and abilities, at all age levels. These studies have been the focus of large-scale meta-analyses; one of them used data from more than 100 studies, testing 3 million persons (Hyde, Fenema, & Lamon, 1990; Hyde et al., 2008). Overall, the average effect size was $d = 0.05$—that is, the difference in average math test scores was basically zero. When the analysis was done by age, the results indicated that there is no gender difference in math performance in elementary or middle school, but a significant difference emerges in high school. These results flatly reject the hypothesis that there are innate differences in ability, and are entirely consistent with the hypothesis that girls and boys are being socialized to believe there is a difference, and that that cultural belief increasingly affects math performance as females progress through the school system. It is not differential ability, but differential socialization that results in few women in top positions in science.

Another explanation for the underrepresentation of women at top levels of science is that it reflects their lifestyle choices—to have children and spend time with family—not discrimination. This explanation was put forward in a paper in the prestigious *Proceedings of the National Academy of Science* (Ceci & Williams, 2011). It was widely covered by major media outlets. The problem is that there are no data supporting the hypothesis (Barnett & Rivers, 2011). The authoritative scientific report is "Beyond Bias and Barriers" (Committee, 2007). It cites more than 500 sources of data showing that women face widespread discrimination in science and engineering. This discrimination is evident in the results of an experiment (Moss-Racusin et al., 2012). Science faculty at major universities rated the application materials of a student, who was randomly assigned either a male or female name. Faculty rated the male more competent and more hireable, selected a higher starting salary, and offered more mentoring to him. Such differential treatment, i.e., discrimination, gives male scientists' careers a boost compared to females with the same qualifications, another reason why women are underrepresented in the scientific professions.

escalator." Either way, the dominance of one gender in the occupation is maintained.

Differences in work performed or in job titles often result in large differences in pay. In 2016, the median weekly earnings (in current dollars) of White women employed full-time was $749, whereas the median for White men was $915 (U.S. Bureau of Labor Statistics, 2017). Thus, the median annual earnings of a White woman was $38,948, whereas the median for a White man was $47,580—a difference of $8,632. Thus, overall, women's earnings are, on average, 82 percent of men's earnings; this is referred to as the *gender earnings ratio*. An analysis of local labor markets found that the more segregated a labor market was, the larger the ratio (Cohen, 2003).

There are also differences in earnings by race and ethnicity. In 2016, the median weekly earnings of Black women was $641, whereas the earnings of Hispanic women was $586. Thus, Black women earned $108 per week less than White women, and the White/Hispanic difference was $163. The median earnings of Black men was $718, and of Hispanic men $663. The White/Black difference was $197 per week and the White/Hispanic gap was $252. (U.S. Bureau of Labor Statistics, 2017). Asian men and women enjoy the highest average weekly earnings in the U.S., $1,058 and $831 respectively. A percentage of these gaps is due to differences in occupations by race and gender, reflecting differences in (access to) education and training. Note that the rank of salaries by race/ethnicity (Asian, White, Black, Hispanic) is the same as the rank by educational attainment (Table 17.2). However, as much as 40 percent is due to gender discrimination (Joint Economic Committee, 2016), not to differences in measures of workers' skills.

**Social Networks.** We have seen that socioeconomic background, ability, educational attainment, and earlier jobs influence occupational attainment over the life course. In part, this is because differences in experiences create differences in an individual's aspirations and abilities to cope with the occupational world. Varied experiences also move people into different social networks. This exposes them to varied social contacts, which have an important effect on their upward mobility. This section considers some of the ways in which position in social networks affects the person.

Networks provide channels for the flow of information, including information about job opportunities. What types of networks are likely to provide information on finding new jobs? You might think it is networks characterized by strong ties, such as families or peer groups. Surprisingly, employment opportunities are often found through networks characterized by weak ties—relationships involving infrequent interaction and little closeness or emotional depth (Marsden & Campbell, 1984). Those to whom our ties are weak are involved in different groups and activities than we are. Consequently, they will be exposed to information that is different from the information we and our friends already have. For this reason, new information is more likely to come via a weak tie than via a strong one. In one study, of those who found jobs through contacts, only 17 percent were obtained through strong ties (Granovetter, 1973).

A study of the hiring process in a midsized high-tech organization gathered information on all 35,229 applicants over a 10-year period (1985–1994). The results indicated that there were only small differences in hiring by gender, and they were accounted for entirely by age and education. For ethnic minorities, on the other hand, some of the differences were accounted for by referral method; members of minority groups lacked access to the informal networks that were associated with success in getting hired (Petersen, Saporta, & Seidel, 2000).

We noted earlier that women are less likely than men to experience upward occupational mobility during their careers. Might this occur in part because men and women differ in their access to networks that carry job information? Earlier in the chapter, we saw that men have greater education and earnings than women, and that Whites enjoy greater education and earnings than minorities. Thus, the gender and racial composition of a person's social networks should be related to the information about jobs available to the person. Analysis of data from a national survey found that people who belong to networks composed of White males received twice as many unsolicited job leads in one year (McDonald, 2011b). Because occupations are segregated, and people prefer homophilous social networks, most respondents were in race and gender homophilous networks, giving White men an advantage. Assistance in finding a job in the past year was more likely to be reported by those in networks comprised of persons of the same gender. Other research finds that men, but not women, are more likely to be informally recruited into a new job as they gain experience in an occupation (McDonald, 2011a). Apparently, men are in networks that allow greater access to information about and opportunities for advancement. Contemporary researchers refer to access to organizational networks as *bridging social capital* to highlight its value as an influence on one's resources (Coffe & Geys, 2008).

Social networks also contribute to mobility within one's workplace. A longitudinal study of employees in one high-tech firm found that having a large network of informal ties was associated with promotions and salary increases (Podolny & Baron, 1997).

It is common to advise people seeking jobs to network, to seek information and assistance from people they know, in person, online, or through networking sites. Thus, men are likely to network with men and women with women, so women are often networking with people who have lower-paid jobs in gender-segregated firms. This, of course, perpetuates gender segregation in employment and the earnings gap between men and women (Munsch, 2013).

## INDIVIDUAL VALUES

Last year, Fred, José, and Marie were each approached by a labor union organizer. Fred, the sales representative, was approached by a member of Retail Clerks International. The organizer explained that under a union contract, Fred would spend fewer days on the road and would receive a travel allowance from his employer. José was approached by a representative of the Teamsters. The organizer sympathized with the problems of independent service station owners and urged José to let the Teamsters represent his interests in dealing with his supplier. Marie was approached by the president of United Health Care Workers; she was promised higher wages and greater respect from physicians if she would join.

Fred flatly rejected the invitation, believing that a union contract would limit his freedom and perhaps reduce his income. José's reaction was mixed. On the one hand, he felt he was at the mercy of "Big Oil." On the other hand, he was also a self-employed businessman; like Fred, he didn't want to join a labor organization that might limit his ability to determine his prices and the pace at which he worked. Marie reacted very favorably to her invitation and began to attend union meetings "to see what they are like." She felt that a union might lead to higher pay and might force the hospital to give her more freedom in determining the pace at which she worked.

In making their decisions, Fred, José, and Marie used their personal **values**, which are enduring beliefs that certain patterns of behavior or end states are preferable to others (Rokeach, 1973). All three were concerned with protecting or enhancing their freedom and income. These values provided criteria for making decisions. Thus, each person weighed the potential effect of joining a union on freedom and income. Fred felt that the effect on both would be negative. José was sure that union membership would limit his freedom but uncertain about its effect on his income. Marie perceived a potential gain in both freedom and income, so she decided to explore union membership.

An important theory of values has been developed by Schwartz (1992, 1994). He identifies 10 motivationally distinct values; these are portrayed in Figure 17.2. Surveys using instruments to assess these values in 32 countries have generally confirmed the structural model displayed in the figure (Bilsky, Janik, & Schwartz, 2011). In 17 countries, including Belgium, Denmark, Germany, Poland, and the United Kingdom, data were collected in three rounds between 2002 and 2007; the results indicated that the structure varied somewhat between countries, but was stable within each country over that period. Schwartz and

Rubel-Lifschitz (2009) investigated gender differences in values, using data from probability samples in 25 countries. Generally, men attribute more importance to power, achievement, hedonism, stimulation, and self-direction, whereas women attribute more importance to benevolence, universalism, and security. Using a measure of gender equality in each country, they also found that as gender equality increased, the importance of benevolence, universalism, self-direction, hedonism, and stimulation increased for both men and women. They speculate that increases in wealth, education, and autonomy that accompany increasing equality allow both men and women to express these values.

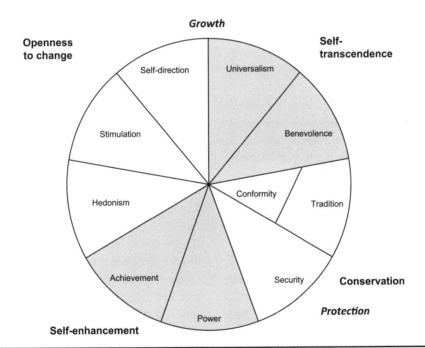

**FIGURE 17.2** The Structure of Basic Values

A theory of values developed by Schwartz (1992) identifies 10 motivationally distinct types of values. Each value is defined in terms of its central goal. The theory also specifies a structure of relationships among the values. Values that lead to actions that conflict with each other are located opposite each other; complementary values are located close to each other. Thus, actions that provide hedonistic rewards often conflict with social norms and traditions; actions that conform to social norms enhance security. The values can be thought of as lying along two dimensions, from self-enhancement to self-transcendence, and from conservation to openness to change.

Source: The structural organization of human values: Evidence from three rounds of the European Social Survey (ESS). (2011). By Bilsky, Janik, & Schwartz, *Journal of Cross-Cultural Psychology*, 42, 759–776.

Because values are general, they can provide integration or coherence across the many roles an individual plays (Hitlin, 2003). Although general, they influence many specific attitudes, choices, and behaviors as well. For example, values are related to our attitudes toward public policy. Thus, the importance one places on personal property and on social equality is related to one's attitudes toward paying higher taxes to help the poor (Tetlock, 1986). Those who place greater value on property will oppose higher taxes, whereas those who place greater importance on equality will favor increasing taxes to help the poor. Those who feel these values are equally important should find it hard to decide.

Values are related to choices. A study of university students assessed their values and asked them to respond to 10 hypothetical scenarios. Each scenario required a choice between two options, each representing a different value. The respondents' choices were consistent with their values (Feather, 1995).

Values are related to preference for convenience or fast foods. A sample of adults responsible for food purchasing and preparation in Thessaloniki, Greece, were interviewed (Botanaki & Mattas, 2010). Their values were measured based on the Schwartz model, as were their attitudes toward convenience in the domains of meal planning, shopping, preparation, and consumption. Pro-convenience food attitudes were positively associated with values of stimulation and achievement—that is, seeking new experiences and acting independently. Valuing conservation and self-transcendence were associated with negative attitudes toward convenience foods.

How do value systems arise? They are influenced by our location in the social structure. This section examines two aspects of social position that affect individual values: occupational role and education.

## Occupational Role

We spend up to half of our waking hours at work, so it is not surprising that our work influences our values. But occupational experiences vary tremendously. To determine their effect on values, we must identify the basic differences among occupations. Three important characteristics have been suggested (Kohn, 1969). The first is closeness of supervision—the extent to which the worker is under the direct surveillance and control of a supervisor. As a traveling salesman, Fred is rarely under close supervision, whereas Marie's work is supervised by the director of nursing and various physicians. The second occupational characteristic is routinization of work—the extent to which tasks are repetitive and predictable. Much of José's work is routine—pumping gas, tuning engines, relining brakes. But his work is not highly predictable. From one day to the next, he never knows what kind of auto breakdown he will encounter or what unusual request some customer may make. The third characteristic is substantive complexity of the work—how complicated the work tasks are. Work with people is usually more complex than work with data or work with objects. Marie's occupation as a nurse is especially complex because she must constantly cope with the problems posed by other nurses, doctors, patients, and families.

All three of these characteristics were measured in several studies of employed men to determine the impact of occupational role on values and personality (Kohn & Schooler, 1983). The results of these studies show a relationship between particular occupational characteristics and particular values: men whose jobs were less closely supervised, less routine, and more complex placed especially high value on responsibility, good sense, and curiosity. Men whose work was closely supervised, routine, and not complex were more likely to value conformity. Thus, the occupational conditions that encourage self-direction—less supervised, nonroutine, complex tasks—are associated with valuing individual qualities that facilitate adjustment and success in a self-directed environment: responsibility, curiosity, and good sense. Occupational conditions that encourage adherence to a prescribed routine— close supervision and routine and simple tasks, such as bolting bumpers on new cars—are associated with qualities that facilitate success in that environment, such as neatness and obedience. This pattern has emerged in studies of employed men and women (Miller, Schooler, Kohn, & Miller, 1979) and in studies conducted in several countries including the United States, Japan, and Poland (Slomczynski, Miller, & Kohn, 1981).

Early studies of the relationships between workers' values and their occupational conditions revealed that workers exposed to particular conditions hold particular values. However, these studies were unable to determine with certainty whether adjustment to occupational conditions actually caused people to value particular qualities. Perhaps men who value curiosity and desire responsibility select occupations that allow them to exercise these traits (Kohn & Schooler, 1973). In attempting to identify the causal order, researchers compared the men's values and occupational conditions in 1974 with their values and occupational conditions 10 years earlier (Kohn & Schooler, 1982). What they found indicated causal effects in both directions between values and occupational conditions. Men who had valued self-direction highly in 1964 were more likely to be in work roles that were more complex,

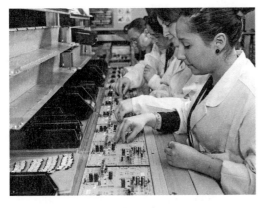

Workers on an assembly line often experience alienation. Assembly-line jobs are monotonous, do not allow workers to exercise initiative, and give them no influence over working conditions.
© gerenme/iStock

less routine, and less closely supervised 10 years later. Thus, values influenced job selection. At the same time, men who were in occupations that allowed or required self-direction in 1964 placed greater value on responsibility, curiosity, and good sense in 1974. Thus, their earlier job conditions influenced their later values.

Do these effects persist into later life? Men and women interviewed in 1974 were interviewed again in 1994 (Schooler, Mulatu, & Oates, 2004). The results replicated those in the original 10-year longitudinal study. Persons high in self-direction in 1974 were more likely to work in jobs that encourage self-direction in 1994, and scored higher on measures of self-direction and intellectual flexibility. Jobs providing greater independence and self-direction—physician, lawyer, professor, accountant, CEO—are higher in social status, providing their occupants with greater advantages.

A review of research on cross-national psychological differences concludes that opportunities for self-direction in one's work are consistently associated with differences in values in a number of countries (Schooler, 1996).

## Education

Are differences in education also related to differences in an individual's values? The research by Kohn and his colleagues described in the preceding section demonstrated that men in jobs that are nonroutine, substantively complex, and not closely supervised value self-direction, whereas men in jobs with the opposite characteristics value conformity. Education is associated with the value one places on these characteristics; the higher one's education, the greater the value placed on self-direction.

Substantively complex occupations involve working independently with people, objects, or data. Such work requires intellectual flexibility, the ability to evaluate information or situations, and the ability to solve problems. These abilities should be related to educational attainment, so education should be related to intellectual flexibility. Analyses of data from a sample of 3,101 men indicate that as education increases, so does intellectual flexibility (Kohn & Schooler, 1973). Thus, education influences both the value placed on self-direction and the abilities needed for success in substantively complex occupations.

## SOCIAL INFLUENCES ON HEALTH

Most of us attribute diseases to biological rather than social factors. But the transmission of disease obviously depends on people's interactions, and our physical susceptibility to disease is influenced by our lifestyles. This is true, for instance, with a disease such as AIDS. Similarly, our mental health is influenced by our relationships with relatives, friends, lovers, professors, supervisors, and so on. Thus, social position affects both physical and mental health. This section examines the impact of occupation, gender, marital role, and social class on physical health. It also considers the relationship between these factors and mental health.

### Physical Health

**Occupational Roles.** What do the physician addicted to oxycodone, the executive with an ulcer, the coal miner with black lung disease (chronic obstructive pulmonary disease), and the factory worker with chronic back pain all have in common? The answer: health problems that may be due largely to their occupational roles.

Occupational roles affect physical health in two ways. First, some occupations directly expose workers to health hazards. Miners who are exposed to coal dust, workers exposed to chemical fumes, and workers who process grain often suffer damage to lung tissue. Wait-staff, bartenders, and kitchen workers exposed to cigarette smoke may develop lung cancer. Workers exposed to various toxic chemicals may die of bladder cancer. Occupational conditions caused 4,836 deaths in 2015 (U.S. Bureau of Labor Statistics, 2016a), and 2.9 million injuries and illnesses (U.S. Bureau of Labor Statistics, 2016b). The highest death rates are in transportation (especially road-related incidents), followed by construction and manufacturing. The highest injury and illness rates are in trade/transportation, followed by education/health. Turning to suicide, the highest rates are in farming, fishing and forestry, followed by construction (McIntosh, 2016).

Second, many occupational roles expose individuals to stresses that affect physical health indirectly. Each of the roles we play carries a set of obligations or duties. Meeting these demands requires time, energy, and resources. When these demands exceed the person's perceived ability to meet them, the result is stress (Lazarus, 1991).

Work is a major source of stress for many adults. There are several types or sources of stressors with different consequences (Thoits, 2010). A common type is *stressful life events*. Upcoming exams, a major project deadline, an acute illness, and a move within the same city are all events that cause some stress; their effects are generally short-lived, and end following the event. In one study, researchers asked adults to report the amount of stress in their lives and their health problems 20 times over a 6-month period. Those who reported higher levels of stress also reported more health problems, including sore throats, headaches, and flu. Increased stress was associated with more ailments on the same day and on subsequent days (DeLongis, Folkman, & Lazarus, 1988). The connection between stress and physical health is the body's immune system. A study of college students found that as their reports of stress increased, the concentration of antibodies in their saliva decreased (Jemmott & Magloire, 1988). The lower the level of antibodies, the more susceptible one is to illness.

Another perspective on stress considers *daily hassles* of life and their effect on health. The

Daily Inventory of Stressful Events (Almeida, Wethington, & Kessler, 2002) assesses whether the person has experienced each of a broad range of stressors, including arguments about various personal and family issues, work or school overload or difficulties, or issues involving one's residence (money, needing repairs). Interviews with a national sample ($N = 1,031$) found that respondents reported at least one hassle on 40 percent of the days and multiple hassles on 11 percent of them. Respondents who reported more frequent interpersonal stressors and concerns regarding the self (the way you feel about yourself, the way others feel about you) were more likely to report daily physical symptoms.

A third source is *chronic stressors*. Insufficient income to support the family, caring for a chronically ill (for example, with AIDS) or disabled person, and living in a dangerous neighborhood (Boardman, 2004) are all examples. Chronic conflict leading to a breakup and chronic unemployment are also examples. These conditions are continuous over time, and so is the stress associated with them. Chronic stress may lead to serious physical illness. Excellent evidence of this link comes from a longitudinal study of two samples of adults (140 and 190 persons, respectively) employed at a large company (Maddi, Bartone, & Puccetti, 1987). Each person's level of stress was assessed by a carefully designed measure of stressful life events. Then, 1 or 2 years later, each person completed a questionnaire regarding illness that included both mild (for example, influenza) and serious (for example, heart attack) conditions. There were strong associations between the level of stress experienced initially and reported illness 1 or 2 years later. Research indicates that the impact of cumulative or chronic stress on health is greater than the impact of life events, and that females, members of minority groups, and poor and working-class persons experience significantly more chronic stress (Thoits, 2010). Chronic stress can be indexed

by *allostatic load*, "the cumulative wear and tear on the body's systems owing to repeated adaptations to stressors" (Geronimus, Hicken, Keene, & Bound, 2006, p. 826). It is reflected in the levels of various substances in the blood stream, including epinephrine, cortisol, and DHEA-s, and measures such as blood pressure.

A fourth source is *traumas*, extreme threats to the person's psychological or physical well-being. Examples include physical or sexual assault, military combat experiences, and involvement in a natural disaster. An earthquake and its aftershocks may last only one day. But the devastation and disruption experienced by survivors may affect them for months. Data from numerous countries document the association of earthquakes with subsequent increased cardiovascular risks, such as pulmonary embolism (Dimsdale, 2008).

Many people spend energy, time, and money jogging, playing tennis, or working out. Does it do any good? There is evidence that people who are physically fit are less likely to experience stress-related illness. One study of students obtained self-reports of time spent per week in each of 14 fitness activities. The researchers also assessed fitness directly, measuring blood pressure, aerobic capacity, and endurance. Higher levels of self-reported fitness were associated with higher levels of health. Greater fitness as measured directly was associated with fewer visits to the student health center (Brown, 1991b). However, whereas stress is related to health, it is not related to self-reported fitness (Roth, Wiebe, Fillingian, & Shay, 1989). Fitness does not reduce the amount of stress one experiences, but it does reduce illness. A review of literature, including randomized clinical trials of physical-activity interventions, concludes that persons who engage in regular physical activity are less likely to experience several diseases, and have a better quality of life (Penedo & Dahn, 2005).

The most widely studied relationship between job characteristics and physical

Traumatic events, like hurricanes, earthquakes, tornadoes, or major floods, may cause high levels of stress in survivors, lasting for years. Rebuilding one's residence, one's financial base, and re-establishing daily routines may take several years, or more. © Leif Skoogfors/FEMA

health is the impact of occupational stress on coronary heart disease. As one's workload increases—including perceived demands and number of hours worked—so does the incidence of coronary heart disease (Dimsdale, 2008). Heart attacks are associated with a high level of serum cholesterol in the blood. Several studies report that the level of serum cholesterol rises among persons under high work-related stress (Chandola, Brunner, & Marmot, 2006). This suggests another tangible link between role demands and physical health. Furthermore, some studies suggest that the job-stressed individual may hyperrespond to stressors outside the work environment.

An important aspect of jobs that are associated with an increased risk of heart attack is the lack of control over work pace and task demands (Dimsdale, 2008). Occupations associated with the highest risk include cooks, waitstaff, assembly-line operators, and gas station attendants. These jobs are characterized by high demand—heavy workload and rapid pace—over which the worker has little or no control. Cashiers and waiters are four to five times more likely to have a heart attack than foresters or civil engineers. One study assessed the contribution of lack of control on the job to coronary heart disease, controlling for other factors, including individual risk factors and the availability of social support (Marmot et al., 1997). Longitudinal data were obtained from 7,372 employed men and women at three points in time. A reported lack of control at Time 1 was associated with increased incidence of self-reported chest pain and angina, and doctor-diagnosed angina or heart attack, at Times 2 and 3.

**Gender Roles.** Who is more likely to experience an accident, cirrhosis of the liver, or coronary heart disease—men or women? You probably picked men, and if you did, you are right. Men are three times more likely to die from cirrhosis than women, and twice as likely to die in an accident. More generally, research consistently finds that women live longer than men but suffer from more illnesses in many countries around the world (Read & Gorman, 2010). Although there is evidence that genetic and hormonal factors play a role, traditional role expectations for men and women and occupational role segregation are also significant factors.

Some gender differences in health are associated with reproductive roles (Macintyre, Hunt, & Sweeting, 1996). Health problems related to reproduction, such as premenstrual syndrome and pregnancy-related conditions, are most likely among women of childbearing age. Men exposed to various chemicals, heat, or radiation, usually on the job, may experience reduced sperm production, abnormal sperm types, or impaired sperm transfer (National Institute of Occupational Safety and Health, 2002). Hormonal changes at menopause affect the physical health of some women, causing osteoporosis and an increased likelihood of broken bones. Older men are very likely to experience enlarged prostate glands, and may die of prostate cancer.

The top three causes of death are the same for men and women in the United States: heart disease, cancer, and respiratory diseases. However, age-adjusted death rates indicate that males are at greater risk for all three (1.6 to 1.3) (National Center for Health Statistics, 2012). One analysis suggests that the greater likelihood of male death from these illnesses is related to smoking (Case & Paxson, 2004). There is also variation by ethnicity. Blacks have the highest age-adjusted death rates of heart disease, cerebrovascular disease, and cancer, while Hispanics have the lowest rates of these three, with Whites intermediate. Research on Black/White differences in mortality suggests that differences in social class—education, income, and job complexity—are responsible

(Warner & Hayward, 2006). These differences have persisted for 50 years (Syme, 2008), indicating that we need new approaches to reducing these disparities.

**Role overload**, in which the demands of one's role(s) exceed the amount of time, energy, and other resources one has, is associated with coronary heart disease. Professionals such as physicians, lawyers, and accountants are especially vulnerable to overload; until recently, the persons holding these positions have been primarily men. Other studies have shown that heart attacks are correlated with certain personality traits known as *coronary-prone behavior patterns* (Jenkins, Rosenman, & Zyzanski, 1974). People who exhibit these behavior patterns are work-oriented, aggressive, competitive, and impatient. They often initiate two or more tasks simultaneously (Kurmeyer & Biggers, 1988). Men are much more likely to be characterized by this behavior pattern than women.

We documented above the differences in income of men and women in the contemporary United States (and it is found in many other countries as well). Women's lower earnings limit their access to health-related resources compared to men (Read & Gorman, 2010).

Men are more prone than women to have cirrhosis of the liver because they are more likely than women (1.7 to 1) to be heavy drinkers (Schoenborn, 2004). Until recently, men were much more likely to smoke cigarettes and, therefore, more likely than women to contract lung cancer and emphysema. Men are 2.5 times more likely to die in auto accidents (National Center for Health Statistics, 2012), both because of higher rates of driving under the influence of alcohol (4 of 5 arrests for driving under the influence (DWI) are of men) and because of poor driving habits (Waldron, 1976).

Clearly, certain behaviors increase the risk of illness or death. The transmission of these health risk behaviors, such as not eating an adequate diet, smoking, and drinking, was the focus of a study of 330 teenagers and their parents. The results showed that the father's lifestyle affected only boys and the mother's lifestyle affected only girls (Wickrama, Conger, Wallace, & Elder, 1999). Thus, gendered health risk behaviors may be learned as part of gender role socialization.

These generalizations highlight overall differences between men and women, but we need to recognize that gender roles vary by culture and subculture—and that gender roles are changing (Watkins & Whaley, 2000); for example, increasing numbers of women are smoking, and so the gender gap in deaths due to lung cancer will gradually get smaller.

**Marital Roles.** Marriage is associated with physical health. Married men and women are less likely to report conditions such as back pain and headaches, and limitations on activity (Schoenborn, 2004). They experience fewer acute and chronic health conditions (Ross, Mirowsky, & Goldsteen, 1990). On a variety of indicators, widowed persons are more likely than the divorced or separated to experience health problems. These patterns are found in Whites, Blacks, and Hispanics.

Why is it that being married protects people against illness and accidents? The most likely explanation is that married persons are less likely to engage in behaviors that expose them to illness and accidents. They probably eat and sleep better than unmarried persons. They are less likely to smoke and drink (Schoenborn, 2004). They may take fewer risks, reducing the likelihood they will be involved in accidents. Finally, they may be more likely to seek medical care when ill (Verbrugge, 1979).

This explanation suggests that the health advantage of married people is the result of living with another person. To test this interpretation, data were analyzed from a national sample of women. Measures of illness included the number of days spent in bed and the number of doctor visits in the past year. Women who lived with another adult reported no more illness than married women, regardless of whether they were single, separated, divorced, or widowed (Anson, 1989). When another adult is present, they can provide emotional support, help identify illness early, and provide care that encourages rapid recovery.

Is merely being married sufficient to reduce risk? Perhaps. But being happily married is even more beneficial. According to one study, married men and women who were satisfied with their marital roles reported better physical health than those who were dissatisfied (Wickrama, Conger, Lorenz, & Matthews, 1995). On the other hand, marital conflict has been shown to have direct negative influences on cardiovascular, immune, and other physiological systems. Marital stress also has indirect consequences for health by increasing depression and by negatively affecting health behaviors (Kiecolt-Glaser & Newton, 2001).

In contemporary U.S. society, some marriages end in divorce; we discussed in Chapter 3 the difficulty of estimating a divorce rate, and recent declines in the rate among young couples. Most divorced persons remarry. How do these transitions—which are often stressful—affect health? A longitudinal study of the relationship between marital status and mortality in a sample of 12,484 people shows that the longer one is married, the greater one's life expectancy. Women especially benefit from not being single. On the other hand, any transition—to (re) marriage, divorce, or widowhood—increases the risk of death (Brockmann & Klein, 2002).

What about cohabiting couples? Do they enjoy the same health advantage as married persons? Research suggests they do not. Comparisons of the health of men and women living in same-sex and different sex relationships found that cohabiters had higher odds of poorer health than married couples (Denney, Gorman, & Barrera, 2013). Among different-gender couples, women experienced a greater disadvantage compared to their married counterparts. There was little difference between same-sex cohabiting men and women.

**Social Class.** We noted earlier that status has a major impact on lifestyle. One aspect of this is the effect of social class on health. A model of the influences on health is presented in Figure 17.3 (Williams, 1990). In this model, socioeconomic status is one of three major influences.

Whether education, occupation, or income is used as the indicator of status, lower-socioeconomic-status groups in the United States experience poorer health. Differences in health between groups defined by various social characteristics are referred to as *health disparities*. Using five nationally representative data sets, researchers examined differences by income and education on five indicators of child health and mortality, and six indicators

of adult health and mortality (Braveman et al., 2010). The results indicated that those with the least income and education had the worst health/highest death rates, the wealthiest and most educated had the best health/lowest death rates, and the health of those with intermediate levels of income and education fell in between. Gradients from highest to lowest health by class were found among both Black and White children and adults, but less consistently among Hispanics. Rates of infant mortality are negatively related to social class; the rate of mortality among Black infants is between 1.6 and 2.8 times greater compared to White infants. Blacks have higher death rates, tend to become ill at younger ages (for

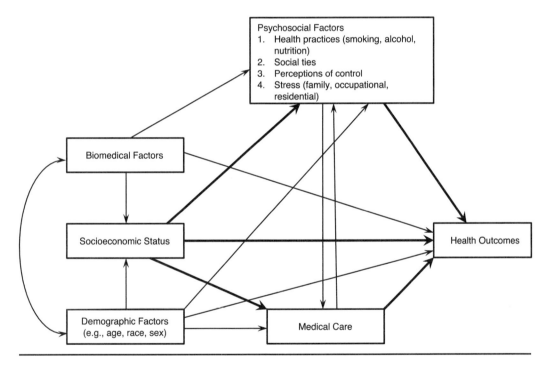

**FIGURE 17.3** A Model of the Influences on Health

There are several influences on a person's physical and mental health. Biomedical, socioeconomic (such as occupation), and demographic (including age, race, gender, and marital status) factors all influence health, both directly and indirectly. All influence such immediate psychosocial factors as health practices and stress. Socioeconomic status is the major influence on the amount and quality of medical care available to the person: the availability of medical care, in conjunction with the other factors, influences how physically and mentally healthy one is.

*Source:* From "Socioeconomic Differentials in Health: A Review and Redirection" (1990) by David R. Williams, *Social Psychology Quarterly*, 53(2), 82. Used with permission from the American Sociological Association.

example, Black women are more likely to be diagnosed with breast cancer before age 40) and some diseases progress faster in Blacks than Whites (for example, chronic kidney disease) (Williams, 2012). Racism and minority persons' experiences of discrimination are certainly a factor in these elevated risks; these experiences are stressful, and may occur on a daily basis, causing chronic stress.

Several factors have been identified as causes of the negative relationship between class and health. First, persons with higher status are more likely to be employed full-time, to have subjectively rewarding jobs, and to have higher income. They are more likely to have health insurance, providing them with access to medical care. Second, higher-status persons are more likely to have a sense of control on the job and of control over their lives and health, reducing stress. Finally, higher-status persons are less likely to engage in health risk behaviors—smoking and heavy drinking—and more likely to eat properly, exercise, and use health-care services. In other words, social class is associated with several of the factors discussed earlier. Analyses of data from two national probability samples found that full-time employment, sense of control on the job, and lifestyle were all related to self-reported health (Ross & Wu, 1995).

Class differences in physical health vary across the life course (House et al., 1994). Differences in health associated with class are small in early adulthood (25 to 44), then increase with age (45 to 54) until late in life, when they become small again (75 and older). The large differences in later adulthood reflect greater exposure of lower-class persons to risk factors such as poverty, occupational health hazards, lack of control on the job, alcohol consumption, and number of stressful life events.

In sum, the relationship between social status and physical health is complex. Occupational roles may expose men and women directly to health risks, causing illness and death, or to the stressful effects of lack of control on the job.

Gender differences in reproductive roles lead to differences in health risks. Role overload is associated with some occupations and differentially affects men and women due to occupational segregation. Being married or living with another adult reduces one's health risk compared to being single. Social class is also associated with differences in mortality, due to its association with occupation and lifestyle. The bottom line is that improving the physical health of people in the United States requires interventions that improve the socioeconomic circumstances and occupational conditions within which all people live (Syme, 2008).

## Mental Health

At the beginning of this chapter, we introduced José, who owns a service station, works long hours, and earns about $65,000 per year. He has two children, a large mortgage on his home, and he has trouble making ends meet. He comes home from work every day exhausted. He worries about the economy and the gradually declining price of gasoline over the past two years, which is cutting into his profits.

Like many Americans, José finds that his life situation is very demanding. His customers expect him to do high-quality repair work at low prices, his wife expects him to support the family and spend time with her, and his children want more toys and electronics than he can afford. At times, the demands made on him by others exceed his ability to cope with them, causing psychological stress. People who are under stress often become tense and anxious, are troubled by poor appetite, or experience insomnia. A widely used questionnaire designed to measure stress-related symptoms is reproduced in Box 17.2. Many of the items on this scale measure behavior, thoughts, and feelings associated with depression.

Stress is a major influence on mental health. Short-term stressors, such as final exam week or an approaching deadline, may produce a

## BOX 17.2 Test Yourself: How Do You Respond to Stress?

Stress is a discrepancy between the demands on a person and their ability to successfully respond to those demands. Individuals under stress experience a variety of physical and psychological symptoms. A widely used measure of these symptoms is reproduced here. Read the instructions and complete the scale.

Here is a list of ways you might have felt or behaved in the past week. Read each of the following statements and then circle the appropriate number to the right of the statement to indicate how often you have felt this way during the past week.

These questions measure depression, a common response to stress. This is the CES-D (Center for Epidemiological Studies Depression) scale.

**Scoring:** You can determine your score by adding up the numbers you circled (0, 1, 2, or 3) for all of the items except items 4, 8, 12, and 16. Notice that these four items refer to positive feelings, whereas the other items refer to negative ones. To score items 4, 8, 12, and 16, give yourself 0 if you circled 3, 1 if you circled 2, 2 if you circled 1, and 3 if you circled 0. Total scores on the scale may range from 0 to 60. If your score is more than 16 points, you could be diagnosed as depressed.

| DURING THE PAST WEEK | RARELY OR NONE OF THE TIME (LESS THAN 1 DAY) | SOME OR A LITTLE OF THE TIME (1–2 DAYS) | OCCASIONALLY OR MODERATE AMOUNT OF THE TIME (3–4 DAYS) | MOST OR ALL OF THE TIME (5–7 DAYS) |
|---|---|---|---|---|
| 1. I was bothered by things that usually don't bother me. | 0 | 1 | 2 | 3 |
| 2. I did not feel like eating; my appetite was poor. | 0 | 1 | 2 | 3 |
| 3. I felt I could not shake off the blues even with help from my family and friends. | 0 | 1 | 2 | 3 |
| 4. I felt that I was just as good as other people. | 0 | 1 | 2 | 3 |
| 5. I had trouble keeping my mind on what I was doing. | 0 | 1 | 2 | 3 |
| 6. I felt depressed. | 0 | 1 | 2 | 3 |
| 7. I felt that everything I did was an effort. | 0 | 1 | 2 | 3 |
| 8. I felt hopeful about the future. | 0 | 1 | 2 | 3 |
| 9. I thought my life had been a failure. | 0 | 1 | 2 | 3 |
| 10. I felt fearful. | 0 | 1 | 2 | 3 |
| 11. My sleep was restless. | 0 | 1 | 2 | 3 |
| 12. I was happy. | 0 | 1 | 2 | 3 |
| 13. I talked less than usual. | 0 | 1 | 2 | 3 |
| 14. I felt lonely. | 0 | 1 | 2 | 3 |
| 15. People were unfriendly. | 0 | 1 | 2 | 3 |
| 16. I enjoyed life. | 0 | 1 | 2 | 3 |
| 17. I had crying spells. | 0 | 1 | 2 | 3 |
| 18. I felt sad. | 0 | 1 | 2 | 3 |
| 19. I felt that people disliked me. | 0 | 1 | 2 | 3 |
| 20. I could not "get going." | 0 | 1 | 2 | 3 |

temporary increase in stress-related symptoms or depression. As soon as the exams are over or the deadline passes, mood may return to normal. Long-term stressors, such as the continuing economic worries that José experiences, or chronic illness, may produce impaired psychological functioning. Neuroses, depression, and posttraumatic stress disorder (PTSD) are among the mental illnesses associated with chronic, severe stress. The experience of stress and impaired psychological functioning varies by occupation, by gender, by marital and work roles, by membership in social networks, and by social class. Some events have an impact on large numbers of people simultaneously. Box 17.3 provides an example of such a stressful event.

**Occupational Roles.** Work-related stress not only affects physical health but also can affect mental health. We noted earlier that occupations that involve heavy workloads and in which workers have little or no control over their work pace are stressful. Physicians are under high levels of stress; they are expected to treat patients quickly, heal them, to be compassionate, and to be cost-effective. These expectations are internalized by most physicians, and they may be exacerbated by personal traits such as perfectionism. The high rates of suicide, depression, substance abuse, and marital problems among physicians appear to result from these stresses (Miller & Megowen, 2000).

Beyond the stresses associated with specific occupations, one's economic circumstances are an important source of stress (Voydanoff, 1990). Economic hardship—insufficient income to meet basic needs—is stressful. Interviews with more than 2,000 adults showed that not having enough money to provide food, clothing, and medical care for self or family was the major variable associated with depression scores (Pearlin & Johnson, 1977).

Economic uncertainty—concern over one's prospects of finding or keeping a job— is also stressful. A study of 7,095 workers found that the level of unemployment in an industry as a whole is associated with the level of distress experienced by employed workers in that industry (Reynolds, 1997). The relationship was stronger for workers in complex, rewarding jobs. Unemployment is especially debilitating (Vinokur, Price, & Caplan, 1996). It is associated with anxiety, depression, and admission to mental hospitals (Voydanoff, 1990), and with an increased risk of death (Voss et al., 2004). In addition to economic rewards, one's work is a highly salient role identity for many people. The meaning the individual attaches to work influences its importance to psychological well-being (Simon, 1997). The impact of unemployment is greater on men than on women, probably because the work role identity is more salient for men.

In some instances, the stress associated with unemployment leads to violence. Each year, there are incidents in which a fired employee returns to the workplace with guns or rifles, often seeking the person(s) believed responsible for their being fired. By one estimate, nearly 2 million Americans experience workplace violence each year (OSHA, 2002). These incidents can lead to injuries and deaths, and to suicide by the former employee.

**Gender Roles.** Adult women in the United States have somewhat poorer mental health than men. On measures of distress, women attain significantly higher scores than men. For example, Macintyre, Hunt, and Sweeting (1996) found that women report greater malaise (sleep problems, difficulty concentrating, worry, and fatigue) than men at all ages. Are women under greater stress? Or are they more likely to report symptoms of distress than men? One study assessed the frequency of experiencing emotions such as anger, sadness, and happiness and the levels of distress in men and women (Mirowsky & Ross, 1995). The results indicated that women expressed emotions more freely than men, but this did not fully account for the differences in stress scores. Overall, women experienced stress about 30 percent more often than men.

In an attempt to identify sources of chronic stress in women's lives, researchers asked female students, professionals, and mothers to write items representing stressful situations for women. A factor analysis yielded five factors, including fear of being unattractive, of victimization, and of failing to be nurturing (Watkins & Whaley, 2000). These sources of stress may be unique to women.

There also may be a gender difference in how people respond to stress. Whereas men experiencing high stress report higher rates of substance use and abuse, women experiencing high stress report higher rates of impaired psychological functioning. In a survey of 3,131 adults, stress was measured by the number of life events experienced by the person, or by someone close to them, in the prior 6 months. Respondents were also asked questions about participation in various behaviors and psychological functioning. Men experiencing stress were more likely to report alcohol or drug use or dependence, whereas women experiencing stress reported increased anxiety and emotional disorders (Armeli, et al., 2000).

**Marital Roles.** Just as married men and women are physically healthier than people who are not married, they are characterized by greater psychological well-being and less depression than single, separated, divorced, or widowed persons (Ross et al., 1990). Again, it appears that it is the presence of another adult in the residence—rather than being married per se—that is associated with being healthy.

Of course, it might be that people who have higher levels of well-being are more likely to marry or cohabit, whereas persons with lower levels remain single. A longitudinal study of 18- to 24-year-old men and women, some of whom married whereas others remained single, found that marriage did improve

well-being (Horowitz, White, & Howell-White, 1996). Another study with data from a national sample compared persons who were stably married with those who experienced separation or divorce. Persons who experienced a loss reported increased symptoms on the CES-D (see Box 17.2); the effect was greater on persons who believed marriage should be a lifelong commitment (Simon & Marcussen, 1999).

The greater well-being of married persons reflects the beneficial effects of social support. A spouse can provide social support—care, advice, and aid in times of stress—and emotional support. Do husbands and wives share equally in receiving these benefits? Apparently not. Married men are characterized by better mental health than married women (Kurdek, 1991).

A study of a representative sample of more than 13,000 adults assessed the relationship between roles and mental health in four ethnic groups (Jackson, 1997). Occupying the spousal role was associated with greater well-being among Blacks, Mexican Americans, Puerto Ricans, and non-Hispanic Whites. Occupying other family roles, especially sibling, was related to better mental health in all groups except Puerto Ricans.

Some researchers focus on the interrelations of work and family roles. Of particular interest is work/family conflict—the extent to which the demands associated with one role are incompatible with the other. One common circumstance is **spillover**, in which the stress experienced at work or in the family is carried into the other domain (Bolger, DeLongis, Kessler, & Wethington, 1989). A study of air traffic controllers and their wives documented the impact of work stress on marital interaction (Repetti, 1989). As the controllers' daily workload increased (larger number of planes handled, poorer visibility), wives reported that the men were more withdrawn at home. A longitudinal study of 166 married couples obtained completed diaries from both

## BOX 17.3  The Impact of Large-scale Traumas on Psychological Functioning

On July 20, 2012, about 12:30 a.m., a young man dressed in tactical clothing entered a crowded movie theater in Aurora, Colorado. He activated two canisters which released gas and smoke, and then started firing in turn a shotgun, a semi-automatic weapon, and a handgun. The shooting lasted two minutes, and resulted in 12 deaths and 70 injuries.

The research summarized in this chapter indicates that relatively common, "everyday" stressors such as moving, starting a new job, changes in relationships, and conflict with family or coworkers affect individuals' physical and mental health, in some cases seriously. Occasionally, a large group or a population experiences extreme situations—events that Dohrenwend (2000) terms *fateful*. **Fateful events** share several characteristics: they are beyond the individual's control, unpredictable, often life-threatening, and often large in magnitude, and they disrupt people's usual activities. Such events have consequences far beyond those of everyday stressors. The Aurora theater shooting affected several hundred people directly and hundreds of others indirectly. There are the immediate stresses of death and injury, and impacts on family, friends, and coworkers. Because the event and its consequences were uncontrollable, thousands of people in the community experienced fear, anger, and rage that could not be channeled into effective action.

A wide variety of responses are seen in adults following such traumatic events. In addition to the emotions just listed, they include disbelief, irritability, anxiety, depression, sleep disturbances, and increases in alcohol and other substance use. For most individuals, these acute traumatic stress symptoms resolve over time. For some, however, the intensity and duration of the symptoms justify the diagnosis of posttraumatic stress disorder (PTSD) (Norwood, Ursano, & Fullerton, 2002).

The most researched such event in the United States was the terrorist attacks on September 11, 2001, on the World Trade Center and the Pentagon. More than 2,800 people were killed, affecting hundreds of workplaces and thousands of families. There was the immediate stress of the deaths and destruction, the continuing stress for persons in New York and Washington due to the disruption of their lives, and the continuing stress for most Americans due to the uncertainty about further attacks.

Excellent data on the impact of the terrorist attacks come from the longitudinal National Tragedy Survey conducted by the National Opinion Research Center (NORC) at the University of Chicago (Rasinski, Berktold, Smith, & Albertson, 2002). Two weeks after the attacks, a probability sample of 1,013 Americans and a probability sample of 406 residents of New York City were interviewed. Four to six months later, in January to March 2002, re-interviews were completed with 805 Americans (79 percent of the original sample) and 296 residents of New York City (73 percent).

To begin, consider national pride. One goal of the terrorist attacks was to demoralize the American population. However, measures of pride taken 2 weeks after September 11 either remained the same or increased compared to previous NORC surveys. For example, 97 percent of those surveyed said they would rather be a citizen of America than of any other country. On the other hand, confidence in major institutions, including the executive branch, Congress, and banks and financial institutions, fell by 7 to 13 percent; the exception was confidence in the U.S. military, which remained at pre-attack levels (81 percent).

The interview included questions assessing the experience of stress. In the first survey, respondents were asked which of 15 symptoms they had experienced following the attacks. Nine symptoms were reported by 20 percent or more of the national sample; the five most common were crying (60.3 percent), trouble sleeping (51.2 percent), feeling nervous or tense (49.9 percent), feeling dazed and numb (45.7 percent), and feeling more tired than usual (37.5 percent). In the sample of New York City residents, 12 symptoms were reported by 20 percent or more; the five most common were crying (74.1 percent), feeling nervous or tense (62.5 percent), trouble sleeping (59.4 percent), feeling more tired than usual (47.6 percent), and not feeling like eating (46.4 percent). Not surprisingly, New York City residents were somewhat more likely to report specific symptoms. Clearly, the impact of the attacks was substantial, measured by the numbers who experienced symptoms of stress.

At the re-interview 4 to 6 months later, reports of symptoms experienced in the past 2 weeks were generally lower than in the initial survey. In the national sample, the numbers reporting crying declined 40 percent, those reporting trouble sleeping declined 20 percent, feeling tense and nervous 22 percent, and feeling dazed and numb 33 percent. Comparable declines were observed in the reports of New York City residents. These longitudinal results indicate a trend toward recovery—that is, reduced incidence of stress. Declines were greatest among those who reported that they knew someone who had been hurt or killed in the attacks. African Americans, on the average, reported fewer symptoms in September, but showed little decline in the follow-up interviews. Slower recovery was also observed in persons with less than a high school education and with family incomes less than $40,000 per year. The follow-up interview included a standard measure of PTSD. Among the New York City residents, 15 percent scored in the range indicative of the disorder. In the national sample, the percentage scoring in this range was 8 percent. The highest PTSD scores were observed among those with poor general health, less education, and less income.

These results suggest that those of vulnerable social status have more or longer-lasting adverse reactions to fateful events. Research on a broad variety of disasters, including natural disasters such as earthquakes (Seplaki, Goldman, Weinstein, & Lin, 2003) and hurricanes, finds that persons of low SES in that society (whether the country is rich or poor), people who are socially isolated, and people who are directly affected by the disaster report higher levels of depressive symptoms. Several hypotheses have been offered to account for the increased vulnerability of low-SES persons. First, such persons may be more likely to have suffered as a result of the event due to poor housing or inadequate public services. Second, economic assets and education can enhance recovery because the individual has access to resources. Third, persons who are of low SES may also be socially isolated, lacking the social support that family and friends can provide. According to one observer, "disasters most often exacerbate social inequality" (de Waal, 2006).

In response to the rise in reports of symptoms and of widespread PTSD after traumatic events, debriefing has become standard clinical practice. Debriefing involves group sessions in which those affected by a fateful event are encouraged to process their emotional reactions. Following many traumatic events, such as 9/11 and the Northern Illinois University shooting (February, 2008), large numbers of persons have participated in debriefings. Do they help persons cope with traumatic events? An expert panel assembled by the National Institute of Mental Health (2002), having reviewed the empirical evidence, concludes that early interventions such as debriefing do not reduce the risk of later or continuing disorder. Research, such as the surveys following the 9/11 attacks, shows that most people are resilient; relying on their own resources, social support networks, and community services, they will recover (van Emmerik, Kamphuis, Hulsbosch, & Emmelkamp, 2002). Psychological services should be available for those whose personal resources are not sufficient or who do not recover on their own.

partners for either 28 or 42 consecutive days. Each person reported on stressors at work (too much to do, arguments with coworkers) and at home (too much to do, arguments with spouse, arguments with child). For both husbands and wives, increased stress at work was associated with increased stress at home (Bolger et al., 1989).

Stress associated with marital roles can influence work role performance. The research by Bolger and colleagues (1989) also found that for husbands, increased stress at home was associated with increased stress at work. Forthofer, Markman, Cox, Stanley, and Kessler (1996) analyzed data from a study of 8,098 persons aged 15 to 54; they focused on 1,431 employed married men and 1,138 employed married women. The results indicated that problems within the marriage were related to the number of days the person was "unable to function" in the preceding month among both men and women.

If marital strains can lead to reduced performance at work, can positive experiences at home enhance work experience? Two studies suggest that the answer is yes. Barnett (1994) studied 300 full-time employed women in dual-earner couples. Positive experiences in the roles of partner or parent buffered the effects of negative job experiences on distress. A longitudinal study found that increases/decreases in marital satisfaction are related to increases/decreases in work satisfaction among employed men and women, but not the reverse (Rogers & May, 2003).

Work/family conflict can affect the quality of the marital relationship by influencing the couple's interaction. Research demonstrated that, and the resulting distress affects two dimensions of marital interaction: hostility and warmth. As distress increases, both the person and the spouse report greater hostility and less warmth (Matthews, Conger, & Wickrama, 1996). Work/family conflict also is related to alcohol consumption. A study of employed adults aged 35 to 65 found that higher levels of marital disagreement (regarding spending money or household tasks) and stress at work (too much to do, conflicting demands) were each related to reports of problem drinking. Positive spillover from family (talking at home, expressions of love) to work was associated with less frequent reports of problem drinking; interestingly, both positive and negative spillover from work to family were associated with greater problem drinking (Grzywacz & Marks, 2000).

Another type of spillover involves the worker using behavior patterns acquired or reinforced at work in interactions with family members. This possibility was explored in a study that linked occupational conditions to the use of violence by a man against his female partner. The results showed that men in violent (for example, law enforcement) and dangerous (for example, construction) occupations were more likely to engage in violence directed at the partner (Melzer, 2002). This may reflect a spillover of the stress associated with these occupations, or the violence-supportive attitudes learned on the job.

How do people cope with work/family conflict? They use one or more of several strategies. In one study, wives reported the use of planning and cognitive restructuring—changing their definition of the situation—for example, deciding the house does not need to be cleaned every week. Husbands reported restructuring and withdrawing from interaction (Padden & Buehler, 1995). In a study of 221 managers, both men and women reported the use of prioritizing, reducing their personal standards (restructuring), asking others for help, and ending involvement in one or more roles (for example, resigning from community organizations) (Kirchmeyer, 1993).

Thus, the relationships among occupational, gender, and marital roles and psychological well-being are complex (Ross et al., 1990). The demands of work roles may lead to distress; this is especially likely when work demands are high and not under the person's control. Economic hardship and unemployment cause distress. Men typically have somewhat better mental health than women, in part because men react to stress by drug and alcohol use, whereas women react psychologically. Married men report greater well-being than married women, apparently because wives are more likely to experience family-related strains (Mennino, Rubin, & Brayfield, 2005). Stresses experienced at work can spill over and affect marital relationships; conversely, strain at home can produce losses at work. In any case, the social roles one occupies are major influences on mental health.

**Minority Status.** A daily hassle experienced frequently by many residents of the United States is discrimination. *Microaggressions*, acts of disregarding the person based on biased beliefs, are experienced often, and require management of anger and emotional upset. These are common experiences for members of racial and ethnic minorities. An inability to successfully resolve these issues causes race-related stress (Franklin, Boyd-Franklin, & Kelly, 2006). It is not surprising, therefore, that a study of 6,082 African Americans, Caribbean Blacks, and Whites found that African Americans and Caribbean Blacks have substantially higher rates of chronic major depressive disorder, and are more likely to report that it is severe and disabling (Williams et al., 2007). Microaggressions are also experienced by LGB persons and especially by trans people.

**Social Networks.** Up to this point, we have reviewed evidence showing that our relationships with others—that is, our membership in social networks—can be major sources of stress. At the same time, social networks can serve as an important resource in coping with stress (Wellman & Worley, 1990).

First, a network of close friends and kin eases the impact of stressful events by providing various types of support (Cooke, Rossmann, McCubbin, & Patterson, 1988; House, 1981). One type is emotional support—letting us know that they care for and are concerned about us. Emotional support is an important buffer for negative psychological states like depression (Harlow & Cantor, 1995). A second type is esteem support—providing us with positive feedback about our abilities and worth as a person. A poor grade, for example, is less stressful if our friends let us know they think we are good students. Informational support from others prepares us to avoid problems or to handle them when they arise. Advice from friends on how to handle job interviews, for example, improves our ability to cope with this situation. Finally, network members provide each other with instrumental support—money, labor, and time. Research shows that people who report poor well-being tend to seek out others who can provide the type of support they need (Harlow & Cantor, 1995).

The presence or absence of support is a major determinant of the impact of a stressful life event. A study of 882 women seeking an abortion obtained longitudinal data from 615 of them. Before the abortion, each woman rated the degree to which she received positive (expressed concern, offered help) and negative (argued, criticized) support from her partner, mother, and friends. Perceptions of positive support from each source were associated with greater well-being following the abortion (Major et al., 1997).

Research has documented the impact of supportive relationships on the individual's ability to cope with stress. A longitudinal study of a representative sample of 900 adults focused on the relationship between social network membership and physical health (Seeman, Seeman, & Sayles, 1985). Persons who reported in the initial interview that they had instrumental support available (that is, persons who, when ill, had others who would call, express concern, and offer help) were in better physical health one year later. Another longitudinal study assessed the impact of family support on mental health (Aldwin & Revenson, 1987). The sample consisted of 245 men and 248 women from randomly selected families in an urban area. The availability of support from one's family at the time of the initial survey was associated with better psychological adjustment one year later. Other research indicates that individuals with family support are more likely to cope with stressful events by using active strategies rather than avoidance or withdrawal strategies (Holahan & Moos, 1990). A longitudinal study of the relation between coping strategies and mental health found that people who used active strategies at the time of the initial survey reported fewer psychological symptoms on the second survey (Aldwin & Revenson, 1987). Finally, using active behavioral coping strategies is associated with shorter duration of several types of stressful events (Harnish, Aseltine, & Gore, 2000).

A second way in which social networks reduce stress is by teaching us strategies for coping with stressful events or crises when they occur. When members of a group are all subjected to similar stressors, the group may develop coping strategies. A study of interns and residents in a hospital found that they were subjected to long hours of demanding work in often poor facilities (Mizrahi, 1984). These physicians coped with stress by minimizing the time spent with each patient, by limiting interaction with patients to "relevant topics," and by treating patients as nonpersons—for example, by focusing exclusively on their illness. These strategies were passed on from experienced group members to new ones.

Several types of relationships can provide support, including primary kin (parents, siblings, and adult children), secondary kin, and friends and neighbors. The kind of support provided depends on the type of relationship.

Persons to whom we have strong ties provide emotional support and companionship. Primary kin provide us with financial aid and services, whereas friends and neighbors give us services and emotional support (Wellman & Worley, 1990). Research indicates that, among Blacks, kin primarily provide services such as transportation and child care, whereas among Whites, kin are more likely to provide financial support; however, the data suggest that this difference may have more to do with social class than with race (Sarkisian & Gerstel, 2004). Also, Black women are more likely to engage in reciprocal exchanges of services, and White women to engage in reciprocal exchanges of emotional support. Research on provision of support among low-income families suggests that these exchanges of services provide an important resource for coping with daily demands (Henley, Danziger, & Offer, 2005).

There is evidence that neighborhood disadvantage is associated with poorer mental health among residents. These are neighborhoods characterized by poor access to health services, transportation, quality housing, jobs, and desirable partners. There may also be significant rates of crime and violence. These conditions may create chronic stress in residents, leading to depressive symptoms and fearful anxiety (Hill, Ross, & Angel, 2005). These, in turn, create distress, which negatively affects health. Supportive social networks, close relationships with nearby kin and neighbors, mediate the relationship between neighborhoods and symptoms by providing emotional support and services, reducing depressive symptoms (Haines, Beggs, & Hurlbert, 2011).

Recognizing the significance of supportive relationships, an innovative approach—social network mapping—is being used to assess the support available to organ transplant recipients (Lewis et al., 2000). The map both increases the person's awareness of the resources available and enables health professionals and social workers to work with the person more effectively.

Family members help us to cope with stressful events, such as the death of a relative or a close friend. They are an important source of emotional support and may help by temporarily taking over some of our role obligations. © Rubberball/iStock

**Social Class.** The lower a person's socioeconomic status, the greater the amount of stress reported (Mirowsky & Ross, 1986). According to data from interviews with a representative sample of U.S. adults, 8.7 percent of persons with incomes below the federal poverty level, 5.1 percent of those with incomes 100 percent above it, and 1.2 percent of those earning 400 percent or more above it are characterized by serious psychological distress (Weissman, Pratt, Miller, & Parker, 2015). Education, occupation, and income are the principal measures of socioeconomic status. An analysis of data from surveys of eight quite diverse samples (Kessler, 1982) shows that each contributes separately to stress. The relative importance of these three components as sources of stress is different for men and women. For men, income appears most important; for women (employed or not), education appears to be the most important component. Occupational attainment is the least important determinant of stress for both genders.

How does education affect stress? Research shows that people who are well educated have lower levels of distress, primarily because of paid work and financial resources (Ross & Van Willigen, 1997). The evidence suggests that the relationship between social class and health also reflects lifestyle differences; persons higher in socioeconomic status are more likely to have a healthy diet, exercise regularly, and get adequate sleep, and less likely to smoke (Mulatu & Schooler, 2002).

In the United States, a large percentage of the lower class are Black. As a result, one might expect Blacks to have poorer mental health than Whites. However, the results of research comparing the psychological functioning of Blacks and Whites are inconsistent; whereas some studies find higher average symptom scores among Blacks, others do not (Vega & Rumbaut, 1991).

Further analyses have sought to identify the causes of the negative relationship between social status and stress. Are lower-class persons exposed to greater stress, or are they simply less able to cope effectively with stressful events? The answer is, both (Kessler & Cleary, 1980). On the one hand, lower-class persons are more likely to experience *economic hardship*—not having enough money to provide adequate food, clothing, and medical care (Pearlin & Radabaugh, 1976). They also experience higher rates of a variety of physical illnesses (Syme & Berkman, 1976).

Both economic hardship and illness increase the stress that an individual experiences. Furthermore, persons who are low in income, education, and occupational attainment lack the resources that would enable them to cope with these stresses effectively. Low income reduces their ability to cope with illness. Moreover, low-status persons are less likely to have a sense of control over their environment, and they have less access to political power or influence. For this reason, they are less likely to attempt to change stressful conditions or events.

Resilience to economic adversity—that is, no increase in distress scores in response to hardship—is provided by several resources. A longitudinal study of 558 rural youths and their families began when the youths were in seventh grade. Resilience among the parents was associated with marital support, effective problem-solving skills, and a sense of mastery. Resilience among the youths was promoted by nurturance (support) by parents and support by older siblings (providing warmth, not drinking alcohol) and friends (Conger & Conger, 2002).

If stress increases as socioeconomic status decreases, we would expect persons lower in status to have poorer mental health. Research over the past 60 years has consistently confirmed this expectation; there is a strong correlation between social class and serious mental disorders (Eaton, 1980). This correlation has been found in studies conducted in numerous countries (Dohrenwend & Dohrenwend, 1974). In general, persons in the lowest socioeconomic class have the highest rates of mental illness (Hudson, 2005).

The differences by social class in rates of mental disorders are due in part to differences in stress. Persons in low-status occupations are more likely to experience lack of control over work. They may also experience economic uncertainty due to risk of layoff or seasonal variations in employment opportunities. This stress is likely to spill over into family interaction patterns, causing familial relations to become an added source of stress rather than a buffer. Research indicates that the shift from adequate to inadequate employment, involuntary part-time work, or low-wage jobs is associated with increased depression, and the shift to unemployment is related to even higher depression scores (Dooley, Prause, & Ham-Rowbottom, 2000). Unemployment is especially stressful, and rates of unemployment are highest among the least educated (U.S. Bureau of Labor Statistics, 2012). Finally, the members of the social networks of the least educated have fewer economic and emotional resources.

For a discussion of the relationships between stress/strain and deviant behavior, and how it varies by race and class, see Chapter 13.

## ALIENATION

Jim dragged himself out of bed and headed for the shower. As the water poured over him, he thought, "Thursday . . . another 10-hour shift . . . if the line doesn't shut down, I'll bolt 500 bumpers . . . sick of car frames . . . I'd rather do almost anything else . . . if only I'd finished high school . . . damn the money! . . . Let 'em take the job and shove it . . . but what else pays a guy who quit school $17.36 an hour?"

Jim is experiencing **alienation**—the sense that one is uninvolved in the social world or lacks control over it, a sense of separation or disconnect from one's social surroundings (Nair & Vohra, 2012). Several types of alienation have been identified (Seeman, 1975). Two will be discussed here: self-estrangement and powerlessness. An analysis of scales measuring alienation verified that these two dimensions are central ones (Lacourse, Villeneuve, & Claes, 2003).

### Self-Estrangement

Jim's hatred for his job reflects **self-estrangement**—the awareness that he is engaging in activities that are not rewarding in themselves. Work is an important part of one's waking hours. When work is meaningless, the individual perceives the self as devoting time and energy to something unrewarding—that is, something "alien." Whereas social background and individual characteristics have some influence, alienation from work is primarily determined by the occupational and organizational conditions of work (Mortimer & Lorence, 1995).

What makes a job intrinsically rewarding? Perhaps the most important feature is autonomy. Work that requires the individual to use judgment, exercise initiative, and surmount obstacles contributes to self-respect and a sense of mastery. A second feature is variety in the tasks that the person performs. Jim has no autonomy; his job does not allow him to exercise judgment or initiative. It also has no variety; it is monotonous and boring.

Four features of industrial technology produce self-estrangement. First, self-estrangement will be higher if the worker has no connection with the finished product itself. Second, it will be higher if the worker has no control over company policies. Third, it will be higher if the worker has little influence over the conditions of employment—over which days, which hours, or how long they work. Finally, it will be higher if the worker has no control over the work process—for example, the speed with which they must perform tasks (Blauner, 1964). Notice that alienation, like stress, is caused by lack of control over the conditions of work. Research indicates that persons from high SES backgrounds are more likely to experience alienation under these conditions (Nair & Vohra, 2012), probably because such environments are inconsistent with their values and skills (see earlier discussion of Occupational Roles).

These features are especially characteristic of assembly-line work, in which each person performs the same highly specialized task many times per day. Thus, workers on assembly lines should be more likely to experience self-estrangement than other workers. A study testing this hypothesis (Blauner, 1964) compared assembly-line workers in textile and automobile plants with skilled printers and chemical industry technicians. As expected, assembly-line workers were more alienated than skilled workers who had jobs that were more varied and involved the exercise of judgment and initiative.

Work in bureaucratic organizations—like large insurance companies or government agencies—may also produce self-estrangement. In many bureaucratic organizations, workers have little or no control over the work process and do not participate in organizational decision making. Thus, workers at the lowest levels of such organizations should experience self-estrangement or dissatisfaction with their work. Conversely, workers who are involved in decision making should be less alienated. A survey of 8,000 employees in 100 companies located in the United States or Japan found that workers involved in participatory decision-making structures had higher commitment to their work (Lincoln & Kalleberg, 1985). Such workers were willing to work harder and were proud to be employed by and wanted to remain with the company.

More generally, the extent to which workers are alienated depends on the system of production in which they work. Hodson (1996) identifies five systems: craft, where each worker produces a product; direct supervision; assembly line; bureaucratic; and participatory. A review of studies of all five types of workplaces reveals a U-shaped relationship between workers' attitudes and the system of production (see Figure 17.4). Both craft and participatory systems are associated with high job satisfaction and pride in one's work; direct supervision is the most alienating system. Results such as these have led many large firms, such as General Motors, to introduce participatory systems.

As noted earlier, individual characteristics do influence reactions to work (Mortimer & Lorence, 1995). Surveys indicate that job satisfaction and involvement are most stable among workers aged 30 to 45. Women are as committed to work as men, though they place greater emphasis on the quality of interpersonal relations in the workplace. Among those holding comparable jobs, Blacks are as committed as Whites to their jobs and employers.

According to the theory developed more than a century ago by Karl Marx (Bottomore, 1964), whether a person will experience self-estrangement is determined by their relation to the means of production. The most alienated employees are hypothesized to be those who have no autonomy, who do not have the freedom to solve nonroutine problems, and who

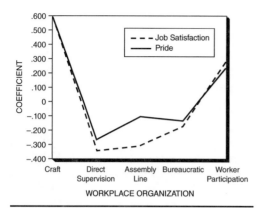

**FIGURE 17.4** Systems of Production and Alienation from Work

The way in which work is organized, or the system of production, is a major influence on people's attitudes toward their work. Historically, five different systems of production have been used: craft, where each worker has considerable autonomy; direct supervision, where another person monitors one's work; assembly line, where the work activity is determined by the organization and speed of the line; bureaucratic, where many aspects of work are governed by impersonal rules; and participatory organization, where teams of managers and workers make decisions.

A review of the research literature suggests that the pride workers have in their work and their job satisfaction vary depending on the system in which they work. The graph displays these variations, indicating that although participative systems are less alienating than the assembly lines and bureaucratic forms they replaced, they are not as satisfying as the craft system of production.

*Source:* Hodson, "Dignity in the Workplace under Participative Management," *American Sociological Review*, 61(5), 730 (1996). Used with permission of the American Sociological Association.

have no subordinates. Marx referred to such workers as the *proletariat*. In contemporary society, assembly-line workers, sales clerks, file clerks, and laborers are all in occupations that have these characteristics. A survey of 1,499 working adults found that 46 percent were in jobs of this type (Wright et al., 1982). Several studies have found that men whose jobs are characterized by lack of autonomy and complexity typically have high scores on measures of self-estrangement (Kohn, 1976) and low

scores on measures of job involvement (Lorence & Mortimer, 1985).

There is some evidence that the characteristics of the work environment influence psychological well-being. One researcher assessed the common environment of office workers by averaging the ratings of all of those employed in each of 37 branch offices; each worker's own ratings were used as a measure of their immediate environment (Repetti, 1987). Workers who rated their branches more positively (on interpersonal climate and support and respect from coworkers) reported lower levels of anxiety and depression. Aggregate ratings by the workers of the environment in the branch were also related to anxiety and depression scores.

**Powerlessness**

Consider the facts that vandalism is widespread in certain sections of large cities, that many adults do not vote in presidential elections, and that some people on welfare make no effort to find a job. These facts all have something in common. They reflect, at least in part, people's sense of **powerlessness**—the sense of having little or no control over events.

Powerlessness is a generalized orientation toward the social world. People who feel powerless believe they have no influence on political affairs and world events; this is different from feeling a lack of control over events in day-to-day life. A typical measure of powerlessness includes items like "This world is run by a few people in power and there is not much the little guy can do about it." Agreement with such statements indicates powerlessness. Most people's scores on measures of powerlessness are quite stable over a period of many years (Neal & Groat, 1974). There is some evidence that a sense of powerlessness develops during childhood (Seeman, 1975). Research with a sample of high school students identified powerlessness as a significant factor in alienation in adolescence (Lacourse

The graffiti gracing walls and buildings in American cities are responses to alienation. Spray-painted messages, sometimes including the painter's initials, reflect the lack of control over their lives that many youth feel.
© stevegeer/iStock

et al., 2003). Interestingly, a sense of powerlessness is not associated with social class—that is, income, occupation, or education.

Statements that measure powerlessness, such as "People like me have no say" and "Politicians don't care what I think," were included in several surveys between 1952 and 1980. Analysis of patterns of agreement with these items shows that powerlessness or political alienation declined from 1952 to 1960, rose steadily from 1960 to 1976, and then declined (Rahn & Mason, 1987). The increase in the 1960s and 1970s was associated with increased concern about such political and social issues as civil rights for Blacks, the war in Vietnam, and the Watergate political scandal. Thus, fluctuations in powerlessness reflect, at least in part, events in the larger society.

Although the sense of powerlessness is found in all classes, upper and lower classes may have different means of expressing it. Middle-class and upper-class persons may be more likely to stay home on election day or to feel apathetic about political affairs or organizations that influence public policy. Lower-class persons may be more likely to have a hostile attitude toward city officials and to vandalize city buses, subway trains, and businesses in their neighborhoods. Thus, how an individual expresses frustration over their lack of influence on the world may depend on their social position.

## SUMMARY

This chapter considers the impact of social structure on four areas of a person's life: achievement, values, physical and mental health, and sense of belonging in society. Social structure influences the individual through the expectations associated with one's roles, the social networks to which one belongs, and the status associated with one's positions.

**Status Attainment.** An individual's status determines their access to resources—money, lifestyle, and influence over others. Three generalizations can be made about status in the United States. (1) An individual's status is closely tied to their occupation. (2) Occupational attainment is influenced directly by the individual's educational level and ability and indirectly by socioeconomic background. Among women, occupational status and earnings are limited by gender segregation. (3) Information about job opportunities is often obtained via social networks, especially those characterized by weak ties.

**Individual Values.** Two aspects of the individual's position in society influence their values (1) Particular values are reliably associated with certain occupational role characteristics. Men and women whose jobs are closely supervised, routine, and not complex value conformity whereas those whose jobs are less closely supervised, less routine, and more complex value self-direction. (2) Higher education is associated with placing greater value on self-direction and with greater intellectual flexibility.

**Social Influences on Health.** Physical health is influenced by occupation, gender, marital roles, and social class. (1) Occupational roles determine the health hazards to which individuals are exposed and whether they experience role overload. (2) The traditional role expectations for men and women make men more vulnerable than women to illnesses such as coronary heart disease. (3) Long-term committed relationships protect both men and women from illness and premature death. (4) Members of lower-status groups and Blacks experience higher rates of illness, disability, and premature death.

Mental health is also influenced by social factors. (1) Economic hardship, uncertainty, and unemployment are associated with poor mental health. (2) Women have somewhat poorer mental health than men. (3) Long-term committed relationships are associated with reduced stress for both men and women. Working adults may experience spillover of stress from work into family relationships. (4) Social networks are an important resource in coping with stress; they provide the person with emotional, esteem, and informational support, as well as instrumental aid. (5) Lower-class persons report greater stress and experience a higher incidence of mental illness.

**Alienation.** Two types of alienation are self-estrangement and powerlessness. (1) Self-estrangement is associated with work roles that do not allow workers a sense of autonomy, such as assembly-line jobs. (2) Powerlessness is a generalized sense that one has little or no control over the world.

### Critical Thinking Skill:
### Thinking as Hypothesis Testing

In everyday life, we function like intuitive scientists. Events occur and we want to explain and perhaps control them. To do that, we use the same skills as a scientist testing a hypothesis: (1) we accumulate observations; (2) we formulate hypotheses or explanations; (3) we use the information to see if it confirms or disconfirms the hypothesis.

A common experience for many people today is stress—feeling tense, anxious, overworked. Stress may result in depressed mood, feeling overwhelmed and unhappy with life. When we experience stress, we usually want to reduce it or escape from it. To do that successfully, we need to determine the source of the stress. The research summarized in this chapter identifies several sources of stress in contemporary life. Your stress may reflect economic hardship, being overworked at school or work (which can spill over at home), problems in an intimate relationship, or lack of a supportive social network. Obviously, to cope with stress effectively requires identifying the source(s) of it. Often, we look around and focus on the most obvious or most recent person or event. If you have a partner, that person is perhaps the most obvious, especially if you have been fighting. But your fights may be a result of economic hardship, your overload at work, or stresses at school, not problems with the relationship. In fact, breaking up with your partner will probably add to your stress rather than reduce it.

A better strategy is to think like a scientist. Accumulate some observations. In what situation(s) do you feel more stress—at work, at home? When do you feel most stressed—during the week, on the weekend, when you pay the bills? Does the stress fluctuate from week to week? If so, is that associated with the deadlines at work, or arguments with a superior, or your partner, or visits with family? If you observe systematically, you will hopefully identify some patterns that suggest a hypothesis. Suppose you observe that the stress is greatest when you pay bills, when there is an unexpected expense, when your partner asks for extra money. That suggests economic hardship, not your partner,

as the source. Collect some data over the next several weeks. Note each time you feel stress and the events that occurred recently. This process will take some time. You might want to keep some notes.

If your observations verify the hypothesis, you can turn to the question of how to cope with the problem. If you think it is economic hardship, there are two general strategies you can use: increase your income, or decrease your expenses. There are several ways to implement each strategy. You could increase income by taking a second or third job. Note, however, that this will add to your stress unless you cut back on school, work, or time spent with your partner or friends or family. You could borrow money, or take out a loan. Or you could reduce your expenses. Sometimes it is relatively easy. Three Starbucks per day cost on average $9.75; three coffees from McDonald's cost $4.47. Maybe you can rent videos from your cable company instead of going to the theater. If you are in a relationship, you will want to communicate with your partner about your observations and choices of strategy. If you adopt a strategy and the hypothesis is correct, your stress should gradually decline. If the stress doesn't decline, like a scientist, you need to start over again and develop a new hypothesis.

# A

**Accommodation** A constructive response to a potentially destructive act by a partner in a romantic relationship. (Ch. 14)

**Accounts** Explanations people offer after they have performed acts that threaten their identities. Accounts take two forms—excuses that minimize one's responsibility and justifications that redefine acts in a more socially acceptable manner. (Ch. 5)

**Action units** A configuration of facial muscles or a discernible movement originating from them. (Ch. 6)

**Actor-observer difference** The bias in attribution whereby actors tend to see their own behavior as due to characteristics of the external situation, whereas observers tend to attribute actors' behavior to the actors' internal, personal characteristics. (Ch. 7)

**Affect** A subjective positive or negative evaluation of an object, which can vary in direction, intensity, and activity. (Ch. 6)

**Affect theory of social exchange** A theory that focuses on the genesis of emotion during social exchange and the cognitive and behavioral effects of that emotion. (Ch. 16)

**Affective aggression** Aggression resulting from aversive affect (negative emotion that people seek to reduce or eliminate). More common among persons who believe that acting aggressively will make them feel better. (Ch. 12)

**Aggravated assault** An attack by one person on another with the intent of causing bodily injury. (Ch. 12)

**Aggression** Behavior that is intended to harm another person and that the other wants to avoid. (Ch. 12)

**Aggressive pornography** Explicit depiction—in film, video, photograph, or story—of sexual activity in which force is threatened or used to coerce a person to engage in sex. *See also* Nonaggressive pornography. (Ch. 12)

**Alienation** The sense that one is uninvolved in the social world or lacks control over it. (Ch. 17)

**Aligning actions** Actions people use to define their apparently questionable conduct as actually in line with cultural norms, thereby repairing identities, restoring meaning to situations, and reestablishing smooth interaction. (Ch. 5)

**Altercasting** Tactics we use to impose roles and identities on others that produce outcomes to our advantage. (Ch. 5)

**Altruism** Actions performed voluntarily with the intention of helping someone else that entail no expectation of receiving a reward or benefit in return (except possibly an internal feeling of having done a good deed for someone). (Ch. 11)

**Anomie theory** The theory that deviant behavior arises when people striving to achieve culturally valued goals find they do not have access to the legitimate means of attaining these goals. (Ch. 13)

**Archival research** A research method that involves the acquisition and analysis (or reanalysis) of existing information collected by others. (Ch. 2)

**Attachment** A warm, close relationship with an adult who provides an infant with a sense of security and stimulation. (Ch. 3)

**Attitude** A predisposition to respond to a particular object in a generally favorable or unfavorable way. (Ch. 8)

**Attitude change** A change in a person's attitudes about some issue, person, or situation. (Ch. 10)

**Attitude inoculation** A process that helps a target person to resist persuasion attempts by exposing them to a weak version of the arguments. (Ch. 10)

**Attitudinal similarity** The sharing by two people of beliefs, opinions, likes, and dislikes. (Ch. 14)

**Attractiveness stereotype** The belief that "what is beautiful is good"; the assumption that an attractive person possesses other desirable qualities. (Ch. 14)

**Attribution** The process by which people make inferences about the causes of behavior or attitudes. (Ch. 7)

**Authority** The capacity of one group member to issue orders to others—that is, to direct or regulate the behavior of other members by invoking rights that are vested in their role. (Ch. 10)

**Availables** Those persons with whom we come into contact and who constitute the pool of potential friends and lovers. (Ch. 14)

**Aversive affect** Negative emotion that people seek to reduce or eliminate. (Ch. 12)

**Aversive event** In intergroup relations, a situation or event caused by or attributed to an outside group that produces negative or undesirable outcomes for members of the target group. (Ch. 15)

# B

**Back-channel feedback** The small vocal and visual comments a listener makes while a speaker is talking, without taking over the speaking turn. This includes responses such as "Yeah," "Huh?" "M-hmn," head nods, brief smiles, and completions of the speaker's words. Back-channel feedback is crucial to coordinate conversation smoothly. (Ch. 9)

**Back regions** A setting used to manage appearances. In back regions, people allow themselves to violate appearances while they prepare, rehearse, and rehash performances. Contrasts with front regions, where people carry out interaction performances and exert efforts to maintain appropriate appearances. (Ch. 5)

**Balance theory** A theory concerning the determinants of consistency in three-element cognitive systems. (Ch. 8)

**Belief perseverance** A tendency to continue to view an initial assumption as correct despite evidence to the contradictory. (Ch. 7)

**Birth cohort** A group of people who were born during the same period of one or several years and who are, therefore, all exposed to particular historical events at approximately the same age. (Ch. 3)

**Body language (kinesics)** Communication through the silent motion of body parts—scowls, smiles, nods, gazes, gestures, leg movements, postural shifts, and so on. Because body language entails movement, it is also known as *kinesics*. (Ch. 9)

**Borderwork** Interaction across gender boundaries that is based on and strengthens such boundaries. (Ch. 3)

**Bystander effect** The tendency for bystanders in an emergency to help less often and less quickly as the number of bystanders present increases. (Ch. 11)

**Bystander intervention** In an emergency situation, a quick response by a person witnessing the emergency to help another who is endangered by events. (Ch. 11)

# C

**Career** A sequence of roles—each role with its own set of activities—that a person enacts during their lifetime. People's most important careers are in the domains of family and friends, education, and work. (Ch. 3)

**Categorization** The tendency to perceive stimuli as members of groups or classes rather than as isolated entities; the act of encoding stimuli as members of classes. (Ch. 7)

**Catharsis** The reduction of aggressive arousal by means of performing aggressive acts. The catharsis hypothesis states that we can purge ourselves of hostile emotions by intensely experiencing these emotions while performing aggression. (Ch. 12)

**Cautious shift** In group decision making, the tendency for decisions made in groups after discussion to be more cautious (less risky) than decisions made by individual members prior to discussion. *See also* Risky shift. (Ch.16)

**Cognitions** An element of cognitive structure. Cognitions include attitudes, beliefs, and perceptions of behavior. (Ch. 8)

**Cognitive dissonance** A state of psychological tension induced by dissonant relationships between cognitive elements. (Ch. 8)

**Cognitive processes** The mental activities of an individual, including perception, memory, reasoning, problem solving, and decision making. (Ch. 1)

**Cognitive structure** Any form of organization among a person's concepts and beliefs. (Ch. 1)

**Cognitive theory** A theoretical perspective based on the premise that an individual's mental activities (perception, memory, and reasoning) are important determinants of behavior. (Ch. 1)

**Collective task** A task that requires group members to take into account the views of other group members to achieve a successful outcome. (Ch. 16)

**Collectivist cultures** Cultures that emphasize group over individual. The focus is on the interconnectedness of individuals, particularly the interdependent nature of their social relationships and identities. *See also* Individualist cultures. (Ch. 4)

**Communication** The process through which people transmit information about their ideas and feelings to one another. (Ch. 9)

**Communication accuracy** The extent to which the message inferred by a listener from a communication matches the message intended by the speaker. (Ch. 9)

**Communication-persuasion paradigm** A research paradigm that conceptualizes persuasion attempts in terms of source, message, target, channel, and impact—that is, who says what to whom by what medium with what effect. (Ch. 10)

**Communicator credibility** In persuasion, the extent to which the communicator is perceived by the target audience as a believable source of information. (Ch. 10)

**Comparison level (CL)** A standard used to evaluate the outcomes of a relationship, based on the average of the person's experience in past relevant relationships. (Ch. 14)

**Comparison level for alternatives (CLalt)** A standard specifying the lowest level of outcomes a person will accept in light of available alternatives; the level of profit available to an individual in their best alternative relationship. (Ch. 14)

**Complexity-extremity effect** The bias where less complex schemas lead to more extreme judgments and evaluations. (Ch. 7)

**Compliance** In social influence, adherence by the target to the source's requests or demands. Compliance may occur either with or without concomitant change in attitudes. (Ch. 10)

**Conditioning** A process of learning in which, if a person performs a particular response and if this response is then reinforced, the response is strengthened. (Chs. 1 and 16)

**Confirmation bias** The tendency to focus on information relevant to a belief and ignoring or downplaying information that is inconsistent with that belief. (Ch. 7)

**Conformity** Adherence by an individual to group norms so that behavior lies within the range of tolerable behavior. (Ch. 15)

**Content analysis** A research method that involves a systematic scrutiny of documents or messages to identify specific characteristics and then making inferences based on their occurrence. (Ch. 2)

**Contingencies (of self-esteem)** Characteristics of self or categories of outcomes on which a person stakes their self-esteem. (Ch. 4)

**Control theory** The theory that an individual's tendency to engage in deviant behavior is influenced by their ties to other persons. There are four components of such ties: attachment, commitment, involvement, and belief. (Ch. 13)

**Cooling-out** A response to repeated or glaring failures that gently persuades an offender to accept a less desirable though still reasonable alternative identity. (Ch. 5)

**Cooperative principle** The assumption conversationalists ordinarily make that a speaker is behaving cooperatively by trying to be (1) informative, (2) truthful, (3) relevant to the aims of the ongoing conversation, and (4) clear. (Ch. 9)

**Correspondence** The degree to which the action, context, target, and time in a measure of attitude is the same as those in a measure of behavior. (Ch. 8)

**Cultural routines** Recurrent and predictable activities that are basic to day-to-day social life. (Ch. 3)

# D

**Definition of the situation** In symbolic interaction theory, a person's interpretation or construal of a situation and the objects in it. An agreement among persons about who they are, what actions are appropriate in the setting, and what their behaviors mean. (Ch. 5)

**Dependent variable** In an experiment, the variable that is measured to determine whether it is affected by the manipulation of one or more other variables (independent variables). (Ch. 2)

**Deterrence hypothesis** The view that the arrest and punishment of some individuals for violation of laws deters other persons from committing the same violations. (Ch. 13)

**Deviant behavior** Behavior that violates the norms that apply in a given situation. (Ch. 13)

**Deviant subculture** A group of people whose norms encourage participation in a specific form of deviance and who regard positively those who engage in it. (Ch. 13)

**Differential association theory** The theory that deviant behavior occurs when people learn definitions favorable to the behavior through their associations with other persons. (Ch. 13)

**Differential susceptibility hypothesis** The belief that some people are genetically predisposed to be more susceptible to social influence and environmental conditions than others.

**Diffuse status characteristics** Social attribute of a person that influences evaluations and beliefs about that person's general competence. *See also* Specific status characteristics. (Ch. 16)

**Diffusion of responsibility** The process wherein a bystander does not take action (e.g., in an emergency situation) because there are other bystanders who share the responsibility for intervening. (Ch. 11)

**Disclaimer** A verbal assertion intended to ward off any negative implications of impending actions by defining these actions as irrelevant to one's established social identity. By using disclaimers, a person suggests that although the impending acts may ordinarily imply a negative identity, theirs is an extraordinary case. (Ch. 5)

**Discrepant message** In persuasion, a message advocating a position that is different from what the target believes. (Ch. 10)

**Discrimination** Overt acts, occurring without apparent justification, that treat members of certain out-groups in an unfair or disadvantageous manner. (Ch. 15)

**Displaced aggression** Aggression toward a target that exceeds what is justified by provocation by that target. Often occurs because aggression instigated by a different source is displaced onto a less powerful or more available target who had no responsibility for the negative response. (Ch. 12)

**Display rules** Cultural norms that dictate how we must modify our facial expressions to make them fit particular situations. (Ch. 6)

**Dispositional attribution** Attributing a behavior to the internal state(s) of the person who performed it rather than to factors in that person's environment. *See also* Situational attribution. (Ch. 7)

**Distributive justice principles** A criterion in terms of which group members can judge the fairness and appropriateness of the distribution of rewards. Three of the most important are the equality principle, the equity principle, and the relative needs principle. (Ch. 16)

**Dyadic withdrawal** The process of increasing reliance on one person for gratification and decreasing reliance on others. (Ch. 14)

# E

**Ebonics** A variety of American English spoken by many Blacks, with distinctive pronunciation of some words; African-American Vernacular English (AAVE). (Ch. 9)

**Egoism** Helping behavior motivated by a helper's own sense of self-gratification. (Ch. 11)

**Embarrassment** The feeling that people experience when interaction is disrupted because the identity they have claimed in an encounter is discredited. (Ch. 5)

**Emotion work** Efforts to change the intensity or quality of feelings to bring them into line with the requirements of the occasion. (Ch. 6)

**Emotional deviance** When individuals project an emotion that is inappropriate or too high or low in intensity for a particular situation. (Ch. 6)

**Emotional intelligence** One's ability to read, understand, and respond to others' emotional cues and behavior. (Ch. 6)

**Emotional labor** Emotion work that is done as an occupational requirement or expectation. (Ch. 6)

**Emotional socialization** Cultural forces influence emotions. For example, cultural values influence how children are socialized to experience and express emotions. (Ch. 6)

**Emotions** Short-lived reactions to a stimulus, a type of affect. The four components of an emotion are (1) a situational stimulus, (2) physiological changes, (3) expressive gesturing of some kind, and (4) a label to identify a cluster of the first three. (Ch. 6)

**Empathy** An emotional response to others as if we ourselves were in that person's situation; feeling pleasure at another's pleasure or pain at another's pain. (Ch. 11)

**Encoder-decoder model** A theory that views communication as a linear process in which the message is encoded by a transmitter, transmitted, and decoded by a receiver. (Ch. 9)

**Equitable relationships** A relationship in which the outcomes received by each person are equivalent. (Ch. 14)

**Equity** When people receive rewards in proportion to the contributions they make toward the attainment of group goals. (Ch. 1)

**Ethnocentrism** In intergroup relations, the tendency to regard one's own group as the center of everything and to evaluate other groups in reference to it; the tendency to regard one's in-group as superior to all out-groups. (Ch. 15)

**Evolutionary psychology** A theoretical perspective positing that predispositions toward some social behaviors are passed genetically from generation to generation and shaped by the process of natural selection. (Ch. 1)

**Experiment** A research method used to investigate cause-and-effect relations between one variable (the independent variable) and another (the dependent variable). In an experiment, the investigator manipulates the independent variable, randomly assigns participants to various levels of that variable, and measures the dependent variable. (Ch. 2)

**External validity** The extent to which it is possible to generalize the results of one study to other populations, settings, or times. (Ch. 2)

**Extraneous variable** A variable that is not explicitly included in a research hypothesis but has a causal impact on the dependent variable. (Ch. 2)

**Extrinsically motivated behavior** A behavior that results from the motivation to obtain a reward (food, praise) or avoid a punishment (spanking, criticism) controlled by someone else. (Ch. 3)

# F

**Facial feedback hypothesis** States that facial muscles not only reflect emotion, but can also influence the emotion we feel. (Ch. 6)

**Fateful events** Events that are beyond an individual's control, unpredictable, often life-threatening, often large in magnitude, and that disrupt people's usual activities. (Ch. 17)

**Feeling rules** Norms that dictate which emotions are appropriate for particular roles in a social context. (Ch. 6)

**Field study** An investigation that involves the collection of data about ongoing activity in everyday settings. (Ch. 2)

**Five-factor model** A psychological model that takes a wide variety of personality traits and organizes them into five factors, or categories. These factors and examples of associated traits are agreeableness (warmth, friendliness), conscientiousness (efficiency, dependability), extraversion (outgoingness, assertiveness), openness (curiosity, insight), and neuroticism (confidence, sensitivity). Also called the "Big Five." (Ch. 10)

**Focus-of-attention bias** The tendency to overestimate the causal impact of whomever or whatever we focus our attention on. (Ch. 7)

**Formal social controls** Agencies that are given responsibility for dealing with violations of rules or laws. (Ch. 13)

**Frame** A set of widely understood rules or conventions pertaining to a transient but repetitive social situation that indicate which roles should be enacted and which behaviors are proper. (Ch. 5)

**Front regions** A setting used to manage appearances. In front regions, people carry out interaction performances and exert efforts to maintain appropriate appearances. Contrasts with back regions, where they allow themselves to violate appearances while they prepare, rehearse, and rehash performances. (Ch. 5)

**Frustration** The blocking of goal-directed activity. According to the frustration-aggression hypothesis, frustration leads to aggression. (Ch. 12)

**Frustration-aggression hypothesis** The hypothesis that every frustration leads to some form of aggression and every aggressive act is due to some prior frustration. (Ch. 12)

**Fundamental attribution error** The tendency to underestimate the importance of situational influences and to overestimate personal, dispositional factors as causes of behavior. (Ch. 7)

# G

**Game stage** Mead's second stage of social experience, in which children enter organized activities and learn to imagine the viewpoints of several others at the same time. (Ch. 4)

**Gender role** The behavioral expectations associated with gender. (Ch. 3)

**Gender schema** Characteristics and behavior that we expect from men versus women. (Ch. 7)

**Generalized other** A conception of the attitudes and expectations held in common by the members of the organized groups with whom one interacts. (Ch. 4)

**Goal isomorphism** In groups, a state in which group goals and individual goals held by a member are similar in the sense that actions leading to the attainment of group goals also lead simultaneously to the attainment of individual goals. (Ch. 15)

**Group** A social unit that consists of two or more persons and has the following characteristics: shared goal(s), interaction (communication and influence) among members, normative expectations (norms and roles), and identification of members with the unit. (Ch. 15)

**Group cohesion** A property of a group, specifically the degree to which members of a group desire to remain in that group and resist leaving it. A highly cohesive group will maintain a firm hold over its members' time, energy, loyalty, and commitment. (Ch. 15)

**Group goal** A desirable outcome that group members strive collectively to accomplish or bring about. (Ch. 15)

**Group polarization** In group decision making, the tendency for group members to shift their opinions toward a position that is similar to but more extreme than the positions they held prior to group discussion; both the risky shift and the cautious shift are instances of group polarization. (Ch. 16)

**Groupthink** A mode of thinking within a cohesive group whereby pressures for unanimity overwhelm the members' motivation to realistically appraise alternative courses of action. (Ch. 16)

# H

**Halo effect** The tendency of our general or overall liking for a person to influence our assessment of more specific traits of that person. The halo effect can produce inaccuracy in our ratings of others' traits and performances. (Ch. 7)

**Helping** Any behavior that has the consequences of providing some benefit to or improving the well-being of another person. (Ch. 11)

**Heuristics** Mental shortcuts that allow individuals to quickly select and apply schemas to new or ambiguous situations. (Chs. 1 and 7)

**Homogeneous** Similar in important qualities. (Ch. 16)

**Hypothesis** A conjectural statement of the relation between two or more variables. Some hypotheses are explicitly causal in nature, whereas others are noncausal. (Ch. 2)

# I

**Identity** The categories people use to specify who they are—that is, to locate themselves relative to other people. (Ch. 4)

**Identity control theory** Proposes that an actor uses the social meaning of their identity as a reference point for assessing what is occurring in the situation. (Ch. 4)

**Identity degradation** A response to repeated or glaring failures that destroys the offender's current identity and transforms them into a "lower" social type. (Ch. 5)

**Illusion of out-group homogeneity** The tendency among in-group members to overestimate the extent to which out-group members are homogeneous or all alike. (Ch. 15)

**Imitation** A process of learning in which the learner watches another person's response and observes whether that person receives reinforcement. (Ch. 12)

**Implicit personality theory** A set of unstated assumptions about which personality traits are correlated with one another. (Ch. 7)

**Imposter phenomenon** A sense of phoniness, that one is undeserving of one's successes or accolades and thinks they may have been achieved based on luck or error. (Ch. 16)

**Impression formation** The process of organizing diverse information into a unified impression of a person. (Ch. 7)

**Independent variable** In an experiment, the variable that is manipulated by the investigator to study the effects on one or more other (dependent) variables. (Ch. 2)

**Individualist cultures** Cultures that emphasize the individual and value individual achievement. *See also* Collectivist cultures. (Ch. 4)

**Individualistic emotion competence** "Ego-focused" emotions, like anger and pride, that support children's independence. (Ch. 6)

**Informal social control** The reactions of family, friends, and acquaintances to rule violations by individuals. (Ch. 13)

**Informational influence** In groups, a form of influence that occurs when a group member accepts information from others as valid evidence about reality. Influence of this type is particularly likely to occur in situations of uncertainty or where there are no external or "objective" standards of reference. (Ch. 15)

**Informed consent** Voluntary consent by an individual to participate in a research project based on information received about what their participation will entail. (Ch. 2)

**Ingratiation** The deliberate use of deception to increase a target person's liking for us in hopes of gaining tangible benefits that the target person controls. Techniques such as flattery, expressing agreement with the target person's attitudes, and exaggerating one's own admirable qualities may be used. (Ch. 5)

**Instinct** An innate behavior that seems to emerge even without socialization or training. (Ch. 12)

**Institutionalization of deviance** The process by which members of a group come to expect and support deviance by another member over time. (Ch. 13)

**Instrumental conditioning** The process through which an individual learns a behavior in response to a stimulus to obtain a reward or avoid a punishment. (Ch. 3)

**Intentionalist model** A theory that views communication as the exchange of communicative intentions and views messages transmitted as merely the means to this end. (Ch. 9)

**Intergroup conflict** A state of affairs in which groups having opposing interests take antagonistic actions toward one another to control some outcome important to them. (Ch. 15)

**Intergroup contact hypothesis** A hypothesis holding that in intergroup relations, increased interpersonal contact between groups will reduce stereotypes and prejudice and, consequently, reduce antagonism between groups. (Ch. 15)

**Internal validity** The extent to which research findings are free from contamination by extraneous variables. (Ch. 2)

**Internalization** The process through which initially external behavioral standards become internal and subsequently guide an individual's behavior. (Ch. 3)

**Interpersonal attraction** A positive attitude held by one person toward another person. (Ch. 14)

**Interpersonal spacing (proxemics)** Nonverbal communication involving the ways in which people position themselves at varying distances and angles from others. Because *interpersonal spacing* refers to the proximity of people, it is also known as *proxemics*. (Ch. 9)

**Intersubjectivity** The information that each participant in an interaction needs about the other participant(s) in order for communication to be successful. (Ch. 9)

**Interview survey** A method of research in which a person (i.e., an interviewer) asks a series of questions and systematically records the answers from the respondents. *See also* Questionnaire survey. (Ch. 2)

**Intrinsically motivated behavior** A behavior that results from the motivation to achieve an internal state that an individual finds rewarding. (Ch. 3)

# L

**Labeling theory** The view that reactions of, and characterizations by, others are an essential element in deviance. (Ch. 13)

**Learned helplessness** Occurs when individuals focus on past failures and conclude that they are incapable of achieving success. (Ch. 7)

**Learning structure** An environment in which an individual can learn the information and skills required to enact a role. (Ch. 13)

**Legitimate means** Those ways of striving to achieve goals that are defined as acceptable by social norms. (Ch. 13)

**Life course** An individual's progression through a series of socially defined, age-linked social roles. (Ch. 3)

**Life event** An episode marking a transition point in the life course that provokes coping and readjustment. (Ch. 3)

**Likert scale** A technique for measuring attitudes that asks a respondent to indicate the extent to which they agree with each of a series of statements about an object. (Ch. 2)

**Linguistic intergroup bias** Subtle and systematic differences in the language we use to describe events as a function of our group membership and the group to which the actor or target belongs. (Ch. 9)

**Locus of control** The perceived cause of events in one's life. (Ch. 7)

**Looking-glass self** The term coined by Cooley that describes the self-schema we create based on how we think we appear to others. (Ch. 4)

**Love story** A script about what love should be like; it has characters, plot, and theme. (Ch. 14)

# M

**Majority influence** The process by which a group's majority pressures an individual to adopt a specific position on some issue. (Ch. 15)

**Mass media** Those channels of communication (TV, radio, newspapers, and the Internet) that enable a source to reach and influence a large audience. (Ch. 3)

**Matching hypothesis** The hypothesis that each person looks for someone to date who is of approximately the same level of social desirability. (Ch. 14)

**Mere exposure effect** Repeated exposure to the same stimulus that produces a positive attitude toward it. (Ch. 14)

**Meta-analysis** A statistical technique that allows the researcher to combine the results from all previous studies of a question. (Ch. 2)

**Methodology** A set of systematic procedures used to conduct empirical research. Usually these procedures pertain to how data will be collected and analyzed. (Ch. 2)

**Middle-range theories** Narrow, focused, theoretical frameworks that explain the conditions that produce some specific social behavior. *See also* Theoretical perspectives. (Ch. 1)

**Minimal group paradigm** Placing people into arbitrarily defined groups that have no important meaning is sufficient to trigger in-group and out-group processes and produce intergroup discrimination. (Ch. 15)

**Mood** A general psychological condition that characterizes an individual's experience and emotional orientation for hours or even days. Considerably less specific than an emotion. (Ch. 6)

**Moral development** The process through which children become capable of making moral judgments. (Ch. 3)

**Moral foundations** Targets vary in their perceptions of what distinguishes right from wrong. (Ch. 10)

# N

**Nonaggressive pornography** Explicit depictions—in film, video, photograph, or story—of adults engaging in consenting sexual activity. *See also* Aggressive pornography. (Ch. 12)

**Nonstandard speech** A style of speech characterized by limited vocabulary, improper pronunciation, and incorrect grammar. The use of this style is associated with low status and low power. *See also* Standard speech. (Ch. 9)

**Norm** In groups, a standard or rule that specifies how members are expected to behave under given circumstances; expectations concerning which behaviors are acceptable and which are unacceptable for specific persons in specific situations. (Chs. 3 and 15)

**Norm of homogamy** A social norm requiring that friends, lovers, and spouses be characterized by similarity in age, race, religion, and socioeconomic status. (Ch. 14)

**Norm of reciprocity** A social norm stating that people should (1) help those who have previously helped them and (2) not help those who have denied them help for no legitimate reason. (Ch. 11)

**Normative influence** In groups, a form of influence that occurs when a member conforms to group norms in order to receive the rewards or avoid the punishments that are contingent on adherence to these norms. (Ch. 15)

**Normative life stage** A discrete period in the life course during which individuals are expected to perform the set of activities associated with a distinct age-related role. (Ch. 3)

**Normative transition** Socially expected changes made by all or most members of a defined population. (Ch. 3)

# O

**Observational learning** The acquisition of behavior based on the observation of another person's behavior and of its consequences for that person. Also known as *modeling*. (Ch. 3)

**Opportunity structure** An environment in which an individual has opportunities to enact a role, which usually requires the assistance of those in complementary roles. (Ch. 13)

**Overreward** A situation in which an individual's outcomes are too high relative to their inputs. *See also* Underreward. (Ch. 16)

# P

**Panel study** A method of research in which a given sample of respondents is surveyed at one point in time and then resurveyed at a later point (or several later points). Also known as a *longitudinal survey*. (Ch. 2)

**Paralanguage** All the vocal aspects of speech other than words, including loudness, pitch, speed of speaking, pauses, sighs, laughter, and so on. (Ch. 9)

**Passionate love** A state of intense longing for union with another and intense physiological arousal. (Ch. 14)

**Personal norms** Feelings of moral obligation to perform specific actions that stem from an individual's internalized system of values. (Ch. 11)

**Perspective-taking model** A theory that views communication as the exchange of messages using symbols whose meaning is created by the interaction itself. (Ch. 9)

**Persuasion** An effort by a source to change the beliefs or attitudes of a target person through the use of information or argument. (Ch. 10)

**Play stage** Mead's first stage of social experience, in which young children imitate the activities of people around them. (Ch. 4)

**Population** A set of all people whose attitudes, behavior, or characteristics are of interest to the researcher. (Ch. 2)

**Position** A designated location in a social system. (Ch. 17)

**Power** One's ability to direct or influence the behavior of others. (Ch. 16)

**Power and prestige order** A structure of influence that emerges in task groups, with those of lower status often deferring to those of higher status and those of higher status taking the lead in decision making. (Ch. 16)

**Powerlessness** The sense of having little or no control over events. (Ch. 17)

**Prejudice** A strong like or dislike for members of a specific group. (Ch. 8)

**Primacy effect** The tendency, when forming an impression, to be most influenced by the earliest information received. The primacy effect accounts for the fact that first impressions are especially powerful. (Ch. 7)

**Primary group** A group with strong emotional ties and bonds that endure over time. This type of group tends to be more informal and intimate than other groups that individuals belong to. *See also* Secondary group. (Ch. 15)

**Primary relationship** An interpersonal relationship that is personal, emotionally involving, and of long duration. (Ch. 17)

**Priming** An implicit cognition effect, whereby exposure to one stimulus influences a response to another stimulus. (Ch. 15)

**Primitive belief** A belief based on our own personal experience or from a credible authority. (Ch. 8)

**Procedural justice** Perceptions of fairness of processes or procedures used to determine distributions. (Ch. 16)

**Promise** An influence technique that is a communication taking the general form, "If you do X (which I want), then I will do Y (which you want)." *See also* Threat. (Ch. 10)

**Prosocial behaviors** A broad category of actions considered by society as being beneficial to others and as having positive social consequences. A wide variety of specific behaviors qualify as prosocial, including donation to charity, intervention in emergencies, cooperation, sharing, volunteering, sacrifice, and the like. (Ch. 11)

**Prototype** In person perception, an abstraction that represents the "typical" or quintessential instance of a class or group. (Ch. 7)

**Punishment** A painful or discomforting stimulus that reduces the frequency with which the target behavior occurs. (Ch. 3)

## Q

**Qualitative methods** Broadly refer to those that rely on verbal or textual materials to represent the phenomenon of concern. (Ch. 2)

**Quantitative methods** Information collected in ways that produce numbers which can then be analyzed by applying statistical techniques. (Ch. 2)

**Questionnaire survey** A method of research in which a series of questions appear on a printed questionnaire and the respondents read and answer them online at their own pace. Usually no interviewer is present. *See also* Interview survey. (Ch. 2)

## R

**Random assignment** In an experiment, the assignment of participants to experimental conditions on the basis of chance. (Ch. 2)

**Reactance** Resistance to persuasion attempts that occurs when the persuasion attempt threatens the independence or freedom of the target. (Ch. 10)

**Realistic group conflict theory** A theory of intergroup conflict that explains the development and the resolution of conflict in terms of the goals of each group. Its central hypothesis is that groups will engage in conflictive behavior when their goals involve opposition of interest. (Ch. 15)

**Recency effect** The tendency, when forming an impression, to be most influenced by the latest information received. (Ch. 7)

**Reciprocity theory** An exchange theory that focuses on conflict, risk, and the expressive value of exchange. (Ch. 16)

**Reflexive self** The ability to act toward oneself, taking the role of both the subject and the object in a situation; a uniquely human trait. (Ch. 1)

**Reinforcement** Any favorable outcome or consequence that results from a behavioral response by a person. Reinforcement strengthens the response—that is, it increases the probability it will be repeated. (Ch. 12)

**Reinforcement theory** A theoretical perspective based on the premise that social behavior is governed by external events, especially rewards and punishments. (Ch. 3)

**Relation** A connection between two people, with people contributing benefits and potentially deriving them from interactions with each other. (Ch. 16)

**Relational emotion competence** "Other-focused" emotions, like sympathy and shame, are taught to children in many East Asian cultures. (Ch. 6)

**Relationship churning** A situation in which a couple is neither together nor stably broken up. Two churning states are at least temporary reconciliation following a separation or breakup, or engaging in sexual activity with an "ex." (Ch. 14)

**Relative deprivation** A gap between the expected level and the actual level of satisfaction of the individual's needs in which the level expected by the individual exceeds the level of need satisfaction experienced. (Ch. 13)

**Reliability** The degree to which a measuring instrument produces the same results each time it is employed under a set of specified conditions. (Ch. 2)

**Response rate** In a survey, the percentage of people contacted who complete the survey. (Ch. 2)

**Risk-benefit analysis** A technique that weighs the potential risks to research participants against the anticipated benefits to participants and the importance of the knowledge that may result from the research. (Ch. 2)

**Risky shift** In group decision making, the tendency for decisions made in groups after discussion to be riskier than decisions made by individual members prior to discussion. *See also* Cautious shift. (Ch. 16)

**Role** A set of functions to be performed by a person on behalf of a group of which they are a member; a cluster of rules indicating the set of duties to be performed by a member occupying a given position within a group; the set of expectations governing the behavior of an occupant of a specific position within a social structure. (Chs. 16 and 17)

**Role differentiation** The emergence of distinct roles within a group; the division of labor within a group. (Ch. 16)

**Role identities** Individuals' concept of self in specific social roles. (Chs. 3 and 4)

**Role overload** The condition in which the demands placed on a person by their roles exceed the amount of time, energy, and other resources available to meet those demands. (Ch. 17)

**Role taking** In symbolic interaction theory, the process of imaginatively occupying the position of another person and viewing the situation and the self from that person's perspective; the process of imagining the other's attitudes and anticipating that person's responses. (Chs. 1 and 4)

**Role theory** A theoretical perspective based on the premise that a substantial portion of observable, day-to-day social behavior is simply persons carrying out role expectations. (Ch. 1)

**Romantic love ideal** Five beliefs regarding love, including the belief (1) in love at first sight, (2) that there is one and only one true love for each person, (3) that love conquers all, (4) that our beloved is (nearly) perfect, and (5) that one should follow one's heart. (Ch. 14)

**Routine activities perspective** A theory that considers how deviant behavior, such as crime and substance abuse, emerges from the routines of everyday life. (Ch. 13)

**Rule breaking** Behavior that violates social norms. (Ch. 13)

**Rumination** Self-focused attention toward one's distress and the possible causes and consequences of the distress rather than ways to overcome it. (Ch. 12)

# S

**Salience** The relative importance of a specific role identity to the individual's self-schema. The salience hierarchy refers to the ordering of an individual's role identities according to their importance. (Ch. 4)

**Schema** A specific cognitive structure that organizes the processing of complex information about other persons, groups, and situations. Our schemas guide what we perceive in the environment, how we organize information in memory, and what inferences and judgments we make about people and things. (Chs. 1 and 7)

**Secondary deviance** Deviant behavior employed by a person as a means of defense or adjustment to the problems created by others' reactions to rule breaking by them. (Ch. 13)

**Secondary group** A group that is formal and impersonal, often organized around instrumental goals. *See also* Primary group. (Ch. 15)

**Self** The individual viewed as both the active source and the passive object of reflexive behavior. (Chs. 1 and 4)

**Self-awareness** A state in which we take the self as the object of our attention and focus on our own appearance, actions, and thoughts. (Ch. 4)

**Self-disclosure** The process of revealing personal information (aspects of our feelings and behaviors) to another person. Self-disclosure is sometimes used as an impression-management tactic. (Ch. 5)

**Self-discrepancy** The state in which a component of the individual's actual self is the opposite of a similar component of the ideal self or the ought self. (Ch. 4)

**Self-esteem** The evaluative component of the self-concept. The positive and negative evaluations people have of themselves. (Chs. 3 and 4)

**Self-estrangement** The awareness that one is engaging in activities that are not rewarding in themselves. (Ch. 17)

**Self-fulfilling prophecy** When persons behave toward another person according to a label (impression) and cause the person to respond in ways that confirm the label. (Chs. 7 and 13)

**Self-presentation** All conscious and unconscious attempts by people to control the images of self they project in social interaction. (Ch. 5)

**Self-reinforcement** An individual's use of internalized standards to judge their own behavior and reward the self. (Ch. 3)

**Self-schema** The organized structure of information that people have about themselves; the primary influence on the processing of information about the self. (Ch. 4)

**Self-serving bias** In attribution, the tendency for people to take personal credit for acts that yield positive outcomes and to deflect blame for bad outcomes by attributing them to external causes. (Ch. 7)

**Sentiment** The social aspect of emotion. Components of human responses that separate them from analogous responses animals would have. (Ch. 6)

**Sexual assault** Sexual touching or intercourse without consent, accomplished by coercion, manipulation, or either the threat or use of force. The greater the force used or the resulting injury, the more severe the assault. (Ch. 12)

**Shaping** The learning process in which an agent initially reinforces any behavior that remotely resembles the desired response and subsequently requires increasing correspondence between the learner's behavior and the desired response before providing reinforcement. (Ch. 3)

**Significant others** People whose views and attitudes are very important and worthy of consideration. The reflected views of a significant other have great influence on the individual's self-concept and self-regulation. (Chs. 1 and 4)

**Simple random sample** A sample of individuals selected from a population in such a way that everyone is equally likely to be selected. *See also* Stratified sample. (Ch. 2)

**Situated identity** A conception held by a person in a situation that indicates who they are in relation to the other people involved in that situation. (Chs. 1 and 5)

**Situated self** The subset of self-concepts that constitutes the self people recognize in a particular situation. Selected from the person's various identities, qualities, and self-evaluations, the situated self depends on the demands of the situation. (Ch. 4)

**Situational attribution** Attributing a behavior to environmental forces facing the person who performed it rather than to that person's internal state. *See also* Dispositional attribution. (Ch. 7)

**Situational constraint** An influence on behavior due to the likelihood that other persons will learn about that behavior and respond positively or negatively to it. (Ch. 8)

**Social class** Persons who share a common status in society. One's class standing may be based on occupational prestige and income. (Ch. 17)

**Social-emotional specialist** In groups, a person who strives to keep emotional relationships pleasant among members; a person who initiates acts that ease the tension and soothe hurt feelings. (Ch. 16)

**Social emotions** Emotions that cannot be understood or defined without reference to the social world; emotions that (1) involve an awareness of oneself in the social context, (2) emerge out of interaction with at least one other actor, and (3) are often experienced in reference to some kind of societal standard. (Ch. 6)

**Social exchange theory** A theoretical perspective, based on the principle of reinforcement, that assumes that people will likely choose actions that maximize rewards and minimize costs. (Ch. 1)

**Social identity** A definition of the self in terms of the defining characteristics of a social group. (Ch. 4)

**Social identity theory of intergroup behavior** A theory of intergroup relations based on the premise that people spontaneously categorize the social world into various groups (specifically, in-groups and out-groups) and experience high self-esteem to the extent that the in-groups to which they belong have more status than the out-groups. (Chs. 1 and 15)

**Social impact theory** A theoretical framework, applicable to both persuasion and obedience, stating that the impact of an influence attempt is a function of strength, immediacy, and number of sources that are present. (Ch. 10)

**Social influence** An interaction process in which one person's behavior causes another person to change an opinion or to perform an action that they would not otherwise do. (Ch. 10)

**Social learning theory** A theoretical perspective maintaining that one person (the learner) can acquire new responses without enacting them simply by observing the behavior of another person (the model). This learning process, called *imitation*, is distinguished by the fact that the learner neither performs a response nor receives any reinforcement. (Ch. 12)

**Social networks** The sets of interpersonal relationships associated with the social positions a person occupies. (Ch. 17)

**Social perception** The process through which we construct an understanding of the social world out of the data we obtain through our senses; more narrowly defined, the processes through which we use available information to form impressions of people. (Ch. 7)

**Social psychology** The field that systematically studies the nature and causes of human social behavior. (Ch. 1)

**Social responsibility norm** A widely accepted social norm stating that individuals should help people who are dependent on them. (Ch. 11)

**Social structure** The ordered and persisting relationships among the positions in a social system. (Ch. 17)

**Socialization** The process through which individuals learn skills, knowledge, values, motives, and roles appropriate to their positions in a group or society. (Ch. 3)

**Sociolinguistic competence** Knowledge of the implicit rules for generating socially appropriate sentences that make sense because they fit the listener's social knowledge. (Ch. 9)

**Source** In social influence, the person who intentionally engages in some behavior (persuasion, threat, promise) to cause another person to behave in a manner different from how they otherwise would. *See also* Target. (Ch. 10)

**Specific status characteristics** Attributes that influence performance expectations for tasks that are relevant to that attribute (e.g., mathematical ability on a math test). *See also* Diffuse status characteristics. (Ch. 16)

**Speech act theory** The theory that verbal utterances both state something and do something. (Ch. 9)

**Spillover** Stress experienced at work or in the family is carried over into the other domain. (Ch. 17)

**Spoken language** A socially acquired system of sound patterns with meanings agreed on by the members of a group. (Ch. 9)

**Standard speech** A speech style characterized by diverse vocabulary, proper pronunciation, correct grammar, and abstract content. The use of this style is associated with high status and power. *See also* Nonstandard speech. (Ch. 9)

**Status** The social ranking of a person's position relative to others. (Chs. 1 and 17)

**Status characteristic** Any property of a person around which evaluations and beliefs about that person come to be organized; properties such as race, occupation, age, sex, ethnicity, education, and so on. (Ch. 16)

**Status construction** The process in which our beliefs about status are formed and reinforced in interaction. (Ch. 16)

**Status generalization** A process through which differences in members' status characteristics lead to different performance expectations and, hence, affect patterns of interaction in groups; the tendency for a member's status inside a group to reflect their status outside that group. (Ch. 16)

**Status value** Like attributes, objects can also acquire status value. Objects that are associated with high-status actors become more valuable than those linked to low-status actors. (Ch. 16)

**Stereotype threat** The suspicion a member of a group holds that they will be judged based on a common stereotype of the group. (Ch. 7)

**Stereotypes** Fixed sets of characteristics that are attributed to all the members of a group; simplistic and rigid perceptions of members of one group that are widely shared by others. (Ch. 7)

**Stigma** Personal characteristics that others view as preventing competent or morally trustworthy behavior. (Ch. 5)

**Stratified sample** In survey research, a sampling design whereby researchers subdivide the population into groups according to

characteristics known or thought to be important, select a random sample of groups, and then draw a sample of units within each selected group. *See also* Simple random sample. (Ch. 2)

**Stress** The condition in which the demands made on the person exceed the individual's ability to cope with them. (Ch. 3)

**Subtractive rule** When making attributions about the influence of personal dispositions on a behavior, the observer subtracts the perceived impact of situational forces from the personal disposition implied by the behavior itself. (Ch. 7)

**Subtyping** A process through which perceivers create subcategories of stereotyped groups who serve as exceptions to the rule without threatening the overarching stereotype. Cognitive strategies like these help people explain away contradictory information and preserve their stereotypes. (Ch. 7)

**Summons-answer sequence** The most common verbal method for initiating a conversation, in which one person summons the other as with a question or greeting, and the other indicates their availability for conversation by responding. This sequence establishes the mutual obligation to speak and to listen that produces conversational turn taking. (Ch. 9)

**Superordinate goal** In intergroup conflict, an objective held in common by all conflicting groups that cannot be achieved by any one group without the supportive efforts of the others. (Ch. 15)

**Supplication** An impression-management tactic that involves convincing a target person that you are needy and deserving. (Ch. 5)

**Symbolic interaction theory** A theoretical perspective based on the premise that human nature and social order are products of communication among people. Also known as *symbolic interactionism*. (Ch. 1)

**Symbols** Forms used to represent ideas, feelings, thoughts, intentions, or any other object. Symbols represent our experiences in a way that others can perceive with their sensory organs—through sounds, gestures, pictures, and so on. (Ch. 9)

# T

**Tactical impression management** The selective use of self-presentation tactics by a person who wishes to manipulate the impressions that others form of them. (Ch. 5)

**Target** In social influence, the person who is affected by a social influence attempt from the source. In aggression, the person toward whom an aggressive act is directed. *See also* Source. (Chs. 10 and 12)

**Task specialist** In groups, a member who pushes the group toward the attainment of its goals; a person who contributes many ideas and suggestions to the group. (Ch. 16)

**Theoretical perspectives** Theories that make broad assumptions about human nature and offer general explanations of a wide range of diverse behaviors. *See also* Middle-range theories. (Ch. 1)

**Theory** A set of interrelated propositions that organizes and explains a set of observed facts; a network of hypotheses that may be used as a basis for prediction. (Chs. 1 and 2)

**Theory of cognitive dissonance** A theory concerning the sources and effects of inconsistency in cognitive systems with two or more elements. (Ch. 8)

**Theory of speech accommodation** The theory that people express or reject intimacy with others by adjusting their speech behavior (accent, vocabulary, or language) during interaction. They make their own speech behavior more similar to their partner's to express liking, and more dissimilar to reject intimacy. (Ch. 9)

**Threat** An influence technique that is a communication taking the general form, "If you don't do X (which I want), then I will do Y (which you don't want)." *See also* Promise. (Ch. 10)

**Trait centrality** A personality trait has a high level of trait centrality when information about a person's standing on that trait has a large impact on the overall impression that others form of that person. The warm-cold trait, for instance, is highly central. (Ch. 7)

**Trust** The belief that a person is both honest and benevolent. (Ch. 14)

**Two-factor theory of emotion** Schachter's theory on the social roots of emotions proposes that emotional experience results from a

two-step process: (1) an event in the environment produces a physiological reaction; (2) we notice the physiological reaction and search for an appropriate explanation. (Ch. 6)

## U

**Ultimate attribution error** A perceptual bias occurring in intergroup relations. Negative behaviors by out-group members are attributed to stable, internal factors such as undesirable personal traits or dispositions, but positive behaviors by out-group members are attributed to unstable, external factors such as situational pressures or luck. As a result, in-group observers will blame the out-group for negative outcomes but will not give it credit for positive outcomes. (Ch. 15)

**Underreward** When a person's outcomes are too low relative to their inputs. *See also* Overreward. (Ch. 16)

**Upward mobility** Movement of a person from an occupation lower in prestige and income to one higher in prestige and income. (Ch. 17)

## V

**Values** Enduring beliefs that certain patterns of behavior or end states are preferable to others. (Ch. 17)

**Victim-blame** When responsibility for a sexual assault is placed on the victim rather than the perpetrator. (Ch. 12)

## W

**Weapons effect** A cognitive priming effect, when the sight of a weapon makes more accessible or primes aggression-related concepts or scripts for behavior. (Ch. 12)

Abbassi, A., & Aslinia, S. D. (2010). Family violence, trauma and social learning theory. *Journal of Professional Counseling, Practice, Theory, & Research, 38*(1), 16.

Abbey, A. (2002). Alcohol-related sexual assault: A common problem among college students. *Journal of Studies on Alcohol and Drugs, 14,* 118–128.

Abbey, A. (2011). Alcohol's role in sexual violence perpetration: Theoretical explanations, existing evidence and future directions. *Drug and Alcohol Review, 30,* 481–489.

Abbey, A., Jacques-Tiura, A. J., & LeBreton, J. M. (2011). Risk factors for sexual aggression in young men: An expansion of the confluence model. *Aggressive Behavior, 37*(5), 450–464.

Abbey, A., McAuslan, P., & Ross, L. T. (1998). Sexual assault perpetration by college men: The role of alcohol, misperception of sexual intent, and sexual beliefs and experiences. *Journal of Social and Clinical Psychology, 17*(2), 167–195.

Abbey, A., McAuslan, P., Zawacki, T., Clinton, A. M., & Buck, P. O. (2001). Attitudinal, experiential, and situational predictors of sexual assault perpetration. *Journal of Interpersonal Violence, 16*(8), 784–807.

Abele, A. E. (2003). The dynamics of masculine–agentic and feminine–communal traits: Findings from a prospective study. *Journal of Personality and Social Psychology, 85,* 768–776.

Abelson, R. P. (1981). The psychological status of the script concept. *American Psychologist, 36,* 715–729.

Aberson, C. L., Healy, M., & Romero, V. (2000). Ingroup bias and self-esteem: A meta-analysis. *Personality and Social Psychology Review, 4,* 157–173.

Abouserie, R. (1994). Sources and levels of stress in relation to locus of control and self esteem in university students. *Educational Psychology, 14*(3), 323–330.

Abrams, D., Marques, J., Brown, N., & Henson, M. (2000). Pro-norm and anti-norm deviance within and between groups. *Journal of Personality and Social Psychology, 78,* 906–912.

Abrams, D. E., & Hogg, M. A. (1990). *Social identity theory: Constructive and critical advances.* New York: Springer-Verlag.

Acock, A., & Scott, W. (1980). A model for predicting behavior: The effect of attitude and social class on high and low visibility political participation. *Social Psychology Quarterly, 43,* 59–72.

Adachi, P. J., & Willoughby, T. (2011). The effect of video game competition and violence on aggressive behavior: Which characteristic has the greatest influence? *Psychology of Violence, 1*(4), 259–274.

Adachi, P. J., & Willoughby, T. (2013). Demolishing the competition: The longitudinal link between competitive video games, competitive gambling, and aggression. *Journal of Youth and Adolescence, 42*(7), 1090–1104.

Adams, J. S. (1963). Toward an understanding of inequity. *Journal of Abnormal and Social Psychology, 67,* 422–436.

Adams, J. S., & Jacobsen, P. R. (1964). Effects of wage inequities on work quality. *Journal of Abnormal and Social Psychology, 69,* 19–25.

Adelman, R., & Verbrugge, L. (2000). Death makes news: The social impact of disease on newspaper coverage. *Journal of Health and Social Behavior, 41,* 347–367.

Adelmann, P. K., & Zajonc, R. B. (1989). Facial efference and the experience of emotion. *Annual Review of Psychology, 40,* 249–280.

Aderman, D., & Berkowitz, L. (1983). Self-concern and the unwillingness to be helpful. *Social Psychology Quarterly, 46*(4), 293–301.

Adler, P. A., & Adler, P. (1995). Dynamics of inclusion and exclusion in preadolescent cliques. *Social Psychology Quarterly, 58,* 145–162.

Adlerfer, C. P. (1982). Problems in changing White males' behavior and beliefs concerning race relations. In P. Goodman (Ed.), *Change in organizations* (pp. 122–165). San Francisco: Jossey-Bass.

Agnew, R. (1992). Foundation for a general strain theory of crime and delinquency. *Criminology, 30,* 47–87.

Agnew, R., & White, H. R. (1992). An empirical test of general strain theory. *Criminology, 30,* 475–499.

Ahl, R. E., Fausto-Sterling, A., Garcia-Coll, C., & Seifer, R. (2013). Gender and discipline in 5–12-month-old infants: A longitudinal study. *Infant Behavior and Development, 36,* 199–209.

Ahlfinger, N. R., & Esser, J. K. (2001). Testing the groupthink model: Effects of promotional leadership and conformity predisposition. *Social Behavior and Personality: An International Journal, 29*(1), 31–41.

Aiken, L. R. (1992). Some measures of interpersonal attraction and group cohesiveness. *Educational and Psychological Measurement, 52*(1), 63–67.

Ainsworth, M. (1979). Infant–mother attachment. *American Psychologist, 34,* 932–937.

Ajzen, I. (1982). On behaving in accordance with one's attitudes. In M. Zanna, E. Higgins, & C. Herman (Eds.), *Consistency in social behavior: The Ontario symposium* (Vol. 2, pp. 131–146). Hillsdale, NJ: Erlbaum.

Ajzen, I. (1991). The theory of planned behavior. *Organizational Behavior and Human Decision Processes, 50*(2), 179–211.

Ajzen, I. (2005). *Attitudes, personality, and behavior.* Maidenhead: McGraw-Hill Education.

Ajzen, I., & Fishbein, M. (1977). Attitude-behavior relations: A theoretical analysis and review of research. *Psychological Bulletin, 84,* 888–918.

Ajzen, I., & Holmes, W. H. (1976). Uniqueness of behavioral effects in causal attribution. *Journal of Personality, 44,* 98–108.

Ajzen, I., & Sexton, J. (1999). Depth of processing, belief congruence, and attitude-behavior correspondence. In S. Chaiken & Y. Trope (Eds.), *Dual-process theories in social psychology* (pp. 117–138). New York: Guilford.

Akers, A. Y., Cohen, E. D., Marshal, M. P., Roebuck, G., Yu, L., & Hipwell, A. E. (2016). Objective and perceived weight: Associations with risky adolescent sexual behavior. *Perspectives on Sexual and Reproductive Health, 48*(3), 129–137.

Akers, R. L., Krohn, M., Lanza-Kaduce, L., & Radosevich, M. (1979). Social learning and deviant behavior: A specific test of a general theory. *American Sociological Review, 44,* 636–655.

Akers, R. L., LaGreca, H. J., Cochran, J., & Sellers, C. (1989). Social learning theory and alcohol behavior among the elderly. *Sociological Quarterly, 30,* 625–638.

Albarracín, D. (2002). Cognition in persuasion: An analysis of information processing in response to persuasive communications. *Advances in Experimental Social Psychology, 34,* 61–130.

Aldag, R. J., & Fuller, S. F. (1993). Beyond fiasco: A reappraisal of the groupthink phenomenon and a new model of group decision processes. *Psychological Bulletin, 113,* 533–552.

Aldwin, C., & Revenson, T. (1987). Does coping help? A reexamination of the relationship between coping and mental health. *Journal of Personality and Social Psychology, 53,* 337–348.

Alexander, C. N., & Rudd, J. (1984). Predicting behaviors from situated identities. *Social Psychology Quarterly, 47,* 172–177.

Alexander, C. N., & Wiley, M. G. (1981). Situated activity and identity formation. In M. Rosenberg & R. Turner (Eds.), *Social psychology: Sociological perspectives* (pp. 269–289). New York: Basic Books.

Alkiş, N., & Temizel, T. T. (2015). The impact of individual differences on influence strategies. *Personality and Individual Differences, 87,* 147–152.

Allard, M. D. (2008). How high school students use time: A visual essay. *Monthly Labor Review, 131*(11), 51–57.

Allard, M. D. (2011). Asians in the U.S. labor force: Profile of a diverse population. *Monthly Labor Review, 134*(11), 3–22.

Allen, J. A., Diefendorff, J. M., & Ma, Y. (2014). Differences in emotional labor across cultures: A comparison of Chinese and U.S. service workers. *Journal of Business and Psychology, 29*(1), 21–35.

Allen, V. L., & Levine, J. M. (1969). Consensus and conformity. *Journal of Experimental Social Psychology, 5,* 389–399.

Allen, V. L., & Levine, J. M. (1971). Social support and conformity: The role of independent assessment of reality. *Journal of Experimental Social Psychology, 7,* 48–58.

Allen, V. L., & Van de Vliert, E. (1982). A role theoretical perspective on transitional processes. In V. L. Allen & E. Van de Vliert (Eds.), *Role transitions: Explorations and explanations* (pp. 3–18). New York: Plenum.

Allison, R., & Risman, B. J. (2013). A double standard for "hooking up": How far have we come toward gender equality? *Social Science Research, 42*(5), 1191–1206.

Allison, S. T., McQueen, L. R., & Schaerfl, L. M. (1992). Social decision making processes and the equal partitioning of shared resources. *Journal of Experimental Social Psychology, 28,* 23–42.

Allport, F. H. (1924). *Social psychology.* Cambridge, MA: Houghton Mifflin.

Allport, G. W. (1935). Attitudes. In C. Murchison (Ed.), *Handbook of social psychology* (pp. 798–844). Worcester, MA: Clark University Press.

Allport, G. W. (1954). *The nature of prejudice.* Reading, MA: Addison-Wesley.

Allport, G. W. (1961). *Pattern and growth in personality.* New York: Holt, Rinehart and Winston.

Allport, G. W., & Postman, L. J. (1947). *The psychology of rumor.* New York: Holt, Rinehart and Winston.

Almeida, D., Wethington, E., & Kessler, R. (2002). The daily inventory of stressful events: An interview-based approach for measuring daily stressors. *Assessment, 9,* 41–55.

Altman, I., & Taylor, D. A. (1973). *Social penetration: The development of interpersonal relationships.* New York: Holt, Rinehart and Winston.

Alvarez, K., & Leeuwen, E. (2015). Paying it forward: How helping others can reduce the psychological threat of receiving help. *Journal of Applied Social Psychology, 45*(1), 1–9.

Alwin, D. F. (1986). Religion and parental child-rearing orientations: Evidence of Catholic–Protestant convergence. *American Journal of Sociology, 92,* 412–440.

Alwin, D. F. (1990). Cohort replacement and changes in parental socialization values. *Journal of Marriage and Family, 52,* 347–360.

Amato, P. R. (1990). Personality and social network involvement as predictors of helping behavior in everyday life. *Social Psychology Quarterly, 53*(1), 31–43.

Amato, P. R. (2001). The consequences of divorce for adults and children. In R. Milardo (Ed.), *Understanding families into the new millennium: A decade in review* (pp. 488–506). Minneapolis, MN: National Council on Family Relations.

American Association of University Women. (1992). *The AAUW report: How schools shortchange girls.* Washington, DC: Author.

American Psychiatric Association. (1981). *Diagnostic and statistical manual of mental disorders* (3rd ed.). Washington, DC: Author.

American Psychological Association. (1993). *Summary report of the APA Commission on Violence and Youth.* Washington, DC: Author.

American Society for Aesthetic Plastic Surgery. (2015). Highlights of the ASAPS 2015 Statistics on Cosmetic Surgery. www.surgery.org/sites/default/files/2015-quick-facts.pdf (Accessed February 24, 2017).

Anderson, B. A., & Silver, B. D. (1987). The validity of survey responses: Insights from interviews of married couples in a survey of Soviet emigrants. *Social Forces, 66,* 537–554.

Anderson, C. A. (2001). Heat and violence. *Current Directions in Psychological Science, 10,* 33–38.

Anderson, C. A., Anderson, K. B., & Deuser, W. E. (1996). Examining an affective aggression framework: Weapon and temperature effects on aggressive thoughts, affect, and attitudes. *Personality and Social Psychology Bulletin, 22*, 366–376.

Anderson, C. A., Anderson, K. B., Dorr, N., DeNeve, K. M., & Flanagan, M. (2000). Temperature and aggression. *Advances in Experimental Social Psychology, 32*, 63–133.

Anderson, C. A., Benjamin, A. J., & Bartholow, B. D. (1998). Does the gun pull the trigger? Automatic priming effects of weapon pictures and weapon names. *Psychological Science, 9*, 308–314.

Anderson, C. A., Berkowitz, L., Donnerstein, E., Huesmann, L. R., Johnson, J., Linz, D., et al. (2003). The influence of media violence on youth. *Psychological Science in the Public Interest, 4*, 81–110.

Anderson, C. A., & Bushman, B. J. (2002). Human aggression. *Annual Review of Psychology, 53*(1), 27–51.

Anderson, C. A., Shibuya, A., Ihori, N., Swing, E. L., Bushman, B. J., Sakamoto, A., et al. (2010). Violent video game effects on aggression, empathy, and prosocial behavior in eastern and western countries: A meta-analytic review. *Psychological Bulletin, 136*(2), 151–173.

Anderson, E., & McCormack, M. (2015). Cuddling and spooning: Heteromasculinity and homosocial tactility among student athletes. *Men and Masculinities, 18*, 214–230.

Anderson, K. B., Cooper, H., & Okamura, L. (1997). Individual differences and attitudes toward rape: A meta-analytic review. *Personality and Social Psychology Bulletin, 23*(3), 295–315.

Anderson, W. P. (2006). A procedure for coding self-regard from narrative self-descriptions. *Psychological Reports, 99*, 879–893.

Andrews, B., & Brewin, C. R. (1990). Attributions of blame for marital violence: A study of antecedents and consequences. *Journal of Marriage and Family, 52*(3), 757–767.

Anson, O. (1989). Marital status and women's health revisited: The importance of a proximate adult. *Journal of Marriage and Family, 51*, 185–194.

Anwar, F., Fry, D. P., & Grigaitytė, I. (2018). Aggression prevention and reduction in diverse cultures and contexts. *Current Opinion in Psychology, 19*(1), 49–54.

Appleton, W. (1981). *Fathers and daughters*. New York: Doubleday.

Araji, S. K. (1977). Husbands' and wives' attitude-behavior congruence on family roles. *Journal of Marriage and Family, 39*(2), 309–320.

Archer, D., & Akert, R. (1977). Words and everything else: Verbal and nonverbal cues in social interpretation. *Journal of Personality and Social Psychology, 35*, 443–449.

Archer, J. (1991). Human sociobiology: Basic concepts and limitations. *Journal of Social Issues, 47*(3), 11–26.

Archer, J. (2000). Sex differences in aggression between heterosexual partners: A meta-analytic review. *Psychological Bulletin, 126*(5), 651–680.

Archer, J. (2006). Cross-cultural differences in physical aggression between partners: A social-role analysis. *Personality and Social Psychology Review, 10*(2), 133–153.

Archer, R. L. (1980). Self-disclosure. In D. M. Wegner & R. R. Vallacher (Eds.), *The self in social psychology* (pp. 409–427). New York: Oxford University Press.

Arditti, J. A. (1999). Rethinking relationships between divorced mothers and their children: Capitalizing on family strengths. *Family Relations, 48*, 109–119.

Arendt, H. (1965). *Eichmann in Jerusalem: A report on the banality of evil*. New York: Viking.

Aries, E. (1996). *Men and women in interaction*. New York: Oxford University Press.

Arkin, R. M., & Duval, S. (1975). Focus of attention and causal attributions of actors and observers. *Journal of Experimental Social Psychology, 11*(5), 427–438.

Armeli, S., Carney, M. A., Tennen, H., Affleck, G., & O'Neil, T. P. (2000). Stress and alcohol use: A daily process examination of the stressor–vulnerability model. *Journal of Personality and Social Psychology, 78*, 979–994.

Armstrong, E. A., Hamilton, L., & Sweeney, B. (2006). Sexual assault on campus: A multilevel, integrative approach to party rape. *Social Problems, 53*(4), 483–499.

Aron, A., Norman, C., Aron, E., McKenna, C., & Heyman, R. (2000). Couples' shared participation in novel and arousing activities and experienced relationship quality. *Journal of Personality and Social Psychology, 78*, 273–284.

Aronfreed, J., & Reber, A. (1965). Internalized behavior suppression and the timing of social punishment. *Journal of Personality and Social Psychology, 1*, 3–16.

Aronson, E., Ellsworth, P. C., Carlsmith, J. M., & Gonzales, J. H. (1990). *Methods of research in social psychology* (2nd ed.). New York: McGraw-Hill.

Asch, S. E. (1946). Forming impressions of personality. *Journal of Abnormal and Social Psychology, 41*, 258–290.

Asch, S. E. (1951). Effects of group pressure upon the modification and distortion of judgments. In H. Guetzkow (Ed.), *Groups, leadership, and men* (pp. 177–190). Pittsburgh, PA: Carnegie Press.

Asch, S. E. (1955). Opinions and social pressure. *Scientific American, 193*, 31–35.

Asch, S. E. (1957). An experimental investigation of group influence. In *Symposium on preventive and social psychiatry* (pp. 15–17). Washington, DC: Walter Reed Army Institute of Research.

Aseltine, R., Gore, S., & Gordon, J. (2000). Life stress, anger and anxiety, and delinquency: An empirical test of general strain theory. *Journal of Health and Social Behavior, 41*, 256–275.

Asendorpf, J. B. (1987). Videotape reconstruction of emotions and cognitions related to shyness. *Journal of Personality and Social Psychology, 53*, 542–549.

Ashforth, B., & Lee, R. (1990). Defensive behavior in organizations: A preliminary model. *Human Relations, 43*, 621–648.

Ashmore, R. D. (1981). Sex stereotypes and implicit personality theory. In D. L. Hamilton (Ed.), *Cognitive processes in stereotyping and intergroup behavior* (pp. 37–81). Hillsdale, NJ: Erlbaum.

Attrill, A., & Jalil, R. (2011). Revealing only the superficial me: Exploring categorical self-disclosure online. *Computers in Human Behavior, 27*, 1634–1642.

Aubrey, J. S., & Harrison, K. (2004). The gender-role content of children's favorite television programs and its links to their gender-related perception. *Media Psychology, 6*, 111–146.

Augoustinos, M., & Innes, J. M. (1990). Towards an integration of social representations and social schema theory. *British Journal of Social Psychology, 29*(3), 213–231.

Augustine, A. A., & Hemenover, S. H. (2009). On the relative effectiveness of affect regulation strategies: A meta-analysis. *Cognition and Emotion, 23*(6), 1181–1220.

Austin, W. (1980). Friendship and fairness: Effects of type of relationship and task performance on choice distribution rules. *Personality and Social Psychology Bulletin, 6*, 402–408.

Austin, W., & Walster [Hatfield], E. (1974). Participants' reactions to "equity with the world." *Journal of Experimental Social Psychology, 10*, 528–548.

Averill, J. R. (1983). Studies on anger and aggression: Implications for theories of emotion. *American Psychologist, 38*, 1145–1160.

Aviezer, H., Hassin, R., Ryan, J., Grady, C., Susskind, J., Anderson, A., et al. (2008). Angry, disgusted, or afraid? Studies on the malleability of emotion perception. *Psychological Science, 19*, 724–732.

Babcock, M. K., & Sabini, J. (1990). On differentiating embarrassment from shame. *European Journal of Social Psychology, 20*(2), 151–169.

Back, M. D., Penke, L., Schmukle, S. C., Sachse, K., Borkenau, P., & Asendorpf, J. B. (2011). Why mate choices are not as reciprocal as we assume: The role of personality, flirting, and physical attractiveness. *European Journal of Personality, 25*, 120–132.

Backman, C. (1990). Attraction in interpersonal relationships. In M. Rosenberg & R. Turner (Eds.), *Social psychology: Sociological perspectives* (pp. 235–268). New Brunswick, NJ: Transaction.

Backman, C., & Secord, P. (1962). Liking, selective interaction, and misperception in congruent interpersonal relations. *Sociometry, 25*, 321–325.

Badie, D. (2010). Groupthink, Iraq, and the war on terror: Explaining US policy shift toward Iraq. *Foreign Policy Analysis, 6*(4), 277–296.

Bailey, W. C. (1990). Murder, capital punishment, and television: Execution publicity and homicide rates. *American Sociological Review, 55*, 628–633.

Baker, K., & Raney, A. (2007). Equally super? Gender-role stereotyping of superheroes in children's animated programs. *Mass Communications and Society, 10*, 25–41.

Baker, T., & Piquero, A. R. (2010). Assessing the perceived benefits—criminal offending relationship. *Journal of Criminal Justice, 38*(5), 981–987.

Bales, R. F. (1950). *Interaction process analysis: A method for the study of small groups.* Cambridge, MA: Addison-Wesley.

Bales, R. F. (1970). *Personality and interpersonal behavior.* New York: Holt, Rinehart and Winston.

Balk, S. J., Fisher, D. E., & Geller, A. C. (2013). Teens and indoor tanning: A cancer prevention opportunity for pediatricians. *Pediatrics, 131*, 772–785.

Balkwell, J. W. (1991). From expectations to behavior: An improved postulate for expectation states theory. *American Sociological Review, 56*, 355–369.

Ball, D. W. (1976). Failure in sports. *American Sociological Review, 41*, 726–739.

Balliet, D., Mulder, L. B., & Van Lange, P. A. (2011). Reward, punishment, and cooperation: A meta-analysis. *Psychological Bulletin, 137*(4), 594–615.

Baltes, P., & Willis, S. (1982). Plasticity and enhancement of intellectual functioning in old age: Penn State's adult development and enrichment project. In F. Craik & S. Trehub (Eds.), *Aging and cognitive processes* (pp. 353–389). New York: Plenum.

Banaji, M., & Prentice, D. (1994). The self in social contexts. *Annual Review of Psychology, 45*, 297–332.

Bandura, A. (1965). Influence of models' reinforcement contingencies on the acquisition of imitative responses. *Journal of Personality and Social Psychology, 1*, 589–595.

Bandura, A. (1969). Social-learning theory of identificatory processes. In D. Goslin (Ed.), *Handbook of socialization theory and research* (pp. 213–262). Chicago: Rand McNally.

Bandura, A. (1973). *Aggression: A social learning analysis.* Englewood Cliffs, NJ: Prentice Hall.

Bandura, A. (1982). Self-efficacy mechanism in human agency. *American Psychologist, 37*, 122–147.

Bandura, A., Ross, D., & Ross, S. (1961). Transmission of aggression through imitation of aggressive models. *Journal of Abnormal and Social Psychology, 63*, 575–582.

Barker, G. (1998). Non-violent males in violent settings: An exploratory qualitative study of prosocial low-income adolescent males in two Chicago (USA) neighborhoods. *Childhood, 5*(4), 437–461.

Barker, R. G., Dembo, T., & Lewin, K. (1941). Frustration and aggression: An experiment with young children. *University of Iowa Studies in Child Welfare, 18*, 1–34.

Barlett, C. P., & Anderson, C. A. (2011). Reappraising the situation and its impact on aggressive behavior. *Personality and Social Psychology Bulletin, 37*(12), 1564–1573.

Barlett, C. P., Harris, R. J., & Baldassaro, R. (2007). Longer you play, the more hostile you feel: Examination of first person shooter video games and aggression during video game play. *Aggressive Behavior, 33*(6), 486–497.

Barlett, C. P., Harris, R. J., & Bruey, C. (2008). The effect of the amount of blood in a violent video game on aggression, hostility, and arousal. *Journal of Experimental Social Psychology, 44*(3), 539–546.

Barnes, C. D., Brown, R. P., & Osterman, L. L. (2012). Don't tread on me: Masculine honor ideology in the U.S. and militant responses to terrorism. *Personality and Social Psychology Bulletin, 38*(8), 1018–1029.

Barnett, M. A. (1987). Empathy and related responses in children. In N. Eisenberg & J. Strayer (Eds.), *Empathy and its development* (pp. 146–162). New York: Cambridge University Press.

Barnett, R. C. (1994). Home-to-work spillover revisited: A study of full-time employed women in dual-earner couples. *Journal of Marriage and Family, 56*, 647–656.

Barnett, R., & Rivers, C. (2011). Flawed study dismissing job bias thrills media. www.womensenews.org/story/women-in-science/110218

Baron, R. A. (1971). Reducing the influence of an aggressive model: The restraining effects of discrepant modeling cues. *Journal of Personality and Social Psychology, 20*, 240–245.

Baron, R. A. (1977). *Human aggression*. New York: Plenum.

Baron, R. A. (1983). The control of human aggression: An optimistic perspective. *Journal of Social and Clinical Psychology, 1*(2), 97–119.

Baron, R. S. (2005). So right it's wrong: Groupthink and the ubiquitous nature of polarized group decision making. *Advances in Experimental Social Psychology, 37*, 219–253.

Baron, R. S., Vandello, U. A., & Brunsman, B. (1996). The forgotten variable in conformity research: Impact of task importance on social influence. *Journal of Personality and Social Psychology, 71*, 915–927.

Barrett, K. C. (1995). A functionalist approach to shame and guilt. In J. P. Tangney & K. W. Fischer (Eds.), *Self-conscious emotions: The psychology of shame, guilt, embarrassment, and pride* (pp. 25–63). New York: Guilford Press.

Barrett, L. F. (2012). Emotions are real. *Emotion, 12*(3), 413.

Barrett, L. F., & Kensinger, E. A. (2010). Context is routinely encoded during emotion perception. *Psychological Science, 21*(4), 595–599.

Barrett, R. (2008). Linguistic differentiation and Mayan language revitalization in Guatemala. *Journal of Sociolinguistics, 12*, 275–305.

Bartlett, M. S., Littlewort, G., Frank, M., Lainscsek, C., Fasel, I., & Movellan, J. (2006, April). Fully automatic facial action recognition in spontaneous behavior. In *Automatic Face and Gesture Recognition*. FGR 2006. 7th International Conference on Automatic Face and Gesture Recognition (pp. 223–230). IEEE.

Bartley, S., Blanton, P., & Gilliard, J. (2005). Husband and wives in dual-earner marriages: Decision-making, gender role attitudes, division of household labor, and equity. *Marriage and Family Review, 37*, 69–93.

Bartoli, A. M., & Clark, M. D. (2006). The dating game: Similarities and differences in dating scripts among college students. *Sexuality and Culture, 10*, 54–80.

Basil, D. Z., Ridgway, N. M., & Basil, M. D. (2008). Guilt and giving: A process model of empathy and efficacy. *Psychology & Marketing, 25*(1), 1–23.

Basso, K., dos Santos, C. P., & Gonçalves, M. A. (2014). The impact of flattery: The role of negative remarks. *Journal of Retailing and Consumer Services, 21*(2), 185–191.

Bastaits, K., & Mortelmans, D. (2016). Parenting as mediator between post-divorce family structure and children's well-being. *Journal of Child and Family Studies, 25*(7), 2178–2188.

Bates, E., O'Connell, B., & Shore, C. (1987). Language and communication in infancy. In J. Osofsky (Ed.), *Handbook of infant competence* (2nd ed., pp. 149–203). New York: Wiley.

Batson, C. D. (1987). Prosocial motivation: Is it ever truly altruistic? In L. Berkowitz (Ed.), *Advances in experimental social psychology* (Vol. 20) (pp. 65–122). New York: Academic Press.

Batson, C. D. (1991). *The altruism question: Toward a social psychological answer*. Hillsdale, NJ: Erlbaum.

Batson, C. D. (2011). *Altruism in humans*. New York: Oxford University Press.

Batson, C. D., Cochran, P. J., Biederman, M. F., Blosser, J. L., Ryan, M. J., & Vogt, B. (1978). Failure to help when in a hurry: Callousness or conflict? *Personality and Social Psychology Bulletin, 4*(1), 97–101.

Batson, C. D., & Coke, J. S. (1981). Empathy: A source of altruistic motivation for helping? In J. P. Rushton & R. M. Sorrentino (Eds.), *Altruism and helping behavior* (pp. 167–187). Hillsdale, NJ: Erlbaum.

Batson, C. D., Duncan, B. D., Ackerman, P., Buckley, T., & Birch, K. (1981). Is empathic emotion a source of altruistic motivation? *Journal of Personality and Social Psychology, 40*(2), 290–302.

Batson, C. D., & Oleson, K. C. (1991). Current status of the empathy–altruism hypothesis. In M. S. Clark (Ed.), *Review of personality and social psychology: Vol. 12. Prosocial behavior* (pp. 62–85). Newbury Park, CA: Sage.

Batson, C. D., O'Quin, K., Fultz, J., Vanderplas, M., & Isen, A. M. (1983). Influence of self-reported distress and empathy on egoistic versus altruistic motivation to help. *Journal of Personality and Social Psychology, 45*, 706–718.

Baudson, T. G., & Preckel, F. (2013). Teachers' implicit personality theories about the gifted: An experimental approach. *School Psychology Quarterly, 28*(1), 37–46.

Baumeister, R. F. (1982). A self-presentational view of social phenomena. *Psychological Bulletin, 91*, 3–26.

Baumeister, R. F. (1998). The self. In D. Gilbert, S. Fiske, & G. Lindzey (Eds.), *The handbook of social psychology* (4th ed., Vol. 1, pp. 680–740). Boston: McGraw-Hill.

Baumeister, R. F., Stillwell, A. M., & Heatherton, T. F. (1994). Guilt: An interpersonal approach. *Psychological Bulletin, 115*(2), 243–267.

Baumrind, D. (1980). New directions in socialization research. *American Psychologist, 35*, 639–652.

Bavelas, J., Coates, L., & Johnson, T. (2000). Listeners as co-narrators. *Journal of Personality and Social Psychology, 79*, 941–952.

Beall, A., & Sternberg, R. (1995). The social construction of love. *Journal of Social and Personal Relationships, 12*, 417–438.

Bearman, P., Moody, J., & Stovel, K. (2004). Chains of affection: The structure of adolescent romantic and sexual networks. *American Journal of Sociology, 110*, 44–91.

Beaulieu, C. (2004). Intercultural study of personal space: A case study. *Journal of Applied Social Psychology, 34*, 794–805.

Beck, S. B., Ward-Hull, C. I., & McLear, P. M. (1976). Variables related to women's somatic preferences of the male and female body. *Journal of Personality and Social Psychology, 34*, 1200–1210.

Becker, H. S. (1963). *Outsiders: Studies in the sociology of deviance*. New York: Free Press.

Beckett, K. (1994). Setting the public agenda: "Street crime" and drug use in American politics. *Social Problems, 41*, 425–447.

Beebe, L. M., & Giles, H. (1984). Speech accommodation theories: A discussion in terms of second language learning. *International Journal of the Sociology of Language, 46*, 5–32.

Bell, R. (1979). Parent, child, and reciprocal influences. *American Psychologist, 34*, 821–826.

Bellavia, G., & Murray, S. (2003). Did I do that? Self-esteem related differences in reactions to romantic partners' moods. *Personal Relationships, 10*, 77–95.

Bellezza, S., Gino, F., & Keinan, A. (2014). The red sneakers effect: Inferring status and competence from signals of nonconformity. *Journal of Consumer Research, 41*(1), 35–54.

Belsky, J. (2006). Early child care and early child development: Major findings of the NICHD study of Early Child Care. *European Journal of Developmental Psychology, 3*, 95–110.

Belsky, J., Bakermans-Kranenburg, M. J., & van IJzendoorn, M. H. (2007). For better and for worse: Differential susceptibility to environmental influences. *Current Directions in Psychological Science, 16*(6), 300–304.

Bem, D. J. (1970). *Beliefs, attitudes, and human affairs.* Belmont, CA: Brooks/Cole.

Bem, S. (1974). The measurement of psychological androgyny. *Journal of Consulting and Clinical Psychology, 42*, 155–162.

Bender, A. (2012). Secrets and magic pills: Constructing masculinity and sexual "normalcy" following spinal cord injury. In L. Carpenter & J. DeLamater (Eds.), *Sex for life: From virginity to Viagra, how sexuality changes throughout our lives* (pp. 198–214). New York: New York University Press.

Bennett, M. (1990). Children's understanding of the mitigating function of disclaimers. *Journal of Social Psychology, 130*, 29–37.

Bennett, M., & Dewberry, C. (1989). Embarrassment at others' failures: A test of the Semin and Manstead model. *Journal of Social Psychology, 129*, 557–559.

Benson, M. L. (1989). The influence of class position on the formal and informal sanctioning of white-collar offenders. *Sociological Quarterly, 30*, 465–479.

Benson, M. L., & Fox, G. L. (2004). When violence hits home: How economics and neighborhood play a role, Research in Brief. NCJ, 205004.

Benson, M. L., & Walker, E. (1988). Sentencing the white-collar offender. *American Sociological Review, 53*, 294–302.

Ben-Ze'ev, A. (2000). *The subtlety of emotions.* Cambridge, MA: MIT Press.

Bergen, D., & Williams, J. (1991). Sex stereotypes in the United States revisited: 1972–1988. *Sex Roles, 24*, 413–423.

Berger, J., Cohen, B. P., & Zelditch, M. (1972). Status characteristics and social interaction. *American Sociological Review, 37*, 241–255.

Berger, J., Fişek, M. H., Norman, R. Z., & Wagner, D. G. (1998). Formation of reward expectations in status situations. In J. Berger & M. Zelditch (Eds.), *Status, power, and legitimacy* (pp. 121–154). New Brunswick, NJ: Transaction.

Berger, J., & Webster Jr., M. (2006). Expectations, status, and behavior. In P. J. Burke (Ed.), *Contemporary social psychological theories* (pp. 268–300). Palo Alto, CA: Stanford University Press.

Berger, L., Brooks-Gunn, J., Paxson, C., & Waldfogel, J. (2008). First-year maternal employment and child outcomes: Differences across racial and ethnic groups. *Children and Youth Services Review, 30*, 365–387.

Berger, P. L., & Luckmann, T. (1966). *The social construction of reality: A treatise in the sociology of knowledge.* Garden City, NY: Anchor Books.

Berkowitz, D., & Marsiglio, W. (2007). Gay men: Negotiating procreative, father, and family identities. *Journal of Marriage and Family, 69*, 36–381.

Berkowitz, L. (1972). Frustrations, comparisons, and other sources of emotion arousal as contributors to social unrest. *Journal of Social Issues, 28*(1), 77–91.

Berkowitz, L. (1978). Whatever happened to the frustration–aggression hypothesis? *American Behavioral Scientist, 21*, 691–708.

Berkowitz, L. (1989). Frustration–aggression hypothesis: Examination and reformulation. *Psychological Bulletin, 106*, 59–73.

Berkowitz, L., Klanderman, S. B., & Harris, R. (1964). Effects of experimenter awareness and sex of subject and experimenter on reactions to dependency relationships. *Sociometry, 27*, 327–337.

Berkowitz, M. W., Mueller, C. W., Schnell, S. V., & Pudberg, M. T. (1986). Moral reasoning and judgments of aggression. *Journal of Personality and Social Psychology, 51*, 885–891.

Berlin, L. J., Ispa, J. M., Fine, M. A., Malone, P. S., Brooks-Gunn, J., Brady-Smith, C., et al. (2009). Correlates and consequences of spanking and verbal punishment for low-income White, African American, and Mexican American toddlers. *Child Development, 80*, 1403–1420.

Bernstein, I., Kelly, W., & Doyle, P. (1977). Societal reaction to deviants: The case of criminal defendants. *American Sociological Review, 42*, 743–755.

Bernstein, I., Kick, E., Leung, J., & Schulz, B. (1977). Charge reduction: An intermediary stage in the process of labelling criminal defendants. *Social Forces, 56*, 362–384.

Bernstein, W. M., Stephan, W. G., & Davis, M. H. (1979). Explaining attributions for achievement: A path analytic approach. *Journal of Personality and Social Psychology, 37*, 1810–1821.

Bernuth, K. (2006, October 22). Amnesia victim, Al, struggles to bring past into present. *Denver Post.* www.denverpost.com/news/ci_4530616.

Berscheid, E., & Reis, H. (1998). Attraction and close relationships. In D. Gilbert, S. Fiske, & G. Lindzey (Eds.), *The handbook of social psychology* (4th ed., Vol. 2, pp. 193–281). Boston: McGraw-Hill.

Berscheid, E., & Walster [Hatfield], E. (1978). *Interpersonal attraction* (2nd ed.). Reading, MA: Addison-Wesley.

Bertenthal, B. I., & Fischer, K. (1978). Development of self-recognition in the infant. *Developmental Psychology, 14*, 44–50.

Bessenoff, G. (2006). Can the media affect us? Social comparison, self-discrepancy, and the thin ideal. *Psychology of Women Quarterly, 30*, 239–251.

Bianchi, S. M., & Robinson, J. (1997). What did you do today? Children's use of time, family composition, and the acquisition of social capital. *Journal of Marriage and Family, 59*, 332–344.

Biblarz, T., & Stacy, J. (2010). Does the gender of parents matter? *Journal of Marriage and Family, 72*, 3–22.

Bickman, L. (1971). The effect of social status on the honesty of others. *Journal of Social Psychology, 85*(1), 87–92.

Biddle, B. J. (1979). *Role theory: Expectations, identities, and behaviors.* New York: Academic Press.

Biddle, B. J. (1986). Recent developments in role theory. In A. Inkeles, J. Coleman, & N. Smelser (Eds.), *Annual Review of Sociology* (Vol. 12, pp. 67–92). Palo Alto, CA: Annual Reviews.

Bienenstock, E., & Bianchi, A. (2004). Activating performance expectations and status differences through gift exchange: Experimental results. *Social Psychology Quarterly, 67,* 310–318.

Billari, F. C., & Liefbroer, A. C. (2016). Why still marry? The role of feelings in the persistence of marriage as an institution. *British Journal of Sociology, 67,* 516–538.

Bilsky, W., Janik, M., & Schwartz, S. H. (2011). The structural organization of human values: Evidence from three rounds of the European Social Survey (ESS). *Journal of Cross-Cultural Psychology, 42,* 759–776.

Binder, J., Zagefka, H., Brown, R., Funke, F., Kessler, T., Mummendey, A., et al. (2009). Does contact reduce prejudice or does prejudice reduce contact? A longitudinal test of the contact hypothesis among majority and minority groups in three European countries. *Journal of Personality and Social Psychology, 96,* 843–856.

Birdwhistell, R. L. (1970). *Kinesics in context: Essays on body motion communications.* Philadelphia: University of Pennsylvania Press.

Bjorkvall, A., & Karlsson, A. (2011). The materiality of discourses and the semiotics of materials: A social perspective on the meaning potentials of written texts and furniture. *Semiotica, 187,* 141–165.

Black, D. (1980). *The manners and customs of the police.* New York: Academic Press.

Blackwell, D., & Lichter, D. (2004). Homogamy among dating, cohabiting, and married couples. *Sociological Quarterly, 45,* 719–737.

Blair, S., & Roese, N. J. (2013). Balancing the basket: The role of shopping basket composition in embarrassment. *Journal of Consumer Research, 40,* 676–691.

Blair-Loy, M. (2003). *Competing devotions: Career and family among women executives.* Cambridge, MA: Harvard University Press.

Blake, R. R., Shepard, H. A., & Mouton, J. S. (1964). *Managing intergroup conflict in industry.* Houston, TX: Gulf.

Blanck, P. D., & Rosenthal, R. (1982). Developing strategies for decoding "leaky" messages. In R. S. Feldman (Ed.), *Development of nonverbal behavior in children* (pp. 203–229). New York: Springer Verlag.

Blascovich, J., Mendes, W. B., Hunter, S., Lickel, B., & Kowai-Bell, N. (2001). Perceiver threat in social interactions with stigmatized others. *Journal of Personality and Social Psychology, 80,* 253–267.

Blass, T. (1991). Understanding behavior in the Milgram obedience experiment: The role of personality, situations, and their interactions. *Journal of Personality and Social Psychology, 60,* 398–413.

Blau, P. (1964). *Exchange and power in social life.* New York: Wiley.

Blauner, R. (1964). *Alienation and freedom.* Chicago: University of Chicago Press.

Blom, J. P., & Gumperz, J. J. (1972). Social meaning and linguistic structure: Code-switching in Norway. In J. J. Gumperz & D. Hymes (Eds.), *Directions in sociolinguistics* (pp. 407–434). New York: Holt, Rinehart and Winston.

Bloom, B. S. (1956). *Taxonomy of educational objectives: The classification of educational goals. Handbook 1: Cognitive domain.* New York: David McKay.

Blumberg, S. J., & Luke, J. V. (2012). Wireless substitution: Early release of estimates from the National Health Interview Survey, January–June 2012. Washington, DC: National Center for Health Statistics. www.cdc.gov/nchs/nhis.htm (Accessed June 20, 2018).

Blumer, H. (1958). Race prejudice as a sense of group position. *Pacific Sociological Review, 1*(1), 3–7.

Blumer, H. (1962). Society and symbolic interactionism. In A. M. Rose (Ed.), *Human behavior and social processes* (pp. 179–192). Boston: Houghton Mifflin.

Blumer, H. (1969). *Symbolic interactionism: Perspective and method.* Englewood Cliffs, NJ: Prentice Hall.

Blumstein, P. W. (1974). The honoring of accounts. *American Sociological Review, 39,* 551–566.

Boardman, J. S. (2004). Stress and physical health: The role of neighborhoods as mediating or moderating mechanisms. *Social Science and Medicine, 58,* 2473–2483.

Bobo, L. (1999). Prejudice as group position: Microfoundations of a sociological approach to racism and race relations. *Journal of Social Issues, 55,* 445–472.

Bochner, S., & Insko, C. A. (1966). Communicator discrepancy, source credibility, and opinion change. *Journal of Personality and Social Psychology, 4,* 614–621.

Bodenhausen, G. V., & Lichtenstein, M. (1987). Social stereotypes and information processing strategies: The impact of task complexity. *Journal of Personality and Social Psychology, 52,* 871–880.

Bogle, K. A. (2007). The shift from dating to hooking up in college: What scholars have missed. *Sociology Compass, 1*(2), 775–788.

Bohn, A. (2003). Familiar voices: Using Ebonics communication techniques in the primary classroom. *Urban Education, 38,* 688–707.

Bohra, K. A., & Pandey, J. (1984). Ingratiation toward strangers, friends, and bosses. *Journal of Social Psychology, 122,* 217–222.

Bolger, N., Davis, A., & Rafaeli, E., (2003). Diary methods: Capturing life as it is lived. *Annual Review of Psychology, 54,* 579–616.

Bolger, N., DeLongis, A., Kessler, R. C., & Wethington, E. (1989). The contagion of stress across multiple roles. *Journal of Marriage and Family, 51,* 175–183.

Bollen, K. A. (1989). *Structural equations with latent variables.* New York: Wiley.

Bollen, K. A., & Hoyle, R. H. (1990). Perceived cohesion: A conceptual and empirical examination. *Social Forces, 69,* 479–504.

Bollen, K. A., & Phillips, D. P. (1981). Suicidal motor vehicle fatalities in Detroit: A replication. *American Journal of Sociology, 87,* 404–412.

Bond, R., & Smith, P. B. (1996). Culture and conformity: A meta-analysis of studies using Asch's line judgment task. *Psychological Bulletin, 119*, 111–137.

Bord, R. J. (1976). The impact of imputed deviant identities in structuring evaluations and reactions. *Sociometry, 39*, 108–116.

Bornstein, R. (1992). Subliminal mere exposure effects. In R. Bornstein & T. Pittman (Eds.), *Perception without awareness: Cognitive, clinical, and social perspectives* (pp. 101–210). New York: Guilford Press.

Bornstein, R. F., & Pittman, T. S. (1992, March). *Perception without awareness: Cognitive, clinical, and social perspectives.* Paper presented at "Perception without Awareness: Cognitive, Clinical and Social Perspectives" Conference, Gettysburg College. Gettysburg, PA: Guilford Press.

Bosker, B. (2013, January 1). Affectiva's emotion recognition tech: When machines know what you're feeling. *Huffington Post.* https://www.huffingtonpost.com/2012/12/24/affectiva-emotion-recognition-technology_n_2360136.html (Accessed June 20, 2018).

Boswell, A. A., & Spade, J. Z. (1996). Fraternities and collegiate rape culture: Why are some fraternities more dangerous places for women? *Gender & Society, 10*(2), 133–147.

Botanaki, A., & Mattas, K. (2010). Revealing the values behind convenience food consumption. *Appetite, 55*, 629–638.

Bottomore, T. B. (Ed.). (1964). *Karl Marx: Early writings.* New York: McGraw-Hill.

Boulding, K. E. (1981). *Ecodynamics: A new theory of societal evolution.* Beverly Hills, CA: Sage.

Bourhis, R. Y., Giles, H., Leyens, J. P., & Tajfel, H. (1979). Psycholinguistic distinctiveness: Language divergence in Belgium. In H. Giles & R. N. St. Clair (Eds.), *Language and social psychology* (pp. 158–185). Oxford: Blackwell.

Bowlby, J. (1965). Maternal care and mental health (1953). In J. Bowlby (Ed.), *Child care and the growth of love.* London: Penguin.

Brackett, M. A., & Mayer, J. D. (2003). Convergent, discriminant, and incremental validity of competing measures of emotional intelligence. *Personality and Social Psychology Bulletin, 29*(9), 1147–1158.

Bradford, S., Feeney, J., & Campbell, L. (2002). Links between attachment orientations and dispositional and diary-based measures of disclosure in dating couples: A study of actor and partner effects. *Personal Relationships, 9*, 491–506.

Bradley, G. W. (1978). Self-serving biases in the attribution process: A reexamination of the fact or fiction question. *Journal of Personality and Social Psychology, 36*, 56–71.

Braithwaite, J. (2002). *Restorative justice & responsive regulation.* Oxford: Oxford University Press.

Brand, R. J., Bonatsos, A., D'Orazio, R., & DeShong, H. (2012). What is beautiful is good, even online: Correlations between photo attractiveness and text attractiveness in men's online dating profiles. *Computers in Human Behavior, 28*(1), 166–170.

Brauer, M. (2001). Intergroup perception in the social context: The effects of social status and group membership on perceived out-group homogeneity and ethnocentrism. *Journal of Experimental Social Psychology, 37*, 15–31.

Braveman, P. A., Cubbin, C., Egerter, S., Williams, D. R., & Pamuk, E. (2010). Socioeconomic disparities in health in the United States: What the patterns tell us. *American Journal of Public Health, 100*, S186–S196.

Brehm, J. W. (1956). Postdecision changes in the desirability of alternatives. *Journal of Abnormal and Social Psychology, 52*, 384–389.

Brehm, J. W., & Cohen, A. (1962). *Explorations in cognitive dissonance.* New York: Wiley.

Brehm, P. (1966). *A theory of psychological reactance.* New York: Academic Press.

Breiding, M. J., Smith, S. G., Basile, K. C., Walters, M. L., Chen, J., & Merrick, M. T. (2014). Prevalence and characteristics of sexual violence, stalking, and intimate partner violence victimization, National Intimate Partner and Sexual Violence Survey, United States, 2011. *MMWR: Surveillance summaries, 63*(SS-8), 1–18.

Brenner, P., & DeLamater, J. (2016). Measurement directiveness as a cause of response bias: Evidence from two survey experiments. *Sociological Methods and Research, 45*, 348–371.

Brewer, M. B. (1979). In-group bias in the minimal intergroup situation: A cognitive–motivational analysis. *Psychological Bulletin, 86*, 307–324.

Brewer, M. B. (1986). The role of ethnocentrism in intergroup conflict. In S. Worchel & W. G. Austin (Eds.), *Psychology of intergroup relations* (2nd ed., pp. 88–102). Chicago: Nelson-Hall.

Brewer, M. B., & Brown, R. J. (1998). Intergroup relations. In D. Gilbert, S. Fiske, & G. Lindzey (Eds.), *The handbook of social psychology* (4th ed., Vol. 2, pp. 554–594). New York: McGraw-Hill.

Brewer, M. B., & Lui, L. (1984). Categorization of the elderly by the elderly: Effects of perceiver's category membership. *Personality and Social Psychology Bulletin, 10*, 585–595.

Brewer, M. B., & Miller, N. (1984). Beyond the contact hypothesis: Theoretical perspectives on desegregation. In N. Miller & M. B. Brewer (Eds.), *Groups in contact: The psychology of desegregation* (pp. 281–302). Orlando, FL: Academic Press.

Briggs, J. L. (1970). *Never in anger: Portrait of an Eskimo family* (Vol. 12). Cambridge, MA: Harvard University Press.

Brim, O. G., & Ryff, C. (1980). On the properties of life events. In P. Baltes & O. G. Brim (Eds.), *Life-span development and behavior* (Vol. 3, pp. 368–388). New York: Academic Press.

Briñol, P., & Petty, R. E. (2012). A history of attitudes and persuasion research. In A. W. Kruglanski & W. Stroebe (Eds.), *Handbook of the history of social psychology* (pp. 283–320). New York: Psychology Press.

Brockmann, H., & Klein, T. (2002). Love and death in Germany: The marital biography and its impact on health (Working Paper 2002–15). Rostock, Germany: Max Planck Institute.

Brockner, J., & Wiesenfeld, B. M. (1996). An integrative framework for explaining reactions to a decision: The interactive effects of outcomes and procedures. *Psychological Bulletin, 120*, 189–208.

Brody, E. M. (2004). *Women in the middle: Their parent care years.* New York: Springer.

Brody, G. H., Chen, Y. F., Murry, V. M., Ge, X., Simons, R. L., Gibbons, F. X., et al. (2006). Perceived discrimination and the adjustment of African American youths: A five-year longitudinal analysis with contextual moderation effects. *Child Development, 77*, 1170–1189.

Bronfenbrenner, U., McClelland, P., Wethington, E., Moen, P., & Ceci, S. (1996). *The state of Americans: This generation and the next.* New York: Free Press.

Broverman, I., Vogel, S., Broverman, D., Clarkson, F., & Rosenkrantz, P. (1972). Sex-role stereotypes: A current appraisal. *Journal of Social Issues, 28*(2), 59–78.

Brown, J. D. (1991a). The professional ex-: An alternative for exiting the deviant career. *Sociological Quarterly, 32*, 219–230.

Brown, J. D. (1991b). Staying fit and staying well: Physical fitness as a moderator of life stress. *Journal of Personality and Social Psychology, 60*, 555–561.

Brown, J. D., Collins, R. L., & Schmidt, G. W. (1988). Self-esteem and direct vs. indirect forms of self-enhancement. *Journal of Personality and Social Psychology, 55*, 445–453.

Brown, R. (1965). *Social psychology.* Glencoe, IL: Free Press.

Brown, R. (1988). *Group processes: Dynamics within and between groups.* Oxford: Basil Blackwell.

Brown, R., & Fraser, C. (1963). The acquisition of syntax. In C. Cofer & B. Musgrave (Eds.), *Verbal behaviour and learning* (pp. 43–79). New York: McGraw-Hill.

Brown, R. P., Osterman, L. L., & Barnes, C. D. (2009). School violence and the culture of honor. *Psychological Science, 20*(11), 1400–1405.

Brown, T., & Warner, D. (2008). Divergent pathways? Racial/ethnic differences on older women's labor force withdrawal. *Journal of Gerontology: Social Sciences, 63B*, S122–S134.

Brownell, C. A. (2013). Early development of prosocial behavior: Current perspectives. *Infancy, 18*, 1–9.

Browning, C. R., & Cagney, K. A. (2003). Moving beyond poverty: Neighborhood structure, social processes, and health. *Journal of Health and Social Behavior, 44*(4), 552–571.

Brunstein, J. C., Dangelmayer, G., & Schultheiss, O. C. (1996). Personal goals and social support in close relationships: Effects on relationship mood and marital satisfaction. *Journal of Personality and Social Psychology, 71*, 1006–1019.

Bryant, W. K., Jeon-Slaughter, H., Kang, H., & Tax, A. (2003). Participation in philanthropic activities: Donating money and time. *Journal of Consumer Policy, 26*, 43–73.

Brym, R., & Lenton, R. (2001). *Love online: A report on digital dating in Canada.* https://www.researchgate.net/publication/237605184_Love_Online_A_Report_on_Digital_Dating_in_Canada (Accessed June 11, 2018).

Bryson, B. (1996). "Anything but heavy metal": Symbolic exclusion and musical dislikes. *American Sociological Review, 61*(5), 884–899.

Buchwald, E., Fletcher, P. R., & Roth, M. (Eds.). (2005). *Transforming a rape culture* (p. XI). Minneapolis, MN: Milkweed Editions.

Buffington, C., Cerf, B., Jones, C., & Weinberg, B. A. (2016). STEM training and early career outcomes of female and male graduate students: Evidence from UMETRICS data linked to the 2010 census. *American Economic Review, 106*, 333–338.

Bugenthal, D. E. (1974). Interpretations of naturally occurring discrepancies between words and intonation: Modes of inconsistency resolution. *Journal of Personality and Social Psychology, 30*, 125–133.

Buhrmester, M., Kwang, T., & Gosling, S. D. (2011). Amazon's Mechanical Turk: A new source of inexpensive, yet high-quality data? *Perspectives on Psychological Science, 6*, 3–5.

Bui, K.-V. T., Peplau, L. A., & Hill, C. T. (1996). Testing the Rusbult model of relationship commitment and stability in a 15-year study of heterosexual couples. *Personality and Social Psychology Bulletin, 22*, 1244–1257.

Burger, J. M. (1999). The foot-in-the-door compliance procedure: A multiple-process analysis and review. *Personality and Social Psychology Review, 3*, 303–325.

Burger, J. M., & Petty, R. E. (1981). The low-ball compliance technique: Task or person commitment? *Journal of Personality and Social Psychology, 40*, 492–500.

Burgess, R. L., & Akers, K. L. (1966). A differential association–reinforcement theory of criminal behavior. *Social Problems, 14*, 128–147.

Burke, P. (2004). Identities and social structure: The 2003 Cooley-Mead Award Address. *Social Psychology Quarterly, 67*, 5–15.

Burke, P. J. (1991). Identity processes and social stress. *American Sociological Review, 56*, 836–849.

Burke, P. J., & Reitzes, D. (1981). The link between identity and role performance. *Social Psychology Quarterly, 44*, 83–92.

Burke, P. J., & Stets, J. E. (2009). *Identity theory.* Oxford: Oxford University Press.

Burn, S. M. (2009). A situational model of sexual assault prevention through bystander intervention. *Sex Roles, 60*(11–12), 779–792.

Burns, D. (2009). The experience and expression of anger and aggression in dating relationships for male college athletes in contact and non-contact sports. Doctoral dissertation, Oklahoma State University.

Burnstein, E., Crandall, C., & Kitayama, S. (1994). An evolved heuristic for altruism: Evidence for a human propensity to calculate inclusive fitness. *Journal of Personality and Social Psychology, 67*, 773–789.

Burt, M. R. (1980). Cultural myths and supports for rape. *Journal of Personality and Social Psychology, 38*(2), 217–230.

Burton, L. M., Bonilla-Silva, E., Ray, V., Buckelew, R., & Freeman, E. H. (2010). Critical race theories, colorism, and the decade's research on families of color. *Journal of Marriage and Family, 72*, 440–459.

Bushman, B. J. (1988). The effects of apparel on compliance: A field experiment with a female authority figure. *Personality and Social Psychology Bulletin, 14*, 459–467.

Bushman, B. J. (2002). Does venting anger feed or extinguish the flame? Catharsis, rumination, distraction, anger, and aggressive responding. *Personality and Social Psychology Bulletin, 28*, 724–731.

Bushman, B. J., Baumeister, R. F., & Phillips, C. M. (2001). Do people aggress to improve their mood? Catharsis beliefs, affect regulation opportunity, and aggressive responding. *Journal of Personality and Social Psychology*, *81*(1), 17.

Bushman, B., Baumeister, R., & Stack, A. (1999). Catharsis, aggression, and persuasive influence: Self-fulfilling or self-defeating prophecies. *Journal of Personality and Social Psychology*, *76*, 367–376.

Bushman, B. J., Bonacci, A. M., Pedersen, W. C., Vasquez, E. A., & Miller, N. (2005). Chewing on it can chew you up: Effects of rumination on triggered displaced aggression. *Journal of Personality and Social Psychology*, *88*(6), 969.

Bushman, B. J., & Huesmann, L. R. (2001). Effects of televised violence on aggression. In D. G. Singer & J. L. Singer (Eds.), *Handbook of children and the media* (pp. 223–254). Thousand Oaks, CA: Sage.

Buss, D. M. (1994). *The evolution of desire: Strategies of human mating*. New York: Basic Books.

Buss, D. M. (1999). *Evolutionary psychology*. Boston: Allyn and Bacon.

Buss, D. M., & Kenrick, D. T. (1998). Evolutionary social psychology. In D. Gilbert, S. Fiske, & G. Lindzey (Eds.), *The handbook of social psychology* (4th ed., Vol. 2, pp. 982–1026). Boston: McGraw-Hill.

Butterfield, F. (2002, August 21). Father steals best: Crime in an American family. *New York Times*.

Buunk, B., Dijkstra, P., Fetchenhauer, D., & Kenrick, D. (2002). Age and gender differences in mate selection criteria for various involvement levels. *Personal Relationships*, *9*, 271–278.

Buunk, B. P., & van der Eijnden, R. (1997). Perceived prevalence, perceived superiority, and relationship satisfaction: Most relationships are good but ours is the best. *Personality and Social Psychology Bulletin*, *23*, 219–228.

Byrne, D. (1961a). The influence of propinquity and opportunities for interaction on classroom relationships. *Human Relations*, *14*, 63–69.

Byrne, D. (1961b). Interpersonal attraction and attitude similarity. *Journal of Abnormal and Social Psychology*, *62*, 713–715.

Byrne, D. (1971). *The attraction paradigm*. New York: Academic Press.

Byrne, D., & Clore, G. L. (1970). A reinforcement model of evaluative responses. *Personality: An International Journal*, *1*, 103–128.

Byrne, D., Ervin, C., & Lamberth, J. (1970). Continuity between the experimental study of attraction and real-life computer dating. *Journal of Personality and Social Psychology*, *16*, 157–165.

Byrne, D., & Kelley, K. (1984). Introduction: Pornography and sex research. In N. M. Malamuth & E. Donnerstein (Eds.), *Pornography and sexual aggression* (pp. 1–15). Orlando, FL: Academic Press.

Byrne, D., & Nelson, D. (1965). Attraction as a linear function of proportion of positive reinforcements. *Journal of Personality and Social Psychology*, *1*, 659–663.

Caballero, M., Lumpkin, J., & Madden, C. (1989). Using physical attractiveness as an advertising tool: An empirical test of attraction phenomenon. *Journal of Advertising*, *29*, 16–22.

Cacioppo, J. T., Petty, R. E., Feinstein, J. A., & Jarvis, W. B. G. (1996). Dispositional differences in cognitive motivation: The life and times of individuals varying in need for cognition. *Psychological Bulletin*, *119*, 197–253.

Cadinu, M. R., & Rothbart, M. (1996). Self-anchoring and differentiation processes in minimal group settings. *Journal of Personality and Social Psychology*, *70*, 661–677.

Cahill, S. E. (1999). Emotional capital and professional socialization: The case of mortuary science students (and me). *Social Psychology Quarterly*, *62*, 101–116.

Callero, P. (1985). Role-identity salience. *Social Psychology Quarterly*, *48*, 203–214.

Cameron, D. (1998). Gender, language, and discourse: A review essay. *Signs: Journal of Women in Culture and Society*, *23*, 945–973.

Cameron, J., & Ross, M. (2007). In times of uncertainty: Predicting the survival of long-distance relationships. *Journal of Social Psychology*, *147*, 581–606.

Campbell, D. T. (1965). Ethnocentric and other altruistic motives. In D. Levine (Ed.), *Nebraska Symposium on Motivation* (Vol. 13, pp. 283–311). Lincoln: Nebraska University Press.

Campbell, D. T. (1967). Stereotypes in the perception of group differences. *American Psychologist*, *22*, 817–829.

Campbell, H. (2008). Female drug smugglers on the U.S.–Mexico border: Gender, crime, and empowerment. *Anthropological Quarterly*, *81*, 233–267.

Campbell, J. D. (1990). Self-esteem and clarity of self-concept. *Journal of Personality and Social Psychology*, *59*, 538–549.

Campbell, W. K., & Sedikides, C. (1999). Self-threat magnifies the self-serving bias: A meta-analysis integration. *Review of General Psychology*, *3*, 23–43.

Cano, I., Hopkins, N., & Islam, M. R. (1991). Memory for stereotype-related material: A replication study with real-life social groups. *European Journal of Social Psychology*, *21*, 349–357.

Cantor, J., & Wilson, B. J. (2003). Media and violence: Intervention strategies for reducing aggression. *Media Psychology*, *5*, 363–403.

Caplan, F., & Caplan, T. (1973). *The power of play*. New York: Doubleday.

Caporeal, L. R. (2001). Evolutionary psychology: Toward a unifying theory and a hybrid science. *Annual Review of Psychology*, *52*, 607–628.

Caprara, G. V., Schwartz, S., Capanna, C., Vecchione, M., & Barbaranelli, C. (2006). Personality and politics: Values, traits, and political choice. *Political Psychology*, *27*, 1–28.

Carden, R., Bryant, C., & Moss, R. (2004). Locus of control, test anxiety, academic procrastination, and achievement among college students. *Psychological Reports*, *95*(2), 581–582.

Carless, S. A., & De Paola, C. (2000). The measurement of cohesion in work teams. *Small Group Research*, *31*(1), 71–88.

Carli, L. L., LaFleur, S. J., & Loeber, C. C. (1995). Nonverbal behavior, gender, and influence. *Journal of Personality and Social Psychology*, *68*, 1030–1041.

Carlson, M., Marcus-Newhall, A., & Miller, N. (1990). Effects of situational aggression cues: A quantitative review. *Journal of Personality and Social Psychology, 58*, 622–633.

Carlson, M., & Miller, N. (1987). Explanation of the relation between negative mood and helping. *Psychological Bulletin, 102*(1), 91.

Carmalt, J. H., Cawley, J., Joyner, K., & Sobal, J. (2008). Body weight and matching with a physically attractive romantic partner. *Journal of Marriage and Family, 70*, 1287–1296.

Carmichael, S., Langton, L., Pendell, G., Reitzel, J., & Piqure, A. (2005). Do the experiential and deterrent effect operate differently across gender? *Journal of Criminal Justice, 33*, 267–276.

Carnevale, P. J., Pruitt, D. G., & Carrington, P. I. (1982). Effects of future dependence, liking, and repeated requests for help on helping behavior. *Social Psychology Quarterly, 45*(1), 9–14.

Carr, J. L., & VanDeusen, K. M. (2004). Risk factors for male sexual aggression on college campuses. *Journal of Family Violence, 19*(5), 279–289.

Carrington, C. (1999). *No place like home: Relationships and family life among lesbians and gay men.* Chicago: University of Chicago Press.

Carroll, J. M., & Russell, J. A. (1996). Do facial expressions signal specific emotions? Judging emotion from face in context. *Journal of Personality and Social Psychology, 70*, 205–218.

Carron, A. V., Colman, M. M., Wheeler, J., & Stevens, D. (2002). Cohesion and performance in sport: A meta analysis. *Journal of Sport and Exercise Psychology, 24*(2), 168–188.

Cartwright, D. (1968). The nature of group cohesiveness. In D. Cartwright & A. Zander (Eds.), *Group dynamics* (3rd ed., pp. 91–109). New York: Harper & Row.

Cartwright, D. (1973). Determinants of scientific progress: The case of research on the risky shift. *American Psychologist, 28*, 222–231.

Case, A., & Paxson, C. (2004). Sex differences in morbidity and mortality (Working Paper w10653). Cambridge, MA: National Bureau of Economic Research.

Caspi, A., & Herbener, E. S. (1990). Continuity and change: Assortative marriage and the consistency of personality in adulthood. *Journal of Personality and Social Psychology, 58*, 250–258.

Catalano, R., Novaco, R., & McConnell, W. (1997). A model of the net effect of job loss on violence. *Journal of Personality and Social Psychology, 72*(6), 1440–1447.

Cate, R., Levin, L., & Richmond, L. (2002). Premarital relationship stability: A review of recent research. *Journal of Social and Personal Relationships, 19*, 261–284.

Ceci, S. J., & Williams, W. M. (2011). Understanding current causes of women's underrepresentation in science. *PNAS, 108*, 3157–3162.

Centers, R. (1975). Attitude similarity–dissimilarity as a correlate of heterosexual attraction and love. *Journal of Marriage and Family, 37*, 305–312.

Chaiken, S. (1980). Heuristic versus systematic information processing and the use of source versus message cues in persuasion. *Journal of Personality and Social Psychology, 39*, 752–766.

Chaiken, S. (1986). Physical appearance and social influence. In C. P. Herman, M. P. Zanna, & E. T. Higgins (Eds.), *Physical appearance, stigma, and social behavior: The Ontario Symposium* (Vol. 3, pp. 143–177). Hillsdale, NJ: Erlbaum.

Chaiken, S., Giner-Sorolla, R., & Chen, S. (1996). Beyond accuracy: Defense and impression motives in heuristic and systematic processing. In P. M. Gollwitzer & J. A. Bargh (Eds.), *The psychology of action: Linking cognition and motivation to behavior* (pp. 553–578). New York: Guilford Press.

Chaiken, S., & Maheswaran, D. (1994). Heuristic processing can bias systematic processing: Effects of source credibility, argument ambiguity, and task importance on attitude judgment. *Journal of Personality and Social Psychology, 66*, 460–473.

Chaiken, S., & Yates, S. (1985). Affective-cognitive consistency and thought-induced polarization. *Journal of Personality and Social Psychology, 49*, 1470–1481.

Chambliss, W. J. (1994). Policing the ghetto underclass: The politics of law and law enforcement. *Social Problems, 41*, 177–193.

Chandola, T., Brunner, E., & Marmot, M. (2006). Chronic stress at work and the metabolic syndrome: Prospective study. *British Medical Journal, 332*, 521–525.

Chang, A., & Bordia, P. (2001). A multidimensional approach to the group cohesion–group performance relationship. *Small Group Research, 32*(4), 379–405.

Chao, R. (1994). Beyond parental control and authoritarian parenting style: Understanding Chinese parenting through the cultural notion of training. *Child Development, 65*, 1111–1119.

Chaplin, W., Phillips, J., Brown, J., Clanton, N., & Stein, J. (2000). Handshaking, gender, personality, and first impressions. *Journal of Personality and Social Psychology, 79*, 110–117.

Chapman, J. (2006). Anxiety and defective decision making: An elaboration of the groupthink model. *Management Decision, 44*(10), 1391–1404.

Chapman, R. S., Streim, N. W., Crais, E. R., Salmon, D., Strand, E. A., & Negri, N. A. (1992). Child talk: Assumptions of a developmental process model for early language learning. In R. S. Chapman (Ed.), *Processes in language acquisition and disorder* (pp. 3–19). Chicago: Mosby/Year Book.

Charon, J. M. (1995). *Symbolic interactionism: An introduction, interpretation, and integration* (5th ed.). Englewood Cliffs, NJ: Prentice Hall.

Check, J. V., & Malamuth, N. M. (1983). Sex role stereotyping and reactions to depictions of stranger versus acquaintance rape. *Journal of Personality and Social Psychology, 45*(2), 344–356.

Chen, H. C., Reardon, R., Rea, C., & Moore, D. J. (1992). Forewarning of content and involvement: Consequences for persuasion and resistance to persuasion. *Journal of Experimental Social Psychology, 22*, 23–33.

Cherlin, A. J. (2010). Demographic trends in the United States: A review of research in the 2000s. *Journal of Marriage and Family, 72*, 403–419.

Chiricos, T., & Waldo, G. (1975). Socioeconomic status and criminal sentencing: An empirical assessment of a conflict proposition. *American Sociological Review, 40*, 753–772.

Chowdhury, T. G., Ratneshwar, S., & Mohanty, P. (2009). The time-harried shopper: Exploring the differences between maximizers and satisficers. *Marketing Letters, 20*(2), 155–167.

Christopher, F. S., & Roosa, M. (1991). Factors affecting sexual decisions in the premarital relationships of adolescents and young adults. In K. McKinney & S. Sprecher (Eds.), *Sexuality in close relationships* (pp. 111–133). Hillsdale, NJ: Erlbaum.

Cialdini, R. B. (1993). *Influence: Science and practice* (3rd ed.). New York: HarperCollins.

Cialdini, R. B. (2001). *Influence: Science and practice* (4th ed.). Boston: Allyn and Bacon.

Cialdini, R. B., Borden, R., Thorne, A., Walker, M., & Freeman, S. (1976). Basking in reflected glory: Three (football) field studies. *Journal of Personality and Social Psychology, 34*, 366–375.

Cialdini, R. B., Cacioppo, J. T., Basset, R., & Miller, J. A. (1978). Low-ball procedure for producing compliance: Commitment, then cost. *Journal of Personality and Social Psychology, 36*, 463–476.

Cialdini, R. B., Kenrick, D. T., & Baumann, D. J. (1982). Effects of mood on prosocial behavior in children and adults. In N. Eisenberg (Ed.), *The development of prosocial behavior* (pp. 339–359). New York: Academic Press.

Cialdini, R. B., Schaller, M., Houlihan, D., Arps, K., Fultz, J., & Beaman, A. L. (1987). Empathy-based helping: Is it selflessly or selfishly motivated? *Journal of Personality and Social Psychology, 52*(4), 749–758.

Clance, P. R., & Imes, S. A. (1978). The imposter phenomenon in high achieving women: Dynamics and therapeutic intervention. *Psychotherapy: Theory, Research and Practice, 15*(3), 241–247.

Clark, E. V. (1976). From gesture to word: On the natural history of deixis in language acquisition. In J. S. Bruner & A. Gartner (Eds.), *Human growth and development* (pp. 85–120). Oxford: Clarendon.

Clark, J. K., Wegener, D. T., Habashi, M. M., & Evans, A. T. (2012). Source expertise and persuasion: The effects of perceived opposition or support on message scrutiny. *Personality and Social Psychology Bulletin, 38*, 90–100.

Clark, M. S., Gotay, C. C., & Mills, J. (1974). Acceptance of help as a function of the potential helper and opportunity to repay. *Journal of Applied Social Psychology, 4*, 224–229.

Clark, R. D., & Maass, A. (1990). The effects of majority size on minority influence. *European Journal of Social Psychology, 20*(2), 99–117.

Clark, R. D., & Word, L. E. (1972). Why don't bystanders help? Because of ambiguity? *Journal of Personality and Social Psychology, 24*, 392–400.

Cloward, R. (1959). Illegitimate means, anomie, and deviant behavior. *American Sociological Review, 24*, 164–176.

CNN. (2012, March 20). 911 calls paint picture of chaos after Florida teen is shot. http://news.blogs.cnn.com/2012/03/20/911-calls-paint-picture-of-chaos-after-florida-teen-is-shot/.

CNPAAEMI (Council of National Psychological Associations for the Advancement of Ethnic Minority Interests). (2000). *Guidelines for research in ethnic minority communities*. Washington, DC: American Psychological Association.

Coffe, H., & Geys, B. (2008). Measuring the bridging nature of voluntary associations: The importance of association size. *Sociology, 42*(2), 357–369.

Cognard-Black, A. (2004). Will they stay, or will they go? Sex-atypical work among token men who teach. *Sociological Quarterly, 45*, 113–139.

Cohen, A. (1966). *Deviance and control*. Englewood Cliffs, NJ: Prentice Hall.

Cohen, B. P., & Zhou, X. (1991). Status processes in enduring work groups. *American Sociological Review, 56*, 179–188.

Cohen, C. E. (1981). Person categories and social perception: Testing some boundaries of the processing effects of prior knowledge. *Journal of Personality and Social Psychology, 40*, 441–452.

Cohen, D. (1996). Law, social policy, and violence: The impact of regional cultures. *Journal of Personality and Social Psychology, 70*, 961–978.

Cohen, D., Nisbett, R. E., Bowdle, B. F., & Schwarz, N. (1996). Insult, aggression, and the southern culture of honor: An "experimental ethnography." *Journal of Personality and Social Psychology, 70*(5), 945–960.

Cohen, E. G. (1980). Design and redesign of the desegregated school: Problems of status, power, and conflict. In W. G. Stephan & J. Feagin (Eds.), *School desegregation* (pp. 251–280). New York: Academic Press.

Cohen, E. G., & Roper, S. (1972). Modification of interracial interaction disability: An application of status characteristic theory. *American Sociological Review, 37*, 643–657.

Cohen, L., & Kluegel, J. (1978). Determinants of juvenile court dispositions: Ascriptive and achieved factors in two metropolitan courts. *American Sociological Review, 43*, 162–176.

Cohen, L. J., & DeBenedet, A. T. (2012, July 17). Penn State cover-up; groupthink in action. *Time Magazine*. Retrieved July 2, 2017, from http://ideas.time.com/2012/07/17/penn-state-cover-up-group-think-in-action/

Cohen, M. J., & Wade, T. J. (2012). Individual differences in first and fourth year college women's short term mating strategy preferences and perceptions. *Psychology, 3*(11), 966–973.

Cohen, P. (2003). Occupational segregation and the devaluation of women's work across U.S. labor markets. *Social Forces, 81*, 881–908.

Cohn, E. G., & Rotton, J. (1997). Assault as a function of time and temperature: A moderator-variable time-series analysis. *Journal of Personality and Social Psychology, 72*(6), 1322–1334.

Cohn, E. G., & Rotton, J. (2005). The curve is still out there: A reply to Bushman, Wang, and Anderson's (2005) Is the curve relating temperature to aggression linear or curvilinear? *Journal of Personality and Social Psychology, 89*(1), 67–70.

Cohn, R. M. (1978). The effect of employment status change on self-attitudes. *Social Psychology, 41,* 81–93.

Cole, T. (2001). Lying to the one you love: The use of deception in romantic relationships. *Journal of Social and Personal Relationships, 18,* 107–129.

Coleman, J. W. (1987). Toward an integrated theory of white-collar crime. *American Journal of Sociology, 93,* 406–439.

Coleman, L. (2004). *The copycat effect: How the media and popular culture trigger the mayhem in tomorrow's headlines.* New York: Paraview.

Coleman, R. P., & Neugarten, B. (1971). *Social status in the city.* San Francisco: Jossey-Bass.

Collett, J. L., & Avelis, J. (2011). Building a life together: Reciprocal and negotiated exchange in fragile families. *Advances in Group Processes, 28,* 227–254.

Collett, J. L., Kelly, S., & Sobolewski, C. (2010). Using *Remember the Titans* to teach theories of conflict reduction. *Teaching Sociology, 38,* 258–266.

Collett, J. L., & Lizardo, O. (2010). Occupational status and the experience of anger. *Social Forces, 88*(5), 2079–2104.

Collett, J. L., Vercel, K., & Boykin, O. (2015). Using identity processes to understand persistent inequality in parenting. *Social Psychology Quarterly, 78,* 345–364.

Collett, P. (1971). On training Englishmen in the nonverbal behavior of Arabs: An experiment in intercultural communication. *International Journal of Psychology, 6,* 209–215.

Colley, A., Mulhern, G., Maltby, J., & Wood, A. M. (2009). The short form BSRI: Instrumentality, expressiveness and gender associations among a United Kingdom sample. *Personality and Individual Differences, 46*(3), 384–387.

Collins, N. L., & Miller, L. C. (1994). Self-disclosure and liking: A meta-analytic review. *Psychological Bulletin, 116,* 457–475.

Committee on Maximizing the Potential of Women. (2007). *Beyond bias and barriers: Fulfilling the potential of women in academic science and engineering.* Washington, DC: National Academy Press.

Compton, J., & Pfau, M. (2004). Use of inoculation to foster resistance to credit card marketing targeting college students. *Journal of Applied Communication Research, 32*(4), 343–364.

Comstock, G. (1984). Media influences on aggression. In A. Goldstein (Ed.), *Prevention and control of aggression: Principles, practices, and research* (pp. 241–272). New York: Pergamon.

Condon, J. W., & Crano, W. D. (1988). Inferred evaluation and the relation between attitude similarity and interpersonal attraction. *Journal of Personality and Social Psychology, 54,* 789–797.

Condon, W. S., & Ogston, W. D. (1967). A segmentation of behavior. *Journal of Psychiatric Research, 5,* 221–235.

Conger, R., & Conger, K. (2002). Resilience in Midwestern families: Selected findings from the first decade of a prospective, longitudinal study. *Journal of Marriage and Family, 64,* 361–373.

Connell, R. W. (2005). *Masculinities.* Berkeley: University of California Press.

Consedine, N., Sabag-Cohen, S., & Krivoshekova, Y. (2007). Ethnic, gender, and socioeconomic differences in young adults' self-disclosure: Who discloses what to whom? *Cultural Diversity and Ethnic Minority Psychology, 13,* 254–263.

Conte, R., & Castelfranchi, C. (1995). Understanding the functions of norms in social groups through simulation. In N. Gilbert & R. Conte (Eds.), *Artificial societies: The computer simulation of social life* (pp. 252–267). London: UCL Press.

Conway, M., DiFazio, R., & Mayman, S. (1999). Judging others' emotions as a function of the others' status. *Social Psychology Quarterly, 62*(3), 291–305.

Cook, K. (Ed.). (1987). *Social exchange theory.* Newbury Park, CA: Sage.

Cook, K. S., Cheshire, C., Rice, E. R., & Nakagawa, S. (2013). Social exchange theory. In J. D. DeLamater & A. Ward (Eds.), *Handbook of social psychology* (pp. 61–88). Dordrecht: Springer Netherlands.

Cook, K. S., & Emerson, R. M. (1978). Power, equity and commitment in exchange networks. *American Sociological Review, 43,* 721–739.

Cooke, B., Rossmann, M., McCubbin, H., & Patterson, J. (1988). Examining the definition and measurement of social support: A resource for individuals and families. *Family Relations, 37,* 211–216.

Cooley, C. H. (1902). *Human nature and the social order.* New York: Scribner.

Cooley, C. H. (1909). *Social organization: A study of the larger mind.* New York: Scribner.

Cooper, A., & Smith, E. L. (2011). *Homicide trends in the United States, 1980–2008.* Bureau of Justice Statistics. BiblioGov.

Cooper, K. (2015). A woman's advantage. https://theblog.okcupid.com/a-womans-advantage-82d5074dde2d#.tbx58818b

Cooper, K., Quayle, E., Jonsson, L., & Svedin, C. G. (2016). Adolescents and self-taken sexual images: A review of the literature. *Computers in Human Behavior, 55,* 706–716.

Cooper, W. H. (1981). Ubiquitous halo. *Psychological Bulletin, 90,* 218–244.

Coopersmith, S. (1967). *The antecedents of self-esteem.* San Francisco: Freeman.

Cornelis, E., Cauberghe, V., & De Pelsmacker, P. (2014). Being healthy or looking good? The effectiveness of health versus appearance focused arguments in two-sided messages. *Journal of Health Psychology, 19*(9), 1132–1142.

Correll, J., Hudson, S. M., Guillermo, S., & Ma, D. S. (2014). The police officer's dilemma: A decade of research on racial bias in the decision to shoot. *Social and Personality Psychology Compass, 8*(5), 201–213.

Correll, J., Park, B., Judd, C. M., Wittenbrink, B., Sadler, M. S., & Keesee, T. (2007). Across the thin blue line: Police officers and racial bias in the decision to shoot. *Journal of Personality and Social Psychology, 92*(6), 1006.

Correll, S. (2004). Constraints into preferences: Gender, status and emerging career aspirations. *American Sociological Review, 69,* 93–113.

Correll, S. J. (2001). Gender and the career choice process: The role of biased self-assessments. *American Journal of Sociology, 106*(6), 1691–1730.

Correll, S. J., Benard, S., & Paik, I. (2007). Getting a job: Is there a motherhood penalty? *American Journal of Sociology, 112*(5), 1297–1339.

Corsaro, W. A. (2011). *The sociology of childhood* (3rd ed.). Los Angeles, CA: Sage.

Corsaro, W. A., & Eder, D. (1995). Development and socialization of children and adolescents. In K. S. Cook, G. A. Fine, & J. S. House (Eds.), *Sociological perspectives on social psychology* (pp. 421–451). Boston: Allyn and Bacon.

Corsaro, W., & Fingerson, L. (2003). Development and socialization in childhood. In J. DeLamater (Ed.), *Handbook of social psychology* (pp. 125–165). New York: Kluwer—Plenum.

Corsaro, W., & Molinari, L. (2000). Priming events and Italian children's transition from preschool to elementary school: Representations and actions. *Social Psychology Quarterly, 63,* 16–33.

Corsaro, W. A., & Rizzo, T. A. (1988). *Discussione* and friendship: Socialization processes in the peer culture of Italian nursery school children. *American Sociological Review, 53,* 879–894.

Cortese, A. J. (2016). *Provocateur: Images of women and minorities in advertising* (4th ed.). Lanham, MD: Rowan & Littlefield.

Coser, L. A. (1967). *Continuities in the study of social conflict.* New York: Free Press.

Costa, M., Dinsbach, W., & Manstead, A. (2001). Social presence, embarrassment, and nonverbal behavior. *Journal of Nonverbal Behavior, 25,* 225–240.

Costa Jr., P. T., & McCrae, R. R. (1992). *Revised NEO Personality Inventory (NEO-PI-R) and NEO Five-Factor Inventory (NEO-FFI) manual.* Odessa, FL: Psychological Assessment Resources.

Cota, A. A., & Dion, K. L. (1986). Salience of gender and sex composition of ad hoc groups: An experimental test of distinctiveness theory. *Journal of Personality and Social Psychology, 50,* 770–776.

Cota, A. A., Evans, C. R., Dion, K. L., Kilik, L., & Longman, R. S. (1995). The structure of group cohesion. *Personality and Social Psychology Bulletin, 21,* 572–580.

Cowan, P. A. (1991). Individual and family life transitions: A proposal for a new definition. In D. A. Cowan & M. Hetherington (Eds.), *Family transitions* (pp. 3–30). Hillsdale, NJ: Erlbaum.

Cox, C. L., Wexler, M. O., Rusbult, C. E., & Gaines, S. O. (1997). Prescriptive support and commitment processes in close relationships. *Social Psychology Quarterly, 60,* 79–90.

Coyne, S. M., Nelson, D. A., Graham-Kevan, N., Tew, E., Meng, K. N., & Olsen, J. A. (2011). Media depictions of physical and relational aggression: Connections with aggression in young adults' romantic relationships. *Aggressive Behavior, 37*(1), 56–62.

Cozby, P. C. (1972). Self-disclosure, reciprocity, and liking. *Sociometry, 35,* 151–160.

Cramer, R., McMaster, M., Bartell, P., & Dragna, M. (1988). Subject competence and minimization of the bystander effect. *Journal of Applied Social Psychology, 18,* 1132–1148.

Crano, W. D. (1977). Primacy versus recency in retention of information and opinion change. *Journal of Social Psychology, 101*(1), 87–96.

Crano, W. (1997). Vested interests, symbolic politics, and attitude-behavior consistency. *Journal of Personality and Social Psychology, 72,* 485–491.

Crawford, K. (2017). Health care fraud sentencing. *Georgetown Law Journal, 105,* 1079–1106.

Crisp, R. J., & Turner, R. N. (2011). Cognitive adaptation to the experience of social and cultural diversity. *Psychological Bulletin, 137*(2), 242–266.

Crocker, J., & Major, B. (1989). Social stigma and self-esteem: The self-protective properties of stigma. *Psychological Review, 96,* 608–630.

Crocker, J., Thompson, L. L., McGraw, K. M., & Ingerman, C. (1987). Downward comparison, prejudice, and evaluations of others: Effects of self-esteem and threat. *Journal of Personality and Social Psychology, 52,* 907–916.

Crocker, J., Voelkl, K., Testa, M., & Major, B. (1991). Social stigma: The affective consequences of attributional ambiguity. *Journal of Personality and Social Psychology, 60,* 218–228.

Crocker, J., & Wolfe, C. (2001). Contingencies of self-worth. *Psychological Review, 108,* 593–623.

Crosnoe, R., & Cavanagh, S. E. (2010). Families with children and adolescents: A review, critique, and future agenda. *Journal of Marriage and Family, 72,* 594–611.

Cuddy, A. J., Fiske, S. T., & Glick, P. (2007). The BIAS map: Behaviors from intergroup affect and stereotypes. *Journal of Personality and Social Psychology, 92*(4), 631–648.

Cuddy, A. J., Glick, P., & Beninger, A. (2011). The dynamics of warmth and competence judgments, and their outcomes in organizations. *Research in Organizational Behavior, 31,* 73–98.

Cuddy, A. J., Rock, M. S., & Norton, M. I. (2007). Aid in the aftermath of Hurricane Katrina: Inferences of secondary emotions and intergroup helping. *Group Processes & Intergroup Relations, 10*(1), 107–118.

Cummings, K. M., Sciandra, R., Davis, S., & Rimer, B. (1989). Response to anti-smoking campaign aimed at mothers with young children. *Health Education Research, 4,* 429–437.

Cunningham, M. R. (1986). Measuring the physical in physical attractiveness: Quasi-experiments on the sociobiology of female facial beauty. *Journal of Personality and Social Psychology, 50,* 925–935.

Cunningham, M. R., Barbee, A. P., & Pike, C. L. (1990). What do women want? Facial metric assessment of multiple motives in the perception of male physical attractiveness. *Journal of Personality and Social Psychology, 59,* 61–72.

Cunningham, M. R., Steinberg, J., & Grev, R. (1980). Wanting to and having to help: Separate motivations for positive mood and guilt-induced helping. *Journal of Personality and Social Psychology, 38*(2), 181.

Cutrona, C. E. (1982). Transition to college: Loneliness and the process of social adjustment. In L. A. Peplau & D. Perlman (Eds.), *Loneliness: A resource book of current theory research and therapy* (pp. 291–309). New York: Wiley.

Dabbs, J. M., & Leventhal, H. (1966). Effects of varying the recommendations in a fear-arousing communication. *Journal of Personality and Social Psychology, 4,* 525–531.

Daher, D. M., & Banikiotes, P. G. (1976). Interpersonal attraction and rewarding aspects of disclosure content and level. *Journal of Personality and Social Psychology, 33,* 492–496.

Dahmen, N., & Cozma, R. (2009). *Media takes: On again.* Sacramento, CA: International Longevity Center–USA and Aging Services of California.

Daly, K. (1987). Discrimination in the criminal courts: Family, gender, and the problem of equal treatment. *Social Forces*, *66*, 152–175.

Daly, M., & Wilson, M. (1998). *The truth about Cinderella: A Darwinian view of parental love.* New Haven, CT: Yale University Press.

Darley, J. M., & Batson, C. D. (1973). From Jerusalem to Jericho: A study of situational and dispositional variables in helping behavior. *Journal of Personality and Social Psychology*, *27*, 100–108.

Darley, J. M., & Fazio, R. H. (1980). Expectancy confirmation processes arising in the social interaction sequence. *American Psychologist*, *35*, 867–881.

Darley, J. M., & Latané, B. (1968). Bystander intervention in emergencies: Diffusion of responsibility. *Journal of Personality and Social Psychology*, *8*, 377–383.

Darley, J. M., Teger, A. I., & Lewis, L. D. (1973). Do groups always inhibit individuals' response to potential emergencies? *Journal of Personality and Social Psychology*, *26*, 395–399.

Darwin, C. (1998). *The expression of the emotions in man and animals.* Oxford: Oxford University Press.

Davies, S., & Tanner, J. (2003). The long arm of the law: Effects of labeling on employment. *Sociological Quarterly*, *44*, 385–404.

Davis, D., & Perkowitz, W. T. (1979). Consequences of responsiveness in dyadic interaction: Effects of probability of response and proportion of content-related responses on interpersonal attraction. *Journal of Personality and Social Psychology*, *37*, 534–550.

Davis, F. (1961). Deviance disavowal: The management of strained interaction by the visibly handicapped. *Social Problems*, *9*, 120–132.

Davis, J. A., Smith, T. W., & Marsden, P. V. (2000). *General social surveys, 1972–2000.* Ann Arbor, MI: Inter-University Consortium for Political and Social Research. www.icpsr. umich.edu:8080/ICPSR-STUDY/03197.xml

Davis, J. D. (1976). Self-disclosure in an acquaintance exercise: Responsibility for level of intimacy. *Journal of Personality and Social Psychology*, *33*, 787–792.

Davis, K. (1947). Final note on a case of extreme isolation. *American Journal of Sociology*, *52*, 432–437.

Davis, K. E. (1985, February). Near and dear: Friendship and love. *Psychology Today*, *22*, 22–30.

Davis, L. R., & Harris, O. (1998). Race and ethnicity in US sports media. In L. A. Wenner (Ed.), *MediaSport* (pp. 154–169). London: Routledge.

Davis, M. H., & Franzoi, S. L. (1986). Adolescent loneliness, self-disclosure, and private self-consciousness: A longitudinal investigation. *Journal of Personality and Social Psychology*, *51*, 595–608.

Davis, S. (1990). Men as success objects and women as sex objects: A study of personal advertisements. *Sex Roles*, *23*(1–2), 43–50.

Dawes, R. M. (1998). Behavioral decision making and judgment. In D. Gilbert, S. Fiske, & G. Lindzey (Eds.), *The handbook of social psychology* (4th ed., Vol. 1, pp. 497–548). New York: McGraw-Hill.

Dawkins, R. (1982). *The extended phenotype.* San Francisco: Freeman.

De Castro, B. O., Veerman, J. W., Koops, W., Bosch, J. D., & Monshouwer, H. J. (2002). Hostile attribution of intent and aggressive behavior: A meta-analysis. *Child Development*, *73*(3), 916–934.

De Fina, A. (2007). Code-switching and the construction of ethnic identity in a community of practice. *Language in Society*, *36*, 371–392.

de Jong-Gierveld, J. (1987). Developing and testing a model of loneliness. *Journal of Personality and Social Psychology*, *53*, 119–128.

De Waal, A. (2006). An imperfect storm: Narratives of calamity in a liberal-technocratic age. *Items and Issues*, *5*, 1–8. (Social Science Research Council).

Dean, K. E., & Malamuth, N. M. (1997). Characteristics of men who aggress sexually and of men who imagine aggressing: Risk and moderating variables. *Journal of Personality and Social Psychology*, *72*(2), 449–455.

Deater-Deckard, K., & Dodge, K. (1997). Externalizing behavior problems and discipline revisited: Nonlinear effects and variation by culture, context, and gender. *Psychological Inquiry*, *8*, 161–175.

Deaux, K., & Martin, D. (2003). Interpersonal networks and social categories: Specifying levels of context in identity processes. *Social Psychology Quarterly*, *66*, 101–117.

DeBono, K. G., & Telesca, C. (1990). The influence of source physical attractiveness on advertising effectiveness: A functional perspective. *Journal of Applied Social Psychology*, *20*, 1383–1395.

Debras, C., & Cienki, A. (2012). Some uses of head tilts and shoulder shrugs during human interaction, and their relation to stancetaking. *International Conference on Privacy, Security, Risk and Trust* (PASSAT), *136*, 932–937.

Deci, E. (1975). *Intrinsic motivation.* New York: Plenum.

Degelman, D., & Price, N. (2002). Tattoos and ratings of personal characteristics. *Psychological Reports*, *90*, 507–514.

DeGue, S., & DiLillo, D. (2004). Understanding perpetrators of nonphysical sexual coercion: Characteristics of those who cross the line. *Violence and Victims*, *19*(6), 673–688.

DeLamater, J. (1974). A definition of "group." *Small Group Behavior*, *5*(1), 30–44.

DeLongis, A., Folkman, J., & Lazarus, R. S. (1988). The impact of daily stress on health and mood: Psychological and social resources as mediators. *Journal of Personality and Social Psychology*, *54*, 486–495.

Del-Teso-Craviotto, M. (2006). Language and sexuality in Spanish and English dating chats. *Journal of Sociolinguistics*, *10*, 460–480.

DeMaris, A., Benson, M. L., Fox, G. L., Hill, T., & Van Wyk, J. (2003). Distal and proximal factors in domestic violence: A test of an integrated model. *Journal of Marriage and Family*, *65*(3), 652–667.

Demo, D. H. (1992). The self-concept over time: Research issues and directions. *Annual Review of Sociology*, *18*, 303–326.

Demo, D. H., & Acock, A. C. (1988). The impact of divorce on children. *Journal of Marriage and Family*, *50*, 619–648.

Demo, D., & Cox, M. (2001). Families with young children: A review of research in the 1990s. In R. Milardo (Ed.),

*Understanding families into the new millennium: A decade in review* (pp. 95–114). Minneapolis, MN: National Council on Family Relations.

Demo, D. H., & Hughes, M. (1990). Socialization and racial identity among Black Americans. *Social Psychology Quarterly, 53*, 364–374.

Denney, J. T., Gorman, B. K., & Barrera, C. B. (2013). Families, resources and adult health: Where do sexual minorities fit? *Journal of Health and Social Behavior, 54*, 46–63.

Denson, T. F., Pedersen, W. C., & Miller, N. (2006). The displaced aggression questionnaire. *Journal of Personality and Social Psychology, 90*(6), 1032.

Dentler, R., & Erikson, K. (1959). The functions of deviance in groups. *Social Problems, 7*, 98–107.

Denton, K., & Krebs, D. (1990). From the scene to the crime: The effect of alcohol and social context on moral judgment. *Journal of Personality and Social Psychology, 59*, 242–248.

Denzin, N. (1977). *Childhood socialization: Studies in the development of language, social behavior, and identity.* San Francisco: Jossey-Bass.

DePaulo, B. M. (1992). Nonverbal behavior and self-presentation. *Psychological Bulletin, 111*, 203–243.

DePaulo, B. M., & Fisher, J. D. (1980). The costs of asking for help. *Basic and Applied Social Psychology, 1*, 23–35.

DePaulo, B. M., Lassiter, G. D., & Stone, J. T. (1982). Attentional determinants of success at determining deception and truth. *Personality and Social Psychology Bulletin, 8*, 273–279.

DePaulo, B. M., & Rosenthal, R. (1979). Ambivalence, discrepancy, and deception in nonverbal communication. In R. Rosenthal (Ed.), *Skill in nonverbal communication* (pp. 204–248). Cambridge, MA: Oelgeschlager, Gunn and Hain.

DePaulo, B. M., Rosenthal, R., Eisenstat, R. A., Rogers, P. L., & Finkelstein, S. (1978). Decoding discrepant nonverbal cues. *Journal of Personality and Social Psychology, 36*, 313–323.

DePaulo, B. M., Stone, J. I., & Lassiter, G. D. (1985). Deceiving and detecting deceit. In B. R. Schlenker (Ed.), *The self and social life* (pp. 323–370). New York: McGraw-Hill.

Der-Karabetian, A., & Smith, A. (1977). Sex-role stereotyping in the United States: Is it changing? *Sex Roles, 3*, 193–198.

Derlega, V. J., & Grzelak, J. (1979). Appropriate self-disclosure. In G. J. Chelune et al. (Eds.), *Self-disclosure: Origins, patterns, and implications of openness in interpersonal relationships* (pp. 151–176). San Francisco: Jossey-Bass.

Derlega, V. J., Metts, S., Petronio, S., & Margulis, S. T. (1993). *Self-disclosure.* Newbury Park, CA: Sage.

Desmet, P. T., De Cremer, D., & van Dijk, E. (2010). On the psychology of financial compensations to restore fairness transgressions: When intentions determine value. *Journal of Business Ethics, 95*, 105–115.

Deutsch, M. (1985). *Distributive justice: A social psychological perspective.* New Haven, CT: Yale University Press.

Deutsch, M. (2000). Justice and conflict. In M. Deutsch & P. T. Coleman (Eds.), *The handbook of conflict resolution: Theory and practice* (pp. 41–64). San Francisco: Jossey-Bass.

Deutsch, M., & Gerard, H. B. (1955). A study of normative and informational social influences upon individual judgment. *Journal of Abnormal and Social Psychology, 51*, 629–636.

Devine, J. A., Sheley, J. F., & Smith, M. D. (1988). Macroeconomic and social-control policy influences on crime-rate changes, 1948–1985. *American Sociological Review, 53*, 407–420.

Devine, P. C. (1989). Stereotypes and prejudice: Their automatic and controlled components. *Journal of Personality and Social Psychology, 56*, 5–18.

Dew, J., & Wilcox, B. W. (2013). Generosity and the maintenance of marital quality. *Journal of Marriage and Family, 75*(5), 1218–1228.

DeWall, N. C., & Bushman, B. J. (2009). Hot under the collar in a lukewarm environment: Words associated with hot temperature increase aggressive thoughts and hostile perceptions. *Journal of Experimental Social Psychology, 45*(4), 1045–1047.

Dickey, D., & Pearson, C. (2005). Recency effect in college student course evaluations. *Practical Assessment, Research and Evaluation, 10*(6), 1–10.

Diekman, A. B., Eagly, A. H., Mladinic, A., & Ferreira, M. C. (2005). Dynamic stereotypes about women and men in Latin America and the United States. *Journal of Cross-Cultural Psychology, 36*, 209–226.

Dietert, M., & Dentice, D. (2013). Growing up trans: Socialization and the gender binary. *Journal of GLBT Family Studies, 9*, 24–42.

Digman, J. M. (1990). Personality structure: Emergence of the five-factor model. *Annual Review of Psychology, 41*, 417–440.

Dillard, J. P., & Shen, L. (2005). On the nature of reactance and its role in persuasive health communication. *Communication Monographs, 72*(2), 144–168.

DiMaggio, P., & Mohr, J. (1985). Cultural capital, educational attainment, and marital selection. *American Journal of Sociology, 90*, 1231–1257.

Dimsdale, J. (2008). Psychological stress and cardiovascular disease. *Journal of the American College of Cardiology, 51*, 1237–1246.

Dinas, E. (2013). Does choice bring loyalty? Electoral participation and the development of party identification. *American Journal of Political Science, 58*, 449–465.

Dion, K. L. (1979). Intergroup conflict and intragroup cohesiveness. In W. G. Austin & S. Worchel (Eds.), *The social psychology of intergroup relations* (pp. 211–224). Monterey, CA: Brooks/Cole.

Dion, K. L. (2000). Group cohesion: From "field of forces" to multidimensional construct. *Group Dynamics: Theory, Research, and Practice, 4*, 7–26.

Dion, K., Berscheid, E., & Walster [Hatfield], E. (1972). What is beautiful is good. *Journal of Personality and Social Psychology, 24*, 285–290.

Dion, K. L., & Schuller, R. A. (1991). The Ms. stereotype: Its generality and its relation to managerial and marital status stereotypes. *Canadian Journal of Behavioural Science, 23*, 25–40.

DiPrete, T. (2007). Is this a great country? Upward mobility and the chance for riches in contemporary America. *Research in Social Stratification and Mobility, 25*, 89–95.

Dishion, T. J., & Dodge, K. A. (2005). Peer contagion in interventions for children and adolescents: Moving towards an understanding of the ecology and dynamics of change. *Journal of Abnormal Child Psychology, 33*, 395–400.

Ditto, P. H., Liu, B., Clark, C. J., Wojcik, S. P., Chen, E. E., Grady, R. H., & Zinger, J. F. (2017). *At least bias is bipartisan: A meta-analytic comparison of partisan bias in liberals and conservatives.* SSRN. https://doi.org/10.2139/ssrn.2952510

Dixon, J., Gordon, C., & Khomusi, T. (1995). Sexual symmetry in psychiatric diagnosis. *Social Problems, 42*, 429–448.

Dodge, K. A., Coie, J. D., & Lynam, D. (2006). Aggression and antisocial behavior in youth. In N. Eisenberg, W. Damon, & R. L. Lerner (Eds.), *Handbook of child psychology: Vol. 3. Social, emotional, and personality development* (pp. 719–788). New York: Wiley.

Dodson, L., & Dickert, J. (2004). Girls' family labor in low-income households: A decade of qualitative research. *Journal of Marriage and Family, 66*, 318–332.

Dohrenwend, B. P. (1961). The social psychological nature of stress: A framework for causal inquiry. *Journal of Abnormal and Social Psychology, 62*, 294–302.

Dohrenwend, B. P. (2000). The role of adversity and stress in psychopathology: Some evidence and its implications for theory and research. *Journal of Health and Social Behavior, 41*, 1–19.

Dohrenwend, B. P., & Dohrenwend, B. S. (1974). Social and cultural influences on psychopathology. *Annual Review of Psychology, 25*, 417–452.

Doliński, D., Grzyb, T., Folwarczny, M., Grzybała, P., Krzyszycha, K., Martynowska, K., & Trojanowski, J. (2017). Would you deliver an electric shock in 2015? Obedience in the experimental paradigm developed by Stanley Milgram in the 50 years following the original studies. *Social Psychological and Personality Science, 8*(8), 927–933.

Dollard, J., Doob, J., Miller, N., Mowrer, O., & Sears, R. (1939). *Frustration and aggression.* New Haven, CT: Yale University Press.

Donald, M. (1991). *Origins of the modern mind: Three stages in the evolution of culture and cognition.* Cambridge, MA: Harvard University Press.

Donnerstein, E. (1984). Pornography: Its effect on violence against women. In N. M. Malamuth & E. Donnerstein (Eds.), *Pornography and sexual aggression* (pp. 53–81). Orlando, FL: Academic Press.

Donnerstein, E., & Barrett, G. (1978). The effects of erotic stimuli on male aggression toward females. *Journal of Personality and Social Psychology, 36*, 180–188.

Donnerstein, E., & Berkowitz, L. (1981). Victim reactions in aggressive erotic films as a factor in violence toward women. *Journal of Personality and Social Psychology, 41*, 710–724.

Donnerstein, E., and Linz, D. (1998). Mass media, violence and the male viewer. In M. E. Oden and J. Clay-Warner (Eds.), *Confronting rape and sexual assault* (pp. 181–198). Wilmington, DE: SR Books/Scholarly Resources.

Donovan, D. M., & O'Leary, M. R. (1978). The drinking-related locus of control scale. Reliability, factor structure and validity. *Journal of Studies on Alcohol, 39*(5), 759–784.

Dooley, D., Prause, J., & Ham-Rowbottom, K. (2000). Underemployment and depression: Longitudinal relationships. *Journal of Health and Social Behavior, 41*, 421–436.

Douglas, K. M., & Sutton, R. M. (2004). Right about others, wrong about ourselves? Actual and perceived self–other differences in resistance to persuasion. *British Journal of Social Psychology, 43*(4), 585–603.

Dovidio, J. F. (1984). Helping behavior and altruism: An empirical and conceptual overview. In L. Berkowitz (Ed.), *Advances in experimental social psychology* (Vol. 17, pp. 362–427). New York: Academic Press.

Dovidio, J. F., Allen, J. L., & Schroeder, D. A. (1990). Specificity of empathy-induced helping: Evidence for altruistic motivation. *Journal of Personality and Social Psychology, 59*, 249–260.

Dovidio, J. F., & Ellyson, S. L. (1982). Decoding visual dominance: Attributions of power based on relative percentages of looking while speaking and looking while listening. *Social Psychology Quarterly, 45*, 106–113.

Dovidio, J. F., & Gaertner, S. L. (1981). The effects of race, status, and ability on helping behavior. *Social Psychology Quarterly, 44*, 192–203.

Dovidio, J. F., & Gaertner, S. L. (1996). Affirmative action, unintentional racial biases, and intergroup relations. *Journal of Social Issues, 52*(4), 51–75.

Dovidio, J. F., Gaertner, S. L., Isen, A. M., & Lowrance, R. (1995). Group representations and intergroup bias: Positive affect, similarity, and group size. *Personality and Social Psychology Bulletin, 21*, 856–865.

Dovidio, J. F., Piliavin, J. A., Gaertner, S. L., Schroeder, D. A., & Clark, R. D. (1991). The arousal/cost–reward model and the process of intervention: A review of the evidence. In M. S. Clark (Ed.), *Review of personality and social psychology: Vol. 12. Prosocial behaviour* (pp. 86–118). Newbury Park, CA: Sage.

Dovidio, J. F., Piliavin, J. A., Schroeder, D. A., & Penner, L. (2006). *The social psychology of prosocial behavior.* Hillsdale, NJ: Erlbaum.

Draghi-Lorenz, R., Reddy, V., & Costall, A. (2001). Rethinking the development of "nonbasic" emotions: A critical review of existing theories. *Developmental Review, 21*(3), 263–304.

Drass, K. A., & Spencer, J. W. (1987). Accounting for pre-sentencing recommendations: Typologies and probation officers' theory of office. *Social Problems, 34*, 277–293.

Dreben, E. K., Fiske, S. T., & Hastie, R. (1979). The independence of evaluative and item information: Impression and recall order effects in behavior-based impression formation. *Journal of Personality and Social Psychology, 37*, 1758–1768.

Drew, P. (2003). Precision and exaggeration in interaction. *American Sociological Review, 68*, 917–938.

Drews, D., Allison, C., & Probst, J. (2000). Behavioral and self-concept differences in tattooed and nontattooed college students. *Psychological Reports, 86*, 475–481.

Duckworth, A. (2016). *Grit: The power of passion and perseverance.* New York: Simon and Schuster.

Dudovitz, R.N., Chung, P. J., Nelson, B.B., & Wong, M.D. (2017). What do you want to be when you grow up? Career aspirations as a marker for adolescent well-being. *Academic Pediatrics, 17*, 153–160.

Dukes, R. L., & Stein, J. A. (2011). Ink and holes: Correlates and predictive associations of body modification among adolescents. *Youth and Society, 43*, 1547–1569.

Dunbar, R. (1996). *Grooming, gossip, and the evolution of language.* Cambridge, MA: Harvard University Press.

Duncan, S., & Fiske, D. W. (1977). *Face-to-face interaction: Research methods and theory.* Hillsdale, NJ: Erlbaum.

Duneier, M. (2001). *Sidewalk.* New York: Farrar, Straus, and Giroux.

Duran, R. L., & Prusank, D. T. (1997). Relational themes in men's and women's popular nonfiction magazine articles. *Journal of Social and Personal Relationships, 14*, 165–189.

Durkheim, E. (1897) [1951]. *Suicide: A study in sociology.* New York: Free Press.

Durlak, J. A., Weissberg, R. P., Dymnicki, A. B., Taylor, R. D., & Schellinger, K. B. (2011). The impact of enhancing students' social and emotional learning: A meta-analysis of school-based universal interventions. *Child Development, 82*(1), 405–432.

Dutton, D., & Aron, A. (1974). Some evidence for heightened sexual attraction under conditions of high anxiety. *Journal of Personality and Social Psychology, 30*, 510–517.

Dutton, D., & Lake, R. (1973). Threat of own prejudice and reverse discrimination in interracial situations. *Journal of Personality and Social Psychology, 28*, 94–100.

Dweck, C. (2007) *Mindset.* New York: Ballantine Books.

Eagly, A. H., Ashmore, R. D., Makhijani, M. G., & Longo, L. C. (1991). What is beautiful is good, but . . . : A meta-analytic review of research on the physical attractiveness stereotype. *Psychological Bulletin, 110*, 109–128.

Eagly, A. H., & Chaiken, S. (1975). An attribution analysis of the effects of communicator characteristics on opinion change: The case of communicator attractiveness. *Journal of Personality and Social Psychology, 32*, 136–144.

Eagly, A. H., & Crowley, M. (1986). Gender and helping behavior: A meta-analytic review of the social psychological literature. *Psychological Bulletin, 100*, 283–308.

Eagly, A., & Steffen, V. J. (1984). Gender stereotypes stem from distribution of women and men into social roles. *Journal of Personality and Social Psychology, 46*, 735–754.

East, P. L. (1998). Racial and ethnic differences in girls' sexual, marital, and birth expectations. *Journal of Marriage and Family, 60*, 150–162.

Eaton, A. A., & Rose, S. (2011). Has dating become more egalitarian? A 35 year review using *Sex Roles. Sex Roles, 64*, 843–862.

Eaton, W. (1980). *The sociology of mental disorders.* New York: Praeger.

Eckert, P., & McConnell-Ginet, S. (1999). New generalizations and explanations in language and gender research. *Language in Society, 28*, 185–201.

Eckes, T. (1995). Features of situations: A two-mode clustering study of situation prototypes. *Personality and Social Psychology Bulletin, 21*, 366–374.

Edelmann, R. J. (1985). Social embarrassment: An analysis of the process. *Journal of Social and Personal Relationships, 2*, 195–213.

Edelmann, R. J. (1987). *The psychology of embarrassment.* Chichester, U.K.: Wiley.

Edelmann, R. J., Evans, G., Pegg, I., & Tremain, M. (1983). Responses to physical stigma. *Perceptual and Motor Skills, 57*, 294.

Edelmann, R. J., & Iwawaki, S. (1987). Self-reported expression and consequences of embarrassment in the United Kingdom and Japan. *Psychologia, 30*, 205–216.

Eder, D. (with Evans, C. C., & Parker, S.). (1995). *School talk: Gender and adolescent culture.* New Brunswick, NJ: Rutgers University Press.

Edwards, C. P., Knoche, L., & Kumru, A. (2001). Play patterns and gender. In J. Worell (Ed.), *Encyclopedia of gender* (pp. 809–816). San Diego, CA: Academic Press.

Edwards, K. (1990). The interplay of affect and cognition in attitude formation and change. *Journal of Personality and Social Psychology, 59*, 202–216.

Edwards, K. M., Turchik, J. A., Dardis, C. M., Reynolds, N., & Gidycz, C. A. (2011). Rape myths: History, individual and institutional-level presence, and implications for change. *Sex Roles, 65*(11–12), 761–773.

Egebark, J., & Ekström, M. (2011). Like what you like or like what others like? Conformity and peer effects on Facebook. Stockholm: Research Institute of Industrial Economics IFN Working Paper, 866.

Eibl-Eibesfeldt, I. (1979). Human ethology: Methods and limits. *Behavioral and Brain Sciences, 2*(1), 50–57.

Eid, M., & Diener, E. (2001). Norms for experiencing emotions in different cultures: inter- and intranational differences. *Journal of Personality and Social Psychology, 81*(5), 869.

Eisenberg, N., Cumberland, A., Guthrie, I., Murphy, B., & Shepard, S. (2005). Age changes in prosocial responding and moral reasoning in adolescence and early adulthood. *Journal of Research on Adolescence, 15*, 235–260.

Eisenberg, N., & Fabes, R. A. (1991). Prosocial behavior and empathy: A multimethod developmental perspective. In M. S. Clark (Ed.), *Review of personality and social psychology: Vol. 12. Prosocial behavior* (pp. 34–61). Newbury Park, CA: Sage.

Eisenberg, N., & Miller, P. A. (1987). The relation of empathy to prosocial and related behaviors. *Psychological Bulletin, 101*, 91–119.

Eisend, M. (2006). Two-sided advertising: A meta-analysis. *International Journal of Research in Marketing, 23*(2), 187–198.

Eisend, M. (2007). Understanding two-sided persuasion: An empirical assessment of theoretical approaches. *Psychology & Marketing, 24*, 615–640.

Eiser, J. R. (Ed.). (1984). *Attitudinal judgment.* New York: Springer Verlag.

Eitle, D., & Turner, R. J. (2003). Stress exposure, race, and young adult male crime. *Sociological Quarterly, 44*, 243–269.

Ekman, P. (1972). Universal and cultural differences in facial expression of emotion. In J. R. Cole (Ed.), *Nebraska Symposium on Motivation, 1971* (Vol. 19, pp. 207–283). Lincoln: Nebraska University Press.

Ekman, P. (1992). An argument for basic emotions. *Cognition and Emotion, 6*(3–4), 169–200.

Ekman, P., & Friesen, W. V. (1969). Nonverbal leakage and clues to deception. *Psychiatry, 32,* 88–106.

Ekman, P., & Friesen, W. V. (1971). Constants across cultures in the face and emotion. *Journal of Personality and Social Psychology, 17,* 124–129.

Ekman, P., & Friesen, W. V. (1974). Detecting deception from the body or face. *Journal of Personality and Social Psychology, 29,* 288–298.

Ekman, P., & Friesen, W. V. (1975). *Unmasking the face: A guide to recognizing emotions from facial cues.* Englewood Cliffs, NJ: Prentice Hall.

Ekman, P. and Friesen, W. V. (1978). *Facial action coding system: A technique for the measurement of facial movement.* Palo Alto, CA: Consulting Psychologists Press.

Ekman, P., & Friesen, W. V. (1986). A new pan-cultural facial expression of emotion. *Motivation and Emotion, 10*(2), 159–168.

Ekman, P., & Friesen, W. V. (1987). Single Judgment Emotion Task. *Journal of Personality and Social Psychology, 53,* 712–717.

Ekman, P., Friesen, W. V., & Ellsworth, P. (2013). *Emotion in the human face: Guidelines for research and an integration of findings.* Burlington, MA: Elsevier.

Ekman, P., Friesen, W. V., & O'Sullivan, M. (1988). Smiles when lying. *Journal of Personality and Social Psychology, 54,* 414–420.

Ekman, P., Friesen, W. V., & Scherer, K. R. (1976). Body movements and voice pitch in deceptive interaction. *Semiotica, 16,* 23–27.

Ekman, P., & O'Sullivan, M. (1991). Who can catch a liar? *American Psychologist, 46,* 913–920.

Ekman, P., O'Sullivan, M., & Frank, M. (1999). A few can catch a liar. *Psychological Science, 10,* 263–266.

Ekman, P., Sorenson, E. R., & Friesen, W. V. (1969). Pan-cultural elements in facial displays of emotion. *Science, 164*(3875), 86–88.

Elder, G. H. (1975). Age differentiation and the life course. In A. Inkeles, J. Coleman, & N. Smelser (Eds.), *Annual Review of Sociology* (Vol. 1, pp. 165–190). Palo Alto, CA: Annual Reviews.

Elder, G. H., & O'Rand, A. M. (1995). Adult lives in a changing society. In K. S. Cook, G. A. Fine, & J. S. House (Eds.), *Sociological perspectives on social psychology* (pp. 452–475). Boston: Allyn and Bacon.

Elkin, F., & Handel, G. (1989). *The child and society: The process of socialization* (5th ed.). New York: Random House.

Elliott, G. C., & Meeker, B. F. (1986). Achieving fairness in the face of competing concerns: The different effects of individual and group characteristics. *Journal of Personality and Social Psychology, 50,* 754–760.

Ellis, L., & Ratnasingam, M. (2006). Gender, sexual orientation and occupational interests: Evidence of androgen influences. *Mankind Quarterly, 53,* 36–80.

Ellison, L., & Munro, V. E. (2010). Getting to (not) guilty: Examining jurors' deliberative processes in, and beyond, the context of a mock rape trial. *Legal Studies, 30*(1), 74–97.

Ellison, N. B., Hancock, J. T., & Toma, C. L. (2011). Profile as promise: A framework for conceptualizing veracity in online dating self-presentations. *New Media & Society, 14,* 45–62.

Ellison, N., Heino, R., & Gibbs, J. (2006). Managing impressions online: Self-presentational processes in the online dating environment. *Journal of Computer-Mediated Communication, 11,* 415–441.

Ellsworth, P. C., Carlsmith, J. M., & Henson, A. (1972). The stare as a stimulus to flight in human subjects. *Journal of Personality and Social Psychology, 21,* 302–311.

Emerson, R. M. (1962). Power-dependence relations. *American Sociological Review, 1,* 31–41.

Emerson, R. M. (1972). Exchange theory, part II: Exchange relations and networks. *Sociological Theories in Progress, 2,* 58–87.

Emerson, R. M. (1981). Social exchange theory. In M. Rosenberg & R. Turner (Eds.), *Social psychology: Sociological perspectives* (pp. 30–65). New York: Basic Books.

Emmons, R. A., & Diener, E. (1986). Situation selection as a moderator of response consistency and stability. *Journal of Personality and Social Psychology, 51,* 1013–1019.

Emmons, R. A., Diener, E., & Larsen, R. J. (1986). Choice and avoidance of everyday situations and affect congruence: Two models of reciprocal interactionism. *Journal of Personality and Social Psychology, 51,* 815–826.

Engelman, M., & Jackson, H. (2017). Gradual change or punctuated equilibrium? Reconsidering patterns of health in later life. University of Wisconsin-Madison: Center for Demography and Ecology, Working Paper 2017-01.

Erikson, E. H. (1968). *Identity: Youth and crisis.* New York: Norton.

Erikson, K. (1964). Notes on the sociology of deviance. In H. Becker (Ed.), *The other side: Perspectives on deviance* (pp. 307–314). New York: Free Press.

Erikson, K. (1966). *The wayward Puritans.* New York: Wiley.

Erol, R. Y., & Orth, U. (2011). Self-esteem development from age 14 to 30 years: A longitudinal study. *Journal of Personality and Social Psychology, 101,* 607–619.

Esser, J. K. (1995). *Groupthink from Pearl Harbor to the Challenger: Failure of decision-making groups.* Beaumont, TX: Lamar University-Beaumont.

Esser, J. K. (1998). Alive and well after 25 years: A review of groupthink research. *Organizational Behavior and Human Decision Processes, 73*(2), 116–141.

Ettinger, R. F., Marino, C. J., Endler, N. S., Geller, S. H., & Natziuk, T. (1971). Effects of agreement and correctness on relative competence and conformity. *Journal of Personality and Social Psychology, 19,* 204–212.

Evans, C. R., & Dion, K. L. (1991). Group cohesion and performance: A meta-analysis. *Small Group Research, 22,* 175–186.

Evans, G., & Wener, R. (2007). Crowding and personal space invasion on the train: Please don't make me sit in the middle. *Journal of Environmental Psychology, 27,* 90–94.

Fader, J. J. (2011). Conditions of a successful status graduation ceremony: Formerly incarcerated urban youth and their tenuous grip on success. *Punishment and Society, 13,* 29–46.

Falci, C. D. (2011). Self-esteem and mastery trajectories in high school by social class and gender. *Social Science Research*, *40*, 586–601.

Farina, A., Gliha, D., Boudreau, L. A., Allen, J. G., & Sherman, M. (1971). Mental illness and the impact of believing others know it. *Journal of Abnormal Psychology*, *77*, 1–5.

Farnworth, M., & Leiber, M. J. (1989). Strain theory revisited: Economic goals, educational means, and delinquency. *American Sociological Review*, *54*, 263–274.

Farris, C., Treat, T. A., Viken, R. J., & McFall, R. M. (2008). Sexual coercion and the misperception of sexual intent. *Clinical Psychology Review*, *28*(1), 48–66.

Fazio, R. H. (1990). Multiple processes by which attitudes guide behavior: The MODE model as an integrative framework. In L. Berkowitz (Ed.), *Advances in experimental social psychology* (Vol. 23, pp. 75–109). New York: Academic Press.

Fazio, R. H. (1995). Attitudes as object-evaluation associations: Determinants, consequences, and correlates of attitude accessibility. In R. E. Petty and J. A. Krosnick (Eds.), *Attitude strength: Antecedents and consequences* (pp. 247–282). Hillsdale, NJ: Erlbaum.

Fazio, R. H., Powell, M., & Herr, P. (1983). Toward a process model of the attitude-behavior relation: Accessing one's attitude upon mere observation of the attitude object. *Journal of Personality and Social Psychology*, *44*, 723–735.

Fazio, R. H., Sanbonmatsu, D. M., Powell, M. C., & Kardes, F. R. (1986). On the automatic activation of attitudes. *Journal of Personality and Social Psychology*, *50*, 229–238.

Fazio, R. H., & Towles-Schwen, T. (1999). The MODE model of attitude-behavior processes. In S. Chaiken and Y. Trope (Eds.), *Dual-process theories in social psychology* (pp. 97–116). New York: Guilford.

Fazio, R. H., & Williams, C. J. (1986). Attitude accessibility as a moderator of the attitude-perception and attitude-behavior relations: An investigation of the 1984 presidential election. *Journal of Personality and Social Psychology*, *51*, 505–514.

Fazio, R. H., & Zanna, M. (1981). Direct experience and attitude-behavior consistency. In L. Berkowitz (Ed.), *Advances in experimental social psychology* (Vol. 14, pp. 161–202). New York: Academic Press.

FBI homicide data (2013). Crime in the United States 2013. Retrieved from https://ucr.fbi.gov/crime-in-the-u.s/2013/crime-in-the-u.s.-2013/offenses-known-to-law-enforcement/expanded-homicide (Accessed June 12, 18).

Feather, N. T. (1967). A structural balance approach to the analysis of communication effects. In L. Berkowitz (Ed.), *Advances in experimental social psychology* (Vol. 3, pp. 99–165). New York: Academic Press.

Feather, N. T. (1995). Values, valences, and choice: The influence of values on the perceived attractiveness and choice of alternatives. *Journal of Personality and Social Psychology*, *68*, 1135–1151.

Feeney, J. A. (1999). Adult romantic attachment and couple relationships. In J. Cassidy & P. R. Shaver (Eds.), *Handbook of attachment: Theory, research, and clinical applications* (pp. 355–377). New York: Guilford.

Feeney, J. A., & Noller, P. (1990). Attachment style as a predictor of adult romantic relationships. *Journal of Personality and Social Psychology*, *58*, 281–291.

Feijten P., & van Ham, M. (2010). The impact of splitting up and divorce on housing careers in the UK. *Housing Studies*, *25*, 483–507.

Feinberg, M., & Willer, R. (2015). From gulf to bridge: When do moral arguments facilitate political influence? *Personality and Social Psychology Bulletin*, *41*(12), 1665–1681.

Feinberg, M., Willer, R., & Keltner, D. (2012). Flustered and faithful: Embarrassment as a signal of prosociality. *Journal of Personality and Social Psychology*, *102*, 81–97.

Feinberg, M., Willer, R., Stellar, J., & Keltner, D. (2012). The virtues of gossip: Reputational information sharing as prosocial behavior. *Journal of Personality and Social Psychology*, *102*(5), 1015–1030.

Fejfar, M. C., & Hoyle, R. H. (2000). Effect of private self-awareness on negative affect and self-referent attribution. *Personality and Social Psychology Review*, *4*, 132–142.

Feldman, D. C. (1984). The development and enforcement of group norms. *Academy of Management Review*, *9*, 47–53.

Felfe, C., & Hsin, A. (2012). Maternal work conditions and child development. *Economics of Education Review*, *31*, 1037–1057.

Felipe, N. J., & Sommer, R. (1966). Invasions of personal space. *Social Problems*, *14*, 206–214.

Felmlee, D., Sprecher, S., & Bassin, E. (1990). The dissolution of intimate relationships: A hazard model. *Social Psychology Quarterly*, *53*, 13–30.

Felson, M. (1994). *Crime and everyday life: Insights and implications for society*. Thousand Oaks, CA: Pine Forge Press.

Felson, R. B. (1985). Reflected appraisal and the development of self. *Social Psychology Quarterly*, *48*, 71–78.

Felson, R. B. (1989). Parents and the reflected appraisal process: A longitudinal analysis. *Journal of Personality and Social Psychology*, *56*, 965–971.

Felson, R. B., Liska, A. E., South, S. J., & McNulty, T. L. (1994). The subculture of violence and delinquency: Individual vs. school context effects. *Social Forces*, *73*, 155–173.

Felson, R. B., & Reed, M. (1986). The effects of parents on the self-appraisals of children. *Social Psychology Quarterly*, *49*, 302–308.

Felson, R. B., & Zielinski, M. A. (1989). Children's self-esteem and parental support. *Journal of Marriage and Family*, *51*, 727–735.

Fernández-Dols, J. M., & Ruiz-Belda, M. A. (1995). Are smiles a sign of happiness? Gold medal winners at the Olympic Games. *Journal of Personality and Social Psychology*, *69*(6), 1113–1119.

Fessler, D. M., Pisor, A. C., & Holbrook, C. (2017). Political orientation predicts credulity regarding putative hazards. *Psychological Science*, *28*(5), 651–660.

Festinger, L. (1954). A theory of social comparison processes. *Human Relations*, *7*, 117–140.

Festinger, L. (1957). *A theory of cognitive dissonance*. Stanford, CA: Stanford University Press.

Festinger, L., & Carlsmith, J. (1959). Cognitive consequences of forced compliance. *Journal of Abnormal and Social Psychology, 58*, 203–210.

Festinger, L., Schachter, S., & Back, K. W. (1950). *Social pressures in informal groups.* New York: Harper & Row.

Field, T., Diego, M., Pelaez, M., Deeds, O., & Delgado, J. (2011). Breakup distress in university students: A review. *College Student Journal, 45*, 461–480.

File, T., & Ryan, C. (2014). Computer and Internet use in the United States: 2013. American Community Survey Reports, ACS-28. U.S. Census Bureau, Washington, DC.

Fine, G. A. (1995). Building blocks and the quadrant of action. In K. S. Cook, G. A. Fine, & J. S. House (Eds.), *Sociological perspectives on social psychology* (pp. 1–7). Boston: Allyn and Bacon.

Fine, G. A. (2000). Games and truths: Learning to construct social problems in high school debate. *Sociological Quarterly, 41*, 103–123.

Fink, E. L., & Cai, D. A. (2013). Discrepancy models of belief change. In J. P. Dillard & L. Shen (Eds.), *Handbook of persuasion: Developments in theory and practice* (2nd ed., pp. 84–103). Thousand Oaks, CA: Sage.

Fink, E. L., Cai, D. A., Kaplowitz, S. A., Chung, S., Van Dyke, M. A., & Kim, J. N. (2003). The semantics of social influence: Threats vs. persuasion. *Communication Monographs, 70*(4), 295–316.

Fischer, C. S. (1984). *The urban experience* (2nd ed.). San Diego, CA: Harcourt Brace Jovanovich.

Fişek, M. H. (1974). A model for the evolution of status structures in task-oriented discussion groups. In J. Berger, T. L. Conner, & M. H. Fişek (Eds.), *Expectation states theory* (pp. 55–83). Cambridge, MA: Winthrop.

Fişek, M. H., & Hysom, S. J. (2008). Status characteristics and reward expectations: A test of a theory of justice in two cultures. *Social Science Research, 37*(3), 769–786.

Fishman, P. M. (1980). Conversational insecurity. In H. Giles & W. P. Robinson (Eds.), *Language: Social psychological perspectives* (pp. 127–132). New York: Pergamon.

Fishman, P. (1983). Interaction: The work women do. In B. Thorne, C. Kramerae, & N. Henley (Eds.), *Language, gender, and society* (pp. 89–101). Rowley, MA: Newbury House.

Fisicaro, S. A. (1988). A reexamination of the relation between halo error and accuracy. *Journal of Applied Psychology, 73*, 239–244.

Fiske, S. T. (1998). Stereotyping, prejudice, and discrimination. In D. Gilbert, S. Fiske, & G. Lindzey (Eds.), *Handbook of social psychology* (4th ed., Vol. 2, pp. 357–411). New York: McGraw-Hill.

Fiske, S. T., Cuddy, A. J., & Glick, P. (2007). Universal dimensions of social cognition: Warmth and competence. *Trends in Cognitive Sciences, 11*(2), 77–83.

Fiske, S. T., Cuddy, A. J., Glick, P., & Xu, J. (2002). A model of (often mixed) stereotype content: Competence and warmth respectively follow from perceived status and competition. *Journal of Personality and Social Psychology, 82*(6), 878–902.

Fiske, S. T., Lin, M., & Neuberg, S. L. (1999). The continuum model: Ten years later. In S. Chaiken and Y. Trope (Eds.), *Dual-process theories in social psychology* (pp. 231–254). New York: Guilford.

Fiske, S. T., & Linville, P. (1980). What does the schema concept buy us? *Personality and Social Psychology Bulletin, 6*, 543–557.

Fiske, S. T., & Neuberg, S. L. (1990). A continuum model of impression formation, from category-based to individuating processes: Influence of information and motivation on attention and interpretation. In M. P. Zanna (Ed.), *Advances in experimental social psychology* (Vol. 23, pp. 1–74). San Diego, CA: Academic Press.

Fiske, S. T., & Taylor, S. E. (1991). *Social cognition* (2nd ed.). New York: McGraw-Hill.

Fitzpatrick, M. J., & McPherson, B. J. (2010). Coloring within the lines: Gender stereotypes within contemporary coloring books. *Sex Roles, 62*, 127–137.

Flack Jr., W. F., Daubman, K. A., Caron, M. L., Asadorian, J. A., D'Aureli, N. R., Gigliotti, S. N., et al. (2007). Risk factors and consequences of unwanted sex among university students hooking up, alcohol, and stress response. *Journal of Interpersonal Violence, 22*(2), 139–157.

Flavell, J., Shipstead, S., & Croft, K. (1978). *What young children think you see when their eyes are closed.* Unpublished report, Stanford University.

Flora, J., & Segrin, C. (2000). Relationship development in dating couples: Implications for relational satisfaction and loneliness. *Journal of Social and Personal Relationships, 17*, 811–825.

Follman, M., & Andrews, B. (2015). How Columbine spawned dozens of copycats. *Mother Jones.* www.motherjones.com/politics/2015/10/columbine-effect-mass-shootings-copycat-data (Accessed May 26, 2017).

Forbes, G. (2001). College students with tattoos and piercings: Motives, family experiences, personality factors, and perception by others. *Psychological Reports, 89*, 774–786.

Forbes, G. B., Adams-Curtis, L. E., White, K. B., & Hamm, N. R. (2002). Perceptions of married women and married men with hyphenated surnames. *Sex Roles, 46*(5–6), 167–175.

Fordham, S. (1999). Dissin' "the standard": Ebonics as guerrilla warfare at Capital High. *Anthropology and Education Quarterly, 30*, 272–293.

Forgas, J. P. (2011). Can negative affect eliminate the power of first impressions? Affective influences on primacy and recency effects in impression formation. *Journal of Experimental Social Psychology, 47*(2), 425–429.

Form, W. H., & Nosow, S. (1958). *Community in disaster.* New York: Harper.

Formoso, D., Gonzales, N., Barrera, M., & Dumka, L. (2007). Interparental relations, maternal employment, and fathering in Mexican American families. *Journal of Marriage and Family, 69*, 26–39.

Forsyth, D. R. (1999). *Group dynamics* (3rd ed.). Belmont, CA: Wadsworth.

Forsyth, D. R., Berger, R. E., & Mitchell, T. (1981). The effects of self-serving vs. other-serving claims of responsibility on attraction and attribution in groups. *Social Psychology Quarterly, 44*, 59–64.

Forthofer, M. S., Markman, H. J., Cox, M., Stanley, S., & Kessler, R. C. (1996). Associations between marital distress and work loss in a national sample. *Journal of Marriage and Family, 58*, 597–605.

Foster, C., & Campbell, W. K. (2005). The adversity of secret relationships. *Personal Relationships, 12*, 125–143.

Fox, G. L., & Benson, M. L. (2006). Household and neighborhood contexts of intimate partner violence. *Public Health Reports, 121*(4), 419–427.

Fox, K. (2013). Incurable sex offenders, lousy judges, and the media: Moral panic sustenance in the age of new media. *American Journal of Criminal Justice, 38*, 160–181.

Francis, L. (1997). Ideology and interpersonal emotion management: Redefining identity in two support groups. *Social Psychology Quarterly, 60*, 153–171.

Franiuk, R., Cohen, D., & Pomerantz, E. (2002). Implicit theories of relationships: Implications for relationship satisfaction and longevity. *Personal Relationships, 9*, 345–367.

Frank, M., Everett, D. L., Fedorenko, E., & Gibson, E. (2008). Number as a cognitive technology: Evidence from Piraha language and cognition. *Cognition, 108*, 819–824.

Franklin, A., Boyd-Franklin, N., & Kelly, S. (2006). Racism and invisibility: Race-related stress, emotional abuse, and psychological trauma for people of color. *Journal of Emotional Abuse, 6*, 9–30.

Franks, D., & Marolla, J. (1976). Efficacious action and social approval as interacting dimensions of self-esteem. *Sociometry, 39*, 324–341.

Fraser, C., Gouge, C., & Billig, M. (1971). Risky shifts, cautious shifts, and group polarization. *European Journal of Social Psychology, 1*, 7–30.

Freedman, J., & Fraser, S. (1966). Compliance without pressure: The foot-in-the-door technique. *Journal of Personality and Social Psychology, 4*, 195–202.

Freedman, J. L., & Sears, D. O. (1965). Warning, distraction, and resistance to influence. *Journal of Personality and Social Psychology, 1*, 262–266.

Freese, J., & Shostak, S. (2009). Genetics and social inquiry. *Annual Review of Sociology, 35*, 107–128.

French, J. R. P., & Raven, B. (1959). Bases of social power. In D. Cartwright (Ed.), *Studies in social power* (pp. 150–167). Ann Arbor: University of Michigan.

Freud, S. (1930). *Civilization and its discontents*. London: Hogarth Press.

Freud, S. (1950). Why war? In J. Strachey (Ed.), *Collected papers* (Vol. 5, pp. 195–216). London: Hogarth Press.

Freud, S. (1962). *Three essays on the theory of sexuality* (Trans. James Strachey). New York: Basic Books.

Frey, D. L., & Gaertner, S. L. (1986). Helping and the avoidance of inappropriate interracial behavior: A strategy that perpetuates a nonprejudiced self-image. *Journal of Personality and Social Psychology, 50*, 1083–1090.

Frey, K. S., & Ruble, D. N. (1985). What children say when the teacher is not around: Conflicting goals in social comparison and performance assessment in the classroom. *Journal of Personality and Social Psychology, 48*, 550–562.

Friedlmeier, W., Corapci, F., & Cole, P. M. (2011). Emotion socialization in cross-cultural perspective. *Social and Personality Psychology Compass, 5*(7), 410–427.

Friedrich-Cofer, L., & Huston, A. C. (1986). Television violence and aggression: The debate continues. *Psychological Bulletin, 100*, 364–371.

Fries, A., & Pollak, S. (2004). Emotion understanding in post-institutionalized Eastern European children. *Development and Psychopathology, 16*, 355–369.

Frieze, I., & Weiner, B. (1971). Cue utilization and attributional judgments for success and failure. *Journal of Personality, 39*, 591–605.

Frijda, N. H., & Mesquita, B. (1994). The social roles and functions of emotions. In S. Kitayama & H. R. Markus (Eds.), *Emotion and culture: Empirical studies of mutual influence* (pp. 51–87). Washington, DC: American Psychological Association.

Frisby, B. N., & Booth-Butterfield, M. (2012). The "how" and "why" of flirtatious communication between marital partners. *Communication Quarterly, 60*, 465–480.

Fritzsche, B. A., Finkelstein, M. A., & Penner, L. A. (2000). To help or not to help: Capturing individuals' decision policies. *Social Behavior and Personality, 28*, 561–578.

Fry, R. (2016, May). For first time in modern era, living with parents edges out other living arrangements for 18- to 34-year-olds. Washington, DC: Pew Research Center.

Fultz, J., Batson, C. D., Fortenbach, V. A., McCarthy, P. M., & Varney, L. L. (1986). Social evaluation and the empathy–altruism hypothesis. *Journal of Personality and Social Psychology, 50*, 761–769.

Furnham, A. (1986). The robustness of the recency effect: Studies using legal evidence. *Journal of General Psychology, 113*(4), 351–357.

Furnham, A. (2010). A parental locus of control scale. *Individual Differences Research, 8*(3), 151–163.

Furstenberg, F., & Kiernan, K. (2001). Delayed parental divorce: How much do children suffer? *Journal of Marriage and Family, 63*, 446–457.

Gaertner, S. L., Dovidio, J. F., Rust, M. C., Nier, J. A., Banker, B., Ward, C. M., et al. (1999). Reducing intergroup bias: Elements of intergroup cooperation. *Journal of Personality and Social Psychology, 76*, 388–402.

Gallo, M. M. (2015). *"No one helped": Kitty Genovese, New York City, and the myth of urban apathy*. New York: Cornell University Press.

Galton, M. (1987). An ORACLE chronicle: A decade of classroom research. *Teaching and Teacher Education, 3*, 299–313.

Gardner, L., & Shoemaker, D. J. (1989). Social bonding and delinquency: A comparative analysis. *Sociological Quarterly, 30*, 481–500.

Garfinkel, H. (1956). Conditions of successful degradation ceremonies. *American Sociological Review, 61*, 420–424.

Garfinkel, I., & McLanahan, S. S. (1986). *Single mothers and their children: A new American dilemma*. Washington, DC: Urban Institute.

Garner, B., & Grazian, D. (2016). Naturalizing gender through childhood socialization messages in a zoo. *Social Psychology Quarterly, 79*, 181–198.

Garrett, P., & Baquedano-Lopez, P. (2002). Language socialization: Reproduction and continuity, transformation and change. *Annual Review of Anthropology, 31*, 339–361.

Garrido, C. O., Adams, R. B., Nelson, A. J., Hess, U., & Kleck, R. E. (2013). Age-related facial markers as mechanisms driving attributions of sadness to neutral elderly faces. Presentation at the Association for Psychological Science Annual Convention. Washington, DC. May 24.

Gartner, R. (1990). The victims of homicide: A temporal and cross-national comparison. *American Sociological Review*, 55, 92–106.

Gawronski, B., & Strack, F. (2004). On the propositional nature of cognitive consistency: Dissonance changes explicit, but not implicit attitudes. *Journal of Experimental Social Psychology*, 40, 535–542.

Gecas, V. (1990). Contexts of socialization. In M. Rosenberg & R. Turner (Eds.), *Social psychology: Sociological perspectives* (pp. 165–199). New Brunswick, NJ: Transaction.

Gecas, V., & Burke, P. J. (1995). Self and identity. In K. S. Cook, G. A. Fine, & J. S. House (Eds.), *Sociological perspectives on social psychology* (pp. 41–67). Boston: Allyn and Bacon.

Gecas, V., & Schwalbe, M. (1983). Beyond the looking-glass self: Social structure and efficacy-based self-esteem. *Social Psychology Quarterly*, 46, 77–88.

Geis, M. L. (1995). *Speech acts and conversational interaction*. New York: Cambridge University Press.

Gelfand, D. M., & Hartmann, D. P. (1982). Response consequences and attributions: Two contributors to prosocial behavior. In N. Eisenberg (Ed.), *The development of prosocial behavior* (pp. 165–196). New York: Academic Press.

Geller, V. (1977). The role of visual access in impression management and impression formation. Unpublished doctoral dissertation, Columbia University, New York.

Gerber, A. S., Huber, G. A., Doherty, D., Dowling, C. M., & Panagopoulos, C. (2013). Big five personality traits and responses to persuasive appeals: Results from voter turnout experiments. *Political Behavior*, 35(4), 687–728.

Gergen, K. J., Ellsworth, P., Maslach, C., & Siepel, M. (1975). Obligation, donor resources, and reactions to aid in three cultures. *Journal of Personality and Social Psychology*, 31, 390–400.

Geronimus, A. T., Hicken, M., Keene, D., & Bound, J. (2006). "Weathering" and age patterns of allostatic load scores among Blacks and Whites in the United States. *American Journal of Public Health*, 96, 826–833.

Gesell, A., & Ilg, F. (1943). *Infant and child in the culture of today*. New York: Harper & Row.

Ghaziani, A. (2004). Anticipatory and actualized identities: A cultural analysis of the transition from AIDS disability to work. *Sociological Quarterly*, 45, 273–301.

Gibbons, F. X., Smith, T. W., Ingram, R. E., Pearce, K., Brehm, S. S., & Schroeder, D. J. (1985). Self-awareness and self-confrontation: Effects of self-focused attention on members of a clinical population. *Journal of Personality and Social Psychology*, 48, 662–675.

Gibbs, J., Ellison, N., & Heino, R. (2006). Self-presentation in online personals: The role of anticipated future interaction, self-disclosure, and perceived success in Internet dating. *Communication Research*, 33, 152–177.

Gibson, S. (2014). Discourse, defiance, and rationality: "Knowledge work" in the "obedience" experiments. *Journal of Social Issues*, 70(3), 424–438.

Gifford, R. (1982). Projected interpersonal distance and orientation choices: Personality, sex, and social situation. *Social Psychology Quarterly*, 45, 145–152.

Giles, H. (1980). Accommodation theory: Some new directions. In S. de Silva (Ed.), *Aspects of linguistic behavior* (pp. 105–136). York: York University Press.

Giles, H., & Coupland, N. (1991). *Language: Contexts and consequences*. Pacific Grove, CA: Brooks/Cole.

Giles, H., Hewstone, M., & St. Clair, R. (1981). Speech as an independent and dependent variable of social situations: An introduction and new theoretical framework. In H. Giles & R. St. Clair (Eds.), *The social psychological significance of speech*. Hillsdale, NJ: Erlbaum.

Gill, V. T., & Maynard, D. W. (1995). On "labeling" in actual interactions: Delivering and receiving diagnoses of developmental disabilities. *Social Problems*, 42, 11–37.

Gilligan, C. (1982). *In a different voice*. Cambridge, MA: Harvard University Press.

Ginorio, A., Gutierrez, L., Cauce, A. M., & Acosta, M. (1995). Psychological issues for Latinas. In H. Landrine (Ed.), *Bringing cultural diversity to feminist psychology: Theory, research, and practice* (pp. 241–263). Washington, DC: American Psychological Association.

Giordano, P., Cernkovich, S., & Rudolph, J. (2002). Gender, crime, and desistance: Toward a theory of cognitive transformation. *American Journal of Sociology*, 107, 990–1064.

Glasman, L. R., & Albarracín, D. (2006). Forming attitudes that predict future behavior: A meta-analysis of the attitude-behavior relation. *Psychological Bulletin*, 132(5), 778–822.

Glass, J., Bengston, V. L., & Dunham, C. (1986). Attitude similarity in three-generation families: Status inheritance or reciprocal influence? *American Sociological Review*, 51, 685–698.

Glenn, N., & Marquardt, E. (2001). *Hooking up, hanging out, and hoping for Mr. Right*. New York: Institute for American Values. www.americanvalues.org/search/item.php?id=18

Glenn, T., & Monteith, S. (2014). New measures of mental state and behavior based on data collected from sensors, smartphones, and the Internet. *Current Psychiatry Reports*, 16(12), 1–10.

Glick, P., & Fiske, S. T. (2001). An ambivalent alliance: Hostile and benevolent sexism as complementary justifications for gender inequality. *American Psychologist*, 56(2), 109–118.

Glick, P., Fiske, S. T., Mladinic, A., Saiz, J. L., Abrams, D., Masser, B., & López, W. L. (2000). Beyond prejudice as simple antipathy: hostile and benevolent sexism across cultures. *Journal of Personality and Social Psychology*, 79(5), 763–775.

Gocłowska, M. A., Baas, M., Elliot, A. J., & De Dreu, C. K. (2017). Why schema-violations are sometimes preferable to schema-consistencies: The role of interest and openness to experience. *Journal of Research in Personality*, 66, 54–69.

Godley, A., & Escher, A. (2012). Bidialectical African American adolescents' beliefs about spoken language expectations in English classrooms. *Journal of Adolescent and Adult Literacy*, 55, 704–713.

Goffman, A. (2015). *On the run: Fugitive life in an American city*. New York: Picador.

Goffman, E. (1952). Cooling the mark out: Some adaptations to failure. *Psychiatry, 15*, 451–463.

Goffman, E. (1956). Embarrassment and social organization. *American Journal of Sociology, 62*(3), 264–271.

Goffman, E. (1959a). The moral career of the mental patient. *Psychiatry, 22*, 125–169.

Goffman, E. (1959b). *The presentation of self in everyday life.* Garden City, NY: Anchor/Doubleday.

Goffman, E. (1963a). *Behavior in public places.* New York: Free Press.

Goffman, E. (1963b). *Stigma: Notes on the management of spoiled identity.* Englewood Cliffs, NJ: Spectrum/Prentice Hall.

Goffman, E. (1967). *Interaction ritual.* Chicago: Aldine.

Goffman, E. (1974). *Frame analysis.* New York: Harper & Row.

Goffman, E. (1983). Felicity's condition. *American Journal of Sociology, 89*, 1–53.

Goldberg, W., Prause, J., Lucas-Thompson, R., & Himsel, A. (2008). Maternal employment and children's achievement in context: A meta-analysis of four decades of research. *Psychological Bulletin, 134*, 77–108.

Goldstein, B., & Oldham, J. (1979). *Children and work: A study of socialization.* New Brunswick, NJ: Transaction.

Goleman, D. (1996). *Emotional intelligence.* London: Bloomsbury.

Goleman, D. (2006). *Emotional intelligence.* New York: Random House.

Gonos, G. (1977). "Situation" vs. "frame": The "interactionist" and the "structuralist" analysis of everyday life. *American Sociological Review, 42*, 854–867.

Gonzales, M. H., Davis, J. M., Loney, G. L., Lukens, C. K., & Junghans, C. M. (1983). Interactional approach to interpersonal attraction. *Journal of Personality and Social Psychology, 44*, 1192–1197.

Goodchilds, J. D., & Zellman, G. L. (1984). Sexual signaling and sexual aggression in adolescent relationships. In N. M. Malamuth & E. Donnerstein (Eds.), *Pornography and sexual aggression* (pp. 234–243). Orlando, FL: Academic Press.

Gooden, A. M., & Gooden, M. A. (2001). Gender representation in notable children's picture books: 1995–1999. *Sex Roles, 45*, 89–101.

Goodman, P. S., & Friedman, A. (1971). An examination of Adams' theory of inequity. *Administrative Science Quarterly, 16*, 271–288.

Goodwin, C. (1987). Forgetfulness as an interactive resource. *Social Psychology Quarterly, 50*, 115–131.

Goodwin, R. (1991). A re-examination of Rusbult's responses to dissatisfaction typology. *Journal of Social and Personal Relationships, 8*, 569–574.

Goodwin, S. A., Gubin, A., Fiske, S. T., & Yzerbyt, V. Y. (2000). Power can bias impression processes: Stereotyping subordinates by default and by design. *Group Processes and Intergroup Relations, 3*, 227–256.

Gordon, C. (1968). Self-conceptions: Configurations of content. In C. Gordon & K. J. Gergen (Eds.), *The self in social interaction I: Classic and contemporary perspectives* (pp. 115–136). New York: Wiley.

Gordon, P. (2004). Numerical cognition without words: Evidence from Amazonia. *Science, 306*, 496–499.

Gordon, R. A. (1996). Impact of ingratiation on judgments and evaluations: A meta-analytic investigation. *Journal of Personality and Social Psychology, 71*(1), 54–70.

Gordon, S. (1990). Social structural effects on emotion. In T. D. Kemper (Ed.), *Research agendas in the sociology of emotion* (pp. 145–179). Albany: State University of New York Press.

Gosling, S. D., Craik, K. H., Martin, N. R., & Pryor, M. R. (2005). Material attributes of personal living spaces. *Home Cultures, 2*, 51–88.

Gove, W., Hughes, M., & Geerken, M. R. (1980). Playing dumb: A form of impression management with undesirable effects. *Social Psychology Quarterly, 43*, 89–102.

Graham, J. M. (2011). Measuring love in romantic relationships: A meta-analysis. *Journal of Social and Personal Relationships, 28*, 748–771.

Gramling, R., & Forsyth, C. J. (1987). Exploiting stigma. *Sociological Forum, 2*, 401–415.

Grammar, K., Kruck, K., Juette, A., & Fink, B. (2000). Nonverbal control as courtship signals: The role of control and choice in selecting partners. *Evolution and Human Behavior, 21*, 371–390.

Grandey, A. A. (2003). When "the show must go on": Surface acting and deep acting as determinants of emotional exhaustion and peer-rated service delivery. *Academy of Management Journal, 46*(1), 86–96.

Granovetter, M. S. (1973). The strength of weak ties. *American Journal of Sociology, 78*, 1360–1380.

Grant, P. R., & Holmes, J. G. (1981). The integration of implicit personality schemas and stereotype images. *Social Psychology Quarterly, 44*, 107–115.

Grasmick, H. G., & Bursik Jr., R. J. (1990). Conscience, significant others, and rational choice: Extending the deterrence model. *Law and Society Review, 24*, 837–861.

Gray, J. (1992). *Men are from Mars, women are from Venus: A practical guide for improving communication and getting what you want in your relationships.* New York: HarperCollins.

Gray-Little, B., & Hafdahl, A. (2000). Factors influencing racial comparisons of self-esteem: A quantitative review. *Psychological Bulletin, 126*, 26–54.

Grayshon, M. C. (1980). Social grammar, social psychology, and linguistics. In H. Giles, W. P. Robinson, & P. M. Smith (Eds.), *Language: Social psychological perspectives* (pp. 155–169). New York: Pergamon.

Green, J. A. (1972). Attitudinal and situational determinants of intended behavior toward Blacks. *Journal of Personality and Social Psychology, 22*, 13–17.

Greenbaum, P., & Rosenfeld, H. (1978). Patterns of avoidance in response to interpersonal staring and proximity: Effects of bystanders on drivers at a traffic intersection. *Journal of Personality and Social Psychology, 36*, 575–587.

Greenberg, J. (1996). *The quest for justice on the job: Essays and experiments.* Thousand Oaks, CA: Sage.

Greenberg, J., & Folger, R. (1983). Procedural justice, participation, and the fair process effect in groups and organizations. In P. B. Paulus (Ed.), *Basic group processes* (pp. 235–256). New York: Springer-Verlag.

Greenberg, J., & Scott, K. S. (1996). Why do workers bite the hands that feed them? Employee theft as a social exchange process. In B. M. Staw & L. L. Cummings (Eds.), *Research in organizational behavior* (Vol. 18, pp. 111–156). Greenwich, CT: JAI Press.

Greenberg, M., & Frisch, D. (1972). Effect of intentionality on willingness to reciprocate a favor. *Journal of Experimental Social Psychology, 8*, 99–111.

Greenberg, M. S., & Westcott, D. R. (1983). Indebtedness as a mediator of reactions to aid. In J. D. Fisher, A. Nadler, & B. M. DePaulo (Eds.), *New directions in helping: Vol. 1. Recipient reactions to aid* (pp. 85–112). San Diego, CA: Academic Press.

Greenberger, E., & Steinberg, L. (1983). Sex differences in early labor force participation. *Social Forces, 62*, 467–486.

Greenfield, E. A., & Marks, N. F. (2004). Formal volunteering as a protective factor for older adults' psychological well-being. *Journal of Gerontology, 59B*, 258–264.

Greenwald, A., & Farnham, S. (2000). Using the implicit association test to measure self-esteem and self-concept. *Journal of Personality and Social Psychology, 79*, 1022–1038.

Greenwald, A. G., Nosek, B. A., & Banaji, M. R. (2003). Understanding and using the implicit association test: I. An improved scoring algorithm. *Journal of Personality and Social Psychology, 85*(2), 197–216.

Greenwald, A. G., Poehlman, T. A., Uhlmann, E. L., & Banaji, M. R. (2009). Understanding and using the implicit association test: III. Meta-analysis of predictive validity. *Journal of Personality and Social Psychology, 97*(1), 17–41.

Gregory, S. W., & Webster, S. (1996). A nonverbal signal in voices of interview partners effectively predicts communication accommodation and social status perceptions. *Journal of Personality and Social Psychology, 70*, 1231–1240.

Greitemeyer, T., & Cox, C. (2013). There's no "I" in team: Effects of cooperative video games on cooperative behavior. *European Journal of Social Psychology, 43*(3), 224–228.

Grice, P. H. (1975). Logic and conversation. In P. Cole & J. L. Morgan (Eds.), *Syntax and semantics, Vol. 3: Speech acts* (pp. 41–58). New York: Academic Press.

Grieve, R., Indian, M., Witteveen, K., Tolan, G. A., & Marrington, J. (2013). Face-to-face or Facebook: Can social connectedness be derived online? *Computers in Human Behavior, 29*, 604–609.

Griffin, D., Gonzalez, R., & Varey, C. (2001). The heuristics and biases approach to judgment under uncertainty. In A. Tesser & N. Schwarz (Eds.), *Blackwell handbook of social psychology: Intraindividual processes* (pp. 207–235). Oxford: Blackwell.

Griggs, R. A., & Whitehead III, G. I. (2015). Coverage of Milgram's obedience experiments in social psychology textbooks: Where have all the criticisms gone? *Teaching of Psychology, 42*(4), 315–322.

Grimshaw, A. D. (1973). On language in society. Part 1. *Contemporary Sociology, 2*, 575–585.

Grimshaw, A. D. (1990). Talk and social control. In M. Rosenberg & R. Turner (Eds.), *Social psychology: Sociological perspectives* (pp. 200–232). New Brunswick, NJ: Transaction.

Gross, A. E., & Latané, J. G. (1974). Receiving help, reciprocation, and interpersonal attraction. *Journal of Applied Social Psychology, 4*, 210–223.

Gross, A. E., & McMullen, P. A. (1983). Models of the help seeking process. In B. M. DePaulo, A. Nadler, & J. D. Fisher (Eds.), *New directions in helping: Vol. 2. Help seeking* (pp. 47–73). New York: Academic Press.

Gross, E., & Stone, G. P. (1970). Embarrassment and the analysis of role requirements. In G. P. Stone & H. A. Farberman (Eds.), *Social psychology through symbolic interaction* (pp. 1–15). Waltham, MA: Ginn-Blaisdell.

Grossman, A. H., D'Augelli, A. R., & Salter, N. P. (2006). Male-to-female transgender youth: Gender expression milestones, gender atypicality, victimization, and parents' responses. *Journal of GLBT Family Studies, 2*, 71–92.

Gruenenfelder-Steiger, A. E., Harris, M. A., & Fend, H. A. (2016). Subjective and objective peer approval evaluations and self-esteem development: A test of reciprocal, prospective, and long-term effects. *Developmental Psychology, 52*, 1563–1577.

Grzywacz, J., & Marks, N. (2000). Family, work, work–family spillover, and problem drinking during midlife. *Journal of Marriage and Family, 62*, 336–348.

Guadagno, R. E., & Cialdini, R. B. (2007). Gender differences in impression management in organizations: A qualitative review. *Sex Roles, 56*, 483–494.

Gueguen, N. (2012). Tattoos, piercings, and sexual activity. *Social Behavior and Personality, 40*, 1543–1548.

Guerrero, L., Jones, S., & Burgoon, J. (2000). Responses to nonverbal intimacy change in romantic dyads: Effects of behavioral valence and degree of behavioral change on nonverbal and verbal reactions. *Communication Monographs, 67*(4), 325–346.

Guimond, S., Begin, G., & Palmer, D. L. (1989). Education and causal attributions: The development of "person-blame" and "system-blame" ideology. *Social Psychology Quarterly, 52*(2), 126–140.

Guimond, S., & Palmer, D. L. (1990). Type of academic training and causal attributions for social problems. *European Journal of Social Psychology, 20*(1), 61–75.

Gully, S. M., Devine, D. J., & Whitney, D. J. (1995). A meta-analysis of cohesion and performance: Effects of level of analysis and task interdependence. *Small Group Research, 26*, 497–520.

Gumperz, J. J. (1976). The sociolinguistic significance of conversational code-switching. In J. Cook-Gumperz & J. J. Gumperz (Eds.), *Papers on language and context* (pp. 1–34). Berkeley, CA: University of California, Language Behavior Research Laboratory.

Gurevitch, Z. D. (1990). The embrace: On the element of non-distance in human relations. *Sociological Quarterly, 31*, 187–201.

Guryan, J., Hurst, E., & Kearney, M. (2008). Parental education and parental time with children (Working Paper 13993). Cambridge, MA: National Bureau of Economic Research.

Gustafson, R. (1989). Frustration and successful vs. unsuccessful aggression: A test of Berkowitz's completion hypothesis. *Aggressive Behavior, 15*(1), 5–12.

Hagood, M. (2011). Quiet comfort: Noise, otherness, and the mobile production of personal space. *American Quarterly, 63*, 573–589.

Hahlweg, K., Heinrichs, N., Bertram, H., Kuschel, A., & Widdecke, N. (2008). Corporal punishment: Prevalence and impact on psychological development of preschool children. *Kindheit und Entwicklung, 17*, 45–56.

Haidt, J. (2012). *The righteous mind: Why good people are divided by politics and religion.* New York: Pantheon Books.

Haidt, J., & Keltner, D. (1999). Culture and facial expression: Open-ended methods find more expressions and a gradient of recognition. *Cognition and Emotion, 13*(3), 225–266.

Haines, V. A., Beggs, J. J., & Hurlbert, J. S. (2011). Neighborhood disadvantage, network social capital, and depressive symptoms. *Journal of Health and Social Behavior, 52*, 58–73.

Halberstam, D. (1979). *The powers that be.* New York: Knopf.

Hall, E. T. (1966). *The hidden dimension.* Garden City, NY: Doubleday.

Hall, J. A., Carter, S., Cody, M. J., & Albright, J. M. (2010). Individual differences in the communication of romantic interest: Development of the Flirting Styles Inventory. *Communication Quarterly, 58*, 365–393.

Hall, J., & Friedman, G. (1999). Status, gender, and nonverbal behavior: A study of structured interactions between employees of a company. *Personality and Social Psychology Bulletin, 25*, 1082–1091.

Halpern, D. F. (1998). Teaching critical thinking for transfer across domains: Dispositions, skills, structure training, and metacognitive monitoring. *American Psychologist, 53*(4), 449–455.

Halpern, D. F. (2002). Teaching for critical thinking: A four-part model to enhance thinking skills. In W. J. McKeachie, S. F. Davis, C. L. Brewes, & W. Buskist (Eds.), *The teaching of psychology: Essays in honor of Wilbert J. McKeachie and Charles L. Brewer* (pp. 91–106). Mahwah, NJ: Erlbaum.

Halpern-Meekin, S., Manning, W. D., Giordano, P. C., & Longmore, M. A. (2013). Relationship churning in emerging adulthood: On/off relationships and sex with an ex. *Journal of Adolescent Research, 28*, 166–188.

Hamilton, D. L. (1979). A cognitive-attributional analysis of stereotyping. In L. Berkowitz (Ed.), *Advances in experimental social psychology* (Vol. 12, pp. 53–85). New York: Academic Press.

Hamilton, M. C., Anderson, D., Broaddus, M., & Young, K. (2006). Gender stereotyping and under-representation of female characters in 200 popular children's books: A twenty-first century update. *Sex Roles, 55*, 757–765.

Hamilton, W. (1964). The genetical evolution of social behavior, I & II. *Journal of Theoretical Biology, 7*, 1–52.

Hanni, R. (1980). What is planned during speech pauses? In H. Giles, W. P. Robinson, & P. M. Smith (Eds.), *Language: Social psychological perspectives* (pp. 321–326). New York: Pergamon.

Harasty, A. (1997). The interpersonal nature of social stereotypes: Discussion patterns about in-groups and out-groups. *Personality and Social Psychology Bulletin, 23*, 270–284.

Hardy, C., & van Vugt, M. (2006). Nice guys finish first: The competitive altruism hypothesis. *Personality and Social Psychology Bulletin, 32*, 1402–1413.

Harkins, S. G., & Petty, R. E. (1981). The effects of source magnification of cognitive effect on attitudes: An information processing view. *Journal of Personality and Social Psychology, 40*, 401–413.

Harkins, S. G., & Petty, R. E. (1983). Social context effects in persuasion: The effects of multiple sources and multiple targets. In P. B. Paulus (Ed.), *Basic group processes* (pp. 149–175). New York: Springer Verlag.

Harkins, S. G., & Petty, R. E. (1987). Information utility and the multiple source effect. *Journal of Personality and Social Psychology, 52*, 260–268.

Harlow, R. E., & Cantor, N. (1995). To whom do people turn when things go poorly? Task orientation and functional social contacts. *Journal of Personality and Social Psychology, 69*, 329–340.

Harnish, J., Aseltine, R., & Gore, S. (2000). Resolution of stressful experiences as an indicator of coping effectiveness in young adults: An event history analysis. *Journal of Health and Social Behavior, 41*, 121–136.

Harris, M. B. (1974). Mediators between frustration and aggression in a field experiment. *Journal of Experimental Social Psychology, 10*, 561–571.

Harris, P., & Sachau, D. (2005). Is cleanliness next to godliness? The role of housekeeping in impression formation. *Environment and Behavior, 37*, 81–101.

Harris Poll. (2016). Tattoo takeover: Three in ten Americans have tattoos, and most don't stop at just one. www.theharrispoll.com/health-and-life/Tattoo_Takeover.html (Accessed November 15, 2016).

Harrison, A. (1977). Mere exposure. In L. Berkowitz (Ed.), *Advances in experimental social psychology* (Vol. 10, pp. 39–83). New York: Academic Press.

Harrison, M. A., & Gilmore, A. L. (2012). U txt WHEN? College students' social contexts of text messaging. *Social Science Journal, 49*, 513–518.

Hartwick, C., Desmarais, S., & Hennig, K. (2007). Characteristics of male and female victims of sexual coercion. *Canadian Journal of Human Sexuality, 16*(1/2), 31.

Harvey, J. H., Weber, A. L., & Orbuch, T. L. (1990). *Interpersonal accounts.* Oxford: Blackwell.

Haskell, M. R., & Yablonsky, L. (1983). *Criminology: Crime and criminality* (3rd ed.). Boston: Houghton Mifflin.

Haslam, S. A., & McCarty, C. (2004). Experimental design and causality in social psychology research. In C. Sansone, C. C. Morf, & A. T. Panter (Eds.), *The Sage handbook of methods in social psychology* (pp. 237–264). Thousand Oaks, CA: Sage.

Hass, R. G. (1981). Effects of source characteristics on cognitive responses in persuasion. In R. E. Petty, T. M. Ostrom, & T. C. Brock (Eds.), *Cognitive responses in persuasion* (pp. 141–172). Hillsdale, NJ: Erlbaum.

Hassin, R., & Trope, Y. (2000). Facing faces: Studies on the cognitive aspects of physiognomy. *Journal of Personality and Social Psychology, 78*, 837–852.

Hastorf, A. H., Wildfogel, J., & Cassman, T. (1979). Acknowledgment of a handicap as a tactic in social interaction. *Journal of Personality and Social Psychology, 31,* 1790–1797.

Hatfield, E. (1982). What do women and men want from love and sex? In E. R. Allgeier & N. B. McCormick (Eds.), *Changing boundaries: Gender roles and sexual behavior* (pp. 106–134). Palo Alto, CA: Mayfield.

Hatfield, E., & Sprecher, S. (1986). Measuring passionate love in intimate relationships. *Journal of Adolescence, 9,* 383–410.

Hatfield, E., & Walster, G. W. (1978). *A new look at love.* Lanham, MA: University Press of America.

Hauch, V., Sporer, S., Michael, S. W., & Meissner, C. A. (2016). Does training improve the detection of deception? A meta-analysis. *Communication Research, 43,* 283–343.

Haugtvedt, C. P., & Petty, R. E. (1992). Personality and persuasion: Need for cognition moderates the persistence and resistance of attitude changes. *Journal of Personality and Social Psychology, 63*(2), 308–319.

Hauser, R. M., & Warren, J. R. (1997). Socioeconomic indexes for occupations: A review, update, and critique. *Sociological Methodology 1997* (pp. 177–298). Cambridge, MA: Basil Blackwell.

Hawkes, D., Senn, C., & Thom, C. (2004). Factors that influence attitudes toward women with tattoos. *Sex Roles, 50,* 593–604.

Hawkins, A. (2004). Reflections on body hair. *Off Our Backs, 34,* 40–41.

Hayashi, A., Karasawa, M., & Tobin, J. (2009). The Japanese preschool's pedagogy of feeling: Cultural strategies for supporting young children's emotional development. *Ethos, 37*(1), 32–49.

Hayduk, L. A. (1978). Personal space: An evaluation and orienting review. *Psychological Bulletin, 85,* 117–134.

Haynes-Maslow, L., Auvergne, L., Mark, B., Ammerman, A., & Weiner, B. J. (2015). Low-income individuals' perceptions about fruit and vegetable access programs: A qualitative study. *Journal of Nutrition Education and Behavior, 47*(4), 317–324.

Haynie, D. (2001). Delinquent peers revisited: Does network structure matter? *American Journal of Sociology, 106,* 1013–1057.

Hazan, C., & Shaver, P. (1987). Romantic love conceptualized as an attachment process. *Journal of Personality and Social Psychology, 52,* 511–524.

Heard, H. (2007). Fathers, mothers, and family structure: Family trajectories, parent gender, and adolescent schooling. *Journal of Marriage and Family, 69,* 435–450.

Hebl, M., & Dovidio, J. (2005). Promoting the "social" in the examination of social stigmas. *Personality and Social Psychology Review, 9,* 156–182.

Hechter, M., & Opp, K. (2001). *Social norms.* New York: Russell Sage Foundation.

Heffernan, K. (2010). Mumbling is macho: Phonetic distinctiveness in the speech of American radio DJs. *American Speech, 85,* 67–90.

Heffernan, M. E., Fraley, R. C., Vicary, A. M., & Brumbaugh, C. C. (2012). Attachment features and functions in adult romantic relationships. *Journal of Social and Personal Relationships, 29,* 671–693.

Hegtvedt, K. A. (1990). The effects of relationship structure on emotional responses to inequity. *Social Psychology Quarterly, 53,* 214–228.

Hegtvedt, K. A., & Isom, D. (2014). Inequality: A matter of justice? In J. D. McLeod, E. J. Lawler, & M. Schwalbe (Eds.), *Handbook of the social psychology of inequality* (pp. 65–94). New York: Springer.

Heider, E. R., & Olivier, D. (1972). The structure of the color space in naming and memory of two languages. *Cognitive Psychology, 3,* 337–354.

Heider, F. (1944). Social perception and phenomenal causality. *Psychological Review, 51,* 358–374.

Heider, F. (1958). *The psychology of interpersonal relations.* New York: Wiley.

Heimer, K., & Matsueda, R. (1994). Role-taking, role commitment, and delinquency: A theory of differential social control. *American Sociological Review, 59,* 365–390.

Heise, D. R. (1979). *Understanding events: Affect and the construction of social action.* New York: Cambridge University Press.

Heise, D. R., & Calhan, C. (1995). Emotion norms in interpersonal events. *Social Psychology Quarterly, 58,* 223–240.

Heiss, J. (1981). Social roles. In M. Rosenberg & R. Turner (Eds.), *Social psychology: Sociological perspectives.* (pp. 94–132). New York: Basic Books.

Heiss, J. (1990). Social roles. In M. Rosenberg & R. Turner (Eds.), *Social psychology: Sociological perspectives* (pp. 94–129). New Brunswick, NJ: Transaction.

Hendrick, C., & Hendrick, S. (1989). Research on love: Does it measure up? *Journal of Personality and Social Psychology, 56,* 784–794.

Hendrick, S., & Hendrick, C. (1992). *Liking, loving, and relating* (2nd ed.). Pacific Grove, CA: Brooks/Cole.

Henley, J., Danziger, S., & Offer, S. (2005). The contribution of social support to the material well-being of low-income families. *Journal of Marriage and Family, 67,* 122–140.

Hennessy, D. A., & Wiesenthal, D. L. (2001). Gender, driver aggression, and driver violence: An applied evaluation. *Sex Roles, 44*(11–12), 661–676.

Henningsen, D. D., Braz, M., & Davies, E. (2008). Why do we flirt? Flirting motivations and sex differences in working and social contexts. *Journal of Business Communication, 45,* 483–502.

Henretta, J. C., Frazier, C., & Bishop, D. (1986). The effect of prior case outcome on juvenile justice decision-making. *Social Forces, 65,* 554–562.

Henrich, J., Heine, S. J., & Norenzayan, A. (2010). The weirdest people in the world. *Behavioral and Brain Sciences, 33*(2–3), 61–83.

Hepburn, C., & Locksley, A. (1983). Subjective awareness of stereotyping: Do we know when our judgments are prejudiced? *Social Psychology Quarterly, 45,* 311–318.

Herek, G. M., & Capitanio, J. P. (1996). "Some of my best friends": Intergroup contact, concealable stigma, and heterosexuals' attitudes toward gay men and lesbians. *Personality and Social Psychology Bulletin, 22,* 412–424.

Heritage, J., & Greatbatch, D. (1986). Generating applause: A study of rhetoric and response at party political conferences. *American Journal of Sociology, 92,* 110–157.

Hess, T. M., & Slaughter, S. J. (1990). Schematic knowledge influences on memory for scene information in young and older adults. *Developmental Psychology, 26,* 855–865.

Hess, U. (2013). Smiling and angry wrinkles: The impact of aging on the clarity of emotional facial expressions. Presentation at the Association for Psychological Science Annual Convention. Washington, DC. May 24.

Hetherington, E. M. (1999). Should we stay together for the sake of the children? In E. M. Hetherington (Ed.), *Coping with divorce, single parenting, and remarriage: A risk and resiliency perspective* (pp. 93–116). Mahwah, NJ: Erlbaum.

Hewitt, J., & Alqahtani, M. (2003). Differences between Saudi and U.S. students in reaction to same- and mixed-sex intimacy shown by others. *Journal of Social Psychology, 134,* 233–242.

Hewitt, J. P. (2000). *Self and society: A symbolic interactionist social psychology* (8th ed.). Boston: Allyn and Bacon.

Hewitt, J. P., & Stokes, R. (1975). Disclaimers. *American Sociological Review, 40,* 1–11.

Hewstone, M. (1990). The "ultimate attribution error"? A review of the literature on intergroup causal attribution. *European Journal of Social Psychology, 20,* 311–335.

Heyl, B. S. (1977). The Madam as teacher: The training of house prostitutes. *Social Problems, 24,* 545–555.

Hibbing, J. R., Smith, K. B., & Alford, J. R. (2014). Differences in negativity bias underlie variations in political ideology. *Behavioral and Brain Sciences, 37*(3), 297–307.

Higbee, K. L. (1969). Fifteen years of fear arousal: Research on threat appeals, 1953–1968. *Psychological Bulletin, 72,* 426–444.

Higgins, C., & Judge, T. (2004). The effect of applicant influence tactics on recruiter perceptions of fit and hiring recommendations: A field study. *Journal of Applied Psychology, 89,* 622–632.

Higgins, E. T. (1989). Self-discrepancy theory: What patterns of self-beliefs cause people to suffer? In L. Berkowitz (Ed.), *Advances in experimental social psychology* (Vol. 22, pp. 93–136). New York: Academic Press.

Higgins, E. T., & Bargh, J. A. (1987). Social cognition and social perception. *Annual Review of Psychology, 38,* 369–425.

Higgins, E. T., & Bryant, S. L. (1982). Consensus information and the fundamental attribution error: The role of development and in-group versus out-group knowledge. *Journal of Personality and Social Psychology, 47,* 422–435.

Higgins, E. T., Klein, R., & Strauman, T. (1985). Self-concept discrepancy theory: A psychological model for distinguishing among different aspects of depression and anxiety. *Social Cognition, 3,* 51–76.

Higuchi, M., & Fukada, H. (2002). A comparison of four causal factors of embarrassment in public and private situations. *Journal of Psychology, 136,* 399–406.

Hill, C., Rubin, Z., & Peplau, L. (1976). Breakups before marriage: The end of 103 affairs. *Journal of Social Issues, 32*(1), 147–168.

Hill, K. D. (2009). Code-switching pedagogies and African American student voices: Acceptance and resistance. *Journal of Adolescent and Adult Literacy, 53,* 120–131.

Hill, S. E., & Durante, K. M. (2011). Courtship, competition, and the pursuit of attractiveness: Mating goals facilitate health-related risk taking and strategic risk suppression in women. *Personality and Social Psychology Bulletin, 37,* 383–394.

Hill, T. D., Ross, C. E., & Angel, R. J. (2005). Neighborhood disorder, psychophysiological distress, and health. *Journal of Health and Social Behavior, 46,* 170–186.

Hines, M., Golombok, S., Rust, J., Johnson, K., Golding, J., et al. (2002). Testosterone during pregnancy and gender role behavior of preschool children: A longitudinal, population study. *Child Development, 73,* 1678–1687.

Hinkle, S., & Schopler, J. (1986). Bias in the evaluation of in-group and out-group performance. In S. Worchel & W. G. Austin (Eds.), *Psychology of intergroup relations* (2nd ed., pp. 196–212). Chicago: Nelson-Hall.

Hiroto, D. S. (1974). Locus of control and learned helplessness. *Journal of Experimental Psychology, 102*(2), 187–193.

Hirschi, T. (1969). *Causes of delinquency.* Berkeley: University of California Press.

Hirsh, J. B., Kang, S. K., & Bodenhausen, G. V. (2012). Personalized persuasion: Tailoring persuasive appeals to recipients' personality traits. *Psychological Science, 23*(6), 578–581.

Hirt, E. R., & Markmann, K. D. (1995). Multiple explanation: A consider-an-alternative strategy for debiasing judgments. *Journal of Personality and Social Psychology, 69,* 1069–1086.

Hitlin, S. (2003). Values as the core of personal identity: Drawing links between two theories of self. *Social Psychology Quarterly, 66,* 118–137.

Ho, D., Fu, W., & Ng, S. (2004). Guilt, shame and embarrassment: Revelations of face and self. *Culture and Psychology, 10,* 64–84.

Hochschild, A. R. (1983). *The managed heart: Commercialization of human feeling.* Berkeley: University of California Press.

Hodson, R. (1996). Dignity in the workplace under participative management. *American Sociological Review, 61,* 719–738.

Hoelter, J. W. (1983). The effects of role evaluation and commitment on identity salience. *Social Psychology Quarterly, 46,* 140–147.

Hoelter, J. W. (1984). Relative effects of significant others on self-evaluation. *Social Psychology Quarterly, 47,* 255–262.

Hoelter, J. W. (1986). The relationship between specific and global evaluations of self: A comparison of several models. *Social Psychology Quarterly, 49,* 129–141.

Hoffman, C., Lau, I., & Johnson, D. (1986). The linguistic relativity of person cognition: An English-Chinese comparison. *Journal of Personality and Social Psychology, 51,* 1097–1105.

Hoffman, M. L. (2001). *Empathy and moral development: Implications for caring and justice.* Cambridge: Cambridge University Press.

Hoffmann, J. (2002). The community context of family structure and adolescent drug use. *Journal of Marriage and Family, 64,* 314–330.

Hofling, C. K., Brotz, E., Dalrymple, S., Graves, N., & Pierce, C. M. (1966). An experimental study of nurse–physician relationships. *Journal of Nervous and Mental Disease, 143,* 171–180.

Hogg, M. A. (2001). A social identity theory of leadership. *Personality and Social Psychology Review, 5*(3), 184–200.

Hogg, M. A. (2006). Social identity theory. In P. J. Burke (Ed.), *Contemporary social psychological theories* (pp. 111–136). Palo Alto, CA: Stanford University Press.

Hogg, M. A. (2013). Intergroup relations. In J. D. DeLamater & A. Ward (Eds.), *Handbook of social psychology* (2nd ed., pp. 533–561). New York: Springer.

Hogg, M. A., & Hains, S. C. (1998). Friendship and group identification: A new look at the role of cohesiveness in groupthink. *European Journal of Social Psychology, 28*(3), 323–341.

Hogg, M. A., Terry, D. J., & White, K. M. (1995). A tale of two theories: A critical comparison of identity theory with social identity theory. *Social Psychology Quarterly, 58*, 255–269.

Holahan, C. J., & Moos, R. H. (1990). Life stressors, resistance factors, and improved psychological functioning: An extension of the stress resistance paradigm. *Journal of Personality and Social Psychology, 58*, 909–917.

Holland, A. S., & Roisman, G. I. (2010). Adult attachment security and young adults' dating relationships over time: Self-reported, observational, and physiological evidence. *Developmental Psychology, 46*, 552–557.

Hollander, E. P., & Julian, J. W. (1970). Studies in leader legitimacy, influence, and innovation. In L. Berkowitz (Ed.), *Advances in experimental social psychology* (Vol. 5, pp. 33–69). New York: Academic Press.

Hollinger, R. C., & Clark, J. P. (1983). Deterrence in the workplace: Perceived certainty, perceived severity, and employee theft. *Social Forces, 62*, 398–418.

Holmes, D. S. (1971). Compensation for ego threat: Two experiments. *Journal of Personality and Social Psychology, 18*, 234–237.

Holmes, J. G., Miller, D. T., & Lerner, M. J. (2002). Committing altruism under the cloak of self-interest: The exchange fiction. *Journal of Experimental Social Psychology, 38*(2), 144–151.

Holst, V. F., & Pezdek, K. (1992). Scripts for typical crimes and their effects on memory for eyewitness testimony. *Applied Cognitive Psychology, 6*(7), 573–587.

Holt, C. L., & Ellis, J. B. (1998). Assessing the current validity of the Bem Sex-Role Inventory. *Sex Roles, 39*(11–12), 929–941.

Homans, G. C. (1958). Social behavior as exchange. *American Journal of Sociology, 63*(6), 597–606.

Homans, G. C. (1961). *Social behavior: Its elementary forms.* Oxford: Harcourt-Brace.

Homans, G. C. (1974). *Social behavior: Its elementary forms* (2nd ed.). New York: Harcourt Brace Jovanovich.

Hopcroft, R. L. (2009). Gender inequality in interaction – An evolutionary account. *Social Forces, 87*, 1845–1872.

Horne, C. (2004). Collective benefits, exchange interests, and norm enforcement. *Social Forces, 82*, 1037–1062.

Horney, J., Osgood, D. W., & Marshall, I. H. (1995). Criminal careers in the short-term: Intra-individual variability in crime and its relation to local life circumstances. *American Sociological Review, 60*, 655–673.

Hornstein, G. (1985). Intimacy in conversational style as a function of the degree of closeness between members of a dyad. *Journal of Personality and Social Psychology, 49*, 671–681.

Hornstein, H. A. (1978). Promotive tension and prosocial behavior: A Lewinian analysis. In L. Wispe (Ed.), *Altruism, sympathy, and helping* (pp. 177–207). New York: Academic Press.

Horowitz, H. V., White, H. R., & Howell-White, S. (1996). Becoming married and mental health: A longitudinal study of a cohort of young adults. *Journal of Marriage and Family, 58*, 895–907.

Horowitz, R. (1987). Community tolerance of gang violence. *Social Problems, 34*, 437–450.

Hostetler, A., Sweet, S., & Moen, P. (2007). Gendered career paths: A life-course perspective in returning to school. *Sex Roles, 56*, 85–103.

House, J. S. (1977). The three faces of social psychology. *Sociometry, 40*, 161–177.

House, J. S. (1981). *Work stress and social support.* Reading, MA: Addison-Wesley.

House, J. S., Lepkowski, J. M., Kinney, A. M., Mero, R. P., Kessler, R. C., & Herzog, A. R. (1994). The social stratification of aging and health. *Journal of Health and Social Behavior, 35*, 213–234.

Hovland, C. I., Janis, I. L., & Kelley, H. H. (1953). *Communication and persuasion: Psychological studies of opinion change.* New Haven, CT: Yale University Press.

Howard, J. (2000). Social psychology of identities. *Annual Review of Sociology, 26*, 367–393.

Howe, N., & Strauss, W. (2009). *Millennials rising: The next great generation.* New York: Vintage.

Hsin, A., & Felfe, C. (2014). When does time matter? Maternal employment, children's time with parents, and child development. *Demography, 51*, 1867–1894.

Hu, Y., & Sundar, S. S. (2010). Effects of online health sources on credibility and behavioral intentions. *Communication Research, 37*, 105–132.

Huang, J. L., & Ford, J. K. (2012). Driving locus of control and driving behaviors: Inducing change through driver training. *Transportation Research Part F: Traffic Psychology and Behaviour, 15*(3), 358–368.

Hudson, C. G. (2005). Socioeconomic status and mental illness: Tests of the social causation and selection hypotheses. *American Journal of Orthopsychiatry, 75*, 3–18.

Huesmann, L. R. (1986). Psychological processes promoting the relation between exposure to media violence and aggressive behavior by the viewer. *Journal of Social Issues, 42*(3), 125–139.

Huesmann, L. R., & Moise, J. (1996). Media violence: A demonstrated public health threat to children. *Harvard Mental Health Letter, 12*(12), 5–7.

Hughes, D., & Surra, C. (2000). The reported influence of research participation on premarital relationships. *Journal of Marriage and Family, 62*, 822–832.

Hughes, M., & Demo, D. H. (1989). Self-perceptions of Black Americans: Self-esteem and personal efficacy. *American Journal of Sociology, 95*, 132–159.

Hultsch, D., & Plemons, J. (1979). Life events and life span development. In P. Baltes & O. G. Brim (Eds.), *Life-span development and behavior* (Vol. 2, pp. 1–36). New York: Academic Press.

Hundleby, J. D., & Mercer, G. W. (1987). Family and friends as social environments and their relationship to young adolescents' use of alcohol, tobacco, and marijuana. *Journal of Marriage and Family, 49,* 151–164.

Hunter, C. H. (1984). Aligning actions: Types and social distribution. *Symbolic Interaction, 7,* 155–174.

Hunzaker, M. F. (2016). Cultural sentiments and schema-consistency bias in information transmission. *American Sociological Review, 81*(6), 1223–1250.

Hyde, J., Fenema, E., & Lamon, S. (1990). Gender differences in mathematics performance: A meta-analysis. *Psychological Bulletin, 107,* 139–155.

Hyde, J., Lindberg, S., Linn, M., Ellis, A., & Williams, C. (2008). Gender similarities characterize math performance. *Science, 321,* 494–495.

Hyde, J. S. (2005). The gender similarities hypothesis. *American Psychologist, 60*(6), 581–592.

Hyde, J. S., & Else-Quest, N. (2012). *Half the human experience* (8th ed.). Belmont, CA: Wadsworth/Cengage.

Hymes, D. (1974). *Foundations in sociolinguistics.* London: Tavistock.

Iervolino, A., Hines, M., Golombok, S., Rust, J., & Plomin, R. (2005). Genetic and environmental influences on sex-typed behavior during the preschool years. *Child Development, 76,* 826–840.

Institute for Diversity and Ethics in Sports. (2016). The National Football League Racial & Gender Report Card (RGRC). Retrieved from www.tidesport.org/nfl-rgrc.html (May 25, 2017).

Ishii, K., Reyes, J. A., & Kitayama, S. (2003). Spontaneous attention to word content versus emotional tone differences among three cultures. *Psychological Science, 14*(1), 39–46.

Israelashvili, M., Kim, T., & Bukobza, G. (2012). Adolescents' over-use of the cyber world – Internet addiction or identity exploration? *Journal of Adolescence, 35,* 417–424.

Ivory, J. D., & Kalyanaraman, S. (2007). The effects of technological advancement and violent content in video games on players' feelings of presence, involvement, physiological arousal, and aggression. *Journal of Communication, 57*(3), 532–555.

Jaccard, J. (1981). Toward theories of persuasion and belief change. *Journal of Personality and Social Psychology, 40,* 260–269.

Jackson, L. A., Hunter, J. E., & Hodge, C. N. (1995). Physical attractiveness and intellectual competence: A meta-analytic review. *Social Psychology Quarterly, 58,* 108–122.

Jackson, P. B. (1997). Role occupancy and minority mental health. *Journal of Health and Social Behavior, 38,* 237–255.

Jackson, P. B., Kleiner, S., Geist, C., & Cebulko, K. (2011). Conventions of courtship: Gender and race differences in the significance of dating rituals. *Journal of Family Issues, 32,* 629–652.

Jackson, T., Chen, H., Guo, C., & Gao, X. (2006). Stories we love by: Conceptions of love among couples from the People's Republic of China and the United States. *Journal of Cross-Cultural Psychology, 37,* 446–464.

Jackson-Jacobs, C. (2004). Hard drugs in a soft context: Managing trouble and crack use on a college campus. *Sociological Quarterly, 45,* 835–856.

Jacobson, N. S., & Gottman, J. M. (1998). *When men batter women: New insights into ending abusive relationships.* New York: Simon and Schuster.

Jacques, J. M., & Chason, K. (1977). Self-esteem and low status groups: A changing scene? *Sociological Quarterly, 18,* 399–412.

Jafar, A. (2017). Asking the right questions: Teaching about Islam and globalization. *Teaching Sociology, 45*(4), 379–387.

Jaffee, S., & Hyde, J. S. (2000). Gender differences in moral orientation: A meta-analysis. *Psychological Bulletin, 126,* 703–726.

James, W. (1890). *Principles of psychology.* New York: Holt, Rinehart and Winston.

Janis, I. L. (1982). *Groupthink* (2nd ed.). Boston: Houghton Mifflin.

Janis, I. L., & Mann, L. (1977). *Decision making: A psychological analysis of conflict, choice, and commitment.* New York: Free Press.

Jemmott, J. B., & Magloire, K. (1988). Academic stress, social support, and secretory immunoglobulin. *Journal of Personality and Social Psychology, 55,* 803–810.

Jenkins, C., Rosenman, R., & Zyzanski, S. (1974). Prediction of clinical coronary heart disease by a test for coronary prone behavior pattern. *New England Journal of Medicine, 290,* 1271–1275.

Jensen, G., Erickson, M., & Gibbs, J. (1978). Perceived risk of punishment and self-reported delinquency. *Social Forces, 57,* 57–78.

Jessor, R., Costa, F., Jessor, L., & Donovan, J. (1983). Time of first intercourse: A prospective study. *Journal of Personality and Social Psychology, 44,* 608–626.

Jewkes, R., Sen, P., & Garcia-Moreno, C. (2002). Sexual violence. In E. G. Krug, L. L. Dahlberg, J. A. Mercy, A. B. Zwi, & R. Lozano (Eds.), *World report on violence and health* (pp. 149–181). Geneva: World Health Organization.

Johnson, B. T. (1991). Insight about attitudes: Meta-analytic perspectives. *Personality and Social Psychology Bulletin, 17,* 289–299.

Johnson, B. T., & Eagly, A. H. (1989). Effects of involvement on persuasion: A meta-analysis. *Psychological Bulletin, 106,* 290–314.

Johnson, C. (1994). Gender, legitimate authority, and leader-subordinate conversations. *American Sociological Review, 59,* 122–135.

Johnson, D. J., & Rusbult, C. E. (1989). Resisting temptation: Devaluation of alternative partners as a means of maintaining commitment in close relationships. *Journal of Personality and Social Psychology, 57,* 967–980.

Johnson, D. W., & Lewicki, R. J. (1969). The initiation of superordinate goals. *Journal of Applied Behavioral Science, 5*(1), 9–24.

Johnson, J. T., & Boyd, K. R. (1995). Dispositional traits versus the content of experience: Actor/observer differences in judgments of the "authentic self." *Personality and Social Psychology Bulletin, 21,* 375–383.

Johnson, K. J., Lund, D. A., & Dimond, M. F. (1986). Stress, self-esteem, and coping during bereavement among the elderly. *Social Psychology Quarterly, 49,* 273–279.

Johnson, M., & Leslie, L. (1982). Couple involvement and network structure: A test of the dyadic withdrawal hypothesis. *Social Psychology Quarterly, 45,* 34–43.

Johnson, R. E. (1979). *Juvenile delinquency and its origins.* New York: Cambridge University Press.

Johnson, R. R. (2007). Race and police reliance on suspicious non-verbal cues. *Policing: An International Journal of Police Strategies & Management, 30,* 277–299.

Johnson-George, C., & Swap, W. (1982). Measurement of specific interpersonal trust: Construction and validation of a scale to assess trust in a specific other. *Journal of Personality and Social Psychology, 43,* 1306–1317.

Joint Economic Committee. (2016) *Gender pay inequality: Consequences for women, families and the economy.* United States Senate. https://www.jec.senate.gov/public/_cache/files/0779dc2f-4a4e-4386-b847-9ae919735acc/gender-pay-inequality---us-congress-joint-economic-committee.pdf

Jones, E. E. (1964). *Ingratiation: A social psychology perspective.* New York: Appleton-Century-Crofts.

Jones, E. E. (1979). The rocky road from acts to dispositions. *American Psychologist, 34,* 107–117.

Jones, E. E., & Davis, K. E. (1965). From acts to dispositions. In L. Berkowitz (Ed.), *Advances in experimental social psychology* (Vol. 2, pp. 219–266). New York: Academic Press.

Jones, E. E., Farina, A., Hastorf, A. H., Markus, H., Miller, D. T., & Scott, R. A. (1984). *Social stigma.* New York: Freeman.

Jones, E. E., Gergen, K. J., Gumpert, P., & Thibaut, J. (1965). Some conditions affecting the use of ingratiation to influence performance evaluation. *Journal of Personality and Social Psychology, 1,* 613–626.

Jones, E. E., & Goethals, G. R. (1971). *Order effects in impression formation: Attribution context and the nature of the entity.* Morristown, NJ: General Learning Press.

Jones, E. E., & Harris, V. A. (1967). The attribution of attitudes. *Journal of Experimental Social Psychology, 3,* 1–24.

Jones, E. E., & McGillis, D. (1976). Correspondent inferences and the attribution cube: A comparative reappraisal. In J. H. Harvey, W. J. Ickes, & R. F. Kidd (Eds.), *New directions in attribution research* (Vol. 1, pp. 389–420). Hillsdale, NJ: Erlbaum.

Jones, E. E., & Nisbett, R. (1972). The actor and observer: Divergent perceptions of the causes of behavior. In E. E. Jones, D. E. Kanouse, H. H. Kelley, R. E. Nisbett, S. Valins, & B. W. Weiner (Eds.), *Attribution: Perceiving the causes of behavior* (pp. 79–94). Morristown, NJ: General Learning Press.

Jones, E. E., & Pittman, T. S. (1982). Toward a general theory of strategic self-presentation. In J. Suls (Ed.), *Psychological perspectives on the self* (Vol. 1, pp. 231–262). Hillsdale, NJ: Erlbaum.

Jones, E. E., & Wortman, C. (1973). *Ingratiation: An attributional approach.* Morristown, NJ: General Learning Press.

Jones, R. M., Taylor, D. E., Dick, A. J., Singh, A., & Cook, J. L. (2007). Bedroom design and decoration: Gender differences in preference and activity. *Adolescence, 42,* 539–553.

Jones, W. H., Briggs, S. R., & Smith, T. G. (1986). Shyness: Conceptualization and measurement. *Journal of Personality and Social Psychology, 51,* 629–639.

Jong, P. (1999). Communicative and remedial effects of social blushing. *Journal of Nonverbal Behavior, 23,* 197–217.

Jöreskog, K. G., & Sörbom, D. (1979). *Advances in factor analysis and structural equation models.* Cambridge, MA: Abe Books.

Joseph, N., & Alex, N. (1972). The uniform: A sociological perspective. *American Journal of Sociology, 77,* 719–730.

Joule, R., & Azdia, T. (2003). Cognitive dissonance, double forced compliance, and commitment. *European Journal of Social Psychology, 33,* 565–571.

Jourard, S. M. (1971). *Self-disclosure.* New York: Wiley.

Jung, H. S., & Yoon, H. H. (2011). The effects of nonverbal communication of employees in the family restaurant upon customers' emotional responses and customer satisfaction. *International Journal of Hospitality Management, 30,* 542–550.

Jussim, L., Coleman, L., & Nassau, S. (1987). The influence of self-esteem on perceptions of performance and feedback. *Social Psychology Quarterly, 50,* 95–99.

Kacmar, K. M., Carlson, D., & Bratton, V. (2004). Situational and dispositional factors as antecedents of ingratiatory behaviors in organizational settings. *Journal of Vocational Behavior, 65,* 309–331.

Kahn, A. S., Mathie, V. A., & Torgler, C. (1994). Rape scripts and rape acknowledgment. *Psychology of Women Quarterly, 18*(1), 53–66.

Kahne, M., & Schwartz, C. (1978). Negotiating trouble: The social construction and management of trouble in a psychiatric context. *Social Problems, 25,* 461–475.

Kahneman, D., & Tversky, A. (1973). On the psychology of prediction. *Psychological Review, 80,* 237–251.

Kalmijn, M., & De Graaf, P. M. (2012). Life course changes of children and well-being of parents. *Journal of Marriage and Family, 74*(2), 269–280.

Kane, R. (2006). On the limits of social control: Structural deterrence and the policing of "suppressible" crime. *Justice Quarterly, 23,* 186–213.

Kao, G., & Joyner, K. (2004). Do race and ethnicity matter among friends? Activities among interracial, interethnic, and intraethnic adolescent friends. *Sociological Quarterly, 45,* 557–573.

Kaplan, H. B., Johnson, R., & Bailey, C. A. (1987). Deviant peers and deviant behavior: Further elaboration of a model. *Social Psychology Quarterly, 50,* 277–284.

Kaplan, H. B., Martin, S. S., & Johnson, R. J. (1986). Self-rejection and the explanation of deviance: Specification of the structure among latent constructs. *American Journal of Sociology, 92,* 384–411.

Kaplan, M. F., & Miller, C. E. (1987). Group decision making and normative versus informational influence: Effects of type of issue and assigned decision rule. *Journal of Personality and Social Psychology, 53*(2), 306.

Karraker, A., & DeLamater, J. (2013). Past year sexual inactivity among older married persons and their partners. *Journal of Marriage and Family, 75,* 142–163.

Kashdan, T. B., Barrett, L. F., & McKnight, P. E. (2015). Unpacking emotion differentiation transforming unpleasant experience by perceiving distinctions in negativity. *Current Directions in Psychological Science, 24*(1), 10–16.

Katz, D. (1960). The functional approach to the study of attitudes. *Public Opinion Quarterly, 24*, 163–204.

Katz, I. (1981). *Stigma: A social psychological analysis.* Hillsdale, NJ: Erlbaum.

Katz, I., Wackenhut, J., & Glass, D. C. (1986). An ambivalence–amplification theory of behavior toward the stigmatized. In S. Worchel & W. G. Austin (Eds.), *Psychology of intergroup relations* (2nd ed., pp. 103–117). Chicago: Nelson-Hall.

Katz, J. (1988). *Seductions of crime: Moral and sensual attractions in doing evil.* New York: Basic Books.

Katzner, K. (1995). *The languages of the world* (3rd ed.). London: Routledge.

Kauffman, D. R., & Steiner, I. D. (1968). Some variables affecting the use of conformity as an ingratiation technique. *Journal of Experimental Social Psychology, 4*, 400–414.

Kaufman, J., & Johnson, K. (2004). Stigmatized individuals and the process of identity. *Sociological Quarterly, 45*, 807–833.

Kelley, H. H. (1950). The warm–cold variable in first impressions. *Journal of Personality, 18*, 431–439.

Kelley, H. H., Berscheid, E., Christensen, A., Harvey, H. H., Huston, T., Levinger, G., et al. (1983). *Close relationships.* New York: Freeman.

Kelley, H. H., & Michela, J. L. (1980). Attribution theory and research. *Annual Review of Psychology, 31*, 457–501.

Kelley, H. H., & Thibaut, J. W. (1978). *Interpersonal relations: A theory of interdependence.* New York: Wiley.

Kelman, H. C. (1974). Attitudes are alive and well and gainfully employed in the sphere of action. *American Psychologist, 29*, 310–324.

Kelman, H. C., & Hamilton, V. L. (1989). *Crimes of obedience: Toward a social psychology of authority and responsibility.* New Haven, CT: Yale University Press.

Kelmer, G., Rhoades, G. K., Stanley, S., & Markman, H. (2013). Relationship quality, commitment, and stability in long-distance relationships. *Family Process, 52*, 257–270.

Keltner, D. (1996). Evidence for the distinctness of embarrassment, shame, and guilt: A study of recalled antecedents and facial expressions of emotion. *Cognition and Emotion, 10*(2), 155–172.

Kemper, T. D. (1973). The fundamental dimensions of social relationship: A theoretical statement. *Acta Sociologica, 6*, 41–57.

Kemper, T. D. (1978). *A social interactional theory of emotions.* New York: Wiley.

Kendall, D. E. (2011). *Framing class: Media representations of wealth and poverty in America* (2nd ed.). Lanham, MD: Rowman & Littlefield.

Kendon, A. (1970). Movement coordination in social interaction: Some examples described. *Acta Psychologica, 32*, 100–125.

Kendon, A., Harris, R. M., & Key, M. R. (1975). *Organization of behavior in face-to-face interaction.* The Hague: Mouton.

Kennedy, S., & Ruggles, S. (2014). Breaking up is hard to count: The rise of divorce in the United States, 1980–2010. *Demography, 51*, 587–598.

Kenrick, D. T. (1995). Evolutionary theory versus the confederacy of dunces. *Psychological Inquiry, 6*, 56–62.

Kenrick, D. T., McCreath, H. E., Govern, J., King, R., & Bordin, J. (1990). Person–environment intersections: Everyday settings and common trait dimensions. *Journal of Personality and Social Psychology, 58*, 685–698.

Kent, G., Davis, J., & Shapiro, D. (1978). Resources required in the construction and reconstruction of conversations. *Journal of Personality and Social Psychology, 36*, 13–22.

Kerber, K. W. (1984). The perception of nonemergency helping situations: Costs, rewards, and the altruistic personality. *Journal of Personality, 52*, 177–187.

Kerckhoff, A. C. (1974). The social context of interpersonal attraction. In T. Huston (Ed.), *Foundations of interpersonal attraction* (pp. 61–78). New York: Academic Press.

Kessler, R. C. (1982). A disaggregation of the relationship between socioeconomic status and psychological distress. *American Sociological Review, 47*, 752–764.

Kessler, R. C., & Cleary, P. (1980). Social class and psychological distress. *American Sociological Review, 45*, 463–478.

Ketelaar, T., & Ellis, B. J. (2000). Are evolutionary explanations unfalsifiable? Evolutionary psychology and the Lakatosian philosophy of science. *Psychological Inquiry, 11*, 1–21.

Khan, A. Y., & Kamal, A. (2010). Exploring reactions to invasion of personal space in university students. *Journal of Behavioral Sciences, 20*, 80–97.

Khanna, N. (2004). The role of reflected appraisals in racial identity: The case of multiracial Asians. *Social Psychology Quarterly, 67*, 115–131.

Khazan, O. (2013). A psychologist's guide to online dating. *The Atlantic.* https://www.theatlantic.com/health/archive/2013/12/a-psychologists-guide-to-online-dating/282225/?utm_source=SFFB (Accessed February 27, 2017).

Kiecolt-Glaser, J. K., & Newton, T. L. (2001). Marriage and health: His and hers. *Psychological Bulletin, 127*, 472–503.

Kiesler, S., Siegel, J., & McGuire, T. W. (1984). Social psychological aspects of computer-mediated communication. *American Psychologist, 39*, 1123–1134.

Kiesling, S. (2004). Dude. *American Speech, 79*, 281–305.

Kilham, W., & Mann, L. (1974). Level of destructive obedience as a function of transmitter and executant roles in the Milgram obedience paradigm. *Journal of Personality and Social Psychology, 29*, 696–702.

Kim, J., Collins, K., Schooler, D., Sorsoli, C. L., Zylbergold, B. A., & Tolman, D. (2007). From sex to sexuality: Exposing the heterosexual script on primetime network television. *Journal of Sex Research, 44*, 145–157.

Kim, Y. J., & Hollingshead, A. B. (2015). Online social influence: Past, present, and future. *Annals of the International Communication Association, 39*(1), 163–192.

Kimmel, A. J. (2004). *Rumors and rumor control: A manager's guide to understanding and combatting rumors.* New York: Routledge.

Kiparsky, P. (1976). Historical linguistics and the origin of language. *Annals of the New York Academy of Sciences, 280,* 97–103.

Kirchmeyer, C. (1993). Nonwork-to-work spillover: A more balanced view of the experiences and coping of professional men and women. *Sex Roles, 28,* 531–552.

Kitayama, S., & Burnstein, E. (1988). Automaticity in conversations: A reexamination of the mindlessness hypothesis. *Journal of Personality and Social Psychology, 54,* 219–224.

Kitayama, S., Mesquita, B., & Karasawa, M. (2006). Cultural affordances and emotional experience: Socially engaging and disengaging emotions in Japan and the United States. *Journal of Personality and Social Psychology, 91*(5), 890.

Kitsuse, J. (1964). Societal reaction to deviant behavior: Problems of theory and method. In H. Becker (Ed.), *The other side: Perspectives on deviance* (pp. 87–100). New York: Free Press.

Kleck, R. E., & Strenta, A. (1980). Perceptions of the impact of negatively valued physical characteristics on social interaction. *Journal of Personality and Social Psychology, 39,* 861–873.

Kleider, H. M., Parrott, D. J., & King, T. Z. (2010). Shooting behaviour: How working memory and negative emotionality influence police officer shoot decisions. *Applied Cognitive Psychology, 24*(5), 707–717.

Klein, O., Snyder, M., & Livingston, R. W. (2004). Prejudice on the stage: Self-monitoring and the public expression of group attitudes. *British Journal of Social Psychology, 43,* 299–314.

Kling, K. C., Hyde, J., Showers, C., & Buswell, B. (1999). Gender differences in self-esteem: A meta-analysis. *Psychological Bulletin, 125,* 470–500.

Knapp, M. L., Stafford, L., & Daly, J. A. (1986). Regrettable messages: Things people wish they hadn't said. *Journal of Communication, 36,* 40–58.

Kohlberg, L. (1969). Stage and sequence: The cognitive-developmental approach to socialization. In D. Goslin (Ed.), *Handbook of socialization theory and research* (pp. 347–380). Chicago: Rand McNally.

Kohn, M. (1969). *Class and conformity: A study in values.* Homewood, IL: Dorsey Press.

Kohn, M. (1976). Occupational structure and alienation. *American Journal of Sociology, 82,* 111–130.

Kohn, M. L. (1989). Social structure and personality: A quintessentially sociological approach to social psychology. *Social Forces, 68*(1), 26–33.

Kohn, M., Naoi, A., Schoenbach, C., Schooler, C., & Slomczynski, K. M. (1990). Position in the class structure and psychological functioning in the United States, Japan, and Poland. *American Journal of Sociology, 95,* 964–1008.

Kohn, M., & Schooler, C. (1973). Occupational experience and psychological functioning: An assessment of reciprocal effects. *American Sociological Review, 38,* 97–118.

Kohn, M., & Schooler, C. (1982). Job conditions and personality: A longitudinal assessment of their reciprocal effects. *American Journal of Sociology, 87,* 1257–1286.

Kohn, M., & Schooler, C. (with Miller, J., Miller, K., Schoenbach, S., & Schoenberg, R.). (1983). *Work and personality: An inquiry into the impact of social stratification.* Norwood, NJ: Ablex.

Konecni, V. J. (1979). The role of aversive events in the development of intergroup conflict. In W. G. Austin & S. Worchel (Eds.), *The social psychology of intergroup relations* (pp. 85–102). Monterey, CA: Brooks/Cole.

Kothandapani, V. (1971). Validation of feeling, belief, and intention to act as three components of attitude and their contribution to prediction of contraceptive behavior. *Journal of Personality and Social Psychology, 19,* 321–333.

Kozielecki, J. (1984). Rodzaje samoprezentacji [Types of self-presentation]. *Psychologia Wychowawcza, 27,* 129–137.

Krahé, B. (2013). Violent video games and aggression. In K. E. Dill (Ed.), *The Oxford handbook of media psychology* (pp. 352–372). New York: Oxford University Press.

Krauss, R. M., & Fussell, S. K. (1996). Social psychological models of interpersonal communication. In E. T. Higgins & A. Kruglanski (Eds.), *Social psychology: Handbook of basic principles* (pp. 655–701). New York: Guilford Press.

Krauss, R. M., Morrel-Samuels, P., & Colasante, C. (1991). Do conversational hand gestures communicate? *Journal of Personality and Social Psychology, 61,* 743–754.

Kraut, R. E., & Poe, D. (1980). Behavior roots of person perception: The deception judgments of customs inspectors and laymen. *Journal of Personality and Social Psychology, 39,* 784–798.

Kreager, D. A., Rulison, K., & Moody, J. (2011). Delinquency and the structure of adolescent peer groups. *Criminology, 49*(1), 95–127.

Krebs, D. L. (1982). Psychological approaches to altruism: An evaluation. *Ethics, 92,* 147–158.

Kreider, R. M., & Ellis, R. (2011). *Living arrangements of children: 2009.* Household Economic Studies, U.S. Census Bureau.

Kreig, G. (2016). 12 times Donald Trump declared his "respect" for women. *CNN Politics.* Retrieved from www.cnn.com/2016/10/07/politics/donald-trump-respect-women/ (January 14, 2017).

Krieglmeyer, R., Wittstadt, D., & Strack, F. (2009). How attribution influences aggression: Answers to an old question by using an implicit measure of anger. *Journal of Experimental Social Psychology, 45*(2), 379–385.

Krohn, M. D. (1986). The web of conformity: A network approach to the explanation of delinquent behavior. *Social Problems, 33,* 581–593.

Krohn, M. D., Massey, J. L., & Zielinski, M. (1988). Role overlap, network multiplexity, and adolescent deviant behavior. *Social Psychology Quarterly, 51,* 346–356.

Kruger, D. J. (2001). Inclusive fitness and judgments of helping behaviors: Adaptations for kin directed altruism. *Social Behavior and Personality, 29,* 323–330.

Krull, D. S., & Dill, J. C. (1996). On thinking first and responding fast: Flexibility in social inference processes. *Personality and Social Psychology Bulletin, 22,* 949–959.

Kucharski, A. (2016). Post-truth: Study epidemiology of fake news. *Nature, 540*(7634), 525.

Kuhn, M. H., & McPartland, T. (1954). An empirical investigation of self-attitudes. *American Sociological Review, 19,* 68–76.

Kulik, J. A., & Brown, R. (1979). Frustration, attribution of blame, and aggression. *Journal of Experimental Social Psychology, 15*, 183–194.

Kumkale, G. T., & Albarracín, D. (2004). The sleeper effect in persuasion: A meta-analytic review. *Psychological Bulletin, 130*, 143–172.

Kurdek, L. A. (1991). The relation between reported well-being and divorce history, availability of proximate adult, and gender. *Journal of Marriage and Family, 53*, 71–78.

Kurmeyer, S. L., & Biggers, K. (1988). Environmental demand and demand engendering behavior: An observational analysis of the Type A pattern. *Journal of Personality and Social Psychology, 54*, 997–1005.

Kurtines, M. M. (1986). Moral behavior as rule governed behavior: Person and situation effects on moral decision-making. *Journal of Personality and Social Psychology, 50*, 784–791.

Kuyper, L., Wit, J., Adam, P., & Woertman, L. (2012). Doing more good than harm? The defects of participation in sex research on young people in the Netherlands. *Archives of Sexual Behavior, 41*, 497–506.

Kwang, T., & Swann Jr., W. B. (2010). Do people embrace praise even when they feel unworthy? A review of critical tests of self-enhancement versus self-verification. *Personality and Social Psychology Review, 14*, 263–280.

Kyjonkova, H., & Lacinova, L. (2010). Private speech and activity type in preschool children. *Ceskoslovenska Psychologie, 54*, 342–356.

Kyratzis, A. (2004). Talk and interaction among children and the co-construction of peer groups and peer culture. *Annual Review of Anthropology, 33*, 625–649.

Labov, W. (1972). *Sociolinguistic patterns*. Philadelphia: University of Pennsylvania Press.

Lachman, S. J., & Bass, A. R. (1985). A direct study of halo effect. *Journal of Psychology, 119*, 535–540.

Lacourse, E., Villeneuve, M., & Claes, M. (2003). Theoretical structure of adolescent alienation: A multigroup confirmatory factor analysis. *Adolescence, 38*, 639–650.

LaFrance, M., & Mayo, C. (1978). *Moving bodies: Nonverbal communication in social relationships*. Monterey, CA: Brooks/Cole.

Lakoff, R. T. (1979). Women's language. In O. Buturff & E. L. Epstein (Eds.), *Women's language and style* (pp. 139–158). Akron, OH: University of Akron.

Lamb, M. E. (1979). Paternal influence and the father's role: A personal perspective. *American Psychologist, 34*, 938–993.

Lamm, H., & Schwinger, T. (1980). Norms concerning distributive justice: Are needs taken into consideration in allocation decisions? *Social Psychology Quarterly, 43*, 425–429.

Land, K. C., McCall, P. L., & Cohen, L. E. (1990). Structural correlates of homicide rates: Are there invariances across time and social space? *American Journal of Sociology, 95*, 922–963.

Landis, D., & O'Shea, W. (2000). Cross-cultural aspects of passionate love: An individual differences analysis. *Journal of Cross-Cultural Psychology, 31*, 752–777.

Landrine, H., Klonoff, E., & Brown-Collins, A. (1995). Cultural diversity and methodology in feminist psychology: Critique, proposal, empirical example. In H. Landrine (Ed.), *Bringing cultural diversity to feminist psychology: Theory, research, and practice* (pp. 55–75). Washington, DC: American Psychological Association.

Laner, M. R., Benin, M. H., & Ventrone, N. A. (2001). Bystander attitudes toward victims of violence: Who's worth helping? *Deviant Behavior, 22*(1), 23–42.

Langan, D., Hannem, S., & Stewart, C. (2016). Deconstructing accounts of intimate partner violence: Doing interviews, identities, and neoliberalism. *Applied Linguistics, 37*, 219–238.

Lange, C. G., & James, W. (1922). *The emotions* (Vol. 1). Baltimore, MD: Williams and Wilkins.

Lansford, J. E., Skinner, A. T., Sorbring, E., Di Giunta, L., Keater-Deckard, K., Dodge, K. A., et al. (2012). Boys' and girls' relational and physical aggression in nine countries. *Aggressive Behavior, 38*, 298–308.

Lantz, D., & Steffire, V. (1964). Language and cognition revisited. *Journal of Abnormal and Social Psychology, 69*, 472–481.

Lantz, H., Keyes, J., & Schultz, M. (1975). The American family in the preindustrial period: From base lines in history to change. *American Sociological Review, 40*, 21–36.

Lantz, H., Schultz, M., & O'Hara, M. (1977). The changing American family from the preindustrial to the industrial period: A final report. *American Sociological Review, 42*, 406–421.

LaPiere, R. (1934). Attitudes versus actions. *Social Forces, 13*, 230–237.

Lareau, A. (2011). *Unequal childhoods: Class, race, and family life* (2nd ed.). Berkeley: University of California Press.

Larimer, M. E., Lydum, A. R., Anderson, B. K., & Turner, A. P. (1999). Male and female recipients of unwanted sexual contact in a college student sample: Prevalence rates, alcohol use, and depression symptoms. *Sex Roles, 40*(3–4), 295–308.

Larson, E. B., & Yao, X. (2005). Clinical empathy as emotional labor in the patient–physician relationship. *JAMA: Journal of the American Medical Association, 293*(9), 1100–1106.

Larzelere, T., & Huston, T. (1980). The dyadic trust scale: Toward understanding interpersonal trust in close relationships. *Journal of Marriage and Family, 42*(3), 595–604.

Latané, B. (1981). The psychology of social impact. *American Psychologist, 36*, 343–356.

Latané, B., & Darley, J. M. (1970). *The unresponsive bystander: Why doesn't he help?* New York: Appleton-Century-Crofts.

Latané, B., & Nida, S. (1981). Ten years of research on group size and helping. *Psychological Bulletin, 89*(2), 308–324.

Latané, B., Nida, S. A., & Wilson, D. W. (1981). The effects of group size on helping behavior. In J. P. Rushton & R. M. Sorrentino (Eds.), *Altruism and helping behavior* (pp. 287–313). Hillsdale, NJ: Erlbaum.

Latané, B., & Rodin, J. (1969). A lady in distress: Inhibiting effects of friends and strangers on bystander intervention. *Journal of Experimental Social Psychology, 5*(2), 189–202.

Lau, R. R. (1989). Individual and contextual influences on group identification. *Social Psychology Quarterly*, *52*, 220–231.

Lau, R. R., & Russell, D. (1980). Attributions in the sports pages. *Journal of Personality and Social Psychology*, *39*, 29–38.

Lauderdale, P. (1976). Deviance and moral boundaries. *American Sociological Review*, *41*, 660–676.

Laumann, E. O., Gagnon, J. H., Michael, R. T., & Michaels, S. (1994). *The social organization of sexuality*. Chicago: University of Chicago Press.

Lavoie, F., Hebert, M., Tremblay, R., Vitaro, F., Vezina, L., & McDuff, P. (2002). History of family dysfunction and perpetration of dating violence by adolescent boys: A longitudinal study. *Journal of Adolescent Health*, *30*, 375–383.

Lawler, E. J. (2001). An affect theory of social exchange. *American Journal of Sociology*, *107*, 321–352.

Lawler, E. J., & O'Gara, P. W. (1967). Effects of inequity produced by underpayment on work output, work quality, and attitudes toward work. *Journal of Applied Psychology*, *51*, 403–410.

Lawler, E. J., Thye, S. R., & Yoon, J. (2000). Emotion and group cohesion in productive exchange. *American Journal of Sociology*, *106*, 616–657.

Lawler, E. J., Thye, S. R., & Yoon, J. (2008). Social exchange and micro social order. *American Sociological Review*, *73*, 519–542.

Lawler, E. J., & Yoon, J. (1996). Commitment in exchange relations: Test of a theory of relational cohesion. *American Sociological Review*, *61*(1), 89–108.

Lawson, K. M., Crouter, A. C., & McHale, S. M. (2015). Links between family gender socialization experiences in childhood and gendered occupational attainment in young adulthood. *Journal of Vocational Behavior*, *90*, 26–35.

Lawton, C. A., Blakemore, J. E. O., & Vartanian, L. R. (2003). The new meaning of Ms.: Single, but too old for Miss. *Psychology of Women Quarterly*, *27*(3), 215–220.

Lazarus, R. S. (1991). *Emotion and adaptation*. New York: Oxford University Press.

Lazer, D., Baum, M., Grinberg, N., Friedland, L., Joseph, K., & Mattsson, C. (2017). Combating fake news: An agenda for research and action. Harvard Kennedy School Shorenstein Center Report. Retrieved from https://shorensteincenter.org/combating-fake-news-agenda-for-research/ (Accessed June 11, 2018).

Le, B., Dove, N. L., Agnew, C. R., Korn, M. S., & Mutso, A. A. (2010). Predicting nonmarital romantic relationship dissolution: A meta-analytic synthesis. *Personal Relationships*, *17*, 377–390.

Leander, K. (2002). Silencing in classroom interaction: Producing and relating social spaces. *Discourse Processes*, *34*, 193–235.

Leaper, C., Anderson, K., & Sanders, P. (1998). Moderators of gender effects on parents' talk to their children: A meta-analysis. *Developmental Psychology*, *34*, 3–27.

Leaper, C., & Smith, T. E. (2004). A meta-analytic review of gender variations in children's language use: Talkativeness, affiliative speech, and assertive speech. *Developmental Psychology*, *40*(6), 993–1027.

Lear, D. (1997). *Sex and sexuality: Risk and relationships in the age of AIDS*. Thousand Oaks, CA: Sage.

Leary, M. R. (1995). *Self-presentation: Impression management and interpersonal behavior*. Madison, WI: Brown & Benchmark.

Leary, M. R., & Kowalski, R. M. (1990). Impression management: A literature review and two-component model. *Psychological Bulletin*, *107*, 34–47.

Leary, M., Tchividjian, L., & Kraxberger, B. (1994). Self-presentation can be hazardous to your health: Impression management and health risk. *Health Psychology*, *13*, 461–470.

Ledvinka, J. (1971). Race of interviewer and the language elaboration of Black interviewees. *Journal of Social Issues*, *27*, 185–197.

Lee, B., & Porfeli, E. J. (2015). Youths' socialization to work and school within the family. *International Journal for Educational and Vocational Guidance*, *15*, 145–162.

Lee, B. A., Farrell, C. R., & Link, B. G. (2004). Revisiting the contact hypothesis: The case of public exposure to homelessness. *American Sociological Review*, *69*, 40–63.

Lee, H. (2006). Privacy, publicity, and accountability of self-presentation in an on-line discussion group. *Sociological Inquiry*, *76*, 1–22.

Lee, H. S., & Park, J. S. (2012). Cultural orientation and the persuasive effects of fear appeals: The case of anti-smoking public service announcements. *Journal of Medical Marketing: Device, Diagnostic and Pharmaceutical Marketing*, *12*, 73–80.

Lee, J. (2009). Escaping embarrassment: Face-work in the rap cipher. *Social Psychology Quarterly*, *72*(4), 306–324.

Lee, S. W., & Schwarz, N. (2010). Washing away postdecisional dissonance. *Science*, *328*(5979), 709.

Lefcourt, H. M. (1979). Locus of control for specific goals. In L. C. Perlmuter & R. A. Monty (Eds.), *Choice and perceived control* (pp. 209–220). Hillsdale, NJ: Erlbaum.

Lefcourt, H. M. (1981). The construction and development of the multidimensional–multiattributional causality scales. In H. M. Lefcourt (Ed.), *Research with the locus of control construct* (pp. 245–277). New York: Academic Press.

Lefcourt, H. M. (1991). Locus of control. In J. P. Robinson, P. R. Shaver, & L. S. Wrightsman (Eds.), *Measures of personality and social psychological attitudes* (pp. 413–499). New York: Academic Press.

Leffler, A., Gillespie, D. L., & Conaty, J. C. (1982). The effects of status differentiation on nonverbal behavior. *Social Psychology Quarterly*, *45*, 153–161.

Lemert, E. (1951). *Social pathology*. New York: McGraw-Hill.

Lemert, E. (1962). Paranoia and the dynamics of exclusion. *Sociometry*, *25*, 2–20.

Lenhart, A., Rainie, L., & Lewis, O. (2001, June 20). Teenage life online: The rise of the instant-message generation and the Internet's impact on friendships and family relationships. Pew Internet and American Life Project. www.pewinternet.org/~/media//Files/Reports/2001/PIP_Teens_Report.pdf

Lenhart, A., Smith, A., Anderson, M., Duggan, M., & Perrin, A. (2015). Teens, technology and friendships. Pew

Research Center. http://pewinternet.org/2015/08/06/teens-technology-and-friendships/(Accessed June 11, 2018).

Lennon, M. C., Link, B. G., Marbach, J. J., & Dohrenwend, B. P. (1989). The stigma of chronic facial pain and its impact on social relationships. *Social Problems, 36*, 117–134.

Leone, R., & Barowski, L. (2011). MPAA ratings creep: A longitudinal analysis of the PG-13 rating category in US movies. *Journal of Children and Media, 5*(01), 53–68.

Lepper, M., Greene, D., & Nisbett, R. (1973). Undermining children's intrinsic interest with extrinsic reward: A test of the "overjustification" hypothesis. *Journal of Personality and Social Psychology, 28*, 129–137.

Leventhal, G. S. (1979). Effects of external conflict on resource allocation and fairness within groups and organizations. In W. G. Austin & S. Worchel (Eds.), *The social psychology of intergroup relations* (pp. 237–251). Monterey, CA: Brooks/Cole.

Leventhal, G. S., Karuza Jr., J., & Fry, W. R. (1980). Beyond fairness: A theory of allocation preferences. In G. Mikula (Ed.), *Justice and social interaction* (pp. 167–218). New York: Springer-Verlag.

Leventhal, G. S., & Lane, D. W. (1970). Sex, age, and equity behavior. *Journal of Personality and Social Psychology, 15*, 312–316.

Leventhal, G. S., Michaels, J. W., & Sanford, C. (1972). Inequity and interpersonal conflict: Reward allocation and secrecy about reward as methods of preventing conflict. *Journal of Personality and Social Psychology, 23*, 88–102.

Leventhal, G. S., Weiss, T., & Long, G. (1969). Equity, reciprocity, and reallocating the rewards in the dyad. *Journal of Personality and Social Psychology, 13*, 300–305.

Leventhal, H. (1984). A perceptual-motor theory of emotion. *Advances in Experimental Social Psychology, 17*, 117–182.

Lever, J., Grov, C., Royce, T., & Gillespie, M. A. (2008). Searching for love in all the "write" places: Exploring Internet personals' use by sexual orientation, gender, and age. *International Journal of Sexual Health, 20*, 233–246.

Levin, J., & Arluke, A. (1982). Embarrassment and helping behavior. *Psychological Reports, 51*, 999–1002.

Levin, S., van Laar, C., & Sidanius, J. (2003). The effects of ingroup and outgroup friendships on ethnic attitudes in college: A longitudinal study. *Group Processes and Intergroup Relations, 6*, 76–92.

Levine, J. M., & Moreland, R. L. (1998). Small groups. In D. Gilbert, S. Fiske, & G. Lindzey (Eds.), *The handbook of social psychology* (4th ed., Vol. 1, pp. 415–469). Boston: McGraw-Hill.

Levine, J. M., Saxe, L., & Ranelli, C. J. (1975). Extreme dissent, conformity reduction, and the bases of social influence. *Social Behavior and Personality, 3*, 117–126.

Levine, M., Prosser, A., Evans, D., & Reicher, S. (2005). Identity and emergency intervention: How social group membership and inclusiveness of group boundaries shape helping behavior. *Personality and Social Psychology Bulletin, 31*, 443–453.

LeVine, R. A., & Campbell, D. T. (1972). *Ethnocentrism: Theories of conflict, ethnic attitudes, and group behavior.* New York: Wiley.

Levinger, G. (1976). A social psychological perspective on marital dissolution. *Journal of Social Issues, 32*(1), 21–47.

Levinson, R., Powell, B., & Steelman, L. C. (1986). Social location, significant others, and body image among adolescents. *Social Psychology Quarterly, 49*, 330–337.

Levitin, T. E. (1975). Deviants are active participants in the labeling process: The visibly handicapped. *Social Problems, 22*, 548–557.

Lewis, G. H. (1972). Role differentiation. *American Sociological Review, 37*, 424–434.

Lewis, I., Watson, B., Tay, R., & White, K. M. (2007). The role of fear appeals in improving driver safety: A review of the effectiveness of fear-arousing (threat) appeals in road safety advertising. *International Journal of Behavioral Consultation and Therapy, 3*(2), 203.

Lewis, K., Winsett, R., Cetingok, M., Martin, J., & Hathaway, D. (2000). Social network mapping with transplant recipients. *Progress in Transplantation, 10*, 262–266.

Lewis, M., & Brooks-Gunn, J. (1979). Toward a theory of social cognition: The development of self. In I. Uzgiris (Ed.), *Social interaction and communication during infancy. New directions for child development* (Vol. 4, pp. 1–20). San Francisco: Jossey-Bass.

Lewis, S. A., Langan, C. J., & Hollander, E. P. (1972). Expectation of future interaction and the choice of less desirable alternatives in conformity. *Sociometry, 35*, 440–447.

Lex, B. W. (1986). Measurement of alcohol consumption in fieldwork settings. *Medical Anthropology Quarterly, 17*, 95–98.

Liang, X. (2006). Identity and language functions: High school Chinese immigrant students' code-switching dilemmas in ESL classes. *Journal of Language, Identity, and Education, 5*, 143–167.

Lickel, B., Hamilton, D. L., Wieczorkowski, G., Lewis, A., Sherman, S. J., & Uhles, A. N. (2000). Varieties of groups and the perception of group entitativity. *Journal of Personality and Social Psychology, 78*, 223–246.

Lieberman, A., & Chaiken, S. (1992). Defensive processing of personally relevant health messages. *Personality and Social Psychology Bulletin, 18*, 669–679.

Lieberman, A., & Chaiken, S. (1996). The direct effect of personal relevance on attitudes. *Personality and Social Psychology Bulletin, 22*, 269–279.

Lieberman, P. (1975). *On the origins of human language: An introduction to the evolution of human speech.* New York: Macmillan.

Likert, R. (1932). A technique for the measurement of attitudes. *Archives of Psychology* (Whole no. 142).

Lilienfeld, S. O., Sauvigne, K. C., Lynn, S. J., Cautin, R. L., Latzman, R. D., & Waldman, I. D. (2015). Fifty psychological and psychiatric terms to avoid: A list of inaccurate, misleading, misused, ambiguous, and logically confused words and phrases. *Frontiers in Psychology, 6*, 1100.

Lin, N., & Xie, W. (1988). Occupational prestige in urban China. *American Journal of Sociology, 93*, 793–832.

Lincoln, J., & Kalleberg, A. (1985). Work organization and workforce commitment: A study of plants and employees in the United States and Japan. *American Sociological Review, 50*, 738–760.

Lind, E. A., Kanfer, R., & Earley, P. C. (1990). Voice, control, and procedural justice: Instrumental and noninstrumental concerns in fairness judgments. *Journal of Personality and Social Psychology, 59*(5), 952.

Lind, E. A., & Tyler, T. (1988). *The social psychology of procedural justice.* New York: Plenum Press.

Lindberg, L. D., & Singh, S. (2008). Sexual behavior of single adult American women. *Perspectives on Sexual and Reproductive Health, 40*, 27–33.

Linder, D. E., Cooper, J., & Jones, E. (1967). Decision freedom as a determinant of the role of incentive magnitude in attitude change. *Journal of Personality and Social Psychology, 6*, 245–254.

Link, B. G. (1982). Mental patient status, work, and income: An examination of the effects of a psychiatric label. *American Sociological Review, 47*, 202–215.

Link, B. G. (1987). Understanding labelling effects in the area of mental disorders: An assessment of the effects of expectations of rejection. *American Sociological Review, 52*, 96–112.

Link, B. G., Cullen, F. T., Struening, E., Shrout, P. E., & Dohrenwend, B. (1989). A modified labeling theory approach to mental disorders: An empirical assessment. *American Sociological Review, 54*, 400–423.

Link, B. G., & Phelan, J. C. (2001). Conceptualizing stigma. *Annual Review of Sociology, 27*, 363–385.

Link, B. G., Struening, E. L., Rahav, M., Phelan, J. C., & Nuttbrock, L. (1997). On stigma and its consequences: Evidence from a longitudinal study of men with dual diagnosis of mental illness and substance abuse. *Journal of Health and Social Behavior, 38*, 177–190.

Linville, P. W. (1982). The complexity–extremity effect and age-based stereotyping. *Journal of Personality and Social Psychology, 42*, 193–211.

Linville, P. W., Fischer, G. W., & Salovey, P. (1989). Perceived distributions of the characteristics of in-group and out-group members: Empirical evidence and a computer simulation. *Journal of Personality and Social Psychology, 57*, 165–188.

Linville, P. W., & Jones, E. E. (1980). Polarized appraisals of out-group members. *Journal of Personality and Social Psychology, 38*, 689–703.

Lipe, M. G. (1991). Counterfactual reasoning as a framework for attribution theories. *Psychological Bulletin, 109*, 456–471.

Lister, J. G. (2015, April 15). The poor are treated like criminals everywhere, even at the grocery store. *Washington Post.* Retrieved from https://www.washingtonpost.com/posteverything/wp/2015/04/01/the-poor-are-treated-like-criminals-everywhere-even-at-the-grocery-store (Accessed June 11, 2018)

Littlepage, G., & Pineault, T. (1978). Verbal, facial, and paralinguistic cues to the detection of truth and lying. *Personality and Social Psychology Bulletin, 4*, 461–464.

Lizardo, O., & Collett, J. L. (2013). Embarrassment and social organization: A multiple identities model. *Social Forces, 92*(1), 353–375.

Lloyd, S. A., & Emery, B. C. (2000). The context and dynamics of intimate aggression against women. *Journal of Social and Personal Relationships, 17*(4–5), 503–521.

LoBue, V., Nishida, T., Chiong, C., DeLoache, J. S., & Haidt, J. (2011). When getting something good is bad: Even three-year-olds react to inequality. *Social Development, 20*, 154–170.

Locke, K. D., & Horowitz, L. M. (1990). Satisfaction in interpersonal interactions as a function of similarity in level of dysphoria. *Journal of Personality and Social Psychology, 58*, 823–831.

Logan, T. K., Walker, R., Cole, J., & Leukefeld, C. (2002). Victimization and substance abuse among women: Contributing factors, interventions, and implications. *Review of General Psychology, 6*(4), 325.

Lois, J. (2003). *Heroic efforts: The emotional culture of search and rescue volunteers.* New York: New York University Press.

Longmore, M. A., Manning, W. D., & Giordano, P. C. (2006). Identity exploration and adolescents' high risk sexual behaviors: A longitudinal analysis (Working Paper No. 06–16). Center for Family and Demographic Research, Bowling Green State University.

Lonsdale, A. J. (2009). The social psychology of music and musical taste. Doctoral dissertation, Heriot Watt University, U.K. www.ros.hw.ac.uk/handle/10399/2275

Lonsdale, A. J., & North, A. C. (2012). Musical taste and the representativeness heuristic. *Psychology of Music, 40*(2), 131–142.

Lopes, P. N., Salovey, P., Côté, S., Beers, M., & Petty, R. E. (2005). Emotion regulation abilities and the quality of social interaction. *Emotion, 5*(1), 113–118.

Lord, C. G., Lepper, M. R., & Mackie, D. (1984). Attitude prototypes as determinants of attitude-behavior consistency. *Journal of Personality and Social Psychology, 46*, 1254–1266.

Lordan, G., & Pischke, J. S. (2016). *Does Rosie like riveting? Male and female occupational choices* (No. w22495). Cambridge, MA: National Bureau of Economic Research.

Lorence, J., & Mortimer, J. (1985). Job involvement through the life course: A panel study of three age groups. *American Sociological Review, 50*, 618–638.

Lorenz, K. (1966). *On aggression.* New York: Harcourt Brace Jovanovich.

Lorenz, K. (1974). *Civilized man's eight deadly sins.* New York: Harcourt Brace Jovanovich.

Lorenzo, G. L., Biesanz, J. C., & Human, L. J. (2010). What is beautiful is good and more accurately understood: Physical attractiveness and accuracy in first impressions of personality. *Psychological Science, 21*, 1777–1782.

Lott, A., & Lott, B. (1965). Group cohesiveness as interpersonal attraction: A review of relationships with antecedent and consequent variables. *Psychological Bulletin, 64*, 259–309.

Lott, A., & Lott, B. (1974). The role of reward in the formation of positive interpersonal attitudes. In T. Huston

(Ed.), *Foundations of interpersonal attraction* (pp. 171–192). New York: Academic Press.

Lottes, I. L., & Kuriloff, P. J. (1994). The impact of college experience on political and social attitudes. *Sex Roles, 31,* 31–54.

Lovaglia, M. J., Lucas, J. W., & Thye, S. R. (1998). Status processes and mental ability test scores. *American Journal of Sociology, 104,* 195–228.

Lucas, J. W., & Lovaglia, M. J. (1998). Leadership status, gender, group size, and emotion in face-to-face groups. *Sociological Perspectives, 41*(3), 617–637.

Lucas-Thompson, R. G., Goldberg, W. A., & Prause, J. (2010). Maternal work early in the lives of children and its distal associations with achievement and behavior problems. *Psychological Bulletin, 136,* 915–942.

Luchins, A. S. (1957). Experimental attempts to minimize the impact of first impressions. In C. I. Hovland (Ed.), *The order of presentation in persuasion* (pp. 62–75). New Haven, CT: Yale University Press.

Luhman, R. (1990). Appalachian English stereotypes: Language attitudes in Kentucky. *Language in Society, 19,* 331–348.

Lundman, R. J. (1974). Routine police arrest practices: A commonweal perspective. *Social Problems, 22,* 127–141.

Lurigis, A. J., & Carroll, J. S. (1985). Probation officers' schemata of offenders: Content, development, and impact on treatment decisions. *Journal of Personality and Social Psychology, 48,* 1112–1126.

Lussier, P., Corrado, R., & Tzoumakis, S. (2012). Gender differences in physical aggression and associated developmental correlates in a sample of Canadian preschoolers. *Behavioral Sciences and Law, 30,* 643–671.

Lutfey, K., & Mortimer, J. (2003). Development and socialization through the adult life course. In J. DeLamater (Ed.), *Handbook of social psychology* (pp. 183–202). New York: Kluwer-Plenum.

Lynch, J. C., & Cohen, J. L. (1978). The use of subjective expected utility theory as an aid to understanding variables that influence helping behavior. *Journal of Personality and Social Psychology, 36,* 1138–1151.

Maass, A., & Arcuri, L. (1992). The role of language in the persistence of stereotypes. In G. R. Semin & K. Fiedler (Eds.), *Language, interaction, and social cognition* (pp. 129–143). Newbury Park, CA: Sage.

Mace, R. (2014). When not to have another baby: An evolutionary approach to low fertility. *Demographic Research, 30,* 1074.

Macintyre, S., Hunt, K., & Sweeting, H. (1996). Gender differences in health: Are things really as simple as they seem? *Social Science and Medicine, 42,* 617–624.

Mackie, D. M., & Goethals, G. R. (1987). Individual and group goals. In C. Hendrick (Ed.), *Group processes* (pp. 144–166). Newbury Park, CA: Sage.

Macmillan, R. (2001). Violence and the life course: The consequences of victimization for personal and social development. *Annual Review of Sociology, 27,* 1–22.

Maddi, S., Bartone, P., & Puccetti, M. (1987). Stressful events are indeed a factor in physical illness: Reply to Schroeder and Costa (1984). *Journal of Personality and Social Psychology, 52,* 833–843.

Maddux, J. E., & Rogers, R. W. (1983). Protection motivation and self-efficacy: A revised theory of fear appeals and attitude change. *Journal of Experimental Social Psychology, 19,* 469–479.

Madon, S., Jussim, L., & Eccles, J. (1997). In search of the powerful self-fulfilling prophecy. *Journal of Personality and Social Psychology, 72,* 791–809.

Mahon, N. E. (1982). The relationship of self-disclosure, interpersonal dependency, and life changes to loneliness in young adults. *Nursing Research, 31,* 343–347.

Major, B., Schmidlin, A. M., & Williams, L. (1990). Gender patterns in social touch: The impact of setting and age. *Journal of Personality and Social Psychology, 58,* 634–643.

Major, B., Zubek, J. M., Cooper, M. L., Cozarelli, C., & Richards, C. (1997). Mixed messages: Implications of social conflict and social support within close relationships for adjustment to a stressful life event. *Journal of Personality and Social Psychology, 72,* 1349–1363.

Malamuth, N. M. (1984). Aggression against women: Cultural and individual causes. In N. M. Malamuth & E. Donnerstein (Eds.), *Pornography and sexual aggression* (pp. 19–52). Orlando, FL: Academic Press.

Malamuth, N. M., Addison, T., & Koss, M. (2000). Pornography and sexual aggression: Are there reliable effects and can we understand them? *Annual Review of Sex Research, 11*(1), 26–91.

Malamuth, N. M., Heavey, C. L., & Linz, D. (1993). Predicting men's antisocial behavior against women: The interaction model of sexual aggression. In G. C. N. Hall (Ed.), *Sexual aggression: Issues in etiology, assessment, and treatment* (pp. 63–97). Washington, DC: Taylor and Francis.

Malamuth, N. M., Linz, D., Heavey, C. L., Barnes, G., & Acker, M. (1995). Using the confluence model of sexual aggression to predict men's conflict with women: A 10-year follow-up study. *Journal of Personality and Social Psychology, 69*(2), 353–369.

Malamuth, N. M., Sockloskie, R. J., Koss, M. P., & Tanaka, J. S. (1991). Characteristics of aggressors against women: Testing a model using a national sample of college students. *Journal of Consulting and Clinical Psychology, 59,* 670–681.

Mallozzi, J., McDermott, V., & Kayson, W. A. (1990). Effects of sex, type of dress, and location on altruistic behavior. *Psychological Reports, 67,* 1103–1106.

Malti, T., Gasser, L., & Gutzwiller-Helfenfinger, E. (2010). Children's interpretive understanding, moral judgments, and emotion attributions: Relations to social behavior. *British Journal of Developmental Psychology, 28,* 275–292.

Maner, J. K., & Gailliot, M. T. (2007). Altruism and egoism: Prosocial motivations for helping depend on relationship context. *European Journal of Social Psychology, 37*(2), 347–358.

Manis, M., Shedler, J., Jonides, J., & Nelson, T. E. (1993). Availability heuristic in judgments of set size and frequency of occurrence. *Journal of Personality and Social Psychology, 65,* 448–457.

Mann, C. R. (1996). *When women kill.* Albany: State University of New York Press.

Mann, E., & Abraham, C. (2006). The role of affect in UK commuters' travel mode choices: An interpretative phenomenological analysis. *British Journal of Psychology*, *97*, 155–176.

Mannheim, B. F. (1966). Reference groups, membership groups, and the self-image. *Sociometry*, *29*, 265–279.

Mannheimer, D., & Williams, R. M. (1949). A note on Negro troops in combat. In S. A. Stouffer, E. A. Suchman, L. C. DeVinney, S. A. Star, & R. M. Williams (Eds.), *The American soldier* (Vol. 1, pp. 486–599). Princeton, NJ: Princeton University Press.

Manning, P. K., & Cullum-Swan, B. (1992). Semiotics and framing: Examples. *Semiotica*, *92*, 239–257.

Manning, W. D. (2013). *Trends in cohabitation: Over twenty years of change, 1987–2010.* Family Profile –11–12. National Center for Family & Marriage Research, Bowling Green, OH. www.bgsu.edu/content/dam/BGSU/college-of-arts-and-sciences/NCFMR/documents/FP/FP-13-12.pdf

Manning, W. D., Brown, S. L., & Payne, K. K. (2014). Two decades of stability and change in age at first union formation. *Journal of Marriage and Family*, *76*, 247–260.

Manning, W. D., Brown, S. L., & Stykes, J. B. (2016). Same-sex and different-sex cohabiting couple relationship stability. *Demography*, *53*, 937–953.

Mannix, E. A., Neale, M. A., & Northcraft, G. B. (1995). Equity, equality, or need? The effects of organizational culture on the allocation of benefits and burdens. *Organizational Behavior and Human Decision Processes*, *63*, 276–286.

Mantymaki, M., & Najmul Islam, A. K. M. (2016). The Janus face of Facebook: Positive and negative sides of social networking site use. *Computers in Human Behavior*, *61*, 14–26.

Manucia, G. K., Baumann, D. J., & Cialdini, R. B. (1984). Mood influences on helping: Direct effects or side effects. *Journal of Personality and Social Psychology*, *46*(2), 357–364.

Manz, C. C., & Sims, H. P. (1982). The potential for "groupthink" in autonomous work groups. *Human Relations*, *35*, 773–784.

Marangoni, C., & Ickes, W. (1989). Loneliness: A theoretical review with implications for measurement. *Journal of Social and Personal Relationships*, *6*, 93–128.

Marchman, V. A. (1991). The acquisition of language in normally developing children: Some basic strategies and approaches. In I. Pavao-Martins, A. Castro-Caldas, H. Van Dongen, & A. Van Hout (Eds.), *Acquired aphasia in children* (pp. 15–24). Dordrecht: Kluwer.

Marcus, D. K., Wilson, J. R., & Miller, R. S. (1996). Are perceptions of emotion in the eye of the beholder? A social relations analysis of judgments of embarrassment. *Personality and Social Psychology Bulletin*, *22*(12), 1220–1228.

Marcus-Newhall, A., Pedersen, W. C., Carlson, M., & Miller, N. (2000). Displaced aggression is alive and well: A meta-analytic review. *Journal of Personality and Social Psychology*, *78*(4), 670–689.

Margolin, L. (2015). Unpacking the invisible knapsack: The invention of white privilege pedagogy. *Cogent Social Sciences*, *1*(1). Doi: 10.1080/23311886.2015.1053183.

Marion, S. B., & Burke, T. M. (2016). Altruistic lying in an alibi corroboration context: The effects of liking, compliance, and relationship between suspects and witnesses. *Behavioral Sciences & the Law*, *35*, 37–59.

Mark, K. P. (2014). The impact of daily sexual desire and daily sexual desire discrepancy on the quality of sexual experience in couples. *Canadian Journal of Human Sexuality*, *23*, 27–33.

Markey, P. M., & Markey, C. N. (2007). Romantic ideals, romantic obtainment, and relationship experiences: The complementarity of interpersonal traits among romantic partners. *Journal of Social and Personal Relationships*, *24*, 517–533.

Markowitz, D. M., & Hancock, J. T. (2015). Linguistic obfuscation in fraudulent science. *Journal of Language and Social Psychology*, *35*, 435–445.

Markowitz, F. (2001). Modeling processes in recovery from mental illness: Relationships between symptoms, life satisfaction, and self-concept. *Journal of Health and Social Behavior*, *42*, 64–79.

Markus, H. (1977). Self-schemas and processing information about the self. *Journal of Personality and Social Psychology*, *35*, 63–78.

Markus, H. (1983). Self-knowledge: An expanded view. *Journal of Personality*, *51*(3), 543–565.

Markus, H., & Wurf, E. (1987). The dynamic self-concept: A social psychological perspective. *Annual Review of Psychology*, *38*, 299–337.

Markus, H. R., & Kitayama, S. (1991). Culture and the self: Implications for cognition, emotion, and motivation. *Psychological Review*, *98*, 224–253.

Markus, H. R., Kitayama, S., & Heiman, R. J. (1996) Culture and "basic" psychological principles. In E. T. Higging & A. W. Kruglanski (Eds.), *Social psychology: Handbook of basic principles* (pp. 857–913). New York: Guilford Press.

Markus, H. R., Smith, J., & Moreland, R. L. (1985). Role of the self-concept in the perception of others. *Journal of Personality and Social Psychology*, *49*, 1494–1512.

Marmot, M. G., Bosma, H., Hemingway, H., Brunner, E., & Stansfeld, S. (1997). Contribution of job control and other risk factors to social variations in coronary heart disease. *The Lancet*, *350*, 235–239.

Marsden, P., & Campbell, K. (1984). Measuring tie strength. *Social Forces*, *63*, 482–501.

Marsh, H. W., Barnes, J., & Hocevar, D. (1985). Self-other agreement on multidimensional self-concept ratings: Factor analysis and multitrait-multimethod analysis. *Journal of Personality and Social Psychology*, *49*, 1360–1377.

Martin, C. L. (1987). A ratio measure of sex stereotyping. *Journal of Personality and Social Psychology*, *52*, 489–499.

Martin, J., Pescosolido, B., & Tuch, S. (2000). Of fear and loathing: The role of "disturbing behavior," labels, and causal attributions in shaping public attitudes toward people with mental illness. *Journal of Health and Social Behavior*, *41*, 208–223.

Martin, K., Leary, M., & Rejeski, W. J. (2000). Self-presentational concerns in older adults: Implications for health and well-being. *Basic and Applied Social Psychology*, *22*, 169–179.

Marwell, G., Aiken, M. T., & Demerath, N. J. (1987). The persistence of political attitudes among 1960s civil rights activists. *Public Opinion Quarterly*, *51*, 383–399.

Mason, W., & Suri, S. (2012). Conducting behavioural research on Amazon's Mechanical Turk. *Behavioral Research*, *44*, 1–23.

Matsueda, R. (1982). Testing control theory and differential association: A causal modeling approach. *American Sociological Review*, *47*, 489–504.

Matsueda, R., Kreager, D., & Huizinga, D. (2006). Deterring delinquents: A rational choice model of theft and violence. *American Sociological Review*, *71*, 93–122.

Matsueda, R. L. (1992). Reflected appraisals, parental labeling, and delinquency: Specifying a symbolic interactionist theory. *American Journal of Sociology*, *97*, 1577–1611.

Matsumoto, D. (1990). Cultural similarities and differences in display rules. *Motivation and Emotion*, *14*(3), 195–214.

Matthews, L. S., Conger, R. D., & Wickrama, K. A. S. (1996). Work–family conflict and marital quality: Mediating processes. *Social Psychology Quarterly*, *59*, 62–79.

Maurer, T., Pleck, J., & Rane, T. (2001). Parental identity and reflected-appraisals: Measurement and gender dynamics. *Journal of Marriage and Family*, *63*, 309–321.

Mayer, J. D., Rapp, H. C., & Williams, L. (1993). Individual differences in behavioral prediction: The acquisition of personal-action schemata. *Personality and Social Psychology Bulletin*, *19*, 443–451.

Maynard, D. W. (1983). Social order and plea bargaining in the court. *Sociological Quarterly*, *24*, 215–233.

Maynard, D. W., & Whalen, M. R. (1995). Language, action, and social interaction. In K. S. Cook, G. A. Fine, & J. S. House (Eds.), *Sociological perspectives on social psychology* (pp. 149–175). Boston: Allyn and Bacon.

Mazur, J. E. (1998). *Learning and behavior* (4th ed.). Upper Saddle River, NJ: Prentice Hall.

McAdoo, H. P. (1997). Upward mobility across generations of African-American families. In H. P. McAdoo (Ed.), *Black families* (3rd ed., pp. 139–162). Thousand Oaks, CA: Sage.

McArthur, L. Z., & Post, D. L. (1977). Figural emphasis and person perception. *Journal of Experimental Social Psychology*, *13*, 520–535.

McCabe, D. L., Treviño, L. K., & Butterfield, K. D. (2001). Cheating in academic institutions: A decade of research. *Ethics & Behavior*, *11*(3), 219–232.

McCall, G. J. (2013). Interactionist perspectives in social psychology. In J. D. DeLamater & A. Ward (Eds.), *Handbook of social psychology* (pp. 3–29). Dordrecht: Springer Netherlands.

McCall, G. J., & Simmons, J. L. (1978). *Identities and interactions*. New York: Free Press.

McCall, P., Parker, K., & MacDonald, J. (2008). The dynamic relationship between homicide rates and social, economic, and political factors from 1970 to 2000. *Social Science Research*, *37*, 721–735.

McCarthy, J. D., & Hoge, D. R. (1984). The dynamics of self-esteem and delinquency. *American Journal of Sociology*, *90*, 396–410.

McCauley, C. (1989). The nature of social influence in groupthink: Compliance and internalization. *Journal of Personality and Social Psychology*, *57*, 250–260.

McCauley, C., Stitt, C. L., & Segal, M. (1980). Stereotyping: From prejudice to prediction. *Psychological Bulletin*, *87*, 195–208.

McDonald, S. (2011a). What's in the "old boys" network? Accessing social capital in gendered and racialized networks. *Social Networks*, *33*, 317–330.

McDonald, S. (2011b). What you know or who you know? Occupation-specific work experience and job matching through social networks. *Social Science Research*, *40*, 1664–1675.

McDowell, W. C., Boyd, N. G., & Bowler, W. M. (2007). Overreward and the impostor phenomenon. *Journal of Managerial Issues*, *19*, 95–110.

McFarland, C., & Ross, M. (1982). The impact of causal attributions on affective reactions to success and failure. *Journal of Personality and Social Psychology*, *43*, 937–946.

McFarland, D. (2004). Resistance as a social drama: A study of change-oriented encounters. *American Journal of Sociology*, *109*, 1249–1318.

McGarty, C., Yzerbyt, V. Y., & Spears, R. (Eds.). (2002). *Stereotypes as explanations: The formation of meaningful beliefs about social groups*. Cambridge: Cambridge University Press.

McGuire, W. J. (1964). Inducing resistance to persuasion: Some contemporary approaches. In L. Berkowitz (Ed.), *Advances in experimental social psychology* (Vol. 1, pp. 191–229). New York: Academic Press.

McGuire, W. J. (1985). Attitude and attitude change. In G. Lindzey & E. Aronson (Eds.), *The handbook of social psychology* (3rd ed., Vol. 2, pp. 233–346). New York: Random House.

McGuire, W. J., & McGuire, C. (1982). Significant others in self-space: Sex differences and developmental trends in the social self. In J. Suls (Ed.), *Psychological perspectives on the self* (Vol. 1, pp. 71–96). Hillsdale, NJ: Erlbaum.

McGuire, W. J., & McGuire, C. (1986). Differences in conceptualizing self versus conceptualizing other people as manifested in contrasting verb types used in natural speech. *Journal of Personality and Social Psychology*, *51*, 1135–1143.

McGuire, W. J., & Padawer-Singer, A. (1976). Trait silence in the spontaneous self-concept. *Journal of Personality and Social Psychology*, *33*(6), 743–754.

McIntosh, W. L. (2016). Suicide rates by occupational group—17 States, 2012. MMWR. Morbidity and mortality weekly report, 65.

McKelvey, K., DiGrazia, J., & Rojas, F. (2014). Twitter publics: How online political communities signaled electoral outcomes in the 2010 US House election. *Information, Communication, and Society*, *17*, 436–450.

McLanahan, S., & Booth, K. (1989). Mother-only families: Problems, prospects, and politics. *Journal of Marriage and Family*, *51*, 557–580.

McLeod, J. M., Price, K. O., & Harburg, E. (1966). Socialization, liking, and yielding of opinions in imbalanced situations. *Sociometry*, *29*, 197–212.

McLoyd, V., Cauce, A. M., Takeuchi, D., & Wilson, L. (2001). Marital processes and parental socialization in families of color: A decade review of research. In R. Milardo (Ed.), *Understanding families into the new millennium: A decade in review* (pp. 1070–1093). Minneapolis, MN: National Council on Family Relations.

McLuhan, A., Pawluch, D., Shaffir, W., & Haas, J. (2014). The cloak of incompetence: A neglected concept in the sociology of everyday life. *American Sociologist, 45,* 361–387.

McMahon, S. (2010). Rape myth beliefs and bystander attitudes among incoming college students. *Journal of American College Health, 59,* 3–11.

McPherson, M., Smith-Lovin, L., & Cook, J. (2001). Birds of a feather: Homophily in social networks. *Annual Review of Sociology, 27,* 415–444.

McWayne, C., Downer, J. T., Campos, R., & Harris, R. D. (2013). Father involvement during early childhood and its association with children's early learning: A meta-analysis. *Early Education and Development, 24,* 898–922.

Mead, G. H. (1934). *Mind, self, and society.* Chicago: University of Chicago Press.

Mehrabian, A. (1972). *Nonverbal communication.* New York: Aldine-Atherton.

Mehrabian, A., & Ksionzky, S. (1970). Models for affiliative and conformity behavior. *Psychological Bulletin, 74,* 110–126.

Meier, R. F., & Johnson, W. T. (1977). Deterrence as social control: The legal and extralegal production of conformity. *American Sociological Review, 42,* 292–304.

Meier, S. (2006). *The economics of non-selfish behaviour.* Northampton, MA: Edward Elgar.

Melzer, S. (2002). Gender, work, and intimate violence: Men's occupational violence spillover and compensatory violence. *Journal of Marriage and Family, 64,* 820–832.

Mennino, S. F., Rubin, B., & Brayfield, A. (2005). Home-to-job and job-to-home spillover: The impact of company policies and workplace culture. *Sociological Quarterly, 46,* 107–135.

Merriam-Webster. (2017). The real story of 'fake news.' Retrieved from https://www.merriam-webster.com/words-at-play/the-real-story-of-fake-news (Accessed June 11, 2018).

Merton, R. (1957). *Social theory and social structure.* Glencoe, IL: Free Press.

Mesoudi, A. (2009). The cultural dynamics of copycat suicide. *PLoS One, 4*(9), e7252.

Mesquita, B., & Karasawa, M. (2002). Different emotional lives. *Cognition and Emotion, 16*(1), 127–141.

Messner, S. F., & Krohn, M. D. (1990). Class, compliance structure, and delinquency: Assessing integrated structural-Marxist theory. *American Journal of Sociology, 96,* 300–328.

Metts, S., & Cupach, W. R. (1989). Situational influence on the use of remedial strategies in embarrassing predicaments. *Communication Monographs, 56,* 151–162.

Meyer, P. (2000). The sociobiology of human cooperation: The interplay of ultimate and proximate causes. In J. M. G. van der Dennen, D. Smillie, & D. R. Wilson (Eds.), *The Darwinian heritage and sociobiology* (pp. 49–65). Westport, CT: Praeger.

Meyrowitz, J. (1985). *No sense of place: The impact of electronic media on social behavior.* New York: Oxford University Press.

Miall, C. E. (1986). The stigma of involuntary childlessness. *Social Problems, 33,* 268–282.

Michaels, J. W., Edwards, J. N., & Acock, A. C. (1984). Satisfaction in intimate relationships as a function of inequality, inequity, and outcomes. *Social Psychology Quarterly, 47,* 347–357.

Michaelson, A. (2009). *The foreclosure of America: The inside story of the rise and fall of Countrywide Home Loans, the mortgage crisis, and the default of the American dream.* New York: Penguin.

Michener, H. A., & Burt, M. R. (1974). Legitimacy as a base of social influence. In J. T. Tedeschi (Ed.), *Perspectives on social power* (pp. 310ff.). Chicago: Aldine-Atherton.

Michener, H. A., Plazewski, J. G., & Vaske, J. J. (1979). Ingratiation tactics channeled by target values and threat capability. *Journal of Personality, 47,* 36–56.

Milardo, R. M. (1982). Friendship networks in developing relationships: Converging and diverging social environments. *Social Psychology Quarterly, 45,* 162–172.

Milburn, M. A., Mather, R., & Conrad, S. D. (2000). The effects of viewing R-rated movie scenes that objectify women on perceptions of date rape. *Sex Roles, 43*(9–10), 645–664.

Milgram, S. (1963). Behavioral study of obedience. *Journal of Abnormal and Social Psychology, 67,* 371–378.

Milgram, S. (1965). Some conditions of obedience and disobedience to authority. *Human Relations, 18,* 57–76.

Milgram, S. (1974). *Obedience to authority.* New York: Harper and Row.

Milgram, S. (1976). Obedience to criminal orders: The compulsion to do evil. In T. Blass (Ed.), *Contemporary social psychology: Representative readings* (pp. 175–184). Itasca, IL: Peacock.

Milgram, S. (1977). *The individual in a social world: Essays and experiments.* Reading, MA: Addison-Wesley Publishing.

Milgram, S., Liberty, H. J., Toledo, R., & Wackenhut, J. (1986). Response to intrusion into waiting lines. *Journal of Personality and Social Psychology, 51,* 683–689.

Miller, A. G. (1976). Constraint and target effects on the attribution of attitudes. *Journal of Experimental Social Psychology, 12,* 325–339.

Miller, A. G. (Ed.). (1982). *In the eye of the beholder: Contemporary issues in stereotyping.* New York: Praeger.

Miller, A. G., Collins, B. E., & Brief, D. E. (1995). Perspectives on obedience to authority: The legacy of the Milgram experiments. *Journal of Social Issues, 51*(3), 1–19.

Miller, D. L. (2000). *Introduction to collective behavior and collective action.* Prospect Heights, IL: Waveland Press.

Miller, G. (1991). Family as excuse and extenuating circumstance: Social organization and use of family rhetoric in a work incentive program. *Journal of Marriage and Family, 53,* 609–621.

Miller, J., Schooler, C., Kohn, M., & Miller, K. (1979). Women and work: The psychological effects of occupational conditions. *American Journal of Sociology, 85,* 66–94.

Miller, M., & Megowen, K. R. (2000). The painful truth: Physicians are not invincible. *Southern Medical Journal, 93*, 966–972.

Miller, R. S. (1987). Empathic embarrassment: Situational and personal determinants of reactions to the embarrassment of another. *Journal of Personality and Social Psychology, 53*, 1061–1069.

Miller, R. S. (1992). The nature and severity of self-reported embarrassing circumstances. *Personality and Social Psychology Bulletin, 18*, 190–198.

Miller, S., Olson, M., & Fazio, R. (2004). Perceived reactions to interracial romantic relationships: When race is used as a cue to status. *Group Processes and Inter-group Relations, 7*, 354–369.

Miller, S. A. (2016). "How you bully a girl": Sexual drama and the negotiation of gendered sexuality in high school. *Gender & Society, 30*, 721–744.

Miner, J. B. (2002). *Organizational behavior: Foundations, theories, and analyses.* Oxford: Oxford University Press.

Minnigerode, F., & Lee, J. A. (1978). Young adults' perceptions of sex roles across the lifespan. *Sex Roles, 4*, 563–569.

Miranne, A. C., & Gray, L. N. (1987). Deterrence: A laboratory experiment. *Deviant Behavior, 8*, 191–203.

Mirowsky, J., & Ross, C. (1986). Social patterns of distress. In A. Inkeles, J. Coleman, & N. Smelser (Eds.), *Annual Review of Sociology* (Vol. 12, pp. 23–45). Palo Alto, CA: Annual Reviews.

Mirowsky, J., & Ross, C. E. (1995). Sex differences in distress: Real or artifact? *American Sociological Review, 60*, 449–468.

Mischel, W., & Liebert, R. (1966). Effects of discrepancies between deserved and imposed reward criteria on their acquisition and transmission. *Journal of Personality and Social Psychology, 3*, 45–53.

Misuraca, R., & Teuscher, U. (2013). Time flies when you maximize: Maximizers and satisficers perceive time differently when making decisions. *Acta Psychologica, 143*(2), 176–180.

Mitchell, A., Castellani, A., Herrington, R., Joseph, J., Doss, B., & Snyder, D. (2008). Predictors of intimacy in couples' discussions of relationship injuries: An observational study. *Journal of Family Psychology, 22*, 21–29.

Miyamoto, S. F., & Dornbusch, S. (1956). A test of interactionist hypotheses of self-conception. *American Journal of Sociology, 61*, 399–403.

Mizrahi, T. (1984). Coping with patients: Subcultural adjustments to the conditions of work among internists-in-training. *Social Problems, 32*, 156–166.

Modigliani, A. (1971). Embarrassment, face-work, and eye contact: Testing a theory of embarrassment. *Journal of Personality and Social Psychology, 17*, 15–24.

Molm, L. D. (1997). *Coercive power in social exchange.* Cambridge: Cambridge University Press.

Molm, L. D. (2006). The social exchange framework. In P. J. Burke (Ed.), *Contemporary social psychological theories* (pp. 24–45). Palo Alto, CA: Stanford University Press.

Molm, L. D. (2010). The structure of reciprocity. *Social Psychology Quarterly, 73*(2), 119–131.

Molm, L. D., Collett, J. L., & Schaefer, D. R. (2006). Conflict and fairness in social exchange. *Social Forces, 84*, 2331–2352.

Molm, L. D., Collett, J. L., & Schaefer, D. R. (2007). Building solidarity through generalized exchange: A theory of reciprocity. *American Journal of Sociology, 113*(1), 205–242.

Molm, L. D., Peterson, G., & Takahashi, N. (2001). The value of exchange. *Social Forces, 80*(1), 159–184.

Molm, L. D., Peterson, G., & Takahashi, N. (2003). In the eye of the beholder: Procedural justice in social exchange. *American Sociological Review, 68*, 128–152.

Molm, L. D., Schaefer, D. R., & Collett, J. L. (2009). Fragile and resilient trust: Risk and uncertainty in negotiated and reciprocal exchange. *Sociological Theory, 27*(1), 1–32.

Molm, L. D., Whitham, M. M., & Melamed, D. (2012). Forms of exchange and integrative bonds: Effects of history and embeddedness. *American Sociological Review, 77*(1), 141–165.

Money, J., & Ehrhardt, A. (1972). *Man and woman, boy and girl.* Baltimore, MD: Johns Hopkins University Press.

Mongrain, M., & Vettese, L. (2003). Conflict over emotional expression: Implications for interpersonal communication. *Personality and Social Psychology Bulletin, 29*, 545–555.

Moore, J. C. (1968). Status and influence in small group interaction. *Sociometry, 31*, 47–63.

Moore, M. M. (1985). Nonverbal courtship patterns in women: Context and consequences. *Ethology and Sociobiology, 6*, 237–247.

Moore, M. M., & Butler, D. L. (1989). Predictive aspects of nonverbal courtship behavior in women. *Semiotica, 76*, 205–215.

Moore, R. (2004). Managing troubles in answering survey questions: Respondents' uses of projective reporting. *Social Psychology Quarterly, 67*, 50–69.

Moorhead, G., Ference, R., & Neck, C. P. (1991). Group decision fiascoes continue: Space shuttle *Challenger* and a revised groupthink framework. *Human Relations, 44*, 539–550.

Moorhead, G., & Montanari, J. R. (1986). An empirical investigation of the groupthink phenomenon. *Human Relations, 39*, 399–410.

Moran, G. (1966). Dyadic attraction and orientational consensus. *Journal of Personality and Social Psychology, 4*, 94–99.

Morgan, K., & Smith, B. (2008). The impact of race on parole decision-making. *Justice Quarterly, 25*, 411–435.

Morgan, W., Alwin, D., & Griffin, L. (1979). Social origins, parental values, and the transmission of inequality. *American Journal of Sociology, 85*, 156–166.

Moriarty, T. (1975). Crime, commitment, and the responsive bystander: Two field experiments. *Journal of Personality and Social Psychology, 31*, 370–376.

Morris, W. N., & Miller, R. S. (1975). The effect of consensus-breaking and consensus-preempting partners on reduction of conformity. *Journal of Experimental Social Psychology, 11*, 215–223.

Morse, K., & Neuberg, S. (2004). How do holidays influence relationship processes and outcomes? Examining the instigating and catalytic effects of Valentine's Day. *Personal Relationships, 11*, 509–527.

Mortimer, J. T., & Lorence, J. (1995). Social psychology of work. In K. S. Cook, G. A. Fine, & J. S. House (Eds.),

*Sociological perspectives on social psychology* (pp. 497–523). Boston: Allyn and Bacon.

Mortimer, J. T., & Simmons, R. (1978). Adult socialization. In R. Turner, J. Coleman, & R. Fox (Eds.), *Annual Review of Sociology* (Vol. 4, pp. 421–454). Palo Alto, CA: Annual Reviews.

Moscovici, S., & Zavalloni, M. (1969). The group as a polarizer of attitudes. *Journal of Personality and Social Psychology, 12*(2), 125.

Moskowitz, G. B., Skurnik, I., & Galinsky, A. D. (1999). The history of dual-process notions, and the future of preconscious control. In S. Chaiken and Y. Trope (Eds.), *Dual-process theories in social psychology* (pp. 12–36). New York: Guilford.

Moskowitz, G. B., Stone, J., & Childs, A. (2012). Implicit stereotyping and medical decisions: Unconscious stereotype activation in practitioners' thoughts about African Americans. *American Journal of Public Health, 102*(5), 996–1001.

Moss-Racusin, C. A., Dovidio, J. F., Brescoll, V. L., Graham, M. J., & Handelsman, J. (2012). Science faculty's subtle gender biases favor male students. *Proceedings of the National Academy of Sciences, 109*(41), 16474–16479.

Muedeking, G. D. (1992). Authentic/inauthentic identities in the prison visiting room. *Symbolic Interaction, 15*, 227–236.

Mulatu, M. S., & Schooler, C. (2002). Causal connections between socio-economic status and health: Reciprocal effects and mediating mechanisms. *Journal of Health and Social Behavior, 43*, 22–41.

Mullen, B., & Copper, C. (1994). The relation between group cohesiveness and performance: An integration. *Psychological Bulletin, 115*, 210–227.

Mullen, B., & Hu, L. (1989). Perceptions of ingroup and outgroup variability: A meta-analytic integration. *Basic and Applied Social Psychology, 10*, 233–252.

Munsch, C. L. (2013). Women's jobs, men's jobs: How networking can lead women to lower paying jobs. Stanford University: The Clayman Institute for Gender Research. https://gender.stanford.edu/news-publications/gender-news/womens-jobs-mens-jobs (Accessed June 11, 2018).

Murphy, K. (2013). Ma'am, your burger has been paid for. Available: www.nytimes.com/2013/10/20/opinion/sunday/maam-your-burger-has-been-paid-for.html (Accessed October 20, 2013).

Murray, J. P., & Kippax, S. (1979). From the early window to the late night show: International trends in the study of television's impact on children and adults. In L. Berkowitz (Ed.), *Advances in experimental social psychology* (Vol. 12, pp. 253–320). New York: Academic Press.

Murray, S. L., Holmes, J. G., & Griffin, D. W. (1996a). The benefits of positive illusions: Idealization and the construction of satisfaction in close relationships. *Journal of Personality and Social Psychology, 70*, 79–98.

Murray, S. L., Holmes, J. G., & Griffin, D. W. (1996b). The self-fulfilling nature of positive illusions in romantic relationships: Love is not blind, but prescient. *Journal of Personality and Social Psychology, 71*, 1155–1180.

Mussweiler, T., Strack, F., & Pfeiffer, T. (2000). Overcoming the inevitable anchoring effect: Considering the opposite compensates for selective accessibility. *Personality and Social Psychology Bulletin, 26*, 1142–1150.

Mustanski, B. (2001). Getting wired: Exploiting the Internet for the collection of valid sexuality data. *Journal of Sex Research, 38*, 292–301.

Myers, D. G., & Lamm, H. (1976). The group polarization phenomenon. *Psychological Bulletin, 83*, 602–627.

Myers, D. J., & Caniglia, B. S. (2004). All the rioting that's fit to print: Selection effects in national newspaper coverage of civil disorders, 1968–1969. *American Sociological Review, 69*, 519–543.

Myers, M. A., & Hagan, J. (1979). Private and public trouble: Prosecutors and the allocation of court resources. *Social Problems, 26*, 439–451.

Myers, M. A., & Talarico, S. M. (1986). The social contexts of racial discrimination in sentencing. *Social Problems, 33*, 236–251.

Myrstol, B. A. (2012). The alcohol-related workload of patrol officers. *Policing: An International Journal of Police Strategies & Management, 35*, 55–75.

Nadler, A. (1987). Determinants of help-seeking behaviour: The effects of helper's similarity, task centrality and recipient's self esteem. *European Journal of Social Psychology, 17*(1), 57–67.

Nadler, A. (1991). Help-seeking behavior: Psychological costs and instrumental benefits. In M. S. Clark (Ed.), *Review of personality and social psychology: Vol. 12. Prosocial behavior* (pp. 290–311). Newbury Park, CA: Sage.

Nadler, A., & Fisher, J. D. (1984). Effects of donor-recipient relationships on recipients' reactions to aid. In E. Staub, D. Bar-Tal, J. Karylowski, & J. Reykowski (Eds.), *Development and maintenance of prosocial behavior: International perspectives on positive morality* (pp. 397–418). New York: Plenum.

Nadler, A., & Fisher, J. D. (1986). The role of threat to self-esteem and perceived control in recipient reaction to help: Theory development and empirical validation. In L. Berkowitz (Ed.), *Advances in experimental social psychology* (Vol. 19, pp. 81–122). New York: Academic Press.

Nadler, A., Halabi, S., Harapz-Gorodeisky, G., & Ben-David, Y. (2010). Helping relations as status relations. In M. Mikulincer and P. R. Shaver (Eds.), *Prosocial motives, emotions, and behavior: The better angels of our nature* (pp. 181–200). Washington, DC: American Psychological Association.

Nair, N., & Vohra, N. (2012). The concept of alienation: Towards conceptual clarity. *International Journal of Organizational Analysis, 20*, 25–50.

Nakao, K., & Treas, J. (1994). Updating occupational prestige and socioeconomic scores: How the new measures measure up. In P. Marsden (Ed.), *Sociological methodology* (Vol. 24, pp. 1–72). Washington, DC: Basil Blackwell.

Nathanson, A. I., & Cantor, J. (2000). Reducing the aggression-promoting effect of violent cartoons by increasing children's fictional involvement with the victim. *Journal of Broadcasting and Electronic Media, 44*, 125–142.

National Center for Health Statistics. (2012). Deaths: Final data for 2010. *National Vital Statistics Reports, 61*(4). Washington, DC.

National Endowment for the Arts. (2008). Survey of public participation in the arts 2008 [MRDF]. Washington, DC: National Endowment for the Arts [producer]. Princeton, NJ: Cultural Policy and the Arts National Data Archive [distributor].

National Institute of Mental Health. (2002). Mental health and mass violence: Evidence-based early psychological intervention for victims/survivors of mass violence (NIH Publication No. 02–5138). Washington, DC: U.S. Government Printing Office.

National Institute of Occupational Safety and Health (NIOSH). (2002). The effects of workplace hazards on male reproductive health (NIOSH Publication No. 96–132). Washington, DC: Author.

National Public Radio. (2002, October 14). How pitchmen sell their wares at state fairs. *Morning Edition* [Program transcript]. Washington, DC: Public Broadcasting Service.

National Television Violence Study. (1996). *National Television Violence Study* (Vol. 1). Thousand Oaks, CA: Sage.

Navarro, M. (2005, April 24). When you contain multitudes. *New York Times*, pp. 1–2.

Neal, A. G., & Groat, H. (1974). Social class correlates of stability and change in levels of alienation: A longitudinal study. *Sociological Quarterly*, 15, 548–558.

Neal, J. W. (2010). Hanging out: Features of urban children's peer social networks. *Journal of Social and Personal Relationships*, 27, 982–1000.

Nelson, T. D. (2002). *The psychology of prejudice*. Boston: Allyn and Bacon.

Nemeth, C., Brown, K., & Rogers, J. (2001). Devil's advocate versus authentic dissent: Stimulating quantity and quality. *European Journal of Social Psychology*, 31(6), 707–720.

Neuendorf, K. A., Gore, T. D., Dalessandro, A., Janstova, P., & Snyder-Suhy, S. (2010). Shaken and stirred: A content analysis of women's portrayals in James Bond films. *Sex Roles*, 62(11–12), 747–761.

Neugarten, B. L., & Datan, N. (1973). Sociological perspectives on the life cycle. In P. Baltes & K. Schaie (Eds.), *Life-span developmental psychology: Personality and social processes* (pp. 96–113). New York: Academic Press.

Newcomb, T. M. (1943). *Personality and social change*. New York: Dryden.

Newcomb, T. M. (1971). Dyadic balance as a source of clues about interpersonal attraction. In B. Murstein (Ed.), *Theories of attraction and love* (pp. 31–45). New York: Springer Verlag.

Nguyen, N. T., Seers, A., & Hartman, N. S. (2008). Putting a good face on impression management: Team citizenship and team satisfaction. *Journal of Behavioral and Applied Management*, 9(2), 148.

NICHD Early Child Care Research Network. (1997a). Familial factors associated with the characteristics of non-maternal care for infants. *Journal of Marriage and Family*, 59, 389–408.

NICHD Early Child Care Research Network. (1997b). The effects of infant child care on mother–infant attachment security: Results of the NICHD Study of Early Child Care. *Child Development*, 68, 860–879.

NICHD Early Child Care Research Network. (2002). Early child care and children's development prior to school entry: Results from the NICHD Study of Early Child Care. *American Educational Research Journal*, 39, 133–164.

Nickerson, R. S. (1998). Confirmation bias: A ubiquitous phenomenon in many guises. *Review of General Psychology*, 2(2), 175–220.

Nikolajeva, M. (2012). Guilt, empathy and the ethical potential of children's literature. *Barnboken—Journal of Children's Literature Research*, 35, 35.

Nisbett, R. E., Caputo, C., Legant, P., & Maracek, J. (1973). Behavior as seen by the actor and as seen by the observer. *Journal of Personality and Social Psychology*, 27, 154–164.

Norenzayan, A., & Nisbett, R. E. (2000). Culture and causal cognition. *Current Directions in Psychological Science*, 9, 132–135.

Norton, M. I., Dunn, E. W., Carney, D. R., & Ariely, D. (2012). The persuasive "power" of stigma? *Organizational Behavior and Human Design Processes*, 117, 261–268.

Norwood, A., Ursano, R., & Fullerton, C. (2002). *Disaster psychiatry: Principles and practice*. American Psychiatric Association. www.psych.org/pract_of_psych/principles_and_practice3201.cfm

Novelli, D., Drury, J., & Reicher, S. (2010). Come together: Two studies concerning the impact of group relations on "personal space." *British Journal of Social Psychology*, 49, 223–236.

Oakes, P. J., & Turner, J. C. (1980). Social categorization and intergroup behavior: Does minimal intergroup discrimination make social identity more positive? *European Journal of Social Psychology*, 10, 295–301.

Ohbuchi, K. I., Kameda, M., & Agarie, N. (1989). Apology as aggression control: Its role in mediating appraisal of and response to harm. *Journal of Personality and Social Psychology*, 56(2), 219–227.

Okamoto, D. G., & Smith-Lovin, L. (2001). Changing the subject: Gender, status, and the dynamics of topic change. *American Sociological Review*, 66, 852–873.

Olver, R. (1961). Developmental study of cognitive equivalence. Unpublished doctoral dissertation, Radcliffe College, Cambridge, MA.

Open Science Collaboration. (2015). Estimating the reproducibility of psychological science. *Science*, 349(6251). 10.1126/science.aac4716.

Operario, D., & Fiske, S. T. (1999). Integrating social identity and social cognition: A framework for bridging diverse perspectives. In D. Abrams and M. A. Hogg, *Social identity and social cognition* (pp. 26–54). Malden, MA: Blackwell.

Oppenheimer, V. K. (1970). *The female labor force in the United States*. (Population Monograph Series No. 5). Berkeley, CA: Institute of International Studies.

Orbuch, T., Veroff, J., Hassan, H., & Horrocks, J. (2002). Who will divorce? A 14-year longitudinal study of Black couples and White couples. *Journal of Social and Personal Relationships*, 19, 549–568.

Orcutt, J. (1975). Deviance as a situated phenomenon: Variations in the social interpretation of marijuana and alcohol use. *Social Problems*, 22, 346–356.

O'Rourke, J., Barnes, J., Deaton, A., Fulks, K., Ryan, K., & Rettinger, D. (2010). Imitation is the sincerest form of cheating: The influence of direct knowledge and attitudes on academic dishonesty. *Ethics and Behavior, 20,* 47–64.

Osgood, C. E., Suci, G., & Tannenbaum, P. (1957). *The measurement of meaning.* Urbana: University of Illinois Press.

Osgood, D. W., Wilson, J. R., O'Malley, P. M., Bachman, J. G., & Johnston, L. D. (1996). Routine activities and deviant behavior. *American Sociological Review, 61,* 635–655.

OSHA (2002) *OSHA Fact Sheet: Workplace violence.* https://www.osha.gov/OshDoc/data_General_Facts/factsheet-workplace-violence.pdf

Oswalt, P. (2014). Why I quit Twitter—and will again. *Time* (September 8–15), 28.

Otten, C. A., Penner, L. A., & Waugh, G. (1988). That's what friends are for: The determinants of psychological helping. *Journal of Social and Clinical Psychology, 7*(1), 34–41.

Oyserman, D., Fryberg, S. A., & Yoder, N. (2007). Identity-based motivation and health. *Journal of Personality and Social Psychology, 93,* 1011–1027.

Padden, S. L., & Buehler, C. (1995). Coping with the dual-income lifestyle. *Journal of Marriage and Family, 57,* 101–110.

Pager, D. (2003). The mark of a criminal record. *American Journal of Sociology, 108,* 1249–1291.

Pantin, H. M., & Carver, C. S. (1982). Induced competence and the bystander effect. *Journal of Applied Social Psychology, 12*(2), 100–111.

Park, B., & Rothbart, M. (1982). Perception of out-group homogeneity and levels of social categorization: Memory for the subordinate attributes of in-group and out-group members. *Journal of Personality and Social Psychology, 42,* 1051–1068.

Parke, R. (1969). Effectiveness of punishment as an interaction of intensity, timing, agent nurturance, and cognitive structuring. *Child Development, 40,* 213–235.

Parke, R. (1970). The role of punishment in the socialization process. In R. Hoppe, G. Milton, & E. Simmel (Eds.), *Early experiences and the processes of socialization* (pp. 81–108). New York: Academic Press.

Parke, R. D. (1996). *Fatherhood.* Cambridge, MA: Harvard University Press.

Parker, C. B. (2016, May 9). Perceived threats to racial status drive white Americans' Tea Party support, Stanford scholar says. Retrieved from https://news.stanford.edu/2016/05/09/perceived-threats-racial-status-drive-white-americans-support-tea-party-stanford-scholar-says/ (Accessed June 11, 2018).

Parrott, W. G., & Smith, S. F. (1991). Embarrassment: Actual vs. typical cases, classical vs. prototypical representations. *Cognition and Emotion, 5,* 467–488.

Parsons, L. M. (2003). Is accounting information from non-profit organizations useful to donors? A review of charitable giving and value-relevance. *Journal of Accounting Literature, 22,* 104–129.

Pascoe, C. J. (2012). *Dude, You're a fag.* Berkeley: University of California Press.

Patrick, S. L., & Jackson, J. J. (1991). Further examination of the equity sensitivity construct. *Perceptual and Motor Skills, 73,* 1091–1106.

Paul, E. L., & Hayes, K. A. (2002). The casualties of casual sex: A qualitative exploration of the phenomenology of college students' hookups. *Journal of Social and Personal Relationships, 19*(5), 639–661.

Paulhus, D. (1983). Sphere-specific measures of perceived control. *Journal of Personality and Social Psychology, 44*(6), 1253.

Payan, J. M., & McFarland, R. G. (2005). Decomposing influence strategies: Argument structure and dependence as determinants of the effectiveness of influence strategies in gaining channel member compliance. *Journal of Marketing, 69*(3), 66–79.

Pearce, P. L. (1980). Strangers, travelers, and Greyhound terminals: A study of small-scale helping behaviors. *Journal of Personality and Social Psychology, 38,* 935–940.

Pearlin, L., & Johnson, J. (1977). Marital status, life-strains and depression. *American Sociological Review, 42,* 704–715.

Pearlin, L., Nguyen, K., Schieman, S., & Milkie, M. (2007). The life-course origins of mastery among older people. *Journal of Health and Social Behavior, 48,* 164–179.

Pearlin, L., & Radabaugh, C. (1976). Economic strains and the coping functions of alcohol. *American Journal of Sociology, 82,* 652–663.

Peirce, K. (1993). Socialization of teenage girls through teen-magazine fiction: The making of a new woman or an old lady? *Sex Roles, 29,* 59–68.

Pelham, B., Mirenberg, M., & Jones, J. (2002). Why Susie sells seashells by the seashore: Implicit egotism and major life decisions. *Journal of Personality and Social Psychology, 82,* 469–487.

Pendry, L., & Carrick, R. (2001). Doing what the mob do: Priming effects on conformity. *European Journal of Social Psychology, 31,* 83–92.

Penedo, F., & Dahn, J. (2005). Exercise and well-being: A review of mental and physical health benefits associated with physical activity. *Current Opinion in Psychiatry, 18,* 189–193.

Pennebaker, J. W. (1980). Perceptual and environmental determinants of coughing. *Basic and Applied Social Psychology, 1*(1), 83–91.

Penner, L. A. (2002). Dispositional and organizational influences on sustained volunteerism: An interactionist perspective. *Journal of Social Issues, 58*(3), 447–467.

Penner, L. A., Dovidio, J. F., Piliavin, J. A., & Schroeder, D. A. (2005). Prosocial behavior: Multilevel perspectives. *Annual Review of Psychology, 56,* 365–392.

Perilloux, C., & Buss, D. (2008). Breaking up romantic relationships: Costs experienced and coping strategies deployed. *Evolutionary Psychology, 6,* 164–181.

Perlman, D. (1988). Loneliness: A life-span family perspective. In R. Milardo (Ed.), *Families and social networks* (pp. 190–220). Newbury Park, CA: Sage.

Perlow, L., & Weeks, J. (2002). Who's helping whom? Layers of culture and workplace behavior. *Journal of Organizational Behavior, 23*(4), 345–361.

Perry, B. (2011). The labeling paradox: Stigma, the sick role, and social networks in mental illness. *Journal of Health and Social Behavior, 52*, 460–477.

Petersen, T., Saporta, I., & Seidel, M. L. (2000). Offering a job: Meritocracy and social networks. *American Journal of Sociology, 106*, 763–816.

Petrunik, M., & Shearing, C. D. (1983). Fragile façades: Stuttering and the strategic manipulation of awareness. *Social Problems, 31*, 125–138.

Pettigrew, T. F. (1979). The ultimate attribution error: Extending Allport's cognitive analysis of prejudice. *Personality and Social Psychology Bulletin, 5*, 461–476.

Pettigrew, T. F. (1997). Generalized intergroup contact effects on prejudice. *Personality and Social Psychology Bulletin, 23*, 173–185.

Pettigrew, T. F., & Tropp, L. R. (2006). A meta-analytic test of intergroup contact theory. *Journal of Personality and Social Psychology, 90*, 751–783.

Pettigrew, T. F., and Tropp, L. R. (2013). *When groups meet: The dynamics of intergroup contact.* New York: Psychology Press.

Petty, R. E. (1995). Attitude change. In A. Tesser (Ed.), *Advanced social psychology* (pp. 195–255). New York: McGraw-Hill.

Petty, R. E., & Brock, T. C. (1981). Thought disruption and persuasion: Assessing the validity of attitude change experiments. In R. E. Petty, T. M. Ostrom, & T. C. Brock (Eds.), *Cognitive responses in persuasion* (pp. 55–79). Hillsdale, NJ: Erlbaum.

Petty, R. E., & Cacioppo, J. T. (1979). Issue involvement can increase or decrease persuasion by enhancing message-relevant cognitive responses. *Journal of Personality and Social Psychology, 37*, 1915–1926.

Petty, R. E., & Cacioppo, J. T. (1986). *Communication and persuasion: Central and peripheral routes to attitude change.* New York: Springer Verlag.

Petty, R. E., & Cacioppo, J. T. (1990). Involvement and persuasion: Tradition versus integration. *Psychological Bulletin, 107*, 367–374.

Petty, R. E., Cacioppo, J. T., & Goldman, R. (1981). Personal involvement as a determinant of argument-based persuasion. *Journal of Personality and Social Psychology, 41*, 847–855.

Petty, R. E., & Wegener, D. T. (1999). The elaboration likelihood model: Current status and controversies. In S. Chaiken & Y. Trope (Eds.), *Dual-process theories in social psychology* (pp. 41–72). New York: Guilford.

Pew Research Center. (2015). *Multiracial in America: Proud, diverse, and growing in numbers.* Washington, DC.

Pfau, M., Van Bockern, S., & Kang, J. G. (1992). Use of inoculation to promote resistance to smoking initiation among adolescents. *Communications Monographs, 59*, 213–230.

Pham, M. T., Geuens, M., & De Pelsmacker, P. (2013). The influence of ad-evoked feelings on brand evaluations: Empirical generalizations from consumer responses to more than 1000 TV commercials. *International Journal of Research in Marketing, 30*(4), 383–394.

Phillips, D. P. (1974). The influence of suggestion on suicide: Substantive and theoretical implications of the Werther effect. *American Sociological Review, 39*, 340–354.

Phillips, D. P. (1979). Suicide, motor vehicle fatalities, and the mass media: Evidence toward a theory of suggestion. *American Sociological Review, 84*, 1150–1174.

Piacentini, M., & Mailer, G. (2004). Symbolic consumption in teenagers' clothing choices. *Journal of Consumer Behavior, 3*, 251–262.

Piaget, J. (1954). *The construction of reality in the child.* New York: Basic Books.

Piaget, J. (1965). *The moral judgment of the child.* New York: Free Press.

Piferi, R. L., Jobe, R. L., & Jones, W. H. (2006). Giving to others during national tragedy: The effects of altruistic and egoistic motivations on long-term giving. *Journal of Social and Personal Relationships, 23*(1), 171–184.

Piff, P. K., Kraus, M. W., Côté, S., Cheng, B. H., & Keltner, D. (2010). Having less, giving more: The influence of social class on prosocial behavior. *Journal of Personality and Social Psychology, 99*(5), 771–784.

Piliavin, I. M., & Briar, S. (1964). Police encounters with juveniles. *American Journal of Sociology, 70*, 206–214.

Piliavin, I. M., Rodin, J., & Piliavin, J. A. (1969). Good samaritanism: An underground phenomenon. *Journal of Personality and Social Psychology, 13*(4), 289–299.

Piliavin, J. A., & Callero, P. L. (1991). *Giving blood: The development of an altruistic identity.* Baltimore, MD: Johns Hopkins University Press.

Piliavin, J. A., Dovidio, J. F., Gaertner, S. L., & Clark, R. D. (1981). *Emergency intervention.* New York: Academic Press.

Piliavin, J. A., Grube, J. A., & P. L. Callero. (2002). Role as resource for action in public service. *Journal of Social Issues, 58*, 469–485.

Piliavin, J. A., & LePore, P. C. (1995). Biology and social psychology: Beyond nature versus nurture. In K. S. Cook, G. A. Fine, & J. S. House (Eds.), *Sociological perspectives on social psychology* (pp. 9–40). Boston: Allyn and Bacon.

Piliavin, J. A., & Unger, R. K. (1985). The helpful but helpless female: Myth or reality? In G. O'Leary, R. K. Unger, & B. S. Wallston (Eds.), *Women, gender, and social psychology* (pp. 149–189). Hillsdale, NJ: Erlbaum.

Pilling, M., & Davies, I. (2004). Linguistic relativism and colour cognition. *British Journal of Psychology, 95*, 429–455.

Pipher, M. (1994). *Reviving Ophelia: Saving the selves of adolescent girls.* New York: Ballantine Books.

Pirkis, J. E., Burgess, P. M., Francis, C., Blood, R. W., & Jolley, D. J. (2006). The relation between media reporting of suicide and actual suicide in Australia. *Social Science and Medicine, 62*, 2874–2886.

Plagens, P., Miller, M., Foote, D., & Yoffe, E. (1991, April). Violence in our culture. *Newsweek, 51*, 46–52.

Planalp, E. M., & Braungart-Rieker, J. M. (2016). Determinants of father involvement with young children: Evidence from the Early Childhood Longitudinal Study-Birth Cohort. *Journal of Family Psychology, 30*, 135–146.

Plant, E. A., & Peruche, B. M. (2005). The consequences of race for police officers' responses to criminal suspects. *Psychological Science, 16*(3), 180–183.

Plant, E. A., Peruche, B. M., & Butz, D. A. (2005). Eliminating automatic racial bias: Making race nondiagnostic for responses to criminal suspects. *Journal of Experimental Social Psychology, 41*(2), 141–156.

Pleck, J. H. (1976). The male sex role: Definitions, problems, and sources of change. *Journal of Social Issues, 32*(3), 155–164.

Podolny, J. M., & Baron, J. N. (1997). Resources and relationships: Social networks and mobility in the workplace. *American Sociological Review, 62*, 673–693.

Pollard, M., Green, H. D., Kennedy, D., Go, M-H., & Tucker, J. S. (2013, May). Adolescent friendship networks and trajectories of binge drinking. Rand Corporation Working Papers, WR-998.

Porter, J. R., & Washington, R. E. (1993). Minority identity and self-esteem. *Annual Review of Sociology, 19*, 139–161.

Powell, K. L., Roberts, G., & Nettle, D. (2012). Eye images increase charitable donations: Evidence from an opportunistic field experiment in a supermarket. *Ethology, 118*(11), 1096–1101.

Powell, M. A., & Parcell, T. L. (1997). Effects of family structure on the earnings attainment process: Differences by gender. *Journal of Marriage and Family, 59*, 419–433.

Powers, C. J., & Bierman, K. L. (2013). The multifaceted impact of peer relations on aggressive–disruptive behavior in early elementary school. *Developmental Psychology, 49*(6), 1174–1186.

Powers, K. E. (2017). Killing in the age of drone warfare: Psychology, distance, and civilian casualties. Presented at the Annual Meeting of the International Studies Association, Baltimore, MD.

Powers, T. A., & Zuroff, D. C. (1988). Interpersonal consequences of overt self-criticism: A comparison with neutral and self-enhancing presentations of self. *Journal of Personality and Social Psychology, 54*, 1054–1062.

Poyatos, F. (1983). *New perspectives in nonverbal communication: Studies in cultural anthropology, social psychology, linguistics, literature, and semantics.* Oxford: Pergamon.

Prager, I. G., & Cutler, B. L. (1990). Attributing traits to oneself and to others: The role of acquaintance level. *Personality and Social Psychology Bulletin, 16*, 309–319.

Pratkanis, A. R., & Greenwald, A. G. (1989). A sociocognitive model of attitude structure and function. In L. Berkowitz (Ed.), *Advances in experimental social psychology* (Vol. 22, pp. 245–285). New York: Academic Press.

Pratt, T. C., Cullen, F. T., Sellers, C. S., Winfree Jr., L. T., Madensen, T. D., Daigle, L. E., et al. (2013). The empirical status of social learning theory: A meta-analysis. *Justice Quarterly, 27*, 765–802.

Praxmarer, S. (2011). How a presenter's perceived attractiveness affects persuasion for attractiveness-unrelated products. *International Journal of Advertising, 30*(5), 839–865.

Prentice-Dunn, S., & Rogers, R. W. (1980). Effects of deindividuating situational cues and aggressive models on subjective deindividuation and aggression. *Journal of Personality and Social Psychology, 39*(1), 104–113.

Previti, D., & Amato, P. (2003). Why stay married? Rewards, barriers, and marital stability. *Journal of Marriage and Family, 65*, 561–573.

Price, H. E., & Collett, J. L. (2012). The role of exchange and emotion on commitment: A study of teachers. *Social Science Research, 41*(6), 1469–1479.

Price, V., Nir, L., & Cappella, J. N. (2006). Normative and informational influences in online political discussions. *Communication Theory, 16*(1), 47–74.

Priest, R. T., & Sawyer, J. (1967). Proximity and peership: Bases of balance in interpersonal attraction. *American Journal of Sociology, 72*, 633–649.

Priester, J. R., & Petty, R. E. (1995). Source attributions and persuasion: Perceived honesty as a determinant of message scrutiny. *Personality and Social Psychology Bulletin, 21*(6), 637–654.

Prince-Gibson, E., & Schwartz, S. H. (1998). Value priorities and gender. *Social Psychology Quarterly, 61*, 49–67.

Pryor, J. B., McDaniel, M. A., & Kott-Russo, T. (1986). The influence of the level of schema abstractness upon the processing of social information. *Journal of Experimental Social Psychology, 22*(4), 312–327.

Pugh, M. D., & Wahrman, R. (1983). Neutralizing sexism in mixed-sex groups: Do women have to be better than men? *American Journal of Sociology, 88*, 746–762.

Quattrone, G. A. (1986). On the perceptions of a group's variability. In S. Worchel & W. G. Austin (Eds.), *Psychology of intergroup relations* (2nd ed., pp. 25–48). Chicago: Nelson-Hall.

Quick, B. L., Shen, L., & Dillard, J. P. (2013). Reactance theory and persuasion. In J. P. Dillard & L. Shen (Eds.), *The Sage handbook of persuasion: Developments in theory and practice* (pp. 167–183). Thousand Oaks, CA: Sage.

Quillian, L., & Campbell, M. (2003). Beyond black and white: The present and future of multiracial friendship segregation. *American Sociological Review, 68*, 540–566.

Quinn, D. M., & Chaudoir, S. R. (2009). Living with a concealable stigmatized identity: The impact of anticipated stigma, centrality, salience, and cultural stigma on psychological distress and health. *Journal of Personality and Social Psychology, 97*, 634–651.

Quinney, R. (1970). *The social reality of crime.* Boston: Little, Brown.

Rabbie, J. M., & Bekkers, F. (1978). Threatened leadership and intergroup competition. *European Journal of Social Psychology, 8*, 9–20.

Rabow, J., Neuman, C. A., & Hernandez, A. (1987). Cognitive consistency in attitudes, social support, and consumption of alcohol: Additive and interactive effects. *Social Psychology Quarterly, 50*, 56–63.

Rafaeli, S., & Ariel, Y. (2008). Online motivational factors: Incentives for participation and contribution in Wikipedia. In A. Barak (Ed.), *Psychological aspects of cyberspace: Theory, research, applications* (pp. 243–267). New York: Cambridge University Press.

Rahn, J., & Mason, W. (1987). Political alienation, cohort size, and the Easterlin hypothesis. *American Sociological Review, 52*, 155–169.

Rahn, W. M. (1993). The role of partisan stereotypes in information processing about political candidates. *American Journal of Political Science, 37*(2), 472–496.

Ramirez, A., & Broneck, K. (2009). "IM me": Instant messaging as relational maintenance and everyday communication. *Journal of Social and Personal Relationships, 26*, 291–314.

Rank, S. G., & Jacobson, C. K. (1977). Hospital nurses' compliance with medication overdose orders: A failure to replicate. *Journal of Health and Social Behavior, 18*, 188–193.

Rashotte, L. S. (2002). What does that smile mean? The meaning of nonverbal behaviors in social interaction. *Social Psychology Quarterly, 65*, 92–102.

Rasinski, K. A., Berktold, J., Smith, T. W., & Albertson, B. L. (2002). *America recovers: A follow-up to a national study of public responses to the September 11th terrorist attacks*. Chicago: National Opinion Research Center.

Ratzan, S. C. (1989). The real agenda setters: Pollsters in the 1988 presidential campaign. *American Behavioral Scientist, 32*, 451–463.

Raven, B. H. (1992). A power/interaction model of interpersonal influence: French and Raven thirty years later. *Journal of Social Behavior and Personality, 7*, 217–244.

Raven, B. H., & Kruglanski, A. W. (1970). Conflict and power. In P. Swingle (Ed.), *The structure of conflict* (pp. 68–109). New York: Academic Press.

Raven, B. H., & Rietsema, J. (1957). The effects of varied clarity of group goal and group path upon the individual and his relation to the group. *Human Relations, 10*, 29–44.

Rea, L., & Parker, R. (1997). *Designing and conducting survey research: A comprehensive guide* (2nd ed.). San Francisco: Jossey-Bass.

Read, J. G., & Gorman, B. K. (2010). Gender and health inequality. In K. Cook & D. S. Masse (Eds.), *Annual Review of Sociology* (Vol. 36, pp. 371–386). Palo Alto, CA: Annual Reviews.

Rees, C. R., & Segal, M. W. (1984). Role differentiation in groups: The relations between instrumental and expressive leadership. *Small Group Behavior, 15*, 109–123.

Regan, D. T., & Fazio, R. (1977). On the consistency between attitudes and behavior: Look to the method of attitude formation. *Journal of Experimental Social Psychology, 35*, 21–30.

Regan, P. (2000). The role of sexual desire and sexual activity in dating relationships. *Social Behavior and Personality, 28*, 51–59.

Reis, H. T., Senchak, M., & Solomon, B. (1985). Sex differences in the intimacy of social interaction: Further examination of potential explanations. *Journal of Personality and Social Psychology, 48*, 1204–1217.

Rempel, J. K., Holmes, J. G., & Zanna, M. P. (1985). Trust in a close relationship. *Journal of Personality and Social Psychology, 49*, 95–112.

Renfrow, D. (2004). A cartography of passing in everyday life. *Symbolic Interaction, 27*, 485–506.

Renninger, L., Wade, T., & Grammar, K. (2004). Getting that female glance: Patterns and consequences of male nonverbal behavior in courtship contexts. *Evolution and Human Behavior, 25*, 416–431.

Rentfrow, P. J., & Gosling, S. D. (2007). The content and validity of music-genre stereotypes among college students. *Psychology of Music, 35*(2), 306–326.

Repetti, R. (1987). Individual and common components of the social environment at work and psychological well-being. *Journal of Personality and Social Psychology, 52*, 710–720.

Repetti, R. (1989). Effects of daily workload on subsequent behavior during marital interaction: The roles of social withdrawal and spouse support. *Journal of Personality and Social Psychology, 57*, 651–659.

Reskin, B., & Padavic, I. (1994). *Women and men at work*. Thousand Oaks, CA: Pine Forge Press.

Rettinger, D. A., & Kramer, Y. (2009). Situational and personal causes of student cheating. *Research in Higher Education, 50*, 293–313.

Reyers, A., & Matusitz, J. (2012). Emotional regulation at Walt Disney World: An impression management view. *Journal of Workplace Behavioral Health, 27*(3), 139–159.

Reynolds, J. R. (1997). The effects of industrial employment conditions on job-related distress. *Journal of Health and Social Behavior, 38*, 105–116.

Rhodes, N., & Wood, W. (1992). Self-esteem and intelligence affect influenceability: The mediating role of message reception. *Psychological Bulletin, 111*, 156.

Richeson, J. A., & Ambady, N. (2003). Effects of situational power on automatic racial prejudice. *Journal of Experimental Social Psychology, 39*, 177–183.

Richman, S. B., & Mandara, J. (2013). Do socialization goals explain differences in parental control between Black and White parents? *Family Relations, 62*, 625–636.

Rickford, J. R., Duncan, G. J., Gennetian, L. A., Gou, R. Y, Greene, R., Katz, L. F., et al. (2015). Neighborhood effects on the use of African-American Vernacular English. *PNAS, 112*, 11817–11822.

Rideout, V. J., Foehr, U. G. & Roberts, D. F. (2010). Generation M2: Media in the Lives of 8- to 18-year-olds. Menlo Park, CA: Kaiser Family. Retrieved from https://files.eric.ed.gov/fulltext/ED527859.pdf (Accessed June 12, 2018).

Rideout, V., & Hamel, E. (2006). *The media family: Electronic media in the lives of infants, toddlers, preschoolers and their parents*. Menlo Park, CA: Kaiser Family Foundation.

Ridgeway, C. L. (1987). Nonverbal behavior, dominance, and the basis of status in task groups. *American Sociological Review, 52*, 683–694.

Ridgeway, C. L. (2006). Status construction theory. In P. J. Burke (Ed.), *Contemporary social psychological theories* (pp. 301–323). Palo Alto, CA: Stanford University Press.

Ridgeway, C. L. (2011). *Framed by gender: How gender inequality persists in the modern world*. New York: Oxford University Press.

Ridgeway, C. L., & Correll, S. J. (2004). Unpacking the gender system: A theoretical perspective on gender beliefs and social relations. *Gender and Society, 18*(4), 510–531.

Ridgeway, C. L., & Johnson, C. (1990). What is the relationship between socioemotional behavior and status in task groups? *American Journal of Sociology, 95*(5), 1189–1212.

Ridgeway, C. L., & Smith-Lovin, L. (1999). The gender system and interaction. *Annual Review of Sociology, 25*, 191–216.

Ridgeway, C. L., & Walker, H. A. (1995). Status structures. In K. S. Cook, G. A. Fine, & J. S. House (Eds.), *Sociological perspectives on social psychology* (pp. 281–310). Boston: Allyn and Bacon.

Riggio, R. E., & Friedman, H. S. (1983). Individual differences and cues to deception. *Journal of Personality and Social Psychology, 45*, 899–915.

Rigney, J. (1962). A developmental study of cognitive equivalence transformations and their use in the acquisition and processing of information. Unpublished honors thesis, Radcliffe College, Cambridge, MA.

Riketta, M. (2005). Cognitive differentiation between self, ingroup, and outgroup: The roles of identification and perceived intergroup conflict. *European Journal of Social Psychology, 35*, 97–106.

Riley, M. (1987). On the significance of age in sociology. *American Sociological Review, 52*, 1–14.

Rindfuss, R., Swicegood, C. G., & Rosenfeld, R. (1987). Disorder in the life course: How common and does it matter? *American Sociological Review, 52*, 785–801.

Rinehart, A. J., & Dunwoody, P. T. (2005, April). Groupthink in the Bush administration's decision for Operation Iraqi Freedom. Poster session presented at the annual Western Pennsylvania Undergraduate Psychology Conference, Chatham College, Pittsburgh, PA.

Riordan, C. (1978). Equal-status interracial contact: A review and revision of the concept. *International Journal of Intercultural Relations, 2*, 161–185.

Riordan, C., & Ruggiero, J. A. (1980). Producing equal-status interracial interaction: A replication. *Social Psychology Quarterly, 43*, 131–136.

Riordan, C. A., Marlin, N. A., & Kellogg, R. T. (1983). The effectiveness of accounts following transgression. *Social Psychology Quarterly, 46*, 213–219.

Robertson, J. F., & Simons, R. L. (1989). Family factors, self-esteem, and adolescent depression. *Journal of Marriage and Family, 51*, 125–138.

Robinson, D. T., Smith-Lovin, L., & Tsoudis, O. (1994). Heinous crime or unfortunate accident: The effects of remorse on responses to mock criminal confessions. *Social Problems, 73*, 175–190.

Robinson, J. W., & Preston, J. D. (1976). Equal-status contact and the modification of racial prejudice: A reexamination of the contact hypothesis. *Social Forces, 54*, 911–924.

Rochat, F., & Modigliani, A. (1995). The ordinary quality of resistance: From Milgram's laboratory to the village of Le Chambon. *Journal of Social Issues, 51*, 195–210.

Rochat, P. (2010). The innate sense of the body develops to become a public affair by 2–3 years. *Neuropsychologia, 48*, 738–745.

Rodriguez, J., Cargile, A., & Rich, M. (2004). Reactions to African-American Vernacular English: Do more phonological features matter? *Western Journal of Black Studies, 28*, 407–414.

Rogers, M., Miller, N., Mayer, F. S., & Duval, S. (1982). Personal responsibility and salience of the request for help: Determinants of the relation between negative affect and helping behavior. *Journal of Personality and Social Psychology, 43*(5), 956–970.

Rogers, S., & May, D. (2003). Spillover between marital quality and job satisfaction: Long-term patterns and gender differences. *Journal of Marriage and Family, 65*, 482–495.

Rohrer, J. H., Baron, S. H., Hoffman, E. L., & Swander, D. V. (1954). The stability of autokinetic judgments. *Journal of Abnormal and Social Psychology, 49*, 595–597.

Rokeach, M. (1973). *The nature of human values.* New York: Free Press.

Romano, E., & De Luca, R. V. (2001). Male sexual abuse: A review of effects, abuse characteristics, and links with later psychological functioning. *Aggression and Violent Behavior, 6*(1), 55–78.

Rommetveit, R. (1955). *Social norms and roles.* Minneapolis: University of Minnesota Press.

Root, M. (1995). The psychology of Asian American women. In H. Landrine (Ed.), *Bringing cultural diversity to feminist psychology: Theory, research, and practice* (pp. 241–263). Washington, DC: American Psychological Association.

Rose, A., & Rudolph, K. (2006). A review of sex-differences in peer relationship processes: Potential trade-offs for the emotional and behavioral development of girls and boys. *Psychological Bulletin, 132*, 98–131.

Rose, H., & Rose, S. (2000). *Alas poor Darwin: Arguments against evolutionary psychology.* New York: Harmony Books.

Rose, S., & Frieze, I. H. (1993). Young singles' contemporary dating scripts. *Sex Roles, 28*, 499–509.

Rosen, L., Principe, C., & Langlois, J. (2013). Feedback seeking in early adolescence. *Journal of Early Adolescence, 33*, 363–377.

Rosen, S. (1984). Some paradoxical status implications of helping and being helped. In E. Staub, D. Bar-Tal, J. Karylowski, & J. Reykowski (Eds.), *Development and maintenance of prosocial behavior: International perspectives on positive morality* (pp. 359–377). New York: Plenum.

Rosenbaum, M. E. (1986). The repulsion hypothesis: On the nondevelopment of relationships. *Journal of Personality and Social Psychology, 51*, 1156–1166.

Rosenberg, L. A. (1961). Group size, prior experience, and conformity. *Journal of Abnormal and Social Psychology, 63*, 436–437.

Rosenberg, M. (1965). *Society and the adolescent self-image.* Princeton, NJ: Princeton University Press.

Rosenberg, M. (1973). Which significant others? *American Behavioral Scientist, 16*, 829–860.

Rosenberg, M. (1990). The self-concept: Social product and social force. In M. Rosenberg & R. Turner (Eds.), *Social psychology: Sociological perspectives* (pp. 593–624). New Brunswick, NJ: Transaction.

Rosenberg, M., & Pearlin, L. (1978). Social class and self-esteem among children and adults. *American Journal of Sociology, 84*, 53–77.

Rosenberg, M., Schooler, C., & Schoenbach, C. (1989). Self-esteem and adolescent problems: Modeling reciprocal effects. *American Sociological Review, 54*, 1004–1018.

Rosenberg, M., Schooler, C., Schoenbach, C., & Rosenberg, F. (1995). Global self-esteem and specific self-esteem: Different concepts, different outcomes. *American Sociological Review, 60*, 141–156.

Rosenberg, M., & Simmons, R. (1972). *Black and White self-esteem: The urban school child.* Washington, DC: American Sociological Association.

Rosenberg, M. J., & Abelson, R. (1960). An analysis of cognitive balancing. In C. Hovland & M. Rosenberg (Eds.),

*Attitude organization and change* (pp. 112–163). New Haven, CT: Yale University Press.

Rosenberg, S. V., Nelson, C., & Vivekananthan, P. S. (1968). A multidimensional approach to the structure of personality impressions. *Journal of Personality and Social Psychology, 9*, 283–294.

Rosenberg, S. V., & Sedlak, A. (1972). Structural representations in implicit personality theory. In L. Berkowitz (Ed.), *Advances in experimental social psychology* (Vol. 6, pp. 235–297). New York: Academic Press.

Rosenblatt, A., & Greenberg, J. (1988). Depression and interpersonal attraction: The role of perceived similarity. *Journal of Personality and Social Psychology, 55*, 112–119.

Rosenblatt, A., & Greenberg, J. (1991). Examining the world of the depressed: Do depressed people prefer others who are depressed? *Journal of Personality and Social Psychology, 60*, 620–629.

Rosenfeld, M. J. (2014). Couple longevity in the era of same-sex marriage in the United States. *Journal of Marriage and Family, 76*, 905–918.

Rosenfeld, M. J., & Thomas, R. J. (2012). Searching for a mate: The rise of the Internet as a social intermediary. *American Sociological Review, 77*, 523–547.

Rosenhan, D. L. (1973). On being sane in insane places. *Science, 179*, 250–258.

Rosenhan, D. L., Salovey, P., & Hargis, K. (1981). The joys of helping: Focus of attention mediates the impact of positive affect on altruism. *Journal of Personality and Social Psychology, 40*(5), 899–905.

Rosenkoetter, L. I., Rosenkoetter, S. E., & Acock, A. C. (2009). Television violence: An intervention to reduce its impact on children. *Journal of Applied Developmental Psychology, 30*(4), 381–397.

Rosenkoetter, L. I., Rosenkoetter, S. E., Ozretich, R. A., & Acock, A. C. (2004). Mitigating the harmful effects of violent television. *Journal of Applied Developmental Psychology, 25*, 25–47.

Rosenthal, R. (1966). *Experimenter effects in behavioral research.* New York: Appleton-Century-Crofts.

Rosenthal, R. (1980). Replicability and experimenter influence: Experimenter effects in behavioral research. *Parapsychology, 11*, 5–11.

Rosenthal, R., & Jacobson, L. (1968). *Pygmalion in the classroom: Teacher expectation and pupils' intellectual development.* New York: Rinehart and Winston.

Ross, A. S. (1971). Effect of increased responsibility on bystander intervention: The presence of children. *Journal of Personality and Social Psychology, 19*(3), 306.

Ross, C. E., Mirowsky, J., & Goldsteen, K. (1990). The impact of the family on health: The decade in review. *Journal of Marriage and Family, 52*, 1059–1078.

Ross, C. E., & Van Willigen, M. (1997). Education and the subjective quality of life. *Journal of Health and Social Behavior, 38*, 275–297.

Ross, C. E., & Wu, C. (1995). The links between education and health. *American Sociological Review, 60*, 719–745.

Ross, L. (1977). The intuitive psychologist and his shortcomings: Distortion in the attribution process. In L. Berkowitz (Ed.), *Advances in experimental social psychology* (Vol. 10, pp. 173–220). New York: Academic Press.

Ross, L., Lepper, M. R., & Hubbard, M. (1975). Perseverance in self-perception and social perception: Biased attributional processes in the debriefing paradigm. *Journal of Personality and Social Psychology, 32*(5), 880–892.

Ross, M., & Fletcher, G. (1985). Attribution and social perception. In G. Lindzey & E. Aronson (Eds.), *The handbook of social psychology* (3rd ed., Vol. 1, pp. 73–122). New York: Random House.

Ross, M., & Lumsden, H. (1982). Attributions of responsibility in sports settings: It's not how you play the game but whether you win or lose. In H. Hiebsch, H. Brandstatter, & H. H. Kelley (Eds.), *Social psychology* (pp. 34–37). East Berlin: Deutscher Verlag der Wissenschaften.

Rotenberg, K. J., & Mann, L. (1986). The development of the norm of the reciprocity of self-disclosure and its function in children's attraction to peers. *Child Development, 57*, 1349–1357.

Roth, D. L., Wiebe, D. J., Fillingian, R. B., & Shay, K. A. (1989). Life events, fitness, hardiness, and health: A simultaneous analysis of proposed stress-resistance effects. *Journal of Personality and Social Psychology, 57*, 136–142.

Rothbart, M. (1996). Category-exemplar dynamics and stereotype change. *International Journal of Intercultural Relations, 20*(3), 305–321.

Rothbart, M., Fulero, S., Jensen, C., Howard, J., & Birrell, B. (1978). From individual to group impressions: Availability heuristics in stereotype formation. *Journal of Experimental Social Psychology, 14*, 237–255.

Rotheram-Borus, M. J. (1990). Adolescents' reference group choices, self-esteem, and adjustment. *Journal of Personality and Social Psychology, 59*, 1075–1081.

Rotter, J. B. (1966). Generalized expectancies for internal versus external control of reinforcement. *Psychological Monographs: General and Applied, 80*(1), 1.

Rotton, J., & Cohn, E. G. (2004). Outdoor temperature, climate control, and criminal assault: The spatial and temporal ecology of violence. *Environment and Behavior, 36*(2), 276–306.

Ruback, R. (1987). Deserted (and nondeserted) aisles: Territorial intrusion can produce persistence, not flight. *Social Psychology Quarterly, 50*, 270–276.

Ruback, R. B., Pape, K. D., & Doriot, P. (1989). Waiting for a phone: Intrusion on callers leads to territorial defense. *Social Psychology Quarterly, 52*, 232–241.

Rubin, M., & Hewstone, M. (1998). Social identity theory's self-esteem hypothesis: A review and some suggestions for clarification. *Personality and Social Psychology Review, 2*, 40–62.

Rubin, Z. (1970). Measurement of romantic love. *Journal of Personality and Social Psychology, 16*, 265–273.

Rubin, Z. (1974). From liking to loving: Patterns of attraction in dating relationships. In T. Huston (Ed.), *Foundations of interpersonal attraction* (pp. 383–402). New York: Academic Press.

Rubin, Z., Hill, C., Peplau, L., & Dunkel-Scheker, C. (1980). Self-disclosure in dating couples: Sex roles and the ethic of openness. *Journal of Marriage and Family, 42*, 305–317.

Ruiter, R. A. C., Kok, G., Verplanken, B., & van Eersel, G. (2003). Strengthening the persuasive impact of fear appeals:

The role of action framing. *Journal of Social Psychology, 143,* 397–400.

Rusbult, C. E. (1983). A longitudinal test of the investment model: The development (and deterioration) of satisfaction and commitment in heterosexual involvements. *Journal of Personality and Social Psychology, 45,* 101–117.

Rusbult, C. E., Johnson, D. J., & Morrow, G. D. (1986). Predicting satisfaction and commitment in adult romantic involvements: An assessment of the generalizability of the investment model. *Social Psychology Quarterly, 49,* 81–89.

Rusbult, C. E., Verette, J., Whitney, G. A., Slovik, L. A., & Lipkus, I. (1991). Accommodation processes in close relationships: Theory and preliminary empirical evidence. *Journal of Personality and Social Psychology, 60,* 53–78.

Rusbult, C. E., Zembrodt, I. M., & Gunn, L. K. (1982). Exit, voice, loyalty, and neglect: Responses to dissatisfaction in romantic involvement. *Journal of Personality and Social Psychology, 43,* 1230–1242.

Rushton, J. P., Russell, R. J., & Wells, P. A. (1984). Genetic similarity theory: Beyond kin selection. *Behaviour Genetics, 14,* 179–193.

Rutchick, A. M., McManus, R. M., Barth, D. M., Youmans, R. J., Ainsworth, A. T., & Goukassian, H. J. (2017). Technologically facilitated remoteness increases killing behavior. *Journal of Experimental Social Psychology, 73,* 147–150.

Ryan, K. (1988). Rape and seduction scripts. *Psychology of Women Quarterly, 12,* 237–245.

Ryan, K. M. (2011). The relationship between rape myths and sexual scripts: The social construction of rape. *Sex Roles, 65*(11–12), 774–782.

Ryder, N. B. (1965). The cohort as a concept in the study of social change. *American Sociological Review, 30,* 843–861.

Sacks, H., Schegloff, E., & Jefferson, G. (1978). A simplest systematics for the organization of turn-taking in conversations. In J. Schenkein (Ed.), *Studies in the organization of conversational interaction* (pp. 696–735). New York: Academic Press.

Saegert, S. C., Swap, W., & Zajonc, R. B. (1973). Exposure, context, and interpersonal attraction. *Journal of Personality and Social Psychology, 25,* 234–242.

Safdar, S., Friedlmeier, W., Matsumoto, D., Yoo, S. H., Kwantes, C. T., Kakai, H., & Shigemasu, E. (2009). Variations of emotional display rules within and across cultures: A comparison between Canada, USA, and Japan. *Canadian Journal of Behavioural Science/Revue canadienne des sciences du comportement, 41*(1), 1.

Sagarin, E. (1975). *Deviants and deviance.* New York: Praeger.

Saito, Y. (1988). Situational characteristics as the determinants of adopting distributive justice principles: II. *Japanese Journal of Experimental Psychology, 27,* 131–138.

Sakurai, M. M. (1975). Small group cohesiveness and detrimental conformity. *Sociometry, 38,* 340–357.

Salmivalli, C., & Nieminen, E. (2002). Proactive and reactive aggression among school bullies, victims, and bully-victims. *Aggressive Behavior, 28*(1), 30–44.

Salovey, P., Mayer, J. D., & Rosenhan, D. L. (1991). Mood and helping: Mood as a motivator of helping and helping as a regulator of mood. In M. S. Clark (Ed.), *Review of personality and social psychology: Vol. 12. Prosocial behavior* (pp. 215–237). Newbury Park, CA: Sage.

Sammon, S., Reznikoff, M., & Geisinger, K. (1985). Psychosocial development and stressful life events among religious professionals. *Journal of Personality and Social Psychology, 48,* 676–687.

Sampson, R. J., & Laub, J. H. (1990). Crime and deviance over the life course: The salience of adult social bonds. *American Sociological Review, 55,* 609–627.

Sanday, P. R. (1981). The socio-cultural context of rape: A cross-cultural study. *Journal of Social Issues, 37*(4), 5–27.

Sanday, P. R. (2003). Rape-free versus rape-prone: How culture makes a difference. In C. B. Travis (Ed.), *Evolution, gender, and rape* (pp. 337–362). Cambridge, MA: MIT Press.

Sande, G. N., Goethals, G. R., & Radloff, C. E. (1988). Perceiving one's own traits and others': The multifaceted self. *Journal of Personality and Social Psychology, 54,* 13–20.

Sarbin, T., & Rosenberg, B. (1955). Contributions to role-taking theory IV: A method for obtaining a qualitative estimate of the self. *Journal of Social Psychology, 42,* 71–81.

Sarkisian, N., & Gerstel, N. (2004). Kin support among Blacks and Whites: Race and family organization. *American Sociological Review, 69,* 812–837.

Sassler, S. (2010). Partnering across the life course: Sex, relationships, and mate selection. *Journal of Marriage and Family, 72:* 557–575.

Sassler, S., Michelmore, K., & Holland, J. A. (2016). The progression of sexual relationships. *Journal of Marriage and Family, 78,* 587–597.

Sawdon, A. M., Cooper, M., & Seabrook, R. (2007). The relationship between self-discrepancies, eating disorder and depressive symptoms in women. *European Eating Disorders Review, 15,* 207–212.

Sawyer, A. (1973). The effects of repetition of refutational and supportive advertising appeals. *Journal of Marketing Research, 10,* 23–33.

Scanlon, M., & Wassink, A. B. (2010). African American English in Seattle: Accommodation and intraspeaker variation in the Pacific Northwest. *American Speech, 85,* 205–224.

Schachter, S. (1964). The interaction of cognitive and physiological determinants of emotional state. *Advances in Experimental Social Psychology, 1,* 49–80.

Schachter, S., & Singer, J. (1962). Cognitive, social, and physiological determinants of emotional state. *Psychological Review, 69*(5), 379–399.

Schaible, L. M., & Gecas, V. (2010). The impact of emotional labor and value dissonance on burnout among police officers. *Police Quarterly, 13*(3), 316–341.

Schaller, M., & Cialdini, R. B. (1988). The economics of empathic helping: Support for a mood management motive. *Journal of Experimental Social Psychology, 24*(2), 163–181.

Schank, R. C., & Abelson, R. P. (1977). *Scripts, plans, goals, and understanding.* Hillsdale, NJ: Erlbaum.

Schau, H., & Gill, M. (2003). We are what we post? Self-presentation in personal web space. *Journal of Consumer Research, 30,* 385–404.

Scheff, T. (1966). *Being mentally ill.* Chicago: Aldine.

Scheff, T. J. (2011). *What's love got to do with it? Emotions and relationships in popular songs.* New York: Routledge.

Scheff, T. J., & Retzinger, S. M. (2001). *Emotions and violence: Shame and rage in destructive conflicts.* Lincoln, NE: iUniverse.

Schegloff, E. (1968). Sequencing in conversational openings. *American Anthropologist, 70,* 1075–1095.

Scherer, K. R. (1979). Nonlinguistic vocal indicators of emotion and psychopathology. In C. E. Izard (Ed.), *Emotions in personality and psychopathology* (pp. 493–529). New York: Plenum.

Scherer, S. E. (1974). Proxemic behavior of primary school children as a function of their socioeconomic class and subculture. *Journal of Personality and Social Psychology, 29,* 800–805.

Schiffenbauer, A., & Schiavo, R. S. (1976). Physical distance and attraction: An intensification effect. *Journal of Experimental Social Psychology, 12,* 274–282.

Schkade, D., Sunstein, C. R., & Kahneman, D. (2000). Deliberating about dollars: The severity shift. *Columbia Law Review,* 1139–1175.

Schlenker, B. R. (2003). Self-presentation. In M. R. Leary & J. P. Tangney (Eds.), *Handbook of self and identity* (pp. 492–518). New York: Guilford.

Schlenker, B. R., & Weigold, M. F. (1992). Interpersonal processes involving impression regulation and management. *Annual Review of Psychology, 43,* 133–168.

Schlenker, B. R., Weigold, M. E., & Hallam, J. K. (1990). Self-serving attributions in social context: Effects of self-esteem and social pressure. *Journal of Personality and Social Psychology, 58,* 855–863.

Schmidtke, J. M. (2007). The relationship between social norm consensus, perceived similarity, and observer reactions to coworker theft. *Human Resource Management, 46,* 561–582.

Schmitt, D. P., & Buss, D. M. (1996). Strategic self-promotion and competitor derogation: Sex and context effects in the perceived effectiveness of mate attraction tactics. *Journal of Personality and Social Psychology, 70,* 1185–1204.

Schneider, D., Harknett, K., & McLanahan, S. (2016). Intimate partner violence in the Great Recession. *Demography, 53*(2), 471–505.

Schneider, S. L. (2008). Anti-immigrant attitudes in Europe: Outgroup size and perceived ethnic threat. *European Sociological Review, 24*(1), 53–67.

Schnittker, J. (2000). Gender and reactions to psychological problems: An examination of social tolerance and perceived dangerousness. *Journal of Health and Social Behavior, 41,* 224–240.

Schnittker, J. (2002). The self-esteem of Chinese immigrants. *Social Psychology Quarterly, 65,* 56–76.

Schnittker, J. (2013). Social structure and personality. In J. D. DeLamater & A. Ward (Eds.), *Handbook of social psychology* (pp. 89–115). Dordrecht: Springer Netherlands.

Schoenborn, C. (2004, December 15). Marital status and health: United States, 1999–2002. (Advance Data from Vital and Health Statistics No. 351). Hyattsville, MD: National Center for Health Statistics.

Schooler, C. (1996). Cultural and social–structural explanations of cross-national psychological differences. *Annual Review of Sociology, 22,* 323–349.

Schooler, C., Mulatu, M. S., & Oates, G. (2004). Occupational self-direction, intellectual functioning, and self-directed orientation in older workers: Findings and implications for individuals and societies. *American Journal of Sociology, 110,* 161–197.

Schrauger, J. S., & Schoeneman, T. (1979). Symbolic interactionist view of self-concept: Through the looking glass darkly. *Psychological Bulletin, 86,* 549–573.

Schroeder, D. A., Penner, L. A., Dovidio, J. F., & Piliavin, J. A. (1995). *The psychology of helping and altruism: Problems and puzzles.* New York: McGraw-Hill.

Schrum, W., & Creek, N. A. (1987). Social structure during the school years: Onset of the degrouping process. *American Sociological Review, 52,* 218–223.

Schultz, E. J. (2016). Coke replaces "Open Happiness" with "Taste the Feeling" in major strategic shift. *Advertising Age.* Retrieved from www. adage. com/article/cmo-strategy/coke-debuts-taste-feeling-campaign-strategic-shift/302184 (Accessed January 12, 2017).

Schultz, P. W., Tabanico, J. J., & Rendón, T. (2008). Normative beliefs as agents of influence: Basic processes and real-world applications. In W. D. Crano & R. Prislin (Eds.), *Attitudes and attitude change* (pp. 385–409). New York: Psychology Press.

Schuman, H., & Johnson, M. (1976). Attitudes and behavior. In A. Inkeles, J. Coleman & N. Smelser (Eds.), *Annual Review of Sociology* (Vol. 2, pp. 161–207). Palo Alto, CA: Annual Reviews.

Schutte, J., & Light, J. (1978). The relative importance of proximity and status for friendship choices in social hierarchies. *Social Psychology, 41,* 260–264.

Schutte, N. S., Kendrick, D. T., & Sadalla, E. K. (1985). The search for predictable settings: Situational prototypes, constraint, and behavioral variation. *Journal of Personality and Social Psychology, 49,* 121–128.

Schwartz, B. (2004, December). The tyranny of choice. *Scientific American Mind.* Retrieved from www.scientificamerican.com/article/the-tyranny-of-choice (Accessed June 11, 2018).

Schwartz, C., & Graf, N. (2007). Assortative matching among same-sex and different-sex couples in the United States, 1990–2000 (Working Paper No. 2007–21). Madison, WI: Center for Demography and Ecology.

Schwartz, S. H. (1978). Temporal instability as a moderator of the attitude-behavior relationship. *Journal of Personality and Social Psychology, 36,* 715–724.

Schwartz, S. H. (1992). Universals in the content and structure of values: Theoretical advances and empirical tests in 20 countries. In M. Zanna (Ed.), *Advances in experimental social psychology* (Vol. 25, pp. 1–65). Orlando, FL: Academic Press.

Schwartz, S. H. (1994). Are there universal aspects in the content and structure of values? *Journal of Social Issues, 50,* 19–45.

Schwartz, S. H., & Clausen, G. T. (1970). Responsibility, norms, and helping in an emergency. *Journal of Personality and Social Psychology, 16*(2), 299–310.

Schwartz, S. H., & Fleishman, J. (1978). Personal norms and the mediation of legitimacy effects on helping. *Social Psychology, 41,* 306–315.

Schwartz, S. H., & Gottlieb, A. (1976). Bystander reactions to a violent theft: Crime in Jerusalem. *Journal of Personality and Social Psychology*, *34*(6), 1188–1199.

Schwartz, S. H., & Howard, J. A. (1981). A normative decision-making model of altruism. In J. P. Rushton & R. M. Sorrentino (Eds.), *Altruism and helping behavior* (pp. 189–211). Hillsdale, NJ: Erlbaum.

Schwartz, S. H., & Howard, J. A. (1984). Internalized values as motivators of altruism. In E. Staub, E. Bar-Tal, J. Karylowski, & J. Reykowski (Eds.), *Development and maintenance of prosocial behavior: International perspectives on positive morality* (pp. 229–255). New York: Plenum.

Schwartz, S., & Rubel-Lifschitz, T. (2009). Cross-national variation in the size of sex differences in values: Effects of gender equality. *Journal of Personality and Social Psychology*, *97*, 171–185.

Schwarz, N., Groves, R., & Schuman, H. (1998). Survey methods. In D. Gilbert, S. Fiske, & G. Lindzey (Eds.), *The handbook of social psychology* (4th ed., Vol. 1, pp. 143–179). Boston: McGraw-Hill.

Scott, M., & Lyman, S. (1968). Accounts. *American Sociological Review*, *33*, 46–62.

Scott, R. (1976). Deviance, sanctions, and social integration in small-scale societies. *Social Forces*, *54*, 604–620.

Scott, S., Hinton-Smith, T., Harma, V., & Broome, K. (2012). The reluctant researcher: Shyness in the field. *Qualitative Research*, *12*, 715–734.

Scotton, C. M. (1983). The negotiation of identities in conversation. *International Journal of the Sociology of Language*, *44*, 115–136.

Searle, J. R. (1979). *Expression and meaning: Studies in the theory of speech acts*. Cambridge: Cambridge University Press.

Sears, D., Fu, M., Henry, P. J., & Bui, K. (2003). The origins and persistence of ethnic identity among the "New Immigrant" groups. *Social Psychology Quarterly*, *66*, 419–437.

Sedikides, C., & Anderson, C. A. (1994). Causal perceptions of intertrait relations: The glue that holds person types together. *Personality and Social Psychology Bulletin*, *20*(3), 294–302.

Sedikides, C., & Jackson, J. M. (1990). Social impact theory: A field test of source strength, source immediacy, and number of targets. *Basic and Applied Social Psychology*, *11*, 273–281.

Seeman, M. (1975). Alienation studies. In A. Inkeles, J. Coleman, & N. Smelser (Eds.), *Annual Review of Sociology* (Vol. 1, pp. 91–123). Palo Alto, CA: Annual Reviews.

Seeman, M., Seeman, M., & Sayles, M. (1985). Social networks and health status: A longitudinal analysis. *Social Psychology Quarterly*, *48*, 237–248.

Segal, B. E. (1965). Contact, compliance, and distance among Jewish and non-Jewish undergraduates. *Social Problems*, *13*, 66–74.

Sellers, C. S., Cochran, J. K., & Branch, K. A. (2005). Social learning theory and partner violence: A research note. *Deviant Behavior*, *26*(4), 379–395.

Semin, G. R., & Manstead, A. S. R. (1982). The social implications of embarrassment displays and restitution behaviour. *European Journal of Social Psychology*, *12*, 367–377.

Semin, G. R., & Manstead, A. S. R. (1983). *The accountability of conduct: A social psychological analysis*. London: Academic Press.

Seplaki, C., Goldman, N., Weinstein, M., & Lin, Y.-H. (2003). Before and after the 1999 Chi-Chi earthquake: Traumatic events and depressive symptoms in an older population (Working Paper No. 2003–02). Princeton University: Office of Population Research.

Serpe, R. T. (1987). Stability and change in self: A structural symbolic interactionist explanation. *Social Psychology Quarterly*, *50*, 44–55.

Sewell, W. H., & Hauser, R. M. (1975). *Education, occupation, and earnings: Achievement in the early career*. New York: Academic Press.

Sewell, W. H., & Hauser, R. M. (1980). The Wisconsin longitudinal study of social and psychological factors in aspirations and achievements. *Research in Sociology of Education and Socialization*, *1*, 59–99.

Sewell, W. H., Hauser, R. M., & Wolf, W. (1980). Sex, schooling, and occupational status. *American Journal of Sociology*, *86*, 551–583.

Shapiro, S. P. (1990). Collaring the crime, not the criminal: Considering the concept of white-collar crime. *American Sociological Review*, *55*, 346–365.

Sharkey, W., Kim, M., & Digs, R. (2001). Intentional embarrassment: A look at embarrassors' and targets' perspectives. *Personality and Individual Differences*, *31*, 1261–1272.

Sharkey, W. F., & Stafford, L. (1990). Responses to embarrassment. *Human Communication Research*, *17*, 315–342.

Shaver, P., Schwartz, J., Kirson, D., & O'Connor, C. (1987). Emotion knowledge: Further exploration of a prototype approach. *Journal of Personality and Social Psychology*, *52*(6), 1061–1086.

Shaver, P. R., Wu, S., & Schwartz, J. C. (1992). *Cross-cultural similarities and differences in emotion and its representation*. Newbury Park, CA: Sage.

Shaw, B. A., Liang, J., & Krause, N. (2010). Age and race differences in trajectories of self-esteem. *Psychology and Aging*, *25*, 84–94.

Shaw, M., & Costanzo, P. (1982). *Theories of social psychology* (2nd ed.). New York: McGraw-Hill.

Shaw, M. E., & Shaw, L. M. (1962). Some effects of sociometric grouping upon learning in a second grade classroom. *Journal of Social Psychology*, *57*, 453–458.

Shell, R. M., & Eisenberg, N. (1992). A developmental model of recipients' reactions to aid. *Psychological Bulletin*, *111*, 413–433.

Sheng, S., Holbrook, M., Kumaraguru, P., Cranor, L. F., & Downs, J. (2010, April). Who falls for phish? A demographic analysis of phishing susceptibility and effectiveness of interventions. In *Proceedings of the 28th international conference on human factors in computing systems* (pp. 373–382). New York: ACM.

Shepherd, M. (2007). *The art of civilized conversation: A guide to expressing yourself with style and grace*. New York: Broadway Books.

Sherif, M. (1935). A study of some social factors in perception. *Archives of Psychology*, *27*(187), 1–60.

Sherif, M. (1936). *The psychology of social norms*. New York: Harper & Row.

Sherif, M. (1966). *In common predicament*. Boston: Houghton Mifflin.

Sherif, M., Harvey, O. J., White, B. J., Hood, W. R., & Sherif, C. W. (1961). *Intergroup cooperation and competition: The Robbers Cave experiment*. Norman, OK: University Book Exchange.

Sherman, J. W., Lee, A. Y., Bessenoff, G. R., & Frost, L. A. (1998). Stereotype efficiency reconsidered: Encoding flexibility under cognitive load. *Journal of Personality and Social Psychology, 75*(3), 589–606.

Sherman, P. (1980). The limits of ground squirrel nepotism. In G. Barlow & J. Silverberg (Eds.), *Sociobiology: Beyond nature/nurture?* (pp. 505–544). Boulder, CO: Westview.

Sherman, S. J., Judd, C. M., & Park, B. (1989). Social cognition. *Annual Review of Psychology, 40*, 281–326.

Sherwood, J. J. (1965). Self-identity and referent others. *Sociometry, 28*, 66–81.

Shestowsky, D., Wegener, D. T., & Fabrigar, L. R. (1998). Need for cognition and interpersonal influence: Individual differences in impact on dyadic decisions. *Journal of Personality and Social Psychology, 74*(5), 1317–1328.

Shibutani, T. (1961). *Society and personality*. Englewood Cliffs, NJ: Prentice Hall.

Shihadeh, E. S. (1991). The prevalence of husband-centered migration: Employment consequences for married mothers. *Journal of Marriage and Family, 53*, 431–444.

Shotland, R. L., & Stebbins, C. A. (1983). Emergency and cost as determinants of helping behavior and the slow accumulation of social psychological knowledge. *Social Psychology Quarterly, 46*, 36–46.

Shotland, R. L., & Straw, M. K. (1976). Bystander response to an assault: When a man attacks a woman. *Journal of Personality and Social Psychology, 34*, 990–999.

Shott, S. (1979). Emotion and social life: A symbolic interactionist analysis. *American Journal of Sociology, 84*(6), 1317–1334.

Shover, N., Novland, S., James, J., & Thornton, W. (1979). Gender roles and delinquency. *Social Forces, 58*, 162–175.

Sidanius, J., Levin, S., van Laar, C., & Sears, D. O. (2008). *The diversity challenge: Social identity and intergroup relations on the college campus*. New York: Russell Sage Foundation.

Sidanius, J., & Pratto, F. (2001). *Social dominance: An intergroup theory of social hierarchy and oppression*. Cambridge: Cambridge University Press.

Sidanius, J., Pratto, F., van Laar, C., & Levin, S. (2004). Social dominance theory: Its agenda and method. *Political Psychology, 25*(6), 845–880.

Sidnell, J. (2007). Comparative studies in conversation analysis. *Annual Review of Anthropology, 36*, 229–244.

Siebenhaar, B. (2006). Code choice and code-switching in Swiss-German Internet relay chat rooms. *Journal of Sociolinguistics, 10*, 481–506.

Sigall, H., & Landy, D. (1973). Radiating beauty: The effects of having a physically attractive partner on person perception. *Journal of Personality and Social Psychology, 28*, 218–224.

Silberman, M. (1976). Toward a theory of criminal deterrence. *American Sociological Review, 41*, 442–461.

Simas, E. N. (2016). Perceptions of the heterogeneity of party elites in the United States. *Party Politics*, 1354068816668676.

Sime, J. D. (1983). Affiliative behavior during escape to building exits. *Journal of Environmental Psychology, 3*, 21–41.

Simmel, G. (1902). The number of members as determining the sociological form of the group. I. *American Journal of Sociology, 8*(1), 1–46.

Simmons, R. G. (1991). Presidential address on altruism and sociology. *Sociological Quarterly, 32*, 1–22.

Simon, R. (1997). The meanings individuals attach to role-identities and their implications for mental health. *Journal of Health and Social Behavior, 38*, 256–274.

Simon, R., & Marcussen, K. (1999). Marital transitions, marital beliefs, and mental health. *Journal of Health and Social Behavior, 40*, 111–125.

Simon, W., & Gagnon, J. H. (2003). Sexual scripts: Origins, influences and changes. *Qualitative Sociology, 26*(4), 491–497.

Simons, R. L., Lei, M. K., Beach, S. R., Brody, G. H., Philibert, R. A., & Gibbons, F. X. (2011). Social environment, genes, and aggression: Evidence supporting the differential susceptibility perspective. *American Sociological Review, 76*(6), 883–912.

Simpson, J. A. (1987). The dissolution of romantic relationships: Factors involved in emotional stability and emotional distress. *Journal of Personality and Social Psychology, 53*, 683–692.

Simpson, J. A. (1990). Influence of attachment styles on romantic relationships. *Journal of Personality and Social Psychology, 59*, 971–980.

Simpson, J. A., Gangestad, S. W., & Lerum, M. (1990). Perception of physical attractiveness: Mechanisms involved in maintenance of romantic relationships. *Journal of Personality and Social Psychology, 59*, 1192–1201.

Simpson, J. A., & Rholes, W. S. (2010). Attachment and relationships: Milestones and future directions. *Journal of Social and Personal Relationships, 27*, 173–180.

Sims, J. P. (2016). Reevaluation of the influence of appearance and reflected appraisals for mixed-race identity: The role of consistent inconsistent racial perception. *Sociology of Race and Ethnicity, 2*, 569–583.

Sims, R. R., & Sauser, W. I. (2013). Toward a better understanding of the relationships among received wisdom, groupthink, and organizational ethical culture. *Journal of Management Policy and Practice, 14*(4), 75.

Sinclair, S., Dunn, E., & Lowery, B. S. (2005). The relationship between parental racial attitudes and children's implicit prejudice. *Journal of Experimental Social Psychology, 41*, 283–289.

Sjöström, A., & Gollwitzer, M. (2015). Displaced revenge: Can revenge taste "sweet" if it aims at a different target? *Journal of Experimental Social Psychology, 56*, 191–202.

Skinner, B. F. (1953). *Science and human behavior*. New York: Macmillan.

Skinner, B. F. (1957). *Verbal behavior*. New York: Appleton-Century-Crofts.

Skowronski, J. J., & Carlston, D. E. (1989). Negativity and extremity biases in impression formation: A review of explanations. *Psychological Bulletin, 105*, 131–142.

Skvoretz, J., & Willer, D. (1993). Exclusion and power: A test of four theories of power in exchange networks. *American Sociological Review*, 801–818.

Slade, E. P., & Wissow, L. S. (2004). Spanking in early childhood and later behavior problems: A prospective study of infants and young toddlers. *Pediatrics, 113*, 1321–1330.

Slater, M. D., Henry, K. L., Swaim, R. C., & Anderson, L. L. (2003). Violent media content and aggressiveness in adolescents. A downward spiral model. *Communication Research, 30*, 713–736.

Slater, P. (1963). On social regression. *American Sociological Review, 28*, 339–364.

Sloane, D., & Potrin, R. H. (1986). Religion and delinquency: Cutting through the maze. *Social Forces, 65*, 87–105.

Slomczynski, K. M., Miller, J., & Kohn, M. (1981). Stratification, work, and values: A Polish–United States comparison. *American Sociological Review, 46*, 720–744.

Small, K. H., & Peterson, J. (1981). The divergent perceptions of actors and observers. *Journal of Social Psychology, 113*, 123–132.

Smardon, R. (2007). "I'd rather not take Prozac": Stigma and commodification in antidepressant consumer narratives. *Health: An Interdisciplinary Journal for the Social Study of Health, Illness, and Medicine, 12*, 67–86.

Smith III, A. C., & Kleinman, S. (1989). Managing emotions in medical school: Students' contacts with the living and the dead. *Social Psychology Quarterly, 52*(1), 56–69.

Smith, D. A. (1987). Police response to interpersonal violence: Defining the parameters of legal control. *Social Forces, 65*, 767–782.

Smith, E. R., Fazio, R. H., & Cejka, M. A. (1996). Accessible attitudes influence categorization of multiply categorizable objects. *Journal of Personality and Social Psychology, 71*, 888–898.

Smith, E. R., & Henry, S. (1996). An in-group becomes part of the self: Response time evidence. *Personality and Social Psychology Bulletin, 22*, 635–642.

Smith, E. S., Powers, A. S., & Suarez, G. (2005). If Bill Clinton were a woman: The effectiveness of male and female politicians' account strategies following alleged transgressions. *Political Psychology, 26*, 115–134.

Smith, P. B., & Bond, M. H. (2003). Honoring culture scientifically when doing social psychology. In M. A. Hogg and J. Cooper (Eds.), *Sage handbook of social psychology* (pp. 43–61). Thousand Oaks, CA: Sage.

Smith-Lovin, L. (1990). Emotions as the confirmation and disconfirmation of identity: An affect control model. In T. D. Kemper (Ed.), *Research agendas in the sociology of emotion* (pp. 238–270). Albany: State University of New York Press.

Smith-Lovin L. (1995). The sociology of affect and emotion. In K. S. Cook, G. A. Fine, & J. S. House (Eds.), *Sociological perspectives on social psychology* (pp. 118–148). Boston: Allyn and Bacon.

Smith-Lovin, L., & Robinson, D. (2006). Control theories of identity, action and emotion: In search of testable differences between affect control theory and identity control theory. In K. A. McClelland & T. J. Fararo (Eds.), *Purpose, meaning, and action: Control systems theories in sociology* (pp. 163–188). New York: Palgrave Macmillan.

Sniczck, J. A., & May, D. R. (1990). Conflict of interests and commitment in groups. *Journal of Applied Social Psychology, 20*, 1150–1165.

Snippe, E., Jeronimus, B. F., Bos, E. H., de Jonge, P., & Wichers, M. (2017). The reciprocity of prosocial behavior and positive affect in daily life. *Journal of Personality.* doi:10.1111/jopy.12299

Snyder, C. R., Higgins, R. L., & Stucky, R. J. (1983). *Excuses: Masquerades in search of grace.* New York: Wiley.

Snyder, C. R., Lassegard, M. A., & Ford, C. E. (1986). Distancing after group success and failure: Basking in reflected glory and cutting off reflected failure. *Journal of Personality and Social Psychology, 51*, 382–388.

Snyder, M. (1981). On the self-perpetuating nature of social stereotypes. In D. L. Hamilton (Ed.), *Cognitive processes in stereotyping and intergroup behavior* (pp. 183–212). Hillsdale, NJ: Erlbaum.

Snyder, M., & Swann, W. B. (1978). Hypothesis-testing processes in social interaction. *Journal of Personality and Social Psychology, 36*, 1202–1212.

Snyder, M., Tanke, E. D., & Berscheid, E. (1977). Social perception and interpersonal behavior: On the self-fulfilling nature of social stereotypes. *Journal of Personality and Social Psychology, 35*, 656–666.

Solano, C. H., Batten, P. G., & Parish, E. A. (1982). Loneliness and patterns of self-disclosure. *Journal of Personality and Social Psychology, 43*, 524–531.

Sommer, B. (2001). Menopause. In J. Worell (Ed.), *Encyclopedia of women and gender* (Vol. 2, pp. 729–738). San Diego, CA: Academic Press.

South, S., Trent, K., & Shen, Y. (2001). Changing partners: Toward a macrostructural-opportunity theory of marital dissolution. *Journal of Marriage and Family, 63*, 743–754.

Spano, R., Freilich, J., & Bolland, J. (2008). Gang membership, gun carrying, and employment: Applying routine activities theory to explain violent victimization among inner city, minority youth living in extreme poverty. *Justice Quarterly, 25*, 381–410.

Spencer, J. W. (1987). Self-work in social interaction: Negotiating role-identities. *Social Psychology Quarterly, 50*, 131–142.

Spitz, R. (1945). Hospitalism. *Psychoanalytic Study of the Child, 1*, 53–72.

Spitz, R. (1946). Hospitalism: A follow-up report. *Psychoanalytic Study of the Child, 2*, 113–117.

Spitzmuller, M., & Van Dyne, L. (2013). Proactive and reactive helping: Contrasting the positive consequences of different forms of helping. *Journal of Organizational Behavior, 34*(4), 560–580.

Sporer, S. L., & Schwandt, B. (2007). Moderators of nonverbal indicators of deception: A meta-analysis synthesis. *Psychology, Public Policy, and the Law, 13*, 1–34.

Sprecher, S., & Metts, S. (1989). Development of the "Romantic Beliefs Scale" and examination of the effects of gender and gender role orientation. *Journal of Social and Personal Relationships, 6*, 387–411.

Sprecher, S., & Regan, P. (1998). Passionate and companionate love in courting and young married couples. *Sociological Inquiry, 68*, 163–185.

Sprecher, S., Schmeeckle, M., & Felmlee, D. (2006). The principle of least interest: Inequality in emotional involvement in romantic relationships. *Journal of Family Issues, 27*, 1–26.

Spreitzer, G. M., & Sonenshein, S. (2004). Toward the construct definition of positive deviance. *American Behavioral Scientist, 47*, 828–847.

St. C. Oates, G. (2004). The color of the undergraduate experience and the Black self-concept: Evidence from longitudinal data. *Social Psychology Quarterly, 67*, 16–32.

Staats, A. W., & Staats, C. (1958). Attitudes established by classical conditioning. *Journal of Abnormal and Social Psychology, 57*, 37–40.

Stack, S. (1987). Celebrities and suicide: A taxonomy and analysis, 1948–1983. *American Sociological Review, 52*, 401–412.

Stafford, L., & Canary, D. J. (1991). Maintenance strategies by romantic relationship type, gender, and relational characteristics. *Journal of Social and Personal Relationships, 8*, 217–242.

Stamou, A. G. (2011). Speech style and the construction of social division: Evidence from Greek television. *Language and Communication, 31*, 329–344.

Stanford History Education Group. (2016). Evaluating information: The cornerstone of civic online reasoning. November 22. Retrieved from https://sheg.stanford.edu/upload/V3LessonPlans/Executive%20Summary%2011.21.16.pdf (Accessed January 12, 2017).

Stang, D. J. (1972). Conformity, ability, and self-esteem. *Representative Research in Social Psychology, 3*, 97–103.

Stangor, C., & Schaller, M. (2000). Stereotypes as individual and collective representations. In C. Stangor (Ed.), *Stereotypes and prejudice: Essential readings* (pp. 64–82). Philadelphia, PA: Psychology Press.

Stanhope, E., & Stanhope, P. (1774). *Letters written by the late Right Honourable Philip Dormer Stanhope, Earl of Chesterfield, to his son, Philip Stanhope, Esq. late envoy extraordinary at the court of Dresden: Together with several other pieces on various subjects: In two volumes.* London: Dodsley.

Stanlaw, J., Adachi, N., & Salzmann, Z. (2017). *Language, culture, and society: An introduction to linguistic anthropology* (7th ed.). New York: Routledge.

Stanton, G. (2015). What is the actual divorce rate and risk? *Public Discourse.* www.thepublicdiscourse.com/2015/12/15983/ (Accessed June 11, 2018).

Stapel, D., & Semin, G. (2007). The magic spell of language: Linguistic categories and their perceptual consequences. *Journal of Personality and Social Psychology, 93*, 23–33.

Stasser, G. (1992). Pooling of unshared information during group discussion. In S. Worchel, W. Wood, & J. Simpson (Eds.), *Group process and productivity* (pp. 48–67). Newbury Park, CA: Sage.

Stasser, G., & Titus, W. (1987). Effects of information load and percentage of shared information on the dissemination of unshared information during group discussion. *Journal of Personality and Social Psychology, 53*, 81–93.

Steele, C. M. (1997). A threat in the air: How stereotypes shape the intellectual identities and performance of women and African-Americans. *American Psychologist, 52*, 613–629.

Steele, C. M. (1999, August). Thin ice: "Stereotype threat" and Black college students. *Atlantic Monthly, 284*(2), 44–47, 50–54.

Steele, C. M. (2010). *Whistling Vivaldi: And other clues to how stereotypes affect us.* New York: W. W. Norton.

Steele, C. M., & Aronson, J. (1995). Stereotype threat and the intellectual test performance of African-Americans. *Journal of Personality and Social Psychology, 69*, 797–811.

Steffensmeier, D., & Demuth, S. (2000). Ethnicity and sentencing outcomes in U.S. federal courts: Who is punished more harshly? *American Sociological Review, 65*, 705–729.

Steffensmeier, D. J., & Allan, E. (1996). Gender and crime: Toward a gendered theory of female offending. *Annual Review of Sociology, 22*, 459–487.

Steffensmeier, D. J., & Terry, R. M. (1973). Deviance and respectability: An observational study of reactions to shoplifting. *Social Forces, 51*, 417–426.

Steffy, L. (2005, January 12). CEOs are playing dumb in attempts to get off hook. *Houston Chronicle.* www.chron.com/disp/story.mpl/business/steffy/2988866.html

Stein, J. A., Newcomb, M. D., & Bentler, P. M. (1987). An eight-year study of multiple influences on drug use and drug use consequences. *Journal of Personality and Social Psychology, 53*, 1094–1105.

Steiner, D. D., & Rain, J. S. (1989). Immediate and delayed primacy and recency effects in performance evaluation. *Journal of Applied Psychology, 74*, 136–142.

Steiner, I. D., & Rogers, E. (1963). Alternative responses to dissonance. *Journal of Abnormal and Social Psychology, 66*, 128–136.

Stemple, L., & Meyer, I. H. (2014). The sexual victimization of men in America: New data challenge old assumptions. *American Journal of Public Health, 104*, e19–e26.

Stephan, W. G., & Renfro, C. L. (2002). The role of threat in intergroup relations. In D. M. Mackie & E. R. Smith (Eds.), *From prejudice to intergroup emotions: Differentiated reactions to social groups* (pp. 191–207). New York: Psychology Press.

Stephenson, W. (1953). *The study of behavior.* Chicago: University of Chicago Press.

Steptoe, A., & Wardle, J. (2001). Locus of control and health behaviour revisited: A multivariate analysis of young adults from 18 countries. *British Journal of Psychology, 92*(4), 659–672.

Stermer, S. P., & Burkley, M. (2012). Xbox or seXbox? An examination of sexualized content in video games. *Social and Personality Psychology Compass, 6*(7), 525–535.

Sternberg, R. (1996). Love stories. *Personal Relationships, 3*, 59–79.

Sternberg, R. (1998). *Love is a story: A new theory of relationships.* New York: Oxford University Press.

Stets, J. E. (2003). Emotions and sentiments. In J. DeLamater (Ed.), *Handbook of social psychology* (pp. 309–335). New York: Kluwer/Plenum.

Stets, J. E., & Burke, P. (2000). Identity theory and social identity theory. *Social Psychology Quarterly, 63*, 224–237.

Stets, J. E., & Carter, M. J. (2011). The moral self: Applying identity theory. *Social Psychology Quarterly, 74*(2), 192–215.

Stevenson, M. B., Ver Hoeve, J. N., Roach, M. A., & Leavitt, L. A. (1986). The beginning of conversation: Early patterns of mother–infant vocal responsiveness. *Infant Behavior and Development, 9*, 423–440.

Stewart, A. (2000). Uses of the past: Toward a psychology of generations. Paper presented at the University of Michigan, Ann Arbor.

Stewart, A. (2002). Gender, race, and generation in the psychology of women. Paper presented at the Annual Meeting of the American Psychological Association, Chicago, IL.

Stewart, A. J., Henderson-King, D., Henderson-King, E., & Winter, D. G. (2000). Work and family values: Life scripts in the Midwest in the 1950s. Paper presented at Conference on Work and Families, San Francisco, CA.

Stewart, A. M., & Craig, J. L. (2001). Predicting pro-environmental attitudes and behaviors: A model and a test. *Journal of Environmental Systems, 28*, 293–317.

Stewart, S., Stinnett, H., & Rosenfeld, L. (2000). Sex differences in desired characteristics of short-term and long-term relationship partners. *Journal of Social and Personal Relationships, 17*, 843–853.

Sticca, F., & Perren, S. (2013). Is cyberbullying worse than traditional bullying? Examining the differential roles of medium, publicity, and anonymity for the perceived severity of bullying. *Journal of Youth and Adolescence, 42*(5), 739–750.

Stiff, J. B. (1986). Cognitive processing of persuasive message cues: A meta-analytic review of the effects of supporting information on attitudes. *Communication Monographs, 53*, 75–89.

Stiles, A., & Raney, T. (2004). Relationships among personal space boundaries, peer acceptance, and peer reputation in adolescence. *Journal of Child and Adolescent Psychiatric Nursing, 16*, 29–40.

Stiles, W., Orth, J., Scherwitz, L., Hennrikus, D., & Vallbona, C. (1984). Role behaviors in routine medical interviews with hypertensive patients: A repertoire of verbal exchanges. *Social Psychology Quarterly, 47*, 244–254.

Stokes, J. P. (1985). The relation of social network and individual difference variables to loneliness. *Journal of Personality and Social Psychology, 48*, 981–990.

Stokes, J., & Levin, I. (1986). Gender differences in predicting loneliness from social network characteristics. *Journal of Personality and Social Psychology, 51*, 1069–1074.

Stolzenberg, L., & D'Alessio, S. J. (2008). Co-offending and the age–crime curve. *Journal of Research in Crime and Delinquency, 45*, 65–86.

Stone, G. P. (1962). Appearances and the self. In A. Rose (Ed.), *Human behavior and social processes* (pp. 86–118). Boston: Houghton Mifflin.

Stone, J., Lynch, C. I., Sjomeling, M., & Darley, J. M. (1999). Stereotype threat effects on Black and White athletic performance. *Journal of Personality and Social Psychology, 77*(6), 1213–1227.

Stoner, J. A. F. (1968). Risky and cautious shifts in group decisions: The influence of widely held values. *Journal of Experimental Social Psychology, 4*, 442–459.

Storms, M. D. (1973). Videotape and attribution process: Reversing actors' and observers' points of view. *Journal of Personality and Social Psychology, 27*, 165–175.

Strauman, T. J., Vookles, J., Berenstein, V., Chaiken, S., & Higgins, E. T. (1991). Self-discrepancies and vulnerability to body dissatisfaction and disordered eating. *Journal of Personality and Social Psychology, 61*, 946–956.

Straus, M., & Field, C. (2003). Psychological aggression by American parents: National data on prevalence, chronicity, and severity. *Journal of Marriage and Family, 65*, 795–808.

Straus, M., & Stewart, J. (1999). Corporal punishment by American parents: National data on prevalence, chronicity, severity, and duration, in relation to child and family characteristics. *Clinical Child and Family Psychology Review, 2*, 55–70.

Strenze, T. (2007). Intelligence and socioeconomic success: A meta-analytic review of longitudinal research. *Intelligence, 35*, 401–426.

Strodtbeck, F. L., Simon, R. J., & Hawkins, C. (1965). Social status in jury deliberations. In I. D. Steiner & M. Fishbein (Eds.), *Current studies in social psychology* (pp. 333–342). New York: Holt, Rinehart and Winston.

Stroebe, W., Thompson, V., Insko, C., & Reisman, S. R. (1970). Balance and differentiation in the evaluation of linked attitude objects. *Journal of Personality and Social Psychology, 16*, 38–47.

Struthers, C. W., Eaton, J., Santelli, A. G., Uchiyama, M., & Shirvani, N. (2008). The effects of attributions of intent and apology on forgiveness: When saying sorry may not help the story. *Journal of Experimental Social Psychology, 44*(4), 983–992.

Stryker, S. (1980). *Symbolic interactionism: A social structural version.* Menlo Park, CA: Benjamin/Cummings.

Stryker, S. (1987). The vitalization of symbolic interactionism. *Social Psychology Quarterly, 50*, 83–94.

Stryker, S. (2001). Social psychology. In P. B. Baltes & N. J. Smelser (Eds.), *International encyclopedia of the social and behavioral sciences* (pp. 14409–14413). Oxford: Pergamon.

Stryker, S., & Burke, P. J. (2000). The past, present, and future of an identity theory. *Social Psychology Quarterly, 63*(4), 284–297.

Stryker, S., & Gottlieb, A. (1981). Attribution theory and symbolic interactionism: A comparison. In J. H. Hawes, W. Ickes, & R. F. Kidd (Eds.), *New directions in attribution theory* (Vol. 3, pp. 425–458). Hillsdale, NJ: Erlbaum.

Stryker, S., & Serpe, R. (1981). Commitment, identity salience, and role behavior: Theory and research example. In W. Ickes & E. Knowles (Eds.), *Personality, roles, and social behavior* (pp. 199–218). New York: Springer Verlag.

Stryker, S., & Serpe, R. (1982). Towards a theory of family influence in the socialization of children. In A. Kerckhoff (Ed.), *Research in sociology of education and socialization* (Vol. 4, pp. 47–71). Greenwich, CT: JAI Press.

Stryker, S., & Serpe, R. T. (1994). Identity salience and psychological centrality: Equivalent, overlapping, or complementary concepts? *Social Psychology Quarterly, 57*(1), 16–35.

Stuart, F. (2016). *Down and out and under arrest: Policing and everyday life in Skid Row.* Chicago: University of Chicago Press.

Stucky, T. D., Payton, S. B., & Ottensmann, J. R. (2016). Intra- and inter-neighborhood income inequality and crime. *Journal of Crime and Justice, 39*, 354–362.

Substance Abuse and Mental Health Services Administration. (2012). *The NSDUH Report: Monthly variation in substance use initiation among adolescents.* Rockville, MD: Center for Behavioral Health Statistics and Quality.

Sudman, S., & Bradburn, N. M. (1974). *Response effects in surveys.* Chicago: Aldine.

Sueda, K., & Wiseman, R. L. (1992). Embarrassment remediation in Japan and the United States. *International Journal of Intercultural Relations, 16*(2), 159–173.

Suls, J., Lemos, K., & Stewart, H. L. (2002). Self-esteem, construal, and comparisons with self, friends, and others. *Journal of Personality and Social Psychology, 82,* 252–261.

Suls, J. M., & Miller, R. (Eds.). (1977). *Social comparison processes: Theoretical and empirical perspectives.* New York: Wiley.

Summers, L. (2005, January 14). Remarks at NBER Conference on Diversifying the Science & Engineering Workforce at the Wayback Machine (archived January 30, 2008). www.harvard.edu/president/speeches/summers_2005/nber.php

Sumner, W. G. (1906). *Folkways.* New York: Ginn.

Sumter, S. R., Vandenbosch, L., & Ligtenberg, L. (2017). Love me Tinder: Untangling emerging adults' motivations for using the dating application Tinder. *Telematics and Informatics, 34,* 67–78.

Surra, C. (1990). Research and theory on mate selection and premarital relationships in the 1980s. *Journal of Marriage and Family, 52,* 844–865.

Surra, C., & Longstreth, M. (1990). Similarity of outcomes, interdependence, and conflict in dating relationships. *Journal of Personality and Social Psychology, 59,* 501–516.

Sussman, N. M., & Rosenfeld, H. M. (1982). Influence of culture, language, and sex on conversational distance. *Journal of Personality and Social Psychology, 42,* 66–74.

Sutherland, E., Cressey, D., & Luckenbill, D. (1992). *Principles of criminology* (11th ed.). Dix Hills, NY: General Hall.

Suttles, G. (1968). *The social order of the slum.* Chicago: University of Chicago Press.

Swann, W. B. (1987). Identity negotiation: Where two roads meet. *Journal of Personality and Social Psychology, 53,* 1038–1051.

Swann, W. B., & Predmore, S. C. (1985). Intimates as agents of social support: Sources of consolation or despair? *Journal of Personality and Social Psychology, 49,* 1609–1617.

Swann, W. B., & Schroeder, D. G. (1995). The search for beauty and truth: A framework for understanding reactions to evaluations. *Personality and Social Psychology Bulletin, 21,* 1307–1318.

Sweeney, P. D. (1990). Distributive justice and pay satisfaction: A field test of an equity theory prediction. *Journal of Business and Psychology, 4,* 329–341.

Swigert, V., & Farrell, R. (1977). Normal homicides and the law. *American Sociological Review, 42,* 16–32.

Sykes, G. M., & Matza, D. (1957). Techniques of neutralization: A theory of delinquency. *American Sociological Review, 22,* 664–670.

Syme, L. (2008). Reducing racial and social-class inequalities in health: The need for a new approach. *Health Affairs, 27,* 456–459.

Syme, S. L., & Berkman, L. (1976). Social class, susceptibility, and sickness. *American Journal of Epidemiology, 104,* 1–8.

Symons, D. (1992). On the use and misuse of Darwinism in the study of human behavior. In J. Barkow, L. Cosmides, & J. Tooby (Eds.), *The adapted mind: Evolutionary psychology and the generation of culture* (pp. 137–159). New York: Oxford University Press.

Tagler, M. J., & Cozzarelli, C. (2013). Feelings toward the poor and beliefs about the causes of poverty: The role of affective-cognitive consistency in help-giving. *Journal of Psychology, 147*(6), 517–539.

Tajfel, H. (1981). *Human groups and social categories: Studies in social psychology.* Cambridge: Cambridge University Press.

Tajfel, H. (1982a). *Social identity and intergroup relations.* Cambridge: Cambridge University Press.

Tajfel, H. (1982b). Social psychology of intergroup relations. *Annual Review of Psychology, 33,* 1–39.

Tajfel, H., & Billig, M. (1974). Familiarity and categorization in intergroup behavior. *Journal of Experimental Social Psychology, 10,* 159–170.

Tajfel, H., & Turner, J. C. (1979). An integrative theory of intergroup conflict. In W. G. Austin & S. Worchel (Eds.), *The social psychology of intergroup relations* (pp. 33–47). Monterey, CA: Brooks/Cole.

Tajfel, H., & Turner, J. (1986). The social identity theory of intergroup behavior. In S. Worchel & W. G. Austin (Eds.), *Psychology of intergroup relations* (2nd ed., pp. 7–24). Chicago: Nelson-Hall.

Tanford, S., & Penrod, S. (1984). Social influence model: A formal integration of research on majority and minority influence processes. *Psychological Bulletin, 95,* 189–225.

Tangney, J. P. (1995). Shame and guilt in interpersonal relations. In J. P. Tangney & K. W. Fisher (Eds.), *The psychology of guilt, shame, embarrassment and pride* (pp. 114–139). New York: Guilford.

Tangney, J. P., Miller, R. S., Flicker, L., & Barlow, D. H. (1996). Are shame, guilt, and embarrassment distinct emotions? *Journal of Personality and Social Psychology, 70*(6), 1256–1269.

Tannen, D. (1991). *You just don't understand: Women and men in conversation.* New York: Morrow.

Tashiro, T., Frazier, P., & Berman, M. (2006). Stress-related growth following divorce and relationship dissolution. In M. Fine & J. Harvey (Eds.), *Handbook of divorce and relationship dissolution* (pp. 361–384). Mahwah, NJ: Erlbaum.

Tatangelo, G., McCabe, M., Mellor, D., & Mealey, A. (2016). A systematic review of body dissatisfaction and sociocultural messages related to the body among preschool children. *Body Image, 18,* 86–95.

Taylor, D. A., & Belgrave, F. Z. (1986). The effects of perceived intimacy and valence on self-disclosure reciprocity. *Personality and Social Psychology Bulletin, 12,* 247–255.

Taylor, D. M., & Moghaddam, F. M. (1987). *Theories of intergroup relations: International social psychological perspectives.* New York: Praeger.

Taylor, D. M., & Royer, L. (1980). Group processes affecting anticipated language choice in intergroup relations. In H. Giles, W. P. Robinson, & P. M. Smith (Eds.), *Language: Social psychological perspectives* (pp. 185–192). New York: Pergamon.

Taylor, S. E. (1981). A categorization approach to stereotyping. In D. L. Hamilton (Ed.), *Cognitive processes in stereotyping and intergroup behavior* (pp. 83–114). Hillsdale, NJ: Erlbaum.

Taylor, S. E., & Crocker, J. (1981). Schematic bases of social information processing. In E. T. Higgins, C. P. Herman, & M. P. Zanna (Eds.), *Social cognition: The Ontario symposium* (Vol. 1, pp. 89–134). Hillsdale, NJ: Erlbaum.

Taylor, S. E., & Fiske, S. T. (1978). Salience, attention, and attribution: Top of the head phenomena. In L. Berkowitz (Ed.), *Advances in experimental social psychology* (Vol. 11, pp. 249–288). New York: Academic Press.

Taylor, S. E., Fiske, S. T., Etcoff, N. L., & Ruderman, A. J. (1978). The categorical and contextual bases of person memory and stereotyping. *Journal of Personality and Social Psychology, 36*, 778–793.

Taylor, S. P. (1967). Aggressive behavior and physiological arousal as a function of provocation and the tendency to inhibit aggression. *Journal of Personality, 35*, 297–310.

Taylor, V. A., Halstead, D., & Haynes, P. J. (2010). Consumer responses to Christian religious symbols in advertising. *Journal of Advertising, 39*, 79–92.

Teachman, J. (1987). Family background, educational resources, and educational attainment. *American Sociological Review, 52*, 548–557.

Tedeschi, J. T., Schlenker, B. R., & Lindskold, S. (1972). The exercise of power and influence: The source of influence. In J. T. Tedeschi (Ed.), *The social influence processes* (pp. 287–345). Chicago: Aldine-Atherton.

Terry, D. J., & Hogg, M. A. (1996). Group norms and the attitude-behavior relationship: A role for group identification. *Personality and Social Psychology Bulletin, 22*, 776–793.

Tesser, A., & Campbell, J. (1983). Self-definition and self-evaluation maintenance. In J. Suls & A. G. Greenwald (Eds.), *Psychological perspectives on the self* (Vol. 2, pp. 1–31). Hillsdale, NJ: Erlbaum.

Teti, D. M., & Lamb, M. E. (1989). Socioeconomic and marital outcomes of adolescent marriage, adolescent childbirth, and their co-occurrence. *Journal of Marriage and Family, 51*, 203–212.

Teti, D., Lamb, M., & Elster, A. (1987). Long-range socioeconomic and marital consequences of adolescent marriage in three cohorts of adult males. *Journal of Marriage and Family, 49*, 499–506.

Tetlock, P. E. (1986). A value pluralism model of ideological reasoning. *Journal of Personality and Social Psychology, 50*, 819–827.

Tetlock, P. E., & Manstead, A. S. R. (1985). Impression management versus intrapsychic explanations in social psychology: A useful dichotomy? *Psychological Review, 92*, 59–77.

Thakerar, J. N., Giles, H., & Cheshire, J. (1982). Psychological and linguistic parameters of speech accommodation theory. In C. Fraser & K. R. Scherer (Eds.), *Advances in the social psychology of language* (pp. 205–255). Cambridge: Cambridge University Press.

Thibaut, J., & Kelley, H. (1959). *The social psychology of groups*. New York: Wiley.

Thibaut, J. W., & Walker, L. (1975). *Procedural justice: A psychological analysis*. New York: Wiley.

Thibaut, J. W., & Walker, L. (1978). A theory of procedure. *California Law Review, 66*, 541–566.

Thoits, P. A. (1985). Self-labelling processes in mental illness: The role of emotional deviance. *American Journal of Sociology, 91*, 221–249.

Thoits, P. A. (1989). The sociology of emotions. *Annual Review of Sociology, 15*, 317–342.

Thoits, P. A. (1990). Emotional deviance: Research agendas. *Research Agendas in the Sociology of Emotions, 180*, 203.

Thoits, P. A. (1995). Social psychology: The interplay between sociology and psychology. *Social Forces, 73*(4), 1231–1243.

Thoits, P. A. (2005). Differential labeling of mental illness by social status: A new look at an old problem. *Journal of Health and Social Behavior, 46*, 102–119.

Thoits, P. A. (2010). Stress and health: Major findings and policy implications. *Journal of Health and Social Behavior, 51*(S), 41–53.

Thoits, P. A. (2011). Resisting the stigma of mental illness. *Social Psychology Quarterly, 74*(1), 6–28.

Thomas, E., & Reaser, J. (2004). Delimiting perceptual cues used for the ethnic labeling of African American and European American voices. *Journal of Sociolinguistics, 8*, 54–87.

Thomas, W. I., & Thomas, D. S. (1928). *The child in America: Behavior problems and programs*. New York: Alfred A. Knopf.

Thomas, W. I., & Znaniecki, F. (1918). *The Polish peasant in Europe and America* (Vol. 1). Boston: Badger.

Thompson, E. H., & Pleck, J. H. (1986). The structure of male role norms. *American Behavioral Scientist, 29*, 531–543.

Thompson, L. E., Barnett, J. R., & Pearce, J. R. (2009). Scared straight? Fear-appeal anti-smoking campaigns, risk, self-efficacy and addiction. *Health, Risk & Society, 11*(2), 181–196.

Thompson, T. L., & Zerbinos, E. (1995). Gender roles in animated cartoons: Has the picture changed in 20 years? *Sex Roles, 32*, 651–673.

Thomsen, C. T., & Borgida, E. (1996). Throwing out the baby with the bathwater? Let's not overstate the overselling of the base rate fallacy. *Behavioral and Brain Sciences, 19*, 39–40.

Thorlundsson, T. (1987). Bernstein's sociolinguistics: An empirical test in Iceland. *Social Forces, 65*, 695–718.

Thornberry, T. D., & Christenson, R. L. (1984). Juvenile justice decision-making as a longitudinal process. *Social Forces, 63*, 433–444.

Thorndike, E. L. (1920). A constant error in psychological ratings. *Journal of Applied Psychology, 4*, 25–29.

Thorne, B. (1993). *Gender play: Girls and boys in school*. New Brunswick, NJ: Rutgers University Press.

Thornhill, R., & Grammar, K. (1999). The body and face of woman: One ornament that signals quality? *Evolution and Human Behavior, 20*, 105–120.

Thornton, B., Lovley, A., Ryckman, R. M., & Gold, J. A. (2009). Playing dumb and knowing it all: Competitive orientation and impression management strategies. *Individual Differences Research, 7*, 265–271.

Thye, S. R. (2000). A status value theory of power in exchange relations. *American Sociological Review, 65,* 407–432.

Tittle, C., Broidy, L., & Gertz, M. (2008). Strain, crime, and contingencies. *Justice Quarterly, 25,* 283–312.

Tjaden, P. & Thoennes, N. (2000). Full report of the prevalence, incidence, and consequences of violence against women. Washington, DC: U.S. Department of Justice.

Toch, H. (1996). The violence-prone police officer. In W. A. Geller & H. Toch (Eds.), *Police violence: Understanding and controlling police abuse of force* (pp. 94–112). New Haven, CT: Yale University Press.

Toma, C., Hancock, J., & Ellison, N. (2008). Separating fact from fiction: An examination of deceptive self-presentation in online dating profiles. *Personality and Social Psychology Bulletin, 34,* 1023–1036.

Tormala, Z. L., Briñol, P., & Petty, R. E. (2007). Multiple roles for source credibility under high elaboration: It's all in the timing. *Social Cognition, 25*(4), 536–552.

Touhey, J. (1979). Sex-role stereotyping and individual differences in liking for the physically attractive. *Social Psychology Quarterly, 42,* 285–289.

Towers, S., Gomez-Lievano, A., Khan, M., Mubayi, A., & Castillo-Chavez, C. (2015). Contagion in mass killings and school shootings. *PLOS ONE* 10(7), e0117259. Doi:10.1371/journal.pone.0117259.

Triandis, H. C. (1989). The self and social behavior in differing cultural contexts. *Psychological Review, 96,* 506–520.

Triandis, H. C. (1995). *Individualism and collectivism.* Boulder, CO: Westview Press.

Triandis, H. C., McCusker, C., & Hui, C. H. (1990). Multimethod probes of individualism and collectivism. *Journal of Personality and Social Psychology, 59,* 1006–1020.

Trice, A. D., & Woods, P. J. (1979). The role of pretest and test similarity in producing helpless or reactant responding in humans. *Bulletin of the Psychonomic Society, 14*(6), 457–459.

Trivers, R. L. (1971). The evolution of reciprocal altruism. *The Quarterly Review of Biology, 46*(1), 35–57.

Trope, Y., & Cohen, O. (1989). Perceptual and inferential determinants of behavior-correspondent attributions. *Journal of Experimental Social Psychology, 25*(2), 142–158.

Trope, Y., Cohen, O., & Maoz, Y. (1988). The perceptual and inferential effects of situational inducements on dispositional attribution. *Journal of Personality and Social Psychology, 55*(2), 165–177.

Trotter, P. B. (2010). The influence of parental romantic relationships on college students' attitudes about romantic relationships. *College Student Journal, 44,* 71–83.

Trouilloud, D., & Amiel, C. (2011). Reflected appraisals of coaches, parents and teammates: A key component of athletes' self? *International Journal of Sport Psychology, 42,* 97–114.

Truman, J. L., & Langton, L. (2015). *Criminal victimization, 2014.* Bureau of Justice Statistics. U.S. Department of Justice. NCJ 248973. https://www.bjs.gov/content/pub/pdf/cv14.pdf

Turner, J. C. (1981). The experimental social psychology of intergroup behavior. In J. C. Turner & H. Giles (Eds.), *Intergroup behavior* (pp. 66–101). Oxford: Blackwell.

Turner, J. C. (1987). *Rediscovering the social group: A self-categorization theory.* Oxford: Blackwell.

Turner, J. S. (2011). Sex and the spectacle of music videos: An examination of the portrayal of race and sexuality in music videos. *Sex Roles, 64,* 173–191.

Turner, R. H. (1978). The role and the person. *American Journal of Sociology, 84,* 1–23.

Turner, R. H. (1990). Role change. In W. R. Scott & J. Blake (Eds.), *Annual Review of Sociology* (Vol. 16, pp. 87–110). Palo Alto, CA: Annual Reviews.

Tversky, A., & Kahneman, D. (1974). Judgment under uncertainty: Heuristics and biases. *Science, 185,* 1124–1131.

Twenge, J. M. (2000). The age of anxiety? Birth cohort change in anxiety and neuroticism, 1952–1993. *Journal of Personality and Social Psychology, 79,* 1007–1021.

Twenge, J., & Crocker, J. (2002). Race and self-esteem: Meta-analyses comparing Whites, Blacks, Hispanics, Asians, and American Indians and comment on Gray-Little and Hafdahl (2000). *Psychological Bulletin, 128,* 371–408.

Twenge, J. M., Zhang, L., & Im, C. (2004). It's beyond my control: A cross-temporal meta-analysis of increasing externality in locus of control, 1960–2002. *Personality and Social Psychology Review, 8*(3), 308–319.

Tyler, T., & Lind, E. A. (1992). Relational model of authority in groups. In M. P. Zanna (Ed.), *Advances in experimental social psychology* (Vol. 25, pp. 115–191). San Diego, CA: Academic Press.

Tyler, T. R., Boeckmann, R. J., Smith, H. J., & Huo, Y. J. (1997). *Social justice in a diverse society.* Boulder, CO: Westview Press.

Tyler, T. R., & Sears, D. O. (1977). Coming to like obnoxious people when we must live with them. *Journal of Personality and Social Psychology, 35,* 200–211.

Uggen, C., & Thompson, M. (2003). The socioeconomic determinants of ill-gotten gains: Within-person changes in drug use and illegal earnings. *American Journal of Sociology, 109,* 146–185.

Umberson, D., Anderson, K., Glick, J., & Shapiro, A. (1998). Domestic violence, personal control, and gender. *Journal of Marriage and Family, 60*(2), 442–452.

Umberson, D., Williams, K., & Anderson, K. (2002). Violent behavior: A measure of emotional upset? *Journal of Health and Social Behavior, 43*(2), 189–206.

Unamuno, V. (2008). Multilingual switch in peer classroom interaction. *Linguistics and Education, 19,* 1–19.

U.S. Bureau of Labor Statistics. (2012). Unemployment in 2012. https://www.bls.gov/opub/ted/2012/ted_20120710.htm

U.S. Bureau of Labor Statistics. (2016a). 2015 Survey of occupational injuries & illnesses: Summary estimates charts package. https://www.bls.gov/iif/oshwc/osh/os/osch0057.pdf

U.S. Bureau of Labor Statistics. (2016b). Employment characteristics of families – 2015. Washington, DC: U.S. Department of Labor, USDL-16-0795.

U.S. Bureau of Labor Statistics. (2016c). Fatal occupational injuries. https://www.bls.gov/iif/oshwc/cfoi/cfch0015.pdf

U.S. Bureau of Labor Statistics. (2017) Labor force statistics from the current population survey. https://www.bls.gov/cps/earnings.htm

U.S. Bureau of the Census. (2010). *Households and families: 2010 Census brief.* Washington, DC: Bureau of the Census.

U.S. Bureau of the Census. (2014). America's Families and Living Arrangements, Table C3. www.census.gov/hhes/families/data/cps2014C.htm

U.S. Department of Health and Human Services. (2010). *Code of federal regulations, Title 45, Part 46, "Protection of Human Subjects."* www.hhs.gov/ohrp/humansubjects/guidance/45cfr46.htm

U.S. Department of Justice. (2017, June 16). Sexual assault. Retrieved from https://www.justice.gov/ovw/sexual-assault

Utne, M. K., & Kidd, R. F. (1980). Equity and attribution. In G. Mikula (Ed.), *Justice and social interaction: Experimental and theoretical contributions, from psychological research* (pp. 63–93). New York: Springer Verlag.

Vaccaro, C. A., Schrock, D. P., & McCabe, J. M. (2011). Managing emotional manhood: Fighting and fostering fear in mixed martial arts. *Social Psychology Quarterly, 74*(4), 414–437.

Valle, V. A., & Frieze, I. H. (1976). Stability of causal attributions as a mediator in changing expectations for success. *Journal of Personality and Social Psychology, 35,* 579–589.

van Aken, M., van Lieshout, C., & Haselager, G. (1996). Adolescents' competence and the mutuality of their self-descriptions and descriptions of them provided by others. *Journal of Youth and Adolescence, 25,* 285–306.

van Baaren, R., Holland, R., Kawakami, K., & van Knippenberg, A. (2004). Mimicry and prosocial behavior. *Psychological Science, 15,* 71–74.

van Baaren, R., Holland, R., Steenaert, B., & van Knippenberg, A. (2003). Mimicry for money: Behavioral consequences of imitation. *Journal of Experimental Social Psychology, 39,* 393–398.

Van Cappellen, P., Corneille, O., Cols, S., & Saroglou, V. (2011). Beyond mere compliance to authoritative figures: Religious priming increases conformity to informational influence among submissive people. *International Journal for the Psychology of Religion, 21*(2), 97–105.

Vandell, D. L., Belsky, J., Burchinal, M., Steinberg, L., & Vandergrift, N. (2010). Do effects of early child care extend to age 15 years? Results from the NICHD Study of Early Child Care and Youth Development. *Child Development, 81,* 737–756.

van Dellen, M. R., Campbell, W. K., Hoyle, R. H., & Bradfield, E. K. (2011). Overcompensating, resisting, and breaking: A meta-analytic examination of theoretical models of reactions to self-esteem threat. *Personality and Social Psychology Review, 15,* 51–74.

van De Rakt, M., Nieuwbeerta, P., & Apel, R. (2009). Association of criminal convictions between family members: Effects of siblings, fathers and mothers. *Criminal Behavior and Mental Health, 19,* 94–108.

Vanderlaan, D. P., & Vasey, P. L. (2012). Relationship status and elevated avuncularity in Samoan fa'afafine. *Personal Relationships, 19*(2), 326–339.

van Emmerik, A., Kamphuis, J., Hulsbosch, A., & Emmelkamp, P. (2002). Single session debriefing after psychological trauma: A meta-analysis. *The Lancet, 360,* 766–771.

van Leeuwen, M. H. D., & Maas, I. (2010). Historical studies of social mobility and stratification. In K. Cook & D. S. Masse (Eds.), *Annual Review of Sociology,* (Vol. 36, pp. 429–451).

Van Maanen, J. (1991). The smile factory: Work at Disneyland. In P. J. Frost, L. Moore, M. Louis, C. Lundberg, & J. Martin (Eds.). *Reframing organizational culture* (pp. 58–76). Newbury Park, CA: Sage.

Van Noorden, R. (2011). The trouble with retractions. *Nature, 478*(7367), 26–28.

van Prooijen, J. W. (2017). Why education predicts decreased belief in conspiracy theories. *Applied Cognitive Psychology, 31*(1), 50–58.

Vega, V., & Malamuth, N. (2007). The role of pornography in the context of general and specific risk factors. *Aggressive Behavior, 33,* 104–117.

Vega, W. A., & Rumbaut, R. G. (1991). Ethnic minorities and mental health. *Annual Review of Sociology, 17,* 351–383.

Verbrugge, L. (1979). Marital status and health. *Journal of Marriage and Family, 41,* 267–285.

Vespa, J., Lewis, J.M., & Kreider, R.M. (2013). America's families and living arrangements, 2012. *Current Population Reports,* P20-570. Washington, DC: U.S. Census Bureau.

Vinokur, A. D., Price, R. H., & Caplan, R. D. (1996). Hard times and hurtful partners: How financial strain affects depression and relationship satisfaction of unemployed persons and their spouses. *Journal of Personality and Social Psychology, 71,* 166–179.

Vishwanath, A. (2014). Negative public perceptions of juvenile diabetics: Applying attribution theory to understand the public's stigmatizing views. *Health Communication, 29,* 516–526.

Vittengl, J., & Holt, C. S. (2000). Getting acquainted: The relationship of self-disclosure and social attraction to positive affect. *Journal of Social and Personal Relationships, 17,* 53–66.

Volling, B. L., & Belsky, J. (1991). Multiple determinants of father involvement during infancy in dual career and single-earner families. *Journal of Marriage and Family, 53,* 461–474.

von Baeyer, C. L., Sherk, D. L., & Zanna, M. P. (1981). Impression management in the job interview: When the female applicant meets the male (chauvinist) interviewer. *Personality and Social Psychology Bulletin, 7,* 45–51.

von Hippel, W., Hawkins, C., & Schooler, J. (2001). Stereotype distinctiveness: How counterstereotypic behavior shapes the self-concept. *Journal of Personality and Social Psychology, 81,* 193–205.

Vonk, R. (2002). Self-serving interpretations of flattery: Why ingratiation works. *Journal of Personality and Social Psychology, 82,* 515–526.

Voss, M., Nylén, L., Floderus, B., Diderichsen, F., & Terry, P. (2004). Unemployment and early cause-specific mortality: A study based on the Swedish Twin Registry. *American Journal of Public Health, 94,* 2155–2161.

Voydanoff, P. (1990). Economic distress and family relations: A review of the eighties. *Journal of Marriage and Family, 52*, 1099–1115.

Vygotsky, L. S. (1962). *Thought and language.* Cambridge, MA: MIT Press.

Wagner, S. H. (2013). Leadership and responses to organizational crisis. *Industrial and Organizational Psychology, 6*(2), 140–144.

Waldron, I. (1976). Why do women live longer than men? *Social Science and Medicine, 10*, 349–362.

Walker, L. L., & Heyns, R. W. (1962). *An anatomy for conformity.* Englewood Cliffs, NJ: Prentice Hall.

Wallin, P. (1950). Cultural contradictions and sex roles: A repeat study. *American Sociological Review, 15*, 288–293.

Wallis, C. (2010). Performing gender: A content analysis of gender display in music videos. *Sex Roles, 64*, 160–172.

Wallston, K. A. (2005). The validity of the multidimensional health locus of control scales. *Journal of Health Psychology, 10*(5), 623–631.

Walsh, E. J., & Taylor, M. (1982). Occupational correlates of multidimensional self-esteem: Comparisons among garbage collectors, bartenders, professors, and other workers. *Sociology and Social Research, 66*, 252–258.

Walster [Hatfield], E., Aronson, E., & Abrahams, D. (1966). On increasing the persuasiveness of a low prestige communicator. *Journal of Experimental Social Psychology, 2*, 325–342.

Walster [Hatfield], E., Aronson, V., Abrahams, D., & Rottman, L. (1966). The importance of physical attractiveness in dating behavior. *Journal of Personality and Social Psychology, 4*, 508–516.

Walster [Hatfield], E., Berscheid, E., & Walster, G. W. (1973). New directions in equity research. *Journal of Personality and Social Psychology, 25*, 151–176.

Walster [Hatfield], E., Walster, G. W., & Berscheid, E. (1978). *Equity: Theory and research.* Boston: Allyn and Bacon.

Walster [Hatfield], E., Walster, G. W., & Traupmann, J. (1978). Equity and premarital sex. *Journal of Personality and Social Psychology, 36*, 82–92.

Walters, J., & Walters, L. (1980). Parent–child relationships: A review, 1970–1979. *Journal of Marriage and Family, 42*, 807–822.

Walther, J. B. (2007). Selective self-presentation in computer-mediated communication: Hyperpersonal dimensions of technology, language, and cognition. *Computers in Human Behavior, 23*, 2538–2557.

Ward, L. M. (2003). Understanding the role of entertainment media in the sexual socialization of American youth: A review of empirical research. *Developmental Review, 23*, 347–388.

Ward, L. M., & Friedman, K. (2006). Using TV as a guide: Associations between television viewing and adolescents' sexual attitudes and behavior. *Journal of Research on Adolescence, 16*, 133–156.

Ward, L., Hansbrough, E., & Walker, E. (2005). Contributions of music video exposure to Black adolescents' gender and sexual schemas. *Journal of Adolescent Research, 20*, 143–166.

Warner, D. F., & Hayward, M. D. (2006). Early-life origins of the race gap in men's mortality. *Journal of Health and Social Behavior, 47*, 209–226.

Watkins, P. L., & Whaley, D. (2000). Gender role stressors and women's health. In R. Eisler & M. Hersen (Eds.), *Handbook of gender, culture, and health* (pp. 43–62). Mahwah, NJ: Erlbaum.

Watson, D. (1982). The actor and the observer: How are their perceptions of causality divergent? *Psychological Bulletin, 92*, 682–700.

Watts, B. L., Messe, L. A., & Vallacher, R. R. (1982). Toward understanding sex differences in pay allocation: Agency, communion, and reward distribution behavior. *Sex Roles, 8*, 1175–1187.

Webb, E. J., Campbell, D. J., Schwartz, R. D., & Sechrest, L. (1981). *Unobtrusive measures: Nonreactive research in the social sciences* (2nd ed.). Chicago: Rand McNally.

Webb, E. J., Campbell, D. J., Schwartz, R. D., & Sechrest, L. (1999). *Unobtrusive Measures, Revised Edition* (Vol. 2). Thousand Oaks, CA: Sage.

Weber, R., & Crocker, J. (1983). Cognitive processes in the revision of stereotypic beliefs. *Journal of Personality and Social Psychology, 45*, 961–977.

Webster, M., & Foschi, M. (1988). *Status generalization: New theory and research.* Stanford, CA: Stanford University Press.

Wee, S. (2013). Development and initial validation of the willingness to compromise scale. *Journal of Career Assessment, 21*(4), 487–501.

Wegner, D. M., Lane, J. D., & Dimitri, S. (1994). The allure of secret relationships. *Journal of Personality and Social Psychology, 66*, 287–300.

Weigand, B. (1994). Black money in Belize: The ethnicity and social structure of black-market crime. *Social Forces, 73*, 135–154.

Weigel, D., & Murray, C. (2000). The paradox of stability and change in relationships: What does chaos theory offer for the study of romantic relationships? *Journal of Social and Personal Relationships, 17*, 425–449.

Weigel, R. H., & Newman, L. (1976). Increasing attitude-behavior correspondence by broadening the scope of the behavioral measure. *Journal of Personality and Social Psychology, 33*, 793–802.

Weinberg, J. D., Freese, J., & McElhattan, D. (2014). Comparing data characteristics and results of an online factorial survey between a population-based and a crowdsource-recruited sample. *Sociological Science, 1*, 292–310.

Weinberg, M. (1976). The nudist management of respectability. In M. Weinberg (Ed.), *Sex research: Studies from the Kinsey Institute* (pp. 336–345). New York: Oxford University Press.

Weiner, B. (1985). An attributional theory of achievement motivation and emotion. *Psychological Review, 92*, 548–573.

Weiner, B. (1986). *An attributional theory of motivation and emotion.* New York: Springer Verlag.

Weiner, B., Amirkhan, J., Folkes, V. S., & Verette, J. A. (1987). An attributional analysis of excuse giving: Studies of a naive theory of emotion. *Journal of Personality and Social Psychology, 52*, 316–324.

Weiner, B., Heckhausen, H., Meyer, W. U., & Cook, R. E. (1972). Causal ascriptions and achievement behavior: A conceptual analysis of effort and reanalysis of locus of control. *Journal of Personality and Social Psychology*, *21*, 239–248.

Weiner, B., Perry, R. P., & Magnusson, J. (1988). An attributional analysis of reactions to stigmas. *Journal of Personality and Social Psychology*, *55*, 738–748.

Weinstein, E. A., & Deutschberger, P. (1963). Some dimensions of altercasting. *Sociometry*, *26*, 454–466.

Weiss, R. S. (1973). *Loneliness: The experience of emotional and social isolation*. Cambridge, MA: MIT Press.

Weissman, J. S., Pratt, L. A., Miller, E. A., & Parker, J. D. (2015). *Serious psychological distress among adults, United States, 2009–2013*. U.S. Department of Health and Human Services, Centers for Disease Control and Prevention, National Center for Health Statistics.

Weitzer, R. (1991). Prostitutes' rights in the United States: The failure of a movement. *Sociological Quarterly*, *32*, 23–41.

Weitzman, L. J., Eifler, D., Hokada, E., & Ross, K. (1972). Sex role socialization in picture books for pre-school children. *American Journal of Sociology*, *77*, 1125–1150.

Welles, B. F., & Contractor, N. (2014). Individual motivations and network effects: A multilevel analysis of the structure of online social relationships. *Annals, AAPSS*, *659*, 180–190.

Wellman, B., & Worley, S. (1990). Different strokes from different folks: Community ties and social support. *American Journal of Sociology*, *96*, 558–588.

Werkman, W., Wigboldus, D., & Semin, G. (1999). Children's communication of linguistic intergroup bias and its impact on cognitive inferences. *European Journal of Social Psychology*, *29*, 95–104.

Werner, C., & Parmelee, P. (1979). Similarity of activity preferences among friends: Those who play together stay together. *Social Psychology Quarterly*, *42*, 62–66.

Western, B. (2002). The impact of incarceration on wage mobility and inequality. *American Sociological Review*, *67*, 526–546.

Westfall, J., Judd, C. M., & Kenny, D. A. (2015). Replicating studies in which samples of participants respond to samples of stimuli. *Perspectives on Psychological Science*, *10*, 390–399.

Weyant, J. (1996). Application of compliance techniques to direct-mail requests for charitable donations. *Psychology and Marketing*, *13*, 157–170.

Whalen, M. R., & Zimmerman, D. H. (1987). Sequential and institutional contexts in calls for help. *Social Psychology Quarterly*, *50*, 172–185.

White, G. (1980). Physical attractiveness and courtship progress. *Journal of Personality and Social Psychology*, *39*, 660–668.

White, K. M., Hogg, M. A., & Terry, D. J. (2002). Improving attitude-behavior correspondence through exposure to normative support from a salient ingroup. *Basic and Applied Social Psychology*, *24*(2), 91–103.

Whitt, H. P., & Meile, R. L. (1985). Alignment, magnification, and snowballing: Processes in the definition of symptoms of mental illness. *Social Forces*, *63*, 682–697.

Whitty, M. (2004). Cyber-flirting: An examination of men's and women's flirting behaviour both offline and on the Internet. *Behaviour Change*, *21*, 115–126.

Whorf, B. L. (1956). Language, mind, and reality. In J. B. Carroll (Ed.), *Language, thought, and reality* (pp. 245–270). Cambridge, MA: MIT Press.

Wicklund, R. A. (1975). Objective self-awareness. In L. Berkowitz (Ed.), *Advances in experimental social psychology* (Vol. 8, pp. 233–275). New York: Academic Press.

Wicklund, R. A., & Brehm, J. (1976). *Perspectives on cognitive dissonance*. Hillsdale, NJ: Erlbaum.

Wicklund, R. A., & Frey, D. (1980). Self-awareness theory: When the self makes a difference. In D. M. Wegner & R. R. Vallacher (Eds.), *The self in social psychology* (pp. 54ff.). New York: Oxford University Press.

Wickrama, K., Conger, R. D., Lorenz, F. O., & Matthews, L. (1995). Role identity, role satisfaction, and perceived physical health. *Social Psychology Quarterly*, *58*, 270–283.

Wickrama, K. A. S., Conger, R., Wallace, L. E., & Elder, G. H. (1999). The inter-generational transmission of health-risk behaviors: Adolescent lifestyles and gender moderating effects. *Journal of Health and Social Behavior*, *40*, 258–272.

Wickrama, K. A. S., Lorenz, F. O., Conger, R. D., & Elder, G. H. (1997). Marital quality and physical illness: A latent growth curve analysis. *Journal of Marriage and Family*, *59*, 143–155.

Wiepking, P. (2010). Democrats support international relief and the upper class donates to art? How opportunity, incentives and confidence affect donations to different types of charitable organizations. *Social Science Research*, *39*(6), 1073–1087.

Wiepking, P., & Heijnen, M. (2011). The giving standard: Conditional cooperation in the case of charitable giving. *International Journal of Nonprofit and Voluntary Sector Marketing*, *16*, 13–22.

Wiepking, P., & van Leeuwen, M. H. (2013). Picturing generosity: Explaining the success of national campaigns in the Netherlands. *Nonprofit and Voluntary Sector Quarterly*, *42*(2), 262–284.

Wiggins, J. S., Wiggins, N., & Conger, J. C. (1968). Correlates of heterosexual somatic preference. *Journal of Personality and Social Psychology*, *10*, 82–90.

Wike, T. L., & Fraser, M. W. (2009). School shootings: Making sense of the senseless. *Aggression and Violent Behavior*, *14*(3), 162–169.

Wilder, D. A. (1981). Perceiving persons as a group: Categorization and intergroup relations. In D. L. Hamilton (Ed.), *Cognitive processes in stereotyping and intergroup behavior* (pp. 213–257). Hillsdale, NJ: Erlbaum.

Wilkins, A. C. (2008a). "Happier than non-Christians": Collective emotions and symbolic boundaries among Evangelical Christians. *Social Psychology Quarterly*, *71*(3), 281–301.

Wilkins, A. C. (2008b). *Wannabes, Goths, and Christians: The boundaries of sex, style, and status*. Chicago: University of Chicago Press.

Willer, D., & Walker, H. A. (2007). *Building experiments: Testing social theory*. Stanford, CA: Stanford University Press.

Willer, R., Conlon, B., Rogalin, C. L., & Wojnowicz, M. T. (2013). Overdoing gender: A test of the masculine overcompensation thesis. *American Journal of Sociology, 118*, 980–1022.

Willer, R., Feinberg, M., & Wetts, R. (2016). Threats to racial status promote Tea Party support among white Americans. Available at SSRN: https://ssrn.com/abstract=2770186 or http://dx.doi.org/10.2139/ssrn.2770186

Williams, D., Gonzalez, H., Neighbors, H., Nesse, R., Abelson, J., Swetman, J., & Jackson, J. (2007). Prevalence and distribution of major depressive disorder in African Americans, Caribbean Blacks, and Non-Hispanic Whites. *Archives of General Psychiatry, 64*, 305–315.

Williams, D. R. (1990). Socioeconomic differentials in health: A review and redirection. *Social Psychology Quarterly, 53*, 81–99.

Williams, D. R. (2012). Miles to go before we sleep: Racial inequities in health. *Journal of Health and Social Behavior, 53*, 279–295.

Williams, L. S. (2002). Trying on gender, gender regimes, and the process of becoming women. *Gender and Society, 16*, 29–52.

Williams, R. M. (1977). *Mutual accommodation: Ethnic conflict and cooperation*. Minneapolis: University of Minnesota Press.

Wills, T. A. (1992). The helping process in the context of personal relationships. In S. Spacapan & S. Oskamp (Eds.), *Helping and being helped: Naturalistic studies* (pp. 17–48). Newbury Park, CA: Sage.

Wilson, B. J., Smith, S. L., Potter, W. J., Kunkel, D., Linz, D., Colvin, C. M., & Donnerstein, E. (2002). Violence in children's television programming: Assessing the risks. *Journal of Communication, 52*(1), 5–35.

Wilson, E. O. (1971). *The insect societies*. Cambridge, MA: Belknap.

Wilson, E. O. (1975). *Sociobiology: The new synthesis*. Cambridge, MA: Harvard University Press.

Wilson, E. O. (1978). *On human nature*. Cambridge, MA: Harvard University Press.

Wilson, J. (2000). Volunteering. *Annual Review of Sociology, 26*, 215–240.

Wilson, J., & Janoski, T. (1995). The contribution of religion to volunteer work. *Sociology of Religion, 56*(2), 137–152.

Wilson, J., & Musick, M. (1997). Who cares? Toward an integrated theory of volunteer work. *American Sociological Review, 62*(5), 694–713.

Wilson, T. D., Houston, C. E., Etling, K. M., & Brekke, N. C. (1996). A new look at anchoring effects: Basic anchoring and its antecedents. *Journal of Experimental Psychology: General, 125*, 387–402.

Winsler, A., Carlton, M. P., & Barry, M. J. (2000). Age-related changes in preschool children's systematic use of private speech in a natural setting. *Journal of Child Language, 27*, 665–687.

Witte, K., & Allen, M. (2000). A meta-analysis of fear appeals: Implications for effective public health campaigns. *Health Education & Behavior, 27*(5), 591–615.

Wolff, P., & Holmes, K. J. (2011). Linguistic relativity. *WIREs Cognitive Science, 2*, 253–265.

Won-Doornink, M. J. (1979). On getting to know you: The association between the stage of a relationship and the reciprocity of self-disclosure. *Journal of Experimental Social Psychology, 15*, 229–241.

Won-Doornink, M. J. (1985). Self-disclosure and reciprocity in conversation: A cross-national study. *Social Psychology Quarterly, 48*, 97–107.

Wong, J. (2002). What's in a name? An examination of social identities. *Journal for the Theory of Social Behavior, 32*, 451–463.

Wood, W., Kallgren, C. A., & Preisler, R. M. (1985). Access to attitude-relevant information in memory as a determinant of persuasion: The role of message attributes. *Journal of Experimental Social Psychology, 21*, 73–85.

Wood, W., & Quinn, J. M. (2003). Forewarned and forearmed? Two meta-analysis syntheses of forewarnings of influence appeals. *Psychological Bulletin, 129*(1), 119.

Worchel, S. (1986). The role of cooperation in reducing intergroup conflict. In S. Worchel & W. G. Austin (Eds.), *Psychology of intergroup relations* (2nd ed., pp. 288–304). Chicago: Nelson-Hall.

Worchel, S., Lind, E., & Kaufman, K. (1975). Evaluations of group products as a function of expectations of group longevity, outcome of competition, and publicity of evaluations. *Journal of Personality and Social Psychology, 31*, 1089–1097.

World Bank. (2008). The road to good health: HIV prevention in infrastructure projects. Section 6: Curriculum for commercial sex workers. http://siteresources.worldbank.org/INTEAPREGTOPTRANSPORT/Resources/573802-1163017279494/3138417-1239142047073/5_Curriculum_for_CSWs.pdf (Accessed May 25, 2017).

Wortman, C. B., & Linsenmeier, J. A. (1977). Interpersonal attraction and techniques of ingratiation in organizational settings. In B. M. Staw & G. R. Salancik (Eds.), *New directions in organizational behavior* (pp. 133–178). Chicago: St. Clair Press.

Wright, B., Caspi, A., Moffit, T., & Paternoster, R. (2004). Does the perceived risk of punishment deter criminally prone individuals? Rational choice, self-control, and crime. *Journal of Research in Crime and Delinquency, 41*, 180–213.

Wright, E. O., Costello, C., Hachen, D., & Sprague, J. (1982). The American class structure. *American Sociological Review, 47*, 709–726.

Wright, E., Gronfein, W., & Owens, T. (2000). Deinstitutionalization, social rejection, and the self-esteem of former mental patients. *Journal of Health and Social Behavior, 41*, 68–90.

Wright, K. (2001). Generosity vs. altruism: Philanthropy and charity in the United States and United Kingdom. *Voluntas: International Journal of Voluntary and Nonprofit Organizations, 12*(4), 399–416.

Wright, K. B. (2005). Researching Internet-based populations: Advantages and disadvantages of online survey research, online questionnaire authoring software packages, and web survey services. *Journal of Computer-Mediated Communication, 10*(3). Doi: https://doi.org/10.1111/j.1083-6101.2005.tb00259.x.

Wu, Z., Schimmele, C. M., & Hou, F. (2015). Family structure, academic characteristics, and postsecondary education. *Family Relations, 64*, 205–220.

Wyer, R. S. (1966). Effects of incentive to perform well, group attraction, and group acceptance on conformity in a judgmental task. *Journal of Personality and Social Psychology, 4*, 21–26.

Wyer, R. S., & Srull, T. K. (Eds.). (1984). *Handbook of social cognition* (Vols. 1–3). Hillsdale, NJ: Erlbaum.

Wylie, R. C. (1979). *The self-concept: Theory and research on selected topics* (rev. ed., Vol. 2). Lincoln: University of Nebraska Press.

Ybarra, M. L., Diener-West, M., Markow, D., Leaf, P. J., Hamburger, M., & Boxer, P. (2008). Linkages between Internet and other media violence with seriously violent behavior by youth. *Pediatrics, 122*(5), 929–937.

Ybarra, M. L., Mitchell, K. J., Hamburger, M., Diener-West, M., & Leaf, P. J. (2011). X-rated material and perpetration of sexually aggressive behavior among children and adolescents: Is there a link? *Aggressive Behavior, 37*(1), 1–18.

Zagefka, H., & James, T. (2015). The psychology of charitable donations to disaster victims and beyond. *Social Issues and Policy Review, 9*(1), 155–192.

Zagefka, H., Noor, M., Brown, R., de Moura, G. R., & Hopthrow, T. (2011). Donating to disaster victims: Responses to natural and humanly caused events. *European Journal of Social Psychology, 41*(3), 353–363.

Zajonc, R. (1998). Emotions. In D. Gilbert, S. Fiske, & G. Lindzey (Eds.), *The handbook of social psychology* (4th ed., Vol. 1, pp. 591–632). New York: McGraw-Hill.

Zajonc, R. B. (1968). The attitudinal effects of mere exposure. *Journal of Personality and Social Psychology, 9* (Monograph Suppl. no. 2, Pt. 2), 1–27.

Zanna, M. P., & Hamilton, D. L. (1977). Further evidence for meaning change in impression formation. *Journal of Experimental Social Psychology, 13*, 224–238.

Zarate, M. A., Garcia, B., Garza, A. A., & Hitlan, R. T. (2004). Cultural threat and perceived realistic group conflict as dual predictors of prejudice. *Journal of Experimental Social Psychology, 40*(1), 99–105.

Zebrowitz, L. A., Andreoletti, C., Collins, M. A., Lee, S. Y., & Blumenthal, J. (1998). Bright, bad, babyfaced boys: Appearance stereotypes do not always yield self-fulfilling prophecy effects. *Journal of Personality and Social Psychology, 75*, 1300–1320.

Zechmeister, J. S., Garcia, S., Romero, C., & Vas, S. N. (2004). Don't apologize unless you mean it: A laboratory investigation of forgiveness and retaliation. *Journal of Social and Clinical Psychology, 23*(4), 532–564.

Zelditch, M. (1969). Can you really study an army in the laboratory? In A. Etzioni (Ed.), *A sociological reader on complex organizations* (pp. 528–539). New York: Rinehart and Winston.

Zey, M. (1993). *Banking on fraud: Junk bonds and buyouts.* New York: Aldine De Gruyter.

Zhao, S. (2005). The digital self: Through the looking glass of telecopresent others. *Symbolic Interaction, 28*, 387–405.

Zhu, D. H. (2013). Group polarization in board decisions about CEO compensation. *Organization Science, 25*(2), 552–571.

Zillmann, D. (1978). Attribution and misattribution of excitatory reactions. In J. H. Harvey, W. J. Ickes, & R. F. Kidd (Eds.), *New directions in attribution research* (Vol. 2, pp. 335–368). Hillsdale, NJ: Erlbaum.

Zillmann, D. (1979). *Hostility and aggression.* Hillsdale, NJ: Erlbaum.

Zimbardo, P. G. (1973). On the ethics of intervention in human psychological research: With special reference to the Stanford prison experiment. *Cognition, 2*(2), 243–256.

Zimmerman, D. H., & West, C. (1975). Sex roles, interruptions, and silences in conversations. In B. Thorne & N. Henley (Eds.), *Language and sex: Difference and dominance* (pp. 105–129). Rowley, MA: Newbury House.

Ziol-Guest, K. M., & Dunifon, R. E. (2014). Complex living arrangements and child health: Examining family structure linkages with children's health outcomes. *Family Relations, 63*, 424–437.

Zuckerman, M., DePaulo, B. M., & Rosenthal, R. (1981). Verbal and nonverbal communication of deception. In L. Berkowitz (Ed.), *Advances in experimental social psychology* (Vol. 14, pp. 59ff.). New York: Academic Press.

Zuckerman, M., Koestner, R., & Alton, A. O. (1984). Learning to detect deception. *Journal of Personality and Social Psychology, 46*, 519–528.

Please note that page references to Figures or Photographs will be in **bold**, while references to Tables are in *italics*. References to Boxes will be followed by the letter 'b' in *italics*.